Airlines
of the Jet Age

Signpost at Christchurch, New Zealand, with mileage to London in both directions reflects the global extent of the world's airlines. (Davies, ca. 1975)

Airlines of the Jet Age

A History

R.E.G. Davies

A Smithsonian Contribution to Knowledge

Published in cooperation with
ROWMAN & LITTLEFIELD PUBLISHERS, INC.

Smithsonian Institution
Scholarly Press

WASHINGTON, D.C.
2011

Published by
SMITHSONIAN INSTITUTION SCHOLARLY PRESS
P.O. Box 37012, MRC 957
Washington, D.C. 20013-7012
www.scholarlypress.si.edu

In cooperation with
ROWMAN & LITTLEFIELD PUBLISHERS, INC.
A wholly owned subsidiary of The Rowman & Littlefield Publishing Group, Inc.
4501 Forbes Boulevard, Suite 200, Lanham, Maryland 20706
www.rowmanlittlefield.com

Estover Road
Plymouth PL6 7PY
United Kingdom

Compilation copyright © 2011 by Smithsonian Institution

All rights reserved. This publication may not be reproduced, stored in a retrieval system,
or transmitted in any form or by any means, electronic, mechanical, photocopying, recording,
or otherwise, without the prior permission of the publisher.

Cover image: Double-decked Airbus A380 (2007). Sunil Gupta/Lockon Aviation Photography.

British Library Cataloguing in Publication Information Available

Library of Congress Cataloging-in-Publication Data:
Davies, R. E. G. (Ronald Edward George)
Airlines of the Jet Age / R.E.G. Davies.
p. cm.
Includes bibliographical references and index.
ISBN-13: 978-0-9788460-8-4 (hardcover : alk. paper)
ISBN-10: 0-9788460-8-7 (hardcover : alk. paper)
1. Airlines—History. 2. Jet transports—History. 3. Aeronautics,
Commercial—History. I. Title.
TL720.D28 2010
387.7—dc22   2010043061

Printed in the United States of America

∞ The paper used in this publication meets the minimum requirements of the American National Standard
for Permanence of Paper for Printed Library Materials Z39.48–1992.

*To my wife, Marjorie
whose patience and forbearance over the years
enabled me to write this book.*

CONTENTS

FOREWORD *by Christopher H. Sterling* ix

PREFACE xi

ACKNOWLEDGMENTS xiii

IMAGE CREDITS xv

PART ONE: PISTON-ENGINE PRELUDE
Chapter 1   Air Transport Infancy   1
Chapter 2   Airline Adolescence   9
Chapter 3   Wartime Hiatus—And Opportunity   24
Chapter 4   Post-War Recovery   27
Chapter 5   Worldwide Expansion   32

PART TWO: THE FIRST JET AGE
Chapter 6   The First Jets and Turboprops   36
Chapter 7   Turboprop Ascendancy   43
Chapter 8   The First Big Jets   50
Chapter 9   The Short-Haul Jets   55
Chapter 10   Proliferation   63
Chapter 11   Emergence of the Middle East   71
Chapter 12   Development of a Second Line   82
Chapter 13   The Commuter Airlines   92
Chapter 14   Restoring the Balance   98

PART THREE: THE SECOND JET AGE
Chapter 15   Wide-Bodied Jets   108
Chapter 16   Supersonic Digression   113
Chapter 17   Development of the Breeds   117
Chapter 18   Redefining the U.S. Second Line   122
Chapter 19   Regional Airlines Worldwide   129

PART FOUR: AIRLINE DEREGULATION
Chapter 20   The United States Sets the Pace   139
Chapter 21   The Airline World Deregulates   142
Chapter 22   Russian Metamorphosis   150
Chapter 23   Decline of the American Giants   158
Chapter 24   Birth of the Low-Fare Generation   171

PART FIVE: TRANSFORMATION IN EUROPE
Chapter 25   Low-Fare Revolution   187
Chapter 26   British Airways Ascendancy   194
Chapter 27   France Consolidates   199
Chapter 28   Germany Regains a Leading Role   202
Chapter 29   European Airline Attrition   209
Chapter 30   Jet Wings over the Mediterranean   217
Chapter 31   Farthest North with the Scandinavians   227
Chapter 32   Europe Unites   236

PART SIX: RISE OF ASIA AND THE PACIFIC RIM
Chapter 33   The Growth of China   240
Chapter 34   India Awakes   246
Chapter 35   The Subcontinent Fragments   251
Chapter 36   Eastern Asia Emergent   259
Chapter 37   Budget Fares for Southeast Asia   281

PART SEVEN: THE COMMONWEALTH ADJUSTS
Chapter 38   Airlines of Australia   285
Chapter 39   New Zealand and the Pacific   291
Chapter 40   Canada Reorganizes   303

PART EIGHT: A CONTINENT MADE FOR AIR TRANSPORT
Chapter 41   The Sleeping Giant Awakes   313
Chapter 42   Down Mexico Way   322
Chapter 43   Around the Caribbean   328
Chapter 44   Central America   340
Chapter 45   Airlines of the Andes   347
Chapter 46   Farthest South   362

PART NINE: AFRICA
Chapter 47   Across the Mediterranean   371
Chapter 48   Sub-Saharan Contradictions   376
Chapter 49   End of the Empire Airlines   392
Chapter 50   To the Cape and Beyond   399

PART TEN: TRANSITIONS
Chapter 51   The Third Jet Age Begins   408
Chapter 52   A New Competitor—High Speed Rail   412
Chapter 53   A New Age Beckons   417

APPENDIX 1: SELECTED AIRCRAFT SPECIFICATIONS   421

APPENDIX 2: NOTABLE EVENTS AND FACTS   426

APPENDIX 3: MONETARY CONVERSION FROM 1940 TO 2010   427

APPENDIX 4: THE FIVE FREEDOMS OF THE AIR   427

APPENDIX 5: THE WORLD'S LARGEST AIRLINES   428

BIBLIOGRAPHY   429

INDEX   431

ABOUT THE AUTHOR   463

FOREWORD

"... after studying this book [few] will doubt that the airlines are destined to make as remarkable progress between now and the year 2000 as they did in their first 40 years."

—Peter Brooks, review of
A History of the World's Airlines (1964)

Brooks's words were prescient indeed, considering what has taken place since R. E. G. Davies's landmark air transport history first appeared 45 years ago—vastly more airlines and routes, thousands more aircraft, and millions more people flying in them. Trying to track this expansive and expanding activity over decades of change seems to be a nearly impossible task.

Yet this fact-filled and readable volume does exactly that. It also makes clear that only an informed and diligent researcher can fully understand and so clearly explain the many long-term changes in global air transport. Doyen of the world's air transport historians for a half century, Davies has accomplished what few others would have the nerve (let alone the energy) to attempt: a detailed survey of how airlines around the world have developed during nearly six decades of what the author terms the "Jet Age." The magnitude of the task he faced and overcame is made plain with just one stark statistic—when he completed his book in 1964, some 270 airlines operated worldwide. As this new study appears 45 years later, the number of scheduled airlines has burgeoned four-fold to more than a thousand.

The sheer number of disparate facts that make up this account is evident in the index, but that only hints at the concerted research effort involved. Preparing this history has involved nearly a decade of dedicated archival research, writing, and creating Davies's signature maps and charts. That productivity builds on his varied career spent in different parts of the industry: the British Air Ministry, then British European Airways, then airline market research in both Britain and the U.S., followed by nearly three decades as curator of air transport at the Smithsonian's National Air and Space Museum. To this background he has added travel to more than 120 countries—and 25 books on air transport history. The result of this unparalleled experience and effort is the first truly comprehensive assessment of how airlines adapted to the arrival of jet aircraft, why some carriers failed along the way, and what all this has meant to the flying public.

Readers will better understand from these pages why commercial aviation has become such a brutally competitive industry, one of thin profits (if not huge losses), rising fuel prices, ever-changing ticket systems reliant on complex computer-based "yield management" strategies, and for the last three decades, a marketplace defined by substantial deregulation. One sad result: airline careers lack the excitement (and income) they generated decades ago. What was once a glamorous career has become just another job. The aircraft are safer (far fewer passengers are hurt or killed per thousand people flying each year), but traveling as a passenger has totally lost its one-time romance. A domestic economy-class trip in the U.S. is now one with far less personal space and more security worries than an inter-city bus. Full aircraft, charges for so many things that used to be free, and sometimes being caught on grounded aircraft for hours at a time—these have come to characterize the world of flying for many of us. Except for the few in first-class (about one percent of all traffic), food service today barely approaches fast-food coffee shops.

Modern airports are usually efficient places, but their parking lots grow ever larger, and one has to thread long ticket and onerous security lines to reach the departure gate. During the Jet Age, once-empty terminals have become shopping malls to generate operating income.

In one important aspect, Peter Brooks's prediction has not been fulfilled: Today's airliners rarely "get you there" any faster than they did a half century ago. Routine trips can be even slower because of air traffic control issues, air or ground congestion, or weather delays. For trips of up to 300–400 miles, many travellers are rediscovering trains which take them between city centers faster than any airline, usually at considerable savings over airfare. Davies is a strong supporter of these rail options, especially the high-speed services long enjoyed in east Asia and western Europe since 1964.

In one chapter, Davies strongly criticizes the wrongheaded and pricy experiment with supersonic transport (SST), which he makes clear, was a technical marvel but financial disaster for all concerned. A monument to the pioneering British-French effort, the handsome Concorde can now be seen only in museums. Throughout its years of widely promoted service, steadily improved (though less heralded) workhorse subsonic airliners carried the world's millions.

Particularly valuable in this account are descriptions of numerous airlines and routes that may be new to many readers. Famous global flag carriers such as Pan American, KLM, and British Airways, and the trunk routes that they travelled (including the bellwether North Atlantic run) are described and analyzed here. So, too, are more unusual stories of creating services to exotic and off-the-beaten-track locations, the so-called "thin routes" of more limited use or appeal that help to make up the worldwide picture of air transport. The growth of Asian services is especially dramatic. So is the work performed by important airline innovators and entrepreneurs such as Skytrain's Freddie Laker, and India's Tata family, among others often unknown outside of the airline business. Davies has met many of these industry leaders, adding to the value of this chronicle.

This well-balanced history melds elements of technology (improving aircraft and systems), economics (as in trying to fly airplanes as full as possible), government regulation (largely limited to safety concerns after about 1980), and foreign affairs (obtaining landing rights, or dealing with fluctuating oil costs that often parallel political crises in the Middle East). More important, this is a history concerning people (those who work for the aircraft manufacturers or airlines and the millions who regularly fly); labor relations (including unions of pilots, flight attendants, and aircraft controllers, among others); culture (for example, the reversal of business versus leisure shares of the total market); and daily management decision-making. Here and there, anecdotes remind us of the lighter human aspects of an intensely serious business. All of these elements have created the modern air transport system, efficient and impersonal, without which much of the world's commerce and life styles would grind to a halt.

To better understand how the airline world we know came to be, pack this volume in your carry-on next time you fly.

Christopher H. Sterling
Washington, D.C.
March 2010

PREFACE

The British de Havilland Comet astounded the world of aviation when British Overseas Airways Corporation flew it from London to Johannesburg on 2 May 1952, halving the journey time. Gloomy forecasts predicted that jet engines would be too fuel-hungry for economic operations, but they were proved wrong. Even so, the episode ended in tragedy, because of hitherto unrecognized structural problems. British leadership in the airline industry was overtaken by U.S. manufacturers, led by Boeing, whose Model 707 went into service in 1958. By 1960, Pan American Airways had circled the world with them. The Jet Age had emphatically begun.

The Jet Age, as it is conveniently called, began in 1952, but it was founded on a technical and operational infrastructure that dates back to 1914. I covered those pioneering years of aviation in my first book, *A History of the World's Airlines* (Oxford University Press, 1964), and for the convenience of readers unable to obtain it, I have summarized this essential background material in the early chapters of this volume.

This book is about airlines, but the main tools of the trade—the jet airliners—are also reviewed. I have avoided listing airlines in the form of a catalog of names, dates, and events, and instead have chronicled the causes and effects or political and social influences that have generated the worldwide expansion of one of the world's great industries. I have given credit where it is due: to the British and the German inventors for introducing the technology, to the American for developing it, to the French for refining it, and to the Soviet Union for its contributions. (Often forgotten is that the Soviet Aeroflot had initiated jet services before Pan American Airways.)

The Jet Age can be divided into three segments, based on the stages of development of the superb airliners that represented them. My first book ended, and this one begins, with the First Jet Age, with the single-aisled Comets, Boeing 707s, and Douglas DC-8s. Wide-bodied, twin-aisled Boeing 747s, DC-10s, and Airbuses mark the Second Jet Age. The double-decked Airbus A380 has ushered in the Third Jet Age. The airlines of the world have benefitted from this astonishing technological progress by offering better service to the public. The first 36-seat Comets could not cross the oceans. Now, 600-seat A380s and their smaller Boeing competitors fly half-way round the world nonstop.

Few tourists were able to fly in those first-class-only businessmen's Comets, but marketing innovations during the 1960s and 1970s, backed by the efficiency of the jet airliners, ushered in a new era. Led by airlines once on the fringe, cheap fares have brought the pleasures of air travel to almost everyone, at least in the world's leading industrial nations. Airlines today concentrate on providing travel opportunities, rather than competing for culinary honors. They have discovered—finally—that high load factors, achieved by bargain-fare offerings, without expensive amenities, achieve better financial viability than did, for example, the supersonic Concorde, a technological miracle, but an economic disaster.

This book notes the geographical change in the world's balance of traffic. The First and Second Jet Ages were launched across the North Atlantic. The Third Jet Age was inaugurated from Europe to Asia, reflecting the growth of population—increasing in number and affluence—of the countries on the western Pacific Rim. Once politically isolated from the rest of the world, China now ranks (by traffic productivity) second only to the United States among the world's airline nations.

Also noted is the emergence of a new source of competition for the airlines, at least in short-haul operations. In 1964, realizing the airlines could not cope with the 40-million-per-year passenger demand on the world's busiest air route (Tokyo-Osaka), Japan introduced the Shin Kan-sen high-speed railroad (H.S.R.). Its original 110-mph cruising speed—since improved to 150-mph—created an entirely new mode of transport. Today, 28 countries are operating, building, or in the advanced planning stages of establishing H.S.R. In Europe, airline service has ceased on some short-haul routes that are serviced by rail. China is developing a nation-wide system. The United States, alone among the world's industrial nations, is not in the vanguard of H.S.R.

During the more than a half-century Jet Age, the world's airlines have earned an astonishing record of achievement and safety, thanks to the admirable reliability of airliner engines and airframes. In my first book, I quoted the Soviet writer Ilya Ehrenburg, who in 1958 (as trans-Atlantic jet service began) wrote "Let aircraft carry tourists, and never again shall we see aircraft carry bombs." The airlines endeavor to fulfill that wish.

R.E.G. Davies
June 2010

ACKNOWLEDGEMENTS

"Plagiarism" is defined as copying someone else's work and claiming it to be one's own; copying several people's work is, satirically, held to be research. I have not deliberately copied the work of others, but this book embraces the work of countless individuals who have preserved the history of this great industry. Air transport is an essential component of the economic machinery that holds the nations of the world together. Its history has been chronicled by hundreds of writers in dozens of magazines and pamphlets, many scores of books, and by the airlines themselves. It also draws upon countless interviews that I have been privileged to make from airline owners, executives, and administrators, to office workers and engineers on the shop floors. These have been gleaned during half a century of world-wide travel. This book is a synthesis of notes and writings collected since 1950, and which are now lodged in dossiers in the Archives of the National Air and Space Museum in Washington, D.C.

The books are listed in the bibliography. Some deserve special mention. I could not have done without Ben Gutterey's *Encyclopaedia of African Airlines*. In a vastly different style, Philip Schleit's *Shelton's Barefoot Airlines* is a classic combination of biography and corporate history. Peter Brooks's analyses of commercial airliner design development were invaluable. Transcending all books about air transport, however, are the authoritative volumes produced by the late John Stroud, who has been a tower of strength as an airline historian since his days with the pre-war Imperial Airways. In his wake have been Bill Gunston, who fell into Stroud's shoes, Gunter Endres, prolific assembler of reliable fleet lists, and many others, particularly those of the Croydon Airport Society.

Outstanding as reliable magazine references for innumerable details have been *Aviation Week, Air Transport World, Airliners*, and especially *Airways*. John Wegg, long-time editor of those last two publications, might well have written this book, if he could have spared the time from producing *Airways*. I have drawn on the writings in these and other journals, notably by Jon Proctor, the late Terry Waddington, David Forward, and George Hamlin, who have all written extensively about the airlines.

This book is also the result of personal interviews and discussions with fellow historians, many of whom I have been privileged to meet during more than half a century of global travel. I have also thereby been able to confirm or correct, with "old-timers" and executives alike, some of the episodes and developments that have been controversial. Many of the anecdotes that will remind readers of the human side of officialdom were obtained firsthand, from the Brazilian Amazon jungles to the Siberian tundra; from the snows of Spitzbergen to the ice fields of Antarctica.

Members of the Latin American Aviation Historical Society have generously shared their knowledge with me, and I am indebted to Dan Hagedorn, John Davis, Gary Kuhn, Carlos Dufriche (Brazil), and Anthony Sapienza (Paraguay). Similarly, my membership of the Washington Airline Society has paid unexpected dividends, with help from Robin Dunn, George Hamlin, Bill Grella, and especially Roger Bentley and Brian McDonough, who supplied dozens of photographs to punctuate the sometimes long passages of text. Bobby Booth and Gianfanco Beting, independent Latin American specialists, have helped too. Eiichiro Sekigawa, veteran writer and historian ensured the accuracy of much of the Japanese content, as did Anthony Lawler for South Africa, Anthony Vandyke for the Middle East and some of Africa, and Jim Mason and Bruce Ellsworth for Canada.

The contribution of the former Soviet Union is also recognized, and I am grateful for the hospitality and help of Yuri Salnikov, television documentary producer; Aeroflot's Tatiana Vinogradova; Vasily Karpy, magazine editor; and Oleg Borisov, former Aeroflot correspondent in Khabarovsk.

The output of British writers has been recognized and respected by all students, enthusiasts, and aficionados of airline news, reports, and history. Air Britain, which started as a small group in England in 1945, is now a worldwide group and, through John Davis, has been a constant source of reference. M.J. Hardy and Peter Berry, little known in the United States, have compiled precise records of air travel.

As I have stated in my Preface, this has been a Smithsonian book. Its writing represents only the proverbial part of the iceberg that shows. Its foundation lies in the extensive airline archives of the National Air and Space Museum. These are constantly maintained by a conscientious group of volunteers, whom I am happy to call my "team." During the past few years, they have comprised Samuel Vick Smith, airplane specialist and pilot; Guy Halford-McLeod, former airline executive and current author; and Bill Shumann, also a pilot and formerly with the F.A.A., *Aviation Week*, and the *Washington Post*—all meticulous proofreaders. Previously, Carroll Adams, ex–Pan American 747 pilot; Stan Dosik, world-travelled businessman; "Buzz Piggot," experienced foreign traveler; and pilots Ron Hunter and Mark Weiss: all were valued members of the team. Collectively, they have kept, and are still keeping, up to date, for public access, a continuous record of the major events in airline history as they occur.

Dr. Christopher Sterling has proofread and copyedited the text and saved me the embarrassment of a mistaken typographical error or lapse of memory. Bob van der Linden oversaw the strenuous timetable of writing the book. Editor Ginger Strader has been patient, tolerant, and helpful. They and countless others whose names are too numerous to list, who have helped me, in a specialized field of literature, to preserve the wish of James Smithson "to increase and diffuse knowledge."

IMAGE CREDITS

Images from the Smithsonian Institution's National Air and Space Museum Archive

Smithsonian Archive Number(s)	
SI-83-16525 / NASM-00087776	United Technologies Corp. Archive via National Air and Space Museum, Smithsonian Institution.
SI-96-15351 / NASM-3B00081	Lufthansa via National Air and Space Museum, Smithsonian Institution.
SI-77-9914 / NASM-00058352	National Air and Space Museum, Smithsonian Institution.
NASM-00046973 / NASM-00046880	National Air and Space Museum, Smithsonian Institution.
NASM-9A08076	National Air and Space Museum, Smithsonian Institution.
NASM-A-47645 / NASM-00138742	National Air and Space Museum, Smithsonian Institution.
NASM-A-1799 / NASM-00048294	National Air and Space Museum, Smithsonian Institution.
SI-75-12118 / NASM-00014150	National Air and Space Museum, Smithsonian Institution.
SI-2003-25387 / NASM-00037232	National Air and Space Museum, Smithsonian Institution.
SI-89-12437	National Air and Space Museum, Smithsonian Institution.
NASM-7A39330	National Air and Space Museum, Smithsonian Institution.
SI-99-40767 / NASM-7A31718	National Air and Space Museum, Smithsonian Institution.
SI-77-5809 / NASM-00014394	National Air and Space Museum, Smithsonian Institution.
SI-91-13253 / NASM-00058509	National Air and Space Museum, Smithsonian Institution.
SI-98-15060 / NASM-3B03933	U.S. Air Force via National Air and Space Museum, Smithsonian Institution.
SI-80-14393 / NASM-00046070	Lufthansa photo no. Dlh 3050-1-3 via National Air and Space Museum, Smithsonian Institution.
NASM-9A08178	National Air and Space Museum, Smithsonian Institution.
SI-97-16607 / NASM-00094619	National Air and Space Museum, Smithsonian Institution.
NASM-A-3854 / NASM-00039110	National Air and Space Museum, Smithsonian Institution.
NASM-00132334	National Air and Space Museum, Smithsonian Institution.
NASM-00096048	National Air and Space Museum, Smithsonian Institution.
SI-2003-4837 / NASM-7A41466	National Air and Space Museum, Smithsonian Institution.
NASM-00096053	National Air and Space Museum, Smithsonian Institution.
NASM-9A08078	National Air and Space Museum, Smithsonian Institution.
NASM-9A08079	National Air and Space Museum, Smithsonian Institution.
NASM-9A08080	National Air and Space Museum, Smithsonian Institution.
NASM-00131619	National Air and Space Museum, Smithsonian Institution.
NASM-9A08081	National Air and Space Museum, Smithsonian Institution.
NASM-9A08082	National Air and Space Museum, Smithsonian Institution.
SI-95-2351	Photo by R.E.G. Davies. National Air and Space Museum, Smithsonian Institution.
NASM-9A08085	National Air and Space Museum, Smithsonian Institution.
SI-96-15335	National Air and Space Museum, Smithsonian Institution.
NASM-9A08176	National Air and Space Museum, Smithsonian Institution.
NASM-9A08179	National Air and Space Museum, Smithsonian Institution.
NASM-9A08088	National Air and Space Museum, Smithsonian Institution.

Images from Personal Collections

Caption Identifier	
Davies	From the personal collection of R.E.G. Davies.
Dunn	Robin Dunn Collection. Reproduced with permission of Robin Dunn.
McDonough	Reproduced with permission of Brian McDonough.
Szura	Reproduced with permission of Arue Szura.

Images from Personal Collections

Caption Identifier	
Bentley	Reproduced with permission of J. Roger Bentley.
J. Laker	Reproduced with permission of Lady Jacqueline Laker.
Davies 1992	From *Aeroflot: An Airline and Its Aircraft—An Illustrated History of the World's Largest Airline* (Paladwr Press, 1992), by R. E. G. Davies. Reprinted with permission of R. E. G. Davies.
Graboske	Reproduced with permission of Fred Graboske.
Sunil Gupta/Lockon Aviation Photography	Reproduced with permission of Sunil Gupta.
Samuel Smith	Reproduced with permission of Samuel V. Smith.
Michel Gilliand	Reproduced with permission of Michel Gilliand.
Photo by Jean Marie Magendie	Reproduced with permission of Jean Marie Magendie.
CSR Sifang Locomotive & Rolling Stock Company	Reproduced with permission.

Images from Other Sources

Smithsonian Archive Number(s)	
NASM-7A45020	LZ-Archiv FN, LZF 10-23. Archives of the Luftschiffbau Zeppelin GmbH Friedrichshafen. Reproduced with permission.
SI-91-7082	American Airlines photo no. A00-127. American Airlines. Reproduced with permission.
SI-79-10980	The Flight Collection, ref. 10347. Reproduced with permission.
SI-94-13380	BAE SYSTEMS Neg. no. DH5412A, Comet 1 BOAC livery G-ALZK 02-APR-1951. Reproduced with permission of BAE SYSTEMS.
SI-91-2442	Viscount Capital Airlines. Reproduced with permission of BAE SYSTEMS.
NASM-00016437	BAE SYSTEMS Neg. no. 1175-1306. Britannia BOAC. Reproduced with permission of BAE SYSTEMS.
NASM-9A08175	BAE SYSTEMS Neg. no. DH12201G, Comet 4 BOAC G-APDR 17-JUL-1959. Reproduced with permission of BAE SYSTEMS.
NASM-9A08083	Boeing photo P37643. Copyright © Boeing Company. Reproduced with permission.
NASM-9A08087	Boeing photo P42929. Copyright © Boeing Company. Reproduced with permission.

PART ONE: PISTON-ENGINE PRELUDE

Chapter 1: Air Transport Infancy

The Concept of Air Transport—Lighter-Than-Air

During the first few years after the epoch-making flight of the Wright brothers on 17 December 1903, little thought was given to the idea that heavier-than-air flying machines (airplanes, or aeroplanes) could earn an honest living by carrying people or goods, for peaceful purposes or for war, at any time during the then foreseeable future. The concentration at the beginning of the 20th century was on lighter-than-air flying machines (airships, and particularly dirigibles). As early as 16 November 1909, the **Hamburg-Amerikanische Packetfahrt A.G. (HAPAG)**, trading as the Hamburg-Amerika Line, was registered to operate passenger services within Germany, using the products of the Luftschiffbau Zeppelin GmbH (the Zeppelin factory), founded by the resourceful Count Ferdinand von Zeppelin on 8 September 1908.

Starting with the LZ 10 *Schwaben* on 15 July 1911, four Zeppelin airships flew within Germany until the outbreak of the Great War of 1914–18. They carried 34,028 passengers (of whom 10,179 paid for the privilege) on 1,588 flights, either on local sight-seeing jaunts or sometimes between German cities. These were not on scheduled services—the airships cruised at about 40 mph and offered no competition with surface transport—but HAPAG's pioneering effort was an impressive achievement. No lives were lost, and the lighter-than-air operation created an enthusiastic spirit of national airmindedness. This would generate encouragement that would be given to future German airlines, from local city communities as well as from Berlin and the local state governments.

Using the more practicable airplanes, air transport was set in motion on both sides of the Atlantic. Several isolated, and certainly experimental, mail-carrying flights had been made before the First World War, mainly in England, Italy, France, and the United States. But outstanding among these ventures was the mail service in India, which lasted for a week from 18 February 1911. A French aviator, Henri Piquet, carried a sack of mail from Allahabad to a nearby rail junction. This is accepted by philatelists as the world's first aerial post. But these pioneers had proved only that an aircraft could carry a sack, and little more. The experiments were not repeated or extended for a few more years.

The First Scheduled Airline

The question of "which was the first airline?" has to be qualified by precise definitions. Omitting the qualification of a sustained operation, i.e., more than a few months' service duration, pride of place must go to the **St. Petersburg-Tampa Airboat Line**, founded by Percy Fansler in St. Petersburg, Florida, toward the end of 1913. This diminutive company began on 1 January 1914, flying across Tampa Bay with equally diminutive Benoist flying boats, most of them seating only a single passenger. Had

The Schwaben *was one of HAPAG's fleet of airships that operated sight-seeing flights in Germany from 1911 to 1914. (NASM-7A45020)*

This Benoist XIV flying boat operated the world's first airline service across Tampa Bay in 1914. (Davies)

the pilot, Tony Jannus, not been killed later in Russia, he would have become as famous as Charles Lindbergh. The distance between St. Petersburg and Tampa was 17 miles, and the air trip saved a 40-mile circuitous road or rail journey around the perimeter of Tampa Bay. This operation, of which the clientele was mainly wintering vacationers from the north, lasted only three months. But Fansler deserves lasting credit for having put the new invention to commercial rather than sporting or military use only a decade after the epoch-making flight of the Wright brothers in 1903. He set an example that would be followed by others; and his tentative exploits would lay the foundations for a worldwide industry.

The First Transport Airplane

In Russia, a far-sighted designer, Igor Sikorsky, with the cooperation of Mikhail Shidlovsky, chairman of the Russo-Baltic Wagon Company at St. Petersburg, built the world's first four-engined aircraft. At first called *Le Grand* or the *Bolshoi Baltiskiy (Great Baltic)*, it first flew on 15 March 1913 and was renamed the *Russkiy vityaz (Russian Knight)*, which flew on 23 July. It was then redesigned with four tractor engines mounted on the lower

*St. Petersburg-Tampa Airboat Line
(The World's First Scheduled Airline)*

The Chaplin Air Line

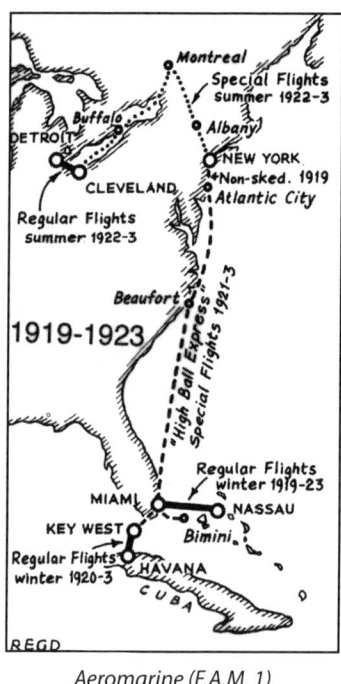
Aeromarine (F.A.M. 1)

*Florida West Indies Airways
(First U.S. Post Office Foreign Air Mail Contract)*

*Edward Hubbard (Boeing)
(F.A.M. 2)*

Merrill Riddick (F.A.M. 3)

The First Airlines in the United States

The Russian Il'ya Muromets was the world's first four-engined transport aircraft. (SI-83-16525)

of the 92-foot biplane wings. It went into final production as the Il'ya Muromets.

Reports of this giant of its time were met with a certain skepticism in western Europe, and it was quite unknown in America. But Sikorsky forged ahead, improving the design and structure. Then, on 30 June 1914, with a crew of three, Igor flew from St. Petersburg to Kiev, a distance of 660 miles, with one stop, arriving in triumph in the afternoon of the next day. On 12 July, it returned home in only 13 hours. Far from being, as the skeptics thought, a transitory and overambitious experiment, it was the greatest advance in aircraft technology since the Wright *Flyer* of 1903. A month after the flight to Kiev, the Great War broke out. About 80 Il'ya Murometses were used as bombers on the eastern front and gave a good account of themselves. A few sporadic commercial flights were made after the War ended in 1918, but the Russian Revolution put an end to all further developments and Sikorsky, finding himself on the wrong side of the political fence, immigrated to the United States.

By a remarkable coincidence, the first cautious steps toward the foundation of a great new industry were made in two cities of the same name: the first regularly scheduled airline in St. Petersburg, Florida, and the first successful load-carrying airplane, as a transport vehicle, in St. Petersburg, Russia.

Resumption of Momentum

The outbreak of war in 1914 halted aeronautical development for commercial purposes, as the aircraft manufacturers concentrated on military applications. Considerable advances were made, and by the end of the Great War, fighter and bomber aircraft had exceeded all expectations. By 1917, some aircraft were being used, on both sides of the conflict, for armed forces mail service. An Italian mail service from Turin to Rome, starting on 22 May, lasted a week; and the idea was pursued in over-water flights from the Italian mainland to Sardinia, Sicily, and across the Adriatic Sea to Albania during the summer. Later in the year, the Germans were flying mail regularly between Berlin and Cologne, the French between Paris and St. Nazaire, and the British on the Western Front. Pride of place could possibly go to the soon-to-be dismantled Austro-Hungarian Empire. On 11 March 1918, a service opened between Vienna and Kiev, directed by A.R. von Marvil, a former fighter pilot. The purpose was to organize supplies of

Air Transport Infancy

AEG biplanes operated the first airline services in Germany in 1919. (SI-96-15351)

Table 1. SIX IMPORTANT FIRST FLIGHTS IN CIVIL AIR TRANSPORT

Date	Airline	Route	Qualifications					
			Regular	Civil	Daily	Passenger	International	Sustained
1 Jan. 1914	St. Petersburg-Tampa Airboat Line	Tampa-St. Petersburg	✓	✓	✓	✓		
20 Mar. 1918	Austro-Hungarian Military Line	Vienna-Kiev	✓	✓			✓	✓
15 May 1918	United States Post Office	Washington-New York	✓	✓	✓			✓
22 Feb. 1919	Deutsche Luft Reederei	Berlin-Weimar	✓	✓	✓	✓		✓
22 Mar. 1919	Farman	Paris-Brussels	✓	✓		✓	✓	✓
25 Aug. 1919	A.T. & T.	London-Paris	✓	✓	✓	✓	✓	✓

grain from the Ukraine to Austria. The service was never opened to the public, but did operate with a degree of regularity.

On the other side of the Atlantic, the U.S. Post Office began air mail service between Washington and New York on 15 May 1918. At first operated under contract by the U.S. Army Air Corps, using Curtiss JN-4H biplanes, and later by the Post Office's own Standard biplanes, the beginnings were fraught with mishaps; but this enterprise laid the foundations for a nationwide air mail network from coast to coast. This, in turn, was the blueprint for the contracted air mail routes that established the airline system of the United States in the mid-1920s.

The world's first sustained passenger airlines started in Europe in 1919. In Germany, **Deutsche Luft Reederei (D.L.R.)**, an ancestor of the present-day Lufthansa, opened for business, on a Berlin-Weimar route, with AEG biplanes, on 5 February. This was short-lived, but other routes followed, all within Germany, until fuel shortages forced suspension on 1 August. The German national airline carries D.L.R.'s "flying crane" symbol to this day.

The first regular international service was by the French company Farman, from Paris to Brussels on 22 March with its Goliath converted bombers. Flown only once a week, no customs formalities were required, but passengers were advised to carry passports. Then the British stepped in with a claim—all the qualifying adjectives are necessary—to have started the world's first regularly scheduled and sustained daily international passenger airline service. George Holt Thomas's **Aircraft Transport and Travel (A.T.& T.)**, founded during the Great War in 1916, began a London-Paris service, with de Havilland D.H.4 biplanes, on 25 August 1919. It soon gained a fine reputation, to exceed all others, for regularity and reliability.

One day before A.T.&T.'s effort, the German company **DELAG** revived interest in the lighter-than-air mode of aerial transport by starting a service from the Zeppelin works at Friedrichshafen to Berlin, using the rigid airship *Bodensee*. But this had to be terminated on 1 December, because the Treaty of Versailles had forbidden the resumption of the airships that had been used so effectively as bombers during the War.

Europe Leads the Way

Europe seized the initiative to inaugurate air services. The victorious Allies were able to use bomber aircraft, converted to civilian use, most prominently by the British company Handley Page, which joined A.T.&T. on the cross-Channel routes using its own bombers, converted for passenger use. Similarly, the French, using aircraft such as the Goliath, deployed several airlines for cross-Channel work. Defeated Germany was forbidden to operate any multi-engined aircraft, or any aircraft powered by an engine of more than 125 horsepower. The unexpected sequel provided a good example of the axiom that necessity is the mother of invention. The Junkers company produced the six-seat Junkers-F 13, the first all-metal aircraft to be specially designed and put into widespread service. Any possible Russian initiative, using the Il'ya Muromets (see above) had meanwhile fallen victim to the chaotic situation in Russia, resulting from the Bolshevik Revolution.

In Britain, other airline companies were formed, notably by the Daimler car hire firm, and four of them merged on 31 March 1924 to create **Imperial Airways** as a national commercial airline, and the world's first "chosen instrument" with government encouragement and support. Its main objective was to develop swift communication for mail and passengers to the British Empire, India, southeast Asia, Australia, and southern Africa. It inherited a small fleet of mostly de Havilland types, steel-framed, doped fabric-covered, but Imperial scrapped many aircraft that, after two years' use, were too unreliable to be trusted.

In Germany, dozens of small companies were formed, some by individual cities or states, some by industrial organizations such as the Nord-Deutscher Lloyd shipping line. The Junkers aircraft manufacturer, restricted by the severe terms of the Versailles Treaty, established airlines in foreign countries. In a complicated series of maneuvers during the period until 1925, the Lloyd companies merged into the **Deutscher Aero Lloyd**; while the Junkers group formed international consortia such as the **Trans-Europa Union** and the **Ost-Europa Union**. An understanding was reached as early as 1922 and this culminated in a merger on

Europe's first air routes were launched by Germany, France, and Great Britain.

The Junkers-F 13 of 1919 was the world's first all-metal transport aircraft. (SI-77-9914)

During the 1920s, the steel-framed, mainly-wooden, Fokker F-VIIb/3m was a popular transport aircraft in Europe. (NASM-00046973)

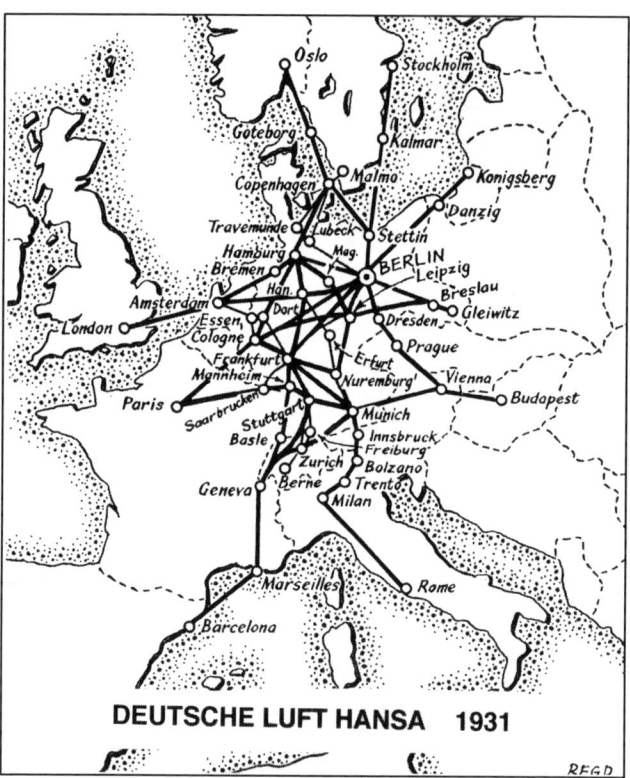

During the early years of European air transport, Deutsche Luft Hansa dominated.

6 January 1926 to form **Deutsche Luft Hansa**. This airline, well managed and well supported by the German Government and other financial sources, was to dominate the airways of Europe until—and even during—the Second World War. In manufacturing, Junkers was joined by others, mainly Dornier.

In France, the establishment of a national airline was not achieved until 1933. However, by the end of 1920, no fewer than eight companies were operating, including Farman. Two of them vied for the cross-Channel traffic from Paris to London: the **Compagnie des Messageries Aériennes (C.M.A.)**, backed by several French aircraft manufacturers, was joined by the **Compagnie des Grands Express Aériens (C.G.E.A.)**. The two cross-Channel companies merged in January 1923 to form **Air Union**, and developed routes to southern France, leaving those to the Low Countries to the **Société Générale de Transport Aérien (S.G.T.A.)**, the new name for Farman. Unfettered by foreign restrictions, the **Lignes Aériennes Latécoère**, founded by the manufacturing company of that name, pioneered a route to north and west Africa; while the **Compagnie Franco-Roumaine de Navigation Aérienne (C.F.R.N.A.)** inaugurated an aerial Orient Express, reaching Constantinople (Istanbul) by 1922. Such enterprise culminated in the creation of Air France in 1933. The French companies used mainly steel-frame and wood/fabric construction, for single-engined and multi-engined types. The manufacturers, such as Potez, Blériot, Breguet, and Latécoère, were invariably closely associated with the airlines that used them.

Other European countries followed, notably the Netherlands and Belgium. **Koninklijke Luchtvaart Maatschappij voor Nederland en Kolonien (K.L.M.)** began service in May 1920 and quickly established a fine reputation. By the early 1930s, with great flair, it was to inaugurate a route to Batavia, Dutch East Indies (now Jakarta, Indonesia), which at the time was the longest air route in the world. The Belgians worked from both ends of its colonial empire, also starting in May 1920 with a forerunner of the **Société Anonyme Belge d'Exploitation de**

Air Transport Infancy

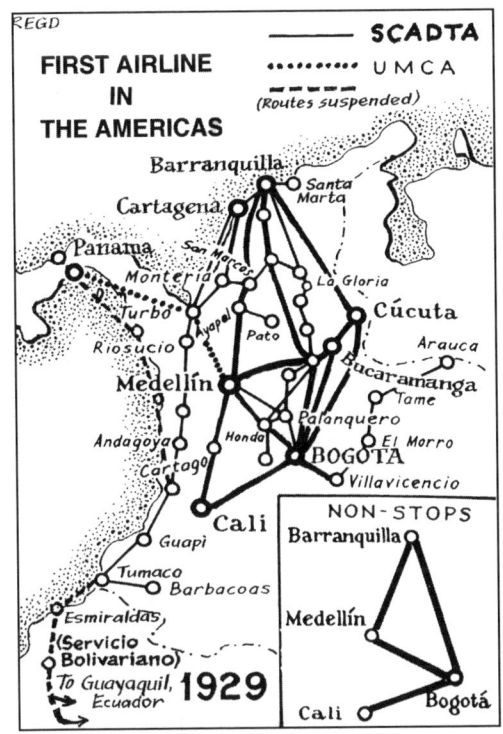

The Colombian SCADTA was the ancestor of today's AVIANCA, which can thus claim to be America's oldest airline.

By 1930, almost every major city in South America was served by Pan American Airways and its associated PANAGRA.

la Navigation Aérienne (**SABENA**) in Brussels, and the first air route in Africa, the **Ligne Aérienne du Roi Albert (LARA)** in the Belgian Congo.

K.L.M. used aircraft built by the Dutch company Fokker. Anthony Fokker had been a successful constructor of fighter aircraft for the German Air Force during the Great War, and quickly adapted his construction methods to a succession of commercial types, first single-engined then multi-engined. Of the latter, the Fokker F-VIIb was the most successful and was the best transport aircraft in Europe until surpassed by the Junkers-Ju 52/3m. The basic difference between the two was that the Fokker was built almost entirely of wood, with a thick-chord wing; the Junkers was built entirely of metal (aluminum alloy), corrugated for lateral strength.

Italy—surprisingly, considering its prowess in aircraft construction—did not establish sustained airline service until 1926. But almost every other country did. These were, in chronological order, Denmark (1920); the Danzig Free State (surrogate for German interests) and Spain (1921); Estonia, Switzerland, and Poland (1922); Austria, Hungary, the Soviet Union, and Czechoslovakia (1923); and Finland (1924). Significantly, most of these countries turned to Junkers, which either sponsored the creation of the airlines, or supported their establishment.

Packhorse to Plane in Latin America

While the United States was establishing a fairly comprehensive coast-to-coast air mail service, Europe was constructing a network of passenger airlines from Madrid to Moscow, from

Junkers metal float-planes, such as this W34, pioneered air routes in Colombia during the 1920s. (NASM-9A08076)

Stockholm to Istanbul, and the empire nations of Europe were beginning to think about linking their overseas empires to the homelands by air routes. Enterprising ideas were being explored to create air services in areas of the world where surface transport was either non-existent or, at best, slow or even primitive. In Latin America, the first airline was **Transports Aériens Guyanais (T.A.G.)**, in French Guiana, which started as early as 12 October 1919. Other Latin American countries entered the field in 1920: **Compañía Colombiana de Navegación Aérea (C.C.N.A.)** and **Compañía Aérea Cubana**. These services were experimental, intermittent, and short-lived; but T.A.G. did begin regular flights on 12 October 1920 and continued these until 30 October 1922.

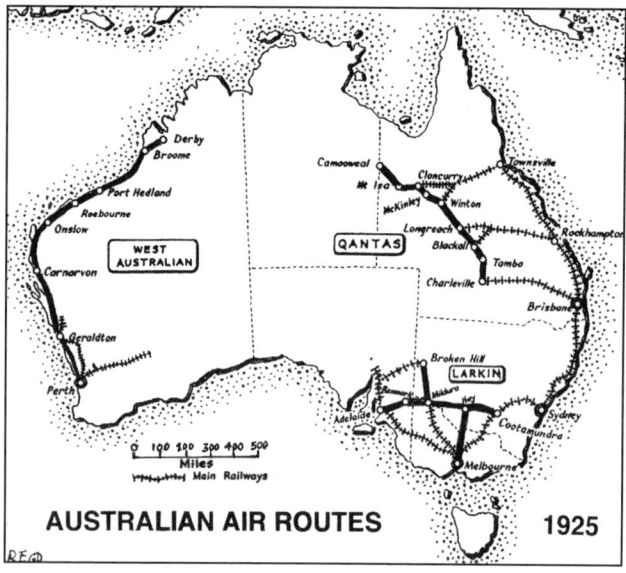

Because of its dispersed urban population, Australians quickly became the world's most air-minded.

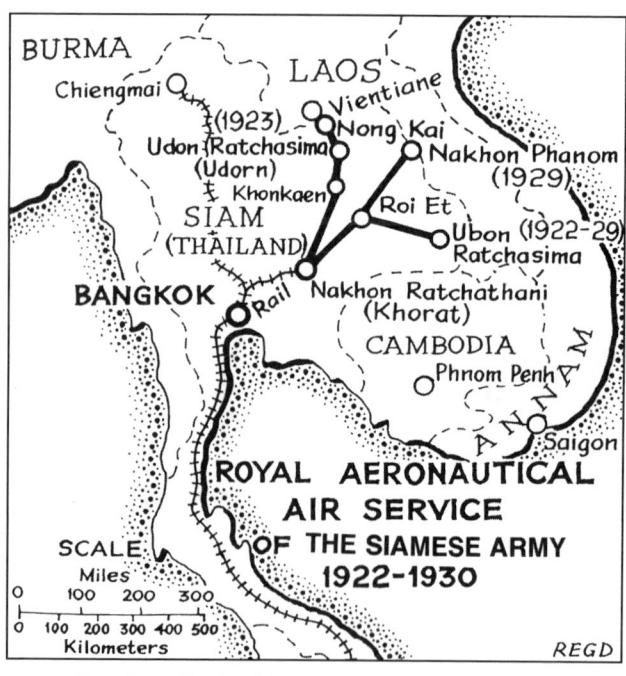

Siam (now Thailand) began air mail services in 1922, the first in Asia.

The **Compañía Mexicana de Transportación (C.M.T.A.)** started in 1921, on a route from the Mexican capital to Tampico; this was taken over on 16 August 1924 by **Compañía Mexicana de Aviación (C.M.A.)**, which subsequently expanded as Mexico's national flag-carrier, and survives to this day. Pride of place among the Latin American pioneers must go, however, to **Sociedad Colombo-Alemana de Transportes Aéreos (SCADTA)**, which began services on 19 September 1921. Founded in 1919 by a partnership of Colombian nationals and German immigrants, and later becoming **AVIANCA**, this was the first regular and sustained airline service in *all* the Americas.

Of particular note also is the **Compañía Río-Platense de Aviación**, founded in 1919 as the River Plate Aviation Company by an Englishman, Major Shirley Kingsley, who merged his operation with a French concern to operate an air service from Buenos Aires to Uruguay, to avoid a circuitous land journey. This service began on 17 December 1921 (to Villa Colón), and was the first international service in all the Americas. It was short-lived, ending in 1923. Another early airline was **Lloyd Aéreo Boliviano (L.A.B.)**, founded mainly by German immigrants in 1925, and which started regular services on 25 December 1925. L.A.B. has the distinction of being the oldest airline in all the Americas to have operated continuously under the same name. Much of the early development of commercial aviation in Latin America resulted from German initiatives, particularly by the Condor Syndikat, which exported substantial numbers of Dornier and Junkers types. The little Ju-F 13, and the -W 33 and -W 34 developments especially, won their spurs, the metal construction proving to be a measure of resistance to tropical climates that other aircraft could not match. Later, in the 1930s, most of these pioneer airlines fell under the control of Pan-American Airways, which was to dominate the whole of Latin America, from the Rio Grande to the Rio de la Plata, until after the end of the Second World War.

Stirrings Down Under

Australia was quick to recognize the potential of air transport, especially in the vast "outback." Almost all its population was concentrated in big cities, and other communities were separated by long distances, and often almost isolated. No national railroad system existed—each state had its own and they had different track gauges. Located as it was at the far end of Britain's overseas empire, and several weeks away by the fastest ocean shipping lines, the idea of an air service from London to Australia was appealing. As early as 1919, the Australian Government had offered a handsome prize—£10,000, or about 20 times that amount in today's equivalent currency value—for the first to fly that distance. Captain Ross Smith and Lieutenant Keith Smith, in a Vickers Vimy bomber, flew from London to Darwin, almost 12,000 miles, to win the prize, and to create a high level of airmindedness in Australia that has persisted to this day. The government encouraged airline development by generous mail contracts. The first went to **West Australian Airways**, which provided service along the coast of West Australia, northward from the railhead at Geraldton, starting on 5 December 1921. This was followed by **Queensland and Northern Territory Aerial Services (QANTAS)**, which linked the three railheads in western Queensland, to provide, from 3 November 1922, a service to Brisbane for the outback farmers and miners. QANTAS is the second oldest airline in the world (after K.L.M.—see above) to be operating continuously under its own name. The third contract was to the **Larkin Aerial Supply Company (LASCO)**, to link Adelaide with Sydney, and this started

Air Transport Infancy

on 2 June 1924. This ended in 1928, because this was the one area of Australia where the railroads provided adequate transport.

Early Airlines in Asia

Other than India, which can claim a brief entry in the aviation record books, only China made attempts to begin air services immediately after the end of the First World War. The Peking Syndicate, representing Handley Page, imported six converted H.P. 0/400 bombers, and made a trial flight to Tientsin on 6 December 1919. A rival faction, the Aeronautics Department of the Chinese Government, also imported converted British bombers, a number of Vickers Vimys, and engaged Colonel F.V. Holt, of the Royal Air Force, to establish a service from Peking to Shanghai. He started on 1 July 1921, but the aircraft only reached Tsinan, because of disruption by the rival local war-lords. He tried again from 18 July to 15 August, and also briefly from Peking to Peitaiho, on the Gulf of Chihli; but the political unrest between the warring factions in China during the early 1920s prevented the development of air services, indeed, the development of almost any nationwide commerce, for several years.

Next on the Asian commercial air transport calendar was the **Siamese Aeronautical Service**. Showing considerable initiative and planning capability, several air mail routes, starting on 1 June 1922, radiated from the railroad terminus at Nakhon Ratchasima (Khorat) into northeast Siam (Thailand). Using Breguet 14 single-engined biplanes, and French-trained Siamese pilots, this service operated for nine years, carrying several thousand passengers, 25,000 bags of mail, and about 30 tons of freight, as well as ambulance missions. This commendable pioneering achievement came to an end, partly because railroads were built, but mainly because the Siamese Government decided to set up a completely commercial airline, formed on 7 July 1930.

Simultaneously with Siam, there was a stirring of airline activity in Japan, already in the ascendancy as Asia's most powerful industrial nation. All the main cities, accounting for about 70% of the population, were served by an efficient railway system, so that there was little incentive for overland flights. But on 4 June 1922, Mr. **Choichi Inouye**, of the Itoh Flying School, founded the **Nippon Koku Yuso Kenkyujo (N.K.Y.K.)** (Japan Air Transport Research Institute). On 15 November he started floatplane flights from Sakai City, a suburb of Osaka, to Tokushima, across Osaka Bay, on the island of Shikoku. This was extended along the shores of the beautiful Inland Sea.

The United States Moves into Action

While Europe and other countries were developing air services of all kinds, the United States was slow off the mark. It concentrated on establishing air mail services, at first under the jurisdiction of the **United States Post Office**. On 15 May 1918, using Curtiss JN-4H training aircraft, it opened an historic mail service between Washington and New York, and this gradually expanded into a coast-to-coast system, inaugurated on 8 September 1920. By 1921 the standard aircraft equipment was the converted British light bomber, the de Havilland DH-4B, large

Japan's Pioneer Airlines

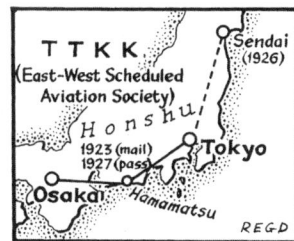

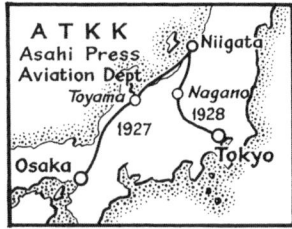

numbers of which had been built in the U.S.A. toward the end of the Second World War.

During 1922 and 1923, the Lighted Airway, a system of regularly spaced high-intensity beacons (averaging about 20 miles apart) was constructed. This enabled the pilots, who had been able to fly only by daylight, to follow the transcontinental route, like a car being guided by street lamps, at night as well as by day. By well-organized relays, the mail could be carried from New York to San Francisco in about 35 hours. By 1930, all the main routes were studded with the powerful beacons. Also, the Post Office had built airfields, and had set disciplinary standards that were to reap benefits in subsequent years of airline operations. It established a principle—as true today as it was then—and subsequently voiced by a prominent airline promoter, Clement Keys: "ninety percent of aviation is on the ground."

The de Havilland DH-4B was a civil conversion of a Great War light bomber, and comprised the main fleet of the pioneer U.S. Post Office air mail service of the early 1920s. (NASM-A-47645)

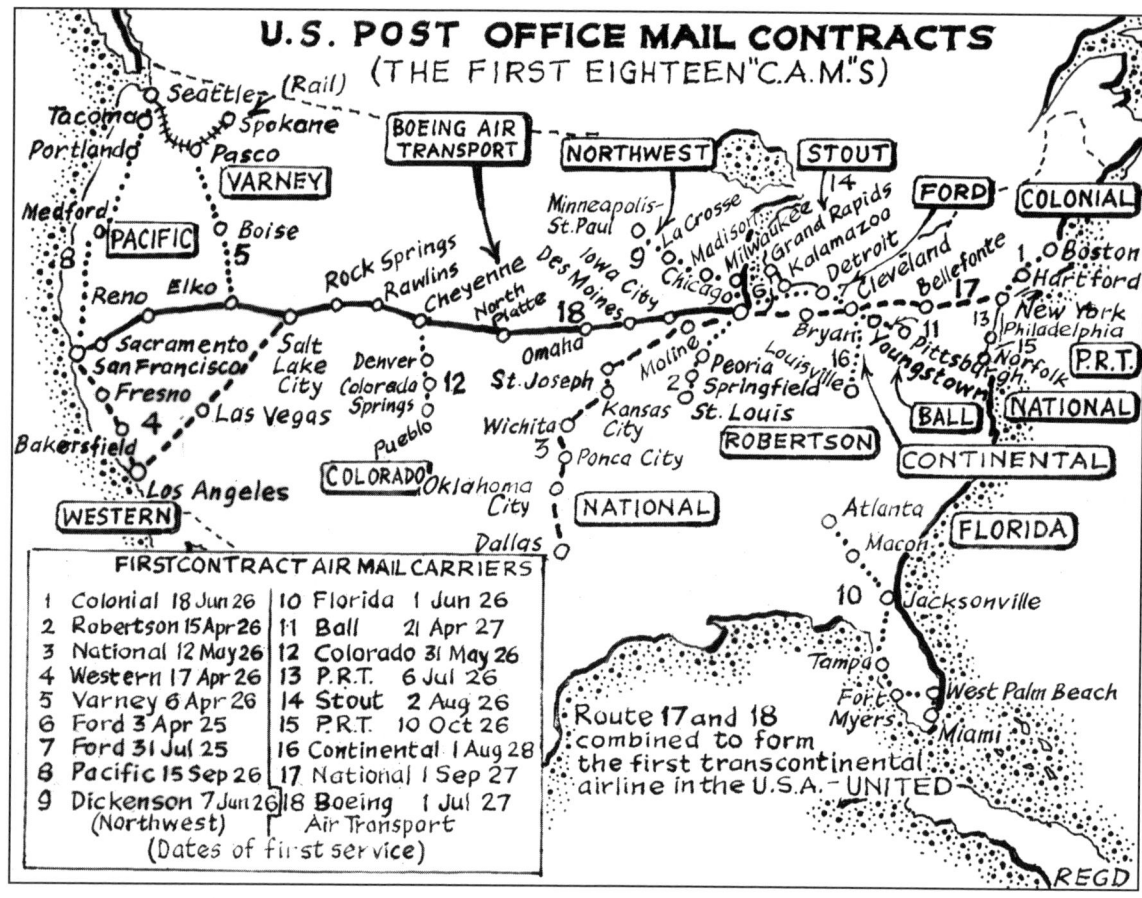

By the late 1920s, most of the United States had air mail service, by commercial airlines under contract to the U.S. Post Office.

While the U.S. Post Office was making great strides, private enterprise was also seeking to exploit the new mode of transport. Great credit should be given to Inglis Uppercu, a New York motor car distributor, who founded **Aeromarine Airways** in 1919, and equipped it with flying boats built by his own Aeromarine Plane and Motor Company, notably the Curtiss 75, a 14-seat conversion of the military F-5L. Both Aeromarine and **Aero Ltd.** had been using such craft to fly thirsty U.S. citizens from Florida to the Bahamas or Cuba after the passing of the Prohibition Act of 30 June 1919. Uppercu acquired a Post Office Foreign Air Mail (FAM) contract—the very first one—to carry the mails from Key West to Havana, starting on 15 October of that year. Aeromarine was the leading airline during this period of U.S. airline infancy. Before surrendering to economic pressures and closing down in 1923, it had carried 17,000 passengers in Florida, the Great Lakes, and locally from New York.

Other such contracts were granted to Eddie Hubbard (FAM 2) from Seattle to Victoria, B.C., and Merrill Riddick (FAM 3) from New Orleans to Pilottown, at the mouth of the Mississippi delta. These last two met, respectively, trans-Pacific and trans-Caribbean/Gulf or Mexico ships, and saved a day's transit time for the mails. Curiously, later on, in 1926, FAM 1 was allocated to Colonial Air Transport, while FAM 4 went to Pan American Airways, discussed later. Other short-lived companies were sustained for more than a few weeks or months. On 4 July 1919, Syd Chaplin, elder brother of the famous actor, started a passenger service from the port district of Los Angeles to Avalon, the Catalina Island resort, 34 miles away. This lasted only three months, but was resurrected by various operators and the route is still a popular local air service to this day.

All the early U.S. air services, mail or passenger, were flown by waterborne aircraft, floatplanes or flying boats. The competition was relatively slow-moving ships against which aircraft, even at only 90 miles per hour, could comfortably compete. Not until 1925 did the first passenger airline service begin on an overland route. On 1 March of that year, the **Ryan Airline**, using war-surplus Standard biplanes modified by Claude Ryan's own company, started scheduled service from San Diego to Los Angeles. The fare was $17.50 single, a tidy sum in those days, enabling Ryan to break even, with free ground transport included, by carrying only one passenger per flight. He abandoned the service in 1927, concentrating on building aircraft.

Chapter 2: Airline Adolescence

The United States Creates an Air Transport System

By the mid-1920s, air transport in the United States was effectively non-existent, except for the Post Office air mail system, which did not carry people. A tremendous stimulus was given by Congress in 1925, when, on 19 April, it approved the Air Mail Act, known as the "Kelly" Act, after its main sponsor. This created a system of contracted air mail carriers (the term lives on to denote an operating airline even today) that were paid varying rates, amounting to an indirect subsidy. They were typically restricted to regions, with no single-carrier transcontinental route nor any complete border-to-border north-south routes. The majority, however, collectively comprised the nucleus of what was to become the trunk airline system of today.

Equally important was the passing of the Air Commerce Act of 1926, signed by President Coolidge on 20 May. This set up, for the first time, a regulatory framework against which the new companies could operate, with provisions for airways, airfields, and communications networks. The air mail contracts were amended to payments by weight, and the fledgling airlines did very well. But they did not constitute a national airline system, which was perceived to be ponderous and inefficient by Walter F. Brown, the Postmaster General appointed under President Hoover in 1929. He studied the situation carefully and at length, and decided that a complete overhaul was necessary. The result was the Air Mail Act of 1930, known as the "McNary-Watres" Act after its sponsors, approved by Congress on 29 April.

The main provision of this landmark piece of legislation was to replace the method of mail payments by load carried to payments according to space offered. This encouraged the use—and therefore the construction—of larger aircraft. This not only offered more space for mail; it offered space for passengers. Instead of having to sit in a cramped cockpit, often on mail bags, they were able to travel in cabins, albeit noisy and not exactly comfortable. The most popular airplane of choice was the metal-construction Ford Tri-Motor, which became the flagship of a dozen airlines that competed for the lucrative mail contracts.

With the realization that air transport could lead to big business, after the Kelly Act and especially after the sudden enthusiasm for and promotion of aviation by Charles Lindbergh's dramatic solo flight across the Atlantic Ocean in 1927, airlines converged into amalgamations and affiliations, and airline stocks sold at a premium. The resultant corporations survived the Wall Street Crash of 1929, and the largest ones became a trio of powerul transcontinental airline systems. Their financial backing and consequent stature was considerable, and their combined strength enabled the United States to overhaul other countries. By 1929, U.S. airline traffic went from strength to strength to dominate the world.

The transcontinental trio that emerged from all the in-fighting consisted of: (1) **United Air Lines**, formed by the amalgamation of four of the contract mail carriers. Backed by the Boeing Company, its coast-to-coast route linked San Francisco directly with New York via Chicago and intermediate

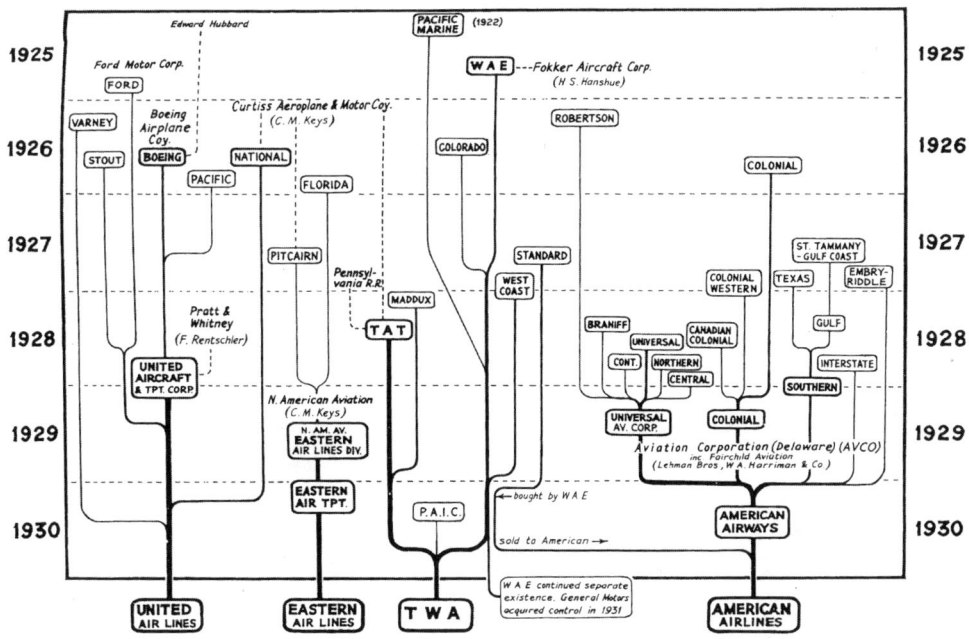

By the early 1930s many of the U.S. pioneer airlines had formed large companies, which became known as the "Big Four."

During the early 1930s, the all-metal Ford Tri-Motor was the airlines' main flagship. This picture was taken at Columbus, Ohio, when Charles Lindbergh was the pilot of one of T.A.T.'s inaugural flights. (NASM-A-1799)

In 1933, United Air Lines introduced the Boeing 247. With its monocoque fuselage, and engines mounted on the wing, it has been recognized as the world's first "modern" airliner. (SI-75-12118)

points, using, predictably, Boeing aircraft types. (2) **American Airways**, the merger, under the control of the Aviation Corporation of America (AVCO), of three airline groups, each of which had been formed by the merger of, or as subdivisions of, several smaller mail contract carriers. Aircraft used were of many different types, from many manufacturers. (3) **Transcontinental and Western Air (T.W.A.)** was the result of the merger of Western Air Express and Transcontinental Air Transport (T.A.T.) because Walter Brown, the Postmaster General, would not approve mail contracts to two airlines competing on the same route.

Boeing had produced what aviation historians agree was the first "modern" airliner. The Boeing 247 incorporated several refinements. It had only two engines, which, however, produced the same power as the Ford Tri-Motor's three, and eliminated the excessive vibration and noise in the cabin caused by the engine in the nose of the fuselage. The engines were mounted into, rather than attached to the wing, and this feature alone added about 25 mph to the speed because the landing gear could be retracted, reducing the airflow drag. The radial engines were cowled, also reducing drag as well as improving the cooling. Altogether, the Boeing 247 was about 60% faster than the Ford, which was quickly seen to be obsolescent.

Such was the competitive margin, because it cut the transcontinental flying time to less than 24 hours, that Boeing tried to turn this to its own advantage. It allocated all the early delivery positions to its own airline, United, and indicated that deliveries to other airlines would be delayed for a considerable time. T.W.A.'s Frye was furious. He prepared a specification for an even better transport aircraft, and sent it to five other manufacturers. The winner of this special competition was Douglas Aircraft Company, with its DC-1, a prototype that quickly went into production as the Douglas DC-2. It had 14 seats, compared to the 247's 10, flew just as fast, and its cabin was far more comfortable, mainly because the wing spars did not go through it. If the 247 was the first modern transport airplane, the DC-2, with its

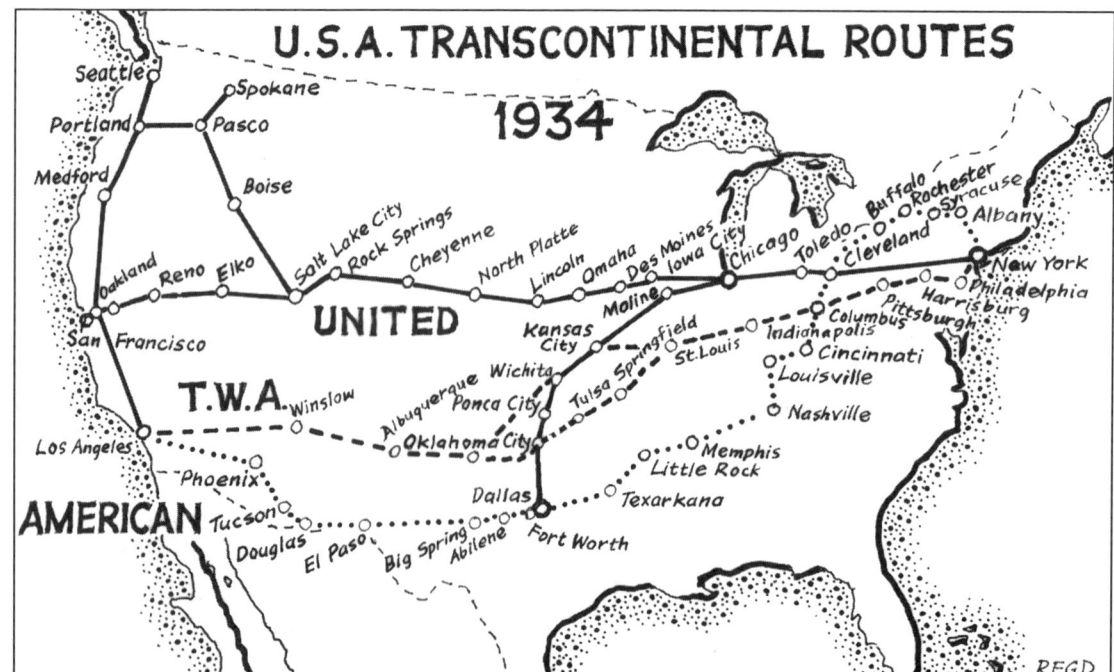

At the time of the "Air Mail Crisis" of 1934, three of the "Big Four" were operating transcontinental air routes.

In the early 1930s, Boeing was closely associated with United Air Lines, to which the first 60 747s were allocated. In 1934, T.W.A. countered with the superior Douglas DC-2, ancestor of the famous DC-3. (SI-2003-25387)

American Airlines introduced the DC-3 in 1936. The first few to be delivered were Douglas Sleeper Transports (D.S.T.s) on the transcontinental route. But all subsequent deliveries were 21-seat DC-3s. (SI-91-7082)

comfortable cabin, was the first that could justify the use of the word *airliner*.

Scandal and Crisis

Such technical progress was overshadowed, however, during the early 1930s, by what became known as the Air Mail Scandal. The air transport system of the United States had taken shape and substance because of the visionary plan devised by Postmaster General Walter F. Brown. The airline route map was logically simple, based on the transcontinental trio, United, American, and T.W.A., intersected by north-south links, for example Western along the Pacific coast, and Eastern along the Atlantic. The list of certificated mail carriers was completed by a dozen or so smaller operators, all of whom depended on mail payments that amounted to indirect subsidies, paid by the government, and therefore guaranteed.

Some of Brown's actions appeared to smack of favoritism, and some of the independent non-mail airlines turned this into a political debate that reached the highest level and created a serious crisis. Much was made of the so-called Spoils Conferences—meetings called by Brown in Washington in which sundry mail contracts were handed down in an alleged atmosphere of a "smoke-filled room." The furore became so strident that, on 26 September 1933, the Senate set up a special committee, chaired by Senator Hugo Black, to investigate the allegations. On the evidence submitted, and on the recommendation of Karl Crowley, the new Postmaster General James Farley's solicitor, President Roosevelt cancelled all the air mail contracts, arousing the ire of all the recipient airlines, Charles Lindbergh himself, and the unofficial voice of the Republican Party, *Fortune* magazine.

Roosevelt asked General Benjamin Foulois, Chief of the Army Air Corps, if they could carry the mail. Woefully unprepared, flying across the Rockies in the worst winter for half a century, 11 pilots were killed within a few weeks during February–March 1934. The publicity was so intense that Roosevelt quickly reversed his decision. New contracts were assigned, almost all of them for routes like the old ones. On 12 June, Congress passed the Air Mail Act of 1934, which essentially consolidated the foundations of an air mail system that Walter Brown had planned five years previously.

During the remaining years of the 1930s, the United States airlines continued to receive an indirect subsidy in the form of mail payments, and prospered to the extent that, measured in passenger-miles flown, it accounted for about 55% of the world's total. Of the airline fleets operated by the U.S. airlines, 85% of the capacity was provided by Douglas twin-engined airliners, mostly by the Douglas DC-3, outstanding successor to the DC-2.

The Empire Routes

Before the Second World War, many European countries still reigned over overseas territories, as colonies administered from the homeland, or protectorates, or as self-governing dominions. The term *empire* was still politically correct, and the biggest empire of them all was the British, "on which the sun never set." **Imperial Airways**, formed in 1924, began hesitantly, initially to reach the Persian Gulf, where British commercial and strategic interests needed to be supported. Aircraft used were the tri-motored Armstrong-Whitworth Argosy, the de Havilland Hercules, and, for the Mediterranean crossing, the Short Calcutta flying boat. A notable step was made on 30 March 1929, when the British route was extended to Karachi then in India. The journey time was scheduled at 7½ days, and though seldom achieved with regularity, this was a commendable achievement, saving as it did several weeks of transit by ship through the Suez Canal and the Red Sea. In 1931, the Handley Page HP 42, a slow (100 mph) four-engined 40-seat landplane, was introduced.

Beyond Karachi, Imperial employed the Armstrong-Whitworth Atalanta, a sturdy all-metal type, able to carry 17 passengers, in what was then considered to be "four-engined safety." The Indian administration, conscious of its status as a self-governing dominion, insisted on the establishment, on 21 June 1933, of **Indian Transcontinental Airways** for the routes within India. The first Atalanta reached Calcutta on 8 July and Rangoon on 23 September, but it was a struggle. **K.L.M.** was flying mail to Batavia, in the Dutch East Indies, with monotonous regularity with Fokker high-winged monoplanes—steel-framed but otherwise of wooden construction, particularly in the thick-chord wing. One of the great days in the history of air transport was when, on 1 October 1931, a Fokker F-XII, fitted with four

In Europe the accent was on comfort, not speed. The average inter-city distance was short. Across the English Channel, Imperial Airways operated the 90 mph, 40-seat, Handley Page HP-42 bi-plane. (SI-79-10980)

luxury reclinable seats, opened a regular passenger service from Amsterdam to Batavia, in journey time of 10 days. In 1932, the larger eight-seat Fokker XVIII supplemented the XII.

1934—A Banner Year

In the United States, the politically inspired crisis described above had changed the course of air transport. Simultaneously a new era had begun in the development of the modern airliner design. Boeing had produced the Model 247, which entered service in 1933, but the following year, T.W.A. introduced the Douglas DC-2, a 14-seat 165-mph all-metal airliner, demonstrably superior. Its successor, the 21-seat Douglas DC-3, quickly became the flagship of every major U.S. airline. A total of 16,000 of these aircraft were built, including those overseas under license. A few are even earning their keep today.

In the eastern hemisphere, the year had started encouragingly for the British. On 18 January 1934, in an arrangement somewhat similar to the one in India, the Australian airline **QANTAS** joined with Imperial to form **Qantas Empire Airways**, which undertook the responsibility of the route from Singapore to Brisbane. On 8 December, an Atalanta delivered the first Christmas air mail from London to Brisbane, in 12 days.

By this time, however, a severe wake-up call was delivered to the British. Sponsored by an enterprising Australian businessman, Sir MacPherson Robertson, the 1934 England–Australia Air Race was a dramatic and spectacular entry in the annals of aviation history. From Mildenhall, Suffolk, to Melbourne, the race was won by pilots Campbell and Black in a specially designed de Havilland D.H. 88 Comet, *Grosvenor House*. But to the admiration, and indeed the astonishment of the aviation community throughout the world, second place went to a standard Douglas DC-2, flown by K.L.M.'s K.D. Parmentier and J.J. Moll, in a point-to-point time of 3 days, 18 hours, 17 minutes. The significance of the effort—K.L.M. carried three passengers and 191 kg (400 lb) of mail—was profound. It emphasized the inferiority of the previous types of aircraft used on the empire routes, and clearly demonstrated the superiority of American technology. The world beat a pathway to Douglas's door and opened the way for an American export industry that ultimately was to dominate the world.

The British had to do something, and did so, with alacrity. On behalf of Imperial Airways, the government ordered "off the drawing board" 29 Short S-23 flying boats. These had adequate performance to match the Douglases on all the routes to the Far East and Australasia. They did not have trans-Atlantic range, but did provide a superior level of comfort, with a "promenade lounge" at an upper level, where long-distance passengers could stretch their legs and enjoy a drink. Additionally, on 20 December 1934, the British Post Office introduced the Empire Air Mail Scheme, whereby all letters within the British Empire would be carried by air at the same rate as that previously charged for surface mail. This was started on 23 February 1938, and encouraged bigger loads—to the extent that at Christmas time, there was often no room for some of the passengers.

Imperial–K.L.M. Rivalry

Imperial's S-23s started to make their mark in 1937, first as far as Alexandria, on 8 February then on 7 October, to Karachi, in four days, accelerated on 10 April 1938 to three days. Singapore was reached in five and a half days, and Sydney in nine and a half. The S-23 was faster than the DC-3 but the latter, being a landplane, could make quicker transit times at the intermediate stops; and it maintained a better record of regularity and punctuality. **Koninklijke Nederlandsch-Indische Luchtvaart Maatschappij (K.N.I.L.M.)** had been established on 15 October 1928 in

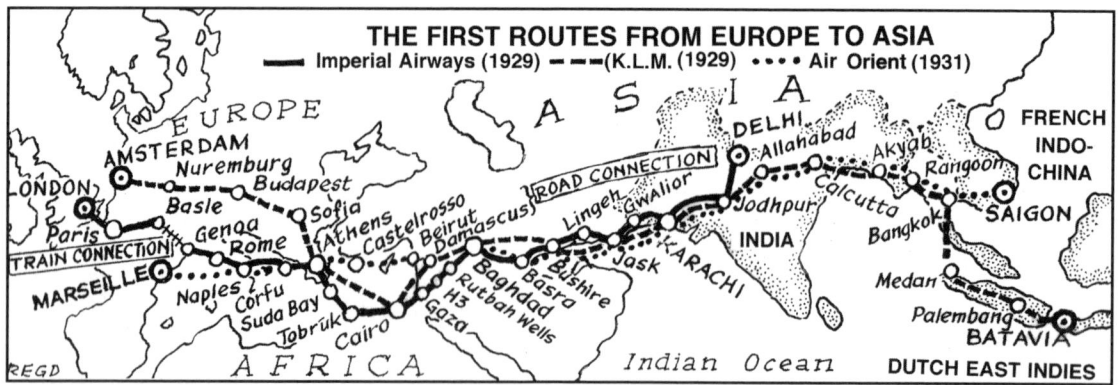

Imperial Airways reached India in 1929. By the same year, K.L.M. was serving the Dutch East Indies (with a branch to Singapore), and Air France reached Indo-China in the same year. The flights stopped several times and took several days.

Airline Adolescence

In the 1934 England-Australia air race, K.L.M. was a close second, flying a standard Douglas DC-2, complete with passengers and mail. This picture was taken as it refueled at Karachi. (Davies)

Batavia by Dutch business interests as a partner to the Amsterdam airline. In partnership with K.L.M., it would extend the Dutch route to Darwin. By 1939, both Imperial and K.L.M., with the aid of their partners, were linking Europe with Australia in eight days.

Routes to Africa

In the "Scramble for Africa" during the latter part of the 19th century, and settled by the Berlin Conference of 1884-85, the major European powers had annexed territories throughout the continent, and administered them as colonies or protectorates. Some were later granted semi-autonomous and self-governing status. Mostly blocked by the Sahara (desert) the overland journey to them was so arduous and time-consuming that the standard means of travel was by ship.

These territories, relatively isolated from their homelands, were thus slow to embrace the advantages of air travel. Much credit should be given to Belgium, which, immediately after the end of the First World War, tried to launch an air service in the then Belgian Congo, a huge colonial territory that had few roads or railways. Most inland travel was by riverboats, and these were impeded by waterfalls along the Congo River. But as early as 1 July 1920, **LARA** opened a service along the Congo with Levy Lepen hydroplanes. It did not last very long, and many years were to pass before a Belgian airline was able to reach its far-flung empire.

Great Britain and France had been the main beneficiaries from the Berlin Conference; and indeed Britain enjoyed a contiguous "Cape to Cairo" territorial strip, except for German East Africa; and even this became a British mandate after the First World War. The way seemed to be open for pioneeering an air service. And the word *pioneer* was apt. Airfields had to be built, local hostilities dealt with, maintenance installations located, and problems of climate and terrain (some parts of the route were more than 6,000 feet above sea level) overcome. Survey flights were made south of Egypt in the 1920s, notably by the famous aviator Sir Alan Cobham. On 28 February 1931, Imperial Airways started a regular mail service as far as Mwanza, on the Tanganyika shore of Lake Victoria. The first air mails reached Cape Town on 20 January 1932, and passenger service began on 27 April of that year. The journey took 11 days. The return fare was £234—a good year's salary for the average working man in those days; but the privileged passengers could enjoy overnight stops in Imperial rest-houses along the way.

The intrepid passenger of 1932 was required to make 33 separate stops (not including emergency or non-scheduled ones) and to make eight changes of vehicle. Flying boats and landplanes of several different types were used, all multi-engined, and in spite of the technical improvements in engines and propellers of that era, average speeds were no more than about 100 mph.

Imperial speeded up in 1937, at the same time adding to the comfort standards. The famous C Class Short S-23 "Empire" flying boats came into service on 2 June 1937, cutting the London-Durban (marine base) time to 6½ days then, on 10 April 1938, to 4½ days. These were the halcyon years of British pre-war airline development, for the Short boats could match the landplanes in speed, and excel them in comfort. Nevertheless, the ground services were a problem. Alighting on the River Nile was sometimes a hazardous exercise, not only in piloting skills, but also in dodging waterborne craft, avoiding floating debris, and, for the passengers, transferring via small boats to the shore.

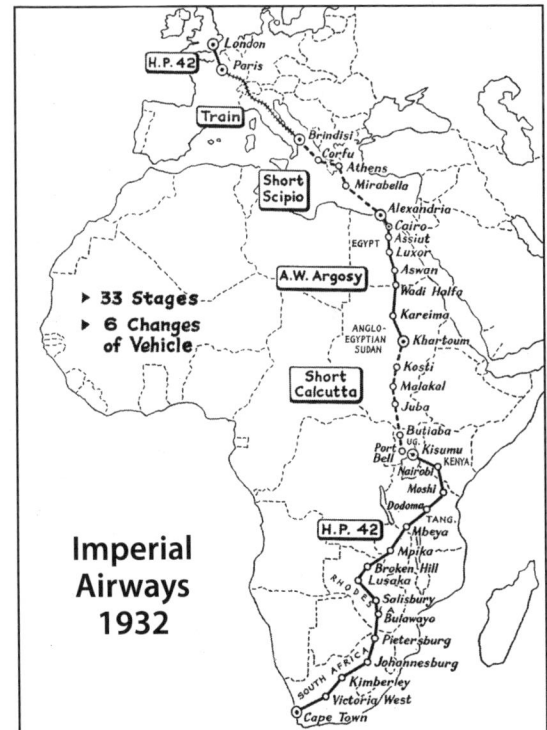

Imperial's Short "Empire" S-23 Capella is seen taxiing along the River Nile at Cairo. (Davies)

The British were able to establish the Cape-to-Cairo air service, in air space over their own territories, and thus with no international negotiation necessary for overflying traffic rights. The French covered most of the Algerian Sahara, French West and Equatorial Africa, and Madagascar. **Air France** had taken over the route to Dakar, originally pioneered by Latécoère and Aéropostale, at its formation in 1933. Another airline, **Air Afrique**, began mail service to Brazzaville, on the Congo River, on 7 September 1934, and passenger service on 27 April 1935, using tri-motored Bloch 120s. This line was extended to Elizabethville (now Lubumbashi) on 9 December 1935 and by the associated Régie Malgache to Madagascar on 19 April 1936.

Belgium had been the first pioneering airline nation in Africa (see above) but its national airline, **SABENA**, was unable to connect the Belgian Congo with Brussels until 23 February 1935, using Fokker F-VIIs on a 5½-day schedule to Leopoldville (now Kinshasa) on 23 February 1935. The delicate issue of flying rights across the French Sahara was achieved by a mutually beneficial agreement with Air Afrique. The French allowed transit rights to SABENA and, in turn, the Belgians allowed Air Afrique/Régie Malgache reciprocal rights across the Belgian Congo. SABENA, meanwhile, upgraded its fleet with Savoia-Marchetti SM-73s.

One other European country opened a trans-Sahara service before the Second World War. Italy's east African colonies, Eritrea and Somaliland, were linked with Rome on 11 December 1935—the need to stop at Cairo and Khartoum en route may have eased Imperial's problems in stopping at points in Italy. When the Italians occupied Ethiopia in 1936, the Linee Imperiale of **Ala Littoria** went to Addis Ababa, using Cant Z506s and Savoia-Marchetti SM-73s.

Pan American Conquers the Oceans

While the European nations were linking their empires with their respective homelands, the United States had adopted—or had been cajoled into the acceptance of—a "chosen instrument" to develop an overseas network. The instrument was **Pan American Airways**, an airline that had been formed and expanded, with remarkable efficiency and élan, by Juan Trippe, entrepreneur extraordinary. It had been founded in 1927 and made its first scheduled mail flight from Key West, Florida, to Havana, a 90-mile hop, on 28 October 1928.

With astonishing speed, Trippe negotiated traffic rights and, backed by a cooperative U.S. Post Office Department with lucrative mail contracts, expanded his route network, first encircling the Caribbean then southward through South America. The United States had no sovereignty over all the independent countries of Latin America. But Trippe was a wily negotiator, and ways were found to circumvent any difficulty. For the west coast (Pacific) route, an agreement was made with the W.R. Grace shipping and trading company to form the **Pan American-Grace Corporation (PANAGRA)**, and the line reached Buenos Aires, the Argentine capital then known as the "Paris of South America," on 12 October 1929. Meanwhile, however, a rival enterprise,

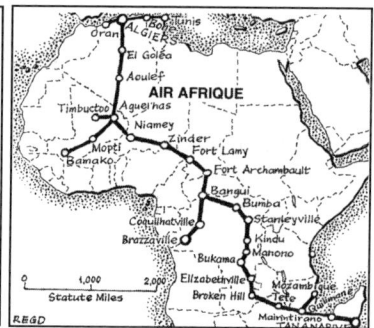

Before the Second World War, most of Africa had been colonized by European countries. Swift air service provided essential links with the homelands. These maps show the routes other than the British "Cape to Cairo" route to South Africa (see previous map).

the **New York, Rio and Buenos Aires Line (NYRBA)** had pioneered the east coast (Atlantic) route, also to Buenos Aires, and with superior equipment. Trippe swept this aside by purchasing NYRBA on 15 September 1930, having secured the precious U.S. mail contract, which was essential for viable operations. As well as consolidating a complete dominance of the airways of the whole of Latin America, Pan American inherited a fleet of fine 22-seat Consolidated Commodore flying boats to replace the sturdy but small Sikorsky S-38s, which, along with various

In the late 1920s, Pan American Airways encircled the Carribbean Sea with flying boats, because landing strips in Central America and in the islands were inadequate. The initial aircraft were Sikorsky S-38s, this one photographed at the Dinner Key base at Miami. (SI-89-12437)

Airline Adolescence

With the Sikorsky S-42, Pan American Airways made the world's first trans-ocean airline survey flight in 1935. (NASM-7A39330)

Fairchilds and Ford Tri-Motors, had hitherto comprised Trippe's aircraft inventory.

He had much wider ambitions. First he consolidated the Latin American route network, by introducing larger aircraft. The 40-seat Sikorsky S-40 was the first of the famous Pan American Clipper flying boats, introduced in 1931, and this was eclipsed by the Sikorsky S-42, introduced in 1934. It flew affluent Americans down to Rio and was used for important survey flights across both the Pacific and Atlantic Oceans. Even as he encircled South America, Juan Trippe dreamed of putting an aerial girdle around the earth; within a decade, he had almost achieved it. On 22 November 1935, a Pan American Martin 130, the *China Clipper*, left San Francisco, carrying mail across the Pacific Ocean, to arrive in Manila a week later. Passenger service started on 21 October 1936. Just as the colonial powers in the eastern hemisphere had had to prepare landing grounds and flying boat bases in remote areas of desert and jungle, Pan American had to construct transit stations at tiny isolated atolls.

One of the most famous flights in air transport history: Pan American's Martin 130 flying boat, the China Clipper, *opened Trans-Pacific air mail service in 1935, and passenger service in 1936. (SI-99-40767)*

In 1939, Pan American opened trans-Atlantic services, via Bermuda and the Azores, with 40-seat Boeing B-314s. (SI-77-5809)

The Atlantic was a bigger challenge. Half the size of the Pacific, the trans-ocean flight was nevertheless more hazardous, mainly because of the worse weather, especially in winter. The Martin's range was marginal on the 2,400-mile San Francisco-Honolulu segment of the Pacific route—all flights were limited to nine passengers, and sometimes the aircraft had to turn back—but it could not be risked at all on the 1,850-mile headwind-plagued Newfoundland-Ireland segment of the route from New York to London or Paris. Pan American's answer was a bigger and better flying boat; and the incomparable Boeing 314 opened the world's first sustained trans-Atlantic air service, by the northern route, on 20 May 1939, terminating at Marseilles, and flown via the Azores and Lisbon. The Boeing carried a ton of mail, and the northern route to Southampton opened on 24 June. Passenger service began to Marseilles and Southampton on 28 June and 8 July, respectively. The one-way fare was $375.00, which in today's equivalent currency would be about $8,000.00. Undoubtedly, air travel before the Second World War was available only to the rich or the specially privileged.

Twilight of the Flying Boats

At the outbreak of European hostilities, on 3 September 1939, the world had become a much smaller place. British travelers could reach Australia in a week, instead of three or four weeks by ship. Africa was within a few days of the governments in Europe, which ruled most of the continent. Except for K.L.M., the colonial airlines had relied on flying boats. Germany had had to surrender all its colonies, and **Deutsche Luft Hansa (D.L.H.)** had been handicapped in its route development by the political and social effects of the aftermath of the First World War. Its technical prowess was unmatched. With a fleet consisting mainly of the reliable Junkers-Ju 52/3m, its European route network was as big as those of all the other airlines put together. Germany had abandoned the use of lighter-than-air technology, even though the *Graf Zeppelin* dirigible airship had maintained a service to South America during the mid-1930s. But after the larger *Hindenburg* had provided a regular service across the North Atlantic during the summer of 1936, the tragic disaster at Lakehurst, New Jersey, on 6 May 1937, put an end to such aspirations.

The Junkers-Ju 52/3m became the most-used airliner in Europe before the Second World War. Not as fast, nor as big as the Douglas DC-3, it was nevertheless reliable and could use small airfields. (SI-91-13253)

The Hindenburg *was the finest airship ever built. However, its tragic disaster when it exploded in flames at Lakehurst, New Jersey, in 1937 marked the end of the era when lighter-than-air aircraft were thought to be the solution for long-distance air travel. (SI-98-15060)*

If the Hindenburg *was the end of one era, this airliner, the Focke-Wulf Fw 200 was the beginning of the next. In 1938 it made a round trip between Berlin and New York nonstop in both directions. This picture was taken on its triumphant return to Berlin. (SI-80-14393)*

But D.L.H. displayed many other initiatives to cross the Atlantic, for example by the use of depot ships, which acted as aircraft carriers and stationed in mid-ocean. Then, in another epochal event, on 10 August 1938, a Focke-Wulf Fw 200 Condor landplane flew nonstop from Berlin to New York (with two crews only) and three days later flew back again, also nonstop. This was a clear demonstration that the days of flying boat supremacy were numbered.

Australasian Development

One of the first countries in the world to establish scheduled air services was Australia. The reason for its success was simply a matter of geography. The vast emptiness of the "outback" precluded surface transport, which was near to being non-existent. All of Australia's large cities were (and still are) on the coast, and the outback population was sparse. To build an extensive network of roads and railways was neither economical nor practical. And so airlines flourished, as the construction of the infrastructure was cheap and the services could be tailored to the demand more efficiently. Tourism to the Barrier Reef and Ayers Rock was still half a century away.

One interesting feature "down under" was the development of airline service in New Guinea, the large island to the north of Australia. In the mid-1920s, gold was discovered there, but the sites were in dense jungles and in mountainous country. Native carriers took two weeks to trek through areas inhabited by wild tribesmen, and each man could carry only 50 lb. **Guinea Airways** came to the goldminers' aid, and with a fleet of metal-built Junkers aircraft, particularly the Junkers-G 31, hauled supplies, and even the components of huge gold-dredgers, to the isolated gold mines. Such was the effort of this early demonstration of the transport airplane as an aerial freighter that, during the peak years in the late 1920s, Guinea Airways was carrying more tonnage of air freight than the total of all the other airlines of the world.

In New Zealand, a few small companies operated sporadic flights in the early 1930s, but the first regular airline service, by **Air Travel (N.Z.)**, did not start until 31 December 1934. As in Australia, this service was made in an area where no railway existed. In due course, several small local companies were taken over by **Union Airways of New Zealand**, which emerged as the leading airline after starting a service on 15 January 1936 to link the North and South Islands. This British dominion was at the opposite side of the earth from its homeland, and following the precedent set by QANTAS, **Tasman Empire Airways** was formed in Auckland in April 1940, with the home country holding 50% of the stock, Australia 30%, and British Overseas Airways Corporation (B.O.A.C.), the newly formed British state airline, 20%. Trans-Tasman service began with Short flying boats, modified for the 1,200-mile crossing, on 30 April 1940.

Airlines in the Cape and in Cairo

In another extremity of Britain's far-flung empire, **Union Airways** (unconnected with the one of the same name in New Zealand) was founded in South Africa on 26 August 1929, mainly to carry mail between the main cities of that dominion. Except for Johannesburg, they too were on the coast, but railway connections were circuitous. Before the Second World War, Union's fleet consisted mainly of the sturdy Junkers all-metal aircraft, which stood up to the hot or cold, wet or dry, climates, and could cope with the primitive landing conditions, in the underdeveloped corners of the world.

The map of Africa before the Second World War was notable in that, with one exception, there was not a single truly independent country. Liberia was, effectively, a commercial outpost of the United States, with the Firestone tire company operating rubber plantations. Ethiopia had been annexed by Mussolini's Italy. Egypt was nominally independent, with a king of its own, but in almost every other sense it was a British protectorate. An indigenous African airline, **Misr Airwork**, was formed on 7 June 1932, with the Misr Bank of Cairo holding 85% of the capital and the British Airwork general aviation company holding 10%. It operated a route up the Nile Valley, to other points in the eastern Mediterranean, and was the first airline to carry pilgrims to Medina, for the Hajj pilgrimage, on special flights in 1937.

Foreign Rivalry in China

Asia was also largely dominated by colonial powers. The British Indian Empire—the "Jewel in the Crown"—then stretched from the Gulf of Oman to the Malayan Peninsula. It is now

Airline Adolescence

fragmented into six countries. The Dutch ruled over what is now Indonesia, and the French over Indo-China, now Vietnam. The British and French still had leased territories here and there, notably Hong Kong, and the Federated Malay States shared the peninsula with the Straits Settlements, including the great entrepot of trade, Singapore. The Philippines was a territory of the United States. According to the maps and political correctness, China was independent; but in commerce and trade, on which the country depended, it was a foreign shareholding, with several nations controlling every aspect of business, in mutually understood spheres of influence. This situation was reflected in the airlines, which China needed, as its railways were a collection of uncoordinated separate entities.

Surprisingly, the colonial nations did nothing to develop air transport in China, except, as early as 1920, two British companies made a few attempts, but were frustrated by the belligerent activities of the many local war-lords. In Peking (Beijing) the Emperor was powerless and amid much strife, the Kuomintang party, headed by Chiang Kai-shek, gained control during the late 1920s and established a seat of government in Nanking. This opened the way for foreign companies to make approaches to start airlines in China. The British were firmly based in Shanghai and Hong Kong, and traded through Treaty Ports all along the Yangtse River as far as Chungking in Szechwan; the French were influential in the southwest; but neither sought to expand their airline networks into the Chinese heartland. This was left to the United States and Germany, both with commercial acumen more sharply defined.

After much wrangling and negotiating, first off the mark was nominally Chinese. It was called the Shanghai-Chengtu Air Mail Line, and started on 8 July 1929, but it never flew west beyond

EURASIA 1931–1940

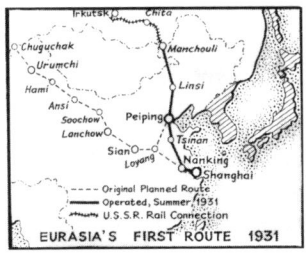
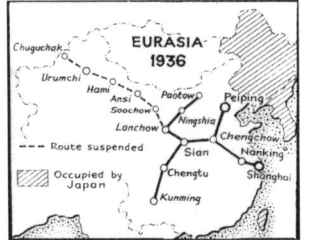
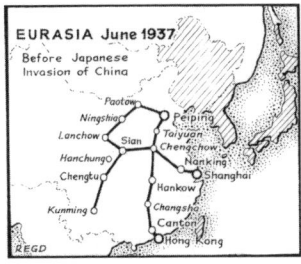
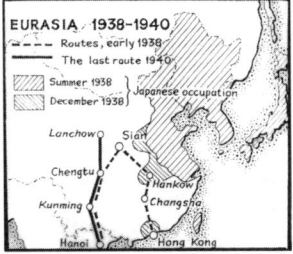

Before the Second World War, Deutsche Lufthansa established the ground infrastructure for a future route to the Far East by founding an airline in China. In these maps, the shaded areas show the extent of Japanese occupation.

CNAC 1933–1946

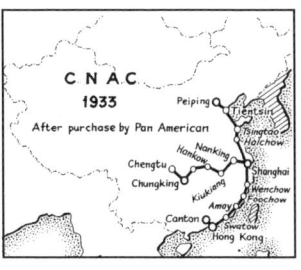

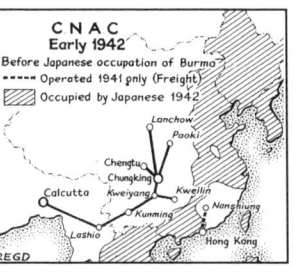
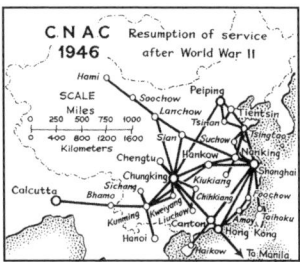

Pan American Airways bought a Curtiss-Wright Chinese subsidiary in 1933. When Japan invaded China, the airline was forced to move to Chungking, whence it provided essential service over the Himalayan "Hump" to India during the Second World War.

Nanking. It had been created to oppose the efforts being made by the United States Curtiss interests, which had, under the direction of Clement Keys, negotiated the creation of the **China National Aviation Corporation (C.N.A.C.)** on 12 April 1929. Frustrated by bureaucratic procrastination, Curtiss had had to set up **China Airways Federal** and started service on 21 October 1929 up the Yangtse River as far as Hankow, but had to terminate this on 15 December. Finally, a compromise was devised to satisfy all parties. A new C.N.A.C. was incorporated on 8 July 1930 and it proceeded to develop air routes between the main cities of China.

Meanwhile, enterprising German interests were persevering in the north. Facing economic and commercial difficulties because of unsympathetic international attitudes continuing after the enmities of the First World War, airline development and expansion had to be achieved in creative ways. A route from Berlin to the Far East via the traditional itinerary through the Near and Middle East, with the Indian Empire as a political barrier, was circumvented by an attempt to develop a service through the Soviet

One of C.N.A.C.'s four Douglas DC-2s flying over Shanghai's Whang-pu River in the mid-1930s. (NASM-9A08178)

Union. Eventually, however, on 21 February, the Chinesisch-Deutsche Luftverkehrs-gesellschaft, familiarly known as **Eurasia**, was formed and started service with the trusty old Junkers-F 13s on 1 June 1931. Its routes were mainly in the north of China, but competed to some extent with C.N.A.C.

The turning point in early Chinese air transport came on 31 March 1933, when **Pan American Airways** bought control of the Curtiss interests in C.N.A.C. Under the direction of William Langhorn Bond, the U.S. "chosen instrument" viewed a strong foothold in China as an essential link in the chain of bases that the visionary Juan Trippe needed to establish a trans-Pacific airline service. Bond was a good organizer, and quickly learned how to work with the Chinese. Pan American provided full support, including, in 1935, the supply of four Douglas DC-2 airliners, the most modern in the world. Even so, C.N.A.C. and Eurasia were strictly domestic airlines, although the former was connected directly with its American parent at Hong Kong. China's first international route was inaugurated on 10 July 1936 by a small airline, the South-Western Aviation Corporation, from Canton (Guangzhou) to Hanoi, French Indo-China.

Japan Spreads Its Wings

All these adventurous enterprises almost came to a halt in the summer of 1937. Japanese commercial expansion had been intensifying, and in 1931, it became aggressive, with Japan annexing Manchuria as a puppet protectorate. **Manshu Koko Kabushiki Kaisha (M.K.K.K.)** was formed on 18 February 1932 and within a few years built an efficient airline network throughout the mineral-rich and industrial Manchukuo, as Japan had renamed the Chinese northern province. Military units edged southwestward further into China, and "incidents" in August 1937 gave Japan a pretence for invasion. The country was in a state of war. The airlines suspended service and resumed only with difficulty, acting more as support for the Chinese government and armed service than as orthodox airlines.

In keeping with its growing industrial strength, and with economic and territorial ambitions in the western Pacific, Japan built up a network of air routes to maintain communications, much in the same way in which the European airlines had connected their empires. On 20 October 1928, the **Nihon Koku Yuso Kabushiki Kaisha (N.K.Y.K.K.) (Japan Air Transport Company)** was formed as a national airline, clearly with imperialist intentions. It took over other small airlines and proceeded to pioneer routes to Korea and Manchukuo, where a puppet government had been contrived and an airline established (see above). Direct service from Tokyo to Mukden (Shenyang) started on 28 December 1931, using Fokker F-VIIs and Universals. Many of these were built under license in Japan, as were some Dornier Wals for overseas routes, and some British Airspeed Envoys for the route to Manchukuo.

Japan was rapidly learning from the West. It started to build Douglas DC-2s, under license to Nakajima, and these replaced the Fokkers on the trunk route; while in Japan a lighted airway was established between Tokyo and Osaka. On 8 October 1935, service began from Fukuoka to Taipei—the Japanese had annexed Taiwan in 1910. With the invasion of China in 1937, a route to Shanghai opened on 2 October of that year, and to Peking (Beijing) in January 1938.

On 28 November 1938, **Dai Nippon Koku (D.N.K.) (Greater Japan Airlines)** was formed as a private company, superseding N.K.Y.K.K. This was reorganized as a joint stock company on 31 August 1939, and on 1 October took over all the remnants of small private enterprises, even that of Choichi Inouye, who had remained rigorously independent. By 1940, Japan's airline activity, measured in passenger-miles, was the fourth largest in the world; surpassed only by the United States, the Soviet Union, and, by a small margin, Australia.

Brazil Takes to the Air

Reference has already been made to the pioneer airlines in Latin America, when small companies boldly began flying commercially in Colombia, Mexico, Cuba, Guyana, Argentina, and Bolivia. Oddly, the largest Latin country, Brazil, and the one most in need, was almost the last to enter the airline lists. The first initiative was by the French. On 14 January 1925, the Latécoère Mission made an experimental flight, piloted by Paul Vachet and crew, in a Breguet 14 biplane, along the coastal ports, often stopping on beaches as there were no airfields.

The French lost the political game in Brazil, when the German Condor Syndikat started some experimental flights, called the *Linha da Lagôa*, on 3 February 1927, in the southernmost state, Rio Grande do Sul, in which much of the population had German roots, and many were German-speaking. This line developed to become the **Syndicato Condor**, which began operations on 1 July 1927, and soon expanded northward. Additionally, German immigrant interests founded **Viação Aérea Rio-Grandense (VARIG)**, which took over the *Linha* route and concentrated on local services within the southern State, starting on 22 June of the same year. These airlines used Junkers or Dornier equipment.

The French finally got under way on 14 November 1927, after the great patriot, Marcel Bouilloux-Lafont, had purchased the Lignes Latécoère and subsequently renamed it **Aéropostale**, and continued to expand French aeronautical influence all over South America.

Vigorous competition for Brazilian airline skies then ensued. In addition to the French and German airline empire-building, U.S. interests, in the shape of NYRBA, entered the fray. Promoted aggressively by Ralph O'Neill, and obliged to set up a Brazilian subsidiary, NYRBA got under way on 1 August 1929, with a shuttle service across the River Plate, and finally completed its route to Miami (not New York) on 25 February 1930. O'Neill introduced the fine Consolidated Commodore flying boats, but was outmaneuvered by the wily Juan Trippe of Pan American Airways, which absorbed NYRBA on 15 September, and changed the name to **Panair do Brasil** on 21 November of the same year.

Within Brazil, the only other airline of consequence before the Second World War was **Viação Aérea São Paulo (VASP)**, founded by the City, the State, and the Bank of the rapidly growing metropolis of São Paulo. It too used German aircraft, introducing the ubiquitous Junkers-Ju 52/3m to Brazilian air travelers.

Much importance was placed on the need for air services to Europe; for in spite of the influence of the United States, millions of South American immigrants were from Europe, and they still retained family and business connections across the south Atlantic. The competition between German and French interests was considerable. Aéropostale made possible the first services, starting on 1 March 1928, using fast packet-boats for the oceanic segments of the journey, as no aircraft of the early 1930s had the necessary range with payload. **Syndicato Condor,** in association with Deutsche Luft Hansa, provided a similar service on 22 March 1930, with their Dornier Wal flying boats linking up with German ocean liners, and then, from February 1934, with great ingenuity, stationing special depot ships in mid-Atlantic, for refueling the Wals. Additionally, the Germans persevered with lighter-than-air craft, the famous Zeppelin dirigible *Graf Zeppelin*, which, with increasing frequency, provided the world's most luxurious passenger service until the tragedy of the *Hindenburg* disaster in 1937.

Latin America Adopts Air Transport

While Brazilian progress was outstanding, other countries in South America were also adopting air transport, and the construction of new railroads almost ceased. Much of the activity was promoted or sponsored by foreign interests, other than those of the United States, mainly by France and Germany. Some countries, like Colombia, desperately needed air transport because their mountainous terrain created formidable, often insurmountable, challenges for the railroad and road builders. In Peru, for example, pioneer air services clung to the coast, while the far reaches of the country, to the upper Amazon basin, were served by Peruvian Navy floatplanes.

French interests were ambitiously promoted. **Aeroposta Argentina**, a subsidiary of Bouilloux-Lafont's organization, developed domestic routes from Buenos Aires from 13 January 1929, and other small companies emerged in the latter 1930s with sporadic efforts to supplement the comprehensive network of Argentine railroads. The French entrepreneur sought to extend routes along the west coast, but early in 1929 Chile started its own **Línea Aéropostal Santiago-Arica** (later to become LAN-Chile), in cooperation with Aéropostale. For a short while, the French company linked Arica with Tacna, across the border in Peru. Early in 1930, it also started another subsidiary in Venezuela, which branched out to Trinidad on 9 January 1931, by which time Aéropostale or its associated subsidiaries served nine countries in South America. Interestingly, the Venezuelan airline, **Línea Aeropostal Venezolana (L.A.V.)** has preserved that honored name to this day. But when Air France was created in 1933, French ambitions were curtailed to the South Atlantic.

The Germans were not only ambitious; they were motivated in an industrial-economic capacity. Having lost an overseas empire as the sequel to the First World War, much effort was directed toward commerce and trade, especially in South America, where many Germans had sought a new life. These expatriates

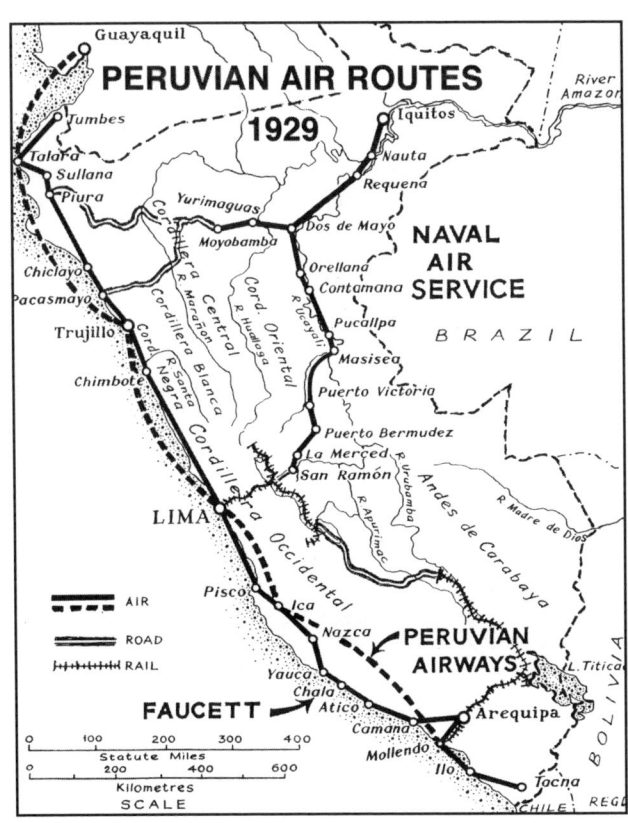

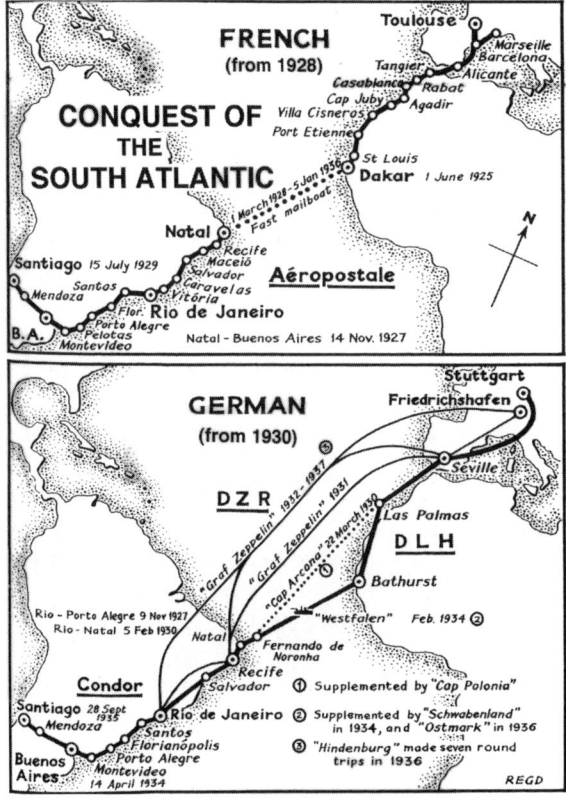

stimulated and sponsored airlines all over the continent. In addition to the initiatives in Colombia and Bolivia, and Brazil, footholds were gained in Peru, where an overseas division of the German flag carrier, **Deutsche Lufthansa Sucursal Perú**, began service on 24 May 1938, to complete an ingenious transcontinental route from Lima to Rio de Janeiro—Pacific to Atlantic, in cooperation with Bolivia's L.A.B. and Brazil's Syndicato Condor. Additionally, with Lufthansa's help, an airline was established in Ecuador, the **Sociedad Ecuatoriana de Transportes Aéreos (SEDTA)**, for domestic services within that country.

In Mexico, Pan American Airways's associate, Cía Mexicana de Aviación, had been in control of the airways since 1924. But in the mid-1930s, a flurry of small companies emerged, serving local communities in different states all over the country. Much credit should go to these entrepreneurs, notably Francisco Sarabia and his brother Jesús, Gordon Barry, "Peck" Woodside, Daniel Fort, Francisco Buch, Julio Zinzer, Alfredo Zarate, Luis Melgosa, Francisco Mancilla, and Carlos Panini. They were all short-lived, either because of insufficient funds or because they were taken over by other airlines. Of that happy band of true pioneers, Manuel Gonzales and Diaz Lombardo had founded **Aeronaves de México**, to start a service on 14 September from the Mexican capital to the embryo coastal resort Acapulco. Of all the pioneering companies, this one was to survive, when acquired by a former president of Mexico, Miguel Alemán, to challenge Pan Am's Mexicana for control of the Mexican skies.

Canada Catches Up

Canada seemed to have been left behind in the global development of air transport. The reasons were logical. There were two excellent transcontinental railroads (the United States had none); the population west of the Great Lakes was limited mainly to a few medium-sized cities; and both the climate and the terrain of most of the country favored only bush-type operations, which had no pretensions to qualify as regular air services. The earliest to carry regular air mail was **Laurentide Air Services**, serving the Rouyn gold fields, early in 1924. Other small companies operated sporadically, from the Gulf of St. Lawrence to the Yukon Territory, but none of these was sustained for more than a year or two.

Eventually, on 10 April 1937, **Trans Canada Airlines (T.C.A.)** was formed as a national flag-carrier, with the stock invested in the Canadian National Railways. Transcontinental service for passengers, after trial mail and freight flights, was inaugurated on 1 April 1939, from Montreal to Vancouver, using Lockheed L.10 Electras, with the larger L.14s added in 1940.

Air Transport in the Soviet Union

Often overlooked by aviation historians is the activity in European Russia and Asiatic Siberia, which, from 1919 onward, came under communist rule as the U.S.S.R, the Soviet Union. During the immediate years following the Bolshevik Revolution, the situation was chaotic, and the historic achievements of Igor Sikorsky before and during the First World War, were almost neglected. His Il'ya Muromets had demonstrated, with an epic flight from St Petersburg to Kiev in the summer of 1914, the world's first transport airplane. A few of the type were used in 1921, but regular commercial airline flights did not start until 1 May 1922, when the Soviet–German joint company **Deruluft** flew Fokker F.IIIs from Konigsberg to Moscow.

Air services across the vast Soviet territory, extending across no less than 11 time zones, gradually got under way. The main artery of surface communication was the famous Trans-Siberian Railway, but the journey from Moscow to Vladivostok, the outpost port on the Pacific, took about two weeks. The Soviet Union clearly needed an airline; but the political confrontation with the West handicapped technical development. Thus, resulting from the 1922 Treaty of Rapallo, technical support came from Germany in the shape of Junkers aircraft built under license in Moscow, and aeronautical influence on Soviet aircraft designers.

At first, in 1924, the state airline, **Dobrolot**, made exploratory flights in Central Asia, partly for propaganda reasons, but on 21 August 1928, a regular service began from Irkutsk, on the Trans-Sib Railway to Yakutsk, an isolated city in eastern Siberia, also serving some gold mines en route. Serious airline business started on 15 May 1929, from Moscow to Irkutsk, with Kalinin K-5 aircraft, and the trans-Siberian air route was completed on 15 December 1933.

Meanwhile, progress was being made under the auspices of the Zhukovsky Institute in Moscow, where a group of Russian designers was learning the trade. Prominent among them was Andrei Tupolev, whose ANT-9 tri-motor made some impressive demonstration flights around Europe during the late 1920s.

A decade later than in the United States, T.C.A. (now Air Canada) started transcontinental air service with Lockheed L.10 Electras in 1937. (Dunn)

The tri-motor ANT-9 prototype Krylya Sovyetov *(Soviet Wings) at Berlin Airport in July 1929, during Mikhail Gromov's second attention-gathering European tour. (SI-97-16607)*

These were piloted by Mikhail Gromov, one of many aviators who helped to create a nationwide airline system by their skilled, and often heroic, achievements. They demonstrated the advances made by flying four ANT-6 and one ANT-7 transport aircraft to the North Pole, arriving on 21 May 1937; while Valery Chkalov flew an ANT-25 nonstop across the Pole from Moscow to Vancouver, Washington State, on 20 June of the same year. Gromov did even better, on 14 July, landing at San Jacinto, California.

Such flights were intended to remind the rest of the world that Soviet aviation was in the ascendancy. Dobrolot was expanding steadily and reorganized as **Aeroflot**. By the mid-1930s, it had spread its wings to the far corners of the U.S.S.R., and to several major cities of western Europe. Working in parallel and in a far more demanding and challenging environment, **Aviaarktika,** founded at Krasnoyarsk on 1 September 1930, managed to bring the advantages of air travel and supply of goods by air to the remote villages of northern Siberia, beyond the Arctic Circle.

By the outbreak of the Second World War, the estimated output of the Soviet airlines, measured in passenger-kilometers flown, was equal to Germany's, and second only to the grand total of the United States.

Aborted Take-Off

As the 1930s came to an end, the world of air transport had changed in a manner that could never have been foreseen when the industry took its first faltering steps 20 years earlier. It had overcome the unreliability of piston engines. No longer did pilots and their passengers take a calculated risk with every flight. Improved design had increased the speed and comfort of modern airliners. Airlines had also improved the economics of their operations. Subsidy was still needed, but had been substantially reduced. Airlines were close to being able to stand on their own.

The London-Paris or New York-Washington trip was no longer an adventure; it was almost routine. No longer did passengers chew gum to alleviate the pressure in their ears or wear

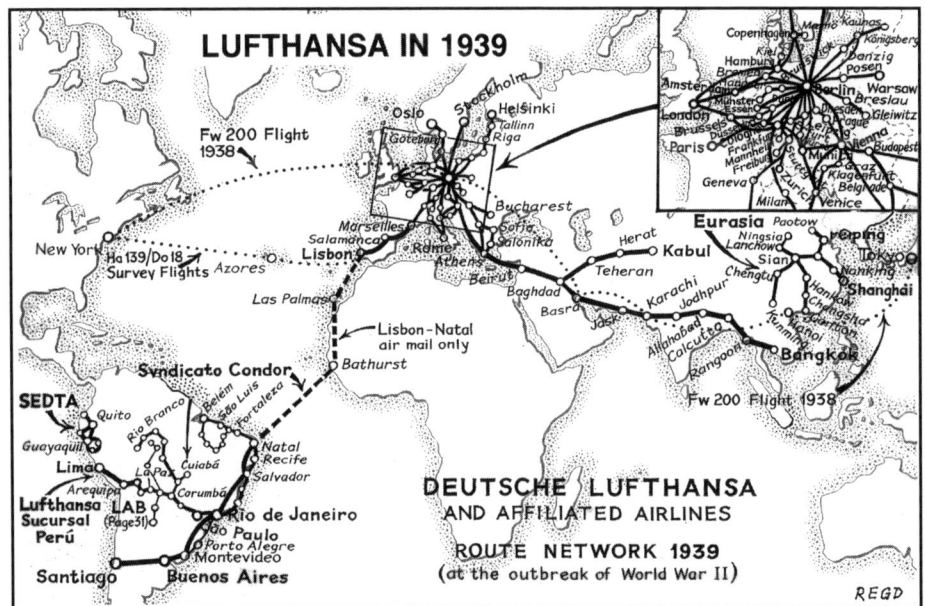

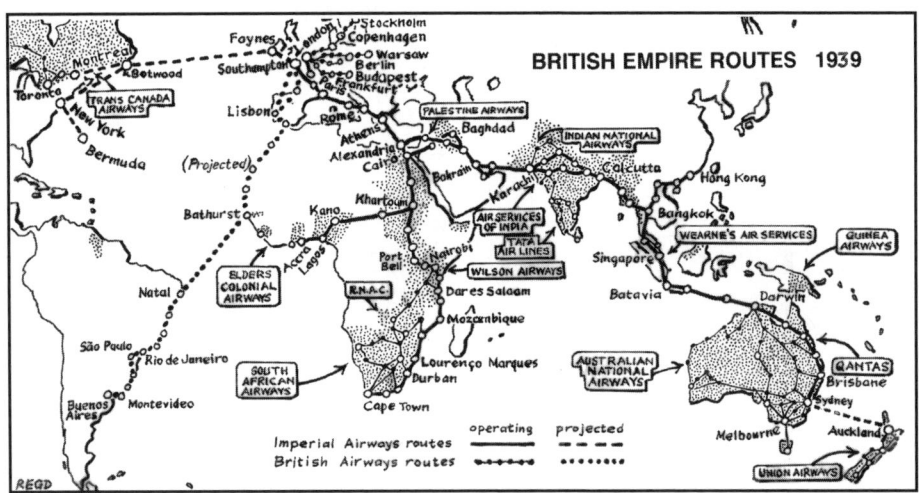

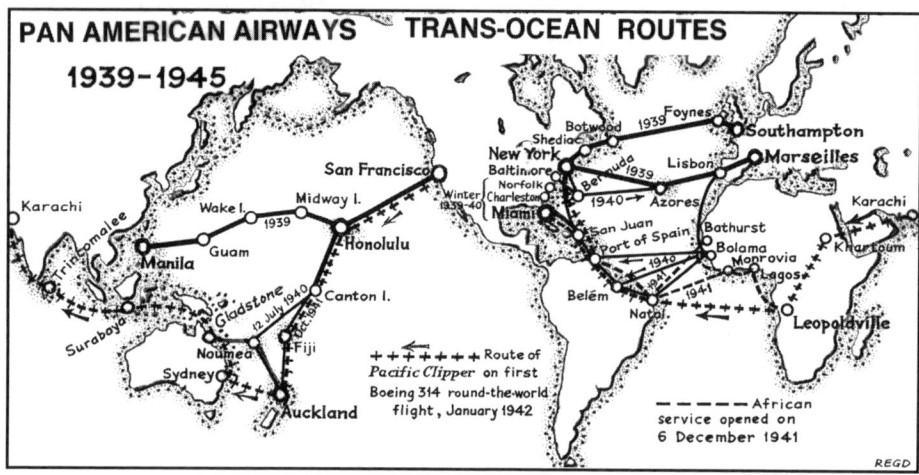

ear-plugs to obliterate the deafening cabin noise. The western United States was only a day away from the east; European nations could reach their far-flung empires in less than a week; the oceans had been conquered. Technological advances had been astonishing. All-metal tri-motors, then more efficient twins, had given confidence to air travelers who could afford the high fares. Four-engined flying boats, in the vanguard of long-distance flying, linked the six continents. Four-engined German and American landplanes were about to supersede them.

Even so, except for the introduction, in 1940, of the world's first pressurized airliner, the Boeing 307, air transport almost came to a standstill. Europe concentrated on war machines. Great Britain, especially, put aside promising airliner projects. The United States was comparatively isolated, while Pan American maintained limited services within a finely balanced neutral environment.

In Europe, the dreams of 1939 were shattered as it plunged into a Second World War. Great Britain's proud claim that it ruled "an empire upon which the sun never set" was, at the outbreak of war, echoed by the network of Imperial Airways. It was maintained sporadically during the six-year conflict, and survived as B.O.A.C. (See Chapter 3.) In contrast, Deutsche Lufthansa, on the threshold of worldwide technical pre-eminence, was devastated. But for the war, it could have demonstrated its Focke-Wulf, Heinkel, Junkers, and Dornier superiority throughout the world. Germany's airline would have to wait three decades for its rehabilitation, on the eve of the Jet Age.

Chapter 3: Wartime Hiatus—And Opportunity

Disruption of a World System

On 3 September 1939, when the world was poised to consolidate an inter-connecting airline system, the nations divided themselves into warring factions, extending far beyond the confines of Europe. By 1941, Europe was under the control of the Berlin–Rome Axis, with Great Britain hanging on precariously to its independence from fascist rule. Sweden, Switzerland, Ireland, and Portugal preserved an uneasy neutrality, with Lisbon a zone of contact between the airlines of the belligerents. The Irish flying-boat base at Foynes was, for the wartime years, the aerial crossroads of the world. South America was almost unaffected by the war, and air transport made progress there; but even so, German expansionist ambitions were frustrated.

Most intercontinental air services then were by flying boats, with Pan American setting the pace. Its fine Boeing 314s carried the U.S. flag across the Atlantic and the Pacific Oceans. When the Second World War broke out in Europe, Pan American had just begun scheduled services across the North Atlantic, and it continued to expand during the next two years. The British were trying to catch up with developments of its Short S-23 "Empire" boats; the French Latécoères were almost ready; and the Germans had served notice, with the Focke-Wulf Fw 200 Condor, that the years of flying-boat ascendancy were numbered.

A group of the largest U.S. airlines had sponsored the design of a large airliner as early as 1936. The result was the Douglas DC-4E, which United Air Lines put into experimental service, briefly, on 1 June 1939. This gave way to a smaller version, the DC-4, which first flew on 14 February 1942, by which time the United States was at war, and the aircraft was at first produced as the C-54 military transport.

Recognizing the imminent replacement of the time-honored flying boats with more efficient long-range landplanes, the British were taking steps to keep up with the international competition. In the summer of 1939, several designs were on the drawing boards at Fairey, Shorts, Miles, and others. But all were cancelled. Britain had to concentrate on building fighter aircraft to defend itself, and bombers to hit back. This was not the result of any agreement with the United States concerning shares of aircraft production. It was simply a matter of national necessity. The United States, on the other hand, with military commitments far from its shores, needed transport aircraft for logistical reasons.

Britain's frustration in its rivalry with the United States for technical leadership in piston-engined long-range airliner fleets may have accelerated the post-war development of the Jet Age. Had the British been able to match, or even come close to matching, in 1946, the American DC-4s or Constellations with their Fairey FC-1s or Short 14/38s, the need for the Comet might not have existed. The timing was the result of Great Britain's

One of the series of biplanes produced during the 1930s by de Havilland, the DH-89A Dragon Rapide was popular in the U.K., and sold well all over the world. (Davies)

desperation, born of the handicaps imposed on it by the devastations of the Second World War, to keep pace with the field.

The British Secure the Empire Links

The Second World War began only one month after the Royal Assent had been given to the British airlines to form a State Corporation, the **British Overseas Airways Corporation (B.O.A.C.)**, on 4 August 1939. This combined the former "chosen instrument," Imperial Airways, with the privately invested British Airways, but excluded a number of smaller domestic airlines whose operations were, on 5 May 1940, coordinated by the formation of the **Associated Airways Joint Committee (A.A.J.C.)**. When Britain declared war on 3 September 1939, all Imperial's services were suspended, but some were resumed briefly as long as it was safe to fly them.

By 1940, Great Britain was isolated, effectively separated from the homeland by the U-Boats on the Atlantic, Italian naval strength through the Mediterranean, and German armies across the whole of Europe. The last flying boat crossed Europe on 11 June 1940, the day after Italy declared war. The sea lanes were under constant threat. The need for the national airline to maintain contact with the Empire was vital.

B.O.A.C. began to operate from Poole Harbour, in Dorset, as its base at Southampton was under constant attack by the Luftwaffe. It also flew landplanes from Bristol, as London was under even more destructive bombing. De Havilland D.H.91 Albatrosses started service to Lisbon on 4 June, and the Short S-23 boats on 19 June. Three months later, the boats began a link to West Africa, and these were supplemented on 26 May 1941 by Boeing 314s, which the airline had managed to acquire from the U.S. manufacturer, and by the Short S-26 G-Class improved "Empire" boats. Connections were made from Accra and Lagos across Africa to Khartoum, whence the old Imperial routes were restored to the Middle East, and across southern Arabia to India and beyond.

In 1939, Imperial Airways introduced the de Havilland DH-91 Albatross. Its clean aerodynamics were in complete contrast with the design of the Handley Page HP-42 of 1931. It was fast but built entirely of wood, and only a few were built. (Davies)

This operation was greatly assisted by **Pan American Airways**, as the result of an agreement forged in London between Prime Minister Churchill and Pan Am's Juan Trippe in June 1941. The U.S. airline undertook the modernization of the trans-Africa route, from dirt strips to paved runways (mainly with the newly developed P.S.P. [Pressed Steel Plate]), and contributed considerably to the British war effort by providing the necessary infrastructure for a vital logistics supply route from the industrial strength of the United States across the Atlantic to General Montgomery's forces defending Cairo.

This route was then developed, enterprisingly, into what became known as the Horseshoe Route (because of its geographical shape), to connect the whole of the British Enpire in the eastern hemisphere. Curiously, in southern Africa, German Junkers Ju 52 tri-motors and the fast Ju 86s were in the service of the British, as they were commandeered for the Allied cause by the Defence Department from South African Airways.

This addition to the airline map did not last long. When Japan declared war on the United States and the Allies on 7 December 1941—the notorious "date that will live in infamy"—all flights beyond Calcutta were immediately at risk. More than that, several S.23s were lost to Japanese dive-bombing after the last service to Singapore on 3 February 1942. The British commercial airlines then resorted to an unusual solution to maintain an air route to Australia. On 10–11 July 1943, the Australian **QANTAS Empire Airways** inaugurated the world's longest nonstop air route, one that would keep that record for many years. From Colombo, Ceylon (now Sri Lanka), to Perth, West Australia, it was 3,513 miles long, and was flown by Consolidated PBY-5 Catalina flying boats. The journey took more than 30 hours and became known as the Double Sunrise Service. This was supplemented on 30 October 1943 by Consolidated Liberator landplanes, terminating at Exmouth Gulf, 600 miles north of Perth. These trans-Indian Ocean services, which could never carry much payload, except important mail and packages and very important personages, ended on 8 April 1946.

Deutsche Lufthansa Withdraws into Its Shell

In September 1939, the German national airline, **Deutsche Lufthansa A.G. (D.L.H.)**, was on the verge of regaining a leading role in the world of intercontinental airlines. It had maintained the route to South America, and with the Focke-Wulf Fw 200 Condor, it had an airliner that could dispense with the depot ships that had acted as commercial mid-ocean refueling stops. This record-breaking aircraft was ready to open landplane service to North America, but was frustrated by political barriers. Though technically neutral, the United States, under the leadership of President Roosevelt, was not about to welcome aircraft

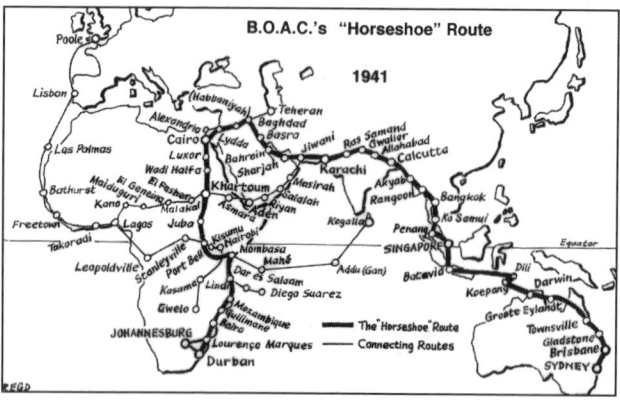

During the Second World War, before Japan occupied southeast Asia, B.O.A.C. continued to serve the British Empire with its C-Class "Empire" flying boats.

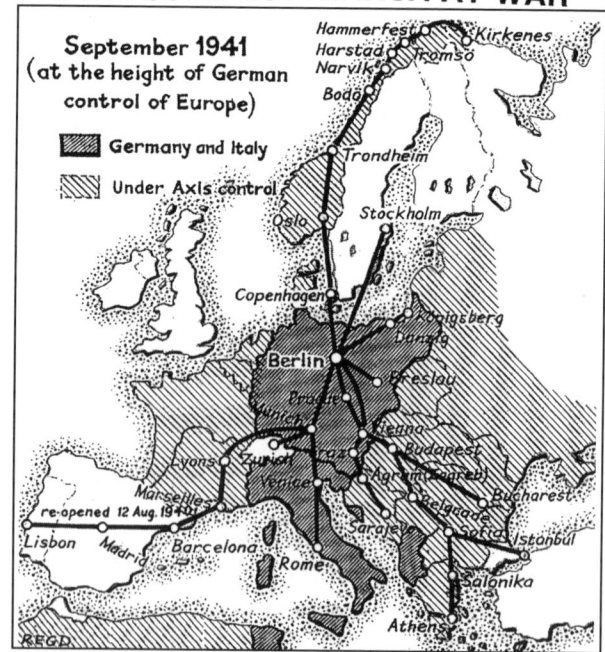

During most of the Second World War, Deutsche Lufthansa could carry important passengers to northern Norway and to Portugal and the Mediterranean.

on a regular basis with the swastika symbol of Nazi oppression on their tails. The veteran Junkers-Ju 52/3m was ubiquitous throughout the airways of Europe and, in the summer of 1939, had opened service to the far east, terminating at Bangkok—a failed effort due to the outbreak of war. The 200-mph 40-seat four-engined Junkers-Ju 90 was in service on the main routes of Europe, and the fine four-engined Heinkel He-116 was due for delivery in 1940. Deutsche Lufthansa was in good shape.

All routes beyond the Mediterranean and those to the west of the western frontier of Germany were immediately suspended in 1939. When Germany over-ran most of Europe in 1940, Lufthansa was able to extend its route network to the farthest north of Norway and to neutral Lisbon, through Vichy France and friendly Spain. The exigencies of war, as in Britain, demanded that passenger lists included only military, political, or administrative personnel. Many flights were quasi-military support missions. But the Lufthansa fleet, mainly *Tante Ju* Junkers tri-motors, did a fine job throughout the conflict.

As the Allies gradually closed in from both sides to squeeze the Third Reich into eventual submission, Lufthansa continued to maintain its vital communications role. As late as April 1945, by which time the American and British armies were closing in on Berlin from the west and the Soviet Red Army was advancing rapidly from the east, it was still possible for an important passenger to fly from Tromso, north of the Arctic Circle, to Lisbon via Berlin, Munich, and Barcelona. But the airline headquarters was transferred to Warnemunde, on the Baltic on 22 April then to Flensburg, in Schleswig-Holstein, on 30 April. The last flights into this last bastion of Nazi Germany were a Fw 200 from Oslo on 3 May and a Ju 52/3m from Aalborg on 5 May. Canadian troops entered Flensburg on 6 May, and Germany surrendered the next day. D.L.H. was officially liquidated on 1 January 1951, and final settlements were made in 1965. It was the end of a career in airline leadership and innovation that, in technical merit, was unequalled. It had led the way in landplane development—it had abandoned the idea of flying boats as a long-term solution to intercontinental travel—and only the American innovation of pressurization, pioneered by the Boeing 307, excelled German aeronautical technology.

Japan Builds an Airline Empire

Almost in parallel with the expansion of German airline dominance in Europe, the Japanese had expanded its domain over the Pacific Rim of eastern Asia. When Japan entered the Second World War on 7 September 1941, its airlines were ready to overwhelm the countries of southeast Asia and the islands of the western Pacific. In addition to the continuance of the services of **Dai Nippon Koku,** military transport services were developed by the Japanese Army and the Japanese Navy. The army also created a secondary unit, strategically based at Singapore, Nanpo Koku Yosubo (Southern Air Transport Command), which provided air services throughout the former Dutch East Indies (now Indonesia). For its part, the navy served the same countries, and also flew as far afield as Kwajalein and Rabaul.

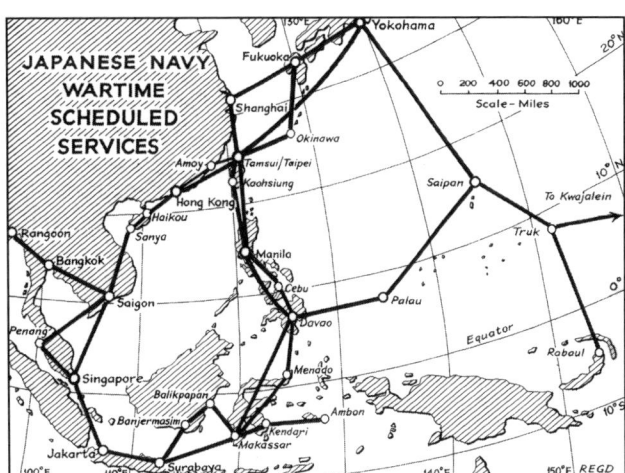

When Japan enforced the Second World War, it quickly over-ran south-east Asia and established an airline network.

All activities ended dramatically on 6 August 1945, when the atomic bomb laid waste the city of Hiroshima. On 24 August, all civil flying was banned, and the Second World War came mercifully to its end on 2 September. Dai Nippon resumed domestic services on 14 September, and the army and the navy—at last—cooperated. But on 9 October 1945, all services ceased by order of the Supreme Commander Allied Powers, General Douglas MacArthur. The last flight, Sapporo to Matsudo, near Tokyo, was on 31 October, when Dai Nippon Koku was liquidated.

The United States Matures

When the United States was plunged into the Second World War on 7 December 1941, the airlines had already made preparations. United Air Lines had begun to train airline personnel at Oakland in October 1940. Pan American had constructed airfields in British territories in the Caribbean, as part of the Lend-Lease program. T.W.A. established its Eagle Nest flight training center at Albuquerque in June 1941. Pan Am also formed Atlantic Airways on 21 June, to ferry aircraft to the European war zones, formed Pan American Africa on 15 July and Pan American Air Ferries on 24 July. The Africa operation was especially notable, as in effect the airline was participating directly in the war before the United States was. As mentioned above, it upgraded Imperial's trans-Africa chain of airfields, and opened its own service to Khartoum on 21 October 1941.

The entire domestic airline industry was also mobilized immediately. First off the mark was Northeast Airlines, which in January 1942 surveyed a trans-Atlantic route via Greenland and Iceland, to reach Stornoway, Scotland, on 4 July 1942. Northwest Airlines had begun service to Alaska on 29 March, soon to be joined by Western Airlines and, on 15 May, by United Air Lines. T.W.A. complemented Pan American across the Atlantic with its four-engined Boeing 307 Stratoliner landplanes. To fly the longer ranges, the pressurization equipment was exchanged for extra fuel tankage. Eastern Air Lines's first overseas flight was to Trinidad on 1 May, extending it to South America, and on 1 June

1944, across the South Atlantic, from Natal to west Africa via Ascension Island. With Douglas C-54s (military DC-4s), United joined Pan Am on the vital supply routes across the Pacific on 23 September 1942. With VS-44 flying boats, **American Export Airlines (A.E.A.)** joined Pan Am across the Atlantic on 26 May. American Airlines supplemented the other airlines everywhere, to Alaska, Greenland, Africa, and China. Back in the U.S., **Pennsylvania-Central Airlines (P.C.A.)**, **Chicago & Southern Airlines (C.&S.)**, and **Delta Air Lines** all contributed to the war effort by transferring most of their fleets to the U.S. Army for troop transports, with extensive training programs, and by modifying thousands of military aircraft after delivery from the manufacturers.

Eastern's South Atlantic route had introduced the Curtiss C-46, a twin-engined aircraft, and because of the exigencies of war, its testing period was curtailed, but it carried twice as much payload as the veteran Douglas DC-3 and it became the workhorse of the India-China supply route across the southeastern Himalayas, the notorious "Hump," which claimed scores of aircraft fatalities.

The U.S. domestic airlines emerged from the war with much accumulated experience. Although their fleets were robbed by the military, they flew in a wartime seller's market, achieving load factors exceeding 80%. Much to Pan American's annoyance, their outstanding contribution to the war effort was rewarded by generous overseas route awards, their domestic route networks were augmented, and their post-war fleets, unlike Europe's, were modern, most of them only a year or less off the production lines. Europe's airline fleets were, by comparison, military conversions or pre-war time-expired types. The U.S.A. was ready and able to dominate the post-war world of air transport.

SUMMARY OF U.S. DOMESTIC TRUNK AIRLINES DURING IMMEDIATE POST-WAR PERIOD
(Those underscored still operating in 2010)

The "Big Four"	
<u>American Airlines</u>	Formerly American Airways, reorganized under new name, 11 Apr. 34
<u>United Air Lines</u>	Reorganized 1934, renamed United Airlines, 1974
Trans World Airlines	Formerly Transcontinental & Western; reorganized on 17 Apr. 34
Eastern Air Lines	Formerly Eastern Air Transport; reorganized under new name, 31 Apr. 34
Other Trunk Airlines	
Northwest Airlines	Formerly Northwest Airways; reorganized under new name, 16 Apr. 34; merged with Delta Air Lines, 2009
Western Airlines	Formerly Western Air Express, renamed briefly as General Air Lines, 8 May – 29 Dec 34; renamed 17 Apr. 41. (Inland Air Lines operated as autonomous division until 9 Apr. 52)
<u>Delta Air Lines</u>	Formerly Delta Air Service / Delta Air Corporation; renamed, July 34
National Airlines	Formerly National Airline System; renamed during Second World War
Northeast Airlines	Formerly Boston-Maine Airways; renamed 19 Nov 40
Braniff Airways	Formerly Paul R. Braniff, Inc., reorganized 3 Nov 30
Colonial Airlines	Formerly Colonial Division of American Airlines; renamed 1 May 42
Chicago & Southern Air Lines	Formerly Pacific Seaboard Air Lines; renamed 1 Feb 35
<u>Continental Air Lines</u>	Formerly Varney Air Transport; renamed 1 July 37
Pennsylvania-Central Airlines	Formed by merger of Pennsylvania Airlines and Central Airlines, 1 Nov 36; name changed to Capital Airlines 21 Apr 48
Mid-Continent Airlines	Formerly Hanford's Tri-State Airlines; renamed Aug 38
Other	
Wilmington-Catalina Airline	Single route sold by Western Air Express. 1932. Renamed Catalina Air Transport 22 July 41

Chapter 4: Post-War Recovery

A New Era Begins

Toward the end of 1945, the world gradually returned to its senses. In Europe, the former enemy countries, mainly Germany and Great Britain, began massive programs of reconstruction of their devastated cities. The Soviet Union mourned the loss of 20 million people, military and civilian, and tried to restore its weakened centralized economy. Japan was on its knees, to be rehabilitated by a visionary and compassionate approach by the American occupying force to a return to normal life. China was relieved of the oppression of Japanese rule, but was immediately submerged in a civil war that would, in 1949, result in a massive change of government, from the last of the war lords to a communist regime that would, for a few years, ally itself with the Soviet Union.

Compared to Europe and Asia, the United States was fortunate. It emerged from the Second World War as the world's dominant industrial power. It did not have the problem of reconstruction, as it had never been bombed. The mighty industrial machine, which had superbly refined the methods of mass production, slowed down, but the apparatus of manufacturing strength remained, unharmed. Before the war, the U.S.A. was matching, but not exceeding, the combined economic strengths of the European countries and their supportive overseas empires. Now there was a new global environment. On the one hand, east of the Atlantic, a desperate process of rehabilitation sapped the potential national stamina; west of the Atlantic, the U.S.A. was able to review its new-found strength, and to build on it. Great Britain and its Empire, which had formerly ruled the Seven Seas, and had been the major influence in steering the world's economy, had to face the ignominy of having to devalue the British pound sterling, and the American dollar became the most desirable trading currency in the global markets.

In no individual industry was this change of fortune more apparent than in the manufacture of commercial transport aircraft. The Germans, Italians, and Japanese were out of business. The French factories went dormant for a few years. The British, as noted above, had concentrated on building fighter and bomber aircraft, to the exclusion of almost everything else, and a switch to building airliners could not be achieved overnight. Reputable manufacturers such as Avro, Bristol, Vickers-Armstrong, and Armstrong-Whitworth soon discovered that converting military types to carry passengers in acceptable comfort was not as easy as it looked. As for Short Brothers, the age of flying boats was in its twilight years. The British aircraft industry tried to "make do" with bomber conversions, but several years would elapse before it could even begin to match the design strength, production quality, and marketing know-how of the Americans.

Avro had built a transport aircraft, the York, and it converted its famous Lancaster bomber to the Lancastrian, while Handley Page produced the Hermes, but these were woefully inadequate and clumsy, compared even to the American Douglas DC-4, now reconverted from its wartime C-54 role as the backbone of the U.S. armed forces logistics effort. Vickers supplied the short-haul Viking, used extensively by British European Airways (see below) but it was no better than the venerable Douglas DC-3, large numbers of military versions of which had already been produced in several huge factories and could be purchased cheaply from war-surplus stocks. The thousands of DC-3s, in fact, were a factor in curtailing any potential exports that Britain might have developed in the immediate post-war years, with useful aircraft such as the "ugly duckling" Bristol Freighter/Wayfarer. The Avro Tudor, at first thought to be a potential competitor, was woefully inadequate; and two disastrous tragedies, in which two Tudors disappeared without a trace across the Atlantic Ocean, were a death sentence. Meanwhile, the Lockheed Constellation, a 300-mph trans-Atlantic pressurized American airliner, was setting the pace everywhere in the world.

Great Britain entered the post-war years with civil conversions of military types. The Avro York, tail-wheeled and unpressurized, served B.O.A.C. until it was able to acquire new airliners from the U.S.A. and new generations of turboprops and jets. (Davies)

As noted above, the age of the flying boat was ending, which was unlucky for excellent manufacturers such as Shorts and Saunders-Roe. During the war, military versions of the Short boats, the S.25 Sunderlands, had been produced in large numbers (720 v. 216 American Consolidated Coronados); but although the British intercontinental airline kept the Sandringham conversions in service for a few post-war years, they were doomed to rapid retirement. Saunders-Roe produced a very large flying boat, the Princess, but this was (like other predecessor giants such as the Dornier Do-X and the Hughes H-4 "Spruce Goose") a failure.

War-time development of airfields led to vast improvement over pre-war grass or dirt fields. Before the war in Europe, only six cities had airfields with hard runways, all in the north, where the depredations of permafrost transformed unpaved areas into marshes with the spring snow-melt. In the States, Ford's innovative concrete at Dearborn and New York's Floyd Bennett Field had been followed in 1940 by La Guardia in New York and the National Airport in Washington. Elsewhere in the world, the

British European Airways (B.E.A.) was faced with operating Douglas DC-3s (ex-U.S. Air Force C-47s) and even ex-D.L.H. Junkers-Ju 52s until Vickers produced its Vikings. The geodetic construction was based on that of the Wellington bomber. (Davies)

The Douglas DC-4 became the military C-54 but was quickly converted back to commercial use. Spurred on by Lockheed's L-049 Constellation, Douglas had to produce the pressurized DC-6 series, of which the DC-6B was acknowledged to be the thoroughbred. (NASM-A-3854)

bombers had demanded a solid base for their heavy wheel loads. The war ended with a world network of airfields that soon became airports.

United States Dominance

In contrast with the European airlines that were struggling to find their feet again, the airlines of the United States never had it so good. By the standards of the day, their output was prodigious. In the first full post-war year, passenger traffic doubled, from six million boardings in 1945 to 12 million in 1946. The five leading trunk airlines were each boarding more than a million each every year. **American Airlines**, **United Air Lines**, and **T.W.A.** controlled the transcontinental skies; **Eastern Air Lines** dominated the area east of the Mississippi; and **Capital Airlines**, which emerged in the northeast, was a substantial competitor. Meanwhile, under Juan Trippe's brilliant leadership, **Pan American Airways** dominated intercontinental air routes. The airlines were supported by a steady supply of new efficient airliners. The Lockheed Constellation, sponsored mainly by Howard Hughes's T.W.A., had set a fast pace. Douglas had to match its speed and pressurized comfort by extending the fuselage length of the DC-4 and pressurizing it, to produce the thoroughbred DC-6B; and the two manufacturers competed intensely during the next decade with improved variants, ultimately reaching their respective zeniths with the Douglas DC-7C "Seven Seas" and the Lockheed L-1649A Starliner, which made their debuts in the mid-1950s, just as the Jet Age was about to render them obsolescent.

An Atlantic Highway

Nowhere in the world was the dramatic post-war giant stride in air transport expansion more evident than on the North Atlantic route. Engine and airframe technology had produced aircraft that were quite capable of flying across the oceans. At first, the route from America to Europe had been via land bases in northeast Canada, Greenland, and Iceland; but these "stepping stones" were gradually dispensed with. The flying boats, mainly those of Pan American, continued in service, via Foynes, a village at the mouth of the Shannon River in Ireland, which had been, for six wartime years, an aerial crossroads. The delivery of bomber aircraft, first to reinforce the British war effort then to establish the U.S. Air Force in wartime Europe, had become a constant flow. As observed above, the American industrial strength had the necessary production capability to supply the airline world with trans-Atlantic flying equipment.

The expansion of airline traffic across the North Atlantic during the immediate post-war years was little short of phenomenal.

THE FIRST AIRLINES ON THE NORTH ATLANTIC ROUTE
*Dates of first scheduled passenger services
(not including 'Polar' or 'Arctic' routes)*

	AIRLINE	DATE	ROUTE	AIRCRAFT
1.	Pan American Airways	8 July 1939	New York-Southampton, via Bermuda, Lisbon	Boeing 314
2.	B.O.A.C.	4 May 1941[1]	Montreal-Blackpool, via Gander	Liberator
		1 July 1946	London-New York, via Shannon, Gander	L.049
3.	American Export Airlines[2]	26 May 1942	New York-Foynes, via Gander	VS-44
		24 Oct 1945	New York-Hurn, via Gander, Shannon	DC-4
4.	T.C.A.	July 1943[3]	Montreal-London, via Goose Bay, Reykjavik	Lancaster
		1 May 1947	Montreal-London, via Reykjavik	DC-4M
5.	T.W.A.	5 Feb 1946	New York-London, via Gander, Shannon	L.049
6.	K.L.M.	21 May 1946	Amsterdam-New York, via Prestwick, Gander	DC-4
7.	Air France	24 June 1946	Paris-New York, via Shannon, Gander	L.049
8.	S.A.S.	16 Sept 1946[4]	Stockholm/Copenhagen-New York, via Prestwick, Gander	DC-4
9.	SABENA	4 June 1947	Brussels-New York, via Shannon, Gander	DC-4
10.	Loftleidir	25 Aug 1948[1]	Copenhagen-New York, via Reykjavik, Gander	DC-4
11.	Swissair	29 April 1949	Zürich-New York, via Geneva, Shannon, Gander	DC-4
12.	L.A.I.[5]	13 July 1950	Rome-New York, via Shannon, Gander	DC-6[6]
13.	El Al	16 May 1951	Tel Aviv-New York, via European points, London, Shannon, Gander	L.749
14.	Iberia	2 Sept 1954	Madrid-New York	L.1049E
15.	Lufthansa	8 June 1955	Hamburg-New York, via Dusseldorf, Shannon	L.1049G
16.	QANTAS	14 Jan 1958	New York-London	L.1049G
17.	Aerlinte Eireann	28 April 1958	Shannon-New York	L 1049H[7]
18.	B.W.I.A.	29 April 1960	Trinidad-London, via Barbados, New York	Britannia[8] 312
19.	Air India International	14 May 1960	Bombay-New York, via Beirut, London	B.707-420
20.	Pakistan International	5 May 1961	Karachi-New York, via London	B.707-320[9]

Notes:
1. 'Return Ferry Service'.
2. Became American Overseas Airlines; acquired by P.A.A. 25 Sept 1950.
3. Wartime V.I.P. service.
4. Earlier Boeing B.17 flights by SILA not on regular schedule.
5. Merged with Alitalia August 1957.
6. Leased from FAMA.
7. Leased from Seaboard & Western.
8. Leased from B.O.A.C.
9. Leased from P.A.A.
10. Service suspended 1950-2.

The *Hindenburg* disaster of 1937 had laid to rest any hopes of lighter-than-air transport, quite apart from the complete impracticality of expansion beyond one or two services a day. Pan American Airways had already led the way in 1939 with its inaugural Boeing 314 flying boat services, which it gallantly maintained during the wartime years. But Deutsche Lufthansa had demonstrated the efficiency of the long-range landplane with the Focke-Wulf Condor flight in 1938, and Douglas had built the C-54 military transport, based on the DC-4 commercial design promoted by the leading U.S. airlines. The British had stepped up to the mark in 1939, with several promising designs, but these had to be abandoned. But for the demanding priorities of the war, Great Britain and Germany might have had the production capability to supply the airline world with trans-Atlantic landplanes, and France also had developed trans-Atlantic flying boats.

Transcending all these efforts, however, was the dramatic nonstop transcontinental flight in 1944 of the Lockheed Constellation, piloted by T.W.A.'s Howard Hughes and Jack Frye. This new airliner was pressurized, thus offering better comfort for the passengers and comparative serenity for the pilots; and it could fly faster and farther than any other airliner. Historian Peter Brooks shrewdly described it as "America's Secret Weapon." The metaphor was completely apt. Its superiority over the competition was such that Douglas had to produce a pressurized version of the DC-4, the DC-6, on a crash program, to match Lockheed. And the world's leading airline nations rushed to put the "Connie," as it soon became affectionately known, into service as soon as they could.

Within two years of the cessation of hostilities, nine airlines were operating scheduled services between European points and the eastern seaboard of North America. Eight of these were to New York, the other, by the Canadian **T.C.A.**, to Montreal. Three were United States flag carriers, and the British B.O.A.C. was joined by the national airlines of the Netherlands, France, the Scandinavian countries, and Belgium. The Americans, B.O.A.C., and Air France were able to operate the impressive and elegant Lockheed Constellations, but the unpressurized Douglas DC-4 and the Canadian-built, Rolls-Royce-engined DC-4M also provided much-needed seat capacity as the demand for air service began to challenge that for ocean-going ships. The post-war progress of the North Atlantic Air Highway is illustrated in the chart on the previous page.

Global Control

To avoid confrontations and disputes, regulations controlling navigation and territorial sovereignty had been ironed out at an epochal conference in Chicago, held between 1 November and 7 December 1944. The foundations were laid for the establishment of the **International Civil Aviation Organization (I.C.A.O.)**, with its head office in Montreal. To this day, this agency has maintained cooperation throughout an airline world that has been, all too often, disrupted by many local and regional wars. To their credit, the airlines have always been a symbol of peaceful pursuit. In all the wars, they were invariably the last business enterprises to stop before the fighting started, and the first to show up when the carnage ended.

I.C.A.O. was an organization of governments and government agencies. The airlines also wanted their own independent group, although many of their goals, such as safety measures and accounting procedures, were much the same. But the **International Air Transport Association (IATA)**, formed on 19 April 1945, became identified mainly for its control of international air fares. Many were the debates about the ethics of such control. The defendants stressed that, without such supervision, the state airlines or their "chosen instruments" could dominate the world's airways, and smaller nations, including many that had gained their post-colonial independence, would have no chance to a share in the lucrative markets. They were probably right at the time. Pan American Airways dominated the world's air routes, with the best equipment and the best organizational strength. The IATA opponents maintained that it was a price-fixing agency, and that there should be an "open skies" policy. Most of the latter group argued from strength, but they did not prevail for many years. Some of the opponents sought ways to evade the IATA restrictions and—though this was not the intention—laid the groundwork for the creation of the world's charter airlines and the inclusive tour business.

The Chicago Conference had established the foundation for what became known as the Five Freedoms of the Air. These allowed all airlines to have overflying, transit, and emergency or refueling rights, and seldom were these ever disputed. The Third and Fourth Freedoms, invariably taken together, allowed airlines to set down or to pick up passengers in foreign countries. Customarily, two countries would mutually agree to exchange rights reciprocally, following a precedent of the conditions agreed: the Bermuda Agreement between the United States and Great Britain, signed on 11 February 1946 and approved by the U.S. Attorney General on 18 June, became a model for future bilateral agreements.

One bone of contention was the Fifth Freedom, which allows an airline to provide full services between two countries other than its own; another was cabotage rights, which would allow an airline of one nation to operate a domestic service wholly within the frontiers of another nation. Such rights were jealously guarded and, in a few cases only, invariably agreed to only by small countries that had no airline of their own. To this day, no foreign airline, except by a U.S. subsidiary, can operate between two points within the United States.

The First Bargain Fares

One small country and one entrepreneur deserve great credit for their ingenuity in circumventing the restrictive shackles of the Fifth Freedom. In Iceland, **Loftleidir**, one of its small airlines that operated domestically (the country was only just building its first roads) and to Europe, took a huge gamble. Following the initiative of its president, Alfred Eliasson, the airline opened a service to New York on 25 August 1948. At first it was not successful and suspended operations between 1950 and 1952.

Great credit must be given to the Icelandic airline Loftleidir, which seized the opportunity during the early 1950s to introduce trans-Atlantic fares that were cheaper than the cartel-style IATA's. The DC-4s were unpressurized and stopped in Iceland, but passengers appreciated a bargain. (NASM-00132334)

But the germ of an idea had been planted. On 12 June 1953, in partnership with the Norwegian airline, Braathens S.A.F.E., Loftleidir started a service between New York and European points, via Reykjavik, Iceland's capital, at lower fares than the IATA standard agreed by all its members. On 1 January 1953, Eliasson lowered them still further. He had broken no law, political or IATA-promoted. Loftleidir had simply combined Third and Fourth Freedom rights, neatly evading the Fifth Freedom requirements, to create a "Sixth Freedom" device. Passengers simply bought two tickets and flew on two separately numbered flights. Such initiative was the harbinger of wide-spread thought and decision making throughout the airline world, including IATA's, which had introduced tourist-class fares on the North Atlantic route on 1 May 1952. But Loftleidir's were still cheaper, and the little Icelandic airline had made its mark and gained a place in airline history.

Airline Consortia

Interestingly, Loftleidir's main competition was derived from a source other than IATA per se, and one which had also set a precedent. The three countries of Scandinavia, Sweden, Norway,

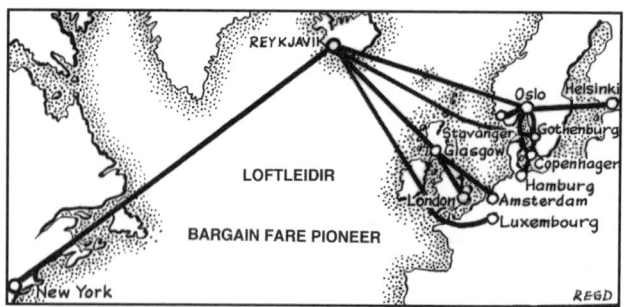

This map illustrates the geographical advantage that enabled Loftleidir to offer one-stop service from the U.S.A. to western Europe.

and Denmark, had come to an agreement to form a consortium. They had realized that, in the post-war European world, even without Germany, and with a weakened Italy, each would face strong competition from its southern neighbors. The three pre-war national airlines therefore amalgamated, on 31 July 1946, into the **Scandinavian Airline System (S.A.S.)**, with shares proportional to population: three-sevenths to Sweden, two-sevenths each to Norway and Denmark. The arrangement was successful and has survived, with S.A.S. making valuable innovations, especially in the operation of routes in the Polar regions that have benefitted the world of airlines as a whole.

Such an initiative, promoted by three countries that were far from impoverished, should have been an example for others to follow. But nationalistic motives seemed to over-rule economic necessity. In Africa, there were consortia that certainly met the conditions and gained the advantages of partnership. The British African territories formed **East African Airways Corporation (E.A.A.C.)** on 1 January 1946. Similarly, Southern Rhodesia (now Zimbabwe), Northern Rhodesia (now Zambia), and Nyasaland (now Malawi) formed **Central African Airways (C.A.A.)** on 1 June 1946. The end of the British colonial empire resulted in an instinctive desire for individual national identities, and these consortia broke up into their separate state-sponsored airlines, as did the French west African colonies after forming **Air Afrique**. (See Chapter 48.)

Surge in Commercial Airliner Development

During the post-war decade from 1945 to 1955, tremendous advances were made in the development of what could be called thoroughbred airliners. The power of the piston engines had increased substantially, and their reliability had reached unprecedented levels. The American Pratt & Whitney and Curtiss-Wright manufacturers, together with, mainly, the British Rolls-Royce and Bristol companies, kept up a steady competitive pace of increasing horsepower that permitted the airframe manufacturers to build bigger and better airliners. The engine companies also matched the increases in power with improvements in efficiency, so that the airliners could fly longer ranges with full payloads.

One notable advance was made by the Wright company, which, in the early 1950s, built the R-3400, which produced 3,400 horsepower. This permitted Douglas, with its DC-7 series, and Lockheed, with its Super Constellations, to develop bigger and better versions of their well-established types. Boeing, with its Model 377 Stratocruiser, also reentered the commercial market. The increment in horsepower was welcomed, but the problems of the turbo-compound design were not. The additional power was gained by recycling unburned exhaust gases through the engine, but this involved design complications that resulted in more frequent engine shut-downs and increased maintenance costs. Nevertheless, the resultant extra productivity of the later designs, the "stretched" DC-7s and Constellations, was put to good use, in particular with nonstop transcontinental services in the United States, and with what, in terms of airline prestige, was the ultimate goal: nonstop trans-Atlantic service from the U.S. east coast to the major capitals of Europe. New York-London and New York-Paris became the "Blue Riband" routes of the airline world.

The domination of American technology was complete. British engines such as the famous Rolls-Royce Merlin and the Bristol Hercules generated only about 1,750 horsepower; and the airframes that they powered could not match the thoroughbred products of Lockheed, Douglas, Boeing, and Convair. The state-owned British Overseas Airways Corporation (B.O.A.C.) was obliged to buy American airliners, as the British manufacturers, which had built superb military aircraft during the Second World War, were unable to adjust to the needs of the post-war airlines. Commercial variants of well-tried bomber designs, such as the Handley Page Halton (Halifax conversion) or the Avro Lancastrian (Lancaster conversion) were demonstrably inadequate. The Bristol Brabazon, potentially a 100-seat giant airliner, was a failure. Handley Page produced a new type, the Hermes, which was not up to B.O.A.C.'s standard requirements, and Avro's Tudor went through several stages of redesign, none of them successful, and was out of the running after some mysterious disappearances over the Atlantic. Nevertheless, the British authorities had planned for a future that would aim to emulate the United States in civil aircraft production.

During this post-war period, other countries could not contribute. The defeated nations, Germany, Italy, and Japan, were denied the opportunity to make use of their aeronautical knowledge, while the French industry was still struggling to regain its severely depleted strength.

What Happened to the Propeller?

Throughout the early decades of airline history, from the 1920s to the 1950s, there had been constant advances in airframe design, by improved aerodynamics, refined structures, and the use of stronger metallic alloys. In parallel, dramatic improvements in engine technology provided ever-increasing power, reliability, and economy. Another element in technological development was the design of the propeller, an essential prerequisite to complement the increasing engine power.

Even as early as the mid-1920s, wooden propellers, laminated for strength, had been superseded by metal-bladed ones, notably the Hamilton-Standard types that, from 1926, were fitted to such early transport airplanes as the Fords and the Fokkers. These were, at first, adjustable on the ground, for coarse or fine pitch, according to the climate or weather conditions. In 1933, Hamilton introduced the variable-pitch propeller, which permitted the pilot to alter the pitch while in flight: fine pitch for take-off, coarse pitch for cruise. A further refinement was introduced in 1935. The constant-speed propeller's blade angle changed automatically with the variation in propeller speed (r.p.m.), and this was put to good use in long-distance missions. This innovation was perfected in 1937 by the hydromatic propeller, using oil pressure, rather than the mechanically operated counter-weights in the hub of the blades. The system was more responsive, and easier for the pilot to feather the propeller in the case of an engine failure. Another method to achieve the constant-speed advantage was the Curtiss electric propeller in 1936, which used magnets in the hub instead of oil pressure.

During the Second World War, some British aircraft were fitted with Dowty-Rotol constant-speed propellers that were made of laminated wood, combined with the use of composite materials, the highly refined structural products of the emerging plastics industry. After the war, a further elaborate refinement was reversible pitch, for slowing down the airliner after landing. The advent of jet power, which was marked by the absence of propellers, did not, however, mean an end to their use. An alternative technology—turbo-prop(eller) or prop-jet—combined the power of a turbine engine mainly to drive a propeller, with only residual thrust. Starting with the British Viscount in 1953—which made its debut a year after the Comet, the world's first jet airliner—this method of propulsion, compared to piston engines, was found to be economical in fuel consumption and maintenance. But propeller speed was limited to avoid self-destructive supersonic speed at the blade tips.

As the Jet Age developed, propellers were at first disdained by much of the traveling public, who felt that they were somehow old-fashioned. But the use of turboprops, especially for very short-haul operations such as commuter networks, continued to remain an essential segment of the world's airline industry.

Piston-Engined Postscript

The technological revolution that swept across the airline industry during the 1950s did not result in the complete replacement of all the airliners that were still equipped with piston engines. The jet and turboprop aircraft at first made their mark in the main centers of industry in the well-developed countries. Some nations, however, were still in the process of full development. In Brazil, for example, most of the country, larger than the U.S. 48 States, with inadequate railroads, still awaited the benefits of air transport. To service the small communities throughout the land, where airfields were usually short dirt strips, the veteran DC-3s were welcome.

Many airlines were formed by inventive entrepreneurs to supplement the established VARIG, Cruzeiro do Sul, and VASP intercity networks. **Redes Estaduais Aéreas, Ltda. (REAL)**, in fact, vigorously promoted by Linneu Gomez, expanded everywhere until the construction of a connecting road, and before its demise and acquisition by VARIG, its number of boarding passengers, often to fly only a few miles, climbed to rank tenth in the world.

Chapter 5: Worldwide Expansion

Technological Revolution and a Global Industry

The disruption of the world's airline system because of the Second World War has been described in earlier chapters. Operational losses were, however, compensated for by dramatic and far-reaching technical advances in airliner construction, mainly in the U.S., to open up new horizons for air transport.

British stop-gap measures with pre-war aircraft and modified bomber designs were joined by new projects (see Chapter 4) that resulted from the recommendations of the wartime visionary Brabazon Committees. These were of five specific types. The first, the 100-seat Brabazon, was for trans-Atlantic traffic, expected to increase exponentially—a correct forecast—but the aircraft failed. The second resulted in the turboprop Vickers Viscount, as a short-medium-haul workhorse to replace the DC-3. With more than 450 built, this was Britain's most successful airliner. For this specification, the Airspeed Ambassador, an excellent piston-engined airliner, was outperformed by the Viscount, and only 20 were built. The third type specification, later subdivided into the M.R.E. (Medium-range Empire) and L.R.E. (Long-range Empire), was for the turboprop Bristol Britannia, which could have been a great success, had it not been for delays caused by engine problems—"flame-outs"—and the International Air Transport Association (IATA) denial of flexible passenger tariffs for turboprops against jets. Fourth on the list was for a fast jet, for mail and perhaps a few expensive seats, and which was developed by de Havilland as the Comet. Finally, for the feeder-line market, the Miles Marathon was a disaster, but the de Havilland Dove was a great success, with sales exceeding 600. Another British post-war success was the Bristol 170 Freighter (Wayfarer in its passenger version), which, among its cargo-lift roles, pioneered car ferry services across the English Channel. With more aggressive marketing, the 170 could have sold several hundreds.

Clairvoyant in much of their content though the Brabazon recommendations were, and partially successful in their eventual evolution, the British industry never reached its full potential. The designs were as good as, if not better than, the Americans' but the mass production capability was inadequate. Even worse were the shortcomings in product support. Airlines had problems with spares supply while manufacturers' advice and expertise with operating airliner fleets was often lacking. Britain could have benefitted too from greater cooperation between manufacturers, operators, airlines, and government, to give momentum to a coordinated industry. In contrast, in France, the Sud-Est Caravelle, which pioneered the fuselage-mounted airliner design, was promoted as a national effort. In Britain, the production and marketing of the Airco (de Havilland–Hawker Siddeley) Trident, the world's first short-haul tri-jet, for example, was handicapped by product mismanagement and a lack of industry partnership. Britain was outmaneuvered in the creation of the European Airbus. But for Sir Arnold Hall's efforts to retain Hawker-Siddeley as a subcontractor, to build the Airbus wings (which it still does), the British commercial aircraft manufacturing industry would have collapsed.

The first target of the airlines was the North Atlantic route, linking the world's major industrial concentrations, the United States and Europe. They constituted the necessary basis of spending power to support air travel, which, in the post-war period, was expensive. Operating costs of even the best airliners were still at a level that required first-class fares to be charged to the public so that the airlines could stand a chance of breaking even. The expansion spread by leaps and bounds far beyond the Pacific and North Atlantic Oceans, where Pan American had been the aerial trail-blazer in 1935 and 1939, respectively. The South and Central Atlantic routes now beckoned, and the routes from Europe to Asia and Australasia were revitalized. Of special significance was the additional participation of more and more airlines, not only from Europe, but also from the more affluent countries in other continents.

Measured by the number of passengers boarded, mainly in DC-3s, REAL ranked, briefly, as the tenth largest airline in the world.

The South and Central Atlantic

The South Atlantic crossing (geographically the Central Atlantic) was shorter than the North. Consequently, during the 1930s, the range problem was solved by lighter-than-air dirigible airships, in which the German company Zeppelin excelled. The French had responded with fast ships to cover the over-ocean segment of the journey to South America. The German **Deutsche Luft Hansa (D.L.H.)** solved the range problem by stationing special depot ships in the middle of the ocean, from which the Dornier Wal flying boats could refuel. In partnership, D.L.H. and **Air France** maintained a mail-only weekly schedule during the latter 1930s, with the French introducing the long-range Farman 2200 in 1938—recognizing the superiority of landplanes. It was left to the Italian airline, **Linee Aeree Transcontinentali Italiane (LATI)**, to start the first passenger service from Europe to South America, on 21 December 1939. Savoia Marchetti S.M. 83A 16-seat landplanes were modified with extra tankage and reduced payload capacity to cross the ocean. A few hundred passengers were carried during the limited service life, which was abruptly terminated on 11 December 1941, when Italy entered the Second World War.

Pan American and **T.W.A.** flew thousands of trans-Atlantic flights during the war. A route across the North Atlantic was established by constructing modern airfields in Newfoundland, Labrador, Greenland, and Iceland. The Azores was an important mid-Atlantic hub, and Foynes, in southwest Ireland, became an essential trans-Atlantic aerial hub. Across the South Atlantic, a refueling airfield stop was established on the remote—and hitherto barren—British possession, Ascension Island.

When the war ended, the European airlines, especially, were anxious to resume commercial contacts with South America. First to enter post-war service was **British South American Airways (B.S.A.A.)**, with Avro Yorks and Lancastrians, on 15 March 1946. The British had hitherto stood aloof from South American aviation, even though they had strong commercial and trading ties with Argentina. A consortium of shipping lines had formed British Latin American Airlines (BLAIR) in January 1944, changing the name to B.S.A.A. in January 1944.

Next was the Dutch **K.L.M.**, with a route to its Caribbean colony, Curaçao, on 10 April 1946. Two weeks later, on 27 April, **Panair do Brasil** became the third South Atlantic operator, taking over the responsibility from its then parent company, Pan American Airways. This was the first time that any airline outside Europe and North America had inaugurated a trans-ocean route or any intercontinental route, except for the Australian QANTAS and the Indian Transcontinental Airways, as pre-war Imperial Airways partners. Brazil had already demonstrated considerable enterprise in building up an extensive domestic airline network, and it was now showing its flag overseas. **Air France** resumed on 24 June 1946, and Argentina's **Flota Aérea Mercante Argentina (FAMA)** joined the fray on 22 September. Within a few years, nine airlines were to compete for the South Atlantic traffic.

A new element appeared in the pattern of trunk route arteries between Europe and South America. The southern termini had always been the big cities on the eastern seaboard: Rio de Janeiro, Buenos Aires, and the fast-growing metropolis São Paulo. But after the war, other countries south of the Rio Grande emerged as destinations in their own right, with claims for direct service. Thus, by the early 1950s, airlines such as K.L.M. began to serve Mexico via Canada and the U.S.A. **B.S.A.A.** had served the British islands of the Caribbean from 2 September 1947. Caracas, Venezuela, became a Central Atlantic terminus for **Iberia** and **Alitalia**; while from the American side, the Mexico's **Aerovías Guest**, **Cubana**, the Colombian **AVIANCA**, and the Venezuelan **L.A.V.**, had earlier provided the Europeans with some indigenous Latin American competition. The DC-4 could make trans-Atlantic flights, stopping at Bermuda, or the Azores, or both.

Trans-Polar Routes

By the early 1950s, yet another choice of major trans-Atlantic routes became available through the initiative of an airline that was already noted for its ingenuity. The **Scandinavian Airline System (S.A.S.)** had been formed as an international corporate consortium, so as to draw upon the resources of three medium-sized European countries to match those of larger ones. After technical analysis of Arctic climate and meteorological conditions, and some enterprising survey flights to determine special navigational techniques, S.A.S. opened a Douglas DC-6B route from Copenhagen to Los Angeles on 15 November 1954. It was

Post-War South Atlantic Airlines
Dates of First Post-War Passenger Scheduled Services

1	British South American	15 Mar 46	6	S.A.S.	22 Feb 47
2	Panair do Brasil	Apr 46	7	Alitalia	26 May 48
3	Air France	24 Jun 46	8	Swissair	27 May 54
4	K.L.M.	6 Aug 46	9	Lufthansa	15 Aug 56
5	Iberia/FAMA (Argentina)	22 Sep 46			

Post-War Central Atlantic Services

Date	Airline	Route	Aircraft
10 April 1946	K.L.M.	Amsterdam-Curacao, via Dakar Paramaribo-Port of Spain	C-54
2 Sept 1947	B.S.A.A.	London-Azores-Bermuda-Kingston-Barranquilla-Lima-Santiago	Lancastrian
Jan 1948	Guest	Mexico City-Madrid, via Miami, Bermuda, Azores, Lisbon	DC-4
14 April 1949	Cubana	Havana-Madrid, via Bermuda, Azores, Lisbon	DC-4
17 April 1949	Iberia	Madrid-Caracas, via Las Palmas, Sal Island, San Juan	DC-4
Mar 1950	AVIANCA	Bogota-Hamburg, via Barranquilla, Bermuda, Azores, Lisbon, Madrid, Paris, Frankfurt	DC-4
3 July 1950	Alitalia	Rome-Caracas, via Milan, Lisbon, Sal Island	DC-4
22 Jan 1953	Air France	Paris-Bogota, via Lisbon, Azores, Fort de France, Caracas	L.749
Oct 1953	L.A.V.	Caracas-Rome, via Azores, Lisbon, Madrid	L.749
3 Feb 1962	C.S.A.	Prague-Prestwick-New York*-Havana	Britannia

*Technical stop only

the first direct service to the west coast of North America, and was made possible by stopping at Sondre Stromfjord, in Greenland, and at Winnipeg, Manitoba. This "great circle" route was much shorter to California than by the previous itinerary via Europe and the North American east coast, thence connecting with a transcontinental service. And after a few years, the improved versions of the Douglas and Lockheed mainliners enabled other airlines to start "Polar" services. The two U.S. flag carriers, Pan American and T.W.A., added their weight with direct California-London flights in 1957.

S.A.S. pioneered yet another long-distance intercontinental route group, this time by flying almost directly over the North Pole (Sondre Stromfjord's latitude was close to the Arctic Circle, but not exactly Polar). Anchorage, Alaska, was about half-way to Tokyo, which, by the latter 1950s, was reestablishing itself as one of the world's great cities, with memories of the Second World War receding in the world of commerce—and soon in the world of tourism. There were already signs that, led by Japan, eastern Asia would become a major industrial and commercial world region, and therefore a good generator of airline traffic. On 14 February 1957, S.A.S. chalked up another historic first, when a DC-7C opened service from Copenhagen to Tokyo via Anchorage. This innovative route was almost (see below) the last of several great achievements of the piston-engined era. Chronologically, they occurred after the first airline jet services began from 1952 to 1954. But the pioneering de Havilland Comet had to "go back to the drawing board" because of a structural deficiency revealed by two tragic crashes. In October 1958, the reintroduction of North Atlantic jet services revolutionized the course of air transport development (see Chapter 6).

POLAR SERVICES (EUROPE-CALIFORNIA)

Date	Airline	Route	Aircraft
15 Nov 1954	S.A.S.	Copenhagen-Los Angeles, via Sondre Stromfjord, Winnipeg	DC-6B
3 June 1955	C.P.A.	Vancouver-Amsterdam, via Sondre Stromfjord	DC-6B
11 Sept 1957	Pan Am	Los Angeles-London, via San Francisco	DC-7C
2 Oct 1957	T.W.A.	Los Angeles-London, via San Francisco	L.1649A
20 Oct 1960	B.O.A.C.	London-Los Angeles	B.707

POLAR SERVICES (EUROPE-FAR EAST)

Date	Airline	Route	Aircraft
24 Feb 1957	S.A.S.	Copenhagen-Tokyo, via Anchorage	DC-7C
10 April 1958	Air France	Paris-Tokyo, via Anchorage	L.1649A
1 Nov 1958	K.L.M.	Amsterdam-Biak, via Anchorage, Tokyo	DC-7C
7 June 1961	J.A.L.	Tokyo-London, via Anchorage	DC-8

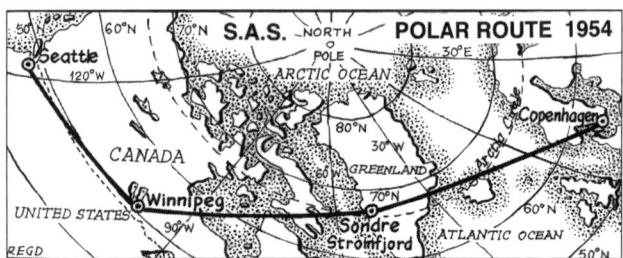

S.A.S.'s route to the American west coast was not strictly "polar," but it did cross the Arctic Circle.

The Silk Road to the Far East

The three European countries that, before the Second World War had pioneered airline service to southern and eastern Asia, quickly went back to business soon after hostilities ended in Europe and Japan's wartime occupation of its "Greater Southeast Asia Co-Prosperity Sphere" ended. With its traditional flair, the Dutch **K.L.M.** was first off the mark with passenger service. On 28 November 1945, it resumed to Batavia, Dutch East Indies—soon to be renamed Jakarta, when independence came to Indonesia. The old reliable Douglas C-54 was used at first, to be supplemented by the Lockheed Constellation. K.L.M. extended its eastern service to Tokyo on 4 December 1951 and to Sydney on 7 December of that year.

Two days after the Dutch inaugural, **B.O.A.C.**, which had opened mail-only service on 31 May 1945, went one better with a through service to Sydney, with a branch to Hong Kong on 24 August 1946. The equipment was the converted Lancaster bomber, the Lancastrian, whose performance—2½ days to Sydney—was impressive. But the standard of comfort was not. Passengers sat sideways along the left side of the narrow fuselage, and the capacity was usually limited to 12 seats. With few amenities and little opportunity for sleep, the patrons needed as much time to recover from the journey as from the flight itself. Except for the Atlantic, many of the British routes in the post-war recovery period were still flown by flying boats. Short Sandringhams, converted from the wartime Sunderlands, opened B.O.A.C.'s first service to Japan in March 1948 with the terminal at Iwakuni, on the beautiful Inland Sea. Service to Tokyo began in August 1948.

Completing the trio of pre-war airlines that hastened to regain a foothold in Asia was **Air France**. Douglas DC-4 service to Saigon, still French Indo-China, started on 18 June 1946. This was extended to Noumea, New Caledonia, on 21 September 1949 and to Tokyo on 24 November 1952 with Constellations. The first new airline to participate in this important intercontinental trans-Asian route, and also the first non-European or

The Avro Lancastrian, converted from the famous Lancaster bomber, flew from England to Australia in 2½ days. Passengers sat sideways along the cabin, with little chance to sleep. (Davies)

Worldwide Expansion

American airline to do so, was **Philippine Air Lines (P.A.L.)** which, with DC-4s leased from Transocean Airlines, began service from Manila to Madrid on 3 May 1947. But this enterprising development terminated in 30 March 1954, when the airline had to tighten its financial belt. Symbolizing its country's realization of independence from U.S. territorial status, P.A.L. enjoyed some years of pride. In addition to extending to London on 24 July 1948, it had also, with DC-6s, opened a trans-Pacific route to San Francisco on 31 July 1946. It was the first Asian airline to achieve intercontinental status. Thereafter, this traditional trunk air route, the "Silk Road," became one of the world's great highways. Pan American Airways, with its prestigious Flights PA1 and PA2, entered the fray on 17 June 1947, as part of its round-the-world service, and by the early 1950s, a dozen airlines were competing for the traffic.

Trans-Saharan African Routes

Until the latter 1960s, almost the entire continent of Africa was under colonial rule. Only Liberia, which had been founded with the support and instigation of the United States (but was commercially dependent on it because of its rubber industry), and Ethiopia, which had suffered Italian colonial rule for a few pre-war years, had enjoyed political independence since the "Struggle for Africa" in the latter years of the 18th century. As summarized in Chapter 2, the colonialist empires regarded air transport as an essential element to maintain communications and travel between the overseas territories and the homelands in Europe.

When the Second World War ended, and as in the case of the trans-Asian "Silk Road," the nations reestablished African connections. Britain's **B.O.A.C.** had inherited the Imperial Airways "Cape-to-Cairo" pioneering flying boat service. This had, in pre-war days, been more of a glorious adventure for the affluent passengers, with pleasant overnight or transit stops at places on the Nile, in the safari country of East Africa, or at the Victoria Falls. With the technical developments accelerated by wartime necessity, and with the continent moving from colonial infancy into early nation-conscious adolescence, the manner of the transport links, and the character of the passengers, began to change. Colonial administrators were joined by businessmen, and early tourists were joined by African negotiators as the colonies moved toward independence.

The airlines followed the flag—and still carried it proudly. The first to establish post-war services from Europe to Africa was the Belgian **SABENA**. It had participated in wartime logistics services for the Allies, and on 8 July 1945, it consolidated these as a public airline service from Brussels to Leopoldville (now Kinshasa), the capital of what was still the Belgian Congo. The equipment was the Lockheed Model 18 Lodestar, which had been introduced into Africa during the war. B.O.A.C followed in the same way. On 16 April 1944, it had taken over, from the Royal Air Force, the West African service to Lagos, Nigeria, still using flying boats. Then, on 10 November 1945, it resumed the traditional trunk route to Johannesburg via Egypt and east Africa, using Avro Yorks. Not the most handsome of transport airplanes, nor the most comfortable, they were complemented by Short Solent flying boats on 4 May 1948. On 7 November 1950, Handley Page Hermes landplanes provided a modest, but short-lived, improvement.

Remarkably, four more airlines had joined the trans-Saharan contingent by the end of 1946, a bare 18 months after the end of hostilities. In June, the Swedish airline, SILA (which was to become part of S.A.S.) flew from Stockholm to Addis Ababa, using ex-wartime converted Boeing B-17 bombers. On 8 July, **South African Airways** flew to London with Douglas DC-4s. On 18 July, **Air France** resumed to Equatorial Africa, with DC-3s, extending to Madagascar on 3 December; and on 31 December, the Portuguese airline **T.A.P.**, also with DC-3s, established the first commercial air link with its African colonies. By the end of 1952, all the other leading European airlines, except Lufthansa (which had to reestablish itself in a peacetime world), were participating in the African market

With the exception of South Africa, a thriving British dominion, rich in minerals, including gold and diamonds, Africa had never had an indigenous airline. When the Second World War ended, the entire continent, except, as previously noted, Liberia and Ethiopia, was still under European colonial rule. In many ways, ranked among all the continents, Africa had been something of a poor relation, with the Europeans and their airlines interested only in serving their overseas administrations, businesses, affluent safari hunters, and armed forces. Except for Johannesburg, not a single city south of the Mediterranean hinterland could be regarded as a viable destination in its own right. But a new infrastructure had been established, partly because of wartime necessity. The tide of nationalism among the host of small embryo countries was to take a few years to grow in strength and momentum, but the need for efficient communications and travel for people, mail, and cargo was, during the 1950s, growing at an alarming rate. Railroad construction had lost its momentum. Promising lines drawn hopefully on the map remained broken. The ambitious Cape-to-Cairo railway was never completed. Road construction was sporadic and inadequate. The continent was thus poised for further airline development on a grand scale; and in May 1952, this is what happened, in a manner that was to be one of the most far-reaching single events in the history of air transport.

Part Two: The First Jet Age

Chapter 6: The First Jets and Turboprops

New Source of Power

The technological revolution that was created by the invention of the jet engine represented the single biggest advance in aeronautical science since the Wright brothers demonstrated, in 1903, the basic principles of lift and control that would enable mankind to fly. Before the Second World War, airplanes had achieved the leadership over the lighter-than-air airships, whose fate was sealed with the disastrous explosion of the *Hindenburg* at Lakehurst, New Jersey, on 6 May 1937. True, by the late 1930s, the 100-mph sport and military aircraft of the 1920s had been developed into 150-mph transports and bombers. And after the war, refinements had increased the speed to 300 mph, and the airliners had progressed from the ubiquitous 21-seat DC-3s to the elegant 90-seat pressurized Constellations. But a plateau of maximum technical achievement seemed to have been reached. Engines of about 3,000 horsepower seemed to be the ultimate practical limit for propulsion; and the prospects for airliners with more than 100 seats seemed to be remote, because of the need for a multiplicity of engines to provide the necessary power. Also, during the early post-war decades, the operating costs of the piston-engined airliners were such that the airlines could turn in a profit only by charging high fares. And this meant that only the higher echelons of the traveling public, predominantly expense-paid businessmen, and later, in the main, the upper middle-class, could afford the luxury of air travel. By 1950, the technical barriers seemed to impede, or at least decelerate economic and commercial progress in air transport to a slow rate of development and growth.

By this time, however, the jet engine had been invented. Working quite independently, Frank Whittle, in England, and Hans von Ohain, in Germany, had found solutions to adapting the principles of turbine power, as in maritime use, to refined designs for aero-engines. Whittle was handicapped and delayed through lack of official support or encouragement, but von Ohain found a sponsor in Ernst Heinkel, the aircraft manufacturer. At the end of the Second World War, both had seen their inventiveness take practical shape. The German Messerschmitt 262, powered by Junkers jet engines, actually saw service during the closing weeks of the war, while a developed variant of Whittle's engine equipped the Gloster Meteor fighter, which did not see combat service.

The victorious Allies acted speedily in peacetime to make the best use of this new source of power. Whittle's engine had been sent to the United States, where engine manufacturers such as Westinghouse and General Electric worked to refine the design. Rolls-Royce and other British engine makers did the same. The result was a steady stream of jet-powered fighter and bomber aircraft that quickly demonstrated the potential of the jets, whose thrust enabled the aircraft to fly faster than any of their propeller-driven predecessors.

The jet engines did not use gasoline. Early experiments had quickly shown that this petroleum product, highly refined with high octane-ratings, had improved the performance of piston engines. But this was dangerous, even lethal, if used as the fuel for jet engines, which were subjected to strong compressed air pressure and ignition. The engines simply blew up. The solution was to use kerosene, a fuel that, though refined from crude oil, like gasoline, was less volatile, and more managable for the apparatus of jet engine design. Even so, the fuel consumption rates were high. The jet engines were greedy, and the operational range of the new, faster, military jet aircraft was invariably limited, simply because they did not have the design capacity to carry enough fuel for sustained flights. A 600-mph fighter, spectacular in performance, was typically limited to flights of an hour or so, while the bombers could fly for only a few hours.

For this reason, little attention was paid—except in one admirable case—to the idea of applying jet power to transport aircraft, or airliners. Engineers and designers alike concluded that the rate of fuel consumption would be unacceptable because the airlines would require more range than the military aircraft needed; and the fuel load required would demand an excessive

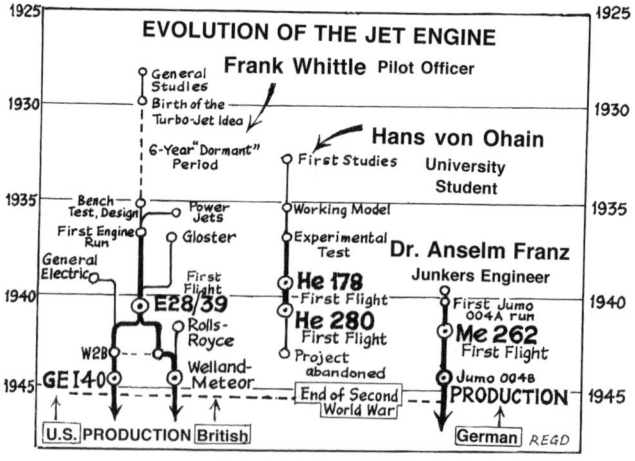

Jet airline service began in 1952, but the origins of what became known as the Jet Age began with the invention of the jet engine during the 1930s. Working independently, Frank Whittle and Hans von Ohain were successful in achieving flight experience at the beginning of the Second World War. The first jet-powered aircraft to see active military service was the Messerschmidt Me 262, powered by Anselm Franz's Jumo engine.

percentage of the carrying capacity of the airliners. Even more important, such a heavy fuel load would be costly, and jet airliners would therefore be hopelessly uneconomical to operate. The leading aircraft manufacturers in the United States, such as Douglas, Lockheed, Convair, and Martin, as well as the smaller companies in Britain, subscribed to this opinion.

At the same time, piston-engined technology did make some progress. Continual improvements in engine design, larger, more powerful, and aimed at better efficiency through leaner fuel consumption, permitted the major airliner builders to produce bigger and better versions of well-tried thoroughbred designs. As mentioned above, Douglas, for example, "stretched" the DC-6 into the DC-7, culminating in the long-range, nonstop trans-Atlantic DC-7C "Seven Seas," while Lockheed stretched its famous Super-Constellation to the L-1649A Starliner; and both competed for supremacy on the world's intercontinental air routes.

But by this time—the DC-7C went into service with Pan American Airways in May 1956—a new sound was to be heard on the world's airways. The English manufacturers had not been in accord with the global industry in its views on the applicability of jet propulsion to airliner design. Both in airframe and engine design and output, they had fallen far behind the American giants, partly because of wartime exigencies, partly because American production technology was far superior. To overcome the recognized handicap, several companies, notably de Havilland at Hatfield, and Vickers at Weybridge, knew that revolutionary approaches were vitally necessary, involving an element of risk. In spite of the doubters, they went ahead to demonstrate that all things were possible, given ingenuity of thought and the determination to make every effort to overcome apparent difficulties. The outcome of their approach was airliners that were so far ahead of their time that the aviation world was shaken to its foundations.

The First Turboprop (Prop-Jet) Airliner

There were two schools of thought among the engine designers as to how to harness the potential power for commercial use. The high fuel consumption necessary to achieve the required thrust was, during the immediate post-war years, recognized as a barrier to economical operations by airlines that had to place profitability above performance. This was especially critical for short- and medium-haul flights—up to 1,000 miles—where too much of the ramp-to-ramp time was taken up by taxiing at the airports and the time taken to climb to and descend from cruising height. Another solution was seen to be the turbo-prop or prop-jet engine design, in which most of the thrust developed by the jet efflux was used by the turbine to drive the propeller. The residual thrust added to the power (the combination of which was defined as effective horsepower, ehp) instead of the standard horsepower (hp).

The earliest application of this technology was the result of collaboration between the distinguished engine manufacturer Rolls-Royce, one of the British aircraft manufacturers, Vickers-Armstrongs, and one of the British state airline corporations, **British European Airways (B.E.A.).** An order by the Ministry of Supply in December 1946 for two Vickers VC-2 Viceroys, to be powered by four Armstrong-Siddeley Mamba turboprop engines, was the group's first initiative. When the first prototype airliner, the Vickers V.630 (now renamed the Viscount), made its first flight on 16 July 1948, it was powered by four Rolls-Royce Darts, which had been specified on 27 August 1947. This 32-seater made its debut in airline service on 29 July 1950, when B.E.A. operated the world's first turbine-powered airline service, from London (Northolt) to Edinburgh (Turnhouse) and, later the same day, from London to Paris (Le Bourget). During the next four weeks, until 23 August, the V.630 flew 127 hours and carried 1,815 passengers on experimental flights.

Encouraged by B.E.A.'s managing director Peter Masefield, ably supported by chairman Lord Douglas of Kirtleside, the V.630 design gave way to a larger version, designed by Sir George Edwards: the Viscount V.700. The model was ordered by the Ministry of Supply on 24 February 1949, and B.E.A. ordered 20 of the new 40–48-seat airliner on 3 August 1950.

Further route-proving and engine-proving were still required, for this was the first example in aviation history of new airframe and engine designs being launched commercially without military or other previous experience. Accordingly, in the summer of 1951, two vintage Douglas Dakotas (ex–Royal Air Force versions of the famous Douglas DC-3) were fitted with two Dart engines each. Flying at 20,000 feet altitude—much to the astonishment of other pilots who spotted the old Gooney Bird well above its normal 8,000 feet—the B.E.A. Dart-Dakotas went into service as freighters on the London (Northolt)-Brussels-Hanover route on 15 August 1951. This was the first scheduled freight service to be operated by a turbine-powered aircraft, and lasted for almost a year, until 30 April 1952. From 25 February until 13 April 1952, the Northolt-Amsterdam-Copenhagen route was added, and a Northolt-Paris-Milan freight service started on 20 April.

Such operations were vital. No amount of bench-testing is a substitute for day-in, day-out scheduled operation, with the demands of near-perfect regularity and punctuality. B.E.A. and Rolls-Royce learned some hard lessons with the Dart-Dakotas, solving problems of de-icing at high altitudes, water-methanol systems, and new technologies. Their patience and determination had their reward. On 16 April 1953, B.E.A. opened the

In 1950, British European Airways ordered the 40-seat Vickers Viscount turboprop (prop-jet). It became Britain's most successful commercial airliner. (NASM-00096048)

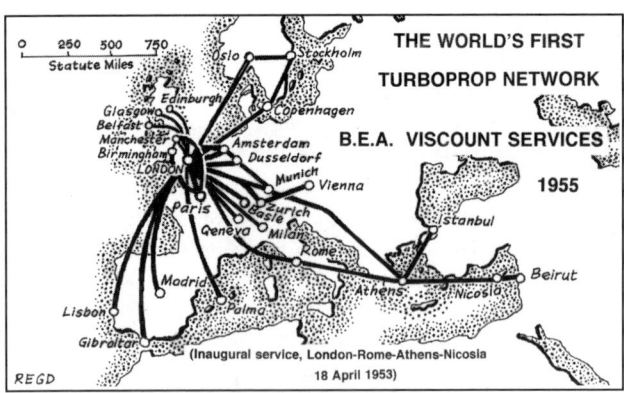

Starting scheduled services in 1953, B.E.A. soon replaced most of its European-route aircraft with the turboprop Viscounts.

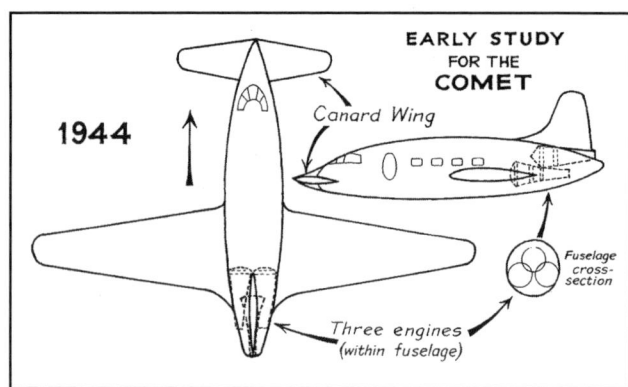

world's first sustained scheduled turboprop service, from London to Nicosia, Cyprus via Rome and Athens.

Drawing-Board Jet

By the time the British short-haul airline had had its hour of glory, its companion state-owned **British Overseas Airways Corporation (B.O.A.C.)** and de Havilland Aircraft, of Hatfield, England, had been able to bask in the limelight of even greater achievement. De Havilland had, toward the end of the First World War, produced the D.H.4 light bomber, which could outpace the best fighter. In 1943, it produced the twin-Merlin-engined Mosquito. Chief designer Ron Bishop, chief aerodynamicist Richard Clarkson, engine designer Frank Halford, and others will never forget the Royal Aircraft Establishment's blessing of the Mosquito: 387 mph (23 mph faster than the famous Spitfire). Also present was David Newman, Clarkson's deputy, and C.C. Walker, the company's chief engineer. The intuitive Clarkson also recalled a tea-time discussion hosted by Sir Geoffrey de Havilland toward the end of that year. Reviewing the projected D.H.100 Vampire jet fighter, Walker observed, as they reviewed aspects of design that would match the jet engine performance and speculating on the remarkable long-term prospects: "you could have all this in a civil airliner." His words were prophetic, for this is exactly what de Havilland set out to do, ignoring the forecasts of excessive fuel consumption and myriad other negative facets of contemporary conventional opinion.

After the war in Europe came thankfully to its end, Clarkson was a member of the British technical delegation which, along with rivals from the United States and the Soviet Union, descended on Germany in the summer of 1945 to glean the secrets of Hitler's jet aircraft and of his advanced rocketry. On his return, Clarkson was convinced that a swept wing was essential for the high speed flight that jet engines could generate. Early studies concentrated on designing a fast trans-Atlantic mail-plane, with only a few passenger seats. The wing, with a 20° sweep, was as far as Clarkson was prepared to go, with the knowledge available at the time.

The curious mail-carrier was first transformed into the D.H.108, with the Vampire's fuselage, a swept wing, but still no horizontal tail. The power of its jet engine was hoped to give Britain the honor of being the first to fly supersonically. Tragically, young Geoffrey de Havilland lost his life in the attempt. Nevertheless, the 108 had given the company an insight into the special difficulties of achieving speeds twice that of conventional postwar transport aircraft.

Bishop's team had firmed up the D.H.106 specification. The aircraft had grown to a 40-seat airliner powered by four de Havilland Ghost jet engines, each developing 5,500 lb. of thrust. Chief engine designer Frank Halford had produced a centrifugal-compressor jet engine that, while not comparable to those that soon followed, was more economical in fuel consumption.

The engines were buried in the wings, not in nacelles or pods. It was the first production airliner to have multiple wheels in the main landing gear, the first to have pressure refueling, and the first to have full power controls, with simulated "feel" for the pilots. These new steps had to be taken: wing position for aerodynamic cleanliness, extra wheels to spread the load on the runways, pressure refueling to reduce ground time, and power controls to overcome the tremendous forces when moving elevators and rudders against a force equivalent to a 500-mph wind. Previous piston-engined airliners were pressurized to 3 lb. per cubic inch, but the D.H.106 was tested to 8¼. In 1950, soon after the first flight, a fuselage section was put through 16,000 pressure reversals in the water tank, from the equivalent of ground level to 40,000 feet and back. This was something that had never been done before, or even come close to, for any previous commercial aircraft design.

The Magnificent False Start

All this innovative work was done in almost complete secrecy. Insiders knew that "something was going on" inside the hangar at Hatfield, but speculation was wide of the mark. Eventually, on 27 July 1949, the prototype de Havilland D.H.106 was rolled out. The London press corps was invited, but did not wait to see it take off on its maiden flight. Chief pilot John Cunningham waited until he felt the aircraft was ready, which was in the evening when the press had gone home. So the first flight of the world's first jet airliner was almost a private affair for the de Havilland staff.

The First Jets and Turboprops

The D.H.106, soon to be called the Comet then carried out exhaustive testing, which Cunningham reported as being amazingly satisfactory. On 25 October 1949, he flew from London to Tripoli, 1,468 miles, in 3 hours 23 minutes, at an average speed of 458 mph, almost twice that of front-line piston-engined airliners at the time. The Comet received its Certificate of Airworthiness on 22 January 1952, and entered service with **British Overseas Airways Corporation (B.O.A.C.)** on the route from London to Johannesburg on 2 May of that year. Against all contemporary opinion, from Seattle, Long Beach, and Burbank (Boeing, Douglas, and Lockheed) to other centers of aviation knowledge in Europe, de Havilland had pulled it off. B.O.A.C.'s Sir Miles Thomas announced that, in its first year, Comet operations were profitable. It was not only operationally superior—not difficult, because of its speed—it was also (albeit with first-class fares) economically viable. The airline world beat the proverbial path to de Havilland's door.

Jet Engine Efficiency

Halford's engine had proved itself, and although the Ghost was to be superseded by the Rolls-Royce Avon, it was still an impressive performer in terms of fuel consumption. It gave the Comet the speed that placed the jet in an entirely new category in the airliner hierarchy. Even more important was the Ghost's reliability, compared to that of even the best of the piston engines. The all-important T.B.O. (Time Between Overhaul) was

The de Havilland D.H.106 Comet 1 introduced the world to jet travel. (SI-94-13380)

the criterion of technical excellence by which all engines were judged, as this was a major item of maintenance cost, one that brought the aircraft back into the hangars for days at a time, costing precious revenue.

Right from the start, T.B.O.s took on a new dimension. Previously, this was measured in hundreds of hours—800 hours was quite acceptable for commercial piston engines. The problem was that the pistons changed direction abruptly hundreds of times per minute, on bearings that had to stand the strain. Spark plugs had to be changed constantly. Cylinders would "blow," especially when exposed to severe climatic conditions. All this changed after the Comet demonstrated the efficiency of the jet engine, which had no reciprocating parts, no complicated electrics for ignition, no plugs, no cylinders. Everything in the engine just went round and round, with negligible wear and tear on the bearings. As long as the lubrication system worked—and oil consumption in the jets was dramatically lower than that of the piston engines—the wear and tear was negligible. Thus, the authorized T.B.O. began to creep up, passing the 1,000 mark then ascending to levels undreamed of only a year earlier. This added efficiency was matched by the reduction of time needed for maintenance.

Another unforeseen benefit was the effect on the airframes of the smooth running jet engine turbines. The reciprocating action of piston engines causes vibration. Passengers and the airframe were subjected to constant vibration as long as the engines were running. Basic repairs of an almost primitive nature were sometimes required, such as replacing popped rivets. The net result was that piston-engined aircraft, with the possible exception of the legendary Douglas DC-3, tended quite simply to wear out after 10–12 years of concentrated use.

Another source of vibration was the propellers, at least two per aircraft, and on all long-haul airliners, four ("four-engined safety" was a familiar promotional slogan). They were driven by complex reduction gears from the engines, made necessary to reduce the rotation speed of the blades, which could reach supersonic level at the tips, with disastrous consequences. Any damage to a propeller would demand "feathering" of that propeller (i.e., changing the angle of the blade to align with the direction of flight) and loss of power. Propellers were complicated and costly. The jet engines did not need them; the smooth-running turbines and lack of propellers did not torture the airframes. Airliners

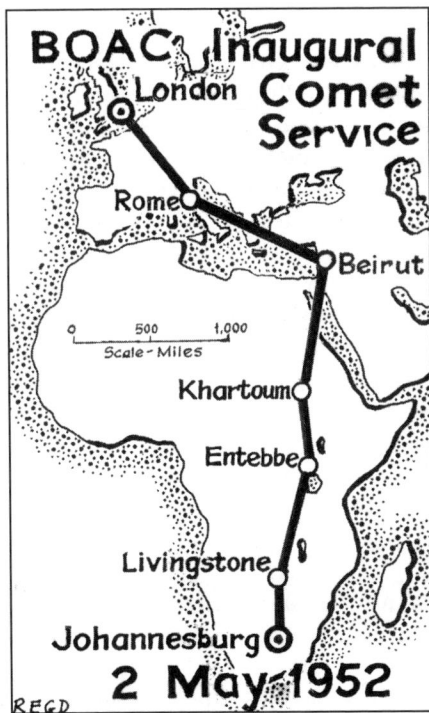

B.O.A.C.'s Inaugural Service from London to Johannesburg was dramatic. It halved the journey time by the best piston-engined airliners and put to rest the doubts that other manufacturers had had of de Havilland's bold innovation.

began to last longer. Instead of having to be retired after about 10 years of faithful service. One of the unseen yet revolutionary benefits the introduction of jet engine propulsion bestowed upon the commercial airline industry was service life that reached 12, 15, 20 years or more. Underlying these various technical benefits was the cost of fuel. The jets did not burn gasoline, as did piston engines. They burned kerosene, which was much cheaper. Thus the engineering efficiency that Halford introduced to jet engine design was complemented by reduced fuel cost.

Jet Engine Development

As experience was gained in jet engine design, axial compressor flow emerged as the superior choice versus Halford's centrifugal. First off the mark was the Rolls-Royce Avon, revealed publicly at the Farnborough Air Show in 1948. The design fitted neatly into the Comet's wing, with the air intakes and jet pipes enlarged to match the greater volume of air needed for the extra thrust. The next year, the Avon-powered English Electric Canberra made its debut as Britain's first tactical bomber, and on 21 February 1951, made the world's first jet-powered crossing of the Atlantic, from Aldergrove, Northern Ireland, to Gander, Newfoundland. The Avon was to power several British military aircraft.

The sixth Comet airframe to come off the production line was fitted with Avons, to be designated the Comet 2. John Cunningham flew it for the first time on 16 February 1952. The Avon was cleared up to 5,000 lb. thrust, compared to the Ghost's 4,450 lb., and this permitted more range because of the extra fuel load that could be carried: 2,500 miles, compared to the first Comet's 1,500 miles. B.O.A.C. placed a launch order for 11 aircraft and British Commonwealth Pacific Airlines (B.C.P.A.) also ordered them. This latter airline was a consortium shared by the Australian, British, and New Zealand governments and was intended for trans-Pacific jet service, but the airline was disbanded when the national airlines of Australia and Canada, and later New Zealand, went their own separate ways. When B.O.A.C. cancelled the Comet 2 fleet, following the Comet 1 disasters in 1954, the Royal Air Force took delivery of them, but flew them, unpressurized, for highly secret specialized intelligence-gathering duties.

The Comet Sets the Pace

During 1952 and 1953, the Comet was a new shape in the skies of the eastern hemisphere. It did not have trans-ocean range, but it was able to set a cracking pace elsewhere. On 11 August 1952, B.O.A.C. began service to Colombo, Sri Lanka via the Persian Gulf (Bahrain), Karachi, and Bombay. Two months later, it reached Singapore via Karachi, Delhi, Calcutta, and Rangoon; on 3 April 1953 it flew into Tokyo via Bangkok, Manila, and Okinawa. The well-known "Speedbird" emblem that had graced the pre-war Imperial Airways flying boats was now to be seen on the tails of the jets flying three times as fast as the Empire Boats, with journey times measured in hours rather than days.

These were proud times for the British aircraft industry, and especially for de Havilland. The company had, entirely from the resources of its own design team, done what none had dared to try, much less to do. The supreme accolade came on 20 October 1952, when the great Pan American Airways, symbol of the United States' technical supremacy across the world's airways, placed an order for the Comet 3, a developed version of the Comet, able to cross the Atlantic Ocean. Tragedy was to come later; but for a few glorious months, de Havilland had the world at its feet.

Next to offer jet airline service was the French independent **Union Aéromaritime de Transport (U.A.T.)**. It had three Comet 1As (increased all-up weight, permitting 44 seats rather than 36) and opened service from Paris and Marseille to West Africa on 19 February 1953. Reaching Johannesburg on 2 November, U.A.T.'s jets were serving nine cities in Africa. South Africans could now fly to Paris direct, instead of taking B.O.A.C's faster service via London.

South African Airways could not tolerate competition on its European routes from two jet airlines against its Lockheed Constellations, and it had to lease two Comet 1s from B.O.A.C. for its Johannesburg-London service, starting on 4 October 1953. Thus three airlines were operating to Europe from the South African commercial and industrial center, where the Comet's take-off performance was equal to the "hot-and-high" airport conditions there and at Entebbe and (very hot) at Khartoum, Cairo, and Kano.

The fourth jet airline was **Air France**. The French national flag-carrier obtained them in an unusual way. De Havilland was negotiating with a U.S. Supplemental (non-scheduled) airline, Overseas National Airways (O.N.A.), which intended to scoop its rivals in spectacular fashion. But the U.S. Civil Aeronautics Authority (C.A.A.) would not accept the credentials of its British counterpart. Air France picked up the delivery positions of O.N.A.'s two Comet 1As and put them into service on 26 August 1953, on a route to Beirut via Rome. Algiers, Cairo, and Casablanca were added in September, and early in 1954, Stockholm was earmarked for jet service.

Canadian Pacific Airlines had ordered two Comet 1As, but one of these crashed at Karachi on its delivery flight, and the

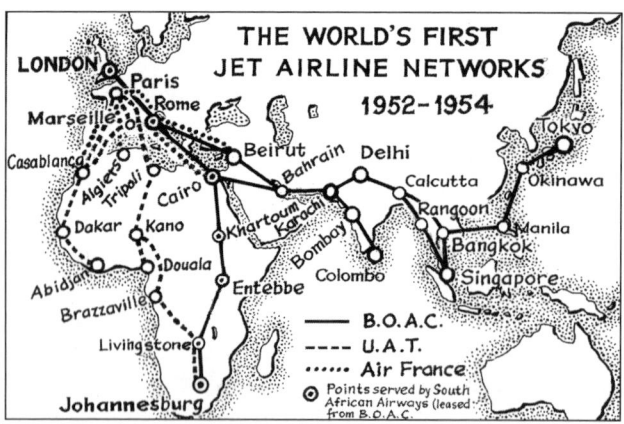

Before Pan American Airways introduced the Boeing 707 in 1958, the D.H. Comet was flying across Africa and Asia, with four airlines serving thirty cities.

other was transferred to B.O.A.C., which promptly leased it to South African Airways (see above). Two other Comet 1As were sold to the Royal Canadian Air Force, but the end had come for the airliner that had completely and irrevocably changed the aviation world's perspective of the direction of technical invention and innovation. It paid a crippling penalty for its own innovations. At the beginning of 1954, de Havilland was on a pedestal, so its fall was devastating.

The Comet Disasters

Like any new airliner entering service, there had been some incidents and crashes, and discrepancies in design or system function were detected. An accident at Rome on 26 October 1952 and another at Karachi on 2 March 1953 (see above) were caused by a high angle on take-off, and the problem was quickly rectified. A Comet disappeared near Calcutta on 2 May 1953 during a violent thunderstorm, presumably because of abnormal stresses that could have happened to any airliner. The disaster of 10 January 1954 was different. A Comet plunged into the Mediterranean Sea near the island of Elba, and there seemed to be no clear-cut explanation; it had taken off from Rome and apparently exploded without warning. The B.O.A.C. pilots had some misgivings, and there was even a suspicion of sabotage, but the Comets went back into service on 23 March. Alas, on 8 April, another Comet crashed into the sea near the island Stromboli. Both aircraft had taken off from Rome; both had been climbing, at about the same altitude; both had logged about the same hours of airframe life. The coincidence was too obvious to ignore and the Comets were again withdrawn from service on 12 April. An agonizing reappraisal of the entire program of construction, concentrating on the structural integrity of the Comet's design, was initiated. The Royal Navy was called in to help, and a salvage operation was able to dredge substantial portions of the Comet wreck from the shallow waters near Elba. These were taken to the Royal Aircraft Establishment (R.A.E.) at Farnborough, England, and reassembled like an enormous three-dimensional jigsaw puzzle. An intensive enquiry was instigated, under the direction of Professor Arnold Hall, who produced a comprehensive report that was accepted as the authentic explanation of why an airliner, constructed under the most severe contemporary standards of the time, should suddenly explode without warning.

A new phrase suddenly received much attention in the language of aeronautical terminology: metal fatigue. The phenomenon was already known, but it had hitherto never been a problem, as no case had ever been recorded of an airliner's structure being affected by it. But the Comet was different. Its cruising height was in the region of 40,000 feet—twice that of propeller-driven Constellations or DC-6s and 7s. The differential in atmospheric pressure was far greater, and the Comet was pressurized to more than 8 lb. per square inch, compared to the conventional 3 lb. per square inch. Sir Arnold's report revealed that this was not enough. His examination team had discovered cracks on top of the fuselage in the frame of the ADF inspection hatch (and later

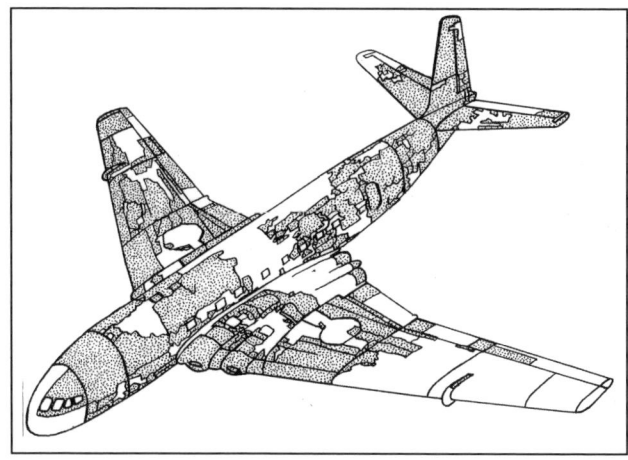

After two disastrous crashes in the Mediterranean in 1954, the remains of a Comet 1 were salvaged (shaded area). The Royal Aircraft Establishment in England revealed a flaw in construction, caused by a hitherto unrecognized result of metal fatigue.

in a cabin window frame), and the cause was concluded to be metal fatigue. This occurs when metal is bent repeatedly, and its molecular structure disintegrates and ultimately breaks.

The effect on the proud de Havilland was close to disaster. It had either to abandon the Comet program, which had held such high hopes for worldwide success, or go back to the drawing board. The difficult decision was made in favor of the latter, but this was no easy task, as a new metal gauge had to be selected and all the windows redesigned. Much was discussed at the time—and since—to the effect that the Comet's windows should have been round, not rectangular, but this was hardly logical at the time, as other manufacturers had moved away from round windows—for example, the Douglas DC-4's oval shapes gave way to the DC-6's rectangulars.

The irony of the sad episode was that de Havilland had gone to extraordinary lengths to offset the dangers inherent in crossing the proverbial thresholds of technology in building the world's first jet airliner. A fuselage section had been subjected to 2,000 cycles from zero to 8 lb. per square inch, and a forward section of the fuselage to 16,000 cycles, equivalent to about 40,000 hours of flying. This testing was far more severe than any that had been done to any airliner ever before. The Comet's wing was still used, half a century later, on the military Nimrod maritime reconnaissance aircraft. Four years were to pass before the reengineered Comet went into service. Meanwhile, another jet airliner was taking center stage.

Soviet Surprise

During the first decade following the end of the Second World War, the western powers drew apart from their wartime ally, the Soviet Union (U.S.S.R.). The "Iron Curtain," as Winston Churchill termed it, was drawn along the western frontiers of eastern European countries that were effectively colonies of Moscow. They were strictly controlled—politically, economically, and socially—by the Kremlin. Industrial and commercial progress beyond the curtain was slow, and living standards were known to be far below those in the West. But in some fields of technology, Soviet strength was anything but slow, and they too, as well as the United States and Great Britain, had gained from German advances in rocketry and in jet engine design. These disciplines were presumed by the West to be directed exclusively toward military requirements. **Aeroflot**, the Soviet state airline, was still, in the early 1950s, operating Ilyushin 12s and 14s as its flagships. These aircraft were, at best, comparable only with Convair 240s or Martin 404s, which were by then second-line aircraft in the United States.

Therefore, on 22 March 1956, when a Soviet delegation arrived at London's Heathrow Airport in a jet airliner, it caught the aviation world by storm. Journalists descended on the airport in droves. At first dismissing the aircraft, a Tupolev Tu-104, as a one-off version of the Tu-16 (or Tu-88) jet-powered bomber, they were nonplussed when, next day, two more arrived with more members of the delegation. The twin-engined airliner was slimmer than the Comet, but its two engines were also placed in the wings, like the Comet's, and although its military ancestry was evident, its commercial conversion was not in doubt. This was not a one-off. The Soviets were in the jet airliner business, although clearly the Tupolev was intended neither for long range nor transocean capability. The Soviet Union was a land-mass, and its minions overseas, political satellites though they may have been, did not justify the development of a long-range jet. At least not yet.

Nevertheless, after the sensational debut in London, Aeroflot did not waste time. Six months later, on 15 September 1956,

Often forgotten in western aviation circles, the Tupolev Tu-104 opened service from Moscow to Siberia in 1956—two years before the jet inaugurals across the Atlantic. (SI-2003-4837)

it opened scheduled Tu-104 service from Moscow to Irkutsk, in central Siberia via Omsk. The seven-hour journey cut the previous 17 hr. 50 m. time of the Ilyushin twins by almost two-thirds. The airline never looked back and can claim to have inaugurated the first *sustained* jet service in the world. By the end of the year, Aeroflot had extended its jet services to Prague and Beijing, and in 1957 to Khabarovsk and Petropavlovsk-Kamchatsky, in the Russian Far East. Also, on 9 December 1957, the Czechoslovak airline, **Ceskoslovenske Statni Aerolinie (C.S.A.)**, with an improved version of the Tupolev, the Tu-104A, with 70 seats instead of only 50, became the sixth airline in the world to enter the Jet Age. During the late 1950s, Aeroflot extended jet service to its eastern European satellites and during the late 1950s, to Delhi, India, while C.S.A. went to Cairo and to Bombay. In future, Soviet airliners were to play a role in spreading the image of communist technology and consequent political prestige around the world, especially in underdeveloped countries.

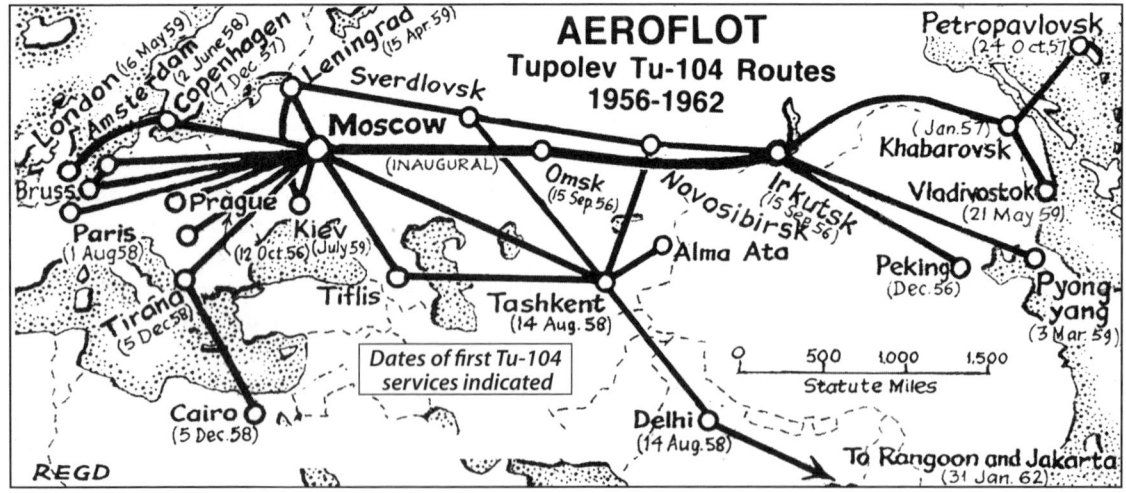

Two years after the Comet disasters, Aeroflot opened jet service from Moscow to Irkutsk. It subsequently added routes to all the main cities of the Soviet Union, and also to Cairo and southern Asia.

Chapter 7: Turboprop Ascendancy

Days in the Sun for the Viscount

The impact of the Viscount on the launching customer's fortunes and prestige was unprecedented. The passenger appeal of turboprop propulsion, vigorously advertized by the manufacturer, the operator, and indirectly through the press, was such that **British European Airways'** market share on its main routes throughout Europe went up by leaps and bounds. The Vickers Viscount changed the balance of power in that context, and from its introduction on 16 April 1953, it ruled the European skies for several years.

At the beginning, it did not have all its own way. B.E.A. had acted with caution, because another excellent short-haul airliner was in production. Piston-engined though it was, the Airspeed AS-57 Ambassador, designed by Arthur Hagg, at Christchurch, England, had many design features that could give the Viscount a good run for its money. Powered by two Bristol Centaurus engines, it flew smoothly, and its high wing and large windows were especially attractive for the passengers, all of whom enjoyed uninterrupted views. Cruising at 240 mph, against the Viscount's 302, and with about the same capacity of 47 seats, it was more economical than the Viscount on the short ranges, especially the cross-Channel routes to Paris, Brussels, and Amsterdam. And because of the high wing, on which the engines were mounted, the propeller clearance and landing gear allowed the fuselage to be much lower when the aircraft was on the ground. Only a few steps were needed for the passengers to enter the aircraft.

Thus, the Ambassador, renamed the Elizabethan class by B.E.A., and ordered on 22 September 1948, entered service on 13 March 1952, on the prestigious Silver Wing service from London to Paris. It was handicapped by the average stage distance for its assigned routes of less than 500 miles, whereas the Viscount's was more than 800, with consequent advantages of being lower down the cost-per-seat-mile curve. By the turn of fate, its life in front-line airline service was relatively short. De Havilland was still on the crest of a production wave for its Comet 1s and 2s, and had already acquired Airspeed as a division of the parent company, making Comet components. Only 20 Ambassadors were built, and because of powerful competition from the Convairliners, de Havilland closed down the line. With no development in view, and with the limitations of manufacturer support, B.E.A. concentrated on the Viscount. It retired its Elizabethans on 30 July 1958.

B.E.A.'s main rival was traditionally **Air France**. Their respective ancestors had competed on the 220-mile London-Paris route since the beginning of airline operations in Europe in 1919. Linking the two biggest and wealthiest cities on the European continent, competition from the railroads was not significant until the construction of the Channel Tunnel. The French national airline lost no time. It recognized the Viscount's obvious superiority, ordered a dozen aircraft in October 1951, and put them into service on 15 September 1953—only five months after B.E.A. The Irish **Aer Lingus** followed on 11 April 1954, to put Dublin into the turbine-powered era, and other airlines placed orders, with **Trans-Australia Airlines (T.A.A.)** taking the Viscount into the southern hemisphere on 18 December 1954.

Important though these welcome orders were, none was more significant than that from **Trans Canada Airlines (T.C.A.)**. Its order for 15 Viscounts in December 1952 was a landmark in the history of British aircraft production. For the first time since the early 1920s, when de Havilland D.H.4s were license-built in the U.S.A. (as DH-4Bs) for the Post Office air mail service, a British manufacturer broke into the American market. This was an important dollar-currency sale for Great Britain, just at a time when its balance of trade needed such assistance. No doubt Canada's commonwealth affiliation affected the decision in a small way, but the airplane sold itself, especially when it was able to comply with the strict regulations imposed on all airliners by the U.S. Federal Aviation Administration.

The first turbine-engined airliner service in America was in 1955 by Trans Canada Airlines (T.C.A., now Air Canada) with the Vickers Viscount. (NASM-00096053)

The biggest export success for Britain's airliner industry was the Vickers Viscount sale to the U.S. Capital Airlines, which opened service in 1955 soon after T.C.A. (SI-91-2442)

T.C.A. opened the first turbine-powered airline service in the Americas on 1 April 1955, with a Montreal-Toronto-Winnipeg service, extended transcontinentally to Vancouver on 1 November. The Viscount displayed the maple-leaf insignia in New York on 4 April, and for the first time the Canadian airline left its U.S. competitors in its wake.

Such success did not go unnoticed in the United States. The Big Four (United, American, T.W.A., and Eastern) remained loyal to their national suppliers—and were confirmed in their faith when Pan American placed its dramatic order for 45 big jets in 1955. But the other trunk airlines were anxious to seize a larger slice of the total air transport cake, of which about 70% was in the hands of the Big Four. Prominent among these was **Capital Airlines**, whose market was almost entirely in the northeast of the U.S.A. Measured in passenger boardings (but not in passenger-miles, because of its short average stage length), it was the fifth largest airline in the world, ranking after only its big American rivals. Its president, James "Slim" Carmichael, joined the queue of airline executives who, during the initial introductory stages of the Viscount, visited B.E.A. in London to review the results. They were all mightily impressed, none more so than Carmichael. Capital's route structure was remarkably similar to B.E.A.'s in the distribution of its segments by stage length. What was a clear-cut success for B.E.A. in Europe could be echoed in the northeastern U.S.A. In May 1954, Capital ordered three Viscounts then arranged the financing for 37 more in August, and another 20 in November. Such a sale of an all-British product to the United States had never been achieved before.

Capital Airlines introduced the Viscount on its Washington-Chicago route on 26 July 1955 and followed with an intensification of service frequencies from the northeastern U.S. to all points south and west. Everywhere it flew (with the airline promoting the Rolls-Royce name in its advertising) it gained over the competition. The Viscounts resisted all challenges, and Carmichael ordered 15 more, such was the demonstrated superiority of the turboprop airliner. He even made a provisional order for 14 Comet 4s.

By mid-1957, three-quarters of Capital's seat-miles were flown by Viscounts, but Capital had over-reached itself. Perhaps it misjudged the traffic projections and underestimated the ability of its competitors to remain strong. More important, under the regulatory Civil Aeronautics Board authority, all new route extensions had to be argued at great length, with the incumbent airlines resisting all attempts by newcomers to penetrate their territories. Capital desperately needed longer routes. The lucrative markets to Florida were delayed until September 1958. Capital's finances took a plunge. It could not make its progress payments to Vickers, which foreclosed on the debt. On 1 June 1961, the airline was purchased by United, which continued to fly the Viscounts for several years after the takeover.

Meanwhile, B.E.A. augmented its fleet with twelve 62-seat Viscount Series 801s, later modified to Series 802s, and put them into service on 13 February 1957. The world's first turboprops were winning converts worldwide. Furthermore, the Rolls-Royce Dart engine proved to be a winner, demonstrating great reliability and ease of maintenance, to the extent that it attracted the attention of other manufacturers that were aspiring to build the elusive "DC-3 Replacement" for feeder airline work.

The Whispering Giant

Reference has already been made to the disastrous effect of the Second World War on British efforts to develop modern airliners to match the highly efficient types emerging from the American production lines. The DC-3 had already been sold in substantial numbers all over the world; in 1940, Boeing's pressurized airliner, the Model 307 Stratoliner, had gone into service. Douglas produced the long-range four-engined DC-4, which proved itself as the military Skymaster transport, and Lockheed's superb Constellation transcended all previous standards of airliner design, passenger comfort, and appeal.

Fortunately for Britain, the Brabazon Committee had made some visionary and critically important recommendations, listing several airliner types that ranged from the small feeder aircraft, the de Havilland Dove, to the trans-Atlantic jet mail-plane, which took shape as the de Havilland Comet. Among others listed were the large four-engined "Empire" types, originally designated the M.R.E. and the L.R.E., Medium-Range Empire and Long-Range Empire, respectively. These four-engined designs were variants of the Bristol 175, which became known as the Britannia. It was supposed to be powered by four Bristol Centaurus engines, but it was later modified to have four Bristol Proteus turboprop engines (originally intended for the Saunders-Roe Princess flying boat, victim of the demise of the flying boat era). The Britannia was bigger than the Constellation or other piston-engined types—five abreast seating instead of four—and faster—400 mph instead of 300. However, when the 550-mph de Havilland Comet 4 entered service in 1958, the Britannia had to take a back seat. **B.O.A.C.** tried to establish a fare structure that would recognize jet speed as appropriate to first-class fares and turbo-prop or propeller speeds as tourist class, but this could not be agreed by the International Air Transport Association (IATA).

The Bristol Britannia 100 Series (the M.R.E.) made its first flight on 16 August 1952, and should have entered service early

For longer ranges, the "Whispering Giant" Bristol Britannia was originally designed as a "Medium-Range or Long-Range Empire" airliner. It did not enter service until 1957, because of problems with the Proteus engines. (NASM-00016437)

Turboprop Ascendancy

in 1954. But there were frustrating delays. B.O.A.C. insisted on stringent high-altitude flight testing in the "hot-and-high" conditions of East Africa, and the aircraft met some hitherto undetected engine problems. Instructed to find heavy cloud conditions, the pilots experienced engine "flame-outs," subsequently found to be caused by insufficient air reaching the burners. This was because the Proteus engine had been designed with air intakes at the back, so as to avoid water ingestion by the Princess flying boat at take-off. This was fine at the Princess's 250–300 mph, but at the Britannia's 400 mph, the engines were starved of air. By the time the problem was solved by "glow plugs" to provide reignition, precious time had been lost.

The Britannia 100 finally went into service to Johannesburg on 1 February 1957 and to Australia on 2 March, cutting about 10 hours off the Constellation's two-day schedule from London to Sydney. For two years, the Bristol airliner set the pace on all the eastern routes across Asia. Then, on 19 December 1957, just in time for Christmas, B.O.A.C. put the Britannia 310 "Whispering Giant" into service to New York. For the first time, a British-built airliner could fly regularly across the Atlantic and, with some justification (though challenged by the Douglas DC-7C and the Lockheed L-1649A), could claim to be the first airliner to fly nonstop between the United States and Britain or Europe in both directions and in all seasons.

B.O.A.C. energetically expanded the Britannia network. It flew to the Far East, the Caribbean, and, on 6 May 1958, to San Francisco—the first time California saw a British airliner, except for demonstration flights. Negotiations began for a trans-Pacific service, but the inauguration was delayed by objections from Northwest Airlines to the U.S. Civil Aeronautics Board. A little diplomacy (and possibly the threat of sanctions against Pan American in British locations around the world) permitted the start of a San Francisco-Honolulu-Tokyo Britannia service on 22 August 1959, connecting with the Comet 4s to establish an all-British round-the-world service.

The Britannia's period of ascendancy was short-lived, but together with the new Comets, it helped to modernize B.O.A.C.'s ageing fleet in a hurry. The Constellations were retired on 26 October 1958, and the Stratocruisers on 31 May 1959. The Douglas emblem still survived for a while. The Argonaut (the Canadian-built Merlin-engined DC-4) lasted another year, until 8 April 1960, and the DC-7C, purchased to ameliorate the setbacks of the Britannia production delays, continued in service as the last of the B.O.A.C. piston-engined fleet. Had the Britannia been produced a year earlier, it might have made its mark more indelibly in the annals of airliner success stories. The view that turboprop propulsion was more economical than that of the pure jet was still held by many aviation leaders. In 1958, Howard Hughes, owner of T.W.A., and always eager to challenge Juan Trippe and Pan American, might well have ordered the Bristol airliner had its builder been able to build an extra dozen aircraft in about nine months. But even with better advance notice, British production methods and resources could not match those of the mighty American industry.

A few Britannias did find their way into a variety of world markets. Possibly the most effective was the Israeli airline, **El Al**. It put the Britannias on the Atlantic route on 22 December 1957, only three days after B.O.A.C., and promptly gave the British airline something to think about. In its scheduling, by astute meteorological analysis, it cut half an hour off its competitor's time. It emphasized the nonstop capability with the slogan "No Goose, No Gander," a clever reference to the omission of Newfoundland's Gander airport and Labrador's Goose Bay as refueling stops.

The Mexican airline, **Aeronaves de Mexico**, introduced the Britannia 300 on a nonstop route from Mexico City to New York, one day before B.O.A.C.'s trans-Atlantic Britannia inaugural, on 18 December 1957, and immediately set up good times. It also leased the aircraft to the other Mexican airline, **Compañía Mexicana de Aviación (C.M.A.)**, for its prestigious Los Angeles-Acapulco route, starting service on 21 November 1958. One day later, **Compañía Cubana de Aviación** started to set record flight times between Havana and New York, but soon afterward, Dr. Fidel Castro's communist revolution led to an abandonment of the service. The Cuban airline, already well respected in airline circles, and operating Constellations to Madrid, was faced with the problem of obtaining spare parts and with basic maintenance; and it solved this by arranging with the friendly **Ceskoslovenske Statni Aerolinie (C.S.A.)** to perform

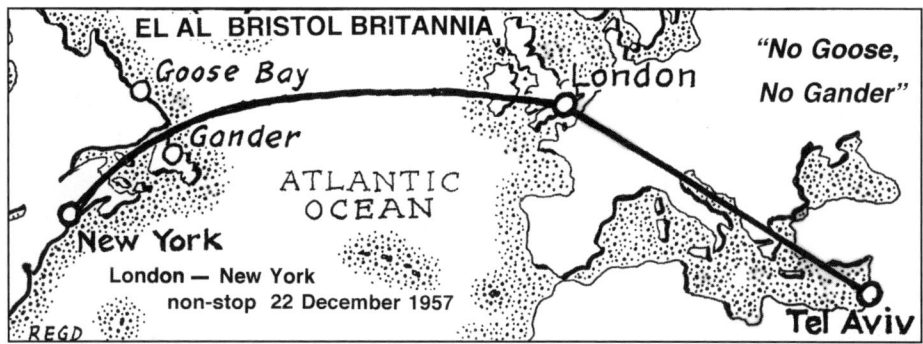

Although outclassed by the Boeing 707s and DC-8s that entered service in 1958 and 1959, the Israeli airline El Al made good use of the Britannia in 1957, with its one-stop service from Tel Aviv to New York, and with a neat slogan.

these tasks. This resulted in C.S.A. itself operating a Havana-Prague service jointly with Cubana, from 3 February 1963.

The Britannia was also an important element in upgrading the fleet and services of **Canadian Pacific Airlines (C.P.A.)**. By a combination of shrewd initiative and the conservative policy of the national airline Trans Canada Airlines (T.C.A.), C.P.A. had built a worldwide network that included trans-Atlantic, trans-Pacific, and South American routes. Based in Vancouver, it put the long-range Britannia on its Polar service to Amsterdam on 1 June 1958, cutting the DC-6B time of about 20 hours by almost a third. On 24 August of that year, it achieved a similar time-saving on the route to Tokyo and Hong Kong. C.P.A. had aspired to compete with T.C.A. on the trans-Canada air route, but after a consultant's report to the Canadian government, it received only a modest share of that market. But in spite of being required to stop at Winnipeg and Toronto en route to Montreal, it transferred its Polar Britannias to that route on 29 July 1959, and followed this with a service to Rome on 1 March 1960.

Several British independent airlines also operated the Britannias; notably Harold Bamberg's **British Eagle International Airways**, with considerable success. Eagle had evaded the restrictions on long-haul services by nonstate operators by setting up overseas companies, and operated Viscounts from New York to Bermuda from 2 June 1958. Then, in 1960, Bamberg made an agreement with the Cunard shipping line, which now saw the writing on the wall for trans-Atlantic shipping, to form **Cunard-Eagle Airways (C.E.A.)**. The Britannias started to fly from London to Bermuda, the Bahamas, and Miami on 15 October 1960. This promising challenge to B.O.A.C. ended when, in an astonishing reversal, Cunard suddenly joined up with the state airline on 7 June 1962, and abandoned Eagle, in what was widely regarded as a shameful betrayal of the principles of private enterprise. B.O.A.C. did make good use of its Britannias, even as the new Comet 4s came into services—particularly on routes to West Africa through leasing agreements with **Ghana Airways** and **Nigeria Airways**. Ghana, the first independent African state, chartered Britannias then bought two of its own, replacing Stratocruisers to fly from Accra to London on 4 February 1961. Nigeria had already made the transition to the big turboprop on Lagos-London on 16 April 1959.

Lockheed's Electra

The U.S. aviation industry decided to follow the British lead and confirm that, for short-haul airline work, there should be a competitive American airliner, if only to prevent an invasion of foreign-built equipment from across the Atlantic. **American Airlines**, under the leadership of C.R. Smith, had recognized the threat from Capital Airlines's Viscounts on many of its prestige routes, especially New York-Chicago. It outlined the specification for a four-engined type that would outclass the British turboprop. The request was met by Lockheed, famous for its Constellations, with the four-engined L-188 Electra, which answered Smith's requirements. It was twice as big as the Viscount, and its Allison 501 engines made it faster—400 mph instead of

In the United States, the Lockheed L-188 Electra was the answer to Britain's lead with turboprop (prop-jet) technology. It too suffered manufacturing problems, leading to crashes, but it eventually became a popular airliner in the U.S.A. and overseas. (NASM-9A08078)

300 mph. It was more than adequate for all the main inter-city routes of the United States, except for the transcontinental nonstops, which were the province of the Douglas and Boeing jets.

Lockheed built the Electra with remarkable speed, It made its first flight on 6 December 1957, and the first production aircraft was delivered to American on 5 December 1958, only 364 days later, an unprecedented rate of service introduction and development. By a twist of fate, Smith did not preside over the inaugural service of the first American turboprop airliner. His pilots went on strike for three weeks from 19 December until after the New Year, and **Eastern Air Lines** opened Electra service on its "gravy run" winter vacation route from New York to Miami on 12 January 1959. American followed on 23 January on its main route against Capital's Viscounts, New York-Chicago, and pressed home the advantages of capacity and speed.

Other U.S. airlines followed quickly, **National** on 26 April, to compete with Eastern; **Braniff** on 15 June; **Western** on 1 August; and **Northwest** on 1 September. The rate of delivery was about two every week, typical of American production efficiency, and was in stark contrast with the Britannia's, which was about two every month. But perhaps Lockheed should have put the aircraft through more stringent testing, and perhaps for a longer time. For whatever reason, a serious problem was soon evident.

On 3 February 1959, an American Electra crashed at New York's LaGuardia Airport, but this drew no special attention. There were soon two more crashes, by Braniff on 28 September and by Northwest on 17 March 1960. Both aircraft had broken up in flight, and the F.A.A. stepped in. There was much understandable pressure to ground the Electras, but F.A.A.'s "Pete" Quesada surprisingly did not do so. Instead, with the problem revealed as a cyclic vibration caused by the long shaft between engine and propeller at the high speed cruise level, services were permitted to continue at a speed reduced from 400 to 316 then to 295 mph. Lockheed spent about $25 million in fixing the problem, the F.A.A. restored the full certificate on 31 December 1960, and the aircraft returned to service on 24 February 1961 as Electra IIs. But the market prospects were severely compromised. Unlike its Constellation, which had forced foreign airlines to buy from Lockheed because of rival competition, the Electra sales were subsequently sluggish. The Australian **QANTAS** bought it for the Tasman Sea route to New Zealand, and the latter's **Tasman Empire Air Lines (TEAL)** had to follow suit. In Europe, only the Dutch **K.L.M.** joined the customer list, and in Latin America, it found favor with only the Brazilian **VARIG**.

Nevertheless, the rejuvenated Electra did well. It had comfortable seating and became popular with passengers. It excelled at shorter routes. Eastern introduced it on its famous New York-Washington and New York-Boston no-reservation Shuttle services, where the 200-mile stage lengths did not permit the jets to take full advantage of a higher cruising speed that could be sustained for only about 10 minutes. The Electra cruised at a lower height, and its block time was only a few minutes more than the jets'. VARIG was particularly pleased with it on the Rio de Janeiro-São Paulo shuttle service (the one that had preceded Eastern's by two years, in 1958). In California, the intra-state airline, **Pacific Southwest Airlines (P.S.A.)**, famous—or notorious, in the eyes of its trunk airline competitors—for its bargain-basement fare levels, was able to operate the Electra profitably, sound proof of the airliner's excellent low operating costs. Altogether, the Lockheed turboprop's broad-bladed propellers were a familiar sight at many of the world's busiest airports for many years to come.

Turboprops in Decline

The Bristol Britannia might well have had a much better future, had it not been for a surprising choice by **British European Airways** for its Viscount successor. European traffic was booming, and by the mid-1950s, a bigger airliner was clearly necessary. The Britannia was having problems with the Proteus engine icing. B.E.A. was encouraged to respond to strong promotion from Vickers, builders of the highly successful Viscount, to stay with that manufacturer. Sir George Edwards' team had designed a four-engined turboprop that had a certain appeal because, like the Lockheed Electra, it was never intended for long-haul routes. The Vickers Vanguard was powered by four Rolls-Royce Tyne engines and could carry 114 passengers, a few more than the Electra. B.E.A. ordered 20 on 20 July 1956, and Vickers was confident that, with an order for 20 more from **Trans Canada Airlines (T.C.A.)** soon afterward, the prospects of worldwide sales, matching the Viscount's record, were good but did not materialize.

The Vanguard made its first flight on 22 April 1959 and went into service on 22 February 1961 with B.E.A. on its London-Paris service, adding much-needed capacity on one of the world's busiest inter-city routes. T.C.A. started on 1 April 1961, on routes from Montreal to Tampa, Nassau, and other Caribbean vacation destinations. In the case of B.E.A., the pure-jet competition from the French Caravelle induced it to match the Gallic short-haul jet with a jet airliner of its own, without waiting for the de Havilland Trident. Hatfield produced a short/medium-haul version of the Comet, in the classic trade-off between range and payload, exchanging fuel for extra seats (101 against B.O.A.C.'s Comet 4's 81), with a slightly longer fuselage. The de Havilland Comet 4B went into B.E.A. service on 1 April 1960 and was successful in warding off the Caravelle, especially on the routes to the Mediterranean. It was even deployed on short-haul routes across the Channel and on domestic routes from London.

The launching of the Vanguard was a major mistake of long-term planning on a national basis. The British industry had underestimated the strength and quality of United States competition. It should not have been fragmented into manufacturing plants that could not keep up with the staggering pace of the giants on the United States West Coast. The Britannia and the Electra did prove to be competent and economic in service and for many years maintained a presence, globally and within the States. But the success of the jet airliners was so outstanding that the public began to view any airliner with propellers as old-fashioned. By the mid 1960s, turboprop airliners were relegated to secondary routes and services, or from scheduled to non-scheduled service, in which category speed was not necessarily the critical operational factor.

Soviet Workhorse

The two major manufacturers of the Soviet Union, Andrei Tupolev and Sergei Ilyushin, were respected by their peers in the Soviet sphere of influence—as were the United States' Donald Douglas, Alan Lockheed, and William Boeing—and vied with each other for pride of place in Moscow. Tupolev had taken the lead in 1956 with the Tupolev Tu-104 series, and Illyushin's team followed with a very successful four-engined turboprop.

The Ilyushin Il-18, at first called the Moskva, went into service with **Aeroflot** on 20 April 1959, on the Moscow-Adler route. Adler is on the Black Sea, one of the popular vacation resorts, especially favored during Soviet times. Other routes followed, to Alma Ata then the capital of Kazakhstan, and to other major cities of central Asia. Aeroflot had taken over **Aviaarktika**, the airline organization that had been established to specialize in operations in the frigid north, especially in Siberia; and on 10 January 1961, the Il-18 brought a modern touch to the northern route from Moscow to Magadan, on the Sea of Okhotsk via Tiksi, at the mouth of the Lena River, on the Arctic Sea coast.

Such versatility in coping with all climates was emphasized at the end of the same year, when, on 15 December 1961, it was selected to make the first flight by a commercial airliner to the

The Ilyushin IL-18 was the Soviet equivalent of the Britannia or Electra. It was popular in eastern Europe and in China, and it also flew within the Antarctic continent. (Davies)

THREE LARGE FOUR-ENGINED TURBOPROPS COMPARED

First Service Date	Aircraft Type	Dimensions-m(ft)		Speed km/h (mph)	Mixed Class Seating	MTOW kg (lb)	Normal Range km (mi)	First Airline	No. Built
		Length	Span						
19 Dec 1957[1]	Bristol Britannia 310	38 (124)	43 (124)	620 (385)	110	84,090 (185,000)	6,000 (3,750)	B.O.A.C.	85[3]
12 Jan 1959	Lockheed 188 Electra	32 (105)	30 (99)	650 (405)	85	52,700 (116,000)	4,000 (2,500)	Eastern Airlines	170
20 Apr 1959	Ilyushin 11-18	36 (118)	37 (123)	640 (400)	100	61,200[2] (135,000)	4,425[2] (2,750)	Aeroflot	565

Notes: [1] The medium-range Britannia 102 entered service on 1 Feb 1957. [2] The Ilyushin 11-18D had a range of 6,500km (4,000mi). [3] All Britannias including 100 Series.

Last Continent, Antarctica. Extra tankage was provided for this flight, from Maputo, Mozambique, to the Soviet scientific station, Molodezhnaya, whence connections were made to other Soviet stations in the vast Antarctic frozen wastes. As shown in the accompanying tabulation of the three main four-engined turboprop airliners, the Il-18's performance and characteristics were about halfway between those of the Britannia and the Electra. In one respect, it differed—substantially. More than twice as many Il-18s were built, mostly for Aeroflot, as all the Britannias and Electras added together. It was a true workhorse for what was, by the 1960s, the largest airline in the world, and it remained in service for at least two decades, well into the 1980s, as a versatile airliner, working in climates and at low-grade airports that were inhospitable to the sleeker, faster, but more demanding jet airliners. It was used extensively in China, and one was Foreign Minister Chou En-lai's personal aircraft.

The Supreme Turboprop

The Soviets had a record of building large aircraft, partly for propaganda purposes. The ANT-20 *Maxim Gorky*, an eight-engined giant of a plane, had flown in 1934 and was equipped with a printing press and other accoutrements for spreading the Soviet gospel. The modified ANT-20bis only saw limited service between 1939 and 1940. The next big Soviet airliner was different and answered a different call. During the late 1950s, the Soviet Union was energetically spreading its communist message all over the world. The Ilyushin Il-18 was doing a good job, but Moscow needed something more spectacular. Soviet jet technology was not yet capable of producing a trans-ocean jet airliner, and there was not yet much pressure to do so. The design bureau in Moscow had supplied Aeroflot with the capacity to serve the far reaches of the vast Soviet land empire, but trans-ocean, or even nonstop trans-Asian long range was not an absolute necessity.

Andrei Tupolev (the "ANT" of the pre-war aircraft manufacturing nomenclature) came up with a solution that was both ingenious and technically sound, providing the necessary power for a large airliner with extensive range, without the use of powerful pure jet engines. At speeds of more than about 380 mph, the tips of large propellers could reach supersonic levels, with the accompanying risk of their falling apart because of the consequent excessive vibration. Tupolev solved the problem by reducing the diameter of the propellers, thus avoiding supersonic risk, but having more of them. The 200-seat Tupolev Tu-114 Rossiya had the conventional four engines, but each one drove two propellers, with a complex counter-rotating mechanism. The resultant power gave this aircraft speeds of 500 mph for the long domestic network and 478 mph for intercontinental routes. Its main shortcoming was its

Propeller-driven airliners were normally restricted to a maximum speed of little more than 320 mph because the propeller tip speed could be supersonic—with disastrous results. Tupolev solved the problem by fitting smaller propellers but more of them—eight in the 420 mph Tu-114. (NASM-9A08079)

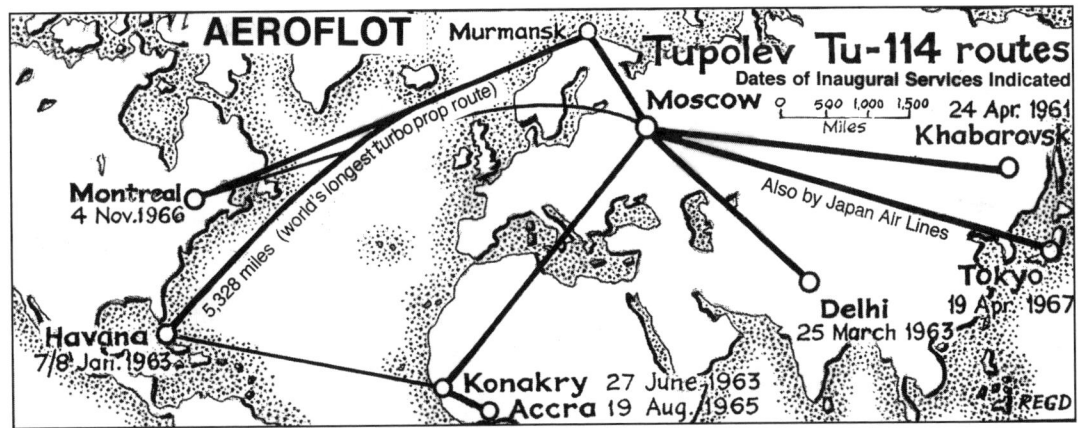

The Tupolev Tu-114 had extremely long range. It was also the only Soviet airliner to fly in the colors of a non-communist airline—by Japan Air Lines to Tokyo, where Aeroflot's flight crew was joined by J.A.L.'s flight attendants.

long landing gear, placing the main deck 16 feet off the ground and requiring passengers to climb the equivalent of two flights of stairs to board or disembark. It went into scheduled service with Aeroflot on 24 April 1961, flying nonstop from Moscow to Khabarovsk, in the Russian Far East. Scheduled service to Havana began on 7 February 1963. Carrying only 60 passengers, a stop had to be made at Murmansk, because it was not allowed to fly across Norway, home to NATO defense deployments. The 5,328-mile Murmansk-Havana segment was shorter than Moscow-Havana, but was still a very long distance at that time.

On 25 March 1963, the Tu-114 started service to Delhi, and on 27 June to the new state of Guinea, in western Africa, with an extension to Ghana on 19 August 1965. Further successes followed, demonstrating to the capitalist world by opening service to Montreal, Canada, on 4 November 1966. Then, after delicate negotiations and survey flights, a joint service began nonstop between Moscow and Tokyo on 19 April 1967. This was a notable achievement, for the aircraft carried the markings of **Japan Airlines**, as well as Aeroflot's, the first time that a Soviet airliner appeared in the colors of a non-communist airline of world stature. K.L.M. also used an Ilyushin IL-62 on its Atlantic route.

Only 33 Tupolev Tu-114s were built, but it made its mark. It was larger than the contemporary jets, with a gross weight of 170 tons, compared to the Boeing 707-300's 168 tons; and for more than a decade, until the advent of the Boeing 747, it was the largest airliner in the world.

Chapter 8: The First Big Jets

Enter Boeing

By the time the redesigned Comet 4 was ready for service, and before the Tu-104A could be further developed, the United States had made its move. Boeing, famous for its wartime B-17 Flying Fortress bomber, had addressed the problem of jet transport aircraft. At first the objective was for a jet-powered tanker to flight-refuel the bombers, the Boeing B-47s and the B-52s, which could not carry both enough fuel and enough bombs to be effective over long ranges. The prototype, designated the Model 367-80 (familiarly known as the Dash Eighty) first flew on 15 July 1954. Unlike the Comet, its engines were suspended from the wing by short pylons, and the wings had a higher degree of sweep, permitting a higher cruising speed—in excess of 600 mph, against the Comet's 500.

The U.S. Air Force liked what they saw, but asked Boeing to widen the fuselage, for more fuel capacity, and this was done, with a consequent order for a production batch in March 1955. By this time, Douglas, with a long and highly respected track record of producing thoroughbred airliners, was planning, at first, a large long-range turbo-prop airliner and then switched to a pure jet, the DC-8. This had a fuselage that could accommodate six-abreast seating, which was an obvious advantage over the Boeing transport, which was only five abreast. Boeing acted promptly, matched Douglas with a second widening of the fuselage, and the commercial Boeing 707 was born.

The first of the famous line, the Series 100, made its first flight on 15 July 1954—while the de Havilland team was working day and night to revive the now endangered Comet—and on 13 October 1955, Boeing made its breakthrough into the commercial airline market, hitherto dominated by Douglas, Lockheed, Convair, and Martin. Previously, for different reasons, it had failed. The 1933 Boeing 247, the 1939 Boeing 314 flying boat, the post-war Boeing 377 Stratocruiser were all good airplanes, but they never sold in substantial numbers. With the Boeing 707, this was to change dramatically and permanently.

Pan American Steals the Jet Age Thunder

In 1955 an airliner order from **Pan American Airways** was a breakthrough. Its determined president, the now legendary Juan Trippe, continued his visionary leadership by recognizing the need for a jet airliner with productivity far exceeding that of previous generations. As a safety measure, he had placed a provisional order for the Comet 3, a 78-seat version that made its first flight on 19 July 1954, and was flown around the world in December 1955 by John Cunningham, including Australia-Canada across the Pacific Ocean. The Boeing 707 was bigger, faster, and altogether better than the Comet series, its designers having learned from de Havilland's bitter experience and having several years of accumulated progress in both airframe and engine manufacture technology.

The redesigned de Havilland Comet 4 started the first trans-Atlantic jet service on 4 October 1958, but three weeks later, London-New York service was overtaken by Pan American's Boeing 707. (NASM-9A08175)

Pan American's order was for 25 Douglas DC-8s and 20 Boeing 707s. Trippe hedged his bets by introducing a competitive edge to the procurement pattern. Douglas had the solid reputation for building excellent airliners, but it had lost time by considering turboprop solutions for the generation to follow its piston-engined thoroughbreds. The Boeing 707-100 made its first flight on 20 December 1957 and delivered the first one to Pan American on 15 August 1958. The airline had a dozen aircraft in service before the first Douglas DC-8 was delivered, on 7 February 1961. By this time, Pan Am's Boeing 707s had girdled the globe, and Trippe reduced the DC-8 order to 19.

British technical leadership was lost. The Comet, having proven to the world that jet airliners could work, was being surpassed. Furthermore, de Havilland's concentration on solving the original Comet's problems handicapped full development of the series, and Vickers-Armstrongs, Great Britain's other major manufacturer, abandoned the larger Vickers V-1000. Several vital years were to pass before Vickers launched its VC-10, with performance potentially on par with that of the DC-8 and the 707 and increasing in popularity with the trans-Atlantic flying public.

De Havilland came out of its corner bruised but still fighting. The de Havilland Comet 4 was an improved version of the Comet 3, with the all-important trans-Atlantic range. A special production and certification effort gave B.O.A.C. the privilege of opening the world's first trans-ocean jet airline service on 4 October 1958, from London to New York. Pan American followed shortly thereafter, on 26 October, with a Boeing 707 New York-Paris service. This was flown every day, whereas the Comet flew on only three days a week. Pan Am never looked back, and though it faced competition from the British airline on the trans-Atlantic route, and B.O.A.C. did well with its jets too, the U.S. airline soon stood clear of the pack. T.W.A. had not matched Pan Am's enthusiasm for the revolutionary airliners and lost its second-place ranking to B.O.A.C., whose Comets, though inferior to the 707s in size and speed, were demonstrably superior to T.W.A.'s Lockheed L-1649A Starliners, perhaps the ultimate in propeller-driven

The First Big Jets

piston-engined airliners. T.W.A.'s owner, Howard Hughes, had procrastinated in joining the queue to order the big jets.

Pan American did not simply introduce jet transport into the airline market; it dominated it. The other airlines on the North Atlantic route hastened to catch up. Except for B.O.A.C., which was obliged to supplement its Comets with the American jet, the leading European flag-carriers lost no time in placing orders with Boeing. Recognizing that their individual shares of the total market were relatively small, compared to Pan Am's, they ordered no more than two or three each, enough to match Juan Trippe's aggressive expansion program on the direct services from New York to the European capitals, joined by T.W.A. on 21 November 1959. The Belgian airline **SABENA** was first in the queue, starting its own 707 service to New York on 23 January 1960; followed by **Air France** on 2 February, and the rejuvenated **Lufthansa** on 17 March. B.O.A.C.'s 707s joined its Comets on 27 May. The Irish airline **Aerlinte** entered the scene on 1 January 1961 with a smaller variant of the 707, the 720.

Already joining the European jet set, however, was a group of airlines that had long been faithful customers of the veteran Douglas company, the one that had launched the legendary DC-3 and the DC-6/7 series of long-distance four-engined post-war airliners. The group was led by the Dutch airline, **K.L.M.**, which had proudly claimed—correctly—that it had operated every production Douglas airliner, even the rare DC-5. Amsterdam-New York service began on 16 April 1960, with the new Douglas DC-8, and it was followed by the Scandinavian consortium, **S.A.S.**, on 1 May, **Swissair** on 30 May, **Alitalia** on 1 June, and **Iberia** on 2 July of 1961. Douglas had demonstrated that the production line at Long Beach was not about to be overwhelmed by the newcomer from Seattle.

Interestingly, as the Jet Age dawned on the North Atlantic, the participation had extended beyond the conventional and customary holders of the normal 3rd and 4th Freedoms bestowed upon airlines by the I.C.A.O. These were (in addition to the 1st—the right to overfly—and the 2nd—the right for a non-traffic stop for fuel or emergency) the rights to set down and pick up traffic in a foreign country. The 5th Freedom—the right of an airline to carry traffic *between* two foreign countries—was jealously guarded but seldom granted by those countries. On the North Atlantic, however, some airlines from beyond the ocean's shores had negotiated these rights, by hard bargaining on an exchange-of-rights basis. Thus, one of the earliest trans-Atlantic airlines was the Australian **QANTAS**, which entered the fray as early as 5 September 1959, as part of its round-the-world service. On 14 May 1960, **Air India**'s "Little Maharaja" gave the Atlantic an oriental flavor, and **Pakistan International** came in on 5 May 1961. Canada's **T.C.A.** was the third North American airline, on 1 June 1960.

These dates and airline names may seem to be an unnecessary catalog, but it is intentional. It emphasizes the amazing speed with which the Jet Age really began. B.O.A.C.'s de Havilland Comet may have operated the world's first jet airline service; the Soviet Union's Aeroflot may have operated the first *sustained* jet service; but the Jet Age began in earnest when Pan American's 707 started to fly every day across the Atlantic in October 1958 and the whole world rushed to jump on to the Big Jet band wagon.

The United States Embraces the Jet Age

In the late 1950s, the impact of the Boeing 707s and DC-8s was revolutionary. All over the world, the airlines were anxious to be part of the Jet Age. A substantial segment of the airline industry

On 26 October 1958, Pan American's daily Boeing 707 service from New York to Paris was the beginning of the sustained launching of the Jet Age for intercontinental air services. (NASM-9A08080)

The Douglas Company's first jet, the DC-8, started service with Delta Air Lines on 18 September 1959, almost a year later than Pan Am's Boeing 707 inaugural. (NASM-00131619)

was the United States domestic market, accounting for about half of the world's total passenger miles. The U.S. manufacturing and operating industries reached their peak, and their share would gradually increase to about two-thirds. By the year 2000, U.S. domestic travel reached almost saturation levels; everyone traveled by air, with long-distance railroads only a memory.

Of the U.S. domestic airlines, first off the mark was **National Airlines**, the Miami-based trunk line, presided over by the salty Ted Baker. By no means one of the larger airlines, it had made an agreement with Pan American to exchange stock, and as a practical and economic device, Baker arranged to have Pan American lease some of its aircraft to National during the winter months, when Pan Am's traffic dropped off dramatically but National's soared as northeasterners, particularly New Yorkers, sought the sun of Florida. National borrowed a Boeing 707 from Pan Am and, on 10 December 1958, operated the first jet service in the Americas, from New York to Miami.

First to operate with its own aircraft was **American Airlines**, which put the 707 on its transcontinental service on 25 January 1959. Another member of the "Big Four," T.W.A., took a gamble and, starting on 20 March, operated New York-San Francisco for a whole month with only one 707, without a single cancellation. This was a tribute not only to its maintenance staff but to the integrity of the Boeing design—new aircraft are notorious for experiencing "teething troubles" during the initial few months of day-in, day-out commercial operations.

On 18 September 1959, two of Douglas's regular customers, **Delta Air Lines** and **United**, both inaugurated their first jet services. With the first DC-8 series, with 119 seats, Delta claimed to be the first, on its New York-Atlanta route, gaining the slender advantage because United's transcontinental flight took off from San Francisco three hours later, because of the time zone difference. By the end of the year, eight U.S. domestic airlines were operating jets. The fourth member of the Big Four, **Eastern Air Lines**, had delayed its jet order, uncertain as to the choice between jet and turboprop, but finally entered the field on 24 January 1960, at long last to be on a technical par with National on the key New York-Miami route.

Boeing surpassed Douglas when its 707 started service almost two years before the Douglas DC-8. But the decades of the latter manufacturer's construction and marketing experience meant that all was not lost. Boeing sold more than 800 707s, compared to about 450 DC-8s, but Douglas developed its product more successfully, by "stretching" the fuselage beyond the earlier -30s and -50s. The DC-8-61 had much greater seating capacity than any of the Boeings; the DC-8-62 had much greater range; and the DC-8-63 combined both. Later, a further development was the DC-8-70 series, built independently from Douglas by Cammacorp, with CFM56 engines to provide substantially increased range. Well into the 21st century, a few DC-8s were still earning their keep as freighters, while 707s were no longer in regular service anywhere.

Ideal North Atlantic Jet Scheduling

The North Atlantic route was ready-made for commercial jet operations. Before the Comet 4 and Boeing 707s made their dramatic entry on the scene in October 1958, a trans-Atlantic air journey between New York and London, Paris, or Frankfurt, even nonstop in a Lockheed Super Constellation or DC-7C, could take between 12 or 14 hours, depending on the winds, invariably westerlies. With the time zone difference of five or six hours, this was operationally inconvenient for the airline schedulers; and the long hours were not too pleasant for the passengers either. The airlines' emphasis on catering standards and on ways to entertain the travelers was a reflection on a combination of less-than-ideal conditions for economical trans-ocean operations.

The introduction of jet airliners revolutionized the entire basis of trans-Atlantic service. Average speeds in excess of 550 mph permitted an eastbound journey in a comfortable seven hours, and westbound in about eight—because of the prevailing winds. This meant that, eastbound, an evening departure would arrive in any European capital at breakfast-time; while westbound, a morning departure would arrive soon after lunch. One airplane could make the round-trip neatly within a 24-hour day, accumulating about a dozen flying hours in the process, thus achieving the desirable high level of aircraft utilization demanded for profitable operation. Also, the flights were less demanding of the crews who previously faced (as they did on the U.S. transcontinental trips) limitations on the permissible continuous time on duty, customarily eight hours. Suddenly, with the jets, an aircraft would be back at its maintenance base only a day after it had more than earned its keep; and the pilots too were well rested, overnighting at the destination, and back home soon afterward.

Dates of Sustained Jet Aircraft Debuts on Ten Major Trunk Air Routes

1. North Atlantic	B.O.A.C.	4 Oct 1958	Pan American	26 Oct 1958
2. U.S. Domestic	—	—	National*	10 Dec 1958
(U.S. Transcontinental)	—	—	American	25 Jan 1959
3. Europe-East Asia	B.O.A.C.	—	Pan American	10 Oct 1959
4. South Atlantic	Aero. Argentinas	19 May 1959	Air France	16 Aug 1960
5. North-South America	Aero. Argentinas	7 June 1959	Pan American	20 July 1959
6. Trans-Pacific	—	—	QANTAS	29 July 1959
7. Trans-Polar	—	—	Pan American	27 Aug 1959
8. Europe-Australia**	—	—	QANTAS	15 Oct 1959
9. Europe-Africa	B.O.A.C.	2 Dec 1959	T.A.I./U.A.T.***	10 Sep 1960
10. Central Atlantic	—	—	Air France	20 June 1960

*Aircraft leased from Pan American. ** Big Jet service preceded Comet 4.
*** DC-8. All other Big Jets are Boeing 707.

The First Big Jets

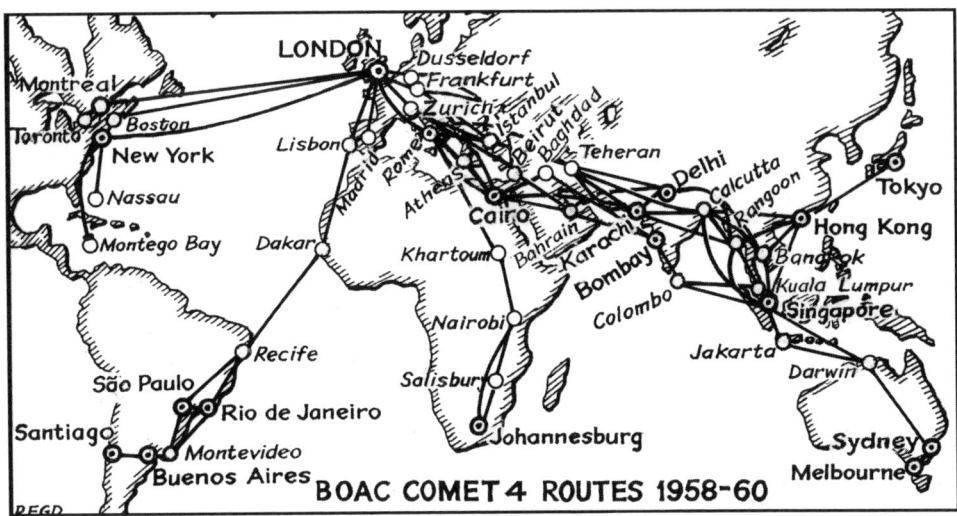

After the Comet 4's debut on the North Atlantic, B.O.A.C. soon expanded its jet services, backed by its Britannia turboprops, all over the world.

Stimulated by the introduction of Economy Fares in April 1959, North Atlantic air traffic grew by leaps and bounds. During the five years following the introduction of the jets, passenger numbers doubled, and then quadrupled in a decade. To suggest that the introduction of jet airliners across the Atlantic Ocean was a factor in consolidating the "special relationship" between the two English-speaking nations, and that it encouraged better understanding between the nations on both sides of the ocean, may be no exaggeration.

The Jets Girdle the Earth

Belatedly, the Comet 4 was able to make its mark in those areas where the Boeing 707 was still restricted because of the limitations of its airfield performance. Overpowered for its size and with more wing area, it could use almost any airport that would accept a Constellation or a DC-7C. This was of great advantage in the eastern hemisphere, where the airfields were not as developed as the international airports of the U.S.A. and Europe. This

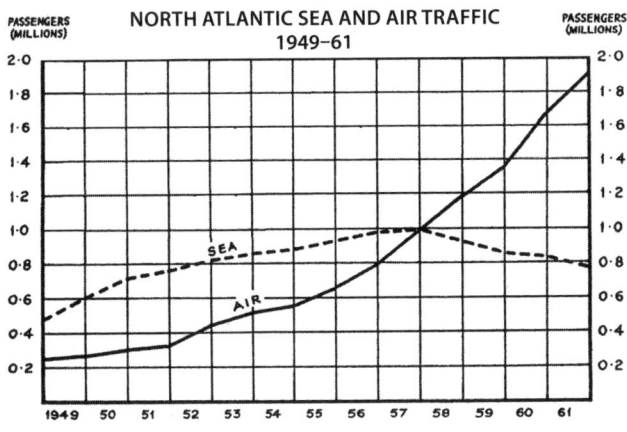

did not last long. All the airline countries of the world cheerfully laid down concrete to extend and to strengthen runways to accept the Boeing 707s and the DC-8s.

In the meantime, **B.O.A.C.** introduced the Comet 4 on its routes to eastern Asia and proceeded to deploy them over its whole network. By mid-1960, when it had its full complement of 20 aircraft, it was serving the six inhabited continents, including 36 countries and 46 cities. Service to Singapore via the Indian subcontinent, began on 1 April 1959, to Australia on 1 November, to South Africa on 2 December, and across the South Atlantic to Buenos Aires on 25 January 1960. By this time, however, another Comet 4 operator had started jet services. **Aerolíneas Argentinas** began its own South Atlantic service to Europe on 19 May 1959, and the first jet service to link the two Americas, with a Buenos Aires-New York service on 2 June. Across Africa, the Comet's excellent field performance was especially useful on traditional routes, where "hot and high" airfields at Nairobi and Johannesburg and extremely hot fields at Cairo and Khartoum were deterrents for full operations by the Big Jets. **Central African Airways (C.A.A.)**, from Southern Rhodesia (now Zimbabwe), leased Comets from B.O.A.C. for a route from Salisbury (now Harare) to London on 4 December 1959, and **East African Airways Corporation (E.A.A.C.)** linked Nairobi with London on 17 September.

The proliferation of jet airline services throughout the world was phenomenal. Within two or three years of the historic trans-Atlantic inaugurations of October 1958, a dozen airlines were crossing Asia and a dozen to South Africa. Almost as many were crossing the South Atlantic, eight or nine across the Pacific, the Central Atlantic, and even the North Pole. Five airlines, led by the Boeing 707s of Australia's **QANTAS** on 15 October 1959, linked Europe with the Antipodes, with time savings measured in days rather than hours. The Jet Age thus encompassed the

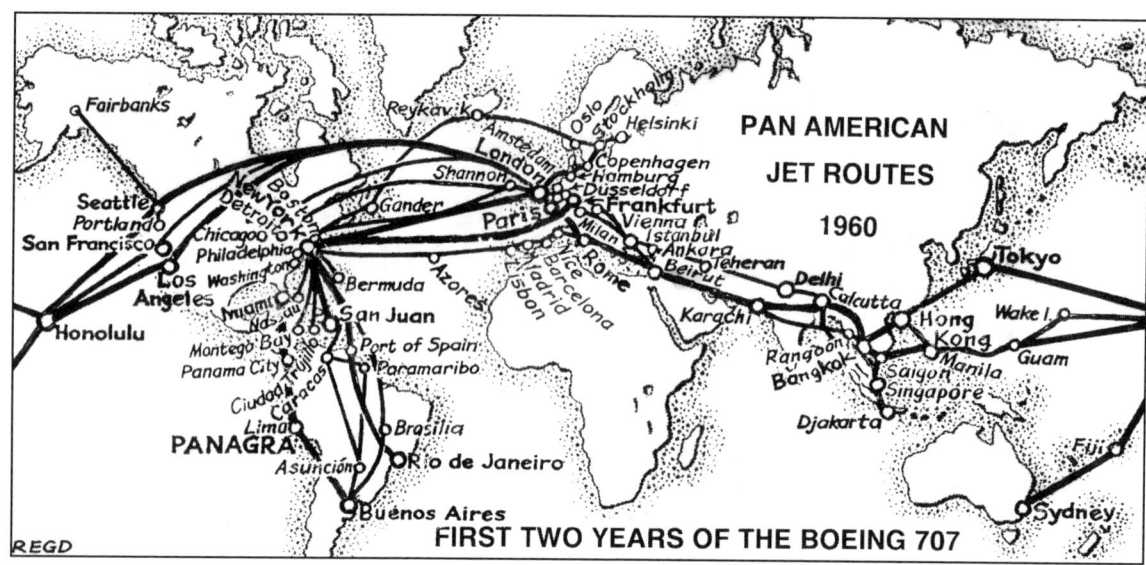

Pan American Airways' rapid expansion of its Boeing 707 routes was impressive. Within two years they embraced the globe. Flights PA1 and PA2 round the world became the airline standard for schedule and service reliability.

world, and in many ways transformed it. The DC-4s and Constellations brought nations of the world closer together, and the Stratocruisers added a touch of ocean-liner luxury. The larger jets made those nations near neighbors.

This Jet Age that began in 1958 also changed the balance of power among the aircraft manufacturers. The Comet 1 crashes in 1954 effectively wounded de Havilland to such an extent that the Comet 4s were only a postscript to its innovative initiative. Mistaken decisions by the other British manufacturers, with restricted resources, ensured their eventual demise and departure from the arena of commercial air transport construction.

In the United States, the balance of power changed too. Boeing achieved supremacy over the other manufacturers: Douglas, Lockheed, and Convair, which hitherto fought for and shared the market for commercial airliners. Boeing's past efforts to enter the fray had, for different reasons, failed to make a serious imprint. Now it swept the field. The Boeing name became identified with the Jet Age, superseding Douglas, which ruled supreme since the DC-2 of 1934. And apart from any technical considerations, such was its imprint on society as a whole that *Boeing Boeing* was a box-office success for theater-goers during the 1960s. The Seattle manufacturer became a household word, epitomizing the transport revolution that became known universally as "the Jet Age."

Twilight of the Mainline Turboprops

The ascendancy of the turboprop generation to front-line flagship status lasted for barely a decade. By the 1960s, any airliner that was propeller-driven was regarded as old fashioned. There were a few exceptions: the Soviet Tupolev Tu-114, which appeared in comparative isolation on the world's air routes as late as 1963; the Lockheed Electra, which could still operate efficiently on the shorter domestic routes of the U.S.A.; and the Ilyushin Il-18, not subject to being outclassed in the Soviet Union or in its satellite nations, where competition was not an issue. The Bristol Britannia ruled the Atlantic air for a brief couple of years, but the jet airliners were so efficient and productive that the widespread inauguration of jet services in 1958 marked the beginning of a swift end to the front-line career of the long-range aircraft.

On 10 March 1987, the Ilyushin Il-62 flew nonstop from Moscow to Khabarovsk, then to New York on 15 July 1968. (NASM-9A08081)

Chapter 9: The Short-Haul Jets

France Steps Up to the Plate

During the introductory years of the first jet airliners, the manufacturers and operators overcame the initial skepticism that fuel-hungry engines would deny the airline industry the opportunity to make a profit. Many benefits of jet propulsion indirectly compensated for the high fuel consumption. After the demonstrated success in 1952 of the B.O.A.C. Comet 1s and 2s—and there was better to come—the idea that jet airliners would ply short-haul routes was still the subject of skepticism. During the 1950s, the British went back to the drawing board; the Americans took the plunge with the first "big" jets; the Soviets struggled to catch up with the West; while the German, Italian, and Japanese aircraft manufacturers were still restrained by the consequences of the Second World War on their industries as a whole.

After 1945, France had characteristically recovered, with great determination from the hardships of war. France sustained its aircraft industry, even during the war, either by manufacturing under German control or by surreptitiously keeping design work alive. During the post-war years, companies were reorganized and amalgamated into state corporations, though many retained traditional names. They produced some useful original designs, such as the Breguet Deux-Ponts, a good load-carrying double-decker transport, but acquired a reputation of producing many new ideas that were not commercially viable.

In 1955, the Sud-Est company, based in Toulouse, gave the world's industry something to think about. Just as the de Havilland Comet had been a new shape in the sky, so too was the SE-210 Caravelle, a completely new departure from all previous approaches to the technology of marrying engines to airframes. The Caravelle's engines were not mounted on, in, or under the wing; they were mounted at the rear of the fuselage. This unprecedented departure from convention and custom was at first regarded as yet another prototype that was destined only for the history books, but Sud-Est was on to something. The Comet's wing, with its buried engines, presented not only a construction problem, but a maintenance one as well. By taking the revolutionary step of rear-mounting the engines, the designers "cleaned up" the wing, which was now relieved of any potential aerodynamic handicaps from extrusions that might be required to accommodate engines. This was also beneficial for the passengers, for the noise of the engines, usually quite distinct for those seated in line with, or even near, the engines, was now confined to only the last seat row or two.

All these advantages were put to the test when the Caravelle made its first flight on 27 May 1955. The airline world took little notice at first, and when **Air France** ordered 12 aircraft in November 1955, this was assumed to be a simple case of patriotic support for a state manufacturer by a state airline. (The critics seemed oblivious of the fact that this procedure was no different

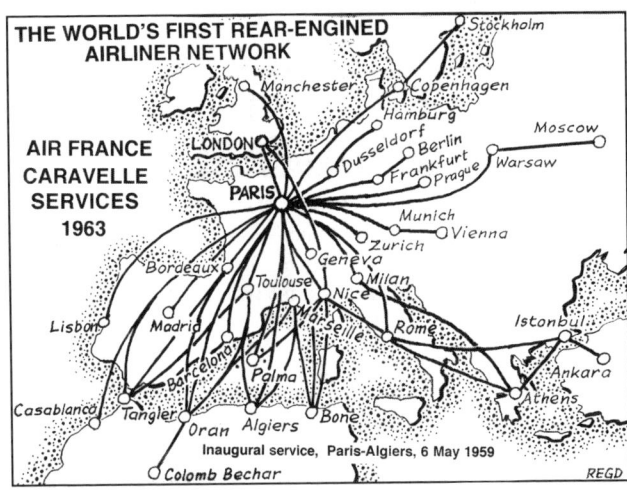

In the 1960s, Air France's Caravelles were flying all over Europe.

from the nationalistic support displayed in other countries.) The Toulouse salesmen had nothing to add to the order book for 18 months. Yet Air France kept the faith, and on 21 June 1956—by traditional standards, remarkably soon after the first flight—it started an experimental service for freight only on 21 June 1956, from Paris to Algiers via Marseilles.

Air France put the Caravelle into full service on 6 May 1959, on the Paris-Rome-Istanbul route, by which time 50 of the new short-haul jet had been ordered. The French airline also deployed it on much shorter routes, even including the 220-mile prestigious cross-Channel Paris-London link. The airline world finally took notice, even though in Britain, the idea of building the Caravelle under license (it did have Rolls-Royce Avon engines and the Comet nose) by Bristol was not pursued, partly because of a reluctance to share manufacture with another country and partly because of parochial conceit. Sud-Est's second customer was **Scandinavian Airlines System (S.A.S.)**, which at that time was in a technical alliance with Swissair. They were to help Air France set new standards of short-haul jet transport in Europe, and, through Sud-Est (which merged with Breguet-Nord to become Sud), give the French aircraft manufacturing industry a place in the commercial market, just as Marcel Dassault (formerly Bloch) had put it on the forefront of military fighter technology.

With the exception of the Dutch K.L.M. and the German Lufthansa, every major airline in western Europe bought Caravelles. With Air Algérie, Royal Air Maroc, and Air Liban, all based in francophile nations, the Mediterranean airways became almost exclusively Caravelle-dominated. But New York had an unusual introduction to the resurgent French technology. On 12 December 1959 the Brazilian airline **Viação Aérea Rio-Grandense (VARIG)**, only the third to open service with the short-haul jet, took a gamble while waiting for delivery of

Against much adverse worldwide technical opinion, The French Sud-Est company demonstrated the efficiency of mounting engines at the rear of the fuselage. This produced a "clean" wing. Air France started scheduled passenger services on 21 June 1956. (NASM-9A08082)

its Boeing 707s. It linked its home city, Porto Alegre, with New York, with stops at São Paulo, Rio de Janeiro, Port of Spain, and Nassau, and on 20 January 1960 it consolidated the service to include Brazil's new capital, Brasilia. Whether or not this unusual debut had any effect on the U.S. domestic airlines is uncertain. Fiercely patriotic, firm believers in American technological supremacy, they had invariably bought only American airliners. When Capital Airlines, the fifth largest airline at the time, had bought the British Viscounts, the action was viewed almost as a betrayal of the U.S. manufacturing industry. Now, in an astonishing move, one of the "Big Four," and the biggest airline in the world at the time, broke ranks.

In 1960 **United Air Lines** ordered 20 Caravelles and put them into service on the New York-Chicago route on 14 July 1961. They were not the first jets on the route, but they were attractive to passengers because the rear-mounted engines ensured a quiet cabin. The subsequent pattern of airline purchases differed, however, from the Viscount experience. Several other airlines had followed Capital to buy the new turboprop, but there was no rush to buy Caravelles. **Trans World Airlines (T.W.A.)** did order 20 Mark 10A versions on 7 September 1961, but the order was cancelled in May 1962. Pressure to buy American products was strong.

Ultimately, 256 Caravelles were built, a creditable record, in the light of the intense competition and even political opposition from the world in general. But the achievement was more than that. Full credit must be accorded to Sud-Est for one of the few genuine design innovations in airliner history. The French aviation industry had risen from the ashes of the Second World War and in producing the first short-haul jet in the world, had given fresh impetus to the entire world of jet airliner manufacture

Realignment in Europe

Several years were to pass before the largest pre-war airlines, Deutsche Lufthansa and Ala Littoria, could regain leading rankings in the European airway system, but eventually they did. The 1960s was a decade when many of Europe's other airlines reached a fairly even balance of relative size and strength.

Because of its status as a nonbelligerent nation, Italy was quickly off the mark. At first, two airlines had been able to establish service as early as 1946, **Alitalia**, with close association and partial control by British European Airways, and **Linee Aeree Italiane (L.A.I.)** with the American T.W.A. Alitalia became a state airline on 1 September 1957, and took over L.A.I. on 6 October of that year. It made rapid progress, and was one of the earlier purchasers of the Caravelle, putting it into service on 23 May 1960, from Rome to London. Soon after, on 1 June, it put Douglas DC-8s on the Atlantic route.

Germany's reentry into the commercial airline field took a little longer. A whole decade went by while the scars of war and the bitterness of Europe simmered down toward the country that had bred Nazi-ism. Not until 1 April 1955 did the once-familiar flying crane insignia (oldest in the airline industry, dating back to 1919) reappear in European skies. Three years later, after Convairliners, the new **Lufthansa** introduced the Viscount (the larger V-800 series); in 1960, after Constellations, it introduced its first long-range jet, the Rolls-Royce-engined Boeing 707-430. Unlike Alitalia, it deferred interest in short-range jets until 12 April 1964, when the versatile Boeing 727 went into service.

During the transitional post-war years, with Italy and Germany having to start again from scratch, other European airlines made impressive gains, taking advantage particularly of the resurgence of German industry and commerce. This remarkable phenomenon, which later became known as the German Economic Miracle, generated traffic at all the larger German cities, such as Hamburg, Munich, Frankfurt, Cologne, and Dusseldorf. For a few years, some of the smaller national airlines in Europe enjoyed healthy traffic increases at the expense of the defeated nations. This development, commercially fortuitous though it may have been, enabled airlines such as S.A.S., SABENA, and Swissair, to enter the Jet Age earlier than normal economic conditions would have allowed.

Another European airline to join the ranks of Caravelle short-haul jet operations was **Iberia**. The Spanish airline had had to work hard to rejuvenate itself. Not only had it been obliged to mark time as a neutral country during the 1939–45 conflict, it had to recover from the tragic Spanish Civil War, which had drained the country of its strength, dignity, and pride. But the beaches of the Spanish coast generated a burgeoning traffic demand from sun-starved holiday makers from northwestern Europe. Palma, on the island of Majorca, became one of the busiest airports in Europe, and the Spanish national airline shared in the tourist trade bounty. By the late 1960s, it had taken its place among the top 25 airlines of the world, overtaking SABENA and Swissair, whose status declined with the rebirth of Lufthansa.

British Vacillation

If ever a country was poised to take advantage of the efficiency of jet airline operations on short- and medium-haul routes, this was Great Britain. In spite of the devastating experience of the Comet 1 disasters, the lessons had been learned and the later Comet 4 Series performed creditably, in spite of being

The Short-Haul Jets

On 1 April 1964, B.E.A. eventually opened service with its redesigned Trident tri-jet, but Boeing had already introduced its 727. (Davies)

overwhelmed by the larger and more efficient Boeing 707s and Douglas DC-8s. Rolls-Royce was still in the forefront of jet engine technology. **British European Airways (B.E.A.)** was the largest intra-European airline, and the British people were the most air-minded nation in Europe. They still had to cross the Channel to reach the Continent, so that the air routes from London to Paris, Brussels, Amsterdam, and Frankfurt were among the busiest in the world. The same inconvenience of taking a ferry-boat, either by train or by car, was an incentive to fly to Spain's Costa Brava or the French and Italian Rivieras.

The British aviation manufacturers and B.E.A. therefore began seriously to examine designs for a short-haul jet. By 1958, the competition was between Bristol, with its Type 200 100-seat twin-jet design, and de Havilland's Type 121 tri-jet, of similar capacity. B.E.A. favored the latter, and work began on the D.H.121, soon to be named the Trident, in 1959. Then ensued what must be recorded as one of the most extraordinary errors of marketing judgment in the history of commercial airliner manufacture.

Work on the first Trident design was well under way. Market forecasts for a 100-seat jet aircraft with a range of up to 1,500 miles confidently predicted future sales of many hundreds. The size was right, according to most airlines consulted. 100 seats was the minimum required for the American market, if de Havilland (becoming Hawker Siddeley, by merger, in 1960) expected trans-Atlantic sales.

B.E.A. had ordered 24 100-seat Trident 1s in 1959, but in 1960, it became alarmed at a slump in traffic and demanded the seating be reduced to 84. Ignoring the detailed analysis of its own market research, Hawker Siddeley capitulated and embarked on a complete modification of the Trident, cutting out three seat rows. Not only did this increase the vital cost-per-seat-mile level, it added to cost of production and almost two years of production time. In the highly competitive environment of airliner marketing, Hawker Siddeley shot itself in the foot. Three weeks later, Boeing visited de Havilland to inspect the plans, ostensibly to discuss a licensed production. It then launched the Boeing 727, a tri-jet remarkably similar, with the same fuselage cross-section as its successful Boeing 707, and with 100 seats. Hawker Siddeley had shot itself in the other foot, and B.E.A. did not introduce the Trident until two months after the 727.

The Boeing 727

With the outstanding production levels of the plant at Seattle, the Boeing 727 was launched with efficient enthusiasm. The company had already produced more than 900 military C-97 transports/commercial type 377 Stratocruisers and was well on its way to matching that number with Boeing 707s. The British could not come close to the superiority of the United States aircraft manufacturing industry. The de Havilland heritage was still highly respected, and the Hatfield firm did resist the might of Boeing for a short while. Boeing's larger aircraft—identical in size to original Trident design—won the day because its seat-per-mile costs and guaranteed delivery schedules and volume output were unmatched.

Eastern Air Lines put the first Boeing 727 into service on the Philadelphia-Washington-Miami service on 1 February 1964. This was followed five days later by United Air Lines, and by American Airlines on 12 April. This tri-jet was thus in service with the three largest airlines in the world even before the Trident opened service with British European Airways. Within a year, 727s were to be seen at every major airport in the United States, and the overseas sales quickly built up. Lufthansa, rapidly finding its feet again as it reestablished its preeminent European status, started 727 service on 12 April 1964. On 1 August 1965, **Japan Air Lines** introduced the 727 on its heavily traveled domestic trunk routes, and its competitor, **All Nippon Airways**, followed soon afterward. The timing for Boeing could not have been better; during the 1960s, as Japan began to assert itself as a major industrial power, air traffic growth reached a phenomenal 20% annual growth level for several years, and often exceeded it.

During the 1960s and 1970s, the world's average air traffic growth rate was sustained at 15%, only declining to lower levels in the 1980s. This meant a doubling of airline traffic every five years, and the world demand for new airliners was almost insatiable. Boeing had the right airplane for the job. Very shortly it developed the Boeing 727-200 series, stretching the fuselage of the -100 to about the same length as that of the previous generation's 707. The first -200 went into service with **Northeast Airlines** on 14 December 1967, on the busy New York-Miami route. The Boeing 727 was a superb airliner, versatile in range

Almost identical to de Havilland's original design for the Trident, the Boeing 727 was introduced by Eastern Air Lines on 1 February 1964. (Copyright © Boeing; NASM-9A08083)

De Havilland Trident sales were eclipsed by the Boeing 727, but it sold well in China, where trading with the United States was limited by the communist government. This one is at Nanning. (SI-95-2351)

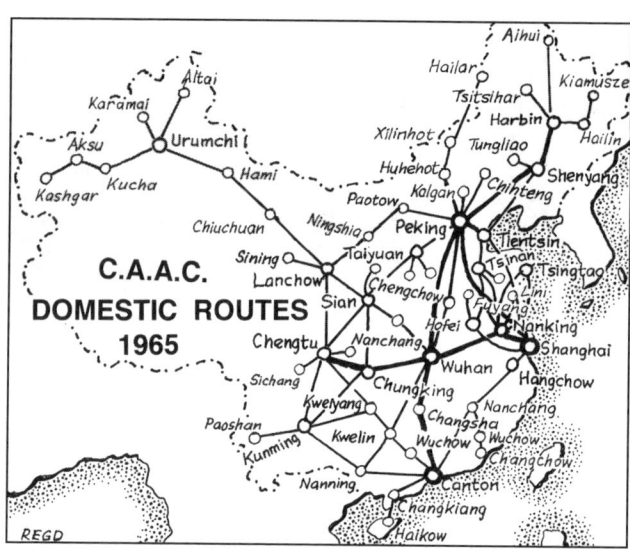

By the mid-1960s, C.A.A.C. was beginning to build a nationwide network, to link all the main provincial cities. Tridents replaced the older Soviet airliners.

and able to turn in a profit for its operators even at comparatively short ranges, for example, on Eastern Air Lines's Air-Shuttle in the dense Boston-New York-Washington air corridor. Ultimately, 1,932 aircraft were delivered, almost exactly twice as many as the previously creditable record set by the 707/720. The Seattle manufacturer was on the crest of a wave.

Tridents to China

Almost two years late, B.E.A. put the Trident 1C into service on 1 April 1964, and operated it successfully against the European competition, consisting mainly of Caravelles. It had already replaced, on many routes, a variant of the Comet, the 4B, which had first flown on 27 June 1959, as a short-haul version of the pioneer type, trading off fuel tankage for additional seating in a longer fuselage. B.E.A. had put its first Comet—and its first pure-jet airliner—into service on 1 April 1960.

Except for small orders from the Middle East (Kuwait, Iraq, Cyprus, and Pakistan), the only substantial Trident order was from the People's Republic of China, whose C.A.A.C. (Civil Aviation Adminstration of China) was disinclined to buy any product of the United States, with whom relations of all kinds—commercial, social, and diplomatic—were still frigid in the extreme. Its order was for the Trident 2E, a longer-ranged version of the Trident 1E, itself slightly larger than the Trident 1C. This was the version that had eventually been delivered to B.E.A., which continued to support the aircraft program with repeat orders. These included 26 Trident 3Bs, whose lengthened fuselage added 30 extra seats, and placed it in the same category as the Boeing 727-200. But to provide the increased power, beyond the capability of the Rolls-Royce Spey engines, a supplementary booster engine was added at the base of the vertical stabilizer's trailing edge. This small but powerful Rolls-Royce RB162 power plant ran during the brief time when maximum power was needed on take-off. But such devices were no match for the Boeing 727s worldwide dominance, and production of the British tri-jet petered out in 1972.

The Chinese state airline needed much coaching. Between November 1972 and June 1978, 33 Tridents were delivered to C.A.A.C. Until then, the only modern aircraft in its fleet were Soviet types, notably the Ilyushin Il-18 and Antonov An-24 "workhorse" turboprops, and the Ilyushin Il-62 four-engined jet. It had also taken delivery of a few Vickers Viscount turboprops, the last off that successful British production line. But the airline was not versed in the kind of efficient usage and deployment of an airline fleet that was customary in the western capitalist world. Although Soviet manufacturing and design technology was donated to the Chinese during the period of Sino-Soviet friendship, operational efficiency was not.

The Tridents, therefore, were something of a mixed blessing to C.A.A.C. The airline was able to cope with the engineering and maintenance, but scheduling was not its strong point. One round-trip on a single route was a typical day's work for one aircraft, and the Trident was no exception. Reservations procedures were primitive as exchange of data by telex or other automatic systems was almost non-existent. The main airports witnessed tired citizens waiting hopefully, sometimes all day or all night, for an available seat. On the other hand, the Tridents, like the Viscounts, could be supported by spare parts and maintenance from Hong Kong, much nearer than Moscow, and far more obliging and efficient. C.A.A.C.'s Tridents, most of them based at Guangzhou, next door to Hong Kong, therefore served to advance the basic knowledge of standard airline operating procedures and how to maximize resources, for example in improving the annual utilization of the airline fleet.

The transformation of Chinese commercial aviation from the struggles of the 1970s to the explosive growth that accelerated only two decades later has been a phenomenal development. (See Chapter 33.)

The British Second Force

The extraordinary decision of Hawker Siddeley to reduce the size of the Trident, against the advice of its market research department, was then compounded on a national scale. A twin-jet airliner was developed that competed with the British tri-jet and that was sponsored by independent initiative. The two amalgamations of the many small aircraft manufacturers in Britain had, in addition to Hawker Siddeley, also produced the British Aircraft Corporation (B.A.C.), from the combined resources of Vickers, Bristol, and English Electric, all with fine traditions of pioneering and creativity. The British airline industry also needed attention. The independents were far too numerous, often competing with each other rather than collectively competing with B.O.A.C. and B.E.A. The politicians took a time-honored step: it formed a committee.

The proposals recommended by the Edwards Committee, appointed by the British government in 1967 were far-reaching. Its Report, published on 1 April 1969, was a blue-print for the creation of what was referred to as a "Second Force." It was an instrument to restore common sense to a situation that had threatened imminent chaos.

Among those privileged to share the scheduled services was **British United Airways (B.U.A.)**, formed in July 1960 by the merger of Airwork and the Hunting-Clan group, and strongly backed by shipping interests. The managing director was Freddie Laker, who had brought his company Air Charter company into the amalgamated group. In January 1962, it purchased the Britavia group. Only Skyways, Harold Bamberg's British Eagle, and a few other stalwart, mainly local, airlines, had remained completely independent. Eagle had ceased operations.

Of those airlines that depended solely on non-scheduled operations, the one that emerged prominently during the 1960s was **Caledonian Airways**, led by Adam Thomson. It fashioned the inclusive tour system into a fine art, and benefitted too from general charters and trooping contracts. On 16 January 1968, Caledonian had joined the Jet Set with an inaugural 189-seat Boeing 707-320C service from London's Gatwick Airport to New York. By selling the whole aircraft capacity to travel agents and tour-group organizers (chess clubs, bird-watchers, baseball fans, theater-goers, and all kinds of people, Thomson offered round-trips to the United States at fares less than the International Air Transport Association (IATA) carriers could charge for a single trip. The £186 round-trip from Los Angeles to London was less than B.O.A.C.'s IATA-ordained £224 one-way economy fare. When Caledonian added Singapore to its long-haul destinations, the flights were all non-scheduled, but usually left at the same time each day.

Edwards recommended that the Second Force could be formed by marrying Caledonian's flair for innovative marketing with B.U.A.'s established scheduled route pattern, to be centered on Gatwick as a solid technical base, with easy access to central London. The merger took place on 30 November 1970, appropriately St. Andrew's Day. Caledonian purchased B.U.A. for £6,900,000, and on 31 March 1971, **British Caledonian Airways,** soon to be known as **B-Cal**, became Britain's Second Force airline. It was granted permission for the coveted trans-Atlantic routes and began scheduled service to New York on 1 April 1973. It then consolidated its presence on the routes to the Far East by quasi-scheduled flights to Singapore, in what was known as the Exempt Charter Service.

During the early 1970s, B-Cal expanded its domestic hub system from Gatwick to major domestic and cross-Channel city destinations, but just as it was getting into its stride, it suffered from the worldwide OPEC oil crisis, and found itself restricted in European expansion opportunities. In 1974, Thomson reduced its routes—including those to New York and Los Angeles—its fleet, and personnel. But under the new Labour government, it was offered additional destinations in the United States and in South America, under the dual-designation provisions of the "Bermuda Two" bilateral agreement, signed on 23 June 1977. The two prime U.S. destinations that he had surrendered were reallocated to Thomson's old rival, Freddie Laker.

Thomson and B-Cal struggled back into the ring, but it was not a fair fight. Prime Minister Margaret Thatcher was dictating all British policy, and instead of favoring independent enterprise, all the best opportunities seemed to fall to British Airways. The state airline lost £545 million during 1983, partly by cutting fares to match those of the independents and partly by not cutting matching costs, including staff numbers. B-Cal prepared a strong case for the allocation of more routes, and Thomson stated, "Under the circumstances it must be nonsense for a government dedicated to supporting private enterprise to create an instrument that will undoubtedly undermine those who have built the existing independent sector." Ultimately, all it received was an increase of the British worldwide market share from 13% to 15%. With 85% still in the hands of Britain's chosen instrument, the cries for a Second Force were reduced to a whimper.

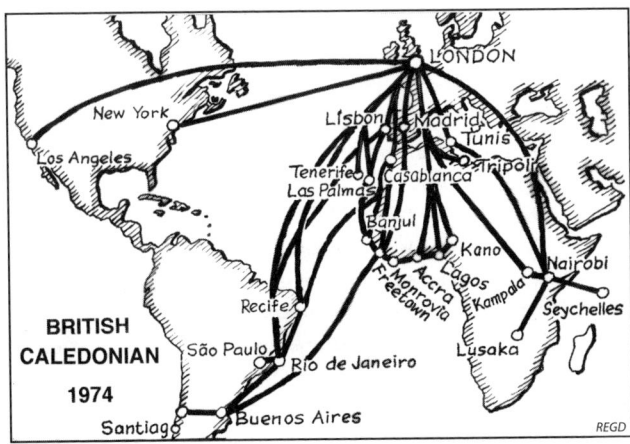

Britain's "Second Force" airline received only a small percentage of international route allocations, but in the 1970s it did develop networks in Africa, South America, and the United States.

Following the success of the Sud-Est Caravelle, the British industry introduced the twin-engined BAC One-Eleven. It went into service with B.U.A. (later B-Cal) on 9 April 1965. (NASM-9A08085)

The BAC One-Eleven

Before Freddie Laker left B.U.A., where he was the managing director, he had been instrumental in working with the B.A.C. for the production of a twin-jet airliner to succeed the French Caravelle. The progenitor was a design from one of the companies that had joined Bristol, Vickers, and English Electric to form B.A.C. Hunting Aircraft had a design, the H.107, a 50-seat short-haul jet, and this became the inspiration for the 80-seat BAC One-Eleven, to be built at the Vickers component of the new corporation. Its engines were the same as the Trident's Rolls-Royce Speys, and from the national point of view, efforts should have been made to pursue even more commonality of the two types, as well as joint marketing efforts. But the spirit of obstinate independence prevailed and the two British companies faced the strength of U.S. manufacturing by competing with each other as well.

The design specification appeared to be exactly right, and Sir George Edwards, chief designer of the Concorde, was a good promoter. Like the Trident, the aircraft had the T-tail (to avoid aerodynamic problems with the rear-mounted engines on the fuselage), the engines were from a famous line, and the size was right—almost as many seats as the Trident's and the Boeing 727-100's, but with only two, not three, engines. By the time the BAC One-Eleven made its first flight on 20 August 1963, orders for about 60 aircraft had been placed. The order from Braniff, soon to be followed by one from Mohawk, was the first for British jet airliners by U.S. operators.

The One-Eleven Series 200 (there was no -100) went into service with B.U.A. on 9 April 1965 and was widely accepted, especially by the burgeoning British inclusive tour operators. Its speed allowed it to make two round-trips every 24 hours to all the popular Mediterranean destinations; and its size was conveniently the equivalent to two bus-loads, an important consideration for the package tour business.

With increased power ratings from the Spey engines, B.A.C. developed the basic design in the traditional manner. The Series 300 had additional range but this soon evolved into the Series 400, with restricted gross weight to meet U.S. restrictions at the time for two-crew operation. American Airlines ordered 30 of the -400s, impressive for a foreign manufacturer competing with the production lines on the West Coast. Then a further improvement was made. The Series 500 version had the fuselage lengthened by 13.5 feet, and it could carry 119 passengers. The biggest customer was B.E.A., which later on added to the fleet when it bought British Caledonian.

The Douglas DC-9

Almost the first airline to take an interest in the BAC One-Eleven was Western Air Lines, based in Los Angeles, close to Santa Monica—original home of the great Douglas Aircraft Company. After a flirtation with Sud Aviation, with the idea of building the Caravelle under license, Douglas revived an almost-discarded project and, in April 1963, announced a twin jet, with two Pratt & Whitney JT8D engines. B.A.C. had already set the pace, and the One-Eleven made its first flight only four months after Douglas brushed the dust off its drawings. When the 80-seat DC-9 Series 10, remarkably similar to the British twin-jet, made its first flight on 22 February 1965, British United put its One-Eleven into service only two months later.

Such a lead was no great deterrent to a manufacturer of the stature of Douglas, which in 1967 had become a division of the McDonnell Douglas Aircraft Corporation, with McDonnell exerting control. To exploit the enormous United States domestic market, it had several significant advantages over the British rival, not least an inherent natural patriotism of all Americans to buy the home-built product. A long tradition of commercial airliner know-how went back to the first (Douglas Commercial) DC-1 of 1934. Generations of thoroughbred designs followed, of which the DC-9 was simply the newest. During three decades, mutual trust had developed to the extent that multi-million-dollar orders were confirmed by a telephone call or a handshake. In the case of the DC-9, an additional factor was the emphasis on easy maintenance, with the ground engineer's needs recognized to be as important as the pilot's.

C.E. Woolman of **Delta Air Lines** placed an order for the DC-9-10 in April 1963 (no doubt over the telephone to Donald Douglas, Sr.). This was the beginning of a flood of orders, with U.S. airlines leading the field. Such was the intensity of air travel in the United States by the late 1960s and early 1970s that airlines no long ordered planes in single digits; they ordered by the dozens. With the DC-9, Douglas was at last able to halt the threat of a complete dominance of the short-medium-range airliner category by Boeing's 727.

The DC-9, like the BAC One-Eleven, was also attractive to the U.S. Regional airlines—they now called themselves by that name, as it seemed more dignified than the official term, Local Service, under which they had been created by the Civil Aeronautics Board. (This development is dealt with later on in this book). The larger companies of that group of what could be termed the "Second Level" found that the traffic demand on many of their routes justified a small jet, and North Central Airlines from Minneapolis, Bonanza Airlines from Las Vegas, and West Coast Airlines from Seattle helped to augment the Douglas order book.

The Short-Haul Jets

Just as the Boeing 727 tri-jet followed the Trident and enjoyed far greater sales, Douglas followed the BAC One-Eleven with the DC-9 twin, and also achieved worldwide success. (SI-96-15335)

European and other foreign airlines also liked the Douglas product. The Dutch **K.L.M.**, which had operated every DC model since the DC-2, could be expected to retain its confidence in a thoroughbred tradition; and it was joined by reputable flag carriers such as S.A.S., Alitalia, and Iberia, all of which were able to intensify their European networks. DC-9s, mainly the most popular -30 series, were to be seen everywhere throughout the continent, from the Arctic isolation of Spitzbergen (S.A.S.) to every Mediterranean resort, where, in addition to Spain and Italy, Yugoslavia was benefitting from the surge of vacationers from the cooler north. In addition to the state airline, **Jugoslovenski Aerotransport (J.A.T.)**, the enterprising Slovenian airline **Inex-Adria** chose the DC-9, and such was the combined success of operator and aircraft that it was able to maintain firm contracts with major German tour operators, against local competition from German airlines.

While the Douglas salesmen ranged around the world, competing vigorously with Boeing especially, they were not quite so successful in the other continents. Japan was a Boeing fortress, and while **Japan Air Lines** and **All Nippon Airways** bought quantities of Boeing 727s, Douglas had to be content with the third airline, **Toa Domestic Airlines**. Sales were made in South Korea, and in Indonesia, Garuda, serving a vast country comprised of many large islands and hundreds of smaller ones. Its president, Wiweko, found the DC-9 to its liking, and bought them regularly for several years. In Australia, the Ansett group preferred it, and in South America, sales were made in Venezuela and Argentina, but not in Brazil, where Boeing held the reins, and where the BAC One-Eleven was preferred by Transbrasil, led by the charismatic Omar Fontana. The DC-9 was developed beyond all expectations and was "stretched" to the extent that the -80, or the MD-80, had more than twice as many seats as the original version.

Soviet Short-Haul

The Soviet designers had already demonstrated they were capable of producing, on a large scale if necessary, technically efficient aircraft. They kept pace with the aircraft production lines of the United States and Europe. For military purposes, the Soviet Air Force's fighters and bombers were as good as any. For commercial airline needs, however, the demand was different in one respect. The market was confined to one customer: the monolithic state airline, **Aeroflot**. No capitalist-based airline would ever buy a Soviet airliner, but the flag carriers of communist or satellite countries would invariably follow Aeroflot's lead. Only occasionally, as in the case of Czechoslovakia's involvement in improving the Tupolev Tu-104, did they make any significant contribution to manufacturer-customer relationships.

This is not to state that the element of competition in the Soviet Union was absent; it was different. Although Aeroflot was the only customer for which a new airliner could be launched, it was a large customer. Once decided on a selected design, and fully approved of its decision, Aeroflot bought that type by the hundreds. On the other hand, if it did not approve a design or type (or possibly was obliged to take it, as in the case of the supersonic Tupolev Tu-144), that effectively killed the project. To win a competition for Aeroflot was a guarantee of success—unlike the case in the West, where a substantial order book from several airlines was necessary to justify a viable production line.

By the late 1950s, Aeroflot's fleet was beginning to look impressive in sheer numbers. But most of these were still propeller-driven aircraft. Only about 200 (or one-tenth) of the fleet was jet-powered by the Tupolev Tu-104. Most of the work was being done by the turboprop workhorses, the 100-seater Ilyushin Il-18s (first called the Moskva), and the 85-seat Antonov An-10 (Ukraina). The main policy objective for Soviet commercial aviation had hitherto been to concentrate on long-distance domestic operations, to bring the regions of Siberia closer to Moscow and European Russia in a reasonable journey time—a few hours to the eastern Urals, Tashkent, or Novosibirsk, or a day's flight from the far eastern cities of Khabarovsk and Vladivostok. The Trans-Siberian Railway was destined to become mainly a freight railroad, and eventually to carry tourists rather than representing a standard means of transport for the majority of Soviet citizens.

The Soviet government, which controlled all industrial activity, stirred itself. The designers too were aware of the increasing momentum and volume of travel within the vast frontiers of the U.S.S.R. Rather than take the train, the Soviet people were taking to the air, encouraged by Aeroflot's cheap fares. The demand for medium- and short-haul airliners was urgent. Government officials demanded to fly by jet the 400 miles between Moscow and Leningrad or Kiev or Sverdlovsk; and citizens wanted to fly to the Black Sea resorts of Sochi or Yalta.

The first response to this demand was from the Tupolev design bureau. The Tu-104 had been able to provide essential inter-city needs since 1956, but was not suited to serve the many short-haul routes radiating from Moscow to dozens of destinations that were only an hour's flight away. Cities such as Riga, Minsk, Kazan, or Kuybyshev (Samara) were population centers that did not individually generate enough traffic to justify frequent jet service with the Tu-104. Thus, a derivative, shorter-fuselaged, version, the Tupolev Tu-124, made its debut on 2 October 1962, on the Moscow-Tallinn (Estonia) route. The 44- to 56-seat short-haul jet trailed the Caravelle by more than three years, but was ahead of both the BAC One-Eleven and the Douglas DC-9 by a similar margin.

Like the pioneer de Havilland Comet team, however, Andrei Tupolev recognized that the wing-root-mounted engine design of the 104 and the 124 was inferior to other ways of installing engines, either in pods suspended from the wing or mounted on the rear of the fuselage, like the ground-breaking Caravelle. Accordingly, on 9 September 1967, the Tupolev Tu-134 entered service with Aeroflot. It differed from the five-abreast seating of the BAC One-Eleven and the Douglas DC-9 in that its fuselage was narrower (of Tu-104 dimension) with only four-abreast seating. But it was an immediate success in the Communist world, as it performed well. More than 700 were delivered to Aeroflot and it was exported to the satellite nations of eastern Europe, which needed short-haul jets to compete with, and to improve their image against the better-equipped western airlines.

The "Six-Pool"

The accessibility of a Soviet airliner that could at least match the western airlines' short-jets in performance, if not in profitability, was welcomed in the eastern European countries beyond the Winston Churchill–defined "Iron Curtain." Yugoslavia, under Marshal Tito, had broken clear from Moscow's grip, but the others were tied to the Soviet system of politics and trade. Under vast international bartering arrangements, exports and imports were concentrated, almost confined, to trading with the U.S.S.R. Hungary, for example, whose Ikarus omnibus manufacturer produced excellent vehicles, exported them by the thousands in exchange for oil and gas, pumped through pipelines direct from northwestern Siberia. Czechoslovakia did the same with street-cars, and all the countries were involved in and irrevocably tied to the reciprocal trading in agricultural and industrial products.

They also traded with each other. Bulgaria and Rumania, for example, benefitted from east German, Polish, and Czech vacationers seeking the sunshine and beaches of the Black Sea, while Budapest was a favorite spot for Berliners. Czech streetcars were the standard for the capital cities of the six eastern European countries, and Ikarus buses were everywhere. Such standardization was perceived to be ideal for the airlines, and on 8 June 1957, LOT (Poland), C.S.A. (Czechoslovakia), MALEV (Hungary), Interflug (East Germany), TAROM (Romania), and TABSO (Bulgaria) signed a provisional agreement to cooperate on matters of air transport. This arrangement became known as the "Six-Pool" as it integrated the six airlines by multilateral agreements covering routes, flights, fares, and liabilities for damages. On 27 October 1965, the eastern Six, together with Aeroflot and Mongolia, signed an "Agreement for the Cooperation of Air Traffic

The Soviet industry's short-haul jet to succeed the Tupolev Tu-104 and -124 was the Tu-134. It had four-abreast seating, compared to five in western twin-jets, but it served well within the Soviet sphere of influence. A Polish LOT's is pictured here at Warsaw. (Davies)

Enterprise in Operational, Commercial, and Financial Areas," the so-called Berlin Accord, and on 6 October 1966, in Brno, Czechoslovakia, a second agreement adopted all the provisions of the Accord pertaining to air transport.

One result of the pooling was to guarantee cheaper airline fares to all citizens of the member countries—about half of those normally charged by western standards, thus echoing the custom in the Soviet Union, where Aeroflot's fares were extremely low, even for people whose income was also low, compared to the pockets of westerners. Payments were made through a clearing house, similar to that initiated many years earlier by the IATA, based in London.

The establishment of such a regulatory system was timely, as within a year of the Brno agreement, the Tupolev Tu-134 became available and it was ideally matched to the main traffic flows in eastern Europe. During the late 1960s, all except one of the Six-Pool airlines purchased (or traded for) the new Soviet 72-seat short-haul jet. First was **Balkan Bulgarian Airlines**, in 1967, not long after Aeroflot, followed by Hungary's **Magyar Legikozlekedesi Vallalat (MALEV)**, east Germany's **Interflug**, and **Polskie Linie Lotnicze (LOT)** in 1969. **Ceskoslovenske Statni Aerolinie (C.S.A.)** had acquired the Tu-124 in 1964 for its short-haul jet services and so did not obtain the Tu-134 until 1971. But chinks were beginning to appear in the Iron Curtain. Limited trading had begun with western Europe. For example, Czechoslovakia was printing high-quality books for western export, and western vacationers were discovering the Black Sea resorts as well as those in the Adriatic. In line with this easing of political adhesion to Moscow, **Transporturile Aeriene Romine (TAROM)** abstained from the Tu-104 list, in favor of the BAC One-Eleven, which was the result of negotiations to build the aircraft under license in Romania.

Chapter 10: Proliferation

Tourism Changes the Balance

The 1960s witnessed the beginning of a subtle shift in what could be described as the balance of power among the world's leading airlines. In 1960, 13 of the top 25 airlines of the world were in North America, and these included the leading five giants: the so-called Big Four U.S. domestic companies (United, American, T.W.A., and Eastern) and Pan American, which still dominated the world's intercontinental air routes. Nine airlines were in Europe, led by Air France, Britain's B.O.A.C. and the Dutch K.L.M. Two others, Germany's Lufthansa and Italy's Alitalia, were still recovering from the effects of the Second World War but were systematically rebuilding. Australia's QANTAS ranked 22nd, and its domestic airline Trans-Australia Airlines (T.A.A.) was 23rd. From the other continents, only Japan Air Lines (J.A.L.) appeared, ranking 24th, arising phoenix-like from the ashes of a nation severely stricken by the war. In South America, Brazil's VARIG had dropped off the top-25 list, and Africa's airlines were mainly embryonic flagships of still-fragmented emerging colonies not yet able to sustain airlines of international standards.

The Spanish national airline **Iberia** joined the ranks of the leading European airlines, benefitting from the rapidly increasing popularity of Spain's tourism industry, as the beaches of Majorca, the Costa Brava, Costa Blanca, and Costa del Sol and the attractions of the Canary Islands. Businessmen's inter-city routes between the cities of northern Europe were matched and often exceeded in traffic density by the tourism routes from sun-starved Scandinavia, Britain, and Germany to the sunny Mediterranean. The hotels in Italy, Greece, and Yugoslavia shared in the burgeoning vacation traffic, but Spain was the main beneficiary.

National corporations such as B.E.A., SABENA, and S.A.S. shared in the spoils, but most of the stimulation came from the independents, in spite of regulations that denied them the rights to operate scheduled services. This resulted in much creative thought among the innovative airline entrepreneurs, who, in Britain, for example, suffered from a slanted interpretation of the phrase "material diversion" from B.E.A.'s routes. They had participated in military logistics work, and had struggled to survive with charter flights, including inclusive tours, which saved the travelers the time and trouble of arranging the details of vacation trips. The travel agents booked hotels and airplanes for a whole season, thus obtaining bargain-basement tariffs, a benefit passed on to grateful sun-seekers.

In 1949, a mandate allowed the independents to fly limited scheduled services as associates of the state airlines. In 1952 this was extended when the British Conservative government took office. A ground swell began to develop in the air tourist industry, which organized inclusive tours on an increasingly wider scale. These offered a package in which the air trip, the ground transport, the hotel, and (possibly the most important) the services of a guide were included in a single combined tariff. The Establishment tried to restrict these by enforcing the definition of a "closed group," which could not be formed for the purposes of air travel. Suddenly, many ingenious package programs were offered to chess clubs, football supporters, and ornithological societies. One agency specialized in tours for the Civil Service Clerical Association, which could hardly be defined as being formed to sponsor travel, but with half a million members, provided a good market for Whitehall Travel.

B.E.A. had patronizingly described this movement as "aiming at a section of the population for whom Continental travel is something new and strange," but later had to admit that "almost all the traffic increase on some routes has been in Inclusive Tours." The newly formed Air Transport Licensing Board began to take a more generous view of airline applications for inclusive tour programs, and in 1965, the Minister of Aviation removed almost all the restrictions. One effect of this was to introduce the element of "survival of the fittest." In Britain, the 70 post-war companies had already been reduced in numbers, mostly by demise but also by merger, to about half a dozen. Harold Bamberg's **British Eagle** and **British United Airways (B.U.A.)**—a merger of Air Charter, Airwork, and Hunting Clan—were, in the early 1960s, operating piston-engined aircraft such as Vickers Vikings, Douglas DC-3s, and various others handed down from the state corporations. Burgeoning traffic demanded improved service. No longer were passengers asked to fly in aircraft of doubtful vintage; they were pleasantly surprised to find B.U.A. operating Viscounts and British Eagle operating Britannias.

In Germany, **Condor Luftreederei** had been formed in 1961 by a merger, with Lufthansa participation, and was joined in 1963 by **Sudflug** and later by several others, including

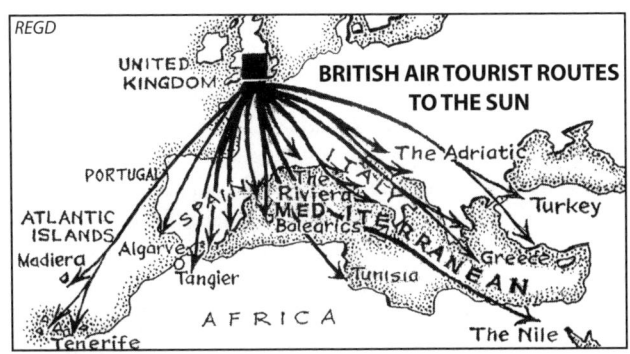

During the 1960s and 1970s, jet travel accelerated journeys from northwest Europe to the sunnier south. From Great Britain especially, inclusive tour traffic expanded as far as north Africa.

Lufttransport Unternehmen (L.T.U.). The German air charter business was characterized by the complete involvement of the major travel agencies, many of which were operated by large department stores, such as Neckermann. In Scandinavia, the initiative was taken, curiously, by a Danish pastor, Ejlif Krogager, who enterprisingly expanded his local parish motor-coach trips into a more ambitious operation. In 1962, he formed **Sterling Airways**, which was so successful that, within a few years, it became the largest charter operator in Europe. Elsewhere, other than Great Britain, Germany, and Scandinavia, which combined to account for three-quarters of the air tour activity in Europe, the Dutch **Martinair** was successful. And one of the several dozen European independents in other countries was located in the destination country, rather than the customary country of tourist origin. The Spanish **Spantax** grew to become, by the mid-1970s, another large European charter airline.

The success and growth of the inclusive tour and charter industry during the 1960s and 1970s was spectacular. During the latter 1960s, the annual traffic growth rate exceeded 35% per annum for several years. Some charter airlines were almost as large as the flag carriers of some of the smaller nations. By 1970, the revenue passenger-mile total of non-scheduled intra-European air traffic surpassed that of the scheduled airlines; in spite of difficulties caused by the oil crisis of the early Seventies, they maintained this lead. In addition to the Inclusive Tour Charter (ITC), other devices were introduced to circumvent restrictive regulations, such as the Advanced Booking Charter (ABC), and the Travel Group Charter (TGC). But the definition between scheduled and non-scheduled was becoming blurred. Popular ITC routes such as London-Palma or Copenhagen-Malaga operated at the same time every day, and some of the independents would remark that their services ran more frequently on time than did many of those of the scheduled airlines.

By the mid-1970s, the European independents owned 300 jet airliners, and all European charter services were operated by some 60 Caravelles, 40 BAC One-Elevens, 20 Douglas DC-9s, about 60 Boeing 737s and 727s, and a few Fokker F-28s. The British **Dan-Air** bought every de Havilland Comet it could locate, correctly calculating that the higher direct operating costs could be offset by very low second-hand purchase prices.

Throughout the remarkable evolution of the European air charter industry, one common denominator had been the low fares. Because of the mass marketing principles, the air fare was part of an entire package and was effectively lower (and often much lower) than the lowest scheduled economy fare. But standards of operations, service, and safety matched those of the scheduled airlines. No longer were the independents regarded as the poor relations of the air transport industry. Fighting regulations that a few years later, with airline deregulation, would be regarded as ludicrous, they had won their spurs, had become a respected group, flying by its own standards, and whose instincts for improvisation and ingenuity would in due course contribute to the technical development of world air transport and the airliner manufacturing industry.

Main European Passenger Charter Airlines 1975

Country	Airlines (passengers, 1975 (millions)) Large	Airlines (passengers, 1975 (millions)) Others	Aircraft in Service
Austria	—	Austrian AirTpt (0.1)*	(leased from Austria Airlines)
Belgium	—	Sobelair (0.5)*, Trans-European (0.5)	B707, Caravelle, B707/720, A300B
Finland	—	Kar-Air (0.1)*	DC-8 (And from Finnair)
France	—	Aeromaritime (0.1)* Air Charter (0.3) Catair (0.1) Europe Air Service (0.1) Euralir (0.1)	(leased from U.T.A.) B727, Caravelle Caravelle HP Herald, Vanguard Caravelle
Germany	Condor (1.9)* B707, 727, 747	Bavaria (0.6) Germanair (0.6) Hapag-Lloyd (0.4) LTU (0.6)	BAC-One Eleven A300B, F-28, BAC 111 B727 Caravelle, L-1011
Italy	—	S.A.M.	(Leased operations, 1974)
Netherlands	—	Martinair (0.6)* Transvavia (0.8)	DC-8, DC-10, F-28 B707, B737, Caravelle
Scandinavia	Sterling (1.9) 727, Caravelle	Braathens (0.4) Conair (0.6) Maersk (0.5) Scanair (0.7)*	B737, F-28, F-27 B720 B720, F-27 DC-8, 727
Spain	Spantax (1.6) DC-8, DC-9, CV990	Aviaco (0.9)* TAE (0.4) Trans Europa (0.4)	DC-8, DC-9, Caravelle, F-27 DC-8, Caravelle Caravelle
U.K.	Britannia (2.3) B737 Dan-Air (2.3) HS-748, B707, B727, BAC-111, DH Comet, Viscount, Laker (1.0), DC-10, B707, BAC-111	Bristish Air Tours (0.8)* British Caledonian (0.6) British Midland (0.2) Monarch (0.8)	B707 B707, BAC 111 B707, Viscount, HP Herald B720, BAC 111, Britannia
Jugoslavia	—	Air Jugoslovia (0.3)* Aviogenex (0.2) Iexadria (0.6)	(leased from JAT) Tu-134 DC-9

*Indicates subsidiary of the country's flagship airline

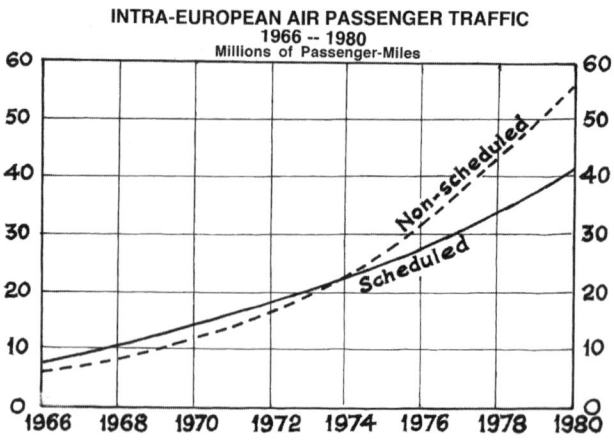

By the mid 1970s, the volume of non-scheduled air passenger traffic in Europe had exceeded that of the intra-European scheduled routes.

Proliferation

U.S. Supplemental Airlines (in order of operating revenues) 1967

Airline (and base city)	Authority	Jet Aircraft Fleet	Remarks
World Airways (Oakland)	Domestic, World-Wide	B707(9) B727 (6)	Largest Supplemental. Logair contract. Large maintenance base, supported Berlin Airlift.
Universal Airlines (Ypsilanti, Michigan)	Domestic, Canada, Mexico	DC-8 (2)	Specialist for automotive cargo from Detroit manufacturers. Logair contract U.S. Navy Quick-trans.
Trans International Airlines (T.I.A.) Oakland	Domestic, World-Wide	DC-8 (4) B-727 (2)	Large and Profitable operator
Capital International Airlines (Nashville)	Domestic, Atlantic Caribbean	DC-8 (7)	Major trans-Atlantic charter business. Maintenance base at Wilmington, Delaware.
Saturn Airways (Oakland)	Domestic Atlantic Caribbean	DC-8 (4)	Second Largest Supplemental cargo airline Logair contract.
Overseas National Airways (O.N.A.) (New York)	Domestic Atlantic Caribbean	DC-8 (3) DC-9 (4)	Large trans-Atlantic charter business. Logair contract. U.S. Navy Quicktrans.
Southern Air Transport (Miami)	Domestic Pacific	B-727 (2)	Livestock cargo. Contract with C.I.A.
Standard Airway (Seattle)	Domestic North American	B-707 (3)	Mainly cargo
American Flyers Airline (Ardmore, Ok)	Domestic Atlantic North America	B-727 (2)	Expanding trans-Atlantic business
Modern Air Transport (Miami)	Domestic North America	Convair 980 (5)	New York-Florida charters. Intra-European contract, based in Berlin.
Johnson Flying Service (Missoula, Montana)	Domestic, Canada	—	Specialized fixed-base operator, including veteran types (B247, Ford, DC-2)
Purdue Airlines (Lafayette, Indiana)	Domestic, Canada	—	Specialized fixed-base operator (small aircraft)
Vance International Airways (Seattle)	Domestic Canada, Mexico	—	Specialized fixed-base operator (small aircraft)

The U.S. Supplementals

In the post-war United States, the restrictions on airline charter services were no less stringent than those in Europe, and in many ways the restrictors were similar in principle and in intent to the restricted. In Europe, especially in Great Britain, the newly formed state airlines shut the door on any possible scheduled competition, but the independents found chinks in the regulatory curtain. In the U.S.A., the plethora of small companies, founded by retirees from the armed forces, were able to fly only under a special exemption of the Civil Aeronautics Act of 18 October 1938; this effectively ruled out any reasonably viable operation. Also, as in Europe, the restrictions were government controlled and fully supported by the incumbent airlines, through their lobbying group, the Air Transport Association (A.T.A.).

Some dents were made in the contrived shell of protection. In 1947, Letters of Registration were granted by the Civil Aeronautics Board (C.A.B.) for non-scheduled airlines—the large and small "Irregulars"—to operate inter-city services in the 48 contiguous states on an infrequent basis. In times of national emergency, such as the Berlin Airlift and the Korean War, the maligned irregulars had come in useful, so their stature was enhanced during the 1960s and the larger ones were recognized as a distinctive airline category, the "Supplementals." In 1966, the group consisted of 13 airlines of varying size that were certified for inclusive tour charters (ITCs), the leading Supplementals for trans-Atlantic routes.

Predictably, this action was challenged by the established airlines, in defense of "grandfather rights" conferred upon them in 1938, but in spite of continued litigation, during which the Supplementals' case was strengthened by their role in airlifting logistics in the Vietnam War, full freedom was not achieved until the Airline Deregulation Act of 1978. Throughout the entire 40-year period of C.A.B.–controlled regulation of the U.S. airline industry, only one airline without the rights conferred in 1938 was ever granted a full certificate: the Washington, D.C.–based Trans-Caribbean Airlines, operating between Puerto Rico and the northeastern cities.

Many had tried to breach the bureaucratically defended walls. One episode was the case of **North American Airlines**. During the 1950s, a group of the despised non-scheduled airlines in California had banded together and established North American as a travel agency. It overcame the 8-per-month city-pair scheduling restriction by combining booked seats on four different airlines, and provided transcontinental air services at half the scheduled airline fares. With minimum administration and overhead costs, North American could still break even, while the certificated airlines were still benefitting from airline subsidies. In 1951, a Senate Committee report noted "constant harassment" and frowned upon the C.A.B.'s "ever-narrowing interpretation of its regulations, designed to limit (the non-skeds) almost entirely to non-common carrier operations." In the famous 1953 Denver Service Case, the C.A.B. found North American "unfit, unwilling, and unable" to perform the services. This statement was what Winston Churchill would have described,

COMPARISON OF TRAVEL COST—COAST TO COAST

TRAVELING BY....	TIME	FARE AND TAX	FOOD & SERVICE TIPS	VALUE OF TIME at $10 per day	TOTAL
NORTH AMERICAN AIR COACH	12 to 14 Hours	$99.00 14.85 $113.85	Tipping not permitted	$5.00	$118.85
BUS	4 Days	$49.80 7.47 $57.27	$24.00	$40.00	$121.27
RAIL COACH	3 Days	$88.81 13.32 $102.13	$18.00	$30.00	$150.13
PREMIUM-FARE AIR LINES	11 to 12 Hours	$157.85 23.68 $181.53	Tipping not permitted	$5.00	$186.53
PULLMAN	3 Days	$140.70 21.10 $161.80	$18.00	$30.00	$209.80

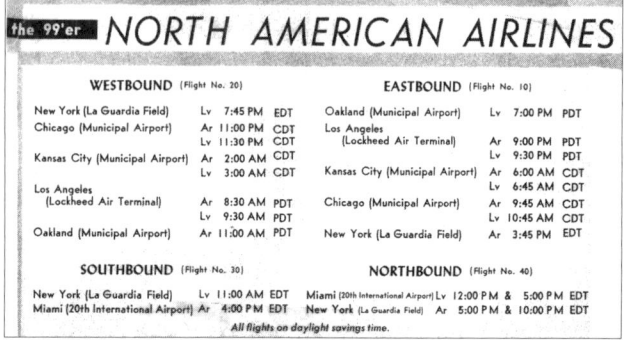

The North American Airlines transcontinental schedule during the 1950s was not competitive in terms of journey time. But as the above extracts from their timetables show, its $99.00 fare (not including taxes) was hard to beat. (Davies)

During the 1970s, the Supplemental airlines soon grew out of their rather dated propeller-driven image and acquired jet airliners, such as this Douglas DC-10 of World Airways. (McDonough)

politely, as a terminological inexactitude. Under the leadership of Stanley Weiss, North American had operated efficiently, and obviously had the public's support and sympathy. In 1955 it carried 275,000 passengers and made a profit. But in 1957, the Supreme Court—the litigation had reached those heights—denied Weiss's appeal, and a pioneer airline of cheap air travel was a martyr to a just cause.

Another pioneer was Orvis Nelson, an ex–United Air Lines wartime captain who joined the ranks of the non-scheduled independents when the war ended. His **Transocean Airlines (TALOA)** specialized in long-distance charters, with the slogan "We Fly Anything, Anywhere." He had contracts for humanitarian airlifts, refugee flights, military support airlifts, including Korea, and various other charter work, culminating in a scheduled service in the U.S. Micronesian Trust Territory and a Stratocruiser service from San Francisco to Hawaii. His Oakland Maintenance Base had performed most of the C-54 overhauls for the Berlin Airlift, but the C.A.B. still decreed that Transocean was neither fit, nor willing, nor able, in spite of overwhelming evidence to the contrary. Orvis closed his airline down in 1960.

One Supplemental had more success. **World Airways** had been founded by the irrepressible Ed Daly, who had operated a few of Pan American Airways' retired Boeing Clipper flying boats. It had distinguished itself during various missions, including the Hungarian refugee airlift. After winning a Logistics Airlift (LOGAIR) contract in 1960 for carrying military personnel, World grew rapidly, and, in June 1962, Daly ordered three Boeing 707-320s. He was the first to order the -320C long-range version of this thoroughbred line of airliners, a reflection on the growing stature of the Supplementals. World Airways participated with distinction in the Vietnam War, and Daly himself was something of a hero, described by his crew as "a man of rare qualities, a fist of iron, balls of brass, and a heart of gold." With the Deregulation of 1978, World Airways at last won a route award, from California to New York and Washington, and started service in 1979, followed by trans-Atlantic service in 1980. But the scheduled airlines had suddenly found ways to reduce their fares, and the supreme irony was that World Airways, which, with other "nonskeds," had fought to introduce low fares for a wider public market, was forced into submission by the scheduled competition.

A Continent in Transition

The permanent start of the Jet Age coincided with a worldwide political development in which commercial aviation played a part. The first decade following the end of the Second World War was characterized by the erosion of the former European-based empires, whose colors, with the exception of South America, had decorated the atlases of the world, from west Africa to the tiny islands of the Pacific Ocean. Until the mid-1970s, the sun never did set on the British Empire (and even today, a flimsy claim could be made for that assertion); and until 1960 most of Africa was still ruled from London, Paris, Lisbon, or Brussels, with minor links with Spain. Only Ethiopia, released from Italian rule by the war, and Liberia, were independent. The latter was never colonized, except by American business interests.

Stan Weiss (left) headed the group that founded North American Airlines and fought (unsuccessfully) for its survival before deregulation would have permitted it. Orvis Nelson (right) did the same with Transocean Airlines internationally. (left: Davies; right: Szura)

All this changed as the wave of nationalism swept across Africa. The word *empire* gave way in London to the more acceptable *commonwealth*, in which the master-and-servant relationship was consigned to history and local administration was strengthened, mainly by political evolution, sometimes by resistance movements bordering on revolution. One manifestation of the growing political freedom, and the urge to gain recognition in the eyes of the world, was to form indigenous airlines. These offered swift communication with the rest of the world, and provided an element of pride and prestige as the beflagged airliners took their places on the ramps of some of the world's leading intercontinental airports, especially at London and Paris.

This continent-wide political movement got under way simultaneously with the onset of the Jet Age, and as a consequence, progress was far from smooth. Coincidentally with B.O.A.C.'s and Pan American's historic trans-Atlantic jet service inaugurations in October 1958, the first country to achieve complete independence, Ghana (other than Sudan, which had special connections with both Britain and Egypt—see below), had just started its own airline. Formerly the British Gold Coast, this was a symbol of its newfound stature. Shortly afterward, the first airline to break clear of the French empire (see below) was Air Guinea, which started in 1960. In the years that followed, a multiplicity of new republics shook off their colonial heritage and, almost without exception, hastened to form airlines just as the richer and experienced flag carriers of Europe were augmenting their fleets with modern jets. The new infant nations were thus at a disadvantage in the competitive world of international air transport. Until the early 1950s, almost every airline service—13 in all—linking Europe with the sub-Saharan countries was European, with the United States represented only by Pan American and T.W.A.

Erosion of Empires

The one major exception was **South African Airways (S.A.A.)**, the flag carrier of the richest state on the continent. South Africa had gained self-governing dominion status in 1910, and became completely independent as a republic in 1961. It had already started its own service to London in 1946, but because of the racist apartheid policies imposed by its government, it was handicapped by the "wind of change" (as Britain's Prime Minister Macmillan phrased it) that was sweeping through the continent. The countries of east Africa refused landing rights at key staging points such as Nairobi, and S.A.A. was obliged to seek an alternative route to London via Luanda, Angola (still Portuguese territory) and more cooperative airports in west Africa.

After the war, the British government had formed three airline consortia as affiliates to B.O.A.C. This was to recognize that its colonies, mandated territories, and protectorates in Africa were too fragmented for each one, independently, to be able to develop viable air services, except short-haul regional and domestic routes. Other than S.A.A., the first sub-Saharan-based airline to open long-range service was **Central African Airways (C.A.A.)**. Originally founded as Rhodesia and Nyasaland Airways (RANA) in 1933 and closely connected with Imperial Airways, it became the Southern Rhodesia Air Service in 1940 then C.A.A.C. in 1946. It represented three British colonies, Southern and Northern Rhodesia, and Nyasaland. Another British ex-colonial association was the **East African Airways Corporation (E.A.A.C.)**, which represented Kenya, Uganda, and Tanzania, until those countries became independent in 1962-63. E.A.A.C. gained an impressive reputation for fine service, until the inexorable "wind of change" overcame it, and the independent nations formed their own airlines.

As a consortium, **West African Airways Corporation (W.A.A.C.)**, as B.O.A.C. affiliate, had represented Nigeria (the most populous country of Africa), the Gold Coast, Sierra Leone, and Gambia, since 1946. It had benefitted from generous leasing agreements with the British state airline. Like the other embryo consortia, W.A.A.C. broke up into separate national airlines, led by **Ghana Airways** (from the renamed Gold Coast), which initially fell under Soviet influence. W.A.A.C. had been predominantly Nigerian, headquartered in Lagos, and the bulk of its operations were taken over in 1958 by the newly formed **Nigeria Airways**, which leased aircraft from B.O.A.C. for the London route. In 1962, **Sierra Leone Airways**, formed in 1958, followed Nigeria and Ghana to London in 1961.

Anglo-Egyptian Sudan, the largest country in Africa, had already become independent in 1956, and **Sudan Airways** had been founded in 1946. In 1959, it leased Vickers Viscounts from the British Airwork (which had been instrumental in founding Egypt's Misrair in the 1930s) to begin the "Blue Nile" service from Khartoum to London in 1959. The destinies of all these African airlines are reviewed in more detail in Part 9 of this book.

The French Disconnection

North of the Sahara, the Mediterranean coast west of Tripoli, known in Arabic as the Maghreb and formerly by Europeans as the Barbary coast, had, by the early years of the 20th century, come under the control or influence of France. Morocco and Tunisia became French protectorates, but Algeria acquired a

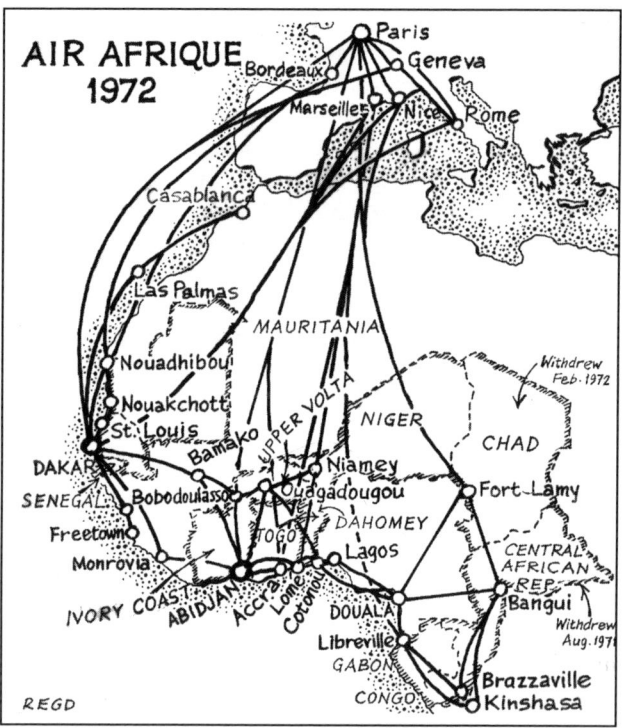

For several years, Air Afrique, based in Senegal, was an airline consortium that represented some of the new countries of Africa that did not have national airlines of their own.

special status. It was neither a colony nor a protectorate, nor was it part of France; the northern provinces sent delegates to the French parliament. Morocco's titular head was the Sultan, and a similar regime existed in Tunis, where European settlers and immigrants were in the minority. But Algerian cities were predominantly French. When Algeria achieved its independence in 1962, under negotiation with President de Gaulle, more than a million French inhabitants left the country.

Air Algérie was founded as Cie. Générale de Transports Aériens (C.G.T.A.) in 1946, as a non-scheduled airline, by the French trans-Atlantic shipping company. It was soon operating regular services from Algiers and Oran to many French cities, and developed domestic connections to outlying points in the southern Saharan region, which were relatively isolated by surface modes of transport. Such was the trans-Mediterranean traffic demand that, among African airlines, it became second in size only to South African Airways and, in 1960 was operating Caravelle jets. In spite of considerable domestic strife—as with many a resilient airline worldwide—the airline continued to flourish. The loss of much passenger demand from the native French was compensated for by a substantial increase in travel by migrant Algerian workers and their relatives to and from France.

Royal Air Maroc also had its origins in the post-war period, when Air Atlas, formed in 1946, and Air Maroc, formed in 1947, merged in 1953 to become the Cie Chérifienne de Transports Aériens (C.C.T.A.), controlled by French shipping lines. The ownership and name was changed in 1957 to the more appropriate title. The city of Casablanca had boomed during the Second World War, as it became the air transport gateway to north Africa, and subsequently expanded rapidly as a commercial center. Geographically closer to the North American continent than any other African city, and with an excellent airport, this gateway was a natural international hub. In 1975, Royal Air Maroc became the first Arabic airline to start trans-Atlantic services, using Boeing 707s, with direct flights from Casablanca to New York and Montreal.

Tunisia became independent of France, under which it was a protectorate, in 1956, and its airline, **Tunisair**, followed a similar course of European route development to those of Air Algérie and Royal Air Maroc. The exodus of Europeans from Tunis was not as great as from Algeria—many of them were Italian emigrants, and Tunisians also joined the north African workforce in the factories and hotels of France, Germany, and Switzerland. Like the other Maghreb countries, it carried pilgrims to Jeddah, Saudi Arabia. Tunisair also enjoyed a healthy tourism clientele, as the habitual sun-seekers from northern climes discovered a new destination, the island of Jerba, as an alternative to the Costa Brava or the Riviera.

Compared to North Africa, the other various territories of the French empire were not as affluent, and because of the geographical distances, were not so closely connected with Paris, socially, diplomatically, or commercially. They were mostly small colonies, and except for one or two which had some natural wealth, such as Gabon, with its rich hardwood forests, their resources for independent development, after the sweeping decolonization policy of Charles de Gaulle in 1962, were slender. To start an airline as a bold demonstration of independence was desirable, it was impracticable for most of the ex-colonies. A bold solution was devised: to form a consortium of 11 of the newly independent republics of the former French West Africa and French Equatorial Africa. In September 1960, the Société pour le Dévelopement du Transports Aériens en Afrique (SODETRAF) was registered in Paris by the French national airline, Air France, and the French independent airline, U.A.T., and with representation from the 11 former French Union colonies.

Events moved quickly. On 26 October, President Houphouet Boigny, of the Ivory Coast, was asked to investigate the proposed terms; and on 28 November, an outline of the scheme was sent to each head of state. On 15–19 December 1960, 12 of them held a second conference in Brazzaville (Congo); from 30 January to 4 February 1961, a scheme was drafted by a survey committee in Dakar (Senegal); and on 28 March 1961, the Treaty of Yaoundé (Cameroon) was signed by all parties to confirm the creation of a new airline that was to represent most of French-speaking west Africa for the next four decades. The airline was officially founded on 26 June 1961, as the Société Multinationale Air Afrique.

The shareholding was 34% by SODETRAF (i.e., Air France and U.A.T.) and 6% by each of the 11 participating states: Senegal, Mauretania, Ivory Coast, Dahomey (now Benin), Upper Volta (now Burkina Faso), Niger, Chad, Congo-Brazzaville, Gabon, and the Central African Republic. Notable absentees were Mali and Guinea, but Togo was added on 1 January 1968. Then Cameroon left on 26 January 1971 and Chad did likewise in February 1972. With the major cities of the consortium as far to the east as Douala, Cameroon, and as far west as Dakar, with trans-Atlantic connecting flights, west Africa had entered the Jet Age.

The full extent of this massive transfer of French sovereignty, accompanied by the creation of dozens of small airlines, simultaneously with the advent of the Jet Age, is also summarized in Part 9.

Farewell to European Control

The continent of Africa had been colonized in the "scramble for Africa" during the latter decades of the 19th century, with the lion's share going to Great Britain and France. As outlined above, the "Cape-to-Cairo" route—all-British after Germany had lost its East Africa territory as part of the First World War reparations—was to spawn several good airlines after the Second World War. The imperial air route to South Africa had achieved in the air what had, on land, been unachievable by railroad. Similarly, the French routes to north and west Africa, and to Madagascar, had given way to independent airlines. In both the British and the French cases, good solutions to the lack of adequate technical resources had often been found by the creation of airline consortia, of which the visionary Air Afrique was to outlive the others.

Of the other European colonists, Italy had been deprived of its African empire in the Second World War, as Germany had in the first. The Spanish territories were very small, with little potential for air traffic. But the Portuguese territories, of which Angola and Mozambique were extensive in area and natural resources, had airlines whose networks were only domestic or flew to close neighbors, and Portugal was not in a rush to release its overseas empire. Independence from Lisbon came a decade after London and Paris had bowed to the inevitable in the early 1960s. But by then, in the mid-1970s, the Jet Age was well under way. Consequently, **Divisão de Exploracão dos Transportes Aéreos (DETA)** was able to start service from Lourenço Marques to Lisbon via Luanda, Angola, on 2 January 1975, with Boeing 707s leased from British Airtours. The airline was to become **Linhas Aéreas de Mozambique (L.A.M.)**, the airline of Mozambique, in 1980. In Angola, **Divisão de Exploracão dos Transportes Aéreos de Angola (D.T.A.)** followed suit on 2 May 1976, with Douglas DC-8-62s leased from Alitalia. By this time, the name of the airline had been changed to **TAAG—Linhas Aéreas de Angola (Angolan Airlines)**.

The Belgian Congo had been, like Portuguese Angola and Mozambique, and the Dutch East Indies, much bigger than the homeland, and the source of much potential wealth. The Belgian surrender of power was accompanied by political and industrial turmoil. The Congo became independent on 30 June 1960, but its first president was murdered, there was widespread violence, and a civil war broke out as the copper-rich province of Katanga tried to break free. Order was not restored until 1965, by which time almost all the Belgian colonists had fled back to Belgium, and the Belgian airline, SABENA, had been deprived of most of its long-distance traffic. **Air Congo** was formed on 28 June 1961, and when the country changed its name to Zaire on 27 October 1971, it too changed its name, to **Air Zaïre.** In spite of the considerable political confrontations, Air Congo was able to start service, in association with SABENA, from Elizabethville (now Lubumbashi) and Leopoldville (now Kinshasa) to Brussels via Rome, with Boeing 707s, right from the start.

The development of the African ex-colonies, as they struggled into responsible airline maturity (and, sadly, many of them did not), is further reviewed in Chapter 48 of this book.

Role Model Independent

Aside from Liberia, a tiny country dependent upon American rubber interests, the only independent country in Africa had been Abyssinia, but its independence was ruthlessly ended when Italy invaded in 1936, to link its colonies of Eritrea and Somaliland into an Italian east African empire. Its national airline had termed its route from Rome to Addis Ababa as the Linee Imperiale, and the new rulers began to modernize the country, by building roads, housing, and public utilities. This included a new airport at Addis Ababa.

Abyssinia was liberated by British forces in 1941, and the country became independent once more, and renamed Ethiopia, following tradition. The British continued to exercise certain controls, especially in travel authority to Ethiopian nationals. Consequently, when a national airline was formed, advice and assistance was sought from overseas, in this case the United States. On 26 December 1945, **Ethiopian Air Lines** was organized, with extensive help from the U.S. airline, T.W.A., which was only too eager to extend its influence overseas, to compete with Pan American's dominance.

As Ethiopia entered the 1970s, its politics moved well to the left, and in 1971, Emperor Haile Selassie made a state visit to China. Late in that year, the first Ethiopian national was appointed general manager, and the T.W.A. management contract was terminated, altogether amicably. The airline was now completely on its own. But it faced a dramatic change in the political

Of the few non-colonial countries in Africa during the post-war years, Ethiopia developed an airline that, operationally and technically, could match all competition. (Copyright © Boeing; NASM-9A08087)

structure of the country. During the early 1970s, Ethiopia ceased to be a kingdom. A Marxist revolutionary party, under Col. Mengistu Haile Mariam, took over the government, and in 1974, the Emperor Haile Selassie was dethroned.

Throughout the unsettled period, the airline maintained a high standard of efficiency, technical expertise, and commercial acumen, on a par with any European or American flag carrier. Ethiopian was one of the few operators of the de Havilland Canada DHC-5 Buffalo, two of which were acquired for cargo flights to Ethiopia's outback. By the mid-1980s, the airline was in full flight, with a near-perfect safety record. London's *Financial Times* described Ethiopian as "an aggressive company, run exclusively by Ethiopians, on strict capitalist lines, within the ambit of one of the world's most rigid, centrally planned, Marxist economies." Quite an achievement.

Survival on the Nile

Another African country in which the national airline's fortunes were inextricably entwined with the country's political upheavals was Egypt. Its airline, **Misrair** (Arabic for "Egypt Air"), founded in 1932 with British assistance, was almost entirely staffed and managed by Egyptians by the 1960s. With the progressive withdrawal of British influence and with the abdication of King Farouk, Egypt had become an independent republic in 1952. Under President Abdel Nasser, who took control in 1954, relations with the West became strained, especially after November 1956, when Britain and France supported Israel by landing armed forces at Suez.

Disenchanted with the West, Nasser turned to the Soviet Union, which demonstrated its willingness for cooperation by completing the Aswan High Dam in 1971, a notable technical achievement (though later to be close to an ecological disaster), and one which influenced Egypt's economic policies, including the procurement of aircraft. Local military conflicts halted tourism temporarily, but the Great Pyramids and the glories of Ancient Egypt further up the Nile were still constant generators of foreign exchange. The hotel trade was dependent on western Europe, even if the Air Force became dependent on Soviet Mach 2 fighters. With very little oil, with only the narrow strip of fertile land along the Nile (4% of Egypt's land area) for agricultural production, the tourist trade was essential for economic well-being.

The national airline was indispensible in its promotion. Misrair had been an early operator of turbine-powered aircraft, with the Vickers Viscount turboprops, and, on 16 July 1960, had introduced de Havilland Comet 4c's on the route to London. In January 1961, the airline's name was changed to **United Arab Airlines (U.A.A.)**, to reflect an ambitious political union with Syria. The network was expanded with Comets flying to Moscow and Tokyo. On 1 August 1965, domestic routes along the Nile and to Athens and Nicosia were hived off the parent airline, involving an indication of a major reorientation toward the Soviet Union. The new domestic airline took its name from the old one, Misrair, but the Soviet aircraft and the route structure were so unprofitable that Misrair's independent status was terminated on 1 January 1968.

Then the Six Day War with Israel, from 5 to 10 June 1967, affected U.A.A.'s traffic so much that it took three years to recover from the decline. In 1971, following the renaming of the country back to Egypt and the abandonment of Nasser's dream of uniting the Arab world, U.A.A.'s name was also abandoned; it became **Egyptair**. Abdel Nasser died in 1970 and was succeeded by Anwar Sadat.

Throughout the ebbs and flows of political turbulence, bureaucratic interference from government, and frequent managerial changes, the Egyptian airline could always depend on certain reliable sources of revenue traffic. The tourists kept coming back to the eternal attraction of the land of the Pharoahs. There was always the annual Hajj—the Muslim pilgrimage to Mecca—in which Egyptair had a good share of the air traffic, because of geographical proximity of Cairo. And there was another annual migration: of teachers. Cairo was the largest city in the Arab world, and it was also the biggest center of education. Its teachers, at every level, were always in demand, and Egyptair carried most of them to the receptive Arab nations. As with the history of the effect of colonization on all African airlines, further details of Egyptair are chronicled in Part 9.

Chapter 11: Emergence of the Middle East

Jump Start in Iran

While Egypt could be regarded as the western fringe of what (in modern parlance, at least) is termed the Middle East, Iran could be said to represent its eastern extremity. Iran is a large country, three times the size of France, with more than 60 million people. Unlike Egypt, however, much of the terrain is mountainous, the largest cities are widely separated, and, in the 1950s, its railroads and roads were inadequate. The country was ideal for an airline route network, and it needed air communication with the outside world, as its railroads did not conveniently connect with those of other countries.

While neighbors Egypt and Israel had recurrent political problems, Iran and Iraq have had problems. These had handicapped Iran's economic progress, even though its oil resources made it potentially affluent. Recovering from the Second World War, during which it had suffered the ignominy of being invaded by British and Soviet armed forces (because it had backed Germany), Iranian industry had been almost wholly dependent upon foreign support. This was true of its airlines. The **Iranian Airways Company (Iranair)**, founded in 1944, had been aided by the American T.W.A., the short-lived Eagle Airlines by B.O.A.C., and Persian Air Services (P.A.S.), which was started in 1958 by SABENA. When Transocean Airlines, which had replaced T.W.A. in support of Iranair in 1955, went bankrupt in 1960 and P.A.S. was in financial difficulty, the two airlines merged on 2 November 1961 to form **United Iranian Airlines**, which is still operating as **IranAir**.

P.A.S. had actually taken the jet initiative when, on 30 October 1960, SABENA leased it a Boeing 707, for service to Brussels, while IranAir was still operating Douglas DC-6 piston-engined airliners and Vickers Viscount turboprops. But under the direction of Major-General Ali Khademi, the new, wholly government-owned, joint airline entered the Jet Age with conviction, even though the winter of 1963–64 was the worst on record. IranAir faced the extremes of Gulf temperatures and humidity in the south, yet had to cross 14,000-foot snow-covered peaks in the north and cope with icy runways.

In March 1964, Khademi negotiated a technical agreement with the world's dominant airline, Pan American Airways, together with a $1.5 million U.S. loan, with the implication to purchase U.S. airliners. Hitherto, all IranAir's mainline and international services had been flown by the Viscounts, but range limitations restricted the routes to the eastern Mediterranean and Bombay via Karachi. A brief Douglas DC-8 jet service to Copenhagen had been flown, with aircraft leased from the Scandinavian S.A.S. This situation changed swiftly, and with Pan American's cooperation, Boeing seized its opportunity to break into what was to be a lucrative market.

On 4 July 1965, IranAir finally entered the Jet Age. Still lagging behind most national airlines, it started to make up for lost time. At first, for its inaugural route to Hamburg via Beirut, Rome, Geneva, and Frankfurt, it operated a Boeing 727-100, leased from Pan American. A year later, the first 727 of its own was delivered, and service to London began on 3 July 1966. Within a few years, the London service frequency was up to 10 per week (two of them via Moscow).

In January 1970, Boeing 707-320s permitted nonstop service to European capitals, and on 24 July 1971, Boeing 737s took over the regional routes. Such was the confidence in Tehran, with the government's oil revenues providing financial guarantees, that IranAir joined the list of supersonic aspirants, ordering three Concordes—but cancelling in 1979 when overland flights were universally outlawed because of the sonic boom. In February 1973, in technical contrast, but far more financially prudent, the airline ordered six Fokker F-27s for domestic routes.

IranAir was on a roll. On 15 May 1976, it began service to New York, at first with the Boeing 707s, but soon to be replaced by Boeing 747SP long-range wide-bodied "jumbo-jets," which permitted nonstop flights from Tehran. But these dizzy heights of trans-Atlantic service were short-lived. On 8 September 1978, martial law was declared to deal with striking oil workers. On 16 January 1979, the Shah abdicated, and on 31 January, the Ayotollah Khomeini named a provisional council to take over the government with emphasis on Islamic ideology.

On 4 November 1979, militants seized the United States embassy and took a large number of hostages. IranAir all but closed down. Boeing's market evaporated, and although the fleet of 707s, 727s, 737s, and 747s was retained, further orders were dropped, as was an order for Airbus A300s. In a delicate military environment, an attempt to rescue the hostages in April 1980 failed. The Shah died in Egypt on 27 July, and on 21 January 1981, an accord was reached for the hostages to be released, and Iranian foreign assets were unfrozen. As for IranAir, hopes of returning to normal were shattered when, on 22 September, war broke out with Iraq, ostensibly over a dispute of rights in the Shatt al-Arab waterway into the Persian Gulf. The war, which was more about religious divisions than economic concerns, dragged on for eight years, and airline activity in the region was at a standstill.

The Airline That Would Not Die

During the first two decades following the end of the Second World War, Beirut, the capital and chief city of Lebanon, emerged as a leading center of commerce and as an attractive resort in the Middle East. The Lebanese had been traders since time immemorial, and their interests spread as far as the East Indies, West Africa, and even Brazil. The commercial acumen was reflected in its airline industry, and during the 1950s, this small country, with a population of only three million and which had been completely independent only since 1946, had four airlines.

The biggest and most influential was **Middle East Airlines (M.E.A.)**, founded in 1945. Under the leadership of Sheikh Najib Alamuddin, it had progressed from humble de Havilland D.H.89A Rapides and Douglas DC-3s to being one of the early operators of the turboprop Vickers Viscount, with a service to London on 18 June 1956. During the Viscount years from 1955 to 1960, M.E.A.'s passenger traffic trebled and its total traffic increased sixfold. This was a period of association with the British B.O.A.C., which had acquired a 39% interest from Pan American Airways in 1955 and which assisted M.E.A. to enter the Jet Age as early as 5 January 1961, with Comet 4C service. Later in that year, on 16 August, and flexing its muscles, the airline severed its links with B.O.A.C., increased its capital, and took over the Mideast Air Service Company (MASCO), the best aircraft and engine servicing depot between Europe and Hong Kong.

During the next five years, during which time comparative tranquility reigned in the eastern Mediterranean, M.E.A. consolidated its position as the leading airline in the region. On 1 October 1961 it took over neighboring Air Jordan, and, with a 35% interest, reorganized it as **Jordan Airways**, but this association ended in 1963, when King Hussein established Royal Jordanian Airways—ALIA. During 1962, M.E.A. did good business in the charter market, with one Comet making 40 Hajj flights for Iran and chartering aircraft to other airlines. Comets also carried 3,000 United Nations troops to Beirut to help maintain a delicate peace.

In March 1963, Air France acquired a 30% interest in M.E.A., and the airline promptly ordered three Sud Caravelle 6N short-haul jets, starting service on 2 May. This was a prelude to a formal merger with the French airline's associated company in Lebanon. It already had a 57% interest in **Air Liban**, and the merger was accomplished in November 1965, with the Lebanese Intra Bank holding a substantial interest. Air Liban had specialized in operating routes between French West Africa and French-speaking Lebanon, and with this merger, M.E.A. was serving 33 points in Europe, west Africa, and Pakistan and India. It had also opened, on 1 January 1965, a route to Addis Ababa via Jeddah and Khartoum, in association with Ethiopian Air Lines, using one of the latter's Boeing 720Bs. Lebanon's main industry was still tourism. Beirut was regarded as the "Paris of the Middle East." In 1965, half a million tourists visited Lebanon, of whom 85% went by air, half of them by M.E.A.

Sheikh Najib was a man of vision. He realized that the productivity of his airline depended on loyal and hard-working staff, and they were able to hold shares in the company. In 1966, he tried to form an Arabic coalition of airlines in the region, to be called the Arab Air Carrier Association, but this never happened. He was overtaken by events that were close to being disastrous. In 1967, the Six Day War between Israel and Egypt did not directly affect Lebanon, but the following year, on 28 December, Israeli commandos attacked Beirut Airport. Three of M.E.A.'s four Comets were destroyed. But such was the resilience of the Lebanese airline that operations were resumed within 12 hours. Aircraft were leased from Kuwait, Morocco, Pakistan, France, and Ethiopia.

One of M.E.A.'s rival airlines was not so lucky. **Lebanese International Airlines (L.I.A.)** had been developed by the Arida brothers in 1953, who took over the airline's single Savoia-Marchetti airliner and a route to Kuwait. At first with Curtiss C-46s then with Douglas DC-7s, it expanded its network from the Persian Gulf, Iraq, and Iran to points in Europe, with a variety of aircraft, including two Convair 990A jets by 1966, purchased from American Airlines. But in the Israeli raid, L.I.A. lost the two Convairs and a DC-7. On 23 April 1969, M.E.A. purchased L.I.A.'s traffic rights and obligations—there being few assets to buy—and emerged as Lebanon's sole passenger-carrying airline.

After temporarily leasing six Convair 990As on 3 August 1968, a contract was signed with Boeing for four 707-320Cs, and in 1972, a plan was adopted for a fleet of 720Bs and 707s. In 1973, fighting broke out between the Lebanese army and the Palestinian Liberation Organization (P.L.O.) that closed the Beirut airport for five days. M.E.A. moved its entire base of operations, including staff, to Cyprus. Ever creative, M.E.A. expanded its network during 1974 into Eastern Europe, even a route to Armenia, and expanded its frequency to London to twice daily. On 24 June, under the direction of operations and planning director, Asad Nasser, at which time the fleet had grown to 16 Boeing 720Bs, the airline ordered three Boeing 747-200Bs, to enter the age of the "jumbo jets."

During this dangerous period, when Beirut was transformed from a vacation resort into a battleground, a crisis was reached in October 1975, when to walk the streets was to invite a cross-fire of bullets. Middle East Airlines struggled to maintain service, even though the normal passenger potential was close to being wiped out. The employees offered to take a 20% pay reduction, and to work overtime at the normal pay scale. The airline's office administration, ticketing, and maintenance staff all moved to the airport, where they "camped out" for months or more at a time. One aircraft was parked at the airport as a "fuel tanker" and the airline's fleet dead-headed to Baghdad and back during the night. Orly Airport in Paris became a temporary operational base, and spare parts or components were sent overland to Damascus, and thence to Paris. This concentration of staff actually improved productivity for a while; with the special effort, 1,450 personnel were able to do the work of 3,900.

In November 1976, Beirut Airport was open for business once again, and M.E.A. began to try to return to normal. In some ways, this was the end of an era, for in December 1977, Sheikh Najib resigned from his chairmanship, for what was described at the time as "personal reasons." No doubt disillusioned and disheartened, he left behind a legacy of wise and courageous leadership, through thick and (mostly) thin; he had introduced jet airline service throughout the Middle East; and most of all had built up staff morale so that it could overcome significant obstacles.

Air Freight Innovator

If M.E.A.'s progress was a miracle of survival, another Lebanese airline succeeded beyond all expectations because of the initiative and ingenuity of its founder. Munir Abu Haidar was a young Lebanese employee of ARAMCO, the huge U.S. oil consortium based in Dhahran, Saudi Arabia. In 1953, with his $600 severance pay from ARAMCO and in the tradition of his distant Phoenician trader ancestors whose ships sailed throughout the Mediterranean and to the shores of Great Britain, Haidar founded **Trans Mediterranean Airways (T.M.A.)**. With two aging Avro Yorks chartered from the British Skyways independent airline, T.M.A.'s main business was carrying perishables, including food, to Dhahran. By 1955, after acquiring three Yorks of its own and the first Douglas DC-4 freighter, T.M.A. started a semi-scheduled route between Tehran, Persia (Iran), and Basle, Switzerland, using Beirut as a Sixth Freedom hub (combining a Tehran-Beirut and a Beirut-Basle route into one, thus evading the strict international regulations concerning direct traffic by an airline between two foreign countries).

The next year, during the Suez crisis, when the Canal was closed for many months, Munir added four more Yorks (air freight is not image-conscious) and began to carry a wider range of goods: gold from London to Dubai, for onward "legitimate smuggling" to Bombay; thoroughbred racehorses from Arabia to Europe; and even dolphins, in a special tank, for a floor show at the Casino du Liban in Beirut. During this period of the mid-1950s, T.M.A. did not have a full operating license from the Lebanese government and operated entirely under contract, at first with Air Liban then with Persian Air Services, and finally with Middle East Airlines. But in 1959 this changed significantly.

On 13 February 1959, T.M.A. was certificated as a Lebanese independent scheduled airline, and was formally incorporated, owned by Haidar and his family. The European route to Basle was extended to Frankfurt, and the following year to London and Amsterdam. Through Beirut, connections were made to points in the Gulf: Dhahran, Bahrain, Doha, and Baghdad. An ambitious route was also given a trial, in support of United Nations requirements in Afghanistan, to Kabul via Kandahar, and several of its DC-4s were converted temporarily into passenger layouts to carry pilgrims to Jeddah during the Hajj.

In 1963, T.M.A. bought its first pressurized airliner, a DC-6, at which time its fleet consisted of eight DC-4s and one remaining York. Two years later, in an all-important decision, the Lebanese Civil Aviation Board approved Munir's application for a route to Hong Kong and Tokyo. He bided his time, meanwhile taking advantage of another closing of the Suez Canal in 1967 and surviving the December 1968 Israeli commando raid on Beirut Airport with the loss of only one DC-4 and one DC-6.

In a little-publicized event of 14 April 1971, T.M.A. inaugurated a once-weekly eastbound round-the-world all-cargo service from Beirut to Beirut via Tokyo, New York, and intermediate points with a Boeing 707-320C that was leased from American Airlines. It was the first Arab airline to open service into the United States, but the significance of the service was more far reaching. One of the main obstacles facing an all-freight airline is that its cargo moves in only one direction. In contrast, with few exceptions, passenger traffic flows are well balanced in both directions. Consequently, air freight operators customarily make

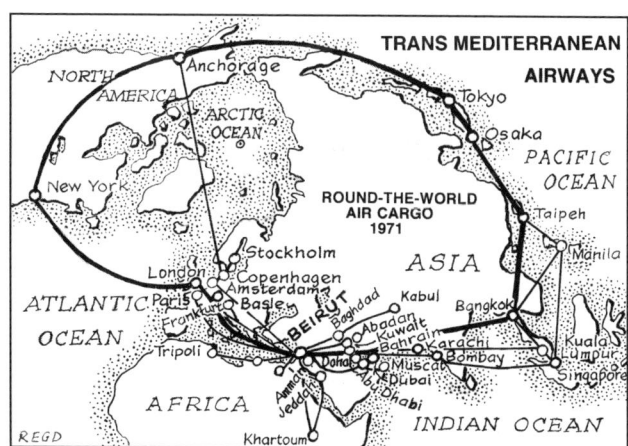

Unlike most passengers, freight traffic does not make round trips. To circumvent the problem of empty back-hauls, T.M.A. inaugurated a round-the-world all-cargo service in 1971.

flights as lightly filled or empty back-hauls. Munir Abu Haikar solved the problem with the single-direction Beirut-to-Beirut flights.

On 15 October 1971, such was the success of the service, a second weekly frequency was added, and in January 1972, a westbound frequency was introduced. T.M.A. was now the world's largest all-freight airline, outside the United States. It also made profits. In only one year, 1968, because of one of the battle-zone periods in the Lebanon, did Haikar fail to be in the black. His airline went from strength to strength, widening its scope, with routes to north and west Africa, added points in southeast Asia, and a route to Scandinavia. By 1975, he had seven 707-320Cs, which flew over 90,000 miles of routes, serving 28 points, with the slogan "Serves the Petro-Dollar World." In that year, this remarkable airline, from little Lebanon, scarred all too frequently by conflict and war, introduced its first wide-bodied jet airliner, a Boeing 747, ex–American Airlines, and which it promptly deployed on its busiest routes to London and other European heavy generators of air freight.

Postscript to the Ottoman Empire

Following the end of the Second World War, the disjointed and slow progress of airlines in the Middle East was inextricably interwoven with the complex politics of the post-war years. With the collapse after the First World War of direct Turkish rule from Constantinople (Istanbul), the political vacuum had been filled by mandated authority of the League of Nations, which effectively ensured that the former Turkish control would be replaced mainly by British and French administrations. Thus Mesopotamia, Trans-Jordan, and Palestine were governed from London, Syria, and Lebanon from Paris.

Mesopotamia gained independence in 1932 as Iraq, but with strong British protection, complete with Royal Air Force bases. Syria and Lebanon gained their independence at the end of the Second World War, in 1946, having already been granted republican status in 1941. Trans-Jordan also became an independent kingdom in 1946, and changed its name to Jordan after the Arab-Israeli war of 1948. The king was of the Hashimite dynasty, which had also, in the early 1920s, ruled the Hejaz after the expulsion of the Turks in 1918. This was the western area of the Arabian peninsula bordering the Red Sea, where the Hejaz had been a short-lived member of the League of Nations until 1924, when it was taken over by an emergent Saudi Arabia.

In the Persian Gulf area, Kuwait had already been free of the Ottomans since 1899, when Great Britain exerted its influence by protecting a local emirate; it declared its full independence in 1961. Bahrain had been a British protectorate since 1861 and became independent in 1971. To the east, on the southern shore of the Persian Gulf, seven small independent emirates, known as the Trucial States, were under the loose protection of Great Britain, whose gunboats were seldom required to keep order, as the main industry was unregulated and unsupervised pearl-smuggling to India. But in 1971, seven emirates (Abu Dhabi, Ajman, Dubai, Fujaira, Ras al-Quaima, Sharjah, and Umm al-Kalwain) amalgamated as the United Arab Emirates (U.A.E.). Qatar became an independent emirate in 1971. Almost unknown throughout the rest of the world, one tiny emirate at least could point to an airline tradition. Back in the early 1930s, the ponderous Handley-Page HP-42 biplanes used to stop at Sharjah for refueling, a process that required expert piercing with a screwdriver of four-gallon tins of gasoline, and hauling them up by hand to the top wing.

In the southeastern quarter of the Arabian peninsula, beyond the dreaded Rub al Khali (the Empty Quarter), Oman, which had enjoyed a vague British protection, including a formal treaty in 1951, became an independent sultanate in 1970. In the deep south, Yemen (land of the biblical Queen of Sheba) declared its independence from the Ottomans in 1918, resisted Saudi conquest, and became a republic in 1962. In 1967, the British Aden colony, used as a coaling station during the years of the British Empire, became South Yemen, and the Hadramaut coast, also looked after by the British, was linked by a union agreement in 1979. Yemen and South Yemen were united in May 1990.

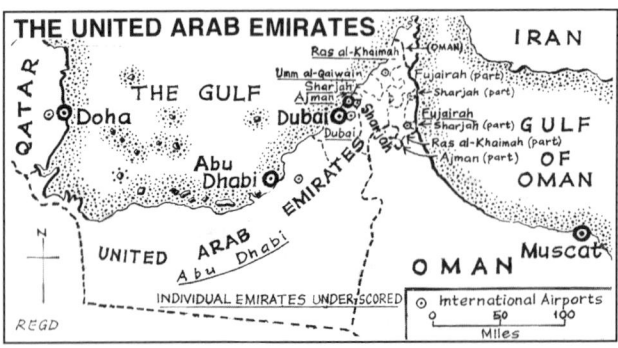

After the Second World War, when oil was discovered in the northeast region of the Arabian peninsula, several small emirates cooperated as the United Arab Emirates. The most affluent were Dubai and Abu Dhabi. Qatar remained independent.

Outside the British and French orbit, and until the mid- and late 1920s, most of the Arabian peninsula—as big as most of western Europe, and one-third of the size of the United States—had been almost entirely desert, much of it completely barren. The acquisitive colonial powers passed it by, as being of no apparent commercial, political, or military value. Then came the discovery of oil. Until the Second World War, Middle Eastern oil production had been mainly in Persia and, to a lesser extent, in Iraq and Bahrain. But in the late 1930s, further exploratory drilling revealed considerable resources throughout the Gulf and especially in Saudi Arabia which, by this time, had spread its sovereignty across most of the peninsula. The main beneficary of the new wells, aside from local territorial claims, was the United States. Through the giant Arabian American Oil Company (ARAMCO), it effectively exerted an economic colonialism through its leadership of the Arabian oil industry, which was itself destined to dominate the world's production.

Airline activity throughout the region was, except for those of Iran and Lebanon, dependent on patronage from the former colonial powers, especially the British through subsidiary companies of the state-owned **British Overseas Airways Corporation (B.O.A.C.)**. These were **British International Airlines (B.I.A.L.)** in 1953, which established Kuwait Airways, and **Associated British Airlines (ABAMEL)** (Middle East), which in 1955 provided the necessary technical and financial backing for Aden (Aden Protectorate), Arab Airways (Jerusalem), Gulf (Bahrain), and M.E.A. (Lebanon). The British position was further consolidated in 1957 by the formation of **B.O.A.C. Associated Companies (B.O.A.C.A.C.)**, whose tentacles extended worldwide and whose objectives were partly to bring British airliners into the region. For many years, this was a successful initiative as British manufacturers recognized the opportunities offered by traditional business and diplomatic connections.

Airlines of the Oil-Rich Gulf

One of the countries within the British sphere of influence was Iraq. Baghdad and Basra came to be regarded in London as important, if not vital, way-stations on the Commonwealth air routes to India, the Far East, and Australia. This applied to both commercial and military operations, and the Royal Air Force had active bases at Habbaniyah, near Baghdad, and at Basra.

Iraqi Airways was one of the first airlines in the Middle East to introduce the turboprop Viscounts, on 16 April 1956, and it entered the Jet Age on 12 October 1965, with the de Havilland Trident—one of the few occasions when the British tri-jet gained an order in competition with the Boeing 727. In the 1970s, the airline fell under the strict control of the Baath Arab Socialist Party, which, under Saddam Hussein, assumed full authority over all aspects of life in Iraq. With international expansionist aspirations and with growing economic strength because of the developing oil industry, Iraqi Airways leased three Boeing 707-321s from Donaldson International and began long-range services on 1 May 1974. Overambitiously, it started service to Rio de Janeiro via Larnaca, Cyprus, and Lisbon and made tentative flights to the Far East, including Singapore, Manila, Tokyo, and Beijing, though never operated as scheduled routes. The airline had to struggle for survival when, on 22 September 1980, war broke out between Iraq and Iran. The Soviet Union was exerting considerable influence. The Iraqi Air Force had fleets of Ilyushin and Antonov transport aircraft that also flew in the airline's colors. Eight years were to pass before the bitter conflict between Baghdad and Tehran ended, by which time Iraqi Airways was government-owned.

One of the interruptions to Ottoman expansion in the Gulf was the founding of the independent state of the Emirate of Kuwait, strategically positioned at the head of the Persian Gulf, just south of the confluence of the Tigris and Euphrates Rivers. This small desert state, about the size of New Jersey, was not part of the British Empire, but was strongly influenced from London in all aspects of foreign affairs. The first airline, **Kuwait National Airways**, founded in March 1954, had been operated by crews, maintenance staff, and DC-3 aircraft supplied by B.I.A.L. set up by B.O.A.C., with minority interests from B.E.A. and Hunting-Clan. A firm aviation business relationship with Great Britain was thus firmly established.

In 1955, the name was changed to **Kuwait Airways**, with the Kuwaiti government holding 50% of the shares, and the routes to neighboring countries extended to Cairo, using equipment handed down from B.O.A.C. By 1959, all scheduled services were operated by Viscount turboprops, and the route network was extended to Bombay and Karachi in the summer of that year. In May 1962, the government bought all outstanding shares, creating the airline as a corporation (K.A.C.), which embarked on an equipment expansion program, and opened a new modern airport.

On 26 June 1962, Kuwait Airways started Comet 4C services, with aircraft leased from Middle East Airlines, and then bought its own Comets, which entered service on 18 January 1963. This was one of the measures by which this small country joined the "big leagues" of airlines. On 31 May, it terminated the technical agreement with B.O.A.C., and in March 1964, opened a thrice-weekly service to London via Geneva, Frankfurt, and Paris. Two months later, it took over Trans-Arabian Airlines, a private Kuwaiti airline, and disposed of its fleet of Douglas DC-6 piston-engined aircraft. No doubt benefitting from financial backing by an oil-rich government, a new maintenance base was constructed and completed in 1966—relieving the airline's dependence on MASCO in war-torn Beirut. In 1966, three Hawker-Siddeley (ex–de Havilland) Tridents were added to the Comet fleet, now four, and curiously, in an aeronautical case of "dignity and impudence," Kuwait also acquired two all-purpose Scottish Aviation Twin Pioneers, small utility aircraft that could land on any piece of level desert the size of a baseball diamond—possibly for special local requirements.

Such expansion was against the background of prodigious wealth. Kuwait has an estimated 20% of the world's oil reserves. Its people enjoy the highest individual personal income in the world, do not pay taxes, and have free healthcare, education, and telephones. The Kuwaiti national airline was able to train its nationals to replace foreign staff at all levels. In November 1968, three new Boeing 707-320Cs were delivered, and these were able to augment the services to London and points in Europe and to India, where Delhi was added to Bombay as a second destination. By 1972, with two more 707s delivered, the Comets and Tridents were sold; Kuwait Airways now had an all-Boeing fleet.

After its aircraft fleet and premises were destroyed when Iraq invaded Kuwait in 1990, Kuwait Airways re-equipped with a fleet of Airbuses. Later, keeping pace with traffic demand, it added (above) a Boeing 747-400M. (McDonough)

Anson to Airbus

East of Kuwait is Bahrain, a tiny state, formerly a small island enclave that dated back to the days of British protectionism as far back as 1871. It regained its independence, as a sheikdom, on 15 August 1971, by which time it already had a thriving airline, which derived most of its business from the oil industry, following the discovery of that lucrative product in 1932. The Cinderella story started with an ex–Royal Air Force pilot, Frederic Bosworth, operating a quasi-airline service in Iraq. He owned and flew a seven-seat Avro Anson to neighboring oil-based cities, mainly Dhahran, and his wife collected the fares as the passengers boarded. Tiring of the frustrating bureaucracy in Iraq, he moved to Bahrain and, with the support of the Sheikh, founded **Gulf Aviation** on 24 March 1950. A year later, when Bosworth died, B.O.A.C. acquired a 51% interest and replaced the Anson and other obsolescent types with de Havilland Doves and Herons. Then, in 1958, with larger aircraft required to meet the growing commercial activity in the Gulf, veteran 28-seat Douglas DC-3s went into service, and Gulf extended its route network from Kuwait to Oman.

Gulf introduced Vickers Viscount turboprops, chartered from Kuwait, in October 1961 to replace chartered Douglas DC-6Bs. Fed by oil industry personnel, from top executives to contract workers from overseas, the airline prospered. For local routes, twin-engined turboprop Fokker F-27 Friendships were added in the late 1960s, and the first jets, BAC One-Elevens, in January 1960. With the booming business, Gulf opened, at Bahrain, its first hotel in the region in 1969 and formed Gulf Helicopters in 1970.

In April 1970 a twice-weekly service to London started, with B.A.C. VC-10s chartered from B.O.A.C., and this offered

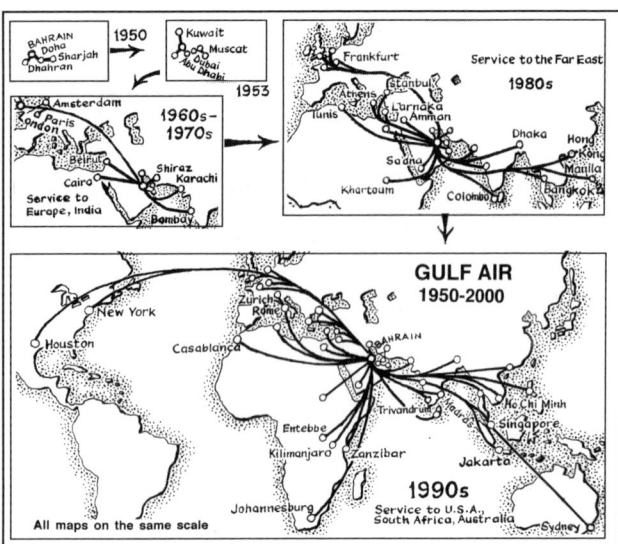

The rapid development of the nations of the northern Arabian peninsula was mirrored by the growth of new airlines. First among these was Gulf Air, which expanded from one small local route in 1950 to a four-continent network by the end of the century.

through service to Abu Dhabi and Dubai. Together with Doha, in Qatar, these cities, formerly small settlements that were often omitted from all but the larger atlas maps, were emerging as sought-after newly affluent bases for the global oil corporations. As Rolls-Royces replaced camels, and high-rise buildings began to rise from the coastline, Gulf's One-Elevens and VC-10s reflected the oil-based industrial revolution that was transforming the Middle East.

One element of the burgeoning oil industry was the need for cheap labor willing to work in the tropical heat, and this was forthcoming from the Indian subcontinent. Late in 1971, Gulf Aviation sent its One-Elevens beyond the Arabian peninsula to Karachi and Bombay. At the other end of the equipment scale, for local commuter service along the Gulf points, four Short Skyvans were obtained to supplement its Beech Queenairs. The waning of British political influence was reflected in B.O.A.C.'s withdrawal from control of Gulf Aviation. In April 1973, the corporate name was changed to **Gulf Air**, and at the end of the year, ownership passed to four Gulf countries. The State of Bahrain, the State of Qatar, the Emirate of Abu Dhabi, and the Sultanate of Oman each had a 25% share of the reconstituted airline. Four VC-10s were promptly ordered, and on 1 April 1974, coinciding with the official date of full airline independence, service was inaugurated between London and Bombay, using the so-called Sixth Freedom interpretation of international law, by which Gulf simply had to make a stop and change flight numbers en route in the Gulf.

Riding the crest of the oil-boom swell, Gulf Air introduced 223-seat wide-bodied Lockheed L-1011 TriStars to replace the VC-10s, and Boeing 737s to replace the One-Elevens. British Airways (successor to B.O.A.C.) had, in 1976, started Concorde service to Bahrain—the world's first-ever supersonic operation—and Gulf Air was a silent, but wisely non-contractual, partner in this initial flirtation with the revolutionary technology. In May 1978, the Gulf Air Company was officially and legally established as a four-nation organization, with headquarters in Bahrain and aircraft registered in Oman.

To describe Gulf Air's growth as a traffic explosion during this heady decade would not be an exaggeration. In 1970, the airline had carried fewer than 100,000 passengers, mostly local and regional. By 1982, it was carrying 2.5 million over routes from western Europe to the far east, where (such was the demand for "guest workers") a Boeing 747 had to be leased to supplement the TriStars. It consolidated its independence further by opening, in April 1987, the Gulf Aircraft Maintenance Company (GAMCO). Gulf Air provided 40% of the financing (Abu Dhabi provided the rest) to replace all heavy maintenance and overhaul previously provided by HAECO of Hong Kong.

Thereafter, intercontinental services were augmented all over the world, and Airbus A320s were added to the fleet. Arrangements were made with the American T.W.A. for through ticketing to New York, test-marketing the route for its own service in the future. But by the early 1990s, even as it prepared to open the first direct service from New York to the Gulf, the airline was to meet its first serious competition from a neighbor. (See Chapter 11.)

The British Take Their Leave

Reference has been made to B.O.A.C.'s affiliations with local airline aspirants in the Middle East during the 1950s. These interests included Kuwait, Bahrain, Lebanon, Cyprus, Jordan, and Aden, reflecting the British political and commercial interests in the region. As time went on, however, with growing affluence and business acumen by local rulers, the British influence was gradually eroded. Meanwhile, the Arab states recognized that their individual airline experience could not match that of the European and U.S. airlines that continued to operate and flourish. They worked together to form their own association. In 1961, the Economic Council of the Arab League approved the establishment of an international Arab Airline Corporation (AACO), which was formed on 25 August 1965 and included almost all the airlines of the Middle East, from the Gulf to Egypt; later, in the early 1970s, it reached across north Africa to Algeria. Possibly because of a changing balance of fortunes, either through explosions of wealth or gunfire between the member nations, the ambitious objectives were never realized, and each country went its own way.

B.O.A.C.A.C., which had successfuly promoted the turboprop Vickers Viscount throughout the region, was left with a minority interest in Gulf Air, and a fast-diminishing interest in the Aden Protectorate, where it owned Aden Airways. This outpost of empire, which had maintained useful links (from the British standpoint) with Bahrain, Cairo, Khartoum, and Nairobi, ceased operations on 30 June 1967, when the Protectorate gave way to the creation of South Yemen, at that time, the Arab world's only

Emergence of the Middle East

Marxist state. Hostility with the northern Yemen, which had become an independent nation in 1918, prevented any effective airline activity until 29 March 1979, when the two countries merged to form a unified state.

Airline Under Siege

Almost as though it is on a distant continent, the Jewish state of Israel has been continually at odds with its Muslim neighbors. Its national airline, **El Al**—Hebrew for "To the Skies"—therefore, has always been relativley isolated, beating a perilous aerial pathway on behalf of its country, to serve as the main channel of communication and travel with the rest of the world. The airline must serve kosher food, which might deter non-Jewish patrons from using the airline, much like Saudia's no-alcohol policy endears it to thirsty Westerners. In recent years, El Al has also had to refrain from flying during the Jewish Sabbath, that is, from sundown on Fridays to sundown on Saturdays.

For a few months in 1958, the Bristol Britannia held its own on the North Atlantic route until the jets took over. (Dunn)

The Israeli airline was in the vanguard of turbine-powered flights across the Atlantic. On 22 December 1957, it followed B.O.A.C.'s Bristol Britannia inaugural (only three days earlier) with a direct Tel Aviv-New York service. It gained attention to the capability of the Britannia 313 with its slogan "No Goose, No Gander," a reference to the nonstop London-New York segment which omitted the hitherto mandatory refueling stops in Labrador and Newfoundland, respectively. (See Chapter 7.)

El Al's technical leadership was short-lived, as the introduction of the faster Boeing 707s and Comet 4Bs in 1958 tolled the death-knell of the 350-mph long-range turboprops. El Al quickly replaced the "Whispering Giants," on 11 June 1961, with Rolls-Royce Conway-powered Boeing 707-420s; in April the following year, these were supplemented by Boeing 720Bs, which at the time were the longest-ranged commercial airliners, able to fly nonstop from Tel Aviv to New York.

During the latter 1960s, Israel's national airline was the target of several terrorist attacks from Arab extremist factions in support of the P.L.O. This led to severe retaliation: a devastating commando raid on Lebanon's Beirut Airport, which was perceived as a terrorist base, and many aircraft were destroyed. Prolonged confrontation compelled El Al to increase security measures, both on the ground and on board the aircraft, with its own highly effective security force and with undercover agents.

Following the Boeing 707s, El Al would buy every type except the 727 from the Seattle production line. On 8 June 1971, the Boeing 747 entered service, and with solid support from New York's loyal Jewish community, it posted a record 95% load factor during the first month of operation.

Because of Israel's differences with its neighbors, however, it was continually at war, preparing for war, or recovering from war. El Al's operational and commercial traffic-generating bases have always been handicapped. A large percentage of its traffic has always been tourism to Jerusalem, for Christians as well as Jews. Efforts to encourage tourism by building hotels on the Mediterranean shore or at Eilat on the Red Sea were too often jeopardized by repeated unrest and military action in the region that discouraged tourists and kept hotel rooms empty.

In November 1980, Abraham Shavit took over the chairmanship from Mordechai Ben-Ari, who had built the airline since its foundation in 1946. Shavit had to take harsh measures to save the airline from bankruptcy. He obtained major wage concessions, dismissed a quarter of the workforce, and eliminated many privileges such as free flights for the staff. Efficiency was considerably improved, and El Al was saved from extinction. Once again, internal strife introduced an unwelcome addition to the effects of international conflict. On 14 August 1982, airline workers confronted ultra-orthodox Jews of the Likud Party who had campaigned to suspend all flights on the Jewish Sabbath. The El Al staff went on strike from September 1982 to January 1983. During that period, an Israeli court placed El Al in temporary receivership. Flights were resumed, but the Sabbath Law remained and included Holy Days, effectively depriving the airline of 20% of its revenues, as much as $50 million per year.

To preserve operational and commercial stability was a constant battle. Nevertheless, El Al continued to maintain technical initiatives. On 24 July 1983, twin-engined Boeing 767s entered service, and in June 1984 (after another strike lasting four months), Boeing 747s started to fly to Los Angeles via Amsterdam and Chicago. Then, in 1985 (almost as an echo of its nonstop Britannia innovation in 1957), Boeing 767s were introduced on the North Atlantic route under the Extended Twin-Engine Operations (ETOPS) regulations permitted by the U.S. Federal Aviation Administration. In 1957, navigation specialist J.E.D. Williams had scheduled El Al's Britannias from London to New York on a schedule that was half-an-hour shorter than B.O.A.C.'s. Now El Al was the pioneer of the more economical efficiency of two engines against four, or even three. This innovation put to rest the hitherto comforting promotion of "four-engined safety," and twin-engined operation across the oceans was quickly adopted by all the world's flagship airlines, using either Boeings or Airbuses.

An Airline for a King

In *A History of the World's Airlines*, the predecessor volume to this book, published in 1964, the airlines of the Middle East rated only a few pages. With the brilliant days of oil-based prosperity only just dawning, **Saudi Arabian Airlines** rated two sentences and a brief tabulation entry. Dhahran, the oil-exporting port in the Gulf was developing quickly, and Jeddah, on the Red Sea, was becoming the gateway for the annual Muslim Hajj to Mecca, but the country as a whole had not yet adjusted its economy to its burgeoning wealth. The flagship airline was still on its learning curve, with the United States's T.W.A. as its head teacher. Its aircraft were headed by Convair 340s and Douglas DC-6s, and its network of routes did not extend beyond neighboring countries.

The airline metaphorically came of age on 19 February 1963, when, by Royal Decree by King Faisal, it became a strictly commercial operation, replacing the arrangement by which it had operated almost as the transport division of the Saudi Arabian Air Force. Already, preparations had been made to modernize the fleet, with an order for two Boeing 720Bs, originally destined for Ethiopian Air Lines, but eagerly transferred to Jeddah in December 1961, and went into service in March 1962.

As yet, the airline sights were set only on destinations not too far across the frontier horizons, and the new jets showed the Saudi flag only as far as Beirut, Amman, and Cairo. Saudi Arabian's expansion got under way in 1967. In that year, it joined the International Air Transport Association (IATA) and demonstrated its emergence into wider fields by starting a service across northern Africa (the Maghreb) to Casablanca in 1967. This was the first direct air link between the eastern and western halves of the Arab world. In the same year, the new Boeings started to fly to London and Frankfurt (for the bankers), calling at Geneva (for the health spas and to escape from the heat of the Arabian desert).

Saudi Arabian Airlines's progress gained further momentum during the 1960s. The first Boeing 707 (of a fleet total of 16) went into service on 15 January 1968, and the European route network was expanded to include Paris and Rome. Three Douglas DC-9s had been introduced for domestic routes on 4 March 1967, but, in the interests of commonality, these gave way to another substantial fleet of Boeing jets, the twin-engined 737s, which came into service early in 1968.

By the 1970s, after a remarkable period of expansion, Saudi Arabia could be said to have joined the big leagues of the Middle East airline fraternity. On 1 April 1972, it changed its operating name to **Saudia** and adopted a new livery. Apart from its new ventures into the international field, it built a network of domestic routes, to connect remote, and often almost isolated, communities with Jeddah, with Dhahran, and especially with the capital, Riyadh. Not only was the population of Saudi Arabia growing, the social conditions were changing in dramatic fashion. The citizens were, only a decade or so previously, mostly desert folk, many of them living at barely subsistence level. Now they were fast becoming urbanized, with Jeddah soon reaching a population of more than a million, and Riyadh, formerly little more than a large town, becoming a large modern metropolis of several million.

The country as a whole was modernizing rapidly, with banks, offices, and luxury homes in the cities, divided highways between all the main centers of population. The camel was usurped as a transport mode, much as the horse had been replaced by motorized transport in the West. The 500-mile link between Riyadh and Jeddah, though well provided for with a good road, was to become one of the busiest air routes in the world. In the early 2000s, Saudi Arabia would join the growing list of countries to invest in high speed rail.

To keep pace with the growing demand for air transport, the Saudi government invested in a modern infrastructure, building new airports, from large termini at the big cities to functional installations at all the regional points, right to the fringes of the Rub al Khali (The Empty Quarter) the featureless desert that covers about one-third of Saudi Arabia. At Jeddah, which had developed into the gateway airport for Mecca, special arrangements had to be made to accommodate the annual Hajj pilgrims, as their numbers were—thanks largely to the advent of air transport—growing at a rapid rate. This was mainly because the speed of the airliners created a completely new dimension in time-saving, compared to sea or land travel. Not only could a Hajji make his pilgrimage in two or three weeks, thus being able to take a reasonable period away from his work or livelihood, but he could afford to travel within a smaller budget, as the airlines could offer cheap fares on capacity-filled aircraft. Also, the Hajj calendar coincided, for several decades during the latter 20th century, with the northern winter season, thus providing opportunities for using otherwise little-used aircraft.

By the mid-1970s, Saudia was able to take the next generation of jet airliner purchases in its stride. At first, it chose the Lockheed L-1011 TriStar, which entered service on 15 August 1975, significantly on the Riyadh-Jeddah domestic trunk route. Such was its impact, spurred by a government decree to reduce domestic fares by 25%, that in that year, Saudi's traffic grew by an unprecedented 60%. And, as will be described later in this book, the growth of the Saudi airline was to take it into the realms of the world's leaders. The last of the veteran Douglas DC-3s was retired after flying the short Dhahran-Bahrain shuttle service when the Fairchild F-27 turboprops replaced them in the spring of 1975. The sight of a DC-3 parked next to a wide-bodied jet was symbolic of the dramatic transition that Saudi Arabia had made, in no more than three decades, from the camel caravan to the luxury

By the early 2000s, the Saudi fleet had grown to 128 Boeing, Douglas, and Airbus airliners, including seven allocated to the Royal Flight. The long-range Boeing 747SP was among those on the nonstop Jeddah-New York route, flying uniquely over four continents. (McDonough)

airliner. The air service ceased when the King Fahd Causeway linked Bahrain with the mainland on 25 November 1986.

An Airline for a Princess

Toward the end of 1963, King Hussein of Jordan, who was an accomplished pilot, took over **Jordan Airways**, which in 1961 had come under the control of Lebanon's Middle East Airlines, changing its name from Air Jordan. In no time at all, the king renamed the airline, on 8 December, **Alia—Royal Jordanian Airlines**. Alia was not, as many assumed, an acronym; it was the name of the King's eldest daughter, meaning in Arabic "the high and exalted one." Fresh impetus to the airline was given by the apppointment of Ali Ghandour, who had sought the King's support, which was enthusiastically given. Services began on 15 December 1963, to Beirut, with a Douglas DC-7 purchased from Lebanon, and two Handley Page Heralds, transferred from the Jordanian Air Force. Routes were added to Cairo, Kuwait, and Jeddah.

The infant airline soon moved into jet operations when, on 1 June 1965, it began Sud Caravelle services with an aircraft leased from Air Algérie, and on 16 July 1965, it opened Alia's first route beyond the Middle East, to Rome. It was the first airline to operate into Jerusalem, in February 1966, with a direct Caravelle service from Rome, and this was, predictably, called "The Holy Route." New European destinations were added, to Paris on 7 July and to London on 6 August, of the same year. Unfortunately, any hopes of further European route expansion were dashed by the Six Day War of 5–10 June 1967, when Israel occupied, among other territories on its borders, the western part of Jordan, which became known as the West Bank. This was the end of service to Jerusalem, and Alia also lost part of its fleet. After becoming an entirely state-owned airline on 3 March 1968, the airline recovered, purchased a third Caravelle, and opened new routes in the Gulf region and to Athens during that year.

Alia added Frankfurt and Munich to its European map in 1969, and signed an order for two Boeing 707-320Cs on 7 December 1969. Service started with this long-range type in February 1971, and the network stretched from Madrid in the west to Karachi in the east. Two Boeing 720Bs (from Pan American) were added on 8 December 1972, and three 727s entered service in July 1974. Within barely two years, 1972–74, benefitting from continued unrest among its neighbors, the Jordanian national airline doubled its traffic, an unprecedented rate of growth by any standards.

Local conflicts, not directly involving Jordan, nevertheless often acted as a deterrent to progress. All the routes out of Amman had to avoid overflying Israel on westbound traffic routes to Europe, adding mileage to the circuitous itineraries via Aqaba in the south and over Syria to the north. Also, Alia suffered a setback on 22 January 1973, when one of its Boeing 707s crashed at Kano, Nigeria, while on a Hajj charter flight, killing 183 on board.

Such was the demand for air freight, especially for perishable fruits and vegetables exported to Europe, that a subsidiary airline was formed in February 1974. **Jordanian World Airways** also catered for tourist charters to visit the places of antiquity, especially Petra, site of the ancient Nabataean city carved in the living rock. Alia also operated to Aqaba, on the small Gulf from the Red Sea, Jordan's only maritime outlet and where it was developing the small port as a vacation beach resort. It had formerly been able to claim that it served the lowest airfield on earth, 1,290 feet below mean sea level, on the Dead Sea. That was abandoned after the Six Day War. On a more positive note, at the long-range end of the operational spectrum, the Boeings began service to New York in 1976, and when Alia moved into the wide-bodied jet age early in 1977, the service was flown nonstop to Amman. In July of that year, this was operated jointly with Syrian Arab Airlines, to add Damascus to the trans-Atlantic route.

Thus, showing much resourcefulness in a far-from-friendly environment, this little country, without sources of affluence such as those enjoyed by the oil-rich Gulf states, had, rather like its Lebanese neighbor, claimed its place among the well-established airlines and as a trans-Atlantic operator of the world's flagship, the Boeing 747.

Turkish Revival

With the exception of Iran, all the airlines that are the collective subject of this chapter are domiciled in countries that were once provinces of the pre-1918 Ottoman Empire. The Turks had an aviation tradition, albeit one that was repeatedly curtailed. It had fought in north Africa as early as 1911, and one of its soldiers could claim the world's first aerial victim when he shot down an Italian aviator. Its air force had participated in the Balkan Wars of 1912–13. And often forgotten is that the Ottomans had sponsored an air race from Constantinople (Istanbul) to Alexandria in 1912. The Curtiss company had actually prepared to produce aircraft in Turkey in the 1920s, but the factory produced motor cars instead—a matter of practical priority for a nation bent on rapid modernization. What remained of that Islamic Caliphate was dissolved in 1924, after the sweeping revolution of Kemal Ataturk, who declared Turkey as a secular republic on 29 October 1923. The disintegrated empire was reduced to a small region of the European Balkans around Istanbul and the whole of Asia Minor. Intrusions by foreign forces—British on the eastern Black Sea shore, French and Italian in the Mediterranean, and Greek in a large area around Izmir—were withdrawn or expelled. The new republic, still as big as France and Italy combined, was slow to emerge as a political power. Between the wars, transport improvement was of high priority but did not include an emphasis on air travel. Far more important was the need for surface modes and gradually Turkey developed a railway network to connect all its main cities. Its national airline, **Devlet Hava Yollari (D.H.Y.)** was founded only in 1933, at first linking the new capital, Ankara, with Istanbul, and then only in the summer, with de Havilland biplanes.

During the Second World War, Turkey was neutral, but held a geographically strategic position, and was the beneficiary of help for the airline in the shape of a fleet of 21 Douglas DC-3s (mostly ex–U.S. Air Force converted C-47s). This enabled D.H.Y. to develop its domestic routes to all the regional centers in Asia

Minor and to introduce international services, to Nicosia, Beirut, and Athena in 1949, with an extension to Cairo in 1950.

D.H.Y. did not modernize until the mid-1950s, when it entered into an agreement with B.O.A.C. to acquire six Vickers Viscount turboprops, and these portrayed more respectability on its overseas routes. In August 1960 it added 10 Fokker/Fairchild F-27s—a sensible move as the Viscounts and Fokkers both had Rolls-Royce Dart engines, the first with four and the other with two each. By this time, the Turkish government had intervened to change the airline's status to a joint state-owned/private company, renamed **Turk Hava Yollari** (**T.H.Y.**).

The 1960s witnessed a new influence that was to revolutionize Turkish aviation. Centred on Istanbul, which was becoming a tourist destination as well as a growing commercial center, T.H.Y. began to expand rapidly, as its traffic was augmented by the ever-increasing flow of Turkish "guest workers" (an euphemism for cheap foreign labor), especially to Germany, where many citizens from Balkan countries and beyond found remunerative employment. Short of funds—the airline had always lost money—it leased a Douglas DC-7B from Sweden and a Douglas DC-9-14 jet from the manufacturer, and in 1968–69 was able to put into service two DC-9-30s of its own. The flow of V.F.R. (visiting friends and relatives) traffic between the guest workers and their families at home demanded larger aircraft, and in January 1971, T.H.Y. received the first of four ex–Pan American 180-seat Boeing 707-321s.

T.H.Y. could be said to have come of age with a vengeance. It had moved into the "big jet" age only in 1971, yet it took delivery of its first 270-seat Douglas DC-10 wide-bodied tri-jet at the end of 1972. It had already had an unfortunate succession of crashes, and on 3 March 1974 it sustained a spectacular one, when, on take-off from Paris en route to London, a door broke off and wrecked the aircraft's control systems. All 340 people on board descended to their death, and tragically, many of them had transferred on to T.H.Y. because of strike action by other airlines. It was a cause célèbre in aviation circles and for many months the repercussions concerning the door locking mechanism reverberated between the press, the airline, the F.A.A., Douglas, and the insurance companies.

In 1974, when the island of Cyprus was split into two between the Turkish and Greek populations, T.H.Y. set up a Cypriot subsidiary, Kibris Turk Hava Yollari (Cyprus Turkish Airlines; see below) and supplied it with jet aircraft to maintain a service to the Turkish mainland. By the mid-1970s, coping with the incessant demands of the emigrant workforces in Europe, T.H.Y.'s fleet had grown to 25 jet aircraft, including eight Boeing 727-200s and nine DC-9-32s. B.O.A.C. had relinquished its minority shareholding, and the airline was almost entirely state-owned.

T.H.Y.'s major trunk route is the inter-city link between the capital, Ankara, and Istanbul, now Europe's most populous city. By the early 2010s, it will meet serious competition from the new high-speed railroad, the first segment of which opened in 2009.

A Small Nation Divided

Until the beginning of the Jet Age, indigenous airline activity in the Middle East, from Istanbul in the west to the Arabian Sea in the east, had been almost entirely dependent upon associations with major airlines of Europe and the United States, partly because of geographical convenience and partly because of political expediency (Cyprus was a British Crown Colony). **B.E.A.** had established a base at Nicosia, Cyprus, and **Cyprus Airways**, founded on 24 September 1947, was in partnership with that airline. On 18 April 1953, when B.E.A. opened the world's first sustained turboprop airline service, with its Vickers V-700 Viscounts, the route was from London to Nicosia via Rome and Athens. The service was operated jointly with Cyprus Airways, and it put this little airline into the record books.

By the mid-1950s, its route network extended to Tripoli, Khartoum, and Bahrain, but it became a victim of the political problems in the region which curtailed its operations, and B.E.A. took over some of the routes, under a charter agreement, on 26 January 1958. Cyprus gained its full independence on 16 August 1960, but the airline retained its association with B.E.A. under a new contract, signed on 26 January 1961, to ensure cooperation as it prepared to provide service in the eastern Mediterranean. This was becoming increasingly competitive airline environment that was vigorously embracing air transport, and receiving encouragement and support from often oil-rich governments.

The association enabled the airline to operate jet aircraft when, on 4 July 1961, it introduced Comet 4Bs, in what would now be called a code-sharing agreement with B.E.A., but further political upheavals brought an end to the emergent tourist trade and consequent loss of traffic. In 1965, a new five-year contract was signed with B.E.A., whereby the British airline continued to operate the trunk route from London, while Cyprus Airways operated local routes radiating from Nicosia, with its own crews. The chronic disturbances related to Palestine were now exacerbated by growing confrontations between Turkey and Greece, which directly affected Cyprus, three quarters of whose population were of Greek origin or spoke Greek.

In September 1969, Cyprus Airways added de Havilland Trident 2 tri-jets and, in January 1972, supplemented them with BAC One-Elevens, but once again the chances of building a solid business base were shattered when, in the summer of 1974, internal friction between the Greek majority, headed by the Orthodox Archbishop Makarios, and the Turkish minority in the northern part of the island, reached a flash point. On 15 July the Cypriot National Guard seized power, Makarios fled the country, and a civil war ensued. A frontier zone was quickly established as Turkish forces occupied northern Cyprus, 40% of the island. This included Nicosia's airport, and all Cyprus Airways services were suspended until 8 February 1975. The airline managed to keep going with two Viscount 800s, leased from British Midland Airways, and transferred its base to Larnaka. On 8 June 1975, the Turkish Cypriots voted to form a separate state, and shortly afterward, on 1 September, Cyprus Airways resumed jet operations with two leased Douglas DC-9-10s.

It made short-term leases then settled down with three BAC One-Elevens and four Boeing 707-120s, and by the end of the decade had resumed service to 10 European and 11 Middle Eastern destinations. In 1983 the Cyprus government took complete ownership of its airline, and in the next year, it showed its mettle by taking delivery of two Airbus A-310 twin-jets.

In 1975, Cyprus was de facto separated into two parts. The northern (Turkish) side of the island had to have its own airline. It was economically as well as politically dependent upon Turkey, and therefore needed efficient communication with its protector. **Kibris Turk Hava Yollari (Cyprus Turkish Airlines) (K.T.H.Y.)** was established and headquartered in Nicosia/Lefkosia, which, like the whole island, was divided in two. K.T.H.Y. leased various jet aircraft from T.H.Y., which owned 50% of the airline, but wore its own colors and initials. It maintained essential air links with the main cities of Turkey, and its aircraft were often interchangeable so that through flights could be operated, for example, to London, to support tourist traffic in competition with its southern neighbor.

A Regional Metamorphosis

Within no more than two decades, the countries of the Middle East asserted their right to be recognized as independent countries, replacing colonial or the former League of Nations mandated rule. Most of them were blessed with oil resources, and this gave them a priceless negotiating tool as they began to assume a greater role in world affairs. This was especially apparent in the airline arena. No longer were the airports of the eastern Mediterranean or the Persian Gulf used by European and U.S. Airlines only as refueling points en route to the subcontinent and the far east. They became traffic hubs in their own right, and the larger countries, Iran and Saudi Arabia, developed substantial domestic route networks, where surface travel had previously been arduous and sometimes dangerous.

As the 20th century drew toward its close, the once almost unknown emirates and sheikdoms of the Gulf States were to emerge, as affluent entities, able to operate their own airlines. They did so with flair and, as will be narrated later in this book, became important, even major actors, on the international airline stage. The nations of the Middle East had shrewdly recognized that the commercial airliner was an instrument through which they could take their place in the modern industrial world. The result was an historic revolution in airline operational achievement, which is described more fully later in this book.

Chapter 12: Development of a Second Line

The Jets Shrink the World

Newspaper headlines, and most of the attention given by the aviation magazines of the 1960s, were directed toward the explosive growth of airline travel and the wonders of rapid communication that was the direct result of the introduction of jet airliners. The long-distance air routes were the obvious beneficiaries because of the significant savings in time. The business traveler could fly westbound across the Atlantic at a convenient departure time and still be in New York in time for dinner, and eastbound flights could be made during the night, saving the equivalent of a working day, even if this meant a day or two recovering from the five-hour jet lag. The 550–600 mph cruising speed permitted an ideal Atlantic scheduling pattern with a complete round-trip within the 24-hour day, and thereby attained maximum use of between 13 and 14 hours. This reflected in the fixed-cost element of the cost-per-seat-mile, the basic foundation of all airline economics. Such advantages were also possible on the Europe–East Asia markets. Although the total volume of traffic did not yet approach that of the North Atlantic, it was beginning to make its mark. Led by Japan, the countries of the Pacific Rim began to take their places in the post-war industrial world. Indeed, by the early 2000s, the volume of Europe–Asia trunk airline traffic was approaching that of the trans-Atlantic operators. The 500-seat double-decked Airbus A380 would make its first scheduled service with Singapore Airlines to London on 18 March 2008, after making its debut to Sydney on 25 October 2007.

The speed of the jet airliners also had a dramatic effect on the leisure travelers, whose horizons expanded to hitherto undreamed-of destinations. During the 20th century, with growing affluence of the middle class populations of the industrial nations of the world, these vistas had expanded out of all recognition from the 19th century days when few people enjoyed the privilege of a vacation, paid or unpaid. Six-day weeks had given way to five working days, and in some enlightened industries—the cotton and woollen workers of northern England, for example—the mills and factories had traditionally closed down for one week in the summer.

By the late 1930s, summer vacations or holidays were almost habitual. Visits to the seaside resorts on the English south coast or to Atlantic City in the United States were within the average family budgets. People in northern Europe were able to fly to French resorts on the Mediterranean, and New Yorkers went to Florida. Post-war 1940s witnessed a gradual expansion of these horizons. The average English family started to go to Paris or Brussels for a weekend, and Americans began to explore the islands of the Caribbean.

Then came the jets. As emphasized above, the technological revolution was not reflected only by the speed and the consequent reduction in journey times; it produced an unanticipated economic benefit because of the sheer efficiency of jet propulsion. Tourist fares worldwide were introduced in 1952, coincidentally with the first jets and turboprops, and followed by economy fares worldwide in 1958, coincidentally with the introduction of the Boeing 707s and the Douglas DC-8s. With jet airplanes, airline operating costs declined, and the tour operators who booked the tickets—for whole airplanes for an entire season—had a cheaper commodity to sell. Down came the fares, producing a rush to the airline booking outlets and an unprecedented boom in leisure air travel. Greece and southern Spain, even north Africa, were now within easy reach of the Scandinavians. "Flying down to Rio" was a practical possibility for many New Englanders, and Bangkok and Singapore hotels filled up with Japanese holiday-makers. For experienced travelers seeking new resorts, islands in the Indian Ocean beckoned, and the travel agents and airlines were happy to fulfill their wishes.

The established airlines were slow to change their ways. They had been used to catering to business travelers, who had hitherto comprised at least three-quarters of their total clientele. Their promotions were directed toward comfort and convenience, particularly on-board catering. They were ill prepared for the onslaught of the non-scheduled airlines that invaded what they had regarded as a protected market. Public pressure from the tourist trade broke down the barriers of international agencies such as the International Air Transport Association (I.A.T.A.) and the United States Civil Aeronautics Board (C.A.B.). Within two decades, the balance of business versus tourist travel reversed itself, and three-quarters of worldwide travelers were tourists.

The airlines eventually met the competition from the charter and non-scheduled airlines with various forms of incentive fares and were pleasantly surprised to find that their balance sheets did not suffer unduly. This was mainly because the average load factors (percentage of seats filled) increased substantially, from typically 55% to 60% during the business-dominated era to 65% or more when holiday-makers filled the seats and were not so demanding for preferred scheduled departure times. The business traveler sought ideal times for his working schedule, and his employer paid the necessary fare; the tourist traveler, especially one with an accompanying family, sought the cheapest fare, and if this demanded a sunrise take-off, a late-evening arrival, and austere on-board catering, this was irrelevant if a few (and often more than a few) pounds, francs, marks, yen, or dollars were saved. Expansion of airline schedules into hitherto unpopular timetable slots permitted higher aircraft utilization and consequent savings in costs.

The net result of these factors was that, during the heady years of the introduction of the Jet Age at the beginning of the 1960s, world air traffic doubled in five years then doubled again—fourfold in 10 years. In the past, even the immortal Douglas DC-3 did not bring air travel to the masses, but in the 1960s, jet airliners introduced the whole world to a vast new market. English coal miners went to the Canary Islands, bank clerks climbed the pyramids in Egypt, civil servants from Bonn enjoyed California's Disneyland, and back-packers from Brooklyn climbed the Eiffel Tower. At no time in history had the nations of the world, whether on business, in politics, or on vacation, come closer together. Jet airliners had made the world smaller.

Another New Market

Contrasting with holiday-bent air travelers, the arrival of the Jet Age coincided with the emergence of what became known as the "guest worker" market. The travelers from southern Asia and beyond were hardly guests, but they were certainly workers, employed by the newly rich Middle Eastern states to build cities, highways, and public utilities. The workers themselves traveled backward and forward at intervals, either to work or to visit families, and the airlines at the origin and destination points enjoyed a healthy business.

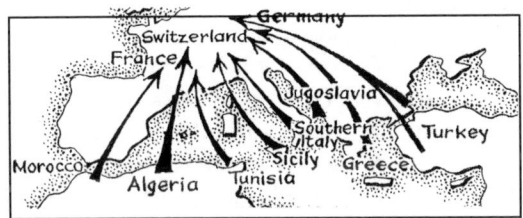

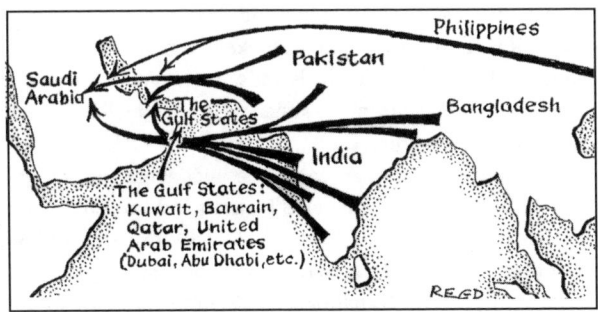

A new source of passenger revenue developed with "guest workers"—a euphemism for cheap labor—expanded considerably from Mediterranean countries to the more affluent industrial northwestern Europe, and from southern and eastern Asia to the Middle East.

Search for a Feeder-Liner

All public transport—land, sea, or air—depends on demographics. Where there are people, there is a potential for travel. An important qualifier is the measure of individual wealth or, more precisely, discretionary income. Also, the propensity for travel is heaviest in urban areas because of occupational necessity. In rural areas, the desire for travel is minimal, especially those of wide expanse, as in Asia, where most of the peasantry live at barely subsistence level. The result is that air travel, just like rail and road travel (and formerly sea travel) proliferates between the large urban centers of the world. In general, the larger and richer the metropolis, the more traffic it generates and attracts. Thus, the world's biggest commercial air traffic centers are among the world's biggest metropolitan concentrations such as New York, Chicago, London, Paris, and Tokyo. By the end of the 20th century, about 55% of the total ton-mileage of all the international airlines was moving into and out of only 25 of the world's busiest airports. By 2008, International Civil Aviation Organization (I.C.A.O.) statistics confirmed that this figure had increased to 75%. The remaining balance of the world's traffic was spread around thousands of other airports. The leading airlines of the world, mainly in America and Europe, secured the lion's share of the densest inter-city traffic. Complementing these, many flag carriers of countries big and small, rich and poor, and lesser companies down the scale competed for the crumbs that were left.

Until the Second World War, these smaller fry were few and far between. Usually, each nation had its own national airline, most of them sponsored and supported, directly or indirectly, by their governments. This was done either by direct subsidy, as a matter of national interest and prestige, as in most European countries, or by generous mail payments and subsidies, as in the United States. Very few countries in the world were able to sustain more than one flag carrier, and the ideal of private enterprise risking its entrepreneurial investments in airline operations was almost unknown. Indeed, such a risk could only be taken at all in large countries where even the established railroads could be challenged by adequate time-saving competition. Thus, in the United States, about 20 privately owned airlines emerged after the war. Brazil witnessed a plethora of opportunist companies, but few survived more than a few years, lacking modern equipment. Australia had a few airlines of varying size and ability. The Soviet Union had a single state airline, and China did too after the 1949 revolution. Some island nations, such as Great Britain and Japan, needed feeder-airline connections to supplement the trunk routes. In the former case, this was done by the state airline, B.E.A.; in the latter, by some enterprising local companies.

Local Service in the United States

In the United States, the extent of the need was vast. The population was affluent. Increased air-mindedness, generated during the war by the armed services and the manufacturing industry alike, stimulated the demand for airline service in every corner of the country. Every community demanded air service, and the government responded through the agency of the C.A.B. During the four immediate post-war years, 1946–50, about 400 new points appeared on the airline map, about half of these awarded to new airlines categorized as Local Service. About 100 were new stations on the existing networks of the trunk airlines. By 1950, no less than 600 cities of the United States had commercial airports served by commercial airlines.

The newcomers drew upon a large reserve of war-surplus Douglas C-47 transports, easily converted to DC-3 standards. They were cheap to buy and, for the density of traffic involved, economical to operate, compared to the larger aircraft of the trunk airlines. But the public wanted something better. The pre-war tail-wheeled design, though operationally serviceable, was non-pressurized and appeared distinctly old-fashioned when lined up with post-war replacement types. These had tricycle landing gears with nose-wheels (and therefore with level flooring when on the ground); most were pressurized and could fly "above the weather;" and they were demonstrably more powerful and faster. The Local Service airlines took notice, and on 2 June 1952, **Pioneer Airlines** put the first modern airliner into service, a Martin 202. On 19 May 1955, President Eisenhower signed a bill granting permanent certificates to the 13 airlines that had survived the experimental period, and the airlines acquired the twin-engined Martins and Convair 240s and 340s.

First of the Twin-Engined Turboprops

After the C.A.B. approved loan guarantees to the Locals on 7 September 1957, Seattle-based **West Coast Airlines** became the first of its category to introduce turbine-engined equipment, when it put its twin-engined Fairchild F-27 (Fokker Friendship, built under license) into service in the northwest—and incidentally was the first operator of this successful "DC-3 Replacement." The turboprop was tremendously successful, as it provided a degree of modernity to airlines that needed to take pride in their image. Its 40 seats (compared to the 28 of the post-war DC-3) was compatible with the traffic demand on the local networks; the Rolls-Royce Dart engines provided a smooth ride; and its high-winged design gave all the passengers the pleasurable experience of always being able to observe the passing countryside.

In Europe, the Irish **Aer Lingus** was first with the Fokker Friendship, and the Dutch manufacturer had great success with its sales campaign. But it was not alone in this burgeoning market. In the 1960s, more than 2,000 DC-3s, of varying ages (but none less than 15 years old) and conditions, were still deployed all over the world, their lives sustained by their ability to land on or take off from almost any grass or dirt strip as short as a thousand yards. Any potential replacement airliner aiming to supplant this veteran Douglas product had to be able to come close to, if not match, this versatile field performance. The Fokker-Fairchilds came close enough to satisfy airlines all over the world, and more than 800 were sold, twice as many as the larger four-engined Viscounts, which had served to launch the Dart engine in the higher echelons of the airline strata.

The Friendship was particularly popular in Asia, and large fleets were to be found in India, Pakistan, Indonesia, and the Philippines. The Fokker's versatility was to be demonstrated in the mountains of northern Pakistan, at Gilgit and Skardu, where, with mixed cargoes of people, produce, and goats, they weaved their way through precipitous mountain passes. They served the mountains of West Irian (formerly the last colony of the Netherlands, before Indonesia's independence), although there were many places in such areas where only the old DC-3s could land and these were replaced by the smaller Canadian de Havilland DHC-6 Twin Otters.

Indonesia is a country of thousands of islands whose geographical extent, east-to-west, is longer than the width of the continental United States. Its island-enforced separation makes it ideal for air transport. The national airline, **Garuda Indonesian Airlines**, was responsible for main-line services to the provincial capitals, operating modern turboprops or jets. In 1983 it handed over the local routes in West Irian to **Merpati Nusantara Airlines** to serve places that were otherwise isolated by impenetrable jungles. It grew quickly, acquiring a variety of airliner types, almost all turboprops, including Vickers Vanguards, to link the colonies of feeder routes in the islands. At its height, Merpati was able to claim service to no less than 128 points which, it wryly observed, was more than Lufthansa's total.

The country was large enough to encourage and to permit others to operate. These included **Bouraq Indonesian**, based at Balikpapan, in Kalimantan (formerly Dutch Borneo); **Seulawah Air Service** and **Mandala Airlines**, which mainly served Sumatra; and **Sempati Air Transport**. These companies were founded in the early 1970s and were able to start service with modern turboprop equipment, ranging from Viscounts and other Dart-engined types to DHC-6 Twin Otters and the smaller Britten-Norman Islanders. One curious exception was **Zamrud Aviation**, which provided service from Jakarta to all the Sunda Islands, and as far as east Timor, with a fleet of the airstrip-friendly Douglas DC-3s. (See Chapter 36 for details of Indonesian airlines.)

In the Indian subcontinent, **Pakistan International Airlines** flew domestically, and until 1971 this meant two separate networks, in west and east Pakistan. The latter was the Muslim-populated area of Bengal, and the separation had resulted from the Partition of India in 1947. **Bangladesh Biman** was founded on 4 January 1972 and was able to start Friendship service from Dhaka to Chittagong as early as 9 March, with aircraft donated by the Indian government. The same airplane was favored by other breakaway states from the former British India: **Union of Burma**

After the end of the Second World War, air-mindedness extended throughout the United States, to small communities as well as to the cities. The C.A.B. created a group of Local Service airlines, which operated to at least 400 points, mostly with Douglas DC-3s converted from military use.

Development of a Second Line

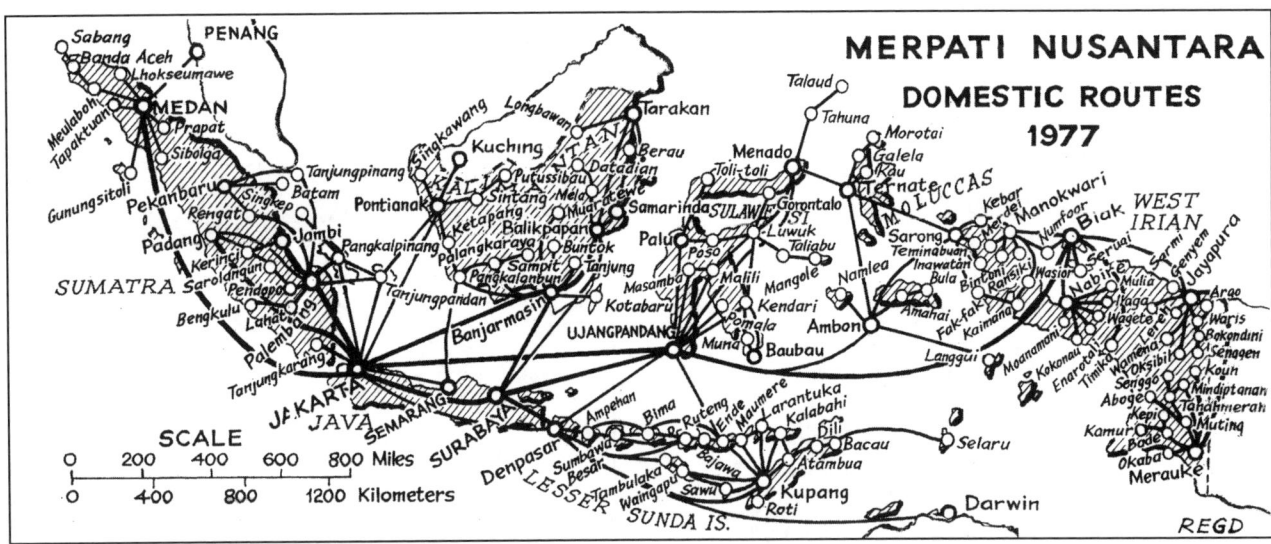

Serving a country that, from west to east, was wider than the United States, Indonesia's Merpati Nusantara reached every corner of the many-islanded country. Its local service network was larger than all routes of the flag airlines of many industrial countries in Europe.

Airways (U.B.A.) in November 1963, **Royal Nepal Airline Corporation (R.N.A.C.)** in April 1966, and even the little **Air Maldives** had one in 1985. (See Chapters 35 and 36.)

In Japan, the Fokker Friendship was well liked by **All Nippon Airways (A.N.A.)**. This airline had grown by merger and acquisition to become Japan's air transport's "second force." **Japan Air Lines** concentrated on international routes and only on the denser inter-city routes of domestic service. All Nippon provided air service from the major Tokyo and Osaka conurbations to the many provincial towns and cities that were not served by the Shin Kan-sen "Bullet Train" lines that began to operate in August 1964. The traffic density on these "Beam" routes, at least during the adolescent years of All Nippon, was ideal for the F-27 Friendship, and when the 25th aircraft was delivered on 8 December 1964, this was the largest fleet of the type in the world. The airline was fast outgrowing its secondary status, at least domestically, to Japan Air Lines. (See Chapter 21.)

Another eastern Asia airline that needed a good replacement for its DC-3s was **Malaysian Airways**, renamed in 1963 from Malayan Airways, after independence from Great Britain was accomplished, as the Federation of Malaysia, in 1957. The Fokker Friendship was used to connect the new capital, Kuala Lumpur, not only with the outlying districts of the Malayan Peninsula, but also with the former northern Borneo colonies, Sarawak and British North Borneo (Sabah). Such was the marketability of the high-winged Friendship that it was used on the shuttle service from "K.L." to Singapore, where a higher frequency with the 40-seater was preferable, until the fast-growing traffic demand justified bigger and faster jets.

Other Asian airlines where the Fokker twin-turboprop found service were **Far-east Air Transport (FAT)** in Taiwan, **Korean Air Lines**, and **Royal Air Cambodge**. Altogether, the Dutch feeder airliner had done well throughout the Asian continent, but it was not without competition. It had a head-start on the only other manufacturers to match its specification. The British Handley Page Herald missed its chance with its initial piston-engined Alvis Leonides engines. The potential customers quickly forced the issue. By the time the 50-seat turboprop Dart-Herald appeared on the scene, and even after some impressive demonstrations in the high Andes (at the 13,400-foot elevation La Paz, Bolivia) and in the high Himalayas (at Leh, Kashmir), too much time had been lost, and the Fokkers were too well entrenched in the feeder-jet "DC-3 Replacement" market. A few Heralds were sold to **Air Manila**, in the Philippines, in November 1965, and to FAT (see above) on 21 February 1966, but this was the limit of Handley Page sales in the Asian market.

Challenger for the Twin-Dart Feeder Market

Far more successful was the Avro (later Hawker-Siddeley) 748. The British company threw its hat into the Twin-Dart feederliner ring. Like the other aspirants, it had to demonstrate that it could at least come close to having the rough-field performance

In the Philippines, many local services were served by the Avro 748s of Philippine Air Lines, Handley Page Heralds of Air Manila, and the 60-seat Nihon YS-11s (above) of Filipinas Orient Airways. (NASM-9A08176)

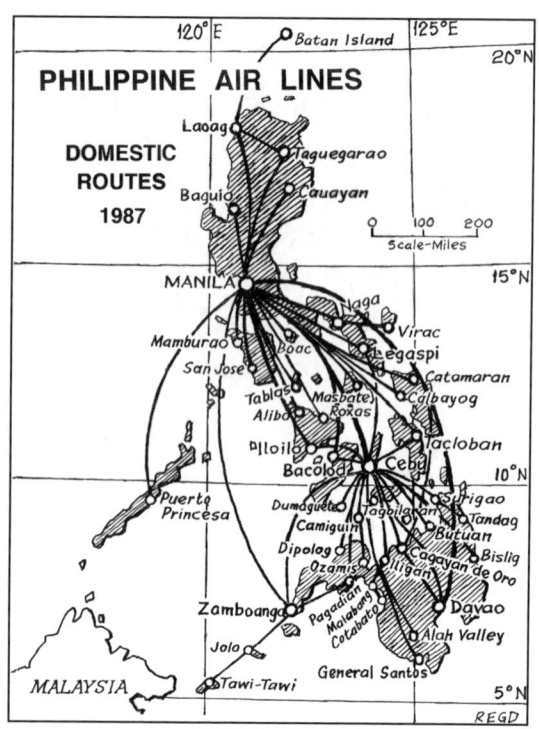

The Philippines are ideally suited for air transport, especially as the maritime ferry services have been slow and unreliable. Both are vulnerable to typhoons, which are frequent in this island country.

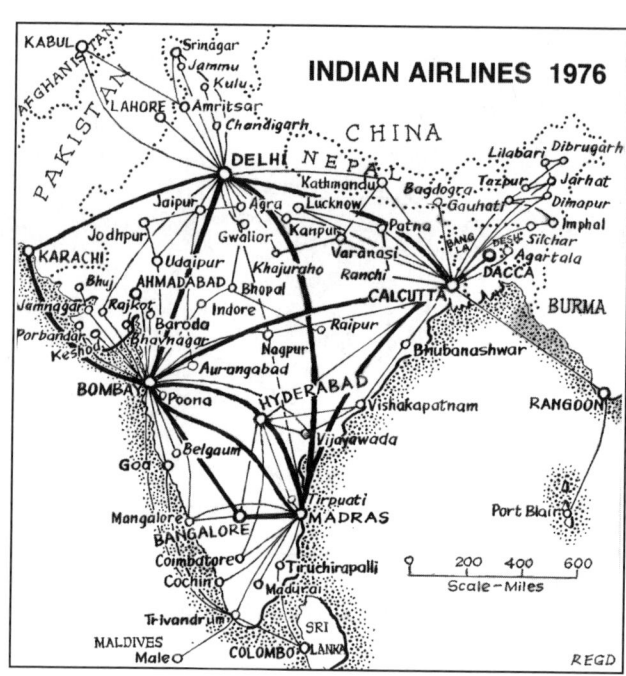

India possesses one of the largest railroad systems in the world, covering long distances and sometimes mountainous terrain. Complementing this, I.A.C. created an extensive feeder network at the northern, eastern, western, and southern extremities of the country.

of the veteran and now legendary Douglas DC-3. Unlike the Friendship or the Herald, the 748's wing was conventionally on the lower fuselage level—requiring special design treatment for the engine positions—but its performance was excellent. It first went into service with Aerolíneas Argentinas (see below) on 2 April 1962 and began to make its mark.

One initiative was to identify the biggest potential market in Asia. Following the cessation of hostilities in India in 1945, dozens of war-surplus Douglas C-47s found their way into the various Indian airlines that amalgamated in 1953 to form the **Indian Airlines Corporation (I.A.C.)**. At one time it counted 74 in its DC-3 fleet. It had already introduced the Vickers Viscount in 1957 and so a Dart-engined twin turboprop was a natural partner for the routes feeding into the Delhi-Bombay-Calcutta "Golden Triangle" of major Indian cities. Avro countered Fokker's lead of proven service by offering to allow the Indians to build the 748 under license. A factory was built at Cawnpore (Kanpur), but this took time. Meanwhile, from necessity, I.A.C. bought some Friendships as well. Eventually, the home-built Avro 748s went into service at the end of 1967.

Avro—now a division of the Hawker-Siddeley Group—claimed that its product was tougher than the Dutch rival, and this appeared to be a valid sales pitch. Under somewhat tragic circumstances, it seemed to be borne out in the Philippines in 1967. On 25 February of that year, a 748 arrived in Manila to demonstrate its capabilities to **Philippine Air Lines (P.A.L.)**. Within four months, three Fokker Friendships had crashed, killing a total of more than 50 people. The die was cast. On 8 July 1967, P.A.L. ordered a fleet of 748s, and its substantial fleet of DC-3s was retired on 14 March 1968. But in spite of the new aircraft's demonstrated versatility, it could not use some of the dirt strips that served some of the southern Philippine towns. The government, under President Marcos, was not prepared to improve the airfields, and the old veteran DC-3 was brought back to soldier on. They were not finally put out to grass, permanently (and literally), until 7 April 1978.

The Avro 748 also found favor in Thailand (formerly Siam). It had a strong and independent tradition of air-mindedness, having supplied personnel, to be trained as pilots, to the Allies in the First World War. This influence had stimulated Siam to start the first sustained air mail service in Asia in 1922. After the Second World War, the Scandinavian Airlines System helped to put Thailand on the international airline map in 1959 when it formed **Thai Airways International (THAI)**. The Thai shares were held by the **Thai Airways Company (T.A.C.)**, which continued to operate domestic routes. By this time, the Thai capital city, Bangkok, was established as a major metropolis in southeast Asia. It was geographically convenient, competing with Singapore as a staging point for all the airlines flying between Europe and the entire western Pacific rim, from Tokyo to Sydney. Thailand was also beginning to emerge as a major tourist destination, for its architectural and cultural heritage, its elephants, its entertainments, and its beaches. Domestic air connections continued with the inevitable DC-3 until, on 1 April 1964, the first HS-748 went into service and brought turbine-engined comfort to this elongated country,

Development of a Second Line

For many years, several manufacturers of 40-seat feeder-liners competed for the local service market in the Philippines. The most successful was the Avro (later Hawker Siddeley) 748 (left), whose rough-field performance was essential for grass and dirt strips. Even so, the veteran Douglas DC-3 (right) was still needed for those fields where improvements had been minimal. (Davies, NASM-9A08177; NASM-9A08179)

but also to neighboring states where the turboprop was more suited to the traffic density and the stage lengths than THAI's jets.

Twin Turboprops in South America

Latin America offered an even more potential opportunity for the introduction of local service airliners. Of the thousands of war-surplus C-47s and other Douglas DC-3 variants, many hundreds were in that continent, where, except in Argentina, railroads were fragmented, rare, or non-existent, and roads often mere dirt tracks. One airline in Brazil had 84 of the Douglas twins, sometimes operating scheduled service over distances of only a few miles, such was the dearth of good roads. One executive ruefully commented that as soon as a Jeep got through to a remote community it would be the end of air service. Steadily, however, local airstrips were improved to be able to accept aircraft larger than a DC-3. Terminal buildings appeared and the dirt, gravel, and grass gave way to asphalt or concrete surfaces on the runways. Nevertheless, the old Gooney Bird did not disappear; it simply passed down the ranks to bush services where even the Jeeps or Land Rovers hesitated to visit.

Meanwhile, the tradition of air-mindedness, born of dire necessity as in the mountains of the Colombian Andes or the upper reaches of the Brazilian Amazon, was alive and well. **Panair do Brasil** and **L.A.V.** in Venezuela had been among the first airlines to order the revolutionary Comet jet airliner in 1951, and Brazil's VARIG had introduced the Caravelle twin-jet as early as 1959. So, in due course, the race was on to replace piston engines with turboprops everywhere south of the Rio Grande. Fokker did not at first have much success, although Venezuela's **AVENSA**, privately owned by Henry Boulton, added five Friendships to its fleet in 1958. But these were usurped by the turbine-engined-powered Convair 580, an airline decision that was no doubt influenced by the commonality with its existing fleet of Convair 340s and 440s, one of the latter of which was converted to the Allison turbine power plant. Other than this sortie into South America, only one F-27 was sold south of the United States, to a small Mexican airline, **Trans Mar de Cortes**, in July 1958. This company had been founded by Alvaro Obregon, a former president of Mexico, who recognized the tourism potential of the Baja Peninsula and the Pacific coast of Mexico and realized that Californian tourists would not appreciate well-worn DC-3s. But he was ahead of his time, and the airline folded in 1962.

The Dutch company had realized that special incentives had to be made to encourage the Local Service airlines of the United States to go overseas to buy their new airplanes, and had shrewdly made a deal with Fairchild, a company in Hagerstown, Maryland, to manufacture the Friendship, under license, and to market them as Fairchild F-27s. The first production prototype was delivered to **Aerovías Ecuatorianas (AREA)** on 9 July 1959, as the first turbine-powered airliner in Ecuador, where the capital of Quito is 9,400 feet above sea level. Unfortunately, this fleet flagship crashed in November 1960, severely damaging the reputation of this high-winged twin-turbine airliner throughout the continent.

The Fokker-Fairchild setback was exacerbated by the marketing efforts of the British company Avro, part of the Hawker-Siddeley group. In 1961, it sold nine of its Model 748 to **Aerolíneas Argentinas**, which, in 1959, had already performed pioneer work with the de Havilland Comets, the first jet airliners in South America. The Avros went into service on routes radiating from Buenos Aires on 15 February 1962 and performed impressively. The manufacturer had always claimed that the 748 could take off from a ploughed field, and this was perhaps no exaggeration. It was solidly built and could out-perform the Fokker twin on short dirt strips. A journalist visiting western Argentina in a 748 was heard to remark that he "had heard of unprepared strips, but this one was taken by surprise."

The 748's success in the continent was wide-spread. Venezuela's other, state-supported, airline, **Aeropostal Venezolana**, also favored the advantages of engine commonality, as it had a fleet of Vickers Viscounts, with the same Rolls-Royce Dart engines as the 748s. Another important customer was the Brazilian Air Force, the Força Aérea Brasileira, whose semi-military **Correio Aéreo Nacional (C.A.N.)** had traditionally played a critical role in the development of air mail services into the distant outback regions of this large country, pioneering routes into jungle strips where the airlines feared to tread. By the 1960s, the airlines replaced the C.A.N., but the military still provided many support services to remote communities, both for the local population and for its own purposes. Buying a substantial fleet of the (now) Hawker-Siddeley 748 was a valuable advertisement for the airplane.

Brazil Tries Them All

The mid-1960s witnessed a widespread introduction of twin-Dart-engined airliners in Brazil. In January 1963, the Brazilian government had created the Rede Integração Nacional (RIN) feeder route system, subsidized as a social service and drawing inspiration from the Local Service networks in the United States. The leading airlines were **Viação Aérea São Paulo (VASP)**, **Viação Aérea Rio Grandense (VARIG)**, and **Cruzeiro do Sul**, but the initiative to upgrade the feeder airline fleet, and to turn Brazil's back on the DC-3, was taken by the fourth largest airline, **Sadia**, named after the meat-packing factory in Concórdia, in the state of Santa Catarina. Omar Fontana, the son of the factory's founder, had, in 1956, started to fly fresh meat to the best butchers in São Paulo then entered the scheduled airline market with DC-3s. After a long fight with the bureaucracy—Omar made 234 round-trips from São Paulo to Rio de Janeiro to gain official permission—and after leasing three Handley Page Dart Heralds from the manufacturer early in 1964, six were purchased and went into sustained service. In June 1972, Fontana changed the name of his airline to **Transbrasil**, and the aircraft carried new colors—about 65 different schemes in the total airline fleet.

Handley Page was only able to break into the fringe of the twin-Dart market, partly because it had been late in adapting to the turbine power (see above). In 1967, Cruzeiro do Sul introduced 12 of the Japanese Nihon YS-11, another twin-Dart airliner, with upgraded engines that permitted a larger fuselage to accommodate 60 passengers, compared to the 40 of the other Dart-engined types. A year later, VASP added eight more YS-11s to the growing number of twin-Darts in Brazil.

Brazil's big airline, VARIG had not stood idly by, and in 1967 also, put the first of a dozen HS-748s into service. And if this did not complicate matters enough, Fairchild decided to try its luck in the Brazilian market. It had done some promising development work with the basic F-27 Friendship. Having taken over the Hiller company, it launched the larger 48-seat Fairchild-Hiller FH-227. It met with moderate success in the United States, and inched into South America at the end of 1967 by selling six of this model to **Paraense**, based at Belém, and specializing in routes throughout the Amazon River basin. But in 1970 three aircraft were lost within a few months, and the airline soon closed down.

The DC-3 Gives Way

The gradual replacement of the apparently ageless DC-3 by the twin-turboprop generation was most clearly defined in Asia and South America. By the mid-1970s, the often-repeated statement that more than 2,000 DC-3s were still in operation was no longer true. Most were retired from service; many were cannibalized for spare parts. Some DC-3s, however, were sold into lower levels of the airline hierarchy, into "bush" operations where they performed valiantly where new airplanes did not dare put down their wheels.

Behind the political "Iron Curtain," a similar piston-to-turbine evolution was evolving in the Soviet Union. The Antonov An-24 was, at least in general appearance, similar to the Fairchild high-winged twin, and it did its duty throughout the vast expanses of the **Aeroflot** network, serving hundreds of communities from the western frontiers in Europe to the far eastern Siberian fastnesses of Kamchatka, Chukotka, and Sakhalin. Including the An-26 and other developments, some 2,500 of the Kiev manufacturer's turboprop twin were put into regular service, more than the combined fleets of all the western twin-Dart types combined.

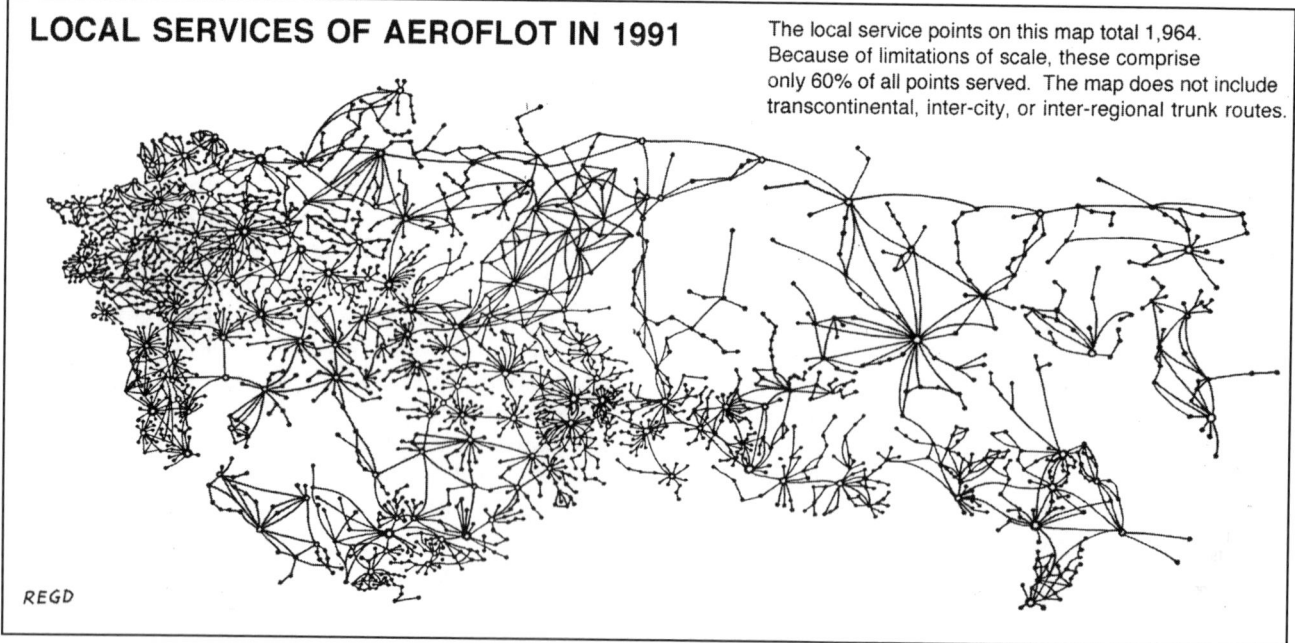

When the all-embracing Aeroflot ceased to exist, it was the largest airline in the world—three times larger than the largest in the western world. Its local route network served almost 2,000 points across eleven time zones. It was so comprehensive that the borders of the Soviet Union are apparent when all points are shown.

Development of a Second Line

The Antonov An-24 market was confined mainly to the communist world. It was a reliable workhorse for feeder services. (NASM-9A08088)

Unrecognized Technical Revolution

The transition from twin-piston to twin-turboprop at these secondary levels was not spectacular, nor was it as visible, to the traveling public as the more dramatic switch by the major airlines from the Constellations, DC-6s and -7s, and Stratocruisers to the first generation of Boeing 707 and Douglas DC-8 jets. But in many ways it was a technical revolution. All over the world, in provincial towns and even in small villages, the local populations could benefit from the better comfort and service of the turboprops. This emergent air-mindedness was widespread. Provincial peoples felt that they were no longer regarded as the second-class citizens of the airline networks (which the operation of pre-war aircraft implied).

Another contemporary development—or perhaps non-development—was that the continued expansion of railroad lines to outback communities slowed to a halt. Ambitious projects for a trans–South American railroad and the African Cape-to-Cairo vision were left on the drawing boards. In an unusual reversal of the trend, Australia was finally to complete the north–south mid-Australian trunk line from Darwin as late as 2003. In China, however, where the construction of a vitally necessary national rail system had never been systematically planned, a comprehensive network was built. This was, at the time, as much for political and military as for commercial reasons, to ensure rapid travel and logistics support to every province of China. But it was also to prove of inestimable value to the future development of the Chinese industrial economy.

THE TWIN-ENGINED TURBOPROPS

First Flight Date	First Service Date	Aircraft Type	Dimensions m(ft) Length	Dimensions m(ft) Span	Speed km/h (mph)	Seats	MTOW kg (lb)	Normal Range km (mi)	First Airline	No. Built
24 Nov 1955	27 Sep 1958	Fokker F.27 (Fairchild F-27)	23 (76)	29 (95)	415 (258)	40	17,900 (39,400)	640 (400)	West Coast	787[1]
11 Mar 1958	17 May 1961	Handley Page Dart-Herald	23 (76)	29 (95)	430 (270)	44	19,500 (43,000)	640 (400)	Jersey Airlines	48
24 Jun 1960	1 Apr 1961	Avro/HS 748	20 (67)	30 (98)	420 (260)	40	20,225 (44,495)	700 (440)	Skyways	381
20 Dec 1959	9 Oct 1962	Antonov An-24	24 (79)	29 (95)	450 (280)	48	21,000 (46,300)	600 (375)	Aeroflot	1,100
30 Aug 1962	20 Sep 1965	NAMC YS-11	26 (86)	32 (105)	450 (280)	64	25,000 (55,000)	1050 (650)	Japan Domestic	182

[1] Includes Dutch-built Friendships, U.S. (Fairchild) F-27s, (Fairchild-Hiller) FH-227. Production continued as Fokker 50.

Regrettably, this aeronautical revolution at the "second level" did not attract the attention of the media as much as did the supersonic Concorde, which went into service in 1976, amid a frenzy of publicity, which continued even after it was retired in 2003. Yet the twin-turboprops have collectively carried tens, perhaps hundreds of millions of airline passengers, at fares that they could afford, improving their lifestyles and, over a period of little more than a decade, helping to create a social transformation in almost every country of the world. The fleet of 14 Concordes, none of which was paid for by the only two airlines that operated it, carried little more than one million well-heeled paying (or non-paying) passengers, over very few routes, during its 27-year supersonic life span. The Concordes are now consigned to museums, but the poor relations, the 40-seat twin turboprops, have continued to serve the world's airlines and the world's peoples, true standard-bearer representatives of the Jet Age, making as important a contribution to the development of the airline industry as the intercontinental Boeings and Airbus jet flagships.

The First Feeder Jets

Even so, the technical resources of the aircraft manufacturing industries were not content to rest on their turboprop laurels. The project engineers and designers in Europe were busy experimenting with ideas for a jet-powered feeder airliner of about the same size as the twin-Dart turboprops. Just as Fokker had, with the Friendship, taken the lead with the first turbine-powered DC-3 Replacement, once again it initiated the first twin-jet of similar size, the Fokker F-28 Fellowship. Intended at first to be a 50-seater, the production model, powered by two Rolls-Royce down-rated Spey engines, had 65 seats, and further developments permitted up to 85 seats in a high-density layout. The first customer, the German **Lufttransport Unternehmen (L.T.U.)**, took delivery in February 1969.

The market for this airliner was marginal, partly because airlines already had adequate fleets of Friendships and 748s, which served them well, and partly because the size of the F-28 was close to that of the Caravelle, the BAC One-Eleven, and the DC-9-10. Nevertheless, with vigorous promotion, Fokker set the pace for future requirement for such a specification slot—something larger and faster than the biggest twin-Dart turboprop, but smaller than any of the main-line short-haul jets. And so they found a niche with secondary domestic route structures, such as with Braathens-SAFE, in Norway, Itavia in Italy, Iberia in Spain, and MacRobertson-Miller in Western Australia. The later variant of the type did particularly well in Indonesia, where the national airline, **Garuda**, found its size to be ideal for the routes radiating from Jakarta to the many islands, where some cities justified 100-seat DC-9s, but many others were too small to generate sufficient passenger traffic. Also, because of the combination of size and frequency, Garuda was able to use the F-28 for a no-reservation shuttle service between Jakarta and Surabaya, Indonesia's second city, at the other end of Java, but with insufficient rail service. Meanwhile, in England, the de Havilland aircraft company, stung by the structural failure of the

For Garuda, the 65-seat Fokker F-28 was ideally sized to link its main regional centers with Jakarta. This one is photographed at Jayapura, West Irian. (Davies)

early Comet, and frustrated by its own weakness in succumbing to pressure by British European Airways to reduce the size of the Trident to an uneconomical level, was working during the 1960s on its own feeder-jet. Inspired by the visionary Richard M. Clarkson, the de Havilland 30-seater DH-126 was deemed, after a world market survey, too small and too short on range. The subsequent 40-seater Hawker-Siddeley HS-136 design was perhaps ahead of its time. Similar airliners were successfully launched in Brazil and Canada 30 years later. Ultimately, and unrecognizable from its ancestor designs, the HS-146, which became the British Aerospace BAe 146, was to enjoy moderate success in specialized markets where short airfield performance was at a premium.

Emergence of Airline Categories

The "second level" 40-seat Convairliners and Martin 404s created a definable niche in the airline hierarchy, and these were replaced in the Jet Age by the BAC One-Elevens, the Douglas DC-9s, and the Boeing 737s. These gave the public what they wanted: the modern image, at all levels, of airplanes without propellers, and with better comfort and a smoother ride. They also gave the airlines aircraft that could be deployed with greater versatility. The speed of the jets was welcomed by all. The large airlines came to realize that they should specialize at the top level and delegate the lower levels to other airlines that would concentrate in that activity; as narrated previously, this led to the creation, in the United States, of a certificated group, the Local Service airlines. The process in the States was assisted and even accelerated by the deliberate lack of focus on passenger railroad travel.

Elsewhere in the world, however, the separation was not as distinct. In Europe, few countries were big enough, or traffic volumes sufficient, to justify a secondary level. But local service airlines did emerge in France (**Air Inter**), Scandinavia (**Linjeflyg**), Italy (**S.A.M.**), and Spain (**Aviaco**). In Great Britain, **B.E.A.** separated its domestic services almost as a subsidiary airline. These European local service companies did acquire jet aircraft in due course. Also, in Europe, the railroads were more efficient, as they were in Japan, and this tended to restrict local airline expansion at the higher pace experienced in the United States.

In India, the domestic state airline, **Indian Airlines Corporation (I.A.C.)**, was able to separate "the Golden Triangle" (Delhi-Calcutta-Bombay) from its other routes. In Japan, which, like Great Britain, had areas, even islands, that made rail transport difficult and time-consuming, local airlines were developed, and some thrived. **Toa Airways**, which had started by serving the small Ryukyu Islands (rather as B.E.A. served the Scottish Hebrides), flourished and eventually promoted itself into the higher ranks. Similarly, **Kita Nihon (North Japan) Airlines**, became well established and later became Japan Domestic Airlines. The progress of the Japanese airlines reflected the unprecedented dynamism of the post-war Japanese economic recovery.

In Australia—a country that, because of its unusual demographics, with more than half of its population living in the five largest cities—the second level was represented by small airlines that struggled to maintain viability, and most of them were absorbed by the Ansett airlines group, whose founder, Reginald Ansett, had started his career as a taxi driver. Butler Air Transport became **Airlines of New South Wales**, while Queensland Airlines and Guinea Airways became **Airlines of South Australia**, representing, respectively, their home states. MacRobertson Miller Aviation in due course also joined the Ansett club, to become **Airlines of Western Australia. East-West Airlines**, based in northern New South Wales, defied the approaches of the Ansett Group and remained aloof until 1987, when the owners of Ansett bought it. It remained operational until 1994. (See also Chapter 38.)

Of the other countries that were large enough to sustain secondary air networks, the Soviet Union's Aeroflot and China's **C.A.A.C.** monopolized all air transport activities. Aeroflot, however, dealt with the secondary route problem by establishing an organization by which the regions of this enormous airline network were given local autonomy, and allocated local fleets, with which they operated the secondary services, reaching every corner of a land three times the size of the United States. China's development was much slower, as its industrial and commercial growth had been restricted by the rigid political policies, including the disastrous "Cultural Revolution."

Thus, during the first few post-war decades, while the flagship airlines of the world were making spectacular headlines with the rapid improvement in intercontinental services that jet technology had made possible, a minor revolution had been evolving at the lower, and less headline-attracting, segments of the industry. With the United States Local Service (Regional) companies leading the way in forming independent secondary airlines, elsewhere in the world some were rigorously independent, some were in partnership with their national flag carriers, and some were actually owned by them. The Jet Age was to witness an organizational transition that was to be characteristic of the airline industry throughout the globe for several decades.

Yet the sustained growth of air travel, stimulated by the increased efficiency of airliner construction and especially by vast improvements in engine technology, would lead to the creation

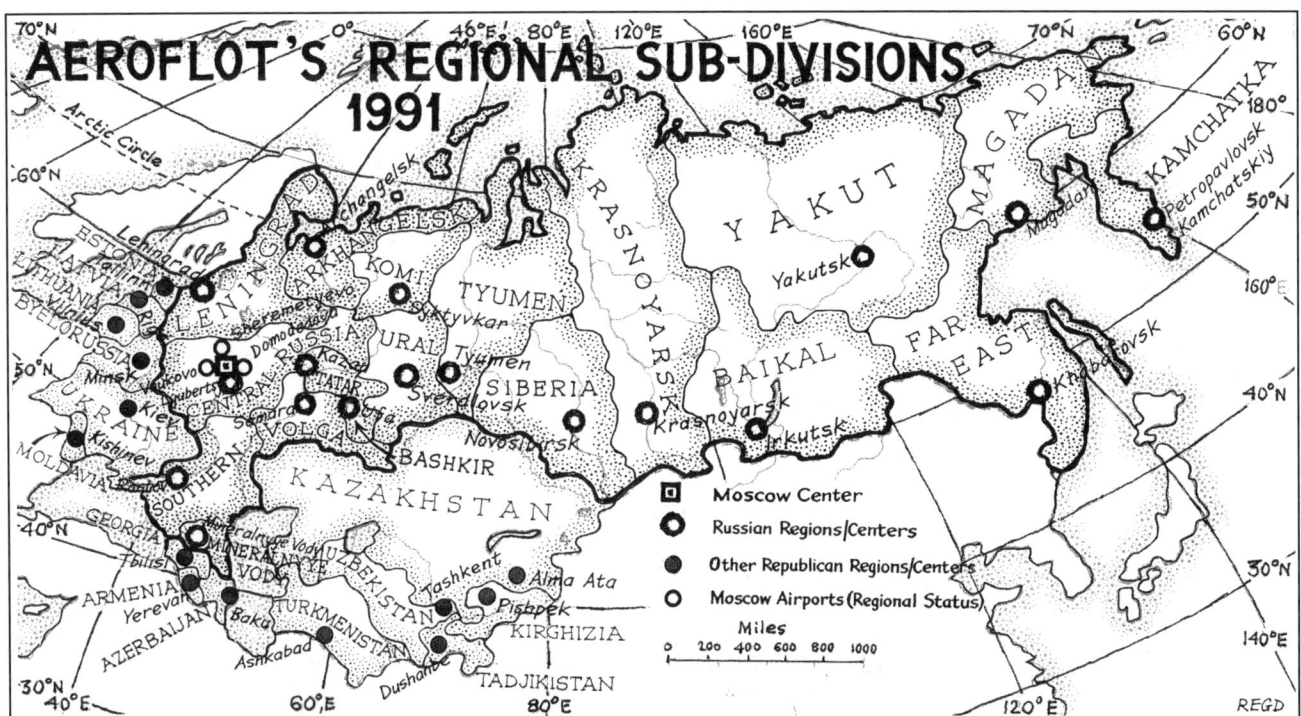

Aeroflot was able to serve the vast extent of the Soviet Union only by creating semi-autonomous subdivisions. Each one was the equivalent of a large regional network and, in some cases, larger than many a national flagship airline.

of an even further airline category subdivision. Almost unnoticed by the industry, the public, and the regulating authorities alike, a new group of airlines would, toward the end of the 1960s, emerge. At first it struggled to survive, but it would eventually become an integral element of airline networks, demand its own special operating conditions, and create the market for new generations of aircraft that were specially designed for its needs.

Chapter 13: The Commuter Airlines

Dignity and Impudence: Scheduled Air Taxi

For many years, the United States Civil Aeronautics Board (C.A.B.) had listed, right at the end of the various airline categories such as trunk, local service, territorial, freight, and supplemental, a miscellaneous group—"Other"—for which special exemption from the normal certification process was given. They emerged from the nationwide group of individualistic fixed-based operators (F.B.O.s), which operated air taxi or charter flights under federal aviation regulations. The C.A.B. had, on 5 May 1947, defined these as Small Irregular Carriers (as opposed to the large ones, which became Supplementals) and restricted them to using only small aircraft, at first of less than 10.000 lb gross take-off weight then, on 5 October 1949, of 12,500 lb., a figure that was popularly thought to be "half a DC-3." In 1952, the C.A.B. granted exemption to these operators to operate scheduled services, and extended this authority in 1965. By this time, the U.S. Federal Aviation Administration (F.A.A.) had begun to keep records of them, under Part 135 of the regulations, for navigational and safety needs. The air taxi companies, scheduled or not, were restricted to VFR (Visual Flight Rules) ruling, but could operate single-engined aircraft, with a single pilot, and did not need an air transport rating, only a commercial one.

Some of them were in a geographical situation whereby the charterers—mainly businessmen, but sometimes everyday folk and occasionally small groups—would demand their services at regular times of the day. These were normally early in the morning, from a small community to a larger city, and returning in the evening. This activity became, de facto if not de jure, a scheduled service and fulfilled special needs that were not met by the scheduled airlines. To its credit, the C.A.B. went along with a common-sense approach and there emerged an elite subdivision of this lowly F.B.O. group, eventually to become classified as Scheduled Air Taxi operators.

Many of these opportunists crossed short stretches of water and linked communities of small population that could never support the operation of even a humble time-expired DC-3. Several of these small companies claimed to have been the first operators in their scheduled class, and pride of place should probably go to Bob Schoen, who founded Orcas Island Air Services in 1947, using Stinson Voyager single-engined aircraft. This became **Island Sky Ferries** and provided essential air service between the San Juan Islands in Washington State's Puget Sound and the local metropolis, Seattle. The islands of New England also provided ready markets for this emerging new category of air transport.

Another early company was the Cutter-Carr Flying Service, which, from 1948, linked the atomic energy center at Los Alamos, New Mexico, with Albuquerque. Not widely advertised for security reasons, this operation was taken over in 1963 by **Carco**

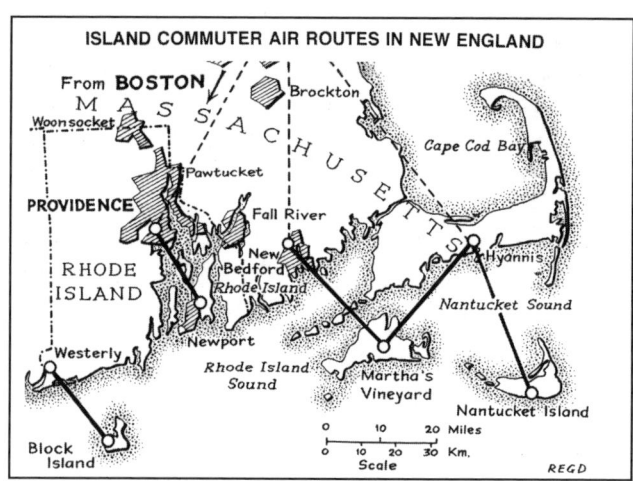

Many early scheduled air taxi operators were formerly fixed base operators (F.B.O.s) who provided regular services, especially over short over-water routes.

Air Service. Illustrating the sometimes loose and debatable question of who was first, and by what definition, one company, under various names, had been serving the Bass Islands in Lake Erie since 1935, flying the eight-mile route from Port Clinton, Ohio. To accommodate the need to fly the island children to school on the mainland, Ralph Dietrick renamed Sky Tours as **Island Air Lines** and made quite a name as the world's surviving scheduled Ford Tri-Motor operator. Another claimant was "Pappy" Chalk, based on the beach at Miami, Florida, and who, for decades, had claimed to be the nation's oldest airline with his service to the Bahamas. His definition of what constituted an airline would not hold up by most criteria, but by 1949, it was flying regularly as **Chalk's Flying Service** to Bimini and Nassau in the Bahamas. Another short-lived operator was Central Transport, which operated small Cessna aircraft in Arkansas during the late 1940s. Founded by Ray Ellis at Fayetteville, Arkansas, to serve the Hot Springs resort, the airline was unable to obtain a certificate, but Ellis did not give up, and it reemerged as **Scheduled Skyways** in 1953 (see below).

One of the most prominent of the scheduled air taxi clan was John Van Arsdale's **Provincetown-Boston Airline (P.B.A.)**. The local geography meant that a surface journey between the two points took about four hours, but P.B.A.'s Cessna Bobcats flying across Massachusetts Bay cut this to half an hour. John's wrestling with bureaucracy was indicative of the regulatory problems involving the Letter of the Law. As many of his passengers were connecting with other flights, the C.A.B. alleged that he was engaging in interstate commerce—not an air taxi operation. Another issue, involving even the State Department, was that the peculiar geography of the route meant that he had to fly outside

The Commuter Airlines

The P.B.A. was so successful that it established a network in Florida, transferring its fleet to adjust to seasonal demand. One of its aircraft was a Douglas DC-3, of complex lineage, that achieved more than 95,000 flying hours. (Bentley)

the acknowledged three-mile limit and was therefore in international air space. Fortunately, common sense prevailed and P.B.A. went on to be a prominent, if specialized, airline.

Another company at this lowly end of the scale of airline status provided air service with equipment matched to the special requirement. **TAG Airlines** (formerly Taxi Air Group) was founded by Ross Miller and began service in 1956 from the Lakefront Airport in Cleveland to the Detroit City Airport. Taking only 38 minutes, downtown to downtown, TAG operated on-the-hour, every hour, charging $14.00 one way against the $10.00 of the certificated trunk scheduled airlines, which flew between the city airports that were far from the business centers. Business travelers avoided the circuitous road route via Toledo, and in 1965 TAG boarded 85,000 passengers—about half the total of the entire scheduled air taxi industry. Sadly, TAG went out of business in 1970 when one of its twin-engined de Havilland Doves (operating just below the 12,500-lb. limit) crashed in Lake Erie.

Jet Age Anomalies

By 1964, when the Jet Age was in full swing, and the Boeing 707 had already been in service for six years, the F.A.A., under whose jurisdiction (Part 135 of operating/maintenance regulations) the air taxis had been able to operate without C.A.B. certification, finally gave grudging admittance to their existence. In 1965, it listed 12 companies in its publication *Scheduled Air Taxi Operators*, and this would henceforth be published annually, and grow rapidly with each issue. The early pioneers in this group of airlines were to swell in numbers. The F.A.A. could not keep pace with the record-keeping process. Other sources of local traffic were emerging too, as Scheduled Skyways, founded by Ray Ellis in Little Rock, Arkansas, on 1 September 1953, discovered. The clientele of his Central Transport service had changed from entertainment to education, connecting the university town of Fayetteville with the Arkansas State capital, and was highly successful until it was absorbed by Air Midwest in 1985.

Third Level to Commuter

By the early 1960s, the widely spread scheduled air taxi operators had established themselves sufficiently to be recognized as a distinct group, and it was left to the journalists to give them an identifiable name. George Haddaway, the Dallas-based magazine publisher of *Flight*, specialized in private, executive, and air taxi operators and their aircraft. One of his staff, E.H. Pickering, wrote a series of eight articles under the title "Needed: A Third Level of Air Service." This visionary commentary and the phrase "third level" were so well received that the magazine was reprinted, and must have been appreciated in official circles, for, in the summer of 1962, the C.A.B. itself used the term *third level* in its Hi-Plains Airways case. The entire industry was booming under the stimulating promotional umbrella of the Jet Age. The Local Service airlines, still enjoying government subsidy, were also prospering. They were reaching out beyond the frontiers of purely local services to small communities, and were beginning to operate inter-city services on short routes. For their part, the trunk airlines were happy to transfer some of their shorter routes to the local service brethren, often made in groups, with full C.A.B. approval. The Locals expanded their route networks considerably, leading eventually to their abandoning the term *local service* in favor of *regional*.

This had been encouraged by the C.A.B., which felt that it was subsidizing some small communities too generously (often

One aircraft favored by the early scheduled air taxi operators was the Beech 18. Most of these seven-seat piston-engine aircrafts were ex-military. This one operated for the Sedalia-Marshall-Boonville Stage Lines. (Bentley)

Described by one early operator as an airplane "that the Wright brothers forgot to finish," the de Havilland Canada DHC-6 Twin Otter was nevertheless highly successful all over the world. Carrying up to 20 passengers, it qualified as a STOL (Short Take-off and Landing) airliner. (Bentley)

One of Dick Henson's Short 330s became part of the fleet of Allegheny Commuter Airlines. (Davies)

The continued development of commuter airlines stimulated manufacturers to supersede their propellers with turbines. The Canadian CRJ-200 was also elevated to regional airline standards, this one by the "connect" affiliate of AirTran. (Bentley)

because of local political pressures). In 1959, it had introduced a "use it or lose it" policy, under which any city that could not generate more than five passengers per day (1,800 per year) would be deleted from the appropriate airline's operating certificate. This helped to open the door for the third-level operators. Rapidly growing in number and never officially accepting the designation of "third level operators," these airlines adopted the more popular and appropriate "commuter airlines." For instance, Dick Henson, a fixed-base operator in Hagerstown, Maryland, began scheduled services to Washington, D.C., on 23 April 1962 using eight-seat Beech 18s, under the name of the **Hagerstown Commuter**. Henson was the first to use the term that set the trend.

In 1963, the term was given legitimacy by the formation of the Association of Commuter Airlines (A.C.A.). Its membership of only six stalwarts grew to become an influential lobbying group. It persuaded the C.A.B. to allow some of its members to carry mail. Some airplane manufacturers adapted executive designs specifically for their scheduled airline needs, and even designed aircraft aimed at the commuter airline market. An important contribution to this effort was the introduction of the Pratt & Whitney PT6 turboprop engine, built in Canada and of an ideal 579 horsepower. It was much lighter than the piston-engines of equivalent power, and thus allowed more pay load, either in passengers or fuel, without exceeding the 12,500-lb. limit. The main beneficiaries of this technical development were de Havilland Canada, with its ubiquitous DHC-6 Twin Otter, and Beech, with its Model 99. The Twin Otter, particularly, with its excellent short-field performance, was to gain popularity all over the world, where it could often provide air service to small airfields that even the DC-3 could not use.

The scheduled air taxi-third level-commuter airline industry grew by leaps and bounds. By 1965, more than 50 airlines were in the official listings, and this did not include some that the officials had not recorded. Neither the F.A.A. nor C.A.B. could keep pace with the seemingly straightforward process of certification, but by 1970, 150 commuter airlines were "on the books" in the official records in Washington. In some areas, particularly California, some companies merged to consolidate their operations. The number of commuter airlines rose to 250 by the early 1970s, but thereafter slowly declined, as the Interstate Highway program brought convenient road access by motor car between almost every city pair that was separated by less than 100 miles.

By the beginning of the 21st century, the commuter airlines had grown to succeed, in some regions, the Regional or Local Service airlines, in an equivalent role. They had also moved with the times technologically, replacing the small turboprop aircraft such as the Swearingen Metros, Beech 99s and 1900s, by jet

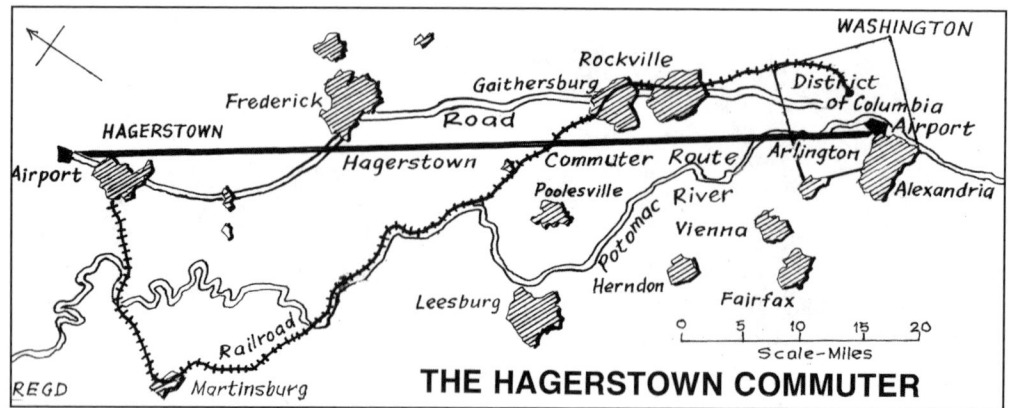

Dick Henson's Hagerstown Commuter was not a long air route, but the road (before the divided highways) and rail connections between Washington and Hagerstown were time consuming.

FORMATION OF GOLDEN STATE AIRLINES 1953–1969

During the early years, some of the F.B.O.s and local companies merged to become commuter airlines of substance.

aircraft with seating ranging from 37 to more than 100. Most of these diminutive airliners have been imported into the United States, where their acknowledged popularity with the public reinforced their marketing success. The Brazilian company Embraer had already established itself as a competitive manufacturer with its 19-seat EMB 110 Bandeirante, at first specifically for the Brazilian market. Its adaptability to bush operations gave it the familiar "Bandit" nickname—an accolade in aviation terminology. This led to the 30-seat EMB 120 Brasilia, and in 1989, the company launched its first jet, the 50-seat ERJ 145, which, after extensive redesign, entered service with Continental Express taking delivery of two aircraft on 19 December 1996. By the early 2000s, Embraer had added jet airliners to its repertoire. Of these, the ERJ-190 has more seats than the first Douglas DC-9 twin-jet, aimed at major inter-city markets in a previous era.

The Canadian industry matched the Brazilians. Bombardier, in 1992, took over the former de Havilland Canada (itself taken over by Boeing in 1986), highly respected for its tradition of building aircraft ideal for commuters and bush operators. These had culminated in the highly successful DHC-6 Twin Otter workhorse, the Dash-7, and the Dash-8. In 1986, Bombardier had taken over Canadair, then making the CL-600 Challenger business-jet. In 1989, it then launched what became the CRJ 200 Regional Jet, a development of the Challenger, to compete with the Embraer jets.

Thus, in the 21st century, the Jet Age not only includes the 500-seat Airbus 380 double-deckers that ply the world's trunk air routes, but also the small 50-100-seat Embraers and CRJ jets. The once-ignored commuter airlines have expanded the application of turbojet technology from long-haul route requirements into the short-haul arena. And turboprop airliners such as the ATRs remind us that the propeller is still more than a museum exhibit.

UNITED STATES COMMUTER AIRLINES 1964–1986

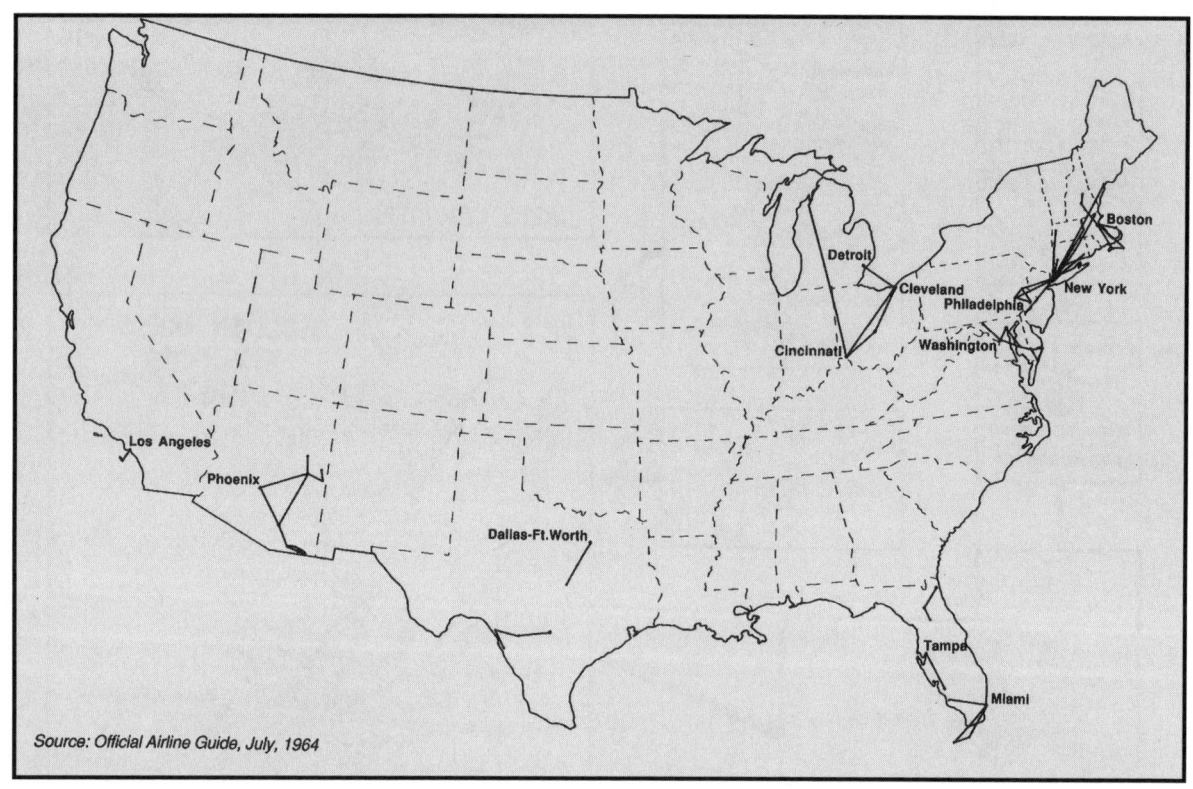

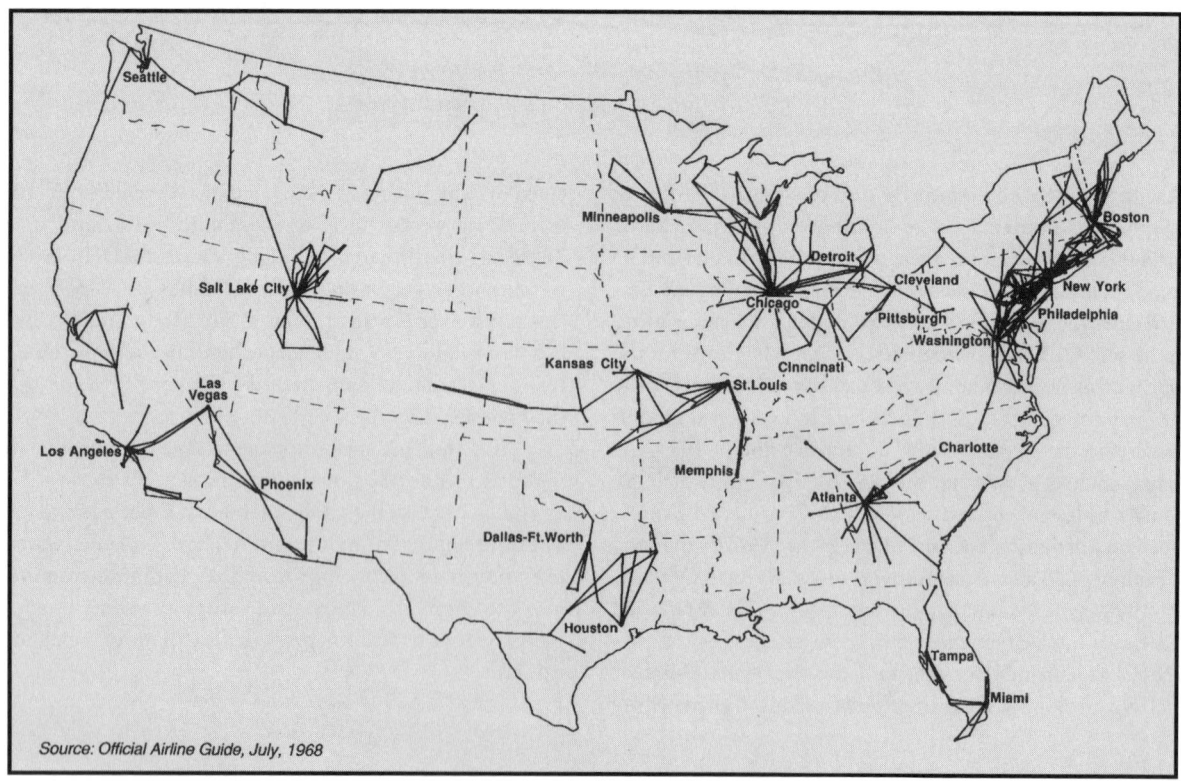

During the 1960s, a few F.B.O.s found that their customers chartered flights at regular times every day, except on weekends. The clientele consisted mostly of businessmen, so that these routes became the basis of what at first were termed Scheduled Air Taxi, or "third level" operators.

The Commuter Airlines

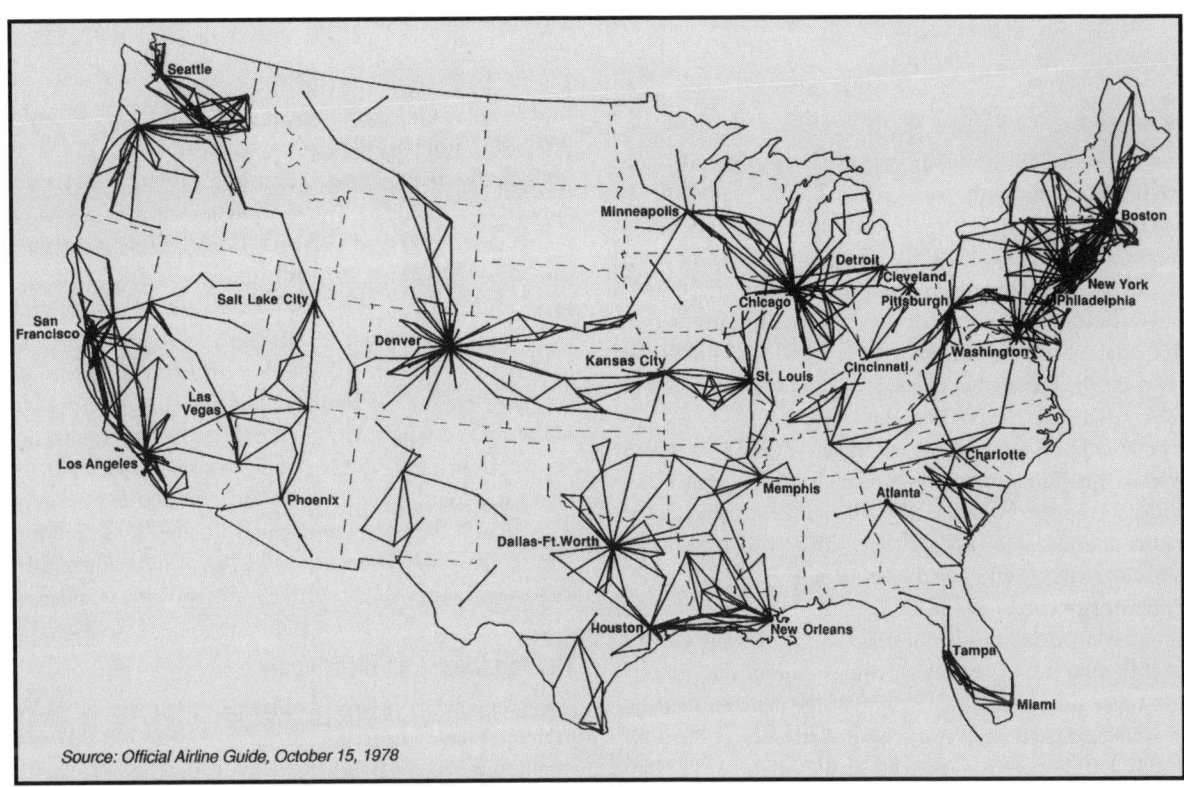

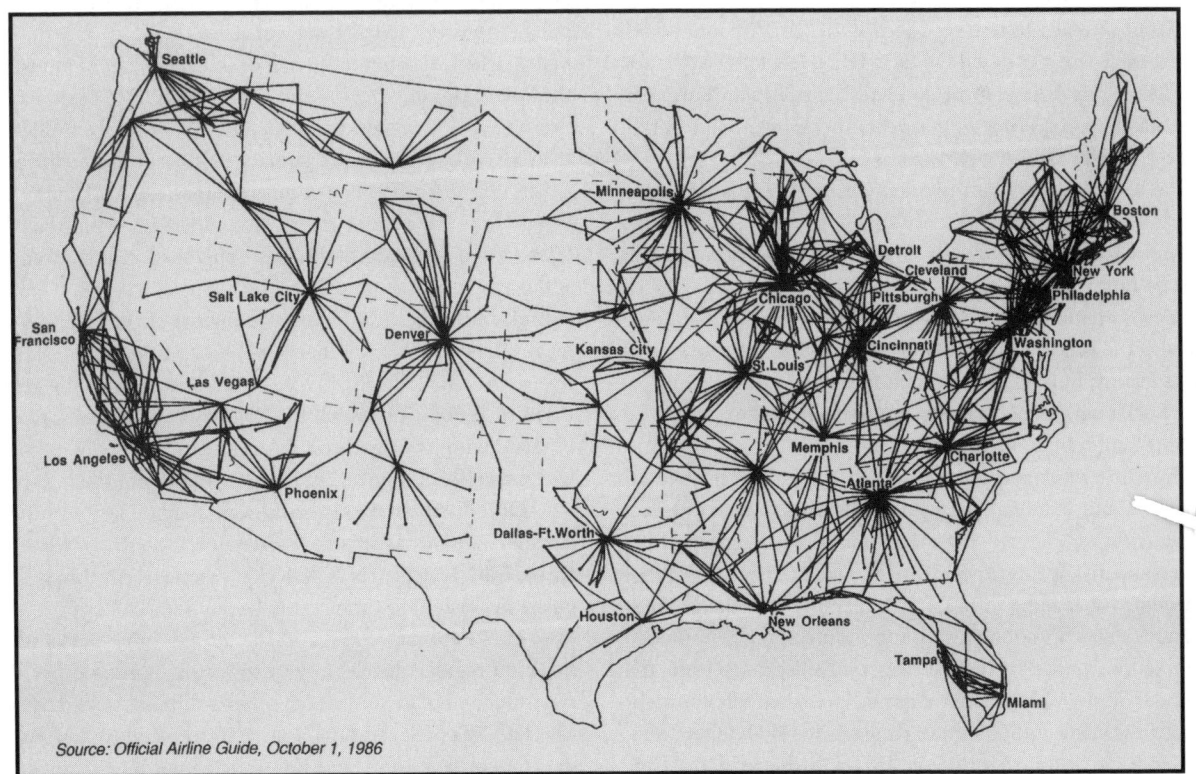

The Scheduled Air Taxi airlines expanded rapidly during the 1970s, both in numbers and in the density of operations. By the 1980s, they comprised the commuter airline industry, and few communities were without a service.

Chapter 14: Restoring the Balance

Europe Regroups

During the immediate post-war period, Germany, Italy, and Japan were forbidden by the victorious Allies to participate in commercial air transport. In 1939, measured in passenger-miles, Germany and Italy led both Great Britain and France, even though the latter's larger networks of intercontinental routes gave them an advantage. In Asia, during 1940, Japan's production exceeded that of any European country and accounted for about two-thirds of the whole of Asia's. The United States was relatively immune from pressures on its airlines.

When the Jet Age swept in permanently in 1958, with Pan American Airways dominating the world's long-haul routes and with British jets and turboprops still challenging America's global dominance, the defeated powers were still at a disadvantage, although Italy, which had ceased hostilities in 1944, was given preferential treatment as a non-belligerent. Two airlines were formed in 1946, **Alitalia** (with 30% B.E.A. shareholding) and **L.A.I.** (with 40% T.W.A. Interest), while some of the pre-war airlines—those that were independent of the state airline, Ala Littoria—amalgamated as **Avio Linee Italiane-Flotte Reunite (A.L.I.-F.R.)**. These were all merged on 1 September 1957 to form **Alitalia-Linee Aeree Italiane (Alitalia)**, which began to grow swiftly. Already inheriting a fleet of Vickers Viscount turboprops from L.A.I., it ordered Douglas DC-8 jets for the Atlantic route, starting on 1 June 1960, and Sud Caravelles for European routes, starting on 23 May of that year. The airline then went on to build a worldwide route network.

The Treaty of Potsdam divided Germany into four zones, under which commercial activity of all kinds, and especially anything related to aviation, was severely restricted. The pre-war Deutsche Lufthansa was formally liquidated on 1 January 1951, and a new initiative got under way, with (officially) no connections with the pre-war airline. On 6 January 1953, a provisional stock company, Luftag, laid the foundations of a new airline, ordering Lockheed Constellations and Convairliners for long-haul and short-haul routes, respectively.

The name was changed on 6 August 1954 to Deutsche Lufthansa A.G., but it traded simply as **Lufthansa**, later Lufthansa German Airlines, to avoid any suggestion of a resurgence of the former company. By this time, British European Airways (B.E.A.) had become the leading intra-European airline with the groundbreaking Vickers Viscount turboprop airliners. It strengthened its hold on the market by introducing, on 15 February 1956, the "stretched" Series 800, and Lufthansa had to match this competition, with the same equipment, starting service in October 1958.

Before the Second World War, D.L.H. had provided a standard of airline service that was arguably unequalled in terms of punctuality, reliability, class of airliner, and cabin service. The new Lufthansa was determined to emulate this bygone reputation. Its initial choice for long-range equipment was the 150-seat Boeing 707-430, a Rolls-Royce Conway-engined variant of that great jet airliner. The flying crane, oldest of all airline insignia, made its appearance in New York for the first time on a jet when Lufthansa inaugurated service on 17 March 1960. Lufthansa supplemented the 707s on 20 May 1961 with 125-seat Boeing 720Bs on routes to South America and Africa.

The tri-jet Boeing 727 was introduced on short-haul routes in Europe and to the Middle East on 12 April 1964. Lufthansa was not only back in business, but was going to set a fast pace. Hitherto, every new American airliner had been introduced by an American airline as the launch customer. The German airline broke the trend. In an historic order, placed in February 1965, it ordered a fleet of twin-engined Boeing 737s, and put them into service on 10 February 1968. Just as it had done during the 1930s, Lufthansa again took the lead during the 1960s.

The Japanese Sun Rises Again

The reemergence of Japan as a leading airline nation had an even more emphatic impact on the industry than did that of the defeated Axis Powers in Europe. In 1939, the rise of Japan Air Lines had gone almost unnoticed, except in the Far East. By 1940, Japan's output was third in the world, exceeded by only the United States, which accounted for half of the entire world industry, and the Soviet Union. After the end of the war in 1945 there was a total ban on aviation of any kind in Japan, and not until an Allied directive (SCAPIN 2106) on 27 January 1951 was the creation of a new airline permitted. The first company, **Japanese Air Lines (J.A.L.)** began domestic service on 25 October 1952, with Martin 202s leased from a United States non-scheduled airline, Transocean. Although it had acquired its own Douglas DC-4s, it jumped a manufacturing generation by ordering two de Havilland Comet 2 jet airliners on 18 November 1952, only a month after starting its first service. It was ready to face the competition on the aerial Silk Road to Europe, on which the British B.O.A.C. had set a cracking pace with its Comets on 3 April 1953. The Comets had to be withdrawn from service, but Japan was ready for the next round.

On 1 October 1953, J.A.L. was reorganized, with full government support as Japan's "chosen instrument," as **Nihon Koku Kabashiki Kaisha (N.K.K.K.)** ("Japanese Air Lines" in English). It wasted no time. Trans-Pacific service began, with DC-6Bs, on 2 February 1954, and the airline immediately made its mark on regular travelers by introducing, among other courtesies, *oshibori* hot towels, which other airlines hastened to provide too. DC-7Cs ("Seven Seas") were introduced to San Francisco on 15 February 1958, and domestic routes and frequencies increased at a rate unknown elsewhere in the world.

J.A.L. entered the Jet Age on 12 August 1960, when Douglas DC-8s replaced the Seven Seas across the Pacific, and the airline continued its special attention to passengers. On the same day, in cooperation with Air France, J.A.L. had block bookings on Air France's Boeing 707 Polar route to Paris; and started its own DC-8 Polar service on 7 June 1961. For its entry on the traditional Silk Road to Europe, it introduced the Convair 880, marginally faster than the DC-8. Passengers who had been accustomed to traditional and somewhat featureless service welcomed the kimono-clad flight attendants and new standards of courtesy that had to be matched by its competitors.

J.A.L., with the fast-growing All-Nippon Airways as a formidable competitor, expanded its domestic routes, to meet the demand of intensive business travel between Japan's big metropolitan areas, particularly the Tokyo-Osaka corridor. Total frequencies reached 30 flights a day in both directions, and high frequencies were also necessary to cope with the traffic demand to the cities of Kyushu in the south and Sapporo in the north. These were to become some of the busiest air routes in the world.

During the 1960s, such were the pressures of traffic demand as a whole throughout a resurgent Japan that airlines simply could not cope. The solution came from the imaginative introduction of a new form of transport, high speed rail. In August 1964, the first *Hikari* express train left Tokyo's Central Station and reached Osaka, 305 miles away, in three hours. This was not just a faster train. The Shin Kan-sen (High Speed Line) was a new form of transport, as far removed from 50-mph express trains, as those were from the stage coaches of the 17th century. The 16-car *Hikari* (two-stop) and *Kodama* (six-stop) trains were able to carry the enormous volume of inter-city traffic. By the early 1970s, more than 40 million people were traveling each year between Tokyo and Osaka, of whom about two million were flying.

Only seven years after opening its first jet service, Japan Air Lines was encouraged to inaugurate its Round-the-World service, on 6 March 1967, using the "stretched" Douglas DC-8-62, and cooperating closely with Air France, Alitalia, and Lufthansa, in a four-airline pool agreement. On 17 April, in an historic agreement with the Soviet airline Aeroflot, J.A.L. was able to take a new and shorter route to Europe via Moscow, flying directly across Siberia. This was achieved by agreeing to use the Tupolev Tu-114, the 400-mph turboprop airliner, in a joint service, piloted by Aeroflot aircrew, with both Russian and Japanese cabin staff. This was the only time in airline history when a front-line Soviet airliner was flown by a major flag carrier of the western world. This service operated successfully, and in 1970 each airline used its own aircraft, J.A.L. the DC-8-62 and Aeroflot the Ilyushin Il-62. On 28 March and 2 June of that year, J.A.L. opened one-stop services to Paris and London, respectively, twice weekly, on the first trans-Siberian route to be operated by any airline except Aeroflot. More services by this short-cut route were to follow, although the Round-the-World service was withdrawn on 7 December 1972.

One more major country needed to be added to complete Japan's global aspirations. Diplomatic relations did not yet exist with mainland China, the People's Republic, or the P.R.C. Memories of the Second World War were particularly acute in China, whose war had begun on 7 July 1937 with the notorious Marco Polo Bridge incident, which led to the Japanese invasion of China, accompanied by much despotism and cruelty. But after a quarter of a century, the diplomatic ice began to thaw, thanks partly to the statesmanship of China's foreign minister, Chou En-lai, with whom, ultimately, a bilateral agreement was signed on 20 April 1974.

The Japanese flag-carrier had to cease operating in Taiwan, which insisted that it was also China, even though realistically it was only a province of China—a designation, curiously, on which both sides agreed. The first DC-8 flew into Beijing on 29 September 1974, and to compensate Taiwan's Republic of China for the loss of the lucrative route to Taipei, J.A.L. founded a wholly owned subsidiary, **Japan Asia Airways (J.A.A.)**, on 9 August, starting Tokyo-Taipei service on 15 September. By the 1980s, Japan's airline traffic, measured in passenger-miles, was surpassed only by the United States and the Soviet Union. Its fleet of Boeing 747s, reaching 90 aircraft at its peak, would dominate trans-Pacific travel. (See Chapter 21.)

Aeroflot Claims Its Place

The world had woken up to the dormant potential of the Soviet aviation industry when, in 1956, the Tupolev Tu-104 made its spectacular debut in London for a diplomatic visit and then entered scheduled service with Aeroflot on 15 September 1956. The West had tended to ignore the capability of the Russian and Ukrainian designers, and of the impressive performance of the Soviet aircraft production lines. During the Second World War, the tank-busting Ilyushin Il-2, the Stormovik (Shturmovik), was produced in greater numbers than any other aircraft in history, and the Yak fighters were a match for Germany's Messerschmitts and Focke-Wulfs.

After the war, however, Tupolev, Ilyushin, and Antonov lagged behind Boeing, Douglas, and Vickers, mainly because the commercial demand for aircraft simply did not exist behind the metaphoric, but extremely rigid and effective "Iron Curtain." During the 1950s, even as the Tu-104 was introduced, the market for Soviet-built airliners was restricted almost entirely to the monopolist state airline, **Aeroflot**. The overseas market for Soviet airliners was restricted to Communist countries or, at best, those with neutral attitudes. Most were emergent countries in Africa. Furthermore, because of the sharp barriers to trading between East and West, Aeroflot itself was inhibited in its international aspirations.

But as tensions diminished during the 1960s, Aeroflot could initiate long-range and trans-ocean routes only with its turbo-propeller airliner, the excellent Tupolev Tu-114 Rossiya, the largest and fastest of that class of airplane ever built. Cruising at about 450 mph, and concerned not with foreign competition with faster jets, but only with establishing air routes to friendly countries, it was Aeroflot's first jet airliner to offer intercontinental air travel. It began service at first on the nonstop route from Moscow to Khabarovsk, in Russia's far east, on 24 April 1961, and opened the first Soviet trans-Atlantic route, to Havana, in

Fidel Castro's Cuba, on 7 February 1963. Services to Delhi, India, and to west Africa followed in 1963, and to Montreal on 4 November 1966. Then, as mentioned previously, it started the route to Tokyo, jointly with J.A.L., on 19 April 1967.

The turboprop Tu-114 was the harbinger of greater things to come. While the Tu-104 had claimed its place as the first jet airliner to operate sustained airline service, its range had restricted it to domestic routes within the Soviet Union and to neighboring countries. Because of the political frigidity with the West, there was simply no need for a long-range jet airliner. But with the approaching thaw, the Ilyushin design bureau developed an aircraft to compete with the American Boeing 707, the Douglas DC-8, and the British VC-10, which were already in service all over the world. The Ilyushin Il-62 was uncannily like the VC-10, with its four engines mounted on the rear of the fuselage. Responding to the allegation that it was a blind copy, Ilyushin observed that the choice of engine position was either in the wing (de Havilland Comet), in pods (707 or DC-8), or at the rear (VC-10). The Il-62 established the Soviet flag-carrier as an important newcomer to the higher echelons of intercontinental air travel. Domestic service with the new airliner began from Moscow to Khabarovsk and to Novosibirsk on 10 March 1967, and international service, to Montreal, began on 15 September. This paved the way for one of the most important events in the history of the Soviet airline: on 15 July 1968, it flew into New York on Aeroflot's first scheduled service to the United States. Flying nonstop from Moscow was beyond its range, so Shannon, Ireland, and Gander, Newfoundland, became regular staging points for the route; even the improved Il-62M still had to make at least one stop between Moscow and New York.

By the 1970s, Aeroflot was able to take advantage of the easing of travel restrictions between the Soviet Union and the western world. The Soviet authorities also recognized the opportunity to exploit the geographical advantages of their airspace, in offering direct air service between western Europe and the far east, flying across Siberia and cutting as much as six hours off the existing polar route. Although international agencies such as the International Air Transport Association (IATA) frowned upon this circumvention of the cherished Five Freedoms (the stop in Moscow created the so-called Sixth Freedom), the introduction of Paris-Moscow-Tokyo Aeroflot service on 29 March 1970 did not lead to international repercussions.

The growth of air traffic within that vast country was no less impressive. In addition to the T-114 and Il-62, the extensive production lines of the aircraft bureaus were also turning out short-haul turboprops and jets in considerable quantities. The venerable Iluyushin Il-18, which had entered service on 20 April 1959, was destined for a long life and wide-ranging service. More than twice as many (585) were built as the Lockheed 188 Electra and Bristol Britannia combined, and they would become the workhorse of Aeroflot's domestic inter-city routes and in China. For secondary services, the Antonov An-24—similar to the Fokker F-27—was deployed everywhere. This 40-seat turboprop twin could be seen lined up at all of Aeroflot's major regional

The Antonov An-24, was—like the Ilyushin Il-18 in a different category of airliner—built in larger numbers than all the western twin engined turboprops combined. These An-26B variants were photographed at Surgut, in western Siberia. (Davies)

centers, where they provided connecting service with the inter-city jets. Including the An-26 and An-32 freighters, no less than 2,500 of this versatile airliner were built.

For every successful U.S. or British jet airliner, the Soviet industry had an equivalent design. Although undoubtedly much was learned, and even copied, from the West, the Soviets were not alone in this respect, as there was much similarity between many of the designs in the U.S. and Europe. The first Soviet short-haul jet was the Tupolev Tu-134, smaller than the Douglas DC-9 or the BAC One-Eleven, and about 700 of them entered service, from 12 September 1967. Significantly, this inaugural was from Moscow to Sochi, a Black Sea seaside resort, and this reflected a growing improvement in the lifestyle of the Soviet citizenry. The political system ensured cheap (if not luxurious) housing, public utilities, and health services, all subsidized by the government. The system also included subsidized transport by all modes, including air transport. Air fares were extremely cheap, by direct comparison with western standards, and they were even quite cheap for the Soviet people. Business travel was non-existent, as there was no business in the centralized Communist system. But the workers were provided with vacation resorts on the Black Sea and elsewhere, which they could visit cheaply in increasing numbers. The airline was—to strike an American analogy—the Greyhound Bus service of the Soviet Union. As a result, by 1967,

The Tupolev Tu-134, smaller than the DC-9 or BAC One-Eleven, was Aeroflot's standard twin-engined jet airliner for several decades. (Davies)

Restoring the Balance

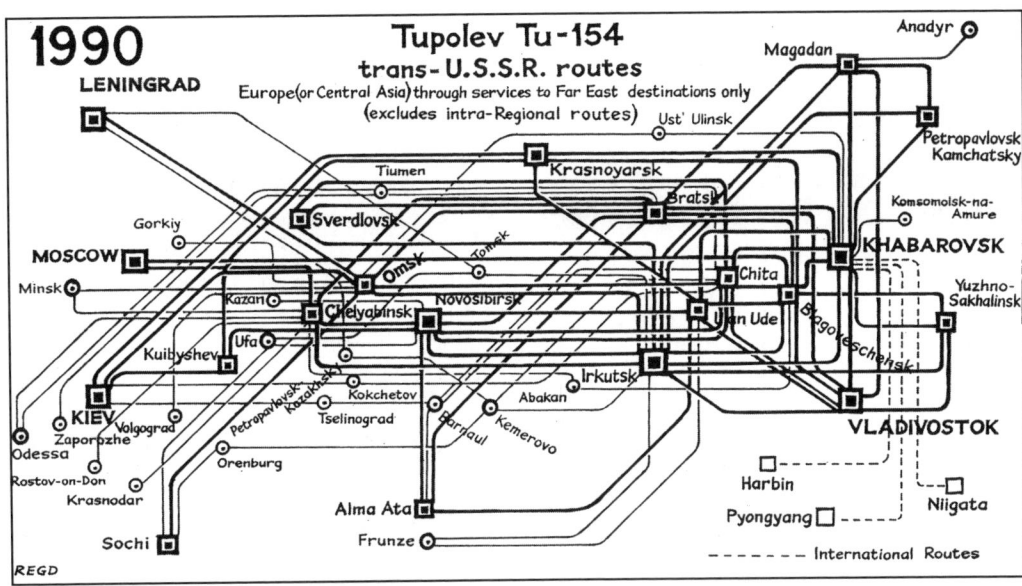

Just before Aeroflot's final disintegration, it was operating about 600 Tupolev Tu-154s on all its main-line routes across the Soviet Union.

measured by passenger numbers or passenger-miles flown, Aeroflot was the largest airline in the world.

In some categories of transport aircraft design, the Soviet manufacturers could not be accused of copying equivalent western types. For its extensive networks of small feeder-line routes, radiating from the larger provincial centers across the 11 time zones of the Soviet Union, the Yakovlev Yak-40 was the first jet airliner small enough to match the modest passenger loads required to serve the small towns and villages hitherto served by the aging Antonov An-2. Uniquely it had three engines. The little 32-seater flew at 500 mph—about four times that of the *Kolkhovniks*—and had a range of more than 300 miles. It went into service with Aeroflot on 30 September 1968, and of the 1,010 aircraft built, 130 were exported to 17 countries, mostly in the Soviet bloc in eastern Europe.

Further down the scale of size and capacity, Moscow turned to one of its aircraft-manufacturing satellite neighbors, Czechoslovakia, for an even smaller aircraft, the Let L410, a 19-seat twin-engined turboprop that could operate in the small grass fields or dirt strips in more remote regions. Of the 1,272 built, 902 of these mini-airliners were exported from late in 1971 to Aeroflot in a form of reverse technology, similar to the good business done by the Hungarian Ikarus bus builder, which exported about 15,000 large buses to the Soviet Union until the latter's collapse.

If the Ilyushin Il-18 had been the outstanding workhorse of the huge Aeroflot network, its jet successor was to emulate it. The Kuznetsov NK-8-engined Tupolev Tu-154, looking remarkably like the Boeing 727, went into service with Aeroflot on 9 February 1972 and became the backbone of the inter-city network. Historian John Stroud described it as having the range of the Il-18, the speed of the Tu-104, and the field performance of the An-10. At first, it was a little short in all three categories, but in

The Tupolev Tu-154 tri-jet was not as economically efficient as the Boeing 727, but it was operationally successful, as evidenced by the map of Aeroflot's main-line routes that it serviced. (Davies)

1974, Soloviev D-30KU turbofans, together with some aerodynamic refinements, turned it into a fine airliner. More than 1,000 aircraft came off the Kuibyshev production line.

Soviet Air Cargo

Often overlooked by western observers, the Soviet aircraft industry was superb in one category of commercial transport manufacture. The Antonov design bureau, based in Kiev, Ukraine, already famous for its Antonov An-2 biplane, began to specialize in ruggedly built freighter aircraft. They had to withstand the continuous punishment encountered on the rough fields of the Siberian outback, not only from the often pot-holed airstrips, but also from the extremes of climate, where ice, snow, and high winds were routinely encountered during the long frigid winters east of the Ural Mountains.

In the West, only one post-war commercial aircraft, the Bristol 170 Freighter, was built specifically for air cargo and ideal for specialized use as a car ferry. Two British independents used

The Bristol 170 was a versatile design, incorporating front-end loading. It was used extensively as a car ferry across the English Channel and as an inter-island freight airline in New Zealand. (Bentley)

them for cross-Channel service. More than 200 were built and with more aggressive marketing (and without hundreds of war-surplus Douglas C-47s and C-54s), this "ugly duckling" could have reached a worldwide clientele. The enterprising Freddie Laker, through his company Aviation Traders, built the Carvair, a conversion of the Douglas DC-4 able to carry five small cars versus the Bristol 170's three, but only a few were built.

In the United States, Douglas attempted to introduce a more modern freighter. The DC-6 was developed into the thoroughbred airliner, the DC-6B, but first off the production line were DC-6A freighters. Few were built, and thereafter the only commercial all-cargo aircraft were derivatives of military types, of which the Lockheed 100, a civil version of the C-130 Hercules, was alone in its class. With more than adequate under-floor cargo capacity in the Douglas DC-8 and the Boeing 707 jets, western airlines had no need for specialized freighters. Also, a major deterrent in the U.S.A. was the efficiency of the railroad freight system, which could deliver almost any kind of cargo to any community in the land within a few days.

In the Soviet Union, the face of Siberia, that vast area beyond the Ural Mountains, almost three times the size of the United States, had, by the 1950s, undergone a complete transformation. No longer was it an area characterized by endless expanses of impenetrable forests and uninhabitable tundra, interrupted only by the Trans-Siberian Railway along the southern fringe. The expanses were still enormous, but no longer endless. First, the evacuation eastward of heavy industry from European Russia and the Ukraine in 1941, forced by the Nazi invasion, transformed the industrial base. Cities such as Sverdlovsk (now, as originally, Ekaterinburg), Chelyabinsk, and Novosibirsk became major manufacturing centers. The Trans-Sib and other railroad arteries became heavy supply lines between the eastern and western extremities of the Soviet Union. Second, the enormous potential mineral wealth of Siberia was being exploited. Noril'sk, near the mouth of the Yenesei River, and north of the Arctic Circle, was the largest source of nickel ore in the world. In the center of the continent were untold riches, including diamonds and other precious stones. In northwestern Siberia were vast deposits of oil and natural gas, and coal mines sprang up everywhere. Gold, silver, platinum, titanium, all these and many others were to be found, often in substantial quantities. But third, the resources of surface transport were almost non-existent in the very areas where the riches were to be found. North of the Trans-Siberian were few railways. There were no roads. The great rivers were frozen over so solidly during the crippling winters that they were able to support heavy vehicles. Air transport was the only solution to providing year-round communication and cargo capacity to the faraway remote regions. The Soviet aviation industry met the challenge.

The prototype for what was to be a succession of heavy-lifters was the military Antonov An-8, a 40-ton turboprop, little known outside its home country. It was designed specifically for cargo, thus with a high wing, landing gear mounted in the fuselage, and a high tail, all to permit the loading and unloading of large items of freight. It was self-supporting, needing no ground equipment, and with four wheels on each leg of the landing gear, it could use rough fields and what are often referred to as unprepared strips. It was even used to land on the scientific ice-stations, on strips prepared in the frozen wastes of the Arctic Ocean. About 100 of these versatile aircraft were built for the armed forces, entering service in 1956, but a commercial variant was also produced as a passenger aircraft, which started to operate on Aeroflot's scheduled routes on 22 July 1959. The larger four-engined Antonov An-10, at first called the *Ukraina* (to mark its origins) differed slightly from its progenitor in that the wings were anhedral, a feature that was to identify all subsequent heavy-lifters that emerged from the Kiev design bureau. Such was the need for air cargo, mainly throughout Siberia, that more than 800 An-10s, 10As, and military An-12s were built.

On 3 February 1960, all the operations of **Aviaarktika**, the organization that was originally formed at Krasnoyarsk on 1 September 1930 to specialize in Arctic aviation, were transferred to Aeroflot. The An-10s began work in the northern wastelands on 5 April 1960 and had the honor, in August of that year, of pioneeering a great circle (geographically direct) route from Moscow to Khabarovsk, an important city in the far east, and connecting Noril'sk and Yakutsk with the mainstream of the Aeroflot network. This latter city had long been an entrepôt of trade on the Lena River in northeastern Siberia, but had hitherto been almost isolated from the rest of the world. It was far from the nearest railroad, and the highway to the nearest port on the Sea of Okhotsk was open during only a few months of the year. The Lena was frozen to the north in the winter and unnavigable to the south, while the only air route was a branch line from Irkutsk. The new air route transformed Yakutsk, whose previous claim to prominence had been as the Soviet headquarters of the Lend-Lease air ferry system during the Second World War. The airport provided a new gateway to the outside world, and the large cargo aircraft rejuvenated the city, to give it a new life. The An-12s mentioned above, able to carry 100 paratroopers, could be termed a product of Siberia. They were built in Ulan Ude, east of Irkutsk, and Tashkent, in Uzbekistan, as well as in Voronezh, in European Russia.

The design team in Kiev had the bit between its teeth. Within a few years, it produced a large aircraft, based on the same design principles as the An-10s and 12s. The Antonov An-22 Antheus

Restoring the Balance

The Antonov An-22 Antheus was a giant load-carrier. Over a short distance, it could carry 100 tons, but was to be superseded by the even larger An–124. (Davies)

The Mil Mi-2 was a small 8-seat helicopter, broadly equivalent in size to the Bell 206 Longranger. It was deployed extensively in the more remote areas of the Soviet Union that lacked airstrips. This one was photographed at Udd Island (renamed Chkalov Island, after the Soviet pilot who landed there on a survey for his trans-polar flight in 1937). (Davies)

(named after a giant Greek god), with four powerful Kuznetzov engines and eight contra-rotating propellers, first flew on 27 February 1965 and made its international debut at the Paris Air Show that year, to the wonderment of the habitually critical western observers of aeronautical progress. It weighed 250 tons, and its payload measured an astonishing 100 tons. It could carry large tanks and incorporated several innovative design features. The rear loading door could not only form the ramp but could also be extended within the fuselage as part of the gantry-crane system, which could lift 10 tons. The floor was of reinforced titanium, a metal that combines the strength of steel with the light weight of aluminum, and in the machining of which the Soviets excelled. Above all, this impressive aircraft could, with its 12-wheel main landing gear, use the same rough strips as its predecessor An-10, even to the extent that the tire pressure could be controlled during flight. As will be described later, the Antheus was to be dwarfed by even larger Antonov freighters.

Soviet Helicopters

The tradition of vertical flight went back a long way in Russia, even to pre-Revolutionary times. Igor Sikorsky had experimented with helicopter designs before he emigrated to the United States in 1917, but 30 years later, Mikhail Mil revived this category of air transport with his first design, the 3-seater Mil Mi-1, which followed the general principles of Sikorsky, incorporating a small tail rotor to offset the induced rotation of the aircraft from the main rotor. This was followed by the larger 8-11-seat Mil Mi-4, which started the first helicopter service in the Soviet Union, from Simferopol to Yalta on 15 December 1958. Further services were added to other resort towns in the Crimea and around the Black Sea, where the mountain terrain was mainly so close to the shore than even the versatile Antonov An-2 was hard pressed to land and take off. Later development led to the introduction of the smaller Mil Mi-2, which was powered by turbine engines mounted above the fuselage, thus permitting more room for passengers, so that it could match the Mil Mi-4's carrying capacity with the size of the Mil Mi-1. It went into Aeroflot service in 1967 and proved to be a versatile and widely used machine throughout the Soviet Union. They were deployed on a variety of missions, including inter-airport links in Moscow; service to offshore oil-rigs in the Caspian Sea; mail service from Moscow's post office to the airports; operations in the Arctic north; or in the mountainous regions of the Central Asian republics, where fixed-wing aircraft flying was extremely hazardous.

The next product of the Mil Design Bureau was met with mixed respect and surprise by western observers. The Mil Mi-6 had five rotor blades, each 17 meters (55'9"). It was longer than a Douglas DC-6B, weighed 40 tons, and could carry a load of six tons. Its electric winch could handle a load of almost 10 tons and, in a fire-fighting role, 10 tons of water. It could carry as many as 75 people or 60 fully equipped soldiers. Deliveries to Aeroflot began in 1961 and it was first used in Turkmenistan on 10 August of that year. The airline had about 100 of the more than 800 produced, most of them used in work at the oil and gas fields of northwestern Siberia. A special variant of this large helicopter was the Mil Mi-10, with a slim fuselage that could carry a bus suspended underneath by means of hydraulic grips attached to the landing gear. The Mil Mi-10K (*Korotkonogiy*, or "Short-Legged") version had a special cabin under the nose, with rearward-facing controls, coordinated with the winching crew. They were used to carry steel pipe sections for the long pipelines linking the oil and gas fields in the remote tundra and taiga with the consumer cities of the south and could carry large sections of the pylons for the electricity grid lines from the huge dams on the great Siberian rivers to the industrial consumers.

Of considerable value for the massive engineering construction programs though they were, the Soviet industry needed a versatile helicopter that combined heavy lift capability of the Mi-6 and Mi-10 with the flexibility of the Mi-4. In 1961 the Mil Mi-8 made its first flight. This helicopter weighed about 12 tons—about the same as the Douglas DC-3—and could carry as big a payload—28 passengers. Like the Mi-6, its fuselage was fitted with clam-shell doors and was thus ideal for air freighting. It went into service with Aeroflot in 1967, and altogether, at least 6,000 Mil Mi-8s were built. They were the workhorses of the extensive pipeline and power transmission lines constructed in western Siberia. The southern base of that operation, Tyumen, was so large that a subdivision, **Tyumen Avia Trans (T.A.T.)** was created. In the 1980s, T.A.T. listed a fleet inventory of some 600 aircraft, of which 450 were helicopters, 300 of which were Mil Mi-8s.

The Mil Mi-8 was used extensively in the exploration and development of the vast mineral resources in Siberia. This one is pictured at an oil rig in the Yamal Peninsula. (Davies)

Most noteworthy in the saga of Soviet helicopter progress was the share in the aerial supply work carried out by Aeroflot in the construction of the Baikal-Amur Magistral (BAM) railroad in eastern Siberia. Begun in the late 1940s, its purpose was to connect the industrial region of central Siberia with the big hydro-electric power stations of the great rivers and to assist in the development of mineral wealth in outlying regions, and also to provide an alternate trunk railroad route to the Pacific Ocean, 200 miles away from the Chinese frontier, regarded as a possible threat to the security of the Union. Almost all the difficult initial survey work was carried out by Mi-8s, until airstrips could be built, at first for the Antonov An-2s, Ilyushin 14s, Yak-40 jets and Antonov An-12 freighters. Without the highly organized battalions of aircraft provided by Aeroflot, the BAM railroad might never have been built.

Mikhail Mil's team was still not finished. It was to produce an even more powerful heavy-lift helicopter, as a highly developed variant of the Mi-6. The Mil Mi-26 first flew late in 1957. Its eight-bladed rotor enabled it to lift 20 tons, aided by an internal gantry crane that could carry two tons.

While the helicopter industry in the Soviet Union was dominated by the Mil Design Bureau, credit must also be given to that of Nikolai Kamov. He solved the problem of a single main rotory wing, that needed an anti-torque tail-rotor, by using co-axial contra-rotating main rotors. The early Kamov designs were quite

Mil Mi-26 has eight rotor blades instead of the Mi-6's five. It can carry 40 tons of cargo. (Davies)

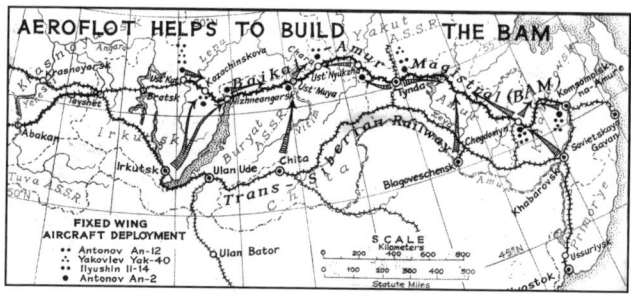

During the latter 20th century, airlines competed with or replaced long-distance railroads. In eastern Siberia, Aeroflot reversed this process. It provided extensive support to the engineering organization that built a parallel line to the Trans-Siberian Railway.

The Kamov helicopter offered flexible versions of the basic design. The detachable rear end of the fuselage could be exchanged for passengers, freight, or other purposes. (Davies)

small, but in response to pressure from the State Scientific Institute, Aeroflot received several hundred Kamov Ka-26s. To quote noted aviation historian John Stroud, Kamov produced "a most ingenious multi-purpose helicopter capable of almost any task except feeding itself." This remark referred to the flexible design that incorporated a twin-boom extension of the fuselage to support the tail unit, and this permitted the fuselage to be split into two, of which the rear half could be either a small passenger unit, or a crop-spraying assembly, or converted for a variety of uses.

Dynamic Growth on the North Atlantic

In Chapter 8, the introduction of jet propulsion, the beginning of the Jet Age, was reviewed, acknowledging that although six airlines had preceded Pan American in the operation of jet airliners, Juan Trippe's company effectively set the seal on a new era. Nowhere was the transformation of travel—in speed, comfort, and economic improvement—demonstrably more effective than on the world's busiest long-haul route group, the North Atlantic. When Pan Am's Boeings first hit the headlines, 16 airlines (all except one—Israel's El Al) were the national airlines from Europe or North America. Ten years later there were 25, and within two decades, there were 41, even though a few had withdrawn. Australia's **QANTAS** and **Japan Air Lines**, for example, had attempted to introduce round-the-world service, but did not continue for long the trans-Atlantic segment, as the loads were minimal. But replacing these were others, from southern Asia, eastern Europe, and additional airlines from the United States when some of the Supplemental (non-scheduled) airlines spread their wings across the oceans.

The volume of passenger traffic increased enormously with the introduction of jet airliners. The North Atlantic route matched their performance perfectly. The aircraft had the range to connect the major cities on both sides of the ocean with nonstop service. Gone were the days when stops at Shannon, Ireland, or Gander, Newfoundland, were necessary. Also, the speed—averaging about 550 mph westbound and 600 eastbound, because of the prevailing wind component—was perfectly matched with a scheduling pattern of daytime westbound and eastbound during the night. London-New York, about 3,500 miles, for example, was customarily flown in about seven or eight hours westbound and six or seven hours eastbound. Thus, any jet airliner could leave a major city in western Europe in the morning, arrive at an east-coast American city in the afternoon, and, after routine maintenance and cleaning, be ready to leave again in the same evening. A round-trip was possible within a convenient 24-hour scheduling pattern, providing maximum aircraft utilization—about 13–14 hours within the 24—which was better than almost any airline could expect with typical route networks elsewhere.

The demographics were also ideal. Travel volumes, whether for business or pleasure, vary directly with the combination of city-pair populations, and indirectly with the distance between them. The formula can vary, depending upon factors such as individual wealth or surface competition, but the basic theory remains true: the more people, the greater the traffic and the further they are apart, the less the traffic, simply because the expense is greater. Thus, on the North Atlantic, the main originating points in America were New York (with 15 million people in its catchment area), Washington, Chicago, Boston, Philadelphia, and Montreal; while in Europe, they were London and Paris (each with more than 10 million), Frankfurt (the hub for several major German cities), Amsterdam, and Copenhagen. Round-trip service could be maintained by the jets with impressive regularity and punctuality on direct routes between all these cities.

By 1980, as a direct reflection of the demographics, the leading airlines on the North Atlantic were both American. **Trans World Airlines (T.W.A.)** had overhauled the pioneering **Pan American Airways** in the late 1960s, and these two American giants each carried more than two million passengers during that year. The United States accounted for about 15% of the total. **British Airways**, which had, in 1972, resulted from the merger of the two state corporations, British Overseas Airways Corporation (B.O.A.C.) and British European Airways (B.E.A.), was a close third (the merger was officially completed on 1 April 1974); followed by the rejuvenated **Lufthansa German Airlines**; **Air Canada**, renamed from Trans Canada Airlines (T.C.A.) in 1964; the Dutch **K.L.M.**; and **Air France**.

The British industry had been slow to catch up with the United States, after the agonizing experience of the Comet disasters. But the new Vickers VC-10, with four engines mounted in the rear of the fuselage was, in its developed Super-VC-10 variant, a superb airliner. Because of the position of the engines, its cabin was very quiet, and it flew smoothly and well. Late as it was—the earlier version entered service to Lagos, Nigeria, in 1964 and was popular throughout Africa because of its superior field performance—the Super started to fly to New York in 1965. The British airline advertised it with élan. Without personal identification, the increased leg-room from the well-designed seats was emphasized by billboards showing Marlene Dietrich's legs (which everyone knew were insured for $1 million), and a neat line from the popular song was converted to "Try a little VC-10-derness."

Unfortunately, the airline's accountants did not match the flair of the publicity staff. The position of the engines meant that the VC-10 had to sacrifice two rows of seats, compared to the layouts of the 707 and the DC-8, and much was made of the higher seat-mile costs. But the higher passenger-mile revenue yields, resulting from the popularity of the 10-derness, were either unrecognized or ignored. The airline felt, wrongly, that the economic balance was inferior to that of its Boeing 707, forgetting that the experienced travelers were enthusiastically transferring from T.W.A. and Pan Am and that the VC-10's load factors were much higher than the 707's. B.O.A.C.'s original order for 42 aircraft, placed in 1959, was reduced to 25, a shattering blow to the manufacturer, which was beginning to make significant inroads into the world market. This apparent adverse commentary by the nation's own airline tolled the death-knell of Britain's minority stake in the long-range commercial airliner manufacturing industry.

The Laker Skytrain and the Twilight of a Cartel

In Chapter 10, the remarkable growth of the charter and non-scheduled airlines of Europe was reviewed, showing that their influence on the progress of commercial aviation generally was considerable. They had been the flag-bearers of cheap air travel. Several of the charter airlines, especially in Great Britain, Germany, the Netherlands, and Scandinavia, grew rapidly to play a significant role in the course of development of the European airline industry as a whole. They forced the scheduled airlines not only to revise their strategy toward vacation traffic, and in several cases to form subsidiary companies of their own to combat the threat from the innovative independents. In 1965, resulting from a more generous approach by the British Air Transport Licensing Board, the Minister of Aviation removed most of the restrictions that had previously inhibited the free growth of the independents. Led by **British United Airlines (B.U.A.)** and **British Eagle**, headed respectively by Sir Adam Thompson and Harold Bamberg, the non-scheduled airlines, which only a decade previously had still been operating time-expired Douglas DC-3s and Vickers Vikings to supplement a few Vickers Viscounts and Bristol Britannias, moved decisively into the Jet Age.

One of the directors of British United was Freddie Laker. From modest beginnings, he had followed wartime service in the Royal Air Force by forming Aviation Traders. He started buying, leasing, and operating aircraft and, as Air Charter, flew cars across the Channel with his DC-4 Carvairs, neatly engineered to supplement his Bristol Freighters (see above). Then, on 1 January 1959, Airwork—a British independent airline of some stature—bought the Laker interests, and Laker joined the Airwork board. On 1 July 1960, Airwork and the Hunting-Clan group joined forces to form **British United Airways (B.U.A.)**. Laker became the managing director (president).

He ordered the fine Vickers VC-10s and claimed, with some justification, to have been the sponsor of Britain's first twin-engined short-haul jet, the BAC One-Eleven, successor to the French Caravelle. He soon found that he could not work with his directors, and left to form his own **Laker Airways**, on 8 February 1966. At first his ebullient personality was thought to be unsuited to orthodox airline direction. But Laker's very unorthodoxy was to be an asset; it resulted in the creation of possibly the finest air service ever offered to the public, and one that has not been emulated since (see below). He bought two travel agencies, and introduced time charters (contracts for a whole year). Before he took delivery of his first three One-Elevens, on 27 February 1967, he had sold the entire capacity for the next two years.

By this time, the inclusive tour market had expanded beyond the confines of Europe and the Mediterranean. Inclusive charters across the North Atlantic increased by leaps and bounds, taking advantage of a loose intrerpretation of the laws controlling affinity groups. By the late 1960s, North Atlantic flights were almost as frequent as those on heavily traveled short-haul routes, such as London-Paris or New York-Washington. Laker realized that it had the potential for a shuttle-service operation, using long-range Boeing 707s. On 15 June 1971, he applied to the Air Transport Licencing Board for the right to operate a no-reservations trans-Atlantic air service, in which the passengers would have to buy their own meals before boarding. He correctly judged that the cheap fares that he proposed—about a quarter of the scheduled airlines' economy fares—would attract a completely new stratum of air travelers. The system was no different than taking a journey by rail, with the same operational simplicity, and Laker called this service, appropriately, **Skytrain**.

The idea of simply going to Victoria Station, buying a ticket, taking the fast train to Gatwick Airport, and jumping on the next airplane leaving for New York was anathema to the scheduled airlines and regulatory authorities on both sides of the Atlantic. The litigation dragged on for six years. Laker meanwhile bought his first wide-bodied airliners, Douglas DC-10s, and put them into service on the Mediterranean routes on 21 November 1972. By this time the British Civil Aviation Authority (C.A.A.) had granted him a license as a designated flag carrier, and the U.S. authorities were obliged to acquiesce. The British Labour government trade secretary, Peter Shore, tried to stop the service but the House of Lords, the High Court, and the Appeals Court ruled against him. Finally, President Carter, an advocate of airline deregulation, signed the necessary legislation on 15 June 1977, and Skytrain was finally launched on 26 September of that year, using 345-seat DC-10s, charging a London-New York single fare of £59. The public flocked to Victoria Station. Some slept all night at Gatwick, happily exchanging the luxury of a reserved seat for all the money they saved. On 3 June 1978, Laker was knighted, to become Sir Freddie Laker. He made huge profits, extended Skytrain to Los Angeles on 26 September 1978, and placed large orders for more DC-10s and Airbus A300s. The Duke of Edinburgh was heard to remark that "Freddie Laker is at peace with his Maker, but with the folks at IATA he's persona non grata."

National protectionism in Europe found ways of making life difficult by imposing operational restrictions. He was frustrated by the Hong Kong authorities, which did not like his flamboyant approach. On the North Atlantic, toward the latter 1980s, there were signs of a traffic recession. The scheduled airlines, which had previously claimed that to offer lower fares was impossibly uneconomic, found a way of doing so. Laker had ordered more aircraft, in dollars, with bank loans. Suddenly, even though he had never defaulted on progress payments (although he had renegotiated the schedule) his bank foreclosed on the loan, and sent in

Freddie Laker, who was later knighted for his contributions to British commercial aviation, introduced a no-reservations trans-Atlantic air service in 1977. Reacting to this competition, the incumbent airlines persuaded his bank to foreclose his account and Freddie's airline closed down. He later sued those airlines under American law. The case was settled out of court for several million dollars. (Davies)

Freddie Laker's introduction of his no reservation Skytrain trans-Atlantic air service was revolutionary. It also reduced costly on-board services to a minimum. (J. Laker)

the bailiffs. Not a single debt was overdue, but Laker Airways was closed down abruptly, without any warning, on 5 February 1982. Long-drawn-out litigation followed. Robert Beckman, Sir Freddie's lawyer, produced substantial evidence that a group of airlines had conspired against his client. In November 1982, he filed an anti-trust suit in the U.S. District Court in Washington for $350 million, which, if settled in the plaintiff's favor, would have amounted to more than $1 billion. Eventually, on 12 June 1985, it was settled out of court for $48 million. British Airways would contribute $32.5 million, and Laker would receive a personal settlement of $8 million. At least $300 million was compensation enough for the thousands of passengers stranded at vacation resorts, and other creditors.

There will probably never be another Skytrain. Laker perfected an air traffic system that the once-denigrated non-scheduled charter airlines had campaigned for during many years. More than any other single airline entrepreneur, Sir Freddie Laker and his Skytrain provided the incisive revolutionary spur that transformed the world airline industry from a business-driven to a popular leisure-driven transport activity. Fifteen years later, as a postscript to the success of Skytrain (measured by the number of passengers boarded), two bargain-fare airlines in Great Britain and Ireland had become the largest in Europe, and Southwest Airlines, once only an intra-state company in Texas, became the largest in the United States.

Part Three: The Second Jet Age

Chapter 15: Wide-Bodied Jets

Pan American Consolidates the First Jet Age

Under the leadership of Juan Trippe, possibly the most visionary of all airline executives in the history of air transport, **Pan American Airways** had been, for several decades, a giant in the international arena. With its famous flying boats, it conquered the Pacific Ocean by using pieces of U.S. territory as stepping stones across that vast expanse of the earth's water. It shared in the development of the finest fleets of long-range flying boats in the world, the Sikorsky S-42s, the Martin 130s, and the Boeing 314s. The British had their elegant Short "Empire" S-23s, but they were no match for Pan Am's Clippers. Only Pan Am could cross the oceans with a useful payload of passengers, and in starting trans-Atlantic service in 1939, it had established itself as the supreme intercontinental airline, and wherever it went, it reminded the world of American technical prowess.

During the Second World War, it continued to pioneer air routes by developing airfields and radio communications around the globe. This included the establishment of a trans-African airway, with modern airfields, as early as 1941, in an agreement with the British government, after a meeting between Trippe and Prime Minister Winston Churchill. Pan Am emerged from the conflict in a dominating position. It possessed the best airliners in the world—fleets of long-range landplanes, including the latest pressurized Lockheed Constellations.

Then, in 1958, it launched the first Jet Age. Britain's **British Overseas Airways Corporation (B.O.A.C.)** had been the first to operate jet airliners, in 1952, but the de Havilland Comet had to be rebuilt following the discovery of a hitherto unknown metallurgical characteristic: metal fatigue. The developed Comet 4 was the first trans-Atlantic jet, starting service from London to New York on 4 October 1958, but Pan American held the trump card with its Boeing 707, bigger and faster than the Comet. It opened service from New York to Paris on 26 October, and within two years, the U.S. flag carrier had encircled the world with a fleet of jet airliners whose productivity was as great as that of all the other intercontinental airlines together. Within a decade, Juan Trippe was ready for the next move. In 1955 he had placed orders with Douglas and Boeing for 45 of the first generation of jet airliners. On 13 April 1966, he repeated this action, by ordering 25 Boeing 747s. These huge airliners could carry 360–450 passengers, depending on the seating layout. They were twice as big as the 707s and DC-8s, and Trippe's association with Boeing served to launch a new jet age.

The Boeing 747 Launches the Second Jet Age

Boeing had to build a completely new factory at Everett, near its home base in Seattle, and with commendable speed and

The wide-bodied Boeing 747 began a new era in the Jet Age when Pan American Airways opened service early in 1970. It could seat as many as 10 in each row, and it had a short upper deck. (Bentley)

production efficiency, it was able to make the 747's maiden flight on 19 February 1969. Less than a year later, on 22 January 1970 (at 1:52 A.M., delayed from the previous evening because of an engine problem), Pan American inaugurated the world's first wide-bodied jet airline service. The airplanes were quickly called Jumbo Jets, or simply Jumbos, because they were big, and not because they operated trunk routes. One attraction was the double-decked design, which was derived from the original military freight transport design, with large clam-shell doors in the nose, with the flight deck above. Climbing the circular stairway into the upper-deck cabin was a special pleasure, akin to the Stratocruiser's lower-deck cocktail lounge of the piston-engined era.

The Boeing 747 was no faster than the 707 or the DC-8 or the VC-10. It was simply bigger. The public liked it, because of its spaciousness. More important, the airlines liked it, because its seat-mile costs, the essential measure of economic excellence, were lower than those of its smaller rivals. Nowhere did the urge to fly on the big airliner catch on more than within the United States. By the end of the year of Pan American's inauguration, nine U.S. domestic operators were advertising the Boeing 747 on their main trunk routes, led by **T.W.A.**, which started on the New York-Los Angeles route on 25 February. **American Airlines** followed on 2 March, but did not retain it as its front-line fleet.

Wherever Pan American went internationally, T.W.A. especially, among other airlines, was sure to follow. On 18 March 1971 its 747s replaced the 707s on the New York-London route, the world's most prestigious inter-city connection. When President Johnson signed the Pacific Route Case on 19 December 1968, just before he left office, T.W.A. emerged with a route to Tokyo and completed its coveted round-the-world service on 31 October 1971 with Boeing 707s. Competition was intense on the trans-Pacific route. The two U.S. airlines suffered by offering excess capacity. Pan American and T.W.A. agreed to a rationalization of routes and frequencies on 16 October 1974, and T.W.A. suspended its Pacific route entirely on 2 March 1975.

The same level of intense competition prevailed on all the North Atlantic air routes, which accounted for at least 30% of all intercontinental passenger air traffic. British Airways, Air France, Lufthansa, K.L.M., and other national airlines in Europe all reacted sternly to the threat of technical dominance by the two U.S. competitors and soon introduced their own jumbo jets. Equally, Japan Air Lines and others in Asia met Pan American head-on, and in due course, J.A.L. was to build the largest fleet of 747s in the world.

The irony of paying the penalty for being first—which had led to the elimination of de Havilland as a world contender when its was devastated by the Comet disasters—now played its part in reducing Pan American's hitherto dominating position in the world's air markets. And the process began as Juan Trippe's airline empire showed signs of crumbling. As part of the deal with Boeing—and both manufacturer and customer were gambling on the immediate success of this great airplane—Trippe had had to place a substantial order: 25 aircraft.

But the number of city pairs to generate sufficient traffic to justify the deployment of such large aircraft was limited. Pan American began to run out of densely traveled air routes. Trippe had handed over the presidency of Pan Am to Harold Gray, the airline's chief pilot, who confirmed the total order of twenty-five 747s. The result was that Pan Am was flying on some routes that generated load factors that were too low to break even. It simply had too many large airliners.

So while Boeing and Pan American Airways ushered in a new era of air transport, the race was on to build and sell a wide-bodied airliner that would be ideal for those routes for which the four-engined 747 was too big. The three other major manufacturers, Douglas, Lockheed, and (the newcomer) European Airbus, each had its candidate. All three had designs ready by the late 1960s. Douglas and Lockheed aimed primarily to cater to the substantial 2,500-mile United States transcontinental market, and designed wide-bodied tri-jets. Airbus saw its main market, at least for initial sales, as Europe, so that its first design was twin-engined, which was better suited to routes such as London-Rome or Paris-Cairo, with a maximum range of about 1,500 miles. Far more important, Airbus was acutely aware that the biggest need for capacity was on very short routes, such as London-Paris or Paris-Lyons. Only a twin-engined 240-seater would be feasible.

The European Airbus

The Airbus consortium was the recognition that no European country could match the mighty industrial strength, in production efficiency and marketing expertise, of the United States. But Europe designers could match the Americans. For all its defects, the first jet airliner, the British de Havilland Comet, had initiated world awareness that turbine power was commercially viable. The British Viscount had led the way in turboprop (prop-jet) technology. The French Caravelle had demonstrated the advantages of mounting the engines in the rear fuselage. Even the de Havilland Trident preceded in design, if not in production or marketing, the highly successful Boeing 727 medium-range airliner.

The single activity in which the United States excelled—as well as in its marketing methods, backed by powerful financial institutions such as the Export-Import Bank—was in mass production. The factories of Great Britain, which had, during the Second World War, produced fighters and bombers by the thousand, were inadequate for the large-scale production of large airliners at the rate that Boeing, Douglas, Lockheed, or Convair could reach. Boeing could roll out as many 727s in a month as de Havilland could produce Tridents in a year. The German industry had been destroyed. The French were in the process of rebuilding their industry by amalgamation of the many small companies, a shortcoming that the British industry had also been slow to recognize and correct. The aircraft manufacturers in Sweden, Italy, the Netherlands, and Spain, though competent, were too small and simply not in the same league, except in niche markets. In contrast, the Americans had perfected production methods on a huge scale and could turn out large airliners almost like a Detroit automobile production line. One British industry executive observed ruefully that, even though its designers and project engineers were no better, the U.S. aircraft industry was better organized (good union contracts), better managed (business oriented), better tooled (efficient machine tools), and better financed (generous banking support) than anywhere in Europe.

Only drastic measures could alleviate Europe's apparent slide into a position of helpless inferiority. And so, during the 1960s, politicians and aircraft industrialists painstakingly worked their way toward a solution. The French and British noted that the American wide-bodied jet airliners were aimed primarily at the long-haul market. Most of the big markets, particularly in Europe, were short-haul, with average stage lengths as low as 400 miles. Market analysis demonstrated that there was a substantial potential market for a wide-bodied airliner designed specifically for short-haul work. Such an aircraft had to be twin-engined, for operating economy, and so the idea was born, on both sides of the English Channel, for a wide-bodied short-haul jet airliner.

At de Havilland, now a division of the Hawker-Siddeley Group, the idea of an "Airbus" was conceived in the project office, under the intuitive encouragement of Richard Clarkson, whose contributions to design aerodynamics had guided the company since before the war. Against much contemporary conservative thinking, market research revealed the need for a 240-seat short-haul design. Meanwhile, the French company Breguet-Nord (national amalgamation was on its way), led by Henri Ziegler, had a similar project. Recognizing that to compete would be self-defeating, the two sides got together. This resulted in cooperative studies for a joint design, the HBN-100. Breguet-Nord then merged with Sud-Est, to become Sud Aviation, and which had its own wide-bodied design, the Galion, following the maritime tradition that had named the SE-210 the Caravelle. Hawker Siddeley then joined Sud Aviation, which became Aerospatiale, to form the Airbus consortium, which then concentrated on the Airbus A300, with design leadership centered at Toulouse.

After extensive market research, the European Airbus consortium consolidated its resources to build the world's first wide-bodied short-haul twin-engine airliner. Air France began a 240-seat A300 service in 1974. (Bentley)

For the American market, especially the nonstop routes between the northeastern U.S.A. and California, a wide-bodied airliner with more range than the A300 was needed. The Boeing 747 was too large for most services. American Airlines introduced the Douglas DC-10-10 wide bodied tri-jet in 1971. (Bentley)

At first, the British and French were the two equal partners, but this was soon modifed to allow the entry of Germany, now fully recovered from the penalties of wartime destruction of its industry. By 1970, the shares were 40% France (Sud), 40% Great Britain (Hawker Siddeley), and 20% Germany (Deutsche Airbus, based in Munich). Then, in an astonishing decision by the Heath government, the British insisted that the A300 should have Rolls-Royce engines exclusively or it would withdraw. The French disagreed, very sensibly, as other engine manufacturers would be only too happy to oblige, and they did. Only by the alertness of Hawker-Siddeley's president, Sir Arnold Hall, did Britain retain a stake (17%) in Airbus, by subcontracting to build the wings. The British shareholding is now 20%, and many Airbuses do have Rolls-Royce engines. Other countries have minor stakes in the European answer to American dominance. Spain and Italy have minority shares, to underscore the developing industrial and political trends toward non-nationalistic Europeanization.

Reaching agreement on standards such as the metric system, metallurgical formulae, and much else, including the need for bi-lingual fluency, all took time. The first Airbus was slow to emerge from the drawing boards at Toulouse, where British and German specialists were learning to work in harmony and with mutual respect. The A300 made its maiden flight on 28 October 1972 and went into scheduled airline service with **Air France** on 23 May 1974. But much time had been lost. The manufacturers in the United States were no slouches when it came to accepting a technical and marketing challenge. Their DC-10 and the L-1011 TriStar contenders duly appeared on the scene in 1970, soon after the Boeing 747's entry into service and two years before the Airbus A300 made its first flight.

The Douglas DC-10

Even though Boeing had achieved success with the supremacy of its products that the company name had become a household word, epitomizing the Jet Age, Douglas was still highly respected in the aviation community. Its commercial series, from the DC-1 to the DC-7, were legends of the piston-engined era, its DC-8 series of long-range jets had run a close second to the Boeing 707s. The Long Beach factory, now a production branch of the McDonnell-Douglas Corporation, announced the Douglas DC-10 wide-bodied tri-jet in 1968. With the efficient concentration that was characteristic of the Douglas tradition and reputation, and setting alarm bells ringing in Europe, the first aircraft made its maiden flight on 29 August 1970. It was about three-quarters of the Boeing 747's size and weight, its capacity was three-quarters the seating, and its three engines produced about three-quarters the power of the 747's four. Its range was in the same ratio, but for the markets for which the DC-10 was primarily aimed, this was not a severe handicap. In 1970, air routes that demanded extreme long range, such as nonstop trans-Pacific, were few. The first DC-10, Series -10, was aimed primarily at the United States domestic market, and while its normal 8- or 9-abreast seating could not quite match the 747's possible 10-abreast, this was not significant. In the traveling public's eye, the aircraft was certainly wide-bodied. In less than a year after its maiden flight, the DC-10-10 went into service, when **American Airlines** introduced it on its Los Angeles-Chicago route on 5 August 1971, to give it a good head-start over its rival tri-jet, the Lockheed L-1011 TriStar and the European Airbus. On 14 August, **United Air Lines** started transcontinental service from San Francisco to Washington (where the traffic demand was better suited to a 270-seater than a 360-seat layout), and, for similar reasons, **National Airlines** put the DC-10-10 on the New York-Miami vacation route on 15 December.

A Major Consortium

Ever since 1934, when the Dutch airline **Koninklijke Luchtvaart Maatschappij** voor Nederland an Kolonien (**K.L.M.**) had bought the DC-2, Douglas's first commercial airliner in full-scale production, it had been a faithful customer, proudly claiming that it had had every subsequent Douglas type through to the DC-7 (except the unique DC-1) and DC-8. Several nations in Europe did not have close aviation industry affiliations to those countries that combined in the Airbus consortium, and whose airlines, therefore, would lean toward their products. Thus, after much negotiation, an agreement was reached between four important European airlines: K.L.M.; **Scandinavian Airlines**

Wide-Bodied Jets

The DC-10-30 (with an extra leg on the main landing gear) was a longer-range version of the tri-jet. (Bentley)

System (S.A.S.), the successful consortium of Sweden, Norway, and Denmark; **Schweizerische Luftverkehr (Swissair)**; and **Union Aeromaritime de Transport (U.A.T.)**, the French independent company. This airline partnership was called K.S.S.U., after the initials of the partners, and the basis of the agreement was to combine in the maintenance and support of a common airliner type, the long-range DC-10-30. Each of the four was responsible for the servicing and the stocking of spare parts of different items, (e.g., engines, airframe, landing gear, or hydraulic and electrical systems) for all the K.S.S.U. members.

In 1958, drawing no doubt on their having refined the delicate organizational machinery of international cooperation, S.A.S. entered into another partnership, this time with Swissair. This was not a complete consortium, but a technical agreement to pool resources for the operation of airliners that they both had, specifically the Sud Caravelle and the Douglas DC-8, to which was added the Convair 880. The pooling arrangements included maintenance, training, and even route scheduling and revenue sharing.

The K.S.S.U. idea was picked up by Boeing, in association with other European airlines, those which, had no special affinity to Douglas, traditionally or technically. Comprising Air France, Portugal's **T.A.P.**, **Lufthansa, Alitalia**, and Belgium's **SABENA**, it was known as the **ATLAS** group, but the lines of manufacturer–customer loyalty were not so clearly drawn, as Douglas also made substantial sales to Alitalia and Lufthansa.

Three engine manufacturers, all with solid records of technical prowess, competed for the wide-bodied airlines market. Boeing's 747s were powered mainly by four 47,000-lb. thrust Pratt & Whitney JT9Ds, and Douglas's DC-10s were powered almost exclusively by 40,000-lb. General Electric CF6-6Ds. For the trans-Pacific route, however, two important airlines felt that the CF-6s did not have the lean fuel consumption that would guarantee nonstop flights to Tokyo and back under all conditions of wind and temperature. **Northwest Airlines** and **Japan Air Lines** selected the Pratt & Whitney alternative. This version of the Douglas wide-bodied tri-jet was designated the DC-10-40. None of the other DC-10 customers followed this example.

The Lockheed L-1011 TriStar

Douglas's southern California rival, based at Burbank but with the main production factory at Palmdale, also announced its wide-bodied tri-jet in 1968. The Lockheed L-1011, named the TriStar, took longer to make its debut, with its maiden flight taking place on 16 November 1970—but only three months behind the DC-10. Lockheed's engine choice was the Rolls-Royce RB-211. This had three compressor stages—against the General Electric's CF-6, which had two—and claimed advanced metallurgical advances, especially in the use of composite materials, which helped to save weight.

But no sooner had the L-1011 taken flight, with encouraging results from the test program, when the engine manufacturer ran into an unprecedented financial crisis. The episode came close to down-grading the famous Rolls-Royce name. On 4 February 1971, Rolls-Royce went into full receivership, after Cooper Brothers had audited the company's accounts and, on 22 January, had conveyed the shattering news to Frederick Corfield, the British Minister of Aviation Supply and Lord Carrington, the Minister of Defence. A flurry of trans-Atlantic activity ensued, as the Lockheed Chairman, Daniel Haughton, had been warned of imminent crisis. He flew to England on 2 February then met the main L-1011 customers, **Delta Air Lines**, **Eastern Air Lines**, and **T.W.A.** Lockheed cut back the production timetable, and laid off 6,500 workers. Rolls-Royce shares dropped to an abysmal low—at one time to a penny—and the British government came to the rescue. A deal was made, requiring a considerable amount of goodwill and faith, as well as hard cash, on both sides of the Atlantic. Rolls-Royce had already trimmed the price of the RB-211 to an impossible low, and many millions of dollars were required to salvage it. The U.K. government eventually put up a $422 million loan, on condition that the U.S. guaranteed the amount. Congress did this (with a majority of one vote) with the Emergency Loan Guarantee Act, on 2 August 1971, and President Nixon signed the bill one week later. On 22 May, Rolls-Royce Ltd. (1971) had become a full commercial entity, and henceforth its affairs would be far more closely scrutinized.

There was also a disturbing revelation made public only after the contracts were signed and approved at the highest level. The eventual collapse of Rolls-Royce had been foreseen at least 16 months before the signing of the Loan Guarantee Act. Under the British Labour government, the Industrial Reorganization Corporation, chaired by Sir Joseph Lockwood, had prepared a devastating report on the state of Rolls-Royce, recommending a complete change of management.

Lockheed's problems were far from over. Three days before the Loan Guarantee Act dug it out of its almost certain grave, the first Douglas DC-10s were delivered, on 31 July, to United Air Lines and American Airlines, and went into service soon afterward (see above). One of the leading L-1011 customers, Delta Air Lines, ordered five DC-10s, but sugared the pill by leasing them from American, and later taking the Lockheeds. Though time was to pass, Lockheed did receive an order from **British European Airways (B.E.A.)**, and Pan American chose it over the DC-10 in 1979. Other orders were from Japan, Saudi Arabia, Canada, and Hong Kong, but these were the subject of desperate measures, some of which involved practices that were shy of normal business ethics.

Competing with Douglas for the wide-bodied tri-jet market, Lockheed suffered a severe setback when its engine supplier, Rolls-Royce, almost went bankrupt. (Bentley)

Ultimately, Lockheed sold 250 L-1011 TriStars, including developed versions to squeeze more range to compete with the DC-10-30 and -40 intercontinental types. But although it had minor design changes and more powerful RB-211-524 engines, the Series -200 and -500 could cross the Atlantic only with a reduced payload, leaving questions as to its economic viability. Douglas had installed an additional central main landing gear on its -30s and -40s, thus permitting a heavier landing weight and a higher payload. This advantage was the main reason why Douglas sold almost twice as many DC-10s as the L-1011 total.

The Ilyushin Il-86

Soviet requirements for an airliner larger than the Ilyushin Il-62 were not as critical as those of western airlines. In the Soviet Union, only a few cities in Siberia were large enough to demand big passenger airplanes, and only Khabarovsk and Vladivostok, and possibly Irkutsk, were far enough away from Moscow to justify the need for long nonstop range. A wide-bodied aircraft design from a Moscow design bureau was therefore delayed for several years. The 747, DC-10, L-1011, and A300 were in airline service before the Ilyushin Il-86 made its first flight. Not that Ilyushin was inexperienced in building large airplanes, having led the Soviet way into trans-Atlantic operations with its Il-62, and the Il-76 heavy freighter had first flown out of Moscow's downtown Khodinka airfield in 1971. It had incorporated a feature of all Soviet types: landing gears with multiple wheels—a total of 14 altogether—to spread the load when landing on poorly

In the West, cargo transport aircraft were later variants of passenger airliners, but the passenger Ilyushin Il-86 followed the cargo Il-76. Its range compared to that of the DC-10-10. (Davies)

A distinctive feature of the Ilyushin Il-86 was on the lower deck, where passengers could deposit carry-on baggage as they boarded the aircraft. This saved time when seating in the cabin. (Davies)

surfaced airstrips that suffered from severe extremes of climate and particularly the effect of permafrost in the northern regions. The Il-76 habitually carried 20-ton loads over 4,000-mile routes to the far east, where it would take-off and land from uneven runways barely a mile long. Such performance was echoed in the completely new design for passengers, not freight.

The first Soviet wide-bodied aircraft got under way in the early 1970s, by which time, Sergei Ilyushin's design leadership had been handed down to Genrikh Novozhilov. The Ilyushin Il-86 made its maiden flight on 22 December 1976. As with all new aircraft types, incidentally, including the Il-76, this took place at Khodinka, the small airfield only a short bus-ride from Red Square. It was then flown, lightly loaded, a few miles to the Zhukovky airfield, where it underwent the customary proving and testing flights. Its size—350 seats—was similar to that of the Douglas DC-10 or the Lockheed L-1011, but it had four wing-mounted engines, in pods, like the Boeing 747s. The Soviet answer to the West had one interesting feature. Passengers entered the airplane through a door to the lower deck—normally reserved for cargo space, climbing only a few steps. They could then deposit their carry-on baggage in luggage racks, climb a few more stairs to the upper deck, needing only those items needed during the flight. Very few Soviet airports had loading bridges as yet, but such inconvenience was compensated for by the ease and speed with which the total boarding or disembarking took place.

Aimed as it was to cater for the big inter-city markets in the Soviet Union, where the first **Aeroflot** service took place on 26 December 1980, from Moscow to Alma Ata, the Il-86 could not fly regularly in both directions from Moscow or Leningrad (soon to be rechristened St. Petersburg) to New York. Its chosen refueling stop was Ireland's Shannon, where a special fuel farm was installed. The Russians appreciated the Irish hospitality and cooperation, including the use of the duty-free shops, and this led to similar amenities being set up by Irish contractors at Moscow's Sheremetyevo Airport.

Chapter 16: Supersonic Digression

Dreams of a New Era

During the 1950s, the world's air transport industry made the biggest technological leap forward during its 30-odd-year history. The infant years were the 1920s; adolescence in the 1930s; coming of age in the 1940s; and maturity achieved with the jets in the 1950s. The aviation world waited for the next era, and in the 1960s, the top-level boards and brains of the manufacturers and airlines began to imagine building a supersonic airliner that would be the natural successor to the 707s and DC-8s of the subsonic generation. The idea was not, in the early stages of the project studies, seen to be outrageous. In the past, airliner technology had always seemed to triumph. Given the inspiration and intuition of visionary designers, the application of sound engineering, and the financial support to guarantee the development costs, there was no reason why a supersonic airliner could not be built. After all, the Soviets had produced Sputnik, the world's first man-made satellite. The Americans set out to put a man on the Moon, and they did. For the Europeans, striving to maintain their place in the hierarchy of flagship airliner construction, this could possibly be an opportunity to make a technological dent in the hitherto American manufacturing dominance which, in the 1960s, accounted for more than 90% of the world's airliner capacity. And so the supersonic airliner was born.

The Concorde

The idea was first put forward by Dr. Morien Morgan in 1954, at the Royal Aeronautical Establishment at Farnborough, England. He was the deputy to Sir Arnold Hall, who was supervising the investigation of the Comet disasters. The manufacturers of the Comet had paid an unfair price for its failure, and Great Britain's aeronautical prestige had suffered badly; but the lessons of jet power had been learned and taken up across the Atlantic by Boeing and Douglas. Now, in a mood almost of desperation, and knowing that the British industry could not match American production capability, a supersonic airliner could, yet again, steal a march on the subsonic Americans.

By November 1956, under Morgan's chairmanship, the Supersonic Transport Aircraft Committee (S.T.A.C.) was able to report that it had nationwide support to launch the project, although it distorted the development cost estimates optimistically at a mere £150 million (ultimately the figure was to be at least £1 billion for Britain's share alone). Design work proceeded, settling on a very advanced delta-shaped wing. The speed was decided to be not much more than Mach 2 (twice the speed of sound) as the friction-induced heat would preclude the use of aluminum at Mach 3. As work went on at Bristol (Type 223), the supersonic airliner also became a political football, and in June 1959, seeking rapprochement with the French, Aubrey Jones, the Minister of Supply, discussed a possible structure of cooperation with the French Minister of Transport. This was because the French were embarking on their own supersonic airliner, provisionally called the Super Caravelle, to be built by Sud Aviation. At first this was a smaller aircraft than the British design, but it grew to be very similar to Bristol's. And so, in 1962, under Macmillan's Conservative government, a cooperation agreement was signed with France for joint production of a supersonic airliner by Aérospatiale and the British Aircraft Corporation (B.A.C.), of which Bristol was now a division. The engines would be Bristol Olympus 593s, rated at almost 33,000 thrust each. Much larger than the original designs, the Concorde would weigh 200 tons, of which half would be fuel. The agreement was an expression of Britain's willingness to join the European Common Market, and henceforth the Concorde was an Anglo-French project.

Cost estimates escalated to £835 million, and in 1964, the Labour government's Harold Wilson tried to cancel the aircraft,

The Concorde's elegant design was described as "A Thing of Beauty and a Joy For Ever." It could also be described as a technical miracle, but it was an economic disaster. (Bentley)

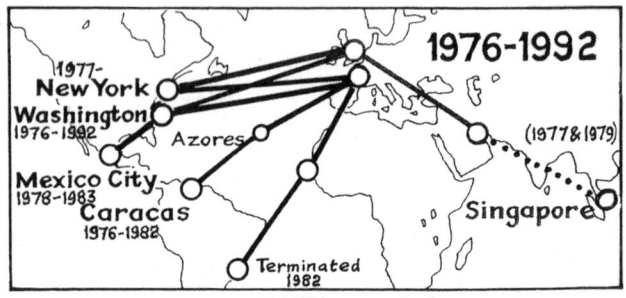
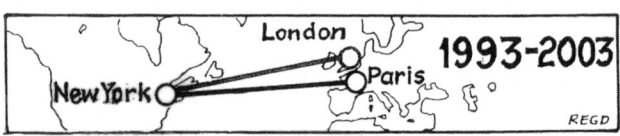

The Anglo-French Concorde entered service in a blaze of promotional optimism. Except for those to New York, the network of trans-Atlantic flagship services lasted only a few years. In 1979-80, Air France extended its service to Dallas, in cooperation with Braniff, but only subsonically. Flights by Singapore Airlines, with British Airways, were brief and intermittent. Some charter flights were made by B.A. to Barbados. Technological breakthroughs had to give way to economic realities. For every seat carried across the Atlantic, the Concorde had to carry a ton of fuel.

but Charles de Gaulle, intent on regaining France's prestige in the commercial and technological world, refused. Confidence exuded from the joint manufacturers, which collected provisional orders not only from the national airlines of their host countries, but also from several major domestic U.S. airlines, Japan Air Lines, and the great Pan American Airways. But by the late 1960s serious doubts had emerged concerning basic physics that turned out to be inescapable. Every time any aircraft accelerated to and continued to fly at more than the speed of sound, the resultant shock wave—the so-called Sonic Boom—left a path of potentially destructive vibration on the ground all along the supersonic aircraft's flight path. In spite of hopes that design modifications could ease the problem, "the Sonic Boom was a physical phenomenon that no sleight of aerodynamic hand could eliminate."

These conclusions were confirmed by extensive testing by the U.S. Federal Aviation Administration (F.A.A.) at Oklahoma City and in Nevada (see below). The effect on the potential customers was devastating. The market was restricted to routes that did not fly over land, and this eliminated about 90% of the world market. The big U.S. trunk airlines withdrew their deposits, as did Japan and other airlines that had grasped at the publicity value of joining the supersonic club. On 31 January 1973, Pan American Airways, which at least had the necessary over-water routes across the Atlantic and Pacific Oceans, cancelled. The market was reduced to commitments only from British Airways and Air France, each of which would receive seven Concordes.

With tremendous aplomb, enormous promotion and publicity, and much flag waving, the world's first supersonic airliner made its first flight on 2 March 1969, from Toulouse, with the second on 9 April, from Bristol. It went into service on 21 January 1976, with **Air France** flying from Paris to Rio de Janeiro and **British Airways** from London to Bahrain. Even though permission was reluctantly granted by the New York authorities for service there in 1976, and flights were already serving Washington, there was no rush from the world's airlines to buy. An experiment by Singapore Airlines came to nothing, and the subsonic Dallas-New York service by the U.S. Braniff Airways was little more than a promotional stunt. Air France services to several places in Latin America lasted only a year or two, as the high fares charged in an effort to break even were not nearly enough to cover the high costs. By the early 1980s, the trans-Atlantic Concorde route network was reduced to two U.S. destinations, New York and Washington, although subsonic extensions were tried for a few years.

The problem was that the high fares could be charged only to a tiny percentage of the traveling public, the highest income bracket, where a $10,000 round-trip ticket could be charged against a bloated expense account. Concorde passengers were typically film stars, television personalities, board chairmen, and diplomats. The big market, consisting of businessmen who had to account for their travel expenses and the enormous volume of leisure travelers, on vacation or on family visits, were not interested in saving a very expensive few hours on the ocean crossing and were much happier taking a 600-mph jet if they had to pay only one-tenth or less of the Concorde fare. The airlines had to face the hard truths of the operating costs. For every seat across the Atlantic, the Concorde had to carry a ton of fuel. Maintenance demanded extensive (and expensive) time on the ground, 10 times more than in the air.

In spite of the unprecedented publicity given to the Concorde, its impact on the world of air travel was negligible. Its complete service record is shown in the accompanying map.

The American SST

Supersonic fever was not confined to Europe. The United States was not about to surrender its national pride to the British or the French—nor to the Soviet Union, which was also in the vanguard of supersonic technology (SST). And so, in May 1958, only five months before Pan American Airways put its first subsonic jet airliner into service, both Douglas and Lockheed announced Mach 2 supersonic design projects, and soon afterward, early in 1959, General Dynamics added a Mach 3 competitor and Boeing joined the fray with its Model 2707. Speed, and speed alone, was at that time considered to be the only objective in aeronautical progress. The engineers and designers ruled. Market forecasts and economic analyses were either ignored or swept under the carpet. Enthusiastic journalists were fed overoptimistic data by the manufacturing industry, and airlines were overanxious to steal a march on their competitors. The atmosphere during the 1960s was irrational to a degree equalled only by religious fanatics, or the flat-earth society.

The Sonic Boom

Throughout the initial development period of the early 1960s, the problem of the sonic boom was either ignored or presumed to be solvable. Manufacturers and politicians tried to brush it off, but the evidence had to be faced. Early in 1964 the results of tests made by the National Operations Research Center of the F.A.A. in Oklahoma City were grim. Further tests at White Sands in December of that year were devastating. The prospect of shattered glass falling on busy city streets, however remote, could not be tolerated under any circumstances.

One measure of the Concorde's operational problems was that an aircraft had to be stationed at New York in case of a maintenance delay by incoming aircraft. For every hour's flying, a dozen were required for essential inspections in Paris. (Bentley)

Such was the influence of the supersonic protagonists that the F.A.A. directive was not promulgated until April 1970. Only then did the world of aviation finally recognize that supersonic airliners would never be permitted to fly over land. Effectively this reduced the market to trans-Atlantic operations. Market research revealed that, with the most optimistic assumptions regarding the world's trunk trans-ocean air routes, and even by stretching the data to their utmost limit, the market for the U.S. SST was no more than two or three dozen aircraft. To fly across the Pacific Ocean at supersonic speeds was a pleasant dream, but crossing the time zones meant that either a departure or an arrival in either direction, even if the aircraft had the necessary 5,000-mile range, would be at a totally inconvenient time, invariably during the night. And the speed of the journey would make no difference to the very real effect of jet lag.

High Cost, Low Market

Then there was the cost involved. Although 21 of the leading airlines of the world reserved 96 delivery positions, the minuscule $100,000 each was worth 10 times that amount in the advertising and publicity budget. On 31 December 1966, the Boeing 2707 was selected, with only Lockheed as the remaining competitor. On 29 April 1967, President Johnson announced that two prototypes would be built, and that these would cost $1.44 billion during the next four years. But as time passed, the estimate for the 300-ton titanium Mach 3 airliner rose to about three times that amount. By this time, the Anglo-French Concorde had made its first flight on 2 March 1969, and the Soviet Tupolev Tu-144 had already taken off on 31 December 1968.

Supersonic flight by large aircraft was also becoming the subject of alarm. Of the only two North American B-70 Mach 3 bombers built, one crashed on 8 July 1966, and the other was put into a museum. General Dynamics built 116 B-58s, costing $3 billion, but 30 were used for testing, and only 86 for military operations. Much had been made of the noise and the boom, so that the environmental objections were strong. Charles Lindbergh, an adviser to Pan American Airways (which would have been the launch customer for the SST) was against it, as was the city of New York, which managed to delay the arrival of Concorde service for many months. Much was made of the possible depletion of the earth's protective ozone layer.

The anti-SST campaign was led by Joseph Califano, later a presidential adviser, and Harvard physicist William Shurcliff, who founded the Citizens League against the Sonic Boom. Paradoxically, their objections, which the Concorde later demonstrated to be of little consequence, were as much the cause of the cancellation of the United States's supersonic airliner program as were the technical challenges of a folding wing (which Boeing had abandoned) or the constantly escalating costs. On 24 March 1971, Congress refused to spend any more of the taxpayers' money on the SST—the Senate turned it down by a single vote. It did the American manufacturing industry, and Boeing specifically, an enormous favor. The Seattle giant was able to concentrate on building profitable subsonic airliners, which were to dominate the world's commercial airliner market for two decades. Not a single Concorde was ever sold. As some British observers gloomily commented, Britain and France waved their flags, but Boeing laughed all the way to the bank.

The Concordski

This colloquial appellation to the Soviet contender for commercial supersonic status was derived from the popular notion that the Tupolev Tu-144 was copied from the Concorde. This was

The Tupolev Tu-144 was a little larger than the 100-seat Concorde, but its wing design did not permit lengthy supersonic flights. This photograph was taken at Alma Ata. (Davies 1992)

AEROFLOT'S TUPOLEV TU-144 ROUTE, 1977-78

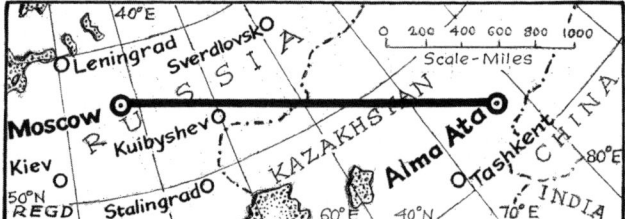

Very few scheduled flights were made by the Soviet supersonic airliner, and these were overland.

only partly true. The Moscow design team may have benefited from some later-discovered industrial espionage, but that direct copying was done is highly doubtful. Rather as, for example, the Douglas DC-9 was similar to the BAC One-Eleven and the Boeing 727 similar to the earlier de Havilland Trident, this was no more than evidence that "great minds think alike," and that, for a given design objective, similar solutions are found. The Tupolev Tu-144 was larger than the Concorde but, with a much higher percentage of titanium in its construction, was no heavier. Its delta wing was larger, but of a different and less efficient shape than the Concorde's. Earlier prototypes had a canard wing, soon discarded, and while attracting much attention from the aeronautical community around the world, it suffered a severe setback when, at the Paris Air Show on 3 June 1973, a demonstration ended in disaster when one crashed into a small community near le Bourget. The so-called black box was never found. At all events, it was a shattering blow for the design bureau. Nevertheless, the Tupolev Tu-144 went into service, from Moscow to Alma Ata, on 26 December 1975, for freight only—Aeroflot, the Soviet national airline, was understandably cautious—and for limited passenger service on 1 November 1977. Services continued intermittently, but ended on 1 June 1978, after only 102 completed flights in scheduled service.

Chapter 17: Development of the Breeds

Stretching the Nine

The highly successful Douglas DC-9 rear-engined twin-jet airliner was reviewed in Chapter 9. It was not the first to have its engines in the rear—the French Caravelle made that significant innovation with Air France in 1959, and the British BAC One-Eleven followed up with British United Airways in April 1965. Although the Europeans had been the innovators, the outstanding resources of design capability and production expertise enabled the United States to dominate the market for this category of airliner.

The DC-9 was not very different from the One-Eleven. The first 80-seat DC-9-10 series went into service with **Delta Air Lines** on 8 December 1965, only seven months after its British predecessor, and it proceeded to dominate the twin-jet market for several years. Douglas's traditional customers bought the DC-9-30 series in substantial numbers, headed by **Eastern Air Lines**, with its first service on 1 February 1967, only 14 months after the launching of the original type.

Just over a year later, drawing upon its long history of cooperation with the European airlines, the Dash-30 series fuselage was lengthened by 15 feet for the Scandinavian **S.A.S.**, which introduced the 125-seat DC-9-40 on 12 March 1968. There was also the -20, specially built for S.A.S., which had a longer wingspan to assist performance from airports with short runways. Then another faithful European Douglas stalwart, **Swissair**, went one better, with the DC-9-50, an additional eight feet longer, with 139 seats, placing it into service on 24 August 1975.

The project office at Douglas was still not satisfied. It went on to produce a design for the ultimate "stretch" of the fuselage, by no less than 14 feet. This DC-9-80 (the number chosen to coincide with the year of introduction) could carry, in all-economy class, 172 passengers, an astonishing achievement—more than double the capacity of the first DC-9-10. It was renamed the MD-80, to reflect the consolidated merger between McDonnell and Douglas.

The first of these efficient airliners went into service with Swissair on 5 October 1980, followed by Austrian Air Lines shortly afterward. The series went on to be the most successful, in terms of numbers sold, of all Douglas jet airliners. One notable feature was a co-production agreement with China, now realigning with the West. Beginning with subassemblies, the Shanghai Aviation Industrial Corporation built 28 MD-83 variants, beginning early in the 1980s and completing the program in 1992.

The development pattern led to the MD-90 series. The engines in this model were International Aero Engines (I.A.E.) V2500s, which improved the direct operating costs, and further refinements were made to the instrumentation and avionics. The MD-90s came in three versions: the -30, with a 155-foot fuselage and 158 standard seating; the -40, 171 feet long and 180 seats; and a short-fuselaged version with 116 seats. The first MD-90 went into service with **Japan Air System** in July 1995. Also, some -30s were built in Shanghai.

The swan-song of this highly successful range of twin-engined jets came during the mid-1990s. Interestingly, the launch customer for the MD-95 (only 100 seats) was **AirTran**, a low-fare, no-frills newcomer to the eastern United States airline scene, which had taken over **ValuJet**, a fellow competitor that had been put out of business when one of its DC-9s crashed because of an exploding oxygen container. This DC-9 variant was not only the last of the breed; it was to lose its designation. On 4 August 1997, the biggest merger (or takeover) in the history of the aerospace industry was to take place, surpassing even the Lockheed-Martin amalgamation. The great Boeing Company of Seattle acquired the McDonnell-Douglas Corporation and proceeded to consolidate the various production assembly lines of both companies. The new MD-95 was promptly redesignated the Boeing 717—neatly filling in the missing numeral in the now-famous 700 series of airliners, one which had originally been allocated to a still-born military version of the Boeing 707.

Unfortunately, it came into the U.S. airline arena just when the airlines had bought too many airliners of all kinds during the 1980s and 1990s. The market for this type of airliner had almost dried up. Boeing had produced its own development of the Boeing 737, and overseas, the European Airbus consortium had produced a strong competitor in the Airbus A320.

The Douglas DC-9 twin-jet airliner series was a classic example of a type development. The first 80-seat DC-9-10s were eventually to be joined by the MD-90s, with up to 180 seats. These photographs are of (left) a 125-seat DC-9-40 and (right) an MD-90-30. (McDonough)

Fat Albert Rules

When Seattle launched the twin-engined Boeing 737-100 in the late 1960s, it seemed to have entered the twin-engined regional jet market rather late. The 737-100 series made its first flight on 9 April 1967 and went into service on 10 February 1968. It broke with tradition in several ways. Not only was its debut more than two years behind Douglas, which, by this time, had built up an impressive DC-9 order book, already surpassing that of the British BAC One-Eleven, but its launch customer was not the customary U.S. airline. The German **Lufthansa** welcomed the 737 as its City Jet, natural partner to its Boeing 727 Europa Jet. Including those delivered to its non-scheduled/charter associate, Condor Flugdienst, Lufthansa would eventually have more than sixty 727s and top this with ninety 737s of various later models.

Contrasting with the DC-9, which followed the Caravelle/BAC design with engines on the rear fuselage, the Boeing 737's engines were mounted like the 707's, in pods, under the wing. At first, this was regarded as a possible problem, as the engines were near the ground and vulnerable on landing or take-off at rough fields to debris thrown up by the nose-wheel, which would enter the engine intakes, with disastrous results. Boeing adroitly fixed deflector plates to the nose-gear and the problem was solved. Compensating for this initial shortcoming was the basic design. The 737 was essentially a reengined short-fuselaged 727, with exactly the same fuselage cross-section. The manufacturer thus enjoyed the commonality of component parts and other aspects of production; it also meant that the 737 offered comfortable six-abreast seating, whereas the DC-9 could only manage five. Boeing built only 30 of the -100 series (of which Lufthansa had 22) but followed Douglas's example of rapid development of the type.

But Douglas had already established a strong foothold in the market, especially with major U.S. airlines such as Delta, **T.W.A.**, and Eastern, as well as many of the Local Service airlines, such as **North Central**, **Bonanza**, and **Ozark**. Air Canada, together with faithful Douglas customers in Europe, such as **K.L.M., Iberia**, S.A.S., Swissair, and **Alitalia**, contributed to an impressive order book for the Long Beach factory—so much so that Douglas ran into severe production difficulties, trying to meet contractual delivery guarantees of DC-9s and DC-8s at the same time. Meanwhile, the order book for the 737-200 seemed sluggish, except for **United Air Lines**—as faithful to Boeing as Delta was to Douglas—and at first, Seattle lagged behind Long Beach by a substantial margin in its sales record.

Toward the late 1970s, the balance changed. Boeing chipped away with a growing list of small orders to a myriad of customers all over the world, such as Ireland's **Aer Lingus**, **South African Airways**, Canada's **Pacific Western**, and Japan's **All Nippon Airways**. And while Douglas had logged the Californian intrastate **Pacific Southwest Airlines (P.S.A.)** and **Air California** into its fold, Boeing had won the order from the Texan **Southwest Airlines**, under the driving (and often colorful) leadership of its president, Herb Kelleher. This was to have enormous consequences in the future as, after the Airline Deregulation Act of 1978, the two Californian airlines were purchased by USAir and American Airlines, respectively, while Southwest went from strength to strength (see below). In a parallel situation, in which non-scheduled airlines in Europe were on the ascendancy, Boeing began to match Douglas in its sales, notably with the British **Britannia Airways**, which built up a large fleet of 737s.

In 1981, Boeing announced its "second-generation" 737-300 series, once again lengthening the fuselage by almost nine feet, with 22,100-lb. thrust GE/SNECMA CFM56 engines replacing the 15,500 lb. Pratt & Whitney JT8Ds. The development of this highly successful airliner was to continue. In November 1993, a third generation Boeing 737-600 appeared on the scene, with an 18-foot longer wing-span and larger empennage. This aircraft, hardly recognizable from the original -100 Series, except in the fuselage cross-section, could fly from California to Hawaii, or transcontinental nonstop across the United States. It went into service with S.A.S. on 25 October 1998. This twin-engined aircraft beat all records for commercial airliner production. The -600 was succeeded by the -700, introduced by Southwest (before the -600) on 18 January 1998; the -800, by Hapag-Lloyd on 24 April 1998; and the -900, by Alaska Airlines on 27 May 2001. Each of these variants was longer than the -600 and was able to achieve the same or better performance than the Boeing

By a consistent policy of charging low fares, Herb Kelleher was the driving force behind the rise of Southwest Airlines from intra-state level to national prominence. (Davies)

When the Boeing 737 was first introduced, its sales were slow. But Boeing's development program in "stretching" its performance was outstandingly successful. One version could fly to Hawaii. (Bentley)

Development of the Breeds

The enterprising Southwest Airlines standardized its fleet on the Boeing 737. It operated more than 400 of the various developments. This one is a 737-7H4. (McDonough)

727 tri-jet, which by this time was fast approaching old age. By the year 2010, more than 6,000 Boeing 737s have been ordered. It has been, in terms of financial turnover, the most successful airliner ever produced.

The Also-Rans

In Great Britain, the sad story of the de Havilland DH 121 Trident tri-jet has already been related in Chapter 9. The design had originally been set by **British European Airways (B.E.A.)** in 1956, and de Havilland had won the competition against the twin-engined Bristol 200 design. But the 100-seater—which could have beaten the Boeing 727 into service by at least a year, and whose seat-mile costs would have been lower—was compromised by the extraordinary demand from B.E.A. to shorten the fuselage to an 84-seat layout, which destroyed the Trident's chances of worldwide success. The Trident 1C, with a take-off weight of 115,000 lb., first flew in 1962 and went into service with B.E.A. in 1964. Other than from the British state airline, only small orders were received from Kuwait, Iraq, Pakistan, Cyprus, and Channel Airways.

By this time, de Havilland had become part of the Hawker-Siddeley Group, and in July 1967, the Trident 2E appeared, with the Rolls-Royce Spey engines upgraded to 11,930-lb. thrust. Of the meager total production of 50 aircraft, 33 went to **Civil Aviation Administration of China (C.A.A.C.)**, the national airline of the People's Republic of China, whose antipathy at that time to anything built in the United States gave the Trident a fortuitous advantage.

The only further development of this airliner was the Trident 3B, which first flew on 11 December 1969. It had a 16-foot longer fuselage, to increase the seating capacity to 146, and the take-off weight to 150,000 lb. This was achieved by fitting an auxiliary engine, a Rolls-Royce RB-162, at the base of the rudder, to be used only for additional take-off power, gaining the aircraft the doubtful distinction of being an underpowered four-engined airliner. The whole production of 26 aircraft was taken up by B.E.A., and two more went to China, with increased weight to 158,000 lb.

This was almost the end of the road for a fine airliner manufacturer that had introduced the world to the Jet Age back in 1952, but had been ruined by forces that it allowed to sabotage its destiny. The Hatfield factory struggled on with its regional HS-146, but the die was cast.

Throughout the 1950s and into the 1960s, the British industry suffered from illusions of grandeur. Its designers and technicians were the equal of any in the United States, but it completely failed to recognize the levels of production that the likes of Boeing, Douglas, and Lockheed could achieve, once a decision was made to go full steam ahead with an aircraft type. Boeing could build and deliver as many 727s in a week as de Havilland/Hawker Siddeley could in three months. The after-sales service, too, was not up to the American standards—even in the 1970s, Douglas would claim to be able to deliver a needed item for any of its in-service aircraft to anywhere in the world within 48 hours.

The corporate attitude in the British industry whether through professional arrogance or ignorance of the market, was a factor in the decline of the British commercial aircraft manufacturing industry, at a time when the first Comet had pointed a clear way forward. Instead of a national coordinated plan, when a rejuvenated Brabazon Committee would have paid handsome dividends in the future course of airliner development, the major companies competed with each other, rather than with the dominant competitors across the Atlantic. The worst example was the construction of the Vickers Vanguard, a four-engined turboprop airliner that was chosen by B.E.A. to succeed the Vickers Viscount. With 123 seats, it was a natural successor to that pioneer turboprop, but the Bristol Britannia and the Lockheed Electra (and even the Ilyushin Il-18) had already supplied enough aircraft of similar specification and performance to meet most of the world's needs, and the initial order of 20 aircraft from B.E.A. was followed only by a further 23 from **Trans Canada Airlines (T.C.A.)** (later Air Canada).

Vickers had, however, won its spurs with the Viscount, and in 1951 the idea emerged for a commercial airliner development of the Valiant bomber, to be the VC-7 or the V-1000, powered by Rolls-Royce Conway turbofan engines. This would have been ordered by both B.O.A.C. and the Royal Air Force, but the project was cancelled by the government in 1955. At first, Vickers proposed a Vanjet, based on the Vanguard, with swept wings and three rear engines, but then turned to a new design, for an aircraft in the Boeing 707/Douglas DC-8 category, but differing in its basic design. The Conway engines were mounted in pairs at the

The Vickers Vanguard should never have been built, as the Bristol Britannia and the Lockheed Electra had already taken up the available market for a medium/long-range turboprop airliner. (Bentley)

rear of the fuselage, and a T-tail, following the tradition started by the Caravelle and developed by the BAC One-Eleven and the Douglas DC-9.

On 30 May 1957, **B.O.A.C.** ordered 35 VC-10s, which was a most encouraging start, worth £68 million, and the contract was signed on 14 January 1958. This was later augmented by 10 Super-VC-10s, which, with upgraded Conways and 335,000 lb. take-off weight, had full trans-Atlantic range. The order was later modified to 15 standard and 30 Supers, and then three of the standards were cancelled. This fine aircraft series suffered from an overemphasis on the importance of Britain's traditional "all-red" empire route to South Africa, dating back to the romantic pre-war days of the flying-boats of Imperial Airways. The VC-10 had to be designed to cope with up to 120°(F) take-offs at Khartoum, and 6,000-foot altitudes at Nairobi and Johannesburg. It was consequently overpowered for the majority of the airports at the world's main airline traffic centers. The position of the engines cost two seat rows in capacity and its cost-per-seat-mile was therefore slightly higher than that of either the 707s or the DC-8's. But its cabin was attractively quiet and the ride was smooth, thanks to the rear-mounted engines. The higher costs were therefore compensated for by higher load factors and resultant higher revenues.

The prototype VC-10 made its first flight on 29 June 1962, by which time, however, the 707 and the DC-8 were already established on all the world's long-haul routes. B.O.A.C. put it into service on the West African route to Accra and Lagos on 19 April 1964. The Super-VC-10s went on to the London-New York route, the world's most prestigious airline trunk artery, on 1 April 1965. To its credit, B.O.A.C.'s advertising excelled itself, with slogans like "Try a Little VC-Tenderness" and billboards emphasizing the better seat spacing with a picture-without-words—Marlene Dietrich's legs. The trans-Atlantic VC-10s attracted unprecedented load factors—as high as 90%—yet, astonishingly, the airline made little attempt to capitalize on its exclusive use of this fine airliner on the North Atlantic. Its analysts concentrated on the high operating costs, some of which admittedly derived from the escalating purchasing price, and a corporate decision was made to favor the Boeing 707s, ordering more of them instead of supporting the British industry, as the French had in supporting theirs by nourishing the Caravelle. B.O.A.C. cancelled 10 of its order on 7 February 1966. This was a cruel blow to the aspirations of Vickers. Coming as the cancellation did, only a year after the Atlantic debut, it delivered a harsh, and certainly undeserved, critique of the airplane, and promising efforts to market the VC-10 were sabotaged.

After this negative turn of events, sales were predictably modest. **British United Airways (B.U.A.)** bought three standard VC-10s, with strengthened floor and freight door, and used them on the West African and South American routes that it had inherited from B.O.A.C. British routes had been reallocated, on the recommendation of the Edwards Committee, whose report was published in May 1969. **Ghana Airways**, of the first British colony (formerly the Gold Coast) in Africa to gain independence, ordered two; and **East African Airways** took five Super-VC-10s, and did very well with them. The production line was reinforced by an order from the Royal Air Force for 14 standard VC-10s. These were used extensively for trooping to distant British garrisons in Hong Kong and Nepal, and they were used during the Falkland Islands War. As late as the early 2000s, R.A.F. VC-10s were still making trips to Belize to supply the small detachment there.

The Last British Main-Line Jet

This left the British Aircraft Corporation (B.A.C.) with only its BAC One-Eleven in production at Weybridge, the home of so many great British airplanes. B.A.C. had correctly judged that world market success depended on breaking into the U.S. airline hierarchy, as in the 1960s, at the beginning of the Jet Age, the Americans still accounted for about half of the world's airline productivity, measured in passenger-miles flown. The company, formerly Vickers-Armstrongs, already had an excellent reputation in the States, as the Viscount turboprop had been the first turbine-powered airliner to enter service there, and was widely praised. So the BAC One-Eleven was at first partially successful, with good initial orders from **Braniff** and **Mohawk** for the basic 80-seat Series 200, which, with two 10,400-lb. thrust Rolls-Royce Spey engines, had a gross take-off weight of 79,000 lb. And an order for 30 from **American Airlines** for the improved Series 400 (in which the gross weight could not be measurably increased because of F.A.A. restrictions for two-crew operations) was encouraging. But other than a small Series 200 order from the Hawaiian **Aloha Airlines**, this was the end of the trans-Atlantic penetration. Other than an order from B.U.A., which was the launch customer, with its first One-Eleven service on 9 April 1965, B.A.C. had to struggle to build up an order book, depending on a multiplicity of small orders all over the world.

British European Airways (B.E.A.), the pre-eminent airline in Europe, now came to B.A.C.'s rescue. Having ruined de Havilland's chances of worldwide success with its insistence on making the Trident smaller, it now reversed its former policy of gloom and sponsored a lengthened-fuselaged version of the One-Eleven, the Series 500, whose take-off weight was increased to 106,500 lb. The additional 13 ft. 6 in. in the cabin permitted 119 seats—ironically what the Trident could have offered, with

The Vickers VC-10 was a superb airliner. During the 1960s, regular trans-Atlantic passengers preferred it to the Boeing 707 or the DC-8. Some were still flying in military support service in 2010. (Davies, NASM-9A07931)

earlier B.E.A. support. The initial order was for 18, and the airline was eventually to have a fleet of 46.

B.E.A. introduced the -500 in June 1969, but once again, the manufacturer had to struggle hard to maintain any momentum of worldwide sales and no further order reached double figures, except one notable exception. Negotiations began during the 1970s with Romania, which was showing signs of resistance against the trading restrictions imposed by the Soviet Union on its communist adherents. Eventually, after the sale of seven -500s to **TAROM**, Romania's national airline, an agreement was signed for, at first sub-assembly then licensed production of the Series 500 to the Romanian ROMBAC. But only a few more were built. B.A.C. closed down the production line of BAC One-Elevens in 1981, after building 264 aircraft.

Except for the BAe 146 short-haul jet, the BAC One-Eleven was the last British airliner to enter service on the world's mainline air routes. It was also built in Romania, under license. (Bentley)

Chapter 18: Redefining the U.S. Second Line

A Question of Definition

In the United States, which for half a century dominated the world of commercial air transport, airlines were strictly regulated by powerful government agencies to ensure that good standards of safety and service were upheld, and that competition, though recognized as desirable, was not allowed to get out of hand and lead to destructive marketing practices. The Civil Aeronautics Board (C.A.B.), established in 1938, was the guardian of such standards in the commercial arena, while the Civil Aviation Authority (C.A.A.)—later the U.S. Federal Aviation Administration (F.A.A.)—watched over navigational and operational requirements—which it still does today, even after deregulation. Early during its 40-year tenure, which ended in 1978 with the Airline Deregulation Act, the C.A.B. responsibly recognized that individual airlines could not be all things to all people; to serve densely traveled routes such as New York-Washington required different aircraft and different infrastructure than a sparsely traveled route in the wheat lands of Kansas or Nebraska, or the Rocky Mountains of Colorado. It had, sensibly, established several categories of airlines. It treated them by different criteria of regulatory practices and, during the early decades, of qualifications for subsidy, either indirectly through mail payments or by direct subsidy.

Thus, by the time the Jet Age arrived, the C.A.B. was listing airlines under several categories such as Trunk, Local Service, International, Territorial, All-Cargo or Freight, Helicopter, and Supplemental. Ultimately, it included a Miscellaneous group, in which most of the airlines became Commuters. **United Air Lines**, **American Airlines**, **T.W.A.**, and **Eastern Air Lines** came to be called the "Big Four"—they accounted for about 75% of the seat-mile output of all U.S. domestic airlines. The Local Service airlines wanted a term that was not diminutive and decided on "Regionals." As described in Chapter 13, the commuter airlines were originally fixed-base operators whose sporadic charter or executive flights gradually congealed into regular services and, therefore, as was obligatory in the post-war years, had to be regulated. They became Scheduled Air Taxis, dubbed Third Level, and ultimately Commuters. This last term was convenient but, in its correct definition, inaccurate. The word derives from the Latin *commutare*, "to exchange." The *Oxford Dictionary* offers several meanings: to interchange (of two things); to buy off (an obligation); to change a punishment (into another less severe); to change one kind of payment for another. In surface transport, as a convenience for both the servicer and the serviced, weekly, monthly, or even six-monthly tickets could be purchased at prices discounted from the rate charged for a single ticket. The fare was thus commuted, and its users became known as "commuters"—the term was adopted in the United States much earlier in the 20th century than it was elsewhere. Those who traveled back and forth from home to work were called commuters, even if they bought single tickets each way every day.

Creation of a New Trunk Airline

In most cases, the introduction of jet airliners into the U.S. regional airlines' fleets coincided with important mergers as the bigger fish swallowed the smaller ones. The most important was the merger between **Allegheny Airlines** and **Mohawk Airlines** on 12 April 1972, to create a larger Allegheny which, on 30 October 1979 was renamed **USAir**. Allegheny had already acquired **Lake Central Airlines** on 1 July 1968. All three had, in the late 1960s, introduced turboprop equipment: Allegheny on 1 June 1965 (Allison-powered Convair 580s), Lake Central on 31 October (the French Nord 262s, followed by 580s on 6 September 1966), and Mohawk on 1 July 1966 (Fairchild-Hiller FH-227s). Mohawk had been one of the first U.S. airlines to introduce jets, with its first BAC One-Eleven service on 15 July 1965, while Allegheny was not far behind, with **Douglas DC-9s** on 1 September 1966. Excluding Allegheny's unsuccessful trials with the Napier-engined Convair 540 at the end of 1959, the upgrading from piston-engined aircraft occurred within the span of only two years in 1965 and 1966, and could be regarded as preparing the surging regionals of the east for the greater corporate expansion in 1972.

The progress had thus been rapid. Allegheny could trace its history (as All-American Aviation) back to the experimental aerial pick-up mail service of 1937. The three airlines had only started scheduled Local Service routes with ex-military 150-mph Douglas DC-3s in the 1940s. Mohawk had begun (as Robinson Airlines) on 12 December 1946, changing its name to reflect its main route, along the Mohawk River, on 23 August 1952. All-American started service on 7 March 1949, and, like Mohawk, adopted the Allegheny name to suit its territory on 1 January 1953. Lake Central had started as Turner Airlines (it was founded by the famous airman Roscoe Turner) on 31 May 1949, changing its name in December 1950. The three airlines, therefore, were matching the trunk airlines with new 300-mph turboprops and 500-mph jets, when only two decades before, they had had to rely on bargain-priced, nonpressurized, tail-wheeled, war-surplus transport aircraft. Toward the latter 1960s also, another eastern airline, Tom Davis's **Piedmont Airlines**, which had started service in the Carolinas on 1 January 1948, upgraded into jets. It had been among the first to operate the successful Fairchild F-27 (license-built from Fokker), on 14 November 1958, and added the larger FH-227s on 15 February 1967. Davis then introduced the 60-seat Japanese Nihon YS-11A on 19 May 1968, and trumped this turboprop ace with Boeing 737 jet service on 1 July 1968. He had already been unfortunate with a bold step in the spring of 1967, with Boeing 727 tri-jets, but had had to withdraw service after a crash. But permanent Boeing

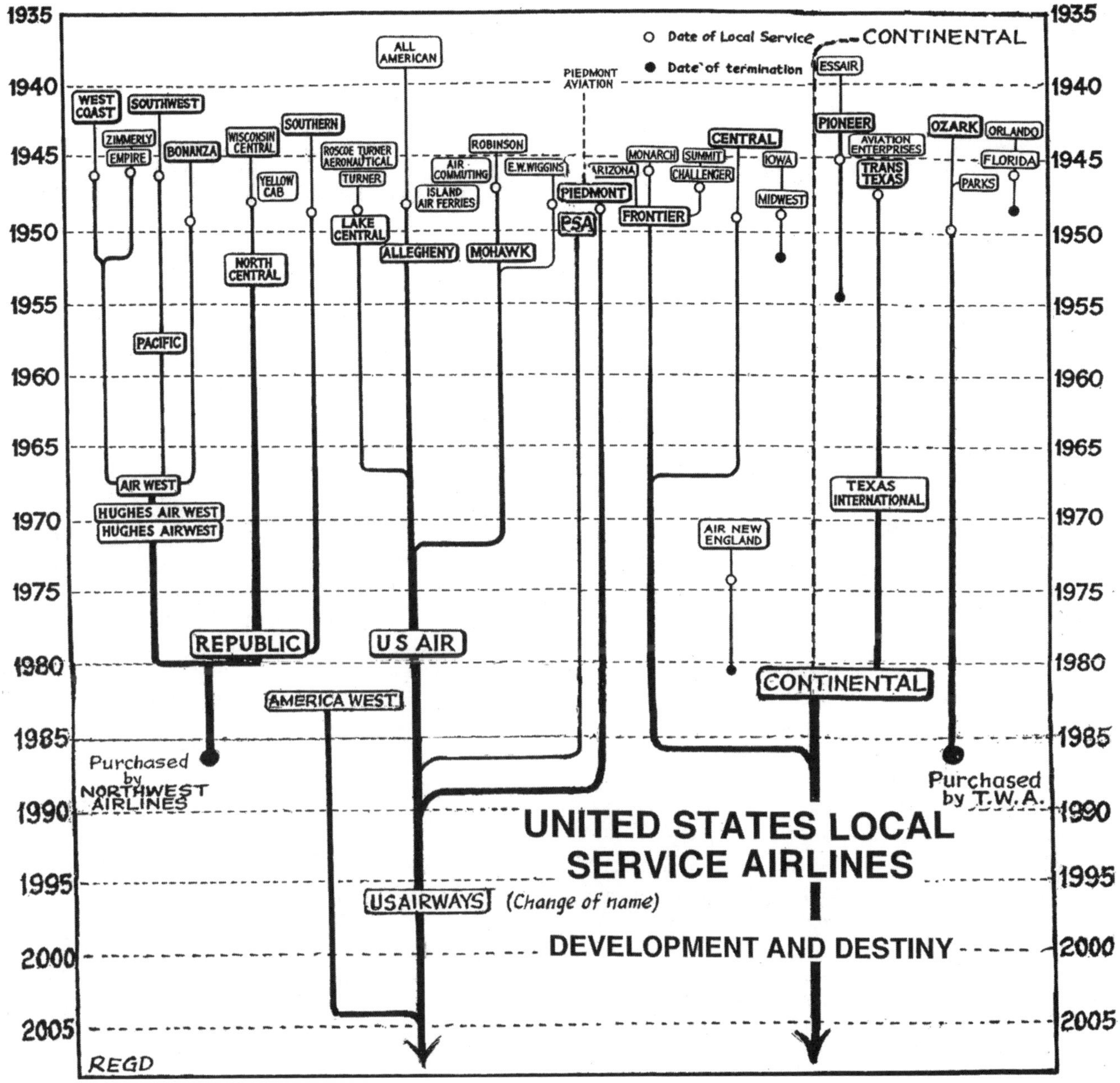

Redefining the U.S. Second Line

Over a period of several decades following the end of the Second World War, the United States Local Service airlines either merged or were absorbed by trunk airlines. During the 1980s they were called Regionals, and by the end of the 20th century they had disappeared altogether.

Piedmont Airlines operated a fleet of Japanese Nihon YS-11 turboprops throughout the Carolinas and nearby states during the 1970s. (Bentley)

727 service, starting on 14 January 1977, was necessary to match the growth on Piedmont's routes, which included several to the booming vacation resorts in Florida.

Surpassing even USAir's achievement in going from DC-3s to DC-9s (via pressurized Convairliners and Martin 404s), Piedmont inaugurated wide-bodied Boeing 767-200s on a trans-Atlantic route from Charlotte to London on 15 June 1987. Only 20 years after its foundation (inevitably with DC-3s), it was operating 120-seat jets. Within 20 years more, it was a trans-Atlantic airline, with twin-aisled 300-seat wide-bodied twin-aisled airliners.

On 5 August 1989, the burgeoning USAir absorbed Piedmont. This was the end to an airline that had pioneered airline service throughout the area east of the Appalachian mountain chain and from which it derived its name.

Creation of a New Western Airline

On the other side of the United States, the Local Service airlines along the Pacific coast were also following a similar pattern of upgrading their aircraft fleets and amalgamating their operations. The distant ancestor of what was to become a major coast-to-coast airline network was a little intra-state airline—no more than a fixed-base operator of a single route. **Zimmerly Air Lines** started to fly 3-seater Cessna Airmasters in Idaho on 11 April 1944, and changed its name to **Empire Air Lines** on 1 March 1946. It moved up to previously owned (as the euphemism has it) Boeing 247Ds on 28 September 1946 then the inevitable DC-3s on 11 March 1948, before being sold to **West Coast Airlines** on 4 August 1952.

West Coast had been founded on 5 December 1946 by Nick Bez. Successful in the salmon-canning business, he had had experience in airlines by operating Alaska Southern Airways. DC-3 service started from Seattle to Portland on 5 December 1946, and local routes in that area expanded to the extent that West Coast was the first airline in the world to operate, from 28 September 1958, a Fokker Friendship, familiarly known in the U.S.A. as the F-27, built under license by Fairchild. Bez elevated the turbine-engined status to that of the pure jet by starting Douglas DC-9 service on 26 September 1966.

In a parallel, almost identical course of adolescent development, Ed Converse's **Bonanza Air Lines** started an intra-state DC-3 route in Nevada from Las Vegas to Reno on 5 August 1946, but his clientele was different from the potato farmers and woodsmen of Zimmerly's route out of Boise. The passengers were mostly businessmen from California seeking wine, women, and song at the flourishing resort cities of Nevada. Bonanza started F-27 service on 29 March 1959, and proudly claimed to be the first all-jet airline in the world when it retired its last DC-3 on 18 November 1960. This was stretching the definition of "jet" a little, but this was rectified on 1 March 1966 with Douglas DC-9 service. Of all the Local Service/Regional airlines, Bonanza had provided the most effective demonstration that anything the trunk airlines could do, the second level could do too. On the busy Los Angeles-Las Vegas route, it went head-to-head with the jets of the trunk airlines and were unbowed.

Another Pacific coast Local Service airline was based in the heart of California, a major traffic-generating area, with its two mega-cities, Los Angeles and San Francisco, along with several medium-sized cities in between. **Southwest Airways** had been founded in 1941 and began DC-3 service along the California Corridor on 2 December 1946. It changed its name to **Pacific Air Lines** on 6 March 1958, and a year later, in April 1959, introduced F-27s. Eschewing the temptations of the popular DC-9s and One-Elevens, president Harry White went for the larger Boeing 727, starting his jet service on 20 July 1966. Pacific had already been an innovator. It had introduced the idea of swift transit stops by keeping one DC-3 engine running while passengers rushed out of and into the waiting airplane. Now, from April to July 1967, in a rather bizarre promotional effort, its publicity chief, Stan Freberg, parodied the instinctive fear-of-flying emotion shared by some passengers by a "sweaty-palms" survival kit issued to Pacific's travelers. It was not a success.

Along the Pacific coast, the route networks of the three airlines, West Coast, Pacific, and Bonanza, overlapped in several market areas. The California Corridor from the San Francisco Bay Area to the Greater Los Angeles metropolitan area was always potentially lucrative, and the connecting services to the gambling casinos and high life of Reno and Nevada were, in the 1960s, expanding rapidly. West Coast's Nick Bez was the driving force behind discussions that led, on 17 April 1968, to a three-way merger, to form a combined airline, **Air West**. A week earlier, President Johnson had given his approval—necessary because foreign routes were involved (West Coast to Canada, Bonanza into Mexico)—following State Department agreement. Combined operations under the new name began on 1 July.

During the next two years, the story behind the merger was a surprising revelation. Apparently, Bez had been acting on behalf of no less than the famous—some would say notorious—Howard Hughes. The billionaire had been eased out of T.W.A. when, on 3 May 1966, he was forced to sell his trustee-held stock for $566 million (the deal took 20 minutes). For all his idiosyncrasies, Hughes, the consummate aviator, had been immersed in the airline business since the late 1930s, and his heart was still with the business of air transport. The ink was hardly dry on the merger contractual documents when, on 12 August, Bez

Bonanza Air Lines introduced frequent service between Las Vegas and Los Angeles with a fleet of Fairchild-Fokker F-27s. (Davies)

announced that the Hughes Tool Company had agreed to buy Air West for $90 million. This raised the hackles of the non–West Coast shareholders, who sensed a contrived sell-out. The deal worked out at $22 per share, and a protracted legal dispute arose, led by Bonanza's Ed Converse, who claimed that the shares were worth at least $40 each. Years later, Converse would come close to his claim, as the Summa Corporation, which had acquired the Hughes interests, paid out at $37 per share. Meanwhile, Nick Bez, the man who had been Hughes's agent, died on 5 February 1969. On 21 July of that year, the C.A.B., with President Nixon's approval, agreed to the acquisition of Air West by the Hughes Tool Company, for $150 million. Litigation still dragged on until the sale was completed on 31 March 1970. This paved the way for the name of the airline to be changed, in July, to **Hughes Air West**. After only four years in exile from the airline world, Howard Hughes was back.

By this time, however, the formerly formidable business tycoon was seriously ill, and he did not live to see his new airline develop into the nationwide force that he would have wished. Howard Hughes died on 5 April 1976, by which time his name was established in the western airline world. On 28 September 1971, a "new look" was given to the airline, with a revolutionary yellow paint scheme which, in spite of certain descriptions of the airliners by critics as "flying bananas," was popular with air travelers. Law suits continued, with Federal Judge Thompson continually throwing out repeated indictments, but the airline pressed on with methodical expansion. On 17 September 1976, already equipped with inherited Douglas DC-9s and early Boeing 727s, Hughes Airwest (it had changed its name slightly) introduced Boeing 727-200s on 15 January 1977, with which it consolidated its route network with nonstop services between major cities and expanded, in 1978, as far east as Milwaukee and Louisville.

Regional to Trunk

An even bigger amalgamation of the Regional airlines was now in the works. During the days of the Local Service airlines, and before they became known as Regionals, the biggest of them all was **North Central Airlines**, based in Minneapolis. It was founded on 15 May 1944 as **Wisconsin Central Airlines**, operating scheduled services with Lockheed L-10 Electras on 24 February 1948, before moving up to Douglas DC-3s in March 1951. Sharing in the generous subsidy payments of that category of airlines, North Central also benefitted from considerable expansion resulting from route awards from the C.A.B. in important reviews of the airline needs of small communities all across the northern prairie states. This was the reason for its change of name on 16 December 1952, after the results of the Seven States Area Case, and it expanded later to the east when it was the leading beneficiary of the Great Lakes Local Service Case. Under Hal Carr's leadership, it also served Toronto and Regina, and later, Winnipeg, in Canada. North Central was thus a force to be reckoned with. On 1 April 1967, it started turboprop service with Allison-powered Convair 580s and, on 8 September, added Douglas DC-9 jets. Throughout the northern midwestern states, North Central jet services competed strongly with those of the trunk airlines, and on 25 April 1976, to meet expanding traffic demand, the larger DC-9-50 series augmented its already large fleet of jets.

On 13 July 1978 (after all the dust had settled in the west), North Central and **Southern Airways** announced their merger. Frank Hulse's airline, based in Atlanta, had served all the small communities in the southeast since 10 June 1949 and was to have the unusual record of being the only U.S. airline never to operate a turboprop airliner. It went straight from the piston-engined Martin 404 (and, of course, the trusty DC-3) to Douglas DC-9s, which it put into service on 15 June 1967. By the time it merged with North Central on 13 July 1978, its network, now linking Chicago and Washington with Miami, was, like its peer airlines, no longer local service and well justified the adoption of the term *regional*. The merged company was also no longer solely north-central, nor was it southern, and it became **Republic Airlines**, with its main base remaining at Minneapolis. The first integrated schedules under the new name started on 1 October 1979.

Republic had no sooner become an airline force in the east and Midwest, when, exactly one year after its formation, it bought Hughes Airwest on 1 October 1980, and joined the ranks of the nationwide trunk airlines, with a substantial fleet of Douglas DC-9s, which had been the preferred choice of jet equipment by all the former airline components, except Pacific. For a few years, Republic held its own at its base at Minneapolis, in spite of the proximity of the headquarters of one of the leading U.S. trunk airlines, and among the leading airlines of the western world, customarily ranking sixth in the passenger-miles ranking lists, and always a good profit maker. **Northwest Orient Airlines**, operating cheek-by-jowl from its own hub at the Twin Cities (Minneapolis-St. Paul) did what all the big fish did in the ocean of competiton: it swallowed the smaller fish. On 23 January 1986, it announced that it had purchased Republic for $884 million. The route networks were combined that year on what had become a traditional date, 1 October.

With the amalgamation of five of the original Local Service airlines to form Republic, and three in the east to form USAir (with Piedmont to be engulfed by the latter), the end was in sight for the few other regional survivors. Once the cold realities of airline deregulation in 1978 had obliterated the comparative security of a regulated fare structure, the aggressively promoted, almost ruthless, momentum toward low fares jeopardized the chances of profitability by small or even medium-sized companies. In the new economic environment, oligopolistic policies alone could florish, and the economics of sheer size now prevailed in the U.S. airline industry and would not change until a new and different threat to a time-honored corporate establishment emerged in the 21st century.

Expansion in the Rockies

One Local Service airline had been in the vanguard of the campaign to change the status to Regional. Lew Dymond, who had taken over the presidency of **Frontier Airlines** in March 1962, was the standard-bearer of the company based at Denver, geographically situated as a potentially national hub in the middle of the country. It had been formed, and named, by an early merger in the late 1940s of three DC-3-operating airlines of the southwestern states, led by Monarch Airlines, which bought Challenger Airlines in December 1949, and then Arizona Airways in April 1950.

If ever an airline justified the description of Local Service, it was Frontier. The area it served was sparsely populated, compared to the United States as a whole. Aside from Denver, the only cities on its network of any size were Phoenix, Tucson, and Salt Lake City. Farmington, at the northwest corner of New Mexico, with a population of 20,000, was a Frontier hub. Its traffic derived from the distance factor, rather than the population it served. It connected by air communities that were far apart and often separated by the rugged Rocky Mountains. But it benefitted from the growing popularity of vacation resorts, including the skiing centers in Colorado, as well as Yellowstone National Park and the Grand Tetons, the latter two through the airport at Jackson Hole, Wyoming.

Late in 1958, the airline had expanded considerably as the result of one of the C.A.B.'s general overhauls of airline route structures, the Seven States Area Case, and by January 1959 had added 24 additional cities to its network. So by this time, the map of Frontier's routes looked impressive, in area covered if not in total population served, and it had attracted the attention of Lewis B. (Bud) Maytag, owner of a well-known refrigerator manufacturing corporation, and who became the major stockholder. Then, in March 1962, in a corporate switch, Maytag moved to take over the National Airlines trunk airline, while its president, Lew Dymond, came to Frontier, which the Goldfield Corporation of San Francisco had bought from Maytag. He took over some of Continental Airlines's routes and, by May 1964, was operating Allison-powered Convair 580 turboprop conversions of the Convair 340. He also ordered five Boeing 727 tri-jets, an aircraft hardly suited to serve places like Farmington, which by now had lost its elevated hub status. Billings, Montana, or Rapid City looked good on the map, but were hardly generators of 727-scale traffic. Nevertheless, on 30 September 1966, Frontier introduced the Boeing 727 and, on 13 June 1967, started nonstop Boeing 727 services from Denver to Kansas City and St. Louis. This challenged the incumbent trunk airline, T.W.A., and predictably met with stern opposition from this incumbent, which added multiple frequencies to put the precocious newcomer in its place—a warning that entering the jet arena could be a risky business.

Meanwhile, however, Dymond's expansionist ambitions took another tack. On 1 October 1967, Frontier acquired **Central Airlines**, one of the smaller Local Service companies, serving mainly the states of Oklahoma and Kansas, and adding Dallas and Fort Worth to his empire. Central had, after Lamar Muse took over as president in May 1965, joined the ranks of turbine-engined operators by adding Rolls-Royce Dart-engined Convair 600s in December of that year. Also, on 1 March 1968, with larger 727-200s, Frontier started nonstop Denver-Las Vegas service,

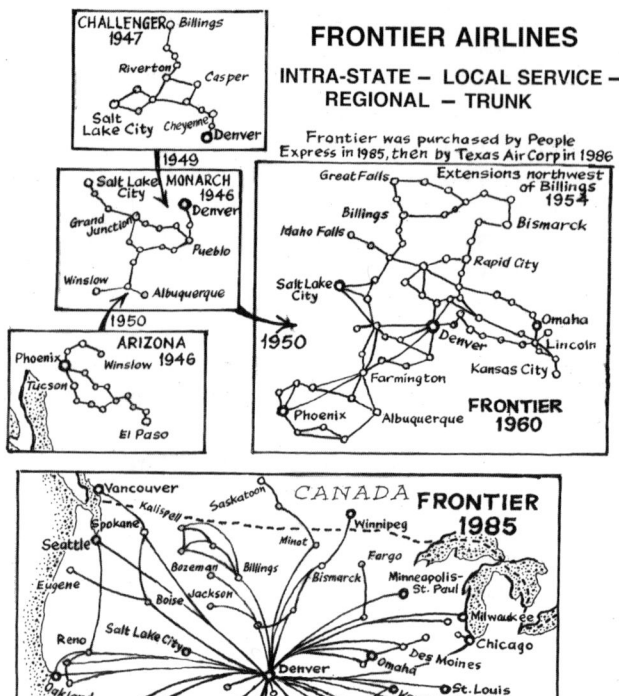

Frontier Airlines was representative of the changing fortunes of the small U.S. airlines that comprised the secondary levels of the route networks. After the Second World War, they served small communities, where road travel was often an adventure. They progressed to serve larger cities, and even to cross frontiers.

thus reaching toward the west coast, and had exchanged the 727s for the smaller twin-engined Boeing 737s in July 1969. The route expansion continued, and reached across the 49th Parallel on 1 July 1974 to serve Winnipeg, in Canada's Manitoba. Then, after the Airline Deregulation Act of October 1978 opened up the floodgates, Frontier moved into several cities on Mexico's Pacific coast and added Vancouver as another Canadian destination. By January 1979, Dymond had almost reached his ambition of becoming a coast-to-coast airline, by offering scheduled service from California's Burbank (serving the Los Angeles metropolis) to Atlanta, Delta's hub in the southeast. Frontier's ultimate destiny is reviewed later, in Chapter 24 ("People Express" and "Revival of an Old Name" sections).

The Mouse That Roared

The Local Service airlines had thrived as long as they were receiving a generous subsidy for serving scores of small communities throughout the United States, and where surface journeys by road or rail were long and arduous, or both. But when in the 1960s the interstate highway network grew by thousands of miles a year, the small towns became less isolated. Direct multi-lane superhighways permitted former all-day trips to be completed in a couple of hours. This eroded much of the need for air mail and cut into the passenger demand for local airline journeys. The days of flying in shaky and draughty old DC-3s, in preference to bumpy rides in beat-up old Chevrolets, or even new ones, were experiences of the past. Some Local Service airlines sought salvation by amalgamating into larger entities, and even challenging the trunk airlines for inter-city traffic. One such airline was **Trans-Texas Airways (T.T.A.)**.

Like all the Locals, it had small beginnings. Founded by Earl McKaughan as Aviation Enterprises in 1940 as little more than a dealership, it was incorporated on 14 November 1944. After being granted a certificate from the C.A.B., it started service to connect small towns to the big Texas cities on 11 October 1947, having changed its name to T.T.A. on 21 June of that year. With the inevitable fleet of DC-3s, it expanded rapidly all across Texas and into neighboring states, and acquired Convair 340s in 1961. These were converted to Rolls-Royce Dart-engined Convair 600 turboprops, which started service on 1 March 1966, and things moved quickly thereafter.

On 17 August 1966, the C.A.B. awarded T.T.A. a route to Vera Cruz, Mexico via Monterrey and Tampico, and shortly afterward the airline marked its international status by starting jet services on 30 October, with Douglas DC-9-10s. These were called "Pamper Jets"—no doubt an effort to erase the popular "Tinker Toy Airways" appendage that had been applied to the DC-3 flights. Such a detracting image was more than removed when the airline was acquired by Minnesota Enterprises in 1968, which disposed of the old tail-sitters, added the larger DC-9-30s, and on 1 April 1969 changed the airline name to **Texas International Airlines (T.X.I.)**. With the jet equipment, the airline began to expand beyond the frontiers of its home state. Nonstop services started from Dallas or Houston or both to Denver on 1 March 1969, to Los Angeles via Albuquerque on 15 January 1970, and to Salt Lake City via Denver on 1 March 1970. The Dallas-Houston-San Antonio "Texas Triangle" was consolidated. At the other end of the airliner capacity spectrum, to maintain a minimum of service to the many small Texas cities in the network, 15-seat Beech 99s were introduced. These were replaced by Swearingen Metros in July 1971, but by now, the image of Local Service was fading fast, especially as inter-state highways were completed all over the largest of the 48 States.

In spite of the change of name and the introduction of the DC-9s, the airline was not doing well financially. In January 1971, its major lender, the Chase Manhattan Bank, alarmed at the mounting losses—$12 million in two years—retained a firm of consultants, the Jet Capital Corporation. This was a partnership between two 31-year-old Harvard Business School graduates, Frank Lorenzo and Robert Carney. Within a few months, they had assessed the situation, drawn upon their financial skills and acumen, and set out to do more than consult; they proceeded to take over the airline.

On 7 June 1971, Jet Capital initiated a refinancing program that included its own investment in T.X.I. to the tune of $1.5 million. On 10 August 1972, the C.A.B. approved the acquisition of T.X.I. by Jet Capital, with Lorenzo and Carney exercising 59% voting control. This was not without risk. By this time, the aggregate losses during the past three years were more than $20 million, the working capital deficit was $18 million, and the net worth was –$7 million. Frank Lorenzo was appointed president, replacing Lloyd Lane, who had resigned in May, and amid much concern and consternation in airline circles, and even on Wall Street, he set about rescuing an airline that had seemed destined for self-destruction. But during the next few years, this hitherto unknown executive, who had gained airline experience only at middle management level with T.W.A. and a Canadian regional airline, set about his task with almost ruthless determination. He had no time for sentiment, for example, for the need to serve small communities that had earlier been the foundation of the Trans-Texas network. He concentrated on the main routes between the big cities, drawing upon the simple demographic principles of providing air service where it was most needed by the most people. By 1976, T.X.I. was able to announce a profit for the year of $3.2 million.

This was an astonishing turnaround. It provided Lorenzo with the financial flexibility to move further forward. His investment into Texas had been a risk, but a well-calculated one. He was a superb manipulator of money, and an astute calculator. He shrewdly applied these skills to an analysis of the T.X.I. operations, recognizing that load factors (the percentage of seats filled) were all-important. High fares were not major revenue-producers if there were too many empty seats. So, in 1977, to the astonishment of the orthodox airline world, accompanied by much skepticism, he introduced "Peanut Fares." These could be bought on certain routes on a limited basis—almost equivalent to stand-bys. The theory was that if bookings on flights still left many seats empty, it was better to sell these cheaply than not to sell them at all. The yield per flight increased, even though the average yield per seat decreased. If the other airlines or the C.A.B. objected, they were mute. Airline deregulation was on the horizon, and soon there would no longer be endless litigation in Washington.

Lorenzo and his Peanut Fares were the pioneers in the U.S. scheduled airline industry of what later became known as deep-discount fares. Late in July 1978, and to the further astonishment of the airline community, he moved to take over National Airlines. This was a case of a second-level regional trying to rise above its status by acquiring a first-level airline. This was regarded as a sign of conceit and little short of arrogance. But the critics underestimated Lorenzo. Already owning 9.2% of National's stock, he wanted 25%, and this alarmed the C.A.B., whose controlling influence, with airline deregulation just around the corner, was waning. (President Carter signed the Act on 24 October.) National's chairman, L.B. (Bud) Maytag, sought the backing of other investors to fend off the threat, but his employees had become disenchanted with the chronic industrial relations problems and published a newsletter, addressing Lorenzo with the offer "Take us, we're yours!" The outcome of the financial sparring was that T.X.I. paid $14.4 million for 20% of National stock, which immediately soared in value. The *Wall Street Journal* noted that this was the first case in regulated airline history in which a certificated airline sought approval of a non-negotiated acquisition of control of another certificated airline. The situation was almost bizarre. **Pan American Airways** had coveted control over National, to link its huge intercontinental network with a transcontinental system, hitherto denied it by the C.A.B. Now, seizing what it perceived as an opportunity, it negotiated to buy National for $350 million, and purchased Lorenzo's T.X.I. shares for $108 million, leaving the latter with $46 million clear profit. It was a textbook case of how a financial specialist could take advantage of a situation that was oversubscribed with sentiment and impulse.

During the next two or three years, the Texas company took full advantage of the liberalization of route control, as the Washington bureaucracy was almost powerless, after deregulation, to deny either the addition or denial of any route segment or air service in the United States. Almost a dozen small communities in Texas and adjacent states lost service, but in their place, Lorenzo added an equal number of other, much larger cities, much further afield. The airline map featured routes, mostly nonstop from Houston and Dallas, as far as St. Louis, Kansas City, and Baltimore, and including a nonstop schedule from Dallas to Los Angeles. The airline's Mexican market was augmented with service to Guadalajara, Mérida, Cozumel, and Cancun. By 1981, its colors were to be seen as far north as Minneapolis, Milwaukee, and Hartford.

On 8 August 1980, to cope with this extensive expansion, T.X.I. purchased twenty 115-seat Douglas DC-9s from Swissair and simultaneously requested the C.A.B.'s permission (though declining in influence, the Board still had some control over major issues) to enter the New York-Washington Air Shuttle market. Lorenzo had always believed in the multiplier theory that the extra traffic generated by the low fares more than compensated for the lower yield per seat. And so, in October 1980, he formed **New York Air**, whose Big Apple insignia on its DC-9s appeared in this high-frequency market on 19 December.

Lorenzo was on the crest of a wave. Just after the tenth anniversary of Lorenzo and Carney's Jet Capital takeover of that maligned little regional airline, T.X.I. began some intense negotiations. Remarkably similar to its participation in the National Airlines affair, it had, by the end of 1980, acquired 4.24% of the stock of another trunk airline, **Continental Airlines**. The airline was ailing. Before deregulation, it had prospered because of its excellent reputation for good service and aggressive promotion. Under Bob Six's popular leadership, it had made consistent profits for decades, but now its competitors had caught up with its high standards, and its staff, through their length of service, were highly paid. It was beginning to lose money, yet almost defiantly (and it was not alone in its spendthrift ways), it expanded its route network considerably in 1981. A net loss of more than $20 million in 1980 rose to $60 million in 1981. Continental Airlines was nakedly vulnerable.

Lorenzo had been increasing his Continental shareholdings and by the fall of 1981, he was in effective control. Although

New York Airways identified its marketing base with its "Big Apple" insignia. (Davies)

many of Robert Six's "old guard" resisted the inevitable, the end came when, with 50.8% of the stock, Lorenzo and T.X.I. took over on 25 November. On 13 July 1982, the stockholders of both companies approved the merger. The operational starting date of the merged airline was 31 October and, from that day, the Texas name disappeared, except in the newly formed Texas Air Corporation, which was the holding company for all Frank Lorenzo's interests. To adopt the Continental name was a shrewd decision, replacing a regional identity with a national one, and at the same time applying some balm to the hurt pride of the acquired staff.

The next event in Lorenzo's headlong business career, however, was not so smooth. Like most in the industry, Continental was losing money heavily. It identified high wages and salaries, especially those of the pilots, represented by their union (ALPA), as a prime source of cost savings. On 14 September 1983, an offer was made to all employees: 35% of the airline's shareholding in exchange for equivalent measures to ensure higher productivity. The pilots procrastinated, and at 6 PM on Saturday, 24 September, Frank Lorenzo closed down the airline under Chapter Eleven of the U.S. Federal Bankruptcy Code. Operations resumed on the following Tuesday, 27 September.

The route network was a shadow of its former self. Most of the medium-range routes were eliminated, along with some major points such as Dallas and Detroit. Staff was slashed from 12,000 to 4,000. Such drastic measures resulted in claims and counterclaims by the opposing factions, but on 17 January 1984, Federal Bankruptcy Court Judge R.F. Wheless, Jr., ruled in Continental Airlines' favor, recognizing its financial distress and that without the Chapter 11 procedure, the results would have been worse. The judge gave the airline "an opportunity to catch its financial breath," while Lorenzo observed that there was "no Chapter 5½."

Before the Chapter 11 filing in September 1983, Continental was losing about $20 million a month. For the second quarter of 1984, its operating profit was $27 million. The litigation had been a landmark in the history of employer–employee relations.

Chapter 19: Regional Airlines Worldwide

A Developing Requirement

The transition in the United States of the Local Service airlines, first into Regional then into the equivalent of Trunk airline status, was the world's prime case of inevitable growth as the Jet Age energized the air transport industry to new heights. Expansion was not confined to the contiguous 48 States. Throughout airline history, there has been a continuous and seemingly almost inevitable pattern of large airlines consuming small ones or, by mergers, creating dominating companies—a process that is common in other industries, the big fish swallowing the minnows. In the modern world of the 20th century, the enormous infrastructure and equipment needed to run an airline, even a small one, required considerable investment. But after the introduction of the more economical jet airliners, such was the momentum of air traffic growth in the 1960s and onward that the sheer demand stimulated unprecedented airline expansion at all levels. And this included those companies whose relative status could be described as the Second Level. Chapter 18 dealt with the outstanding example of the importance of this airline category providing a complementary service to the industry leaders. But the United States was not alone in recognizing the need for such diversification.

For any country to enjoy the luxury of such organized divisions of airline service, it had to be, by geographical necessity, big. The U.S.A. led the world because of its combined size, population, and wealth, but other countries also cherished similar aspirations. Other factors were involved. Even if a country was marginally big enough for a regional airline to take its place as a feeder to the national flag carrier, a good surface transport system sometimes obviated the need. This was especially true in Europe, where the railroad system prevailed, and in India, whose excellent railroads were quite adequate for regional needs, and the national airline also provided regional services.

In the largest country of the world, the Soviet Union, a single state airline, Aeroflot, held a complete monopoly of airline service, at all levels; but a regional system evolved from practical operational necessity within its organization (see below). In China, the world's most populous country, the Jet Age, with all its advantages, was slow to arrive, as the so-called Cultural Revolution that followed the establishment of the People's Republic, combined with the departure of the thousands of Russian technical teams, had left the country in a desperate state by the 1960s. It had, by a Mao Tse-tung decree, undertaken a massive railroad construction program, with the objective or providing adequate rail service from every province of the land to the major cities, especially the capital, Beijing (formerly Peking). But the state airline was little more than a service for Chinese officialdom. Some large countries, however, from their inherent demographic foundations, have been able to sustain regional airlines to complement the national ones.

Second Level in Brazil

Occupying half of the South American continent and slightly bigger than the contiguous 48 States of the U.S.A., Brazil's development into an industrial and commercial power was not fully realized until after the Second World War. But its surface communications were fragmented. Roads were confined to the hinterlands of the large cities, and at least 40 different railroad companies, each with its local catchment area, with no integration with each other, could not be described as a system. The peoples of each region were almost alien to those of the other regions. They were held together mainly by the common Portuguese language, the inheritance of the former colonists, and by their devotion to the national sport, association football, in which Brazil was quite regularly the world champion. The inadequacy of comprehensive surface transport on a national scale provided an ideal environment for a flourishing airline industry, and indeed, Brazil has, since the late 1920s, been one of the most air-minded nations in the world.

The latent potential of natural and creative resources of this vast land were given new impetus in the late 1950s, when President Kubitschek made his dramatic announcement: "I will awaken the Sleeping Giant," and proceeded to match his words with deeds. The most effective of these was to rejuvenate an idea that had been only hinted at, in some atlases for many decades, as the future site of a Federal Capital. It was located in the central heart of hitherto undeveloped land to emphasize to all Brazilians that the country's wealth lay in the interior. As 90% of Canada's population was within about two hours drive from the U.S. border, the same percentage of Brazilians lived only two hours from the Atlantic Ocean.

When the Jet Age arrived, Brazil's air transport was in good shape, with VARIG as its respected flag carrier and São Paulo's VASP and Rio's Cruzeiro do Sul as strong domestic airlines, providing efficient service between all the main cities and to all the provincial towns. Of the smaller domestic airlines at the second level, Omar Fontana's Transbrasil had survived the process of "survival of the fittest," and on 22 May 1975, VARIG had acquired Cruzeiro do Sul, which continued to operate it as a separate entity. They had all profited from the incentives to air transport and travel as Kubitschek's dream of a Federal Capital emerged. With astonishing drive and initiative, the planning and construction of the city of Brasília was accomplished with phenomenal success. Among other domestic immigrants, tens of thousands of civil servants moved in from Rio de Janeiro.

In 1958, such was the volume of traffic between São Paulo and Rio de Janeiro that the world's first air shuttle service was introduced on 6 July 1959. The city of São Paulo, growing to become one of the world's largest metropolitan areas, was emerging as an industrial powerhouse, with German and French car manufacturers moving in to establish large production lines. Thanks to Kubitschek's vision, Brazil had arrived.

By the 1960s, Brazilians were becoming car-minded as well as air-minded, as the industrial momentum included the development of the transport infrastructure. The railroads, with their multiple ownerships and different gauges, was not in the wake-up program. The interior of Brazil was instead opened up, with ambitious interstate highways, which, within a few years, connected all the big cities, and even penetrated the Amazonian jungles to reach Manaus. In the 1950s, it had still been an isolated and dilapidated city that had seen better days, with distant memories of the rubber boom of the early years of the century. By the 1970s, it was speedily recuperating to become a commercial and industrial center.

This nationwide decentralization had a profound effect on the course of development of the airlines; rather as an echo of the experience of the Local Service/Regional airlines in the United States, the development of good roads eliminated many of the travel markets that had hitherto been the exclusive domain of the trunk airlines of Brazil. They had done well as long as the veteran Douglas DC-3s had been in good supply in the post-war years, and they had sustained service with the twin-engined turboprops. But the multiplicity of small communities throughout the country demanded a replacement aircraft that was ideally suited in size for an equal multiplicity of individual routes, and even the HS-748s, F-27s, Heralds, and YS-11s were too large for this type of demand.

On 27 November 1961, with great foresight, the Department of Civil Aviation convened a 12-day conference at the resort city of Petrópolis, to discuss a rationalization of the Brazilian airlines, as the industrialization of the country gained momentum, and Kubitschek's policy to develop the interior of Brazil began to take shape as productive lands were opened up in the interior. Savannah territory was developed for agriculture, jungles were cleared for farming, mineral wealth was exploited in hitherto undiscovered areas, and they all needed to be served by air routes to the big cities. The problem was how to pay for a vast investment in air transport, and this involved the question of government support (i.e., subsidy).

This had led to the creation, on 15 October 1963, of the Rede de Integração Nacional (RIN), which was broadly comparable to the Local Service Airline policy of the United States, aimed to provide a social service, as well as a market-driven service, to all the populated communities of Brazil. The difference was that the services were provided by the existing airlines, operating under strict surveillance by the Department of Civil Aviation to ensure that the proper levels of fares were appropriately allocated so that the subsidy grants were not abused.

At the higher levels of Brazilian air transport, where modern jets reinforced the inter-city traffic demands, including the expansion of the acclaimed shuttle services to Belo Horizonte and Brasília. At the lower levels as the veteran DC-3s wore out, mainly through sheer old age, the turboprop generation could not quite do the same job. They were not only larger than the DC-3, at a time when the fragmentation of Brazil's expanding population required a smaller airplane, but they required better fields than the dirt strips in which the old Gooney Bird felt at home. The Canadian DHC-6 Twin Otter would have been ideal for the purpose, but the Brazilians found their own solution.

Brazilian Third Level and an Aircraft Industry

The industrialization of Brazil led to the foundation of an aircraft manufacturing industry. Brazil itself was inspired to produce an aircraft that not only helped to stimulate the creation of a new segment of the airline hierarchy, but whose quality and suitability to the specialized markets of the third level would gain worldwide recognition and a global clientele. The success of this courageous enterprise would eventually, by technical skill, good marketing, and visionary foresight, lead to Brazil achieving the status of one of the world's commercial airliner manufacturing countries. In parallel with and contributing to this success was the establishment of the Brazilian Regionals.

During the 1950s and 1960s, Brazilian aeronautical engineers had honed their skills and unveiled a small eight-seat turboprop design, the IPD-6505, intended for the use of the Força Aérea Brasileira, whose mission in life included much admirable quasi-civil flying as well as military objectives. The potential of this efficient little airplane was quickly realized, and the Brazilian government provided the initiative to generate the necessary capital to create a manufacturing production line. On 19 August 1969, at São José dos Campos, about 75 miles east of São Paulo, the Empresa Brasileira de Aeronáutica (Embraer) was founded as a joint stock company, with the government holding 51%, to produce the airplane in quantity. This small beginning was eventually to promote Brazil into the hierarchy of commercial aircraft suppliers to the whole world. Embraer's designers and engineers quickly recognized that the IPD-6505 needed to be larger. The redesigned EMB 110 Bandeirante was the result. It made its first flight on 9 August 1972, and the first commercial version, the 110C, went into service with **Transbrasil** on 16 April 1973, soon followed by **VASP** on 4 November, for service to smaller communities in the southern states of Brazil.

On 12 November 1975, another classification of airline was established, the Sistema Integrado de Transportes Aéreos Regional, to complement the domestic trunk and secondary routes. It was, in a direct echo of the U.S. system, a third level of commercial airline operations, but in Brazil's case, a neat formula was devised to provide financial support for routes that were unlikely to be self-supporting. A subsidy came from a special fund, financed by a surcharge on all the tickets sold on the mainline and secondary routes, and distributed according to load factor—effectively a payment for empty seats, but an encouragement for the airlines to promote airline service where it was vital to aid the new pioneers of the Brazilian outback. To encourage integration with the main routes, each new airline would own up to a third of the shareholding of the new airlines created to meet the need.

The country was divided into five regions: the Amazon Basin, the Tocantins-Araguaia Basin, the São Francisco Basin, the West Central Region, and the South Central Region. Six weeks later, the first new airline was in business (it was already

Regional Airlines Worldwide

The EMB 110 (Bandeirante in the 110P version) became a popular 18-seat mini-airliner worldwide, from Alaska to New Zealand. This was one of the first, delivered to TransBrasil in 1973. (Davies)

Nordeste was one of the small airlines in Brazil for which the "Bandit" (as the EMB 110 was affectionately called) was the ideal size.

operating before the new legislation), appropriately in the Amazon Basin, where the need was greatest; but within a year, all five regions had their own airline. By 1977, the five third level companies were serving 121 towns throughout Brazil's 26 states and territories, and operating 60 aircraft, more than half of which were the Bandeirantes, an 18-seat version, the Embraer 110P. It was an impressive achievement. The "Bandits," as the Bandeirantes became known—as an indication of affection and respect when they went into service in overseas markets—served to consolidate and unify Brazil. It has been a brilliant example of how aeronautical technology can contribute to the basic economy of a whole nation. In the production of commercial aircraft, Brazil was to become an exporter, not an importer, and a positive element in the annual balance-of-trade reports. By the early 2000s, Embraer had built 494 Bandeirantes, together with 350 of the 30-seat EMB 120 Brasilias, and had moved on from turboprops to pure jets with the ERJ 145 family of regional jets.

Regional Solutions in the Soviet Union

In the largest country in the world, the Soviet Union, the mere idea of establishing local airlines was anathema to the political creed of communist central control. Nevertheless, even under the communist system, the urge to preserve local identities was still strong in the 1960s and 1970s, and geographical distances presented a practical problem. The Soviet Union stretched over 11 time zones—almost half-way round the world—and communities that were several thousand miles from Moscow felt that they should manage their own local affairs.

The state airline, **Aeroflot**, was charged with overseeing every aspect of non-military air operations, and it acted as the Transport Command for the armed forces also. It was about three times as big as the largest airline in the western world, and operating about 10,000 airliners of various sizes. Among these were about 3,000 versatile Antonov An-2 12-seat biplanes, supplemented by on-going deliveries of 48-seat Antonov An-24 and Czech-built 19-seat Let L410 turboprops, plus 32-seat Yakovlev Yak-40 mini-tri-jets: hundreds of each type.

These were deployed all across the Soviet Union, allocated to Regional Sub-Divisions, according to local requirements. The distribution ranged from the An-24s in the more populous regions of European Russia and the Ukraine to various small types, including jets, in the more sparsely populated areas beyond the Ural Mountains into the far reaches of Siberia, where distances tended to be longer and traffic far less. At the bottom of the scale of demand, the versatile An-2s, which could land on or take off from any grass field. Hundreds of helicopters, mainly the Mil Mi-8, performed vital services where no fixed-wing aircraft would dare to go. The services with old biplanes dropping into farmlands seemed to be defying obsolescence, and were a curious contrast to the modern jets that flew into the regional centers. In the more remote communities of the Siberian east, especially in Yakutia and Chukotka, where the melting permafrost customarily turns airfields into quagmires, any aircraft other that the little Antonov An-2 *Kolkholsnik* biplane would come to grief. And in the northern reaches along the hinterland of the Arctic Ocean coast, people in isolated villages, with no roads within a hundred miles, went shopping in the Mil helicopters to the nearest towns. The system worked very well, partly because there never seemed to be a shortage of aircraft, or of pilots to fly them. A 160-seat Ilyushin Il-62 could arrive at the main airports at Khabarovsk or Yakutsk, and passengers would take a short bus ride to the nearby regional airport to change to one of the smaller airplanes. A Moscovite could leave home in the morning, fly nonstop to the east, partly through the night because of the time zones, and visit a relative somewhere in the far east the next morning.

The vast extent of Aeroflot's service to the Soviet Union is illustrated in the map, which delineates the 32 individual regional subdivisions of Aeroflot. Their dedication in providing air service to every remote corner of the country (an interesting

This was a typical scene in the vast reaches of Siberia. One of Aeroflot's Antonov An-2 is pictured here at Novo Kurovka, a small village north of Khabarovsk. (Davies)

Wide-bodied "Jumbo" jets needed mile-long runways and extensive airport buildings and installations. Some parts of the world were not yet at that level. In the 1980s, this was still a typical scene in Russia's far east (at Nikolayevsk-na-Amuri). (Davies)

comparison with the objective set for the Local Service airlines in the United States) enabled the airline to claim that it served up to 4,000 individual destinations. From the Baltic Sea to the Pacific Ocean, the achievement was unique, and will never be emulated.

China Starts from Scratch

In the most populous country in the world, China's government has been communist since the revolution of 1948 and the establishment of the People's Republic of China (P.R.C.) on 1 October 1949. The creation of a national airline for the P.R.C. had a checkered history. When the Second World War ended in 1944, the German-sponsored Eurasia ceased operations, and the Kuomintang-backed China National Aviation Company (C.N.A.C.), originally controlled by Pan American Airways, was evacuated to Taiwan in 1949, along with the defeated Kuomintang government. Most of its fleet, however, was left in the then-British Hong Kong, and in a remarkable episode, a dozen aircraft, mostly C-47s and C-46s, were flown out to the mainland by Chinese pilots who decided to remain with the communists. Premier Chou En-lai welcomed them in Peking, and the lone Convair 240, named *Beijing*, became the flagship of the line that had been formed on 2 November 1949, the **China Civil Aviation Administration (C.C.A.A.)**, with a mixed collection of ex-military types.

With Soviet help, another airline was formed on 27 March 1950. Known as **SKOGA**, the acronym for the Russian name (translated as the Sino-Soviet Joint Stock Company), it had taken over the wartime Hamiata on 27 March 1950, was heavily backed by the Soviet Union, and received technical support, equipment, and even personnel from that source. It took over the routes of the former Japanese airline in Manchuria and provided connections to Soviet cities in Siberia. In March 1954, the two airlines merged under the jurisdiction of the China Civil Aviation Bureau, and its Chinese name was transliterated as **Minhaiduy**. With its fleet reinforced by a large number of Russian airliners, mostly Lisunov Li-2s (the license-built DC-3s), it consolidated the main inter-city routes in China, and added more cross-border routes to North Korea, to Vietnam, and, on 11 April 1956, to Rangoon, Burma, the first sortie into non-communist territory, during a period when the political policy with the West was strictly isolationist.

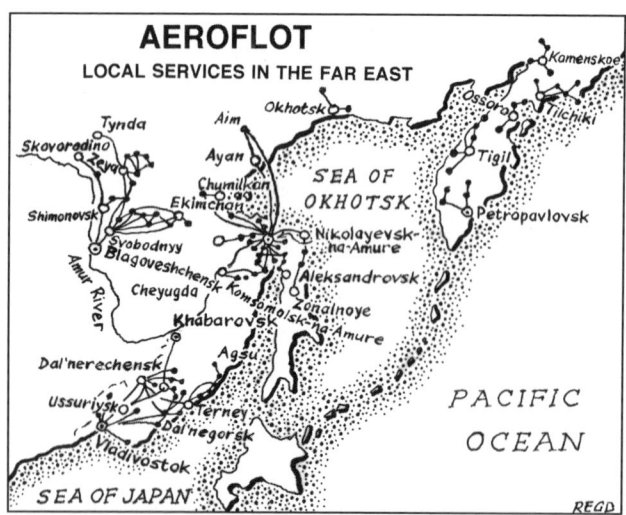

While Aeroflot was developing overseas routes with its Ilyushin Il-62s, it did not neglect social services at the lower levels of the market. This map details the small hub networks flown by Antonov An-2 in the far east.

The full development of a substantial Chinese airline of any kind, much less any thoughts of regional companies, was impeded by several factors. First was the isolationism, which confined the availability of aircraft to Soviet sources, and though initially promising, this was cut off in the early 1960s when the rift with Moscow terminated all Soviet support. This included thousands of technicians who were teaching the Chinese how to build military jet airplanes, and how to fly them. Fortunately, they were good students, and when the Russians left, they had acquired enough technological expertise to build their own aircraft. Even so, this did not extend to the special requirements for civil airliner construction, and China moved into a new era of technology by ordering, in 1961, six British Vickers Viscount 800-series Viscount turboprops. These supplemented the Ilyushin Il-18s, Antonov An-24s, and other Russian types that comprised the fleet.

The second reason for the pedestrian rate of progress of China's national airline was the relative lack of support from the highest government levels. Chairman Mao had perceptively realized that the primitive standards of transport in China was a reason for its former fragmentation into areas that had been de facto semi-autonomous, either controlled, in the 19th and early 20th centuries by colonial powers, and latterly by squabbling warlords, of whom he regarded Chiang Kai-shek, the Kuomintang leader, as one. In the 1950s, there were few roads, and the railways were still fragmented into individual lines. This lack of transport communication with the capital was a severe handicap in controlling the country. Top priority was therefore given to the construction of a national railroad system, connecting every provincial capital with each other and with Beijing (the new name for Peking). In an amazing program of engineering, this ambitious objective was achieved, even in the mountainous areas of western China, within three decades. Only Lhasa, 12,000 feet above sea level, in remote Tibet, remained unconnected by rail to the rest of China; that formidable target of construction was achieved in 2006, with trains that, like aircraft, needed oxygen for the passengers over the high mountains.

The significance of the railroads was shrewdly foreseen as the only way in which the Chinese people as a whole could respond to the sense of nationalism that was to be an essential part of their lives. The majority of the population was peasants, most of them living at subsistence levels. Famine and floods had been their heritage; few had traveled more than a few miles from where they were born. Only in the few big cities was there a potential middle class, mainly bureaucrats. Cheap rail travel, therefore, took priority over airline travel, which was expensive to organize and operate for a public that was not yet ready for it, either socially or financially.

In the 1960s, the isolationism began to diminish, and cautious steps were taken to improve relations with the capitalist West. The Chinese realized that in America and Europe, technological progress was advancing at a brisk pace, whereas theirs was at a standstill, because of new policies, such as the misnamed "Cultural Revolution," which had destroyed much of the inherent inventiveness, craftsmanship, and initiatives of science and technology. In April 1962, the Civil Aviation Bureau became the **Civil Aviation Administration of China (C.A.A.C.)**, continuing as a state monopoly.

In the field of commercial air transport, however, China had a long way to go. Handicapped by an aging aircraft fleet, except for the Viscounts and Il-18s, it was also penalized by the isolationism that had prevented any commercial exchanges with other countries, or the knowledge of even elementary business practices or operational procedures. The combined intelligence of a whole nation had been suppressed, sometimes ruthlessly, unlike that in the Soviet Union, where it had been diverted into different channels. Many years were to pass, therefore, before those responsible for running C.A.A.C. could adapt themselves to the essential elements of airline operational and accounting efficiency.

Thus, while China's airline flag carrier was trying to rise from the ashes of almost self-destruction, the idea of any regional identity within the country was out of the question. Several decades were to pass, and a technical and political revolution of considerable magnitude was to erupt, before the most populous country on the globe would emerge in the 21st century, with an economic miracle. This would match, and in some aspects surpass, that of Japan which, in the 1960s, was sweeping the world while China was just getting back on its feet. Regional airlines would not be possible for many more years. (See Chapter 33.)

Canadian Regionals

The second largest country in the world might have been expected to have been a natural foundation for the initiation and development of regional airlines. But in an important respect it was far different from its neighbor to the south. Its total population was only about one-tenth of that of the United States (or about the same as California's), and 90% of that was within 100 miles of the U.S. border. Traditionally served by two excellent transcontinental railroads, Canada did not even have a national trunk airline until Trans Canada Air Lines (T.C.A.) was founded in 1937—by Canadian National Railways, the government-supported railroad. Until then, all the airlines of Canada had been, by definition, regional, but realistically, mainly local or what could be termed third level.

Because of the distribution of population, relatively sparse except in areas near the United States, these were little more than "bush" operators, or served as feeder routes to the transcontinental trunk railroads and, later, the national airline. The fragmented individuality was rationalized in 1942 when they were amalgamated to become Canadian Pacific Airlines (C.P.A.), owned by the railroad of that name, which had purchased control of Canadian Airways in 1933.

Thus, for many years, even after the end of the Second World War, and in contrast with the United States, the spirit of private enterprise in forming regional airlines was not prominent. A regional airline could not be commercially viable, partly because the population distribution did not permit economic operations, and the two railroads, one state-controlled, the other owned by a transport conglomerate, had other priorities. Consequently, even as late as 1947, only four small airlines in Canada were offering scheduled passenger services. These four, together with a later additional company, were the foundation of a Canadian regional airline system.

On 20 October 1947, the Minister of Transport, J.W. Pickersgill, outlined a policy for the establishment of regional airlines with clearly defined roles that elevated their previous activities as semi-charter companies. They had offered little more than on-demand service to the isolated communities in the Canadian outback, or support for the military demands of the defensive DEW Line outposts in the Arctic north. Additional guidelines were issued by his successor, Donald Jamieson, in August 1969. These designated the specific areas of operation for the five certificated airlines, ensuring that they did not compete on the trunk

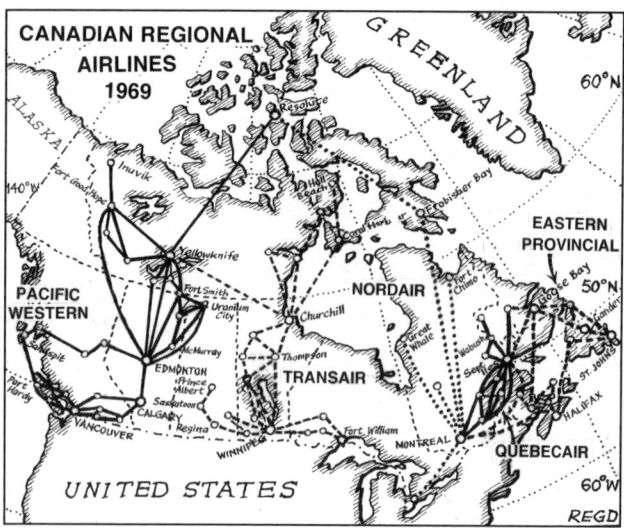

Canada's regional airlines served as feeders to and from the transcontinental flag carriers.

routes of the two national airlines, but giving access to a major metropolitan area to each of the four. The five Canadian regionals were thus created with ministerial blessing.

Pride of ancestry among the privileged five must go to **Eastern Provincial Airways (E.P.A.)**, which could claim a history back to 1941, when Maritime Central Airways was founded to serve the maritime provinces of New Brunswick, Nova Scotia, and Prince Edward Island. These were somewhat detached geographically from the main centers of population in Quebec and Ontario. E.P.A. itself was founded in 1949 in Newfoundland and began scheduled services in 1961 to link St John's, Newfoundland's capital, with the important trans-Atlantic airports at Gander and Labrador's Goose Bay; Halifax, Nova Scotia; and its designated metropolis, Montreal. It progressed steadily, adding turboprop Dart Heralds to its fleet of Douglas DC-3s and assorted de Havilland Canada single-engined bush types in January 1963. Then, in June 1969, it became a jet airline, with services linking the main cities in its network with Montreal with its first Boeing 737-200, leased from United Air Lines.

Another airline in Canada's far east was **Quebecair.** Originally founded in 1946 as Rimouski Aviation Syndicate, and renamed Rimouski Airlines the following year, it provided a much-needed air service to link communities along both sides of the St. Lawrence River downstream from Montreal. It started scheduled services in 1965, when it acquired its new name, having merged with Gulf Aviation in 1953. Subsequently it took over a number of smaller operators in the area and introduced Fairchild F-27s in October 1958, and BAC One-Eleven jets in February 1969.

Also based in Montreal, **Nordair** was formed by the merger of Boreal Airways and Mont Laurier Aviation in 1957, and scheduled services started to Frobisher, on Baffin Island. In December 1968, it put Boeing 737-200 jets, also leased from United, into service and became the first airline to operate jets into Canada's far north. Based in Montreal, and with a route to the Maritime Provinces, its role was primarily as a supply line to isolated outposts, for which it became specialized and, therefore did not carry a substantial volume of commercial traffic.

Further to the west, Great Northern Airways, formed in Winnipeg in 1947, started local scheduled service in 1951 and changed its name to **Transair** in 1956 when it merged with Arctic Wings. Its DEW Line work took it as far north as Churchill, on Hudson Bay, and Resolute, on Cornwallis Island, and it was able to upgrade its piston-engined fleet to turboprop Hawker-Siddeley 748s and Nihon YS-11s, but the population it served in the prairie states of Canada was not sufficient to justify jet airliner service. It also connected with Fort William (now Thunder Bay) on Lake Superior, the port for the export of Canada's wheat from the prairies.

Across the Rocky Mountains and based in Vancouver, Canada's third largest city, **Pacific Western Airlines (P.W.A.)** was the largest of the recognized Canadian regionals. Founded in 1946 as Central British Columbia Airways, it changed its name in 1953, having absorbed several small companion bush operators, and two years later acquired Queen Charlotte Airlines, which was already carrying passengers to the islands of that name. In 1957 and 1959, in a far-reaching decision, the Air Transport Board transferred some of Canadian Pacific Airlines's western network to Pacific Western, and these included routes to the important cities of Calgary and Edmonton. These are the only Canadian cities more than 100 miles north of the 49th parallel, and at the time they were benefitting from the rapidly growing Alberta oil and gas industry. By the mid-1960s, P.W.A. was carrying more passengers than all the other Canadian regional airlines combined. In March 1967, it bought three Convair 640 turboprops and, in December 1968, followed this with three Boeing 737s. Alone among the regionals, it also diversified its activities into the international charter market, and acquired two Boeing 707-138Bs in November 1967. As will be seen in Chapter 40, Pacific Western was poised for greater expansion in future years.

Airlines for an Island Nation

If ever a country was ready-made for the development of regional air services, it was the multi-island nation of Indonesia, formerly the Dutch East Indies. In land area it ranks only 14th in the world, but much of its area is on three islands: Borneo, Sumatra, and half of New Guinea—all are among the world's six largest. More important, Indonesia's population, even in the 1960s, was some 150 million and, since the collapse of the Soviet Union, has grown to be the fourth largest in the world, exceeded only by China, India, and the United States. More significantly, and unlike Japan, its several scores of populated islands cannot be connected by tunnelling, so that inter-island travel, by relatively slow ships, has invited intensive airline development. Except within densely populated Java, inter-city distances called for airline service. Indonesia's unique geography put Medan, in northern Sumatra, further away from Jayapura, in West Irian (New Guinea), than San Francisco is from New York.

The Dutch colonials had established a well-run airline, KNILM, before Indonesia gained independence in 1947, and the Indonesian national airline, Garuda, was quick to reestablish an inter-island network, starting in 1949 and expanding to all the main cities and towns on all the islands. But by 1962, the growth of the nation's economy indicated a requirement for a specialized airline organized to serve the smaller communities. Accordingly, on 6 September of that year, **Merpati Nusantara** was formed and was, like Garuda, government-owned. Its origins dated back to November 1958, when the Indonesian Air Force had provided social services to outlying areas. Under government regulation 19/1962, a transfer of responsibility took place, including the handing over of a small fleet of Canadian DHC-2 Beavers and DC-3s. This action was associated politically with the special status of what had been the Dutch half of the island of New Guinea, and which was still retained after Indonesian independence. It remained as Netherlands New Guinea until 1963; the transfer of sovereignty, along with the local aircraft fleet, was not completed until 1969. The Dutch had given considerable assistance, including much financial help to establish a local network, and this was continued by funds from the United Nations, which, in 1967, also provided some DHC-6 Twin Otters under an aid program.

Merpati grew quickly to serve the whole Indonesian archipelago and became **Merpati Nusantara Airlines** in 1969. It operated short international services, with turboprop twin-engined aircraft, to Singapore and Malaysia, to Kuching in eastern Malaysia (formerly Sarawak), and to Darwin, in northern Australia. It also operated charter services to the Philippines and even across the Pacific to Los Angeles, using Vickers Vanguard four-engined turboprops. Yet at the other end of the scale of airline service, mainly in West Irian (the western half of New Guinea), it still served dozens of small and isolated jungle communities with Canadian Twin Otters. Based in Biak, it even perpetuated the life of the venerable DC-3, using them as freighters to the dirt strips of that province. The men who maintained them claimed that no other aircraft could carry (as could the allegedly time-expired Douglas piston-engined twin) up to four tons of assorted goods into places where the strips alternated between pot-holed tracks when dry and marshy terrain when wet.

Such was Merpati's enthusiasm in its appointed role (which denied it the privilege of operating jet aircraft) that in the mid-1970s it could claim to serve more points than Lufthansa, a total of 128, of which about one-third were the strips in West Irian. But its turboprop fleet measured up quite well to Garuda's short-haul Fokker F-28 and Douglas DC-9 jets, and that airline's chief, Wiweko Supono, felt that Merpati had been given too generous a mandate. During the late 1960s and the early 1970s, he campaigned to terminate, or at least restrict, Merpati's operations, and eventually did succeed, in 1974, in preventing its purchase of jet equipment. Finally, on 26 October 1978, after the turboprop specialist had sustained heavy financial losses, the Indonesian government transferred its Merpati shares to Garuda, and thereafter direct competition on the main routes ceased.

Another vigorous Indonesian regional independent was **Bouraq Indonesian Airlines**, based in Balikpapan, Kalimantan (the Indonesian part of Borneo) and specializing in services to cities in Java and Sulawasi (formerly Celebes). Founded by J.A. "Gerry" Sumendap, who was associated with Porodisa, an extensive timber business, it started operations on 1 April 1970, at first with DC-3s, but quickly moving on to twin-engined turboprops, including 16 Hawker Siddeley 748s, which were quite at home at some of the unprepared strips. These were also operated by a Bouraq subsidiary, **Bali Air**, specializing, as its name implied, in services to that popular island resort. Like Merpati, Bouraq supported the local Indonesian aircraft industry, buying, in November 1978, some Nurtanio 212s, built under license from the Spanish CASA manufacturer. In 1982, the airline became independent from Porodisa, and Sumendap promptly bought four Vickers Viscounts from C.A.A.C., the Chinese airline, in September 1983. It was an astute purchase, as the fleet had not been used intensively, and so were almost as good as new.

While Bouraq specialized in serving Kalimantan and Sulawesi, two other airlines concentrated on the large island, Sumatra. **Mandala Airlines** was founded in February 1970 at Surabaya, Java, and at first served all the main Indonesian islands. It became closely associated with **Seulawah Air Services**, based in Palembang, Sumatra, and the two airlines cooperated closely, under the same management. Like the other regional operators,

Merpati Nusantara connected its mainline routes flown by the Viscounts (left). Elsewhere the versatile de Havilland Canada DH-6 Twin Otters (right) provided air service throughout Indonesia. This one is photographed at Banjermasin. (Davies)

Most of Indonesia's larger cities were in Java, and were served by mainline jets. But airline traffic to smaller communities throughout this large country of islands needed smaller airliners. Shown here among the many different types flown were (top left) a Grumman Albatross of AirFast, photographed at Ujungpandang; (top right) a DC3 of Bouraq at Banjermasim; (lower left) a Britten-Norman BN-3 Trislander of Bali Air at Balikpapan; and (lower right) a Britten-Norman BN-2 Islander of Indonesia Airtransport, also at Balikpapan. (Davies)

it used turboprop aircraft, including Lockheed Electras. Merpati, Bouraq, and Mandala (which absorbed Seulawah), together with **Sempati Air Transport**, founded in 1968, fulfilled the secondary, or regional, airline role in this far-flung island nation well and supplemented Garuda's primary status for many years. Then, in 1989, greater flexibility was granted by the Indonesian government, which removed the restriction for jet operations. Merpati, especially, took over some of Garuda's feeder jets.

A review of the Indonesian regional airlines should not be complete without a reference to a small company that specialized in air services to the small islands that extended eastward from Java as far as Timor. **Zamrud Aviation Corporation**, in a curious time-warp, could be observed, as late as the 1970s, flying Douglas DC-3s, of questionable vintage, to the Nusantara, or Lesser Sunda Islands. Lombok, Flores, Sumbawa, and other island outposts, looked upon this diminutive airline as its local bus company, post office, and general delivery system, providing a service that the other regionals either found impracticable or beneath their dignity.

Regionals Down Under

The Commonwealth of Australia was ideally suited for the establishment of regional airlines, not least because this self-governing dominion of the British Empire had recognized the individuality of the separate states. This was because they had first been founded as separate colonies during the 19th century, and not until 1901 were they federated. Each state retained its own railroad gauge, and the local loyalties remained strong, as evidenced in the intense interstate rivalry in cricket, the national sport. The shape and course of the colonial history was also linked to the special demography of the country. In the 1930s, the total population of Australia was about the same as London's or New York's; yet New South Wales's Sydney and Victoria's Melbourne each had more than a million each, and

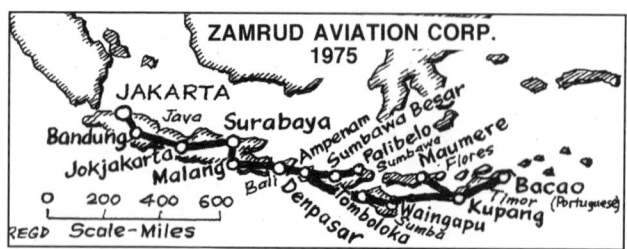

Contrasting with the nationwide network of Merpati Nusantara (see map on page 85), Zamrud Aviation operated refurbished ex-military Douglas DC-3s to the smaller islands of Indonesia.

Contrasting with the modern jet airliners at Jakarta or Surabaya, Zamrud's vintage DC-3s were still, in the 1980s, providing essential air transport between the smaller islands of Indonesia. (Davies)

the other state capitals were also sizable cities, each with its own hinterland. Otherwise, the country was sparsely populated, with vast areas of either farmland or desert. West Australia was not connected by rail to the rest of Australia until 1917.

Almost exactly the same area as the United States, and with relatively inadequate railroads and almost no main highways between the cities and the "outback," the development of the airlines followed a similar pattern to the predecessor railroads. By the mid-1920s, Australia had three airlines: **West Australian**; **QANTAS (Queensland and Northern Territories Air Service)**; and **Larkin**, based in Victoria and serving South Australia. New South Wales had an adequate rail network to the provincial towns, and so did not need an air service at that time. The first inter-state company with nationwide aspirations was not founded until 1930, when the first Australian National Airways was founded by the famous aviator Charles Kingsford-Smith, but this enterprise ended tragically within a year when its flagship crashed.

Until the end of the Second World War, the development of commercial airlines in Australia was haphazard, with many small companies operating, often for only a short while, local services for a limited clientele. One of these, Tasmanian Aerial Services, founded by Ivan Holyman, eventually became a new **Australian National Airways (A.N.A.)**, which by 1937 was operating modern Douglas DC-2s between the major cities of eastern Australia. But in Western Australia, almost isolated from the east, the regional spirit was strong. **MacRobertson-Miller Aviation (M.M.A.)** had replaced the pioneering West Australian Airways to fly the route from Perth to Darwin, to connect with the Empire Air Mail service from London. Meanwhile, QANTAS (see above) had been the regional airline in the northeast since 1919. South Australia's regional had an odd history. Its name was **Guinea Airways**, which had pioneered air routes to the jungle gold mines of New Guinea, made a connection to Adelaide in 1937, and transferred its base there. In New South Wales, C.A. Butler founded **Butler Air Transport,** to serve the western farmlands of that state. In the center of Australia, E.J. Connellan had formed a uniquely social-service company, which became **Connellan Airways** in 1943.

When the Second World War ended in 1945, these airlines, together with several other unsuccessful aspirants, found themselves immersed in a battle for nationwide control. The post-war Labour government appointed a commission on 12 February

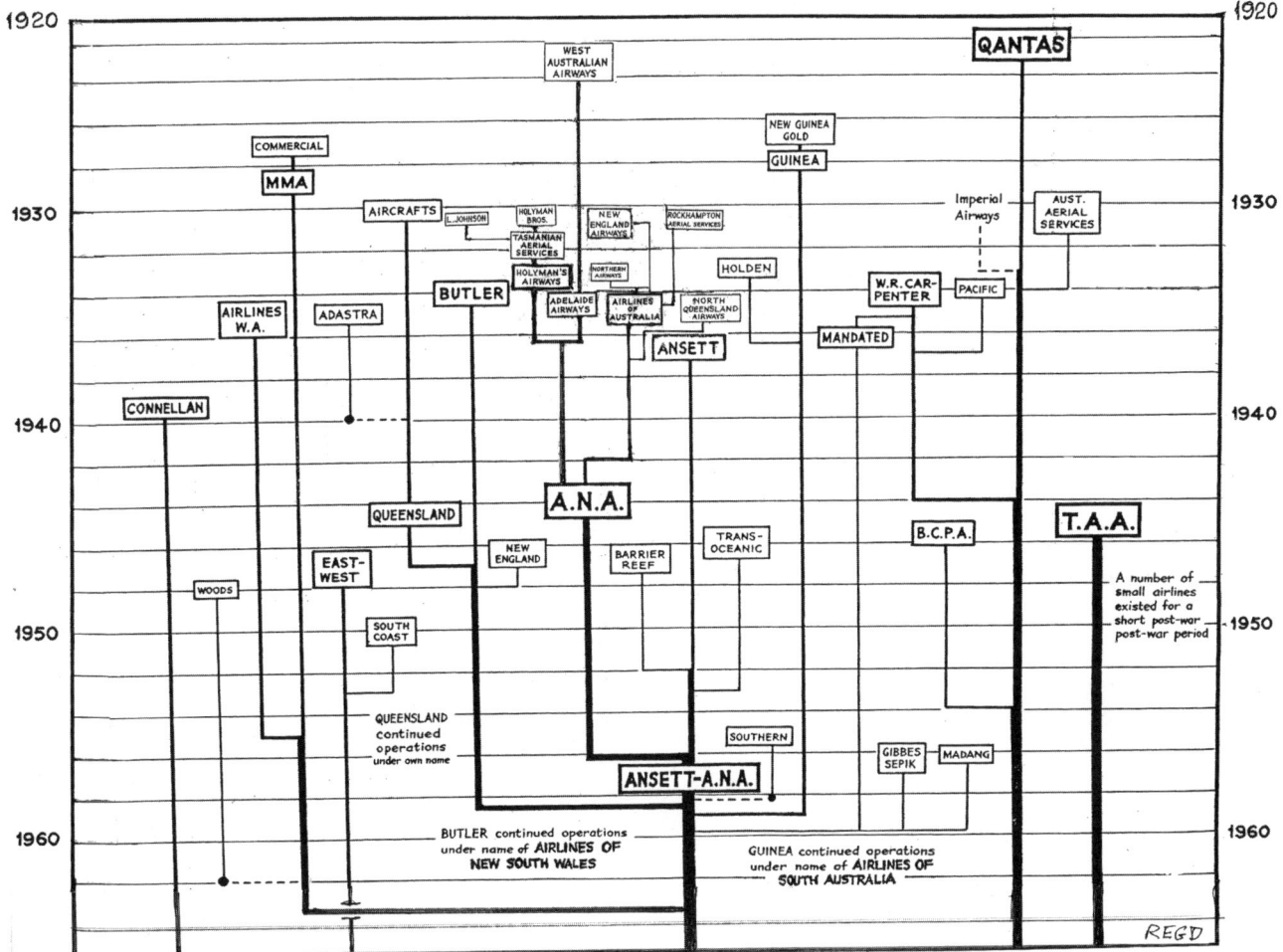

AUSTRALIAN AIRLINES 1920s–1965

1946 to establish regional as well as national airline services. The result was the creation of the state-owned national domestic airline, Trans Australia Airlines (T.A.A.), and this competed with the spirit of free enterprise, Holyman's A.N.A. The two airlines continued as rivals until 18 November 1952, when the Civil Aviation Agreement Act gave them strict equality of operating rights. By this time, T.A.A. had taken over QANTAS's domestic routes in Queensland, together with some routes in other states. The standards of flying equipment had kept pace with world standards. T.A.A. was one of the first airlines to order the British Viscount turboprop, starting service on 18 December 1954, but A.N.A. still operated piston-engined Douglas DC-6Bs. This led to a decline in the latter's fortunes, and on 4 October 1957, it was forced to sell out to Reginald Ansett, whose Ansett Airways had been founded in February 1936, to serve locally in the state of Victoria. Begun modestly with one used aircraft, Ansett's business acumen now placed him in a position to fulfill more ambitious goals; this included the formation of a group of regional airlines, identified along state lines, to operate as feeder or connecting services to his inter-city network. To set up this system, Ansett initiated what can only be termed a mopping-up operation, for by the early 1960s his **Ansett Airlines of Australia** had almost cleared the decks of the former regional companies by buying them up.

First to fall was Butler, which had already built a network in new South Wales and southern Queensland, and which was taken over in 1958. On 17 December 1959, the name was changed to **Airlines of New South Wales**. By this time, earlier in that year, Ansett had acquired Guinea Airways, to cover South Australia, with connections to neighboring states, together with local services in New Guinea. And although a few years were to pass, in April 1963, MacRobertson-Miller, in spite of vigorous opposition from the fiercely independent western Australian state, became **Airlines of Western Australia**. Curiously, therefore, Australia had at last found itself with a recognizable and clearly identifiable regional airline system; paradoxically they were all owned by one conglomerate, Ansett Transport Industries. Connected by Ansett Airlines of Australia, which was an early purchaser of Boeing 727 and Douglas DC-9 jets during the 1960s, the regionals moved into turboprop twins, primarily the Fokker F-27. They were part of an airline empire, over which Sir Reginald (from 1969) presided until his death on 23 December 1981.

Whither the Regionals?

By the 20th century, the distinction between regional and mainline, or trunk, airlines had become blurred. The conditions that had spawned them during the formative years of air transport and their maturity after the Second World War has changed. As reviewed at the beginning of this chapter, only the largest countries of the world, by geographical definition and also by financial resources, could sufficiently support regional distinctions to allow the luxury of such airlines. Yet what has happened to the once-promising and once-proud local companies that have not survived developmental challenges?

The story in the United States has been one of competing transport modes and a political transportation policy that could almost have been designed to eliminate regional airline opportunities or aspirations. The post-war neglect of and consequent decline of a passenger railroad system stimulated regional airline growth for a few years. But under President Eisenhower, the initiation of the Interstate Highway construction program on 29 June 1956 was the beginning of the end. As soon as people could drive 100 miles in two hours without traffic lights or intersections, there was little incentive to take an airplane flight. As the highways grew, first the local railroads then the local airlines felt the pinch. Even after expanding into inter-city markets, they sometimes survived by mergers, but their traffic base evaporated and they were ultimately absorbed by the trunk airlines. Today there some 300,000 miles of multi-lane highways in the United States, and very few communities are more than a short driving distance from an interchange with the old roads.

Elsewhere, similar patterns could be discerned, and more recently the innovative high speed railroad systems in eastern Asia and Europe have presented a new challenge, a warning to regional airline entrepreneurs that a new mode of surface transport has emerged to revolutionize inter-city travel. In Japan and western Europe today, the practical possibilities of establishing new regional airlines seem negligible. The initiatives are directed not to geographic identification but to meeting with and generating more air travel by lowering fare levels, a process that has been accelerated by the deregulation of airlines. These 250 kph (150 mph) high speed rail systems all but eliminated many short-haul regional airlines in Japan and western Europe as soon as they opened service. But elsewhere a different approach for local air travel suggested freedom from government control, to encourage initiatives from entrepreneurs, and to allow market forces to determine the need and to guide the solution. Such a policy began in the United States in 1978 and soon spread around the world.

Part Four: Airline Deregulation

Chapter 20: The United States Sets the Pace

A Changing Traveling Clientele

As the second half of the 20th century witnessed the benefits of the Jet Age for long-haul travel, and (in the United States especially) multi-lane highways offered the same advantages for short-haul journeys, the effect on the traveling public was almost revolutionary. People were traveling more and more. At first, during the early post-war years, the U.S. airlines had depended almost entirely on business travelers, who accounted for about three quarters of the total demand. But the main benefit, with the 1958 introduction of the jets, was not, as superficially promoted and perceived, the speed; it was the operational economy. This was derived from the use of cheaper fuel (kerosene), vastly improved maintenance procedures, and longer aircraft lives. These factors enabled the airlines to continue to lower fare levels, a process that had begun in the late 1940s, with coach class fares. The process continued thereafter, not so much with the published price of the tickets, but with the growing affluence of the American public, for whom, as the years went by, an airline ticket represented a much smaller proportion of individual discretionary income.

Nevertheless, post-war airline travel was not yet the assumed mode of travel for the average "white-collar" office worker, and certainly not for the "blue-collar" manual one. Some middle-class people would take an air trip, but not on a regular basis. Families from New York still drove to Florida, and still took the train to Niagara Falls, and most vacationers in northern Europe did the same to the Mediterranean, with the British filling the cross-Channel ferry boats. And even when taking a summer holiday, people treated an air journey rather like going to the theater or to a special dining occasion: they dressed up for it.

Back in the 1950s, the first-class cabin had occupied as much as one-third of the available seats, still catering mainly to business travelers, but by the 1970s, the balance of the seating arrangements in the airliner cabin was changing significantly. The percentage of leisure travelers, either vacationers, or "VFRs"—visiting friends and relations—or even business men who had their eyes on their budgets, rose rapidly. The effect was to reduce the percentage of first-class seats. To take an air trip was no longer an unusual event for the average traveler, and dressing up for the occasion was less obligatory or conventional. With the younger generation—students now able to fly to college, given special fare discounts—blue jeans and even T-shirts began to appear.

Low Fares Increase Traffic Growth

During this period, and mainly because of the lower fares, air travel as a whole maintained an astonishing level of growth. For almost two decades, the annual increase in passenger-miles in the United States had averaged about 15%, which meant that the total volume doubled every five years. When the Jet Age began, the figure was 40 billion. In 1970 it was 170 billion. The numbers for the first-class market hardly changed, but for all other classes of travel, in sheer numbers alone, the airline industry had undergone a metamorphosis. Air travel for the masses had arrived.

The managements of the certificated scheduled airlines were reluctant to recognize this profound change. Through their Air Transport Association (A.T.A.) lobbying group, and with the compliance of the Civil Aeronautics Board (C.A.B.), the traditional process of setting fares, dating back to 1938, was perpetuated. No airline could reduce fares without going through long-drawn-out procedures in Washington, where the C.A.B. presided over inevitable objections from competitors. The introduction of coach-class fares in 1948 had been an exceptional, almost bizarre, case, in which rival airlines did not object to **Capital Airlines**' low *Nighthawk* fares because they completely underestimated the desire of the general public to have low fares rather than four-course meals or a bar. But subsequently the entire industry was reluctant, even determined, not to allow this to happen again; all the airlines insisted upon standardized meals, the same seating widths and separations, indeed, almost standardized everything. This applied especially to fares, which, set by the C.A.B. with the appoval and compliance of the airlines, acting in unison, varied not according to market demands, but according to the distance traveled, whether to a major city or to a whistle-stop community across the Great Plains.

The five-member C.A.B. went along with the flow, even though many of its staff often recommended a more liberal approach. It defended the status quo by ensuring that no maverick company offering cheap air transport to an eager public would be granted the privilege of a full unrestricted scheduled airline certificate. During the 40 years of its existence, only one such certificate was ever granted, to Trans-Caribbean Airlines, a small but enterprising operator serving the market from San Juan, Puerto Rico, to New York and Washington, and whose owner was based in Washington. Other deserving low-fare aspirants, notably North American Airlines, Transocean Airlines, and World Airways—leading members of the non-scheduled, or Supplemental Airlines fraternity—were kept at arm's length by the bureaucrats and lobbyists in Washington, and denied even an experimental or provisional certificate, even though the necessary qualifications of being "fit, willing, and able" (they had the experience, the enthusiasm, and the fleets to fulfil any demand) were consistently denied. (See Chapter 10.)

Double Discounts

Eventually, however, justice could not be denied. Popular pressure—one of the basic elements of a democratic society—was to have its way. The inadequacies and the shortcomings of the traditional system could, in the long term, no longer resist the incessant demands of the air traveling public for a better deal. The writing was perhaps on the wall, and a few instances occurred when airlines read the writing.

First, early in 1977, under Frank Lorenzo's maverick-style approach, **Texas International** introduced Peanut Fares from Texas to California, a move reminiscent of Capital's innovation in 1948. The reaction was prompt. On 25 April 1977, **American Airlines** offered *Super-Saver* fares ($227 transcontinental); **Eastern** also did the same from the northeast to Florida; and **T.W.A.** matched American with several tempting offers. Coincidentally, on 6 June 1977, the C.A.B. approved Sir Freddie Laker's super–economy fare/no-reservation trans-Atlantic Skytrain. The whole idea was elementary: better to fill otherwise empty seats with cheap fare-paying passengers than to fly them empty.

Meanwhile, the non-scheduled airlines that had, over the years, found ingenious ways of overcoming the restrictions imposed upon them by the bureaucratic array of the A.T.A., the C.A.B., and the Department of Justice. The public did not mind a cramped seat, a 3 A.M. take-off, or a simple meal if it could save money on the fare. Like the reaction of an average shopper, bargain fares were hard to resist. Had the safety regulations allowed, many would have been happy to stand all the way from New York to Chicago in exchange for a fare discount. So, by the mid-1970s, the old order was changing fast. Drastic changes had to be made to an administrative structure that was showing signs of decay.

The Deregulation Act of 1978

When the time came for something to be done, the measures taken were not half-hearted. The political reform that took place was no band-aid solution to a deteriorating ailment. It was in the tradition of some of the past United States actions, reminiscent of the New Deal or the Lend-Lease Act. Time-honored procedures were not simply modified. Under the 1977–81 Carter Administration, there was no patching up a wounded leg suspected of approaching gangrene; the leg was cut off. There was no reorganizing of the respected C.A.B., which, for 40 years, with a maximum of only about 800 staff, had ruled over half of the world's airline productivity. In one piece of legislation, the C.A.B. was to be phased out over five years.

While the C.A.B. took most of the punishment in the avalanche of popular opinion that welcomed the start of a deregulated era, arguably it was the victim of its own connivance with the A.T.A., which had stoutly opposed any intrusion into its bastion of tradition, under the protection of the clauses of the 1938 Act, expressed as "grandfather rights." As early as 1974, a Special Staff on Regulatory Reform, directed by Roy Pulsifer, made a well-conducted study of the competitive situation—or, as it revealed, the non-competitive status quo—and issued its report on 22 July 1975. Its recommendations were largely adopted as the framework of the Deregulation Act that was to come. Sam Brown, the Board's official historian remarked that the C.A.B. was the first regulatory agency to recommend the abolition of its main business.

Pulsifer's report, which clearly exposed the lack of real, as opposed to theoretical, competition, was concurrent with the C.A.B.'s own Advisory Committee on Procedural Reform, established on 21 June 1975. It had addressed the issues of rule-making procedures. Decisions that should have taken only a few months could sometimes be held up for years. It considered the creaking mechanism for granting the entry or exit of airlines in what was supposed to be a free market. And the strict adherence to fare levels that were simply based on distance was questioned. This self-analysis was conducted under the chairmanship of John E. Robson, so that, when Alfred E. Kahn was sworn in as the new C.A.B. chairman on 10 January 1977, the groundwork had already been laid for ruthless action to be taken, and within his own hierarchy, he was preaching to a receptive choir.

The onslaught came on 15 October 1978, when the U.S. Congress enacted into law the Airline Deregulation Act of 1978, which was signed by President Carter on 24 October. Marvin S. Cohen was appointed to succeed Kahn, and Michael Levine was named General Director, a new position of influence and authority. Kahn himself became the chief spokesman to explain the full effect of this revolutionary legislation. This was possibly the most far-reaching since the Civil Aeronautics Act of 1938, which had effectively created an airline club, the membership of which was closed to outsiders, and which had nurtured a strictly controlled government agency that, equally effectively, protected the club and condoned its own self-serving definition of how best to serve the public.

The Floodgates Open

At first, there seemed to be a note of caution in the enactment of the Act's intentions. The policy seemed to be one of gradualness. Each existing airline, in all categories, could add one new route each year, and could protect one of its own routes from a new entrant. But apparently forgotten were several thousand routes that were available but had simply not been applied for,

Frank Lorenzo took over Texas International in 1977 and promptly ignored the practice of rigid-controlled fares. His Peanut Fares was the first move in the industry to offer bargain-priced fares to a welcoming public. (Davies)

and these dormant city pairs were therefore available without infringement on the one-a-year clause.

On 18 October 1978, even before the president signed the Act into law, at 8.30 A.M., the airlines stood in line outside the C.A.B. in Washington, and systematically claimed hundreds of new routes. By the spring of 1979, the field was open. When the old Board's control over route authority ceased on 31 December 1981, open entry by any airline to almost any city pair it had its eyes on was effectively valid. The airlines just did what they wanted and kept the Department of Transport informed of what they had done. This applied internationally as well as within the United States. The once closely guarded overseas privileges, originally a de facto monopoly of Pan American Airways and later injected with post–Second World War new blood, disappeared. The most accessible foreign city, and the one with the biggest traffic potential, London, was besieged with requests for counter space at Gatwick Airport (Heathrow was saturated already), and six U.S. airlines were successful, in addition to the four scheduled incumbents. The pattern was repeated all over the world, and as will be narrated below, such profusion had an effect on the Locals. In the United States, profusion was almost an understatement. By the end of 1978, there were more than 150 aspiring applicants, none of which could be legitimately denied access to the airline air, provided that they were (to use the C.A.B.'s own qualification criteria) fit, willing, and able. But only about 50 measured up to all three of those criteria, mostly because of lack of capital to acquire even a minimum fleet. Of those, even fewer were able to start service. In a ruthless survival-of-the-fittest environment, almost all the brash newcomers soon went under. Only one complete newcomer survived into the next century. This was **America West**, often on the brink of failure, but able to exploit the demographic advantage of its base in Phoenix, the most rapidly growing urban area in the United States. Another star that emerged with conspicuous success was one of the previous intra-state airlines, **Southwest Airlines**, which, under the driving leadership of the popular Herb Kelleher, steadily grew to become, within two decades, one of the nation's largest. This development, and the fate of the other intra-state airlines, is the subject of Chapter 24 in this book.

Price War and a Fight for Survival

In addition to the freedom to add new routes without much hindrance, the other freedom was the removal of restrictions on fare levels, and although the C.A.B. control over fares did not officially come into effect until 31 December 1982, this was irrelevant. The airlines plunged into an orgy of fierce competition. Airline passengers suddenly discovered that they could "wheel and deal." The former seller's market had become a buyer's market, and the public was calling the shots. But there were other aspects of this bonanza both for the travelers and for the airlines.

First, the passengers discovered that the intensive competition for lower fares, applied only to those routes where the traffic volume was high. If a traveler wished to visit a small community, the fare was more likely to be increased or air service was suspended altogether. One example of the anomalies in the new order, at first, was that the cheapest way to fly from California to Philadelphia—not well served at the time—was to fly to New York and then take a taxi.

Second, the airlines faced lower average yields (actual revenue per seat flown). The break-even load factor (percentage of seats filled that were necessary to cover the seat-mile costs) rose alarmingly. Previously this figure had hovered around 60%–65%, but now, even though some flights were filled to capacity, the total revenue from an individual flight was no higher than before. Yet there was a limit to how high the *average* load factor could go. Scheduling patterns had to include flights during hours of the day when many flights were lightly loaded. Most airliners spent the night on the ground, and the daily utilization (revenue hours flown) could not be increased. The net result was that, with costs (fuel, maintenance, salaries, aircraft prices) remaining the same, the yields were declining. Airline balance sheets did not reflect any positive financial results from deregulation. After the initial feast, immediately following October 1978, came the reckoning. By the end of the century, an 80% load factor, once thought to be operationally undesirable, became recognized as the minimum level to break even financially.

As a background to the entire process of deregulation, one fundamental aspect had perhaps been forgotten by the legislators. Airline traffic as a whole, which had once benefitted from the growth generated by first-time travelers and increasing personal discretionary income, had slowed down to a more pedestrian pace. The annual 15% per year growth level was a thing of the past. By the early 1980s, almost everyone who wished to fly by air was already doing so. The airline industry had only to face a bad year or two of total traffic growth for survival-of-the-fittest to be translated into death-to-the-deficient. Older airlines found it difficult to change their ways or to persuade their staff to change. Inevitably, as the 20th century drew to a close, the rate of airline demise, of time-honored airline pioneers that lost touch with the momentum of change, was alarming.

The strong survived. The efficient and the ruthless ones, and those that were able to resist the incursion of manipulative financiers, were able to make the right decisions and, by the development of traffic hubs, to increase their individual shares of the market. Unpredictably and unpredicted, access to strongly protected gates and slots at the busy airports were held by the incumbents, and they were not about to surrender this valuable— and unregulated—asset. Those airlines with long-established "fortress hubs" held strong cards, and they played them well. New airlines were denied easy access to many remunerative markets. This trend had not been anticipated by the designers and supporters of the deregulation process, which they expected would generate more strong airlines rather than fewer. They were wrong. Big fish devoured minnows, or the minnows just died. This complete transformation of the airline industry of the United States, initiated by deregulation, was so far reaching that it is covered in Chapter 21.

Chapter 21: The Airline World Deregulates

A Different Corporate Environment

One major difference between the airlines of the United States and those of the rest of the world is that all the U.S. airlines were completely privately owned. In Europe, Asia, Africa, Australasia, and Latin America, the major airlines were either privately owned, but at the same time regarded by their governments as "chosen instruments" thus given special privileges; alternatively, they were jointly owned by private investors and their governments, or they were completely government-owned.

The other difference was that, as observed in Chapter 19 regarding the development (or non-development) of regional airlines, the United States was, in the 1950s, almost the only country that was big enough to have both the need and the resources to permit a community of several financially healthy airlines. Brazil and Australia struggled to emulate such a system; while the Soviet Union and China were examples of countries whose politics (in which the airlines were effectively government departments) did not apply to ther fragmentation of a quasi-public utility. This factor, simply a matter of geography, meant that an approach to deregulation was invariably interpreted as a means of access to international routes, because few countries were big enough to need more domestic air services. And by the late 1960s, led by Japan, those countries that were industrialized enough to pursue massive expansion of domestic public transport, turned to a completely new form of transport: high speed rail. The effect on the balance of air-versus-rail public transportation was revolutionary and is discussed at the end of this book.

The adherence to internationally agreed fare structures was eroded to the extent that the role of the International Air Transport Association (IATA) as the agency for determining the system changed. Deregulation did not eliminate rigidly agreed fare levels, but it came close. Some airlines, notably several in east Asia, including the powerful All Nippon Airways, were not members of IATA anyway. Deregulation effectively put an end to what many had regarded as a stoutly defended international cartel fortress.

Thus, while the effect of the airline deregulation process in the United States was globally far reaching, the legislative process was not echoed in the same way. Airline corporate structures were different, the recognition and acceptance of the need varied in intensity, and legislative action took different courses. One common element was the perceived impression that the U.S. government had confirmed that private enterprise was to be stimulated, in the interests of free competition, without the handicap of hindrance from bureaucratic brakes or barriers.

In general, the governments of other countries interpreted the action to be taken as a call for a more liberal approach toward this relationship. In Great Britain, the move toward this objective took an extreme form and liberalization became privatization. Such was the revolutionary aspect of this course that neither the verb "to privatize" nor the noun "privatization" had found its way into the *Oxford Dictionary*.

The British Privatize

The idea of a free market (or "market forces") met with receptive ears in Great Britain, where the Conservative government, under the firm hands of Prime Minister Margaret Thatcher, needed little encouragement to de-nationalize several basic industries. Under the post-war Labour government, these had been created as national corporations. The principle involved was that certain industries, especially public utilities, vital to the national interest, needed direct government control. Through Parliament, they were responsible to the public and the idea was to free them from the shortcomings of market forces, however theoretically attractive their advantages might be. The British Overseas Airways Corporation (B.O.A.C.) had been formed, just before the outbreak of the Second World War, for that very reason, by a Conservative government.

Margaret Thatcher set about her privatization program with conviction and enthusiasm. Basic industries such as coal and steel production, British Rail, the telephone system, even London Transport's famous double-decked omnibuses, all went under the parliamentary hammer. In 1980, by Act of Parliament, **British Airways** ceased to be a national corporation. The stock offering ended on 6 February 1987, with buyers oversubscribing more than 11 times.

The Prime Minister had a staunch ally in Lord King, Chairman of British Airways, which had been formed on 7 October 1971 by the merger of B.O.A.C. and British European Airways (B.E.A.). He brought in Colin Marshall as his chief executive, and together they set about changing the administrative direction of the national airline. They could justify draconian measures by pointing to heavy losses—hundreds of millions of pounds sterling—during the 1960s and 1970s, and soon the cold winds of commercial reality began to blow across the airline headquarters at London's Heathrow Airport. Lax financial disciplines were tightened up, duplications of departmental activities were corrected, many areas that came close to being sinecures were abolished. The net result was that, during the years following the privatization, total staff numbers were drastically reduced, at all staff levels, by about 15,000, close to one-third of the total workforce. Yet the productivity of the airline did not suffer. This was the result of the new approach, recognizing that the driving force of any public transport organization was—obvious to an impartial observer—to serve the public. Too much emphasis had previously been placed on technical considerations, and British Airways had tended, often with apparent reluctance, to follow improvements to passenger amenities and convenience set by competitors, rather than, as the biggest European airline, to set those standards itself.

As the Jet Age matured during the 1960s and 1970s, the competition for equipment advantage had all but disappeared. The speed of all the leading airliners—Boeing, Douglas, BAC, or Sud—was about the same, and the new Airbuses were no faster. Also, any advantage gained by preferential access to lucrative markets had also diminished, as the major cities of the world could be reached by a wide selection of competing airlines. British Airways particularly faced competition from vigorous airlines established in former colonies or dominions. By the sheer quality of its passenger service, **Singapore Airlines**, the flag carrier of a tiny country of barely two million people, was voted annually as the world's best airline. It was a hard act to follow, and to its credit, British Airways gradually rebuilt its reputation for good service in every respect.

One big advantage in the private sector was the access to capital. As a state corporation, British Airways had previously had to rely on funds from the Treasury, under the conditions (and often limitations) set by the Public Sector Borrowing Requirements allocations. These levels of capital were ultimately decided by Ministers who were often advised by interests that weighed the merits of other candidates for the public purse. The national airline did not always receive the essential investment for development or expansion, so the removal of this perceived handicap was of great benefit.

Worldwide Collapse of Fare Regulation

One of the main features of the deregulation of airlines in the United States was that it came abruptly—as the process took effect, perhaps too abruptly. Many of the established airlines did not adjust quickly enough or they reacted impetuously in the wrong direction. Elsewhere in the world, airlines had already had to move with the times, particularly in the field of determining the fares structure, individually or collectively. For many years, within Europe and, to a lesser extent, in North America, the scheduled airlines had watched their non-scheduled competitors, the charter airlines, develop low-fare vacation flights. Most non-business travelers would cheerfully exchange the privilege of a five-course meal or an ideal departure or arrival time if they could save 10% on the airline fare. The saving was often as much as a week's hotel bill. So extreme was the differential between the opportunities offered by an inclusive tour package (airline fare plus hotel plus guide services and local transport) that during the winter season, when the operators offered rock-bottom sale prices to keep the airplanes flying and to keep the hotel rooms filled, a coal-miner from Newcastle or a steel-worker from Essen could spend Christmas in Tenerife more cheaply than if he had stayed at home. And he could take his family too.

In the northern countries of Europe—Britain, Germany, the Netherlands, and especially in Scandinavia, where cold winters cast people's eyes to the south—the growth of inclusive tours was intensive. And the same people who made their annual visits to Spain's Costa Brava or the Grecian isles were also the voters, and so governments had to take notice, by the late 1960s, that more intra-European passenger-miles were being flown by the charter companies (which had often been granted scheduled routes as well) than by the national "chosen instrument" airlines.

Following the end of the Second World War, with few exceptions, most of the world's airlines had united to form IATA. This organization performed great service in setting standards of the basic service that airlines should offer to the public in terms of comfort, meals, and fares. Its somewhat dictatorial directives were defended on the basis that its members were merely agents for their parent governments, but IATA was perceived as an international cartel. Therefore, any attempts to break it usually met with public sympathy, which governments were well advised to recognize.

IATA did introduce tourist fares in 1952, and economy fares in 1958. Yet even the latter did not match the low fares that could be offered on long-distance routes by the charter companies, and by pioneers of the so-called Sixth Freedom traffic, such as Iceland's **Loftleidir**. By the late 1960s, the trans-Atlantic market had, to a large extent, self-deregulated, as the charter companies had found ways of evading the strict application of national laws by applying long-distance affinity group fares. Bookings were made through a myriad of different organizations, such as sports or social clubs. A member of the United Kingdom Society of California could make a British Caledonian Airways round-trip from Los Angeles to London more cheaply than to fly one way by scheduled airline to New York. The non-scheduled airlines did a roaring trade, filling their airplanes, even at 3 a.m. This development extended to the populous markets of the northeastern U.S.; to the Great Lakes area, which benefitted from VFR (visiting friends and relations) traffic, especially from western Europe; and to the burgeoning vacation traffic from Europe to sunny Florida and Disneyworld. The travel brochures in London and Cologne offered bargains to Miami as they did to Palma.

The process of deregulation was thus effectively, if not officially, under way at least a decade before the 1978 Act. Even though the upstart "non-skeds" had intruded to take a share of the world market, air travel as a whole was expanding so quickly during the period that other airlines, on both sides of the Atlantic, were anxious to share the lucrative trans-ocean air travel business. This universally held desire became a ground-swell of corporate persuasion and lobbying, which met with agreeable governmental response. This led to a top-level meeting of the minds in an historic collaboration between the United States and the British governments in 1977. This resulted in a far-reaching bilateral agreement that became known as "Bermuda II," as it was regarded as a successor to the first, and famous, Bermuda Agreement of 1946. This had first laid down agreed shares of capacity, frequencies, and other conditions of airline service that protected the signatories from excessive and possibly predatory competition. The main issue—a year before the U.S. deregulation that concerned only the domestic industry—was the admission of additional airlines into the hitherto protected intercontinental domains of Pan American, British Airways, T.W.A., and Northwest.

Some new airline insignias began to appear at the international gateway airports on both sides of the Atlantic and of the Pacific. Resulting from the conclusions of the Edwards Report in 1969, **British Caledonian Airways (B-Cal)** had already been given a limited share of British overseas scheduled air routes, and this included services alongside B.A. to New York and Los Angeles, which were called dual-designation cities. Thus, under Bermuda II, B-Cal was the obvious choice to meet the provisions of the Agreement.

The U.S. Civil Aeronautics Board (C.A.B.), still the airline regulator, acted in a measured manner that was a credit to its awareness of the sensibilities of the regulated. For selected new city pairs, the designated airlines gained reciprocal traffic rights, but protection was assured against predatory moves by the incumbent (by excessive flight scheduling) by awarding exclusive rights to only one company to one of the pairs of cities for a period of three years. This would also provide the opportunity to test the market to ensure that forecasts of traffic increases (possibly designed to support the case for entry) had not been overoptimistic. B-Cal started Douglas DC-10 service to Houston in October 1971 and **Delta Air Lines** began from Atlanta to Gatwick on 30 April 1978. **Continental Airlines** gained a route from Dallas/Fort Worth and, in company with Delta, was obliged to land at Gatwick, London's second airport (and one of Europe's busiest).

The whole process of international deregulation involving the United States was thus not carried out by a single blow of the legislative axe, as had been the case with the domestic routes. Over a period of a few years, the deregulated environment emerged, not at the stroke of a pen, but as the result of several bilateral negotiations that effectively were already part of the underlying objectives of deregulation. And the process continued. The irrepressible Freddie Laker got into the spirit of the Act. After less than two years with its new-found American destinations, B-Cal decided to pull out from New York and Los Angeles, and in 1975 the responsible British Minister cancelled the dual-designation authority. Laker challenged this action, claiming that Peter Shore had "broken his own law," and won the day, giving **Laker Airways** access to New York.

Interestingly, one result of the whole process of liberalizing the scheduled airline structure was that the low-fare differential that had been the main marketing advantage of the charter airlines, including the U.S. Supplementals, was eroded, to the extent that the low-fare traveling public could also find bargains with the established scheduled airlines. The IATA members, responding to what are loosely described as market forces, had achieved their objectives of sustained growth, not by eliminating much of the threat from the group charterers, but by adopting the policy of "if you can't beat 'em, join 'em." Rigid IATA control of international fares was a thing of the past.

Japan's Second Force

One of the most astonishing developments of the Jet Age has been the creation and subsequent rise to prominence of Japan's **All Nippon Airways (A.N.A.).** When the British B.O.A.C.'s de Havilland Comet shattered all airline speed records in May 1952, even A.N.A.'s predecessor companies did not exist. Yet half a century later this airline was to be the launch customer for a new generation of technically advanced commercial airliners.

A.N.A. was formed on 1 March 1958 (only eight months before B.O.A.C and Pan American opened trans-Atlantic jet services) by the merger of **Far Eastern Airlines (Kyokuto Koku)** and **Japan Helicopter and Aeroplane Transport Company (Nihon Herikoputa Yuso Kabushiki Kaisha [N.H.Y.K.K.])**—known familiarly as **Nippeli**—founded respectively on 26 and 27 December 1952. The merged fleet was small in size and type, with de Havilland Doves and the ill-fated Handley Page Marathons operating short-haul routes throughout Japan. The veteran Douglas DC-3 was A.N.A.'s flagship. In August of its first year, a DC-3 crashed, so that the aspirant second-force airline's start was far from auspicious. Its entry into trunk-line service, on 1 April 1959, was modest enough, with DC-3s, but these were soon supplemented, on 10 October of that year, with pressurized Convair 440s, and All Nippon airliners were to be seen at every major city of Japan. On 1 August 1960, in tune with the explosive growth of airline service throughout the country, it introduced turboprop service with four-engined Vickers Viscounts on the trunk routes, and on 10 July 1961, twin-engined Fokker F.27 Friendships on the shorter routes.

Between 1960 and 1964, All Nippon's average annual passenger growth rate was an unprecedented 53%. This reflected the

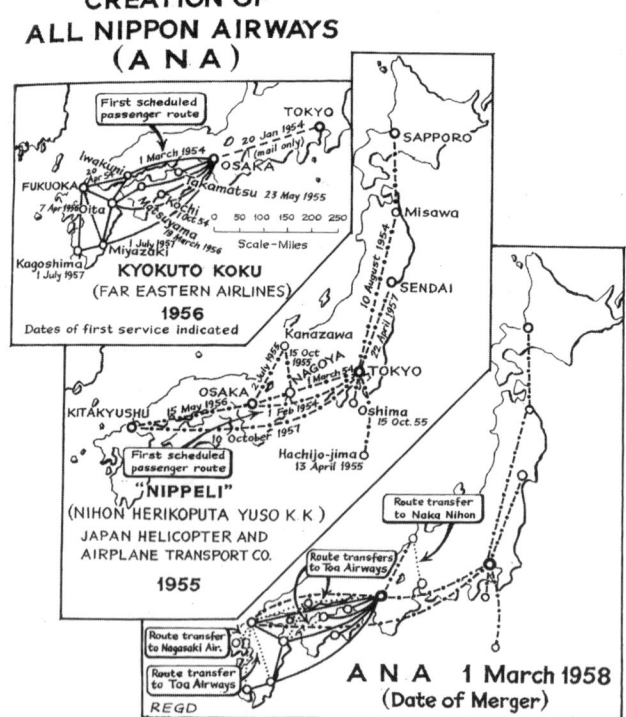

A.N.A. was created in the 1950s. Kyokuto Koku (Far Eastern Airlines) and 'Nippeli' were two small airlines that merged in 1958 to become Japan's second force airline.

The Airline World Deregulates

phenomenal economic growth of Japan as its post-war recovery completed the transformation of the nation from a partly industrial, partly rural or agricultural, society into a world powerhouse, with its cameras, radios, electronics, and soon, motor cars demonstrably superior to all others. In 1960, the prime minister called for the doubling of the gross national product in 10 years. Japan achieved it in five.

Recognizing that efficient airline service, with competitive incentives, was no enemy of industrial growth, the Japanese airline authorities did not, as did the United States's C.A.B., favor the incumbent airline, **Japan Airlines (J.A.L.)**, on domestic services. For international services, it continued to be the "chosen instrument," and a very effective one. J.A.L. had entered an already highly competitive field and not only held its own, but had set a fast pace, introducing new standards of cabin service. If these innovations, which amounted to little more than better attentiveness by the flight attendants, did not put the European and American airlines to shame, they certainly kept them on their toes. J.A.L. carried its flag with honor and pride, and its nation was content to allow it to remain that way, unchallenged from Tokyo, at least for a while.

Meanwhile, during the late 1950s and early 1960s, All Nippon had established its own hub-and-spoke route system in what were termed *beam* routes, as they radiated from Tokyo and Osaka like the beams of the sun; these were operated intensively by the Viscount and Friendship turboprops. The last DC-3 was retired on 15 March, and several events combined to serve notice that A.N.A. was to be a major component in the future development of Japanese commercial aviation. On 25 May 1964, it started pure-jet service with a leased Boeing 727-100 on the Tokyo-Sapporo route, which, partly through such enterprising policies, was to become the busiest in the world. Also, during August and September, it signed partnership agreements with several smaller airlines, including the transfer of a few of its smaller routes to them (an action that would later be termed *code-sharing*), and it purchased **Fujita Airlines** on 1 November 1963, **Central Japan Airlines (Naka Nihon Koku)** on 25 January 1965, and **Nagasaki Airlines** on 1 December 1967.

The historic opening, in August 1964, from Tokyo to Osaka via Nagoya and Kyoto, of the Shin Kan-sen, the world's first high speed railroad—the term belies the fact that start-to-stop speeds in excess of 100 mph effectively created a new form of transport—did not affect A.N.A. as much as it affected J.A.L., of which the domestic system was restricted to the busy trunk routes that the "bullet" trains would serve. Also, on 30 November 1964, A.N.A. not only retired its last piston-engined aircraft,

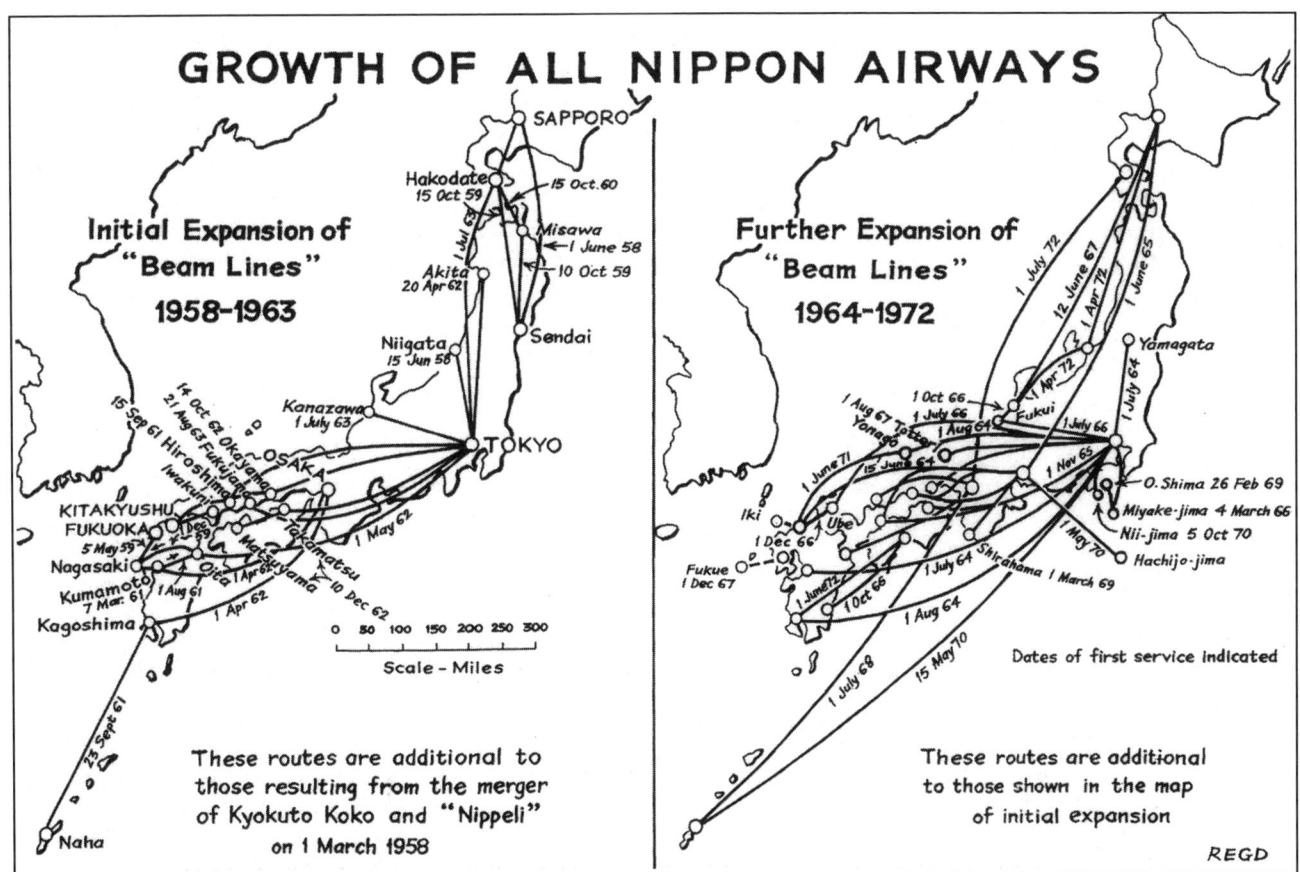

A.N.A. moved ahead with an energetic program of expanding its domestic routes, familiarly known as the "Beam Lines." By a dynamic increase in traffic, A.N.A. ranked, by the 1970s, as one of the world's leading airlines.

the Convair 440, but it introduced, on 20 September 1965, a third turboprop type, the twin-engined Nihon YS-11, which had as many seats as the four-engined Viscount. That the airline launched a home-built product that could be successful in world markets might have been politically useful in its drive toward recognition as an industry leader.

But the way toward such status had to include the operation of international routes, and that way was strewn with obstacles, some from government policy, some from vigorous opposition from J.A.L., whose dominant role in post–Second World War Japan was a latter-day parallel with Pan American Airways' quasi-monopoly role in the pre-war United States. All Nippon had to negotiate this obstacle course toward the fulfilment of international status methodically and opportunistically. It even overcame one or two self-imposed obstacles of its own, as well as facing increased competition on its domestic routes from J.A.L., which moved, with government approval and direction, to claim a share of the homeland business. So in Japan the deregulation process took an entirely different course, a balanced judgment by, on the one hand, a wise aviation administration that guarded against overambitious expansion or self-destructive competition that could be disastrous; on the other hand, courageous and visionary enterprise by an airline that saw its future as something more ambitious than as a second force to a chosen instrument.

An indication that government airline policy was not averse to this objective was the consolidation of airline routes and services within Japan. Far from the fragmentation of airlines that a free-for-all deregulation process would have produced, the opposite course was taken. On 15 April 1964, **Japan Domestic Airlines (J.D.A.)** was formed by the merger of **North Japan Airlines (Kita Nihon Koku)**, **Nitto Airlines**, and **Fuji Airlines.** Kita Nihon, founded on 30 June 1953, had served the north. Its Convair 240s were a familiar sight in Hokkaido. Little Nitto, founded in Osaka on 4 July 1952, had started services across the Inland Sea to Shikoku, with Grumman amphibians. Another small company, **Fuji**, founded on 13 September 1952, operated small Pipers and Beeches to offshore islands.

Discussions were held with a view to A.N.A. merging with Toa Airways (see also later in this chapter), but these were not pursued at the time. J.D.A. was effectively in partnership with J.A.L., which provided technical, commercial, and administrative advice and assistance, and this resulted in J.D.A. becoming a jet operator on 15 March 1966, with ex-J.A.L. Boeing 727-100s. On 20 May of the same year, the Ministry approved the complete merger of the two airlines. But these plans did not reach fruition.

Meanwhile, the Second Force, All Nippon, had not been idle. The understanding had been that, while J.A.L. would operate the trunk routes between the major metropolises, A.N.A. would be responsible for all the feeder routes to secondary cities and other communities. On 4 June 1970 came a breakthrough. An Aviation Committee of the Ministry of Transport announced its Principles of Air Transport Policy, one of the clauses of which stated that "A.N.A. should be given permission to operate short-range international routes in the future." The airline wasted no time. On 1 July—only a month later—permission was received to operate charter flights to South Korea, and before the end of the month, two YS-11 flights were made from Osaka and Fukuoka to Pusan.

All Nippon Airways now had the bit between its teeth. Its expansion on all domestic airline fronts was phenomenal. On 16 August, it carried more than 30,000 passengers in the single day, at a load factor of more than 92%. On 4 November it made a survey flight to Hong Kong and, early in 1971, began charter flights, from Tokyo on 21 February and from Osaka on 21 March. On 3 August Bangkok was linked with Nagoya, and on 31 March 1972 with Kumamoto. By the end of 1971, 24 flights had been completed to Hong Kong, 31 to Bangkok, and the airline was scheduling 15 round-trips per month. During 1972, Jakarta, Kuala Lumpur, and Singapore were added as charter destinations, informal approaches were made to China, and on 28 August 1973, a charter flight was made from Hakodate to Khabarovsk, in the Soviet far east.

Such was the explosive growth of the airline—in the month of August 1972 alone it had carried one million passengers—that it had to undertake an ambitious aircraft procurement program; this involved one of its "self-imposed obstacles." A.N.A.'s traffic levels demanded larger aircraft than the 178-seat Boeing 727-200s, which had gone into service on 1 October 1969, supplementing the smaller Boeing 737s on 20 June. It had to have twin-aisled wide-bodied aircraft. Lockheed demonstrated its L-1011 TriStar on 23 June 1972, and Douglas its DC-10 trimotor three days later. The decision apparently favored Douglas, as its plant at Long Beach, California, allocated six aircraft on its production line to A.N.A. These were ordered through the Mitsui Bank, acting on the airline's behalf, and in which it had a strong financial interest. Following manufacturer-customer tradition, Douglas sent airline support representatives to Tokyo to review maintenance procedures and spares supplies and other technical requirements. Then, one fateful day in September, they were refused admission to the airline's engineering base. No explanation was given, but on 30 October, A.N.A. placed an order for 26 326-seat TriStars. The big aircraft went into service on 10 March 1974, from Tokyo to Okinawa, and was soon deployed on all the densely traveled domestic trunk routes. Kagoshima received the L-1011 on 20 July, only 17 years after its first airline service, with the 8-seater de Havilland Dove—such was the measure of A.N.A.'s spectacular expansion as Japan's Second Force airline, but now claiming something very close to parity.

On 4 February 1976, the deal was revealed to have resulted from a huge bribery scandal at the highest levels of both airline and government. Political influence could have stemmed from a meeting in Honolulu, only a few weeks before the October 1972 announcement, between Prime Minister Tanaka and President Nixon, accompanied by Henry Kissinger. Lockheed desperately needed orders, and its $250 million bank loan had been covered by a U.S. government guarantee. A prominent Japanese businessman committed suicide; Tanaka was arrested on 27 July 1976, and resigned. Lockheed's chairman, Carl Kochian, revealed most of

The Airline World Deregulates

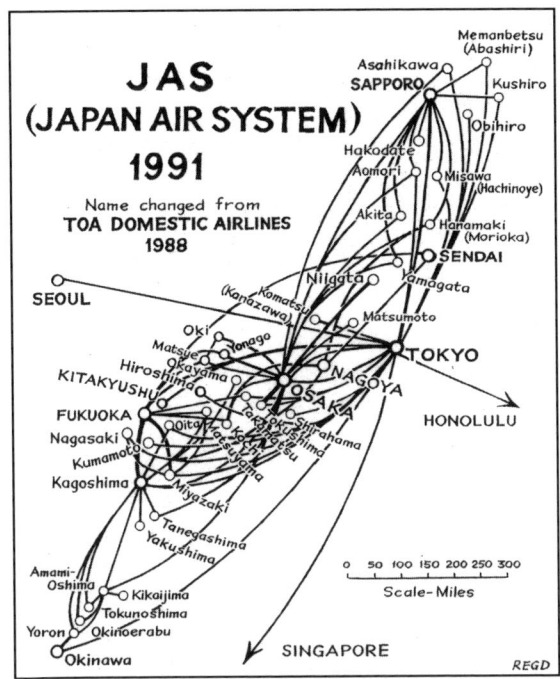

A.N.A. and J.A.L. competed vigorously for the dense traffic on the inter-city trunk routes. Toa and Japan Domestic Airlines competed for the secondary and regional traffic. Eventually, the two merged to form Toa Domestic Airlines, which, in 1988, changed its name to Japan Air System.

the sordid details before the U.S. Securities and Exchange Commission, and the matter was investigated in the U.S. Senate.

All Nippon Airways pursued its destiny. On 19 July 1975, it had applied for permission to fly five international scheduled routes, including one to Taipei and Hong Kong; but was forestalled by J.A.L. establishing **Japan Asia Airways (J.A.A.)**, specifically to serve Taiwan and to avoid a potentially bitter dispute with mainland China when services to the People's Republic could be inaugurated. But A.N.A. had served notice of its ambitions and backed its faith by ordering, on 1 September 1977, three Boeing 747SRs, with an option for eight more. Specially matched to the demands of routes such as Tokyo-Sapporo, Osaka, and Fukuoka (three of the world's five busiest), these double-decked giant airliners were fitted with 528 seats for both A.N.A. and J.A.L.

From its introduction of affinity group charters in 1971, All Nippon had, by 20 May 1978, when Tokyo's new international gateway airport at Narita was opened, carried half a million passengers to almost every eligible tourist destination in east Asia. As if to recognize the irresistible market force of this huge leisure activity, in that year the Ministry of Transport introduced the authority to operate Inclusive Tour Charters (I.T.C.s)—exactly what All Nippon needed. On 29 September it founded **ANA World Tours**. The first charter flight under the new legislation was from Sendai to Beijing on 15 August 1979. During the next few years, ANA World Tours was shepherding flocks of tourists to the Philippines, Malaysia, and Guam, and on 24 September 1984, it flew a full load into Honolulu. By this time also, on 21 June 1983, A.N.A. had introduced the highly efficient Boeing 767 on its domestic network.

Nippon Air Cargo

The potential in Japan, an island nation, for the air freight (or air cargo) business was enormous. Throughout the post-war years, long-range four-engined airliners such as the Lockheed Constellation and the Douglas DC-6 seemed to have the potential for carrying goods as well as people and mail. But optimistic forecasts for a great future in air freighting had come to nought. Airlines such as Flying Tigers and Seaboard & Western had made valiant attempts to establish a permanent foothold in the market, but had been handicapped by the successful development of the passenger airliners, whose carrying capacity allowed a margin for carrying freight, customarily in the lower holds, as well as the revenue passengers. For the big airlines, carrying freight was a welcome bonus, and the flexibility of service destinations provided by their wide-spread route networks gave them a big advantage over the air freight specialists, which had to depend on full or almost-full loads on every route operated. Another, almost fundamental, problem was that most passengers, traveling for business or pleasure, made round-trips. They invariably came home, whereas air freight did not. Consequently, lucrative contracts for delivering export cargoes needed reciprocal contracts to avoid aircraft returning to their bases empty.

By the 1970s, however, the sheer volume of air cargo demand worldwide had grown to the extent that most of the big intercontinental airlines were allocating some of their aircraft—even the first-line types, not only the older ones relegated to the role—to all-cargo services. The basic pattern of the best all-cargo routes comprised the trans-ocean air arteries between North America and Europe (trans-Atlantic), between North America and the far east (trans-Pacific), and between Europe and the far east (trans-Asia). Within the Soviet Union, where much of the land east of the Ural Mountains still lacked surface transport, air cargo flourished.

The big Antonov and Ilyushin freight aircraft provided the life lines of trading and supply throughout the vast areas of Siberia. Yakutsk, the traditional inland trading city of northeastern Siberia, with a population of more than 200,000, did not have a railroad connection to the rest of the country.

Of the non-Soviet air freight arteries, the trans-Pacific ones held the greatest promise. Except for China, still politically introspective, the entire area of eastern Asia, from Korea and Japan in the north to Malaysia and Indonesia in the south was, from the late 1960s, experiencing a dramatic expansion of its industrial base. Led by Japan, factories were established that could manufacture consumer products with labor rates that were often a fraction of those in the developed western world. The result was a booming export trade in a wide variety of commodities, many of which were intrinsically of high value by weight, such as cameras, watches, precision instruments, and radios and televisions.

While larger items such as motor cars went by ship, many of the other products could be flown economically to the biggest market, the United States, by air.

All Nippon Airways founded **Nippon Cargo Airlines (N.C.A.)** on 24 September 1978, and this could be viewed, in retrospect, as the turning point in the parent airline's drive toward world status. For it opened doors that, by international airline convention and tradition, enforced by government or government-supported agreements, had hitherto been closed to it. Eventually, on 3 April 1985, a binding agreement was signed between the controlling government agencies of Japan and the United States. The main features were that J.A.L.'s monopoly of Japanese flights to the United States ended and A.N.A./N.C.A. were designated for trans-Pacific routes. Between Japan and Micronesia—still under U.S. stewardship—two airlines from each country were permitted. A.N.A. had started charter flights to Saipan on 9 July 1984. Most important, and with far-reaching implications, from 1 April 1986, new U.S. destinations would be permitted: Washington (designated to A.N.A.) and Atlanta (to J.A.L.). These supplemented the existing gateways at San Francisco, Los Angeles, New York, Seattle, and Chicago.

There was no stopping A.N.A. now. It completed its scope of the Pacific Rim (as all the countries bordering the ocean had collectively become known) on 24 September 1985 by its first charter flight to Perth (albeit on the Indian Ocean coast); Sydney would soon follow. On 3 March 1986, Japan's Second Force airline started its first scheduled international route (excluding Okinawa) with Tokyo-Guam service, to give notice that its status versus J.A.L. was no longer secondary but was as an equal competitor.

On 16 July 1986, services opened to Los Angeles, followed 10 days later to Washington, prestigiously the capital of the world's biggest industrial power and the seat of government and therefore influence. The Boeing 747 route to Los Angeles was in parallel with Japan Airlines, but the one to the federal capital was different. It was the nonstop capital-to-capital flight between Japan and the United States and was a landmark event. More long-range cities, either by scheduled or charter flights, were added in swift succession during the next two years. On 16 July 1989, All Nippon "invaded" Europe, first with a service to Vienna (purchasing a 9% shareholding in Austrian Air Lines) then, on 22 July, to London, the biggest gateway in Europe. Moscow, Paris, and Brussels followed within a year, and on 9 March 1991, scheduled service opened to New York.

On 1 January 1989, A.N.A. had joined the IATA and was thus subject to the operating conditions that applied to all its members. But by this time, the restrictive levels of fares had become moot. IATA must have been pleased to welcome the Japanese company that had long kept aloof, yet had grown to rank among the world's largest passenger-carrying airlines. On 27 April of that year, it ordered 20 Boeing 747-400s to add to its already large fleet. Such a level of achievement was unprecedented. All Nippon Airways had been born only 31 years previously, and its flagship had been a well-worn DC-3. Now it was a world leader. And in little more than another decade, it was to make its mark on the course of air transport development with an equally unprecedented innovative decision. Not only that, it was a determined survivor. Almost as a textbook proof of private-enterprise success against a government-supported chosen instrument, All Nippon Airways continued normally when Japan Airlines filed for bankruptcy on 20 January 2010.

Japan's Third Force

In the late 1970s, the United States had plunged into a deregulated airline environment in which the immediate consequences were neither immediately apparent nor achieved. The Japanese airlines and their regulators, however, took a different course. This was partly because Japan is a much smaller country and less amenable to regional airline viability, but also because the authorities recognized airlines as a public utility and not simply as just another form of business. The outcome was almost a textbook example of an economic axiom: that the benefits of competition can be realized with only two or, at the most, three competitors. Japan had perhaps learned from watching the process as it developed in the United States, and perhaps, as an island nation like Great Britain, realized that some of its territory did not lend itself to competition at all, because the traffic from outlying communities was just not enough to satisfy such a demand.

On 30 November 1953, **Toa Airways** had been formed in Hiroshima and specialized in providing service to Kagoshima, in southern Kyushu, and further south to the islands of the Ryukyu group, some of which were becoming vacation destinations. During the 1960s, it had made agreements with All Nippon Airways, itself not yet dominant in the domestic arena, for the transfer of routes from Kyushu into southwest Honshu and gave it, most importantly, on 15 June 1964, access to Osaka. Toa's fleet had been quite modest. The island services had been operated mainly by de Havilland Doves and Herons, with Convair 240s connecting the bigger industrial cities of northern Kyushu with Kagoshima and Hiroshima. Its entry into the Jet Age was not spectacular—just a few YS-11 turboprops on order as it quietly added regional routes to its still regional network.

The small airlines were handicapped by the acute shortage of pilots, because of the depredations of the war, during which more than 1,500 had turned themselves into human bombs as kamikazes. The demobilized survivors invariably found employment with Japan Air Lines and All Nippon Airways, which gave the regionals a problem. They had met this by taking advantage of the Japanese aviation laws, which allowed airlines to operate with non-scheduled certificates, flying aircraft with pilots who did not require a full airline ATR rating. This helped the small airlines to become established, but sooner or later, they had to move up technically into the higher echelons of air service. And with the explosive expansion of the Japanese economy in the 1960s, this had to be sooner than later. Thus a natural sequel, from the point of view of both the small operators and the administration, there was an urge to merge.

The Airline World Deregulates

Few airlines in an industrial society could have had a more modest beginning than Toa Airways. This 20-seat de Havilland piston-engined Heron is photographed at Hiroshima. (Bentley)

The first such amalgamation took place on 15 April 1964, when Nitto and Fuji joined the larger Kita Nihon to form Japan Domestic Airlines (J.D.A.) (see above).

All Nippon was charging ahead, so the next step seemed almost inevitable. On 15 May 1971, J.D.A. merged with Toa Airways, apparently closely associated with All Nippon, unofficially if not in corporate terms, to become **Toa Domestic Airlines (T.D.A.)**. J.A.L. had only a minority shareholding, but two of the railroads had 35%, so that this latest amalgamation was, as yet, uncontrolled by the trunk carriers. By this time, incidentally, the development of Japan's innovative high speed railroad, the Shin Kan-sen (effectively, as mentioned earlier, a new form of surface transport, far superior in speed, if not in service standards, to Japan's meter-gauge rail systems) was taking over traffic between the big cities. Yet such was the tremendous growth of travel demand that the airlines still continued to grow at a brisk rate. The railroad interest could have been a means of self-protection.

T.D.A. was quick to spread its wings, riding high on the wave of explosive growth of the Japanese economy. On 1 August 1972, it introduced Boeing 727-100s on the Tokyo-Oita route, on 1 September Tokyo-Kagoshima, and on 1 October, Tokyo-Fukuoka. With further route additions, mainly to points in Kyushu, Japan's third airline was making a statement in the skies of southern Japan. On 4 June 1973, it leased a Douglas DC-9-31 and soon followed, on 1 December, with the larger DC-9-41s, which were fitted with a wide-body interior layout. The inaugural service with this Douglas twin was from Tokyo to Kushiro, in eastern Hokkaido, so that T.D.A.'s name became familiar over the length and breadth of all the Japanese islands.

On 1 March 1975, service began on the Tokyo-Sapporo and Tokyo-Fukuoka trunk routes—two of the world's five busiest air routes. But following the disciplined approach by the Japanese controlling authorities, the competition with the incumbent Japan Air Lines and All Nippon Airways was regulated by standardized fares and negotiated scheduling. The system could be described as organized deregulation. It was not a free-for-all, almost open-skies policy, as practiced in the United States after the sweeping effects of the 1978 Airline Deregulation Act; neither was it like the former tight Australian dual-airline policy. It was an intelligent compromise that encouraged good service, yet prevented wild excesses.

The system worked. In July 1978, T.D.A. began "double-tracking" a number of All Nippon Airways's routes, from Tokyo to Kagoshima, Kumamoto, and Hakodate. These were in parallel with A.N.A.'s beam routes, but the latter did not suffer from the added competition. T.D.A. now had the bit between its teeth and, on 1 March 1981, introduced the 281-seat Airbus A300 on Tokyo-Kagoshima and the 163-seat Douglas DC-9 Super-80 on Tokyo-Oita and Tokyo-Misawa. Finally, on 1 November 1983, T.D.A. entered the Tokyo-Osaka market, linking Japan's two biggest cities.

The airline was no longer taking third place to its two senior partners. Operationally and technologically it was their equal, if not measured in numbers of passengers carried or in the size of its fleet. And further consolidation of its status continued, almost as an echo of All Nippon's rise to prominence a decade earlier. It had, at the other end of the scale from its acquired trunk airline status, established **Japan Air Commuter (J.A.C.)** on 1 July 1983, having ordered the short-strip-friendly 19-seat Dornier 228 in May, and this versatile aircraft started services from Amami-Oshima, one of the larger islands of the Ryukyus, on 10 December 1983.

Ever versatile, T.D.A. offered, from 17 March 1985, helicopter flights to Tsukuba, about 30 miles north of Tokyo, for the Science Expo held there. The route was triangular, linking both the Haneda and Narita airports. But far more important and far-reaching, again echoing A.N.A.'s progress, was flying its first international charter, from Osaka to Seoul, South Korea, on 19 September 1986. As if to announce its elevation to the big leagues, a contract was signed for 300-seat wide-bodied Douglas DC-10s on 28 October, and the next year, on 27 April, T.D.A. joined IATA. To emphasize and to symbolize its achieved ranking into the highest echelons of airline stature, the name of the airline was changed, on 1 April 1988, two days after the first DC-10 was delivered, to **Japan Air System (J.A.S.)**.

The identity of little Toa, respected though it was for its pioneering in the Ryukyus, and hitherto restricted by the very word *domestic*; these memories were now consigned to history. J.A.S. quickly began to spread its wings far beyond the confines of the Japanese homeland. On 1 July 1988, the route to Seoul was upgraded from charter to scheduled status, the commuter subsidiary was operating 60-seat YS-11s, and charter flights began to Honolulu on 17 June 1989, and to Singapore on 3 February 1990. The first Airbus A300B4-600, larger than its predecessor, with 308 seats, was delivered on 29 April 1991. On 3 June of that year, to round off a triumphant progression of events, scheduled service started to Honolulu, which had become a major Japanese tourist destination. This had resulted from the negotiations with the United States, which had brought All Nippon Airways across the Pacific, and with its arrival at the 50th State, 20 years after the Toa–J.D.A. merger, Japan Air System had come of age.

Chapter 22: Russian Metamorphosis

Collapse of a Mighty Airline

In size and stature by almost any measure of comparison, there has never been an airline quite like **Aeroflot**, and there never will be again. When the communist power collapsed at the end of 1991, the disintegration of the Soviet Union's airline was much more; it was the near-destruction of the nation's entire air transport system. In addition to providing airline service between cities, towns, and villages across 11 time zones, equipped with a fleet of about 11,000 aircraft, of which about 3,500 were jets or turboprops, it provided emergency and social services throughout Siberia's Arctic northlands, conducted crop-spraying programs over thousands of square miles, substituted for roads and railroads in the construction of thousands of miles of oil and gas pipelines, and was a key element in building the Baikal-Amur Magistral (BAM) railroad that parallelled the famous Trans-Siberian. It was also the transport arm of the armed forces, the equivalent of the U.S. or R.A.F. Transport Commands, but much bigger.

Suddenly to wipe out such a vast organization was, therefore, an act of such far-reaching consequences that the whole system, from the Baltic Sea to the northern Pacific Ocean, was in danger of complete collapse. The recovery from near disaster could be attributed partly to a disciplined transfer of powers and responsibilities at the governmental administrative level; partly to a latent talent among Russians, Ukrainians, and others, to readjust to a capitalist society and react to traditional sale-and-demand market forces; and partly to an instinctive backs-to-the-wall attitude that had served the Soviet Union so well in its defense against Napoleon in the 19th and Hitler in the 20th century.

The authorities had the good sense not to destroy Aeroflot altogether. Its experience was too valuable an asset. In the 1960s and 70s it had gained an unenviable reputation for poor service, but had thrown away the standard of making air service available to every citizen, rich or poor. When it gradually expanded its route system beyond the boundaries of fellow-traveling nations, it had to improve its attitude toward a more discerning public. By the late 1980s, its main-line services to foreign capitals were able to hold their own against western airlines competition. And so, in the new Russia, a depleted Aeroflot was able to maintain its international services, with a fleet of about 100 airliners, with Ilyushin Il-86 and Il-62s as the long-distance flagships. And sensibly, to avoid too many domestic interchanges, it was able to operate a route network within Russia between all the main cities. Otherwise, however, the vast network of secondary routes, even to some major cities of more than a million population, together with third-level and bush services to the most remote regions of the Arctic hinterland and the Siberian tundra, were peremptorily amputated.

Picking Up the Pieces

The Soviet Union had collapsed with a finality that few politicians, historians, or internationalists could have forecast. First had come the liberating declarations of *glasnost* (open-ness) and *perestroika* (restructuring), delivered dramatically by Mikhail Gorbachev in 1985. This policy was enough to shake the foundations of the Kremlin; indeed, this is what happened. Almost within months, the house of communism came tumbling down, and all across the republics that had comprised the enormous geographical extent of the U.S.S.R., a somewhat bewildered population struggled to pick up the bricks from the rubble and try to rebuild. Boris Yeltsin had effectively usurped Gorbachev and accelerated the pace of the transformation of a centrally based totalitarian regime into a diversified capitalist society. This open-ness was seized upon enthusiastically—and not always too ethically—by former arm-chair industrialists and entrepreneurs who had long been frustrated to observe the successes and consequent riches and private fortunes generated in the West. Independent companies, large and small, sprang up by the thousands. Private manufacturers took over the former production lines of the state industries; small shopkeepers emerged from the former state distribution system; and Muscovites lined up to taste McDonald's hamburgers.

Nowhere was this complete revolution more abrupt or more far-reaching in its transformation than in the dismemberment of the Soviet Union's giant air transport system, Aeroflot. The Ministry of Civil Aviation, the political parent of the organization, itself underwent a transformation. It was confronted with the overwhelming challenge of authorizing the establishment of hundreds of new private airlines. For the Minister of Civil Aviation, Boris Panukov, this was an unenviable task, and an additional aspect of the entire procedure was the break-up of the Soviet Union itself. In one sense, however, the task was at least confined to Russia, as the former semi-autonomous republics in the Baltic, Caucasus, and Central Asian regions broke free from Moscow and became totally independent as sovereign powers.

At the breakup of the once-omnipotent Aeroflot, many of the new airlines simply changed their status from operational divisions of the parent company—there were 34 of them, covering 11 time zones—into companies owned by or controlled by the individual regions, many of which, in Siberia, were bigger than several European countries. In addition, under the new wave of perestroika that was sweeping the land, new independent companies were founded everywhere. In a capitalist society, the requirements of a new company invariably comprise monetary investments by individuals or by other interested companies that were already newly established. Russians, Ukrainians, and others quickly grasped the elements of the new world of finance. In one sense they were aided by the recognition that, without air transport, the vast reaches of Russia especially would be reduced to, at best, a fragmented collection of peoples isolated from their brethren. Ponderous and improvisational though the transferring process was, the massive reorganization got under way.

Russian Metamorphosis

THE NEW CIS AIRLINES

Airline	Base
(Former Aeroflot directorates are shown in bold type)	
Aeroflot – Russian International Airlines (CUMVS)	Moscow-SVO
Aerovolga	Kazan
Air Ukraine	Kiev
Archangelsk CAD	Archangelsk
Armenian Airlines	Yerevan
Azerbaijan Airlines (AZAL)	Baku
Baikalavia	Irkutsk
Bashkir Airlines	Ufa
Belarus CAD	Minsk
Domodedovo PO	Moscow-DME
Far Eastern Avia	Khabarovsk
Georgian CAD	Tbilisi
Goniiga State Scientific and Research Institute	Moscow-SVO
Independent United Air Detachment	Moscow-VKO
Kazakh CAD	Alma-Ata
Kirghizi CAD	Bishkek
Komi Ave	Syktyvkar
Krasnoyarskavia	Krasnoyarsk
Leningrad ACA	St Petersburg
Magadan Avia	Magadan
Mineralvodskoe PO	Mineralnyevody
Moldavian CAD	Kishinev
Nerungri Sakha Corp	Yakutsk
NPO PANKH	Krasnodar
Sibavia	Novosibirsk
Southern Airlines	Rostov-on-Don
Tadzhik CAD	Dushanbe
Tatarstan Airlines	Kazan
Tyumenavia Trans	Tyumen
Transaero	Moscow-SVO
Turkmenavia	Ashkhabad
Ugats	Moscow-Bykovo
Urals CAD	Ekaterninburg
Uzbeki CAD	Tashkent
Vnukovo CAD	Moscow -VKO
Yakutavia	Yakutsk

Notes: ACA: Association of Civil Aviation, CAD: Civil Air Department, PANKH: Aerial Work Detachment, PO: Production Association

DME = Domodedovo
SVO = Sheremetyevo
VKO = Vnukovo

The biggest asset of any airline is its aircraft fleet, and all the new airlines were given generous terms under which they acquired them. The former Aeroflot divisional fleets were simply taken over. These were more than adequate to sustain the newcomers for their introduction to private enterprise during their formative years. The fleets were all Russian or Ukrainian-built, except some Czechoslovak turboprops. Aeroflot had purchased a few Airbuses, but with the collapse of the Soviet Union, production of civil airliners at the factories of Tupolev, Ilyushin, and Yakovlev came to a standstill. In the longer term, the new airlines would have to buy their own, and would have to find ways of raising the necessary capital to do so. This was a real problem, as the low fares established by the Soviet government as a national subsidy to the proletariat were far from adequate to provide a breakeven level of revenue to cover the costs of running an airline. The airlines set higher fares to reconcile the gap between income and expenditure, but soon discovered that this discouraged travel. Also, the huge state-run Soviet industries were grinding to a halt. Unemployment, which theoretically had been nonexistent under Communist rule, was now rampant and few people could now afford to travel by air any more.

The other enormous handicap was the fuel supply. In former days, the headquarter bases of the semi-autonomous regions never had to worry about the bills for gasoline, kerosene, or oil. It was delivered by tanker or by pipeline, and the local director simply signed a receipt for record purposes. This had been the Soviet system. Almost everything, from consumer goods to public utilities, were manufactured and supplied through a centralized chain and for many essentials such as aviation fuel, the accounting did not involve the actual transfer of money. But now, the new companies had to make arrangements with the emergent oil giants such as Yukos and Gasprom, which were enthusiastically taking over the vast riches of the Russian oil and gas-producing wells that constituted the world's second largest source of that vital commodity.

Political Revolution

The unravelling of the Soviet Union that had been fashioned during the early 1920s, following the Russian Revolution of 1917, took place quickly. When the U.S.S.R. was disbanded on 31 December 1991, this was solely an international de jure declaration. The deeds had already been done. The autonomous republics had declared their independent status during the summer and the closing months of that year. Little Lithuania had begun the de facto movement, declaring independence on 11 March 1990—and paid a price for its courage by a mini-invasion of Russian troops. Georgia declared on 9 April 1991, eight more followed during the month of August, and before the official date of the end of the Soviet Union, all 14 of the non-Russian republics were new nations.

For a few years, attempts were made to hold together a loose semi-federation, the Commonwealth of Independent States (C.I.S.), the formation of which was announced on 22 December 1991. But this was never to achieve the level of mutual cooperation or recognition that, for example, had been evolved when the once-cohesive British Empire dissolved after the Second World War and became the British Commonwealth. The effect on the former Soviet airlines in the C.I.S. was another organizational disruption of their independent status. Instead of reporting ultimately to Moscow and controlled, however loosely, by the Russian Ministry of Civil Aviation, they were now completely on their own, having to adapt to new regimes, new (and often inexperienced) administrations, and having to start again almost from scratch. Most of them, Ukraine and Kazakhstan excepted, were in small countries, with little scope for domestic air services, and therefore most of them had to learn the intricacies of international diplomacy regarding air services, operating standards, traffic rights, and the myriad aspects of trading in a competitive world where the hard lessons had already been learned.

The New Airlines

To state that the post-perestroika situation in Russia was chaotic would not be too far from the reality. But to condemn it out of hand would be unfair, for the entire structure of Russian politics, economics, foreign policy, local government, employment, and standards and styles of living had undergone a revolution as far-reaching as that of 1917. It was a complete reversal—and a bloodless one—that cancelled the Communist regime, emphatically centralized in Moscow, and substituted a diversified capitalism. Such a complete transition was overwhelming and took time. Everything in Russian society had to be created anew. Little from the former centralized organization could be easily converted to a new market-oriented economy. True, the local butcher's shop, No. 284, for example, would be taken over by the former state-employed manager, as would some of the staff, who no longer had to be party members to gain favor. Local bus services were not too difficult to change over. People started to go back to church. Young people could go to discos, but large industries—such as banking, insurance, property ownership, oil and gas production, and the vast agricultural base—all had to undergo an often painful transformation. The omnipotent Aeroflot was no exception. Its dissolution took time.

Transaero

While the 34 subdivisions of Aeroflot were "getting their act together" (some of them were alone as big as many a flag carrier of the western world), the spirit of free enterprise rose to break into the restless Russian air. In October 1990, **Transaero** was formed in Moscow as a joint stock company airline, the first of its kind in Russia. Five years had gone by since Mikhail Gorbachev's perestoika, and the wheels had turned slowly in the corridors of power in Moscow. But they did turn, with an element of "who you know" still being at least as important as "what you know." The formation of Transaero heralded the transformation of the Russian air transport industry. This new airline made its first charter flight in November 1991 then the first non-state domestic air service, to Noriilsk, in northern Siberia, in January 1993. In April of that year, it introduced Boeing 737s, on lease from Ireland. This alone was a break-through, as in previous years, western manufacturers had been unable to penetrate the impregnable wall of resistance to defend the massive state commercial aircraft builders that included Tupolev, Ilyushin, Yakovlev, and Antonov.

Transaero also created a sensation, at least in Russia, by catering for businessmen, introducing a better class of service for them than the traditional bus standards. Its Ilyushin Il-86 wide-bodied aircraft had 255 seats, *in mixed class*, an unheard-of innovation for a traveling public that had always had only economy class seating—and even that was usually below that of western standards. Transaero recognized that, in the new Russia, the wealth of the nation as a whole, in a capitalist society, would be spread over income strata that would include a middle class, and even a rich clientele who would demand the amenities of comfortable seats, good on-board service and meals, and even assistance at the airports. All these pleasantries had been conspicuously absent during the austere climate of the old Aeroflot, which was the Soviet Union's nationwide cheap aerial bus service.

In 1994, Transaero made its first foreign flight, to Tel Aviv then to London via Riga, and, in April, to New York. In June 1996, with Douglas DC-10s, leased from American Airlines, it opened nonstop service to Los Angeles, and with a growing fleet that included Boeing 757s and 767s, it claimed to be, measured by annual passenger-miles, the second largest airline in Russia, exceeded only by Aeroflot, which had retained a virtual monopoly on all foreign routes plus domestic connections to all the main cities in Russia. Further expansion continued, but progress was halted with the "Black Monday" national financial crisis on 17 August 1998, when the value of the ruble plummeted. Transaero's business declined considerably for a few years, but began to recover in the early 2000s, led by Olga Pleshakova, the first woman president, or even senior controller, of any big commercial enterprise in the new Russia.

Sibir and Vnukovo

Many of the former divisions of Aeroflot were, as mentioned above, substantial entities and were able to take advantage of their geographical and demographic situations, and especially as they occupied airports and simply took over Aeroflot's previous installations, including passenger terminals and maintenance bases. While, in Moscow, Aeroflot concentrated on Sheremetyvo Airport, the other two airports in the Russian capital, Vnukovo and Domodedovo, set themselves up independently. **Vnukovo Airlines** was established in 1993, and at first was second only to Aeroflot in passenger boardings. Its 50-strong fleet included 22 Ilyushin Il-86 wide-bodies, but the airline experienced many managerial and organizational problems, and some of its aircraft showed signs of wear. In 2001, after some years of negotiation, it suspended operations, and most of its fleet and business were taken over by another ex-Aeroflot division, **Sibir (Siberian Airlines)**, based in Novosibirsk, the largest Russian city east of the Ural Mountains.

Sibir had at first been named Tolmachevo State Aviation Enterprise, and had taken over many of the smaller local regional companies, under an arrangement that was loosely known as the Siberian Treaty. Many of its flights were charters to groups of Siberian city dwellers who were benefitting from better living standards, and Sibir obliged with shopping trips abroad, including to Beijing, with substantial overloads of excess baggage on the return flights.

Transaero's wide-bodied Ilyushin Il-86, with business-class seats, was unprecedented in Russia. The airline then trumped its own ace with Boeing 747s. (Bentley)

The post-Soviet Russian airlines faced a familiar process of attrition as competition increased. Sibir emerged as the dominant airline in Siberia, with Ilyushin Il-86s (above) as its flagships. (Bentley)

In April 1998, Vladislav Filev became director general, and he immediately improved the standards of cabin service and raised wages—an incentive that was relatively novel in Siberia. Sibir bought the first Tupolev Tu-204 (and Tupolev's first sale) in 1999, by which time it was the fifth largest airline in Russia. On 4 October 2001, it suffered a tragic loss when a Tu-134 was shot down by a Ukrainian missile over the Black Sea, but in the same year, it took over Vnukovo Airlines, thus acquiring a second base and operational hub in the nation's capital.

This gave Sibir the rank as the second largest airline in Russia, a remarkable achievement considering that Novosibirsk is not known worldwide as a natural hub. But this does not take into account the vastness of Siberia—twice as large as the United States—and the growing wealth from apparently almost unlimited natural resources in oil and gas, and minerals, including precious stones in abundance. It emphasized its status as a front-runner in Russian air transport by switching its Moscow base to Domodedovo in 2002, but once again, two years later, the mixed fortunes of 2001 were repeated. Another Tu-134 was lost on 24 August 2004 when it crashed after taking off from Moscow, having been sabotaged by two women suicide bombers. Sibir had just taken delivery of its first of three new Airbus A310-300s. It then went from strength to strength. In spite of problems with high import taxes, and a natural desire to support the Russian industry, it continued to modernize its fleet when, in May 2005, it took delivery of its first Boeing 737-500 to replace the aging Tupolev Tu-154s, which had become the workhorses of the post-perestroika era but were now tiring.

Domodedovo Airlines

Back in the 1960s, Moscow's main commercial airport was Vnukovo. It was superseded in the 1970s by Sheremetyovo, which promptly became Aeroflot's base. In the 1980s, however, another Moscow airport came into prominence when, in 1975, Aeroflot's supersonic airliner, the Tupolev Tu-144, took off on its first flight to Alma Ata (now Almaty, in Kazakhstan) from Domodedovo. The subsequent regular service was short-lived, ending in June 1978. In the same year, Aeroflot embarked on the more practical nonstop service, to the farthest reaches of Russia, nine time zones away, at Petropavlovsk-Kamchatski, on the far-off Pacific Ocean rim, using Iluyishin Il-62s. In 1981, Domodedovo became the base for the wide-bodied Ilyushin Il-86s, with scheduled flights to Tashkent, then the fourth largest city in the Soviet Union, and now the capital of Uzbekistan.

As decreed by the government, the joint airline-airport role—its status as a division of the all-embracing Aeroflot—ended, and **Domodedovo Airlines** was established on 12 January 1998. With its fleet including the new wide-bodied Ilyushin Il-96s as well as Il-76 freighters, the new company quickly became a force in the reconstituted airline industry of Russia. In the same year, it took delivery of one of the last of Ilyushin's dependable workhorses, the Il-18 turboprop, built in greater numbers than all the other four-engined airliners in the world combined. It had

Of several Moscow-based airlines founded in post-Soviet Russia, Domodedovo Airlines has been the most successful, based at the airport of the same name. (Bentley)

first entered service 34 years earlier. Domodedovo's rise to prominence has been stimulated by the extension of the metropolitan subway network to connect the airport directly to the city center. Extensive installation improvements, notably to enhance convenience for the passengers, have also attracted much favorable comment.

In parallel with the emergence of the passenger airline, an all-cargo airline of considerable substance, with a fleet of Ilyushin Il-76s, **East Line** had been founded at Domodedovo on 1 January 1991 and was officially established on 17 November 1995. It started passenger services in 1997, with Il-86s and others in 1997, specializing in flights to Europe and the Middle East. It has been (for Russia) uncharacteristically versatile in its activities, leasing aircraft from other airlines when needed, as well as owning them. It has enterprisingly reconstructed and modernized the passenger terminal at Domodedovo, in which it still retains a shareholding interest.

Kras Air

While Moscow had its new Aeroflot, Transaero, and Domodedovo, Siberia had its Sibir, from Novosibirsk; Kras Air, from Krasnoyarsk; and UTair, from Tyumen. A far cry from when Siberia was notorious in Czarist days for its salt-mines, and in Soviet days for the gulag, western Siberia is now a hive of industrial activity, based on its oil and gas riches and extensive mining. The city of Krasnoyarsk was not about to watch Novosibirsk monopolize commercial aviation in the area. Krasnoyarsk Airlines became **Kras Air** in 1992 when it was privatized as a joint stock company. It succeeded one of Aeroflot's major divisions and inherited a strong fleet of Ilyushin Il-62s, Il-76s, and Tupolev Tu-154s, as well as fleets of feeder aircraft. In December 1994, it showed its mettle by being only the second new Russian airline to apply for permission to fly to New York, for which route it obtained two ex-K.L.M. Douglas DC-10s.

But in 1996, it had to pull out of New York, as the traffic demand to and from Siberia had not yet grown to an economic level. Cruises on the Yenesei River and Lake Baikal, local visits to dams that dwarfed the Hoover Dam, were not yet on the tourist circuit. In the same year, an Il-76 crashed in Kamchatka. But two years later, Kras Air took delivery of two Rolls-Royce-powered 175-seat Tupolev 204s. For this bold effort, the airline had much local support, as the acquisition was financed from the Krasnoyarsk

One of the earlier airlines to be hived off the Aeroflot airline monopoly was Krasnoyarskavia, based geographically in the center of Siberia. It inherited Tupolev 154s. (Davies)

regional governor's office, and to ensure continued progress, the new general director, Boris Abramovich, made some important decisions. He reduced the number of aircraft in the fleet from 80 to 50, yet maintained the same level of fleet productivity, and he installed some modern training programs for the staff at all levels, including courses in London and in Korea. Kras Air turned its back on the austere Soviet methods of running an airline.

Expansion of its route network continued, including a direct link with Norilsk, in the far north. More important was the transfer of its Moscow services from Vnukovo to Domodedovo Airport, after completion of a new terminal there. With this rejuvenated link, Kras Air established through connections between Europe and eastern Siberia: Irkutsk (for Lake Baikal), Khabarovsk, and Vladivostok, for which the Krasnoyarsk-Moscow segment was served by a daily Ilyushin Il-86 flight, sometimes with extra sections. This wide-bodied service offered 14 first-class seats in addition to 302 economy class; only Transaero had hitherto introduced comparative luxury to the Russian air traveler.

The Unique Tyumenaviatrans

To use the term *unique* requires extreme caution, yet in this case it is fully justified. Nowhere else in the world has a large airline, measured by its output in the carriage of freight and passengers, had its origins as a helicopter organization, and nowhere in the world has there ever been a helicopter organization that so outstripped all others in size and level of activity as **Tyumenaviatrans**. At its height, immediately before the end of the Soviet Union in 1991, its fleet of aircraft numbered 660, of which no less than 450 were helicopters. Of these, 360 were the versatile Mil Mi-8s, able to carry up to 28 passengers (as in the village services in northern Siberia, and the vacation resorts of the Black Sea). At one time or another, at least 1,000 of these versatile machines, of which more than 6,000 were built, were based at Tyumen.

In addition, based at Tyumen were some of the large 65-seat Mil Mi-6s (hundreds of these were built too), and dozens of its specialized variant, the Mil Mi-10, which had an elongated landing gear and shrunk fuselage to enable it to transport sections of large pipes for the gas fields, subassemblies of electricity transmission towers, or even a truck or a bus. Also to be seen at Tyumen throughout the 1960s and onward were the Mil Mi-26s. These helicopters are truly the mightiest of their type. With eight-bladed rotors, they are equipped with an internal two-ton gantry crane and can lift a payload of 20 tons. With such a formidable fleet of helicopters, Tyumenaviatrans's fixed-wing fleet was almost a marginal branch of its operations. Yet it also had many Antonov An-2s (that remarkable 12-seat biplane that can almost land on a baseball diamond); 40-seat An-26 turboprops; Tupolev Tu-134s and 154s for main routes; and 30-seat Yakovlev Yak-40 tri-jets for local routes.

The airline had been established on 7 February 1967 as the helicopter division of Aeroflot, based at Tyumen, which was ideally located on the Trans-Siberian Railway to serve the oil and gas fields of western Siberia beyond the Ural mountains. The reasons for the choice went back even further, to 1941, during the early years of the exploration of the underground riches, as the maintenance base for the helicopter fleet. These rotor-craft were chosen for the huge logistics problem of transporting the oil and gas from fields that were in the far north. The pipelines were hundreds of miles long, and to build them through the vast area of swamps, lakes, and forests—the taiga and the tundra—would have required a construction effort almost as formidable as the Trans-Siberian itself. So instead of building railways and roads that would be essential to deliver the pipes and the transmission towers for the electric grid lines, large helicopters could provide the necessary logistics directly to the sites. Ultimately a railway was built from Tyumen to the north, but the fleet of Mil helicopters provided the logistic support for all the pioneering construction work.

By the end of the 1990s decade, the Tyumenaviatrans directorate of Aeroflot was carrying more than eight million passenger a year, ranking fifth among the 34 directorates. For the army of workers in the oil and gas fields, it enjoyed almost a monopoly of transport services. Not surprisingly, its 650,000 tons of freight carried in 1990 was the highest in Aeroflot, amounting to a fifth of that airline's total. On 1 July 1992, following the collapse of the Communist system and the fragmentation of Aeroflot, a presidential decree established the State Committee of Property within the new Russian Federation, and on 28 October **Tyumen Avia Trans (T.A.T.)** was formally registered. At first, the former directorate was split into two parts, with **Tyumen Airlines** taking over the main routes to other Russian and C.I.S. cities. But like many such companies that could not cope with the process of attrition that was soon the sequel to the abrupt transformation from a centralized communist state to a capitalist society, this airline was up for sale at the end of 2002. T.A.T. took over the whole Tyumen-based air services, at first under the former Aeroflot director, Vladimir Iliaronov, to oversee the problems of survival, even in an area in which the supply of fuel was not as critical as in many other areas of the former Soviet Union. During the process of readjustment, passenger traffic dropped to only a tenth of what it had been with the monolithic Aeroflot, when people could travel very cheaply, as decreed as far ago as the Soviet Union's Second Five-Year Plan of the early 1930s. This was all changed, and the new airlines had to learn how the books were balanced, with the necessary high fares and the difficulties of obtaining aircraft by buying them, rather than them simply being allocated. Under Iliaronov, T.A.T. spread its organization, with the registered office at Khanty-Mansiysk and operational headquarters at Surgut.

In 1999, Andrei Martirosov was appointed CEO. He restructured T.A.T.; introduced western-style economy measures; and benefitted from some lucrative overseas contracts, sponsored by the United Nations, in countries that needed large helicopters. The big Mil Mi-6s were to be found in South America and Africa, operating in areas that conventional surface transport could not reach. Closer to home, in a revolutionary move for services on the main routes, the Tupolev Tu-154s were fitted with 12 business-class seats, and 18 "economy-comfort" seats—standards that were quite a novelty for Russian air travelers. In January 2001, T.A.T. bought control of the former Aircraft Overhaul Factory No. 26 at Tyumen and, in April 2002, rather as Sibir did to Moscow's Vnukovo, bought a 49% interest in Domodedovo Airlines.

Recognizing that it was no longer a local regional airline and that some of its clientele were overseas oil industrialists, T.A.T. simplified its name to **UTair**, an abbreviation for Ugorsk Transport, this referring to the traditional name for the west Siberian region. Like many of the other airlines freed from the obligation to operate only Russian aircraft, UTair ordered, in August 2004, five ATR 42-300s to replace its aging An-24s.

The Unique Volga-Dnepr Super Freighter

Caution is not needed to use the term *unique* to describe **Volga-Dnepr**. Based at Ulyanovsk, on the Volga River, and using aircraft designed in Kiev, which is on the Dnepr (in the Ukraine at the time of this writing), the name reflects an admirable exercise in political and industrial pragmatism. Alexei Isaikin has steered this remarkable company to a position of respectability throughout the aviation world.

The primary shareholder is Aviastar, a new production company at Ulyanovsk, with other interests from the Antonov Design Bureau of Kiev, its engine company, a bank, and the Central Directorate of International Air Transport. The latter shareholder may well have recognized that Volga-Dnepr would be more than just another airline. Its fleet of specialized freighters would carry the Russian flag to every continent.

The Antonov An-124 Ruslan is the world's biggest transport airplane, originally intended for military logistics, but easily converted for commercial use. It can carry 120 tons of freight, either in multiple pallets or containers of any size, or in awkward bulk loads, such as 50 cars. Its range with maximum payload is 2,400 miles. With the same payload as the Ilyushin Il-76, itself a large wide-bodied freight aircraft, the range is more than 6,000 miles. Even with such a payload-range capability, its speed is a respectable 450 mph. One An-124 can carry as much as nine Hercules (Lockheed C-130s). Volga-Dnepr's initial fleet of 13 aircraft included seven of these giants.

Established in August 1990, Isaikin set out to sell Volga-Dnepr as a unique logistics resource, which, indeed, it has been for several years. Its An-124s have transported turbine assemblies from Barcelona to New Caledonia, equipment for the Channel Tunnel from North Carolina, satellites from France to Guiana, and, on one occasion, 107 cars to Australia for a rally. They carried gold—32 tons of it—from Abu Dhabi to Zurich, and an entire Nimrod marine reconnaissance fuselage for British Aerospace. Boeing and Airbus both used the An-124s for transporting large subassemblies or engines to the production lines at Seattle and Toulouse. Its versatility was later recognized by the United Nations, which, among other humanitarian missions, contracted with Volga-Dnepr for close to 300 flights to Afghanistan, where the giant aircraft's multiple landing gear (28 wheels in the main gear alone) and its front-and-back loading ability made it tolerant of landing fields that were not at top International Civil Aviation Organization (I.C.A.O.) standards. Other notable efforts were to evacuate U.S. personnel from Zaïre in December 1991 and, in August 1993, to carry 230 tons of stage equipment for the singer Michael Jackson on a 10-week world tour.

During the 1990s, in a joint venture, the British company **HeavyLift** worked extensively with Volga-Dnepr, and the An-124 could be seen in the colors of others who ventured to exploit its special payload-range capability. Though spectacular, the need for them, however, was not frequent or regular, and so the utilization of the aircraft tended to be sporadic. Also, there was still an operational hang-over from the old Soviet days, and Isaikin promoted a program of staff training to modernize and westernize the entire structure of his special airline. He introduced incentives for good work, English language classes, and intensive pilot

The Antonov An-124 Ruslan has no equal. With payloads up to 120 tons, the Volga-Dnepr airline enjoys worldwide contracts for specialized cargo. (McDonough)

The Antonov An-124 dwarfed all other cargo transport aircraft. (McDonough)

training. By 1999, Volga-Dnepr was working with **Air Foyle**, a British agency that successfully expanded the world demand so that the An-124 fleet was expanded to eight. Ulyanovsk was not too convenient for essential servicing and maintenance, and bases were set up at Shannon, Ireland; Sharjah, United Emirates; Stansted, near London; Houston, Texas; and Tientsin, China. By 3 August, when two new An-124s were delivered from Aviastar, the aircraft's service life had been extended from a modest 7,500 hours to 24,000, and the engine life from 1,250 hours to 2,400. Quality control and engineering tolerances had changed considerably from the Soviet style, which depended on replacement of whole units rather than servicing or overhaul. On 1 February 2001, the partnership with HeavyLift was dissolved, with Volga-Dnepr operating independently, but with HeavyLift still chartering the An-124s. In June of that year, a new agreement was made with the U.S. company Atlas Air, which was no doubt a business strategy to gain contracts for oversize loads in the United States.

Even such a giant aircraft as the Ruslan could not depend on its unique size alone for extended use, and in November 2001, Volga-Dnepr signed an agreement with the Antonov Design Bureau to upgrade the An-124. Improvements included new avionics and a better flight deck that reduced the crew from six to four. Even more remarkable was the installation of an overhead traveling crane that could cope with a 30-ton load. Such an effort led to another break-through for Isaikin, for in July 2002 he obtained a $29.9 million loan from the I.L.F.C. leasing company to complete an An-124 at Aviastar, to increase the Volga-Dnepr fleet to 10. The key element of this transaction was that it was the first time when an American company had risked an investment in Russia without an ironclad government guarantee.

Early in 2004, thoughts of starting regular, even scheduled, long-haul services between the world's major airline hubs, began to take shape when Volga-Dnepr established **AirBridge Cargo** as a fully owned subsidiary, with two main bases at Moscow and Krasnoyarsk. The selection of the western Siberian city may have been made because of the liberalization of Russian aerospace that permits trans-polar flights between the eastern and western hemispheres. Aircraft flying between, for example, Chicago and Hong Kong can save hours of flight time by following a great circle route and, heavily loaded, can stop for refueling at Krasnoyarsk. AirBridge Cargo subscribes to the trend toward globalization—it has an ex-Alitalia Boeing 747-200 freighter and has ordered two 747-400s, at a price of $450 million. For half a century, many airline and aircraft promoters have dreamed of the emergence of a huge air freight market. Volga-Dnepr seems to be on the way to bringing this dream closer to reality.

Pulkovo Air Enterprise

The second city of the Soviet Union is St. Petersburg, founded by Peter the Great in the 18th century, and which, during the First World War was named Petrograd; then, after the death of Lenin in 1924, was named Leningrad after him. It has the distinction of being the origin point of the world's first long-distance flight by a transport aircraft, when, in 1914, just before the outbreak of the First World War, Igor Sikorsky's *Il'ya Muromets* four-engined biplane made a round-trip to Kiev. Following the collapse of the Soviet Union in 1991, the city reverted to its former name. After a heated campaign, agreement with the authorities was reached to name the reconstituted airline after its airport. Thus, the **Pulkovo Air Enterprise**, as in other situations throughout Russia, combines the airport and airline activities under the same management.

It inherited a balanced fleet of more than 50 airliners, including 21 Tupolev Tu-134s, 15 Tu-154s, and eight wide-bodied Ilyushin Il-86s. These aging types are being replaced by modern Tupolev Tu-334s. The domestic route network extends mainly to the south, with a trunk line to Moscow. Because of its geographic location on the northern edge of the main populated area of European Russia, St. Petersburg's airline traffic includes few passengers transferring between other points. On the other hand, its international traffic benefits from the cultural attractions of the city, which rival those of Moscow.

A New Airline Hierarchy

As the airline world of the former Soviet Union transformed into a capitalist society, it was characterized by competition in its many forms, and by investment—also in many forms. Hundreds of airlines, big and small, that emerged with the downfall of communism, fought for survival. They had all managed to acquire aircraft, with the original 34 semi-autonomous divisions of Aeroflot taking the lion's share, and converting themselves into independent airlines. Others were set up by the new entrepreneurs, but all had to face new problems, especially the supply of fuel, and the scramble for passenger traffic. Before 1991, the people of the Soviet Union benefitted from the edict that ensured cheap air travel. Now, they had to pay the going rate, which depended on the airlines' profit and loss accounts, most of which suffered from shortages of equipment, oil, and—too often—experience.

This unprecedented airline metamorphosis was remarkably similar to the same process that has evolved in the western capitalist world. Much of the reason for such a similarity is one of demographics. Airline traffic varies according to certain basic economic laws of distribution. Where there are people, there is a travel demand. This volume increases directly according to the size of the origin–destination population base, and decreases according to the distance between the two points—although, like all such laws, there are qualifications and exceptions. With air transport, the demographic base is confined to urban populations, as these are the centers for industry and wealth. People in rural areas do not create such a demand, and in any case, travelers tend to go to the main cities.

In the new Russia, a similar pattern to the airline history of the United States has taken shape. Other than Aeroflot, which could be compared to Pan American, half a dozen airlines have reached a stage of maturity that could be related in stature to the former U.S. Big Four, which accounted for about three-quarters of the total U.S. passenger-mile output. The Russian airlines described above could be termed the "Big Six" (Sibir, Transaero, Domodedovo, Kras Air, UTAir, and Pulkovo), with Volga-Dnepr as a unique cargo specialist. These are the elite of the Russian airline industry, and like the American leaders, they account for most of the passenger traffic across the nation's 11 time zones.

The process of attrition during the 1990s and early 2000s witnessed the disappearance of scores of aspirant companies that tried to exist against all the odds. It was a case of too many airlines chasing after too little traffic. The struggle goes on, such is the vast extent of Russia, especially east of the Urals. Many regional airlines manage to serve their respective local communities, and have connecting arrangements with their larger cousins.

New Countries, New Airlines

The dismemberment of the Soviet Union changed the political map of the world to a greater extent than had ever been done before, and in a short time. The development of the United States, the dissolution of the Austro-Hungarian Empire: these changes pale in significance in area, if not in population, compared to the sudden creation of the 14 republics of the C.I.S., as they became known. The biggest in population is Ukraine, with almost 50 million people, including five cities with more than a million each, and an area bigger than any other country in Europe. Kazakhstan, sparse in population, is bigger than the whole of western Europe. Each of the 14 inherited one of the Aeroflot divisions, one for each republic, a legacy that at least gave them a start.

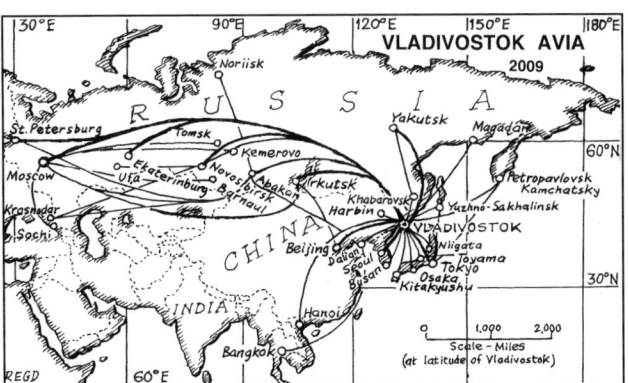

Vladivostok Avia was one of the later additions to the growing list of private companies that supplemented Aeroflot after it ceased to be the monopolistic state airline.

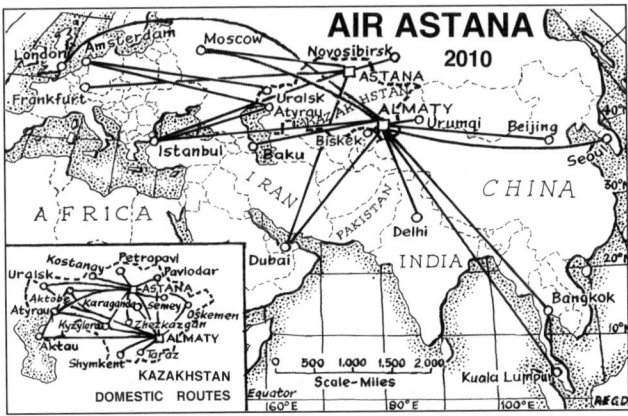

Of the post-Soviet central Asian republics, Kazakhstan is the largest—its area is more than western Europe's. From its new capital, Astana, from which it takes its name, and from Almaty, the largest city, its airline flies to Europe and to eastern and southern Asia.

The course of history often takes strange turns and the boundaries of the new republics in the Caucasus and in central Asia had only been defined during the early years of the Soviet Union. That vast empire was smaller than Czarist Russia, which included Finland, Poland, and what is now Moldova. These regained independence after 1918, as did Georgia, Armenia, and Azerbaijan in the Caucasus. But the new countries of central Asia had never had any real independence in their entire history, except ill-defined states such as Khiva and Bokhara. At the dissolution of the Soviet Union in 1991, therefore, Kazakhstan, Kyrgystan, Uzbekistan, Turkmenistan, and Tajikistan had much political and administrative adjustment to accomplish, a prerequisite to converting Aeroflot's regional airline divisions into independent entities.

There was also the matter of economics. Kazakhstan and Turkmenistan are oil producers, which is a comforting source of finance, as well as fuel, for an embryo airline. Uzbekistan is a significant producer of cotton, the heritage of huge irrigation projects that, regrettably, has laid waste other parts of the region; Tashkent is a large industrial city (where the Soviet variant of the Douglas DC-3 was built). Kyrgystan, without a single railroad, has a vacation resort in the Ysk Kul lake, patronized during Soviet times, but development of this resource will take time. Tajikistan is the most mountainous of this group, and the poorest. Because of its size, therefore, and even with the increase in railroad mileage during the Soviet era, Kazakhstan needed an airline most of all. Its east–west frontiers are as far apart as London and Athens, or New York and Denver.

Chapter 23: Decline of the American Giants

The Other Side of the Deregulation Coin

When Alfred Kahn oversaw the Airline Deregulation Act of 1978 (see Chapter 20), the way seemed clear for a new era to begin. The consequent liberalization would encourage private enterprise and individual creativity, particularly by permitting all airlines to operate routes wherever they wished and to charge whatever fares they chose. The principles (or restrictions) of a sharply regulated industry were instantaneously replaced by the principles of market forces (and sometimes not so principled actions).

But this was a two-edged sword. As described in Chapter 20, the enthusiastic rush to operate new routes was not always backed by careful traffic forecasts or by shrewd financial analyses. As the morning of 18 October 1978 dawned, representatives of the airlines, new and old, stood in line at the headquarters of the Civil Aeronautics Board (C.A.B.) in Washington, to claim the rights to operate on what were termed dormant routes, those that had previously been authorized but had not been put into service by the airline applicants. Some airlines were circumspect. United Air Lines applied for only one route. Other airlines were less cautious, applying for several routes, and many did not seem to appreciate the fact that the previous applicants had not taken up the services simply because they had had second thoughts and decided that their traffic predictions, for one reason or another, had not been fulfilled. One airline in particular threw caution to the winds, and acted so irresponsibly that it seemed to have taken leave of its senses.

The Collapse of Braniff

Until 1965, Texas-based **Braniff Airways** was one of the pioneer companies, founded in the late 1920s, and survived the reorganization of 1934 to retain, with the new legislation of 1938, "grandfather rights" to a route network that concentrated on north–south connections throughout the Midwest. By the standards of the big transcontinentals, it was not an industry leader and had done little of outstanding significance; its name was hardly known on the east coast or in the west. Its airline colors were a conventional and respectable dark blue and red. Then, in 1965, a flamboyant individual, Harding Lawrence, arrived from Continental Airlines to become chairman and CEO. He scoured every surface of Braniff's structure so that, within a year, the airline was unrecognizable from the rather sedate company that was seldom featured in the news, much less in the headlines.

Lawrence realized that, outside Texas, Braniff was little known to airline travelers across the United States, and that orthodox advertising would have a limited effect. In November 1965, realizing that a dramatic news item for the press would be its own advertisement, he devised a scheme that achieved this objective. "The End of the Plain Plane" was a revolutionary aircraft color scheme introduced to an astonished public. Working in partnership with Mary Wells, head of an innovative advertising agency (whom he later married), Braniff aircraft's rather dull colors were suddenly a thing of the past. Each individual airplane was painted all over with one of seven brilliant colors. Deprecatingly described by the public and the industry alike as the "jelly bean" jets, it transformed Braniff's image. This was followed by an equally revolutionary change in the flight attendants' dress style. Superseding the conventional two-piece uniforms were stylish creations by the famous Italian stylist Pucci, which drew instant attention. Braniff became the talk of the town not only in Dallas and Houston, but far and wide from Los Angeles to New York. The team of Lawrence and Wells had transformed Braniff from just another airline into an industry leader.

Flamboyant promotion was one thing; commercial enterprise was another, and Lawrence soon demonstrated that he was adept at both. When he joined the airline, its name was changed, in April 1965, to **Braniff International Airways**, and a month later, it had ordered five Boeing 707s and twelve 727s for $118 million. With substantial interest from financial investors—Greatamerica Corporation had acquired a 58% interest for $42 million on 6 August 1964—Lawrence was on a roll. He now had considerable negotiating stature and was able to confirm that the word *international* in the airline's name was no idle boast. On 19 January 1967, Braniff completed the purchase of Pan American-Grace Airways (PANAGRA), and within two weeks absorbed the western South American network into its system. The C.A.B. had long been concerned about Pan American's virtual monopoly of South American routes, and with the problems of equally shared control of PANAGRA. Now this once-overlooked airline had a substantial stake in the international arena. Again, Lawrence wasted no time. On 4 September 1967, Braniff introduced the Douglas DC-8-62, the long-range version of the "stretched" DC-8, and in 1968, the C.A.B., with Texan President Johnson's approval, awarded several nonstop routes to the airline from the United States to South American capital cities.

Just before leaving office, Johnson approved a package of Braniff routes to Hawaii, even including flights via Mexico City and Acapulco as well as direct from Dallas, but the newly elected President Richard Nixon deferred this award. This promoted some controversy, as Braniff was known to be a strong Democrat supporter. But in the final decision in the extensive Pacific Route Case, Braniff was confirmed (except for the Mexican itinerary) and, on 14 August 1969, inaugurated nonstop service from Dallas to Honolulu. On the home front, Braniff was also active, as on 1 October of that year, it extended its network to Florida in the Southern Tier Case and consolidated its routes from Texas to New York and Washington. Then, on 15 January 1971, in a typical Lawrence foray, Braniff's first Boeing 747 wide-bodied jet was put into service on the nonstop Dallas-Honolulu route. The aircraft, N601BN, humorously referred to as "The Great Pumpkin" or "The Big Orange," paid its dues. Except for periods of maintenance, it averaged a record 18 hours per day flying time.

Now a recognized force in the airline hierarchy, Braniff attracted considerable interest on Wall Street. The LTV Corporation had acquired Greatamerica's controlling interest on 17 November 1967, but during 1971 sold its shares in a public offering, worth $190 million. Other than these transactions, things were, by Lawrence standards, relatively quiet. He was on hand on 22 September 1973 at the inauguration of the new Dallas/Fort Worth International Airport, whose area was more than New York's Manhattan. In true Mary Wells fashion, yet another dramatic airliner color scheme was introduced on 17 November 1975. "The Flying Colors of America" were modern art designs by famous artist Alexander Calder, and again this kept the Braniff name in the forefront.

On 18 March 1978, Braniff opened nonstop service to London, so that the Atlantic Ocean, as well as the Pacific, was now on the Braniff map, and with a solid U.S. transcontinental network, Braniff timetables needed extra pages. Braniff had been able to announce record profits during the early and mid-1970s. But then came the Airline Deregulation Act, signed into law by President Carter on 24 October 1978. Flushed with success, Lawrence seemed to have cast caution to the winds, and looking at his airline's map, possibly felt that, with Pan American showing signs of old age, now was the time to turn Braniff into a worldwide airline, even usurping Pan Am's acknowledged status as the international flag carrier of the United States. To show his intentions, on 12 January 1979, he introduced the Anglo-French supersonic Concorde airliner on the Dallas-Washington route. This enabled Braniff to claim its entry into the supersonic age, even though the aircraft could not exceed the speed of sound on its overland routes. But it was faster, by about 100 mph, than any other airliner in America, and the through route was to London or Paris. The aircraft were British Airways's or Air France's, but some Braniff pilots qualified on the Concorde, the only Americans to do so.

This extravagance, however, hid a deeper and dangerously far-reaching malady within the airline. Lawrence seemed to be overcome with illusions of grandeur, with a vision of becoming the successor to Juan Trippe, who had systematically built up Pan American to become the world's only truly all-powerful intercontinental airline with a combination of shrewd planning, administration, and political acumen. When, on 18 October 1978, dormant routes were up for grabs, most airlines were ambitious but circumspect. As mentioned above, United Air Lines asked for one route. Braniff was less so. It asked for, and received, more than 300 and promptly took steps to activate them. On 15 December, 17 new cities were added to the Braniff map, and by mid-March 1979, 50 new nonstop routes were activated. The indecent haste was not, however, accompanied by careful planning. There were stories of airports greeting a Braniff flight, but with no Braniff staff or office yet installed. The extravagance went from bad to worse. On 3 July 1979, trans-Pacific service was extended from Honolulu to Hong Kong via Guam, on 17 September to Seoul, and on 26 October to Singapore. Lawrence was one of those who failed to appreciate that there were good reasons why those routes were dormant, the main one being that they did not have the potential traffic demand to justify economical operation.

The necessary and vital market research and schedule planning had been cast aside. Harding's illusions had overcome all common sense. The cost of expanding the infrastructure was far in excess of any resultant increase in revenue. Load factors plummeted and Braniff International Airways, only half a decade previously admired for its leadership and success, was suddenly losing money hand over fist. On 1 June 1980, the Concorde service was terminated, and although, on 30 July, the prestigious *Wall Street Journal* proclaimed that "no one expects Braniff to go broke. No major carrier ever has," the writing was on the wall. On 30 December 1980, Harding Lawrence resigned, much to the satisfaction of his senior management, who had suffered through a dictatorial regime, and the junior staff, especially the flight attendants, who dreaded to fly if they knew he would be on board, such were his bad manners.

Vice President John Casey took over temporarily, and in November 1981 Howard Putnam, formerly with Southwest Airlines, became chairman and CEO. But he was far too late. During the previous three years, Braniff had lost close to $350 million, and this was increasing day by day. On 12 May 1982, all operations were suspended, with a total debt estimated to approach $1 billion. Two days later, American Airlines picked up the London route, and Eastern had already picked up the old PANAGRA South American routes in April. Negotiations with Pacific Southwest Airlines (P.S.A.) in California fell through, and on 7 December 1982, Braniff filed for Chapter 11 bankruptcy. In June 1983, Putnam stepped down and on 16 July a revival plan was approved by the U.S. bankruptcy court, with the Hyatt Corporation investing $20 million in exchange for 80% of Braniff stock, and guaranteeing $50 million in loans. On 29 November, Braniff, Inc. was incorporated in Nevada as a subsidiary of the Delfort Corporation, formerly Braniff Airways. On 1 March 1984, operations started with 30 leased Boeing 727-200 aircraft, from Dallas to 18 cities.

Making the same mistake that others had made, the new management stressed its "high-class" marketing strategy, to combat the presumed "low-class" of its local competitor, Southwest Airlines. But on 5 September, this approach having failed emphatically, it changed its policy to a discounted fare structure. On 24 October 1984, the president, William D. Slattery, resigned. After only half a year's operations, the new Braniff had lost $80 million. On 5 November, service was suspended at 10 cities and reduced at eight others. Nine of its 12 gates at Dallas were sold, but attempts to lease aircraft were denied by a bankruptcy judge. It opened service to Boston and Phoenix, and ventured across the southern border, to Mexico City. On 28 April 1986, it opened a new hub at Kansas City, and on 15 January 1988 another hub at Orlando, where, having acquired Florida Express, it proclaimed its own Express commuter network, with Florida's 18 BAC One-Elevens.

But the sands were running out, even though, in June of that year, the Dalfort Corporation sold its controlling interest to BIA-COR Holdings, a financial investment group owned by Jeffrey Chodrow and Arthur Cohen. Six months later, it announced a $3.5 billion agreement with Airbus for the acquisition of 50 A320s, in a complex deal that comprised 26 aircraft from the Irish G.P.A. Group lessors; 5 to be financed by International Aero Engines, 11 by Airbus, and the remaining 8 to be arranged later. The first A320 actually went into service on 28 August 1989, but exactly one month later, Braniff, Inc. went into Chapter 11 bankruptcy and ceased operations on 6 November. But on 1 July 1991, BIA-COR Holdings resurrected Braniff, having acquired the operating certificate of Emerald Air, which was also bankrupt. **Braniff Airlines International** started service from Dallas to Los Angeles, but had to suspend it on 1 August because it could not obtain gate space at LAX. It then switched directions and flew to Fort Lauderdale, and also from Newark to Orlando. On 7 August 1991, yet again, the resurrected Braniff went into Chapter 11 bankruptcy then ceased operations on 2 July 1992. It was an ignominious ending. 3,500 passengers were stranded, and found little help from other airlines that, in previous eras, had come to the rescue. But this was a new era.

Air Florida's Rise and Fall

The demise of Braniff was a warning to all the airlines who thought that deregulation would be a heaven-sent license to spread their wings with abandon. Of the many that entered the competitive arena of the United States, few survived more than a few years. **Southwest Airlines** was an exceptional case of sheer business acumen and visionary planning overcoming the odds, with so many cards stacked against it.

Braniff had traced its history back to the late 1920s, and lasted 60 years before its collapse. Ther next airline to join the ranks of the fallen lasted only 13. **Air Florida** was founded by Eli Timoner as an intra-state airline only in November 1971, to join the ranks of the successful P.S.A., Air California, and Southwest. By 1984, it was gone.

Service began on 27 September 1972, with a leased Boeing 707, on a circular route, Miami-Tampa-Orlando-Miami, with a fixed fare of $12.00 for each segment. Early in 1973, the inappropriate 707 was replaced by three Lockheed L.188 Electra turboprops; a route to the state capital, Tallahassee, began; and the low introductory fare doubled. In 1977, now well capitalized and with its first jet, a Boeing 727, C. Edward Acker, formerly president of a declining Braniff, was appointed chairman, to add his airline experience to Timoner's enterprise. A fleet of Douglas DC-9s replaced the older aircraft, and on 1 October 1978, seven new points within Florida expanded the network.

Airline deregulation gave Acker the opportunity he needed to augment the airline's field of operations. With intra-state restrictions removed, Air Florida opened routes to Washington, D.C. on 1 February, and to four points in the Bahamas and to two in the U.S. Virgin Islands. On 29 April 1979, New York was on the Air Florida map. By the summer of 1980, this upstart airline, with seven Boeing 737s added to the fleet, was flying to Houston, Dallas, and Philadelphia, and to several more places in the Caribbean and Central America. If this was not enough expansion, as early as 28 March 1980, charter flights began to Europe with a wide-bodied Douglas DC-10, leased from Icelandair.

But a year later, the bills came in, and Air Florida had to restructure its long-term debt. Nevertheless, further expansion occurred, with a scheduled DC-10 trans-Atlantic service to London, starting on 1 February 1981, followed by other European cities and further local growth to Belize and Bermuda on 15 September, to Chicago and four major cities in the Great Lakes area on 15 November, and to Boston on 1 December. The fleet had grown to 41 aircraft, some of which were with Air Miami, as the Florida Commuter.

But Ed Acker did not stay to oversee the situation. In 1981 he departed to become chairman of Pan American Airways, where he promptly increased that airline's competitive presence in Florida. David Lloyd-Jones, from American Airlines, took over Air Florida in Miami. With high jet fuel costs, a poor nationwide economy, and a heavy long-term debt, Air Florida needed all the luck it could get. Instead, on 13 January 1982, it was devastated by the crash of a Boeing 737 that plunged into the frozen Potomac River in Washington, killing 78 people, after taking off from the nearby National Airport without having been properly de-iced. In spite of showing a brave face, with service to Providence, Burlington, and Guatemala City starting on 25 April 1982, Air Florida was on its way out. During the next two years, the fleet was reduced to thirteen 737s and a single DC-10, and on 3 May 1984, Lloyd-Jones resigned. Exactly two months later, the airline filed for Chapter 11 bankruptcy, most of the remaining employees were discharged, and the last flight arrived from London. The Air Florida bubble had burst. On 28 September 1984, Midway Airlines acquired the remaining assets for $53 million, and airline service was revived, as Midway Express, on a route from Miami to Chicago.

Even the Mighty Fall

The harsh realities of the effects of airline deregulation took a few years to make themselves fully evident. The erasure of Braniff from the list of domestic trunk airlines did not cause too much alarm at the higher echelons of the U.S. airline world. The general agreement was that the cause of its demise was not deregulation itself, but the headstrong reaction to it by an over-ambitious Harding Lawrence. The coming and going of Air Florida had been put down to the spectacular tragedy of the Boeing 737 crashing into the Potomac River just when it was struggling to reorganize its finances and operations, and in spite of starting a potentially lucrative route to London.

But toward the late 1970s, there were disturbing signs that all was not well in the hallowed corridors of power on the 46th floor of the Pan American Building, astride New York's Park Avenue. **Pan American Airways** could justifiably claim to be The World's Most Experienced Airline. It had pioneered tran-ocean air routes in the 1930s, shared in the development of long-range piston-engined airliners in the 1940s, launched the Jet Age in the late 1950s and the so-called Jumbo-Jet Age in 1970. For half a century, since its formation in 1927, under the shrewd leadership of Juan Trippe, it had dominated intercontinental air transport, to the extent that, whatever decisions it made, the airline world had to take notice. Pan Am had dominated the world, and its round-the-world PA-1 and PA-2 flight numbers were known to all frequent air travelers as the epitome of good airline service.

The beginning of a downward slipping—not yet a slide— can be traced back to the resignation of Najeeb Halaby on 22 March 1972. A distinguished test pilot, and formerly head of the Federal Aviation Administration, he had been chairman of the airline for only two years. He had done some "house cleaning" by terminating a number of vice presidents, directors, and others whose names had filled two pages of Pan Am's annual reports, and who seemed not to have contributed much to the airline's fortunes. He was just settling in when he was replaced by William T. Seawell, formerly with Rolls-Royce's American Division.

At first, Seawell seemed to be on a progressive and expansive course. He organized the Falcon Jet Corporation, jointly with Marcel Dassault, the French executive jet manufacturer, to sell the Falcons; he strengthened the route network with some nonstop connections; and, on 5 December 1973, he opened the new terminal at New York's JFK International Airport, the largest individual installation of its kind in the world. But throughout the mid-1970s, there was a regular succession of route suspensions, as, little by little, the great Pan American trimmed its network. During the first week of January 1974, several Latin American and European cities disappeared from the map and from the schedules. While these were not among the leading generators of passenger traffic, the action was, nevertheless, cause for comment, as Pan Am had seldom abandoned any foothold, once established.

During the next two years, the route network was manipulated, with more suspensions, this time even at prominent cities such as Paris (on 2 March 1975) and Bermuda (on 8 September 1975). On the other hand, it negotiated an amicable agreement with British European Airways for a more efficient sharing of the Internal German routes into beleaguered Berlin, and on 13 February 1976, it began a one-stop route from New York to Johannesburg, South Africa via Rio de Janeiro.

But all was not well. The aircraft procurement policy went astray on 25 April 1976, when it inaugurated nonstop New York service to Tokyo with the Boeing 747SP. The SP stood for Special Performance, in this case, enough range for the 6,754-mile route, but this was achieved at the expense of a payload penalty of between 60 and 74 seats. And the full payload could not be carried in the westbound direction, against the 100-mph jetstream headwinds. Ominously, the competing Japan Airlines did not react by also operating the SP. It simply waited for the inevitable engine improvements that gave its own standard 747s the necessary range as well.

Nothing affects the mood of the air traveling public more than a fatal crash. Usually, the memories pass after a while; but in Pan Am's case, on 27 March 1977, one of its 747s was involved in a tragedy that has a place in the history books and still remains in the public memory. For on that day, at the Spanish island of Tenerife, during low visibility, a Pan Am airplane taxiing on the runway was hit by a Dutch K.L.M. 747 taking off. 576 people were killed, and almost incredibly, thanks partly to some heroic rescues by stewardess Dorothy Kelly, 67 people survived. It remains today the worst air crash in history. And it could not have come at a worse time for a tottering Pan American.

On 29–30 October 1977, Pan Am made a spectacular "pole-girdling" flight with a Boeing 747, which flew the 26,230-mile south-north-south itinerary in 62 hours. While this also went into the record books, it was not exactly the proving flight for a new route. Far more relevant to the airline's fortunes were two decisions made within a period of only four months in 1978. Either one would have been a mistake; taken together they spelled disaster.

On 4 April 1978, Seawell announced an order for twelve 238-seat Lockheed L-1011-500 TriStars, to supplement the fleet of the larger Boeing 747s on routes that did not justify their 360-seat capacity. The first TriStar service was New York-Caracas on 1 May 1980. This policy could possibly have worked, had it not been for the proposal made on 23 August to buy Miami-based National Airlines. The objective was to acquire a domestic network to provide Pan American international service to many more U.S. cities, other than the certificated gateways on the east and west coasts. For decades in the past, even Juan Trippe, who had usually got his own way, had been frustrated in trying to provide through services from the heart of America, without having to change airlines as well as flights at the gateways.

Although President Carter had approved the merger with National on 22 December 1979, which became effective on 7 January 1980, it was flawed for several reasons. First, Pan Am had paid too high a price, thanks to shrewd tactics by Texas Air's Frank Lorenzo (who made $42 million from share dealings); second, with airline deregulation already established in October 1978, it could have spread its wings domestically without recourse to buying another airline; and third, possibly the most far-reaching effect of all, it had purchased an airline whose long-haul flagship was the Douglas DC-10. Pan American's fleet thus included fleets of all three of the long- and medium-haul wide-bodied airliners, and each of the three had a different engine: 747s with Pratt & Whitney, L-1011s with Rolls-Royce; and DC-10s with General Electric. The maintenance problems and spare-parts provision for all three aircraft and all three engines must have contributed to a deteriorating financial situation, which became evident early in 1980.

Some of the blame was placed on the increase in the price of fuel—twice as high in 1980, at 91 cents a gallon, as in 1979. During that summer, Pan Am put on a brave face, with more nonstop routes, and some window-dressing with new flight attendant uniforms and a program of new Clipper names for all the aircraft. But overshadowing such moves was the sale, on 28 July 1980, of the Pan Am Building, which stood astride Park Avenue, above Grand Central Station, and which had not only become a landmark for New York tourists, but had become a symbol of its dominance in the airline's world. At the time, the insurance corporation Metropolitan Life's purchase price of $400 million was the highest real estate transaction for a single building in recorded history.

One month later, Pan American sold 50% of its Falcon Jet Corporation to Avions Marcel Dassault, the French manufacturer, and began to reduce staff numbers. On 26 October, it closed down the National terminal at Kennedy Airport and integrated the two airlines completely. On 26 January 1981, the last Boeing 707 was retired, and two days later, the resumption of service to China marked an historic political as well as commercial event. The resumption of service to Paris on 1 April was made only two days before Juan Trippe, the founder and inspiration of the World's Most Experienced Airline, died, at the age of 81.

Pan American struggled on and announced, on 3 June 1981, an Airline Employee Economic Contribution Plan, which was another way of describing pay cuts and other staff recessions. It sold and leased back some of its Boeing 747s to a leasing company. On 7 July, William Waltrip became president, under Seawell, and he announced a number of operational changes, but these did not materially improve Pan Am's fortunes. On 21 August, Grand Metropolitan, a British hotel corporation, bought the airline's Intercontinental Hotels for $500 million.

On 1 September 1981, Seawell handed over to C. Edward Acker, the former chief of Air Florida (see above), who, having previously also been with Braniff, was familiar with the Latin American scene. He tried to negotiate an agreement with his former airline under which Pan American would operate Braniff's west coast South American services with the Lockheed TriStars. But the C.A.B., still with residual powers, delayed approval, citing its concern about a Pan American monopoly, "thus reversing a U.S. policy of 30 years." Instead, in a rare night meeting on 26 April 1982, it approved the transfer of Braniff's routes to Eastern Air Lines. Although Pan American had opened service to Santiago, Chile, on 15 July 1981, the TriStar fleet, which it should never have bought, was now clearly superfluous, and it was sold, at a loss, on 21 July 1982.

Still struggling, Pan American did not give up easily, even though its financial losses and the removal of its great insignia dominating the view over Fifth Avenue clouded its image among the air traveling public. No longer could it, by superior operating strength, dictate its future almost regally, as in the past, under Juan Trippe. But it added new points on both its domestic and international networks, including, on 4 November 1982, a 747SP nonstop service from Los Angeles to Sydney—7,487 miles, the longest in the world. A nice bonus came in December 1983 when Pan American World Services was selected, again, to operate over the Eastern Test Range, part of the U.S. space program at Cape Canaveral, under a contract worth $615 million. On 23 December 1984, it introduced the Airbus A300B4, wearing a bold new livery, on a network of Caribbean services. The 252-seater was the first twin-engined wide-bodied jet, and an ideal solution to much of Pan American's operational requirements. But this was a case of too little, too late.

On 28 February 1985, after a period of deteriorating relations between the Pan American management and staff, the mechanics, with support from other unions, went on strike. The network was drastically reduced to about one-third of the total operations, serving only major world cities; although services were gradually resumed and the full network restored by 28 April, much damage had been done to the once pre-eminent Pan American image in the eyes of the traveling public.

If this was not bad enough, in an attempt to plug the gap in its perilous financial balance sheets, Ed Acker announced, on 22 April, the sale to United Airlines of the entire trans-Pacific segment, 23% of its worldwide domain. For $750 million, a figure that many industry analysts considered to be worse than a bargain price, all the destinations in east Asia and Australasia—the burgeoning Pacific Rim—disappeared from the Pan American map. The transaction, comprising 18 aircraft, including 11 747SPs, and all the installations, was completed on 11 February 1986. Hawaii was abandoned in April, and the once-omnipotent world airline was left with only the trans-Atlantic system as a potentially sure profit-maker.

Steps were taken to pick up the pieces. On 28 May 1985, an Airbus A310-200, *Clipper Berlin*, made a brave show as it entered service on the Internal German Service, and during the summer, a new hub was established at Washington, D.C. and services expanded at Houston. Following the decision to concentrate on the Atlantic, to feed the New York and Washington gateways, Pan American bought, on 15 April, Ransome Airlines, based in Philadelphia and serving the whole northeastern corridor as far north as Portland. Ransome became the **Pan Am Shuttle**, based at La Guardia, on 1 October, and many more points in Europe were added at the end of April 1986.

In the past, Pan American had invariably got what it wanted; things had changed, not least in the corridors of power in Washington. A requested approval for an Airbus A310 nonstop service from Pittsburgh to London was turned down by the Department of Transportation, the successor decision-maker to the C.A.B., in favor of a Cincinnati-London service by Delta. Juan Trippe would have regarded this as high treason. In August, Pan Am was fined almost $2 million for safety-rule violations, a disciplinary act that could never have been contemplated in the years gone by.

The former aura of omnipotence was gone. No longer did European-bound Americans automatically turn to Pan American to book their seats. The competition from both sides of the Atlantic intensified. The financial loss in 1986 was $463 million. With its world market share halved from 12% in 1980 to 6% in 1986, and with not much else to sell, Acker had to renegotiate the fleet finances so that most of it was under lease agreements. But the banks were no longer generous lenders, and by early 1987, there were already murmurs of impending Chapter 11 bankruptcy.

Efforts to augment service to Europe included a nonstop New York-Berlin service on 29 May 1987. Two days later, the Berlin-Hamburg route became a **Pan Am Express** shuttle service, followed, on 1 November, by ones to Frankfurt and Munich. But these were minor distractions from the chronic problems at the top level of the administration. At the end of the year, a crisis of major proportions developed. In December 1987, a plan was revealed to merge with Braniff, Inc. The Pan American Corporation, the parent company, would retain the Pan Am Shuttle, Pan Am Express, and Pan Am World Services. The deal depended on substantial labor concessions, and a package was negotiated by vice president Martin Shugrue. But this was viewed by chairman Ed Acker as an obstruction to his support of the Braniff offer. Pan American was clearly up for sale, and by the beginning of 1988, the airline industry observed a steady procession of potential buyers, including Kirk Kerkorian, a well-known airline investor. Also, labor relations were described as acrimonious.

The unions drove a hard bargain. They agreed to harsh concessions only if both Acker and Shugrue were ousted, which they promptly were. In January 1988, Thomas G. Plaskett took over the chairmanship in a most unenviable business environment. In November he won $153 million in labor concessions, and sold the orders and options for 50 Airbus A320s for $115 million. But these were band-aid solutions at a time when even more drastic surgery would not have sufficed. And then, in an historic aviation tragedy, on 21 December 1988, a Pan American Boeing 747 exploded in mid-air over the town of Lockerbie in Scotland, killing 270 people. The fact that the cause was a bomb placed on board in Frankfurt that remained undetected at London, did not improve Pan Am's image with the traveling public. It was the final straw for this once-great airline.

Temporary relief came in April 1989, when its Shuttle traffic surged when Eastern went on strike. A move to merge with Northwest Airlines was defeated in June with a better offer by Los Angeles investor Alfred Checchi. In December, discussions with Continental's Frank Lorenzo and T.W.A.'s Carl Icahn came to nought. On 15 May 1990, a Pan Am Express local network based in Miami was only a short-lived positive note that did nothing to stem the downward flow. The Iraqi invasion of Kuwait on 2 August 1990 did nothing but harm. Fuel prices rocketed. Pan Am's routes were vulnerable. Plaskett tried everything he could to save the airline. In September, for $150 million, he sold the Internal German Service to Lufthansa, which was now permitted, with the collapse of the Soviet hegemony and control over eastern Europe, to operate domestic routes. On 23 October, the routes to London, by far the biggest traffic generator in the system, went to United Airlines for $400 million. But by the end of the year, even the Shuttle was losing millions every week. On 9 January 1991, Pan American Airways filed for Chapter 11 bankruptcy, declaring assets of $1.6 billion, and liabilities of $2.6 billion.

On 25 January, Bankruptcy Judge Cornelius Blacksheer approved a $400 million loan from Bankers Trust Corporation to maintain essential operations, conditional on British approval of the sale to United, at that amount, of Pan Am's assets, including the London route. Under the terms of what became known as the "Heathrow Pact," United received the rights into Heathrow, and American Airlines received those of T.W.A. The British did well, gaining Fifth Freedom rights for onward routes beyond the United States, rights from points in Europe to the States, and for a second British airline to serve the U.S.A. from London's Heathrow. Pan American's last flight from this, the world's busiest international airport, was an Airbus A310 service on 3 April 1991, the day United took over.

There followed a period of inter-airline bargaining, which left sad memories. Pan Am's head was on the block, having lost $663 million in 1990. On 11 July 1991, Delta Air Lines agreed to purchase the Pan Am Shuttle and the routes to Europe for $260 million, raising its bid to $310 million at the end of the month. This was approved by the judge on 12 August, and the objective was for Delta and its creditors to own a much-reduced Pan American to operate only on a route network confined to Latin America—ironically the very region where the World's Most Experienced Airline had started. But almost at the last minute, Delta refused to pay the $25 million still outstanding of the $140 million to keep Pan Am flying, alleging some impropriety in Pan Am's bookkeeping.

On 4 December 1991, the inevitable end came. United Airlines emerged as the winner of the auction for Pan Am's assets, paying $135 million for its Latin American routes. The last service was an emotional affair. Flight #436, from Barbados, a Boeing 727 piloted by Captain Mark Pyle, was greeted at Miami, the place of the airline's birth, as he taxied to the terminal, by a rare tribute: an arcade of fire-hosed water spray. There was not a dry eye among the remaining Pan American staff who witnessed the finale of the world's only airline in history that had, in its great years, conquered the world's oceans, sponsored jet airliner dynasties, and, for almost four decades, become a household name.

Another Giant Felled

During the halcyon days of the mid-20th century, **Eastern Air Lines** had dominated the airline scene east of the Mississippi River—about one-third of the United States—to the extent that its name was as familiar in the small towns as much as it was at the Rockefeller Center in New York, where its prestigious headquarters was a second home to its extrovert president, Eddie Rickenbacker. It was not an intercontinental airline, and was thus little known outside the United States. But such was its stature that there were some years in the 1950s and 1960s when, measured in the number of passengers boarded, and before the rise of the Soviet Aeroflot, it ranked as the largest airline in the world.

It managed its business with one of the largest and most modern fleets, dating back to pre-war years, when its Great Silver Fleet (of Douglas DC-3s) seemed to put it in a class of its own. After a period of recovery from the Second World War, in 1956, it acquired Colonial Airlines, and consequent access to Bermuda. Its fleet of piston-engined aircraft grew to include the best versions of the Lockheed Constellations and the Douglas DC series, culminating in the "Golden Falcon" DC-7B, which went into service just before the Boeing 707 jet took the airline world by storm in 1958. Rickenbacker had stayed with the propeller, choosing to meet the threat of Capital Airlines's British Viscount turboprops with the Lockheed Model 188 Electra, of which Eastern was the launch customer, putting them into service on 12 January 1959. Its first jet airliner, the Douglas DC-8-21, was ordered, almost in story-book fashion, during a telephone conversation between Rickenbacker and Donald Douglas, and Eastern entered the Jet Age with service on the "gravy run" from New York to Miami on 24 January 1960.

The airline's planning and scheduling departments were always fully occupied in coping with the intensely concentrated network. Hardly any community with more than 50,000 people—and often fewer—escaped their attention. Over-riding such a requirement, however, was meeting the demands on its densely traveled routes, of which the 220-mile New York-Washington and the 180-mile New York-Boston segments ranked among the busiest air routes in the world. Following the innovation of Brazil's São Paulo-Rio de Janeiro Ponte Aérea (Air Bridge), started on 6 July 1959, Eastern introduced the **Eastern Air-Shuttle** service on 30 April 1961. The standard fare from New York was $12.00 to Boston, $14.00 to Washington. It was strictly a no-reservation service, and tickets could be purchased en route, after standing in line for a boarding pass. One novelty was that the flight was guaranteed. If one airplane was full, a reserve one was immediately available. On one or two occasions, because of this special amenity, Eastern was obliged to carry a single passenger on its 95-seat Constellation. This paid high dividends in the resultant publicity, worth tens of thousands of dollars in advertising.

During the 1960s, during which period Rickenbacker retired, at the end of 1963, Eastern's jet fleet grew substantially, to keep pace with expanding traffic demands in the east, and especially to serve growing vacation resorts and retirement communities in Florida. After the initial score of 23 DC-8s, and 15 Boeing 720s (acquired as an interim measure while waiting for the Boeing 727 tri-jets), orders from the two major manufacturers amounted to 66 of the short-haul 727-100 series, and 102 of the longer-range 727-200s. Additionally, 125 short-haul Douglas DC9s of various series were added, of which Eastern was the launch customer for the -30 series, the most successful of the line. And to cope with the densest routes, 26 "stretched" DC-8-61s and -63s came into service at the end of the decade, just before the wide-bodied jets became available.

The approach to acquiring wide-bodied airliners was cautious. The 360-seat Boeing 747 was ideal in size for the Florida and Puerto Rico routes, and it was introduced on New York-Miami on 21 December 1970. But this was an interim measure. Aircraft were leased from Pan American and T.W.A., and steps were taken to choose a smaller wide-body that would suit the network as a whole, both in size and range capability. The choice was the 270-seat Lockheed L-1011 TriStar, of which Eastern was the launch customer. It bought 50 of these "Whisperjets" and put them into service on 26 April 1972.

During this period, the route system expanded. It became a transcontinental airline on 13 June 1967, but failed in its bid to become a trans-Pacific operator. However, with a route to Los Angeles on 23 September 1969, serving an affluent population as big as Australia's, and a lot closer to home, this was more than adequate compensation for losing out on the South Pacific. On 13 December of the same year, the map also included Kingston, Jamaica, to add to San Juan as a Caribbean destination. The vacation business in the Bahamas was also substantial, and Eastern invested in that market by buying the local Mackey Airlines, by an exchange of stock, on 8 January 1967. Further consolidation to the south came on 15 March 1973, when Caribair was absorbed. This airline had been founded in San Juan, Puerto Rico, in 1939, and it extended Eastern's network as far as Trinidad and Curaçao.

The continuous expansion was beginning to affect Eastern's finances. After Rickenbacker's departure in 1963, Malcolm McIntyre and then Floyd Hall had carried on to guide the airline through years of success, to be followed, in 1974, by ex-astronaut Frank Borman. His appointment was expected to bring in disciplined measures to reduce costs. In an effort to solve the problem of operating short stage lengths, of which, in the main, Eastern's route network was composed, he sought a short-haul wide-bodied airliner. The twin-engined European Airbus A300B4 fitted the bill. The reluctance to seek an aircraft fleet from an overseas source was overcome by a remarkable offer from the Airbus consortium of manufacturers in Toulouse, France. On 25 August 1977, a trial aircraft, followed by three more, were flown over Eastern's routes, with no obligation to buy them. This offer was described as an opportunist deal between "a manufacturer with no customers and an airline with no money." But Eastern liked them, bought them, and put them into service on (inevitably) New York-Miami on 13 December of the same year. 34 of the Whisperliners were added to the fleet, much to the satisfaction of Airbus, which was seeking an entry into the U.S. market. This latter ambition was thus achieved, with further U.S. Airbus orders to follow, and once again, as with the DC-9-30 and the Lockheed TriStar, Eastern had led the way.

Borman took bold steps to trim the flow of red ink. He froze wages of the 32,000-strong workforce and cut the list of vice presidents by half. He restructured the $1.5 billion debt, and eliminated the luxury of, effectively, the dual headquarters: administration in New York, operations in Miami. The Airbus helped to reduce the average direct operating costs, but competition had intensified, after Delta had bought Northeast on 1 August 1972 to provide, among other threats, a third trunk airline on the vital New York/Boston/Washington-Florida artery. Eastern inherited Braniff's South American routes on 14 May 1982 when that airline collapsed, and to supplement the Airbuses and the Boeing 727s, Borman worked with the manufacturer to launch the 185-seat Boeing 757-200. This was a twin-engined version of the highly successful Boeing 727. Borman had persuaded Boeing to enlarge the original size to fit Eastern's needs (the 757-100 was never built) and it went into service on 1 January 1983. With Air Florida's failure (see above) Eastern became a trans-Atlantic operator, picking up the Miami-London route with initial service on 15 July 1985. But the realities of Eastern's financial resources were evidenced by the necessity to lease, rather than buy, three McDonnell-Douglas DC-10s to be able to operate the route, as the TriStars did not have the range.

Predictably, the wage freeze had not been popular. The unions were recalcitrant negotiators, as Borman had to conduct a series of belt-tightening actions during the mid-1980s. By 1985, with heavy competition, both from the established Delta and American Airlines and from low-fare newcomers after airline deregulation in 1978, the financial situation had become critical. The long-term debt amounted to $2.5 billion—a million more than when Borman took over—and after further lay-offs early in 1986, Eastern Air Lines was sold, on 1 October of that year, to the Texas Air Corporation, presided over by Frank Lorenzo.

For a time, there was cautious optimism that he would somehow pull the airline out of its economic crisis. He was well known for his draconian style of harsh measures, especially in union negotiations. He was not known for trying to solve problems with band-aid solutions. His Texas Air, with its Continental Airlines and newly acquired People Express, now controlled about one-fifth of all the airline seats in the western world, and there were indications that a complete merger with Eastern was contemplated.

First, however, something had to be done, and done quickly. In May 1986, slots and gates in the northeastern corridor were sold to Pan American, and in October 1988, the famous Shuttle was sold to real estate developer Donald Trump for $365 million. But in spite of further layoffs, and having eliminated the Kansas City hub on 1 September 1987, the bleeding continued. Eastern lost $718 million in 1988, but the Machinists Union demanded a wage increase and on 9 March 1989, went on strike. The effect on Eastern's fortunes was disastrous. Any ideas of a merger with Continental had to be put aside. The public deserted Eastern in favor of competitors; for several months the operations were reduced; and the Latin American routes were sold to American Airlines on 1 July 1989. There followed a long winter of discontent, and on 13 April 1990, the creditors persuaded a federal judge to take control of the management, a euphemism for "get rid of Frank Lorenzo." On 18 April, the judge appointed ex-Pan American executive Martin Shugrue to take charge for what he termed "for cause, including incompetence." Whatever Lorenzo's alleged shortcomings, this was not one of them, as his successor was soon to find out.

Shugrue had also been president of Lorenzo's Continental for a year, but the two had apparently not got along. Lorenzo had had enough and resigned on 13 August 1990. In spite of palliatives granted by the judge from the escrow fund, Eastern was now losing $2.5 million per day. Cash reserves had run out. On 16 January 1991 the Gulf War erupted, and two days later, Eastern Air Lines closed its doors, 19,000 employees lost their jobs, and Shugrue's only task was to preside over the sale of assets during the long-drawn-out liquidation process.

It was a sad end to a once great airline. Its brave slogan "The Wings of Man" and its claim to "America's Favorite Airline" were hollow memories. A decade later, the unions, including that of the powerful pilots, were accepting far harsher terms than Lorenzo had ever asked for. Solidly successful in the world of high finance, Lorenzo departed the airline scene.

Death of a Great Pioneer

Trans World Airlines (T.W.A.) had weathered the storm of Pan American Airways' dominance of the international airline scene during the 1960s and 1970s, when Juan Trippe's vision and determination had given that airline a position of supremacy that the air transport world had never experienced before. Successively, Pan Am had, in 1959, launched the first Jet Age with the introduction of the Boeing 707 then, in 1970, repeated the triumph with the wide-bodied Boeing 747, the so-called Jumbo Jet. Other airlines had to follow suit and try to keep pace with the technological innovations that the partnership of airline and manufacturer had produced.

Most of them in the United States and elsewhere beat a pathway to Boeing's door, and some to Douglas and Lockheed, even, eventually, to Europe. But as the Jet Age got under way, T.W.A. had to keep up with the world leader internationally, and with the heavy domestic competition. During past years, the financial strength of owner Howard Hughes had always been available to support investment in new airliner fleets, but by the late 1950s, even the funds of the Hughes Tool Company (Toolco) were insufficient to match those of his rivals. He had had to seek help from Wall Street, and this came from Equitable Life, which insisted on a long-term financing plan. This was anathema to Hughes, but his back was to the wall, and he had no choice.

T.W.A. had been able to match the American Airlines introductory 707 schedule on 25 January 1959, the first transcontinental jet service, by a coast-to-coast 707 of its own on 20 March. Such was the efficiency of its engineering organization at Kansas City that it managed to do this for a whole month with only one aircraft. Hughes may have been tightening his belt, but he still directed all the big decisions. After many delays and repercussions at the manufacturer's San Diego plant, T.W.A. added the Convair 880 to its fleet and started service on 12 January 1961, nine months after Delta's inaugural with the same type.

Hughes had staved off the deep financial problems by borrowing from Irving Trust but could not maintain repayments and by 1960, the lenders' patience had run out. They forced him to accept a voting trust to control his 77% stockholding, and demanded as a condition for survival that they be appointed T.W.A.'s key management positions. Ernest Breech, formerly chairman of Ford, became chairman, and Charles Tillinghast became president. Hughes was not the type to surrender easily, and brought an anti-trust suit against the lenders on 30 June 1961. The C.A.B. supported Hughes, who resumed control on 10 July 1964, but the Court of Appeals reversed the decision. Hughes finally capitulated and, on 3 May 1966, sold his stake in T.W.A., the airline he believed he had built into a world-class airline, to challenge the global dominance of Pan American. In 20 minutes, the stock was sold for $566 million.

During this time, as the boardroom battles swayed to and fro, and the lawyers went head-to-head for almost a decade, the airline continued to maintain its stature in the airline world. It introduced the United States, and indeed the world, to the epoch-making Douglas DC-2, which in 1934 had turned Douglas into a manufacturing world leader; it gave airline passengers the benefits of pressurized cabins, to "fly above the weather" with the Boeing 307 Stratoliner in 1940. The name T.W.A., together with that of Hughes himself, was indelibly associated with the Lockheed Constellation, which, from 1946, had set the pace on all the world's major city-pair routes. So even during the times of financial uncertainty, T.W.A.'s head was still high in the hearts and minds of the engineers. On 7 September 1961, 20 Sud Caravelles were ordered from France, but the order was cancelled in May 1962, leaving United Air Lines as the sole operator of the world's first rear-engined jet airliner in North America. On 14 October 1963, T.W.A. joined the list of prospective customers for the Anglo-French supersonic Concorde and hedged its gamble with similar commitment for the Boeing 2707 SST.

Far more important during the 1960s was the mainstream business of operating the workhorses of the airways, the Boeing 727s and Douglas DC-9s. These were ordered in large numbers, almost a hundred of each type, as T.W.A.'s domestic network flourished. Internationally, by the end of 1969, it superseded Pan Am as the leading trans-Atlantic airline, measured by its passenger boardings. T.W.A.'s Boeing 747s went into service on the premier transcontinental route, New York-Los Angeles, on 25 February 1970, and on the premier trans-Atlantic route, New York-London, on 18 March. This airliner came just in time, as its 370 seats, even in mixed class, were worth two Boeing 707s or Douglas DC-8s, and served to ease the congestion at New York's JFK Airport, where the queues to take-off at the peak hours reached 30 or 40 airliners in line. Little heralded, but of benefit to all the airlines, the initiative of T.W.A.'s Mel Brenner led to a common-sense scheduling agreement, agreed by both the C.A.B. and the Justice Department. Airlines could take turns at the preferred 9 A.M. take-off time without harming the principles of fair competition.

The 747 was not deployed on T.W.A.'s round-the-world service, which had started on 31 October 1971, having opened a trans-Pacific route with the faithful Boeing 707s on 1 August 1969. Once again, common sense prevailed, as there was just not enough traffic for both T.W.A. and Pan American to achieve reasonable loads and frequencies. On 16 October 1974, the two airlines entered into a route standardization agreement, and T.W.A. suspended its Pacific operation on 2 March 1975. Subsequently, a few of T.W.A.'s 707s were retired after 30 years of service, each with more than 100,000 flying hours "on the clock."

During the 1970s, a well-equipped T.W.A. seemed to be on an even keel, if not on an expansionist program, with the new brooms of management apparently sweeping clean. To supplement the Boeing 747s on routes that did not generate 370-seat loads, T.W.A. introduced the Lockheed L-1011 TriStar on 25 June 1972. These two wide-bodied airliners were the backbone of the fleet for the next decade, and were supplemented only on 2 December 1982, when the Boeing 767-200 entered service on the Los Angeles-Washington route. On 31 October 1983, the last Boeing 707 flew into Kansas City, to end a remarkable era of sound and safe service covering almost a quarter of a century.

Even during this period in which it had to steer its course very carefully, T.W.A. managed to be in the forefront of innovation in airline service and operations. As long ago as 19 July 1961, it had been the first airline to regularly show motion pictures—the debut was *By Love Possessed*, starring Lana Turner. Now, on 1 February 1985, it was the first U.S. airline to fly a twin-engined airliner, a Boeing 767, across the Atlantic in scheduled passenger service. This was done under the F.A.A.-certified EROPS (extended Range Operations), later renamed ETOPS (extended Twin-Engine Operations) program.

But all was not well. After Howard Hughes was expelled in 1966, the new management, in 1967, purchased the Hilton Hotel chain, to compete with Pan American's Intercontinental Hotels; bought the Canteen Company in 1973 to provide its own on-board catering; and diversified—surprisingly—by acquiring the estate business of Century 21. On 12 October 1978, two weeks before the passing of the Airline Deregulation Act, these various activities were coordinated under a new holding company, the Trans World Corporation.

Diversification has been described by cynics as "abandoning businesses in which you are well experienced, and adopting those about which you know nothing." This may have been the case with the change of corporate management in T.W.A., even though the non-aviation divisions did well. Not enough attention was paid to facing up to the new challenges of deregulated competition. The airline had to tighten its belt. On 1 September 1983, all personnel accepted a 10% pay cut, and on 30 November, the all-powerful Airline Pilots Association (ALPA), which customarily regarded such action as blasphemy, did the same. With lagging sales, a high debt load, and high operating costs, the omens for T.W.A. in the mid-1980s were not encouraging.

The weakened airline was vulnerable to infiltration from speculative financial interests, and on 9 May 1985, a wealthy speculator, Carl Icahn, made the first move by announcing that he held more than 20% of the common stock of T.W.A. There followed a high-level battle between the incumbent shareholders, Icahn, and a familiar contestant, Frank Lorenzo, of the Texas Air Corporation. Carl Icahn won the battle on 7 September, buying stock at $19.50 a share cash, plus residual stock. He seemed to have started well, for on 27 February 1986, he purchased **Ozark Air Lines**, the Regional (once Local Service) airline based in St. Louis, alongside T.W.A.'s main hub. It was a good move, as by this time its network, served by a large fleet of Douglas DC-9s, stretched from coast to coast, and to Florida and Texas. But Icahn's positive influence ended there. He proposed an Employee Stock Ownership Plan (ESOP), but this was never put into practice. Instead, he began to sell off the airline's assets, making a profit on his original investment then, in 1989, selling aircraft and gates at Kansas City and the Chicago-London route to American Airlines. By the summer of 1990, the airline was $3 billion in debt.

After a bizarre offer to buy Pan American Airways, T.W.A.'s proud status on the North Atlantic was devastated. On 21 January 1991, Icahn announced the halving of all services to Europe, and furloughed 2,500 employees. On 14 March, American Airlines bought the routes to London from New York, Los Angeles, and Boston. T.W.A.'s last flight into London's Heathrow Airport was on 1 July 1991, and the effect of the sale was only a temporary reprieve. On 31 January 1992, it filed for Chapter 11 bankruptcy. Massive concessions were made by all employees, in exchange for 45% of the equity of the airline, and on 8 January 1993, Carl Icahn relinquished control. On 3 November, the airline emerged from bankruptcy. The fact that T.W.A. survived at all at this stage of its distinguished history was a tribute to the loyalty and dedication of its entire staff, which made unprecedented deals, saved their jobs, and kept the airline afloat.

Between 1993 and 1997, a succession of chairmen and presidents did their best to restore finances, sustain operations, and encourage staff morale. This last effort was so successful that in 1994 the employees accepted deductions from their pay packets to pay for a new McDonnell Douglas MD-83, appropriately named *Wings of Pride*. But it was an uphill struggle. The creditors were unforgiving and made few concessions. Then, just as the embattled airline seemed at least to be holding its own, and in a remarkably similar occurrence that had been the death warrant for Pan American, a Boeing 747 disintegrated shortly after take-off from New York's JFK Airport on 17 July 1996. The cause of this Flight 800 disaster has been the subject of controversy ever since. Several books have been written, debating whether or not the airliner was hit by a missile or was blown up by a suicide bomber, and challenging the official explanation of a spontaneous ignition and explosion of fuel in the center fuel tank.

Whatever the reason, it did not help T.W.A. in its efforts to stay in business. William (Bill) Compton, who became president on 3 December 1997, and was appointed CEO in May 1999, did his best against considerable odds. The debt to Icahn was restructured only by allowing him to sell tickets through his own ticket agency, thereby depriving T.W.A. itself of much-needed revenues. Old aircraft were retired, and orders placed for 50 new Boeing 717s (formerly McDonnell Douglas MD-95s) and 50 new Airbus 318s. Compton managed to make an agreement with the Machinists Union, to increase wages, effective from 1 August 1999. A show of keeping up with the times was with the start of Boeing 717 service on 2 March 2000 and the retirement of the Boeing 727, with a "pig party" to mark the occasion, on 30 September of the same year. Code-share agreements were made with Chautauqua Airlines, based at Indianapolis, and with American Eagle, at New York, to provide a Trans-World Connection to nine cities in New England, the Great Lakes region, and Montreal.

On 10 January 2001, after several rumors of various approaches, **American Airlines** offered to buy T.W.A. for $500 million, provided it file for Chapter 11 bankruptcy, which it did on the same day. Fighting off other offers by increasing its bid to $742 million, the merger was completed on 9 April 2001. It was a sad end for a great airline, comparable to the demise of Pan American, and a commentary on one of the darker sides of entrepreneurial capitalism. For those two airlines had been responsible for the introduction of important generations of flagship commercial airliners: the Ford Tri-Motor, the Douglas DC-3, the Boeing 307, the Lockheed Constellation, the Boeing 707, and the Boeing 747, not to mention other innovations that were copied by all their competitors. There was no reward for the pioneers from whose achievements and innovations the whole world of airlines had benefitted.

Process of Attrition

During a few years following the Airline Deregulation Act of 1978, in no more than two decades, the shape of the once dominant U.S. airline industry in the eyes of the world changed beyond recognition. The demise of Braniff and Air Florida did not substantially affect the perceived stature of the U.S. airlines and of the air traveling public as a whole, but the disappearance of Pan American, Eastern, and T.W.A. certainly did. Braniff's routes were quickly absorbed by Eastern and Air Florida's by other airlines. But the end of Pan American was another matter.

Under Juan Trippe's astute leadership, Pan American had done more than dominate the intercontinental air routes of the world. It had set such a fast pace that its competitors invariably had to follow Trippe's course in new airliner acquisitions and in inter-city scheduling. Of the four major dynasties of trans-ocean airliners (1930s flying boats; 1940–1950s piston-engined landplanes; 1960s jets; 1970s wide-bodied jets) it created the demand and was the launching customer. Without the confident support of "The World's Most Experienced Airline," the oceans would not have been conquered so soon, and the Boeing jets would not have entered the Jet Age as soon as they did. Thanks to Pan American initiative in the latter 1960s, the Boeing 747 "Jumbo Jets" were still flying as the flag carriers of many national airlines well into the 21st century. It was the first airline to operate completely around the world, and Flights PA-1 and PA-2, used to set the highest standards of regularity, punctuality, and service across the Atlantic, Asia, and the Pacific. They are now, sadly, distant memories of an airline that flew the American flag with pride and with such effect that the Pan American offices in many countries around the world were as important, in their ambassadorial role, as the local U.S. consulates or embassies.

The disappearance of Pan Am and, later, of T.W.A. across the Atlantic and the Pacific removed the dominating influence of U.S. airlines on trans-ocean routes. A score of European and other foreign airlines were more than a match for American, United, Delta, and Continental, which filled the gaps in U.S. flag services across the Atlantic, and for Northwest, United, and Continental, which did so across the Pacific. As a result, where once, across the Atlantic, and led by Pan Am and T.W.A., United States accounted for half the traffic volume, its share declined to only about one-third.

Before it collapsed, Eastern Air Lines had been one of the "Big Four" U.S. domestic airlines, and had been so recognized by the C.A.B. itself. United Air Lines, American Airlines, T.W.A., and Eastern together generated about three quarters of all passenger-miles on internal routes. They were joined by Delta Air Lines, which, having already absorbed Northeast Airlines in 1972, merged with Western Air Lines in 1987, so that there were now the "Big Five." Interestingly, one of the objectives of the Airline Deregulation Act was not realized. Instead of the major traffic flows being distributed among more airlines and deriving the benefits of increased competition, the big ones gathered a greater share of the inter-city traffic than before. With the deaths of Eastern and T.W.A., the surviving United, American, and Delta together enjoy a more complete dominance of the traditional airline markets than before deregulation. The Local Service (Regional) airlines were consigned to the history books. But a new force appeared, at first underestimated, and at first thought to have been submerged under the corporate power of the big airlines. The story of a new breed of airline, which believed that cheap fares would solve all problems, is told in Chapter 24.

Meanwhile, the airlines coped with the changing travel environment and tightened their belts. Management addressed fundamental issues of finance, particularly in the acquisition of expensive airliners, by leasing them from large companies specializing in that business. To some extent, they paid for the new fleets with the money they earned as they went into service. Airline staff were persuaded to accept lower wages and salaries, and even the once-powerful ALPA began to make concessions that, before deregulation, would not have been discussed, much less agreed upon. Those airlines that kept their heads survived, those whose management made bad decisions, or could not come to terms with the unions, did not. When a major airline terminated operations, the survivors gratefully picked up the slack, and the additional cast-off traffic helped to sustain them. This usually contributed to an acceptable equilibrium for a few years, but financial viability depended heavily on the economic health of the United States. As long as the gross national product and the consequent Index of Discretionary Income continued to increase annually, there was enough traffic for all the airlines, but a decline in the economic indicators invariably meant trouble, and as the traveling public postponed business trips or vacations, this led to a case of survival of the fittest. And as the airlines of the United States entered the 21st century, even survival by any means at all became a crisis.

A Marriage of Convenience

This phrase is applied to a domestic situation in which a person with some stature in the community, often inherited, but with few material assets, marries someone with little social standing but whose bank balance is substantial. In an analogous situation, two United States domestic airlines were to echo a meeting at the altar, in which a marriage of convenience was beneficial to everyone.

Of all the post-deregulation newcomers, and excluding those airlines that simply changed their status (e.g., from intrastate or territorial to inter-state or national) and not counting those airlines (e.g., Pacific Southwest or Air California) that were devoured by the larger dominant companies, only one post-deregulation airline of any substance has survived. Like some of its companion new-starts, **America West** defied potential oblivion was partly because its base was Phoenix, Arizona, which for several decades has enjoyed a phenomenal population growth matched only by special cases such as Las Vegas. In 1900, Phoenix's population was about 5,000; in 1950 it was about 100,000; today the metropolitan area has about 3 million people, thanks to the attraction of the year-long sunshine. Geographically, America West was ideally located to distribute traffic from the east to all the cities of California.

Two thousand miles away, in Washington, D.C., another airline of a very different kind was also struggling to keep its place in the scheme of things. When the Deregulation Act was passed, Allegheny Airlines was still classified as a Regional airline, although, having taken over Mohawk, another Regional, it claimed to be the sixth largest airline in the United States. President Carter had hardly signed the new act into law when, under its new president, Edwin Colodny, it extended its route network to Florida and the southern states as far west as Phoenix; and on 28 October 1979, changed its name to **US Air**. During the next few years, it underscored its claim for nationwide recognition by substantial expansion. On 15 March 1983, with nonstop service from its Pittsburgh hub to Los Angeles and San Francisco, it became a transcontinental airline. It brought several commuter airlines into its system, and at the same time established close links with British Airways for code-sharing from Pittsburgh to London.

Substantiating its claim for top-level recognition, US Air bought the once-innovative intra-state Pacific Southwest Airlines (P.S.A.) on 8 December 1986, and a few months later, agreed to buy Piedmont Airlines, a former Local Service airline colleague. This took a while to consummate, but on 5 August 1989, the merger was complete, and by the next morning the name Piedmont had been erased. A new paint scheme was adopted on 24 May 1989, and the Allegheny Commuter network of code-sharing commuters was renamed **US Air Express** on 1 July. For a while, things looked hopeful, and Warren Buffett, the well-known billionaire, acquired a 12% share of the airline in August. Services to San Juan, Puerto Rico, and nonstop service with Boeing 767-200s from Pittsburgh to Frankfurt, starting on 15 June 1990, suggested confidence.

However, the airline had never shaken off its reputation as a high-cost carrier. Many of its routes were monopolies, or near-monopolies. Its had the highest cost-per-seat-mile in the industry, offset by the highest yield. By 1990, the gradual erosion resulting from a general lowering of fare levels everywhere was taking its toll. In August the airline began to furlough some of its pilots, and deferred deliveries of ordered aircraft, and parked some of its fleet as it cut back some schedules. It reported a net loss of $454 million for the year.

Soldiering on, it launched the **US Air Shuttle** on 12 April 1992, taking over the Trump Shuttle, originally the famous New York-Washington/Boston airline service started by Eastern Air Lines in 1960 (see Chapter 24). Hopes were raised when, after US Air Shuttle started Baltimore (Washington)-London and Philadelphia-London services on 1 May 1992 to add to its trans-Atlantic routes, an agreement was signed on 20 July between US Air president Seth Schofield and British Airways' Sir Colin Marshall for the latter to acquire 44% of the ailing American airline. Had this deal gone through, it would have resulted in the world's biggest global alliance. But U.S. law did not allow a foreign company to own more than 25% of the controlling stock. British investment was reduced to just less than that figure, when the two airlines settled on 21 January 1993.

In the fall of 1995, discussions were held between USAir and United Air Lines, the biggest airline in the world, now that the Soviet giant Aeroflot had collapsed along with the Soviet Union. On 21 January 1996, Stephen Wolf, the former United chairman, became the new chairman/CEO of US Air. The next year was eventful. Trans-Atlantic service from Philadelphia was extended to Munich, Madrid, and Rome in May and June. In August, US Air filed suit against British Airways and American Airlines because Wolf claimed British Airways had not fulfilled its financial obligations to US Air. The British solved the problem by selling its US Air shares on 21 May 1997 for $625 million.

On 30 April 1996, Wolf had changed the name of the airline to **US Airways**, at the same time changing the color scheme to a deep blue and medium gray, remarkably similar to that of United Airlines that Wolf had introduced in 1992. In November, an order was announced for no less than 400 aircraft, mostly from Boeing, but also including 120 from Airbus, and this led to litigation with Boeing a year later. The route network was trimmed on 4 September 1997 by suspension of service at many points and the closing of maintenance bases at other stations, but then Wolf reversed direction in favor of expansion, reaffirming the order talks, now for 400 Airbuses, with Boeing for wide-bodied aircraft and adopting a low-fares tariff policy. The company gained complete ownership of the Shuttle service and launched **MetroJet** as a low-fare affiliate, aimed to compete with the aggressive Southwest Airlines. Wolf brought in Rakesh Gangwal as his president/chief operating officer on 18 May 1998 and seemed to be on the expansion course, by ordering 30 Airbus A330s on 2 July, inaugurating Airbus A319 service on 10 November and A320s on 1 February 1999.

While this made the headlines, all was not well within the airline, as the entire staff, with some justification, was not too pleased with being asked to make concessions while Wolf and Gangwal were receiving several million each in salaries, bonuses, and stock options. Strikes were threatened, and settled, but morale was low, and productivity at all levels was even lower. US Airways's cost per seat mile was twice as high as Southwest's, and in the first quarter of 2000, with its stock value falling dangerously, the company lost $218 million.

A big merger seemed imminent. On 23 May 2000, United Airlines offered to buy US Airways for $11.6 billion, at the same time to sell most of US Airways routes at its Washington National Airport hub to Robert Johnson, the founder of Black Entertainment Television. He was planning to start a new airline, DC Air. The deal was engineered by Wolf, and the shareholders approved it on 12 October. Although US Airways lost $269 million in 2000, Wolf's salary doubled and Gangwal's tripled to a combined $24 million. At the beginning of 2001, there was much sparring and maneuvering by airlines, notably American, Continental, and Delta, to purchase shares of US Airways, while Johnson pursued his ambition to start DC Air. But although the European Union agreed to terms for the North Atlantic, the whole idea was raising alarm in government circles at the prospect of what would have resulted in a very large airline, and an oligopoly of only five major U.S. giants. A bill to postpone the deal was introduced in Congress, and on 1 April 2001, after the Justice Department requested more information, the merger was first postponed then, on 27 July, both airlines announced its cancellation, after Justice said it would violate anti-trust law. United paid a $50 million termination fee to US Airways.

On 5 August, by which time the stock had fallen to $18 a share, Global Airlines Corporation offered to buy the airline for $10 billion. But all negotiations came to an abrupt halt when, on 11 September 2001, the World Trade Center in New York was destroyed by terrorists, and another airliner crashed into the Pentagon in Washington, D.C. All commercial flying in the country was suspended for two days. When it resumed, strict security measures were taken at all airports, and air travel declined dramatically as business and pleasure travelers alike were apprehensive. Of all the airlines, US Airways suffered the most, because of its Washington hub, and it later received a loan of $900 million from a contingency fund to compensate for lost revenue while the Ronald Reagan Washington National Airport, alarmingly close to the Pentagon, was closed.

Not until 23 October was the airport reopened; meanwhile, on 17 September, the airline announced plans to cut 11,000 jobs from the workforce and, four days later, revealed plans to shut down Metrojet, its low-fare subsidiary that had been launched on 1 June 1998. Nevertheless, the financial situation was in crisis, with a loss in 2001 of almost $2 billion. On 27 November, Gangwal resigned as president, and on 11 March 2002, David N. Siegel, previously chief of Avis Rent-a-Car, replaced him. He reported to the main board of the airline, not to Wolf, who also moved on elsewhere. Handsome severance payments among the top three retirees amounted to $35 million.

On 11 August 2002, US Airways filed for Chapter 11 bankruptcy protection, and further economies of staff were made, but a life line appeared from David Bronner, whose Retirement Systems of Alabama offered to take a 37.5% stake in the airline—quite a bargain, as the stock had deteriorated to about $4.00 a share. Some measure of cautious confidence was restored, Bronner took over as chairman on 4 April 2003 and with $500 million additional financing, and the airline seemed to be on its feet again, albeit precariously. On 12 May it ordered 170 regional jets, on 31 May it joined the global Star Alliance, and on 2 June it restored the New York-Washington/Boston Shuttle Services.

The financial bleeding continued. Siegel resigned on 19 April 2004, to be replaced by Bruce R. Lakefield, formerly with Lehman Brothers. Siegel received the now customary severance pay ($5 million in this case), but Lakefield cut his salary and refused the "golden handshake." He too faced problems that were deeply fundamental, dating back throughout the entire history of an airline that had enjoyed either captive markets with little competition or markets in which it was almost a monopoly, and had set its fare structure accordingly. Its revenue-per-seat-mile had always been the highest in the industry, and its operating costs reflected that level.

On 4 April, MidAtlantic Airways started a low-fare airline operating between Philadelphia and Pittsburgh, two of US Airways's main hubs. On 10 May Southwest Airlines, now a powerful force in the airline competitive world, opened service from Philadelphia to seven destinations. This effectively put an end to the incumbent's hitherto dominance at Philadelphia. Its reaction was to seek additional concessions from its now-indignant workforce, but the 28,000 employees at all levels were unwilling to negotiate, and the inevitable result was for the airline to seek bankruptcy protection for the second time, which it did on 12 September 2004.

Just before Christmas, computer problems in the baggage-handling system at Philadelphia led to an unprecedented pile-up of luggage. 10,000 pieces were sent to Charlotte so that they could be sorted and eventually returned to their owners. More than 300 flights were cancelled on Christmas Eve and Christmas Day. 2,000 passengers were stranded at Cincinnati because of heavy snow. Morale within the airline was so low that hundreds of employees called in sick over the holiday period.

The end was in sight. US Airways either had to cease operations or it had to merge or be absorbed by another airline, and in the latter case, it had no cards to play. In the spring of 2005, offers were made by speculative investors, and on 19 May, after discussions that had begun tentatively as early as July 2004, a merger was announced between US Air and Phoenix-based America West. This was promptly approved by the Justice Department on 23 June—an indication of a desperate situation that had to be resolved, with no half-measures. The various investments totaled $500 million, and the merged airline ownership was: investors 49%, America West 39%, US Airways creditors, 12%. The US Airways name was retained, but the headquarters went west, to America West, in Tempe, Arizona. The aircraft would receive a new paint scheme, sensibly with white upper fuselages, to reflect the blistering sun at Phoenix and Las Vegas, which, following demographic trends (both cities were the fastest growing in the nation) would become the merged airline's western hubs.

And so a new major airline was salvaged from potential disaster; both airlines had survived two Chapter 11 bankruptcies. One had concentrated on high fare structures, the other had moved into adopting that policy. With the two distribution hubs in the west (Phoenix and Las Vegas) and with corresponding hubs in the east (Pittsburgh, Philadelphia, and Charlotte, not to mention a network throughout the Caribbean), the potential for a new major domestic trunk airline, if not assured, did appear to be encouraging.

Chapter 24: Birth of the Low-Fare Generation

The Post-War Opportunist Pioneers

When the Second World War came to an end, a flood of war-surplus equipment of all kinds, including thousands of aircraft, swept the United States. The military fighters and bombers were out of work and scrapped, but the transport aircraft, mainly Douglas C-47s, C-54s, and Curtiss C-46s, were clearly not so expendable, as long as they could be converted for commercial or other civilian use. Indeed, they had originally been built for the airlines, so this was a case of their being restored to their proper role. The war surplus disposal authorities returned aircraft back to the airlines that had supplied them, and many were sold to entrepreneur companies or to ambitious individuals. The aircraft numbers were matched by a flood of demobilized airmen, pilots, navigators, mechanics, and engineers, all of whom eagerly sought to transfer their skills from the military to the commercial. They established local enterprises that extended the scope of fixed base operators (F.B.O.s) beyond the hitherto accepted levels, so that in the late 1940s, several small independent airlines emerged, able to buy aircraft cheaply, and charge low passenger fares or low air freight tariffs because they operated on the proverbial shoestring. In time, the Civil Aeronautics Board (C.A.B.) put a stop to what it (and the established airlines) regarded as a flagrant abuse by gypsy operators of the rules and conditions of a closely regulated industry.

However, as long as an upstart airline did not fly across state lines, and kept within its own state backyard, it was immune from the strict control of the C.A.B., and could even operate scheduled services, as long as it followed the proper conditions of safety and navigation rulings of the Civil Aeronautics Authority, which later became the Federal Aviation Agency (F.A.A.). Almost by geographical definition, the circumstances for such freedom were limited—a state had to be big enough and populous enough to support enough traffic for viable air service. The clear winner was California, because it was home to two of the largest metropolitan areas of the country, the sprawling Los Angeles area and the Bay Area of San Francisco. They were 340 miles apart, an ideal distance for short-haul air services. The fastest train took all day or all night, and even the new multi-lane freeways did not permit a day's road travel without incurring fatigue or breaking the speed limit.

By the time the Jet Age began, several intra-state airlines were well established. California Central Airlines, the first successful Large Irregular Carrier (as they were designated by the C.A.B.), had enjoyed the blessing of the California Public Utilities Commission from 1948 until 1953, but its $9.99 Los Angeles (Burbank)-San Francisco (Oakland) fare could not sustain it, in spite of having carried 137,000 passengers during 1952. But another bold contender for the California Corridor market did survive.

Poor Sailors' Airline

Pacific Southwest Airlines (P.S.A.) was a force to be reckoned with, because while its management pursued the policy of low fares, it did not go to extremes, and its marketing was remembered for its promotional élan, which included hot-panted stewardesses to compliment simple ticketing procedures. Founded by Kenny Friedkin, who deserves an honored place in the airline Hall of Fame, P.S.A. had started with a single DC-3 in 1949, moved on to four-engined DC-4s in 1955, and prop-jet Lockheed Electras in 1959. Then, when United Air Lines introduced its Boeing 727 *Jet Commuter* $14.50 Los Angeles-San Francisco fare on 27 September 1964, P.S.A., whose financial position was so strong that it did not have to borrow money to buy its own 727s, responded on 9 April 1965 with its own one-way fare of $13.50. During the next decade, the airline never looked back, and its success was so convincing that even the C.A.B. itself began to question its own restrictive regulations, as it observed the popularity of P.S.A., defiantly excelling the incumbent airlines, which should have held all the competitive trump cards.

Quite apart from the attractive flight attendants, the airline was very efficient, streamlining all the irritant aspects of air travel. The aircraft were invariably on time, the ticketing was simple, but above all, the journey itself was always enjoyable. Floyd Andrews always claimed that the fact that the girls were gorgeous was just a coincidence. They all had to pass an extremely strict training course and did their job perfectly. California air travelers loved to fly by P.S.A. because it was an enjoyable experience, not just a boring way to go from one place to another. In short, the airline had that indefinable quality of charisma. It played a trump card when, just before Christmas 1966, it introduced the famous mini-skirts to complement its friendly service.

The whole environment within the airline reflected the service, or was complimentary to it. All the staff enjoyed their work, worked voluntary overtime, and willingly performed duties other than their own. Pilots helped old people to disembark, stewardesses helped with heavy baggage, while management often held informal gatherings, to baptize the Electras, or a party at Las Vegas for all the staff. Not surprisingly, traffic grew in leaps

Pacific Southwest Airlines emphasized its friendly on-board service policy by putting a smile on the face of its Boeing 727s. (Davies)

and bounds. In 1967, the first Douglas DC-9-30s arrived as did the first Boeing 727-200s. P.S.A. was the first airline in the western states to operate the "stretched" version of this successful airliner, and by 1968, it was the tenth largest airline in the United States, ranked by passengers boarded. Another boost to its already popular image came in the spring of 1969 when one of the pilots painted a big smile on the nose of a 727. President Andrews objected at first, but the media reaction was so favorable that he accepted it, and the Smile stayed on the aircraft until P.S.A.'s demise. In June of the same year, the Los Angeles-San Francisco service was the dreamed-of "every hour, on the hour," made economically possible by the speedy 15-minute turn-rounds, thus achieving maximum utilization of the aircraft.

Little by little, however, and in spite of the Smile and the mini-skirts, a subtle change was occurring within the airline, partly because the special qualities of almost personal service had been possible because it was a small, very specialized airline. By the early 1970s, it had expanded service to Oakland, San Jose, Sacramento, Long Beach, Ontario, Fresno, and Stockton. Its fleet was growing—23 Boeing 727s and 737s by this time— and to meet the traffic demand, P.S.A. introduced the 302-seat wide-bodied Lockheed L-1011 TriStar on 1 August 1974. All this was a sign of growing stature, but partly because of the fuel crisis of the early 1970s and partly from possibly mistimed overconfidence, the management ran the risk of overstepping itself. It invested in hotels in San Francisco, San Diego, the Hollywood Park race track, rented space in the *Queen Mary* at Long Beach, attempted to buy its new rival, Air California (see below). Its "Midnight Flyer," introduced on 27 October 1969, was an immediate success for tired businessmen after a long day. Such was its fame in the airline world that an aspirant intra-state airline based in Dallas, Texas, sent a strong, high-level delegation to San Diego to study P.S.A.'s methods, procedures, and recipe for success. This aspirant, Southwest Airlines (see below), was a good pupil.

But luck did not always favor the brave. In 1972, when there was a string of hijackings, P.S.A. had four of them, just as it was ordering the big Lockheeds. The staff morale had changed, and a six-week strike by the Machinists and Teamsters ended only two days before Christmas Day in 1973. The senior management was changing, both in its personnel and its style. The Friedkins had died in 1972–73, and Floyd Andrews, who had taken the helm with great flair, resigned in March 1976 because of failing eyesight. Paul Barkley became the Chief Operating Officer, and the charismatic image of this remarkable airline began to fade. The skirts descended to below the knee, the service lacked the repartee with the customers, the pilots had to make stereotyped announcements (not leaving the public address system on when asking who had the map or the flying instruction book); computers replaced the instant telephone answering service.

Then came the devastating blow. On 25 September 1978, a Boeing 727-200 was involved in a mid-air collision over San Diego. 135 passengers and crew, including 37 P.S.A. personnel, were killed, plus seven on the ground and two in the colliding Cessna 172. It broke a 29-year safety record. The human tragedy

was matched by the shadow it cast on the imminent opportunity for expansion; only a month later, on 24 October 1978, President Carter signed the Airline Deregulation Act that allowed P.S.A. to expand beyond the state boundaries of California. It had already inched its way across. On 4 April 1975, it had obtained permission to serve Lake Tahoe, across the California-Nevada state line, by landing at nearby Douglas County Airport in Nevada, and had recalled some Electras to negotiate the demanding landing and take-off procedures. Throwing caution to the winds on 15 December 1978, it started frequent services from San Diego to Las Vegas, and from San Francisco to Reno. The year's total boardings were almost eight million—not bad for an airline that had started in 1949 with a single DC-3.

Expansion to other destinations continued, including Mexican vacation resorts and, later on, at the end of 1988, to the northwestern States. But the management style had changed under Barkley. He was successful in what he described as "creative financing" in replacing the tri-jet 727s with the "stretched" DC-9-80 twin-jets in November 1980, and, British Aerospace 100-seat BAe 146 four-engined jets in June 1984. But by this time, with deregulation, other low-fare airlines, increased fuel costs, an air traffic controllers strike: these all combined to erode P.S.A.'s former leadership within California. The last gesture was to introduce the PSA Expressway—a flight every half-hour between Los Angeles and San Francisco. Even this turned out to be a dying effort.

The end came suddenly. On 7 December 1987, one of the BAe 146s crashed near San Luis Obispo, killing 43 people. Coincidentally, on the next day the US Air Group proposed a takeover of P.S.A. and its engine overhaul associate. The sale was completed on 24 May but P.S.A. had made its last flight on 8 April. Barkley retired in 1989. All that was left of a great pioneering airline was the remnants of the P.S.A. Group, an oil and gas leasing company, which eventually folded up in the year 2000. A bitter irony was that the one airline that did the most to sow the seed that was to ripen into airline deregulation was among its more prominent victims.

Air California

If ever an airline was launched on the basis of good market research, the one that was to challenge P.S.A. proved the point. The fastest-growing area in the United States—and one of the richest—was to the southeast of the Los Angeles metropolis, centered on Orange County, and it was at that airport, also known as Santa Ana, that **Air California** was born. Not only were the population demographics favorable, but the journeys from Santa Ana or Newport Beach to Los Angeles by road were a perfect example of the "sprawl-and-crawl" that swept across the United States as it turned its back on rail transport, including suburban services, during the latter half of the 20th century.

After the necessary wrangling with the California Public Utilities Commission the brash new airline began services from Orange County to San Francisco on 16 January 1967, with a fleet of three Lockheed L-188 Electra turboprops. These were ideal for the base airport where the runway was marginally short for

Based in affluent Orange County, Air California challenged P.S.A.'s popularity. Its Douglas DC-9s were decorated in bright colors, as were its flight attendants, whose uniforms included Mexican ponchos. (Davies)

jets and there were local objections to their noise. Its answer to P.S.A.'s attractive stewardesses was a striking orange and yellow Mexican-style uniform that was more of a fashion show, complete with poncho. By 1968, after a brief trial with a couple of Douglas DC-9s, Air California leased six Boeing 737s, to compete with P.S.A., which then attempted to merge the two airlines, and a long battle led to the Westgate California Corporation taking control on 10 June 1970. P.S.A. withdrew from the competition. Subsequently the challenger continued to add more points to its intra-state network, taking care to concentrate on routes from its home territory.

During the next few years, the airline continued to operate as an intra-state airline, more-or-less junior to P.S.A., expanding modestly to serve Mammoth Lakes, a popular skiing resort, by buying Holiday Airlines. Then came airline deregulation, and, like P.S.A., immediately began to serve Reno, on 18 December 1978, and Las Vegas, on 1 June 1979, at the same time suspending service to San Diego, its competitor's home base. Then, in May 1980, the airline was sold to two real estate investors, William Lyon and George Argyros, who started to expand Air California more aggressively. On 1 April 1981, the aircraft carried the image of **AirCal**, an abbreviation by which the airline was already known. They bought Douglas DC-9-80s—the "stretched" version—which could carry almost as many passengers as P.S.A.'s 727-200s, but with two engines rather than three, and was more economical to operate; and in 1982, started to operate from Los Angeles to San Francisco nonstop. By the end of 1984, it was concentrating on this important downtown-to-downtown route, and its share of the California Corridor market was 35%—almost as much as the incumbent P.S.A.'s 39%. A dozen Boeing 737-300s were ordered, and such was the success of the two bargain-fare airlines that the well-established veteran United Air Lines was carrying only 17%.

As in the case of P.S.A., the end to Air California came suddenly. In November 1986, American Airlines announced that it would buy it. By 1 July 1987, the Orange County airline was submerged in the flood of takeovers and bankruptcies which had become all too frequent occurrences during the post-deregulation decade. Contrary to the imagined prospects of the deregulation process, and with one outstanding exception, the airlines that had led the way in providing the only significant competition that mattered to the traveling public—low fares—were cynically removed from the United States airline arena.

New York Air

The basic economics lessons of California had been learned elsewhere, specifically in Texas, where, even before deregulation, Frank Lorenzo had, in marketing his Texas International Airlines, launched the audacious "peanuts fares" campaign for a selection of routes that reached far beyond the confines of the airline base in the State of Texas. These were termed "double discount" fares, and the public, predictably, liked them. The system was, quite simply, one in which seats were sold selectively on flights where the load factors were usually low, on the principle that a bargain-basement sale is better than no sale at all—a practice that retail stores have followed since time immemorial. But with a slight difference: once an airline seat is used on a flight, with or without a passenger in it, it is gone. It does not sit on a shelf, awaiting a customer. Later, with advanced computer technology, these otherwise empty seats could be sold under a form of horse-trading that was politely termed "yield management."

When airline deregulation changed the airline playing field in 1978, and as a New Yorker, Lorenzo had long observed, and disparaged, the airline environment in the northeast, where USAir especially had maintained high fare levels on many intercity routes such as New York-Pittsburgh, or from Philadelphia. The Eastern Air Shuttle service catered mainly for business men; and the Amtrak railroad provided a service on the Boston-New York-Washington "Boswash" corridor that was only moderately challenging.

The Airline Deregulation Act of 1978 had failed to deregulate one important factor in the competitive arena. Access to gates at an airport, and their "slots" (the time allotted to one aircraft arrival or departure) were still effectively regulated—by the incumbent airlines. At many airports at the big cities, few slots were available on the open market, and these were invariably at inconvenient travel times, and not particularly desirable. Consequently, the incumbents were in a position to sell their slots at their own price, and at some busy airports, one slot could cost hundreds of thousands of dollars. In fact, the trading of slots would often become an accepted feature of the manipulation of some airline balance sheets; newcomer airlines often found difficulty in starting service.

Lorenzo shrewdly identified an opportunity. At Washington's National Airport, where operations were restricted to short-medium-haul flights, because long-range jets could not take off or land, slots were available. In 1980, the Department of Transportation, taking over from the C.A.B., was considering what to do about the 640 slots available, with 22 airlines applying for them. The incumbents already had 278, half of them Eastern's. Most of the applicants were small, many of them of recent origin, and mostly with little capital or experience. Early in August, Lorenzo's **Texas International Airlines (T.X.I.)** "stunned the industry" (to quote the *Washington Post*) by applying for 44 slots at National and no less than 70 at New York's LaGuardia Airport. To back up the application, Texas had ordered 30 115-seat Douglas DC-9s for $135 million. On 29 October 1980, the D.O.T. cleared the way for T.X.I. to operate nine round-trips per day between the two airports that hosted the famous Eastern Air Shuttle. At the same time, in a reallocation of slots, five incumbents lost 10 of them to allow the entry of Air North, Midway Airlines, Empire Airlines, and Mid-South Airlines, but these were of little consequence, compared to the impact of Frank Lorenzo's initiative.

On 19 December 1980, **New York Air** made its debut. The airline was created as subsidiary of the holding company, Texas Air Corporation, of which T.X.I. was also a fellow subsidiary. With its first DC-9, Flight "Apple 2" took off at 7 A.M. from Washington to New York, to begin the familiar on-the-hour, every-hour service in direct competition with the Eastern Shuttle. The apple insignia, displayed on the tail of the aircraft, was a direct association with the familiar reference to New York as the "Big Apple." More important was the fare. Against Eastern's $60 each way, New York Air charged $49 during the week and $29 at weekends. The pilots' union, ALPA, protested at the non-union rates paid to the crews—$30,000 a year for about 70 hours per month, against ALPA's $75,000 for about 50; but this was of no avail. New York Air was off to a flying start on one of the busiest air routes in the world.

The shuttle from New York to Boston began on 15 February 1981, and to Cleveland on 12 April. Other destinations followed, to points in the Midwest, to Raleigh-Durham (an American Airlines hub) and to Orlando, already a rapidly growing popular resort destination because of Disneyworld, followed by other attractions. Service to Detroit started from LaGuardia on 20 September but an important move was made in February 1982 when this route was switched from LaGuardia to Newark. This was an interesting reflection on ancient history. Before the Second World War, Newark had been New York's commercial airport, and LaGuardia, named after the popular mayor, replaced it in 1940. Now, 40 years later, the advantages of Newark's accessibility to Manhattan were once again realized, as traffic to LaGuardia was congested at the airport, while the ground connections were inadequately served by public transport.

On 2 February 1982, Michael Levine, formerly with the C.A.B. when it was wound down after deregulation, took over as chairman, and changed the policy of New York Air. The flourish with which the airline had entered the market had not been sustained, partly because the Eastern Air Shuttle retained its adherents, particularly the businessmen to whom the fare was immaterial, and to pay the fare, either on arrival at LaGuardia or on board the aircraft, had become a habit. People Express's low-fare emphasis was modified, and service-oriented catering replaced the bag-of-peanuts standards. Several of the destination cities, other than those on the Corridor, were eliminated. Nevertheless, at the end of the year, the airline had to report a net loss of almost $24 million. The airline kept afloat with a redistribution of the capital, by which Texas Air took 5 million shares of the common stock for $17 million.

Careful route expansion continued, when, with 147-seat MacDonnell Douglas MD-80s, a Newark-New Orleans service was added on 4 September 1984, and in Washington, flights started from Dulles International Airport, as well as National, on 1 February 1985.

Trumped

The busy New York-Washington/New York-Boston routes had, since the earliest years of air transport in the United States, been of consuming interest to all the airlines that had been certificated to operate them. Chief among these was Eastern Air Lines, which innovated the no-reservation Shuttle service in 1961. This fell under Frank Lorenzo's control when, in 1986, his Texas Air Corporation bought Eastern. First selling the airport slots and gates to Pan American for $65 million, he then, on 12 October 1988, sold the Shuttle itself, along with 17 165-seat Boeing 727-200s, for $365 million, to real estate developer Donald Trump, who owned hotels and casinos in Atlantic City.

After Eastern's Chapter 11 bankruptcy affairs were cleared on 9 March 1989, the **Trump Shuttle** started operations on 8 June, in competition with the new Pan Am Shuttle. It quickly regained the half-share of the traffic that had been lost to Pan Am during Eastern's problems that included a strike. This was no bargain-fare enterprise. Trump offered guaranteed on-time arrivals and extra on-board amenities to attract discerning business travelers. But the higher revenues that these generated were more than offset by the cost of providing them. In July 1991, a tentative agreement was made with Northwest Airlines to manage the operation. However, Continental Air Holdings (Texas Air Corporation's new name) still retained certain legal rights and blocked the sale.

On 11 July 1991, Delta Air Lines took over the Pan Am Shuttle, when it acquired most of that historic airline's worldwide network, and Northwest withdrew. On 19 December, Trump sold his airline to USAir, and on 12 April 1992, the service became the **USAir Shuttle.**

People Express

Simultaneously with the launching of New York Air, the idea of promoting cheap fares had gained ground at Houston, where Frank Lorenzo's advocacy had reached receptive ears. On 7 April 1980, even before Texas International's notorious slot purchase at Washington and New York, **People Express** was founded in Houston by Donald Burr and two of his colleagues at the Texas airline. Financing was negotiated with the investment firm of Hambrecht and Quist to the extent of $24 million, and this was used to purchase 17 Boeing 727-130s from Lufthansa, with economy-class seating increased from 84 to 118. This was a great bargain, as one new 737 would have cost $13 million, and the German airline's maintenance had been immaculate.

The other key element in the business plan was to locate the airline's hub at Newark, hitherto much underutilized. People Express leased the entire North Terminal, which was vacated when two new terminals were opened. This choice was remarkably visionary, as it was the beginning of the development of Newark, not only as New York's third airport, but, in the course of time, as New York's leading airport in terms of passenger boardings. People Express moved into Newark on 1 January 1981, making surface transport arrangements with the New Jersey Transit express bus service at the Port Authority Bus Terminal in downtown Manhattan, charging only $4.00 for the connection. It adopted the trading title of PEOPLExpress, with the twin "people" profile insignia on the aircraft tails. A good airport-to-downtown passenger service was important. The rise of People Express and the growing recognition of Newark seemed to coincide with the disappearance of the service from 42nd Street to the two airports on Long Island. The Carey Bus had almost become a permanent feature of the New York image, as it often welcomed first-time visitors from overseas.

Scheduled services began on 30 April 1981, from Newark to Columbus, Buffalo, and Norfolk. This was a different marketing policy from New York Air's, eschewing the Shuttle in favor of selected destinations that were inadequately served by other airlines. But in one respect the two airlines agreed. The fare structure was emphatically low, almost half that of the previous incumbents. An advertising slogan was that it was "cheaper than driving." During the next few months, other poorly served cities were added, such as Jacksonville, Syracuse, and Indianapolis, and although the PATCO (air traffic controllers) strike on 3 August slowed up the growth, it did not slow up People Express's spirit of initiative. On 25 October it started to make dawn departures from Newark, thus avoiding the F.A.A. flight restriction period, and also opened service to Sarasota, on the Gulf Coast of Florida, once again foreshadowing an expansion of travel to that area.

Subsequent growth was explosive. Additional points were added in New England and Florida, and, more important, on 3 August 1982, shuttle services did begin to New York from Washington's National Airport, and on 15 November of that year, from the capital's Dulles International Airport. To support this expansion, the first (of five) Boeing 727-200s were delivered. Then, on 6 April 1983, in a move that eclipsed all other airline news of the period, People Express petitioned the United Kingdom Civil Aviation Authority (C.A.A.) for permission to open a route from Newark to London. On 20 May, Harold Pareti (who had replaced Gerald Gitner as one of the original Texas founders) held a press conference in London to announce the plans. The public reaction was unprecedented, as, within a few days, the flights were fully booked for several months ahead. The C.A.A. was obliged, by the force of public opinion, to accelerate the authorization decision, which came only a few hours before the 430-seat economy/premium Boeing 747-227B (ex-Braniff) inaugural service on 26 May 1983. With memories of Sir Freddie Laker's Skytrain, the one-way economy fare was $149.00, or less than £100 sterling.

Just as, in a far different operating environment, Pan American Airways will never be forgotten in the annals of world air transport history, so too will People Express be remembered for having claimed its place. Not only did it revive the popularity of the trans-Atlantic bargain fare; it put Newark back on the map, and that airport has gained in strength ever since.

By the beginning of January 1984, Burr's fleet consisted of 50 Boeing 727-200s and 22 Boeing 737-100s, thus providing the equipment for a major program of further expansion. This included, on 15 June, the first transcontinental service, to Los Angeles, and within a year, People Express had added 18 more destinations, effectively becoming a national trunk airline. Burr had introduced a novel style of management, in which all members of the staff, from branch managers to counter-clerks, were shareholders in the airline and were expected to perform or exchange any duty, and this procedure even included air crew—not that a baggage handler was expected to take the left-hand seat of a 737. But the idea was not a success, even though the intention may have been good. It was a perfect example of the axiom "jack of all trades but master at none." Whether or not this was the reason for his departure, Pareti, whose hour of glory had been the announcement in London of the new Freddie Laker Skytrain successor, resigned on 15 January 1985 and, as narrated below, started his own airline, with a new set of standards.

People Express continued its headlong expansion by acquiring other airlines. The most important was Frontier Airlines, long established since the Local Service airline years of the 1940s and 1950s, and which had a solid hub system based at Denver. Frank Lorenzo had also wished to incorporate Frontier into Continental Airlines, but when, on 22 November 1985, Donald Burr outbid him, Frank sent a congratulatory telegram to Frontier. The purchase had cost $300 million. Whether by intuition or shrewd business acumen, perhaps he knew that Burr was over-reaching himself, and that Frontier would be Continental's in due course.

For People Express did just that. On 31 January 1986, almost before the ink was dry on the Frontier deal, it took over the Provincetown-Boston Airline (P.B.A.), one of the oldest of the commuter airlines and which had fallen from grace with the F.A.A. The main asset was a local network in Florida. This added 14 more points to the People Express map, but the transaction seemed to be counter-productive. The same could be said for the acquisition of Britt Airways on 5 February. The intensive commuter routes serving the Chicago and St. Louis hinterlands again added points geographically, but did not win points among People Express's auditors. For by the time the Britt deal was completed on 26 February, the airline announced a loss of $27.5 million for the 1985 calendar year.

As with many an airline promoter whose downfall is narrated in this book, Donald Burr was a great risk taker. But he underestimated the skills and the ruthlessness of the incumbent airlines to fight for their survival. American Airlines, for example, in the summer of 1986, introduced its Super-Saver program, in which it matched, and in some cases undercut, People Express's fares. The older airlines also had efficient computer systems that could control their business with a yield-management manipulation of fares as and where and when needed; whereas People Express was offering its product in a relatively old-fashioned and ponderous manner, and because of its strange management system, often by inexperienced personnel. Even the Air Bridge—three Boeing 747 flights a day to connect the two big hubs at Newark and Denver, designed to provide connecting service all across the network—did not work well.

On 23 June 1986, Burr announced that People Express was up for sale. It had lost $58 million in the first quarter of the year alone; and the hemorrhaging was getting worse. The stock value was $5.50 a share, half that of the previous month, and the debt was $500 million, much of it incurred by the purchase of airlines. At first, talks were held with United Airlines, but that airline quickly withdrew, and on 24 August all the Frontier operations were halted, followed by Chapter 11 bankruptcy four days later. On 15 September, Frank Lorenzo announced that his Continental Airlines would buy People Express, including Frontier, for a total value of $296.7 million, including an infusion of cash. The Department of Justice encouraged swift action, and on 14 October the Department of Transportation approved the merger.

People Express's last flight was on 31 January 1987 and the whole fleet was integrated with Continental's. The airline's career had been brief, only six years, ranging from an unprecedented rocket-like ascent to success to an equally unprecedented meteoric plunge to failure. But it will be remembered affectionately by the millions of people who had never flown before, and who were introduced to air travel by an airline which, in spite of its idiosyncracies, did much to change the shape of the U.S. industry and travel habits across the Atlantic.

Presidential

The life of the next airline to try its hand at low-fare airline operations was even shorter. Harold Pareti, who had served his apprenticeship with Donald Burr, but had disagreed with the way things were going, adopted his own formula for success in the world of this new breed of airlines, so different from the old. He incorporated **Presidential Airlines** on 5 March 1985 and moved to ensure that one essential requirement for any new airline was adequate financial strength to withstand the slings and arrows of misfortune, or, in the competitive airline business, those of no-holds-barred competitors. He enrolled a groups of investors so that, by September, he was able to announce that Presidential was the best capitalized ever of all the new airlines.

The fleet of four Boeing 737-200s was modest, compared to what People Express had started with, and so the initial network was correspondingly small. The other differences were that Pareti selected as his base Washington's Dulles International Airport and although the fares were low—$39 off-peak to all points—the service was not at a "no frills" level, and first class service, at $99, was offered to all points except Miami. The initial network was also to Boston, Cincinnati, Indianapolis, Hartford, and by the end of the year, Cleveland, West Palm Beach, and Orlando were added. Pareti had clearly identified the Great Lakes States and Florida as potential traffic sources.

On 21 January 1986, an agreement was made with **Gulf Air**, a commuter line that served Massachusetts from Boston and the Bahamas from Florida; and on 21 February, having obtained the necessary exemption from the F.A.A., started international service from Montreal. Presidential's entry into the field was done with a flair. When the new mid-field terminal at Dulles Airport was opened early in the year, the V.I.P. lounge was named The Oval Office, while at the corporate level, Najeeb Halaby, former F.A.A. administrator and former chairman of Pan American Airways, was elected to the board of directors.

Progress continued through the year, and on 4 June Presidential announced an agreement with Pan American Airways for connecting traffic at Miami and Washington. Two weeks later, Pareti selected the 90-seat British Aerospace BAe 146 feeder airliner for operation on routes that did not generate enough traffic for the Boeing 737s. Service to New York's LaGuardia Airport and to Detroit started on 3 July, and following an example set by People Express, Presidential purchased **Colgan Airways**, based in the Washington area, and **Key Airlines**, a contract operator specializing in Caribbean destinations. Colgan was a commuter airline, operating small turboprop aircraft, but Key had eight Boeing 727-100 jets—a strange combination. On 12 January 1987, Pareti announced that Presidential would become a "mezzanine jet feeder carrier," with a 10-year marketing agreement to do business as Continental Express. Continental Airlines bought Presidential's 15-gate mid-field terminal at Dulles Airport, with a long-term lease-back, and soon afterward, Pareti sold Key Airlines to World Airways. In spite of these belt-tightening moves, Presidential's net loss in 1986 was almost $40 million.

The next two years witnessed mixed messages. On the one hand, expansion of the network, on 23 March 1987, to a range of cities from the Dulles hub, mainly to smaller cities in the northeast, connecting with Florida resorts, and using the BAe 146s, suggested solid progress. In June, an order for ten 19-seat BAe Jetstream 31 turboprops suggested careful planning, with the smaller aircraft serving the smaller cities. But on 6 February 1988, the Continental deal was terminated and a similar arrangement was made with United Airlines, as United Express. To underline confidence, starting on 20 February, more cities were added, and by the end of the year, Presidential's network east of the Mississippi was substantial. To prove a point, on 17 November, Pareti ordered 16 Boeing-de Havilland-Canada Dash 8-300s, and on 5 August 1989, his airline was the first in the United States to put this versatile STOL (Short Take-Off and Landing) aircraft into service.

Regrettably, this amounted to little more than putting on a brave face in a business environment of pending disaster. Route expansion and fleet augmentation were not in parallel with a sound financial foundation to support the Presidential dreams. On 2 December 1989, the airline declared Chapter 11 bankruptcy, and the demise was complete.

Pause for Reflection

After only a single decade, the bright future for a new generation of airlines of substance, enabled by the 1978 Airline Deregulation Act, seemed to be in disarray. People Express and

Presidential, which were intended to herald a bright future for bright new entrepreneurs with bright ideas, had somehow failed to prove the theories. Lorenzo's New York Air had to be separated from its Texas Air promoters because of his acquisition of Eastern Air Lines, one of the traditional Big Four of the U.S. airline world. With the departure of these ambitious newcomers, there was no rush by the major airlines to try new ideas. They were able, at least for a while, to breathe a sigh of relief. But there was no room for complacency. Down in Texas, where Frank Lorenzo had originally launched his peanut fares, Herbert Kelleher, a student of the pioneering P.S.A.—the "Poor Sailors Airline" (see above)—put Kenny Friedkin's ideas, with a few of his own, into practice.

Southwest Airlines Settles In

By the early years of the 21st century, **Southwest Airlines**, a former intra-state airline that had picked up where P.S.A. and AirCal left off, was boarding more passengers than any other airline in the world. This is not to rank it as the world's largest airline, because its average stage distance has been short, and the distance traveled by each passenger has to be taken into account in assessing the true ranking. Nevertheless, for a company that started with a single route as recently as mid-1971, this is a remarkable accomplishment. Southwest has succeeded because it stuck to the basic principles of catering to passengers' requirements, rather than trying to outperform competitors in meal service and on-board entertainment. Taking a leaf out of P.S.A.'s book—which it had studied during a six-week visit—it concentrated on frequent scheduling, efficient routines, both at the gate and in the air, with modern equipment, and with élan. This last marketing aspect was achieved largely by equipping its stewardesses with daring red and orange mini-skirts and hot pants, outdoing P.S.A., which dropped the idea.

Realizing the demographic advantages of linking the "Texas Triangle" of Dallas-Fort Worth, Houston, and San Antonio, which were little more than 200 miles apart, though with insignificant ground transport, Rollin King approached attorney Herbert Kelleher in 1966 with a proposal that culminated in the foundation of Air Southwest Company on 15 March 1967. They changed the title to Southwest Airlines on 29 March 1971. This four-year delay was the result of continual negotiations with the Texas Aeronautics Commission and objections from the incumbent airlines, mainly Braniff International, whose history went back to the 1920s and which believed it owned territorial rights in Texas. That this upstart newcomer succeeded when many others had failed was due to the patience and determination of Kelleher—always known as Herb—whose flair for publicity by extrovert party tricks was matched by a keen legal mind, one which would demand much attention during the years to come.

Southwest started service from Dallas's Love Field to Houston and San Antonio on 18 June 1971, and closed the triangular route on 14 November of that year, thus establishing several of the major components of its marketing approach that were to prove themselves in the years to come. The fare, $20.00 one-way on all segments, was simple and cheap, and the night fare was even cheaper: $10.00. The frequency was high: right from the start, every hour to Houston and every other hour to San Antonio. And on 14 November, half of the flights into Houston went to the old Hobby Airport, which, like Dallas's Love Field, was much closer to the downtown business area and indeed far more convenient for most of the other air travelers too. This was so successful that by 14 May 1972, all Houston flights served Hobby.

Such innovative actions were perceived as aggressively competitive to the incumbent airlines, especially Braniff. Kelleher fought many a rearguard action in the courts during the next few years over the use of Love Field, with the Dallas City Council actually passing an ordinance to close the airport to all scheduled services on 15 April 1974. But two days later a judge issued a restraining order against this cavalier decision, and the case went all the way to the U.S. Supreme Court, which upheld his ruling on 16 December 1974.

Intra-State Expansion—and More

When, on the following 27 January, the Supreme Court denied a petition to rehear the Love Field case, Southwest girded its loins for action. On 11 February, it started service to the Rio Grande Valley. By the year's end it had five Boeing 737s in service and had carried more than a million passengers during the 12 months of 1975. In spite of further local Texan litigation, attempting to inhibit its growth, the airline ordered more aircraft, declared a dividend for its shareholders, issued more stock, and increased traffic by 50%. It had the bit between its teeth.

The year 1977 saw solid expansion within Texas, to Corpus Christi on 1 March, to Lubbock and Midland-Odessa on 20 May, to El Paso on 30 June, and to Austin on 15 September. Its traffic increased again by 50%, and it was encouraged to establish a subsidiary company, on 31 January 1978 with the same policy structure, at Chicago's Midway Airport. The C.A.B. gave its blessing on 14 July 1978, for Midway (Southwest) Airway Co. to operate an array of short-haul routes to neighboring cities.

Herb Kelleher had been named interim president when Lamar Muse resigned on 28 March, and he became chairman of the board when Howard Putnam, formerly with United, became president. But with the October 24 1978 Airline Deregulation Act, the idea of the Chicago subsidiary was moot, as Southwest was relieved of its obligations to operate only within Texas. Once again, it wasted no time in seizing its opportunities, and after opening service to Amarillo, it added New Orleans—its first destination outside Texas—on 25 January 1979, and also to Beaumont/Port Arthur on 5 March. Backing its operational expansion, Southwest introduced self-ticketing machines at all its stations, and adopted the slogan of LUV, to reflect both the name of its home base and its attitude toward its clientele.

The Wright Amendment

Defendants of the status quo were not finished yet and fought a rearguard action to preserve what were believed to be the rights of airlines operating from the new Dallas-Fort Worth International

Airport (DFW), and objected to Southwest's decision to concentrate on its services from Love Field, to the exclusion of DFW. American, Continental, Delta, and other previously certificated airlines wished to promote the new airport, which, though bigger in area than New York's island of Manhattan, was quite a distance from both Dallas's and Fort Worth's city centers.

Southwest's reliance on Love Field was paying off. Its fleet totaled 18, and its passenger boardings continued to increase at the brisk rate of about 50% a year—the industry average was only 10% or less—it continued to announce annual profits. They say that "you can't beat City Hall," and in this case, the metaphorical hall did prove to be a thorn in Southwest's side. On 12 December 1979, a U.S. Senate and House Conference Committee unanimously approved a compromise amendment to the International Air Transportation Act that limited service from Love Field (to give DFW preference) to Texas points and to the contiguous states of New Mexico, Oklahoma, Arkansas, and Louisiana. Direct flights beyond those limits were not allowed. Strongly supported by Texan members of the House of Representatives, the amendment was pushed through by a Texan from Fort Worth, Jim Wright, the Speaker of the House, and it subsequently became known as "The Wright Amendment." Naturally, Herb Kelleher and his cohorts at Love Field regarded it at the time as the Wrong Amendment, but it was the law, so that, curiously, Southwest Airlines was the only airline in the United States whose routes were still regulated.

In any case, Southwest was doing well, as its policies promoting goodwill among its passengers were paying off. During 1979, it carried 5 million of them, 42% more than in the previous year—a rate of growth that other airlines could only dream about. A two-week strike by the Machinists' union early in 1980 did not deter the airline, and at the beginning of April 1980, it started service to Oklahoma City, Tulsa, and Albuquerque. In September it was operating seven round-trips a day from Love Field to Houston Intercontinental Airport. Herb Kelleher took the Wright Amendment in stride, and was buying more Boeing 737s by the dozen.

New Hubs, New Procedures

An important move was made on 31 January 1982, when services were inaugurated to and from Las Vegas, Phoenix, and San Diego. Service was offered to 11 cities from each one. Southwest was readjusting to the enforced restrictions of the Wright Amendment. On 4 October 1984, it introduced ticketless travel on the Dallas-Little Rock and Houston-Corpus Christi routes, an experiment that was the harbinger of worldwide acceptance. No longer did a passenger have to go through the somewhat ponderous motions of obtaining an airline ticket, either from the airline or a travel agent, by a visit or by mail. A telephone call was enough, identification with a boarding pass at the gate was all that was necessary, and Southwest's policy of not assigning seats ensured swift boarding of the 737s, with greatly increased aircraft utilization.

The larger and more efficient 737-300s came on the routes on 17 December 1984, and by March 1985, Southwest was operating as far as Denver, San Francisco, St. Louis, and Chicago (Midway). On 25 June of that year, for $60 million, an agreement was signed with **Muse Air**, changing the name briefly to **TransStar**. This airline operated McDonnell Douglas MD-80s, and good aircraft though these were, Kelleher concentrated on a standardized fleet of 737s (which numbered 94 by the end of the year), and MuseAir/TransStar was closed down.

There seemed to be no stopping the maverick airline now. Further extending its route network to include Oakland, Burbank, and Sacramento in California, and Detroit, Nashville, Indianapolis, and Birmingham in the east, Southwest was becoming a powerful competitor, with more than $300 million in the bank and a $250-million line of credit. Such corporate strength was too much for Chicago-based **Midway Airlines**, which suspended operations on 19 November 1991. Ominously, on 15 September, Southwest began its first services from Baltimore to Chicago, charging only $89.00 one way—substantially undercutting the market hitherto dominated by USAir. Consolidating its faith in the Boeing 737, Southwest was instrumental, in November 1993, in sponsoring the designs of the -700 and -800 versions of the airliner. Kelleher did not do things by halves. The initial order was for 63 aircraft, with an option on 63 more. On 4 October 1994, 18 more 737s were added to the fleet when **Morris Air**, based at Salt Lake City, was absorbed. Intra-California schedules were augmented to compete with the incumbent United Air Lines, which countered with its United Shuttle.

One of the cornerstones of Southwest Airlines's operating policies was becoming evident. Instead of challenging the established airlines head-on at their fortress main-line airports, it nibbled away at secondary or satellite airports. It did not serve Chicago's O'Hare International or New York's three airports, just as it eschewed Dallas-Fort-Worth International. Baltimore served Washington, D.C., and low-fares compensated for any access inconveniences. The ticketless travel experiment was a success, and it was expanded throughout the Southwest system by February 1995. Following its choice-of-airport policy, it entered the Florida market early in 1996, avoiding Miami and serving Fort Lauderdale, and adding Orlando and Tampa. By March 1996, it had become the largest Boeing 737 airline in the world, with 229 aircraft delivered, and it swept into New England, not through Boston but through Providence, Rhode Island, trading distance from Boston for on-time regularity because of Providence's lack of congestion, with consequent on-time performance.

Toward the late 1990s, Southwest Airlines made it clear that it was no longer an upstart intra-state that had managed to penetrate the traditional airline markets in the United States. It was setting its own pace, and older airlines were made to react to its innovations. On 6 April 1997, with Nashville-Los Angeles and -Oakland connections, it entered the nonstop long-haul markets. Expanding services at Detroit, it penetrated Northwest Airlines's hub, slashing the latter's fares by almost two-thirds. Manchester, New Hampshire, added a second Boston satellite. On 14 March 1999 came the most important market entry of all. With service to Islip, on Long Island, Southwest entered the New York market

Birth of the Low-Fare Generation

and, with connecting service to Nashville, could offer one-stop service from the Big Apple to California. Sadly, on 19 June 2001, Herb Kelleher was obliged to step down due to ill health as chairman of the airline that he had built into an industry leader.

Then, on 11 September 2001—another date that will, in President Roosevelt's stirring words, "live in infamy"—there was a terrorist attack in New York, with two airplanes being flown into and causing the collapse of each of the twin towers of the World Trade Center. Another airplane was flown into Washington, D.C.'s Pentagon, and another crashed in Pennsylvania. All told, almost 3,000 people were killed. All airliner operations were shut down. For several days, the airlines were paralyzed with complete inactivity, except to strengthen precautions against a repetition of the brutality, for example, intensified baggage inspections and the abolition of on-board silverware. Wider implications of the attacks were far more severe. The public lost its enthusiasm for flying, and traffic and revenue figures of airlines plummeted. The established airlines, which were now called by the somewhat misleading collective term *legacy*, suffered badly because they were slow to change. Overheads were still high compared to new airlines such as Southwest, whose operations were more efficient and less labor-intensive. Airlines such as United, Northwest, and Delta, once pillars of disciplined financial acumen, faced red ink and would resort to Chapter 11 bankruptcy to trim their debt, partly by abandoning staff pension plans. Southwest, along with other new airlines weathered the storm and, though curtailed, continued to show profits.

The old flair was still there, under the leadership of James Parker, as vice chairman and CEO, and Colleen Barrett as president, the first woman to take over a major airline. In September 2002, taking advantage of the increased operational range of the later versions of the airline's only aircraft type (of which it now had a fleet of almost 400), Southwest began nonstop service from Baltimore to Los Angeles, its first transcontinental nonstop service and a harbinger of future policy that made the restrictive Wright Amendment irrelevant. Unlike the "legacy" airlines, its line of credit with the investment banks was still excellent, so it was able to embark on further steps to gain its traffic shares in major markets. On 9 May 2004, Southwest began services from Philadelphia, constituting another blow to the hitherto safely ensconced USAirways. The fare to Chicago was $200 round-trip—half of the competition's—and routes to other destinations were soon added. By October, these numbered 41. Baltimore was already a Southwest hub, and the airline was now carrying more individually boarded passengers than any other airline in the United States. The airline that had started with one route in Texas in 1971 had become an industry leader.

The Cheek of the "Critter"

To trump Herb Kelleher (and Kenny Friedkin of P.S.A. before him) was a challenge to any other innovative airline, but one newcomer came close: **ValuJet**. It was based in Atlanta, which had hitherto been monopolized by Delta Air Lines, which, as long ago as the mid-1930s, had established the industry's first hub operation. It also built its initial network to concentrate on the booming Florida market, concluding that, if the price was right, vacationers (no longer confined only to the affluent among New Yorkers and New Englanders) would not mind changing aircraft at Atlanta. And they did not.

ValuJet was incorporated in Nevada in July 1992 by a triumvirate of Robert Priddy, chairman, Lewis Jordan, president, and Maurice Gallagher, vice chairman. All had airline experience and all believed that, like Southwest, an airline should be low-cost, low-fare, and offer fun and friendly service. Its marketing slogan was "good times, great fares." Armed with this approach, ValuJet's first flight took off to Tampa from Atlanta on 26 October. The initial fleet of six Douglas DC-9-32s was brightly painted in blue, yellow, and white, and featured on their noses a sprightly aircraft cartoon, which became popularly known as "the critter."

Within weeks, ValuJet was operating to four points in Florida, with connections through its hub from Louisville, Memphis, and New Orleans. Flights from Washington started on 12 January 1994, and by the year's end, 20 DC-9s were serving cities as far as Chicago, Philadelphia, and Dallas. Throughout the next two years, ValuJet consolidated its position throughout the east coast, providing air travelers with low-fare competition and the kind of service and frequencies that had formerly been shared between Delta and the defunct Eastern Air Lines. Taking a leaf out of Kelleher's Southwest book, ValuJet lived up to its claim to be fun and friendly to fly with. Boarding the aircraft was in the same relaxed and unregimented style as at Dallas's Love Field. The flight attendants wore polo shirts and sneakers. Valujet's informality added a new dimension—a sense of humor—to an often boring air journey. Its flight attendants' uniforms were more casual, and they offered their clientele some light-hearted games. The passengers were invited to competitions (passing the toilet roll was a favorite), and prizes included "two free tickets to Hawaii—when we open service." The transfers at Atlanta were usually painless, and the customers appreciated the low fares.

Priddy and Jordan did not just sit back and allow the obvious popularity of the "critter" DC-9s to win market shares from Delta, especially, and from USAir. When, on 1 March 1996, ValuJet started service from Atlanta to Charlotte and Pittsburgh, it went on record to describe these destinations as "two of the most monopolistic hubs in the nation." Even so, the fleet of DC-9s was increased to 51 aircraft, ValuJet was flying to 31 destinations, and new gates were being added at Atlanta to deal with their rapidly

ValuJet's MD-95s were not in service very long, but the airline came close to threatening Delta at its home base in Atlanta. (Bentley)

increasing traffic. Further reflecting its success, ValuJet became the launch customer for the ultimate development of the Douglas DC-9 series, the MD-95. On 19 October 1995, it ordered 50, with options on 50 more, valued at a total of $1 billion. Shortly afterward, in the traditional financial move that Wall Street investors approve of, on 21 November, ValuJet's stock was split for the second time. Following a rash of new routes and the expansion of its bases at Boston and Raleigh-Durham, it opened direct service from Atlanta to New York on 1 May 1996 and charged $89–$149 one-way. This was Delta's main route on which, in 1995, half a million passengers had paid $233. Though ValuJet was primed to go head to head with Delta, a crash would alter the balance of affairs in Atlanta.

Low-Fare Disaster

A ValuJet crash on 11 May 1996 seemed to confirm critics' allegations of low standards of operation. Just when Bob Priddy and his happy team seemed to have the eastern airline world at their feet, one of its DC-9s crashed in Florida's Everglades, killing 104 passengers and 5 crew members. On 17 June, the F.A.A. withdrew ValuJet's operating certificate, alleging that the airline's recent record of maintenance procedures had been faulty and that this crash was the inevitable result. The cause of the crash was unusual; it could be described as accidental or negligent, or both, and not directly the fault of the airline but a result of outsourcing selected items of maintenance or supply. In this case, the culprit was an oxygen generator, classified as a hazardous item that should not have been on the aircraft unless it was empty. Those placed on board the DC-9 by a subcontractor were not, and they self-ignited, causing the catastrophic fire that downed the aircraft. The subsequent investigation by the National Transportation Safety Board (N.T.S.B.) reported causes that included a lack of adequate inspection by the airline, the subcontractor (which dismissed some of its mechanics), and the F.A.A. itself. It was described as a chain of errors and emphasized that an airplane disaster is rarely caused for a single reason, although human error, either in the air or on the ground, is usually a common denominator.

On 26 September, the F.A.A. allowed ValuJet to resume service; four days later, it did, to most of its major destinations from Atlanta but on a restricted network and with low-fare incentives. It reduced the number of DC-9 seating variants in its fleet to 3, most of them the popular DC-9-30. Its fleet totaled 43 aircraft and was still solidly based at Atlanta, competing with Delta. The public flocked back to ValuJet, encouraged by its reintroduction of bargain fares, and defying the efforts of Delta Air Lines, which, with the introduction of its own Delta Express low-fare services, tried to build a similar model. ValuJet president Jordan also announced a program of additional Atlanta-based routes to begin throughout October, at introductory low fares. Fifteen of its DC-9 fleet were sold on 4 October, and Joseph Corr was hired as president in November. But the ambitious and confident expansion program was overtaken by a development that would have far-reaching consequences on ValuJet and the U.S. airline scene as a whole.

ValuJet's image had already been seriously damaged, and the critter's cheerful attitude seemed somewhat out of place. On 24 September 1997, Priddy and Jordan dropped the name, as a merger was announced with another low-fare airline. In spite of its shortcomings—and much of the blame of the Everglades tragedy was placed on the F.A.A. and the maintenance subcontractor—ValuJet was not short of cash. It was, however, facing competition from another airline that had a similar low-fare marketing policy—the airline's name was changed by acquiring Orlando-based AirTran Airways, which formed the holding company AirTran Holdings. Joe Corr was to be Chief Executive Officer.

Emergence of AirTran

Compared to ValuJet, **AirTran Airways** was small, and the merger was a case rather akin to a marriage of convenience. ValuJet had money and a large fleet, while AirTran had only 10 Boeing 737s but its name was untarnished. It had started service from Orlando on 6 October 1994 with only two aircraft and serving only five cities. Its parent company, headed by Robert Swenson, had acquired Conquest Sun Airlines the previous June. Its policy was different from ValuJet's. It selected direct routes to cities that were not so well served by other airlines, such as Knoxville, Providence, Syracuse, and Allentown, whereas the critter had challenged the established airlines, especially Delta, with an aggressive policy of low fares on main routes to big cities. On 24 October 1997, AirTran ordered 11 more gates at Atlanta. Route expansion continued and served almost every city east of the Mississippi. Also, on 1 October 1998, the F.A.A. instituted a new airline safety inspection system, the Air Transportation Oversight System (ATOS).

Further consolidating its low-fare ascendancy in the eastern States, AirTran followed the ValuJet flag. Joe Leonard succeeded Corr as chairman and president on 6 January 1999, and Robert Fornaro took over the presidency on 23 March. On 1 July 1999, AirTran opened four flights daily Atlanta-Newark, which was an important Delta route, vying with the one to LaGuardia, and inaugurated service with the new MD-95 (now designated as the Boeing 717, following the purchase of McDonnell-Douglas by Boeing) on 1 August 1997. It then, on 12 December, attacked US Airways on its home ground at its Pittsburgh hub, with service to

Air Tran's Boeing 717s (ex MD-95s) often displayed colorful support for football teams. This one happens to be for the Atlanta Falcons. (McDonough)

New York, Chicago, and Atlanta, following this, on 5 July 2001, with a Pittsburgh-Philadelphia service. This route was US Airways's busiest but would not hold that privilege much longer, such was the magnetic attraction to the flying public of low fares.

AirTran was now an airline force to be reckoned with, and on 21 May 2003, (following the lull in air travel resulting from the 11 September 2001 terrorist attacks) a Boeing 717 started direct service from Atlanta to Denver, signalling a westward expansionist policy beyond the Mississippi. On 1 July, it ordered 50 Boeing 737s, with an option on 50 more (another billion-dollar order), having already leased Airbus A320s from the Irish Ryan International. AirTran started nonstop service from Atlanta to Los Angeles and Las Vegas on 4 June. No longer a low-fare regional airline, it established itself in Washington on 23 October, with direct service to Atlanta, Fort Lauderdale, and Fort Myers, while Atlanta-San Francisco followed on 12 November and Dallas-Las Vegas on 11 February 2004.

To list new airline services or routes may seem unnecessary, but AirTran was invading the territory of the major trunk airlines and infiltrating their fortress hubs. Delta's Atlanta and US Airways's Pittsburgh and Philadelphia hubs had, in the regulated climate before 1978, been almost impregnable. After the Airline Deregulation Act, the airline and airport skies were open to all. AirTran's low fares spread to where the legacy airlines were the most vulnerable and contributed to both US Airways and Delta Air Lines filing for Chapter 11 bankruptcy.

Gone were the days when competition was defined by which airline offered the best meals, had the most imposing headquarters, or had the best airplanes. Reduced fares worked, and the newcomers implemented them. Older airlines that had once scoffed at Freddie Laker's offering of box lunches on Skytrain were now doing the same. Passengers did not mind bringing their own $3 sandwiches if they saved $30 on their fares.

Just as ValuJet had suffered the indignity of being grounded, just when it was about to deal a severe blow to Delta's Atlanta fortress-hub traffic, AirTran was now the beneficiary of an event that it did not foresee. In October 2004, ATA Holdings Corporation, the parent company of low-fare **ATA Airlines**, filed for Chapter 11 bankruptcy. As part of the reorganization demanded by law—invariably drastic cuts in staff or other expenditures—ATA sold its operations and 14 gates at Chicago's Midway Airport to AirTran for $87.6 million. The deal included extra gates at Washington and New York.

The airline that only 10 years before was a newcomer with two airplanes was now taking its place alongside the likes of Southwest Airlines in revolutionizing the airline culture of the country.

JetBlue: A West Wind Blows In

Just when the different marketing strategies between the older established airlines and the brash new low-fare newcomers seemed to be settling down to some kind of equilibrium, yet another contender entered the scene. Whether by careful analysis or by marketing instinct, the new airline had drawn upon the once constant element of airline origin-destination traffic that seemed to have escaped attention: not a single airline, new or old, was based in New York City. With a population in the greater urban area approaching 25 million, together with its status as the largest U.S. commercial center and as a major tourist destination, the demographic factor was unarguable. Chicago was also a substantial center, but with about one-third the population, and United Airlines relied largely on transfer traffic through the geographically natural hub between the east and west coasts. T.W.A. had once benefitted from its position in St. Louis, and Northwest Airlines made much of Detroit, while American Airlines had moved its base from New York to Dallas-Fort Worth, partly for the same reason.

So New York was once again to have an airline of its very own. In February 1999, David Neeleman announced plans for a new airline, provisionally named New Air, certainly an apt choice. Already with airline experience, he had sold Salt Lake City–based Morris Air to Southwest Airlines in 1993 and had been involved with the success of the low-fare Canadian airline WestJet. He had also obtained extra capital by selling his Open Skies, an electronic ticketing system, to Hewlett-Packard. Having gained the essential credit-worthiness with money in the bank, he obtained an additional $130 million from financier George Soros, Weston Presidio Capital, and the Chase Manhattan Bank.

On 14 July 1999, when he launched **JetBlue**, Neeleman simultaneously announced an order worth $4.5 billion for 75 162-seat Airbus A320s. The marketing policy was in the low-fare range, but not in the bargain-basement, and he offered wider seats with more leg-room than the other low-fare operators, and more cabin baggage space. Passengers would enjoy their flights not with games and gimmicks, but with 24-channel live televisions for every seat. Like his predecessors, however, he believed in rapid turnarounds and no assigned seats. Ticketless travel saved staff and expedited airport movements. Neeleman confidently claimed that JetBlue had the four essential ingredients to make a successful new airline: "money, new planes, experienced management, and great routes." This last ingredient stemmed from the choice of New York's JFK International Airport as the base for JetBlue. Neeleman was encouraged by enthusiastic support from New Yorkers, from both the business and the leisure communities. JetBlue was effectively the Big Apple's own airline, just as New York Air had been some years before. Words of support were soon backed by deeds. Only two months after JetBlue was created, it received 75 daily slots at JFK from the Department of Transportation.

The first A320 took off on 11 February 2000 to Fort Lauderdale. Herb Kelleher's policy at Southwest was to concentrate on satellite airports at major urban areas, rather than the congested major hubs. This made it easy to schedule flights, and it invariably avoided congestion. Adopting a similar approach, JetBlue served the winter sunshine of Florida (sometimes described as the sixth borough of New York) as Tampa, Orlando, West Palm Beach, and Fort Myers were quickly added. The JetBlue planners neatly recognized that points in upper New York State had been neglected and quickly lowered the fares to Buffalo (close

Newcomer JetBlue, operating from its base at New York's JFK airport, relied on Airbus A320s for a network that quickly became nationwide. (McDonough)

to Niagara Falls), on 17 February and later to Rochester and Syracuse. Unlike Southwest or AirTran, they were also, from the start, prepared to challenge the long-distance airlines, serving the Los Angeles area at Ontario as early as 21 July, and the Pacific Northwest and the San Francisco Bay area (via Seattle and Oakland, respectively) on 1 May. The biggest urban center of the West Coast was the 12-million-population Los Angeles sprawling metropolis, and JetBlue expanded its Ontario foothold on 29 August by opening service to Long Beach. The catchment area of this airport, in the freeway-connected and affluent southeastern suburb of the vast Los Angeles conurbation, was almost as great as that of Los Angeles International Airport (LAX) itself. Furthermore, on 18 June, Neeleman had already secured 27 of the 41 available slots at Long Beach. Now JetBlue practically owned Long Beach, and there was no interminable queueing for take-offs or landings.

Brisk progress continued. On 28 November, the Federal Capital was added to the map, but the choice this time was Washington's Dulles International Airport, because crowded National Airport was often subject to delays. The initial link was to Fort Lauderdale, and during 2002, service to California was augmented by routes to San Juan, on 31 May, and to Las Vegas, on 10 October. A further flank attack on the incumbent Delta was made with a southern transcontinental route from Fort Lauderdale to Long Beach on 8 May, followed shortly afterward with service to San Diego.

Neeleman announced further airliner orders in 2003. The original A320 order had already been solidified on 18 June 2001 to a total of 131, and was modified on 21 April 2003 to 111 firm orders, with options on 50 more. Contrasting with Southwest's policy of a single-type fleet, however, and only two months later, the reason for the apparent reduction was revealed. JetBlue ordered 100 100-seat Embraer 190s, for $3 billion, to diversify the airline's seat capacity according to the potential demands on individual routes.

By the end of 2004, Jet Blue had, in only four years, won its spurs as the nation's fastest-growing airline. By earning annual revenue exceeding $1 billion, quite comfortably, it qualified officially as a major airline. Such success was unprecedented. At the outset of the 21st century, JetBlue became as powerful an influence on the changing shape of the U.S. airline industry as Kenny Friedkin's P.S.A. had been in the 1950s within the frontier of California and Herb Kelleher's Southwest Airlines had been in Texas. On 5 October 2005, Neeleman played his strongest card, the New York base. JetBlue opened for business at Newark, one of the city's three main-line airports, with service to Fort Lauderdale and Orlando, with further service to the sun at Tampa and Fort Myers two weeks later. A month later, San Juan was even sunnier for damp New Yorkers. And in November the first Embraer 190 entered service. It was named, to reflect the country of its manufacture, *Brazilian Blue*.

Revival of an Old Name

One city that appeared to meet these new-found criteria was Denver, resplendent with a brand-new airport, geographically central in the U.S.A., and growing in prosperity in its own right, partly because it was the biggest ski resort center in the nation—an advantage for winter seasonal scheduling. Many years previously, one of the original Local Service airlines, **Frontier Airlines**, had somehow survived, until taken over by People Express in 1986, and then absorbed by the Texas Air Corporation, to become part of Continental Airlines. But Continental decided to concede the Colorado market to the solidly ensconced United Airlines, which then fell on hard times. Frontier went bankrupt in 1987. Then, on 5 July 1994, it was revived, as some former officers of the company showed faith in the demographic potential, and opened routes to Chicago, San Francisco, and Los Angeles. Simultaneously, a rival Colorado aspirant, **Western Pacific Airlines (W.P.A.)**, started services from nearby Colorado Springs, with both airlines operating Boeing 737s. Founded by Edward Beauvais, W.P.A. was flamboyant in its marketing, specializing in painting its aircraft vividly in a selection of non-airline advertising promotions. It had assumed that Denver's new airport would be too far north of the city and that some of Denver's passenger traffic would switch to Colorado Springs, but this did not occur. On 1 August 1997, W.P.A.'s new president, Robert Peiser, announced an agreement to merge with Frontier, but this idea was dropped in October, as W.P.A.'s finances were weak. Frontier seized the initiative, and with the support of Wexford Management, submitted a bid to the Department of Transportation to take over the failing airline's routes, adding New York (LaGuardia) on 3 December. W.P.A. ceased operations on 4 February 1998.

During that year, Frontier experienced a considerable recovery of its fortunes, repaying the loan to Wexford. Sam Addoms became president/CEO and, in October 1999, initiated a complete fleet replacement. The fleet of twenty 737s would be replaced by 11 new Airbus A318s and A319s, with comparable seating in the 114–132 range. The first A319 went into service on 1 June 2001. Frontier code-shared with both **Great Lakes Aviation** and with **Mesa Airlines**. The airline seemed to enjoy popularity because of its Rocky Mountain–based image and, on 11 April 2004, began nonstop services from Los Angeles to Kansas City, St. Louis, and Minneapolis. With **Horizon Air**, it formed **Frontier Jet Express**, and by the end of the year was operating a fleet of 46 aircraft, 40 of them Airbus A318s and A319s.

Initiative in Indiana

If ever an airline managed to survive riding the crest of a wave then plunging into an abyss, it was **American Trans Air**. It was founded in 1973 in Indianapolis, by a Latvian immigrant, J. George Mikelsons. These were in pre-deregulation days, and opportunities to form new airlines were slender. George's methods overcame bureaucratic hurdles. He started a travel club named Voyager 1000, renamed it Ambassador, and renamed it again to American Trans Air. The travel club's first aircraft, *Miss Indy*, was an ex–Eastern Air Lines Boeing 720. In March 1981, following airline deregulation in 1978, Mikelsons had obtained certification for his company as a common carrier, and soon had a fleet of 10 Boeing 707s and 727s. By 1986, American Trans Air could claim to be the largest charter airline in the United States, with a fleet that included nine Lockheed L-1011 wide-bodied aircraft. In May of that year, the first scheduled services opened to resorts in Florida, to Puerto Rico, and to Las Vegas. Mikelsons had managed to create his own niche market, serving the mid-western population centers east of Chicago and west of Pittsburgh. In 1993, he went overseas to Belfast, Northern Ireland, and—for sentimental reasons perhaps—to Riga, Latvia. In July 1992, it became the first airline to be certificated (with the Pratt & Whitney PW-2000-powered Boeing 757) for ETOPS (Extended Twin-Engine Operations), which might have helped it to win a $47 million contract from Air Mobility Command in 1993 for service to the Mediterranean, the Gulf, and as far east as Manila.

On 9 August of the same year, **Chicago Express** started operations with British Aerospace Jetstream 31 commuter aircraft to provide service to neighboring Midwestern cities and from Midway's new hub at Raleigh, North Carolina; but by 1996, it was codesharing with American Trans Air, which purchased the smaller airline in 1999. Meanwhile, other domestic operations had expanded considerably, even as far as Hawaii, but following the much-publicized ValuJet crash on 11 May 1996 and a $3 million loss, American Trans Air had cut back all its schedules. Some of its fleet of 49 aircraft was returned to the lessor, and 20% of its 5,000 employees were laid off. Such was the heavy competition in the low-fare market that the new airlines, strongly led by Southwest, were competing both with the established airlines and with each other.

American Trans Air was becoming known simply as A.T.A. By 1998, headed by John Teague and with considerable investor support, it appeared to be on the mend. It ordered 37 Boeing 737-300s and ten 216-seat Boeing 757-300s, for a total commitment of almost $3 billion. The first 757 went into service on 1 August 2001, but only a month later, on 11 September, terrorist attacks in New York, Washington, D.C., and Pennsylvania abruptly halted all commercial airline flights for several days.

American Trans Air's roller coaster career continued. More services were added, mainly to vacation resorts in Mexico and the Caribbean. Early in August 2002, founder George Mikelsons resumed control, replacing Teague. The next year, A.T.A. Airlines (officially renamed) contributed 15 Boeing 757s and an L-1011 to the Civil Air Fleet, for military transport services in the second Gulf War.

Nevertheless, in spite of the fortuitous bonuses from military contracts, heavy losses—$90 million in the first six months of 2004—led to A.T.A. filing for Chapter 11 bankruptcy protection on 26 October of that year. It sold, among others, 14 gates at Chicago's Midway Airport to AirTran, and Mikelsons finally retired in August 2005. Then, in October, Southwest Airlines, the dominant leader of the new fraternity of low-fare airlines in the United States, acquired 27.5% of A.T.A. stock (effectively a controlling interest), initiated a code-sharing agreement, and contributed a $47 million loan.

Catching the Spirit

The rise of Las Vegas as a national focal point for entertainment and gambling was made possible because of air conditioning and airline service that expanded accessibility. By the 21st century, it was a thriving metropolis of more than a million people, drawn there not only for the high life, but also for the climate and attractive lifestyle made possible by low housing prices.

Many airlines, big and small, ensured that Las Vegas was on their route networks, but also the marketing and commercial possibilities of such a resort location were echoed elsewhere. In the late 1970s, seaside resort of Atlantic City in New Jersey expanded its entertainment attractions to include legalized gambling. One of the owners of its luxury hotels was Donald Trump, an extrovert real estate developer. On 12 October 1988, Trump purchased the famous Eastern Air Lines Air Shuttle for $365 million, and the **Trump Shuttle** opened for business on 8 June 1989. It served Atlantic City from Boston from 7 August 1990, but in the face of competition from the Pan Am Shuttle on the New York-Boston/Washington routes, it was never a success. This was partly because the shuttle was never a low-fare airline. It depended on a business-oriented clientele. By the 1990s, additional competition came not only from Delta Air Lines, which had bought the Pan Am Shuttle, but also from railroads. Over the same route to Washington, AMTRAK was competitive in city-center journey time, comfort, and passenger fares. On 19 December 1991, Trump sold out to USAir, and its **USAir Shuttle** began operations on 12 April 1992.

Though it did not attract the notoriety or publicity of Donald Trump's activities, another airline was operating without much fanfare behind the headlines, but, partially at least, with a similar objective, to bring well-heeled gamblers to Atlantic City. **Charter One** was founded in Detroit in 1980 by Edward Homfeld as a tour agency to take patrons of the casinos to Las Vegas, Atlantic City, and the Bahamas. On 8 September of that year, and with a business connection with Trump, Homfeld obtained an operating certificate, and in May 1992, changed the company name to **Spirit Airlines**. Its policy was based on low fares, but when, in 1996, in addition to serving several Florida destinations, it tried its luck on the Detroit-Boston market, Homfeld faced a fare war

Another low-fare airline, founded in Detroit in 1980, changed its name to Spirit in 1992 and, like JetBlue, relied on Airbus A320s. (McDonough)

with Northwest Airlines (which had built Detroit as a major hub and described its competitor's tactics as homicidal). By 1999, Spirit's fleet comprised 11 McDonnell Douglas DC-9 variants and was making 50 daily round-trips from Detroit to 14 cities, including Los Angeles, but apparently, the Northwest fortress hub was impregnable, and Homfeld moved his airline to Fort Lauderdale. After 11 September 2001, and like all the other low-fare airlines, his application for a $54-million loan from the Air Transportation Stabilization Board (A.T.S.B.) was rejected.

Under the presidency of Ben Baldanza, Spirit ordered 11 Airbus A320s and four Airbus A321s to add to its fleet of leased A319/321 Airbuses. A year later, when it announced $100 million worth of new financing, it was claiming to be the biggest privately held carrier in the nation. The continued survival, indeed the largely unpublicized success of Spirit Airlines was further confirmation that low fares were the all important, even essential marketing factor in the intensely competitive U.S. airline arena of the 21st century.

Short-Lived Midwest Contender

Many had the Spirit, but the absolute size of the potential market did have its upward limit, and the incumbent airlines, though reluctant to change their ways, were prepared to do so if their backs were to the wall, especially if a serious threat was perceived. Such was the case when Bob McAdoo founded **Vanguard Airlines** in Kansas City on 4 December 1994. He was one of the former officers of People Express who still believed in low fares, and with a fleet of seven 128-seat Boeing 737s, Vanguard opened service on a radius of routes from its base to the west coast and as far east as Cincinnati.

Strong resistance from American Airlines curtailed the expected traffic volume, some services were withdrawn, and John Tague moved from Air South to replace McAdoo. By 1999, the struggle had intensified, especially on the Dallas-Wichita market. American Airlines had established its headquarters and center of operations in Dallas, to the extent that any other airline attempting service there was regarded as a sworn enemy, to be resisted at all costs. Before Vanguard entered the scene, American charged $180 single to Wichita, but after Vanguard's $57 offer, American reduced its fare to $96. On 13 May, the Justice Department alleged that American was in violation of anti-trust legislation, and that "hub carriers cannot be permitted to use predatory tactics to keep new entrants out of their markets." Yet on 27 April 2001, a Federal judge dismissed the Justice Department's lawsuit, seeming to view the situation as no more than fair, if somewhat ruthless, competition and calling into question the definition of "predatory." Vanguard's two modest applications for government-guaranteed loans, following the devastating 11 September New York attack, were rejected, and the airline suspended operations on 30 July 2002.

Short-Term Survival of a Name

One of the oldest airlines in the United States, National Airlines had traced its history back to 1934, when it started a local service in Florida. It grew to become an important trunk-line operator until Pan American Airways bought it in 1979. The name was taken over briefly in 1989 by Overseas National Airways then in 1994 by Private Jet before passing to Carnival Airlines. In 1999, the reconstituted Pan American II sold the National name to Michael Conway for $175,000 who, on 12 April 1995, had founded New Airline, Inc. Strongly backed by a $48.5-million investment from a group of Las Vegas hotel and casino owners, he registered **National Airlines** on 31 July 1998.

Bureaucratic negotiations in obtaining a Certificate of Public Necessity and Convenience from the D.O.T., and then an Air Carrier Operating Certificate from the F.A.A., delayed the start of low-fare scheduled operations until 27 May 1999, with a Boeing 757-200 on the busy Los Angeles-Las Vegas route. By the end of the year, National was serving New York, San Francisco, Dallas, Miami, and Philadelphia. The fleet had grown to twelve 757s.

Even though adding Washington to the Las Vegas–based hub network, National filed for Chapter 11 bankruptcy protection on 6 December 2000. Its application for a $50-million government loan guarantee was rejected because of "excessive low-fare competition in markets served by National." There was a sense that smaller carriers were treated inconsistently in such matters, for instance, USAirways had received conditional approval in four weeks, and reaffirmation the day after filing for Chapter 11 protection.

Sun Seekers

Amidst the many airline failures and loss of employment, the dedication of some airline staff became apparent. In July 1982, a number of ex-Braniff employees, headed by Dick Roberts, joined up with M.L.T. Vacations of Minneapolis to form **Sun Country Airlines**. With a single Boeing 727-227, the first vacation charter flew on 20 January 1983 from Sioux Falls, South Dakota, to Las Vegas. Seeking niche markets, additional aircraft were leased and flights made from St. Louis and Dallas, but Northwest Airlines, ever alert to nip competition in the bud, took over M.L.T. in 1986.

Provisons of the M.L.T. deal still left Sun Country as a separate entity, and it promptly subleased a 300-seat Douglas DC-10 from Northwest, and banker John Barry took over control. The little airline prospered by becoming a member of the Civil Reserve Air Fleet in 1989 and its DC-10 participated in the Desert

Storm military airlift to the Middle East in 1990–91. More aircraft were added and on 25–26 July 1995, Sun Country could claim to be the first airline to be approved for G.P.S. (global positioning system) operations, flying from Boston to the Azores and back.

On 15 April 1997, Bill Macchia, a wholesale travel company owner, took over the airline, but losses continued in spite of special fare offers and because of Northwest competition. On 1 June 1999, Sun Country became a scheduled airline and declared its hand with a Twin Cities-Los Angeles fare of $149, compared to Northwest's $828. Northwest lowered its fare immediately, and adjusted its flight times and frequencies. It was a case of cutthroat competition. In May 2000, Macchia protested before a U.S. Senate panel against predatory practices by Northwest. He did not succeed.

The 11 September New York terrorist attacks did nothing to help any of the airlines, and the small ones, including the latest start-ups, suffered the most. All Sun Country services were terminated, but under new management, operations were reinstated in January 2003.

Much Too Independent

After the solidly established United Airlines filed for bankruptcy in 2002, many observers watched with inquisitive eyes to seek opportunities that might present themselves as fall-outs from the airline's plight. One such opportunity seemed to present itself at Washington's Dulles International Airport, where about 90% of the destinations on the electronic board were United's, and many of them short-haul routes served by **Atlantic Coast Airlines**, as a marketing partner. It owned, or had on lease, 87 Canadian CRJ 200s, which, in short-haul-style operations, relieved the big brother from some of its chores.

Taking the industry somewhat by surprise, on 19 May 2004, under the direction of chief executive Kerry Sheen, Atlantic Coast suddenly began to sell tickets under the name of **Independence Air**, divorcing itself from United, and claiming support from $300 million of invested capital. The first services began on 16 June 2004, from Washington to Chicago, Newark, Boston, Atlanta, and Raleigh/Durham. By 1 September, its network included no less than 34 points, including New York's JFK International, White Plains, and Stewart, as well as Newark.

Several of the main destinations were served at high frequencies, almost on the hour every hour, totaling 300 flights a day, and all at low fares, for example, only $49 to New York or $79 to Chicago. Predictably, United, which did not view Sheen's aggressive advertising too kindly, cut its fares on many routes to match Independence's, which was selling tickets on the Internet under flyi.com.

Right from the start, the airline lost money. In spite of repeated assertions that all would be well, though there were initial setbacks, especially because the small 50-seat CRJs would be supplemented by a fleet of twenty-eight 132-seat Airbus A319s. The first of these was delivered on 8 September and entered service on 23 November 2004. By this time, though, Independence Air was already in deep trouble. Subsequent moves to stem the tide were astonishing. On 10 January 2005, it returned 20 of its 87 regional jets to a major creditor. A month later, it added more routes (it had already added a few in October) and, on 1 May, began transcontinental flights to California and Seattle. Independence had lost $265 million in the past three quarters. It had improving load factors, but these were achieved only by offering fares that undercut low-fare airline competitors and, in some cases, were lower than those of a Greyhound bus.

Too late, the airline started to tighten its operational belt, cutting some service frequencies, postponing delivery of some of the Airbuses, and suspending service altogether at many points, including the transcontinentals. But Independence Air was well past the chances of recovery. It lost almost $100 million in the second quarter of 2005, and most analysts were amazed that it had lasted so long. On 7 November 2005, only 18 months after a brash entry into an already congested arena, it filed for Chapter 11 bankruptcy protection.

Evolution of a New Breed

With Southwest heading the pack, and with AirTran and relative newcomer JetBlue not far behind, by the year 2005 the new bargain-basement airlines had made a severe encroachment upon the preserves of the legacy airlines. The formerly protected preserves were up for grabs; the 1978 Airline Deregulation Act had opened up commercial airline operations to any entrepreneur who wished to risk his or her venture capital.

About 150 aspirant challengers to the establishment had applied to the Department of Transportation for scheduled operating authority, but only about 40 managed to begin service. Most of them soon learned that theory is too often more optimistic than practice. The intra-state airlines joined the throng, but P.S.A. was bought by USAir, and Air California by American Airlines. Texas's Southwest Airlines continued to be a thorn in the older airlines' sides, with increasing success as it rejected traditions of meal service, seating preference, and even carry-on baggage. Two new airlines, People Express and Presidential Airlines, entered the market but did not succeed, and the incumbents appeared to breathe again.

The days of the mid-20th century, when businessmen provided most of the passenger traffic were long gone. Leisure travelers were, in their millions, able to afford family vacations, even just weekends, in sunny Florida and the Caribbean or in Las Vegas. Southwest Airlines had set the pace with innovative marketing that larger airlines could not match. Some of the old and respected names, such as T.W.A., Eastern, and even Pan American, collapsed into bankruptcy.

By 2005, the new breed of low-fare airlines was collectively accounting for about one-third of the passenger boardings in the United States. Interestingly, in a reflection of past history, the newcomers were also developing their own unofficial membership strata. Just as in the past, the Civil Aeronautics Board had recognized the "Big Four" giants among the domestic trunk airlines, Southwest, AirTran, and JetBlue seemed to be emerging as the "Big Three" among new entrants. The public as a whole preferred low fares to full meal service. At the same time, legacy airlines took draconian measures under the protection of the Chapter 11 clause of the bankruptcy legislation, allowing drastic staff reductions, essential salary cuts of up to 30%, and the abolition of pension funds. The situation in 2005 was appalling. Once the bulwark of United States long-distance public transport, the established airlines had, during a period of only two decades, collectively lost about $23 billion.

Those two decades had covered the first years when the airlines had operated under legislative deregulation. Whether or not this complete change of the economic foundation of the industry had been successful could be open to question. Some of the advantages for the traveling public had been explored even before the Airline Deregulation Act of 1978. Frank Lorenzo's experiment with "peanuts" fares in the late 1970s had introduced bargain fares even when all fares were strictly regulated. The industry has come a long way since then.

New low-fare airlines match the older established companies in their industrial strength and influence. For example, on 27 September 2010, Southwest Airlines announced it would acquire AirTran, resulting in further attrition in U.S. airline numbers.

PART FIVE: TRANSFORMATION IN EUROPE

Chapter 25: Low-Fare Revolution

Toward a Complete Union

Back in the 1970s, Freddie Laker had claimed that, within the framework of the liberalized European Common Market, he could legally operate, as a British airline, a scheduled service between any two countries of continental Europe. He was perhaps premature in assuming that principles could be followed by a glorious free for all, ignoring matters of legislation and regulatory control. The ground-swell of airline deregulation that swept the United States after 1978 took several years to adjust to some degree of stability, and that was within a single country. Europe comprised many, and not all of them subscribed to all the provisions of the European Union. So "open skies" from Stockholm to Lisbon or from Dublin to Athens took time to germinate and to evolve as an acceptable state of affairs to the individual authorities that controlled those multi-national skies.

The air transport sector of the European Union, set up as an international commission, gradually moved forward, however, toward the ideal of a completely liberalized European freedom of the air, short-circuiting the traditional rules of the so-called Freedoms of the Air, established by the International Civil Aviation Organization (I.C.A.O.) after the end of the Second World War. The first step toward relaxing the grip of individual countries was taken in the 1960s, when the practice of pooled airline agreements was eroded. No longer could two countries monopolize the airways between them by a pool agreement by their respective national airlines that set the fares, the frequencies, and the capacities, more often than not to the exclusion of other operators.

In June 1990, new provisions extended the rights of airlines to almost complete acceptance of four of I.C.A.O.'s Five Freedoms. These were the Third and the Fourth, that is, traffic rights between two countries. (The First and the Second, already accepted across western Europe, covered overflying and emergency stops.) More important, Fifth Freedom rights, for an airline of any country to operate commercially between two other countries, were accepted. Interestingly, in some cases, this right (or restriction) had been evaded by what became known as the Sixth Freedom: a country that was geographically located between two others could offer Fifth Freedom rights by serving as an intervening stop.

Finally, in July 1992, the door was opened wide, and beginning in January 1993, almost all restrictions were removed. Not only were the Five Freedoms made completely effective; the rule of cabotage, hitherto a form of national protectionism, was abandoned in April 1997. A German or British airline could henceforth operate, for example, between Milan and Rome, or Air France between London and Glasgow. In practice, however, there was no rush. European countries were too small to permit profitable domestic routes, and the improvements in road and rail transport, notably the introduction of high speed rail networks, emphasized the problem.

At last, on the eve of the 21st century, the skies of Europe were completely opened, and a new era of airline development began, echoing airline deregulation that the United States launched in 1978.

Island Mavericks

Kenny Friedkin of Pacific Southwest Airlines in California and Herb Kelleher of Southwest Airlines in Texas had revolutionized the air transport scene in the United States. Tony Ryan, the Irishman who founded an airline that carried his name, did more than that. Within a single decade, he had put **Ryanair** in a position of near-supremacy in the whole of Europe—prevented from absolute domination only by an English company, **easyJet**, started shortly afterward by Stelios Haji-Ioannou. Measured in terms of intra-European passenger miles flown, the airlines founded by these two upstart airline entrepreneurs have overtaken all the former well-established airlines that had taken 80 years to develop.

Their formula for success, blatantly copied from Southwest and its later U.S. protégé ValuJet, was simple: cheap fares and low costs. To achieve complete success in both of these parameters, they overturned all traditional assumptions about efficient airline operation. Cheap fares were possible by filling a much higher percentage of the seats offered, without the restrictions of fare regulation. Low costs were achieved by rejecting marketing organizations and by adoption of computers that came close to abolishing the need for personal sales at ticket offices and by telephone. By taking the lead in such innovations, Ryanair and easyJet have together transformed the airline industry of an entire continent.

Ryanair

The original capital of this astonishing airline was provided early in 1985 by Tony Ryan, who had made a fortune by leasing aircraft, including fleets of Douglas DC-9s, from his base in southern Ireland, the city of Waterford, hitherto known to the outside world for its beautiful crystal. In May of that year, he started ad hoc charters with one 15-seat Embraer Bandeirante—known affectionately by pilots as the Bandit, a name that might have, for the scheduled airlines of that time, described its owner. His entry into the world of scheduled service on 8 July 1985 was hardly noticed.

The route to London's Gatwick Airport was the test-marketing venture for one that soon developed into a hub network to points in Ireland based in Waterford and also from Ireland's capital, Dublin. The London termini of Luton and Stansted replaced Gatwick, as they had the advantage of being less congested, allowing faster turnarounds and higher aircraft utilization. Dublin was also connected to British provincial cities, Liverpool, Cardiff, and Leeds, using at first HS 748 turboprops but upgraded on 1 December by Romanian-built BAC One-Elevens. Fully conventional airline service was offered: first-class sections and meals, but the difference was the fares—only a quarter of those being offered by Aer Lingus, which quickly realized that charging £189 from Dublin to London was a thing of the past.

With the regular injection of further capital from Ryan, the fleet was augmented by more One-Elevens, and three ATR-42s, but while the policy of cheaper fares was being followed, the policy of lower costs was not. During the first four years, **Ryanair** lost almost £18 million. The airline survived only because of Ryan's faith in its ultimate future. Some reorganization took place in 1988 under the P.J. Goldrick, but the complete transformation, the one that launched Ryanair almost into orbit, was initiated by Michael O'Leary, who took over in 1991. An incentive that something had to be done came in February of that year. Aer Rianta, the Irish aviation authority, threatened to place a truck in front of a Ryanair airliner to stop it taking off if the airline did not pay its bills. O'Leary set to work with a vengeance, instituting drastic changes. The full-service policy was abandoned in favor of a Southwest Airlines–style low-fares, no-amenities approach, only more so. Ryanair claimed that the only item free on its aircraft was air. The fleet was replaced in 1994 by eleven 130-seat Boeing 737-200s, bought second-hand from other airlines, to achieve standardization with an aircraft with a well-proved record of operating economy. Ryanair's route network looked good on the map, but O'Leary cut the cities served from 23 to only four, concentrating on only the larger city destinations from Dublin. Seat assignments gave way to simple boarding-pass priority, obtained at the touch of a computer button at the check-in desk, no ticket required.

Within two years, the one-way fare from Glasgow (Prestwick) to London (Stansted) was £19—the price of a dinner in a good restaurant. Flying across the Irish Sea was never the same. Only a few years later, London-Dublin was the busiest route in Europe, outpacing London-Paris, where the Channel Tunnel has made severe inroads to British Airways' and Air France's traffic.

1997 also witnessed the full measure of another of Ryanair's policies, one which had been partly exploited by Southwest in the United States. Serving London through Luton and Stansted, some 30 miles from downtown, had proved the advantages of less airport congestion and lower airport costs compared to the airport queues and the landing fees at Heathrow or Gatwick. Paris was served through Beauvais, Stockholm through Skavsta, and, more convincingly, Brussels through Charleroi (see below). Europeans enjoyed rapid connections from the airports to their homes or businesses in the city centers. Ryanair also opened up direct service to the southwestern corner of Ireland, where the Kerry airport was the gateway to the Lakes of Killarney and the spectacular coastline of the Atlantic. There was little doubt as to the success of this policy. During 1997, Ryanair carried 4 million passengers and became a force to be reckoned with.

Ryan and O'Leary had moved the Irish newcomer into the big leagues. In March 1998, they ordered 45 Boeing 737s, with an option on 20 more. They added more routes throughout Europe, maintaining the policy of serving the market through satellite airports, for example Venice via Treviso, Florence via Pisa, Toulouse via Carcassonne. The total network comprised 28 destinations in seven countries. Six new cities were added in 1999, and five more in 2000, all to airports that had been ignored by the established flagship airlines. At the turn of the century, Ryanair passed Aer Lingus, Ireland's national airline, in its annual passenger boardings.

On 26 April 2001, it established a base at Charleroi—now being called Brussels South—as well as its successful second base at London's Stansted. Four Boeing 737s were based at Charleroi,

Other than the neat "flying harp" logo to connote its Irish identity, Ryanair had no inhibitions in revealing its name to the public. (Bentley)

with the same marketing policies: all flights were point-to-point, with no connecting traffic or baggage transfers, but that was no deterrent to passengers who welcomed the cheap fares across the Channel and to the sunshine of Italian resorts. Ryanair had to settle the question of the legality of the subsidies that the city of Charleroi had granted to the airline. But any skepticism as to the permanency of Ryanair's success was dismissed as, in spite of the widespread effect of the 11 September 2001 terrorist attack in New York, Ryanair carried more than 10 million passengers in that year.

EasyJet

After Ryan came Stelios Haji-Ioannou, whose rise to prominence in the European airline scene was even quicker than his Irish predecessor's. His background was shipping, from which base he no doubt inherited sound business acumen. The foundation of his airline, on 17 March 1995, was based on two main decisions. First, it was based at Luton, which had been renamed London-Luton in 1992 to reflect its easy access to the capital. This was either by the nearby M-1 motorway or by rapid nonstop rail service, for which a special station adjacent to the airport had been built. The second decision was to base the entire operational policy on that of the successful Southwest Airlines. The name of his airline, trading as **easyJet**, also echoed that of another American low-fare maverick, ValuJet.

The inaugural service, on 10 November 1995, was London to Glasgow, and the fare offered was, for advanced bookings, only £29, or about a quarter of the incumbent British Airways's economy fare. All bookings were made on the Internet. The flights were by 148-seat Boeing 737-200s, with the airline's reservations telephone number prominently painted on the sides of the aircraft. All maintenance was outsourced to Monarch Airlines, still a successful charter operator and now fully mature as a scheduled British airline, based at Luton.

In March 1996, Ray Webster was appointed managing director, and by the end of the year, easyJet was serving Scotland well (and strongly challenging British Airways) with service to Aberdeen, Edinburgh, and Inverness. On 24 April, it started its first international route, to Amsterdam, followed by Barcelona and Nice, in June. In October 1997, a second English gateway was initiated at Liverpool. Like other new low-fare airlines, easyJet made no attempt to provide free amenities. The majority of air travelers, especially those flying on short services of an hour or two, willingly exchanged a meal or a free drink for a reduction in the ticket price, and the ease of booking a seat.

In 1998, easyJet acquired a 40% shareholding in the Swiss charter airline **T.E.A.**, based at Basle, and changed the name later to **easyJet Switzerland**, moving its base to Geneva. By the summer, the route network extended to Athens and Madrid, and the airline was selling seats on the fast-growing Internet. In February 1999, easyJet started service to Malaga, tapping the burgeoning tourist market of Spain's Costa del Sol, and by the end of that year, the airline had carried more than 3 million passengers.

In March 2000, eighteen 149-seat Boeing 737-800s were ordered (augmenting the 737 fleet to 32), and Amsterdam was added to Luton, Liverpool, and Geneva as the fourth operational hub. In November, 25% of the share capital was offered to private investors, raising £200 million. More than 7 million passengers were carried in 2001, and in April 2002, four new routes were opened from Paris.

This stellar demonstration of free enterprise was underlined in 2002 when Haji-Ioannou consolidated his growing low-fare empire, first on 6 May by offering to purchase Deutsche B.A. (the British Airways subsidiary in Germany), and then on 1 August, buying **Go**, the same airline's low-fare subsidiary based at Stansted. An indication that easyJet was now in the big league of European airlines was that the price paid was £577 million. Its fleet now consisted of 64 Boeing 737s, which served 48 routes to 11 countries, carrying 14 million passengers in 2002.

When, on 26 November, Haji-Ioannou stepped down as chairman, he had good reason to be satisfied with his entrepreneurial

Rivaling Ryanair, easyJet went further. Telephone and e-mail numbers on its aircraft were effective advertising. (Bentley)

success. EasyJet had just ordered, on 14 October, 120 Airbus A319s (plus another 120 A320s on option) and his airline had announced pre-tax profits of £72 million. Sir Colin Chandler, who took over the chairmanship, was given a good start. His first decision was, on 17 March 2003, to abandon the idea of buying Deutsche B.A. after protracted negotiations and the stagnation of the German market; but any erosion of the potential European market was soon offset by an agreement with the French authorities for a host of airport slots at Orly Airport, with immediate service, on 1 July, from Paris to Toulouse. All was not plain sailing, however, as easyJet became involved in the Ryanair dispute over landing slots and subsidies, particularly at Belgium's Charleroi.

In addition to its three bases in London (Luton, Gatwick, and Stansted) and four other British bases (East Midlands, Liverpool, Newcastle, and Bristol), it was now firmly established at three cities in Europe (Geneva, Paris, and Amsterdam). In October 2004, **Icelandair** purchased a 10% shareholding, to provide a trans-Atlantic connection, and an interesting reminder of the tradition of low fares that had originated in far-off Reykjavik, when Loftleidir (Icelandair's former name) had defied the International Air Transport Association (IATA) cartel by creating a so-called Sixth Freedom service from points in Europe to New York.

By 2009, the easyJet map covered Europe with a web of almost 400 routes that now extended to the east as far as Warsaw, Krakow, Tallinn, and Riga, with more hubs at Berlin's Schönefeld Airport and by forming easyJet Switzerland. The fleet had grown to approach 200 aircraft (142-seat Boeing 737s and 124–185-seat Airbus A319/320/321s). The easyJet name was a household word in Britain, having brought the pleasures of air travel to millions of ordinary people.

The Essence of Competition

There is an economic axiom that claims that all the benefits of competition can be achieved with only two competitors, and that a third participant in an identifiable market is redundant or superfluous, and in any case is doomed to failure or, at best, also-ran status. So it has been with the spectacular rise of the low-fare airlines of Europe. Ryanair and easyJet have been so successful that, in terms of public transport, they have jointly epitomized the objectives of a European Community, transcending political frontiers. The countries of continental Europe have watched the intruders from across the English Channel dominate their own airways.

Others That Tried

One such aspirant was **Debonair**, founded in January 1994 by Franco Mancassola, who had several years of experience in independent airlines. At first, with a leased fleet of five British Aerospace BAe 146s, and a substantial capital from investors that was to total £14.5 million, he intended to operate from London's Gatwick Airport, which had recently witnessed the demise of a long-term independent, **DanAir**, and of a more recent one, **Air Europe**. Although a declared low-fare operator, Mancassola tried to modify the approach from completely no-frills austerity to something a little bit better, to attract businessmen who respected economy but who needed elbow room. This took the

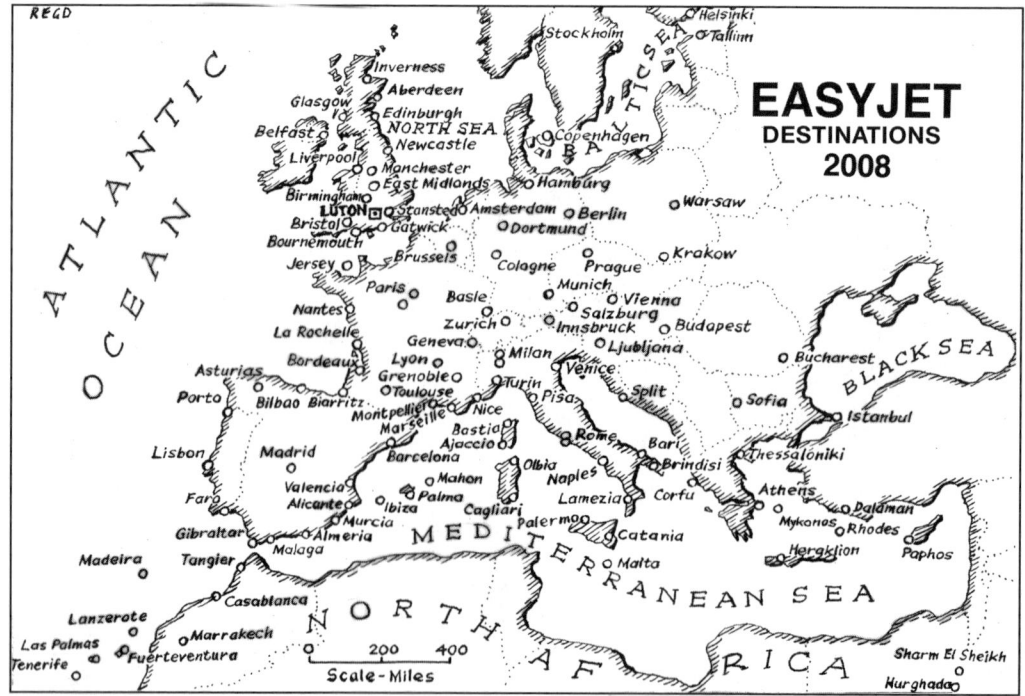

Within a few years, easyJet had proved that bargain fares were the key to airline success. By 2008, it was flying to more than 100 destinations, including a dozen each in Italy, Spain, and France.

form of 33-inch pitch and assigned seating, to avoid the first-come-first-served system, which Franco considered to be undignified for men with briefcases.

British Airways moved into Gatwick in strength, and so Debonair switched to Luton, which was just as convenient by rail to London. On 19 June 1996, services began to Munich, Dusseldorf (at nearby Munchen-Gladbach), and Barcelona. Madrid and Newcastle were added on 10 July, Copenhagen on 7 August, and Rome (Ciampino) in November. By 1998, Debonair was expanding to new destinations in Europe. It also tried to return to Gatwick with flights to the main destination, Barcelona, and leased a 139-seat Boeing 737-300 to supplement its fleet of twelve 90-seat BAe 146s. These plans, though, were little more than gestures, as the operating costs of the four-engine 146s exceeded the low-load-factor revenues. Debonair ceased operations on 1 October 1999.

By the 1990s, Richard Branson, head of Virgin Atlantic Airlines, was the owner of numerous Virgin companies, dealing in all kinds of products; but he still regarded the operation of airlines as his special forte, having based his policies on Sir Freddie Laker's extrovert style of self-promotion, which saved considerable advertising costs and gave him considerable satisfaction. By April 1996, Branson decided to enter the European low-fare airline arena. Instead of creating a new airline from scratch, he looked around to find an existing airline that he could simply buy, and with the acceleration of the formation of the European Union, he did not have to confine his search to Britain.

Accordingly, the Virgin Group acquired 90% of the Brussels-based **Euro-Belgian Airlines** for $60 million and appointed Jonathan Ornstein, ex-president of Continental Express, to head it under the new name, **Virgin Express**. The airline operated a fleet of 12 Boeing 737-300/400s from Brussels to Barcelona, Madrid, Milan, Nice, Rome, and Vienna. Most of the flights were on inclusive-tour charters, but this would change to more scheduled services. The acquisition also included the French company Air Provence, which was renamed, in customary fashion, **Virgin Express France**.

At the end of 1996, an agreement was made with the veteran (but ailing) Belgian flag carrier, SABENA, for a cross-leasing deal to operate the frequent service to London's Heathrow, where the connection was thus made to Virgin Atlantic's trans-Atlantic and intercontinental services. Services were also started from Brussels to London's Stansted, where gates and slots were readily available. To consolidate a position in France, Virgin made a bid to buy into **Air Liberté**, in partnership with the Rivaud bank. Taking advantage of the increasingly liberal opportunities in Europe, Copenhagen was added to the network, and Rome connected with Barcelona and Madrid (in what would once have been a politically impossible Fifth Freedom route).

On 30 March 1997, another agreement was made with **SABENA** for the Brussels-Rome route, with the national airline continuing to offer the traditional fare structure, and Virgin offering the low fares. But early in 1998, Virgin Express declared a financial loss for the year. Branson reacted in typical fashion; to cut losses, he invested in expansion, rather than retraction. In October of that year, an Irish subsidiary, **Virgin Express Ireland**, was formed at Shannon, and on 10 November 1999, service began not only to London, but on to Brussels, Berlin, and Rome. The losses continued, and even though a new route opened to Malaga, an order for 11 new Boeing 737-700s was cancelled and several services were terminated. To shore up the base in Brussels, operations there were merged with those of **SN Brussels Airlines (S.N.B.A.)**, which had been created from Delta Air Transport.

With the demise of SABENA, there was some hope for the continuation of a Brussels-based airline, but the struggle for survival by Virgin Express was a textbook example of the economic realities of competition. Two rivals for a defined market—in this case, the low-fare European airline business—are invariably sufficient to meet the demand. And a third aspirant, even with all the élan and financial resources of the man who created the Virgin empire, could not break Ryanair's and easyJet's grip on the market.

In some cases, veteran airlines, many of them entrenched as part of a firmly established and popularly accepted air travel environment, watched the bold new entrants to the market first with disdain then with growing interest, on to alarm, and eventually to resignation to facts that had been apparent for decades. In Great Britain, the national airline, **British Airways**, with unmatched industrial strength—it was the world's leading international flag carrier at the time—decided to take this unorthodox course by forming a low-fare subsidiary, **Go**, which would prove to be an unfortunate name choice. It was registered on 1 April 1998 (its official name was Go Fly, Ltd.) and based at London's Stansted Airport, with a fleet of leased Boeing 737s, rather than transferring its own aircraft.

Go was headed by Barbara Cassani, formerly with the parent company, who opened service on 22 May 1998 to Milan and Rome, followed in June by a connection to Copenhagen, and then service from Edinburgh and to Bologna on 8 September. The strategy was simple: to compete with the dominant easyJet and Ryanair in offering cheap flights from Britain to the Mediterranean sun. A new destination added to the map every month during the summer.

One aspect of Go's marketing approach was to counter the ostentatious style of easyJet's prominent display of its telephone number and Internet code on its aircraft. The word GO already dominated the tail section of each of its 737s; to this was added, on the sides of the forward section of the fuselage, phrases such as "let's go," or "away we go," or "go for a break." Different colors were used for each aircraft, but such flamboyance came too late. The airline had not made a sufficient intrusion into the vacation market to press its promotion to a wide enough audience.

Ironically, its slogans could have forecast the airline's fate. In June 2001, the airline was sold to the 3i Group for £110 million ($151 million). Then, after protracted skirmishing, including the control of the British Airways German subsidiary, Deutsche B.A., on 6 May 2002, easyJet bought Go for £374 million. Barbara

Cassini could hardly be blamed for mismanagement, and the parent airline had undervalued its subsidiary.

More of the Same

Interestingly, in the world of international politics, the United Kingdom had been reluctant to acknowledge the fact that in the 21st century (and with the construction of the Channel Tunnel) it was irrevocably part of Europe. In the industrial and commercial world, the low-fare airlines of the British Isles had been eager to cross the Channel. Led by Ireland's Ryanair, and quickly joined by England's easyJet, their initiatives to exploit the enormous low-fare air travel demand, released from crippling restrictions by the European Union's edict of April 1987, enabled them to corner the market. At the beginning of the century, only 15 years after what was effectively European airline deregulation, five of the six new entrants were from offshore islands, and the sixth was based in Britain too.

This outsider was founded by Europe's oldest airline, the Dutch **K.L.M.**, which had already hived off its short-haul routes to a subsidiary, **Cityhopper**. In January 2000, it changed the name of its K.L.M. U.K. division (formerly Air U.K.) to **Buzz**, a low-fare subsidiary. Based at London's fast-growing Stansted Airport, it opened seven routes, ranging from Helsinki to Marseilles, with eight ex-K.L.M. BAe 146s. On 26 March, Buzz added three more points, including Jerez in southern Spain, and then proceeded to concentrate on France, serving no less than 12 provincial cities, in addition to Paris, already on the network. But on 30 March 2002, some routes were suspended, and in November of that year, Buzz was divested from the parent K.L.M., while KLM UK merged with Cityhopper. The Dutch airline had paddled in dangerous waters and had done more than get its feet wet. On 1 April 2003, the now-dominant Ryanair acquired Buzz, including its 14 BAe 146s and Boeing 737s, for €24 million ($25.6 million).

The novelty of creating a marketing image with an eye-catching name was becoming popular, and even as Buzz's fortunes were declining, another well-established British airline sought originality in that field by launching its low-fare subsidiary with an outrageous pun. On 20 March 2002, **British Midland International (B.M.I.)** started service from the East Midlands Airport, near Derby (where it had originated in the late 1940s as Derby Aviation), with its *bmibaby*. Its first route was to Malaga on Spain's Costa del Sol, with aircraft from B.M.I.'s main fleet. By the end of the year, B.M.I.'s baby was flying 22 routes from East Midlands, mainly to Spanish destinations. Again following the example set by Ryanair and easyJet, two of its 737s were transferred to Cardiff on 25 October to give the Welsh capital nine vacation routes, and in May 2003, the pattern was repeated at Manchester.

Channel Chameleon

One of the rags-to-riches stories of the British independent airline community during the period of post-deregulation readjustment evolved in the offshore Channel Islands, where local airlines had flourished since the early 1930s. Joining the incumbent operators, which included the still-nationalized British European Airways (B.E.A.), **Intra Airways** was formed in 1969 to operate inter-island services. It served the three main Islands—Jersey, Guernsey, and Alderney—with a fleet of ageing Douglas DC-3s and two 16-seat Britten-Norman Islanders. By the late 1970s, it had added three ex-British Midland Vickers Viscounts, and in November 1979, having taken over Bournemouth-based **Express Air Services**, with its DHC-6 Twin Otters, its name had changed to a more-identifiable **Jersey European Airways (J.E.A.)**.

Like many other small companies at the time, J.E.A. was in deep trouble when, in November 1983, it was rescued by Jack Walker, a millionaire steel magnate who lived in the Islands. His Walker Steel Group owned Spacegrand Aviation, which was founded in 1979 in Blackpool, to serve executives of his company by flying them to the Isle of Man and Dublin, with small executive aircraft. With an injection of much-needed capital to clear $3 million in debt, Walker entered the commercial airline field with enthusiasm, seeking a niche market in July 1985 by linking the vacation markets of the Islands with Belfast, Northern Ireland via Exeter, in southwest England. In October of that year, Spacegrand was absorbed by J.E.A., and the operational base was transferred to the geographically central Exeter, which had adequate hangar space to accommodate a growing fleet of Fokker F-27s, HS-748s, and new Shorts 330s.

Walker took advantage of the liberal policies of airline licensing and route authority which had been introduced by the Conservative government in 1964, and by 1986 J.E.A. was not only linking northern England, Belfast, and Dublin with Jersey and Guernsey, but had opened routes to London's Stansted Airport and to France at Dinard and Paris. The old DC-3s had been replaced by six Fokker F-27s from Australia. The airline did not yet subscribe to the view that airline service should be reduced to bare essentials, and continued to offer on-board catering—a reflection, perhaps, of the old Spacegrand executive approach. The policy seemed to work, as three larger BAe 146s joined the fleet, and by the mid-1990s, J.E.A. was the fourth largest British domestic airline, carrying more than a million passengers annually.

In 1996, already code-sharing with **Air UK**, it moved further into France by a franchising agreement with **Air France**. This was a "wet-leasing" arrangement under which J.E.A. provided the aircraft and crews (Channel Islanders were bi-lingual) and the aircraft flew in Air France colors to Lyons and Toulouse. In the spring of 1999, the airline bought 11 new Dash 8 Q200s, 300s, and 400s from Bombardier, and four Canadian CRJ 200s, to augment the fleet to 25 aircraft. On 18 July 2000, to reflect its wider horizons, J.E.A. became **British European**, adopting the name of the previous state corporation, a move that was not challenged by British Airways. To justify its name, flights were increased from London's City Airport to Paris, and in 2001, the Paris-Birmingham route was extended to Glasgow. More than 2 million passengers were now being carried every year, but the effects of the low-fare giants easyJet and Ryanair were being felt, and a simplified—and lower—fare structure was introduced.

Low-Fare Revolution

Flybe's network of routes serving the outer islands of the United Kingdom is almost identical with B.E.A.'s during the post-war years, and even with those of the pioneer airlines of the 1930s.

Jack Walker died in 2002, just as British European again changed its name on 18 July to **Flybe**, thus joining the ranks of airlines with novel names. The policy of offering business-class seats as well as low-fare economy class was continued, without dire consequences, as evidenced in June 2005 by a $870-million order for fourteen 118-seat Embraer E-195s from Brazil, and in the following year, a code-sharing agreement was signed with **Continental Airlines** to provide code-sharing connections to New York's Newark Airport.

Flybe's fleet now totaled 42 aircraft, with 36 more on order, and it was operating leased Boeing 737-300s. From Intra Airways's 20-mile hop from Jersey to Guernsey in 1969 to 3,400-mile interline flights to New York in 2006, and in less than four decades, this many-faceted airline had undergone a remarkable history of survival and progress.

Brash newcomers, especially easyJet and Ryanair, transformed the British airline industry during the last decades of the 20th century. Of the brave independent airlines that had survived many years—many had collapsed in the face of restrictive legislation—some carried on with previous policies of marketing charter flights and inclusive tours, and took advantage of more liberal governmental and European edicts to move into the world of scheduled services. They offered a range of seating classes and fares. Some were able to maintain the status quo and resisted the temptation to go for broke with all-out, no-frills, bargain-basement fares. The structure of these airlines has been the sequel to the Edwards Report, commissioned by the government in 1969, which set the stage for a consolidation of many of the smaller independents to create a Second Force airline that would offer some kind of competition to the state-owned airlines.

Chapter 26: British Airways Ascendancy

Britain's Flag Carriers Consolidate

Earlier developments in British air transport as the Jet Age unfolded have been reviewed. In Chapter 9, one sequel to the 1969 Edwards Report was the creation of a Second Force airline to end the state-owned **British Overseas Airways Corporation (B.O.A.C.)** monopoly of long-distance scheduled routes. The resultant merger between British United Airways and Caledonian Airways was not, however, a powerful enough force to change the competitive environment within the British airline hierarchy. **British Caledonian (B-Cal)** entered the North Atlantic market in 1968, but B.O.A.C. was too well entrenched throughout the six continents. B-Cal was not given enough of the certificated route network—a maximum of only 15%—to be able to do more than touch the fringe of the incumbent's domain. Its share could be cynically regarded as little more than crumbs from the master's table.

British Overseas Airways Corporation came under further independent attack in the 1970s. A schism in B-Cal's boardrooms had resulted in the departure of its president, Freddie Laker, who then, early in 1966, founded his own airline, **Laker Airways**, and immediately displayed the level of aggressive independence that might have been expected from a freer Second Force. Laker demonstrated that true competition with B.O.A.C. needed more than airline service of the same standards—flight frequencies, aircraft type selection, and meal service being the customarily accepted criteria of competition. His no-reservation, no-frills, bargain-fare London-New York Skytrain service would not, however, start until 1977, and only after much bureaucratic stonewalling by the various certificating authorities did this open a new chapter in the competitive arena. It frightened the North Atlantic airline incumbents so much that they were relieved when, after a sensational international court case, Laker's bankers had foreclosed and shut him down in 1982 (see Chapter 14).

While the political policy-makers were skirmishing in the courts, B.O.A.C. went about its business and moreover campaigned against what it felt, with some justification, was an intrusion into and usurpation of markets that it had spent decades in developing. It also continued to extend its intercontinental routes beyond the realm of the British Commonwealth. On 1 April 1967, it opened service across the South Pacific, in association with QANTAS and Air New Zealand, and at the end of the year augmented services to the Caribbean via New York. On 7 November 1968, closer to home, and less spectacularly, its I.B.M. 360 computer system, abbreviated BOADICEA, revolutionized the reservations system through the network, and over time, permitted better operational economics by ensuring higher average load factors.

On 5 May 1969, a direct Polar Service began, by flying northwest from London to Tokyo via Anchorage, Alaska, and this was improved upon on 2 June 1970 when the Japanese capital was also reached, eastward via Moscow and across Siberia. The Boeing 707-336C made the Moscow-Tokyo 4,667-mile segment in 14 hours. The following month, VC-10 service opened to Philadelphia and Washington, and a direct route to Miami extended the flag-carrier's presence in the United States. Route extensions were only one aspect of the state airline's commercial progress. Management recognized that it could not turn back increasing popularity of low fares, which the independent airlines had exploited through Affinity Charters and Inclusive Tours. On 1 March 1970, B.O.A.C. pioneered the Early Bird low-fare program, available to passengers who paid at least four months in advance, and which came to be known as Advanced Booking Economy (APEX) fares.

Far from adopting a defensive posture, therefore the airline went on the offensive, and in September 1970, established a non–International Air Transport Association (IATA) subsidiary, British Overseas Air Charter Limited, to combat the growing ranks of similarly organized competitors. When this was activated in the following year, the main market to be targeted was the Far East and Australia, with a £360 round-trip fare to Sydney, compared to a £609 standard economy-class tariff. Group Inclusive Tours (GITs), New York-London, at $150 one-way, were to be effective on 1 February 1972, and the APEX system of savings on fares if booked in advance was vigorously promoted.

During its twilight years, B.O.A.C. went about its business, from the day-to-day routine to the revolutionary. Even the routine was extensive. As well as opening routes in 1972 to Addis Ababa, Oman, and the newly independent Bangladesh, one of its services to Japan was routed via the Seychelles, the latest fashionable tourist destination in the Indian Ocean. In January 1973, a true trans-Indian Ocean route, that included Mauritius as well as the Seychelles, opened from Johannesburg. And to embellish the list of the world's trans-ocean crossings, a direct polar service from London to Los Angeles opened on 2 March.

During October and November 1972, though hardly routine, B.O.A.C. carried 3,000 Asian refugees from Uganda to the U.K. As to the revolutionary side of things, on 25 May of that year, it announced an order for five Anglo-French supersonic Concordes. This was expected to open a new chapter in the development of the world's air transport industry, with the United States and the Soviet Union both reacting with supersonic designs of their own. As yet, the problems of sonic booms and high noise levels had not been solved, but hopes remained high. B.O.A.C.'s last annual report included a map of future Concorde routes from London to New York, Tokyo, Sydney, and Johannesburg.

Britain's long-distance national airline had served its country well. It had started in 1940 by amalgamating two international airlines, and now it was itself amalgamated with another.

Britain's Vickers VC-10s was popular with frequent flyers, mainly because of its quiet cabin. (Bentley)

Its original mission had been to serve the British Empire overseas, and with a fine fleet of flying boats it had done the job. Now, after 32 years of service, it was still doing it, and doing it well, with a fine fleet of jet airliners that included the best of the first jet generation, the Vickers Super-VC-10, and of the second, the Boeing 747. It was facing the supersonic future with confidence. But B.O.A.C.'s mission was no longer restricted to the English-speaking nations. It served the entire planet. Britain's post-war intercontinental national airline retired with all flags flying.

Britain Leads Europe

In terms of productivity, **British European Airways (B.E.A.)** was always in the shadow of the worldwide B.O.A.C., as it was geographically restricted to a smaller operational area. Yet it carried far more passengers than its larger cousin and was the dominant scheduled airline of Europe. It had faithfully followed a policy of "Buy British" and had been the launch customer for the Vickers Viscount, which achieved worldwide success, and had also introduced the 84-seat de Havilland Trident tri-jet. British European Airways also sponsored the larger turboprop Vickers Vanguard though that aircraft was purchased by only one other airline, Trans Canada.

By the time the first Trident went into scheduled service on 1 April 1964, the last venerable Douglas DC-3 had been retired in 1962, and the early Viscounts in 1963. In an innovative departure, **B.E.A. Helicopters** was formed as an autonomous division on 1 January 1964 and on 2 May the first Sikorsky S.61N was put into service on the Lands End-Scilly Isles route. It replaced the de Havilland D.H.89 Dragon Rapide biplane of pre-war vintage—the only aircraft able to use the short strip on St. Mary's Island. A heliport opened in Penzance for the new service, which was more convenient for the fast rail service from London than the airport at St. Just.

The state airline was receiving increased competition on its domestic routes, and in February 1965, the Minister of Aviation stated that the independent airlines would not be allowed to make further incursions, and also that B.E.A. would be allowed to extend its activities in the inclusive tour market. On the technical front, on 10 June 1965, B.E.A. made the first fully automatic touchdown on a scheduled airline service, on a Paris-London Trident flight.

During the early 1960s, B.E.A.'s European network expanded, especially to Mediterranean resorts such as Greece's Corfu, Yugoslavia's Dubrovnik, and Portugal's Faro, as well as additional destinations. On 1 April 1969, B.E.A. Germany became a separate profit center (see below) and on 24 April, **B.E.A. Airtours** was formed as a subsidiary charter company, using B.E.A.'s Comet 4Bs. By this move, the airline's policy had had to adjust to the realities of the market as by this time the combined intra-European share of all passengers carried by the non-scheduled airlines was greater than that of their scheduled competitors. Leisure travelers, mainly northern Europeans seeking the sun, outnumbered the businessmen. B.E.A. Airtours made its first commercial flight on 6 March 1970, from Gatwick to Palma; then on 28 June 1971, it announced its intention to buy seven Boeing 707s from B.O.A.C., and these went into full service in 1972.

In spite of the background protectionism that it had enjoyed over the past two decades, B.E.A. had been reluctant to recognize that cheap vacation travel had become the major source of airline revenue throughout Europe. But on 1 February 1972, all first-class fares were abolished, and on 10 April, "instant" half-price fares were introduced on short-haul routes to Paris and Amsterdam and extended to Scandinavia on 5 May. Such marketing initiatives should have been made years previously. The airline that once dominated the airline skies of Europe was almost a lame duck when the two state airlines were merged. In its defense, its designated area of operations, extending beyond Europe only to Mediterranean resorts in North Africa and Lebanon, meant that its average stage distance was only about 350 miles. The economic realities at such a range are that operating costs per seat-mile are inevitably high, and for B.E.A., facing cut-throat competition from aggressive independents, its own fare structure could not produce revenues to match costs. A few new services were still added to the network, all to the Mediterranean, but when B.E.A. ceased to exist on 1 April 1972, its profit for the previous year was only £181,000, and its prospects were hardly encouraging. Altogether it was a sad end to a great airline.

Creation of British Airways

The first step toward the complete amalgamation of the two British state-owned airlines was the creation, on 1 April 1972, of the British Airways Board, which assumed ownership of B.E.A. and B.O.A.C. and their subsidiaries. This had been authorized by the Civil Aviation Act of 1971, which became law on 7 October of that year. David Nicholson, a former management consultant, was appointed chairman of the board, which established seven operating divisions: B.O.A.C., Inc. (British Overseas Air Charter); B.E.A. (including B.E.A. Airtours); British Air Services, subsequently British Airways Regional (including former B.E.A. subsidiaries, Cambrian Airways, Northeast Airlines, Scottish Airways, and Channel Islands Airways); British Airways Helicopters; British Airways Engine Overhaul; British Airways Associated Companies; and International Radio. Such an organization could claim, except for the largest companies in the United States and the Soviet Union's all-embracing Aeroflot, to be the biggest airline in the world—in revenue, passenger-miles flown, aircraft fleet, and staff numbers. Internationally, it was a giant, although its 58,000 staff was estimated to be 20,000 more than was needed, if the conventional advantages of avoiding personnel duplications were to be effected. Its operating hub was at the leading international airport in the world, London's Heathrow Airport, and British Airways prospered from that sound base. Full integration took some time. The Civil Aviation Authority (C.A.A.) was also formed on 1 April 1972, replacing a succession of Ministerial overseers that had exercised governmental stewardship. On 1 January 1973, the names of both B.E.A. and B.O.A.C. were retired, and on 1 April 1974, **British Airways (B.A.)** was officially formed by Act of Parliament. Henry Marking, long-time veteran of B.E.A., became chief executive; Stephen Wheatcroft, also from B.E.A. and an airline economics authority, and Ross Stainton, of B.O.A.C., became deputy managing directors. The aircraft jet fleet ranged from wide-bodied Boeing 747s, long-haul Vickers VC-10s and Boeing 707s, to short-haul Tridents and BAC One-Elevens, with Short Skyvans adding feeder-route impudence to the jet dignity. Wide-bodied tri-jet Lockheed TriStar L.1011s and Anglo-French supersonic Concordes were on order.

Supersonic Dreams

The commercial world of aviation, the British and French governments, the gullible press, and an adoring public, were all captivated with the prospect of flying at twice the speed of sound. All thoughts of the costs of achieving such a prestigious goal were subjugated by the spectacular performance of the airliner produced by the best aircraft designers, engineers, and aerodynamicists at Toulouse and Bristol. The Concorde would be an economic disaster because it could never come close to paying its own way. Meanwhile the national airlines of Britain and France dutifully went on as the chosen flag carriers of their countries.

Operationally and politically, the path was difficult. Concorde operations were handicapped because of the sonic boom—a force of nature that no amount of technology could overcome. Supersonic flights could only be made over water. B.A.'s twice weekly Concorde service to Bahrain, inaugurated on 21 January 1976 (the same day as Air France's service to Brazil) could not be sustained because of the necessity to fly over land. Efforts to find a route to avoid this obligation all the way to Australia via India and Singapore had to be put aside. Any hopes for a world market for the Concorde were dashed by the overland restrictions. This essentially restricted the Concorde only to trans-Atlantic services, and even these were only marginally possible because of payload-range limitations. Trans-Pacific service was out of the question because two intermediate stops would have been obligatory.

British Airways persevered and overcame the political problems involved with the United States, which had abandoned the supersonic commercial dream. Because of the enormous cost estimates, and alleged negative environmental fallout, the Senate had in 1971 voted against an American supersonic design that would have been bigger and faster than the Concorde. The obvious destination for British and French routes, from London and Paris respectively, was New York. Local authorities there objected because of the Concorde's high noise level (unrelated to the sonic boom) and the first trans-Atlantic supersonic airline service, on 24 May 1976, was to Washington, D.C., where the international airport (under Federal authority) was judged to be far enough from the built-up area to permit landings and take-offs. New York eventually relented, and it too accepted the Concorde on 22 November 1977. During the whole operational life of the supersonic fleet, only extremely well-heeled passengers flying between New York or Washington and London or Paris could afford the fares, far more expensive than normal first-class. The two supersonic airlines never came close to covering the direct operating costs, much less the indirect costs, and neither airline had to buy the aircraft.

In December 1977, experimental flights were made to Singapore via Bahrain, but these were never developed, and on 12 January 1979, the New York route was, in cooperation with Braniff International, extended to Dallas—but not supersonically. British Airways recognized that, good flag carriers though they were, the Concordes did have a special place in the scheme of things, but commercial route development was not economically viable. It had to take care of this essential side of airline affairs with its less headline-attracting subsonic fleet.

On its United Kingdom domestic network, for example, on 12 January 1975, B.A. started a seat-guaranteed Shuttle Service from London to Glasgow, using nine 100-seat Trident 1s, and charging a one-way fare for the 420-mile route of £17.00 ($39.00)—quite a contrast with the Concorde's thousands of pounds, but more remunerative on balance with the operating costs. Adjustments to the long-haul route structure were made after a government white paper on future civil aviation policy was published in February 1976. British Caledonian withdrew its route to Los Angeles, but extended its coverage of South America to Caracas, Bogota, and Lima, and was also given the route to East and Central Africa. British Airways brushed off this minor incursion into its now worldwide leadership stature. On 2 May 1979, it ordered nineteen 186-seat Boeing 757s, and on 29 March 1981, the last Vickers VC-10 scheduled service foreshadowed the end of the airliners' buy-British policy.

On with the Show

While litigation over Freddie Laker's innovative air service occupied media headlines for three years, Britain's overseas flag carriers had to sustain operations. Their biggest problem was overstaffing. Merging two large corporations to take advantage of opportunities to avoid duplication was not always straightforward. The process of attrition, even with generous severance pay, could not be done with draconian methods, or a system-wide strike would have resulted. Even so, the 58,000 staff of the 1970s was reduced to 43,000 by the end of 1981. Many services to Europe were withdrawn, and eight stations were closed. All cargo operations were withdrawn.

One satisfactory solution to the economic objectives was in Scotland, where the Highlands Division was threatened with extinction. In April 1982, it was rejuvenated as the staff was cut from 600 to 167 by adopting a multifunctional policy of employment, with incentives. Older four-engine Viscounts were replaced by twin-engine HS 748s.

In 1982, Sir John King took over the chairmanship, and ideas of challenging the low-fare competitors head-on were abandoned. In 1983, he hired Colin Marshall, an experienced executive in consumer marketing, as his chief executive. On 9 February of that year, the first Boeing 757 replaced the Tridents, and in the summer a new logo and new aircraft colors were introduced, with the word *Airways* removed from the name on the aircraft.

These actions, typical of all airlines as they tried to move with the times, were made against the background of yet another government decision, in a report on airline competition policy, published in July 1984. Some long-haul services from Gatwick to Central Africa and Arabia were transferred to British Caledonian; services to a dozen European cities were opened to other British airlines; more freedom to expand domestic services was granted; and limits were imposed on the extent of European charters by B.A. The national airline was having problems of its own, as when, on 4 December, it unveiled new colors that proved unpopular. Also, the Concordes had to have special treatment, as the new paint scheme could not tolerate the high skin temperatures encountered at Mach Two.

A Second Force No More

The Edwards Committee Report of 1969 that had led to the creation of a "Second Force" airline was intended to provide intercontinental competition to B.A. from independent airlines and to erode its monopoly as the state-owned "airline of choice." The result was the merger of British United Airways and Caledonian Airways to produce British Caledonian (B-Cal), headed at first by the resourceful Freddie Laker and later by Sir Adam Thomson. B-Cal's allocated share of the route mileage never exceeded 15% of the total, and B.A.'s ascendancy in the highly competitive international field was never seriously challenged because of the relatively minor stature of the so-called Second Force.

The situation became moot when, late in 1987, the B.A. bought B-Cal for $418 million. B-Cal and its Second Force ceased to exist, and B.A. turned its attention to other developments. For the highly important Atlantic routes, it formed a marketing agreement with United Airlines and, nearer to home, expanded the Highlands Division to expand its routes from Scotland, Manchester, and Birmingham to many points in Europe, especially to Germany.

The decade ended on a high note for B.A. With the addition of the larger and longer-ranged Boeing 747-400, which entered service on the London-Philadelphia-Pittsburgh route on 28 July 1989, the airline underscored its intensions to further penetrate the U.S. market, and on 29 August, this fine airliner began nonstop service to Singapore—despite powerful competition from Singapore Airlines—and thus one-stop service to the main cities of Australia. As B.A. entered the 21st century, it was able to announce a pre-tax profit of $584 million for the 1989–90 fiscal year.

Further Expansion

During the early months of 1991, most airlines were affected, some severely, by the First Gulf War, which occurred athwart the main airway artery between Europe and Asia, and which deterred potential airline travelers everywhere. The coalition forces, headed by the United States, repulsed the Iraqi invasion of Kuwait, but soon afterward, on 20 March 1991, B.A. was indirectly involved in United Air Lines' purchase of the ailing Pan American's route to London. At the same time, American Airlines obtained T.W.A.'s London route. The British received additional onward rights at U.S. stopovers and additional rights from European points to the U.S., while Virgin Atlantic was given the cherished rights for a second British airline to fly to the U.S. from Heathrow. This was some compensation for the traffic loss caused by the Gulf War, but B.A. withdrew its Lockheed TriStar fleet, gave away 50,000 tickets to lure back its passengers, and underscored its inherent financial strength by ordering, in August, 15 313-seat twin-engine Boeing 777s.

Anxious to further penetrate the U.S. market, and possibly to take advantage of U.S. domestic airline weakness, on 20 July 1992, Sir Colin Marshall signed a $750-million provisional agreement with **USAir** for 44% of its stock; but this had to be reduced on 22 December, because of U.S. law that limited foreign shareholdings to 25% of the equity. $300 million was paid on 15 March 1993, and code-sharing on the London route began on 1 May, when an additional $100 million was forthcoming. However, the prospects deteriorated as USAir seemed unable to make a profit, and in June 1996, amid protests from both USAir and Virgin, B.A. began talks with American Airlines, one of the few airlines in the United States whose accounts were not in the red. After further months of discussion, on 10 January 1997, B.A. and American filed a joint application to the U.S. Department of Justice for anti-trust immunity. To help things along, B.A. sold its 18% stake in USAir for $625 million, and on 5 October 1998, negotiations for an "open skies" bilateral agreement began. The long-extended negotiations dragged on and seemed to have little chance of conclusion as long as B.A. protected its dominant share of airport slots (take-off and landing positions) at Heathrow.

Aside from trans-Atlantic considerations, other important decisions were made to consolidate the British position within Europe and elsewhere. In June 1992, B.A. bought 49% of **Deutsche B.A.** (formerly Delta Air). On 26 October, it bought DanAir (Davis & Newman Holdings) for a symbolic £1 price, but assuming its substantial debt, and added 38 aircraft to its fleet. This was the end of one of the original independent companies that were affiliated to B.E.A. in the early 1950s, and it managed to keep flying for more than 40 years. Shortly thereafter, using its financial strength, B.A. tried to buy control of QANTAS, but had to settle for 25% (£304 million) as the Australian government echoed American restrictions on the shareholding percentage permitted for foreign holdings.

1992 results showed a handsome profit, for the eleventh year running, and B.A. was serving 150 destinations in 69 countries and carrying 7% of the world's international passengers. But on 11 January 1993 its image was tarnished when it had to settle a court case. Virgin Atlantic's charismatic owner, Richard Branson, sued B.A. for a "dirty tricks" campaign, in which Lord King did not emerge with dignity. British Airways settled out of court for close to £3 million but brushed off the setback as its financial health continued. In 1993, in a determined effort to cut costs and increase market penetration, it agreed to franchise a number of its domestic and regional services to CityFlyer, which operated the services in B.A. colors but paid it a fee for sales and marketing. The idea caught on, and by 1997, a number of airlines were operating as franchise carriers: **Maersk Air** (U.K.), **Brymon** (already owned by B.A.), **G.B. Airways**, **Manx**, **British Regional**, **British Mediterranean**, **Sun-Air** in Scandinavia, and **Comair** in South Africa. It also acquired a substantial interest in Air Liberté, which, with its existing interest in T.A.T., gave the British about one-fifth of the French domestic traffic market. Air Liberté operated three 325-seat Douglas DC-10s to the French Caribbean and to Réunion, and had code-sharing agreements with several smaller French independents.

Robert Ayling had succeeded Sir Colin Marshall as CEO and, in June 1997, unveiled a new corporate identity for its airliner tail-marking design. The intention was good, as no less than 50 images were painted on the tails, each one representing, by symbolic designs, countries served by B.A. The scheme was a £60 million investment, and although it generated interest in the artistic world, it did little for the marketing image, especially when Branson's Virgin Atlantic responded by emphasizing its British-ness with the Union Jack and other flamboyant marketing. Ayling resigned in March 2000 and was succeeded by Rod Eddington, from Australia's Ansett Airlines, who had spent 18 years with Hong Kong's Cathay Pacific.

National Jet Italia became B.A.'s eleventh franchise operator on 11 July 2000. On 15 August, the Concorde fleet was grounded, as a sequel to a spectacular Air France take-off crash at Paris on 25 July. A modification program included the fitting of Kevlar linings to the fuel tanks. The Concordes went back into service on 7 November 2001, but low load factors led to economic realities being recognized, and the fleet was withdrawn from service on 31 October 2003, by which time the New York-London round-trip fare had increased to $15,000.

Putting its supersonic flag-waving behind, B.A. had to attend to the upstart low-fare, no-frills airlines that were eroding its market throughout Europe. In August 2002, easyJet formally acquired B.A.'s Go for $577 million, making it, after Ryanair, the second largest intra-European airline. British Airways had begun to acquire some of its franchise partners: CityFlyer in 1999, Manx and British Regional in 2002. The next step was to consolidate them as well as Brymon, with its own Manchester- and Birmingham-based regional operations, into a new regional airline, **CitiExpress**. The Manx brand was eliminated, and CitiFlyer aircraft were transferred. The resultant fleet numbered 84 aircraft.

In May 2003, another cost-cutting program was launched to reduce staff numbers by 13,000, reduce ticket-price options, cancel some supplier contracts, use manufacturers' aircraft manuals (instead of creating its own), eliminate some aircraft types, and increase aircraft utilization by night maintenance. These efforts were undertaken without too much industrial strife, but the economy drive continued with the appointment of Willie Walsh (formerly of Aer Lingus) on 3 May 2005 to succeed Rod Eddington. Walsh lost little time. On 30 November, B.A. announced substantial staff cuts at the managerial level, from 1,715 to 1,118. These decisions must have had some effect. British Airways' pre-tax profit in 2005 reached £620 million ($1.2 billion).

The CitiExpress program was improved and modified under the name **B.A. Connect** (launched on 26 March 2006), with the emphasis on low fares but with some on-board catering. Fleet numbers were reduced to 50, with only 4 aircraft types instead of 9. Individual routes were halved, to 50, and total destinations reduced from 49 at 25 airports to 32 at 14. British Airways was certainly feeling the impact of the low-fare, no-frills operators. During the previous five years, passenger boardings on the former regional network had declined from 6 million to less than 4 million.

B.A. European started Boeing 757 flights from Paris to New York on 19 June 2008. Reflecting the liberalized regulations in Europe, these were operated as a fully owned subsidiary. In July, B.A. bought the French airline L'Avion, which merged, on 4 April 2009 with B.A. European as *Open Skies*. A Paris-Washington route started on 3 May 2010.

With national frontiers no longer a barrier to the policy of "open skies," British Airways took advantage of the term to make it their own. This is one of its Boeing 757s. (McDonough)

Chapter 27: France Consolidates

Air France Resilience

The French national flag carrier entered the Jet Age and the jumbo jet age with confidence and style. The French nation has always been able to revive from disaster with impressive efforts. In 1958, its aircraft industry produced the Caravelle, which was to herald a generation of fuselage-engined airliners. Air France flew the first Caravelle scheduled service, from Paris to Las Palmas via Bordeaux, on 7 November 1959. During the 1960s, in company with British Airways, it made its contribution to the Concorde supersonic project. Far more important for the future of its aviation industry, France took over the design leadership of the European Airbus.

With the advent of the Jet Age, **Air France** consolidated its position as France's air transport leader and a front-runner in Europe. Its Boeing 707s of the first Jet Age and its Boeing 747s of the Second matched the long-haul competition in both hemispheres, and did so with the advantage of an on-board French cuisine fit for the most fastidious of gourmets. It did not have a monopoly of all long-distance or intercontinental routes, as (parallel to Great Britain's allocation of routes to British Caledonian as a "Second Force") some routes to Africa and in the Pacific were operated by the independent Union de Transports Aériens (U.T.A.).

By the early 1970s, Air France was flying its 747s nonstop from Paris to Los Angeles, and on 1 April 1973, in cooperation with U.T.A., it began a round-the-world service via Tokyo, Papeete (Tahiti), and Lima. Part of this innovation was, after an agreement with the Soviet Union, the inauguration of a Trans-Siberian link direct to Tokyo, the first western European airline to gain that privilege.

Enter the Airbus

Transcending all other developments, however, was Air France's entry into public scheduled service of the first A300B Airbus on the Paris-London route on 23 May 1974. This was the beginning of Europe's long-prepared challenge to United States dominance of the construction of first-line commercial airliners. Though Airbus's shareholding was European (with Germany and Great Britain with major shares), France deserves credit for its faith, determination, and leadership in the project. The main assembly factory at Toulouse—an extension of Aerospatiale's—was in due course to produce a whole line of Airbus airplanes, ultimately to match the output of Boeing at Seattle. This new force in aviation was proudly launched and energetically promoted by the French-led manufacturer, the French government, and the French national airline. All cooperated to ensure that the first Airbus, the world's first wide-bodied twin-engine short-haul airliner, made its debut without a hitch.

Supersonic Debut

The next few years were dominated by Air France's total commitment to the Concorde (see Chapter 16). The aircraft made its dramatic entry into service on 21 January 1976, flying to Rio de Janeiro, whose airport was named Aeropuerto Supersonico. Undoubtedly, the airline derived much marginal publicity from being one of the only two in the world to operate supersonically, but it was a financial burden, even if the marketing department put on a brave face. One of its seven aircraft had to be on hand permanently as a standby at New York, in case of a technical problem with the arriving aircraft from Paris; and later on, one aircraft was retained for spare parts.

Considering the high cost of the passenger tickets—twice as high as first class—Concorde did well at first, but most of the services to Latin America were soon withdrawn, as few could afford the privilege of flying on it. Also there were warnings, especially concerning the effect of Concorde's 200 mph landing speed had on its tires. On 14 June 1979, for example, a tire blew on take-off from Washington, and wheel parts damaged a wing. Disaster was only averted by an alert passenger who, against objections from the cabin staff, finally managed to warn the pilot. (See also the demise of the Concorde, later in this chapter.)

Another Airbus—and a New Challenge

When Air France introduced the first Airbus A300 service on 23 May 1974, the world of airlines was at first somewhat skeptical as to the future of this, the world's first wide-bodied airliner designed specifically for short-haul work. But with growing success—most airline passengers fly on routes of less than 1,000 miles—the Toulouse factory trumped its own ace by producing the smaller single-aisle Airbus A320 that, with variants, was to challenge the Boeing 737 as the most popular airliner in the world. Air France ordered 25 of them in September 1981. Rather as with the Concorde, this aircraft was also to have its warning when, on 26 June 1988, one crashed on a charter flight, with the blame aimed at the "fly by-wire" (elimination of mechanical

Air France ordered the first Airbus A320s in 1981. It was to become an outstanding success world-wide. By 2010 more than 5,000 of this wide-bodied twin-jet had been ordered. (McDonough)

controls) technology. In due course, the A320 series, including the smaller A319 and A318, and the larger A321, with as many as 200 seats, was to be an outstanding success. By 2010, more than 5,000 had been ordered.

Only one month after the initial A320 order, a competitive challenge arose not from another airline, but from surface transport. Seven years after the Japanese had opened the world's first high speed rail service (more than 100-mph average speed), France was in the European vanguard when it introduced the T.G.V. (Train à Grande Vitesse). The first line, from Paris to Lyon, covered the 250-mile journey in less than two hours and made immediate inroads into Air Inter's traffic, to the extent that the on-the-hour schedule soon dwindled to only two or three flights a day. The early 1980s witnessed France's flagship airline holding on financially, but only marginally so. It had many affiliates, especially in Africa, where French remained the language of commerce in the former colonies, and it owned a prestigious hotel chain and other service-oriented concerns. Even so, in 1982, Air France lost $105 million (much of it no doubt on the Concorde), and it experienced low load factors on all routes except its route to New York. Maintaining the tradition of quick recuperation, it recovered, with stricter cost controls and better scheduling to restore its load factor to better than break-even.

Much of the airline's recovery was under the direction of the new chairman, Bernard Attali, who replaced the ageing fleet of Boeing 727 tri-jets with the more economical 108-seat Boeing 737 twin-jets. Air France's extended interests in other European regional companies, including Euro Berlin, with its 51% shareholding balanced by Lufthansa's 49%. This airline linked Berlin with the main cities of Germany, together with Pan American's Internal German Service, British European Airways, and Air France itself, until the reunification of Germany in 1991.

Acquisition of U.T.A.

Most important, however, was the setting in motion of a complete merger of the state-sponsored and -supported Air France with the independent **Union de Transports Aériens (U.T.A.)** and the internal domestic **Air Inter**. Union de Transports Aériens controlled 36% of Air Inter and Air France 37%. The initial agreement was announced in January 1990 but the final vote to merge did not occur until 29 December 1992. By this time, Air France was losing money heavily—$581 million in 1992 alone—and seeking to make alliances everywhere, while, at the same time, facing opposition from across the Atlantic. The airline's debt rose to $6.2 billion, and the loss for 1993 was $1.3 billion. France's national airline was close to bankruptcy. In January 1994, Christian Blanc was appointed chairman-CEO and was charged with a formidable rescue plan. He faced multiple problems: sales severely below forecast; delay in buying control of Air Inter, and thus losing much traffic feed for long-haul routes; high salaries, low productivity, and complex organization; and a heterogeneous fleet, 154 aircraft comprised 24 types with 33 different cabin layouts.

In March 1994, the rescue plan was announced and met a drastic situation with drastic measures, imposed as a condition of a $3.39 billion capital injection from the government. No job was cut, but salaries were frozen and early retirement helped to reduce staff numbers. The company structure was reorganized into five profit centers, and the growth plan was reduced to 2% per year. Meridien Hotels was sold for $140 million. The struggle was hard ($510 million lost in 1994), and the cards were stacked as the airline tried to manipulate alliances with other airlines, and change route schedules to reduce numbers in favor of more frequencies. All this took place against the background of the European Union's air transport market being completely deregulated as of 1 April 1997.

In June of that year, after agreements with several domestic regional airlines, a promising innovation was La Navette (the Shuttle) in which eighteen 142- to 206-seat Airbus A319/320/321s were allocated to operate from Paris (Orly) to Toulouse, Marseilles, and Nice.

Prelude to a New Era

The sixth president in 12 years was Jean-Cyril Spinetta. He too was destined, at first, to follow a hard road. On 9 April 1998, the first Boeing 777-200 entered service, which helped to improve the fleet's operating economics. Then in June 1998, the pilots went on strike, but eventually agreed to a seven-year salary freeze, just in time for France to host the World Cup. Meanwhile, a combination of the various economy measures had been successful, for Air France made a profit of $273 million in 1998. And this was in spite of the European Court of Justice annulling the French government's massive bailout of the airline in March 1994.

The final decade of the 20th century had not been easy for France's flag-carrier, but aside from all the political wrangling, international negotiations, and political maneuverings, Air France did attend to the essential business of running a good airline. In February 1999 it signed a partnership agreement with **TAM Brazilian Airlines**, the up-and-coming company that was threatening the airline establishment in Brazil and that had ordered 40 twin-engined Airbuses. In the following month, the Navette shuttle was extended to Bordeaux, and during 2000 Air France

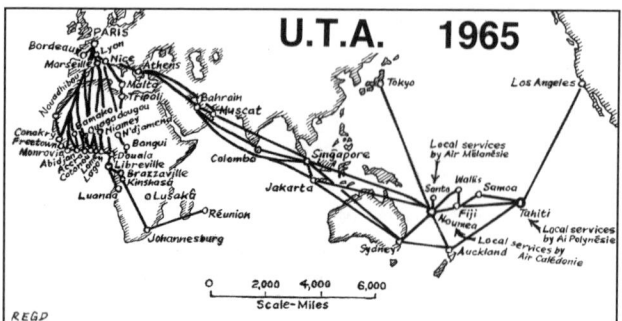

Before its final acquisition by Air France in 1992, U.T.A. (the merger of U.A.T. and T.A.I.) had created a large intercontinental network. Air France retained the Atlantic routes, plus Dakar and Madagascar in Africa. U.T.A. served all the west African French-speaking countries, and French territories in the Pacific.

strengthened its arrangements with the French domestic independents, to consolidate its dominance of the home market. In 1999 this had accounted for more than 26 million passenger boardings, in spite of the growing influence of the T.G.V. high speed inter-city train services.

The 21st century heralded another case of the positive and the negative for Air France. On 22 June 2000, it announced plans to order 10 Airbus A3XX 555-686-seat double-decked giant airliners, following quickly on the heels of Emirates and Singapore Airlines, which had been the launch customers. This decision placed France's airline at the forefront of a new generation of globe-circling airliners, as far-reaching as the introduction of the Boeing 747 had been in 1970. This time, however, there would be no Pan American Airways to dominate the Atlantic skies, and Air France would, in due course, operate the Airbus A380 (as the A3XX would become) on the prestige route between New York and Paris, achieved on 13 November 2009.

Any euphoria that Air France might have enjoyed in the days following this important announcement was quickly dashed as, on 25 July 2000, one of its Concorde supersonic jets was destroyed when, taking off from Paris's Charles de Gaulle Airport, a burst tire, caused by debris on the runway, together with accompanying magnesium shreds from the wheels, caused an instant and devastating fire and the crash of the aircraft. 109 passengers and crew, plus four people on the ground, were killed, and the Concorde fleet was taken out of service for more than a year. It did not return until 7 November 2001; but its days were numbered, and the five remaining aircraft were retired from service on 31 May 2003. Also, British Airways had grounded its fleet on 15 August 2000 and retired its seven aircraft on 24 October 2003 to bring the supersonic era irrevocably to an end.

On 21 December, facing the inevitable trends in the air transport industry that demanded worldwide international groupings, the U.S. Department of Transportation tentatively approved an alliance of Air France, Delta, Alitalia, and the Czech C.S.A., to be known as Skyteam, and including agreements with AeroMexico and Korean Air.

The Great Merger with K.L.M.

Such maneuvers paled into insignificance on 1 October 2003, when Air France announced jointly with **K.L.M.** a deal in which Air France would buy for $909 million the Netherlands airline, which was losing money heavily. This was a merger of enormous magnitude. Just as Air France had close links, amounting to control, with many smaller companies, K.L.M. had a long-standing relationship with Northwest Airlines, fourth biggest in the United States, and a more recent agreement with Continental Airlines. It also owned K.L.M.-U.K., 80% of **Transavia**, and 50% of **Martinair**. The final agreement, under which K.L.M. would continue to operate under its own colors, was signed on 15 October 2003. The combined fleet numbered 556 aircraft, operating to 226 destinations. The merger was completed on 3 May 2004, under which Air France acquired 89% of K.L.M. shares. It thus became the biggest airline in Europe, and the biggest international airline in the world—and a profitable one, making $1.2 billion in 2005.

Air France's financial problems during the late 1900s did not prevent the maintenance of high operational standards. Its fleet of Boeing 747-400s (left) and Airbus A340s (right) ensured that its intercontinental services were among the world's best. (McDonough)

Chapter 28: Germany Regains a Leading Role

Lufthansa Consolidates

Up to 1939, the German national airline had been, by a substantial margin, the biggest airline in Europe, and could boast the most modern airliner fleet in the world. Because of the political residue of the ashes of that war, Germany was not allowed to resurrect Deutsche Lufthansa until 1955, and for its trading name, it diplomatically dropped the first word. To start a national airline again, completely from scratch, was no easy task, and a decade was to pass after the end of the war before the new **Lufthansa** (German Airlines) got into its stride.

The first domestic routes had started on 1 April 1955, and intra-European routes on 15 May, with 44-seat Convair 340s. On 8 June, a Lockheed 1049G Super Constellation opened trans-Atlantic service to New York. By the time the first Boeing 707 opened the first jet service to New York on 17 March 1960, the intercontinental network had already reached South America on 15 August 1956, which, including a pool agreement with Air France, revived memories of pre-war pioneering with that airline. The Middle East was reached on 12 September 1956, and the route was extended to Bangkok on 5 November 1959. Back in Europe, the turboprop Vickers Viscount 802 went into service in October 1958. A steady program of route expansion, flown by the best airliners, and operated efficiently with excellent service standards, soon established a reputation for Lufthansa that was second to none. The route network reached West Africa (Lagos) on 4 March 1962, Johannesburg on 14 May of the same year, and a trans-Polar route to Tokyo opened on 28 May 1964. Nearer home, the first 119-seat Europa Jet, which Lufthansa called its Boeing 727 tri-jets, started service on 12 April 1964.

In February 1965, Lufthansa's technical leadership was confirmed when, for the first time in history, a new airliner type was launched, not by an airline of the United States, but by a foreign airline. Lufthansa became the launching customer for the 103-seat twin-engined Boeing 737. The choice of wing-mounted engines seemed to be going against the then-current preference, initiated by the French Caravelle in 1958, for the power plant to be mounted on the rear of the fuselage. Lufthansa's Boeing 737 City Jets went into service on 10 February 1968. In retrospect, the wisdom of the German airline's analysis and bold decision, made only a decade after the airline, phoenix-like, had begun a new life, was astonishing. For the Boeing 737, at first regarded by the industry as breaking an established design trend, went on, with its technically advanced variants, to break all records in production quantities. During the next 40 years, more than 8,000 of these money makers were to come off the production lines at Seattle.

The consolidation process in Germany had continued unabated. New destinations were added to the Lufthansa map almost every month, often trail-blazing an airline path to places where others had hesitated, such as to the cities of eastern Europe, still within the political and commercial orbit of Moscow, on 26 August 1967; to Bolivia's La Paz on 7 April 1968; to Addis Ababa, Ethiopia; and to Jeddah, Saudi Arabia, on 7 May 1969. The exploding charter market, especially the inclusive air tours, was watched carefully, and on 1 January 1968, **Sudflug** was acquired as a wholly owned subsidiary, to add to **Condor Flugdienst**, the largest German non-scheduled airline that had been owned by Lufthansa since 1961.

An important step in international corporate organization was made when, on 14 March 1969, in response to another (K.S.S.U.) European association, Lufthansa became a leading member of the ATLAS Group, whose other members were Air France, Alitalia, and the Belgian SABENA. The idea behind such groupings was to avoid unnecessary duplication of costly and labor-intensive maintenance. Each member was responsible for selected spares holdings, repair, and overhaul of individual aircraft types and engines that were common to all. In contrast with K.S.S.U., which was based on the commonality of Douglas airliners, ATLAS was based on the products of Boeing.

Lufthansa itself was totally satisfied with both the aircraft and the airline support from Seattle, and reciprocated by taking delivery of its first wide-bodied Boeing 747 and putting it into service, Frankfurt-New York, on 26 April 1970. But it also recognized that this 340-seater (even in generous mixed-class) would only be economical on the densest routes, such as those between the world's major cities, and so backed up the 747s with an order for 270-seat Douglas DC-10-30s on 23 September of the same year, and which went into service in January 1974. (The last Viscount turboprop had been retired on 31 March 1971.)

Later that year, in November, at an International Air Transport Association (IATA) conference in Montreal, Lufthansa made it clear that it was once again a European leader by refusing to agree to a majority view by that worldwide airline agency on a new North Atlantic fares package. As it owned Condor, it could participate in the affinity group market indirectly, and still charge normal rates itself. In fact, this was a trend that was fast becoming acceptable, because air travelers were demanding far more flexibility than the traditional airlines had been willing to offer.

Airbus Sponsorship

The next announcement from the Cologne headquarters clearly confirmed that, for all its support for the products of Boeing and Douglas, Lufthansa was—in consort with the German manufacturing participation in the French, Toulouse-based Airbus—solidly European. On 20 December 1972 it ordered three twin-engined 240-seat wide-bodied Airbus A300Bs, plus four more on option. The first one went into service on 1 April 1976, so that, together with Air France, the two national airlines of the Airbus promoters and builders were thus in solid support of a potential European manufacturing effort to vie with the Americans for the world airliner market

The late 1970s were marked by constant reminders that the German airline was progressing on all fronts. On 14 December 1976, the first long-range Boeing 747SL went into service to Sydney, Australia, almost as a reminder that such a limited-stop route was the answer to the once-alleged advantage of a Concorde service. Lufthansa's plethora of technical and operational planning moves did not include a supersonic venture. By April 1977, all its flights to the United States, west coast as well as east coast, were with wide-bodied equipment. Orders for bigger and better Boeings and Airbuses continued apace, although the most important was on 2 April 1979, for 25 (plus 25 on option) of a smaller Airbus, the A310.

Long-range expansion and high-capacity aircraft fleets did not exclude close attention to markets nearer to home—less spectacular for aviation news headlines, but essential for feeding traffic into the main hubs at Frankfurt, Hamburg, and Munich, On 29 June 1978, Lufthansa bought a controlling interest in **Deutsche Luftverkehr GmbH (D.L.T.)**, which had originally been founded as a local air taxi service at Emden on 11 December 1970. The D.L.T. fleet included such aircraft types as the 50-seat Fokker F-50 and the Shorts S-330 and the Embraer 120, both with 30-seats. Lufthansa had also, during these years, become not only the biggest air cargo operator in Europe, but also the biggest in the whole world. On 10 March 1977, it had recognized the importance of air cargo by founding **German Cargo Services (G.C.S.)** and steadily expanded its scope.

Intermodal Initiative

One of the airline's more visionary operational developments occurred on 27 March 1982, when a new Lufthansa service was introduced on the Frankfurt -Bonn-Cologne-Dusseldorf route. This was an important traffic generator, serving the biggest cities along the Rhine, but clearly with inter-city stages far too short for economic operations by any type of commercial aircraft. The solution was the **Lufthansa Airport Express**, a special train, operated by the Deutsche Bundesbahn, but marketed as a Lufthansa service, and sold with airline tickets. The train station at Frankfurt was at the airport, so that air-to-train transfers could be made with minimum inconvenience. This example of intra-modal transport was an outstanding innovation, for decades later, Germany's Inter City Express (ICE) high speed trains would supersede the airline's bold experiment as, in the 21st century, all of western Europe adopted such trains to span the continent.

The bold incursion into surface transport was welcomed on 1 April 1982 with an important management change, when Heinz Ruhnau became deputy chairman and succeeded Chairman Herbert Culmann three months later. Reinhardt Abraham took over as his deputy. They oversaw the continuation of fleet expansion (more 747s, 737s, and an order for 250-seat Airbus A340-300s on 14 February 1987) and additional routes to big cities near (e.g., Eindhoven by D.L.T. on 1 April 1986) and far (e.g., Washington on 1 April 1987). The map showed 160 destinations in 81 countries. Yet the main task was to be in the political field, as the time was approaching when the two Germanys, west and east, would come together when the Soviet Union collapsed in 1991, and Lufthansa would absorb the east's **Interflug**.

Germany Unites and Lufthansa Moves East

In August 1989, Lufthansa reached an agreement with Air France to form a joint airline, **Aero Berlin** (the name changed soon afterward to **Euro Berlin**) to link Berlin with the main cities in West Germany. In November 1989, to herald the downfall of East Germany, the Berlin Wall, which had been erected as a protective political gesture by the communist regime, began to fall. When the Berlin Wall fell, events moved swiftly for Lufthansa. Early in September, as the great Pan American Airways approached its doom, the German airline bought its Internal German Service (I.G.S.), including its nine Boeing 727-200s, for $150 million. Almost as an anachronism, dating back to the partition of Germany at the end of the Second World War, no German airline had been permitted to serve Berlin, which was isolated within Soviet-controlled territory from West Germany. On 28 October 1990, the flying crane symbol, the oldest airline insignia in the world, once again flew into Berlin's Tegel and Schoenfeld airports, in the former French and Soviet Zones, respectively.

Tightening Belts

The intensive expansion activity had cost a lot of money, as competition intensified, partly because Delta Air Line took over Pan American's routes and was able to offer multiple connections across the Atlantic, at Lufthansa's expense. Domestically too, several independent companies were stealing traffic, and ICE rail services were improving all across Germany. At the end of 1992, Juergen Weber, who had taken over from Ruhnau, announced that the airline had lost $500 million during the previous two years. Almost an indictment on an organization that had prided itself on efficiency, the reasons for the losses were described as an unnecessarily large workforce, excess capacity, and an inefficient network. 3,000 jobs were cut, 26 aircraft were pulled out of service, and routes were consolidated.

Nevertheless, the ICE (not yet truly high speed) rail connection between the Rhineland cities was increased in June 1993 to 16 daily round-trips, with four from Frankfurt to Stuttgart. Overcoming the political problems of Chinese objections to Lufthansa service to Taiwan, the Condor subsidiary opened service to Taipei on 4 July 1993. A few months later, on 4 October, an alliance was signed with United Airlines, with full code-sharing to begin on 15 January the next year. Following a worldwide trend in airline politics, the German cabinet voted, in March 1994, to relinquish its 51% shareholding in its national airline, without, however, suggesting that state ownership had contributed to the recent problems.

Renewed Expansion on All Fronts

More than most other airlines, Lufthansa regarded its air freight services as important sources of revenue, and in April 1996, it

Lufthansa's solidly established organization enabled it to maintain its airline ascendancy as a world leader. Like Air France, its aircraft, such as the Boeing 747-400s, matched all competition. (McDonough)

augmented those to the Indian subcontinent with Douglas DC-8 and Boeing 727s, routed via Sharjah, adding Hyderabad (one of India's "silicon-valley" computer hubs) to the seven other terminals there and ordered five MD-11 freighters to underline its faith in the market. On other fronts, its Cityline became Europe's second-biggest regional airline (Switzerland's Crossair was No. 1), with its fleet of Canadian and Avro feeder-liners carrying more than three million passengers a year to 58 destinations in 23 countries. Franchise arrangements were made with **Augsburg Airways**, **S.A.S.**, and the French **AirLittoral**, and in May 1997, **Lufthansa** became one of the members of the Star Alliance, which combined code-sharing and bilateral agreements with Air Canada, S.A.S., United Airlines, and Thai International. Alliances were also effected in December with Singapore Airlines and in March 1998 with All Nippon Airways.

Meanwhile, in October 1997, in a far-reaching corporate move, the German government sold its remaining 37.5% stake in Lufthansa, which was thus no longer a state-owned or state-controlled corporation, but shared substantial investment by the Deutsche Postbank, the Deutsche Bahn, and the Nordrhein und Westfalen and Muenchener Gesellschaft für Luftverkehrswerke. During 1999, Lufthansa bought a 20% shareholding in British Midland Airways, and made important code-sharing agreements with France's Regional Airlines in the same year and with Air China and Italy's Air One in 2000. Spreading its European net further, it acquired 25% of German regional **Eurowings** early in February and had extended this shareholding to 49% by the end of 2001.

During the closing years of the 20th century, Lufthansa's fleet had been augmented in line with the traffic requirements. In 2000, the airline had 312 airliners, 132 of them Airbuses of all series, 120 Boeing 737s and 747s, also of various series, plus 42 Canadian CRJs and 18 Avro RJ85s with CityLine. But the next purchase was more than just another order; it was a statement of confidence in the future of air transport. On 6 December 2001, Lufthansa confirmed an order for fifteen 550-seat (mixed-class) giant Airbus double-decked A380s, for $12 billion. This was the second largest order for this European competitor to Boeing's hitherto dominance of the commercial airliner market.

Low-Cost Market Erosion

When Wolfgang Mayrhuber took over from Juergen Weber as Lufthansa's chairman in 2002, Lufthansa's main task was to confront the growing threat of the low-cost, no-frills airlines that had successfully exploited the rights of any airline within the European Union to fly almost anywhere they liked between any of the member countries, led by Ryanair and easyJet. Merging retail giant Karstadt-Quelle with air-tour giant Neckermann, Condor Flugdienst, and the age-old British travel agent Thomas Cook to form an airline under the name of the latter had not worked out. In the age of computers, together with the Internet, travel agencies were becoming redundant. So was LSG Skychefs, the world's biggest airline caterer, possibly because in-flight meal service was declining as a traffic-generating amenity. Other diversified assets that were disposed of were Globeground, Amadeus Global Travel, and 25% of DHL International.

One interesting experiment, however, was to try to match traffic demand with capacity offered on some long-haul routes with special attention to the business-passengers who were prepared to pay high fares for comfort, including the fully reclining lounge seats what were gaining popularity. In June 2002, a partnership agreement was made with **Privatair**, a company that specialized in such a market. On behalf of Lufthansa, after some trial flights on the Dusseldorf-New York (Newark) route, service began with 48-seat Boeing Business Jet 2 version of the 737, as well as 48-seat Airbus A319Rs. Privatair also operated from Munich to Newark, and provided a 126-seat shuttle service on a circular route, Toulouse-Hamburg-Bristol (Filton)-Broughton (north Wales) specifically to serve the various sub-assembly plants of the Toulouse-based Airbus production organization. That such a service was justified was a clear measure of the size and stature of the European manufacturer. These were the locations of the sub-assemblies of the new double-decked Airbus A380, and to show its confidence in and preparation for this new airliner dynasty, and recognizing that India was going to need it, Lufthansa cooperated with the authorities at Mumbai to ensure that the airport at that city, with upward of 18 million people, was ready for the giant airliner.

Back to Basics

Lufthansa had thus taken care of the future flag-ship upgrading need by ordering the big Airbus A380 (see above). It was also taking care of future route extension and expansion needs into areas where the entire worldwide balance of economic strength was changing, namely, China and India. On 1 May 2003, Shenzhen, the new city near Hong Kong—only a swamp three decades previously, but now a thriving, 2 million–population industrial center—and Qingdao, home to the famous brewery that the Germans had founded before the First World War, joined the extensive overseas network. Munich was emerging as a major gateway, paralleling Frankfurt, while Charlotte, North Carolina, became the nineteenth North American destination.

Nearer to home, Lufthansa consolidated its dominance of the traditional European market by an historic corporate scoop. On 21 March 2005, an agreement was reached with **Swiss**

International Airlines, the newcomer that had succeeded the bankrupt Swissair, for a joint shareholding status. The German airline could easily afford it, for the €980 million (more than $1 billion) loss in 2003 had been dramatically reversed to a net profit in 2004, and the union was soon approved by the European Competition authorities. Lufthansa's stake was 49% and one condition of the deal was that it had to surrender 64 airport slots in Germany, Scandinavia, Zurich, and Vienna.

Further to secure its European network foundations, and as part of the Zukunft Kont (Future Continental) initiative launched in 2003, to reduce costs and improve European and domestic operations, Hamburg was given a traffic boost. This was done by expanding **Germanwings**, a subsidiary of Eurowings (49% Lufthansa), whose fleet comprised 20 Airbus A319 and A320s.

The Rise of Air Berlin

Following the end of the Second World War, Germany's ruined capital city had been separated from most of the rest of the country. The Soviet Union had created East Germany and controlled the eastern sector of Berlin, which became the capital of the satellite republic. The western sectors of the city were surrounded, and in 1948, only a remarkable airborne logistics operation, the famous Berlin Airlift, saved the city from being absorbed by Moscow's political agent. Thereafter, western Berlin not only survived, but began to restore itself, and though communications with the west were not easy, industry was revived, and the city gradually reasserted itself as a thriving particpant in the capitalist world. Among the new businesses that took the risk of establishment there, and with an optimistic view of the eventual outcome of events, was **Air Berlin**. It was founded in 1978 by former Pan American pilot Kim Lundgren primarily as a charter airline, but unlike most of that category, it did not depend on travel agents; it sold seats individually. It did well, as the people of Berlin eagerly took advantage of cheap flights to the Mediterranean, especially Palma, Majorca.

Its early fleet grew to include Boeing 737s, and by 2005, with 55 aircraft, it could claim to be the third largest low-fare airline in Europe, after Ireland's Ryanair and England's easyJet. In that year, it showed its mettle by ordering 100 Airbus A320s, which could have been a signal for enthusiastic confidence in the future. This was confirmed in August 2006, when it went public and then, in a surprise move, announced the takeover of **Deutsche B.A.** This constituted the emergence of a new player in the upper echelons of the German air transport industry, in which the non-Lufthansa airlines, catering mainly for inclusive tours and closely allied to the travel agencies, were a substantial element.

The German Independents

The independent airlines in Germany, catering for a burgeoning overseas tourist market as the country entered its period of economic growth, contrasted with the trend in Great Britain. The British independents had to fight tooth and nail to overcome government regulations that hindered innovations that might encourage people to fly. Lufthansa, Germany's "chosen instrument," on the other hand, hedged its bets, and far from opposing the idea of non-scheduled charter operations, offered encouragement in many ways—ways which, moreover, were condoned by a pragmatic government administration.

The main contenders for this potentially huge market were drawn from three essential sources. Lufthansa was the existing national airline; Lufttransport Unternehmen (L.T.U.) depended on basic demographics; and Hapag-Lloyd already had a history of transportation, albeit not in aviation but in shipping, and its founders had participated in both heavier-than-air and lighter-than-air pioneering before Lufthansa was formed.

The channel by which Lufthansa put its foot into the door of the charter market was by taking a substantial interest, by direct investment and practical assistance, through **Condor Flugdienst**, formed on 25 October 1961. This had been a merger based on Deutscher Flugdienst GmbH, which had been founded on 21 December 1955 as a small charter airline by Lufthansa, Deutsche Bundesbahn, and the Norddeutscher-Lloyd and Hamburg-Amerika shipping lines. This little company, equipped only with 1940s-vintage Vickers Vikings and, later, Convair 240s, thus set an example of interest in intermodality in an embryo market with airline, railroad, and shipping shareholdings. However, Lufthansa bought all the shares in 1959–60. It then bought another small airline, Condor Luftreederei, from the Oetker group, and merged the two into Condor Flugdienst.

Lufthansa promptly transferred two of its Vickers Viscounts to Condor, which thus became the first German charter airline to operate turbine-powered equipment. These were soon joined by Boeing 727s and Fokker Friendships in 1965, and by 1968, Condor became the first German all-jet airline, with Boeing 707s leased from its parent. It continued to take the lead in the European non-scheduled field of operations by introducing, on 1 May 1971, a 478-seat Boeing 747. This aircraft, named *Fritz*, and its sister ship, *Max*, began the trans-Atlantic route on 14 May 1972.

The authorities cast a blind eye on the subject of the definition of scheduled versus non-scheduled services. Condor flights seemed to take off from Frankfurt at the same time every morning, a situation that would have caused consternation in the corridors of power in London. But the momentum continued, with expansion during 1973 to many destinations in east Asia, even as far as Tahiti in the South Pacific. Eight Boeing 727-200 Series were also purchased. German tourism had by this time become a major industry. Nevertheless, the intense competition for the market inevitably created a "survival of the fittest" condition, and Condor was fortunate in having a rich and favored parent. Others were not so lucky. One challenger had at first appeared to make its mark, but suffered from being undercapitalized and perhaps from over-reaching. **Luftverkehrsunternehmen Atlantis** had been founded, as Nordseeflug-Sylter Lufttransportunterenehmen, on Westerland, on the North Sea island of Sylt, on 20 July 1965, as a modest operator to the mainland with one Douglas DC-3. It changed its name on 25 July 1968, when it decided to enter the international field, with a 104-seat Douglas

DC-7C, and specializing in carrying foreign "guest" workers on a "VFR" (visiting friends and relations) to and from their families back home. Atlantis added DC-8-33 jets in 1968, went public in 1969 (6,300 small shareholders), operated across the Atlantic to justify its name, added Douglas DC-9s in 1970, and embarked on an ambitious program of low fares. Its Frankfurt-New York $140 round-trip (compared to Lufthansa's IATA-based $395 one way) was launched on a wave of explosive tourist growth in Germany; but this did not last. Atlantis ordered two 300-seat Douglas DC-10s in 1971 and tried to obtain authority to operate scheduled services. German inclusive-tour traffic suffered a severe decline in 1972. Atlantis's bubble burst, and it ceased operations in 1973.

Meanwhile, during the 1970s, Condor was consolidating and restructured the fleet. The 747s were ideal for the dense traffic on, for example, Frankfurt-New York, but on a dispersed network, with multiple destinations, the almost-500 seats were too often difficult to fill. They were replaced by 373-seat DC-10-30s and long-range 309-seat Airbus A300s. Then, in 1981, Condor was able to use four of Lufthansa's large order for Boeing 737-200s. By 1988, its share of the German charter market was 25%, about the same as L.T.U.'s, but with Lufthansa behind it, Condor was far more secure in maintaining that level. With the fall of the Berlin Wall the next year, a new market opened, as East Germans were typically not able to travel. Condor's passenger numbers doubled to six million annually, and its market share, by 1995, grew to 33%. To cope with the expansion, an order was placed in September 1996 for twelve 350-seat Boeing 757-300s (with an option for another 12) for delivery in 1999, to augment its fleet of 9 long-range Boeing 767s, 18 earlier 757s, 4 leased 737s, and 5 DC-10s.

To illustrate the key role that the German charter airlines played in the thriving tourist market, Condor observed that one Boeing 757 could "support" 6,000 hotel beds at a typical Mediterranean resort with a thrice-daily service. The distinction between charter and scheduled operations was now quite blurred; a quarter of Condor's flights were listed on a timetable, and it was even offering premier-class seats on some routes. By the close of the century, the need to coordinate the airline services with mass marketing of tourism through recognized agencies had become inevitable. On 18 September 1997, **Condor** merged with Karstadt-Quelle's giant Neckermann-und-Reisen agency in a joint venture, C.&N.–Condor-Neckermann Touristik, which opened for business on 1 January 1998. At the same time, **Condor Berlin** was founded as a subsidiary, with a fleet of 8 Airbus A320s.

Not content with its expansion to the east, C&N looked westward, and in December 2002 took a significant share of the charter-tourist market in Great Britain by acquiring Thomas Cook (U.K.), a famous name in the tourist industry, dating back to the 19th century. The name was temporarily adopted as **C.&N.–Thomas Cook**, but reverted to the Condor marketing name in June 2004. The combined fleet totaled 75 airliners, served by 3,800 travel agencies, with sales of €7.5 billion per year.

The Importance of Demographics

Although Lufthansa's headquarters are in Cologne, the hub of its operations is in Frankfurt. It is one of Germany's larger cities, and, as a banking center, possibly the richest; but it is not among the major population centers. Berlin, Hamburg, and Munich individually are the country's largest, but by far the biggest urban concentration is the group of contiguous cities along the Ruhr River and the nearby Wüpper and Rhine Rivers. Together their population totals about six million, making this conurbation the third largest in western Europe. Intensely industrial, there is much wealth, and thus considerable discretionary income to stimulate travel.

The development of a regional airline network was already under way. In May 1964, the Nord-Rhein-Westphalia (N.R.W.) land (provincial) authorities sponsored a trial period of operations, based at Düsseldorf, and serving Luxemburg, Cologne, Essen, Saarbrücken, and other cities as far as Bremen and Rotterdam. The franchised airlines were Air Lloyd, Condor, and Suddeutsche Flugservice, using small 6-seat Beech Queenairs and Piaggio P-166s. This experiment ended in December 1965, service to smaller airports abandoned, and flights resumed on 1 April 1966 by **Lufttransport Unternehmen (L.T.U.)**.

Founded by Kurt Conle in Frankfurt in 1955, with a modest fleet of small Bristol 170s and Vickers Vikings, and one of 38 airlines founded in West Germany during the "economic miracle" period, L.T.U. had moved to Düsseldorf in 1959. Under the direction of Ernst-Juergen Ahrens, Düsseldorf was identified as the base city for its airport installations and for its proximity to the Ruhr—within an hour's drive on the *autobahn* of 20 million people. L.T.U. quickly developed a healthy charter business for air tourism, as well as the regional routes. The piston-engined aircraft were supplemented by Nord 262 and Fokker F-27 turboprops and in 1965, with Caravelles, becoming the first charter airline anywhere in the world to use new, rather than secondhand airliners.

On 1 April 1966, an agreement was signed with Lufthansa to operate regular regional routes from Düsseldorf, as the national airline found these local operations to be impractical. The provincial government of N.R.W. invested 1.8 million deutschemarks (£190,000) in 1968, to create **Interregional Fluggesellschaft (I.F.G.)** with participation from Lufthansa. Services began to Saarbrücken, Hanover, and Bremen, with Nord 262s and Fokker F-27s. Two other small non-scheduled airlines joined I.F.G.: **Bavaria Fluggesellschaft**, based in Munich, and **General Air**, based in Hamburg. Interestingly, this post–Second World War promotion of regional airlines seemed to echo post–First World War support for air transport, which helped to stimulate the intense air-mindedness that has characterized the German population.

Such was the patronage of L.T.U., so close to its clientele, that it began to publish flight schedules and, in June 1973, took a giant leap by taking delivery of its first 331-seat Lockheed L.1011 TriStar. The timing was bad, however; it coincided with a worldwide economic depression and an increase in fuel prices. Although deliveries of more L-1011s were delayed, relief came when, in June 1976, the U.S. Civil Aeronautics Board authorized flights to the United States. Within a few years, L.T.U. was flying regularly (but not scheduled) to New York, the U.S. west coast, Florida, the Bahamas, the Mediterranean, Sri Lanka, and throughout the Mediterranean—a far cry from local routes in Westphalia.

When it joined IATA in 1990, the Conle family still had a 61% shareholding, while the Westdeutsches Landesbank (WestLB) held 33% of a group that included L.T.U.-Sud in Munich; L.T.E. in Palma, Majorca; L.T.C. Catering; and L.T.I. International Hotels, which operated three ships in Egypt on the Nile. It was operating 26 large airliners: 6 L.1011s, 4 Boeing 767s, 4 McDonnell-Douglas MD-11s, and 12 Boeing 757s. In 1995, it became only the fourth airline to operate the Airbus A330-300.

On 1 January 1999, the powerful SwissAir (SAir) Group acquired a 49.9% share in L.T.U., and WestLB (the largest shareholder of the industrial conglomerate Preussag) was obliged by the German anti-cartel office to sell most of its shares. Known as the European Leisure Group, SAir had substantial shares in Air Europe (Italy), Volair and Sobelair (Belgium), and Balair (Switzerland). Although SAir planned to reduce the total seat capacity of the airline by one-fifth, in May 2000 it ordered 18 A320s and 7 A330s, in a move to standardize the fleet with Airbuses.

In August 2000, the German retail giant Rewe agreed to purchase the SAir Group's share, together with WestLB's remaining 10%. This takeover of two-thirds of the ownership of what was now the second largest airline in Germany (after Lufthansa-Condor) was approved by the government and by the European Commission in January 2001. Even so, L.T.U. reported a €224 million ($202 million) loss for the year 2000. In November 2001, SAir sold its stares to Stadtparkasse Düsseldorf, a partly state-owned savings bank, for €1 (89¢), with the NordRhein state government providing a €102 million guarantee. The WestLB and the city of Düsseldorf were also involved in the rescue plan, with any shortfall backed by Rewe. By the end of 2005, the financial maneuvering was completed with a minimum €200 million package headed by Rewe and the Deutsche Bank.

The Importance of a Name

Similar to Lufthansa's strength being derived from an indisputable history and L.T.U.'s following basic demographics, another well-financed transport group also had immaculate credentials. **Hapag-Lloyd Flug GmbH** was formed in 1970 when two world-renowned German shipping companies North German Lloyd and Hamburg-Amerika merged. Beginning with a small fleet of three 131-seat Boeing 727-100s, the policy was openly directed to challenge the Lufthansa-Condor dominance on a broad front, both in airline operations and in the related air tourism business. During the early 1970s, with 12.37%, Hapag-Lloyd became the largest shareholder of Touristic Union International (T.U.I.), which, in turn, held half of the German charter and vacation business. With another associated shareholder, Wilhelm Scharnow, Hapag-Lloyd had 18% of this huge tourist organization. By 1976, after forming an Air Freight Division, and now with eight Boeings, Hapag-Lloyd was carrying a million tourists a year.

On 1 July 1977, it absorbed the operations of the Schorghuber companies as well as **Germanair** and their 315-seat Airbuses. The main shareholders now included the powerful Deutscher, Dresdner, and Allianz Versicherung banks. Under the direction of managing director Claus Wülfers, and unlike its rivals Condor and L.T.U., Hapag-Lloyd's policy was to concentrate on the short- and medium-haul traffic, mainly to Mediterranean resorts, and to eschew long-haul ambitions. By the 1990s, its fleet comprised seven Airbus A310-200/300 and 17 Boeing 737-400/500, all short-medium-haul airliners. They were carrying more than three million passengers a year, and the airline ranked third among the German air charter airlines, with 16.5% of the market, against Condor's 33% and L.T.U.'s 29%.

Early in September 1997, Hapag-Lloyd was purchased by the huge industrial conglomerate Preussag, in which WestLB was the largest shareholder, and this was approved by the anti-cartel office in March 1998. (See also Preussag's involvement in L.T.U., above.) In April 1998, this third-place German airline was the launch customer of the latest Boeing 737 variant, the 189-seat -800, with a total order for 16.

Air tour operation in Europe had, at the turn of the century, over-reached national boundaries, and had become multinational, with interlocking relationships, associations, and cross-ownerships transcending traditional corporate systems. Hapag-Lloyd was in the mainstream of this trend as, in May 2002, its owner, Preussag, renamed itself **T.U.I.**, after its better-known leading tour operator **Touristic Union International**. With subsidiary branches in Britain (Britannia), Sweden (Nordic), Italy (Neos), France (Corsair), and Poland (White Eagle), as well as its own German airline, it commanded a total combined fleet of 88 airliners, including all the Boeing types, and a few Airbuses. At the end of the year, on 3 December, it launched a companion budget airline, **Hapag-Lloyd Express**, based in Cologne, with a second hub at Hanover, and equipped with 148-seat Boeing 737s and a few Fokker 100s, all leased from Germania.

The Other Lloyd

Not to be confused with Hapag-Lloyd, the charter airline **Aero Lloyd** enjoyed considerable success throughout the developmental years of the German air charter market during the 1960s and onward, and, after an initial small fleet of Caravelles, was a faithful Douglas customer for DC-9s and subsequent variants during the 1980s as it developed a healthy business to all the Mediterranean resorts and the Canary Islands. In 1991, it took delivery of a 323-seat MD-11, and in 1994 was able to report a total of almost 3 million passengers. It then turned to twin-engined Airbuses of the A320 series, but after the first one was delivered in 1996, Aero Lloyd's fortunes declined, and it disappeared from the German air charter scene. A rescue operation by Aero Flight in 2004 was insufficient to prevent its complete demise in November 2005. It was a sad end to a once flourishing charter airline that had taken German vacationers to 40 places in the sun, from the islands of the Aegean to Tenerife and Madeira.

German Third-Level Airlines

While plane-loads of sun-seekers flew south, others were able to enjoy a less glamorous, but nevertheless enjoyable few weeks on beaches that were closer to home. There were some places in

Germany, rather like the Scilly Isles in England or the Orkney Islands in Scotland, where short-distance air travel was convenient, often more comfortable, and, with the right equipment, economically possible. The East and North Frisian Islands, off the North Sea coast, were ideal for weekenders from northwest Germany, and the climate was usually pleasantly warm.

The first initiatives, in the 1970s, were by **Luftverkehr Wilhelmshaven-Friesland** and **Frisia Luftverkehr Norddeich (F.L.N.)**. In April 1968, **Ostfriesische Lufttransport (O.L.T.)** began services from Emden, using small aircraft and expanding—if that is the term for development at this level—to six-seat Britten-Norman Islanders. These pioneering third-level airlines were joined by **Bremerhaven Airline** and **Helgoland Airlines** from Bremerhaven and Wilhelmshaven, respectively. F.L.N. was renamed **Luftverkehr Friesland Harle (L.F.H.)** on 1 October 1983, and continued to thrive. Typically, its airplanes made 10 round-trips a day to the island of Wangerooge, from nearby Harle on the mainland, and its five-minute flight time is unlikely to be challenged as the shortest in Germany.

The widely varying demand for airline service, on the one hand for trans-ocean and intercontinental flights of Lufthansa and the big charter companies, and on the other hand for brief, island routes by third-level airlines like L.F.H., has led to a complex situation in Germany that the liberal policies of implied freedom of entry have done little to clarify. One experiment in satisfying the claims of local independent interests and those of the state corporation was the formation (originally in September 1986 as Interot Airways) of **Augsburg Airways** on 1 January 1996. With its fleet of Bombardier twin turboprops, it operated partly under its own name, but mainly as an affiliate of its larger neighbor in Munich, as TEAM Lufthansa.

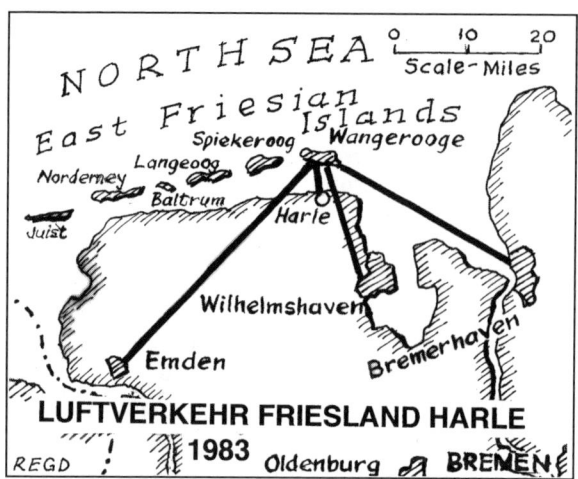

The big jets of Germany's flagship airlines carried tourists across the world's oceans. Meanwhile, on one of the world's shortest air routes, L.F.H. carried a few at a time to the summer sunshine of the North Sea.

Such flexibility in its approach to air transport continues a long tradition of bold initiatives in Germany, some successful, some not, dating back to the introduction of all-metal aircraft in 1919, and the pioneering of trans-Atlantic flying, with airships, depot ships, and both large and long-range landplanes in the 1930s. The range of aircraft, from the 550-seat Airbus 380s to the diminutive types at the lower levels, provide the benefits of air travel to everyone in the country and will be challenged during the 21st century only by the development of the railroad system and the high speed ICE trains—see Chapter 52.

Chapter 29: European Airline Attrition

A Changing Business Environment

From the very beginning of the air transport industry, every country in Europe aspired to own a national airline, as a symbol of their industrial and commercial stature. Because of the realities of economics, flying the flag solely by individual or independent initiatives was impossible without some kind of subsidy so that, in many cases, the airlines were state owned or -supported. The larger countries, Germany, France, Great Britain, and Italy, combined their aerial aspirations with their aircraft production programs. Some smaller countries such as the Netherlands and Belgium, with overseas territories with areas and natural wealth exceeded those of the homelands, developed airlines to serve their distant colonies.

Following the Second World War, however, these empires that characterized much of the political establishment in Europe, fell apart. Competitors for intercontinental air route systems could no longer depend on their overseas territories as a foundation of much of their traffic. The chosen instruments of the larger countries, however, could survive partly because their indigenous populations were sufficient to provide the necessary passenger demands to ensure viability. But as the 20th century drew to a close, with political liberalization over-ruling sovereign rights, and with the national frontiers of Europe effectively disappearing as Europe was federalized, smaller nations could no longer hold their own against larger neighbors. People within the countries of the European Community held common passports and no longer needed visas to visit each other. Except for Great Britain, Switzerland, and the Nordic countries, Europe adopted a common currency. For the airlines, this created a new business environment, one which was not a case, necessarily, of the survival of the fittest. It was the result of the harsh exercise of international political and financial power in the 21st century.

Italy Struggles

A somewhat curious exception to an apparent European airline community dominated by the four biggest countries was Italy. Its population and potential industrial strength were in the same economic stratum as those of Germany, Great Britain, and France. Yet in the post-war era, Italy never seemed to have achieved its full potential, and such a deficiency was reflected in the recurrent tribulations of the national airline, **Alitalia**. Its problems seem not to have been created by any single cause. The country had the necessary infrastructure of population, although the level of affluence of the north was not shared by the south. The elongated geography that linked the main cities of the peninsula, together with the islands of Sicily and Sardinia, should have been ideal for an air transport network. The country is a major Mediterranean tourist destination for the sun-starved nations of northern Europe, and Rome is for Catholics the world over a place to visit some time in their lives. No country can match Italy as a venue for the appreciation of art in all its forms, old and new. But other factors, some of the Italian government's own making, were to cancel out these marketing advantages.

Alitalia had entered the Jet Age full of confidence, with a worldwide network of routes that were parallel to those of all the other intercontinental airlines. In 1964, **Aero Transporte Italiani (A.T.I.)** was hived off as a domestic airline, echoing the system in Britain's and France's B.E.A. and Air Inter, respectively. During the late 1960s, Alitalia was riding the crest of a wave, with a fleet of Douglas DC-8s and DC-9s, Caravelles and Viscounts, with Boeing 747s and even the still-born Boeing 2707 supersonic airliner on order.

On 31 October 1969, Alitalia declared its industry leadership at the annual International Air Transport Association (IATA) international fares conference, held at Lausanne. It denounced the proposed Atlantic "Dallas fare package" for 1970, challenging the accepted cartel-driven rate-fixing device by most of the world's flag-carrying airlines. Alitalia offered lower excursion packages for its Rome-New York route, quickly put these into force on 1 November, and opened wide-bodied Boeing 747 services on 5 June 1970.

Such bold initiatives were not met with success. Like all the world's airlines, the fuel crisis of the early 1970s added to severe financial losses, leading to the appointment, in December 1972, of Umberto Nordio as CEO. On 31 October 1974, he presented a drastic plan to the board that involved the retirement of its 21 DC-8s and 16 Caravelles, to standardize the fleet, and to terminate service to many routes. Approved by the main (75%) shareholder, the Instituto per la Reconstruzione Industriale (I.R.I.). this was followed on 5 December by a recapitalization of the airline, with almost complete ownership by the State, and a large debt was written off.

The country's economy was in trouble, with high unemployment, political chaos (the Communist party was still very strong), and the currency devalued. "Somebody—it was said—was always on strike at Fiumicino [Rome's airport]." Alitalia's overweight and disjointed management structure was overhauled. Boeing 727s were ordered for the short- and medium-haul routes, and within a few years the airline was able to break even. The Airbus A300 wide-bodied twin was introduced on 1 July 1980 and Alitalia showed shrewd foresight in agreeing with British Airways on jointly operated routes in April 1982. All first-class services gave way to the relatively new business class, although 12 seats in the upper deck of the 433-seat Boeing 747s were reserved for Top Class passengers who paid a 20% premium over the first-class rate.

Alitalia held steady during the 1980s. The government refused to allow an increase in domestic fares (the parent airline still flew on all the major routes, with A.L.I. backing up with the secondary ones), but compensated with a $10 million-a-year subsidy. Always a faithful customer of Douglas, Alitalia was responsible for the overhaul and maintenance not only of its own DC-10 tri-jet wide-bodies, but for those of the ATLAS Group (Alitalia, Lufthansa, Iberia, Air France, and SABENA). Douglas subcontracted some of its manufacturing to Italy, and in December 1983, the first "stretched" DC-9 "Super-80" entered service on the routes to Sicily. Of the fleet of 30, six were allocated to A.T.I., and two to the mainly charter operator, **Aeromediterranea**, but the latter was absorbed by the former in 1985.

In addition to its front-line jets, Alitalia also allocated ATR-42s to A.T.I. and Jetstream 31s to **Aliblu** and **Avianova**, at the third level of local route operation. It also worked closely with **Alisarda** in Sardinia, to which island, as well as Sicily, the services were of the frequent and regular shuttle type.

The domestic Rome-Milan trunk route generated about 1.7 million passengers a year, but the mood of the nation still seemed to identify itself with Rome, to the exclusion of sufficient emphasis on the industrial north, the center of Italy's economic wealth. Milan's population, together with that of nearby cities, was almost twice that of Rome, and Turin was the home of Fiat, one of the world's biggest car manufacturers. Yet Alitalia did not allocate sufficient resources to Milan, while the authorities responsible for Milan's airports procrastinated in developing Malpensa, with better long-haul expansion potential, to complement Linate, which was more restricted. Malpensa is 33 miles to the northwest of the city, and unlike London, Paris, Frankfurt, Zurich, and other European air traffic hubs, was not connected to the city center by adequate fast surface transport. Consequently, there developed a "drain" of long-haul air traffic, especially trans-Atlantic, across the Alps from northern Italy to other airlines of northern Europe.

To offset such drainage, Alitalia showed more enterprise in its own backyard, the Mediterranean. In May 1990, it signed a cooperative agreement with Iberia, by which trans-Atlantic flights, north and south, westbound and flights to the Far East, eastbound, were closely coordinated. By 1993, Alitalia was even operating some domestic flights within Spain. Any deserved advantage of such initiatives was cancelled out by the 1990–91 Gulf War, which severely depleted the traffic of all airlines flying to the booming Middle East and beyond. But sensing the need for cooperation with, rather than competition against, its European neighbors, in January 1993 Alitalia acquired a 30% interest in Hungary's MALEV. This was ill judged and did not last long. Land-locked Hungarians could easily drive to the Adriatic shores of Croatia and Slovenia rather than fly to Italy for vacations.

Although Alitalia was the launch customer for the Airbus A321, the larger variant of that twin-engined series, and started service in April 1994, the airline's finances were in bad shape. Once again, the State came to the rescue, with a prompt infusion of $1.6 billion, with more to come later, but with the provision that the airline cut its staff by 12%, and increase its staff productivity by 25%. Alitalia and A.T.I. were to merge—none too soon—and Renato Riverso and Roberto Schisano were put in charge as chairman and CEO, respectively. To offset traffic

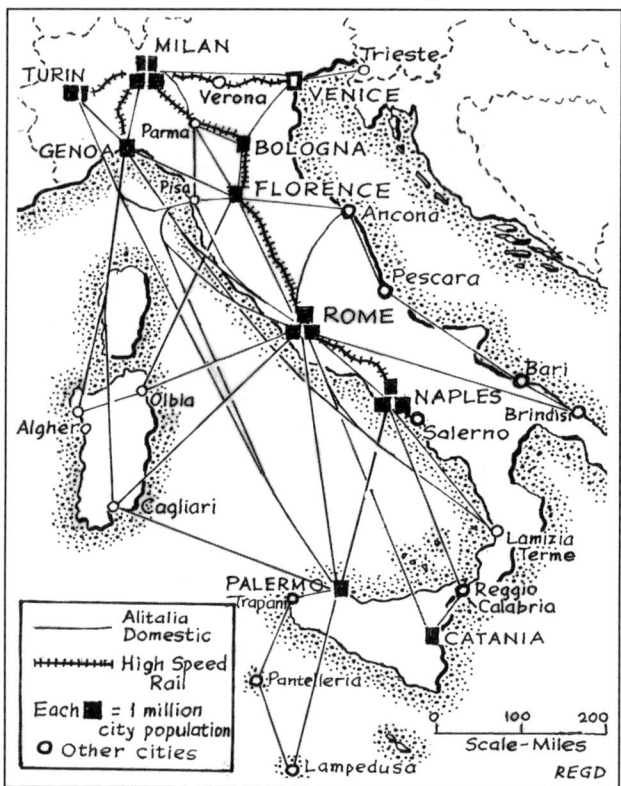

erosion, they created a low-fare division, Alitalia-TEAM; to improve long-haul operating costs, they wet-leased two 231-seat Boeing 767-300ERs from ailing Australian Ansett; and on 31 January 1997, started a code-sharing agreement with Air France. **Avianova** became a new regional affiliate. The state-aided bailout was confirmed by the European Commission, but the problem of Milan, which should by this time have adopted the role as a major European airline hub, was still suffering not only from the "leakage" to the north, but from the inability of the Italian authorities to solve the problem of Malpensa Airport and satisfy all the airlines who wished to serve northern Italy.

Riverso and Schisano were replaced in 1997 by Fausto Cereti and Domenico Cempella, who embarked on a new course in an attempt to join up with another major European airline. Having, on 25 October 1998, stopped service to cities that did not provide enough traffic for viability, such as Bogota, Lima, Manila, and Melbourne, a new agreement was made with the Dutch K.L.M. to replace the one with Air France. The idea was to create a multi-hub system, based on Amsterdam, Milan, and Rome, and at last, in recognition of demographic realities, many routes were transferred from Rome to Milan. By this time, Alitalia had a fleet of 157 airliners, of which 54 were with the Alitalia-TEAM, while **Alitalia Express** was managing the domestic network, complementing Sardinia's Meridiana, Minerva, Azzura Air at Bergamo, and Eurofly at Turin. Eurowings, from Nuremburg, Germany, was also active in the Italian market.

During the early 2000s, Alitalia managed to avoid the fates that beset Swissair and Belgium's SABENA, resisting various reports of mergers or close associations with other European airlines. But operationally, it kept up its standards with aircraft such as the efficient Boeing 777 wide-bodied twin-jet. (McDonough)

The plan was to go into operation on 29 October 1999, for an initial 10-year term, but K.L.M. was running into financial problems, and Milan's airport restructuring was not completed. The planned privatization of Alitalia too was behind schedule. In the spring of 2000, K.L.M. pulled out of the agreement, which it described as "an unacceptable business risk."

Undaunted, the next summer the management tried again, reviving interest in a link with Air France, replacing Amsterdam with Paris as the northern hub of the tripartite hub system. This had the advantage of being part of the Sky Team alliance that the French airline already shared with Delta Air Lines—third largest in the United States, as well as the Brazilian VARIG and the Czech C.S.A. This seemed to the proverbial silver lining, as on 21 December 2001 the U.S. Department of Transportation granted antitrust immunity for the Sky Team to coordinate schedules and fares, while, on 17 June 2002, the European Commission approved a complete restructuring plan for Alitalia, involving recapitalization at €1.43 billion that would incorporate 50% in new shares and 50% convertible bonds, with private investors accounting for 38% of the total.

Milan was given some recognition with a direct service to Washington in March 2003. Revised fleet plans ranked Milan as the main hub in Italy, but its finances were in a terrible state. The government had poured €2.5 billion into Alitalia during the past eight years, but it lost €510 million ($620 million) in 2003, and the net debt rose to €1.44 billion. Once again, on 5 July 2004, the government approved a €400 million ($496 million) credit line to support the draining cash reserves, but this drew a negative reaction from other European airlines to alleged protectionism, by subsidizing Alitalia at the taxpayer's expense, but ignoring the market need for low fares.

The crisis was one of national proportions, with the prestige, even the honor, of Italy's flag carrier at stake. But it apparently ignored foreign protests, and in March 2006, managed to outbid Air One to purchase the bankrupt Volare for €38 million ($48 million). The deal was challenged in the courts.

Whatever the outcome, Alitalia's image in the eyes of the airline world had undergone a disturbing change. Once an aristocrat of the air, the choice for famous film stars, and the provider of the religious equivalent of Air Force One for the Pope's overseas tours, Italy's flag carrier by the second decade of the 21st century became the poor relation of Europe's air transport industry.

European Attrition

The full effects of the American deregulation process was echoed a few years later in Europe, where the legislative program was slower, because of the individuality of its many nations. The timetable of depletion in the ranks was surprisingly similar. The stern rules of what were lightly called "market forces," which were in reality the effects of ruthless competition, resulted in a case of survival of the fittest and of the big fish swallowing the smaller fry.

The term *smaller fry* may be unfair to describe airlines that had their origins in the very birth of the air transport industry. As the end of the 20th century approached, the effects of deregulation began to change the standards of required service and "market forces"—mainly a no-holds-barred urge to lower fares. The value of a large traffic volume from the airline home bases—simple demographics—revealed the weakness of many of the smaller countries of Europe. Germany, France, Great Britain, and Italy all had firm traffic bases of indigenous populations exceeding 50 or 60 million; Spain's population was less, but commanded close to half of the European vacation market; and the three Scandinavian countries had, with commendable foresight, merged their interests after the Second World War. But some of the small countries, however admirable their history, were not so well equipped with the basic need: a big enough native population to sustain a national airline flag carrier. During the early decades of the Jet Age, they held their own, and were even in the vanguard of technical developments. For some, competition became a losing battle, as harsh competitive forces took their toll.

Struggle for Survival in Switzerland

Completely unexpectedly, even for experienced analysts of the industry, the first of the smaller European airlines to fall from grace was **Swissair**. Switzerland was always regarded as the home of impeccable financial solidarity, with the reputation of impregnable Swiss banks reflected in its airline. The downfall, however, was not at first apparent.

Within 10 years of the beginning of the Jet Age, on 31 October 1968, the last Convair 440 made its final flight, and Swissair had an all-jet fleet. Its Douglas DC-8s and DC-9s would soon be joined by wide-bodied Boeing 747s and Douglas DC-10s; its intercontinental network had just been augmented on 1 April with a route to Johannesburg; and its finances were solid, with a capital increase on 25 October 1969 to 273 million Swiss francs, of which 70% was owned by private shareholders. Its stature as a symbol of airline reliability and integrity was enhanced by its membership of the K.S.S.U. Group (formed with K.L.M. and S.A.S., when the French U.T.A. joined on 18 February 1970) whose members were also noted for efficiency.

Among the less positive events at the time were two incidents that were to become more frequent in the airline world as the years went on. On 21 February 1970, a Convair 990 (Swissair had been a leading operator of the type) was destroyed near Zurich by a terrorist bomb; and on 6 September of the same year, a DC-8 was hijacked from a New York flight and forced to land at a desert air strip in Jordan. All on board were released by the P.F.L.P. (Popular Front for the Liberation of Palestine), but the aircraft was destroyed, along with a T.W.A. Boeing 707, a B.O.A.C. VC-10, and a Pan American 747.

In spite of such blows, steady progress continued during the 1970s, under the firm direction of Dr. Walter Berchtold, who was succeeded on 1 January 1972 by Armin Baltensweiler. Boeing 747 service to New York began on 1 April 1971, to be backed up by DC-10s in January 1973. A route to Peking (Beijing) and Shanghai opened on 6 April 1975, and every year during the decade, new points were added to Swissair's map, mainly with its DC-9s, for which successful series it was in the vanguard of variant developments. The longest DC-9, the -81, or the MD-81, went into service on 5 October 1980, and the long-range DC-10-30ER in March 1982. Stoutly maintaining its European identity, however, an order was placed on 14 March 1979 for 10 wide-bodied short-haul 204-seat Airbus A310s, which made its Swiss debut on 21 April 1983.

In 1980, the railway system of Switzerland added a branch line to Zurich Airport, so that air travelers could make their journeys from anywhere in Europe to anywhere in Switzerland by a connection at the airport: a single ride on an escalator, rather than by a tedious bus or taxi connection. This facility was to become an important factor in European transport, as the airports in London, Paris, Brussels, and Frankfurt were also front-runners in intermodal connections, especially as the high speed rail lines were built (in striking contrast with the situation in North America, where city-to-airport connections are still a laborious exercise in patience and price).

Swissair's leadership in cooperating with the airliner manufacturers continued unabated during the 1980s. It put the 172-seat long-range A310-300 into service in January 1986, together with 85-seat Fokker F-100 feeder-liners shortly thereafter, having underscored its loyalty to Douglas in 1985 by ordering 12 MD-11s—stretched versions of the DC-10 that should have been launched by a hesitant manufacturer several years earlier. Although it was a fine airliner, its entry into service in March 1991 was a good example of the harsh penalties for not having "stretched" the DC-10 in the early 1970s.

Baltensweiler had been succeeded as president on 1 May 1982 by Robert Staubli, who, in turn, gave way to Otto Loepfe on 1 August 1988. He was at the helm when a far-reaching decision was made in October 1990. Almost simultaneously with ordering 26 single-aisled 133-seat A320s and 170-seat A321s, Swissair became a member of the European Quality Alliance. Together with S.A.S., Austrian, and Finnair, and with close connections with Singapore Airlines and Delta Air Lines, this association never fulfilled its promise of its slogans, Global or Atlantic Excellence, and was disbanded in 1999. Among the smaller nations of Europe, initiatives for close cooperation, short of merging, were becoming attractive solutions to overcome tight budgets. But there was no common objective, as the individual nations would not combine as a whole, and the situation became uncertain and confused. On 19 May 1992, Swissair began close cooperation with Austrian Airlines, to create a "home market" of common ticket offices and ticket-counters, with bases at Zurich and Vienna, and, from 1993, Geneva, which had been granted long-distance hub status. Another plan to form the Alcazar Group, with K.L.M., S.A.S., and Austrian, failed to succeed because K.L.M. wanted it to be linked with a partnership with the U.S. Northwest Airlines, while the other three wanted to link with Delta Air Lines.

In 1994 Swissair acquired the majority ownership of the Swiss regional airline, Crossair, and the following year changed course again. This time the formula was different. This was not cooperation, it was a capitalist buy-out for control. In January 1995 negotiations began for Swissair to acquire a 49.9% stake in Belguim's SABENA, of which 37.5% was already held by Air France. This $212 million equity holding was confirmed in May and approved by the European Commission in July, with the provision that airport slots at Zurich and Geneva were released to preserve fair competition. As if to confirm this association, these two airlines and Austrian made a combined order for 17 long-range wide-bodied Airbus A330-200s, twin-engined version of the four-engined A340, in December 1996.

The SAir Group

In 1997, Philippe Bruggisser replaced Loepfe, and Swissair appeared to be flexing its financial muscles, even though, in 1996, it had lost $341 million, in spite of increased sales. It restructured its corporate base, establishing the **SAir Group**, as a controlling parent of Swissair, Crossair, and SABENA. In November 1998, the third largest airline in Germany, Lufttransport Unternehmen (L.T.U.), was added by another 49.9% SAir stake purchase. In April of that year, the inter-airline trend was extended by the formation of the Qualiflyer Group, adding Air Portugal, the French A.O.M., and the Turkish airline to the club. But this was more of a marketing initiative, rather than any exchange of shares.

Swissair's solid reputation for reliability and safety had been badly affected during the same year, when, on 3 September, one of its MD-11s had crashed into the sea off the coast of Nova Scotia, after taking off from New York. The cause was judged to be a fault in the wiring of the entertainment electrical circuit, although the only warning to the crew was smoke in the cockpit, and the disintegration of the aircraft was instantaneous. 229 passengers and crew lost their lives.

Back in Zurich, the SAir Group was strengthening its position. In October 1999, the Atlantic Excellence club was disbanded, while SAir took a 37.5% interest in LOT Polish Airlines, and 20% in South African Airways. It transferred most of Swissair's Geneva-based flights to Crossair, which took over most of the routes to the Mediterranean. On 26 May 2000, SAir decided to increase its stake in SABENA to 85%, with the Belgian government holding the remaining 15%. In compensation, the German holding in L.T.U. was sold to the Rewe retail giant. By the end of the year, the Group strengthened its interests in France by similar purchases of control of Air Liberte, Air Littoral, to add to A.O.M. This attempt to form a major French airline was seriously misjudged, partly because all the smaller French airlines were losing money, and traffic on the short-haul routes was being eroded by the success of the T.G.V. (Train a Grande Vitesse) which, for example, on 10 June 2001, cut the 300-mile train time from Paris to Marseilles from 4hr 20m to 2hr 55m.

The Final Blow

The SABENA deal was not working out. The increase in shareholding proposal was exchanged for a €430 million ($366 million) cash injection, and Swisair agreed to take nine Airbuses off the Belgian airline's hands. Bruggisser had been replaced on 23 January 2001 by Moritz Suter, but his stay in office lasted only six weeks. This airline, the symbol of air transport integrity, was suddenly faced with a crisis of sheer survival, as its efforts to control other European airlines were revealed to be an illusion of grandeur.

The axe fell after the closure of all operations to America for the few days after the terrorist attack on New York's World Trade Center on 11 September. On 1 October 2001, the SAir Group collapsed, the Swissair fleet was grounded the next day, and the day after that, almost unbelievably, this former "gold-plate" airline filed for bankruptcy. On 28 October, Crossair had taken over Swissair's operations, and 30 March 2002 was the last day of operation, under that well-respected name, for this pioneer of European air transport.

"The King is Dead, Long Live the King"—so goes a traditional call on the death of a British monarch. And so it was with the Swiss airline. On 31 March, a new airline, officially **Swiss International Airlines**, but trading more simply under the name **Swiss**, took over the reins. But it was hard going. In spite of downsizing the staff and the fleet, and reducing airliner orders, the new airline lost 980 million Swiss francs ($724 million) in 2002. It then had to adopt a low-fares policy—a policy that would have been regarded as treason 20 years earlier—to combat the threat from easyJet and Ryanair which, under liberalized European rules, were invading Switzerland. EasyJet even established an operational hub at Geneva. Domestic routes were terminated, bilateral deals were hastily made, the London route was code-shared with British Airways; but the losses continued: 684 million SF ($537 million) in 2003, and Dose resigned in March 2004.

In January 2005, almost defiantly clinging to the tradition of offering the finest service to Swiss bankers, Swiss inaugurated a business-class-only service from Zurich to New York's Newark Airport, using 56-seat Privatair Boeing 757 Business Jet 2s (BBJ2s). But this was whistling in the wind. Swiss International had to face the harsh realities, and in March that year, it agreed with Lufthansa for the German airline to take it over, and in so doing, become a member of the Star Alliance. In July, Lufthansa increased its Swiss stake to 49% and conceded 164 slots at seven European airports to comply with European Commission conditions.

Belgium Struggles On

When the Jet Age began, the Belgian national airline, **Société Anonyme Belge d'Exploitation de la Navigation Aérienne (SABENA)** could rightly claim to have shared in the operational and technical progression of European air transport as a whole. It had pioneered an admirable helicopter service, linking Brussels with all the neighboring cities, and was the first and only international service of its kind in the world. It was terminated, however, in 1966, as the high costs of such operations were not sustainable.

For some years after the end of the Second World War, SABENA had flourished because of its geographical advantage while Germany was denied the right to operate an airline. But this privilege ended when the new Lufthansa quickly got under way in 1955. More than any other colonial nation, Belgium suffered from the loss of its overseas territories, in this case, the Belgian Congo, many times the size of the homeland. SABENA distinguished itself in 1961, when the wave of African nationalism created a refugee crisis. In only 20 days, more than 34,000 refugees were evacuated from the Congo, where Leopoldville, an oasis of Belgian lifestyle, became Kinshasa, the capital of Zaire.

Such blows could have been demoralizing, but SABENA soldiered on, backed by a government that was determined to hold its own within the European family of airlines. Brussels was the headquarters of the European Common Market and of NATO, the North Atlantic Treaty Organization. It had been the first in Europe to operate the Boeing 707 jet services, and was well respected by trans-Atlantic travelers. Service to Bombay began on 1 November 1967. The Johannesburg service was routed through Nairobi two days later. Keeping up with its bigger rivals, it began a Polar service to Tokyo on 4 April 1969. With Boeing 727s already plying the European and medium-distance routes to Africa, it maintained technical equality in the long-haul by introducing 401-seat Boeing 747 wide-bodies to New York on 1 October 1970, and backing those up with 199-seat Douglas DC-10-30CFs on 7 August 1973. With jet service to all the continents except Australia, Belgium may have been a small country but its airline was no poor relation. In fact, with Boeing 737s coming into service in April 1974, SABENA was able to confirm its ascendancy over other European rivals in services and routes to Africa.

At the other end of the scale, recalling perhaps its helicopter initiatives of the past, it launched a Common Market Commuter

An indication of the changing role of Switzerland's rejuvenated national airline was the employment of smaller aircraft to serve routes where, with Europe's "open skies" policy, competition was intense. This is one of its Embraer twin-jets. The word Swiss is also marked in four languages. (Bentley)

on 3 May 1976, with a Liege-Charleroi-London service, with 12-seat Beech 99s, leased from Publiair, to show that it did not neglect the provincial cities of Belgium. Even so, on the wider front, market forces were closing in on one of the smaller nations of Europe, and the airline that had the reputation of being owned by the government. On 23 May 1978 a royal ordinance was issued, modifying the previous articles of registration and organization, and soliciting investments from Belgian bankers and industrialists. Carlos van Rafelghem, from the Ministry of Finance, was appointed chairman/CEO, and a policy of low fares was introduced. Adjustments were made to the long-haul network, with new routes to the U.S.A., Atlanta, Detroit, and Chicago, during the next two years, while direct service to Mexico City was terminated, and the southern route to Tokyo was suspended. The Boeing 747s and Douglas DC-10s replaced the 707s, the last one of which was retired on 31 October 1981.

SABENA's cost structure was anything but amenable to any drastic measures. Salaries were high—the pilots were among the highest paid in Europe—and the unions were strong, stoutly objecting to lowering wages, resorting to strikes only too often. Following a disastrous business year in 1981, the airline's capital was increased from BF 3,000 million to 9,000 million in 1982. This enabled the airline to carry on without addressing the basic problem. On 25 March 1984, the 203-seat Airbus A310-200 entered service but this aircraft was leased from Aviafin, a company in which SABENA itself had a 27% interest.

And so the financial maneuvering went on as Belgium struggled to keep pace with its more powerful rival neighbors. In 1985 the SABENA Group was formed, comprising the flag carrier, together with the charter airline, Sobelair, and servicing and fuel supply companies as profit centers. The following year, a controlling interest was acquired in **Delta Air Transport (D.A.T.)** to operate short-haul routes from Antwerp, while in March 1987, the new Airbus A310-300 opened service to three new African cities, and Toronto was added to Montreal as a second Canadian destination. On 26 October of that year—once again demonstrating an awareness of Brussels as a geographical hub of western Europe—SABENA cooperated with British Midland's Eurocity Express and started flying into the London City Airport, close to the heart of the city, using de Havilland Dash Sevens.

The Belgian airline was putting on a brave face. At the expense of complete independence, the need to seek additional support was clear; but if the writing was on the wall, SABENA's back was not yet up against it. Preliminary discussions with the Scandinavian S.A.S. in 1986 had not progressed, but in June 1989 a proposal by British Airways and K.L.M. had to be taken seriously. Each airline would have taken a 20% stake in SABENA, with the Belgian government retaining the controlling interest, to create Sabena World Airlines, but the European Commission issued a formal "statement of objection." The British and Dutch withdrew on 31 January 1990.

Next in line for an international partnership was Air France, which, in the early 1990s, took a 37.5% interest in SABENA, but this was never fully implemented, and was sold on 4 May 1995 to Swissair for BF 4 billion ($141 million), plus additional shares for $212 million, worth a 49.5% stake. Belgian investors contributed BF 2 billion ($71 million) to this major revolution in ownership. The official announcement included the statement that "this tie-up also gives SABENA a partner that is renowned for its sound financial health and its sound management," a phrase that with a decade, would become a hollow commentary. As was customary, when the European Commission approved this takeover in July 1995, it insisted on the surrender of certain airport slots by both airlines.

SABENA's position in Europe, once apparently secure, with Brussels geographically well positioned, and the seat of the European Union, had, during the closing decades of the 20th century, deteriorated. Competition from Great Britain had increased not only from British Airways, but also with Sir Richard Branson's Virgin Group, amongst others, casting covetous eyes on Belgium. Most of all, however, the opening on 12 February 1986 of the Channel Tunnel, with high speed trains cutting the surface journey from London by half, was a bitter blow. Like all the national airlines of Europe, the route to London was the most important European destination in the network. In October 1996, a deal closed with Virgin Express for seating allocation on its 737-300s, and similar arrangements were made with other airlines to Barcelona, Rome, and London's Gatwick. The T.G.V. high speed trains led to the cancellation of the air route to Paris.

The Swissair partnership appeared to be advantageous when, on 19 December 1996, the SAir Group's restructuring was approved by all its board members, and SABENA benefitted by a share of a combined order with Swissair and Austrian for 232-seat Airbus A330-200s. On 1 January 1997, the extensive cargo operations were sold to Swissair-Cargo, but the financial situation was still in dire straits. The loss in 1996 was more than BF 8 billion ($218 million), almost exactly the value of the shares sold to Swissair in 1995, in addition to those that it had taken from Air France.

Sabena still struggled on, adding, on 15 May 1997, Cincinnati, Delta's northern U.S. hub, as an extension of its code-sharing trans-Atlantic deal. On 27 April 1998, a similar arrangement was made for connecting flights at Paris's Orly Airport, as the French A.O.M. airline became part of the SAir Group. SABENA also became a founder member of the Swiss-inspired Qualiflyer Group, and things seemed to be looking up, with the last Boeing 747 flight, on 28 October of the same year, signalling a revival of fortunes. Indeed, a modest profit of BF 771 million ($20 million) was made in 1998, the first in 40 years. Never reluctant to innovate, a new route to Madras (now Chennai) was announced on 1 September, with hopes of traffic generation from one of the key cities of India's "Silicon Valley."

Death of a Pioneer Airline

At this stage, the droll response to the admonition "Cheer up, things could be worse" of "So I cheered up, and things were worse," could have fitted the calendar of SABENA's roller-coaster ride toward its eventual demise. In 1999, Delta broke up the

Atlantic Excellence alliance, but SABENA, with Swissair, was able to replace this almost immediately with a similar arrangement with American Airlines, and it was still a member of the Qualiflyer Group. But much of this was window dressing, as it lost $14 million in 1999 and a further $397 million in 2000. Yet again, SABENA was bailed out by the SAir Group and the Belgian government, but in January 2001, the long-haul routes to Newark and Johannesburg were withdrawn, to be followed in October by Washington and Tokyo. Routes in Europe were also cancelled as the fleet was down-sized, and Airbus orders were cancelled.

The final nail in SABENA's coffin came soon after the terrorist attack in New York on 11 September. Over its history it had always been opposed by the unions for any reductions in staff numbers or pay reductions. When the attack occurred, the pilots had just walked off; but they did not have work to do anyway, as all air services worldwide were disrupted for several days. The cash-strapped Swissair fleet was grounded on 2 October, and that once impregnable airline filed for bankruptcy the next day. This was the end of the Swiss-controlled SAir Group, on which SABENA depended, and it too "filed for protection against creditors," which was a euphemism for the same debacle. SABENA's last flight was from Cotonou and Abidjan on 7 November. It was a sad end to the seventh oldest airline in the world.

The Dutch Hang On

To complete a trilogy of the struggle by airlines of the smaller countries of Europe to match the progress and strength of their larger neighbors, **Koninklijke Luchtvaart Maatschappij (K.L.M.)** did manage to avoid for many years the serious straits that its Belgian neighbor seemed to descend into with regularity. Its colonial inheritance was a little larger than SABENA's single African territory, and it managed to retain commercial links with lost territories after they were given up. Its reputation as a world-class airline was second to none, and its anicable relationship with Douglas, dating back to the DC-2s of 1934, continued into the Jet Age. On 27 July 1967, already with a fleet of long-haul DC-8s and short-haul DC-9s, its first Amsterdam-New York service with the "stretched" DC-8-63 (which some said at the time was "the nearest thing to printing your own money," was the first of this variant in the world.

In June 1969, K.L.M. joined with the other partners in the KSSU Group (Swissair, S.A.S., and U.T.A.) to order 36 DC-10 wide-bodied airliners to complement the small Boeing 747B order that was essential for the prestige and highly competitive route to New York. Like SABENA and Swissair, domestic services were almost non-existent in such a small country as the Netherlands, and in most of Europe, competition was heavy. K.L.M. compensated for these difficulties by enterprising developments in other continents, and during the 1970s, its intercontinental route network matched those of its larger and richer European rivals. The familiar blue aircraft became familiar sights throughout Africa, the Middle East—one of the first into Dubai, still in the infant stages of its commercial expansion—and into Chicago, Hong Kong, and Melbourne. During a period of worldwide air traffic growth, when the volume was doubling every five years, K.L.M. rode the crest of a wave, with the Boeing 747's entry into service on 15 February 1971 marking the end of a virtual Douglas–K.L.M. permanent partnership.

In 1973 Sergio Orlandini became president and, with a steady hand, led the airline that had an almost immaculate history of pioneering and contemporary success. K.L.M. was assured of its financial security because of the Dutch government's appreciation and support, when needed, of the manner in which, though partly privately owned, K.L.M. carried the Dutch flag with dignity and assurance throughout the world. Though never arrogant or complacent, as it usually ended each year in the black, the airline's forgivable serenity was shattered on one terrible morning, on 27 March 1977, when several airliners were diverted to use the single runway of Tenerife's Los Rodeos Airport because of suspected terrorist activity at nearby Las Palmas.

On its take-off run, a K.L.M. Boeing 747 crashed into a Pan American 747 that was just taxiing onto the runway. The Dutch airliner tore off the upper part of the Pan Am airplane "like peeling off the lid of a sardine can." 583 passengers and crew were killed. It still remains as the worst disaster in commercial airline history.

Nevertheless, K.L.M. soldiered on, made profits, and in 1983 the government shares were reduced from 65% to 55% of the total. On 1 February, Orlandini introduced a program that was aimed to be customer-oriented, even though his airline already enjoyed a second-to-none reputation for service and operational reliability. The slogan was to be "reliable, punctual, careful, and friendly," and while cynics might ask why such an exhortation was necessary, it seemed to work, as in 1984 the airline made a profit of $97 million.

Orlandini was succeeded in September 1987 by Jan de Soet, who oversaw some diversification of the airline's activities. During the next two years, K.L.M. had created Cityhopper and Nether-Lines for local services, taken a 40% interest in Transavia and a 30% interest in Martinair, two of Europe's most successful charter airlines. It also acquired an initial 15% of Air UK, with the shrewd objective of feeding British provincial traffic to European destinations through Amsterdam.

Downfall of Another Great Pioneer

By 1991, the Dutch government's investment in its national airline was only 38%, so that the forces of private enterprise and private investment controlled its main corporate policies. Discussions with a close alliance, falling short of a merger, with British Airways having failed, K.L.M. turned its eyes across the Atlantic, and identified a prospective partner in the United States. The resultant sparring with Northwest Airlines showed great promise. In July 1989, K.L.M. had already invested $150 million in Wings Holdings, owned by Alfred Checchi, who had put up $400 million to take over control of Northwest. Soon, a joint service was being operated from Minneapolis to Amsterdam, with Boeing 747s of both airlines.

The merger prospects were excellent. Most mergers are effectively takeovers, and the strongest partner usually takes control and its name survives. This one had the merit of a partnership of equals. K.L.M. was, in terms of passenger-miles flown annually, the fourth largest airline in Europe; Northwest was the fourth largest in the U.S.A. K.L.M.'s equity share in Northwest in 1992 was 49% but the U.S. government insisted on the regulatory restriction that a foreign company of any sort could not own more than 25% of the voting stock. However, on 11 January 1993, the two airlines received anti-trust immunity from the Department of Justice, and they began extensive code-sharing on both sides of the Atlantic.

But the Dutch airline's fortunes seemed thereafter to be on a knife-edge of viability. On the one hand, it increased its control of associated European regional airlines, increasing its stake in Air UK, for example to 100%. But in July 1997 it sold back its shareholdings of Northwest (in three annual installments) retaining the operating alliance, but not the equity. Late in September, they signed a 10-year joint-venture agreement. With the Dutch government buying back its investment in July 1998 for $500 million, K.L.M. was able to report a profit for that year of $389 million.

All seemed to be well. In February 1999, a $1.2 billion order was placed with Boeing for four 747-400 combis and 5 737-800s. And on 29 October of that year, a Master Cooperation Agreement (M.C.A.) with Alitalia came close to creating a unified European airline. Part of this deal was for K.L.M. to pay Alitalia (which needed the money badly) €100 million ($107 million) for a substantial investment in the new Malpensa airport at Milan. Still confident, K.L.M. established a low-cost subsidiary, **Buzz**, based at London's Stansted Airport, in January 2000. K.L.M. added quite a few new destinations to its route map, and even now it put on a brave face by taking a 26% stake in Kenya Airways, and collaborating with Malaysian Airlines to make Kuala Lumpur its Far Eastern terminus instead of Sydney.

But the long-term prospects for independent prosperity, profitability, even survival, were now bleak. To the surprise of the entire European airline industry, K.L.M. and Air France, on 15 October 2003, signed a "Final Transaction Agreement" under which the two airlines formed a common parent company, so that they could both continue to operate individually under their own names. This effective merger was ratified by the European Commission on 11 February 2004, with the familiar condition that slots must be relinquished at Amsterdam and Paris to avoid monopolistic practices. On 3 May 2004, Air France was able to sign the purchase agreement under which the French acquired 89% of K.L.M.'s shares. On 1 June, coordination was under way, with an Amsterdam-Paris joint shuttle service, and long-haul rationalization. Together with its American partners, Northwest and Continental, K.L.M. joined the Skyteam Alliance.

This was one major alliance in the airline world that seemed to have worked. Despite soaring fuel costs and unfavorable dollar-euro exchange rates, the joint airline started life with handsome profits. In terms of total revenues, it assumed the world's leadership, although it would face increasing competition within Europe as the high speed rail networks gained strength.

Chapter 30: Jet Wings over the Mediterranean

Spain Recovers

Europe took many years to recover from the devastation of the Second World War, and even neutral countries were not exempt from the struggle. Among these was Spain, which although technically neutral, was widely regarded as a Nazi sympathizer, under fellow traveler General Franco, who had only just won a civil war when hostilities broke out in September 1939. When the postwar **Iberia**, therefore, was established as the national airline on 7 July 1940, its resources were severely limited, especially in the fuel supply. Toward the end of the war, limited domestic services began, with DC-3s supplied by the United States, though long-distance services across the Atlantic were not resumed until 1949. Super-Constellation service to New York began 26 August 1954. The new Iberia had a lot of catching-up to do.

To its credit, it entered the Jet Age, matching its rival airlines with the best equipment: Douglas DC-8s for the long haul in 1961, by which time it had developed a network throughout Spanish-speaking Latin America; Caravelles for the medium-hauls, introduced on 1 June 1962. By 1965 Iberia's well-balanced fleet totaled 57 aircraft, including Convair 440 Metropolitans for its domestic routes. On 30 June 1967, the first Douglas DC-9-30 entered service amd this short-haul jet was to form the backbone of Iberia's fleet for the next two decades. The first "stretched" DC-8-63 was added to the fleet in August 1968.

A Tourism Explosion

Such a recovery was spurred by Spain's sunshine-laden climate, even in the winter, a multiplicity of beaches, and the enterprise of its vacation industry, working in cooperation with package tour operations in northern Europe. During the 1950s, tourist and travel agencies, in Britain, Germany, and Scandinavia especially, had cooperated with independent non-scheduled charter airlines to create an enormous inclusive tour vacation market, in which air fare and hotel charges were bulk-packaged at cheap rates—ironically inspired to do so because the charter airlines were banned from operating scheduled services by the International Air Transport Association (IATA)–protected national airlines. This industry grew exponentially, and of all the countries in the sunny Mediterranean, Spain was far and away the main benefactor. By the mid-1960s it accounted for half of all the traffic originating from northern Europe.

By 1970, non-scheduled European airlines, operating mainly on Mediterranean inclusive tours, were generating more intra-European passenger-miles than all the scheduled flag carriers put together. For the traveling public, bargain fares, and cheap hotels, food, and wine more than compensated for the lack of on-board amenities. During the winter, when Spanish hoteliers slashed the price of rooms just to avoid shutting down, airlines kept flying and cutting fares to avoid grounding the aircraft and laying off the crews. A Scottish coal-miner could take his family on a holiday in Tenerife and spend less than if he had stayed at home.

For Iberia, this was a welcome reversal from the enforced frugality of the wartime and post-war years. During the late 1960s and early 1970s, traffic doubled every four years—faster than most airlines could expect even during prosperous times—and Iberia launched a spending spree that matched those of the richer airlines of Europe. A modest order for three Fokker F-28 Fellowships on 23 April 1970 was eclipsed on 22 October by the delivery of the first Boeing 747-100, which entered service to New York on 4 January 1972. Realizing, however, that this 360-seat could only hope to fly with all seats filled on that route alone, Iberia ordered three 270-seat Douglas DC-10-30s on 15 January 1972, and a month later confirmed an order for four Airbus A300B4s, plus an option on eight more. The first Boeing 727-200 entered service on 2 May of that year, and further orders for 727s and DC-10s followed in 1973. The Spanish airline had, within a few dramatic years, emerged from the margins of European air transport to join the leaders.

In 1974, 35 million tourists visited Spain, and the public as a whole benefitted from the economic "multiplier" effect, as tourist money flowed throughout the country's population, from real estate developers to shop-keepers, even laborers. Spanish domestic travel, served by Iberia's associate Aviaco (see below), as well as by the national airline's own flights, also boomed. Some 800,000 passengers flew on the Madrid-Barcelona route alone, leading to the inauguration, on 1 November of that year, of the first "air bridge" high-frequency shuttle service in Europe. For only twice the $17.00 train fare, a trip that lasted more than seven hours, Spanish businessmen could fly the route in an hour, every hour, on the hour. This remained lucrative until the Spanish railroad introduced high speed rail in 2009.

After the Feast . . .

Such a complete transformation, from rags to riches, could not last. By the time the first A300B4 entered service on 27 February 1981, the financial bubble had burst. After a series of profitable years, Iberia was losing money, and a succession of presidents had not stopped the flow, even though by this time it was serving almost every country in Latin America. Two serious crashes, on 7 December 1983, and on 19 February 1985, killing a total of 240 people, did not help. Then, in May 1990, a shrewd arrangement with Alitalia gave some hope for the future. In a pooling traffic exchange, Iberia would carry Alitalia trans-Atlantic passengers through Madrid, while the Italian airline would reciprocate with Spanish passengers through Rome and on to Bangkok.

The outbreak of the Gulf War in 1991 disrupted operations throughout the Middle East. At the same time, a dispute arose with United States authorities regarding reciprocal traffic rights.

Nevertheless, developments in Latin America continued. Already holding 30% of Aerolíneas Argentinas and 38% of Chile's Ladeco, Iberia now took a 45% share of the Venezuelan VIASA. With El Banco Provincial taking another 15%, the total Spanish investment was $145 million. Hubs were established at Buenos Aires and Santo Domingo, and even in Miami. These initiatives, led by Iberia's chairman Miguel Aguilo, were expensive, and the Spanish government injected no less than $929 million in 1992 to keep Iberia afloat.

The gamble to create an Iberia-led airline empire in Latin America did not succeed. By 1993, when Aguilo was replaced by Javier Sales, steps were taken to stop the flow of precious resources. At the end of 1994, an order for Airbus A321s was cancelled. There were lay-offs and pay cuts. But yet again, the Spanish government bailed out Iberia to the tune of another $870 million, but on the instructions of the European Commission, investments in South American airlines had to be abandoned. It sold its shares in Argentina, reduced those in Ladeco. On 23 January 1997, all VIASA flights were suspended, and on 18 February that airline folded.

Iberia then turned to the pressing affairs nearer home. On 12 May 1997, **Air Nostrum** started operations on behalf of Iberia, using turboprop equipment to save costs on those routes that were uneconomical for jets. Facing heavy competition from high-quality service, Spanair and low-fare **Air Europa**, Iberia took over one-third of the latter's operations in January 1998. The next move, only a month later, was unexpected: a $2.6 billion order was placed for 76 of the Airbus A320 single-aisle series. Later that year, it was revealed that British Airways and American Airlines had each agreed to acquire 10% of Iberia's shares, and this deal was concluded in February 1999. Such confidence encouraged other investors to take another 30% at the end of the year.

By the start of the 21st century, Iberia had pulled out of the route to Tokyo, which looked good on the map but not on the balance sheet. In March 2000, the Sociedad Estatal de Participaciones Industriales (SEPI) launched a public offering for 54% of its shares in Iberia, although on 4 April 2001 it was obliged to lower the price. Iberia's ownership was now 65% by individual shareholders. 8% of these were taken up at a discount for employees, while 35% went to international investors. The turning point was apparently echoed with the managerial style. When, on 13 July 2001, pay disputes with the pilots' union had dragged on, the chairman Xavier de Irala shut down the airline. It started up again shortly thereafter.

Iberia now had a more disciplined management and staff, a well-balanced fleet, and more emphasis on its short/medium-haul routes. The year 2002 was difficult, not only because of the disruption of trans-Atlantic traffic, but Iberia's dispute with its pilots dragged on and had to come to terms with the privatization process. It could no longer lean on the government for financial relief. It joined the OneWorld Alliance and this led to closer cooperation with British Airways, and also with Portugal's T.A.P. All routes to Asia were abandoned, and instead, connections were made through London. At the end of the year, the European Commission approved the partnership with British Airways (which held 9% of Iberia stock), which was described by one observer as "only a few steps short of a merger."

In March 2003, a new route opened to Moscow—a clear sign of a new direction for the Spanish airline. With a much improved financial situation, Iberia was able to order 79 Airbus A320s, for $4.5 billion, to replace its aging fleet of short/medium-haul aircraft and to add long-haul Airbus A340-600s.

The Spanish Second Line

As Spain recovered from its own civil war and from its associations with the Axis powers during the Second World War, concessions were apparently made to counter the suggestion that Madrid-based Iberia would enjoy a monopoly. On 18 February 1948, **Aviacion Y Comercio (A.Y.C.)** more commonly known as **Aviaco**, was founded in Bilbao, center of the Basque region in the north. It had first specialized in freight and car ferry services, but soon established a network of routes, acting as a supplement to Iberia's domestic and international system. In 1955, the Instituto Nacional de Industria (I.N.I.) bought a majority shareholding, transferred the headquarters to Madrid, and during the next few years replaced old aircraft, including, in 1962, Caravelle jets.

The move to Madrid had marked a consolidation with Iberia, which, in 1959, had acquired a two-thirds shareholding in the airline, with the remainder still held by the original founders and by I.N.I. During the next decade, Aviaco continued to operate, if not to flourish, as both an operational and political convenience to Iberia. In March 1973, it purchased six Douglas DC-9-30s and later increased this fleet as well as adding six DC-8-50s for long-haul charters. This latter activity was withdrawn during the 1980s and with a fleet of 21 DC-9s and 9 Fokker F-27-600s, Aviaco was carrying 4 million passengers a year, mostly to connect all the main cities of Spain to Madrid and to each other.

While the charter airlines of northern Europe dominated the annual beach-seeking exodus, Spanish interests gradually entered the field. For two decades, one new airline was initially outstandingly successful. **Spantax** (abbreviated from Spanish Air Taxi) had had a modest beginning. It had been founded on 6 October 1959 by Captain Rodolfo (Rudi) Bay, an ex-Iberia pre-war pilot, together with Marta Estades, an ex-Iberia stewardess. With small British aircraft, they had started flights in 1960 to connect mining interests in the Spanish Sahara with the Canary Islands then expanded into tourist charters with Douglas DC-3s. In 1962, Spantax started flying from Palma, Majorca, which had become the most popular tourist destination in the entire Mediterranean.

Rudi Bay was a charismatic character. As well as being a veteran pilot, he had raced motorcycles and cars. He had also flown in the Nationalist Air Force, and his record in that service is believed to have been to his advantage when developing Spantax, which he did with enthusiasm. He was not alone in Spain during the 1960s in suffering crashes with DC-3s, but at the same time he acquired longer-range Douglas propeller airliners as he began to enter the main tourist market. Then, on 24 February 1967 he bought two Convair 990 jets from American Airlines, stopped flying for Iberia (he had kept his foot in that door), and established a firm base at Palma for the summer season, transferring staff during the winter to Las Palmas, Gran Canaria.

The 149-seat Convair 990s were the fastest commercial airliners in the world, and they had the range necessary to fly from Stockholm to Las Palmas. This fleet was increased to a dozen, and in April 1973, two Douglas DC-8Fs were acquired for longer-range charters, mainly to Palma. A 380-seat wide-bodied Douglas DC-10 was added in 1978 but it crashed on 13 September 1982, killing 51 people. Spantax's level of operations declined thereafter although five Boeing 737-200s entered service in 1983. Three years later, Captain Bay resigned from the presidency, and, with declining fortunes (as other Spanish charter airlines offered stiff competition—see below), control passed to the Patrimonio Nacional, the state holding company. In April 1987, ownership passed to the Aviation Financial Group in Luxembourg and on 29 March 1988, still $80 million in debt, Spantax's short but eventful career came to an end.

Simultaneously with the gradual decline of Aviaco and the decade or so of Rudi Bay, other airline entrepreneurs came and went to exploit the popularity of Spain as the preferred destination for the inclusive-tour business that was thriving across northern Europe. These are reviewed in the tabulation below.

Transformation in Portugal

Though not strictly a Mediterranean country, Portugal has all the characteristics of one, geographically sharing the Iberian Peninsula, and its political and subsequent commercial history have run parallel with its larger neighbor, Spain. Of all European countries that had once owned overseas empires, its decline has been, over the centuries, the most economically harmful. Territory lost in Africa during the post-war period of decolonization—Angola, Mozambique, and Guinea—contrasted in the extremes of size and natural resources with the homeland, similarly to Belgium's loss of the Congo. But in some compensation, like Spain's language commonality with most of Latin America, Portugal shared a common language with Brazil. Unlike Spain, however, it was a small country, and on the mainland, only the Lisbon-Oporto route was long enough to warrant domestic air service, and even that was a marginal operation.

Before the Second World War, airline activity had been conducted almost entirely in association with Air France. Portugal did not form its own "chosen instrument" airline until 1944, when **Transportes Aéreas Portuguesas (T.A.P.)** came into existence as a division of the Civil Aeronautics Department. Almost the entire objective was to link the colonies with Lisbon, and when this was accomplished on the last day of 1946, the fleet was limited to pre-war Douglas DC-3s, which took six days to reach Lourenço Marques. T.A.P. had the curious distinction of operating the longest twin-engined air route in the world. It became a commercial company on 25 April 1953, with banking and shipping interests, but still with support from the government.

By this time it had four-engined Douglases, adding Lockheed Constellations in 1955.

At the beginning of the Jet Age, the airline expanded to Brazil. On 1 December 1960, it formed a special relationship with Panair do Brasil, starting a service to Rio de Janeiro, offering special low fares to the citizens or permanent foreign residents of the two countries. But the route was still served by piston-engined equipment, and T.A.P.'s first jets, Sud Caravelles, did not start until 1 August 1962, at first to European cities and later to Madeira, the Azores, and the Canary Islands. Jet services to Africa followed on 5 October 1963, using Boeing 707s leased from SABENA. Portugal's flag carrier began to mature when, on 22 April 1965, the joint service with Panair do Brasil was terminated. Its own Boeing 707s started, on 22 December of that year, to fly to Luanda, Beira, and Johannesburg and on 17 June 1966, to Brazil. Boeing 727-100s replaced the Caravelles on the main European routes on 30 April 1967, and 707s replaced a blocked-space agreement with Alitalia on the North Atlantic route to New York on 1 April 1968.

One of Portugal's overseas territories was the Azores, the mid-Atlantic island group that had been a vital refueling stop during the pre-war sparring by the United States, Britain, and France for trans-ocean leadership. Now it was supplementing that role as a destination in its own right, for tourists wishing to escape the crowds on the Spanish beaches. An airport at Ponta Delgada was added to the existing Santa Maria, and on 1 April 1972, T.A.P. took a financial interest in the Azores' local airline, **Sociedade Açoriana de Transportes Aéreos (SATA)**, which had linked the islands with Beechcraft and de Havilland Doves since 1947. This date coincided with the entry into service of Boeing 747s, which were able to fly with full loads nonstop from Lisbon to New York or south to Luanda, Angola, introducing the *Navigator* business-class service, which was especially popular when the latter route was extended to Johannesburg in November.

The way seemed clear for further progress, as on 18 July the 20-year 1953 concession (see above) had been renewed for

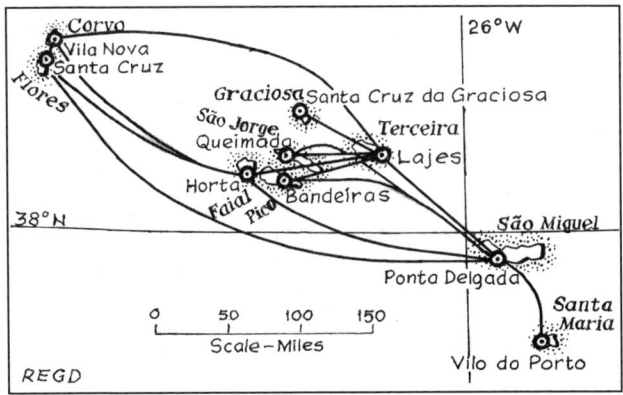

Relatively isolated in the mid-Atlantic, the Azores Island group, about 300 miles from west to east, has its own airline.

10 more years. In April 1973, Oporto was given a direct route to Paris, and a year later, a direct service from Funchal, Madeira, opened to London. Because this island resort destination was almost entirely mountainous, construction of an airport had been difficult. The British Aquila Airways had consequently operated one of the last flying boat services in airline history. In August 1961, T.A.P. had leased a Comet 4B from British European Airways to operate to nearby Porto Santo, the little island 40 miles away, and had put its own Caravelles on this route in 1962. No sooner had the Funchal direct service enhanced the prospects of tourism to the Portuguese Atlantic islands when, three weeks later, on 25 April 1974, the country experienced a bloodless revolution. Long-time dictator Dr. Antonio Salazar was deposed. Within a month, T.A.P. had a new board of directors. Administrative problems were exacerbated by the growing agitation for independence in the African territories. On 15 April, the airline was taken over by the government.

The new management faced a crisis, similar to Belgium's. Nationalistic fervor in the Portuguese colonies was intense, and all the colonists were in such danger of retribution, real or perceived, that a mass evacuation from Angola was undertaken. Between 1 May and 31 August 1975, T.A.P. flew 136,000 Portuguese nationals back to Lisbon, 254 flights on its own 747s, 232 on chartered 707s. Other airlines, Portuguese and foreign, carried an additional 68,000 refugees. Almost 4,000 people were evacuated on one single day. This was a magnificent example of the value of an efficient airline in times of national crisis; but the loss of the colonies depleted T.A.P.'s revenues by 40%.

During the next few years, times were difficult until, in January 1980, new president Fernando Augusto dos Santos Martins undertook a bold recovery program. In 1981, backed by three European banks and the U.S. Export-Import Bank, T.A.P. signed a contract to buy five Lockheed L-1011 TriStars. The government agreed to wipe out past financial losses, caused by the loss of the African territories and the obligation to operate other unprofitable routes. More emphasis was placed on the need to increase air tourism to Portugal, still provided mainly by foreign charter airlines. To enhance its image, the name of the airline would be changed to the more identifiable **Air Portugal**. The big Lockheeds entered service in 1983, and Airbus A310-300s were added. On 16 April 1989, a direct Lisbon-Los Angeles route opened via Terceira, a third en route stop in the Azores.

In the shadow of Spain, its larger neighbor, Portugal was nevertheless taking a welcome share of the flourishing European north–south tourist traffic. Faro, on the Algarve coast in the south, was one of the major destinations. T.AP Air Portugal (an interim name change) now faced competition from seven Portuguese airlines, four of which were charter specialists. But such was the growing business that Airbus A320s were added to the fleet in 1992, four Airbus A340s in December 1995, and the first of 16 Airbus A319s arrived two years later. The maintenance base in Lisbon was one of the finest in Europe, with more than 2,000 staff, and had overhaul contracts with other airlines. Manuel Ferreira Lima took over as chairman in February 1996 and soon after announced Air Portugal recorded its first profit after more than 20 years.

As it entered the 21st century, the Portuguese national airline could reflect on its half-century career with pride. It represented a small country, relatively poor by northern European standards, but with a great tradition in the past of bold exploration worldwide. T.A.P. lived beyond its means, however, and the loss of the African colonies was a devastating blow, while the 1974 revolution made things worse. One of the last measures taken thereafter had been, on 26 October 1998, to cancel flights to Macao, as this remnant of a once extensive empire became part of China. The event was symbolic of an historical pattern. Goa and other enclaves in India had been taken over by Delhi in 1961, and Eastern Timor became independent in 2002. The former T.A.P. had done its job as the transport arm of a colonial empire. The new Air Portugal is now performing a different task: the essential component of a well-organized tourist industry—but it was not alone.

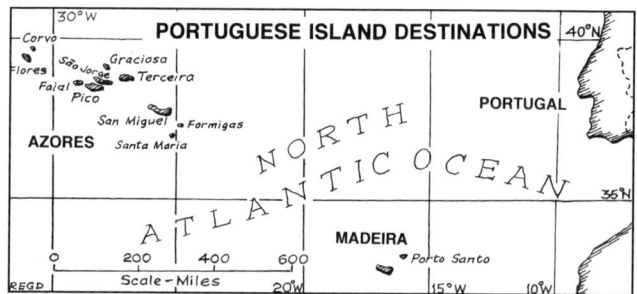

Deprived of an obligation to serve the former Portuguese colonial territories in Africa, the Portuguese airlines still did good business flying to popular island destinations for European tourists.

Portugal was beginning to share in the tourism boom that had effectively changed the lifestyles of Europeans. North of the Alps, people looked upon an annual two weeks or so on southern beaches as part of their way of life; while the people south of the Alps set about catering for the almost continuous exodus. Joining the air tourism business was **Portugália**, founded in Lisbon on 25 July as a joint stock company, with two leased 96-seat Fokker 100s. The first routes, opened on 7 July 1990, were to the country's second city, Oporto, and to Faro, the main tourist destination on the attractive Algarve coast in the south. Charter services were also offered to Funchal, Madeira. Within two years, a fleet of four Fokkers served all the main cities of Europe in a spoke network from Lisbon to provincial cities such as Strasbourg, Cologne, Stuttgart, and Turin. In 1996, to avoid confusion with the acknowledged flag carrier, it changed its name to PGA-Portugália, becoming known simply as **P.G.A.** Six Brazilian Embraer 44-seat EMB-145s enabled the network to expand to many other cities in Europe, as well as Tenerife, and by1998, the number of passengers carried approached a million.

The next year, the Swiss SAir Group purchased 42% of this vigorous newcomer, although the extent of its independence was still regulated, and in 2000, P.G.A. reinstated a previous code-sharing agreement with Air Portugal. Like all other airlines, progress was then severely affected by the terrorist attack in New York on 11 September 2001, and also SIAir collapsed. This thwarted somewhat the launch of P.G.A. Express, which was formed by a wet-leasing agreement with the Omni organization, which supplied 50-seat SAAB 2000s. During its brief history, the Portuguese independent always provided excellent service standards, acclaimed throughout the industry, and this was celebrated by the introduction at the end of 2003 of a shuttle service, operated jointly by Portugal's two airlines, between Lisbon and Oporto.

Post-War Revival in Greece

Before the Second World War, the Greek capital, Athens, had been a vital staging point between Europe and the Middle East, and on to southern and east Asia, for the flag airlines serving their overseas territories. But the small Greek airline, strongly supported by Germany, had operated only short-haul domestic routes. After the Allied victory, commercial air services were slowly revived. Three small airlines (one supported by Scottish Aviation) struggled unsuccessfully to survive, and finally merged. But after continued losses, the Greek government took over on 1 June 1958, and offered the airline for private tender. This was taken up by the big ship owner, Aristotle Onassis, who paid $2.3 million for full ownership. On 6 April 1957, at the threshold of the Jet Age, the new **Olympic Airways** started local services within Greece and to the Aegean islands with a fleet of 14 ex-military Douglas DC-3s, and on 2 June international services with Douglas DC-6Bs leased from the French airline U.A.T.

Still dependent upon foreign technical support, and determined to match all the rich European airlines that used Athens as a refueling stop to the East, Olympic signed a consortium agreement with British European Airways on 1 April 1960. The jet fleet was four 89-seat de Havilland Comet 4Bs, short-haul variants of the Comet 4s used by B.O.A.C., and operated in parallel with B.E.A.'s routes to the eastern Mediterranean. Onassis's shipping fleets, including giant oil-tankers, were to be seen all over the world, and Olympic Airways sought to similarly expand also. With three long-range Boeing 707-320s, trans-Atlantic service from Athens began on 1 June 1966, via Rome and Paris, but with one weekly nonstop flight to New York. Service to Johannesburg via Nairobi, followed on 1 November 1968.

Well financed, and with a free hand since the government had extended his franchise in 1962, Onassis consolidated his airline, terminating the B.E.A. agreement in 1969 as Boeing 727-200s replaced the Comets on European routes, releasing the 707s to fly to Montreal and Chicago. The veteran DC-3s were replaced by the 60-seat Japanese Nihon YS-11s. In 1971, Olympic Aviation was formed as a specialized air taxi/charter division, as well as for local scheduled services, catering for the affluent market which sought individual itineraries to tour the Greek islands.

By 1972, Olympic's main fleet consisted of Boeing 707s, 727-200s, and 720Bs, six of each. On 3 March of that year, a new route opened via Bangkok and Singapore, to Australia, terminating at Melbourne, where the large emigrant Greek population was said to make it the second Greek city in the world.

More aircraft were added, culminating in 389-seat Boeing 747-200s which entered service on 1 July 1973. But shortly thereafter, Olympic's progress was abruptly halted because of labor problems, and the airline shut down. On 1 January 1975, the Greek government, headed by Prime Minister Constantine Karamanlis, took control. Some long-haul routes were abandoned, Airbus A300-B4s were added in 1979, and 18-seat Short Skyvans helped to expand local routes to the islands, which too often had only short airstrips. These were succeeded by 30-seat Short 330s in 1980 and then, on 29 May 1984, by 19-seat Dornier 228-200s. The policy was to extend rapid air service—typically less than an hour from Athens—to every Greek island with a population of more than 1,500. This admirable social objective was pursued at a price, for Olympic lost money heavily, $49 million in 1984 alone. Losses continued and the worsening situation was exacerbated by the outbreak of the Gulf War in August 1990, in which Greece seemed to be too close for the comfort of the European tourist market.

The government was prepared to write off an accumulated debt of $1.8 billion, but this needed the approval of the European Commission, which in 1994 insisted on new management, severe reduction in staff numbers, and the modernization of the fleet. Olympic's progress was intermittent thereafter, as all the staff were civil servants and their jobs were secure under Greek law. A succession of chairmen did their best to resolve the problems, but Europe's "open skies" policy which came into effect in April 1997 cancelled out such efforts. Foreign airlines were now given freer access to the 11-million-strong tourist market, which accounted for 13% of the total Greek gross national product.

Long-range Airbus A340-300s entered service to New York in November 1999, and Boeing 717-200s were leased in January 2000. An attempt for some injection of British capital by Speedwing, British Airways's consultant subsidiary, ended in July 2000. Olympic's survival had been a matter of national pride, rather than emergence as a commercial organization. In December 2003, it was renamed **Olympic Airlines**, in the hope of breaking from its past.

Airlines in the Aegean

The rising tide of airline deregulation finally reached Greece, distant from the heartland of Europe, as it had done in Portugal. As early as 1965, Nick Simigdalás, with a modest fleet of four six-seat Piper Super-Cubs, applied for a license to fly people to the islands, but permission to do this as scheduled services was denied. But his Aegean Aviation survived, and after a decade of successful charter work, he acquired Learjets, obtained a license, and handed over the business to the affluent Vassilakis Group, which owned the biggest Hertz rent-a-car business in Europe. On, 1 January 1999 the government ended Olympic's monopoly, and on 28 May, equipped with two 100-seat BAe RJ-100s, **Aegean Airlines** began service from Athens to five domestic destinations. In October, Aegean acquired **Air Greece**,

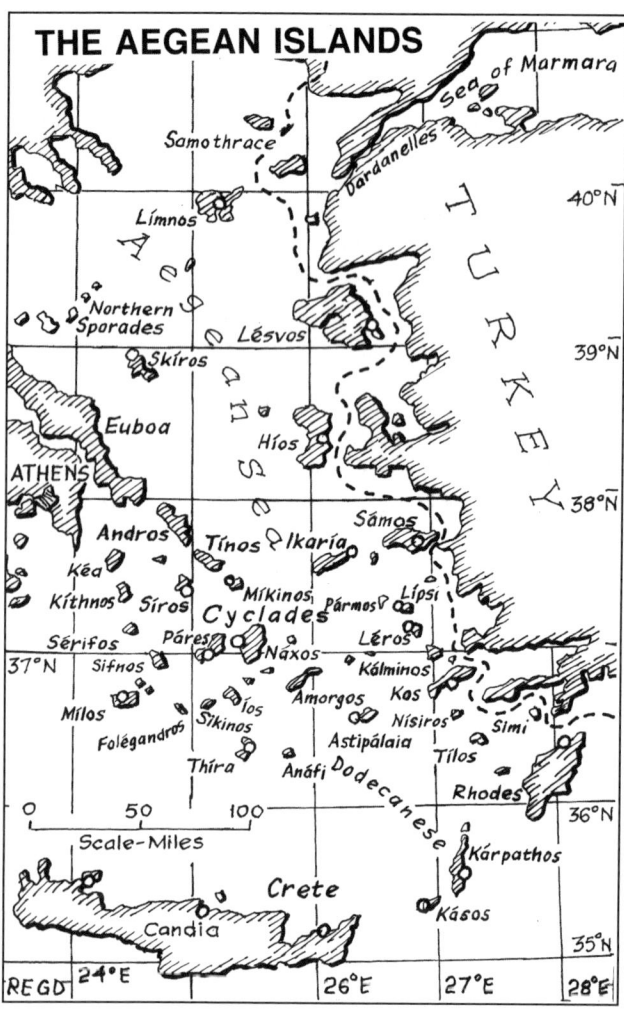

Almost all the many islands of Greece's Aegean Sea now have their own airfields and are directly accessible from Athens by air.

based at Heraklion, Crete, and its fleet of three ATR 72s and two Fokker 100s, and expanded service. This was followed in March 2001 by a merger with **Cronus Airlines**, which operated Boeing 737s to European points.

Opening the Adriatic

Before the Second World War, northern Europeans visited the Mediterranean mostly by train to the French Riviera. Cheap air travel was not yet available, although Mediterranean ship cruises were becoming popular, at least among the upper middle class. Driving a car across the Alps to Italy or Spain was quite an adventure, even an accomplishment. The Adriatic Sea was a branch of the "Med" that was visited only on its western, Italian, shores, as the pre-war roads to and the amenities in the coastal towns of Yugoslavia were little known and seldom frequented.

After the war, this situation began to change. Yugoslavia had become a communist country—a far cry from the Kingdom of the Serbs, Croats, and Slovenes that had been created by the League of Nations in 1918 out of the remnants of the Austro-Hungarian Empire. But under the leadership of the wartime hero Marshal Tito, the multi-racial Balkan country did not join the six countries of eastern Europe as satellites of the Soviet Union, and its relationship with western Europe was cooperative and friendly. One outcome was the development of tourism, made possible by the advent of air travel that was booming from the 1950s onward.

Air service within Yugoslavia resumed sluggishly. **Jugoslovenski Aerotransport (J.A.T.)** was formed on 1 April 1947 with cast-off Douglas DC-3s and Junkers-Ju 52/3m's, but all routes were suspended in 1948 during the uncertain period of the break with the Soviet bloc. Gradually, the airline revived, with cooperation with Swissair, dropping routes to eastern Europe in 1950 and opening routes to western Europe in 1951. The fleet of DC-3s was supplemented in 1954 by Convair 340s and Ilyushin Il-14s in 1957, before J.A.T. finally entered the Jet Age on 1 April 1963 with Sud Caravelles.

By this time, tourists in the north were "discovering" the Dalmatian coast, especially the charming city of Dubrovnik, and J.A.T. began to join the inclusive tour fraternity by forming, on 31 July 1969, **Air Jugoslavia** as a charter subsidiary, which leased Boeing 707s from Pan American Airways. Trading with the West was still difficult, because of the shortage of "hard" currency, but this was overcome by a program of reciprocal trade, under which the value of certain Yugoslav products were exchanged for investment in Douglas airliners. The first DC-9-30 went into service on 13 May 1970; but such was the volume of traffic, especially during the summer tourist season, that larger Boeing 727s entered service on 13 June 1974. J.A.T. established an interesting "hub" operation, in which aircraft from the European cities converged at Zagreb, so that the passengers (who identified their own baggage for the transfers) could connect to the several Dalmatian destinations on the Adriatic coast.

The airline's stature became an effective flag-carrying representative of the nation, many of whose citizens had emigrated to the United States (mainly to build cars in Detroit) and to Australia (to establish a wine industry). J.A.T. served the emigrants who created a flourishing V.F.R. (visiting friends and relations) traffic. Air Yugoslavia's charters were converted into a J.A.T. scheduled service from Belgrade to New York on 15 May 1976, and to Sydney via Kuwait and Singapore, on 1 April 1977. Such was the confidence in continued expansion that on the same day, an order for Boeing 747SPs was announced, but after several weeks of concentrated negotiation, this was changed to three long-range Douglas DC-10-30s. Service with these 270-seat airliners began to New York on 15 December 1978, to Chicago on 1 April 1979, to Beijing on 30 April, and to Melbourne via Sydney, on 19 May of that year.

Under Tito's regime, the Yugoslav airline continued on an even keel from its main base in Belgrade during the next decade, until, with the downfall of the Soviet Union at the end of 1990, things fell apart. A civil war broke out in 1991 and lasted for four years before an uneasy peace was agreed between the various ethnic and religious factions which, dominated by Serbia, had ruled

Jet Wings over the Mediterranean

the country since the fall of its monarchy in the 1940s. The regions had never enjoyed local political autonomy, and they joined in the widespread momentum in eastern Europe to turn its back on communist rule. Croatia and Slovenia became independent countries in the summer of 1991, followed by Macedonia in September. The fighting in the center of Yugoslavia was fierce, but Bosnia-Herzogovina freed itself from Serbian control in 1992. The name Yugoslavia was erased on 4 February 2003, to be succeeded by Serbia-Montenegro, now reduced to little more territory that it had in 1914. The latter land of the Black Mountain seceded in 2006 and subsequently became Kosovo. Somehow, J.A.T. managed to survive, though as a mere shadow of its former self.

Serbian Charter

Yugoslavia's brand of communism was a litle different from that of the Soviet Union, in that a limited amount of commercial activity was permitted, albeit under strict supervision from the Belgrade bureaucracy. Thus Generalexport, a trading company with close associations with Moscow, was able to form, in January 1968, **Aviogenex**, to participate in the burgeoning inclusive tour traffic from northern Europe to the Dalmatian coast, leaving J.A.T. to concentrate on the scheduled market. The initial fleet consisted of two 72-seat Tupolev Tu-134s, and the initial opertions justified replacing these in 1970 with four 80-seat Tupolev Tu-134As. In spite of a fatal crash at Rijeka on 23 May 1971, almost 200,000 tourists were carried in that year, but business subsequently declined and Aviogenex ceased operations.

Slovenian Enterprise

During the post-war decades of communist rule in eastern Europe, all commerce and industry was state-owned, directly, or indirectly via state-owned semi-commercial enterprises. A remarkable exception was to be found in Slovenia, one of the provinces of Yugoslavia, itself distanced from Moscow's control by the determination of Marshal Tito after the Second World War. Here, in the provincial capital, Ljubljana, **Adria Aviopromet** was formed on 14 March 1961 by grants from the local Slovenian administration, and financed by the Slovenian Commercial Bank. The province was Yugoslavia's most prosperous, and had a tradition of going its own way without Belgrade's direct control.

Starting with two Douglas DC-6Bs acquired from K.L.M., its business was entirely non-scheduled, specializing in flights to Germany, on behalf of the growing demand for "guest" workers from southeastern Europe to the car factories in Munich and Stuttgart. At first, the operations were from Zagreb, in the neighboring Croatian province, until the new airport was opened in Ljubljana early in 1964. Such was Adria's service efficiency that it was able to compete effectively and successfully with German charter airlines. It was also permitted to operate a weekly service between Belgrade and Algiers, and to participate in services to Dubrovnik, the delightful Adriatic city that was rapidly becoming a popular vacation destination.

By November 1968, however, it was bankrupt and was taken over by the trading organization, Interexport, which changed the airline's name to **Inex-Adria.** Rejuvenation led to the entry into scheduled service, on 18 August 1969, of the first 110-seat Douglas DC-9-32 jet, on the domestic route from Ljubljana to Titograd and Dubrovnik via Belgrade, in parallel with J.A.T.'s Caravelles. Progress thereafter was steady, with extra DC-9s enabling route expansion to the Middle East as well as to Europe, marred only by a crash near Aden on 19 March 1972.

Inex-Adria added the larger DC-9-50s from 1976, but experienced another tradegy in that year when a DC-9 collided with a British Airways Trident 3 over Zagreb. Fortunes were then mixed as, to meet the traffic demand, the first 172-seat "stretched" DC-9-81 (MD-81) went in to service in June 1981. Sadly, this was followed, on 2 December, by the tenth worst recorded air disaster in history, when one of the new aircraft crashed into the mountains on approach to Ajaccio, Corsica, killing 178 people.

On 24 March 1983, Inex-Adria opened its first international scheduled service, to Larnaka, Cyprus, followed, on 7 December 1984, by flights to Munich. In 1986, Interexport sold its ownership, and the airline changed its name back to **Adria Airways.** By

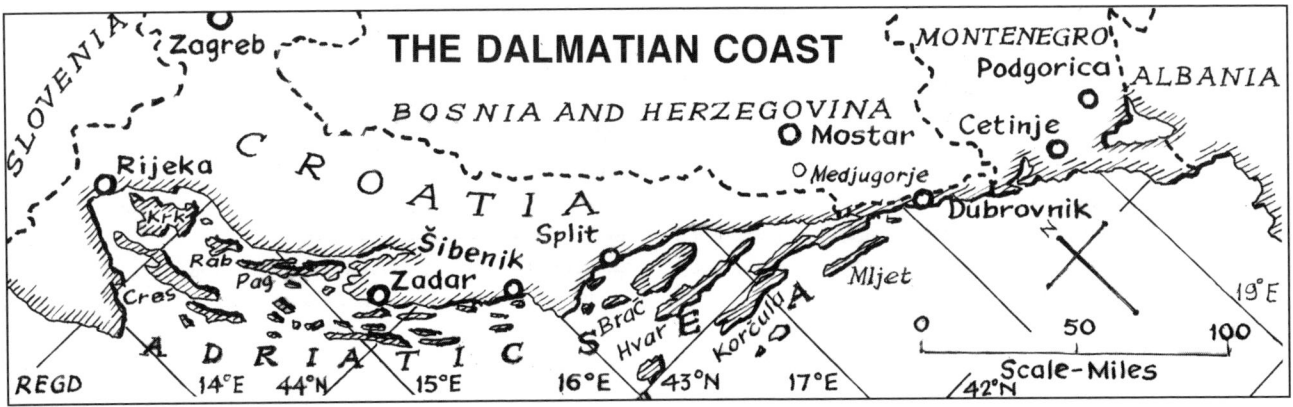

During the 1960s, the Jugoslav airlines, J.A.T. and Inexadria, expanded services to the Dalmatian resorts, especially Dubrovnik. At the Zagreb hub, passengers transferred their own baggage on to the connecting flights.

this time, the fleet comprised 10 DC-9s and two de Havilland Canada Dash Sevens, and in March 1989, it took the bold step of introducing Airbus A320s, becoming, incidentally, the launch customer for the V2500-powered version of that airliner.

Soon afterward, in June 1991, Slovenia declared its independence from the Serbian-dominated Yugoslavia. Although war did not break out, the Yugoslav Air Force raided the Ljubljana airfield. Adria's installations and four of its aircraft were badly damaged, as well as the base itself. On 25 October, its operating certificate was suspended and it returned on 16 January 1992 only by moving its base temporarily to Klagenfurt, across the border in Austria. Picking up the pieces, Adria managed to carry on into the 21st century with a restored fleet, plus five CRJ200 feeder-line aircraft, and maintaining close cooperation with Lufthansa.

Emergence of Croatia

Shortly after the formation of Adria Aviopromet in Slovenia, **Pan Adria** was formed on 25 May 1961 in Zagreb, in the Croatian province of Yugoslavia. It lost out to the other Adria in developing the inclusive tour traffic to the many new resorts on the attractive Dalmatian coast, especially Dubrovnik, and at first had to be content with local taxi and agricultural work with small aircraft. On 3 July 1964, however, it began an enterprising night-mail service from Zagreb to Split and Dubrovnik, followed by a regular passenger service to Mostar and night mail to Belgrade and Skoplje (Macedonia province).

The modest fleet was three Czech-built Moravas, replaced in 1967 by three Aero Commander 500s, and then, in 1970–71 by four Convair 440s. It started an international route to Trieste, Italy, and moved into the European charter market to England, where the Dalmatian coast was becoming very attractive to regular holiday-makers who wished to make a change from the crowded resorts in Spain. Pan Adria moved into the Jet Age when it took delivery of its first Douglas DC-9 on 25 May 1973.

It appears to have ceased operations, replaced by **Trans Adria**, which began service on 7 March 1979, on a network centred on Zagreb, with Fokker F-27s and Swearingen Metros. But although J.A.T. had made Zagreb its hub to distribute European vacationers to the Dalmatian resorts, full recognition of Croat status in the area did not come until the approach of full independence. Croatia soon followed Slovenia in gaining independence "like a child going through a nasty divorce" as David Forward has neatly described the Balkan turmoil in the summer of 1991. Zagal (the abbreviation for Zagreb Airlines) had been formed—almost in anticipation of the break with Serbia—in 1989, and on 23 July 1990 it changed its name to **Croatia Airlines**. It was the first shareholder company in the former Yugoslavia, and started operations to Split on 5 May 1991, with an MD-80 leased from Slovenia's Adria.

During the ensuing conflicts, only a few months later, services were only intermittent, because of the fighting, and tourists had fled. But Croatia bought three Boeing 737-200s from Lufthansa, and in 1993 two ATR42-300s. The diplomatic bargaining for traffic rights between the new ex-Yugoslav republics was difficult, but staffing was less of a problem, because of desertions from J.A.T. And the Dalmatian coast, from Rijeka in the north to Dubrovnik in the south, gave the airline confidence for future traffic potential.

The Maltese Mouse

The diminutive stature of Malta in the European airline arena is certainly true, as its population of some 400,000 hardly suggests the operation of a thriving national airline. Yet that is exactly what the heirs to the Knights of St. John (who once successfully resisted the power of the Ottoman Empire) have accomplished.

Malta remained a British colony after the Second World War. Two companies had been formed, with British independent airline help, but these had given way to partnership with British European Airways (B.E.A.). The surviving Malta Airways was little more than a handling agent for the state corporation until 1963, when **Air Malta** was formed as the national flag carrier of the new republic. B.E.A. continued to lease its aircraft, but the technical support came from Pakistan International Airways, which took 20% of the capital, and supplied two Boeing 720Bs which had become surplus to its requirements, following the loss of East Pakistan to create Bangladesh.

Completely independent operations began on 1 April 1974, with services mainly to London, but also to other northern cities in Europe and to nearby Tripoli. Tourist traffic expanded swiftly, especially during the summer, during which a variety of different aircraft were leased from different companies. More routes were opened, including Cairo and Tunis, and by 1978 Air Malta was boarding more passengers than the country's total population. In that year, it purchased and operated the first aircraft of its own, two 720Bs bought from Western Airlines. Assisted by a local restriction on charter companies, it continued to grow apace. The first of six Boeing 737-200s entered service in March 1983, and B.E.A. stopped its service to Malta in 1989. The network expanded in the north to other cities of Britain and Germany. Airbus A320-200s were added to the fleet in August 1990 and, in 1993, were flying to the Middle East as far as Dubai. In May 1994, Scandinavia was added to the map; Oslo becoming the 36th destination. During the summer of 2000, Air Malta added ambitious flights to New York, with wet-leased Boeing 757-200s from America Trans Air, but not enough American tourists were diverted from the Spanish resorts. Air Malta sensibly withdrew the service.

Across the Straits

Of the British footholds in the Mediterranean, only one remained defiantly British, after Malta and Cyprus became independent. The small, vigorously British community at the foot of the famous Rock of Gibraltar has resisted the sovereignty claims of Spain since 1713, and its naval base was one of the ports essential for the Royal Navy when the British Empire depended on the shipping route through the Mediterranean to reach its far-flung possessions in Asia.

Remarkably, it had an airline. The local Bland Line, which operated local sea and cable car excursions, had interested itself in an airline as early as 1932, to fly the 40 miles across the Straits to Tangier which, at that time, was an unusual city, a community wholly within Morocco, but presided over by an international council of seven European nations. Tangier finally reverted to Morocco in 1956. Gibraltar revived its ambition after the Second World War, and on 15 May 1947, organized **Gibraltar Airways**, in cooperation with British European Airways, which provided the initial fleet of three de Havilland DH-89 Rapides. The flights took 21 minutes, and achieved excellent reliability, even though, against headwinds in the lee of "The Rock," some pilots claimed that they were flying backward.

B.E.A. took over the route with its own DC-3s in October 1953, cutting the time to 10 minutes, and put its Viscounts on the route in 1959, as an extension from London. It operated to London with Vanguards and did much to develop the nearby Costa del Sol, but the introduction of more expensive Tridents coincided with the Spanish closure of the frontier. The Gibraltarians were reluctant to lose the London connection and **Gibair** (as it was popularly called) took over the route, using Tridents at first then chartering Boeing 737s from Britannia Airways. By 1963, the veteran DC-3s were back to Tangier; for such a short route, they were the most flexible and adaptable. Gibair sought to expand service to nearby points in Morocco, but lacked support; and to Spain which, however, in 1969, denied access, as General Franco closed even the road into Spain until 1985.

With the reopening of the frontier, Gibair bought its own aircraft, and expanded its route network to Spain, Morocco, and other Mediterranean points with a small fleet of Airbus A320s. In the mid-1990s, it moved its base to London's Gatwick Airport, and changed its name to **GBairways**, as a British Airways franchised associate. At last, on 16 December 2006, after Spanish claims to Gibraltar had simmered down to a whisper, a landmark flight was made to Madrid, while Iberia reciprocated with one to Gibraltar. It was an historic event, as both airlines were new to the route, which had hitherto been operated only by B.E.A. If Malta's statistics of air passengers versus indigenous population were remarkable, Gibraltar's were sensational. The resident population was less than 3,000, but annual visitors numbered in the millions.

Albanian Rebirth

For the devotees of trivia, the history of Albanian air transport presents an interesting item. Way back in February 1927, first with German sponsorship and Junkers-F 13s, Adria Aero Lloyd operated short domestic routes from Tirana, and these passed to Italian airlines in July 1929. Thereafter, air transport was confined to flights from Italy, as Mussolini's fascist government increased its control of the country, culminating in complete annexation in 1939. Air services within Albania, after its liberation in 1944, did not resume until 1992. The former kingdom of Albania had bypassed whole generations of airliner development, from the DC-3 era to the last of the piston-engined aircraft. It went straight from the world's first transport airplanes to the world's first turbo-props and jets.

Yugoslavia's communist independence from Moscow had been an unusual political circumstance as the countries of Europe emerged from the Second World War. Albania's was even more remarkable, for it allied itself with communist China, whose rulers chose this small Balkan country as a foothold in Europe, for political influence and for trade. The country closed its frontiers. The only air services for about half a century were by China's C.A.A.C., East Germany's Interflug, and Hungary's MALEV. Then the fall of the Berlin Wall in 1989 heralded a political revolution and a primitive democracy.

As is typical of almost every country that emerges from a war or a revolution, after democratic reforms were adopted in 1992, one of Albania's first industrial actions was to form an airline. **Albanian Airlines** was formed in that year by a partnership with Tyrolean Airways, from Austria, which operated the first route to Vienna with two 36-seat de Havilland Canada Dash 8-300s. Progress was slow, and ceased entirely in 1993, when the government took over the bank account, well into red ink. The airline was sustained only by the interest of Mohammed Al-Kharafi, an Egyptian businessman who bought 95% of the company shares and resumed service on 30 June 1995 with a leased Airbus A320. A year later, realizing that an Airbus was too big for the limited market (comprised mainly of emigrants and refugees from the old regime), Albanian Airlines leased Tupolev Tu-134s from Bulgaria and built up a modest network to a few European cities, adding two BAe 146s, a Yakovlev Yak-40, and a larger Tupolev Tu-154A. The country has some potential for building up a tourist industry and, by the 21st century, was successfully emerging from its former isolation from the rest of Europe.

A Divided Island and a Claim to Fame

After the First World War, when Britain took over Cyprus from the Ottoman Empire, it became a crown colony, to join Malta and Gibraltar as strategic outposts of a declining Commonwealth, especially as a base for the Royal Air Force. It was also important for the British state airlines, as a staging point in the eastern Mediterranean, and even as a destination in its own right, as adventurous tourists went beyond Greece in search of the sun and ancient culture. To recognize local sensibilities, **Cyprus Airways** was formed on 24 September 1947, with the Cypriot government (still under a British governor) and British European Airways (B.E.A.) holding 40% each of the shares, and private interests taking up the balance. Services began to Athens on 6 October 1947, at first with B.E.A.'s aircraft and then, from 6 October, with its own Douglas DC-3s. During a period during which Archbishop Makarios led a movement toward union with Greece, the airline nevertheless grew, to serve points in Turkey and the Levant, and by 1950 as far as Bahrain in the Gulf and Khartoum in east Africa.

During the 1950s, Britain's other state airline, B.O.A.C., took shares in Cyprus Airways, and with B.E.A.'s strong support (as it regarded the airline as a surrogate branch of its own operations), Nicosia had the distinction, on 18 April 1953, of being the final destination of the world's first turbojet (propjet) airline service, when a 40-seat Vickers Viscount 700 arrived from London via Rome and Athens.

During the 1950s, not only was there division between the Greek and Turkish ethnic populations; there was also rivalry between the two British state corporations. B.E.A. saw Cyprus as a hub for its eastern Mediterranean routes, while B.O.A.C. regarded the area as within its Middle Eastern sphere of influence. B.E.A. took over all the operations on 26 January 1958, under a charter agreement, and, following the granting of full independence in 1960, a new five-year contract on 26 January 1961 recognized the airline as the national carrier of Cyprus, with Comet 4Bs introduced on 4 July. When the contract was renewed in 1965, all local routes were operated from 1 November by Cyprus Airways on its own account and with its own crews, although B.E.A. still provided technical support and Viscount 800s. But progress toward stability was marred by the constant friction between the Greeks and the Turks to such an extent that Turkey refused to admit flights to Ankara or Istanbul under the Cypriot flag. During the 1960s, an uneasy truce prevailed in Cyprus, and the airline was also handicapped by continual unrest and wars throughout the Middle East. Yet with B.E.A. support, it still began to operate de Havilland 100-seat Trident 2 tri-jets in September 1969.

In January 1972, the airline bought two Trident 2Es from B.E.A., chartered another, and, on 1 June 1974, exchanged one of these for a BAC One-Eleven, but these aircraft were short-lived. Differences between the Greek and Turkish peoples on the island had intensified. Turkish military intervention exacerbated a smoldering ethnic conflict that erupted when, six weeks later, on 15 July, the Cypriot National Guard seized power, and Makarios fled the country. Heavy fighting soon broke out in a civil war and by the end of August, Cyprus Airways' fleet was all but destroyed, and had to be written off. Turkish forces had occupied the northeastern side of the island on 16 August. This was about 40% of the area, and Nicosia, the capital city and the airline's base, was split into two.

Operations resumed on 8 February 1975, with two 73-seat Viscount 810s leased from British Midland, and with the base transferred to Larnaka, in the southern (Greek) side. Recuperation was complex but determined, and essentially Greek as the Turkish Cypriots voted, on 8 June, to form a separate state. Cyprus Airways then managed to defy basic principles of fleet compatibility by adding two DC-9-10s to replaced the Tridents then an assortment that included a DC-8-52, a Bristol Britannia, 3 BAC One-Elevens, 2 Boeing 720s, 2 all-cargo DC-6s, and even a Canadair CL-44. Many flights radiated from Paphos, which became Cyprus's second international airport, but administrative offices remained in Nicosia.

The airline could claim that Resilience is its middle name. By 1978 it had settled down to a fleet of three One-Eleven-500s, and four ex–American Airlines Boeing 707-123Bs. It was operating to 10 European and 11 Middle Eastern points, and by 1983 was entirely Cypriot-owned. Well run, Cyprus Airways has made profits consistently, and at the end of 1984 it took delivery of two Airbus A310s. European tourists too were resilient, as Cyprus had become a popular destination, with the familiar attractions of Mediterranean climate and historic associations. During the 1980s, with continued recovery, further destinations were added, especially in the Gulf. In 1989 it introduced Airbus A320s, of which type it was one of the launch customers.

Ethnic political rivalry was matched by commercial rivalry in the air. While Greek Cyprus Airways could draw upon experienced staff and organization to recover from the civil war, the Turkish north had no such advantage and had to start from scratch. Furthermore, Northern Cyprus was not recognized as a sovereign country and has not been admitted to the United Nations, whose personnel still patrol the border between the two parts of the country. But with the support of THY Turkish Airlines, **Cyprus Turkish Airlines (C.T.A.)** or **K.T.H.Y.** (*Kibris* is Turkish for "Cyprus") managed to begin service to nearby Turkish cities in the late 1970s, using aircraft on a generous lease arrangement from T.H.Y., with which it operated almost as a joint airline. However, as Northern Cyprus was not a member of the United Nations, the airline was not admitted to I.C.A.O., and could not fly directly to Europe. And just as Cyprus Airways had had to establish bases on the southern coast, C.T.A. too had to improvise from airfields other than Nicosia's main airport.

In the spring of 1990, it bought a Boeing 727-200 Advanced from T.H.Y., and proudly repainted it in its own colors. Like its neighbor across the buffer zone, it exploited the tourist market not only in Turkey—Istanbul was a prime destination—but also to London, in conjunction with T.H.Y., as onward flights from Turkey.

Another Cypriot airline was short-lived, and ceased operations for a different reason: a much-publicized crash. In 2004, Libra Holidays had bought **Helios Airways**, formed in 1999, which operated regularly through many points in Europe. It had one Airbus A319 and two Boeing 737-300s. When one of the Boeings crashed near Athens on 14 August 2005, killing all 121 people on board, the name was changed to AJet, or Alpha Jet, but ceased operations in 2006.

Chapter 31: Farthest North with the Scandinavians

...Together We Conquer

Except in southern Sweden, the terrain and population distribution of Scandinavia lends itself to air transport, and all three countries had been in the forefront of aviation development in the earliest years. A strong sense of private enterprise had complemented the government initiative that had led to the formation of S.A.S. Norway's large shipping companies had branched out into aviation, while Denmark, especially, a land of islands, could support local air services in spite of its diminutive size. **Scandinavian Airline System (S.A.S.)** had already, in 1957, taken a half-share of Sweden's Linjeflyg and on 26 February 1971, in partnership with Maersk and Cimberair, formed Dan-Air. (The local/regional airlines of the individual countries are reviewed below.)

Unlike the airlines of southern Europe, where political developments led to enforced fragmentation, the countries of northern Europe beyond the Baltic Sea regained stability after the end of the Second World War. Individually, they sensed that they could not compete with the powerful airlines of the larger countries to the south, and felt that divided, they would almost certainly have fallen. As events unraveled, the S.A.S. emerged as the world's only completely successful airline consortium. Geographically, Scandinavia includes only Norway, Sweden, and Denmark, but Finland and Iceland are also included in the context of the historical review in this book. Cooperation between them all has been consistent, even though commercial rivalries have prevented a closer union. There have been suggestions that a Scandinavian consortium could embrace Finland and Iceland, but the spirit of independence prevailed, and today, Finland, Iceland, and Greenland, and even the little Faroe Islands, have gone their own way.

Presiding over the field of commercial aviation throughout the area, S.A.S. was formed in 1946 by merging the three national airlines, and with the shareholding in proportion to the populations of the three partners: three-sevenths Sweden, two-sevenths each Norway and Denmark. This consortium was given the privilege of exclusive international traffic rights for commercial air services from the three countries. The complications of its multi-national formation obliged it to form a non-operating subsidiary in the U.S.A., to overcome U.S. traffic rights legalities, and its aircraft were progressively registered separately in the three countries. When the Jet Age began, S.A.S. had already pioneered routes across the Arctic Ocean to reduce distances and times between European and American points. Its Great Circle Polar Route inauguration in 1954 was a landmark date in the history of air transport. It was not all smooth sailing (or, more correctly, flying), however, as while in 1959 it had made a shrewd investment in creating Thai International Airways, its venture with Mexico's Aerovías Guest had been a failure. In 1959 also, severe labor disputes had led to the suspension of most S.A.S. services, which demanded substantial financial help from the three national owners in 1961.

By this time, on 15 May 1959, S.A.S. had opened its first jet service, with a Sud Caravelle, from Copenhagen to Cairo via Prague, Budapest, Istanbul, and Damascus—not the shortest route, but one that "showed the flag." Even though most European airlines, led by SABENA, had started trans-Atlantic jet services with the Boeing 707 in 1958-60, the Scandinavians awaited the Douglas DC-8, and began flights to New York on 1 May 1960, soon putting them on the Polar Route, and, on 2 November 1961, to Johannesburg. New routes to Chicago and Montreal on 1 April 1964 reflected a complete financial turnaround, cancelling out its losses of 1961.

In 1965, S.A.S. gained two more places in the record books. It was the first airline in Europe to introduce an electronic reservation system and to hire a female pilot, Norwegian Turi Wideroe, whose family had pioneered the coastal routes along the Norwegian fjords and opened up air service to the Lofoten Islands.

By the mid-1960s, the world's first short-haul jet airliner, the Caravelle, had been overtaken by a second generation. Of the main competitors, Douglas won against the Boeing 737 and the BAC One-Eleven by offering a special variant of its DC-9 series to suit S.A.S.'s special specifications, with the "stretched" 140-seat DC-9-40 and the "shrunk" 80-seat DC-9-20 series. These went into service on 12 March 1968 and 15 January 1969, respectively.

Short Route to the Orient

Meanwhile, S.A.S. had continued its pioneering of innovative long-haul routes. It introduced the DC-8-62 on 22 May 1967. This was a development of the first DC-8, with a lengthened fuselage, mainly to accommodate more fuel for extended range, and the Scandinavian airline showed great initiative by pioneering yet another major long-distance air route. Following negotiations with the Soviet Union for overflying rights, it inaugurated the Trans-Asian Express service on 4 November. The route from Copenhagen to Singapore via Tashkent and Bangkok (where the Thai landing and traffic rights were secure through its association with the Thai airline) was 5,356 miles long, with a total journey time of just over 12 hours. This saved about 3,000 miles over the traditional route via the Middle East and southern Asia, and S.A.S. could offer convenient connections with most of the major European capitals. It was even a good way to travel from London to Australia. Such was the success of this new Great Circle route that, on 28 March 1971, S.A.S. took advantage of its Soviet Union overflying privileges, and an association with Aeroflot, to introduce the Trans-Siberian Express, from Copenhagen to Tokyo via Moscow.

Passengers arriving at Longyearbyen, Spitzbergen, (the northernmost airport in the world) are advised not to stray far. (Davies)

Other policy and organizational changes were not so headline-attractive but nonetheless important. In February 1970, it became a member of the KSSU Group of European airlines, promoted by Douglas, and aimed at sharing maintenance and spares holdings. The other members of the Group were K.L.M., Swissair (with which S.A.S. already enjoyed a close relationship), and the French independent, U.T.A. One sequel to this technical partnership was, in September 1971, to add an order for 250-seat Douglas wide-bodied DC-10s to the 360-seat Boeing 747s, the first of which went into service to New York on 9 April 1971.

The Douglas DC-10 entered service on the Polar Route across the North Pole, direct to Tokyo, on 5 November 1974. Although S.A.S. had to have the larger Boeing 747 for its main long-haul route to the United States, it had become a solid Douglas customer, with reorders for its large fleets of DC-8s and DC-9s. Less publicized was another new route, but of a certain historical

An S.A.S. Douglas DC-9 is photographed at Longyearbyen, Spitzbergen. On the mountainside in the background is one of the Russian coal mines. (Davies)

importance. This was the inaugural flight, with a DC-9-41, on 2 September 1975, to Longyearbyen (Longyear City) on the main island of the Spitzbergen (Svalbard) group, a Norwegian territory in the Arctic Ocean. Braathens, the Norwegian shipping company, had already made charter flights, but S.A.S. was able to claim the operation to the world's most northerly point served by a scheduled air route, only 790 miles from the North Pole.

The next few years were operationally uneventful but the 30th anniversary of the consortium's foundation was celebrated and, in 1978, paid tribute to Knut Hagrup, who had steered S.A.S. through its best years. But as its first Airbus A300B-22 entered service on 18 February 1980, the world's air transport industry was entering a new era, as non-scheduled airlines were making inroads into what had hitherto been regarded as a protected environment for government-owned or state-supported airline flag carriers. S.A.S. sustained its first annual financial loss in 18 years, admitting the effect of low-fare airlines such as Freddie Laker's, and on 1 June 1982, introduced discounted low fares itself. Jon Carlson, the new (ex-Linjeflyg) president, in a statement that reflected the changing situation globally, as well as for S.A.S. alone, announced "The comfortable days under IATA's protection are gone. Now we've got to be more like the street-fighters."

The tradition of innovation was continued—to offset, perhaps, an awareness that the Scandinavian population as a whole (less than half of Germany's, Great Britain's, France's, or Italy's) and without the sunshine-guaranteed tourist destinations such as those of Spain and the Mediterranean, was not enough to sustain a natural indigenous market. In 1984, to cross the narrow strait between Sweden and Denmark, S.A.S. started a hovercraft service from Malmö to Copenhagen's Kastrup Airport, for international airline passengers only from southern Sweden. Even that connection has now been offset by a bridge across the strait. In the same year, it started **Eurolink**, for short-haul commuter services, based at Copenhagen, and connecting cities in Norway and Sweden with Hamburg.

Compensating for its demographic weakness, Carlson sought to rejuvenate commercial links overseas. In 1988, he sought to acquire a 40% interest in Aerolíneas Argentinas, but this idea fell through in the face of local protests, and the investment was transferred to Chile. More promising was an agreement with Frank Lorenzo's Texas Air Corporation, which controlled Continental Airlines and Eastern Air Lines. At the end of the year, S.A.S. purchased a quarter of the stock of the Airlines of Britain group, and by the end of 1990, its overseas alliances comprised the European Quality Alliance, with Swissair, Finnair, and Austrian, together with connections with Thai International, All Nippon, and Canadian International. But the world of commercial airlines had by now fulfilled Carlson's words about street-fighting. The Quality Alliance—known as the Alcazar—did not last long, as Swissair collapsed. A cooperative agreement with Lufthansa was forged in May 1995, while the links with Continental ended with an agreement with United Airlines in December. Deals were made to meet European Union requirements concerning the threat of monopolistic practices, but S.A.S. was meeting much competition

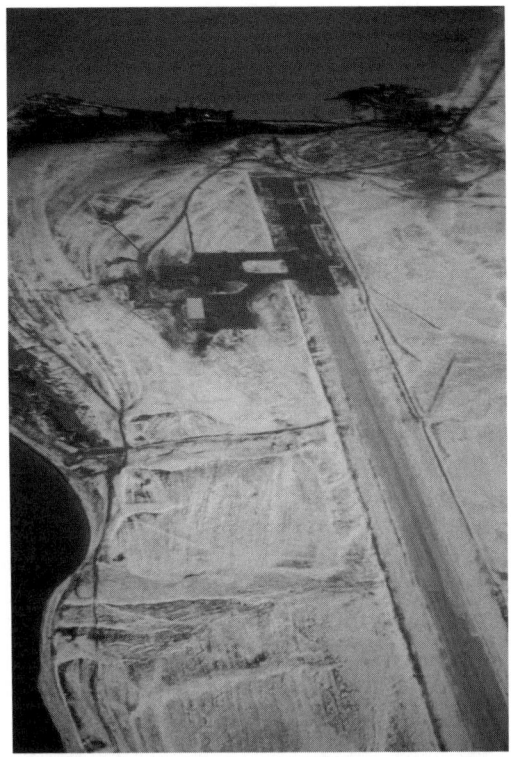

During the 1970s, at the most northerly commercial airport in the world, Longyearbyen, Spitzbergen, the runway was painted white, to reflect the day-long summer sunshine that melted the permafrost. This produced an uneven surface, but the paint was removed as jet aircraft found it difficult to stop when landing. (Davies)

from the former outcasts of the flag carrier hierarchy. Denmark's Sterling Airways (see below) had catered for most Scandinavian southbound sun-seeking tourists, while easyJet and Ryanair would soon lead all European airlines in passenger boardings.

And so the battle for survival went on. In December 1997, S.A.S. took a 29% stake in Wideroe's Flyveselscap to secure its Norwegian base, and consolidated this in May 2001 by acquiring a two-thirds shareholding in Braathens. But it was fined $36 million by the European Commission for entering into a cartel-like agreement with Maersk. By the end of the decade it started to reduce its Douglas fleet. A large order for 55 Boeing 737-600s in September 1998 would replace the DC-9s (and the Fokker 28s), while one for 4 Airbus A330-300s and 6 A340-300s in December 1999 would replace the long-haul Boeing 767-300ERs.

As the reputable Scandinavian flag carrier (always three flags) entered the 21st century, President Jan Sternberg was succeeded, on 8 May 2001, by Joergen Lindegard. The devastating blow to all the world's airlines by the terrorist attack in New York on 11 September 2001 was followed only a month later by another blow to S.A.S. when 114 peopled were killed on one of its MD-87s in Milan, when a business jet crashed into it during dense fog.

Forced by its relative demographic weakness to continue to adopt a cosmopolitan base, a majority stake in Spain's Spanair was acquired in 2002 and on 30 March 2003, S.A.S. launched a low-fare subsidiary, **Snowflake**, equipping it with four of its large Boeing 737-800s. The shape of the airline was undergoing a change from its traditional role of long-haul technical and operational leadership. It now had to react to others, rather than set a pioneering pace. Within the new European "open skies" market, it faced increased low-fare competition right on its own doorstep, when, in April 2003, the ubiquitous Ryanair opened its fourth operating base at Skavsta Airport, 60 miles south of Stockholm, but at no great disadvantage for the ground connection to the city, as S.A.S itself was not exactly downtown. The year 2005 witnessed a further tightening of the belt as the long-haul operations were reduced to five destinations: Washington, New York, Chicago, Bangkok, and Tokyo.

The Power of the Pulpit

At the beginning of the Jet Age, the most effective challenge from the private sector to S.A.S.'s near-monopoly of air transport in Scandinavia came not from the travel agencies or potential airline entrepreneurs, but quite unexpectedly from a minister of the church who initially had nothing to do with aviation at all. In 1950, at Tjaereborg, in southwestern Denmark, Pastor Ejlif Krogager was asked by a group of his parishioners to organize a bus trip to Spain for a summer vacation. The first journey lost money but the idea caught on. The second one was well patronized, and resulted in the formation of Tjaereborg Rejser, Nordisk Bustrafik, as a travel bureau. It eventually built up a fleet of 70 long-distance motor coaches.

Having been deprived of the opportunity to travel abroad for so long during the Second World War, the Danes were eagerly joined by the Swedes and Norwegians whose multi-national airline's intercontinental enterprise did not reach down to the pockets of most of the population, admirable though it was for long-distance business travelers. In May 1962, together with Jorgen Störling, from S.A.S., Krogager formed **Sterling Airways**, with a fleet of two ex-Swissair 93-seat Douglas DC-6Bs. On 7 July it made its first low-fare charter flight from Copenhagen to Las Palmas, in the Canary Islands.

This was the start of the story of unprecedented airline progress. After adding to the DC-6B fleet, Sterling entered the Jet Age in 1965 with two new 131-seat Sud Super Caravelle 10s. The airline's rate of growth during the next few years was phenomenal. Under Anders Helgstrand, it outpaced all the other non-scheduled airlines of Europe, benefitting from the economic prosperity of the Scandinavian nations, whose high discretionary income levels, combined with long vacations, created a booming market. During the next decade, passenger boardings increased by 30% per year—a rate almost impossible by the established industry. By 1971, the Caravelle fleet had grown to 29, including seven of the latest 131-seat Caravelle 12s, which could not only fly nonstop to the Canaries but, by refueling at Keflavik, Iceland, and Gander, Newfoundland, could also fly to the United States, mainly to Hartford, Connecticut.

Such expansion demanded larger aircraft. On 3–4 May 1972, Sterling ordered three 189-seat Boeing 727-200s and three 345-seat Airbus A300Bs. To serve the whole Scandinavian market, two 56-seat Fokker F-27s linked Oslo, Gothenburg, and Stockholm with the Copenhagen hub, while, on 1 October 1973, as the first 727 was delivered, a hydrofoil connection was made to nearby Malmö. Throughout the 1970s, the Danish innovator faced increasing competition from all sides, from new charter operators that seemed to be formed every month by the scheduled airlines which adopted the policy of "if you can't beat 'em, join 'em." S.A.S. created **Scanair** as a non-scheduled subsidiary to challenge Sterling on its home turf. In response, during the late 1980s, the latter bought other tour agencies, and became self-supporting, having been bought out from the Tjaereborg Group. But the bubble of success burst, and late in 1993, Sterling Airways was liquidated.

Further capital injection enabled it to resume as **Sterling European**, with a humble fleet of three Boeing 727-200s, and in 1995 the Norwegian shipping giant, Fred Olsen, bought the airline to operate an air-freighting contract with T.N.T. By the time this contract expired in July 2002, the airline was entirely Norwegian-owned, and in November 2000 it had transformed itself to start scheduled services. The first routes were to Alicante and Malaga, followed by other destinations in the Mediterranean. Still based in Copenhagen, its fleet now comprised six Boeing 737-800s which, exceptionally for a low-fare airline, served meals on board because most of its flights exceeded four or five hours. In 2002, it opened 21 new routes, adding 11 more in 2003 and increasing its fleet from eight to 10 airliners. But competition was now intense, and in September 2005, this once standard-bearing innovator was obliged to merge with Maersk Air, a comparative newcomer (see below) to form **Sterling Airlines**. This company was then sold to the FL Group of Iceland, which owned that country's national airline. It had come a long way, in more ways than one, from the church outing in 1950.

Down to the Sea in Ships (of the Air)

The size of Denmark did not encourage local airline operations, but its island territory was separated by stretches of water that only in recent years have been connected by bridges. Like Norway, and dating back to the 9th century, when the Jutes from Jutland invaded England, the Danes have always Gone Down to the Sea in Ships, Now, in the 20th century, they took to the air. On 1 January 1970, the powerful A.P. Møller group, which operated 150 ships and built giant oil-tankers at Odense, with its **Maersk Air**, began short domestic services in Denmark with Fokker F-27 turboprops. On 1 May 1971, it enterprisingly began flights to the Danish Faroe Islands, with 44-seat de Havilland Canada Dash Sevens. Later in that year it participated in DanAir, in partnership with Cimberair and S.A.S.

Maersk was also active in the burgeoning air charter market, and in 1976 introduced its first Boeing 737, which was also able to use the Faroes' small airfield at Vágar (Vågø). In 1980, the first international service opened, to Stavanger, and in 1984, it took advantage of the new European Economic Commission's directorate for inter-regional services with a new route from Billund to Southend. The former was close to Legoland, home of the famous toy manufacturer, while the latter's rail link with London made it convenient to Britain's capital's financial district.

Maersk's network and fleet grew swiftly during the next few years. Fokker 50s supplemented the 737s in 1988 and in October 1990, scheduled services started to Amsterdam, Brussels, and Stockholm, while the London terminus was transferred to Gatwick. By 1996, it was operating a fleet of 25 Boeing 737s. But by the turn of the century, competition from surface transport was intensifying all across Europe, with the construction of motorways and the development of high speed trains. In 1998, a new bridge across the Øresund linked Sweden with Denmark by land. With most of its conglomerated worldwide business in container ships, Maersk withdrew from the always-marginal airways, and on 30 June 2005, the parent company sold its airline to Iceland's Fons Eigarhaldsfélag, which, in turn, sold the airline, now merged with Sterling Airlines, to the FL Group, owners of Icelandair.

Scandinavian Shipping Strength

Separated from the mainland of Europe by the Baltic Sea and narrow straits, the Scandinavian countries have always been among the leading shipping nations of the world. Before the Second World War, Norway—a country of about four million people—had the third largest fleet in the world. Since the War, Finland too has joined this fraternity, and the shipyards of all four Scandinavian countries have flourished. Not surprisingly, the onset of air transport as a major competitor for their passenger business was met sharply by the individual companies, including their conversion to the idea of operating airlines as well as cruise ships or giant oil tankers.

Great credit is due to the Norwegian Braathens family who, headed by Ludvig Braathen, had founded **Braathens-SAFE** on 26 March 1946. At that time, the emergent S.A.S. was concentrating on developing services across the North Atlantic, and making preliminary plans for a trans-Polar route. Braathens aimed to fill a gap which, at that time, seemed to be leave the airline door open. SAFE was the acronym for South American and Far East, and true to its definition, with Douglas DC-4s, it had started a multi-stop route to Hong Kong in August 1949. It was overcome by

For some years, Braathens retained the memory of former ambitions. This Boeing 737's "SAFE" refers to "South America and Far East." (Bentley)

political motives and was obliged to concede such aspirations to the Scandinavian consortium, and suspended service to the Far East in 1954. Nevertheless, it continued in air transport, operating domestic services in Norway from Oslo to Bergen, Stavanger, and other smaller places where the government had built airstrips. Entry into the Jet Age was with turboprop aircraft, a 40-seat Fokker F-27, replacing smaller de Havilland Herons in December 1958.

As in other countries of Europe, Braathens displayed much initiative in providing air services, other than those allowed by the three S.A.S.-supporting Scandinavian governments and the International Air Transport Association (IATA) international cartel. In 1959, it operated the first charter service to Longyearbyen, Spitzbergen, and cooperated with the Icelandic Loftleidir, which had pioneered the non-IATA so-called Sixth Freedom trans-Atlantic route (see below). Night mail flights, including newspaper deliveries, started in 1962. During the 1960s, inclusive tours expanded the scope of operations. Possibly to respect Norwegian pride, Braathens was able to continue its domestic network, even to expand it, and early in 1969, the first 100-seat Boeing 737 began pure jet service, closely followed by 60-seat Fokker F-28s.

By 1972, the airline was carrying a million passengers a year, and was firmly established as an essential element of air transport in Norway. Accordingly, a new Act of Parliament allocated 60% of the domestic air route system to S.A.S., and 40% to Braathens, effective from 1 April 1975. The former concentrated its flights at Oslo, while the latter concentrated on serving all points along the southern and northern coasts. Braathens also continued to serve Spitzbergen, where, in 1959, a modern airport had been opened, and by 1974 was flying there with the 737s.

When Norway deregulated commercial aviation on 1 April 1994, this determined company (which had ceased to operate ships in 1985) had 52% of the domestic market, possibly unique for a non-flag airline. But the pioneering days were over, and it had to fight for its existence in a newer, highly competitive world. During the 1970s, it had formed **Busy Bee** as a low-fare charter affiliate and, in September 1996, purchased control of **Transwede**, across the border, renaming it Braathens-Sweden a year later. By this time the total fleet numbered 37 Boeing 737s, and the SAFE suffix to its name was finally replaced by the corporate A.S.A. Further expansion was made in August 1998 by acquiring **Malmö Aviation**, merging it with Transwede. Its BAe 146-200s plied between points in Sweden to London's City Airport. But this was the beginning of the end, as Braathens had over-reached itself, and was losing money heavily. In May 2000 S.A.S. agreed to acquire a majority shareholding. At first Norway rejected the idea, but on 27 November accepted the "grim reality." The company was renamed **S.A.S.-Braathens**, along with its other subdivisions in Denmark and Sweden.

The Farthest North Airline

To operate any airline services on a regular basis is a challenge to any aspiring entrepreneur. Braathens was not alone, and shared the business with **Widerøe's Flyveselskap**, which, after assorted charter contracts, specialized in providing the Lofoten Islands with rapid and convenient connections with the mainland and with each other. This was no easy assignment, such as, for example, routes between Florida and the Bahamas. The Lofotens are at the same latitudes as northern Alaska or central Greenland. At the time of its founding by Viggo Widerøe in 1934, Viggo had the rare distinction of being an airline president who was sentenced to 10 years in prison (for anti-German sentiments during the Second World War); less onerous a distinction—Wideröe's was the only airline in the world that operated scheduled services—authorized on 1 April 1954—entirely north of the Arctic Circle. Benefitting, however, from the warmer climate generating from the Gulf Stream Drift current, that community enjoys an active and profitable fishing industry. The islands, however, do not offer much in the way of flat surfaces for airstrips, and those that have been fashioned out of the mountainous terrain offer a sporting journey from the specialized aircraft that provide the air services.

Wideröe had entered the Jet Age with rather a stretched definition of the term. Larger 19-seat de Havilland Canada DHC-6 turboprop Twin Otters succeeded the 10-seat Otters on 1 July 1968 when several small 3,000-foot STOL airstrips had been opened in the north. The aircraft were able to cope with the roller-coaster approaches to fields such as the one at Svolvaer, where the pilot has to steer through a gap in the local peaks and avoid the low clouds that obscure those same peaks. A little different as a "jet" experience, it is certainly as demanding as landing a Boeing 747 at JFK in New York. Essential though such flights were for the social benefits to Norway's far-flung people, the little airline could not pay its own way. To meet this definite need for a public utility, the share capital was substantially increased. The Norwegian ship-owner Fred Olsen acquired 40% of the shares through his **Fred Olsen Flyselskap**, which had owned airliners but had not reached into the airline market as much as Braathens-SAFE (above), which took 17.5%. S.A.S. contributed 22% and other investors the remaining shares. This enabled Wideröe's to expand, by 1977, its chain of 35 STOL-ports all the way to

Wideröe operates local services in northern Norway, mainly serving the Lofoten Islands. The airstrips are usually short, with difficult surrounding terrain. STOL (Short Take-off and Landing) aircraft, such as the de Havilland Canada DHC-6 Twin Otter (foreground) and the Dash Seven, are essential. (Davies)

Honningsvåg, the northernmost village in Europe. De Havilland Dash 7s supplemented the versatile Twin Otters on 4 May 1981.

In 1997, S.A.S. increased its stake in Widerøe's to a controlling interest. As the century ended, this airline, founded in 1934 (the year when the Douglas DC-2 first entered service) had become more than a public utility; it was a national institution. When Viggo died on 8 January 2002, the last Twin Otter was retired two months later, after 32 years' service with the type. It took off from Batsfjord's gravel strip, one of a group of communities north of 70° latitude (as in northern Alaska or Greenland. In the 21st century, Jet Age air service in some places in the world is still at the far end of the scale of airliner size and performance.

Back at the Swedish Ranch

Concentrating as it did in its pioneering work in developing intercontinental air routes, S.A.S. had been criticized for neglecting internal routes within Sweden. The need for air transport was real, for Sweden is larger than Italy, and longer from north to south. One requirement was for newspapers, and thus, on 2 April 1957, the flagship airline took a half-share in founding **Linjeflyg**, with two leading newspapers taking the other half. Its first route started to the island of Gotland on 30 September 1957, and quickly expanded to link most of the provincial cities in Sweden, other than the main routes from Stockholm to Gothenburg and Malmo. It got under way at first with Convair 440 piston-engined airliners, and its entry into the Jet Age was marginal, with 26-seat Nord 262 turboprops on 1 May 1962. This was followed by 65-seat Fokker F-28-1000 jets on 25 April 1973, and as traffic grew, Linjeflyg sponsored the development of this small short-haul feeder-liner to the 85-seat -4000 variant on 14 December 1976.

Finnair

Although closely associated with Scandinavia—for many years, Swedish has been a second language for the Finns—it is not part of that large northern peninsula, and its native language is not of the same group, akin only to Estonian and Hungarian. It has been an independent country only since it was freed from Russian Czarist rule in 1917 during the First World War. Finland lost parts of its territory to the Soviet Union in 1945 because of its wartime alliance with Germany. It is continental Europe's farthest north country with a sparse population—only half that of London or Paris. In aviation, however, its diminutive size has not prevented its national airline, **Finnair**, from steady development parallel to its larger neighbors.

The need for an efficient air service was dictated by geography. Surface routes to the rest of Europe were ponderous, because both rail and road needed circuitous routes that led almost to the Arctic Circle. The shipping route from the capital, Helsinki, to Stockholm, was effectively Finland's commercial lifeline, but even this was only the first segment of a long itinerary to western Europe. Throughout Finnair's history—called **Aero O/Y** until 25 June 1968—it was in the forefront of airliner innovation, and before war erupted in 1939, it had ordered the world's first long-range four-engined landplane, the Focke-Wulf 200 Condor.

Such initiative was matched two decades later, when it was an early operator of the world's first short-haul jet, the 80-seat Sud Caravelle, which opened service to Stockholm and on to Germany on 1 April 1960. This airliner was deployed on a domestic route to the northern city of Oulu on 15 December 1961, and Aero O/Y consolidated the domestic network on 30 November 1962 by the purchase of **Karhumaki**, which had been vigorously operated by the two brothers of that name since 1950. This continued as a charter operator as Kar-Air. On 10 February 1965, Finnair made the first Caravelle 10 landing, with an all-weather system, badly needed in Finland's grim climate, but in the same year, reflecting a growing economy and standard of living, this was not needed for a summer service for tourists to Dubrovnik, on the sunny Adriatic. It opened routes to eastern European points in 1968—it was already operating to Moscow and Leningrad—and when it received its first long-range Douglas DC-8-62CF, its first service, on 28 February 1969, was to Spain's Palma.

This was simply the rehearsal for bigger things. On 15 May 1969, DC-8s opened trans-Atlantic to New York via Copenhagen and Amsterdam, through which it had traffic rights. It then followed the Douglas banner by ordering DC-9-10s on 30 July 1970 to expand its routes in Europe. On 27 March 1975, wide-bodied DC-10s replaced the DC-8s to New York. In November 1976, Finnair went east, to Bangkok via Moscow, and in April 1977, Montreal became a co-terminal in North America. Its subsidiary, **Finnaviation**, which had succeeded Karhumaki, extended its northern route to Tromso, Norway, on 1 June 1979, and this feeder airline introduced 15-seat Embraer Bandeirantes on 8 October of that year, while Fokker F-27s were added on 31 March 1980. At the other end of the range (and size) scale, the 270-seat DC-10s opened service to Los Angeles via Seattle, on 16 May 1981.

By the mid-1980s it had matched its long-established and larger neighbor S.A.S. in equipment standards, service, and route

The 15-seat Embraer Bandeirante is just the right size to serve the small communities in the north of Finland. This one is at Rovaneimi, just a few miles south of the Arctic Circle, and the "gateway" to Lapland. (Davies)

network. On 19 April 1983, with the long-range DC-10-30ER, it inaugurated a nonstop route to Tokyo, routed via the Bering Strait. This was the first nonstop European air service to Japan, and it opened up Helsinki as a gateway to the Far East. Finnair operated almost every DC-9 variant—the -10, -40, -50, MD-82 and -83—but notably not the -30. The 42- to 50-seat ATR-42 entered service on 30 March 1986 and the Airbus A300B4 in 1988, as well as SAAB 340s.

The next few years were marked by more intensive competition and by the collapse of the Soviet Union in 1990. This crippled the substantial trade that had been built up between the two countries, and affected Finnair's progress. The new airlines of Scandinavia had eroded much of the trans-Baltic traffic, and in 1997 (as recounted above, it joined forces with Denmark's Maersk Air, in a code-sharing agreement on the Stockholm-Copenhagen route, S.A.S.'s busiest. It had already, in the previous year, absorbed Finnaviation and had terminated Kar-Air. With the loosening of Fifth Freedom rights in the European Union, it joined the Nord Airline Partners alliance, and in September 1999, became a full member of OneWorld, led by British Airways, with which it has already enjoyed a long-standing relationship. It also established links with Estonian Air and Lithuanian Air. In February 2002, Hong Kong was one of the first additional destinations in eastern Asia that demanded the use of six McDonnell Douglas MD-11s. By 2005, Finnair was the third largest European airline serving mainland China, while its medium-haul fleet comprised 29 Airbus A320s, 18 MD-80 series, and 7 Boeing 757-200s.

Icelandic Initiatives: An Heroic Saga

The rise of Iceland as a powerful civil aviation influence is a modern example of an heroic saga to be told as a lesson to a skeptical audience. The skeptics were more than neutral unbelievers; they were the vested interests which were opposed to the idea of any airline daring to offer cheap fares across the Atlantic Ocean in defiance of the first-class, tourist, and economy levels set by the IATA. This was, in spite of its well-worded protests, effectively a price-fixing cartel. As early as 1948, the then local Icelandic airline, **Loftleidir**, whose only overseas route was to Copenhagen, had successfully applied to the American Civil Aeronautics Board for permission to operate charter flights to New York. The C.A.B. did not appear to fear much competition from this diminutive upstart and at the time nor did IATA. After all, Loftleidir had only one unpressurized Douglas DC-4.

This complacency by the Establishment began to change when, on 12 June 1952 (only two months after the start of the world's first jet service) the services were operated on a regular basis, applying special cut-rate fares, and special packages, in co-operation with Braathens (see above) for connections at Reykjavik to Stavanger, and on to Oslo and Copenhagen. During the next 10 years, Loftleidir's traffic increased, as it extended its route map to other major cities of northern Europe, now with a fleet of five Douglas DC-6Bs. The airline was able to do this because, under internationally accepted ruling by the International Civil Aviation Organization (I.C.A.O.), by combining the Third and Fourth Freedoms of the Air (to board and disembark passengers, respectively, in a foreign country) it could evade the conditions of the Fifth Freedom (to carry onward passengers *between* two foreign countries). It could take advantage of Iceland's geographical position in the North Atlantic. The circuitous route from European capitals to New York was longer, the equipment was older, and the amenities were fewer than the big flag carrier airlines; but the fares were cheap.

Much to its surprise, IATA discovered that a discounted fare attracted far more travelers than five-course meals or free drinks. On 26 May 1962, Loftleidir moved its base from the downtown Reykjavik airport to the larger intercontinental base at nearby Keflavik. The Scandinavian countries and the United Kingdom insisted that the connecting flights should be charged at IATA fare levels, but Loftleidir responded by concentrating the low-fare connections at Luxembourg, which was not an IATA member. This was an example of applied demographic principles, as Luxembourg was within a few hours by train or road to the Low Countries, the German Ruhr conurbation, and even Paris. The tactic was spectacularly successful. Loftleidir's traffic almost quadrupled within a single year.

Even IATA could not ignore this preposterous challenge to its air transport dictatorship, and so, in 1963, it lowered its economy fares. Loftleidir responded to the need to replace its piston-engined aircraft, not by choosing a pure-jet type, but by putting into service, on 29 May 1964, its first Canadair CL-44 four-engined turboprop. This 160-seat airliner flew only in the 300–400 mph range, rather than at the 550–600 mph of the Boeing and Douglas jets; but its seat-mile costs were lower, and the passengers were content to exchange the longer journey time for the cheaper fares. Loftleidir called the aircraft its Rolls-Royce 400s. Such was the intensity of the David-and-Goliath battle that Germany imposed advertising restrictions on the Icelandic maverick, which responded by offering attractive stop-overs in Reykjavik, with excursions to the hot springs, the geyser, and the Gullfoss waterfall, the highest in Europe. Together with the attraction of the duty-free shops, Loftleidir can be credited with laying the foundation of establishing Iceland as an unusual, if not unique, vacation destination.

Already highly air-minded because of the difficulties of surface transport in the mountainous terrain, Icelanders showed their mettle. The apparent strength of IATA did not alarm airline executives. To accommodate tourists (tolerating being called "the hippie airline" because of its popularity with youthful backpackers), Loftleidir opened its own hotel at Reykjavik's airport on 1 May 1966, introduced a 24-hour stop-over in Luxembourg, and sent the CL-44s back to Canada for modification. Upgraded Rolls-Royce Tyne engines allowed the fuselages to be lengthened to accommodate 189 passengers. For a short time, these CL-44Js were the largest airliners on the Atlantic route.

By now, Iceland was no longer on the defensive. On 5 March 1969, Loftleidir acquired **International Air Bahama**, a low-cost airline that also operated briefly with Boeing 707s to Luxembourg. These were replaced by Douglas DC-8-63s (the "stretched" variant) and this was followed by participation, with a Swedish shipping line, in forming, on 4 March 1970, Luxembourg-based **Cargolux Airlines International**, partly by allocating two of its CL-44s—with its rear-end loading capability—to the operation. Back in Reykjavik, the Loftleiðir Hotel increased its accommodation to house up to 434. Loftleidir obviously liked the DC-8. It bought a -55 (standard) and opened its own jet service on 4 November 1971. Now in full cry, it replaced its Swedish terminal with Stockholm the next day, and on 2 May 1973 added Chicago as the second destination in the U.S.A.

Loftleidir's complete success overshadowed the development of Iceland's other airline. Founded at Akureyri in 1937, it was reorganized in 1940 as **Flugfélag Íslands.** After the end of the Second World War, it operated Consolidated Catalina flying boats to Scotland, Douglas DC-3s to Copenhagen, and, assisted by Scottish Aviation, opened service to London in 1949. Unlike the renegade Loftleidir, it joined IATA in 1950, and with DC-4s, flew on its own wings. Adopting the more identifiable name **Icelandair** in 1956, it began Vickers Viscount turboprop services on 3 May 1957. Steady development of routes to Europe included the Faroe Islands' first air service on 23 July 1963. Fokker F-27s improved domestic flights on 14 May 1965 and this was followed by its first Jet Age service, with a Boeing 727-100, on 1 July 1967.

Existence of two airlines in such a small country—its population in the 1970s was barely 200,000—was impracticable, if not uneconomic. Consequently, to avoid self-destructing duplication, on 28 June 1973, the two companies agreed to merge. However, they continued to operate separately under an adminimstrative holding company, **Flugleidir**, effective on 20 July. Members of the board included Alfred Eliasson, Loftleidir's imaginative founder, and Sigurdur Helgason, who was to guide the airline's future. The joint airline consolidated its position in air-minded Iceland by purchasing, on 1 September 1978 (**Arnarflug**) **Eagle Air**, a charter airline, founded on 10 April 1976, and operating two 149-seat Boeing 720Bs.

To emphasize the air-mindedness of the island country, the number of domestic passengers carried in 1977 exceeded Iceland's total population. Meanwhile, its overseas operations joined the big leagues when a wide-bodied 270-seat Douglas DC-10CF entered service to New York on 4 January 1979. In October of that year, the merger of 1973 was completed and the joint airline became known as **Icelandair**. Access to Washington, D.C. via Baltimore's airport began late in 1979, and in an admirable example of inter-modality, free motor-coach service connected Luxembourg with more than half a dozen cities in western Germany. On 21 October 1983, cut-rate railroad tickets were offered to Paris and to Switzerland, and free coach services were extended to Belgium and the Netherlands in September 1984. No longer did this airline represent a legendary episode in world air transport history; it had taken its place as a respected member of the world's airline community. It was still a traveler's bargain—the free coaches picked up passengers who had flown New York-Luxembourg for $149.00. On the other hand, Icelandair's first-class Saga service was equal to that of any of the leading long-established airlines.

In the early 1990s, Icelandair augmented its fleet, first, in April 1990, with the first 189-seat Boeing 757-200 (22 in Saga Class) then, in March 1992, with Fokker 50s. These latter replaced the F-27s that had given reliable service for 27 years, but the newer Fokker tuboprops had enough range to fly to Greenland and Scotland, as well as the Faroes. The domestic services, reaching almost every fishing village around Iceland's fjord-indented rugged coast, were reconstituted as **Air Iceland.** Icelandair held 65% of the stock. It had 4,000 stockholders, and was the largest company in the country, accounting for 3% of the gross national product. In October 2006, half the shares were sold to three Icelandic corporations: Langflug (32%), Naust (11.1%), and Blue-Sky Transport Holding (7.4%).

In February 1986, another example of Icelandic originality emerged with the founding, by Captain Angrimur Johansson and his family, of **Air Atlanta**. The name had nothing to do with the American city; it was named after the hotel they were staying at in Switzerland. The originality was that it did not fly its own network of routes, although in its early years, its aircraft flew in its company colors. It was a contract carrier, and specialized in "wet-leasing," that is, rather than the aircraft alone, chartering its aircraft complete with full flight deck and cabin crew, plus guaranteed maintenance and technical support. It was to become the largest wet-leasing airline in the world, specializing with Boeing 707s at first then, in 1989 with Lockheed L-1011 wide-bodies, and, in April 1993, with Boeing 747s. These were chartered all over the world and were much in demand during the Muslim Hajj seasons.

On 22–23 June 1996, it drew much publicity by leasing one of its L1011s for an airborne wedding, at midnight (though still daylight) above the Arctic Circle. The company was happily prosperous in any case, adding regularly to its fleet of Boeing jets. In November 2002, Magnus Thorsteinsson bought a majority shareholding, and by 2004, now owned by the Avion Group, this leader in the field of wet-leasing had a staff of 900, providing efficient support, on the ground as well as in the air, for a fleet of 16 Boeing 747s and 8 Boeing 767s.

The Ultimate in Air Transport

While Iceland is an outstanding example of how air transport can transform the lifestyle of a nation, the modern history of Greenland (one of Denmark's remaining territories after the secession of Iceland in 1944) is more remarkable. Almost entirely because of the advent of airplanes, the transformation has been phenomenal. The second largest island in the world, it consists almost entirely of an enormous ice cap, thousands of feet thick, with a little ice cap–free land on the coastal margins, and almost none of that cultivable. The Inuit population was, until the mid-20th century, only about 20,000, in isolated communities, mainly on the western coast, and commercial activity limited to fishing, seal hunting, and some cryolite mining.

Until the mid-20th century, limited trade with Denmark or elsewhere was entirely by ship. There were no roads. The Second

World War eventually brought Greenland to the world's attention, when the United States established a few bases for logistic flights to the European theater, and after the war, Sondre Stromfjord became a key transit point for airlines that took the "polar" route between Europe and North America. Subsequently, it was a strategic area during the Cold War, for the U.S. observation/defense stations—the "DEW-Line"—against potential air attacks from the Soviet Union, across the Arctic Ocean.

But even with negligible surface lines of communication, Greenland had no airline of its own until after the beginning of the Jet Age. Only on 7 November 1960, was **Grønlandsfly**, or **Greenlandair** organized, as a joint partnership. The Scandinavian S.A.S., which had pioneered the polar route, owned 25%, and the Greenland administration, the Royal Greenland Trading Company, and the private cryolite mining company had 25% each. The first fleet consisted of two Consolidated Catalina flying boats and two de Havilland DHC-3 Otters. These were soon replaced, in 1963, by two Sikorsky S-55 helicopters, the only aircraft able to cope with the short airfields that had been hacked out of the rocky coastal inlets. Such was the transformation of lifestyle for local Greenlanders that, on 1 June 1965, three larger 24-seat Sikorsky S-61Ns were added, fitted with double heaters.

Their success was amazing. By 1970 Greenlandair was carrying 30,000 passengers a year, more than its indigenous population, and five years later, it was carrying 100,000. This eclipsed Iceland's claim to be the most air-minded nation in the world. The airline now had 14 helicopters and two Douglas DC-6Bs to serve the American base at Thule in the far north, to points on the east coast, and to Copenhagen. In 1979, it introduced its first 50-seat DHC-7, and its first jet, a Boeing 757-200, based in Copenhagen, which it also leased to Scandinavian tour operators. In 2001, it took over Air Alpha, operating two Cessna 208B Caravans in the Disko Bay area, and on 18 April 2002, renamed itself as **Air Greenland.**

On 11 November 2002, it began service with a 241-seat Airbus A330-200, as by this time, the population had grown to 56,000 and Air Greenland was carrying 260,000 passengers a year. Many were tourists, and on 28 April 2003, service began to Akureyri, Iceland, as well as to Reykjavik. The DHC-7 fleet was increased to six, and with improvement to the landing strips, the helicopter fleet, which had been the sole airways mode for its first two decades, was reduced to two.

In June 2007, Air Greenland opened jet service to Baltimore, with leased aircraft. In less than a lifetime, a land that had been visited only by intrepid explorers or climate researchers, now welcomes tourists, although they do not stay long. Lacking experience, the schedules were ill timed for connections, either in the U.S.A. or in Europe, and the innovative service was short-lived.

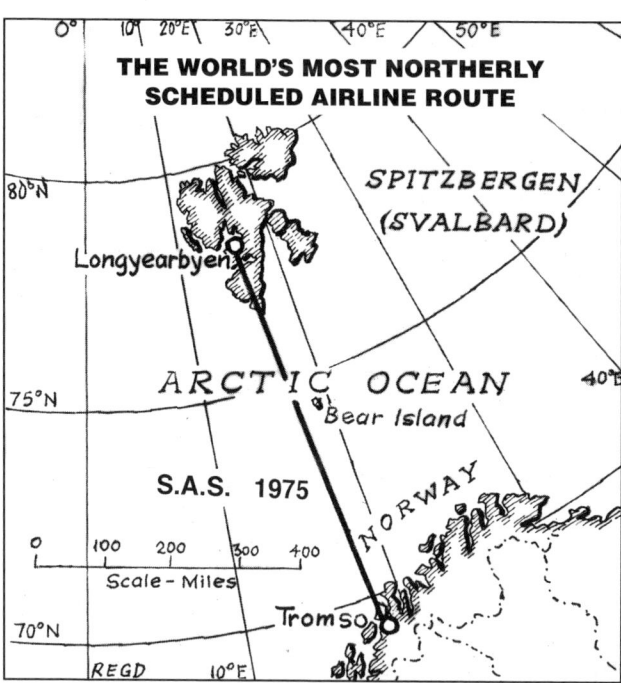

Pioneered by Braathens for special charters, S.A.S. started service to Spitzbergen, less than 900 miles from the North Pole, in 1975.

Chapter 32: Europe Unites

Austria Draws the Iron Curtain Aside

Once one of Europe's most desirable destinations for elite tourists, and one of its finest capitals, Vienna was engulfed in Nazi Germany's occupation of Austria in 1938. Unique to Austria, though, as early as 1918, it had started regular flights between Vienna and Kiev, in the Ukraine. The passengers were officials charged with organizing food supplies for a beleaguered belligerent, but nevertheless this was the world's first international intercity air service. Between the two wars, Austria's airline played an insignificant role in Europe, and Hitler put an end even to that.

Twenty years were to pass after its demise, and its revival—a phoenix from the ashes of the past—was delayed by Austria's occupation until 1955 by the four victorious powers. The rebirth of **Osterreichische Luftverkehr A.G.**, or its pre-war acronym **OLAG**, coincided with the beginning of the Jet Age. The official formation, on 30 September 1957, was delayed by protracted negotiation between two companies that had already been formed: Air Austria, by the Austrian People's Party, aided by K.L.M.; and Austrian Airways, aided by S.A.S. In due course, an amicable political compromise resulted in **Austrian Airlines,** the preferred name in a world of air transport in which English had become the universally accepted common language. The shareholdings were 42% by private investors, 28% by public enterprises, and 15% each by S.A.S. and Fred Olsen Flyselkap, the Norwegian charter company that had replaced K.L.M. The initial fleet was four Vickers Viscount V.779Ds leased from Olsen. Operations began on 31 March 1958 to London via Zurich. Joining the International Air Transport Association (IATA) immediately, it had a modest claim: the world's first all-turbine fleet.

During 1958 and 1959, the route network was expanded energetically and innovatively. Geographically located on the edge of the "Iron Curtain" between capitalist western Europe and communist eastern Europe, Austrian Airlines added stations on both sides of this political frontier. Beginning with Prague on 28 June 1958, all the capital cities in the east were added to the map, except Budapest, which was only a brief road trip or pleasant Danube cruise away from Vienna. The airline acted as an aerial crossroads between east and west, 30 years before the Berlin Wall came down. Not only did it facilitate travel between opposing governments that were sometimes confrontational, it established a true hub-and-spoke route network, many years before that term came into general use within the airline fraternity.

On 28 March 1960, Austrian replaced its leased Viscounts with four of its own Series 837s, and continued its route expansion policy into the Mediterranean and the Middle East, reaching Beirut, Damascus, and Cairo on 5 August 1960. It added two more ex–Capital Airlines Viscount 745s in 1961. The airline was rewarded by a reconstruction plan, effective 21 March 1962. This gave relief from debts incurred by a difficult foundation, and the stock capital was more than doubled. This enabled the airline to acquire its first jets, Caravelle VI-Rs, introduced on 20 February 1963, and to start domestic service to Graz with Douglas DC-3s on 1 May 1963. It had to retract its claim to have an all-turbine fleet, but this was rectified on 6 May 1966 when Hawker-Siddeley HS-748s took over, adding local services to neighboring countries.

The young airline pursued a steady course. On 1 April 1969, (only a decade after its formation) it opened a trans-Atlantic service to New York via Brussels, with a Boeing 707, chartered from SABENA. But this was short-lived. Nevertheless, this must have given special satisfaction to Dr. Anton Heschel and Dr. Hubert Papousek who, unusually in the airline business, were joint managing directors to ease possible political rivalries, and who had steered Austrian to this measure of success. During the next few years, they consolidated the corporate base in Europe, and also formed a charter subsidiary, **Austrian Air Transport**, in 1973, and revived domestic services with **Austrian Air Services**, in 1979, with a minority shareholding. Austria's four main provincial cities shared the balance. The fleet was also strengthened with adherence to the Douglas DC-9 series, which had started in 1971 with the first DC-9-30, augmented by -50s in 1975, and by Super-80s in 1980.

During this period, Austrian continued its policy of adding, almost annually, more stations in Europe. More spectacularly, on 26 March 1989, it added service to New York with its own aircraft, a 172-seat Airbus A310-324, which shortly afterward opened service to Tokyo, on 16 July, via Moscow. It had become adept in the art of international negotiation, in this case, a joint agreement with Aeroflot and All Nippon Airways. Together with Swissair, Finnair, and S.A.S., Austrian formed the European Quality Alliance on 3 May 1990, to create a union of Europe's smaller airlines to compete with the likes of Lufthansa or Air France, with commonality of equipment and route sharing. This led to increased cooperation with Swissair on 1 November 1992, when the two German-speaking neighbors agreed to share customer offices, hotels, telephones, and other marketing services in Austria and Switzerland. Such expansionist activities would have been expected from a much larger airline. Dr. Herbert Bremmer and Mario Rehulka, who succeeded Heschel and Papousek on 19 May 1993, had achieved the impressive route map by careful and efficient management and by offering excellent service. From 10 June 1994, on long flights in the Airbuses, Austrian's Grand Class was as good as, if not better than, the first class or business class of any of its competitors.

Throughout the 1990s, progress along the now well-established lines continued: more destinations, more hub-and-spoke connections, and additional corporate strength. It acquired

Although Austrian Airlines' expansion slowed down in the early 2000s, its membership of the Star Alliance kept it in the airline forefront, as emphasized in this Boeing 767 ER. (McDonough)

42% of Tyrolean Airways in 1994, a minority shareholding in **Ukraine International Airlines (U.I.A.)** on 9 November 1996, and 36% of Lauda Air, on 12 March 97 (all of which see below). The long-haul network was augmented to Chicago in 1992, Beijing and Washington on 26 March 1995, Singapore on 5 October 1996, and Montreal in May 1999. The crest was reached in 2002, by which time—having acquired Lauda Air and renamed Tyrolean as **Austrian Arrows**—the Austrian Airlines Group, operating under a single code number, was serving 123 destinations in 64 countries. Vienna was now as visible on the world airline map in the 21st century, as the Danube city was on the imperialist map in the 19th.

Eventually, a combination of economic trends and increasing competition halted its expansion. Australia was dropped, as well as many destinations throughout Asia. Proud Austrian now had to struggle against an unfavorable tide.

A Champion's Airline

The history of air transport has been marked by the involvement of personalities who were able to introduce entrepreneurial flair to the industry without a flying background. The granting of licenses to compete with Austrian Airlines was such a case. **Lauda Air** was founded in 1976 by Andreas Nikolaus "Niki" Lauda, a former world champion race car driver, for whom the last rites had been read after an horrific car crash in Germany. He started modestly in 1979 with charter flights to Luxembourg with a single Fokker F-27. The company collapsed, and Lauda mortgaged his home, returned to racing, and even won another Formula One title. Undeterred by his initial failure, he started operations again in 1985 with two Boeing 737s and began scheduled services two years later.

By 1989, Lauda was operating long-haul flights to Australia and southeast Asia. On 26 May 1991, a Lauda Boeing 767-300ER crashed in Thailand, killing all 223 on board. Undeterred by this devastating blow, services continued and in 1933 **Lauda Air Italy** (by which time the majority shareholding was held by the Volante organization). The fleet, three Airbus A330s, was still controlled by Niki Lauda. The Italian Lauda ceased operations.

In May 1996, Lauda was one of the first to fly to Ho Chi Minh City (formerly Saigon), as Vietnam began to open up its frontiers. The network and fleet expanded, both inter-continentally and within Europe, with five Boeing 767-300ERs, two 737-400s, and six Canadair CRJs. In September, the first 342-seat Boeing 777 came on line, and with Kuala Lumpur as a transfer hub replacing Singapore, as well as an experiment with on-board casino-type gambling, the champion racing driver—possibly the most popular man in Austria—reached an agreement with the country's national airline.

But for the first time since 1991, Lauda Air did not make a profit. Eventually, after a confrontation with Austrian's joint presidents, Niki resigned on 21 November 2000, but continued as CEO of Lauda Air Italy. In December Lauda Air became a wholly owned subsidiary of Austrian Airlines, which acquired 36% of the shares, while Lufthansa took 20%. Niki retained 30%. On 31 March 2003, Gruppo Ventaglio purchased Volante's shares, and after buying control of Aero Lloyd Austria, the effervescent Lauda launched NL Luftfahrt, his fourth airline venture in 14 years, as a low-cost operator, with two Airbus A320/321.

An Airline for the Alps

Alpine peaks are a deterrent to aspiring airlines. During the early years of air transport, pilots avoided the Alps. Trans-Alpine services were not firmly established until the 1930s. Even after the Second World War, air services to the mountains connected with rail and road at Basle or Lyon or Milan as the perceived safe approach to the Matterhorn or to St. Moritz. One city was better identified with the region, but because of its location, in a valley between two Alpine ranges, standards of operation needed for regular airline services were far more demanding than the average. Indeed, there had been several air tragedies in Innsbruck that were discouraging.

The foundation of an airline to be based there was therefore an act of courage and a defiance of orthodox operational judgment. The risk was great, and needed reserves of capital to take it. This was forthcoming when, in 1958, Aircraft Innsbruck was founded by Gernot Langes-Swarovski and Christian Schwemberger-Swarovski, of the world-famous crystal-glass empire. This became, on 1 April 1980, **Tyrolean Airways**. Its success depended on superb airfield performance at the vulnerable Innsbruck airport, and this was solved by launching the airline with 48-seat de Havilland Canada DHC Dash Seven four-engined turboprops, whose claim for STOL (Short Take-off and Landing) performance had become legendary. They made frequent connections at first to Vienna and Zurich, and within the next few years extended the net widely to many more cities, including four in Austria and three in Germany.

In March 1988, Tyrolean went public, though Gernot still held 92% of the stock. Then, in February 1994, Austrian Airlines acquired 43% of the shareholding, with the Swarovskis holding an equal amount, and Leipnik-Lundenburger Industrie the remaining stock. With the addition of eight Fokker 50s, the fleet had increased to 23 aircraft, and Austrian discontinued its domestic and regional services to both airlines' mutual convenience. The national airline increased its shareholding to 85% in December 1997 and to complete ownership in 1998.

The transformation was absolute. Tyrolean had emerged from its initial status as a high-risk, single-aircraft venture into a successful regional airline, with a constantly growing fleet and widening horizons. In 2003, its name was changed to **Austrian Arrows**, and its livery altered to match Austrian's. It was serving 72 cities throughout Europe, including six in the homeland, and reaching as far as Tripoli, Turkey, and the Caucasian republics. The 54-aircraft fleet included de Havilland Dash 8 Q300s and Q400s, Canadian CRJs (a dozen each of all three); 16 Fokker 100 ized and six Fokker 70s. Innsbruck was now firmly on the Euopean airline map.

Enter the Ukraine

With the collapse of the Soviet Union in December 1990, Ukraine soon declared its independence, and thereby became the largest country in Europe, excluding Russia. Its population was similar to France, Italy, and Great Britain. Only Germany's was larger. In addition to the capital, Kiev, five other cities each had more than a million people. Substantial resources of mineral wealth, including large coalfields, a flourishing steel industry, and agricultural wealth that had been the envy of Europe; these combined to give Ukraine a head start in its newly acquired independence.

Its Antonov aircraft manufacturer had built a series of commercial types that ranged from the little 14- to 20-seat An-2, whose small airfield capability gained worldwide fame; and, at the other end of the scale of size, the four-engined An-124, the largest freighter aircraft in the world, even used by Boeing to ferry major sub-assemblies to Seattle. Inevitably, as with every newly independent state, a national airline was essential for its economy, but in Ukraine's case, a representative national airline did not emerge. There were several, competing with each other.

Even before the statutory break-up of the Soviet Union, in 1989 when Mikhail Gorbachev visited Ukraine, **Antonov Airlines** was the first airline to be formed in the U.S.S.R. since Aeroflot, almost 60 years earlier, possibly because its specialized fleet was the best in its class in the world and therefore a Soviet asset. The 150-ton payload An-124 was such an outstanding heavy freighter that for specialized assignments it was sought all over the world. The Antonov Design Bureau alertly formed joint ventures with the British Air Foyle and **Heavy Lift** companies, and gained contracts for outsize and very heavy air-freighting demands. On one occasion, an An-124 delivered a 115-ton railway locomotive from Canada to Ireland. On 7 May 2001, it even test flew the six-engined, 250-ton payload An-225, which had been specially designed to carry the Soviet "Buran" space shuttle. By this time, the airline had a fleet of eight An-124s, and in July 2003, to broaden its scope into more orthodox markets, it took delivery of its first Boeing 767-300ER.

Ukraine could claim to have deep roots in the field of air transport, for as far back as the 1920s, Ukrvozdukhput had operated for a few years before being absorbed by Aeroflot. On 1 June 1990, a new bilateral agreement between the U.S.S.R. and the United States broadened the scope of air services between the two, allowing six more airlines on each side, with projected routes from New York to Kiev, Tbilisi, Minsk, Riga, Magadan, and Khabarovsk. Accordingly, **Air Ukraine** was formed in December 1990, at first as an associated but completely independent company, from the former Ukraine Division of Aeroflot, and still under the direction of the Ministry of Civil Aviation in Moscow. When the final dismemberment of the Soviet Union occurred at the turn of the year, hundreds of airlines, of all shapes and sizes emerged from the political chaos. Seventy were in Ukraine, but Air Ukraine had had a head start, and, with permission granted from the Ministry, it opened service from Kiev to New York via Shannon, on 11 June 1991, with an Ilyushin Il-62M leased from Moscow's Vnukovo Airport.

The transformation of airline sovereignty was not exactly straightforward, with de facto operations conflicting with de jure control. On one occasion in May, for example, at Toronto on a charter flight, the Air Ukraine insignia was put on the aircraft, but had to be removed when it returned to Moscow. But on 24 August 1991, with complete Ukrainian independence, more than a hundred main-line airliners were transferred from the Aeroflot Division, together with 200 or 300 An-2s and dozens of helicopters. Air Ukraine started to break clear of the new Russia, buying seven Ilyushin 62Ms from Poland's LOT for $15 million, and on 5 May 1992 made the first Kiev-New York service with its own airplane (but still dependent on Aeroflot for technical support). Full operational freedom, with its own crew, and with its own flag, was delayed until 2 November 1993.

Air Ukraine then began to fashion an international route network. During the next few years, it added Beijing and Tientsin, for "shoppmg tours" in China and also to Delhi. Service to Washington, D.C., started on 16 May 1994, followed by Chicago and Tashkent a month later and Toronto the next year.

The political scene in Ukraine was not conducive to the idea of a "chosen instrument" but the government supported a western-oriented **Ukraine International Airlines (U.I.A.)**, formed in 1992, with a fleet of two new Boeing 737-400s, supplied through the Irish leasing company G.P.A. Soon U.I.A. replaced the -400s with used -200s, which were more economical to operate. By 1995, U.I.A. was making a profit. At first, Air Ukraine held 90% of the shares, but on 9 November 1996, Austrian Airlines, Swissair, and the European Bank for Reconstruction acquired control. After the collapse of Swissair in 2002, this passed to the State Property Fund (S.P.F.) (62%), with Austrian retaining 22%. From the start, U.I.A. had reflected its name by adopting a fully international approach, joining IATA and its Clearing House. By the early 2000s, its fleet of 737s was serving a widespread European and Middle East network, and Yak-40s connected the main Ukrainian cities domestically.

The third Ukrainian airline of substance was **AeroSvit**, formed in October 1994, as a private venture, also with Boeing 737s. Its early years were marred in 1998 by the crash in Greece of a Yak-42 on a charter flight, and in January 1999 Gregori Gurtovoi, from the Russian independent airline Transaero, was appointed president. He adopted a policy of cooperation with other airlines, domestic and foreign, to avoid self-destruction by excessive competition in markets of limited traffic. The Boeing fleet included three types of 737, three 757-500s, and one 767-300ER. With this last airliner, AerSvit opened a long-haul route from Kiev to Bangkok in November 2002. On 30 March 2003, service began to New York, and further intercontinental expansion included New Delhi, and Toronto. In 2004, AeroSvit's shareholding comprised Aerotur, the Ukrainian agency for tourism (40%), the State Property Fund (22%), and Gilward Investments, of the Netherlands (38%). The airline was thriving, ordering, in July 2007, seven more Boeing 737s.

Of the other aspirants for a share of the air traffic potential of the Ukraine, Ukrainian-Mediterranian Airlines (UM Air) did not fare well, as one of its Yak-42s crashed in Turkey late in July 2003. Donbasaero ventured into the domestic arena, to emphasize the importance of the Donbas conurbation to the Ukrainian economy as a whole.

Caucasian Contrasts

Of the three former Soviet autonomous republics in the Caucasus, Azerbaijan was by far the richest, as its oil production and reserves, centered on Baku, were among the largest in the world. The national wealth supported a national airline, **Azerbaijan Airlines**, which, by early 1998, was operating flights to western Europe with a Canadair CL-44 "Guppy" specialized cargo-lifter. In October 2000 it received its first Boeing 757-200s, and began services to London, Istanbul, Dubai, and Tel Aviv. Subsequently the fleet expanded with more Boeings, some Soviet types, and some European ATR-42s and -72s. In March 2007, a further order from Boeing included three of the latest Model 787 Dreamliner.

The three Caucasian states were all beneficiaries of the Aeroflot divisions. **Armenian Airlines** inherited, among other types, an Ilyushin Il-76 wide-bodied aircraft, but, like Georgia, was unable to make its mark in the air transport affairs of the region, lacking industrial and financial strength and without adequate tourism attractions to generate traffic.

Airlines on the Baltic Rim

Of the three Baltic republics that were hived off from Czarist Russia after 1918, Estonia, the smallest, appears to have established the most stable airline when it gained its independence from the Soviet Union in 1991. **Estonian Air** was founded by the government in December, taking over some of Aeroflot's Tupolev Tu-134s and Yakovlev Yak-40s. It was privatized in 1995, with Denmark's Maersk Air owning 49% and Baltic Cresco 17% of the shares. In keeping with the political desire to break ties with Moscow, the airline looked to the west for equipment and replaced its Russian types with Boeing 737-500s and Fokker 50s.

Latvia's main economic asset is the thriving port of Riga, formerly supplementing Leningrad (St. Petersburg) as the Soviet Union's maritime outlet to the Baltic Sea and thence to the world. The government-owned post-Soviet airline, **Latavio**, shut down on 1 October 1995, as did **Baltic International**, on the same day. It had begun with a U.S. partnership to replace its Tu-134s with Boeing 727-100s. Initial services were from Riga to Frankfurt and Dusseldorf, Hamburg was added on 29 March 1993, and London on June 22. The two airlines were succeeded in 1995 by **Air Baltic**, of which 53% is held by the state and 47% by the Scandinavian S.A.S., which also provides management and technical services. At first operating smaller airliner types, such as Avro RJ-70s and a SAAB-340, its network in 1996 extended to all the neighboring capital cities and as far as London, Frankfurt, and Kiev. By 2007 its horizons stretched as far as Moscow, St. Petersburg, and Tashkent. Another small airline, Riair, began Boeing 737-200 service to Moscow in September 1994.

Lithuanian Airlines started in December 1991, with a single Boeing 737-200, but by 1996, its fleet consisted of three 737s, two Tu-134s, and eight Yak-42s. The three countries along the eastern shore of the Baltic Sea are among the smallest in Europe. Even with some appeal for historically interested tourists, there is little potential for airline development on a wide scale.

Part Six: Rise of Asia and the Pacific Rim

Chapter 33: The Growth of China

Emerging from the Shadows

When the Jet Age began, under the strict control of Chairman Mao Tsetung's People's Republic communist government, the Chinese state airlines, SKOGA and C.C.A.C., were still in the dark ages of air transport development. Their Soviet aircraft were outdated, and as yet the airlines had little awareness of efficient scheduling or maintenance. Their clientèle were mainly politicians and bureaucrats, as private commerce did not exist, and there was no business traffic. Tourism, either among the Chinese or from overseas, was unknown. The emergence of China into the outside world was a slow and cautious process.

Not until 1961, when relations with the Soviet Union were going sour, and to recognize the need to modernize its aircraft fleet, did Chinese authorities cautiously approach the West. After prolonged negotiations in London—China still had no embassy in Britain— its state purchasing agency ordered six 60-seat Vickers Viscount 843 turboprops. In April 1962, the aviation bureau became the **Civil Aviation Administration of China (C.A.A.C.)**, under which name it would operate for the next 30 years.

The First Jets

The Viscounts entered service in 1963. Then twenty 100-seat Ilyushin 18 turboprops were added in 1965, and these became the workhorses of the fleet, as they had been in the Soviet Union and elsewhere. The first glimpse of a pure jet airliner in China had occurred only a year previously, when **Pakistan International Airlines (P.I.A.)** opened a Boeing 707 service from Karachi and Dacca (now in Bangladesh) to Canton (now Guangzhou) and Peking (Beijing). This was the first foreign airline from the West to enter China. The first European jet service there was by an Air France 707 on 20 September 1966. No doubt, this must have left the name Boeing in the Chinese procurement minds, but many years were to pass before China itself would open discussions with the Seattle manufacturer.

In 1970, C.A.A.C. began to break out of its political isolation from the world of commercial aviation. It ordered five 170-seat Ilyushin Il-62s from Moscow, and opened the first nonstop service from Peking to Canton on 13 May 1971. Still reluctant to do business with the United States—diplomatic relations were frigid—the airline turned to Great Britain and ordered six 140-seat Hawker-Siddeley (formerly de Havilland) Trident 2E trimotor jets, which went into service on several domestic routes on 15 March 1973. Another 20 were then ordered, and on 4 December of the same year, a further 15. But China had to make its mark overseas, and the Ilyushins fell short of the standards required outside the Communist world. On 11 September 1972, with a thaw in the diplomatic corridors, CATIC, the Chinese purchasing agency, ordered 10 Boeing 707s for $26 million. Reports suggested that the delegation to Seattle paid in cash.

C.A.A.C. meanwhile expanded its domestic network considerably, not only to the larger cities, but also introduced jet air service to provincial cities and towns. The Tridents were supplemented by Antonov An-24 40-seat turboprops to extend air service to smaller communities. But operationally, the airline still had much to learn. Reservation systems were still primitive. Round-trip tickets could not be arranged. A typical day's work for a Trident was a single flight from Beijing to Shanghai.

China's first direct air route to western Europe was by an Il-62 to Tirana, Albania. This unlikely destination was politically, not commercially, motivated. It was a gesture of appreciation to the tiny Balkan country that had sponsored China's membership of the United Nations. Then, on 27 October 1974, a C.A.A.C. Boeing 707 flew into Paris, having opened a service to Tokyo on 29 September. China joined the International Civil Aviation Organization (I.C.A.O.) in October. Commercially, as well as diplomatically, China had at last broken the international aviation ice, and other foreign airlines joined P.I.A. and Air France: Ethiopian on 23 February 1973, IranAir in November 1974, Romania's TAROM on 21 December of that year, and Swissair on 7 April 1975, all to start services to China.

China Adapts

Shen Tu became the Director General of C.A.A.C. in 1978 and until his retirement in 1985, he presided over a period of modernization, consolidation, and growth. His first move, on 16 December 1978, was to sign a contract with Boeing for three 747SPs, the long-range version of the successful wide-bodied airliner, and able to fly nonstop from Shanghai to New York. Other routes were opened to Ethiopia and Switzerland, reciprocating the services of those countries, and then to Frankfurt on 3 May 1979, even before Germany's Lufthansa started service to Beijing. Nearer to home, the Tokyo route had been joined by Osaka in 1976, Nagoya and Manila in 1979, and Bangkok in 1980. After much negotiation, the final barriers were broken to Hong Kong (then still British) on 21 June 1980, with five Tridents a day from Shanghai, with two by Cathay Pacific's 707s as its share of the pooled route. C.A.A.C.'s 747SPs had already started to Paris on 1 April 1980, and that route was extended to London on 15 November. Finally, to put a seal on its future status as a worldwide national airline, an SP began service from Beijing and Shanghai to San Francisco and New York on 7 January 1981, adding Los Angeles on 12 April 1982.

By this time, something had to be done for domestic service to modernize the fleet by replacing the Tridents, at the same time to provide a foundation for starting Chinese airliner

The Growth of China

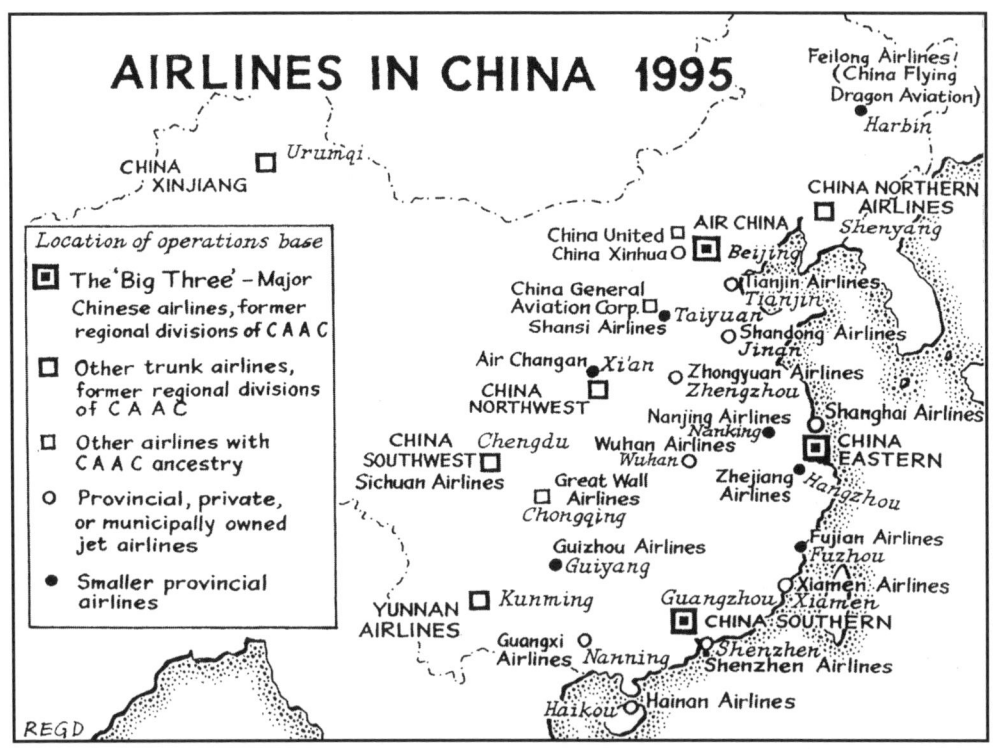

The transformation in China from the single national airline was comprehensive. From the centralized authority of C.A.A.C. in Beijing, every province had its own. The ones in Shanghai and Guangzhou were to grow into international prominence.

production—to remove the obligation of always having to seek help from capitalist countries which only a few years before had not been welcome as trading associates. This idea culminated in an agreement with McDonnell-Douglas, to build twin-engined Douglas DC-9s in the Shanghai Aircraft Factory. At first the factory was on trial to guarantee the quality of its manufacture to supply subassemblies to Douglas at Long Beach, California. The tests were entirely successful, and the agreement progressed for Shanghai to build DC-9-30s. On 4 August 1985 C.A.A.C. put the first of 28 147-seat "stretched" Shanghai-built MD-82s

By the 1980s, Chinese airlines were growing at a furious pace, with a potential total fleet of a thousand jet airliners. Representative of this expansion are (top left) Air China's Boeing 747SP, (bottom left) China Eastern's McDonnell Douglas MD82, (top right) China Southern's Boeing 737-500, and (bottom right) Shanghai Airlines's Boeing 757. (Bentley)

AIRLINES OF CHINA — EX-C.A.A.C.

Airline	Base	Date Formed	Main Aircraft	Remarks
C.A.A.C. Descendents or Affiliates — The Six Major Corporations				
Air China	Beijing	1 Jul 88	Airbus/Boeings (Large fleets)	Took over C.A.A.C.'s international routes as well as main-line domestic routes. Acquired China Southwest, 2001; China National Av. Corp., 2002; Zhejiang, 2004. Owns 51% of Air Macau, Shandong; 30% of Cathway Pacific. World wide network. Fleet of more than 250 aircraft.
China Southern	Guangzhou	1989	Airbus/Boeings (Large fleets)	Began long-haul international service in 1996. Now largest airline in Asia. Acquired Zhongyuan, 2000; China Northern, Xinjiang, 2003. Fleet of more than 300 aircraft.
China Eastern	Shanghai	25 Jun 88	Airbus/Boeings/Embraer (Large fleets)	Acquired Air Great Wall, 2001, China Yuman and China Northwest, 2003. Subsidiaries: China Cargo, Jiangsu, Wuhan, Yunnan. Fleet of 270 aircraft. Singapore holds 24% of shares. Merged, Shanghai Airlines, 2009.
China Northern	Shenyang	1990	MD82 Airbus	Merged into China Southern, 2003.
China Southwest	Chengdu	1987	Boeing/Airbus	Merged into Air China, 2002.
China Northwest	Xi'an	1989	BAe 146 Tu154 Airbus	Merged into China Eastern, 2003.
Other C.A.A.C. and Independents				
China Xinjiang	Urumqi	1985	ATR-72 IL-86 Boeing 737	Routes in Xinjiang and internationally to Central Asian republics. Merged into China Southern, 2003.
China Yunnan	Kunming	1993	CRJ-200 Boeings	Regional routes and to neighboring countries in southeast Asia. Merged into China Eastern, 2003.
China United	Nanyuang (Beijing)	25 Dec 86	Boeing 737	Former military transport division. Shanghai Airlines 80% shares, 2005.
China General	Nanjing	July 89	Yak 42 Boeing 737	General aviation, some charters. Acquired by China Eastern, 1997.
Shanghai Airlines	Shanghai	1985	Boeings	Owned by Shanghai municipal govt. First independently owned airline in China. Began international services, 2002. Merged into China Eastern, 2003. Fleet of 60 aircraft.
Xiamen Airlines	Xiamen	24 Jul 84	Boeings	First airline in China established by private individuals. 60% shareholding by China Southern. Fleet of 50 aircraft.
Shenzhen Airlines	Shenzhen	Nov 92	Airbuses/Boeings	Formed by C.A.A.C. and Sheuzhen govt. Air China holds 25%. Formed Kunpeng Airlines as regional, 2007. Fleet of 90 aircraft.
Hainan Airlines (see also Tianjin)	Haikou	Oct 89	Airbuses/Boeings	Largest privately-owned airline in China. On 30 Nov 2007, four airlines in Hainan group (inc. Shanxi, Chang'an, China Xinhua) merged to form Grand China Air. Fleet of 7 aircraft.
Sichuan Airlines	Chengdu	19 Sept 86	Airbuses Embraer	Shareholders include China Southern (39%), Shandong (10%), Shanghai (10%). Fleet of more than 40 aircraft.
Shandong	Jinan	12 Mar 94	Boeings CRJs	Owned by Air China. Owns 10% of Sichuan. Founded Xinxing (New Star) Alliance, 1997. Fleet of 37.
Tianjin Airlines (see also Hainan)	Tianjin	2004	Fairchild-Dornier 328/Embraers	Operational, 2007 (see Hainan). Name changed from Ground China Express on 10 June 2009. Fleet 472 aircraft.
Wuhan Airlines	Wuhan	1991	Boeing 737	Merged into China Eastern. Fleet of 18.
China Xinhua	Beijing	Aug 92	Boeing 737	Owned by Grand China Air (see Hainan). Fleet of 16.
Zhejiang Airlines	Hangzhou	7 Sep 90	Airbus	Absorbed by Air China, 2004. Fleet of 13.
Shanxi Airlines	Taiyuan	1988	Boeing 737	Merged into Hainan group, 2007. Fleet of 8.
Zhongyuan Airlines	Zhengzhou	17 May 86	Boeing 737	Acquired by China Southern, 2000. Fleet of 7.
Great Wall Airlines	Shanghai	1 Jun 06	Boeing 747	Cargo airline. Owned by China Eastern (51%), Singapore (49%). International routes to U.S.A. and Europe.
Chang'an Airlines	Xi'an	24 Dec 92	Boeing 737	Merged into Hainan group, 2007. Fleet of 4.
China Flying Dragon	Harbin	1981	DHC-6	Local services with small aircraft.
Guizhou Airlines	Guiyang	1991	Boeing 737	Owned 60% by China Southern. Local services.
Guangxi Airlines	Nanning	1994	Boeing	China Southern 35% in 2006.
Fujian Airlines	Fuzhou	8 Aug 93	Boeings	Acquired by Xiamen Airlines, 1996.

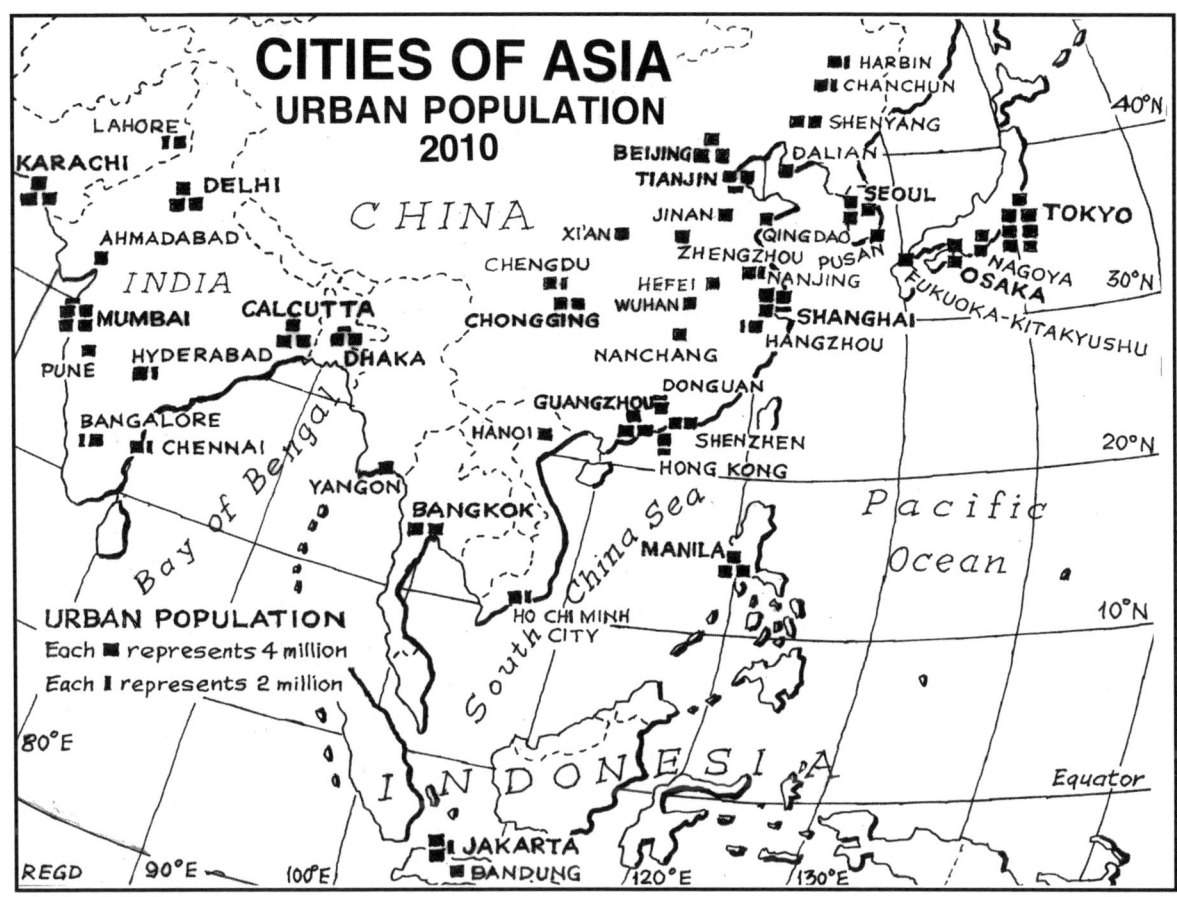

On this map of south and east Asia, each of the 45 cities has a population of more than 4 million. These constitute a vast market for increased international and—especially in China and India—for inter-city air travel.

into service. Boeing had not ignored China. In 1981, it had sent a 737 demonstrator to prove its compatibility with all the required Chinese airports. This included Lhasa, Tibet, at an elevation of 11,600 feet. C.A.A.C. ordered ten 737s in November 1982.

All these far-reaching procurement and operating decisions were made against a bureaucratic background of centralized control. A maintenance engineer at Chengdu would have to obtain clearance from Beijing to change a landing gear. Yet heavier demands were being made for intensified scheduling to meet the rapidly increasing demand for airline seats, as China began to transform itself into a leading industrial nation. The consequent demand was for substantially increased travel, swifter than that on the railroad which, efficient and reliable though it was, offered most inter-city journeys that took up at least a day. The airline's was a few hours. Sadly, in C.A.A.C.'s efforts to make up for lost time, the late 1970s and early 1980s were marred by a series of fatal accidents. China's national airline tightened its state-owned belt and worked hard to adapt to western ways in safety as well as operations.

Decentralization

In September 1984, the State Council in charge of the country's modernization program, announced the formation of four regional airlines to serve domestic routes. These became **China Eastern**, **China Southern**, **China Southwest**, and **China Northwest Airlines**, based in Shanghai, Guangzhou, Chengdu, and Xi'an, respectively. These were supplemented later by **China Northern** and **China Xinjiang**, at Shenyang and Urumchi, and **Yunnan Airlines**, at Kunming. China's international routes were spun off to become **Air China**. In the transformation from state centralization to a market economy (i.e., competition) the establishment of regional airlines, sponsored by individual provinces, was also encouraged.

In April 1985, Shen Tu was succeeded by Hu Yishao, who faced an unprecedented challenge: how to keep up with the growth of Chinese air traffic, at home and overseas, now doubling every two years, reflecting the exploding growth of Chinese industry. The first two 218-seat Airbus A310-200s went into service in 1985 and orders for 10 Tupolev Tu-154s, 10 British Aerospace BAe 146-100s, eight Boeings, a 747-200 Combi, two 767s, and five 737-200s soon followed. The selection was well balanced in terms of capacity requirements and balanced too in the sources of supply. Scheduling and reservations systems were overhauled and competition on some domestic routes was, after approval from Beijing, permitted. Most of all, some attention was given to passenger service, comfort, and convenience, courtesies which, under C.A.A.C., had been of low priority.

As with almost any transport system, state controlled or by free enterprise, relative success depends largely on demographics. The larger a city's population combined with its relative wealth, the larger the traffic base for potential travel demand. Thus, in a process familiar elsewhere in the world of airlines, Air China, China Eastern, and China Southern, based in the three largest cities, emerged as China's leading airlines. Steps were also taken to provide the essential technical support. Guangzhou Aircraft Maintenance Corporation (GAMECO) took over from Hong Kong Engineering Company (HAECO), and Air China formed AMECO Beijing, the former C.A.A.C.–Lufthansa joint venture. The Shanghai Aircraft Factory, which had participated in the joint venture with Douglas, provided support in that city.

A more important factor affecting passenger demand is the rapid urbanization. Workforces that had been primarily agricultural, living in villages and small market towns, have moved to the factories and industrial communities of the big cities. Not only did the larger cities grow at a pace that had never been

GROWTH OF CATHAY PACIFIC 1948-1994

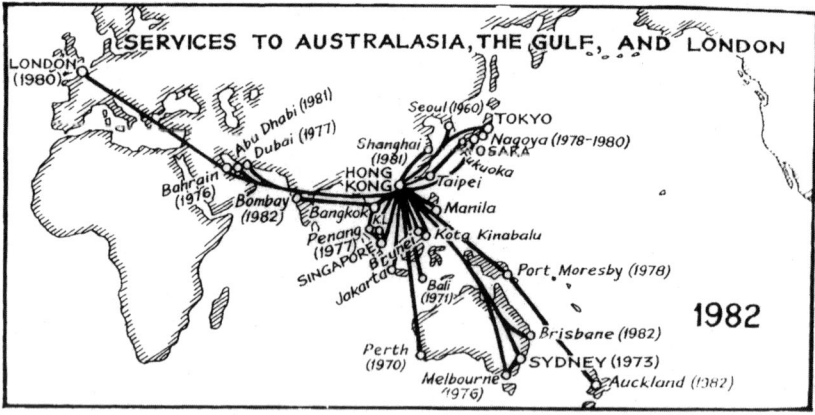
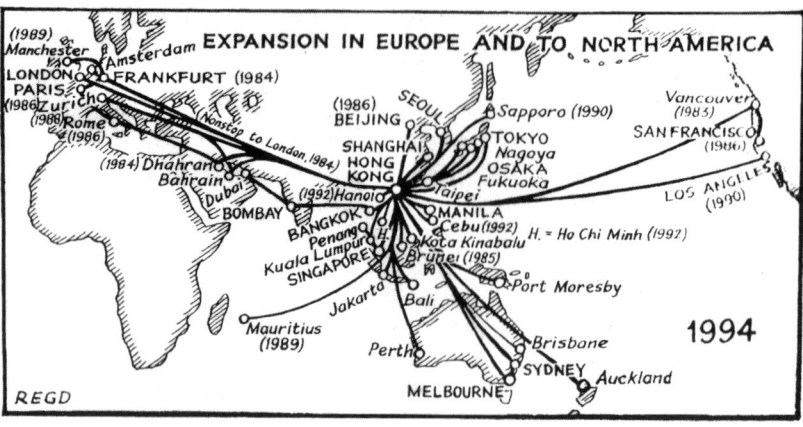

In the area that was formerly centered on Hong Kong, Canton (now Guangzhou) declined in importance internationally during the period when China was almost isolated from the world of commerce. By the 21st Century, the regional revival has been phenomenal. Not only has Guangzhou emerged as China's third city; a completely new city, Shenzhen, has risen from the rice fields north of Hong Kong. The lease of this former British colony expired in 1997, and enjoys special administrative consideration within modern China. Hong Kong's own airline continues to prosper.

witnessed elsewhere; China created new cities as well. By the beginning of the 21st century, more than 50 cities in China each had more than a million inhabitants, including Shenzhen, which had been created in a single decade in the rice fields and marshes north of Hong Kong.

The explosion of urban population, accompanied by growing spending power and a freer economy, demanded an airline industry that would serve provincial cities and towns as well as the large conurbations. Thus, in addition to the major airlines that were hived off from C.A.A.C., other regionals were also established by the provinces, and these were joined during the 1990s by many independents. They sought to serve their own districts in a development process that was similar to that of the local service airlines of the United States after the end of the Second World War. When, in May 1984, Premier Zhao Ziyang called for an end of state monopolies, Shanghai's mayor responded immediately. **Shanghai Airlines** soon set a fast pace for others to follow.

Boeing and Airbus did agree that the potential market for Chinese commercial airliners was enormous. Market forecasters in Seattle and Toulouse both visualized a market in China for 1,500 airliners or more by 2020.

By the beginning of the 21st century, Air China, China Southern, and China Eastern had taken their places among the world's leaders, ranked by passengers boarded or passenger-miles flown. Hong Kong's Cathay Pacific, still categorized separately by the I.C.A.O., is also among the top 25. Such expansion has been welcome for Boeing and Airbus. Boeing has done well, especially with its short/medium haul 737s, while Airbus can point to an order by China Southern for its 550-seat double-decked Airbus 380.

Nevertheless, just as China has rejuvenated a stagnant airline industry, it has built a nationwide network of high speed train routes. Competition from this new revolutionary form of surface transport will decelerate airline growth within China.

Chapter 34: India Awakes

A Flying Start

India entered the Jet Age in great style. Under the shrewd and intuitive leadership of J.R.D. Tata, the head of the great Tata industrial consortium, **Air India International** was recognized as one of the world's finest airlines, with a flair for marketing, under the direction of "Bobby" Kooka, who introduced the cordial *Maharajah* symbol of gracious service. On 15 August 1958, only a few months before Pan American's dramatic trans-Atlantic Boeing 707 inauguration, Air India started service to Moscow via Tashkent, opening an alternative route from the subcontinent to Europe. Its jet debut came on 19 April 1960 with its own 707 service to London on 14 May 1960, having consolidated its market share on the traditional "Kangaroo" London-Australia route by signing the Tripartite Agreement to share the revenues on this lucrative British Commonwealth-based route. Its geographical en-route staging area gave Air India 21%, while B.O.A.C. took 51% (as the major originator of traffic) and Australia's QANTAS 28%.

Steady expansion continued. The London service was extended to New York on 14 May 1961. Agreements were made with Indian Airlines to operate Bombay-Calcutta, and with B.O.A.C., to operate Madras-Singapore on 5 April 1962. On 7 May, the Constellation fleet was withdrawn, so that **Air-India** (renamed on 8 June) became the world's first all-jet operator, and Perth was added as an Australian stop on the route to Sydney. On 2 August 1964, the Australian service was extended to Fiji, where half of the 500,000 population was of Indian descent, and on 2 October 1964, full advantage was taken of its rights through Moscow to open the shortest and fastest service between New York and Delhi. On 1 April 1967, the Tripartite Agreement included provision for a pool that included Malaysian Airways and Air New Zealand. A trans–Indian Ocean route opened to Mauritius on 15 August, and during the next few years, extensions were made in Africa and the Persian (Arabian) Gulf.

Wide-bodied services with the Boeing 747 started to London on 24 May 1971, and New York followed two days later, but the Tripartite Agreement was terminated on 1 April 1972. On 30 May 1976, a 747 "Bullet" service from New York to Bombay gave Americans the fastest services to India, at the same time offering Indians, with growing family ties with emigrants to the U.S.A., the reciprocal privilege.

Farewell to J.R.D.

Until 1974, Air-India had enjoyed an almost unbroken succession of profitable years, but intensive competition on the southern trunk route between Europe and the Far East was now encroaching on India's traffic share. Singapore and Thai International especially were among the airlines of southeast Asia that matched the Indian high standards of cabin service and

J.R.D. Tata, scion of a great Indian industrial enterprise, founded Air India and guided it into worldwide recognition. He was effectively deposed after more than 40 years of inspired leadership. (Davies)

amenities. A prominent casualty of the decline (someone invariably has to take the blame) was J.R.D. himself, who retired as chairman and CEO in 1978, having been effectively replaced by the appointment of a new managing director late in 1976. For Air India, this was the end of an era, for Tata had guided the airline since he founded its direct ancestor on 15 October 1932. Aged 78, he celebrated the 50th anniversary of that historic occasion by reenacting his de Havilland Leopard Moth flight from Karachi to Bombay—in the same airplane.

Disaster and Retrenchment

The financial situation improved with the appointment of ex-banker Raghu Raj as chairman in April 1980, and the Airbus A300B4 was introduced in August 1982, ideally for the routes to the Gulf. But Air-India suffered a heavy blow when one of its 747s dived into the sea off the southern coast of Ireland on 23 June 1985, killing 329 passengers and crew. Subsequent investigations concluded that this was the result of a bomb being planted on board at Montreal, but at the time, just when Air India was trying to maintain viability and stature, its progress was stalled. Commercial interests in Mumbai (Bombay) did not always find approval from the government in Delhi, and the airline seemed to have lost its former sense of leadership. The change in attitudes could perhaps be symbolized by the decision to abandon the friendly Maharajah in Air-India's promotion, as some felt that this indicated subservience, rather than service. This was not so. Air-India had combined western efficiency with eastern hospitality. Its aircraft decor, its sari-clad stewardesses, and its genuine Indian cuisine set an example for other airlines to follow.

India Awakes

The devaluation of the Indian rupee in July 1991 was another setback, and indications of parliamentary uncertainty in Delhi were disturbing. A widespread view was that the end of the dual monopoly of Indian air transport (Air-India and Indian Airlines) was imminent. On 1 January 1994 the Indian government revoked the 41-year-old Air Corporations Act to privatize the two corporations. Top-level resignations followed, and in 1998, Michael Mascarenhas was elevated from commercial director to managing director. Efforts to restore order had been disappointing, even though two Lockheed L-1011-500s and three Airbus A310-300s had been leased, and routes to Canada, South Africa, and Australia had been terminated. On 7 December 1998, the two corporations agreed to merge, under a common holding company, but Delhi promptly disbanded the boards of both companies.

Air-India faced an uphill battle, mainly to fight circumstances beyond its control, and without help from the government. All the cards were stacked against this airline that had once put India in the forefront of the world air transport hierarchy. In 1993, international routes to the Gulf, the source of much traffic from "guest workers" in the Emirates, Kuwait, and Saudi Arabia, had been granted to Indian Airlines. Also, the new generously financed Gulf airlines, Emirates, Qatar, and Oman, as well as the incumbent Gulf Air, were making unprecedented progress. Foreign airlines in Europe and east Asia were also benefitting from the liberalization and expansion of the Indian economy through their 5th and 6th Freedom privileges through India. The wage bill increased, and although overdue, this could not be offset by attrition or layoffs, because of long-held laws against such actions. The fleet was badly balanced, as the ideal payload-range of the Airbuses did not match either the long-range routes or the short hauls to the Gulf.

A New Deal

While the floodgates for the creation of independent airlines were opened (see below), they were not allowed to operate on international routes for five years after starting service. Nevertheless, the time had come to end the bureaucratic wrangling in Delhi. On 15 September 2000, the prime minister confirmed the expansio!n of an India–United States bilateral agreement, to augment Air-India's own initiatives in signing code-sharing agreements with nine foreign airlines. Also announced was the planned sale of the government's 60% holding in Air-India and its 51% in Indian Airlines. But the opposition to a foreign airline taking shares was so strong that the most promising offer, of Singapore Airlines and the powerful Tata Group, to buy 40% of Air India, fell through. Singapore was quoted as mistrusting "the intensity of the opposition," (i.e., political groups, trade unions, and the media).

During the next few years, Air-India operated as a shadow of its former self, as the new independent airlines sorted themselves out, and (as chronicled below) showed a flair for judging the market and making the right decisions—features that had been sadly lacking with the one-time flagship instrument. Eventually, the sleeper awoke—or was awakened—in 2004, when management was given the all-clear to make a long-overdue substantial investment in new aircraft. To provide early relief, three Boeing 777-200ERs were leased early in 2005, along with with two 747-400s, with the prospect of further orders to follow. To "keep up with the Joneses"—with low-fare services—**Air-India Express** was founded on 29 April 2005, to serve mainly southern India, with a fleet of 18 new Boeing 737s, and Air-India was to have 23 300-seat Boeing 777s, and 20 of the revolutionary 260-seat Boeing 787 Dreamliners. The announcement provoked indignant protests from Airbus, which claimed that it had not been given the opportunity to make a counter-offer, but in January 2006, these were cast aside as formal documents were signed for the 777s (eight -200LRs, fifteen -300ERs) and twenty-seven 787-8s, as well as the eighteen 737s for Express.

On 1 March 2007, the effort to merge the two state corporations finally became a reality, nine years after it almost happened, as would have benefitted all concerned. This time, in the face of massive competition from the independents, the government had little choice, as the two airlines' domestic market share had fallen to a mere 17%. One of the newcomers, Jet Airways, already had 27%, after only a few years of existence. This time the merger was between four airlines, including Air-India's Express subsidiary, and Indian Airlines's Alliance. The decline of Air-India, once among the world's top 20 airlines, to rank barely in the top 50, was finally ended. Recovery of its former stature might be possible, but the independents' competition is vigorous, and the flag carrier has a fight on its hands for Indian airline leadership in the 21st century.

The Rise and Fall of Indian Airlines

China's growth has been so spectacular that it has overshadowed the efforts of other Asian countries, especially India, whose population (like China's) now exceeds a billion, and industrially is also expanding at a high rate. Indeed, the Indian economy (gross national product) has been growing at almost the same rate as China's, and in computer services, is probably the world's leader. While India's industrial strength was accelerating, however, the two incumbent airlines dragged their feet. But with the law of 1994, a dozen aspiring newcomers joined the airline ranks, and in a process familiar in many capitalist countries before, the fittest were to survive as the weakest fell by the wayside.

The newcomers faced a well-established incumbent on the domestic front. The **Indian Airlines Corporation (I.A.C.)** had enjoyed a monopoly of scheduled airline services since 1953, and except when augmented in emergencies, had provided the country with adequate, if not inspired, service. On 10 October 1957, it had moved out of the piston-engined Douglas DC-3 era (its fleet had, after the Second World War, exceeded 70 of them) when the 48-seat Vickers Viscount turboprop entered service and quickly linked the main cities, and included Karachi, Rangoon, and Colombo. The Viscounts also took over the historic Night Mail Service, speeding it up from the old DC-4s. I.A.C. moved quickly to augment the Viscounts. In May 1961, 40-seat

Fokker Friendship twin-engined feeder-liners supplemented the four-engined 48-seaters. By this time, early in February 1964, the first 89-seat Caravelle jets added much-needed capacity to a fast-growing market. The fleet improvement program came none too soon. The 1950s had been marred by too many crashes, all involving well-worn DC-3s. Services were seriously interrupted in 1965, with a conflict with Pakistan, and accidents further depleted I.A.C.'s fleet resources. This led to the temporary lease of a Boeing 707 in February 1967.

In September 1967, services were slashed as I.A.C.'s fleet was commandeered during India's border confrontation with China on its northern Himalayan frontier. The corporation did splendid work in air transport support of the Indian defense forces. Pilots, engineers, and maintenance men were "called to arms" in the middle of the night and maintained a vital airlift to the Front until hostilities ended. During the year, the airline dropped the corporation word from its name. In December, 48-seat Hawker-Siddeley 748 turboprops, built under license at Kanpur (Cawnpore), supplemented the Friendships, with the added advantage of being able to use almost any of the airstrips that only the DC-3s had been able to serve.

Seven 126-seat Boeing 737 jets entered service on 1 January 1971. When the war broke out with Pakistan in December 1971, resulting in the creation of Bangladesh, formerly East Pakistan, not surprisingly I.A.C. sustained a financial loss in 1972, and economy measures had to be taken.

The Night Mail Service ended on 12 September 1973, an experiment in rapid mail transfer that was an example to be followed with great success by Federal Express in the U.S.A. a few years later. During that summer, three aircraft were lost, and the Viscounts were withdrawn from service. A labor crisis resulted in a "new deal" in which management was given "the right to manage" and the unions agreed to eliminate wasteful work. During the negotiations, a non-union skeleton staff kept the airline afloat.

A significant step was taken on 18 March 1974 when all the DC-3s were retired, and 16 stations all across the country were closed. These were at smaller communities, or those close to other larger stations, and where the veteran "Gooney Bird" had been able to land but where the modern jets and turboprops could not. Indian Airlines was prepared to leave that responsibility to others, while it aimed to keep pace with the relentless demand of an air traveling public that was growing fast as the urban population of India expanded with its growing industrialization. In April 1975, an order was placed for three 278-seat Airbus A300B-2s, which entered service on 1 December 1976. With politico-economic encouragement from Delhi, with the benefit of increased Airbus capacity, it was given permission in the summer of 1977 to open international routes to neighboring countries, particularly to the Gulf states, where tens of thousands of "guest workers" had created a new class of V.F.R. (visiting friends and relatives) traffic. Officially these were charter services for Air-India, but effectively this was the beginning of a trend that would eventually have far-reaching consequences in the balance of power between the two flag carriers.

Indian Airlines Airbus A300B. (Bentley)

Political stability in India during the 1980s played a role. Prime Minister Indira Gandhi was assassinated on 31 October 1984, and her son, Rajiv, a great supporter of air transport, met the same fate on 21 May 1989. He had approved a large order for Airbus A320s, overturning the intent to buy Boeing 757s. Whatever the political influence on the choice, the need for capacity was not in doubt. In 1988, Indian Airlines was exceeded in annual passenger boardings only by five U.S. and two Japanese airlines. Yet some idea of the massive potential in India was shown by the statistics: in that year the airline had carried, for the first time, more than 10 million passengers, but the Indian railroads carried 11 million *each day*.

The phrase "a chapter of accidents" is often used to describe a series of such events, and nowhere was this more apt than with I.A.C. as it struggled to cope with the inexorable growth of traffic demand. The first "fly by-wire" Airbus A320 entered service on 1 July 1989, and the airline took steps to enquire about Soviet Ilyushin Il-96s and Tupolev 204s. But staff problems when the engineers began to work to rule cost $7 million in lost revenues, and when a second Airbus A320 crashed on 17 February 1990, the fleet was grounded. The subsequent enquiry blamed pilot error, but rumors abounded concerning the original order, with accusations of bribery. On 10 December 1992, the pilots struck for better pay, and Indian promptly wet-leased (i.e., with crews and maintenance) six 180-seat Tupolev Tu-154 tri-jets from Bulgaria and Uzbekistan. This time, luck favored the airline when, only a month later, on 9 January 1993, one of the Uzbek aircraft crash-landed at Delhi, finishing upside-down in three pieces. Miraculously, all 152 passengers and 13 crew survived with only a few injuries.

I.A.C. had had to face competition from independent airlines, and these did little harm, as they were able to serve the smaller communities with feeder services, while Indian Airlines concentrated on the inter-city routes, the main ones which had now almost reached the level of hourly shuttle services. East-West Airlines and Jet Airways were now operating successfully (see below) and they were soon joined by a dozen other aspirants.

Indian Airlines carried on against gradual incursions by the new independents, and to its credit, after eight straight years of financial deficits, made a modest profit of $11.5 million in 1998. But like Air-India (see above) the airlines took a pragmatic, rather than an idealistic view of what the future for Indian air transport held for them. On 7 December of that year, the boards of both airlines agreed to merge, and set up a holding company. They may have looked toward the British action in merging B.O.A.C. and B.E.A., partly to improve joint ticketing and domestic-international transfers. But the announcement was regarded in Delhi as confrontation, and—uncharacteristically—the government moved swiftly. A month later, it disbanded the boards of directors of both airlines. They were now back to square one.

At the end of the year, an A300 was hijacked, and although the release of 184 hostages was welcome news, the crash of a Boeing 737 of Alliance Air (Indian's low-fare subsidiary) on 17 July 2000 was not. *Aviation Week* summed up India's domestic flag airline as "plagued with escalating debt, diminishing profits, and geriatric fleets." Something had to be done, even though the impasse between the operators and the legislators was still a barrier to prompt and effective action.

At the end of 2002, I.A.C. sought approval to buy 43 single-aisle Airbuses, and had carefully selected the balance between the three versions, the A319/320/321, ranging in seating from about 120 to 220. By this time, the leading independents were rapidly increasing their collective penetration of the market. Jet Airways especially was offering low fares, and Indian had to match them. In 2004, with the new Congress Party government in power, the new Minister of Civil Aviation stated that "the pride of India must be preserved" and declared that the industry must be strengthened. In November, the Public Investment Board cleared the $133 million order for the 43 Airbuses.

Rise of the Indian Independents

The creation of the two state airlines by the Air Corporation Act of 1953 allowed almost no room for any other airline activity whatsoever. Not until the 1970s were three small companies, using old equipment, permitted to operate special charter services that the corporations did not want, mainly to provide for the sudden surge for "guest" workers in the Gulf States.

In January 1981, a chink in the protective armour revealed an experiment in coping with the increasing demands for flights to small communities, those that could offer meagre resources in airfields and ground installations, and that would require specialist "third level" airline services, together with specialist management. The solution was a compromise. **Vayudoot** was half private, half owned by Air-India and Indian Airlines. At first it operated to only a few points with two Fokker F-27s from I.A.C., but in 1983, a young executive from Air-India, Harsh Vardhan, took over, and embarked on a continuing expansion policy. Within five years, with a fleet of 27 F-27s, Hawker-Siddeley 748s, and Dornier 228s—the last with excellent short-field performance—almost 100 points were marked on Vayudoot's map and 300,000 passengers carried. I.A.C. maintained the mixed fleet. However, like so many other similar efforts all over the world, Vayudoot outgrew itself, could not pay its way, and the domestic trunk airline took over in 1993.

A few other ventures during the early 1990s were short-lived. India's fast-growing population, combined with its growing spending power, began to exert pressure on the aviation

Boeing 737-700 of Jet Airways. (Bentley)

authorities that led to a change in government policy. In February 1994, the new Minister of Civil Aviation revoked the 1953 Act and opened the door for private enterprise, as already referred to above. Some entrepreneurs had already been permitted to start flying, notably **East-West Airlines**, on 28 February 1982; **Jet Airways** on 5 May 1993, both from Bombay; and **Sahara India Airlines** from Delhi on 2 December 1993. These airlines were the leaders in a new wave of companies that were more soundly capitalized than their failed predecessors; they had learned from their mistakes, benefitted from the collapse of Vayudoot, and boldly entered the Jet Age with fleets of Boeing 737s. Jet Airways especially, headed by Naresh Goyal, was more than ready as its background combined the Tailwinds travel organization with substantial investment from Gulf Air (Bahrain) and Kuwait Airways, each holding 20% of the shares. With excellent cabin service and operational efficiency, the Jet Airways fleet—more than thirty 120-seat Boeing 737s and eight 64-seat ATR-72—was soon able to gain about a quarter of the Indian domestic market.

Even with the accumulated experience, however, all was not plain sailing for the newcomers, who found themselves competing not only with the state corporations, but with each other. East-West was out of business by July 1996. The new authorization restricted the new airlines to domestic routes for five years, after which they were allowed to operate internationally. Also, in December 1994, the Civil Aviation Ministry upgraded six air taxi operators to scheduled airline status, plus three others, provided that their fleets amounted to at least three aircraft.

Low-Fare Turning Point

Such efforts from New Delhi did nothing to alleviate the fundamental problem of the failure of the national airlines, Air-India and Indian Airlines, to provide adequate air services for a population of more than a billion, of whom perhaps at least 10% could, by this time, be classified as "middle class," and desirous of air travel for pleasure and family as well as for business. Ministerial efforts were quite inadequate, and a solution came from a business source. Ex-army officer G.R. Gopinath, known to his friends as Captain Gopi, founded **Air Deccan** in Bangalore, the focal city of India's thriving "Silicon Valley." He had traveled widely and had observed the success of Ryanair and easyJet in Europe, based on an obsessive emphasis on cheap fares at the cost of every on-board amenity except a toilet. He related this success to the potential for air travel in India. He boldly spawned

Air Deccan's nationwide network was based on hub operations from the major cities of India, including the computer centers, Hyderabad and Bangalore.

a flying revolution by starting service on 27 August 2003 from Bangalore to Hubli (a city of about 800,000 people, yet with no air service) with a rock-bottom fare equivalent to $11.00. In a neat contrast with Air-India's former (but now renewed) Little Maharajah symbol of excellent—but expensive—service, Air Deccan's symbolic traveler was a humble *Mr. Citizen*. Gopinath reached out to the railway travelers, and sold tickets on the Internet and in gas stations. In doing so, he did more than offer cheap fares, he broke down social barriers.

The low-fare market that Captain Gopi unleashed then exploded. The example set by Air Deccan spread throughout India like wildfire. In May 2005, **Spice Jet**, at New Delhi, and **GoAir**, at Mumbai, entered the LCC (Low-Cost Carrier) arena, followed by **IndiGo Airlines**, also at New Delhi, founded in August 2006. These companies did not start cautiously with a handful of aircraft. IndiGo stole some headlines at the Paris Air Show in June 2007 by announcing an order for 100 of the Airbus A320/321 series. But the momentum did create its own problems. With their best efforts, the Indian airports, the communities whose airfields had never experienced such activity before, and the air traffic controllers: all were confronted with a myriad of operational problems. The new airlines too were caught up in their evangelical zeal, and did not balance their books too well, most of them losing money heavily in the initial years.

At Coimbatore in southern India, **Paramount Airways** started a first-class and business-class airline with smaller Embraer jets in September 2005. But all the publicity thunder had already been stolen by what was to join Jet Airways and Air Deccan as a major force in the rejuvenation of Indian air transport. On 9 May 2005, **Kingfisher Airlines** started service on a network that, like its predecessors, covered the whole of India. It was founded by Vijay Mallya, the chairman of United Breweries, India's (and indeed one of the world's) largest. Like IndiGo, it announced a huge order at the Paris Air Show that included not only the large long-distance Airbus A330s and A350s, but also five 550-seat double-deck Airbus A380s, the first order by any Indian airline for the giant airliner.

The new privately owned airlines are setting a fast pace and presenting a formidable challenge to the merged state corporations. Under the liberalized regulations, and having served their apprenticeship domestically for the statutory five years, they have been allowed to fly internationally. Jet Airways opened services to Singapore, Kuala Lumpur, and Bangkok in April 2005 and to London on 6 May 2005 with Airbus A340s. It strengthened its position by absorbing Sahara in April 2007, and renaming its operation as **JetLite**, to join the group of low-fare newcomers. Further international connections were made, culminating in a trans-Atlantic Mumbai-New York/Chicago nonstop service on 5 August 2007.

Watch India!

Throughout the history of Indian air transport, one element has always worked against achieving the high levels of staff productivity that have enabled most airlines to operate. Elsewhere, quarrels with labor unions, from hangar-floor mechanics to senior pilots, have invariably been resolved, and compromises reached, to enable the employer to break even and continue to pay the wages. In India, once hired, no government employee can be fired. Thus, in troubled times, the very idea of staff layoffs or redundancy schemes or even dismissals, cannot be implemented, because they are prohibited by law. This has always been an inhibiting factor in Indian airline boardrooms in times of financial difficulty and even crisis. However, now that the independent airlines have provided the necessary stimulus to the industry as a whole, and the positive effects are felt by all, the prospects for growth and prosperity should exceed past trends. Even by the 21st century, only 1% of India's 1.1 billion population had ever flown by airline. However, with the pace of India's economic growth exceeding world averages, its discretionary income is growing fast, especially in the urban areas. Seven of India's largest cities have populations that exceed four million, and some 30 others each top one million. India has the potential of becoming one of the world's largest airline markets. Traffic is already growing at an unprecedented high rate and shows no sign of abating. Led by innovative and visionary entrepreneurs, India will start to regain, at long last, the respected global status that began to evaporate after the leadership of J.R.D. Tata was cast aside.

Chapter 35: The Subcontinent Fragments

A Changing Geography

For the first few decades following the end of the Second World War, southern Asia experienced political adjustments on a grand scale. Too often military action destroyed the lives of millions of people. The entire area between the Arabian Sea and the Malayan Peninsula had, before 1945, been known as the Indian Empire, ruled indirectly from Great Britain through its Viceroy, who represented the monarch. Indian self-government was equivalent to that of dominion status, and the granting of local autonomy to the traditional rulers of "princely states." British India accounted for about 80% of the population of the then worldwide British Empire, and a considerable percentage of its wealth.

Spurred by the pre-war peaceful campaigns for independence by the remarkable Mahatma Gandhi, nationalistic movements arose, even erupted, throughout British India during the latter 1930s and 1940s. Some of these led to separatist nations around India's periphery. Prominent among these was the creation of Pakistan, whose incentive to break away from predominantly Hindu India was religiously inspired by Muslim politicians. This resulted at first, in 1972, in a divided state, most of the area as West Pakistan, bordering on Afghanistan, and as East Pakistan in eastern Bengal. This unsatisfactory arrangement led to tension among the two portions, and the East broke away in 1971 to become Bangladesh.

The island of Ceylon, off the southern tip of India, became independent in 1948, and changed its name to Sri Lanka in 1972. Burma too claimed its independence in 1948, and changed its name to Myanmar in 1989. Myanmar's independence became isolationist, cutting it off from the many benefits of trade, commerce, and tourism enjoyed by its neighbors. These are now collectively grouped as being in the Subcontinent, a politically correct as well as a geographical term for what was formerly the Indian Empire. The Maldives, the group of islands strung out to the south of the Indian peninsula, began as a sultanate in 1965 before becoming a republic in 1968. Nepal, the Himalayan nation, unified as a kingdom in the late 18th century, had never been part of the British Empire, having successfully defended its frontiers when Britain was aggressively empire-building during the 19th century. It continued its mutually dependent relationship with India, in which Britain guaranteed Nepal's frontiers in exchange for the supply of troops to the British Army, the famous Ghurkas, whose record of bravery is unsurpassed. Finally, Bhutan, the other mountainous nation in the eastern Himalayas, was almost unknown to the rest of the world until the Jet Age was well under way. It had no paved roads until 1960, and was off limits to foreigners until 1974.

Throughout the world, symbols of independence have been to fly a new flag, issue a new currency, add new stamps for the philatelists, and to found a new airline. This, however, needs an adequate air travel market for support, not least to pay the wages of the staff. Except for Pakistan, with the benefit of previous Indian sources of staff and experience, the new nations had few resources or travel markets, and did not find it easy.

Tourism was in its infancy. The main destination in the whole area was still India's Taj Mahal, with brave adventurers going to Burma to see the temples and pagodas, or to Ceylon to ride the elephants. Then came the Jet Age. Suddenly, British, Scandinavian, or German tourists could reach Colombo or Kathmandu in a single day or at worst, overnight, instead of making an inconvenient stop in the Middle East. In the 1960s and 1970s, the Subcontinent became as accessible to Europeans as the Mediterranean. By the 1980s, they had been joined by the Japanese and the more adventurous Americans. From the arrival of the first B.O.A.C. Comet in 1952, followed by the Boeing 707s in 1958, jet airliners helped to bring a new source of much-needed income to the new nations of southern Asia.

A New Country Divides

The newly formed **Pakistan International Airlines (P.I.A.)**, created as a Corporation on 11 March 1955, opened its first turboprop service with a Viscount 800 Series between Rawalpindi and Delhi on 31 January 1959, and followed this up little

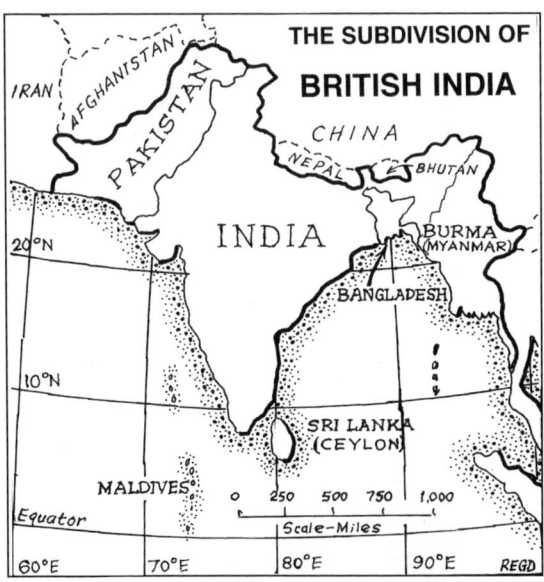

India, Great Britain's former "Jewel in the Crown," began to disintegrate as early as 1937 when Burma became a separate colony. In 1948, it declared its independence. Pakistan (East and West) was created in 1947 after a civil war. East Pakistan became Bangladesh in 1971. Ceylon had broken clear in 1948, as Sri Lanka, followed by the Maldive Islands in 1965. Each of the six republics has its own national airline.

more than a year later with a Boeing 707-320 Series (leased from Pan American) jet service from Karachi to London on 7 March 1960. This was the first jet service by an Asian airline, and announced that P.I.A. may have been a newcomer but did not necessarily need to learn from the incumbents. These steps were initiated by Air Commodore Nur Khan, who became managing director in March 1959, and P.I.A. continued to serve well as a flagship airline.

On 4 October 1960, Lockheed Super-G Constellations, released from the London route, were transferred to the "Inter-Wing" service, Karachi-Dacca, to consolidate the vital communications link between the two halves, East and West, of the divided country. In 1961, with a Boeing 720B, also leased, P.I.A. held, for a short while, the distinction of operating the longest-ranged airliner in the world, and on 5 May of that year, showed its colors in New York. But this service was suspended in 1963 because of the lack of traffic. Much nearer home, a DC-3 "Airbus" service started in East Pakistan on 25 March. This was replaced on 5 November 1963 with Sikorsky S-61N helicopter services to 10 points, and although this ceased in 1966, it took its place as one of the few sustained helicopter services in airline history.

P.I.A. claimed another "first" on 26 April 1964 when it became the first non-communist airline to fly to the People's Republic of China, using its 720Bs on a route from Dacca to Shanghai via Canton (Guangzhou). It followed this on 10 May with direct flights to Europe via Moscow, having traded traffic rights with the Soviet Union. During 1965 the airline suffered three crashes, and Nur Khan stepped down to take charge of Pakistan's Air Force. This was just in time to witness the disruption of Inter-Wing operations when, in September, armed conflict broke out between Pakistan and India. The essential Karachi-Dacca air link was served temporarily via Colombo, but the Lahore-Dacca route was resumed on 9 February 1966 when India gave overflying permission.

In the spring of 1966, P.I.A. was one of the few airlines that bought the Hawker-Siddeley (formerly de Havilland) DH 121 Trident, the -1E variant with more than the original 86 seats of the -1A. Pakistan's choice may have been a strategic move, associated with its liaison with China, which also bought Tridents because of its adverse political stance with the United States during the 1960s. The Tridents were sold to China in 1970.

Enver Jamall took over from Nur Khan and with the Tridents and an extra Boeing, was able to extend the route network to additional points in Europe, to Nairobi, and to four points in the Gulf, where Pakistan was among the suppliers of "guest workers." On 1 April 1967, service began to Bangkok, and in November 1969, this was extended to Manila and Tokyo. Ten F-27 turboprops served all the secondary routes in East Pakistan, and even replaced the DC-3s on the spectacular mountain routes north of Rawalpindi to Gilgit and Skardu.

P.I.A. could now offer service from Europe to the Far East, but hopes of further expansion were dashed when a civil war broke out in 1971 between the East and West Wings of the divided country. The Bengalis in the East Wing felt that they were dominated by the West and all their local affairs were controlled from Karachi (this was before the creation of the new capital at Islamabad). Tensions rose and troops attacked local forces in the East on 25 March. The next day, civil war was declared and the troubles escalated to such an extent that on 3 December, India intervened. The conflict was soon over, as the Pakistani forces were overwhelmed on 15 December 1971 and the independence of Bangladesh was firmly established. A new airline formed, but not without difficulty.

P.I.A. had to take emergency measures to maintain stability, and during the next two years, it did so with a program of commendable initiatives. On 1 April 1972 it opened a thrice weekly Boeing 707 service from Karachi to New York and on 3 November 1972 a *Batik* service to Jakarta via Colombo, Kuala Lumpur, and Singapore. On 20 January 1973 the China service to Shanghai was rerouted via Rawalpindi/Islamabad and Peking (Beijing), eliminating Canton (Guangzhou). This cut almost five hours off the flying time and provided a direct route from Europe, even the United States, to China.

Air freighting was successfully expanded with high-value shipments such as sports equipment, carpets, and surgical instruments. On 1 April 1974, P.I.A.'s experience led to a 20% equity share in Air Malta, a new airline that it helped to establish. The annual Hajj airlift to Mecca increased from 6,000 to 20,000 in November 1975, and the guest worker traffic to the Gulf expanded. The airline even grew its own flowers and ran its own chicken farm.

Through teamwork by the staff, the division of Pakistan had thus been met with unpredictable success. On 4 April 1974 Douglas 270-seat DC-10s replaced the Boeing 707s on the premier route to London, gateway to a large and growing population of Pakistani emigrants in Britain. This was so well patronized that on 5 May 1976 360-seat Boeing 747s were leased from Portugal for the London routes from both Karachi and Rawalpindi. A watershed agreement with India was signed in July 1976; many of the negotiators were old friends. (Jamall recalled the days when the representatives on both sides had been "grease-monkeys.") By 1977, services to India and Bangladesh had been resumed, but the former Inter-Wing route was no longer a vital element of P.I.A.'s route network. In 1978, four Airbus A300Bs were ordered.

Fokker F-27 turboprops replaced veteran DC-3s on the spectacular route into the Himalayan mountains of northern Pakistan.

The Subcontinent Fragments

A period of recession followed, and both Jamall and M.M. Salim, who had guided Air Malta, were succeeded by Major-General Rahim Khan and Air Marshal Wigar Azim. In 1981, belts were tightened, staff reduced (but salaries increased), and the government rescued P.I.A., with an injection of loans and equity. By 1985 the recovery permitted a new route from Islamabad to London via Moscow. Boeing 737s were delivered, and the versatile airliner could even serve Skardu, one of the almost inaccessible communities in the high Himalayas. By 1988, Pakistan's domestic airline network counted 30 stations, including high frequencies from Karachi to Lahore and Rawalpindi/Islamabad. To the international network were added Manchester (close to a large concentration of Pakistani immigrants in northern England); and direct service from Lahore to London. In March 1992, P.I.A.'s 43rd international destination, Tashkent, was the first by a foreign airline into Uzbekistan. Some alarm was sensed in 1996 when Pakistan's new government laid off 1,400 of the P.I.A. staff. In the following year a government spokesman stated that "there was no immediate priority to privatize the airline." Two F-27s crashed, one in June 2004, the second, killing all 45 on board, in July 2006, leading to a decision to replace these veteran turboprop twins with ATR-42s. More spectacular—and more positive—was the Boeing 777-200LR service inauguration on 3 March 2006, nonstop from Toronto to Karachi.

The East Wing Recovers

The creation of the new Bangladesh (Bengali nation) in December 1971 was the result of a civil war between religious factions. Local P.I.A. staff set up an (unnamed) airline service on 2 February 1972 and carried 10 passengers in a Douglas DC-3 from Dacca to Chittagong—hardly consistent with the Jet Age—in full flight around the Bangladesh frontiers. The airplane crashed on 10 February, and all flying stopped. Undeterred, the authorities not only started services to Sylhet and Johore, but, on 4 March, contracted with British Caledonian Airways to fly to London. Flights were under charter regulations, the strict conditions of which were waived by the British authorities on humanitarian grounds. Then the Indian government donated two Fokker F-27-600 turboprops for domestic services, and in April a vital international link with neighboring Calcutta began with Douglas DC-6Bs, leased from a Norwegian charter airline. Worldwide assistance continued, with the Netherlands and Australian governments donating more F-27s to extend domestic flights.

Bangladesh Biman (Air Bangladesh) was officially founded on 27 October 1972. The airline was fully government owned, and the aircrew were all ex-P.I.A. Starting a new airline without any infrastructure was difficult, but scheduled service to London via Bahrain began on 18 June 1973, with Boeing 707-320s leased from Pan American. Gradually, the infant airline grew. On 31 December 1973, service began to London with aircraft purchased from Northwest Airlines, and a route to Bangkok opened in 1974. Funds voted by the United Nations, in association with I.C.A.O., were provided for equipment and to train personnel.

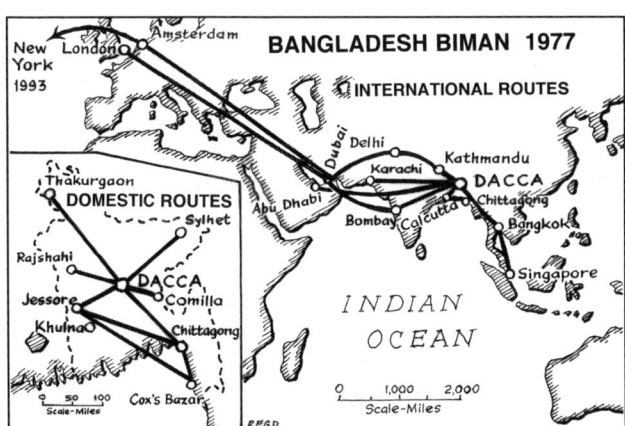

New countries have to have an airline, if only to "fly the flag" overseas. Bangladesh was no exception.

Two more Boeings were acquired in 1975 and 1976, and in June 1976, the airline changed from a semi-autonomous government department to a corporation. Thus strengthened, services began to the Middle East, India, and Singapore.

By the 1980s, the airline had a fleet of five 707s to serve routes that included those for contract workers to the Middle East, catering for annual Hajj pilgrims to Mecca, and supporting massive emigration to Great Britain, where tens of thousands of Bengalis took up residence. Two Fokker F-28-4000s were acquired in June 1980 for domestic and local routes, and in 1983, three Douglas DC-10-30s from Singapore Airlines introduced the Royal Bengal first-class service.

The airline had come a long way, in a single decade, from a local DC-3 service in 1972. Two British ATP turboprops were added in 1990, and in December 1993, Bangladesh Biman proudly opened DC-10 services to New York. In 1996, two Airbus A310s were added, but it was still a struggle. The emigrant population now numbered more than a million as guest workers in the Middle East, while about 250,000 lived in the U.K. and 100,000 in the U.S.A. The airline was not serving them well, though the government deregulated its air industry in 1997. To make matters worse, its poor safety record culminated with the United States and the European Union banning flights in 2003. These were resumed, but more aircraft were written off during the next four years. On 23 July 2007, Bangladesh Biman became a public limited company, renamed **Bangladesh Airline.**

Himalayan Airline

If Bangladesh's low-lying physical geography was a problem, Nepal's was the opposite. Its mountainous land included most of the world's highest peaks, either within its frontiers or on them. **Royal Nepal Air Corporation (R.N.A.C.)**, representing the country's own effort to provide the privilege of air transport, rather than contracting with Indian Airlines, started operations on 1 July 1958. This was the same year when trans-Atlantic jet services started; but because of the formidable terrain, the only aircraft that could cope with airfields on the sides of Nepal's mountains, often at altitudes up to 8,000 feet, was the piston-engined Douglas DC-3.

Turbine power succeeded this ubiquitous veteran in April 1966, when a Fokker F-27 entered service, only to be replaced by the Avro (Hawker-Siddeley) 748 on 26 January 1970, which was even more adaptable to the challenging performance requirements. Started by the F-27s in October 1968, the 748 became popular with its daily "Mountain Flights" from Kathmandu. Uniquely the only flights for which the origin and destination points on the tickets were the same, the one-hour circular aerial tour of the eastern Himalayas includes views of five of the eight highest peaks in the world, including Mount Everest. For the adventuresome, starting in 1971, DHC-6 Twin Otters operate into airfields such as Lukla, where the 6,000-foot sloping runway is at 9,000 feet altitude at the upper end, at the foot of a mountain, and 8,700 feet at the other end, on the edge of a precipice.

R.N.A.C. entered the Jet Age more definitely on 15 September 1972, when the first 120-seat Boeing 727 began service on a flight to Delhi, followed by services to Calcutta and Bangkok, and later, on 16 March 1977, to Colombo. By the 1980s, the world's tourist agencies were "discovering" Nepal as a fascinating destination, with Kathmandu responding with new five-star hotels. The national airline followed in 1987 when, in pool with Lufthansa, it opened a Boeing 757 service to Frankfurt, and the following year bought its own 757s, fitted with 174 economy-class seats, plus 16 "Shangri-La" business class. In September 1989, the Frankfurt route was extended to London, and other destinations included Dubai, Dhaka, and Bombay. By the 1990s, this predominantly agrarian country's biggest employer was R.N.A.C., and the tourist revenue that it generated made it the largest earner of foreign exchange. Paradoxically, its very success worked against it, as the Nepalese authorities liberalized its airline regulations in 1992 so that the national airline was confronted with a bevy of entrepreneurial small operators. **Nepcon Air**, **Nepal Airways**, **Everest Air**, and **Himalayan Helicopters** all entered the domestic airline market with a range of aircraft for which short take-off and landing performance is essential.

R.N.A.C. HS 748s made scenic flights along the eastern Himalayas to Mount Everest (and back). (Davies)

SCHEDULE (OCT–MAY)

RA104	RA101	RA100	FLIGHT NUMBER	RA100	RA101	RA104
HS7	HS7	HS7	TYPE OF AIRCRAFT	HS7	HS7	HS7
DAILY	DAILY	DAILY	DAYS OF OPERATION	DAILY	DAILY	DAILY
0820	0800	0700	D KATHMANDU A	0800	0900	0920

This is the only scheduled airline service in the world in which the departure and arrival cities are the same.

The Many Lives of Sri Lankan

If a cat has nine lives, aviation authorities in Colombo must have ten. The survival of a national airline, following independence from Great Britain in 1948, has been the story of constant internal strife, linked with rival international interests. For many years, Colombo was of strategic value to airlines flying between Europe and the Far East and Australia, but as the range of jet airliners increased, the refueling stop became redundant. Ceylon's (Sri Lanka's from 1972) value was eliminated, and its indigenous airline had to flex its muscles to survive, especially as a continuing civil war did nothing to encourage the normally popular tourism market.

Colombo had its first taste of the Jet Age earlier than most countries, as in the summer of 1953, **Air Ceylon's** Douglas DC-4

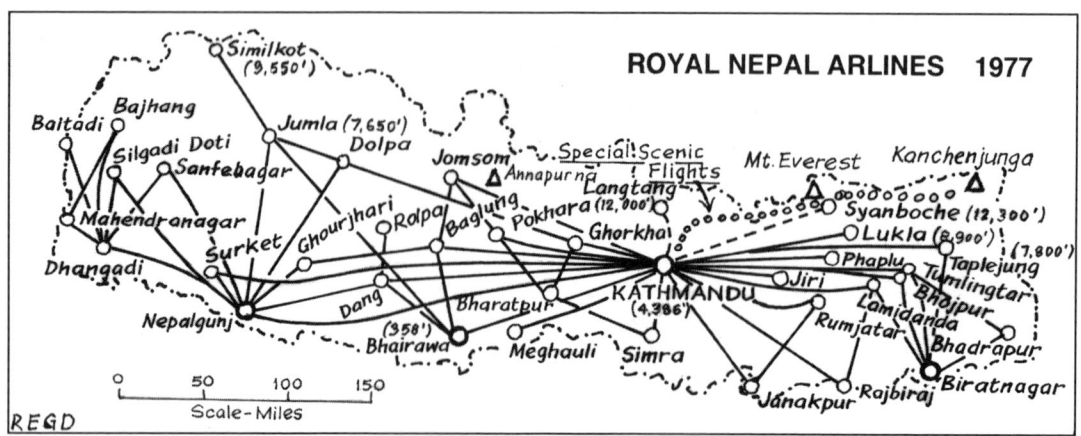

In a mountainous land with no railroads and few roads, an airline is an essential element of the country's economy.

Well into the Jet Age, only small turbo-props can use some airstrips. At Lukla, Nepal, in the high Himalayas, the 1,500-yard strip has a mountain at one end and a precipice at the other, with an 8° slope (top left). An R.N.A.C. Twin Otter lands close to the edge (top right), and parks at the top (bottom left). A Pilatus Porter (bottom right) prepares to take supplies to Syanboche, at 12,300 feet. (Davies)

service to London, started in 1950 with aircraft and technical assistance from Australian National Airlines (A.N.A.), had to be suspended because of B.O.A.C.'s Comet 1 ill-fated, but pioneering, jet service. In November 1955, after the Comet's withdrawal, K.L.M. purchased A.N.A.'s 49% shareholding, and after resuming service to Europe in 1956 with Lockheed Super-Constellations, introduced turbine power on 1 November 1960 with Lockheed Electra turboprops for Air Ceylon's *Sapphire* service—a reference to the island's special mineral wealth. The Dutch agreement lasted only a year, and B.O.A.C. returned on 20 March 1962, this time with a leased Comet 4.

B.O.A.C. cooperation continued for eight years, during which time a 40-seat Hawker-Siddeley (Avro) 748 turboprop started regional service to India on 7 November 1964, and a de Havilland Trident 1E tri-jet for extended routes in the subcontinent on 19 July 1969. But the pool agreement with B.O.A.C. ended on 31 March 1971, and although it was renewed for one year, including the lease of a Vickers VC-10, Air Ceylon sought another partner. (Curiously it had operated all three of the British jet airliners of the time, Comet, Trident, and VC-10.)

The new agreement was with the independent French airline U.T.A., which provided Douglas DC-8-50s for service to London on 6 April 1972, with Singalese cabin decor and cabin crew—just in time for a political change. Ceylon became the Republic of Sri Lanka on 22 May 1972. For the fifth time, the airline changed partners, when the U.T.A. agreement was terminated on 30 September 1976, by which time, the DC-8 was owned, rather than leased. Air Siam entered the field, planning to operate a 270-seat wide-bodied Douglas DC-10—such was the demand for the London traffic—but this offer was still-born, as Air Siam itself ceased operations. The government acted quickly and, on 15 December, appointed Air Vice-Marshal Padwan "Paddy" Mendis as chairman. He declared that Air Ceylon would "go it alone." But the going was not easy, as the wet-leasing agreement with a Boeing 720 from a U.S. company and a DC-8-41 from Canada was over-expensive. Routes to Europe ended on 7 December 1977, and domestic flights were discontinued in September 1978 when—to add to Air Ceylon's many problems—an Avro 748 was blown up by a hijacker.

This time the government decided on a clean sweep. On 11 January 1979 it created a new airline, **Air Lanka**, rather than bail out Air Ceylon. New chairman Captain Wikramanayake ("Captain Wik") entered with Singapore Airlines a loose agreement for all operational, commercial, and engineering services, and crew

Air Ceylon was one of the few operators of the de Havilland Trident tri-jet—forerunner design of the Boeing 727. (Davies)

training. Boeing 707s were leased from Singapore, and the European routes augmented with four points in the Gulf. 250-seat Lockheed L-1011s were leased in 1980 and 1981, and one purchased in March 1981. The next year, the government raised the capital from $15 to $30 million, and assumed almost complete ownership. Routes were added to Hong Kong and Jakarta, and two L-1011-500s were purchased.

In 1983, civil war erupted and was waged at varying levels of intensity until 2009. This severely affected the tourist market and also coincided with the acquisition of two Boeing 747 widebodies from QANTAS in 1984. The airline had to remove them and the L-1011s from service due to a lack of passengers. To make matters worse, on 3 May 1986, one of the L-1011s was destroyed on the ramp at Colombo by a bomb, killing 18 and injuring 41 people on board. Until then, in spite of the ups and downs of a sporadic career, Air Lanka had had a perfect safety record.

Captain Wik was removed on 21 November 1986, and a subsequent commission issued a scathing indictment of his administration; it brought in a new team, introduced economies (but increased salaries), and leased two L-1011s from British Airways in 1991. An ambitious order with Airbus in 1992 for two single-aisle A320s and five twin-aisle long-range wide-bodied A340s met with such controversy that Air Lanka had to cancel a portion of the order. Nevertheless, the small and much troubled airline was, in February 1994, the first airline in Asia to operate the Airbus A340-300. Service to Europe was now nonstop, and although a new route to South Africa was short-lived, things seemed to be on the mend. In 1998, six Airbus A330-200s were acquired to replace the L-1011s.

At long last there seemed to be light at the end of the tunnel of misfortunes. On 1 April 1998, a sixth partner airline and a new name arrived in the form of the Dubai-based Emirates, which acquired a 40% shareholding, and Air Lanka became **Sri Lankan Airlines**. The new management reviewed the route structure. Code-sharing was introduced with Emirates to Singapore, Jakarta, and Stockholm, Royal Jordanian to Amman, Eurofly to Milan, and Indian Airlines to Delhi. The first Airbus A330 was delivered in October 1999, and service to Sydney was resumed, with direct connections to the Maldives, a paradise for tourists, especially Australians.

Inevitably, almost as if cursed, disaster hit Sri Lankan commercial aviation yet again. On 24 July 2001, a raid on the airport at Colombo damaged five aircraft, and destroyed two others, valued at $350 million. Happily, however, this land of tropical beauty, famous for tea plantations, sapphires, and elephants, still retains a magnetic attraction for tourists the world over. The civil war between Sinhalese Buddhists and the minority Tamil Hindus in the north continued, but in 2003, an agreement with the Maldives permitted Sri Lankan to operate directly from Malé to Europe and to Tokyo. This is a welcome reversal of the lessor–lessee relationships that were once the fate of well meaning but inadequately financed airline administrations of the past. Nevertheless, the country and its airline are handicapped by the ethnic division.

The Air Road to Mandalay

Burma's (now Myanmar's) national airline has lacked opportunities for success. The government has, throughout the years of the Jet Age, adopted policies that have not only deterred industrial or social progress, but have too often seemed deliberately to oppose it. A country possessed of mineral and agricultural wealth imposed restrictions on trade, and its considerable potential for encouraging revenue-earning tourism was negated for years by a near total ban on foreign visitors. Against these handicaps, the **Union of Burma Airways (U.B.A.)** did its best. It put the Vickers Viscount into service early in 1958 to show the flag in Hong Kong, Singapore, and Jakarta, and later in Bangkok. Its domestic routes were interrupted in 1962 when rebel forces took over some of the northern provinces, but the old Douglas DC-3s began to be replaced in November 1963 with Fokker F-27 Friendships. In 1969, U.B.A. leased a Boeing 727 to resume service to Hong Kong, which had been suspended 10 years earlier.

In December 1972, the airline's name was changed to the **Burma Airways Corporation (B.A.C.)**, with the managing director reporting directly to the government. In 1974, the tourist visa duration was extended from the obstructive 24 hours to seven days, but there was no rush to fill the hotels in Rangoon (Yangon) or Mandalay, even though their golden pagodas beckoned adventurous tourists. The Hong Kong service had to be suspended again because of Vietnamese overflight restrictions. Burma Airways rationalized its fleet to match the commercial demand. On 1 April 1976, on its main domestic route, it introduced the 65-seat Fokker F-28, and on 2 May put this regional jet airliner onto international routes to Bangkok, Calcutta, Kathmandu, and Singapore. On the smaller domestic services, DHC-6 Twin Otters started to replace the remaining DC-3s on 19 September of the same year. Larger 85-seat F-28-4000s arrived in June 1977, and the last Boeing 727, which had been leased, was sold.

Rangoon and Akyab were the only airfields that could accept the Boeing 727, yet the obvious tourist destination was Mandalay, because of the nearby profusion of pagodas at Pagan, the country's major historical site. By 1985, Burma's airline was reduced to an all-Fokker fleet, three F-28s and six F-27s, which at least maintained air service between Rangoon and Mandalay. The 348-mile journey took less than two hours, compared to 22 hours by train or eight days by boat. But the fare, equivalent to

US$23.90, was about one month's pay for the average Burmese. Three of the Twin Otters had crashed, so the whole fleet was grounded, depriving many communities of any regular transport service at all.

By the end of the 1980s, Burma's self-imposed isolation from the rest of the world loosened. **Myanmar International Airways (M.I.A.)** took over the international air routes in April 1993, with a leased Boeing 757-200ER and investment, technical support, and staff from Singapore-based Highsonic Enterprises; 737s were leased from Royal Brunei Airlines. On 1 April 1989 (when the name of the country was changed to Myanmar, or Myanma), the old Burma Airways survived as **Myanmar Airways** to continue the domestic Fokker services. Two of the F-27s crashed in 1998, but the F-28s and one F-27 continued to provide air services throughout the length and breadth of the country. The original joint venture with Singapore terminated in January 2001, to be replaced by one with Region Air Myanmar (HK) Ltd., with a 49% stake. A local businessman took 11%, while Myanmar Airways retained 40%.

There must have been some strong, though carefully restrained, agitation in Mandalay, conscious of the fact that it was one of the potentially biggest tourist destinations in southeast Asia. For on 6 October 1994, **Air Mandalay** was formed as a joint venture with Myanmar Airways, with a small fleet of two 70-seat ATR 72s. Service started to Yangon (formerly Rangoon) on 18 October, and an international service to Chiangmai, northern Thailand, on 18 September 1995. Services were extended to the Shan States and Phuket. Not to be outdone by a northern challenge, **Yangon Airways** started in 1996 also with ATR 72s, with domestic flights to Mandalay and southern Myanmar. Initially a joint venture with Myanmar Airways and Krong-Sabat Co., a Thai organization, the latter's shares were acquired in 1997 by the MHE Mayflower Company. Services were extended as far north as Myitkyina.

Jets to an Island Paradise

If Myanmar enjoyed the privilege of having a wealth of fascinating places to visit, the island nation of the Maldives had nothing to offer except sun and sand. Few people in the countries that generated tourism on a large scale knew of the islands, which were merely offshore bits of India. For sunny beaches, Europe had the Mediterranean; North America had Florida and the Caribbean; and Japan had Hong Kong, Bangkok, and Bali. All were within a few hours' flight, and until the Jet Age brought about what has been described as the Defeat of Distance, vacation destinations were within a thousand miles of where the tourists lived. By 1960, while the world's leading airlines encompassed the globe, tourists who had already enjoyed the sun and sand of the Costa Brava or Miami Beach discovered that North Africa or Brazil's Copacabana Beach were equally accessible by 600-mph jets, and the extra cost were often offset by cheaper accommodations at little-known resorts. A decade later, adventurous vacationers had begun to "discover" the Seychelles, Aruba, and, in due course, the Maldives.

These islands attained full sovereign status as a Sultanate on 26 July 1965 and became an Islamic Republic three years later. Still "off the beaten track," the first sporadic air service to Malé, the Maldivian capital, did not start until 1967, by Air Ceylon. Regular flights, once every two weeks from Colombo, were not established until November 1971 by the Sri Lankan Air Force, which advised and assisted in the formation of **Air Maldives** early in 1974. On 9 October of that year, two Convair 440s (too early yet for jets) began service to "the sun-kissed islands, not far short of paradise."

Still dependent on Sri Lanka for support, the airline faltered, and although reorganized as Air Maldives Ltd. on 1 June 1976, it ceased operations a year later. The next move was soon, on 2 November, to form **Maldives International Airlines (M.I.A.)** with help from Indian Airlines (already operating Avro 748s), which wet-leased Boeing 737s. Subsequent progress was swift. Air connections to other, even more remote, Maldive islands as far as Gan, 400 miles to the south, began with a Short Skyvan on 3 August 1981. For the overseas market, the airline became **Maldive Airways Limited** on 30 September 1984. Arab interests provided the capital for a fleet of three Douglas DC-8-51s for long-distances and a Fokker F-27 for regionals. On 3 March 1985, service to Madras started, as well as to Trivandrum and Colombo, and to the Gulf States. By the summer of 1986, international flights were suspended. The old **Air Maldives** name was revived to operate inter-island flights.

In spite of the inability to sustain a viable air transport industry of its own, the Maldives continued to prosper as a tourist destination. Foreign airlines, including the newly emerging ones in the Gulf States, continued to provide ever-increasing capacity, while the desire to travel around the islands, to keep pace with the demand, stimulated the foundation of several local airlines. Inter Atoll Air operated a DHC-6 Twin Otter in 1986 (but it failed the following year) while **Hummingbird Helicopters** found a solution from 8 July 1989 with Sikorsky S-61Ns, adding 22-seat Mil-8s in 1991. **Maldivian Air Taxi** entered the field in November 1993, with 14-seat Twin Otters, and by 1997 was able to report that its fleet of 15 carried 300,000 passengers during the year.

The success has not been without tragedy, as two helicopters crashed, with fatalities, in 1999 and 2000. Even so, tourist arrivals in 2001 totaled almost half a million, and within five years,

Indian Airlines helped tourists to "discover" the paradise islands of the Maldives. This is a Boeing 737 at Hulule Airport. (Davies)

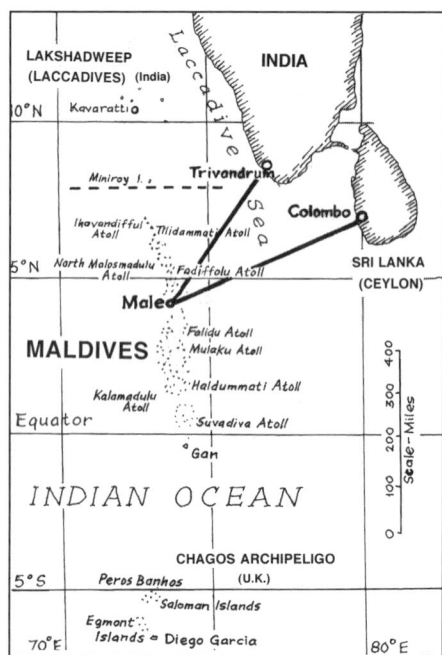

that almost doubled. From its humble status, still as an unknown home for local fishermen when the first Comet jets reached Colombo in 1953, the Jet Age has, only a few decades later, put the Maldive Islands firmly on the pages of travel agency brochures.

Airline to Shangri-La

A famous novel and movie of the 1930s told the fictional story of the discovery of a strange land beyond the Himalayas, cut off from the rest of the world. The arrival of air transport to the tiny country of Bhutan would almost classify as fiction, were it not true. Until the latter years of the 20th century, the only way to visit there was by an arduous journey, little of it on wheels. Nepal had no railways but Bhutan did not have many roads. For decades the king resisted the presence of foreign visitors. On 5 April 1981, when Bhutan finally opened its frontiers, **Druk-Air** was established by royal proclamation.

On 12 February 1983, two 18-seat-Dornier 228 turboprops opened service from Calcutta to Paro, the nearest place to Thimphu, the capital. Paro's altitude is 7,330 feet above sea level, and the closely surrounding mountains of up to 16,000 feet demand good airmanship from the pilots as well as excellent STOL performance from the aircraft. Yet within a few years, Druk-Air was making great progress. In November 1988, it acquired a 72-seat BAe 146 four-engined turbojet, and as the Bhutanese name of the country was confusing, became known also as **Royal Bhutan Airlines**, and added routes to Dhaka, Delhi, Kathmandu, and Bangkok. After improvements to Paro's airfield, a 114-seat Airbus A319 made test flights before opening regular service to this once-remote land on 31 October 2004. Shangri-La is now on the world's doorstep.

High in the Himalayas, the Bhutanese airline Druk-Air started service with Dornier 228 turboprops. (Graboske)

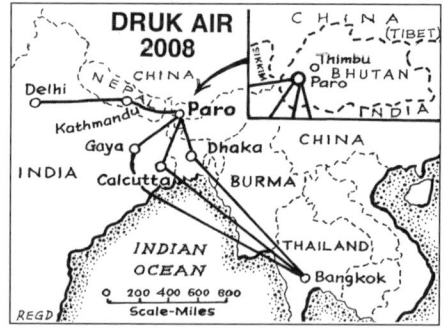

Once almost isolated from the outside world, Bhutan now has its own Airbus service to neighboring countries.

Chapter 36: Eastern Asia Emergent

Farewell to Colonialism

Except for Thailand, the whole of Asia has been under effective colonial control since the 18th century, even though China was ostensibly independent. Before the Second World War, Great Britain, the Netherlands, France, Russia, and even Portugal, collectively extended European rule over vast stretches of territory. Japan invaded and occupied parts of China, whose economic wealth was shared by several countries in mutually agreed areas of commercial control. The Philippines was a United States overseas territory until the Japanese occupation in 1942. By the end of that year, Japan's empire had extended from Burma to New Guinea, and although the indigenous peoples had exchanged European colonialism for Japanese dominance, the Allied victory in 1945 would soon mark the end of foreign control.

As colonies established their own forms of government, one confirmation of liberation—flying a new flag—was soon followed by another—establishing a national airline. Showing the flag on the tail of its aircraft at a foreign airport was a demonstration of pride and achievement. But the emergence from foreign control was a mixed blessing and it took time. While colonial administrations had ensured that natural local wealth was exploited to the advantage of the rulers, they had also introduced forms of justice that were of permanent value. India, for example, is the biggest democracy in the world. Often the pathway to independence is not smooth; industrial progress, sometimes marred by violent changes of power, can be slowed or handicapped. Yet some of the new airlines now rank among their older, more experienced predecessor "empire" corporations. The airlines of Asia as a whole, with those of the southeast among the leaders, are now riding on the crest of the Jet Age wave, while Pan Am is but a receding chapter in airline history; B.O.A.C. is no longer; K.L.M. was absorbed by Air France; and J.A.L. declared bankruptcy early in 2010.

Malaya in the Ascendant

The creation of Malayan Airways on 1 May 1947 occurred before the Federation of Malaya gained complete autonomy in 1948. Still with overseas ownership, mainly B.O.A.C. and QANTAS, Malaya's airline progressed from DC-3s and smaller aircraft to Vickers Viscounts and Bristol Britannias. It entered the pure jet age with a leased de Havilland Comet 4 in 1962, followed by an order for its own Comets in May 1965, after the Federation of Malaysia was formed. This was the political merger of the Federated States with the British colonies in northern Borneo and Singapore, and the airline name was changed accordingly to **Malaysian Airways**. It did not last long. Chairman Loke Wan Tho, who was killed in an air crash in June, did not live to witness the political separation of the city of Singapore from the Malayan mainland in August of that year. Consequently, on 14 May 1968, the two governments renamed the airline as **Malaysian-Singapore Airlines (M.S.A.)**, with each holding 38% of the shares, and B.O.A.C., QANTAS, and Brunei with minority holdings.

This new airline, the flag carrier of two new countries, showed its mettle. Comet services were extended to Australia, in an extensive pooling arrangement with B.O.A.C., QANTAS, Air-India, and Air New Zealand. Boeing 707s, on lease, started service to Tokyo on 1 August 1968. Domestic and regional services were well served by Boeing 737s, from 21 August 1969, while diminutive Britten-Norman Islanders replaced old Scottish Twin Pioneers in the mountains of Sabah. Both governments increased their shares to 43% each, and the airline opened a new 16-story headquarters in Singapore. On 27 April 1971, Malaysian Airways Ltd. (MAL) was formed, but the name was soon changed to **Malaysian Airways System (M.A.S.)**. (The word *mal* means "bad" in French; *mas* means "gold" in Malaysian.) By this time, the airline was able to assert itself, with a Boeing 707 service to London from 2 June plus affinity charters and additional destinations in Europe. Nearer home, Fokker F-27s improved the local routes from 1 June 1972. The airline split officially on 1 October 1972.

Phenomenal Singapore

Easily the biggest center of trade and commerce in the entire region, the citizens of Singapore, mostly of Chinese origin, felt that Kuala Lumpur did not recognize their contribution to the Malaysian economy. Today it is the world's biggest container ship hub. Global air transport followed a similar pattern, as Singapore was an essential B.O.A.C. traffic hub and refueling point for its routes to the Orient and to Australasia. Other European airlines shared this approach, although Bangkok was also to rise in importance.

Singapore incorporated **Mercury Singapore Airlines (M.S.A.)** on 3 February 1972. Agreement had already been reached as to the division of the Malaysian aircraft fleet and installations. Singapore inherited most of the long-range Boeing 707s, together with 727s and two Fokker F-27s. It did not need many of the latter; almost unique among other countries, the little island was too small to have a domestic system. After protest from Kuala Lumpur (as the initials were the same as those of the Malaysian airline), on 30 June, it was renamed **Singapore Airlines (S.I.A.)**.

During the next three decades, S.I.A. grew to a position of leadership in the statistical ranking of global airlines; and this flag carrier of a city-state of four million people set the scene for the airlines of Asia, collectively, to overhaul Europe in operations and fleet ownership and modernity. A superb management team took some calculated and wisely judged risks in operational and financial decision making. Within a month of the renaming, it ordered two 349-seat wide-bodied Boeing 747s for $65 million, and a month later bought four used Boeing 707s. When the break-up with M.S.A. was officially confirmed on 1 October

1972, Singapore was self-sufficient. The F-27s were replaced by Boeing 737s, and flights to London were increased to a daily service, with intermediate stops. By the time the first 747 went into service on 1 October 1973, Singapore was serving 28 cities in 21 countries.

On 15 August 1975, a $13-million engine overhaul base was completed. Chairman J.Y.M. Pillay announced the intention to start a trans-Pacific route and to invest in an enlarged fleet to operate it. He announced an innovative three-class fare structure on the route to Tokyo via Hong Kong and Taipei, and added Seoul as a co-terminus. Progress in the 1970s continued steadily if not spectacularly: new destinations, Paris, Auckland, Dubai; more aircraft, including an order for the Boeing 727-200 Advanced on 30 June 1976; the establishment of Tradewinds Charters in August; an insurance subsidiary in November; and Singapore Aero-Engine Overhaul on 1 April 1977. On 6 July 1977, four 268-seat Douglas DC-10-30s were ordered for $410 million, and three weeks later, a $14-million air freight terminal was opened. These expensive events, though routine, were overshadowed by, first, on 23 September, landing rights granted by the United States, and second, on 21 October, an agreement with British Airways to operate a supersonic Concorde service to London via Bahrain. Boeing 727s started flying on 1 October to Manila, but the first planned Concorde departure, for 9 December, had to be cancelled because Malaysia denied the essential over-flying rights. To underline its financial strength, on 10 May 1978, with an order for 19 Boeing aircraft, worth $900 million, S.I.A. claimed the largest single commercial sale in history. As an early indication of future leadership, it counteracted transit-right problems in June by operating nonstop from Hong Kong to Honolulu, the first airline to do so. Later in the year, S.I.A. provided assistance to the struggling Air Lanka, by assigning about 70 personnel to Colombo, a move that was augmented in September 1979 by the lease of two Boeing 707s, which Air Lanka later purchased.

On 24 January 1979, after the Malaysian authorities relented on the overflying, Singapore did resume Concorde service to London via Bahrain, but judiciously code-shared the flights on British Airways aircraft. The 9½-hour journey time was 6 hours faster than the best subsonic schedule; but this service was terminated on 30 October 1980 because of high costs. Trans-Pacific passenger service started on 4 April 1979, with Douglas DC-10s, but this aircraft gave way to Boeing 747-200s, after a disastrous DC-10 crash at Chicago, which grounded the type worldwide for several weeks. A second U.S. destination, Los Angeles, was added on 2 July 1980, and a direct route, via a single stop at Tokyo, beginning on 11 December, reduced the elapsed time from Singapore to 16½ hours. For its medium-range routes, and departing from the customary choices offered by Douglas and Boeing, the European twin-engined 246-seat Airbus A300 entered service to Jakarta and Kuala Lumpur on 2 February 1981. The aging 707s were sold, as the airline's enhanced reputation gave Airbus a firm presence in southeast Asia. On 1 July 1981, the new international airport at Changi opened. A Boeing 727 landed first, perhaps a sentimental tribute to a fine airliner near retirement.

Singapore Airline's worldwide stature was evident in the official International Civil Aviation Organization (I.C.A.O.) statistics. In 1981, measured by revenue passenger-miles, it was the world's sixth largest international airline. Its on-board service earned it recognition by both business and leisure passengers. In February 1983, at Changi, it completed the world's largest column-free engineering hangar, to provide unmatched maintenance to a modern fleet whose average age was only three and a half years.

On 5 May 1983, it opened the world's first service by the new Boeing 747-300 (or 747-SUD—Stretched Upper Deck) on the Los Angeles route, and on 24 November to London, with a technical stop at Dubai, but often operating nonstop. The Sydney, Perth, and Melbourne Australian services were augmented on 30 March 1984 with Brisbane and Adelaide, as it had now become a major competitor in the Australia-Europe market. It gained headlines on 29 June when the sixth 747-SUD was delivered, 7,261 miles nonstop from Seattle, in less than 16 hours. During the next few years, new points were added to the route map, ranging from Mauritius, in 1985, to Christchurch, in 1986, while the emerging importance of the subcontinent was recognized with increased service to Delhi, Dhaka, and Calcutta in 1986. By the end of the decade, it was placing large orders for Boeing 747s almost every year, and with the latest from Boeing, the 747-400, it inaugurated, on 29 May 1989, permanent and regular nonstop service to London. On 1 July 1990, it joined the International Air Transport Association (IATA). That organization, once a purveyor of patronage, was now a privileged recipient.

Building from strength (in 1990 it was the 13th largest airline in the world), it was one of the first to order, in November 1995, the new Boeing 777 (the "Triple-Seven"), a wide-bodied airliner that combined the twin-aisle feature and long range with power from only two engines, giving it outstanding operating economics. It accelerated the demise of the tri-jet types, but not the four-engined, as Airbus had responded with the A340, the 184-seat -500 variant of which claimed to have the longest range of all airliners. Singapore's May 1998 order for these aircraft was followed in June 1999 by a coup for Boeing, which took in 15 of S.I.A.'s Airbus 340-300s, in exchange for 10 long-range 777ERs. Nevertheless, when, on 3 February 2004, the 181-seat *Raffles* class Singapore-Los Angeles nonstop service opened, followed on 28 June by New York nonstop, these prestigious services were with the Airbus 340-500.

Singapore's global credentials were now firmly established. It joined Lufthansa and United Airlines in the Star Alliance in March 1999. With solid financial strength—backed by a 56% government holding through Temasek Holdings—it also expanded its foreign involvement in overseas investments. Attempts to buy shares of China Airlines and Ansett collapsed but on 31 March 2000, for $970 million, it bought 49% of Virgin Atlantic from Sir Richard Branson. It also acquired a stake in Air New Zealand, which by September 2001 amounted to 34%, when Ansett ceased operations.

World Leadership

On 26 May 2000, Chairman Chew Choon Seng confirmed an order for ten 555-seat Airbus A3XX-100 double-deck giant airliners, which were soon designated as A380s. Second to order, after Emirates, Singapore Airlines was the first to open service. Boeing did not compete in the very-large-airliner market, promoting instead a larger variant of the 747 series. It announced instead the Model 787 Dreamliner, built largely of composite materials rather than metal. This aircraft was less than half the size of the A380 and was aimed at different markets. Singapore signed up for 20 (plus 20 options) in October 2006, following a large order for 31 350-seat Boeing 777-300s on 24 August 2004. Like the A380, the 787 was delayed and did not make its first flight until 22 December 2009.

Singapore took delivery of the first A380, fitted with 471 seats—in a mixed layout that was more attractive than the 555-seat manufacturer's recommendation—on 15 October 2007. It made a ceremonial debut, to Sydney, only 10 days after delivery, on 25 October, and began scheduled A380 service three days later. As noted in Chapter 51 of this book, Singapore's A380 inauguration heralded a new era in air transport history.

Recognizing also that regional services needed individual attention, S.I.A. first established, in 1975, a tour and charter subsidiary, **Tradewinds**. On 25 May 1984, with 16–18-seat Dornier 228s and, later, Shorts Skyvans, and in cooperation with Malaysian Air Charter, it started a daily air shuttle service to nearby Malaya. This infant subsidiary quickly grew and on 21 February 1989 leased a new 160-seat McDonnell Douglas MD-87 to begin scheduled services to resorts in southern Thailand and a route to Brunei. Further extensions soon followed. Boeing 737s were added on 17 August 1990, and the airline was renamed **SilkAir** on 1 April 1992. Leased Airbus 310s in 1993, and Fokker F-28s in 1996 were followed by the purchase of 18 Airbus A319s and 320s in 1997. Though its reputation was marred by a 737 crash on 19 December 1997, the first of its own 320s went in to service to Phuket on 25 September 1998. The last 737 was withdrawn in September 1999, and the last Fokker a year later. By 2002, with a fleet of nine Airbus A319s/320s, SilkAir was operating to 24 destinations, and reaching as far afield as Hyderabad in India and Chengdu in China. As described below, local competition was to intensify.

Malaysia Picks Itself Up

Hiving off Singapore from Malaysia was akin to separating Bangkok from the rest of Thailand. Singapore had been, by a considerable measure, the center of commerce and industry for the former British colony and Straits Settlements. Kuala Lumpur was the largest provincial city, but was not yet ready to take over the reins of government. Singapore emerged from the break-up with all the administrative experience, the engineering base, and the majority of the main-line fleet. The surviving element of the Malaysian Airline System (M.A.S.), however, had to start almost from scratch. Initially in 1973 it was able to maintain flights to London with Boeing 707s wet-leased from QANTAS, and maintained domestic and regional services with its own Boeing 737s and Fokker F-27s. In Sarawak and Sabah (formerly British North Borneo), Britten-Norman BN-2 Islanders operated into the tea plantations in the mountains, where these unpressurized aircraft had to emulate the old Scottish Twin Pioneers in crossing a pass at almost 14,000 feet without oxygen. In contrast with Singapore, M.A.S. had an obligation to operate social services to the outlying parts of the physically divided country, mostly with little prospect of their being commercially profitable.

Gradually, a modern airline developed from an improvised base. M.A.S.'s relations with Singapore Airlines remained businesslike and usually cordial, with few repercussions from the latter's independence, which could have been the source of confrontation. In December 1973 a pooled shuttle service began between the two cities. In October, flights had already started from K.L. (as Kuala Lumpur is familiarly known) to Taipei via Hong Kong, and this route was extended to Tokyo on 1 April 1974, this time with the airline's own 707s. Further intercontinental route expansion continued during the year, with service to London via Dubai, on 1 July, and nonstop to Sydney on 2 October, when M.A.S. was able to announce the fastest England-Australia timetable, with only two stops. Well supported by its government, Malaysian was able to order two 252-seat Douglas DC-10-30s in December 1974 and put these into service to Tokyo on 2 October 1976. On the same day, Perth was added as a third Australian destination, the 707s having already included Melbourne exactly one year earlier.

The new sovereign nation found itself at odds with British authorities that claimed that M.A.S.'s DC-10s would divert traffic from London to Australia on British Airways routes. Final agreement was reached, and on 30 October, M.A.S. introduced the DC-10 to London, and two days later to Sydney. Frankfurt was added on 30 November, and through London-Australia flights were introduced, via Kuwait, in December. The young airline was no longer a poor newcomer but holding its own as an equal.

Malaysia is a predominantly Muslim country and in 1974, it began to work with Lembaga Urusan Tabung Haji (LUTH), the Pilgrims Management and Fund Board, to organize passenger flights on the annual Hajj (pilgrimage) to Mecca. It became one

Singapore Airlines was the first airline to introduce the double-decked Airbus A380 in 2007. (Sunil Gupta/Lockon Aviation Photography)

of the leading airlines in this operation. On 16 November 1974, Airbus A300B4s were introduced on services in Asia and to Australia, and on 2 April 1980, Paris became the fourth destination in Europe. At the other end of the equipment scale, the Rural Air Service, as the local routes were called, added points in Sarawak. On 24 July 1980, a new Air Services Agreement was signed between Malaysia and Singapore, to consolidate cooperation and to permit pooling of aircraft services. Singapore was given authority to serve Penang and East Malaysia, while M.A.S.'s Airbuses became the flagship of the busy Kuala Lumpur-Singapore shuttle service. On 1 November 1982, this international service was on-the-hour, every hour, mainly with Airbuses.

Development from poor relation to worldwide airline status was accomplished in less than a decade, overseen by Saw Huat Lye, general manager retired in 1982, and Abdul Aziz bin Abdul Rahman, the first managing director. On 22 December a joint agreement with Thai International permitted improved service from K.L. and Penang to Bangkok. M.A.S. was by now in the forefront of innovation and aimed at a demanding passenger market. On 1 April 1983, it introduced a "no-baggage check-in counter" for passengers without baggage, who could arrive at the airport only 20 minutes before the flight. A Senior Citizens Travel program offered a 50% discount on all domestic fares, except on the Rural Air Service.

In 1986, another aerial milestone was reached when a twice-weekly trans-Pacific service opened to Los Angeles, eastbound via Tokyo, westbound via Honolulu. In the next year, the proud airline moved into a 34-story office building in Kuala Lumpur, and in October changed its operating (but not its corporate) name from M.A.S. to **Malaysia Airlines**. Journalists and aficionados delight in inventing derogatory meanings to airline abbreviations. In this case, the acronym MAS means "gold" in Malayan; but as a spoken abbreviation, it could also mean "where is the system." This sly humor was misplaced, for in 1988 it received its third Boeing Company's *Pride in Excellence* award for its 737 dispatch reliability. Malaysia was the only airline to be so recognized. Also, the change of name marked the airline's privatization, with the government reducing its former sole-ownership shareholding to 42%.

In 1989, new services opened to Delhi, Karachi, Guangzhou, Fukuoka, Zurich, and Brisbane, with Adelaide soon following in 1990, to make five Australian destinations. Malaysia joined with Singapore, Cathay, China Airlines, and the Philippines to set up the Abacus computerized reservations system, and on 1 July, along with Singapore, Cathay, and Royal Brunei, joined IATA. In October it received its first Boeing 747-400, to add to its already extensive fleet of three earlier variants and wide-bodied airliners. Kuala Lumpur was firmly on the world map. By 1994, the Malaysian fleet totaled 94 airliners, including 53 Boeing 737s, mostly owned and none very old. The acquisition of a large modern fleet reflected financial health. On 3 November 1993, for $27.4 million, Malaysian bought a 25% stake in World Airways, a United States Supplemental airline, whose future development was uncertain. Along with 32% of Malaysian, the World stock was acquired in January 1994 by Malaysian Helicopter Services (M.H.S.), a move that effectively privatized the airline, although the government retained veto rights and power concerning strategic decisions. It soon approved, in 1995, the purchase of 40% of Royal Air Cambodge and 49% of Air Maldives.

During the 1990s, Malaysia's airline grew to cross the South Atlantic and, in 1998, to reach the United States, eastbound and westbound. In April 1997, its first 278-seat Boeing 777-200 flew nonstop, Seattle to Kuala Lumpur, in 16 hours. Sustained financial losses, however, by the turn of the century amounted to $2.4 billion. The airline sold aircraft, reduced service frequencies (and unremunerative stations), and cut staff drastically. The crisis ended on 20 December 2000, when the Malaysian government bought back the M.H.S. shareholding, now 29%, for $17 million, while a new company, Penerbangan Malaysian Berhad (P.M.B) acquired most of the balance, $69 million in what was described as a bailout.

During the next few years, the airline recovered, and recognizing the economic growth of the larger nations of eastern Asia, expanded its services to India and China. By 2004, five cities in India and several new destinations in China and service to Vietnam had been added. On 11 December 2003, Malaysia ordered six 500-seat Airbus A380s, to match the lead of neighboring Singapore.

On 1 August 2006, new regulations controlling domestic routes became effective. Malaysia was allowed to operate only 19 of them, in competition with the new upstart, Air Asia. Of the entire network, only four of its 118 routes were profitable. 25 routes were dropped, and the fleet, already reduced, shrunk from 40 aircraft to 23. It had lost $350 million in only nine months. Several thousand jobs were lost, and government subsidy was no more, though the airline was now 69% state owned.

The recovery was headed by Idris Jala, who joined M.A.S. as CEO on 1 December 2005. He slashed more destinations and recognized the growing importance of tourism, which offered opportunities for Malaysian enterprise. Penang had been a resort for the British expatriates even before Malaysian independence, and it was now becoming a major destination for vacationers far and wide. To combat the erosion of traffic from Air Asia, M.A.S. launched a low-cost subsidiary, **Firefly**, on 3 April 2007, based at Penang, with connections to points in Malysia and to Thailand, with a fleet of Fokker F-50s.

Airlines for an Island Nation

With the possible exception of the Phillipines, no country needs an airline more than Indonesia. Geographically, its 17,000 islands, some ranking among the largest in the world, extend from east to west over a distance of more than 3,000 miles, farther than from Los Angeles to Boston. Formerly the Dutch East Indies, its population ranks as the world's fourth, after China, India, and the United States, and it is the most populous Islamic country. It gained independence on 19 December 1949, and **Indonesian Airways**, a renegade operation during the struggle for nationhood, became the state-owned **Garuda Indonesian**

Airways on 31 March 1950. Its first turbine-powered aircraft, Lockheed L.188 Electras, opened service from Jakarta (formerly Batavia) to Hong Kong on 16 May 1961.

Garuda had a special responsibility beyond "showing the flag" overseas. It had to provide modern communications within its far-flung domain, which reached from northern Sumatra in the west to half-way across the Pacific island of New Guinea in the east. Few places, not even provincial centers, had airfields that could cope with modern piston-engined airliners, much less jets, although the Electras could reach Medan in the north and Biak in the east. Recognizing that these operations were mainly far removed from Jet Age technology, the Indonesian government set up a second state airline, **Merpati Nusantara Airlines**, on 6 September 1962, to specialize in providing domestic services to the furthest reaches of Indonesia (see below).

Garuda's first jets were Convair 990As, introduced on 20 November 1963. During the next few years, routes were opened to neighboring capitals, and on 29 March 1965, after some delicate negotiations with the former colonial ruler, to Amsterdam via other European cities. On 12 August 1966, Douglas DC-8-55s augmented the jet fleet, while Convairliner twins and venerable Douglas DC-3s continued to serve the islands, with the latter still landing and taking off at places where most other commercial airplanes could not go. On 17 February 1968, new management was established under the direction of Air Commodore Wiweko Soepono, who had been a pilot for and the spirit behind Indonesian Airways. Sweeping modernization plans were put into effect, suspending unprofitable routes, promoting more international flights, and encouraging tourism. To replace the aging piston-engined fleets, he ordered Douglas DC-9s for mainline regional jet services, and Fokker F-27s for the feeder routes. These went into service in April 1969, and on 23 November of that year, DC-8s started flying to Sydney via Bali.

Wiweko was a good airline economist and engineer. He realized that the domestic routes of Indonesia were so varied that a jet airliner smaller than the 100-seat DC-9 but larger than the 40-seat F-27 turboprop was needed. The first 60-seat Fokker F-28 was delivered in 1971, and Garuda would build its fleet to be the world's largest of the type. On 1 April 1976, the first of a fleet of six 270-seat wide-bodied Douglas DC-10s went into service on the route to Amsterdam via Jeddah and Paris; and on 1 July DC-9s initiated a no-reservations Air Shuttle service from Jakarta to Indonesia's second city, Surabaya. Starting at eight flights each way per day, this built up to 10, and during peak periods, such as Ramadan or Christmas, even a DC-10 supplemented the Shuttle fleet. A second Shuttle began on 1 July 1977, to Semarang, another major city of Java, with F-28s, building up to eight flights a day.

In 1977, Garuda left the Orient Airlines Association (O.A.A.). Wiweko Soepono did not delegate much responsibility. He might have felt that he could steer by his own ability; he could fly a new airliner, judge its technical level, and analyze the merits in the marketplace. Under his direction, Brussels and Zurich were added as new DC-10 European destinations, and at the other end of the traffic strata, F-28s opened service to Palu, in Sulawesi, in response to a government directive that Garuda must serve all provincial capitals.

On 26 October 1978, the regional airline, Merpati Nusantara Airlines, also government-owned, was transferred to Garuda, Its senior management was dismissed, and staff reduced by half, as the entire organization was centralized. The worldwide grounding of the DC-10 fleet in June 1979 was a blow, as was the devaluation of the Indonesian rupiah by 33%, but route development continued nevertheless. DC-10 service to London began on 9 July 1980, to be upgraded to the larger Boeing 747s on 1 December. Seating was 425, including 18 first class, contrasting with the 544-seat layout for summer's Hajj pilgrims. With the advent of the big Boeing, the DC-10s were used throughout eastern Asia, to Australia, and on domestic trunk routes to Medan, Ujung Padang, and Bali.

On 28 March 1981, a DC-9 was hijacked at Bangkok. In the rescue of 42 hostages, all five hijackers were killed, together with the pilot and one of the commandos.

During 1982, Wiweko selected the Airbus A300, inspected it himself and claimed to have initiated the two-crew flight deck. The wide-bodied twin entered service on the Jakarta-Medan route in January, but the passenger traffic was dealt a blow at the end of the year, when, on 15 November, the exit tax was raised from 25,000 to 150,000 rupiahs (US$27 to $222). Then, on 18 December, in a move hitherto alien to local political custom, the government imposed this tax on all officials, from ministers down, and on all members of the armed forces, regardless of whether the travel was official or personal.

Wiweko's control was almost at an end. His last achievement was to launch, on 1 August 1983, the Tokyo Express, in cooperation with Japan Air Lines, supplementing the existing services. On 18 November 1984, he was replaced by R.A.J. Lumenta, who was one of the few senior executives who had managed to contribute to the airline's progress. With Mohammed Soeparno as president-director, sweeping changes were made to the administration. It adopted a new insignia, renamed the airline **Garuda Indonesia,** and extended cooperation with other airlines. Tightening of belts led to it announcing, in 1988, the first profit in 11 years. But further revolutionary changes, detrimental to the airline's fortunes, were to follow.

In 1990, the Indonesian government deregulated air transport. This allowed the private airlines, previously confined to using turboprop equipment, to fly jets. Garuda, meanwhile, leased a fleet of 124-seat Boeing 737-300s. In a complete reversal of the 1978 decision, all domestic routes except the trunk services to the big cities were transferred back to Merpati Nusantara, free of Garuda control. The latter, however, still maintained its commitment to provide capacity for the annual Hajj. Indonesia is the largest Muslim country (more than 180 million people), but the farthest from Mecca. Garuda allocated 544-seat Boeing 747s and 355-seat Douglas DC-10s to the task. In 1989 it carried 58,000 pilgrims to Jeddah and back.

Commercially, however, the airline struggled. In 1992 it added McDonnell-Douglas MD-11s and service to Guangzhou direct from Medan, but the finances were at a low ebb. The sale of aircraft in 1994 only delayed the inevitable. Carrying a $754-million debt, which the government took over, and with a DC-10 crashing and burning at Fukuoka, the year 1996 witnessed the biggest shake-up in Garuda's 47-year history. One-third of the staff was laid off; 60% of the shares were sold to PT Aerowisata, a luxury hotel and catering group. Although further aircraft were leased, including six Boeing 777s and seventeen 737s, nothing stemmed the tide of declining fortunes.

On 26 September 1997, an Airbus A300 crashed at Medan, killing 234. As the government under President Suharto collapsed, so did the value of the rupiah, by no less than 80%. In June 1998, Robby Djohan, took over the Garuda presidency and enacted even more drastic economy measures: staff numbers reduced, routes cut, and foreign debt renegotiated. Djohan left after only half a year, on 1 December, after he had severed links with seven allegedly corrupt subcontractors and prepared the airline for a major step forward.

On 31 December 1998, with an accumulated debt of $1.8 billion, a Lufthansa and Deutsche Bank management team was appointed to revitalize the airline. Lufthansa Consulting signed a two-year contract to standardize the fleet, to raise domestic fares, and to curb discounting. Yet again, staff numbers were reduced from 13,000 to 9,600 and 17 international routes were shut down. A Singapore bank agreed to restructure the huge debt, and the European Credit Agency permitted an order for six Airbus A330-300s to be paid over 16 years, rather than the conventional 12.

In September 2005 Garuda ordered 10 new Boeing 787 Dreamliners, as well as 18 737-800s. But just as the airline seemed to be stabilizing, Fate struck again. When, on 7 March 2007, one of its 737s over-ran the runway at Yogyakarta, killing 21 people and injuring 50 others, it was the third major fatal incident in Indonesia in 10 weeks, during which a combined 123 people were killed. The United States advised its travelers to avoid flying on Indonesian airlines, setting a rare political precedent. By 2009, however, with a brand new paint scheme and logo for its fleet, Indonesia's flag carrier was showing encouraging signs of rehabilitation.

The World's Largest Regional

To describe **Merpati Nusantara** as a feeder airline extraordinaire was no exaggeration. It was founded on 6 September 1962 to take over a small fleet operated on domestic social services by the air force, and it evolved to serve every sizeable community in a country that was wider than the continental United States and consisted of 17,000 islands, some of which were among the world's largest. Operating with small aircraft, of which the veteran Douglas DC-3s were the flagships, the route structure was expanded throughout the country. This effort included bush routes in the remote mountains of New Guinea (West Irian), taken over from the Dutch de Kronduif when, on 1 January 1963, Indonesia acquired sovereignty on that island. Garuda handed over responsibility for social (and loss-incurring) services, and Merpati was aided by a United Nations aid program to acquire versatile DHC-6 Twin Otters in 1967. Adding *Airlines* to its name in 1969, it entered the Jet Age (at least with turboprops) in April 1970 with two 68-seat Vickers Viscounts acquired from All Nippon Airways. These enabled Merpati to link the small communities to Jakarta and provincial capitals with modern aircraft, backing them up with 60-seat Nihon YS-11s in December 1970, 46-seat Hawker-Siddeley 748s in 1971, and then two 135-seat Vickers Vanguards in March 1972. Fokker F-27s were added in November 1973. All these aircraft were turboprops, whereas Garuda had jets, but Merpati offered better schedules and cheaper fares in a competitive environment.

This was no light matter for A.D. "Joe" Leimena, Merpati's energetic planning director, who described the sparring matches as the "Six Lives." In 1967 Wiweko had tried, unsuccessfully, to have Merpati wound up. In 1969, he tried to restrict Merpati to West Irian, again without success. He was repulsed again in 1971, when Leimena introduced the Vanguard, which was more than a feeder airliner, linking all the provincial capitals with premium service. Wiweko won the next round, by persuading the government to restrict Merpati to propeller-driven aircraft. The fifth round was stalemated, but following Merpati's loss of $3 million in 1978—this was inevitable when operating a vast network of low-level mainly bush services without subsidy—on 26 October, the Minister of Communications transferred the government shares to Garuda. This categorized Merpati as a sister company, and on 1 January 1979 the airline had to withdraw service from the main-line provincial routes, but was allowed to operate international charters. On 5 January, J.A. Lumenta, Garuda's corporate secretary, was appointed president of Merpati. A new life for the world's largest feeder airline was about to begin.

During the next decade, the balance of air transport operations in Indonesia was stable. The domestic/regional airlines, Merpati, Bouraq, and Mandala-Seulawah, though restricted to propeller equipment, were able, alongside Garuda, to serve their country well. As the largest of them, Merpati was a vital element of communication between all the separated communities of the multi-island nation. At its height, it served no less than 128 cities, towns, and villages, about a third of which were inaccessible communities in remote areas of the larger islands, especially West Irian, where there were few roads, or even tracks. Merpati was, for the citizens of Indonesia, the equivalent of the Greyhound bus in the United States.

Then in September 1989, came an upgrading, as Indonesian industrial infrastructure itself progressed. The regional airlines were allowed to operate jet aircraft. Merpati took over two of Garuda's DC-9s and 15 of its Fokker F-28s, to establish local hubs at Surabaya and Balikpapan. At the latter, it expanded routes throughout Kalimantan, so that the regionals were now competing with each other, rather than supplementing Garuda services. By 1990, 40 new routes had been taken over from Garuda, and the fleet included 37 jets. As an indication of self-sufficiency, it was also operating 10 Indonesian-built 40-seat CASA-Nurtanio CN-235 turboprops, with no less than 65 CN-250s on order, plus two Lockheed L-100 (C-130) Hercules, one fitted with 96 seats.

In April 1997, a government decree officially separated Garuda from Merpati. More regulation was introduced to an industry that had somehow survived precariously from administration laissez-faire and personal favoritism. The airlines started to work together, seeking more coordination to eliminate cut-throat competition. This was supervised by the Indonesia National Air Carriers Association (INACA), with a strict policy aimed to reschedule debts and to reduce staff numbers. To stimulate financial stability, it approved a fare increase of 40% on 1 September 1998 followed by another 14% three months later. Within a year, however, Merpati was facing bankruptcy. But its service to the community was such that, with new management, it found ways to sustain its nation-wide routes by government aid. It was able to enter the 21st century with some stability by leasing rather than buying aircraft. By 2005, it was operating 32 aircraft, mainly Boeing 737 and Fokker 100 jets, backed by CASA 212s, CN-235s, and Twin Otters, to take care of the smallest outposts in the jungles, more than a thousand miles from Jakarta.

Indonesia's Second Line

Because of its contribution to the continued unification of the wide-spread and geographically disjointed country, Merpati enjoyed indirect sponsorship from the Indonesian government. But this was not exclusive. On 1 April 1970, **Bouraq Indonesian Airlines** was founded by J.A. "Gerry" Sumendap as a subsidiary of Porodisa Holdings, an extensive timber industry in Kalimantan and Sumatra. Even though the Jet Age was well under way, the first services were modest, with a fleet of Douglas DC-3s based at Balikpapan, geographically in the center of the country. Progress was swift; Nihon YS-11 turboprops were added in May 1971, and Fokker F-27 Friendships in June 1972, to extend the route network to the cities of Java and Sulawesi and also to Singapore and the Philippines.

Political restrictions, both from Jakarta and neighboring countries, were a deterrent to foreign expansion, but in 1973, a sister company, **Nusantara Air Service** (renamed in 1974 as **Bali International Air Services**), ventured into Merpati's airspace. Nusantara is the Indonesian name for the chain of islands east of Java, but Bali is far better known by the foreign tourists, who were beginning to visit in increasing numbers, especially from Australia. Sumendap supplemented his twin-turboprop fleet with another, the 46-seat Hawker-Siddeley 748, which he selected because of its superior airfield capability at the mostly primitive airstrips on the network. Smaller aircraft such as Britten-Norman Islanders and Trislanders served the small communities, but services on the main routes were improved on 24 January 1977, with the introduction of four-engined Vickers Viscounts, and on 2 November 1978 with CASA 212s, license-built in Indonesia by Nurtanio.

In 1982 Bouraq became totally independent, without Porodisa control. In September 1983, in an astute purchase, Sumendap acquired four 60-seat Viscount 843s from China, where they had been sparsely used, and therefore still had a potentially long life. In 1994, the fleet was upgraded by the addition of Boeing 737s. Then, on 29 October 1995, in cooperation with Singapore's SilkAir, international service opened from Ujung Pandang to Singapore. In company with all the airlines of Indonesia, Bouraq was forced, in 1998, to take severe economy measures. It laid off hundreds of employees, and had to return some of its fleet of nine 737s, replacing them later with four MD-82s (the stretched DC-9s, by then marketed by Boeing).

In February 1970, another airline, established under the government policy of 1969, aiming to liberalize and to decentralize domestic civil aviation, was **Mandala Airlines**, based in Surabaya, east Java. Also under the same ownership was **Seulawah Airlines**, based in Palembang, southern Sumatra. Starting operations in June, they connected Jakarta with, under Mandala colors, Sulawesi and Ambon to the east, and, under Seulawah, to the cities of Sumatra as far as Medan, to the northwest. By the early 1980s, the latter airline was merged into Mandala, which continued to operate precariously for the next 20 years. Cardig International became the sole owner in April 2005, but it suffered a severe setback on 5 September of that year when one of its Boeing 737-200s crashed during take-off from Medan, killing 149 people, including some on the ground in a nearby village. Another 737 incident at Tarakan on 3 October 2005 did not bode well for Mandala, but Indigo Partners took 49% of the shareholding in October 2006. Its fleet of six 737s included two -400s, plus two Airbus A320-200s. The airline's survival has largely been helped, as with other aviation enterprises in Indonesia, by the country's need for air transport during the annual Hajj season.

Merpati, Bouraq, and Mandala were, separately, able to provide air services throughout the country. During the 1970s, they

Many different airlines were active everywhere in Indonesia. Bouraq's Nurtanio/CASA C212c (top) and Fokker F-27 (bottom) are pictured at Balikpapan. (Davies)

formed a fairly stable "Second Level," rather on the lines of the Local Service airlines in the United States. Other small companies sought to gain access to this market. The most prominent among these was **Sempati Air Transport**, founded in December 1968, and which started operations as a small charter airline in March 1969 with a single DC-3. With contracts from the oil industry, it was able to acquire six Fokker F-27 turboprops to expand cautiously. When the Indonesian government deregulated air transport in 1990, however, such caution was thrown to the wind. Hasan Soedjono became president, and the Transport name was dropped.

Sempati Air embarked on a program of ambitious expansion, including, in 1991, routes to Singapore, Malaysia, and Australia. Control was in the hands of Mohamad (Bob) Hasan, a large timber merchant, who is said to have "maintained close ties with President Suharto." Orders were placed for seven 103-seat Fokker 100s, and within a few years, six Boeing 737-200s and four Airbus A300B4s. Sempati claimed to be the second largest Indonesian airline, with 26 routes, claiming profits from its policy of guaranteed on-time performance. Then in 1996 a massive Asian financial crisis hit Indonesia hard, with the rupiah's value plummeting against hard currencies. In July 1997, a Sempati F-27 crashed, delaying plans to go public with the shareholdings. With debts of more than $300 million, 19 domestic and five international routes were abruptly closed. The fleet was reduced to a few 737s, the network to three domestic routes, and most of the staff laid off. When, in 1998, President Suharto was ousted from Indonesian leadership, Sempati closed down at the end of May. In June 1999, with debts of $760 million, it filed for bankruptcy.

The rise and fall of airlines in Indonesia has never deterred aspirant entrepreneurs from engaging in air transport that, by the very nature of an island country of continental stature, encouraged risk-taking initiatives. So, apart from the most prominent, a host of other airlines have operated, especially since the deregulation of 1990. To meet the newcomers, the incumbents reacted: Garuda, with Citilink, with Fokker F-28s; Merpati by upgrading with Airbus A300-600s; and Bouraq, with Bali Air as a subsidiary, with Boeing 737s. Mention should also be made of **Pelita Air**, which, as a division of the state Pertamina oil company, continues to operate a great variety of different types, including helicopters.

Some of these—various reports referred to upward of 50 or more airlines formed after deregulation—have added to the Indonesian airline scene; but the definition of what constituted an airline was quite broad. One new company, Lion Air, was founded in October 1999 and adopted the policy of low fares; it was well capitalized and invested in a large fleet. Its rapid growth is described in Chapter 37.

Thai Hub of Southeast Asia

Before the Second World War, only one country in southeast Asia had maintained political independence from the encroachment of European colonial powers. During the First World War, Siam had declared war on Germany and Austria-Hungary in 1917. King Rama had already sent men to France to train as pilots, had ordered aircraft in 1913, and in 1914 had established an air support division for the army and an airfield at Bangkok. The existence of such aviation experience led to the post-war formation of an air-mail service, which began 1 June 1922. Siam can claim to have been the most air-minded country in southeast Asia, if not Asia as a whole.

During the inter-war years, the army's Royal Aeronautical Service operated local routes until 1930, when the Aerial Transport Company of Siam took over until the end of 1941, when Japanese forces over-ran the country. The Siamese Airways Company (S.A.C.) was formed by the Ministry of Communications to resume domestic services on 1 March 1947 and to neighboring countries. On 1 November 1951 it merged with Pacific Overseas Airlines (Siam) to form the **Thai Airways Company (T.A.C.)**.

The need for swift communication was regarded as a national responsibility, as the distance from Chiangmai in the north to Phuket or Haatyai in the south was as far as New York to Chicago, and the railway journey took at least two days via Bangkok. In 1957 Thai Airways introduced Lockheed Constellations, and at first, technical assistance was sought from airlines in the United States. Dissatisfied, Thai sought advice from Hans Erik Hansen, of **Scandinavian Airlines System (S.A.S.)**. The two airlines entered into an agreement on 24 August 1959 for international services, and this was converted on 14 December 1959 with the establishment of a separate **Thai International**, with T.A.C. holding 70% of the shares, and S.A.S. the balance. This was a coup for S.A.S., which had been at a disadvantage for routes to Asia, because the colonial powers had been rigidly protective of traffic and landing rights, especially at Singapore. The first service, Bangkok to Hong Kong, on 1 May 1960, was followed by flights to all the capitals of eastern Asia before the end of the year. By its close association with the Thai airline, S.A.S. was able to create an airline hub at Bangkok, and to compete as far as Tokyo.

Thai International's first jet service was on 18 May 1962, with a 99-seat Convair 990. Henry Jensen, from S.A.S., also undertook a cost-cutting program, partly by reducing the numbers of expensive ex-patriate personnel. On 9 January 1963, he reached a pool agreement with Malayan Airways and Cathay Pacific, to alleviate uneconomic competition on the Hong Kong-Bangkok-Kuala Lumpur-Singapore triangular route system. Then on 1 April 1964, he took the bold step of introducing the 72-seat Sud-Est SE-210 Caravelle to replace the Convair 990, which was uneconomical for the regional routes. The French airliner had only two jets (rear-mounted on the fuselage) and "four-engined safety" was previously considered essential for the predominantly over-water routes. But the Caravelle proved to be economically and operationally successful. At this time, Niels Lumholdt arrived from Copenhagen to preside over the airline's long-term plans.

Simultaneously with Thai International's Jet-Age introduction with the Caravelle, T.A.C. began to replace its piston-engined fleet with 40-seat Hawker-Siddeley 748 turboprops, which it had selected over other twins because of its performance at some airfields, described as unprepared strips. Service began to Bali on 24 December 1967, after protracted negotiations with the Indonesian government. The Caravelles were operating to India in 1968 and such was the whole network's traffic demand that Thai turned to larger aircraft. On 1 February 1969 two 99-seat Douglas DC-9-41s were leased from S.A.S. and on 1 May two 146-seat DC-8-33s from the same source.

After much delay, Thai International received its first indigenous competition from the newly formed **Air Siam**, which started trans-Pacific service on 31 March 1971 with a wet-leased Douglas DC-8-63. This airline had been founded on 15 September 1965 (originally as Varanair Siam) by His Highness Prince Varanand, who had been an officer in the British Royal Air Force for many years. Known as "Prince Nicky," he aspired to give Thailand its own airline, without foreign partnership. With help from British friends, he managed to obtain precious U.S. and British operating rights. To finance this bold venture, he sold property worth several million dollars, but his management was not up to the standards of administration and operations necessary for an airline of intercontinental stature. The trans-Pacific service was suspended on 12 January 1972, and a disillusioned Nicky sold more property to pay off the debts. Sadly he resigned from the failed venture in October.

Air Siam struggled on with a route to Tokyo with a BAC One-Eleven and a Boeing 707, both leased. The airline began service to Honolulu, with a leased Boeing 747, on 1 September 1973. Airbus A-300B service to Hong Kong began on 21 October 1974, by which time the shareholding included the Thai Royal Family 40%, and business interests 55%. On 30 November, Air Siam should have resumed its trans-Pacific service with a DC-10, but the aircraft was stranded at Los Angeles as the necessary landings rights had not been negotiated. On 1 August 1976, Thai International employees demonstrated against Air Siam's growing favors from the government, and then went on strike. Air Siam terminated all services on 12 January 1977, its licenses were revoked on 4 February 1977, and it was liquidated in September 1978.

Though disturbing for Thai International, Air Siam served as little more than an annoying punctuation in the former's own intercontinental progress. Vice presidents Lumholdt and Chatrachai Bunya-Ananta, meanwhile, had concentrated on developing the Australian market, by exploiting Bangkok as a geographical hub to challenge Singapore. Service to Sydney started on 1 April 1971, and this was improved by pioneering a completely new Europe-Asia route, via Moscow as a technical stop, and across central Asia. The Royal Orchid Service was inaugurated in great style on 3 June 1972 in cooperation with S.A.S., with long-range 146-seat DC-8-62s. Further improvements were made when, on 6 November 1973, through service began from London to Sydney, stopping only at Bangkok, in 20 hr. 15 m. Such was the popularity that larger 204-seat DC-8-63s were added to the fleet on 22 March 1974. The two airlines, both with strong government investment, operated independently and cooperated when necessary to avoid possible conflicts of route assignments. Gradually the S.A.S. shareholding in Thai International was reduced: from 30% to 15% on 16 July 1974, and this would be eliminated on 31 March 1977, with the Ministry of Finance acquiring 84%.

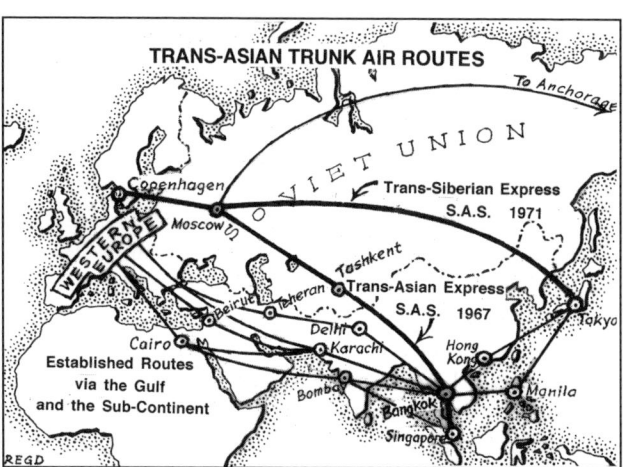

Thai International benefitted from the initiatives of its European partner, S.A.S., which had pioneered trans-Asian trunk routes since 1967. Bangkok was recognized as an important air traffic center to complement the established Singapore and Hong Kong hubs.

On 21 October of that year, the domestic T.A.C. introduced 116-seat Boeing 737-200s. Thailand had become a popular worldwide tourist destination, offering elephant rides in Chiangmai and sunny beaches at Phuket. Bangkok was recognized as a major airline hub for the whole of eastern Asia which, with Australia, was becoming known as the Pacific Rim. The city, with its temples, bargain shopping, excellent hotels, and active night life, was a tourist magnet. A T.A.C. 748 opened service to Hanoi on 17 May 1978, to mark a thaw in international relations with Vietnam. During the first four months, the aircraft were full. To match aircraft to routes and stations with low traffic demand, 30-seat Shorts 330s, with even better field performance, replaced the HS-748s on several routes.

Thai International, meanwhile, had made great strides. Simultaneously with the elimination of S.A.S. shares, the first wide-bodied 270-seat Douglas DC-10 had gone into service in March 1977, followed shortly afterward with Airbus A300B4s on regional routes on 1 November. Its traffic growth had elevated it in world ranking from around 50th to around 20th. It bought 360-seat Boeing 747s to cope with the burgeoning traffic demand. The first one was delivered on 2 November 1979, to concentrate on nonstop services to Europe, and (finally to emulate Air Siam) to begin trans-Pacific service to Los Angeles via Tokyo and Seattle, on 30 March 1980. Service to Melbourne started on

A Thai International Airways Douglas DC-10. (Bentley)

4 April, and the U.S. terminal was changed to Dallas on 5 November. On 2 April 1982, Thai International forged a direct link to the People's Republic of China with service to Guangzhou, but this was superseded on 29 March 1982 by Beijing as the terminus. The first Airbus A300-600, largest and with the most range of all the A300s, was delivered on 30 September 1985.

All was well, with additional services to New Zealand and other destinations, until a change of government in 1988. A much-publicized 737 crash at Phuket on 15 April 1985 did not improve T.A.C.'s image, and may have contributed to a major decision by the Thai politicians. On 1 April 1988, the two airlines were merged, to become **Thai Airways International (THAI)**. This could have led to efficient consolidation, drawing talent from both sides; but the opposite was the case. The reorganized management was simply not up to the job. Schedules were badly affected, and thousands of passengers were stranded. This former text-book story of airline success went through what was described as "The Black Winter." When the politicians came to their senses, they reappointed Chatrachai as president. He stayed on for a while to put things in order—not an easy task at a time when the government itself was coping (which it did harshly) with pro-democracy protesters.

In November 1995, the government ended THAI's monopoly of international services, responding to the growing entrepreneurial strength that was beginning to filter through the southeast Asian airline industry. The fleet was augmented with additional 747s, Airbus A330s, and Boeing 777s, and on 14 May 1997 joined with Lufthansa, United, S.A.S., and Air Canada to form the Star Alliance to extend and consolidate its market through global code-sharing. This action was followed by considerable controversy as 25% of the shares were offered to foreign airlines, but Chatrachai claimed vigorously (and successfully) that Thai investors could take care of such capital needs. Lufthansa, however, transferred its area hub to Singapore.

As THAI entered the 21st century, stature and dignity had been restored. In August 2004, it joined the elite list of airlines that ordered the 550-seat Airbus A380 double-decked wide-bodied airliner. In preparation for this innovation, Bangkok's new international airport, Suvarnabhumi (Golden Land) opened on 28 September 2006. THAI's *New York Silk Express* had already introduced a nonstop Airbus A340-500 Bangkok-New York route on 1 May 2005, competing with Singapore's equivalent 17-hour flights. This venture, however, together with nonstops to Los Angeles, gave way to one-stop service in February 2007, because of high fuel costs.

Independence in Thailand

When the Air Siam interlude ended in 1978 (see above), Thai Airways and THAI would face no competition, even domestic, for almost a decade. The small operators seemed to be of little consequence and serving only a specialized local tourist market. One of these, however, was more enterprising. Sahakol Air had started as an air taxi service in 1969, owned by Dr. Prasert Prasarttong-Osoth, who also acquired land on Koh

Samui Island, about 375 miles south of Bangkok. The delightful resort was 12 hours away from the capital by train and ferry boat and so the enterprising doctor made the obvious move: he started an air service, renaming his taxi service as **Bangkok Airways** in 1985. At first, on 20 January 1986, he started routes to other places with 12-seat Embraer Bandeirantes, then with a larger HS-748, but he had to suspend operations in July 1987. He resumed a year later and gained confidence when his operating license was renewed. On 15 January 1989, the airport at Koh Samui was opened. Service to the resort started on 25 April 1989, with 37-seat de Havilland Canada DHC-8-100s. One crashed there on 21 November 1990, killing all on board, but the airline recovered. Such was its popularity among vacationers that 56-seat DHC-8-300s in 1991 were augmented by a wet-leased 100-seat Fokker 100 in 1992.

When, in January 1994, Bangkok Airways was denied second-carrier status, to replace Air Siam, Virachai Vannukul, took over the management, introduced economy measures, and retained only the beach resorts from an over-expanded network. 70-seat ATR-72-200 turboprops, best fitted to the traffic demand, were added. By 1998, Koh Samui was the fourth busiest

This Bangkok Air Boeing 717 paid tribute to its origins with its name, Samui. (Bentley)

airport in Thailand (after Bangkok, Chiangmai, and Phuket). Direct international service to Koh Samui from Singapore was inaugurated in March 1997, and destinations in Cambodia reinstated in the fall of that year. These latter included Siem Reap, serving the magnificent Angkor Wat temple, and this was so successful that Bangkok Airways established a subsidiary airline, **Siem Reap Airways**, using wet-leased ATRs. Such enterprise heralded even more ambitious expansion. The first 125-seat Boeing 717 (the former McDonnell Douglas MD-95) opened pure jet service on 15 November 2000, and during successive years started routes to China, Vietnam, and Myanmar. 163-seat Airbus A320s arrived in September 2004.

Other than Bangkok Airways, which offered good service at good but not bargain-basement prices, several other companies entered the market but did not last long. **PBAir** and **Angel Airlines** started services in 1998, both with National Carrier status, the latter with Airbus A300B4s and other jets, all leased, on routes to China. More successful was Orient Express Air, which had started in July 1995, taking over some of THAI's routes with Lockheed TriStars and Boeing 747s and 757s, changing its name to **Orient Thai Airlines**. It then, on 3 December 2003, launched Thailand's first true budget airline as **One-Two-Go**, followed by **Thai Air Asia**, a joint venture with Air Asia in Malaysia on 3 February 2004. Such was the impact of the availability of cheap fares that Thai Airways was forced to start its own budget subsidiary. **Nok Air** began 737 service on 23 July 1994 (see the next chapter). **Phuket Air** was founded in January 2001 by Vikrom Aisiri, owner of clubs and hotels in the hinterland. At first, its Boeing 737-200s were based further north, at Ranong, just across the Myanmar frontier, which had a gambling resort. Services to Bangkok began on 19 December, and expanded throughout Thailand during the next two years. It also served Myanmar at Mandalay and, in 2004, Yangon (Rangoon). On 20 May 2004, Phuket Air started a Boeing 757 service to Dubai via Chittagong and topped this on 1 July with service to London via Sharjah. But the route was suspended during the first winter, and even though Amsterdam and Bali were added to the map in March 2005, all long-range routes were terminated in April 2005.

Resurrection in the China Seas

After the People's Republic of China (P.R.C.) was declared in October 1949, Chiang Kai-shek's post-war Kuomintang regime evacuated to the offshore island of Taiwan, to form the Republic of China (R.O.C.), a term which has since been dropped. Along with priceless wealth, some two million Chinese evacuees, with support from the United States, established a prosperous economy, even though its claims to be the real China are not universally recognized, even by the United Nations. While mainland China's airline industry foundered into stagnation, Taiwan managed to pick up the pieces of the former **Civil Air Transport (C.A.T.)**, salvaged from the remnants of wartime air transport services in China at the beginning of 1948. On 15 January 1950, it acquired the shares of the two redundant airlines in China and put together a Taipei-based airline that served military as well

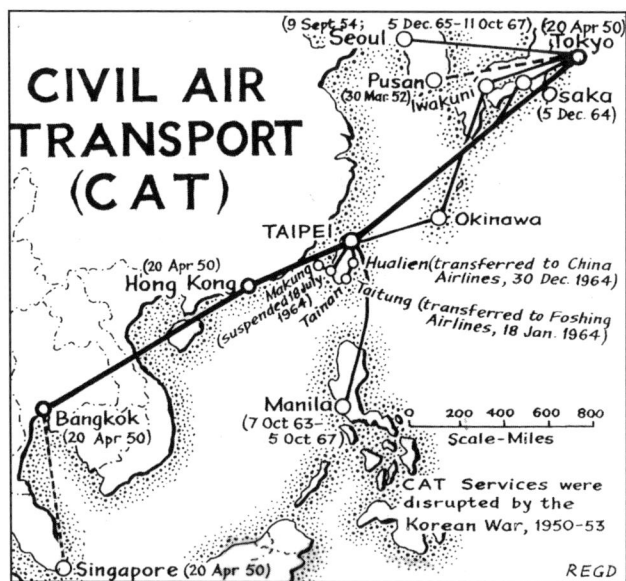

For a few years after Taiwan separated from China in 1949, C.A.T. became its national airline, serving commercial and military requirements alike.

as civil requirements, including the U.S. Central Intelligence Agency (C.I.A.).

During the 1950–53 Korean War, it was an important link for the neighboring non-communist countries. In 1954 the Nationalist government bought a minority shareholding so that C.A.T. became the flag carrier of Taiwan, with routes to Japan, Hong Kong, Bangkok, and Singapore. Compared to the austerity of the P.R.C.'s pedestrian and inefficient C.A.A.C., C.A.T. began to demonstrate a flair for good marketing. Its *Mandarin* service, introduced on 15 October 1958 with Douglas DC-6Bs, set new standards of cabin hospitality, and this was upgraded to jets on 12 July 1961 with Convair 880s. Even so, its status was eroded during the 1960s. Domestic routes were transferred to **Foshing Airlines** on 18 January 1964; and a C-46 crash on 20 June was a serious blow, as one of the 52 passengers killed was a Hong Kong movie magnate. Air America, the C.I.A.'s own airline, took over the route to Okinawa on 30 June 1967. The end was near. The Convair 880 was sold to Cathay Pacific on 10 January 1968, and the death knell was struck on 16 February when the replacement Boeing 727 crashed. All services were suspended on 29 May.

It was replaced by **China Airlines (C.A.L.)**, founded by a group of retired Chinese Air Force officers on 10 December 1959. At first it operated only domestic routes, but clearly ambitious, it had purchased a Lockheed Constellation as early as October 1966, when C.A.T. was struggling. On 1 April 1967, its first Boeing 727s opened services to Tokyo and Hong Kong, quickly followed by all the eastern Asian capitals abandoned by C.A.T. Consolidation quickly followed, with Caravelles taking over domestic routes, and, on 2 February 1970, a trans-Pacific route to San Francisco via Tokyo (and Anchorage westbound) with Boeing 707-320Cs. Such enterprise was curtailed, not by commercial competition or operational shortcomings, but by global politics. On 25 October 1971, the P.R.C. was admitted as a member of the United Nations, as Taiwan's claim to be the legitimate China fell on deaf ears. It became an outcast, automatically expelled from the I.C.A.O. and forced to resign from IATA on 15 September 1974. The latter restriction was not fatal, as China Airlines was in good company—many of the airlines of east Asia were also non-IATA. (At the time world statistics published by IATA did not include them, so that the indicated potential growth of the air transport industry on the Pacific Rim was underestimated.) A further blow, however, was the termination of the Japan-China Air Agreement, which severely reduced high-yield traffic. Japan Air Lines had to bypass Taiwan en route to Hong Kong, while C.A.L. rerouted its Pacific service via Guam.

Taiwan may have been down politically, but commercially it was far from out. Millions of Chinese who chose to move to Taiwan were from the most enterprising levels of an entrepreneurial nation. They set to work with vigor and (in an echo of Germany's post-war "economic miracle") turned this previously unremarkable island into an industrial powerhouse. Taiwan began to manufacture all kinds of goods, including high-tech products, in direct competition, both in quality and price, with Japan, which had also shaken the world of commerce with its ingenious electronics, children's toys, and cameras that were among the world's best. China Airlines supported the economic drive by converting a Boeing 707 to all-cargo configuration. Starting on 1 June 1974, it could carry 65,000 lb. (more than 30 tons, or the equivalent of 2,000 television sets) across the Pacific to an eager market in the United States. In October 1975, flights to Japan were resumed, avoiding confrontation with C.A.A.C. by flying into Tokyo's Haneda Airport instead of Narita. On 31 October 1976, it started service to Saudi Arabia to herald a spectacular year of recovery. Traffic increased 63% over 1975, with profits leaping from $1 million to $6.2 million.

Confidence restored, the trans-Pacific service was enhanced in April 1979 by the introduction of a wide-bodied Boeing 747SP, flying nonstop to San Francisco, with its flight originating in Hong Kong. In January 1981, cargo service was extended to New York via Fairbanks, and on 10 May 1982, to Luxembourg via Singapore and Dubai. China Airlines was re-asserting itself in the competitive world of air transport. On 1 April 1984, it introduced a luxury *Dynasty Class* on all routes, and on 12 April, by opening a Taipei-New York-Amsterdam route, inaugurated a round-the-world service. Though good for public relations, it was like other round-the-world enterprises: uneconomic. Financial rewards were better, if not so headline-catching, nearer to home. Toward the end of the 1980s, travel restrictions between Taiwan and mainland China (the P.R.C.) were gradually relaxed, so that families who had been separated during the 1949 exodus could be reunited, albeit through descendents, after decades of separation. Travel had to be via Hong Kong or Tokyo, and in spite of the Tiananmen Square student protest and brutal repression of 3–4 June 1989, 750,000 Taiwanese visited China in 1990.

Good fortune did not favor China Airlines for long. In 1991, for the first time, it had competition on international routes, with the foundation of Eva Air (see below). Although direct Kaohsiung-Bangkok service started on 28 October 1991, any traffic bonus was cancelled by the termination of flights to Seoul on 14 September 1992, when South Korea established diplomatic relations with China. Then in December the coveted route to Paris was awarded to Eva, while C.A.L. lost a Boeing 747-400 that plunged into the sea near Hong Kong during the same month. To add to the bad news, on 27 April 1994 an A300-600 crashed at Nagoya, killing 264 people.

During the next few years, an extensive campaign emphasized safety, but hopes were again dashed when another A300 crashed during a foggy night at Taipei on 16 February 1998, killing 203. Reacting to widespread safety concerns, Eva Air merged the smaller domestic airlines. On 8 January 1999, negotiations for Singapore Airlines to acquire an interest in C.A.L. collapsed. On 22 August, an MD-11 of Mandarin Air, crewed by C.A.L., crash-landed at Hong Kong during a tropical storm, killing only two, but injuring 211. China Air Lines' reputation continued to deteriorate further as on 25 January 2002, an A340 narrowly missed disaster on take-off at Anchorage, and exactly four months later, a 747-200 crashed in the Taiwan Strait, killing 225. The hitherto tolerant Taiwanese government hardened its view of what had once been a proud flag carrier for the country.

The airline was commendably resilient, rebuilding its air-minded passenger clientele. Early in 2003, Brisbane became its 44th international destination, Seoul and Hanoi were reinstated, direct service started to Honolulu, and code-sharing began with Delta Air Lines. Crowning these network additions was a key date in C.A.L. history, when, on 29 January 2005, an Airbus A330-300 inaugurated service to Beijing. The first of 48 special charters, it was routed via Hong Kong, Wuhan, and Zhengzhou. Yet Fate has never been kind to Taiwan's flag-carrier. On 20 August 2007, a Boeing 737-800 exploded at Okinawa. This time, three of the 165 on board were injured.

Airline Competition in Taiwan

As the Taiwan government eased C.A.L.'s assumption of monopoly airline privileges, the first to claim operating rights was **Far Eastern Air Transport (FAT)**, founded in August 1957 by a rich businessman, T.C. Hwoo, with two brothers in the Air Force and K.T. Siao. Starting with small Beech 18s on various charter missions, it was operating on the Taipei-Kaohsiung trunk route by 1955 with DC-3s. On 21 February 1966, it introduced 50-seat Handley Page Herald twin-engined turboprops, and such was the demand that 80-seat DC-6Bs were added in 1967 and 68-seat Viscount 800s in April 1970. 90-seat Caravelle jets added in April 1974 were still too small for the booming traffic, and the first 128-seat Boeing 737 went into service in June 1976, to be joined by Lockheed 188 Electras in March 1980. FAT and China Airlines together were sharing an every-hour all-day service on one of the world's busiest routes, and by 1988, FAT was carrying two million passengers annually.

In 1995, new investment was made by several financial institutions and China Airlines, and in 1997 the offer of shares opened the way for the introduction of overseas routes, first, in January 1998, to Subic Bay, in the Philippines, and to Palau then in October to Kota Kinabalu. During 2000–2002, more routes opened from Kaohsiung to Phuket, Thailand; Laoag, Philippines; and Denpasar, Bali, and in 2004, to Hanoi, Vietnam. But late in 2007, the new high speed rail line, connecting all the Taiwan west-coast cities, almost wiped out air traffic along that route.

In spite of its commendable spirit of free enterprise and bold financial investment, the progress of commercial aviation in the Chinese offshore island had not been smooth. In particular, all the airlines had suffered from aircraft crashes, and by the late 1990s, the hitherto indulgent regulatory authorities seemed to have had enough and decided to authorize a latecomer on the scene to sort things out. This was no group of ambitious newcomers venturing into the transportation arena. When **Eva Air** was founded in March 1989 in Taipei, it took its name from the Evergreen Marine Corp., one of the world's largest sea freight container shipping lines. It promptly ordered a substantial fleet: 14 McDonnell Douglas MD-11s, 8 Boeing 747s, and 4 767-300ERs. This alone revealed considerable financial resources, and three other important factors contributed to its prospects. China Airlines could not operate to any country that the P.R.C.'s Air China served; Taiwan's economy was surging; and the relaxation of its government's restrictions was releasing a pent-up demand for overseas travel.

Boeing 767-300ER service began on 1 July 1991 to Bangkok, soon followed by Jakarta, Seoul, Kuala Lumpur, Singapore, and other southeast Asia destinations. Trans-Pacific service started to Los Angeles on 12 December 1992, with Boeing 747-400s, whose seating included a 142-seat Economy Deluxe cabin—an innovation that has since been copied by other airlines as premium economy class. On 29 March 1993, London was added, while British Airways responded the next day with its British Asia subsidiary, to avoid political objections from Beijing. Within the next two years, Eva Air added three more destinations in the U.S.A., two more to Europe (including nonstop flights, with special dispensation for Chinese overflying rights), two to Australia, direct services to Canada and Dubai, and even joined the throng on the Taipei-Kaohsiung domstic trunk artery. Access to Hong Kong was achieved in 1996. Seldom, if ever, has a new airline built up such a global route network in such a short time. In April 1996, Eva bought 30% of **Taiwan Airlines**, which had started social community services with small aircraft to Orchid Island in 1970, and 42% of **Makung Airlines**, which late in 1967 had been flying to the local capital of that name in the Penghu islands off Taiwan's west coast. Since September 1990, it had operated 112-seat BAe 146s on domestic routes from its base in Kaohsiung and by 1993 it was flying to Laoag in the Philippines, and to Da Nang in Vietnam. Eva changed Makung's name to **UNI Air**. A third small domestic airline, **Great China Airlines**, had started crop-dusting with helicopters in 1967, and introduced 52-seat de Havilland Canada Dash 8-300s on scheduled routes in 1987. Eva acquired 24% in 1997 and on 1 July 1998 merged the three companies under the UNI Air name.

Meanwhile, Eva's international network, fleet, and traffic continued to grow. New destinations ranged from Honolulu to Vientiane, Laos. The first Boeing 777-300ER went into service on the London route via Bangkok, on 15 September 2005; but it had finally broken its exclusive reliance with Boeing with a large order for Airbus A330-200s. In addition to Hawaii and Anchorage, six other U.S. cities were being served by Eva Air. The airline had, in little more than a decade, claimed a place among the leading airlines of the world.

China Airlines had not been dormant. In 1991, to overcome political sensitivities in Australia and Canada, it founded **Mandarin Airlines** which, with only one Boeing 747-400, was able to provide the necessary links to Sydney and Vancouver. It operated independently and efficiently, adding more aircraft, and in August 1999 merged with **Formosa Airlines**, to comply with the government's wish to simplify the domestic system, and to halt a disturbing succession of crashes by a fragmented industry. Formosa had been founded as a crop-spraying company in 1966 as Yung Shing Airlines, mainly with helicopters, and was renamed on 15 July 1978. It concentrated on routes to the small islands to the west and east of Taiwan, adding a 19-seat Dornier 228 turboprop on 11 February 1983. But it was plagued with crashes, and even though China Airlines acquired 42% of the shares, the tragedies continued, with a Saab 340 fatal accident on 18 March 1998 listed as its sixth in 10 years. The culmination was China Airlines's acquisition in June 1999, and a merger with Mandarin.

Another small company, Foshing Airlines (see above), had taken over the Taiwan east coast route to Taitung on 18 January 1964 and remained precariously in service with mostly irregular flying until 1992, when it was renamed **TransAsia Airlines**. With backing from the Goldsun construction group, it acquired 50-seat ATR42s and 74-seat ATR72s and then Airbus A320s

Eva Air Boeing 747-400. (Bentley)

A Foshing Airline ATR 42. (Bentley)

to add to the frequent airline services on the main Taiwan west coast route. It also offered charter flights to the Philippines and Cambodia. In 2007, China Air Lines, Eva's local subsidiaries, and all the other domestic airlines, were severely battered by the opening of the Taipei-Kaohsiung high speed railroad. It served (into the downtown areas) all the larger cities in Taiwan, and airline service became almost unnecessary.

Philippine Airlines Lives On

Philippine Airlines (P.A.L.), with a proud tradition, has had to fight for survival. Its relationships with its government have fluctuated between support and negligence, and its finances between success and disaster. But at the outset of the Jet Age, possibly influenced by the appearance of B.O.A.C. Comets in 1953, en route to Tokyo, there seemed to be some hope for an airline that had felt to be under siege. On 27 March 1956, Colonel Andres Soriano, the San Miguel beer magnate who had founded P.A.L., ordered two Viscount turboprops while the government announced a 30-million peso program of airport improvements at five main provincial cities. On 1 June 1957, a Viscount 770D opened service to Hong Kong, but as yet, no Philippine airfield other than Manila could accept it. After domestic service was improved with Convair 340s, however, Viscounts started to Cebu on 10 March 1958 and to Davao on 25 August.

Conscious of its need to serve the Philippine people, and to complement the *Rural Air Service*, (introduced on 15 June 1955 with de Havilland Canada DHC-3 Otters) P.A.L. launched the DC-3 *Star* services on 1 April 1959. The fares were at 10 pesos per mile, less than the *El Economico* fares at 13 pesos, and made possible by operating at night, thus incurring only marginal costs. Fortunes in the following year were mixed. On 7 January 1960, the first 8-seat Scottish Aviation Twin Pioneer arrived to replace the Otters, and on 9 March the first 40-seat Fokker F-27 Friendship replaced the Convairs. P.A.L. celebrated by naming the Viscount and Fokker flights as Rolls-Royce services, but the satisfaction was dimmed by two DC-3 crashes at the end of the year, in which 61 people were killed. Both flights were on the *Star* services, and amid widespread public criticisms, Soriano ordered these services to be suspended immediately. He was subjected to intensive cross-questioning by a Senate committee, and had to defend P.A.L.'s maintenance procedures in a confrontational atmosphere. Apparently he felt the adverse publicity to be unfair, for in February 1961 he informed the President of his intention to resign, effective 30 March. (He died on 30 December 1964.)

Eduardo Romueldez was elected president on the next day, while many executives also resigned. When the committee issued its findings on 18 May, its 163-page report criticized Soriano's dictatorial methods and profits by associated companies, but praised the airline's safety record and upheld its monopoly position as the only solution for a sound commercial aviation policy for the Philippines. P.A.L. carried on. On 28 June a *Night Mercury* service started to Bacalod, and the Twin Pioneers were retired. On 11 December, a Boeing 707 was leased from Pan American for the Hong Kong service, to compete with Cathay

After the end of the Second World War, P.A.L. was one of the first airlines to fly between Europe and Asia, but intercontinental service was interrupted for several years.

Pacific's Electras. On 19 January 1962 a new administration under President Macapagal led to the appointment of Renato Barretto as president, with Benigno ("Benny") Toda, a young businessman, as a member of the board, then elected chairman on 29 March. Romueldez's brief reign had served P.A.L. well; he had exerted a firm hand and a fair one. Although the peso was devalued, Barretto negotiated an agreement with the Dutch airline K.L.M., which bought a 112-seat Douglas DC-8-50 and then leased it to P.A.L. On 18 June it made its debut to Hong Kong as a preliminary to reopen, three days later, the trans-Pacific route to San Francisco via Honolulu. On 1 December Oscar Ramos became the first Filipino jet captain.

Barretto strenuously campaigned against domestic competition from local airlines that he said, "skimmed off the cream" by operating only the routes to the provincial cities, while P.A.L. had to maintain all the services to smaller communities. Fleming's FAST DC-4s were operating with cheap fares and full loads. Two fatal DC-3 crashes had not helped P.A.L.'s image, but on 16 March 1964, a low-fare non-scheduled *Maya* DC-4 service was introduced to compete with Fleming. This, and other incursions, are narrated in Chapter 37. Conflicts with Toda led to Barretto's resignation on 5 August 1963, leaving Toda in full control. On 22 April, P.A.L. moved to a new headquarters site in Makati, purchased at a cost of 1.2 million pesos from Toda who, allegedly, had bought it for half the price. On 1 July the Supreme Court declared the airline to be government-controlled, but on 24 August the Government Service Insurance System (G.S.I.S.) announced the sale of shares to Toda. On 18 January 1965, Toda's new Rubicon corporation gained absolute majority control, with 52% of the shares. The balance was still held by the government, with 24%, Pan American 20%, T.W.A. 2%, and others 2%.

On 29 June 1965, in a climatic event that could not have occurred elsewhere in the airline world, a typhoon threatened to dislodge aircraft from their moorings in Manila, and the ground crew "flew" them into the wind, thus saving them from destruction. The Rural Air Service was discontinued at 13 points when the C.A.A. insisted on on-board navigation aids but did not provide the necessary ground equipment. 74-seat BAC One-Eleven jets were ordered, and the Friendship fleet increased. The timing was right, as competition was intensified when the C.A.A. approved Air Manila, Filipinas, Fairways, and Southern Airways to operate unlimited scheduled services in February–March 1965 (see also Chapter 37). Nevertheless, P.A.L. was undeterred. It introduced in-flight movies on its Pacific services on 27 March, the first to do so across the ocean, and increased the frequency. The route to Taipei reopened, with a Viscount, on 15 July; to Sydney, with a DC-8, on 6 October; and to Singapore on 1 November. The non-scheduled *Maya* service was discontinued on 25 February 1966, following protests from Filipinas, but Toda brushed this off. Rubicon held P.A.L.'s management contract, Aeroban was its purchasing agent, and Cibeles its insurers—all branches of Toda's business interests. Progress continued as, on 1 May, One-Eleven *PALjet* services started on the popular routes to Hong Kong and Taipei, and to Cebu, Bacolod, and Davao on 4 May. The last Viscount flight had flown Bacalod-Manila on 10 April, and on 21 April, the *Night Mercury* flights were cancelled after protests by other airlines to President Marcos, who had been installed on 9 November 1965.

All was not well on the domestic services to the second-level cities. Following a DC-3 crash on 29 June 1966, a Fokker Friendship crashed on 28 February 1967 and another, on a demonstration flight, on 27 April. Then on 6 July yet another crashed, effectively ending the type's prospects in the Philippines. For on 25 February, a Hawker-Siddeley HS-748 demonstrator aircraft had arrived to display its excellent rough-field performance—and many of the rural airfields in the country were certainly rough. It went into service on 15 November 1967.

Rubicon's financial strength was evident in 1968. On 28 February it ordered two DC-8-63s for 52 million pesos, almost as much as the entire budget for the city of Manila. A month later, it bought Pan American and T.W.A.'s remaining shareholdings in P.A.L., to bring his total to 74%. On 14 March, all the DC-3s were retired, but this led to public protests and service resumed on 27 May to four of the points where the old Gooney Bird was the best aircraft capable of using the strips. On 12 September, however, in the worst accident in the airline's history, a One-Eleven crashed, a few days after a bomb had exploded in an HS-748. That aircraft landed safely, but one passenger climbed out and fell to his death. Two more crashes occurred in the spring of 1970, but One-Elevens were deployed on more domestic routes.

Another typhoon on 19 November, the strongest in 50 years, caused extensive damage to installations and aircraft at Manila. On 12 December, two-thirds of the pilots resigned, leading to severe disruption of all services. On 11 January 1971, an independent auditor's report revealed large payments to Rubicon companies. Within a month, P.A.L. suspended services at 18 points, 600 employees were laid off, and aircraft orders were cancelled. 13 of the points lost were allocated to Filipinas and Air Manila. Service was nevertheless extended to Frankfurt on 1 April and to Melbourne on 9 September, but in contrast with its profitable 1969, the airline was losing money heavily. On 23 September 1972, President Marcos declared martial law, and the Philippine Air Force was assigned to supervise all the airlines. He ordained that Filipinas and Air Manila should merge into P.A.L., and after much protesting and negotiation, it became, on 1 January 1974, the sole domestic airline and the designated flag carrier. Toda had created a personal public relations coup when, on 13 October 1973, a One-Eleven was hijacked, and he offered himself as a hostage in exchange for the 52 passengers, on condition that he be returned to Manila with presidential amnesty because his action had been illegal. Marcos agreed, but P.A.L. had to employ the hijackers.

On 17 July 1974, with K.L.M.'s help, wide-bodied service began to San Francisco with 250-seat Douglas DC-10s. The U.S. C.A.B. took advantage of the event to settle a long-standing disagreement on trans-Pacific frequencies. It impounded the aircraft until the Philippine authorities agreed to allow increased frequencies by U.S. airlines serving Manila. P.A.L. then enjoyed a healthy financial recovery, aided by the absence of domestic competition, as it had taken over Air Manila and Filipinas. Although two HS-748s were lost, the ex-Air Manila YS-11 fleet was increased to eight.

During the spring of 1976, two One-Elevens were hijacked and a DC-8 destroyed, but new services were inaugurated in 1977 to Kuala Lumpur, to Jakarta on 7 April, and to Port Moresby on 1 September. P.A.L. was doing its job as an airline in spite of dissatisfaction with Toda's behavior. On 19 April 1977, a government report revealed that P.A.L. had paid 55 million pesos to Toda-owned companies, some apparently fictitious, with mysterious write-offs and undefined expenses. A February bill for 2.4 million pesos to President Marcos for chartered aircraft was reported in the press. To avert public confrontation, on 19 October, Toda made a formal offer to sell his 74% shareholding to the government, which, on 17 November, acquired it. As the balance was held by the government insurance agency, Philippine Airlines was now a state-owned corporation. In April 1978, such was the feud with Marcos, Toda's submitted bill was not paid.

The president appointed Ramon Cruz as the new P.A.L. president. Cruz immediately visited the maintenance department and spoke to the staff in Tagalog, the national language, to emphasize that he would not be an absentee president and that the airline would adopt a better Filipino image. All contracts with Toda's companies were cancelled, capital was increased, and Boeing 747s were ordered. On 7 April 1978, the last DC-3 was retired. In December P.A.L. once again took over the Rural Air Service from PATI, the government operator, together with the fleet of ten 10-seat Britten-Norman BN-2 Islanders. At the other end of the aircraft technical scale, a 140-seat Boeing 727 started service to Beijing and Guangzhou, so that the Philippine airline was the first in southeast Asia to be able to serve both Chinas, the mainland P.R.C. and Taiwan. On 4 December an Airbus

A300B started service to Singapore, and on 4 January 1980, Boeing 747s replaced the DC-10s on the trans-Pacific route. The first-class service was the best in the world, with full-size *Skybeds* in the *Cloud Nine* upper-deck lounge, so that (as authorized by the F.A.A.) passengers could sleep through the Honolulu stop. Los Angeles was added to the map on 17 December, and the last DC-8 retired on 26 March 1981.

Eduardo Romualdez (airline president in 1961) took over as chairman on 7 May 1982 and was confronted two weeks later with another One-Eleven hijacking. But by the end of the year, services had started to Brisbane, Dubai, Paris, and Zurich with wide-bodied aircraft. In the spring of 1983, Seoul, Kota Kinabalu, and Bandar Seri Begawan were added, and more important, a new agreement with Japan gave P.A.L. fifth freedom rights through Tokyo, including the route to the U.S.A. On 21 August 1983, a human tragedy overcame the entire life of the nation, including the airline. Former Senator Benigno Aquino, who had been in self-exile in the United States, was assassinated as he arrived at Manila Airport. This affected P.A.L., whose staff was politically mixed. Also, the economy was at a low level because Marcos had devalued the peso, and Muslim insurgence in Mindanao disrupted domestic traffic. Aquino's widow announced her candidacy for the Philippine presidency. On 15 February 1986, Marcos was declared the winner but was met by a massive disobedience movement, which coined the term *People Power*, as huge crowds took to the streets and defied Marcos's military forces. P.A.L.'s Cruz, a Marcos supporter, resigned on 24 February. The next day, all domestic flights were cancelled; the same evening, people marched to the Malacañang Palace; and the next day, Marcos's entire family left by U.S. Air Force helicopters for exile in Hawaii.

Cruz had been an excellent administrator, modernizing the airline, stifling corruption, and giving the staff a new spirit. But his loyalty to Marcos spelled his downfall. Philippine Airlines' fortunes during the next few months were subordinated entirely to the momentous political upheaval that was to change the course of the country's politics for ever, and even to provide an example to the rest of the world in its successful and peaceful protest against potential tyranny. On 27 February, P.A.L. resumed flying and on 6 April a new administration, under the chairmanship of José Gonzales, took over. On 1 July it adopted a new livery to emphasize a new regime, and efforts were made to improve service to the smaller communities by leasing four 36-passenger Shorts SD-300 turboprops on 1 February 1987. Traffic to Cebu, the second largest Philippine city, was graced with 250-seat Airbus A300 service on 21 May. When an HS-748 suffered a crash on 26 June, it was the first fatal accident in 12 years, and even though an SD-360 crashed on 13 December, the tragedy was put in perspective one week later when a ferryboat sank after a collision with a tanker between Marinduque and Mindoro. It was the worst non-natural disaster in Philippine history, as only 24 passengers survived from an estimated overload of 3,000 people.

In August 1988, President Aquino revoked Marcos's one-airline policy, and P.A.L. met the presumed future competition by starting Fokker 50 service on 24 September. Yet another implied need for good air service occurred in October, when another ferryboat sank in a typhoon, with the loss of a thousand lives. Nevertheless, throughout the country, the apparent cavalier approach to public transport safety was met by the formation, on 27 June, of the Air Safety Foundation.

A major change in the airline's structure occurred on 29 January 1992, when the process began to privatize the airline—as it had once been. The bidding was won by Lucio Tan, a Filipino-Chinese beer and tobacco businessman, and Antonio Cojuanco, of PR Holdings, with 40% each; but in the following March, the latter was ousted when the two disputed a large airliner purchase, which culminated in an order for six Airbus A340s, two Boeing 747-400s, and the lease of four more -200s from Singapore Airlines.

Never short of dramatic headlines, on 11 December 1994, a bomb exploded under a Japanese businessman's seat in a trans-Pacific 747. This was suspected to have been set off by the Al Qaeda terrorist group, and may have been a foretaste of more far-reaching terrorist attacks years later. Apart from operational problems, the privatization had not led to better times for the airline as a whole. After several boardroom shake-ups, while presidents came and went, Tan took over as chairman and CEO on 1 January 1995. The fleet of mainly Boeing and Airbus jets was one of the youngest in Asia, and in June 1997, he proclaimed a new slogan: "Asia's sunniest airline." But the sun did not shine warmly on the balance sheet. As the Asian financial crisis hit all the airlines, and the Philippine peso lost half its value, P.A.L. reported a loss of 9 billion pesos on 31 March 1998. On 19 June, it filed for receivership, the fleet was reduced from 53 to 22 aircraft, European services were cancelled, salaries and wages were cut, and staff were laid off. The airline shut down completely on 23 September and Hong Kong's Cathay Pacific took over operations five days later.

The crisis was met by the Philippine President Estrada and the Securities and Exchange Commission which stepped in with a "stand alone" rehabilitation plan to satisfy Airbus, Boeing, and other creditors. Overseas services were partially resumed on 29 October, and an arduous rescue program began. The plan was submitted to the S.E.C. on 7 December 1998 and to fully secured creditors in April 1999. A Cathay Pacific/Regent Star Services advisory team was replaced in June by Lufthansa Consulting, and full domestic services resumed on 10 August.

On 1 September 2000, Tan sold the engineering and maintenance operations of the 31-strong fleet to the Lufthansa's Technik Philippines, and services were improved to some intercontinental and east Asian routes. The airline made a remarkable recovery. During the first year of the rehabilitation plan, projected to lose US$16 million, P.A.L. made $1 million profit. For the fiscal year ending 31 March 2001, the profit rose to $8.6 million. The first 143-seat Airbus A319 service on 20 October 2006 was a prelude to building a fleet of 14, with 260-seat Airbus A330s and 220-seat A340s superseding the larger 433-seat Boeing 747s. On 4 October 2007, the Philippine S.E.C. released its airline flag carrier from receivership, and with new services to Chinese destinations as far away as Chongquing and Chengdu,

Korean Air's Boeing 747-400s have met stiff competition from Asiana Airlines, with the same equipment. (Bentley)

P.A.L. faced the 21st century with far more confidence than it had dared to expect when its turbulent 20th came to an end.

First Steps in Korea

The beginning of the Jet Age, if recognized as the first London-Johannesburg Comet 1 service in 1952, came just a year before the end of the Korean War in 1953, when local services using Stinson trimotors, started by Korean National Airlines in 1949, were reestablished by the Ministry of Defense. A route to Hong Kong eventually began in 1954, and a Lockheed Constellation was purchased in 1960. But by then, K.N.A. was almost bankrupt. The Korean government took it over as Koreanair, and reorganized it as **Korean Air Lines (K.A.L.)**, subscribing 60% of the capital. Domestic services started on 6 December 1962, and 40-seat Fokker F-27 turboprops were added on 23 January 1964, with international routes to Japan during the year. Further routes to Hong Kong via Taipei, prepared the fledgling airline for pure jet service.

The first Douglas DC-9 flew to Osaka on 9 August 1967 then to Hong Kong, but service was suspended on 18 November, as the government retrenched. The airline was turned over to a private corporation, the Hanjin Group, owned by the Cho brothers, on 1 March 1969. To meet fast-growing domestic demand, 60-seat YS-11 turboprops were added on 28 April, and Boeing 720 jets on 29 September 1969. On 2 October the Hong Kong route reopened, with extension to Saigon and Bangkok; and on 26 April 1971, a Boeing 707 started trans-Pacific cargo service to Los Angeles via Tokyo and Honolulu. This was a prelude to passenger service, twice a week, with 707-320Cs, on 19 April 1972. South Korea made its mark in the world's international airline arena within a single decade of its creation as a sovereign nation.

K.A.L. Grows Up

At first, K.A.L. was entirely successful. The Pacific service was soon to be augmented by Douglas DC-8s on 11 December 1972, by the first Boeing 747 wide-bodied airliner on 16 May 1973, and Douglas DC-10 tri-jets on 1 July 1975. Service to New York was added, via Anchorage, on 29 March 1979, nonstop frequencies to Los Angeles on 16 September of that year, and long-range Seoul-New York on 30 March 1985. Closer to home, Boeing 727s supplemented the DC-9s on 13 July 1972, and K.A.L. became one of the earlier customers for the wide-bodied twin from Europe, the Airbus A300B4. The nation's determination to excel by concentrated industrial development was reflected by increased affluence, if not wealth, that, in turn, created a demand for air travel at home and abroad. Such progress, however, was marred by incidents that, at least for a time, damaged Korea's image. On 20 April 1978, a Boeing 707 was forced down by a Soviet fighter near Murmansk, the U.S.S.R.'s ice-free port and Atlantic naval base. The forced landing resulted in only two deaths and 13 injuries; but this was not the case when, on 1 September 1983, a Boeing 747 was shot down by a Soviet fighter over the Sea of Okhotsk, not too far from the Soviet Pacific base at Vladivostok. This time, 269 people were killed, and four years later, a terrorism attack on a Boeing 707 off the Malayan coast killed another 115. K.A.L. survived these setbacks and drew some compensation during the summer of 1988 by becoming the official airline for the Olympic Games, which that year were hosted jointly by Korea and Japan.

By the early 1990s, K.A.L. had created a worldwide route network, equivalent to those of many older and well-established airlines, and had climbed up the world ranking table of annual passenger-mile production. In 1988, it opened services to London and to Canada; and on 1 January 1989, the lifting of restrictions on foreign air travel for Koreans released a pent-up demand. In December 1990, K.A.L. was one of the first operators of the McDonnell Douglas MD-11—the long-delayed DC-10 "stretched" airliner—and new routes included those to Sydney, Australia, and São Paulo, Brazil, so that it served all six continents. On 22 December 1994, four cities in China were added, and on 26 July 1995, Washington joined New York and the Californian gateways as a major U.S. destination.

By the mid-1990s, the K.A.L. fleet totaled 105 modern jets, many of them all-cargo aircraft, as, in support of Korea's industrial expansion and export trade, the airline rose to rank as the world's third largest air cargo operator. But, in a repetition of its tragedies during the 1970s and 1980s, 226 people were killed in a Boeing 747-300 crash at Guam on 6 August 1997, and a series of other incidents, fortunately none fatal, led to the need for a $114-million safety improvement program. A new South Korean airline was prospering and had already eroded some of K.A.L.'s traffic. **Asiana Airlines** was formed in February 1988 as a subsidiary of the Kuk Ho Businesss Group, chaired by Sum Koo Park. Its Boeing 737-300s opened domestic services on 23 December 1988, and extended to Japan on 10 January 1990. During the next few years, it challenged K.A.L., internationally with Boeing 767s to southeastern Asia's main cities and intercontinentally with Boeing 747-400s to Los Angeles. A 737-500 crash on 26 July 1993 did not slow its growth rate, and in November 1993, when it was the launch customer for the Boeing 767E freighter, and after only five years of operations, it carried its 20 millionth passenger. Subsequent additions to the map included routes to Europe, Australia, and China, and the fleet was augmented with Airbus A321s. By the early 2000s, matching K.A.L., it was serving 15 cities in China and 14 in Japan, but, like other airlines in the region, had to slow down and apply severe economy measures to avoid bankruptcy.

Such was the momentum of South Korea's growing industrial strength, reflected in a flourishing economy and increased personal income that the appearance of this powerful rival airline did impinge upon K.A.L.'s progress. The progressive spirit continued, as, in October 2003, the nation's flag carrier ordered five new double-decked wide-bodied 550-seat Airbus A380s; and on 10 April 2005 ordered 10 Boeing 787 Dreamliners. Then on 20 November 2006, it placed a further order to Seattle for 25 airliners, worth US$5.5 billion. **Korean Air Cargo** had become the world's largest, with a fleet of 19 747-400F freighters.

For both K.A.L. and Asiana, the year 2005 heralded the arrival of a strong competitor in the Korean domestic market. In 1964, Japan had solved the problem of moving 40 million passengers a year between Tokyo and Osaka by inaugurating the world's first 100-mph-plus high speed rail system, the Shin Kan-sen, also known as the "bullet train." Now, South Korea became the second country in Asia to do the same, with high speed rail between Seoul and the major provincial cities, each with a population of substantially more than a million. This new form of surface transport eroded passenger demand on main-line domestic air routes.

The Latecomers

However advanced the North Koreans may have been in rocket science and nuclear engineering, its development of fast and efficient domestic transport lagged far behind the West. It lacked the essential equipment and personnel to take a respectable place in the Jet Age. In 1950, a Soviet-North Korean Airline (SOKAO) had been organized jointly to provide limited domestic services as well as between Pyongyang and Vladivostok, Beijing, and Chita, with Lisunov Li-2s (Soviet DC-3s); but services were suspended in June at the beginning of the Korean War. Operations were resumed in 1953 and routes added to several points in northwest China. Renamed UKAMPS (an acronym for the Ministry of Communications of the Korean People's Democratic Republic) in 1954, its fleet was later augmented with Soviet jet and turboprop airliners, including Tupolev Tu-154s and Ilyushin Il-62s. It was also known as the **C.A.A.K.**, the Civil Administration of the Democratic People's Republic of Korea. Within its isolated Soviet-controlled environment, it became more ambitious over the next few years and extended routes to Moscow, East Berlin, Sofia, Khabarovsk, and even to Bangkok. For easier international recognition, in 1993 it adopted the operating name **Air Koryo**. Still intensely introverted and with its government determined to remain confrontational with other neighboring countries, the North Korean airline's restrictive policies have been in striking contrast with those of Korean Air Lines, across its southern frontier.

Mongolia had already had a long history of cooperation with the Soviet Union, having been linked as early as 1926, when Moscow-built Junkers-F 13s of Dobrolot connected Ulan Bator (then called Urga) with Verkne Udinsk (today's Ulan Ude) on the Trans-Siberian Railway. This mainly desert and sparsely cultivated country has little agricultural land. Outlying communities had almost no contact with the capital, although it was connected to China with a branch of the Trans-Siberian Railway via Ulan Bator. But at the end of the Second World War, Polikarkov biplanes replaced the veteran Junkers, and began to fly to some of the remote areas. Airfields were little more than strips in the desert; and only three of the 22 were paved. Winter temperatures could drop as low as minus 20°F.

Flights were maintained by the government until, on 7 July 1956, **Mongolyn Irgeniy Agaaryn Teever (MIAT)** (or Mongolian Airlines) was formed, completely state-owned but closely associated with the Soviet Union's Aeroflot. It extended service to Irkutsk and Beijing with 20-seat Li-2s and 32-seat Ilyushin Il-14s, and linked the small villages with 8-seat Antonov An-2 biplanes and 4-seat Yak-12s. As the airline struggled to mature during the 1970s, it acquired 40-seat Antonov 24 turboprops, and became known as **Air Mongol**. Growing up, on 2 November 1987, it leased a 140-seat Tupolev Tu-154M jet from Aeroflot, and extended services to Moscow and Beijing. This was a prelude to moving even further into the global Jet Age. In 1992, following the demise of the Soviet Union, Korean Air Lines donated a 138-seat Boeing 727-200, to improve the Moscow route and extend it to Berlin; but a crash on 26 May 1998, when 28 people were killed, was a deterrent to over-confidence. Nevertheless, a 214-seat Airbus A310-300 was leased to maintain its international initiative.

A landslide victory for the Mongolian People's Revolutionary Party in 2000 gave further impetus to much-needed development, including more international connections to Seoul, Osaka, Irkutsk, and Hohhot, code-sharing with its Korean Air Lines benefactor. On 19 July 2002, it leased its third jet airliner, a 162-seat Boeing 737-800, which was used mainly for charter flights to Japan. Once a symbol of inaccessibility, Mongolia was becoming a destination for the more adventurous Western tourists who now seek to explore more remote places.

Mongolia was seldom visited by foreigners. It had no airline of its own until 1956, but moved into the Jet Age in 1992. This is its Airbus A310. (Bentley)

Rising from the Ashes

When the Jet Age began in the early 1950s, Vietnam was in a state of uncertainty as to its future. During the Second World War, the colony known as French Indo-China had been controlled by French Vichy forces, allied to the Japanese occupiers. With the end of hostilities, the Chinese moved in, and Ho Chi Minh declared the Democratic Republic of Vietnam. In 1946, the British, in temporary administration, transferred authority to the French, but their reactionary politicians soured relations with the local inhabitants. Even so, as has been the custom since the air age began, the immediate adoption of a national flag was followed by the creation of a national airline. Thus, on 1 October 1951, **Air Vietnam (Hàng-Không Việt-Nam)** was formed to take over the local domestic and regional DC-3 services of Air France, while the French independent companies, Aigle Azur (with ex-T.W.A. Boeing 307 Stratoliners) and SAGETA, continued to provide the link between Saigon and Paris.

But the simmering political uncertainty erupted into military confrontation, culminating, on 8 May 1954, in the capitulation of French forces at Dien Bien Phu, near Hanoi, the capital of Tongking, the northern province of Indo-China. This was followed by the cease fire or Geneva Peace Agreement of 21 July, in which Vietnam was divided into two parts at the 17th parallel of latitude. Air Vietnam's northern terminus became Húe, instead of Hanoi, and on 26 October 1955, the northern Republic of Vietnam was officially proclaimed. It soon established its own airline, and opened service to Beijing.

For more than a decade, Air Vietnam survived precariously as the northern Viet Minh communist forces gathered strength and challenged the south, now strongly supported by the United States, which entered a military conflict that became known as the Vietnam War. Ultimately with disastrous consequences to the South, the outcome remained in the balance. Hope was rekindled in the hearts of the Air Vietnam staff of the southern airline, reorganized in 1958, with the South Vietnam government

As Vietnam established itself in the south of the former French Indo-China, it operated a fleet of Caravelles. (Bentley)

holding 55% of the stock and Air France 33%. Its first jet airliners, Caravelles, supplied through Air France, showed the Vietnamese flag in neighboring countries. Two Boeing 727s were purchased to enter service on 1 March 1968, to replace the Caravelles, and no less than 16 old Douglas and Curtiss piston-engined aircraft were leased from Taiwan. In that year, however, the "Tet Offensive" gave notice that North Vietnam was a serious threat, and further peace talks were held in January 1969. Air Vietnam extended its Taipei route to Japan, while domestic traffic boomed, aided by a low fare policy and considerable patronage from the occupying U.S. armed forces and administrators. For a few months late in 1970, a Boeing 707 was leased, but such ambitions that this may have encouraged were dampened by another massive North Vietnamese offensive. In April 1973, Air Vietnam bought a Boeing 707 from Pan American Airways and, with its 727s, adopted a complete new look by adorning the fleet in a striking red and yellow paint scheme. The old logo, a mythological dragon, was retired.

On 30 April 1975, the South Vietnamese government surrendered to the North Vietnamese. On 2 July 1976, Vietnam was officially reunited and a new era began for this long-stricken land. In November of that year, Vietnam Airlines, which had been a division of the North Vietnam Civil Aviation Department, became a rejuvenated **Air Vietnam**, which promptly linked Hanoi

Following the Geneva Peace Agreement of 1954, air services within the former French Indo-Chinese area were sporadic. They ranged from Air France's Boeing 707 jets to Paris, to the veteran Boeing 307s of 1940s vintage operated by the International Control Commission as a neutral link between north and south Vietnam. This meeting of two generations of Boeing airliners was photographed at Phnom Penh in 1967. (Samuel Smith)

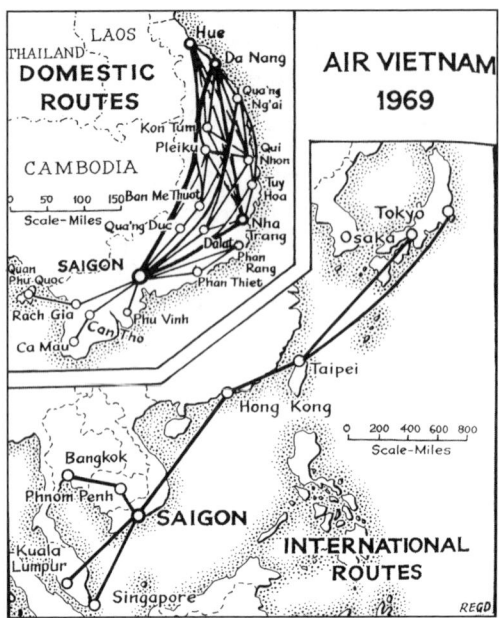

with Ho Chi Minh City (formerly Saigon); Vientiane, Laos; and Phnom Penh, Cambodia—operating with a fleet of Soviet airliners, plus the 707s. During the next few years, Laos and Cambodia achieved independence, and the former Indo-Chinese provinces Tongking and Annam combined to form a new Vietnam. Air Vietnam reflected the Hanoi government's policy of political compromise: agreement with the West in practical matters of commerce and trade, without abandoning its own principles. In 1988, it also suffered a Tupolev Tu-134 crash in Bangkok, killing 81 people. This pragmatic approach—a policy of *doi mo*, similar to the Russian *perestroika*, led to the establishment of a disciplined airline. In February 1990, Hanoi's Air Vietnam became **Vietnam Airlines**. Ownership was transferred from the Ministry of Defence to the Ministry of Transport, Post, and Communications, where it held a semi-autonomous position and was allowed to operate commercially. Attempts to upgrade the fleet with western aircraft were at first frustrated by political objections from the U.S. State Department. On 15 February 1992, two Boeing 737-300s started service and the airline wet-leased (aircraft and crews) two European ATR 72 turboprops from Europe. France's President Mitterrand and Air France Chairman Bernard Attali made a state visit to Vietnam in August 1992 to resume commercial transactions with the West.

Vietnam Airlines, representing a united Vietnam, began services in 1992 with a wet-leased ATR 72 from Britain. (Bentley)

Until then, the fleet of 16 Soviet airliners, of which a dozen were the old Tupolev Tu-134s, had not been the best flag carriers for a resurgent airline. In January 1993, it leased Boeing 767-200ERs and Airbus A300/A310 for flights to Seoul, in agreement with Korean Air Lines. The first 150-seat A320 arrived on 25 October 1993 and was able to open service to Moscow. President Clinton lifted the trade embargo early in February 1994, the U.S. Senate having voted favorably on 27 January. Subsequently, Vietnam's economic recovery was impressive; airline traffic growth averaged 36% annually during the next eight years. The modernized fleet permitted service to Berlin and Paris, and additional western jets were leased. Although another Tu-134 crashed on 3 September 1997, killing 63, the airline carried 3.65 million passengers in the year 2000. For the new, once-embattled Vietnam Airlines, a new era had begun.

In December 2001, casting the legacy of time-expired Russian aircraft far behind, six Boeing 777-200ERs were ordered, followed in August 2002 by five Airbus A320s. Code-share agreements had been signed with several U.S. airlines for trans-Pacific operations. By 2003, and in spite of the outbreak of the SARS virus, which delayed expansion plans, the Vietnamese fleet was as modern as any in the region. That same year, to match its neighbors and to secure its future, Vietnam Airlines ordered six Boeing 787-8 all-composite Dreamliners and followed this on 1 October 2007 with a substantial order from Airbus for another 20 A321s and 10 of the new A350-900XWBs. A far cry from the Vietnam War when aircraft carried soldiers to Da Nang, they now carried tourists.

Cambodian Collapse and Regeneration

Cambodia attained independence from France in 1953, having been a province of the latter's Indo-Chinese colony since 1863. Prince Norodon Sihanouk, the ruler assigned in 1960 by the Japanese when they occupied southeast Asia in 1941, was the first head of state.

On 14 June 1956, an agreement with the French led to the foundation, on 15 October, of **Royal Air Cambodge (R.A.C.)**, ownership shared by the Cambodian government, 38%, Air France, 34%, and 28% by private investors. Its first service, on 20 October, was a far cry from jet technology. It connected Phnom Penh, the capital, and Siem Reap, the airfield close to Angkor Wat, with Bangkok, with a veteran Douglas DC-3. On 2 July 1957, a Boeing 307 Stratoliner, also of pre-war vintage, opened service to Hong Kong. In January 1961, an agreement with Air France took R.A.C. into the Jet Age. During the 1960s, however, the airline's growth reflected the standards of a previous era, with a Douglas DC-4 and a DC-6 adding routes to Vientiane, Hanoi, and Canton (Guangzhou), and as far as Singapore. But the escalation of war between North and South Vietnam destabilized the region. R.A.C. even had a Russian Ilyushin Il-14, presented to Prince Sihanouk by the Soviet Union, but in January 1969, it at last owned its own jet airliner, a Caravelle. The North Vietnamese invaded Cambodia in the spring of 1970, and Sihanouk was exiled to Beijing. Recalling its ancient history, Cambodia became the Khmer Republic.

Royal Air Cambodge entered the Jet Age with Caravelles. (Bentley)

In the mid-1970s, the Khmer Rouge political movement began a vicious civil war, culminating in the surrender of Phnom Penh on 17 April 1975. This was followed by the forcible evacuation of most of its citizens into the "Killing Fields," when perhaps two million Cambodians were executed or died from hardship and privation. On 8 January 1979, the rebel government renamed the country Kampuchea, and on 7 September 1982, **Kampuchea Airlines** began flights to Ho Chi Minh City. A second Vietnamese offensive in 1983 resulted in a state of political and social turmoil until the Vietnamese eventually withdrew their forces in 1991, and the rebels signed a peace agreement with the government. Prince Sihanouk returned from exile. Siam Kampuchea Airlines, operating as **S.K. Air**, was founded with 55% Thai and 45% Kampuchea Airlines shareholding, and operated a Boeing 737-300 leased from Thai Airways. **Phnom Penh Airways** and **Cambodian International Airlines** also flew the same route with a wet-leased Fokker F-28.

Such a competitive environment ended emphatically at the end of 1994, with a change of government. All Cambodia's air services were vested in a new Royal Air Cambodge, and the licenses for the short-lived independents cancelled. On 2 January 1995, the first service, to Kuala Lumpur, with a 146-seat Boeing 737, leased from Malaysia, was followed by routes to Bangkok, Hong Kong, and Singapore. A 70-seat ATR-72 served Ho Chi Minh City, and this versatile turboprop opened domestic routes to outlying communities that had survived the Killing Fields. On 2 November 1996, the new R.A.C. reopened service to Guangzhou. The next year, a more liberal policy permitted the reappearance of Kampuchea Airlines, a joint venture between the Cambodian government and Orient Thai Airways, with a fleet of Lockheed TriStars and Boeing 737s, and which enterprisingly made a success of charter work, especially for the International Organization for Migration (I.O.M.) in rehabilitating refugees from various civil wars around the world.

Siem Reap Airways, representing a national rejuvenation in Cambodia, operated in association with Thailand. This Boeing 717 displays the tourist attraction. (Bentley)

Released from repeated civil wars and genocide, free enterprise in Cambodia appears alive and well. On 25 October 1999, **Royal Phnom Penh Airways**, owned by the son of Prince Sihanouk, began service to provincial towns and, on 28 December 2000, to Bangkok. **Siem Reap Airways** joined in on 3 November 2000, with wet-leased ATR-72s from Bangkok Airways, and later leased a 140-seat Airbus A320, such was the demand by tourists to Angkor Wat. Against such competition, Royal Air Cambodge suspended all its services on 16 October 2001.

Airlines for Laos

In close parallel with events in Cambodia, the fifth province of French Indo-China aproached the 20th century without the advantage of a potential tourist attraction of worldwide repute. The country was land-locked, and had no industry except subsistence agriculture. The main form of transport was river traffic along the Mekong River. Laos had become a French protectorate in 1893, and regained its independence on 19 July 1949, as a constitutional monarchy under Prince Souvanna Phouma. It was one of the poorest countries in the world, but **Air Laos** was founded in 1952, half-owned by Laotians, the other half by Air France (30%) and Aigle Azur (20%), which provided the technical support with a few DC-3s. Service started in December, between Vientiane, the port on the Mekong River, and Luang Prabang, the old capital, to replace the river boats. The airline also called at small towns on a "whistle-stop" service, and Buddhist monks could travel at a 20% discount.

On 21 July 1954, the Geneva conference of foreign ministers led to the Partition of Vietnam at the 17th parallel of latitude. But fighting continued in Laos between the communist Pathet Lao and the pro-western General Novosan. The air route to Hanoi was replaced by one to Da Nang (formerly Tourane), and this was extended to Hong Kong with ex-Aigle Azur Boeing Stratoliners. But fighting continued in Laos, and the United States was still involved in air activities through Air America, operating on behalf of the C.I.A. On 23 July 1958, the Prince was forced out of office, and in 1961, Air Laos ceased operations. Two opposing factions claimed sovereignty, and the dispute was settled by the formation of a coalition government in June 1962, by which time, **Royal Air Lao** had taken over Air Laos's two DC-3s. It operated sporadically with a Douglas DC-4 then a DC-6, in cooperation with Hong Kong's Cathay Pacific. On 21 February 1973, the cease-fire agreement led to the phased withdrawal of Air America and the U.S. Continental Air Services. In 1974, Royal Air Lao leased a Caravelle from Air France, and operated to Bangkok and Canton, but returned the aircraft when the Lao People's Democratic Republic, established on 3 December 1975, removed "Royal" from the airline's name. It continued diplomatic flights to Ho Chi Minh City until a hijacker blew himself up in the cockpit in August 1976.

On 21 December 1977, government-owned **Lao Aviation** resumed air service from the north to the south of this elongated country with 40-seat Antonov An-24 turboprops, and to Bangkok. Gradually adapting to the technical level of its neighbors, the

A Royal Air Lao Caravelle. (Bentley)

airline leased a Boeing 737 and two Tupolev Tu-154s during the 1990s, and a Fokker F-28 in 2002. The name became **Lao Airlines** in 2003. A 140-seat Airbus A320 was leased briefly in that year, but operations expanded mainly to provide good service within Laos. The 70-seat ATR-72s, which became popular everywhere in southeast Asia, were supplemented with four Xian Y-7s (Chinese An-24s) and five 17-seat Harbin Y-12s, also from China. With the aid of airline service, this once remote land is now within an hour or two of the metropolitan cities of southeast Asia, rather than days or even a week or two by boat, jeep, or elephant.

Luxury Airline

If Laos was the poor relation of French Indo-China, one of the former outposts of the British Empire was at the opposite end of the scale of affluence. Since 1909, the Sultanate of Brunei had been a protectorate, had fashioned a state constitution in 1959, and achieved partial independence on 7 January 1979. The total population of about 50,000 benefitted from the wealth from its oil wells, so that the sultan became one of the world's richest men, and his personal income probably equal to the gross national product of Laos. Even before independence, Brunei had an airline with standards of service and amenities reflecting its riches.

Founded on 18 November 1974, government-owned **Royal Brunei Airlines** was first staffed mainly by British expatriates. The next year, it opened service on 14 May with a Boeing 737-200 from Bandar Seri Begawan (formerly Brunei) to Kota Kinabalu (formerly Jesselton, across the Bay in Sabah (formerly British North Borneo), and to Singapore. The next day, Kuching (Sarawak) and Hong Kong were added. With a second 737 delivered on 11 August 1975, service to Manila on 3 April 1977, and Bangkok on 9 December 1977, an efficient airline network linked the Sultanate with all its neighbors. A new hangar, able to accommodate half a dozen 737s and even a Boeing 747, was completed at its home base in 1980, and within two years, Royal Brunei had embarked on an intensive training program for crews and cabin staff.

Full independence for Brunei was achieved on 1 January 1984. Route expansion continued during the 1980s, augmented by the addition of two Boeing 757s in 1986. These were fitted with 142 seats, of which 16 first-class were fully reclining, and the toilets were probably the largest and luxurious in the world, with gold-ornamented fittings. The cuisine and the service were superb. This standard did not apply to the annual Hajj airlift to Mecca, as Royal Brunei contracted with Saudia for as many as 4,000 pilgrims annually. As a Muslim airline, no alcoholic drinks were served.

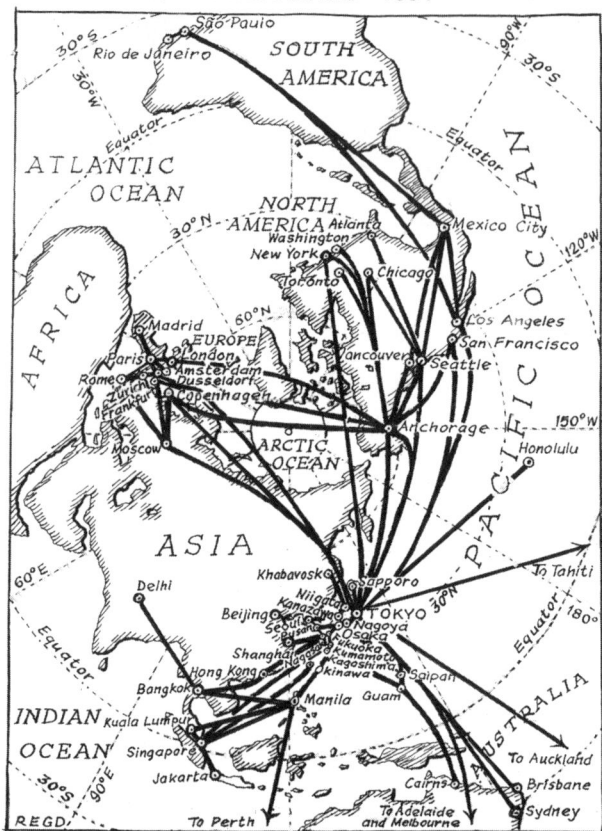

By the end of the 20th century, the Japan Air Lines intercontinental network ranked among the most extensive in the world.

Much publicity was attracted on 10 June 1990, when a Boeing 767-200ER, on a delivery flight, flew nonstop from Seattle to Nairobi in almost 18 hours. Such long range was welcome, as long-haul services started to Frankfurt later that year were followed by London in 1991, and a general expansion included Perth, Bali, Beijing, and Zurich. Regional service was not neglected as in 1995, and two Dornier 228s started local flights to Mulu, Bintulu, and Labuan, in nearby northern Malaysia. Thereafter, Royal Brunei Airlines could afford the luxury of opening services to other faraway destinations, and then terminating them if the loads were not sufficient. With the delivery of two Airbus A319s in 2003 and two A320s in 2005, the long-haul network was much reduced, with London remaining as the main European terminus.

Japan Leads the Asian Resurgence

While the countries of southeast Asia were discovering their industrial potential, and China was self-destructing during the "Cultural Revolution," Japan asserted its strength as, from the 1960s, it experienced a period of unprecedented economic prosperity and growth.

Its national airline reflected the national success. By the end of the 20th century, Japan Air Lines became one of the largest airlines in the world.

Chapter 37: Budget Fares for Southeast Asia

New Perspectives in the Pacific Rim

An intensification of airline activity and usage marked a dramatic aspect of the economic development of all countries, including those of southeast Asia. During the middle of the 20th century—when the colonial powers, Britain, France, and the Netherlands were surrendering their European-governed territories to newly independent nations—the passengers carried on airlines such as B.O.A.C., K.L.M., and Air France were mainly businessmen and government officials. Few were indigenous to the region.

By the first decade of the 21st century, however, changes were visible to any traveler. Not only were the new nations finding their feet, they were in the vanguard of commercial progress, with their low manufacturing costs (compared to those in the U.S.A. or Europe) stimulating healthy export trades. Also, with political stability, the whole region was being "discovered" by western and Australian tourists. Moreover, the progress, if not prosperity, of the region raised the standard of living to the extent that an industrial middle class was emerging in areas that had formally seen little but poverty. Workers in Surabaya could now take a weekend break in Penang or Pattaya.

The entire region, from Japan to Java, welcomed the advent of the bargain-fare airlines. Nowhere was the need greater, for in most countries, the standard of living for the majority of the population was—and in some places still is—low. Except in large cities, typically capitals, people lived at subsistence levels, and parameters such as discretionary income statistics are almost meaningless. Air transport opened up the frontiers for the few in the higher income brackets, business men and politicians; but ordinary people often live their whole lives within a radius of only a few miles from where they were born. They never travel anywhere.

Ambitious innovators such as Malaysia's Fernandes (see below) have added a new dimension to traveling prospects in the far east. The lower fares reached down to bottom levels of the "incomes pyramid," and each step has expanded the potential market exponentially. Until the late 20th century, air travel for the indigenous peoples was a seldom experienced luxury. Air Asia has sponsored the beginning of a social revolution.

Nevertheless, operations have been difficult in those countries that did have an active middle-class whose numbers demanded increased travel opportunities. The routes involved were invariably short- to medium-haul, and the airlines were hard pressed to provide the necessary capacity. Alone among the eastern Asian countries to enjoy a high standard of living and high incomes, Japan faced the problem of serving an extremely densely traveled route. In the 1960s Tokyo's and Osaka's contiguous urban populations were about 20 million and 8 million, respectively; the two cities are only 300 miles apart. The demand for upward of 40 million individual journeys each year—a nightmare for road traffic, and a severe challenge for the excellent trains—was met by opening the world's first high speed railway, the Shin Kan-sen, or "bullet train." It averaged 100 mph, twice the speed of orthodox express trains.

The world woke up to this revolutionary form of surface transport, and in due course, recognized its worth and copied the Japanese enterprise. Worldwide development (see Chapter 52) included successful efforts by some countries in east Asia, notably South Korea, Taiwan, and China. The remarkable Chinese program of a nationwide high speed rail network will undoubtedly affect the shape and course of the growth of its domestic airlines. Elsewhere, Vietnam is reviewing the possibilities of a Hanoi-Ho Chi Minh link; and studies are in hand for a Kuala Lumpur-Singapore line to add to the list.

Thus the surge in airline traffic that, in east Asia, has far exceeded the growth elsewhere in the world, may yet face a challenge from trains that can already match the inter-city speed of airliners over distances of up to 500 miles.

Low Fares in the Philippines

Widespread introduction of budget fares in east Asia trailed well behind that movement in Europe, or within the U.S.A. Yet in the Philippines, cheap air fares were available as early as 1957. They did not appear because of any government direction or private altruism, but because certain intuitive individuals believed that low fares would generate more traffic, hence more revenue, and a good chance of profit. The geography of the Philippines made it a special case. The national flag carrier, Philippine Air Lines (P.A.L.) had the responsibility—an unwritten statute, if not formally expressed by decree—of serving myriad communities scattered around dozens of islands. Some were medium-sized cities, but most were small towns, and some were even villages, with small populations. Independent interlopers seeking to challenge P.A.L. therefore concentrated on the few cities, or, as the incumbent insisted, started to "skim the cream off the top" of the market as a whole.

One such interloper was U.S. citizen James Fleming. He had formed **Fleming Airways System Transport (FAST)**, and after a few non-scheduled flights under a temporary permit on 5 March 1958, and even after a DC-3 crash, he introduced an ex--K.L.M. DC-4 on the main domestic routes to Cebu and Davao, and later to Bacolod, on 5 March 1961. This forced P.A.L. to compete with its own DC-4s with the *Maya* service. Events overtook the challenger, which lost two more crashed DC-3s in 1964-65, and FAST ceased operations on 6 July 1965. P.A.L. terminated the *Maya* flights on 25 February 1966. Fleming left the country.

During this early experimental venture into bringing air fares down, **Cruz Airways** also operated briefly from Manila in 1962, as did **Southern Airways** from Davao in 1965. The latter's aircraft were seized early in 1966, after carrying contraband. Hazardous though these maverick concerns were, they did remind the Filipino traveling public that low fares could be offered, and their presence forced P.A.L. to come to terms with the idea. As for the issue of safety, the local public seemed to accept the risks, partly because the records of the tragedy-prone ferry boats between the islands did not offer much of an alternative.

The Philippines may thus claim to have been the first in the whole of Asia to have introduced low fares, albeit only on domestic routes and in a fashion that could be described as irresponsible. But by the time of Fleming's departure, stronger forces were already at work to erode Philippine Air Lines' presumed monopoly of air services. Late in 1963, after resigning from P.A.L., Renate Baretto and other former associates formed **Filipinas Orient Airways**, and began services on 6 January 1965, confirmed officially as scheduled on 10 March 1965, with eight DC-3s. Shortly afterward, on 14 February 1964, a group of businessmen formed **Air Manila**, and began scheduled services on 30 March 1965. The formation of these two airlines was strongly rumored to have been possible through political maneuvering, as the government reduced its shareholding in P.A.L. from 54% to 24%.

During the first year, even though they suffered three crashes and Filipinas ceased operations twice, the mainly DC-3 fleets carried 350,000 passengers on P.A.L.'s trunk routes, charging cheap fares. During the period from October 1965 to 9 May 1970, P.A.L. endured no less than eight crashes, most of them fatal. During that time, Air Manila and Filipinas were carrying more than 600.000 passengers a year between them, even though the former was grounded three times.

To compete with P.A.L.'s BAC One-Elevens, both airlines acquired turbine-powered airliners, Air Manila with Lockheed Electra turboprops late in 1971, Filipinas Orient with Caravelle twin-jets in November 1972. But the political sands were running out, even though Air Manila was granted permission to operate an international service to Bali with a Boeing 707, leased from T.W.A., and added "International" to its name and "AMI" prominently on the tail of its aircraft. On 12 September 1972 President Marcos ordered a military takeover of all airlines, and in March 1973, Philippine Air Lines was designated as the sole airline, effective from 1 April. All A.M.I. and Filipinas Orient flights ceased on 31 December 1973.

A sad sequel was, on 4 April 1974, the reemergence of **Air Manila International (A.M.I.)**, equipped with two Boeing 707s, to operate non-scheduled charter services within eastern Asia and to the United States. During 1975, it carried 30,500 passengers on affinity flights, mostly to Japan, but also for overseas Filipinos. This sequel to early low-fare competition in the Philippines came to an end on 4 june 1976 when an Electra crashed on take-off from Guam, killing 45 people, and all aircraft were grounded, this time permanently.

For a short time thereafter, **Transasian Airlines**, also known as Sterling Philippines, founded jointly by Filipino interests and the Danish charter company, operated 108-seat Caravelle 10Bs, when President Marcos lifted the travel ban on overseas travel for Filipinos. In October 1977 it began flights for guest workers in the Middle East but the operations were short-lived. Two decades would pass before bargain fares were again available on a large scale in the Philippines. Several enterprising aspirants entered the fray, when, on 1 January 1995, airline deregulation came into force. First off the mark was **Grand Air**, which started service on 16 March 1995, in eponymously grand style with two Airbus A300B4s to Cebu and Davao, following early in 1996 with flights to Hong Kokng and Taipei. By June 1997, it was flying as far as Singapore, but had to suspend operations in September 1998.

Also among the first was **Air Philippines**, founded by William Gatchalian, the local "plastics king," with Lucio Tan, of P.A.L., believed to have some interest. On 1 February 1996, Boeing 737-200s began services to many destinations, but excluding Cebu, the largest provincial city. By 1999, the fleet of seven 737s and five YS-11s was serving 12 points, but further expansion hopes were dashed when, on 19 April 2000, a Boeing crashed near Davao, killing 131.

The Jet Age was not always characterized by wide-bodied 200 to 400-seat airliners, or inter-city networks. In the Philippines, for example, one of the newcomers after deregulation was **Asian Spirit Airlines** which began services in February 1996 with de Havilland Canada Dash Seven 30-seat four-engined turboprops. They called at small island communities, especially those with small airfields, with the new Caticlan resort as the main destination.

Fernandes Sets a Fast Pace

On 17 November 1996, **Air Asia**, operating in Malaysia as Pacific Eagle, started services with a single leased Boeing 737-300, operating from Kuala Lumpur (K.L.) to Taipei via Kota Kinabalu. Such was the impact on the travel business in the region that the airline's application for an operating certificate was delayed for two years to allow the incumbent Malaysia Airlines to recover from the shock and prepare for the competition. On 8 December 2001, 28-year-old Tony Fernandes, who had watched the success of Ryanair and easyJet in Europe, and with three other partners, purchased almost the whole Air Asia stock and its two 737s for 27 cents a share, but assumed $10 million of debt. On 15 January 2002, he launched aggressively a "low fares, no frills" policy, changing the airline livery, and extending the network with more 737s. In April, he introduced ticketless travel, promoted the use of the Internet, and adopted the slogan "Now Everyone Can Fly."

The bargain-fares policy paid off immediately. The $10-million dollar debt was eliminated within seven months. He evaded restrictions at Singapore's Changi Airport by operating to Johor Bahru, on the nearby Malaysian mainland. He took other risks that were even more inventive, promoting business with special sales, for example K.L. to Penang for $2.63, and K.L. to Kota Kinabalu for $13.16. On 3 February 2004, with 49% of the stock, he founded **Thai Air Asia**, after joining with the Shin Corporation to overcome restrictions by the Thai authorities. In

Air Asia's dramatic entry into the east Asian airline world revolutionized air travel there, setting an example with its own slogan displayed (left) on a Boeing 737. It was welcomed by the public, the press, and various authorities, with acknowledged recognition, as displayed on one of its Airbus A320s (right). (McDonough)

December, he did the same with **Indonesia Air Asia**. With an order for 60 Airbus A320s in March 2005, augmented to a total of 100 in 2007, the perceived prospects had not been demonstrated with such confidence even in Europe or the United States. By 2007 the bargain-basement empire was flying to 75 destinations with a fleet of 50 Boeing 737s and Airbuses, and carried 18 million passengers during the year. In January 2008, the A320 order was doubled to 200, a truly astonishing decision for an airline only six years old.

With such aggressive and successful competition, Thai International (THAI) could not rest on its higher-priced laurels. It was forced to enter the market by starting **Nok Air** (*nok* means "bird" in Thai) as a corporation in which it held 39% of the stock, with other Thai financial institutions sharing the balance. Service began on 23 July 2004 from Bangkok to Chiang Mai, Udon Thani, and Hat Yai, with 149-seat Boeing 737-400s leased from Thai Airways. The one-way fare to Chiang Mai was US$15.00. It had to be, with Fernandes setting the pace. But with Thailand's 65 million people growing in prosperity and with vacation resorts increasingly popular among overseas visitors, the market is a gold mine for all the participants.

With a tradition of being in the forefront of airline progress, Thailand was not the front-runner with bargain fares in southeast Asia, although Bangkok Airways was prominent in offering discounts and opening up the resorts of southern Thailand with package deals. The first truly budget airline was **One-Two-Go**, starting service on 3 December 2003, as a division of Orient Thai Airlines (see previous chapter), which had taken over some of THAI's routes in July 1995. Its first service, with a Boeing 757-200, on 3 December 2003, was to Chiang Mai, soon followed by other destinations, including the southern resorts. But the doyen of bargain fares in the area, Tony Fernandes, was not far behind.

He had already "shown the flag" on 8 December with a Boeing 737-300 flight from his Malaysian base, Kuala Lumpur. Two months after One-Two-Go, he had launched domestic routes from Bangkok. Rapid expansion had quickly followed, with routes to Singapore, Penang, Kuala Lumpur, Kota Kinabalu, and Phnom Penh. In April 2005, Fernandes introduced China to the world of bargain fares with a route to Xiamen.

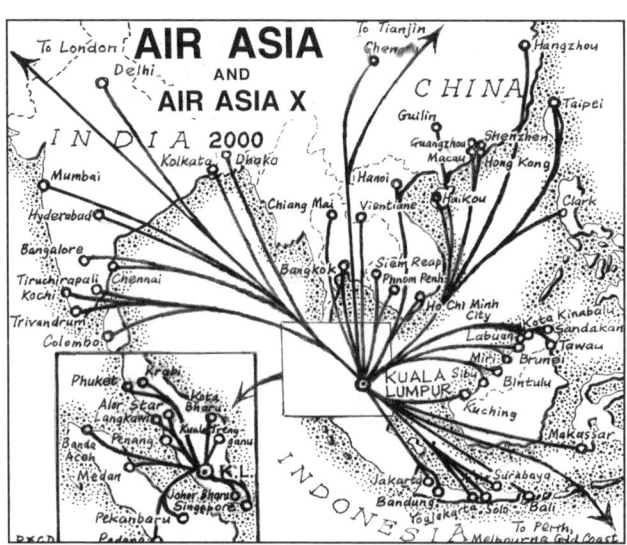

Reaction in Singapore

The reaction in Singapore to the instant success of Air Asia was typical of the entrepreneurial drive that characterizes the economic achievements of that island nation. Rather unexpectedly, the initial move did not come from Singapore Airlines but from another quarter. On 5 May 2004, **Valuair** was founded by Lim Chin Beng, with 11% held by Asiatravel.com Holdings, to start Airbus A320 service to Bangkok. Within a month, Hong Kong and Jakarta were added, and later, Perth, Australia. Not far behind, **JetStar Asia** was founded on 29 September by Australia's Qantas Airways, holding 49% of the shares, with Temasek Holdings, a Singapore government investment group, with 19%, and two private investors with the balance. With a fleet of five 180-seat A320s, service to Hong Kong began on 13 December 2004, and during the following year, the airline quickly added Shanghai, Taipei, Manila, Surabaya, Jakarta, Pattaya, and Bangkok. In an important business venture, these two new airlines, both proving that bargain fares in southeast Asia had come to stay, merged on 24 July 2005, retaining initially the JetStar name.

The powerhouse airline of the whole region was not going to watch this development unmoved. And move it did. On

Tiger Airways Airbus A320. (Bentley)

9 December 2003, with 49%, Singapore Airlines organized **Tiger Airways**. The shares were divided equally between Temasek Holdings (the Singapore government had its airline investments well placed everywhere), Indigo Partners, and Tony Ryan's Irelandia Investments. Indigo's Tony Davis, ex BMI-Baby, was appointed CEO. Tiger launched its first A320 service, to Bangkok, with flair, on 15 September 2004 with a 59¢ fare, only for Thai Air Asia to respond with 29¢. Southeast Asia had no previous experience on this scale in either the competition or the opportunity for cheap travel. Within a year, Tiger had increased its fleet to five aircraft, enabling it to expand its network to Kolkata (Calcutta), Macau, and points in Thailand and Vietnam. In March 2005, the one-way fare to all destinations was on sale at $6.00. A million passengers were carried during the first year of operation, and early in 2006, three more cities were added in China. In July 2007, at the Paris Air Show, Tiger announced an order for 30 more Airbus A320s to add to its fleet of 20, with 20 more on option. During the year, two more destinations in southern India and four in Australia joined the timetable, while further plans were in hand for extensions throughout India.

Indonesian Maverick

Garuda, the chosen instrument airline of Indonesia, has had a checkered career, and like other "second-level" regional airlines such as Merpati Nesantara and Bouraq, it has survived various crises such as the Asian economic recession and a massive devaluation of the rupiah. They would have disappeared but for subsidies from a government that realized that air transport was a vital element of the national economy. After a period of several decades of development that has varied from uncertainty to almost certain disaster, an end-of-the-century newcomer entered the scene. PT Lion Mentari Airlines (**Lion Air**) was established in October 1999 by Rusdi Kirana and family and began operations on 30 June 2000 from Jakarta to Pontianak, with a leased Boeing 737-200. Customer service was high on its priorities, but its main marketing approach was a policy of low fares. During 2000–2003, Kirana acquired 14 MD-82s, the largest of the DC-9 family, from various foreign lessors, and in spite of a crash at Surakarta on 30 November 2004, it had established a solid foundation of routes, and was doing better than breaking even.

On 26 May 2005, Lion Air announced an agreement with Boeing for up to 60 737s, leaving its options open for quantities of individual models. During the following years, orders were firmed up, and on 18 June 2007, at the Paris Air Show, this Indonesian newcomer raised the order to 100, including forty 737-900ERs, of which model it was the launch customer. Lion Air was participating in a minor revolution in air transport across southeastern Asia.

Indonesia's low-fare Lion Air matched Tony Fernandes' Air Asia initiative with its own fleet of Boeing 737s. (Bentley)

Part Seven: The Commonwealth Adjusts

Chapter 38: Airlines of Australia

An Air-Minded Nation

With the absorption of the Dutch K.L.M. by Air France in 2004, Australia's national airline, QANTAS, can now claim to be the oldest in the world with a continuous record of independent and uninterrupted scheduled operations. The reason for its early foundation, in 1919, was the result of demography: the distribution of population in a large country—a continent—that had no integrated railroad system. Even today, almost two-thirds of Australians live in the six largest state capitals, hundreds of miles apart. Except for a single transcontinental line, each state has its own rail system, using different gauges. Australia grew up during the 19th century, after the Industrial Revolution, so that the patterns of distribution and travel were quite different, and on a much wider scale.

Whether for grain or livestock, the farms, or stations (Australian for ranches) were large, with a single station covering a thousand square miles or more. The distribution of their products was not for local consumption but for export to England, a market 10,000 miles away. Thus the lines of distribution were directly to the east coast ports, mainly Sydney. Toward the closing of the 19th century, the discovery of gold and other minerals led to a "gold rush" and the growth of industry. Much of the gold was mined near Melbourne, which grew into a well-planned city to approach Sydney in size.

Australia's flag carrier, **QANTAS (Queensland and Northern Territory Aerial Services)** was founded in 1919 to connect outlying stations with railheads. The "outback" was so sparsely populated that rail extensions would have been uneconomical to build or to operate. An air service, however infrequent, irregular, and expensive to maintain, justified government support. Because of the distances involved, especially in Western Australia, the conditions were ideal for the expansion of airline services. During the early decades of the 20th century, this ex-colony, now a vigorous self-governing dominion, became the most individually traveled nation in the world.

Government Initiatives and Control

Since 1934, QANTAS had flown the Australian flag overseas with distinction, pioneering the long-range route to England in conjunction with Imperial Airways. Yet it was not the country's leader into the Jet Age. This distinction went to the new post-war airline that was created as a state corporation, and provided an example of how success in air transport does not necessarily rest with principles of state-versus-private ownership, but with the abilities of the people who direct the airline fortunes. **Trans-Australia Airlines (T.A.A.)**, headed by L. J. Brain, had, since its first DC-3 service in 1946, matched, if not beaten, its competition, the spirit of which is not lacking in Australia. By the early 1950s, it was operating a fleet of DC-4s and Convair 240s to all the states, having taken over QANTAS's domestic routes and the Adelaide-Darwin north-south link from Guinea Airways. Late in 1952, the Airlines Agreement Act gave the independent Australian National Airways (A.N.A.; see below) equal rights for air mail contracts, interest-free loans, etc. In August of that year, T.A.A. had already ordered 40-seat Vickers Viscounts, only the fourth airline to sign up for the world's first turboprop airliner. It entered service on the Melbourne-Sydney-Brisbane trunk route on 18 December 1954.

The newcomer introduced tourist-class service on 14 October 1955 and ordered Fokker F-27 Friendship turboprops in 1956, as competition intensified. A.N.A. had fallen behind, and on 4 October 1957, was purchased by Ansett Transport Industries (A.T.I.), headed by a former taxi service owner, the dynamic Reginald Ansett. Hitherto, **Ansett Airways**, founded in 1936, had confined itself to Victoria and New South Wales, but was growing in stature as it became, in 1946, a subsidiary of A.T.I. In 1947, it introduced second-class fares, which was against the official policy, but public opinion supported the renegade, and this led to the first steps toward the enactment of a unique form of regulated competition. The aim was political: to balance the state-sponsored airline T.A.A. with the newcomer. **Australian National Airways (A.N.A.)** was a veteran private-enterprise airline that had helped to pioneer commercial aviation in Australia in pre-war years, and it was still respected by the traveling public. T.A.A. had interstate operating privileges, but Ansett's only way to expand was to acquire other companies. In spite of its heritage, A.N.A. had severe financial difficulties, and was sold to the opportunist Ansett on 28 August 1957, to become, formally, **Ansett-ANA** on 4 October.

The Two-Airline System

The threat of self-destructive excess competition was such that the government enacted the Civil Aviation Agreement Act in 1957 to launch what became known as the "Two-Airline System." The legislation's purpose went toward avoiding unnecessary overlap of services and wasteful competition while providing the public with economical services and ensuring appropriate revenues. The agreement provided for conferences between T.A.A. and A.N.A., rationalizing services by setting up a committee constituted by a coordinator who was nominated by the minister and members nominated respectively by the commission (representing T.A.A.) and Ansett.

The two airlines were obliged to deploy their aircraft fleets in parallel, to the extent that on each route operated by both, the same capacity and similar frequencies should be offered, at the same fares. Any deviation of more than one or two percentage

Illustrative of the Two-Airline System are these two Douglas DC-9-30s: Ansett's, at Townsville (left), and TAA's, at Cairns (right). (Davies)

points, through operational necessity, had to be reconciled. Competition was thus reduced to the quality of service, both in the air and at the airports, and surprisingly this apparent excess of regulation worked very well for the Australian air-traveling public, even though on some routes two airliners were flying almost in formation.

T.A.A. operated its first F-27 on 1 May 1959. The Dutch twin had as many seats as the four-engined Viscount 700 series, but on 24 June, the first 60-seat -800 series was delivered, together with the first 100-seat Lockheed Electra. This time, the balance had swung toward Ansett-ANA, which had opened Electra service on 18 March. T.A.A. was not far behind, on 8 July.

On 7 March 1960, the spirit of the Two-Airline System was further emphasized when the Cross-Charter Agreement was put into effect. Three T.A.A. Viscounts were exchanged for two Ansett-ANA DC-6Bs—the seating capacity was equal. Then, on 1 September of that year, T.A.A. took over the New Guinea services of QANTAS, while Ansett-A.N.A. followed in that area by purchasing Mandated Airlines.

Both airlines entered the true Jet Age in 1964, with 100-seat Boeing 727-100 service—T.A.A. and Ansett-A.N.A. on the same day, 2 November. The first 86 seat Douglas DC-9 services were in January 1967 for Ansett and on 17 April 1967 for T.A.A. The airline business in Australia was thriving, and both airlines had to increase their aircraft capacities. In 1969, when Reginald Ansett was knighted, the A.N.A. suffix was dropped from his airline's name, which became **Ansett Airlines of Australia.** T.A.A.'s first 150-seat Boeing 727-200 was delivered on 7 December 1972, and until July 1981, the two airlines operated identical fleets, each with 12 727s and 12 DC-9s. T.A.A. operated its first international route, to New Zealand (Hobart-Christchurch) in December 1980.

Erosion of the Balance

The Two-Airline System did not apply to regional services within the individual states, and Ansett took advantage of the opportunity to encroach on T.A.A.'s regional routes by buying the regional airlines. On 5 February 1958, it had acquired control of Butler Air Transport in New South Wales, which also operated Queensland Airlines. In December 1959, Guinea Airways was also taken over, and Butler and Guinea became **Airlines of New South Wales** and **Airlines of South Australia,** respectively. Ansett tried to repeat the process across the Tasman Sea with South Pacific Airlines of New Zealand (SPANZ) (see Chapter 39) becoming Airlines of New Zealand. This failed, but in April 1963, the veteran MacRobertson-Miller Airlines joined the group, to become **Airlines of Western Australia** in 1981. Ansett's September 1974 service to Lord Howe Island was the last by four-engined flying boats.

After much inter-corporate skirmishing, the control of the holding corporation, Ansett Transport Industries (A.T.I.), had passed to two powerful industrialists, who effectively shared its future direction. Rupert Murdoch headed News Corp., a newspaper conglomerate with worldwide involvement; Sir Peter Abeles headed Thomas Nationwide Transport, Ltd. (T.N.T.). Sir Reginald Ansett continued as chairman, but he died on 23 December 1981. Earlier that year, in March, the new management announced the biggest aircraft purchase (worth $600 million) in Australian history: 21 Boeing 737s, 727s, and 201-seat 767s.

This was to counter T.A.A.'s 238-seat Airbus A300B4s, ordered in October 1981 and put into service soon afterward; while in July, Ansett had taken over the routes of Connellan to become **Airlines of Northern Australia**, later to be changed in 1985 to Ansett NT. On 5 March 1983, the Australian Labor party won a sweeping election victory over the Liberals, and the decision was made not to renew the Two-Airline System. The principles of the policy seemed to be preserved when both airlines received their 767s in June 1983, but they were now fighting for the premium market share of the whole of Australia, and taking decisions without reference to former regulations. James Strong took over as general manager of T.A.A. at the end of 1985 and changed the airline's name to **Australian Airlines** (simply Australian on its aircraft). Ansett ordered 12 more 737s, plus eight (later increased to 12) Airbus A320s, and in February 1986, announced the formation of Ansett Worldwide Aviation Services, to offer technical support, training, and aircraft leasing worldwide.

The next few years were turbulent. Ansett bought Newman's Air, a new airline in New Zealand, and in September 1987 replaced its Fokker F-27s with the larger Fokker 50s. But Australian

Fokker F-28 of Air New South Wales. (Davies)

was doing so well that it led Ansett in market share, which was also increasing. Then in 1989, the government decreed that in all state corporations (such as Australian) the already salary-capped CEOs would have to reapply for their jobs. Strong resigned. On 24 August 1989, the Australian Federation of Air Pilots (AFAP) called a strike, and all except nine of the 547 pilots quit, demanding a 25% pay increase.

Australia's air transport system was in chaos. The Two-Airline System was terminated on 30 October 1990, and the industry was effectively deregulated. Airline services were maintained, using charter carriers, R.A.A.F. Lockheed Hercules converted troop carriers or freighters, and even foreign airlines. In October, Australian started to recruit new pilots. By February 1990, with half of the AFAP pilots returning, it had restored most of its services. On 4 October, in an effort to match the appeal of the name, Ansett was renamed **Ansett Australia**, and embarked on an ambitious expansion program. On 11 September 1993, it ventured to Bali, and in 1994, Ansett International opened services to all the major cities of east Asia, as far north as Seoul, and to Auckland and Nadi, Fiji.

Corporate maneuvering in the southwestern Pacific became complicated in October 1996 when T.N.T. (Abeles) sold its 50% Ansett shareholding to **Air New Zealand (A.N.Z.)**. In July 1997, Ansett, Singapore, and A.N.Z. signed a tripartite alliance, which apparently was not on firm ground, as in June 2000, the New Zealand airline completed the acquisition of Ansett by purchasing the other 50%. In April of that year, though, Singapore Airlines had already bought 24.9% of A.N.Z. On 14 September 2001, Ansett Australia ceased operations. 10,000 staff were thrown out of work, but 3,000 were rehired as, on 29 September, services were resumed on a pruned schedule with only a few Airbus A320s. The New Zealand government continued to hold an 83% stake in Ansett Mark II, and although the two millionaires who formed the "Tesna" Syndicate (Ansett spelled backward) tried to purchase the renewed airline, they were unsuccessful. On 4 March 2002, the Ansett name disappeared entirely from the schedules, and from the historical record.

Qantas Keeps Pace

Qantas (the name was no longer an acronym) was Australia's international flag carrier but was not the country's first airline into the Jet Age, if turboprop (propjet) propulsion is included in the definition. In 1953, when Britain's Comet 4s, together with those of Malysian Airways, were flying to Sydney and Perth, Qantas resisted the temptation to leap into the Jet Age at that time. It "hedged its bets" a little, by acquiring a 29% interest in Malayan on 19 March 1958, and buying Fiji Airways on 24 March. On 23 May it ordered Lockheed Electra turboprops, mainly for the trans-Tasman route to New Zealand. But unlike its rivals, which derived much traffic from on-line passenger demand between Europe and Australia, Qantas depended much more on its indigenous clientele.

On 14 January 1958, it had become the first airline in the world to operate a scheduled service completely around the globe, with the Super Constellations (Pan American could not operate across the continental U.S.A.). Finally, on 29 July 1959, Boeing 707s opened pure jet service across the Pacific, from Sydney to San Francisco via Fiji and Honolulu. Qantas was the first airline outside the United States to operate a large jet airliner. It cut the flying time from Sydney to London, inaugurated on 5 September, from 61 to 28 flying hours. The Electra's first route was to Tokyo via Darwin and Manila, on 18 December. Lockheed's problems with that airliner did not seriously affect Qantas as it operated below the speed limits set by the F.A.A.; but the fleet had to be reengineered and the first flight to Auckland under its own name was on 3 October 1961(see TEAL, below).

Meanwhile, an important political move had been made on the Kangaroo route to London, as en route stops were unavoidable and the countries involved were no longer dependent colonies. In particular, under the leadership of J.R.D. Tata, Air India International was flexing its muscles. On 1 April 1960, a tri-partite agreement went into effect, in which scheduling between Australia and London would be negotiated to permit agreed reasonable shares of the revenues between the three participants, with cross-leasing of aircraft, if needed, to preserve the balance. The Commonwealth policy was clearly directed toward a "chosen instrument" approach, with Qantas concentrating on long-haul intercontinental routes, excluding those to neighboring countries. Accordingly, on 1 September, all New Guinea regional and internal services were transferred to T.A.A.

The westbound route to Europe was secure, but the trans-Pacific route to the U.S.A. presented a range limitation problem for the early Boeing 707-100 series. Qantas overcame this by ordering, in March 1960, three Series -138Bs, which were the result of a shorter fuselage and consequent lower all-up weight, together with additional fuel and therefore range, in exchange for a smaller payload. The Constellations were retired in May 1963. At the end of that year, Boeing and Pratt & Whitney had combined to provide the necessary range for Qantas (as the Series -338C) with the standard Boeing 707 fuselage.

In January 1964, Qantas added its name to the order books for the Concorde—four, and six for the American challenger, the larger and allegedly faster U.S. SST, still on the drawing board at Boeing. However, like other airline speculators, Qantas was sensible enough to emphasize that the orders were subject to guaranteed performances. The Concordes were hopelessly

A Qantas Boeing 707-138B. (Bentley)

uneconomic and Qantas never received any; the U.S. SSTs were never built, and the deposit was refunded in April 1971. More practically, on the trans-Indian Ocean Perth-Johannesburg service via the Cocos Islands and Mauritius, where Electras had replaced the Constellations in April 1963, the long-range 707s cut the journey time from 18 to 13 hours, starting on 28 March 1967.

By the 1960s, Australia liberalized its restrictions on immigrants, and in 1965 alone, Qantas carried almost 30,000 of them on special flights, compared to 20,000 on scheduled flights. The official name of the airline was still Qantas Empire Airways Ltd. (Q.E.A.), but on 1 August 1967, the middle name was dropped, in a somewhat long-delayed statement of independence from London. In October, it was able, following new government policy, to launch long-range affinity charters (once frowned upon by the IATA cartel), and a month later, it placed the largest aircraft order in its history: four wide-bodied Boeing 747s, worth US$123 million. Qantas reinforced its interests in the South Pacific area with a shareholding in New Hebrides Airways in 1968, while Fiji Airways changed its name to Pacific Island Airways. In July 1970, a new airport opened in Melbourne to permit long-distance operations from the Victorian capital that could match Sydney's. The Australian government had revised its policy on international air charters in 1969, so that traffic in this category increased substantially, as did migrant passenger numbers. Further approval was given in August 1971 to operate charters, under competitive pressure from B.O.A.C., which had established a charter subsidiary.

The first 421-seat Boeing 747B wide-bodied service, inaugurated on 17 September 1971, was to Singapore, and extended to London via the Middle East on 25 November. The United States delayed the necessary air transport agreement and service to San Francisco did not start until 10 January 1972. The power of IATA and its members—including Qantas—to control fares and scheduling had almost evaporated, In December 1971, a US$700 round-trip Sydney-London fare was negotiated at a special Geneva conference, and on 1 April 1972, all the airlines on the Europe-Australia route set a one-way fare of US$483, which was $297 below the IATA standard. On 1 April 1973, the trans-Atlantic eastbound route beyond London was abandoned, thus ending the round-the-world route. The trans-Pacific segment, via Mexico City, was withdrawn in August 1974, to be replaced by a route to Vancouver via Tahiti, in January 1975. But this too, together with the trans-Indian Ocean service, was eliminated from the world map in 1976. In April 1975, Belgrade was included on some flights to Europe, because the Yugoslav airline J.A.T. had started direct Douglas DC-10 service via Singapore to Melbourne, the home of tens of thousands of Yugoslav immigrants.

Qantas's last Boeing 707 flight was on 26 March 1979, so that its entire fleet was now 747s. In December 1988, it purchased a 19.5% share of Air New Zealand. By this time, the fleet had been augmented by a dozen Boeing 767-200 and -300ERs. The mass resignations of Australian pilots in August 1989 affected Qantas, but not as severely as on the domestic airlines. The deregulation of all Australian airlines on 1 November 1990, as the Two-Airline

Airbus A300 of Trans Australia (ex T.A.A.). (Bentley)

System was cancelled, did not directly affect international routes; but nevertheless, waning fortunes obliged Qantas to lay off 3,650 employees, or 18% of its workforce, in April 1991.

On 1 June 1992, Qantas merged with **Australian Airlines** (formerly T.A.A.). Chairman William Dix described the event as the single most important event in the aviation history of Australia. On 17 December, British Airways bought a 25% shareholding. This stabilized the situation on the route to London, and on 27 March 1994, the trans-Pacific route was simplified by dropping San Francisco as the U.S. terminus, but increasing frequencies to Los Angeles. In May 1997, Qantas sold its 19.4% share in Air New Zealand (which owned 50% of Ansett) and attracted new investors, worth US$295 million, most of which went into payments for three more Boeing 747-400s, making 23 in the fleet. Things were going well. In 1998, the record annual profit totaled US$183 million and in November of that year, the trans-Pacific route was rationalized with a code-sharing agreement with American Airlines, under the aegis of the OneWorld Alliance. To add to the positive corporate and operational news, Qantas retained its unique record of never having sustained a fatal accident in its entire history.

Into a New Era

As the new millennium began, Australia's flag carrier retained its position in center stage within the industry by becoming one of the earliest airlines to order, in November 2000, the new 500-seat-plus Rolls-Royce Trent-engined Airbus 3XX—in the final development stage, and still awaiting its A380 type number. This was part of a US$4.6-billion order that included 13 Airbus 330s, and six more 747-400s; but it served notice to its transcontinental and trans-ocean competitors. Only Singapore Airlines and Dubai's Emirates would precede Qantas with the inaugural services with this new double-decked airliner generation. The A380 entered service on the trans-Pacific route, Melbourne-Los Angeles nonstop on 20 October 2008.

But affairs within Australia were not so straightforward. Qantas faced competition not only from the veteran Ansett, but also from two new domestic airlines. They were the survivors of the group of newcomers that rushed to enter the market when the airline industry was deregulated on 1 November 1990. Their opportunities were few. All the inter-city routes were flown by Qantas's Australian Airlines. This balance of urban population was so extreme that the sixth largest city, Newcastle, had only one-fifth of that of Adelaide, the smallest of the five capitals, each with more than a million people. The only other cities with more than 100,000 people were Canberra, 200 miles from Sydney (and with reasonable rail service); and Hobart, Tasmania, separated by the Bass Strait. Other than front-line airliners to serve the big cities, therefore, the aircraft market required to serve small towns and the Outback, even for 40-seat turboprops such as the F-27, was meager. Thus an evenly distributed airline system, with first, second, and third level categories, each with airliners whose size was matched to the demand, was not possible.

Before the Second World War, Qantas had managed to serve the small communities in Queensland. Pioneer airlines, including MacRobertson-Miller, had done sterling work in connecting the widely separated small coastal towns between Perth and the cattle country of northern West Australia. Butler built a small network in New South Wales, with Sydney as a hub, and Reginald Ansett did the same in Victoria, based in Melbourne. Guinea Airways linked Darwin in the north with Adelaide. They were complemented by a score or so of individual small companies that, in the United States, would have been classified as Fixed Base Operators (F.B.O.s). None of these survived the war, and a new generation of Australian F.B.O.s came on the scene, under the watchful eye of regulators in Canberra.

Regulation, however, was difficult to impose and loosely applied. Notable companies that emerged during the post-war period were **East-West Airlines**, which was quite successful in New South Wales, and little **Woods Airways**, whose 25-mile route from Perth to Rottnest Island was claimed to be the shortest in the world. East-West, like Butler, had been operating successfully for some few years, and had acquired South Coast Airways in 1953. In 1963, the government finally relaxed its rules and allowed charter companies to operate limited "supplemental services" in country areas. But the bureaucracy in Canberra did not modernize the regulations. A Regional Airline Association was able to do little, and one frustrated member described relations with the regulatory authorities as "swimming in a bowl of porridge." Less colorfully, another described the situation: "our once proud and stable industry is being slowly throttled to death by an autocratic bureaucracy that is accountable to nobody." Little companies came and went, mostly short-lived.

On 1 July 1967, Regulation 203 recognized the creation of Third Level Services, allegedly to rectify a deteriorating situation. Rather than establishing a firm airline structure for small charter airlines, the aviation department still applied exemptions to individual applications (25 in the first year) to operate an airline route or two. With no standard qualification, rules applied to one applicant did not necessarily apply to another. Little companies still came and went, but few survived. Exceptions were **Kendell Airlines**, which had started in Wagga Wagga in 1965, and **Hazelton Airlines**, which had started to carry passengers in 1975. Don Kendell and Max Hazelton were sufficiently determined to weather the slings and arrows of outrageous misfortune from Canberra, but were, like all the other contenders, handicapped by the country's demographics. The most popular aircraft that came close to matching the sparse traffic generated by the small

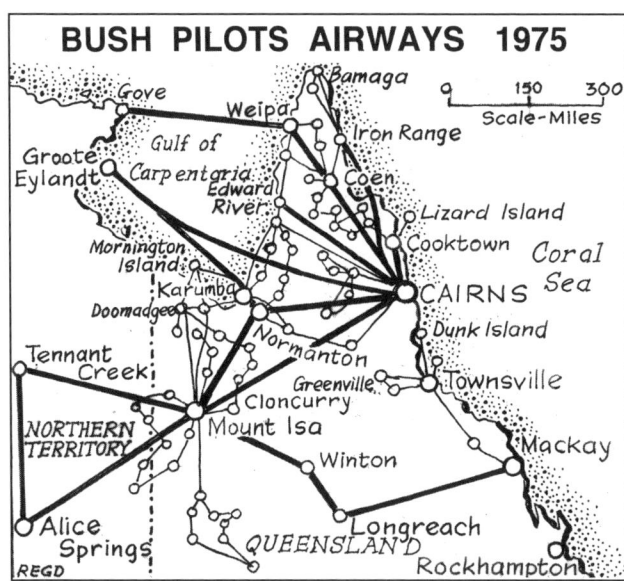

Bush Pilots Airways provided air service to the Queensland Outback, where the farmers were privileged to have an almost "on demand" status.

provincial towns was the eight-seat Cessna 402, supplemented by equally small Beech, Piper, and Embraer aircraft, more suited for private and executive travel than for scheduled operations. Another small airline in Queensland, based at Cairns, was **Bush Pilots Airways**, serving a host of small stations over a wide expanse of the Outback. Owner Syd Williams supplied "piddle-packs" to the farmers who had consumed too many beers while waiting for a loosely scheduled and toilet-less Cessna 402 to arrive.

The somewhat grudging efforts of the administration to overcome the demographic realities were accompanied by the gradual improvement in roads, which offset the reluctance of all the states to extend the rail system—although a Darwin-Alice Springs line completed the central north-south trunk route, almost exclusively for freight. Very few of the newer third-level operators survived an inevitable process of attrition. Two that did were **Opal Air**, named to reflect its main source of business at Coober Pedy, and together with **Pagas Air**, faced competition only from shipping across the Spencer Gulf in South Australia.

Back to Two Airlines

When the Two-Airline System was swept away on 30 October 1990, many aspirants ventured to grasp the opportunity to challenge the two incumbents: Australian, owned by Qantas, and Ansett, the airline branch of an industrial empire. Once again, the realities of the Australian demographics obliged them to compete with front-line jet airliners on the more densely traveled routes between the five major million-population-plus cities. First off the mark, and full of confidence, Bryan Grey, who had airline experience with East-West Airlines, founded **Compass Airlines**. Service opened on the inter-city routes on 1 December 1990, with four leased Airbus A300-600s. This lasted barely a year, and was grounded by the government on 30 December 1991. The reasons given were under-capitalization—new investors were reluctant to take an early risk—and competitors' fare discounting. Compass's low fares were instantly matched and exceeded by the incumbents, who operated the ground installations and facilities at the airports. As in the United States, gates and slots at the airports were still controlled and even owned by Qantas and Ansett, who were not about to offer assistance to an upstart newcomer.

The name was revived in September 1992, when Sam Coates launched Southern Cross Airlines, He bought the Compass name and operated as **Compass Mark II** with five MD-82s and -83s. Its life span was even less than its predecessor's. It ceased operations on 11 March 1993, and its deputy chairman was sentenced to 10 years in jail for false accounting.

The spirit of independence was not quite dead. Late in 1996, it gained incentive when the government introduced slot controls at Sydney, where Qantas and Ansett had dominated the infrastructure. The gates were now opened for another new entrant to the potential Sydney-Melbourne-Brisbane market, which amounted to 40% of Australia's 25 million air passengers. Gerry McGowan had founded the Impulse Transportation Group in 1982, delivering newspapers with small Piper and Beech aircraft. It added passenger services in 1993 when it acquired Oxley Airlines. He took the plunge in 2000 by adding more investment from overseas (which was now allowed under government policy) and on 5 June of that year, launched **Impulse Airlines**, starting with a fleet of five Boeing 717s. The Sydney-Melbourne frequency was 17 round-trips per day, and the fares were as low as A$33 (US$20) on the Sydney-Brisbane route, started on 4 September. A new route to Newcastle was added on 12 February 2001, but the same fate as Compass's awaited this latest challenger to the Australian airline establishment. The foreign investors withdrew, and on 14 May, McGowan joined forces with Qantas, continuing Beech 1900D flights to Newcastle and Canberra as part of the parent company's regional **QantasLink**.

An unwritten rule of competition is that, except in special circumstances, almost all the advantages of such policy can be achieved with only two competitors, and a third contender seldom usurps, or even survives, entry into the market. This was true in air transport in Australia, where the Sydney-Melbourne and Sydney-Brisbane routes were in high demand, but for several decades, regulations strictly enforced the Two-Airlines System. Only in the 1990s were they relaxed, in the face of popular demand and the recognition of the need for fewer regulations.

Even so, when Sir Richard Branson attempted to spread his wings in Australia, the path toward legitimacy was not easy. The existing policy was precariously maintained by Ansett and Impulse, the latter a surrogate of Qantas, which, by the 21st century, was more than just an airline; it was an Australian institution. Nevertheless, Branson—who never took "no" for an answer—formed Virgin Australia on 8 December 1999, and secured approval from the Australian Foreign Investment Review Board. Virgin Atlantic was already 49%-owned by Singapore Airlines,

in good standing in Canberra, and the prospect of an influx of substantial capital investment was viewed positively. On 28 May 2000, Sir Richard announced that the renamed **Virgin Blue**, based in Brisbane, would begin service with Boeing 737s and would be a low-fare airline, charging A$48 one-way from Brisbane to Sydney, which included Internet access, but with charges for meals. The term *Blue* has a positive connotation in Australia, but the Civil Aviation Safety Authority (CASA) failed to grant approval to the new airline. But Branson's staff received their Air Operator's Certificate on 28 August 2000, and Virgin Blue began Brisbane-Sydney service with a 162-seat Boeing 737-400 on 31 August. Brisbane-Melbourne followed, with 22 flights daily—almost as many as the competition's 30. Brisbane to Townsville and Adelaide were soon added, and services from Melboune to Adelaide, in May 2001. In June, Coolangatta (for the fashionable Gold Coast resorts) completed a network serving all the major traffic-generating cities of eastern Australia and to New Zealand. Ansett Airlines closed down on 4 March 2002. By this time, Virgin Blue was in full stride, and had connected transcontinetally with Perth. Almost simultaneously with Ansett's downfall, Branson sold 50% of his new airline to the port and shipping Patrick Corporation for A$ 260 million. With eyes for expansion and sights set also overseas, 10 Boeing 737-800s were ordered in January 2003, and rights to operate beyond New Zealand to Fiji and Vanuatu obtained in August.

To comply with Australian law, as the Virgin name was confined to domestic operations, **Pacific Blue** was launched in Christchurch, New Zealand, on 9 January 2004, and services from Brisbane introduced on 23 January. Melbourne-Christchurch followed on 4 March, by which time, Virgin Blue had attained a 35% share of the Australian domestic market, with a fleet of 44 Boeing 737-700s and -800s, and making a profit of A$159 million in 2004. Such aggressive growth forced Qantas to form **Jetstar** in May 2004, to compete with this new form of two-airline rivalry, while the Patrick Corporation raised its interest in Virgin Blue to 62.5% in March 2005. On 30 October of that year, **Polynesian Blue Airlines** made its first flight to the Pacific islands. By 2006, the Virgin group was serving 30 destinations with 50 737s, and carrying 13 million passengers annually. Its map included 23 cities in Australia, three in New Zealand, and five in the islands as far as Apia, in Western Samoa. In November 2006, eleven 100-seat Embraer 190 regional jets were ordered, Patrick's interest was taken over by Toll Holdings, and an "interline bond" adopted with Hawaiian Airlines for trans-Pacific connections to the United States.

This was a prelude for a Virgin trans-Pacific service of its own, and in July 2007, the Australian Air Services Commission approved a request to operate, as **Virgin Australia**, nonstop flights to the U.S., with Boeing 777-300ERs. The Virgin Blue revenues in that year were A$2.17 billion. This new airline, only seven years old, was already a major force, and a significant member of the Virgin airline empire, completing the circulation of the globe, and a major representative of the multi-product Virgin industrial conglomerate.

Chapter 39: New Zealand and the Pacific

Development in the Antipodes

A long-time member of the British Commonwealth, New Zealand has always been in the shadow of its larger neighbor, Australia. The small twin-island nation's total population is about the same as that of Sydney, Australia's largest city. At the beginning of the Jet Age, there were a dozen sheep for every one of its approximately three million people. Combined with its geographical separation (almost isolation in the Antipodes) from most of the world, indigenous air traffic has never been significant. On the other hand, since the late 1930s, air transport has made Australia more accessible, and the country has been increasingly popular as a tourist destination.

Routes to Australia, 1,400 miles or so distant, and to the Pacific islands, were operated by Short flying boats until 1949, when Douglas DC-4s, chartered from QANTAS, replaced them with landplanes. Local representation was through **Tasman Empire Airways, Ltd. (TEAL)**, which had originally been formed in 1940, jointly with B.O.A.C., QANTAS, and New Zealand's Union Airways. In 1954, Australia took over the British interest, so that it held half of the shareholding. All services were closely integrated between TEAL and QANTAS, whose airline stature was much greater than New Zealand's, held through New Zealand's National Airlines Corporation (N.A.C.).

TEAL moved into the Jet Age when, on 1 December 1959, it opened service from Auckland to Sydney with 100-seat Lockheed Electra turboprops. All flights were closely integrated with QANTAS's own Electras so that the threat of pure jet competition was moot. The last Short Solent flying boats were withdrawn on 14 September 1960. The timing was unfortunate, as in December the Electras had to be successively withdrawn from service and sent back to Lockheed for modification, following some crashes in the United States. On 25 July 1961, New Zealand acquired 100% ownership of TEAL. To ensure a fair distribution of the traffic to Australia, the relationship with QANTAS was still carefully preserved. At first this was 30% of a pooled schedule on the trans-Tasman routes, then increased to 40% on 1 April 1962. The next year, Sir Leonard Isitt, who had headed the airline since 1947, retired. Direct commercial competition became effective as TEAL was renamed **Air New Zealand (A.N.Z.)** on 1 April 1965. Any thoughts of the new airline maintaining its semi-dependence on QANTAS were erased as the first service with its own jet aircraft, on 3 October 1965, from Christchurch to Sydney, was not with Boeing aircraft, QANTAS's flagship choice, but with 160-seat Douglas DC-8-52s. Auckland saw the jets on 24 November 1965, and four days later the DC-8s replaced the Electras on the "Coral Route" to Pago Pago, U.S. Samoa, via Fiji. This attractive Pacific island service had originally started on 27 December 1951 with the Short flying boats to the Cook Islands, a New Zealand dependency, then extended to French Tahiti via Fiji, and later to Tonga on 12 August 1953. The Electras had been able to replace the Shorts, first to Tahiti in February 1961, when the airport was opened at Papeete, and to Pago Pago on 16 September of that year.

No longer a junior partner to QANTAS, A.N.Z. enjoyed a red letter day on 14 December 1965, when it opened trans-Pacific DC-8 service to Los Angeles via Fiji and Honolulu. Service to Asia started in the following year, to Hong Kong and Singapore on 3 and 6 March 1966, respectively, via Sydney. On 12 November 1967, one-stop service from Auckland to the United States was inaugurated, via Tahiti, and the French connection further maintained to Noumea, New Caledonia, which New Zealand had served since 1964. During the next few years, trans-Tasman service was intensified, and when its short airport runway was extended, Wellington, New Zealand's capital, joined the network to Sydney, Melbourne, and Brisbane. Such was the popularity of New Zealand as a tourist destination that, beginning on 5 September 1972, the Los Angeles route was flown every day.

When in 1970, the second Jet Age began with twin-aisle wide-bodied airliners New Zealand's choice was the 270-seat Douglas DC-10, whose capacity matched the traffic demand better than the 360-seat Boeing 747. The first one joined the DC-8s from Auckland to Sydney on 3 February 1973, and on the 6,959-mile trans-Pacific route, with only one stop via Honolulu, on 2 April. In 1974, Air New Zealand DC-10s were flying to London, thus eliminating a cooperative agreement with British Airways to interchange at Los Angeles.

On 1 April 1978, merger with New Zealand's National Airways Corporation (N.A.C.) became effective. This domestic airline had been formed on 7 December 1945 (at first N.Z.N.A.C.) with the merger of three smaller airlines whose combined networks served every urban community and tourist destination in the land, and also, until 4 September 1955, a route to Norfolk Island. Its early mixed fleet included de Havilland DH-89s, DH-86s, and Douglas DC-3s, and these were augmented with 50-seat turboprop Vickers Viscounts 807s on 3 February 1958, supplemented with 40-seat twin-engined Fokker F-27 Friendships on 22 December 1960. N.A.C. kept pace with world standards to modernize its fleet, and in September 1968, received its first Boeing 737. By the time it merged with A.N.Z. on 1 April 1978, it was operating a fleet of nine 100-seat 737s and 18 F-27s between all major cities, from Auckland to Dunedin via Wellington and Christchurch.

The New Zealand government had always encouraged private enterprise as well as recognizing that national interests had to be protected, especially for international operations. One entrepreneur could not be ignored, as he had pioneered road and air sight-seeing services throughout the fiordlands and lakes of the South Island since the early 1920s. Rodolph Wigley had

Mount Cook Airways has the rare distinction of flying (albeit not as a scheduled service) into the world's only airstrip that is constantly on the move: the Tasman glacier near New Zealand's Mount Cook. (Davies)

The versatile Armstrong-Whitworth Argosy, with front and rear loading doors, was put to good use by Safe Air in New Zealand. (Bentley)

become a local legend, and with his son Harry, had founded **Mount Cook Airways** in the 1930s. On 22 September 1955, he made an historic landing on the Tasman Glacier with an Auster, equipped with home-made retractable skis. One early trip was made by world-famous mountaineer, Sir Edmund Hillary, and the flights were soon a regular feature for visitors at the nearby Hermitage resort hotel. This charter service is unique. It lands on the only airstrip in the world that is constantly on the move.

The popularity of the Mount Cook resort encouraged Wigley and his son to connect it with the outside world. On 6 November 1961, with a Douglas DC-3, scheduled service began from Christchurch to the short mountain-ringed airstrip, while a fleet of 6-seat Cessna 185s consolidated the glacier operation. In January 1969, expanding its tourist market, the airline took over Tourist Air Travel (T.A.T.), which flew Grumman Widgeon amphibians to the southern lakes and fjords. On 19 October 1970, it introduced the 44-seat Hawker-Siddeley HS-748 turboprop as Harry Wigley brought the Jet Age to the New Zealand Alps and expanded into the North Island, to the hot springs resort of Rotorua. In 1973, N.A.C. bought a 15% interest in Mount Cook, which then operated its first trunk route, from Christchurch to Auckland via Rotorua. Also, Wigley had, in November 1972, introduced 11-seat Grumman Goose amphibian short flights from Auckland into the Bay of Islands, but these were later handed over to See Bee Air in 1976.

By the time Harry Wigley died in September 1980, he had become Sir Henry but had not lived to see the gradual disappearance of his airline. In 1984, Air New Zealand added a further 15% interest to N.A.C.'s original 15% in Mount Cook Airlines and, on 25 September 1985, a further 47% to gain complete control.

An Exception to the Rule

As if to defy the inexorable pace of technological progress, one airline in New Zealand continued to operate a highly specialized service without jet power. The innovative Airwork corporation of Britain had founded **Straits Air Freight Express (SAFE)** in 1951 to specialize in the swift transfer of goods between the two islands, where the Cook Straits were notoriously hazardous to shipping. A waterfront strike prompted N.A.C. to operate cargo DC-3s and C-46s, but SAFE came up with a better idea. Bristol 170 Freighters, equipped with front-loading doors, were matched with a mechanical ground-loading system, accelerating the entire process. In one year alone, from its base at Blenheim, to Wellington, SAFE carried 55,000 tons of cargo; and in one two-day period, carried 1,000 head of cattle. Racehorses were carried in specially designed horse-boxes. Late in 1967, two of its 14 Bristols began a service to the Chatham Islands, at which time the company changed its name to **Safe Air Ltd**. In 1971, one Bristol started a night express service between Auckland, Wellington, and Christchurch. The following year, N.A.C. bought the airline from Air Holdings, which had acquired Airwork. Operations continued with the addition of two larger turboprop Argosy 222 freighters, which had both front- and rear-loading fuselage-wide doors.

Australian Challenge

New Zealand authorities welcomed innovation and were not averse to overseas interests. This degree of tolerance was evident when, in October 1960, approval was granted for Australia's Ansett to take a large majority shareholding in an airline that had just been founded by two former N.Z.N.A.C. pilots. At their invitation, Ansett invested A$50,000 plus two Douglas DC-3s (ex-Butler and no longer competitive back home) to begin, on 14 December, an inter-island service as **South Pacific Airlines of New Zealand (SPANZ)**. With its old 31-seat DC-3s improved as Viewmasters, with large windows, it quickly developed a network to all the cities and towns served by N.A.C. But in August 1964, Ansett's 40% shareholding was taken over by local interests. The competition had been counter-productive—a case of too much capacity chasing too little traffic—and both airlines lost money in their intense rivalry. SPANZ flew its last service on 28 February 1966.

A World-Class Airline

While domestic changes were being made, Air New Zealand continued to make its mark overseas. In 1979, Western Samoa's Apia, and Raratonga were added to A.N.Z.'s Pacific destinations, but on 28 November of that year, the run of success and expansion was clouded by the loss of a DC-10 on the slopes of Mount

Erebus, Antarctica, on a charter flight, in which 257 people were killed. The tragedy was caused by confused navigational briefing and documentation. Even so, A.N.Z. was on the crest of a wave, with healthy traffic growth, and as MacDonnell-Douglas shirked the challenge of building a "stretched" DC-10, an order was placed in April 1980 for five Boeing 747-200s—and this was in spite of suffering a heavy financial loss, after many years of profits. Norman Geary became the chief executive in December 1981, and 747 service to London began in August 1982, and to Tokyo in September. Things went well. In April 1984, some flights to London were cut to 22 hours, with only one intermediate stop, at Los Angeles. The next year, a record annual profit of NZ$134 million heralded the inauguration of service to Vancouver on 15 November 1985. By this time, 220-seat Boeing 767-200ERs were in service, and a 77% shareholding in the Mount Cook Group, specializing in scenic flights in the South Island with 44-seat HS-748s, consolidated A.N.Z.'s dominance of the domestic market in 1985 (see above). International tourism was booming, with 70% of the traffic now from overseas, compared to only 40% a few years previously. A new European terminus was added at Frankfurt.

Battles for Control Down Under

The New Zealand government did not approve of a near monopoly and allowed the Australian Ansett to start operations in July 1987, at first with de Havilland Canada Dash 7s to serve Rotorua and Queenstown then on to trunk routes with Boeing 737s (see below). Air New Zealand was then privatized. In December 1988, a consortium headed by Brierley Investments, local investors, and QANTAS, with minor shares by American Airlines and Japan Airlines, purchased the flag carrier for NZ$3.3 billion. In 1992, a far-reaching decision was made by the Australian and New Zealand governments to create a Single Aviation Market. The two countries granted rights to carry traffic beyond each other's borders. QANTAS, for example, could fly nonstop from Auckland to Los Angeles, while A.N.Z. could fly nonstop from Los Angeles to Sydney. The latter took full advantage of the agreement. Within two years, it was operating 200 flights a week to Asia from the big cities of eastern Australia and from Cairns. In November 1995, it agreed for T.N.T., a large Australian transport consortium, to buy shares in Ansett Australia, later to become a half-ownership, for A$475 million.

The affairs of the airline giants became more complicated after a memorandum of understanding of 21 June 1997 proposed a regional alliance with Ansett Australia and Singapore Airlines. A.N.Z. became a member of the Star Alliance on 5 April 1999, but shortly afterward, Singapore's plan to buy 50% of Ansett was killed when A.N.Z. refused to surrender its presumptive right to buy the remaining 50% from Rupert Murdoch's News Corporation. This ambition—complete ownership of Ansett—was achieved on 30 April 2000, with Singapore buying 25% of A.N.Z. by August of that year. Gary Toomey took over as CEO and in June 2001, Qantas (no longer an acronymn) proposed a deal. Singapore Airlines would sell its 25% in A.N.Z. in exchange for giving up control of Ansett, while Qantas would buy Brierley Investments's 30%. In September 2001, Singapore and Brierley each increased their equity in A.N.Z. and the former's stake was thus raised to 34%.

Such boardroom battles became irrelevant in Australia. Ansett was grounded on 12 September 2001, and A.N.Z., then its owner, abandoned it. Air New Zealand privatization had been a disaster, and on 4 October, the New Zealand government effectively renationalized the airline by taking over 83% of the shares, and injecting NZ$885 million (US$372 million) in a two-phase loan. Singapore's and Brierley's holdings were reduced to 4.3% and 5.2% respectively. Toomey was replaced by Ralph Norris in February 2002.

The fresh capital enabled A.N.Z. to buy 15 152-seat Airbus A320s, which entered service on the trans-Tasman routes in October 2003, by which time the airline, together with Qantas, was discounting heavily. In December 2002, the two airlines agreed to the Australian flag carrier buying 22.5% of A.N.Z., but both the Australian and New Zealand authorities rejected the plan in the fall of 2003. Undeterred, A.N.Z. continued to invest in new equipment, signing, on 2 June 2004, to buy eight Boeing 313-seat 777-200ERs, and becoming the launch customer for the -9 variant of the new 787 Dreamliner. Now operating efficiently with its 747s and 767s, and with Singapore disposing of its minority shareholding, the airline had achieved the major market shares on all its main routes, except to Hong Kong. Facing increased competition (including Dubai's Emirates) on the important trans-Tasman route group, and in a sequel to the planned Qantas-ANZ shares negotiations of 2002–03, Qantas, A.N.Z. and their affiliated Jetstar and Freedom Air, respectively, all agreed to consolidate their schedules on the Tasman routes in 2006. Already operating to Shanghai from 2006, service to fast-growing China was augmented in 2008 by a route to Beijing, in time for the Olympic Games that year.

Jungle to Jets

The second largest island in the world (excluding Australia), New Guinea was colonized during the 19th century, with the Netherlands occupying the western half. The southern part of the east was a British protectorate, and became the Australian Territory of Papua in 1906. The northern part of the east, with adjoining islands, was the German Kaiser Wilhelmsland until after the end of the First World War, when, in 1919, it was mandated to Australia by the League of Nations. The two parts of the east eventually amalgamated to become independent as Papua New Guinea in 1975. A land of forests and mountains, the indigenous population consists of more than 700 tribes, each with its own language.

Air transport came to this primitive and almost neglected island in 1927, when the discovery of gold in a remote area led to the development of specialist air transport, to supplant a 10-day trek through the jungle by native carriers. Unlike many regions faced with the same predicament, there were no mules, horses, or oxen. At first, several adventurous pilots tried to establish air services into jungle strips, and some even survived a few years.

Guinea Airways led the pack and soon had the distinction, during the 1930s, of carrying more freight than all the other airlines of the world combined. In the 1940s, the same claim was made by the Central American airline TACA, of Honduras. The two countries were able to share this rare characteristic of communication because both administrative capitals—Port Moresby in the case of New Guinea, Tegucigalpa in the case of Honduras—were isolated from the rest of the country by the absence of a railroad. At least Honduras had a few roads, but even as late as the beginning of the Jet Age, and before it had its own airline, New Guinea had only 150 miles fit for a four-wheeled vehicle—and a sturdy one at that.

Inspired by so many bold pilots who tried their luck in New Guinea before the war, the spirit of adventure still lived on after the end of hostilities. Even then, the conditions for true pioneering were little changed. In 1947, Bobby Gibbes started with a single Auster along the Sepik River, where the only other mode of travel was by canoe. In August 1955, his **Gibbes-Sepik** airline imported three 1940s vintage Junkers-Ju 52/3m tri-motors, which, carefully restored, continued to fly in a post-war time warp, along with six Norduuyn Norsemans. Gibbes's efforts ended in November 1958 when the Australian civil aviation authorities pursued their Two-Airline System to the northernmost extent of their jurisdiction On 1 April 1960, this was a rare example of when an airline, still equipped with aircraft designed in the late 1920s, was sold to a modern airline, Mandated Airlines, itself acquired by Ansett, which operated 1960s jets.

The main task of providing essential travel, in a land where any journey held an element of risk, was still maintained by **Territory Air Lines (T.A.L.)**, based at Goroka, and founded by two pilots who started local charter flights in 1952, using de Havilland D.H. 84s. On 1 January 1958, they sold the airline to Dennis Buchanan, who had flown with Gibbes. He expanded the fleet, mostly with small single-engined Cessnas, and early in 1968, acquired the license to operate scheduled services (which he had been doing de facto, if not de jure). With business growing, and as tourists began to "discover" New Guinea, he bought his first 20-seat twin-engine DHC-6 in 1972.

In July 1974, to avoid the territorial reference as New Guinea was about to become independent, Buchanan changed the airline name to **Talair**. A man of action, he had, within a few years, acquired Melanesian Airways (**Macair**) in the Solomon Islands; the local Panga Airways; purchased shares in New Hebrides Airways, when Vanuatu became independent; then Metro Manila, in the Philippines; and Velengair in the Kingdom of Tonga. By the late 1980s, he had more than 70 aircraft, and in 1991, was knighted for his contributions to aviation in the southwest Pacific. But his efforts were not appreciated in the new bureaucracy of New Guinea, as Sir Dennis was no doubt perceived as a representative of the colonial past. As the economy of Papua New Guinea deteriorated, and frustrated with officialdom, his patience was exhausted. He shut down Talair abruptly on 25 May 1993 and moved to Australia, where he died on 29 August 2001.

The independence of 15 September 1975 had not come easily. The local people had scant experience of any form of government, either local or as a nation. But reflecting the post-war global custom, the new nationalism was accompanied by the desire to fly its new flag on an airline of its own. Moves toward this objective were already in hand. In May 1973, a National Airline Commission announced the intention to create **Air Niugini (A.N.G.)**, even using the phonetic pidgin spelling. The Papua New Guinea government held 60% of the A$480,000 shareholdings, with the three Australian airlines, T.A.A., QANTAS, and Ansett, holding the balance. The first official flight was on 1 November 1973, exactly a month before partial self-government was attained, and a local network to outlying points in New Guinea and the adjacent islands was established with 28-seat DC-3s and 36-seat F-27s, took over networks that the Australian airlines had already been operating since the war. In May 1975, the first international flights were made with leased Boeing 727s, from Port Moresby to Honiara, Solomon Islands, Cairns and Brisbane, Queensland, and were operated by the Australians in all but name.

In January 1976, the government purchased the A.N.G. shares of Qantas and T.A.A., leaving only Ansett with 16%. It launched the first intercontinental service, ostensibly its own, once a week to Manila, with a wet-leased Boeing 720B. But its ambition overtook its ability to fulfil its air transport requirements. In January 1977, a route opened to Kagoshima, southern Japan, but this did not last long; and in 1978 neither did flights to Singapore via Jakarta, nor, in 1979, to Honolulu, with two leased Boeing 707s.

Air Niugini certainly had problems at home, trying to meet its obligations to provide air services to all the outlying communities in New Guinea, and to all the offshore islands that were part of the new nation. Its last DC-3 was retired on 31 January 1977, and a new fleet of Fokker F-28s supplemented the F-27s. But altogether the situation—described by independent observers as "disastrous"—led to a huge financial loss of US$6.5 million in 1979–80. The government called in the reputable McKinsey consultants, and in 1981, bought the outstanding Ansett shares. Part of the solution was to participate in a tripartite agreement with Hong Kong's Cathay Pacific Airlines and Air New Zealand for a Hong Kong-Port Moresby-Auckland through service. The three airlines maintained the service in rotation.

Papua New Guinea's national airline thus survived, but it was a struggle. Joseph Tauvasa became the chief executive, and achieved the goal of serving all 19 of the country's provinces (as had Talair). In 1984, the government had the honor of welcoming Pope John Paul II. A.N.G. flew him to Mount Hagen and Honiara, but this event did nothing to improve the balance sheet, nor did the lease of an Airbus A300B, even though it was exchanged for a smaller A310-300 in June 1991. Other setbacks were volcanic activity at Rabaul and militant unrest in Bougainville, which severely diminished the tourist trade. When, on 15 April 1998, the Papua New Guinea government came to the rescue with a US$8.5 million bailout package, the prime minister's verdict was that the airline was the victim of years of mismanagement and political interference. Much of the problem was a mistaken protectionist policy. This was alleviated in August 2002, when Qantas guaranteed to buy blocks of seats on a Boeing 767, which replaced the Airbus; but this was returned to its lessor in December 2007, to be succeeded by two other 767s, leased from Iceland. Meanwhile, the P.N.G. government, in line with most other countries, announced an "open skies" policy in March 2006. With a fleet of Fokker 100s and Bombardier (ex–D.H. Canada) Dash 8s, all leased, its aircraft were now at least better matched to the slender traffic demands of Papua New Guinea's domestic air route system.

Ocean Transformation

Until June 1928, when Australian pilot Charles Kingsford-Smith and his crew made the first airplane crossing of the Pacific Ocean, the widely scattered islands of this vast expanse of sea, twice as big as the Atlantic, were almost unknown to the rest of the world. A notable exception was Hawaii, a U.S. territory, which became a popular destination for affluent tourists who could afford the time and expense to take the Matson Line luxury ships from San Francisco to Honolulu. Except in the little-patronized South Pacific east of Tahiti, this 2,500-mile journey was the longest non-alternate commercial air route in the world, presenting a formidable challenge for any aspiring airline.

Elsewhere, the island groups were isolated from each other by hundreds of miles, and inhabited by local Polynesian or Melanesian peoples. By Western standards, they were regarded as primitive, and in some places they were cannibals. 120 languages were spoken in the Solomon Islands alone. Only Fiji and Samoa shared with Hawaii the status of having populations of more than barely 100,000. Visitors from the outside world were confined to a few missionaries and some enterprising traders from Australia. During the 19th and early 20th centuries, these tropical paradises were annexed as colonies or protectorates by British, French, German, and American empire builders. At the time, they never foresaw any outstanding resources, except a little copra and guano, but they were useful as coaling or radio stations, or for provisioning trans-Pacific shipping, and to add a few names on their world maps.

But all this changed in 1935, when the visionary Juan Trippe, head of Pan American Airways, inaugurated a route for his flying boats to connect North America with China. A few years later, Pan Am pioneered a route across the Southern Pacific. The aviation world became aware of tiny atolls such as Palmyra, Kingman Reef, Canton, and Christmas islands. These were surveyed as possible refueling stops for flying boats, and Pan American had to apply political diplomacy to establish the rights to alight in some of the lagoons. New Zealand, for example, became aware of the strategic value of some of its faraway specks of administered territory.

Fiji Takes a Lead

Prominent in the development of independent local airlines in the Pacific Ocean—an area that became known to geographers as Oceania—was the Fiji Islands, which became independent of Great Britain in 1970, at which time its population was about half a million, half of whom were indentured Indians. As early as 1932, Guinea Airways had tried to start a local airline, but this lasted only a year or two. The idea was revived in 1951 by Harold Gatty, another famous airman, who formed **Fiji Airways**. It began its first service in September, from Suva to Nadi (pronounced "Nandi"), with three de Havilland D.H.89s, and in 1954, added three D.H. Drovers, produced by the Australian branch of de Havilland. Gatty died in August 1957, and his widow sold the airline to Qantas for A£54,000. The purchase was completed on 24 March 1958, and a reconstituted Fiji Airways adopted a policy of extending airline service throughout the islands of the South Pacific. To improve operational feasibility, two four-engined de Havilland Herons were acquired in January 1959.

On 1 January 1960, ownership was changed to equal shares between Qantas, Britain's B.O.A.C., and New Zealand's TEAL. The capital was increased, and Qantas remained responsible for the management. In 1960, a route opened to Tonga, and in November 1961 service began to Honiara, Solomon Islands via Porto Vila, New Hebrides, and to Apia, Western Samoa. A domestic network started in 1962 to some of Fiji's outlying islands, and in July 1964, flights began to Tarawa, the location of the furthest Japanese eastward advance during the Second World War. In March 1965, the Fiji colonial government purchased a 25% shareholding, as the capital was increased further to F£240,000, and with more Herons and a wet-leased DC-3, further local island services were introduced. The airline was on its way to further expansion, and comparative adulthood in the world of airlines in the southern Pacific. For on 22 October 1967, its service to Tarawa, albeit only twice a month, was with a 40-seat Hawker-Siddeley turboprop HS-748, with two chartered DC-3s as back-up. The next year, with the capital increased to F£1,020,000, and with the Kingdom of Tonga and the U.K. Western Pacific High Commission each with a 25% minor shareholding, the Tarawa service was extended to Nauru and the Honiara service to Port Moresby. In 1969, the trend continued, with Nauru, Western Samoa, and the Gilbert and Ellice colony augmenting the international shareholding. Flight frequencies increased, and domestic routes linked some of the Gilbert Islands, with a Heron based at Tarawa. Recognizing the new character of the airline, as Fiji gained its independence, its airline name was changed on 23 September 1970 to Pacific Islands Airways, and further, on 30 July 1971, to **Air Pacific**, by which time the Tonga Service included Niue.

This was the prelude to Fiji entering the Jet Age beyond the turboprop stage. On 2 April 1972, its first twin-jet BAC One-Eleven service linked Nandi with Port Moresby via Port Vila and Honiara, and in June 1973, the service included Brisbane. The jets served Tonga in October of that year, and in May 1974 began a direct service to Auckland. Meanwhile, in November, the Herons on the domestic routes were supplemented by Britten-Norman BN-3 Trislanders. In May 1976, one of these quaint but efficient piston-engined aircraft was sold to the Gilbert and Ellice colony, to operate locally there, where the Gilberts would become the new republic of Kiribati, and the local network would become Air

Tunguru—see below. In 1978, the Fijian government took over control of Air Pacific by acquiring the shares of Qantas, B.O.A.C., and Air New Zealand. It started a service to Sydney in September 1980, by leasing 120 seats (about one-third of the total) on a Qantas Boeing 747. Reaching the largest city in Australia was a vital step in the Fijian airline's progress. It was able to trade its strategic position as an essential stop for Qantas on its trans-Pacific route to the United States for an advantageous agreement for leased airline capacity. Further steps to expand across the Pacific were made to reach Pago Pago, in American Samoa via Apia, and onward to Papeete, Tahiti, French Polynesia.

In 1983, gaining confidence, Air Pacific launched its ambitious Project America, to put into practice the terms of an existing bilateral agreement for the exchange of traffic rights. On 28 September, with a 291-seat leased Douglas DC-10-30, it started flying to Honolulu, at the same time adding Melbourne, but deleting Papeete. This was an admirable objective but was badly timed, as U.S. tourism to Fiji had been decreasing. Foreign airlines were promoting Australia and New Zealand more, and longer-ranged airliners could dispense with the refueling stop at Nadi. By 1984, Fiji's national flag-carrier was in trouble—described later as "technically bankrupt"—and Qantas came to the rescue. Flights to Honolulu were cancelled.

In 1987, Air Pacific withdrew from all points in Fiji, except Nadi, Suva, and Labasa, Vanua Levu, which it served with two ATR-42s. The smaller points continued to be served by Fiji Air and Sunflower Airlines, the larger of many small inter-island operators. This left Air Pacific to concentrate on international services. In August 1990, the Fiji government bought some of Qantas's shares and in turn sold some of these to a Japanese resort enterprise. The administrative headquarters were moved from Suva to Nadi, the operational base. Although unable to buy the wide-bodied aircraft necessary to maintain parity with competitors on the trans-Pacific aerial highway, Air Pacific could pay its way with high-yield passenger revenues, and thus afford to lease aircraft. In July 1990, it leased a 218-seat Boeing 767-200ER for medium-range routes, including one to Tokyo; replaced the ATR-42s with a Boeing 737-500; and, in July 1994, a 433-seat Boeing 747-200, with which it opened service to Los Angeles. On 26 October 1997, in cooperation with Canadian Airlines, it started its longest route, to Vancouver via Honolulu (a city it originally reached in 1983–84).

Ownership of Air Pacific was now 46% by Qantas, 53% by the Fijian government, and small holdings by the South Sea regionals. Fortunes were still in the balance, and a new managing director, Michael McQuay, took stern measures and laid off a dozen senior executives. But aircraft leasing continued, with a 126-seat Boeing 737-700 in November 1998, and the first of two 162-seat NG (New Generation) 737-800s in July 1999. After 14 profitable years, a new leader from Qantas, John Campbell, faced a significant loss in 2000. The culprit was the Fijian government itself, which had to cope with a racially inspired coup in Suva. The news spread quickly around the world, resulting in a severe drop in tourist arrivals in Fiji from Japan, Australia, and New Zealand—about 70% of Air Pacific's international traffic. But after the crisis was over, recovery included the lease from Singapore Airlines of two 458-seat Boeing 747-400s. The airline turned its attention once again to securing a domestic network. In 2008, it acquired Sun Air, one of the two major domestic airlines, renaming it **Pacific Sun**, to operate as its associate, with 9-seat BN-2 Islanders and 14-seat DHC-6 Twin Otters, to supplement the 44-seat ATR-42s.

The Islanders Stake Their Claims

The island groups across the Pacific Ocean were becoming acquainted with aircraft that, to fit demand, had only a few seats. Mostly too small for public service elsewhere, they were used mainly for personal or executive use. Fiji was a case that epitomized this unusual situation. Air Pacific owed its development potential to its geographical location as a trans-Pacific refueling stop for intercontinental airline corporations. A quite different market existed to connect the trunk routes to tiny spots on the map, with short airstrips which only small Cessna, Piper, and similar aircraft could use. Fiji was a fertile area for modest airline entrepreneurs, specializing in serving tourists who sought to "get away from it all" on a deserted, palm-shaded beach, but with the amenities of a star-rated hotel.

Starting operations on 10 July 1967, Air Pacific (not to be confused with the current flag-carrier) was renamed Fiji Air on 29 March 1971, and again as **Air Fiji** in February 1995. Owned by Aviation Investments (55%), the government (11%), and other shareholders, its fleet of 15-19-seaters, including twin-engined EMB-110 Bandeirantes, and Chinese Harbin Y-12s, were deployed on 15 domestic and one route to Funafuti, Tuvalu, about 800 miles north of Fiji. Next to join in the growing market for tourists arriving at Nadi and who needed shuttle service to the local islands, was **Sunflower Airlines**, founded in 1981. Only a 10-minute flight by Britten-Norman BN-2 Islander was Malololailai, where resort hotels with romantic names such as Beachcomber or Castaway welcomed the sun- and beach-seekers. Business boomed enough for Sunflower to invest in larger aircraft, a 30-seat Shorts 330 and a 20-seat DHC-6 Twin Otter, to extend service to the eastern Fiji island of Taveuni, and to offer charter flights to many of the country's numerous islands and islets. As narrated above, Sun Air was acquired by Air Pacific's own domestic subsidiary, Pacific Sun, in 2007.

Air Pacific Embraer Bandeirante. (Davies)

New Zealand and the Pacific

Fiji Air Britten-Norman Islander. (Davies)

Polynesian HS748 photographed at Nadi, Fiji. (Davies)

Most ambitious, and possibly unique in the annals of air transport, was **Turtle Airways**, founded by Richard Evanson, who had prospered in the Californian soft-ware business, and retired to Fiji in 1978. He bought a small island in the Yasawa Group, northwest of Viti Levu, and supplemented this purchase with a small Cessna 206 floatplane so that he could go shopping at Nadi. Realizing the potential, he created Turtle Island as part of a luxury package deal that included the flight and the hotel, carefully designed to reflect local conditions. The luxury was not of the kind associated with five-star hotels. The Island had no shops and no television, but Evanson supplied food, drink, and suntan lotion plus frequent trips to Nadi.

The small airlines listed above were the main ones that survived the changing fortunes of the vacation market as it ebbed and flowed from desirable to avoidable, in parallel with the Fijian economy and its delicate politics. Others that had brief existences were, in the 1980s, Air Coral Coast, Island Air, and Dovair; and, in the early 2000s, Air Katafanga (the site of Harold Gatty's pioneer venture), Air Wakaya, and Pacific Island Air. Large or small, however, from trans-ocean Air Pacific to the short flights to the island paradises, the Fijian airline entrepreneurs had put their little country on the world map, as a sought-after vacation destination, especially for adventurous tourists who had previously only known Hawaii.

The Other South Sea Airlines

With a population almost equal to that of all the other small island nations of the South Pacific combined, Fiji was the clear leader in aspiring to have its own airline. Among the former British- or New Zealand–administered islands, Western Samoa was the next to step forward. It attained its independence from Wellington in 1962—eight years before Fiji—and its **Polynesian Airlines** was founded in 1959 by Australian Sir Reginald Barnewell and Eugene Paul, a Samoan businessman. Services began in January 1960 from the West Samoan capital, Apia, to Pago Pago, in nearby American Samoa, with two Percival Princes.

These aircraft were small enough for the local traffic at the time, but services were suspended at the end of the year because of accidents, and not resumed until 5 July 1963, when a promising opportunity arose. New Zealand's TEAL withdrew its inter-island flying boat route, and a rejuvenated Polynesian replaced it under charter, flying Apia-Aitutaki (Cook Islands)-Papeete with DC-3s. On 13 February 1964, the route was extended to Suva, but new regulations defined the fuel requirements for diversions to alternate airfields (a minimum of 90 minutes flying) which curtailed the DC-3 operation. A four-engined DC-4 was dry-leased but unreliable. Finally, after Fiji Airways had acquired a 21% interest, the first Hawker-Siddeley 40-seat HS-748 turboprop entered service in the spring of 1970. It was chartered from Fiji Airways, but with the Samoan government increasing its shareholding to 51%, Polynesian's own 748 went into service on 2 February 1972.

By the mid-1970s, Niue had been included on the Cook Islands service and the frequency on the local route to the American Pago Pago was eight each day. Raratonga, in the Cooks, was added in November 1978, and the French Wallis Island regained its air service in a joint venture with the intercontinental U.T.A., direct from Paris, connecting also with Tahiti. More dramatic for this small airline was the start of direct flights to Auckland via Tonga, on 24 February 1978, with a Boeing 737 leased from Air New Zealand. The service operated only once a week, but Samoa was now firmly on the South Sea islands network. This was emphasized by introducing the "PolyPass," a code-sharing venture with another island group and Air Vanuatu (see below). Forging ahead, further short-haul aircraft, a BN-2 and an Australian Nomad, were added in 1978; and on 16 October 1979, Polynesian crews started to fly the 737. Service to Los Angeles began on 28 May 1993. Honolulu was added a week later. Polynesian's debts amounted to a quarter of Samoa's annual budget. Richard Gates was hired from Air New Zealand to put things right. He cut the fleet to a single 737, restored order to the balance sheet, and code-shared with A.N.Z., with services only to Australia and New Zealand. A new airline, Polynesian Blue (see previous chapter), was established as a joint venture with the Samoan government and the Australian Virgin Blue.

Fiji/Air Pacific and Polynesian were able to provide connecting services during the 1960s and 1970s, until the smaller island groups attained maturity with independence and desired airplanes with their own flags. Typically, inter-island journeys were several hundred miles long. Boats could take two or three days, and because the populations were small, the services were infrequent. But once the islanders had tasted the advantages of air travel, expectations expanded. Just as, at a different level of modernization, the jet engine revolutionized the world of air

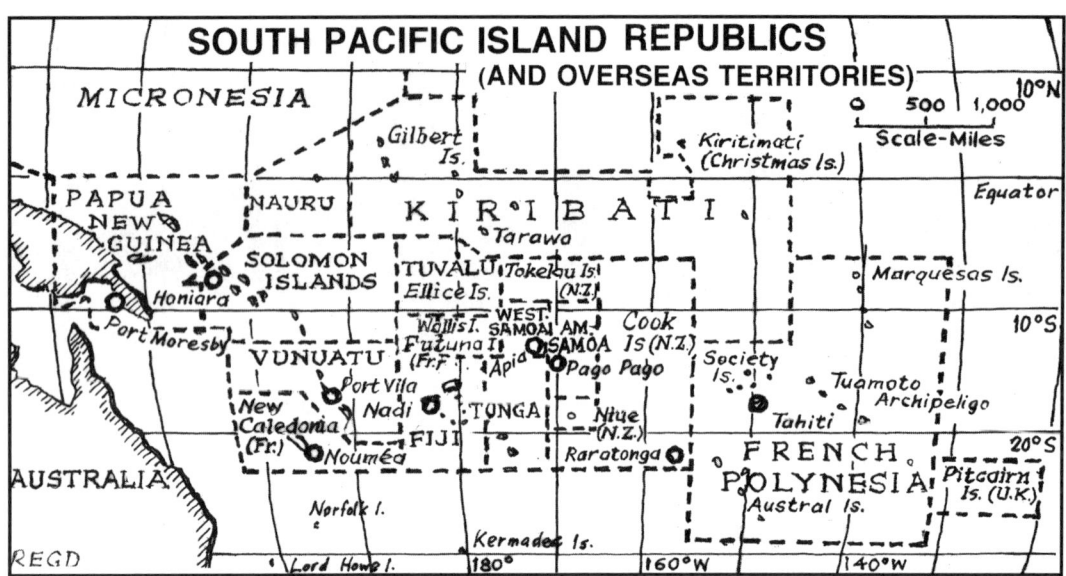

Before the Second World War, the Pacific Ocean was ruled entirely by Great Britain, France, and the United States. Today, the islands and atolls are home to nine small republics, together with some still administered by France, New Zealand, and the U.S.

transport globally, things in the South Pacific were never the same. As first the Britten-Norman Islander, and later the Hawker-Siddeley 748, replaced the boats, the coral island equivalent of the post-war DC-4 replacing the *Queen Mary* on the Atlantic, and later, the Boeing 707 replacing the Constellation. Islands that were near enough to existing operators that could help and those with larger populations were the first to add their names to the South Sea island list. Thus those closest to Fiji and Samoa, as narrated above, were soon served. **Cook Island Airways** was 90%-owned by Air New Zealand, and its BN-2 Islanders that started services in December 1973 put their name into practice. Other than tourists and local administrators, they brought the benefits of medical and education services to a total population of less than 20,000.

Much closer to Fiji were the Tonga Islands, formerly the Friendly Islands, and created as the Kingdom of Tonga. By the often irregular standards of local air networks of the area, they were reasonably served by Fiji Airways and Polynesian. As early as 1974, a hotel owner in Vava'u, northernmost of the Tongas, arranged a BN-2 air service to Nukualofa in an arrangement with the Tongan government, but this was little more than an on-demand charter service. Friendly Island Airways opened regular routes in 1985, became **Royal Tongan Airlines** in May 1991, and began international services in July 1991. Undercapitalized, its Boeing 757 was repossessed in April 2004, and the domestic operation closed down on 18 May 2004. Then the infrequent inter-island ferry boat went aground on 26 May, right at the start of the tourist season. Two new airlines promptly took off. First, on 9 June, was **Peau Vava'u** (Air Waves), with two leased 28-seat DC-3s, the last of this vintage type to be in scheduled service. Then came a leased Convair 580 on 3 May 2005, but flights were suspended in November 2006, when the airline headquarters were destroyed by fire. Service was restored on 14 May 2007 with a leased Jetstream 41. Second to start was **FlyNiu Airlines**, which began on 16 June 2004 with a 37-seat Bombardier Dash 8-200, but the courts decided that the little kingdom could not sustain two airlines, and it closed down on 10 September.

Also near the source of technical support were the Solomon Islands, close to New Guinea. One of the experienced pilots from that severe testing ground for aspirant airlines, Lawrence Crowley, started "regular charter" flights in the Solomons in 1962 with a Piper Aztec. The next year, he founded **Megapode Airways**, with a much-needed inter-island service with a de Havilland Dove, which could take advantage of good ex-military airstrips, a residue from the war. In June 1968, Macair (see the New Guinea chronicle, above) purchased Megapode, renaming it Solomon Island Airways, or **Solair**, and substituting a Beech Baron and an Islander for the Dove. Then Talair, also from New Guinea (above) took over Macair, which connected Solair with its own route to Bougainville. This short connection gave Solair the distinction of being the smallest international airline in the world.

In 1978, the Solomons gained their independence from Great Britain, and Solair branched out to manage Air Tungaru (see below) in the Gilbert Islands. The new government then acquired 49% of the shares, later augmenting this to complete ownership. With increased stature, it started service in April 1980 from Honiara to Brisbane, in a shared BAC One-Eleven operation with Air Pacific. This was consolidated in 1989 with a 98-seat Boeing 737, of which 15 were allocated to Solair, and the seating capacity shared with other South Pacific countries on routes to Australia and connecting Port Moresby with Fiji and New Zealand via Honiara and Port-Vila, Vanuatu. Civil war in the Solomons disrupted this promising experiment in airline cooperation, which was resumed in May 2007, with a 76-seat Embraer ERJ 170 and three DHC Twin Otters.

Even before the Solomons, the island group to the southeast, the New Hebrides, as the Anglo-French condominium was then called, could boast two airlines, though these were primarily small charter companies flying executive aircraft types. New Hebrides Airways, English-speaking, was formed in June 1960; the other, Hebridair, French-speaking, in 1964. Together they operated under the joint name of **Air Melanésiae**. In 1969, Qantas acquired a 51% shareholding, half of which was transferred to B.O.A.C. at the end of the year, when a new partnership was formed with Air Hebrides, a subsidiary of the French independent, U.T.A.

On 30 July 1980, the New Hebrides condominium became an independent republic, Vanuatu, and the airline name changed to **Air Vanuatu**. A month later, the resourceful Dennis Buchanan, of Niugini's Talair and also of Solair, bought a majority shareholding, leading to complete ownership in 1981. The fleet of the faithful Islanders and Trislanders was augmented to include a 20-seat DHC-6 Twin Otter, and later two Fairchild F-27s and an ATR-42, by which time, in December 1987, the Vanuatu government had taken over. By the 1990s, under a code-sharing arrangement with Fiji's Air Pacific, the airline was flying to Sydney, Melbourne, and Brisbane with a Boeing 737-800.

Of the other British or New Zealand territories in the Pacific, few of the tiny atolls were big enough or had enough population to support any kind of transport service, much less scheduled airline flights. This is why, when the courageous individuals or local governments took the risk, it was invariably in cooperation with a larger island group such as Fiji or Western Samoa. Kiribati was such a case. Formerly the Gilbert, Phoenix, and Line Islands, these isolated specks in the ocean were distributed over an area that, east to west, was several hundred miles more than the width of the continental United States. With only 70,000 people, it became independent on 12 July 1979, and desired an inter-island connecting service that did not take several days to complete, as a sea journey did.

Air Tungaru, based at Tarawa, had already started service with a Britten-Norman Tri-Islander on 1 January 1978, with a contract with the Solomons. A year later, in a charter agreement with Air Nauru, a Boeing 727 began flights to Honolulu via Christmas Island. Aiming toward complete independent control, Air Tungaru wet-leased the 727 in January 1980, and then bought a 19-seat de Havilland Heron to replace its Britten-Normans and to open service to Fiji. In the spring of 1981, it bravely bought its own jet, a Boeing 727-100QC, and by starting a route to Papeete, was able to connect Hawaii with Tahiti via Christmas Island (renamed Kiritimati). This was flown once a week in agreement with Hawaii's Aloha Airlines (now defunct).

The other half of the former Gilbert and Ellice Islands British colony, the Ellice group, were tiny coral islands and atolls centered on Funafuti. They became an independent constitutional monarchy as Tuvalu (meaning "eight islands together") on 1 October 1978. It is the fourth smallest country in the world, and cannot justify an airline of its own. But it was able to take a small share in Air Fiji, for three flights a week to Suva, and to initiate other charter arrangements. Its 12,000 people live a somewhat precarious existence, as no place in the islands is more than about 12 feet above sea level, and cyclones have already washed away some of the land.

Airline Tycoon

The flag carrier of a tiny Micronesian island, **Air Nauru**, could be described as a "tycoon." Nauru's population of 8,000 has benefitted economically from the fact that the island's eight square miles is composed almost entirely of rich phosphate, the result of a buildup of sea-bird droppings over millennia. First colonized by Germany in 1888, it became an Australian territory in 1914 then, after the Second World War, was jointly administered by Australia, New Zealand, and Great Britain as a United Nations Trust Territory. It became an independent republic on 31 January 1968, and its relatively wealthy (phosphate-fuelled) government promptly formed its own airline, starting service to Brisbane on 14 February 1970 with a chartered eight-seat Dassault Falcon.

Other than the even smaller Ocean Island (now Banaba), the nearest community was Tarawa, in the Gilberts (now Kiribati), 400 miles away. In the spring of 1971, Air Nauru started service there, and on to Majuro, in the Marshall Islands. The traffic potential was minimal, but the airline astutely realized that there were great possibilities to exploit the so-called Sixth Freedom of the air. This permits an airline to use its geographic position to combine the Third and Fourth Freedoms, i.e., the Fifth Freedom (to originate and receive passengers and freight between two foreign countries). In this way, using its financial advantage over other Pacific island nations, it could spread its wings, just as the Icelandic airline was able to enter the trans-Atlantic market.

In 1972, with a 60-seat Fokker F-28, Air Nauru started service to Japan via Guam and Okinawa, and expanded this initiative in 1974 to offer through service to Australia, adding a Boeing 737-200 in 1975, and a Boeing 727-100 in 1976. Further aircraft were added so that by the 1980s, the number of seats in its nine Boeings equaled one-tenth of Nauru's total population. It then went into decline, partly because the phosphate resources were disappearing, and also because longer-range jet service by major airlines over the 6,000-mile Japan-Australia/New Zealand route did not need a Nauru stop-over.

In 1996, with only one 737-400 left, the government surrendered ownership to the Nauru Air Corporation, which, however, under regulatory control from Australia, could not sustain most of the operations. Its remaining 737 was seized by creditors at Melbourne on 18 December 2005. With assistance from China, another 737-300 was acquired, and the airline started up again on 14 October 2006, renamed as Our Airline.

For a short while during the early 1970s, Air Nauru had provided air service from Australia to Norfolk Island as Norfolk Jet Express, but it went into voluntary liquidation on 4 June 2005. Its old network throughout the South Pacific had disappeared, replaced by the Australian newcomer, Ozjet, and Fiji's Air Pacific.

Like many a tycoon's experience in the business world, Air Nauru's success had been short-lived.

Airlines in Micronesia

There has been a certain irony about the history of air transport in what is now known as Micronesia. Before the First World War, the widely scattered Caroline Islands were part of Germany's fragmented overseas territories in the Pacific, which also included the Marianas, the Marshall Islands, northeastern New Guinea, Nauru, and Western Samoa. In1919, the terms of the Versailles Treaty awarded to Japan the custody of the Carolines, the Marianas, and the Marshalls. In 1947, they combined to become a United Nations Trust Territory, administered by the United States. With the end of hostilities, many small independent companies had seized the opportunity to provide air services between the islands with small aircraft. Most of them, for a year or two, operated from Guam to Saipan and nearby islands. In 1974, **Air Pacific** used a de Havilland Heron and a Piper Navaho, to be succeeded by Island Air in 1976 with Bandeirantes, Cessna 402s, and Nomads. **Freedom Air**, from 1978, lasted longer, first with Cessnas and Piper Cherokees then, after its fleet was wiped out by Typhoon Omar in 1992, with Shorts SD-330s and -360s. It also operated as South Pacific Express between Apia, Western Samoa, and Pago Pago, U.S. Samoa. **Air Guam** flew on the popular inter-island route to Saipan in 1984. At the same time, elsewhere in the Carolines, **Canadair Air** attempted briefly to connect Truk with the neighboring islands with PBY-5A Catalinas.

To the far west of the widespread Caroline Islands, in the late 1970s, Palau had had its own local airline, **Aero Belau**. But like all the other aspirants, local traffic was never enough to sustain them for very long. When Palau became a tiny independent nation in October 1994, however, **Palau Micronesia Air**, with support from Air New Zealand, started a Boeing 737 service to other places in Micronesia, even as far afield as Australia, on 5 August 2004. But independent ambition over-reached itself, and it ceased flying on 23 December of the same year.

Two and a half thousand miles to the east, the Marshall Islands, location of the atomic bomb experiments, were rejuvenated to peacetime conditions, and gained independence in 1986. The **Airline of the Marshall Islands (A.M.I.)** had already opened a route from Majuro, the capital, to Kwajalein and other outer islands with two 12-seat Nomads. No doubt the pilots were master navigators, in the tradition of the Marshall islanders who perfected the art of maritime navigation between the islands by closely interpreting the directions of wave movements. During the late 1980s, in addition to a HS-748 that connected Majuro to other Pacific island groups, A.M.I. leased a Douglas DC-9-62 combi (a "stretched" version of the series). With up to a hundred seats or up to nine pallets, "Little Amy" maintained, for a decade, a route to Honolulu and occasionally to Kiribati's Christmas Island.

Transcending the local short-haul companies at Guam, Palau, and the Marshalls, the whole area of Micronesia was connected by one that was necessarily supported by a major U.S. trunk airline that had ambitions for trans-Pacific service in the area. **Air Micronesia** had been formed in December 1967 by Continental Airlines (30%), the United Micronesia Development Association (60%), and the Hawaiian Aloha Airlines (10%). Before then, sporadic service had been provided by contractors to the Trust territory government with old DC-4s and Grumman SA-16 Albatross amphibians. A new contract was signed on 17 January 1968 with Continental, and "Air Mike" began service on 16 May of that year with a Boeing 727-100 to link Saipan with Honolulu via intermediate island stops, including the U.S. Johnston Island. The amphibians were retired on 2 February 1970, when Ponape built a runway for the jets on reclaimed land. Yap and Palau were added as a single route in December 1972 when a second 727 was added.

Much work was done during the 1970s to construct and improve runways throughout the territory, and with the opening of Saipan International Airport, Air Micronesia opened service to Tokyo on 1 October 1976. Thenceforward, as the president of Air Mike remarked, "Japan (became) the backbone of our

Until a jet runway was constructed at Kosrae, some 400 miles east of Ponape, service there was maintained by the Pacific Missionary air service, with Beech 18s. (Davies)

company" to such an extent that by the mid-1990s, it was carrying more than two million passengers a year, with five additional Japanese cities providing direct connections for vacationers. Boeing 737s supplemented the 727s, and such was the demand from Japanese holiday-makers that two wide-bodied 747s were leased from Continental, followed, in 1998, by four 757s. It had used Douglas DC-10s for a route to Sydney, but that service was short-lived. Continental had increased its shareholding to 91% but when it went into Chapter 11 bankruptcy in 1992, its Pacific Rim affiliate, now based at Guam, changed its name to Continental Micronesia. It had all but abandoned its former base in Saipan, where, on 1 July 2004, **Cape Air** started services in the Marianas under the banner of a Continental Connection. Like many other airlines on the Pacific Rim during this period, Air Mike reduced or cancelled services to some points, including Hong Kong, Bali, and even its first base, Saipan, this last on 15 July 2008. By this time, its fleet of 13 Boeing 737-400s and -800s was operating vigorously to eight cities in Japan.

The French Pacific Connection

During the years of territorial settlement on the islands of the Pacific by the colonial powers during the 19th century, the French flag was not planted as firmly as the British; but its footholds were just as widespread. The Society Islands of Polynesia in the southeastern part of the huge ocean were, until the advent of air transport, well off the proverbial beaten track of the air. The French independent airline **Transports Aériens Intercontinentaux (T.A.I.)** had first connected the Pacific outposts with the home country with Douglas DC-6Bs on 6 January 1956 by an extension of its Indo-China route to Nouméa, New Caledonia, and on to Auckland on 4 February 1957. Then on 28 September 1958, one week before the world's first sustained jet airliner service across the Atlantic, the piston-engined Douglas finally connected Tahiti with the rest of the world. Hitherto, this island had been known to the general public mainly through Gauguin's paintings, but now it was accessible to adventurous travelers. At that time, T.A.I. landed at the island of Bora Bora, as Tahiti had no airstrip, and the connection was made by **Reseau Aérien Interinsulaire (R.A.I.)** at first with 14-seat Consolidated Canso flying boats, and by 1960, with 30-seat Short Sandringhams. This elegant development of the pre-war 1930s design continued to make the link until 1970, and even opened service to other islands. This was almost the last scheduled service in the world by any of the large flying boats (see p. 286), and by this time, the second generation of jets, the Boeing 747, had started service across the Atlantic—a remarkable span of aeronautical design and technology.

T.A.I. took a controlling interest in R.A.I. and in October 1960, and when at last a new airport was built for Tahiti at Papeete, it supplied two DC-4s. For the short seven-minute air ferry service to Moorea, a 20-seat DHC-6 Twin Otter was introduced. To comply with customer preference and recognition, from 1 January 1970, R.A.I. operated as **Air Polynésie**, and added 40-seat Fokker F-27 turboprops, to cope with the growing popularity of the South Seas to compete with Hawaii as a tourist destination. Such popularity was stimulated by movie films. Marlon Brando bought a small island near Tahiti, while the island of Moorea became a desired destination with all the romanticism that tourists desired.

This stimulus had resulted in the founding, in 1968, of two local airlines, **Air Tahiti** and **Air Moorea**, which shared the privilege of operating a frequent air ferry service to Moorea, with 9-seat BN-2 Islanders and other small aircraft. The seven-minute flights were operated every 15 minutes throughout the day, and no reservations were needed. Air Tahiti and R.A.I. merged, and in January 1987, introduced 46-seat ATR-42s. Air Moorea was taken over on 12 April 1989, and Air Tahiti continued to prosper. In April 2007, it started an international route to Raratonga, Cook Islands, by which time the fleet had grown to 10 ATRs, including six 66-seat -72s.

A further stimulant to expanding French Polynesia as a major world tourist destination was the suspension of nuclear testing at some of the outer islands of the group in 1972. Hitherto, access to Tahiti from America, Europe, and the western Pacific

This Short Sandingham of R.A.I. was photographed in April 1970 at Huahine, an island near Tahiti. This was on one of the last flights by a large four-engined flying boat, evoking memories of an era before jet engines were invented. (Davies)

A Piper Cherokee Six of Air Moorea. (Davies)

had been by French and U.S. airlines. Now, the local territorial administration, partnered by local investors, founded **Air Tahiti Nui** (*nui* means "greater") on 31 October 1996. It opened its first long-haul route, to Los Angeles, on 20 November 1996, and two days later, to Tokyo, with a 286-seat Airbus A340. This four-engined twin-aisle airliner, which could fly 8,500 miles, was necessary for the 6,000-mile distances that had to be flown beyond the permitted ETOPS (Extended Twin-Engine Operations) range at the time for twin-engined aircraft. The single aircraft also linked Tahiti with Osaka in April 2000 and with Auckland in August 2000, code-sharing with Qantas, which was able to suspend its own Papeete-Los Angeles trans-Pacific segment. Traffic for the newcomer airline was so good that by 2004 it had four A340s and was code-sharing with Japan Airlines.

Tourism to Tahiti had been of little consequence in the early 1950s, and as narrated above, T.A.I. did not extend its eastern long-haul route across the Pacific until 1958. But two years earlier, it had reached the western Pacific, at New Caledonia. Here there were extensive deposits of chrome and nickel, among the largest in the world outside the Soviet Union, and a good reason for connection to Europe. Rather like R.A.I. in Polynesia, a local Melanesian airline was founded for local service by private interests. **Transpac–Société Caledonienne de Transports Aériens** began operations on 25 September 1955, from Nouméa, the capital, to Koumac, the mining center 200 miles away to the north of the island. During the next few years, with a fleet of de Havilland D.H. 89 Rapides, services to neighboring islands were opened, and traffic grew, to the extent that the local government assumed 70% of the capital and on 30 October 1967, renamed the company **Air Calédonie**.

Traffic grew steadily, with Nouméa becoming an airline hub for the south-western Pacific. The old biplanes were replaced by the 1980s with 19-seat DHC-6 Twin Otters and 9-seat BN-2 Islanders. Some services were made to the Wallis and Fortuna Islands, which were nearer to Fiji than any other French territories in the Pacific. Because of the closer distance to Japan, compared to Tahiti, New Caledonia became a tourist destination, and in April 2000, a leased Airbus A310, with 210 seats, started a service to Osaka, under the name **AirCalin** (short for Air Caledonia International). During the next two years, two Airbus A330s replaced the A310, services opened to Australia and New Zealand, and a 146-seat Airbus A320 added in 2004. By 2007, the tourism trade had declined; Air Calédonie was operating ATR-42s and 72s, economical 40- to 60-seat turboprop aircraft, while AirCalin maintained the connection to Paris, by cooperating with Air France via Seoul, South Korea.

Chapter 40: Canada Reorganizes

Demographic Imbalance

As mentioned in the review of the Canadian Regionals in Chapter 19, Canada's population is about the same as California's; but with an area larger than that of the 48 States, airline development problems north of the border are different—mainly related to the scale of operations. Unlike the U.S.A., which laid the foundations of four transcontinental airlines by the late 1920s, Canada did not have an airline until 1939. There were two main reasons. First, two well-established railroads provided excellent transcontinental service, without change of trains, as in the U.S. Second, the market was quite small by comparison. The well-known statistic—that 90% of Canada's population lived within 100 miles of the U.S. frontier—was compounded by the fact that two-thirds of them lived in Ontario and Quebec, wherein the two large cities, Toronto and Montreal, were only 200 miles apart, with the nation's capital, Ottawa, in between. On the Pacific coast, 3,000 miles away, Vancouver was not the metropolis that it is today, and Alberta's oil and gas riches had yet to be exploited. Canadian transcontinental air service thus had to wait until the formation of a government-promoted airline, as the only private enterprise able to provide it, the Canadian Pacific Railway, was in no hurry to do so.

Impressive State Initiative

The size and distribution of Canada's population did not thus encourage private initiatives to create a transcontinental airline. The few cities of any stature across the vast prairie states could not produce enough traffic to augment the east–west termini. The Canadian Pacific and the Canadian National railroads were so efficient that even travelers from New York to Seattle could make convenient coast-to-coast journeys via Canada. Founded in 1885, the Canadian Pacific, with its steamships, hotels, and other related investments, was an institution of worldwide fame, and the corporation had no incentive to form an airline to compete with its own railroad. Its air transport interests lay in the formation of small local airlines that fed traffic into the main rail artery. The Canadian National Railway, on the other hand, founded in 1922, became an instrument of government policy when, as much to uphold national pride as for commercial objectives, **Trans Canada Airlines (T.C.A.)** was formed on 10 April 1937, with control vested in Canadian National. It had no background of experience, no equipment, and no personnel, so that early development, though methodical, was slow. Transcontinental passenger service, with 10-seat Lockheed L-10A twins, from Montreal to Vancouver, did not start until 1 April 1939, with seven intermediate stops. It became the country's international airline during the Second World War, crossing the Atlantic as a wartime ferry service; and opening post-war scheduled service to London, with Douglas DC-4M North Stars, on 15 April 1947. In 1948, it started service to the Caribbean, which has been a lucrative winter market for chilled Canadians ever since.

The Canadian flag carrier was no sluggard as it won its wings. In 1954, its Super-Constellations matched the standards of all trans-Atlantic operators, but in the following year, it demonstrated the quality of technical leadership more emphatically on its home ground. It introduced the 44-seat Vickers Viscount

This Vickers Viscount of Trans Canada Airlines was the first turbine-powered airliner to start scheduled airline service in North America. (Dunn)

turboprop on 1 April 1955 from Montreal to Winnipeg, and three days later carried the maple leaf flag to New York. T.C.A. was the first airline to operate a turbine-powered airliner in North America. Capital Airlines did not start its Viscount service until the end of July, so that—stretching the definition a little—Canada had beaten the United States into the Jet Age. It eventually had a fleet of 51 of these airliners, and intensified its cross-border services to New York to 10 flights each day from both Toronto and Montreal, and twice daily from Ottawa.

For its international routes (only the trans-Atlantic and to the Caribbean—the reasons for this limitation are narrated below) and its long-distance domestic flights, T.C.A. continued to operate its Constellations until 1960, when its first Douglas DC-8-40s (Rolls-Royce Conway engines) entered service, transcontinental to Vancouver on 1 April and trans-Atlantic on 1 June. 107-seat Vickers Vanguards were introduced on a stopping service to Vancouver on 1 February 1961 and to the Caribbean on 1 April. The North Stars were retired on 30 June of that year.

In 1962 T.C.A. reported a deficit of $12 million, the largest in its history, partly because of the change in the fare structure. In 1960, more than half of its passengers had been business-class, but this declined abruptly to only a fifth in 1961. More emphasis was placed on freight revenue, and on 1 March 1963, a DC-8F Jet Trader was claimed to be the first specially built dual-purpose aircraft in the world to go into service. It could carry 87 passengers and 40,000 lb. of freight in six pallets. On 15 April 1963 T.C.A. transferred much of its route network in the prairie provinces to a local airline, Transair, thus relieving itself of loss-sustaining obligations, and incidentally releasing the last of its veteran Douglas DC-3s.

One bright spot during the early 1960s occurred on 13 October 1964, when T.C.A. flew Queen Elizabeth II from Ottawa to London. This was the first time a non-U.K. airline enjoyed this privilege. Shortly thereafter, in a move to identify its national airline more emphatically, its name was changed to **Air Canada**. Operationally, the next two decades were steady, if not spectacular. The first 72-seat Douglas DC-9 jet went into service on 4 April 1966, and the airline subsequently acquired a large fleet. Part of the transaction involved the partial manufacture of the airliner in Canada. International routes were augmented by additional destinations in the Caribbean; service to Miami on 1 June 1966, following a new U.S.–Canada air agreement; and direct flights to Moscow on 1 November of that year.

Back at headquarters, managerial changes were anything but steady. Since its inception as T.C.A., Air Canada had been directed by Gordon McGregor, who (rather like Pan American's Juan Trippe) had controlled a centralized administration, of which he was both the chief executive and chief operating officer. In the late 1960s, Yves Pratte replaced McGregor. He decentralized management dramatically, to include no less than 22 vice presidents. Orders were placed for wide-bodied airliners: Boeing 747s, which went into service early in 1971, and Lockheed L-1011s, in the summer of 1973. A DC-8 explosion, because of the rupture of a fuel line, on 5 July 1970 at Toronto, was a set-back for an airline whose safety record has been close to immaculate throughout its history; but to compensate, in the winter of 1971, the "Sun Living" program promoted more travel to the Caribbean, while the "Rapidair" service introduced a high frequency timetable between Toronto and Montreal.

An unusual cause for fame (or notoriety) was achieved on 23 July 1983, mainly because of the risk involved in adopting the metric system. A Boeing 767, on a flight from Ottawa, ran out of fuel when only halfway to Edmonton. By a splendid display of airmanship (even though he was reprimanded for failing to spot the problem earlier by inspection), the pilot, Captain Pearson, managed to land the aircraft safely at Gimli, a small airfield in Manitoba. The incident has gone down in the annals of air transport history as "The Gimli Glider."

The year 1988 was one of sweeping changes. In July, Air Canada ordered 34 Airbus A320s (with 20 more on option) to replace much of its ageing fleet, going into service in January 1990. The Public Participation Act in August 1988 led to almost half of its shares being sold to the public, for $246 million; and in June 1989, the 57% balance, then worth $530 million, completed the process of privatization. No longer a direct instrument of the Ottawa government, the Canadian national airline had more freedom for commercial negotiations at any level.

Canada's Second Force

Few airlines in the world have been founded under such unusual circumstances as the one that became **Canadian Pacific Airlines (C.P.A.)**. No less than five years after the founding of Trans Canada Airlines, C.P.A. began as an adjunct to the railway. On 1 July 1942 that company, which had hitherto held shares in small companies (e.g., Canadian Airways and Mackenzie Air Service), announced the formation of C.P.A. It integrated the assets and operations of these two (already merged as United Aircraft Services) with eight more small prairie/bush operators, having already brought their employees onto the Canadian Pacific payroll. One of these was Yukon Southern Airlines, which operated to Canada's far northwest, and whose president was Grant McConachie.

The population of the Yukon and the Northwest territories combined was less than 20,000 of Canada's post-war 14 million. The potential for the future in this direction was dependent on connections at only a few mining centers, which did not suit McConachie's ambitions. Drawing from his familiarity with the Yukon's proximity to Alaska, and with memories of wartime activities, he had become aware of the importance of a route to Japan that, via the Yukon and/or Alaska, was shorter (by the "great circle" itinerary) than the traditional mid-Pacific route via Hawaii. With the merger, he had become the assistant vice-president, C.P.A.'s Western Lines, and he campaigned to expand the company's ambitions beyond that of the bush services. In 1948, he received a grant from Canada's Air Transport Board to open service to Tokyo by the great circle route. It was conditional on operating with DC-4M North Stars and had to serve the South Pacific as well. Accordingly, on 13 July 1949, 36-seat unpressurized North

Canadian Pacific introduced long-range Bristol Britannia turboprops on its intercontinental air routes. (Dunn)

Stars started services from Vancouver to Sydney, Australia, and to Hong Kong via Tokyo. The former route involved refueling overnight in Honolulu, and at Canton Island and Fiji. The latter, on 19 September 1949, also landed at Shanghai, coinciding with the Communist takeover of the Chinese government.

The curious aspect of this, the beginning of a new era in Canadian air transport, was that McConachie gained his trans-Pacific franchise by default. T.C.A. was the government's "chosen instrument" and should have been awarded the route. But at the time, T.C.A. did not believe that the routes would generate enough traffic to be commercially viable. To compete with the pressurized DC-6s of B.C.P.A. (British Commonwealth Pacific Airlines, jointly owned by the governments of Australia, Canada, and Great Britain), C.P.A. ordered two de Havilland Comet 1A jets and four Douglas DC-6Bs as insurance. The caution was justified. En route to Australia to inaugurate the trans-Pacific route, the first Comet crashed at Karachi on 3 March 1953, and so the 6Bs entered service in April.

On 17 October of that year, C.P.A. also started a route to Lima, Peru, via Mexico City, and such was the confidence in de Havilland that in November it ordered three long-range Comet IIs. But once again, crashes in the Mediterranean early in 1954 put an end to the Comet story until 1958. Undaunted, McConachie applied for a trans-Polar route to Europe, and was granted one to Amsterdam, which was duly opened on 4 June 1955. In September, a Toronto-Mexico City service connected Canada's east, as well as the west, with South America; on 16 May 1956, the Lima service was extended to Buenos Aires; and on 23 September 1957, to Santiago. In Europe, service to Lisbon began on 30 May 1957, and extended (until 1976) to Madrid.

Canadian Pacific's map of international routes therefore appeared most impressive. But to some extent, T.C.A.'s conservative approach may have been wise, as it carried far more passengers across the Atlantic and to the Caribbean than did C.P.A. on all its routes. Chairman Gordon McGregor (see above) was reluctant to take risks with the taxpayers' money. McConachie was willing to take a gamble and backed his intuition with a talent for convincing rhetoric. In 1958, he attempted to start a Canadian transcontinental route in direct and equal competition with T.C.A. On the recommendation of the British aviation economist Stephen Wheatcroft, however, he received permission to operate only one daily flight, and this was not nonstop. By this time, to compensate for the loss of the Comets, he had ordered the long-range 89-seat Bristol Britannia turboprops. They started C.P.A. service on 1 June 1958, Vancouver-Amsterdam, and the *Canadian Empress* service, Vancouver-Winnipeg-Toronto-Montreal, on 4 May 1959.

During this period of international expansion, the airline gradually abandoned the local and bush routes that had been its foundation back in 1942. Services in the Gulf of St. Lawrence went to Rimouski in 1948, those in Manitoba and Saskatchewan

By a combination of visionary initiative and opportunism, Grant McConachie developed Canadian Pacific Airlines into a worldwide system, serving five continents.

to Transair in 1957, and the Mackenzie River routes to Pacific Western in 1959. Internationally, Rome was added to the European services on 5 March 1960. Douglas DC-8 jets replaced the trans-Atlantic Britannias on 31 May 1961 and on transcontinental routes on 1 June.

In the spring of 1964, Canada's minister of transport confirmed permanent recognition of the two international airlines' spheres of influence, as operated. McConachie died on 29 June 1965, after an action-filled career. His final effort was, on 25 February, to place a deposit on three U.S. supersonic airliners. On 30 January 1967, a Vancouver-San Francisco route gave direct cross-border access to California. In January 1968, the larger, long-range Douglas DC-8-63 "Spacemasters" began to arrive, and Athens was added to the southern European network on 9 September 1968. In that year, partly to avoid confusion with the abbreviation for Hong Kong's Cathay Pacific Airlines, C.P.A. became **CP Air**.

All went well during the 1970s. The international network was strengthened by extensions to Tel Aviv and the Azores. These were later suspended in favor of Milan, Vancouver-Los Angeles, and three additional points in Mexico, which made a profitable exchange despite labor problems in Mexico City. In 1976, DC-10s were flying nonstop from Vancouver to Lima, 5,000 miles (the longest route on the network and, at that time, one of the longest in the world). Domestically, in March 1967, the government had authorized the airline to operate 25% of the transcontinental schedules, and steady progress was made to reduce the imbalance versus Air Canada. On 1 June 1979, a "no frills" SkyBus service began from Toronto to the British Columbia and Alberta cities, but this ended on 14 December 1981. Internationally, in contrast, a high-yield full-fare economy-level Empress Class was introduced on 26 October 1980.

In a reflection of the manner in which Canadian Pacific Airlines had been born, attention was drawn, during the early 1980s, toward embracing local service airlines. On 24 April 1983, schedules were integrated with Eastern Provincial Airways (E.P.A.), and on 3 October with AirBC. E.P.A. was purchased, together with its affiliate, Air Maritime, on 31 August 1984. Canadian airline deregulation opened the doors for free enterprise. Further additions to the list of what was now termed CP Commuters, were Air Atlantic on 28 February 1986, Norcanair in April, and Nordair Metro on 12 May. Canadian airline deregulation had cleared the way for the spirit of free enterprise to break clear of innumerable restrictions. Additions to the map included a return to Victoria, B.C. (after a 36-year absence), a brief return to Regina and Saskatoon, and more important, a direct service from Vancouver to Shanghai, to take advantage of the improvement in China's growing openness to foreign airlines. These were the last changes to be made under the CP Air name.

On 2 December 1986, after months of rumors, the well-established local service airline, Pacific Western Airlines (P.W.A.), purchased CP Air for C$300 million and promptly renamed it **Canadian Airlines International (C.A.I.)**, after a brief interlude when CP Air had itself reverted to Canadian Pacific, with Canadien Pacifique inscribed on the right side of the aircraft.

The combined fleet numbered 12 Douglas DC-10s and 75 Boeing 737s. One of C.A.I.'s first moves was to buy Nordair, abolishing the name then to tidy up the list of commuters to Time Air (Lethbridge, Alberta), Calm Air (Thompson, Manitoba), Quebecair and Metroliner (Quebec), and Air Atlantic (St. John's, Newfoundland).

Further rationalization came in 1989, when, for C$210 million, the parent corporation, P.W.A., purchased Wardair (see later in this chapter) whose extensive (formerly charter, now scheduled) network, especially to the U.K. and Europe, was integrated with Canadian's (see below). This gave it access to London, Paris, and Frankfurt. The fleet was upgraded to Airbus A320s, Boeing 767-300ERs, and 747-400s. Expansion came at a cost. Wardair had incurred C$595 million debt; then came the Gulf War, and in 1992 alone, Canadian lost C$543 million. With Air Canada also suffering financially, serious discussions were held toward the idea of a complete merger. But after a preliminary agreement on 8 October 1992, Air Canada withdrew on 3 November. The battle lines were drawn up. P.W.A./Canadian revived the idea of an alliance with American Airlines, with A.A. taking a 25% shareholding, and planned to sue Air Canada for predatory pricing. On 29 December, in what was described as "an unparalleled style of aggressiveness," the AMR Corporation (A.A.) agreed to invest $196 million in Canadian for a 34% share (but only 25% voting rights). A deal was finally signed on 27 April 1994. Canadian was saved from bankruptcy by the conversion of C$700 million debt into equity; wage concessions of C$200 million; C$246 capital injection from AMR; and withdrawal from Air Canada's Gemini computer system for AMR's Sabre.

A new U.S.–Canada bilateral agreement was signed on 24 February 1995 and opened up the hitherto restricted frontier to expand cross-border traffic by airlines of both countries. Canadian received most of the available slots at Chicago and New York; the U.S. was restricted at Montreal, Toronto, and Vancouver, but only for three years. Canadians were suddenly given access to almost any major city the United States. With Toronto as its main hub, Air Canada was able to expand far more than Canadian, which nevertheless was able to turn a C$187 million loss in 1996 into a modest C$5.4 million profit in 1997. One contribution was the addition, on 28 October 1996, of Manila, and on 26 October 1997, of Fiji, to augment the Pacific network.

A Major Merger

The first indications of a proposed merger between Air Canada and C.A.I. came on 24 August 1999, when Toronto's Onex Corporation (in which American Airlines's AMR had invested C$335 million) bid C$1.8 billion to acquire Air Canada. On 6 August Robert Milton had succeeded R. Lamar Durrett as Air Canada's president. Patriotically viewing the offer as an example of United States presumed control over its northern neighbor, he had Onex's offer declared illegal, and, on 4 December, recruited Star Alliance to bid C$1.8 billion on Air Canada's behalf in retaliation. The Canadian Airlines shareholders recommended approval of the Air Canada offer, an action which

A Canadian Bombardier CRJ-200 ER of Jazz, Air Canada's regional subsidiary. (McDonough)

Milton summarized as "ending 62 years of duplication and losses." Now with a fleet of 243 aircraft, the inevitable consolidation process led to thousands of layoffs from the 40,000 staff, and the threat of strikes by the unions. But now, in terms of productivity, among the top 20 airlines of the world, the amalgamated company set about coming to terms with the new market forces that had developed while the two former companies had been conducting their high-level wrangling.

One of the forces was the demonstrated success of the policy of bargain-fare offers to the public in exchange for reductions of on-board amenities to a minimum. On 1 October 2001, Air Canada introduced **Tango**, as a wholly owned affiliate, to charge C$99 (or US$63) one way for the busy Toronto-Montreal segment, a 60% reduction in the economy rate. In April 2002, it announced Zip, which, by the time it started 737-200 operations on 22 August 2002, Air Canada had completed the consolidation of the regional airlines that it had taken under its wings: AirBC, Air Nova, Air Ontario, and Canadian Regional. Favoring short and eye-catching names, this commuter-style group was named **Jazz**.

By guiding Air Canada through troubled waters, Milton did not, however, emerge high and dry. The long-delayed merger hardly had time to work out its consolidation problems when the airline world was plunged into shock by the 11 September 2001 terrorist aircraft disasters in the United States. The price of jet fuel rose, the war in Iraq affected world airline traffic, and the SARS outbreak in east Asia wrecked the air routes across the Pacific. On 3 April 2003, the airline filed for bankruptcy in both the Canadian and U.S. courts. Once again, Milton fought back. He negotiated a refinancing debtor-in-possession deal with the banks, worth C$700 million, and in June—with both sides in desperation mood—persuaded the pilots' unions to a new contract that was worth as much. In November, Victor Y.K. Li, a Hong Kong businessman and Canadian citizen, offered a more than C$500 million investment into Air Canada. On 19 December, now with solid equity, 90 commuter aircraft were ordered from Bombardier and Embraer, and on 1 October 2004, the airline emerged from bankruptcy, after a refinancing package worth C$1.1 billion.

The pattern of alternative ups and downs of Air Canada's career continued. An order on 25 April 2005 for 96 Boeings, including the new 787 Dreamliner project, suggested confidence in the future. But in January 2008, partial ownership of Jazz was released, and the year-end financial picture was discouraging—a loss of about C$1 million. Milton became the president of ACE Aviation Holdings, the parent company of the airline, and handed over Air Canada's fate to others. As in the United States, Europe, Australia, and throughout Asia, another threat had made itself emphatically known: the traveling public's demand for cheap fares, rather than additional on-board amenities.

The role of **Pacific Western Airlines (P.W.A.)** in the consolidation of Canada's air transport industry has been outlined above. Of the five regional airlines that had been officially authorized to develop local hub networks, it was the only one whose stature matched the Local Service airlines south of the border. Its strength was derived partly because surface transport in the mountainous terrain of British Columbia and Alberta was necessarily slow; and partly because the natural resources of the region, derived from oil, gas, and minerals, promoted the need for air transport and which could be met by growing discretionary income.

In 1963, for example, having already absorbed some of Canadian Pacific's local routes in 1957, it had introduced its Chieftain Airbus non-reservation service between Calgary and Edmonton, based on the successful Eastern Airlines Shuttle and the Brazilian Rio de Janeiro-São Paulo pioneer of that system. By 1969, P.W.A. was carrying 250,000 a year on this route alone, and by 1984, the service ran at 15 flights a day. This regional airline had become, at least in western Canada, a force to be reckoned with.

It did more than simply expand its passenger route network. During the early 1970s, four Lockheed L-100 Hercules freighters were doing good business all round the world, carrying electronics from Japan, and cattle (dehydrated for the journey) in the reverse direction. Another innovation, in 1976, to circumvent its failure to obtain a Canadian transcontinental route to Toronto, was to offer "charters" to Buffalo, across the U.S. border, and bus the passengers free to their Ontario destinations. By this time, the Alberta provincial government had bought P.W.A., and moved the headquarters to Calgary. In 1977 it bought Transair, another regional, based at Winnipeg, to extend its operating area across the prairie states. In 1989, flights under the P.W.A. name ceased, but the parent company bought Wardair (see above).

P.W.A.'s apparent vision of challenging Air Canada's major share of the nation's airline business developed into a series of

By 1990, Pacific Western, one of Canada's early regionals, had become a national airline, by an astute series of purchases of other airlines. This is one of its Boeing 737s. (Bentley)

financial maneuvers that led to the full integration with CP Air. Purchase of that prestigious airline on 2 December 1986 was an historic achievement. The long-drawn-out process of the subsequent merger with Air Canada is summarized earlier in this chapter. Air Canada had taken over the substantial innovative airline interests from the west, and this could have resulted in a monopoly. Many new small companies had arisen from the ashes of the regional group of five that had been absorbed by CP Air and Air Canada in the 1970/80s, but they were not a threat.

Canada Gets a Third Force

One new airline appeared to repeat what Canada's third largest airline, P.W.A., might have done, had it not pursued a different course by taking over Canada's second largest, and merging with Air Canada. Whether by neglect, misjudgment, or bad management, the new and apparently all-powerful Air Canada overlooked a trend that was beginning to emerge in air transport throughout the world. Just across the border to the south, bargain-fare airlines were no longer on the margins of the industry. Led by Southwest, they were demonstrating that the traveling public, given the choice between more comfortable (and more costly) seats or a discount on the fare, they preferred the latter. The airline that offered these, even without a meal, turned in a profit because more seats were filled at less expense.

In western Canada, following in the wake of P.W.A., this trend was observed close at hand by a local real estate developer, Clive Beddoe. Disliking the habit of paying $600 to fly from Vancouver to Calgary, he decided to form an airline. With three other investors, and with advice from David Neeleman, of Morris Air (a successful bargain-fare U.S. airline), he enlisted enough capital from the Ontario Teachers Fund to form **WestJet**, which began a deeply discounted service on 29 February 1996, with three leased 120-seat Boeing 737-200s from Vancouver to Calgary and Edmonton. Concentrating on efficient, if not luxurious, service, and with a profit-sharing policy for the staff, it was off to a good start, but most observers expected it to follow the fate of other contemporary aspirants, and collapse after a few months. The regulatory authority, Transport Canada, did not help, threatening to suspend its operating license because of unacceptable maintenance records. Beddoe shut down the airline for 17 days to correct the paperwork. To everyone's surprise, Westjet carried 760,000 passengers in the first year, and made a small profit.

This upstart maverick then acted decisively on two fronts. Many years previously, the U.S. Civil Aeronautics Board (C.A.B.) had introduced a "use it or lose it" policy to ensure adequate support from individual communities to support the Local Serice airlines. Beddoe now did the same at a different level. He started service to Winnipeg, but when that city appeared to lack enthusiasm for Westjet, he transferred the service to Regina and Saskatoon. Victoria and Kelowna were added, and Winnipeg returned to the fold in March 1999. He also drew upon a precedent set by Southwest in the U.S., and airlines in Europe: Westjet developed Abbotsford, an outer suburb of Vancouver, 45 miles to the east, thus avoiding congestion at the city's main airport, and guaranteeing on-time departures. By the end of that year, new routes to the north of British Columbia and to Thunder Bay, Ontario, were being served by a dozen 737s, after a public offering had been made in July. Coincidentally, further encouragement stemmed from Air Canada's taking over Canadian (see above), and the demise of three small start-ups, CanJet and Royal (sold to Canada 3000), and Roots, which lasted only 39 days.

Clearly aspiring to become a transcontinental airline, and now under a more deregulated administration, WestJet moved further eastward, once again employing the satellite airport device to gain access to Canada's biggest city and airline market, Toronto. In March 2000, it opened service to Hamilton, 45 miles away, and offered free bus connection to downtown Toronto. A month later, the Dominion capital, Ottawa, and Moncton, New Brunswick, completed a coast-to-coast network. By this time, the 737 fleet had grown to 23, and WestJet was on the crest of a wave. In September 2000, it ordered 26 140-seat Boeing 737-700s, leased 10 more, and took options for 58 more (at $42 million each). The first -700 delivery on 25 May 2001 heralded transcontinental nonstops from Alberta to Hamilton and Saskatchewan to Ottawa.

There was no stopping WestJet. By the end of 2003, Montreal and Newfoundland were on the map, and with the new trans-border liberalization, seven cities in the U.S.A. were added in 2004. The 737 fleet grew to more than 50, with 20 more on order. The airline seemed to do everything right. Then, in November, just after starting service to sunny Florida, an anonymous telephone revealed that it had done something very wrong. Air Canada and Jetsgo alleged that a WestJet executive had obtained access to Air Canada's web site, and had obtained detailed information—in 243,630 computer bytes, no less—of his rival's traffic. WestJet could use Air Canada's route statistics for its own planning. This example of industrial espionage did not go unpunished. The plaintiffs sued for C$220 million damages, and settled, on 29 May 2006, for C$5.5 million in costs, and C$10 million donation to charities.

WestJet admitted that its methods were unethical and unacceptable, and although it failed to make its customary profit in 2004, it went about its business. Public condemnation of WestJet's ethical misconduct was not harsh, possibly because it simultaneously offered cheap flights to Nassau, Bahamas, to penetrate Air Canada's monopoly of the winter season Caribbean-bound vacation traffic. More destinations to the south followed in 2007, and a route to Hawaii started in 2009, with 166-seat Boeing 737-800s. By the end of 2009 its fleet was approaching 100, mostly the latest variants of that hugely successful airliner. It had grown to serve 34% of the Canadian domestic market and 11% of the transborder traffic into the U.S. It was serving every large or mid-sized city in Canada, 17 in the U.S.A., six in Mexico, and 14 in the Caribbean-Mexico region, including three in Cuba. Its operating costs were 36% lower per employee than Air Canada's, which supported its claim to be the most profitable airline in the whole of North America.

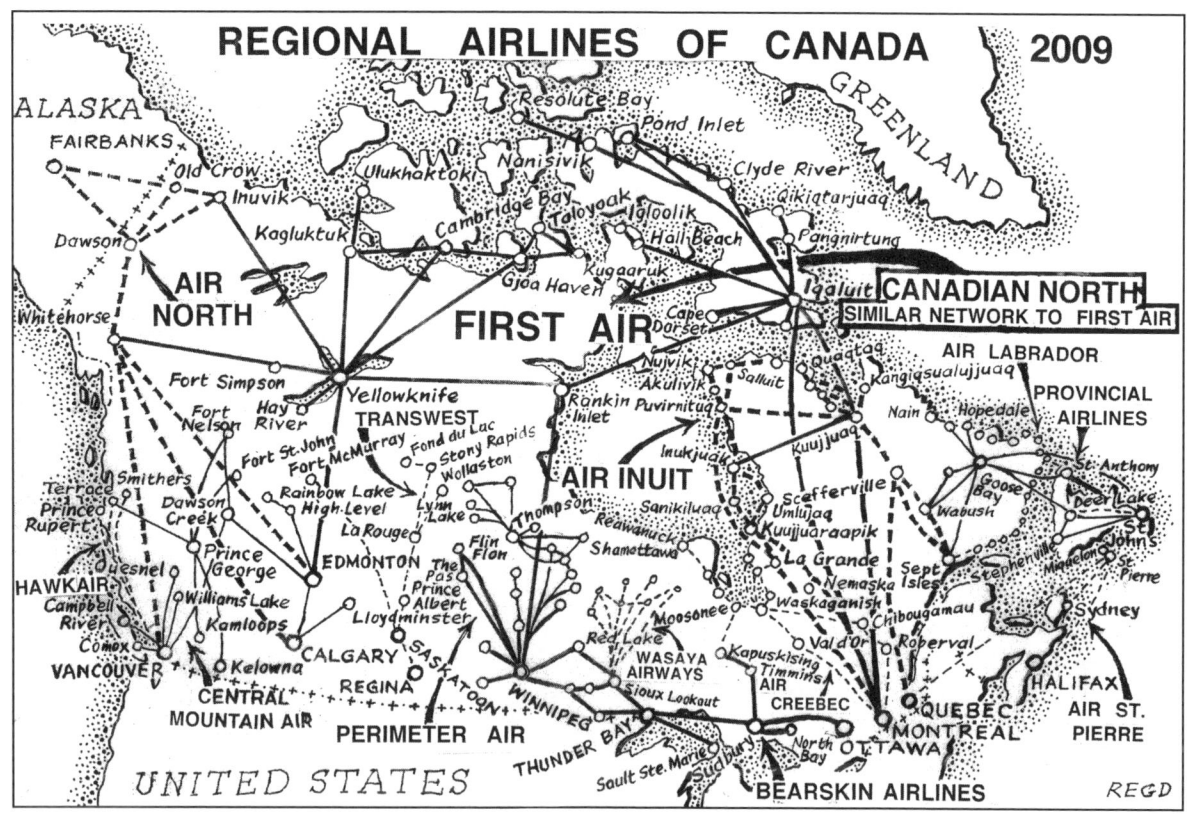

The route patterns of the local service airlines, founded at the end of the 20th century and afterward, were remarkably similar to those of the earlier Canadian locals.

An Industry of Many Parts

Throughout its history, Canada's peoples have been divided sharply between the sparsely populated north, the moderately populated southern prairie provinces, and the more densely populated eastern provinces with the country's two mega-cities, Toronto and Montreal. As the 20th century progressed, British Columbia, centered on Vancouver, gained in stature, and by the 21st century, the oil and gas industry in Alberta stimulated Calgary and Edmonton's population growth. But in the Yukon and in the Northwest Territories (NWT), where gold and other mineral resources, including uranium, were sporadically mined, there was little incentive for urban growth. Even by 2000, NWT's capital, Yellowknife, was a town of barely 20,000 people.

Nevertheless, because very few places enjoyed the convenience of roads, much less railroads, air transport was at a premium, as the only way to travel was by boat on the rivers and lakes in the summer or by dog-sled in the winter. In the mid-1920s, a few bush pilots began to offer air transport services. They were a special breed, flying their aircraft into poorly laid gravel strips or, preferably, on to lakes, big and small. Some of them established routes that could be identified as regular (but seldom qualifying as scheduled) services. The most successful of these were absorbed into what became Canadian Pacific Airlines.

The post-war years witnessed a surge of aviation activity on three main fronts. The de Havilland company in Canada produced a series of sturdy aircraft, designed especially for the northern wilderness, or the frozen north; the end of the war released a surfeit of pilots to fly the aircraft; and to ensure safety and the proper conduct in commercial aviation affairs, the Canadian government enforced—or tried to enforce—regulations. Operating certificates were in nine categories of carriers. Those affecting the bush pilots and their companies were (1) Scheduled; (2) Regular specific point air carriers, serving "with some degree of regularity"; (3) Irregular specific points from a designated base; and (4) Charter. Other classifications were (5) Contractors; (6) Flying Clubs; (7) Speciality purposes—training, photography, mapping, advertising, surveying, etc.; (8) International scheduled; and (9) International non-scheduled.

As the United States' C.A.B. discovered in Alaska when it tried to apply strict standards, aviation in the north did not necessarily fit a formula. During the fierce winters, scheduling to a timetable, day-in, day-out (#1) was impossible; while in the summer, many an on-demand, irregular, or charter, service (#2, #3, and #4) often resolved into a de facto schedule, as the aircraft tended to fly each day at the same time between the same points. The rules and regulations were characterized more by their omission than by their observation, and to its credit, the regulators in faraway Ottawa seemed to overlook infringements in favor of the unwritten "common sense" category.

The bush operators in the north grew out of pre-war conditions of expediency, when many a flight had too often become an adventure. The national trunk airlines, T.C.A. and Canadian Pacific, kept pace with their powerful neighbors to the south, but at the same time contracted with the small companies in the north, which were still obliged to operate into dirt strips. During the 1970s, the market as a whole had grown to justify the introduction of regional airlines (see Chapter 19). They did more than simply provide connections from the north to the main transcontinental airline arteries in the south. The Canadian de Havilland DHC-2 Beaver and the DHC-3 Otter became workhorses to replace the dozens of small pre-war types (except, of course, the Douglas DC-3, which resisted oblivion, even into the 21st century). When the Jet Age arrived, they were supplemented by turbine-engined turboprops. The most popular of these was the Avro, later Hawker-Siddeley, 748, which could not only take-off and land from most of the dirt strips; its Rolls-Royce Dart engines would start at temperatures as low as minus 40° Fahrenheit—when piston engines seldom could.

The ubiquitous operations of the small Canadian airlines at the dawn of the Jet Age, including the bush-pilot survivors, are listed in the tabulation, and a few warrant special mention. Prominent in the east for many years was **Austin Airways.** Founded in 1934 at Timmins, in northern Ontario, it was able to operate scheduled services in 1958. By the 1970s, it could justly claim to be the oldest continuously operated airline in Canada.

Its workhorse fleet grew from the small bush aircraft, via DC-3s and 11 DHC-6 Twin Otters, to 14 Hawker-Siddeley 748s. Its routes reached as far north as Cape Dorset, Baffin Island, and as far south, across the border, to Minneapolis and Cleveland. It bought Stan Deluce's White River Air Service in 1973, and other small operators including Superior Airways in 1981. It merged with **Air Ontario**, based in London, in June 1987, and under that name made a different claim: "Canada's largest regional"—which with 53 aircraft altogether, including Cessna 402s, Convair 580s, and Fokker 28s was probably correct. In 2001, it became part of Air Canada's Jazz.

A challenger to Austin for its "oldest" claim would be **Wheeler Airlines**, from St. Jovite, Quebec. Starting regular services in 1957, including charters to Europe with DC-4s, it had 42 aircraft (including Cansos and helicopters) and advertised as the "oldest air service in Canada." Far away to the northwest, beyond the Territories, **Air North**, founded on 1 February 1977 and based in Whitehorse, was promoted as "Yukon's Airline." Its fleet included the usual DC-3s, a DC-4, HS-748s, and a Boeing 737-200. Along with Air Ontario, **Air BC** was another small operator that was eventually taken over by Air Canada into its regional Jazz affiliate. Founded in Vancouver on 1 November 1980, it was adopted by CP Air on 3 October 1983 then by Air Canada on 26 April 1987, followed by Jazz on 27 March 2002. It specialized in flying throughout British Columbia, to the fishing lakes and especially to the offshore islands. It had more than 100 small aircraft, mostly floatplanes. Incidentally, it should not be confused with **B.C. Airlines**, from 1953, which became part of Pacific Western, when that airline began its expansion (see above). It too had a claim to aviation fame. It was the first (and for many years claimed to be) "the only Canadian airline to carry a reigning British monarch." In the late 1950s, when Queen Elizabeth II was touring Canada, she took a much-needed break and flew with B.C. Airlines to one of the lakes, to be "away from it all."

Other small Canadian airlines were hardly bush operators. **CanJet Airlines**, from Halifax, was one of the discount-fare companies, starting in April 2000. Its fleet of six Boeing 737s connected all the major cities as far west as Winnipeg. It succumbed to the fierce competition in September 2006. **First Air**, founded as Bradley Air Services, also has a modern fleet that not only included DC-3s, Twin Otters, and 748s, but also ATR-72s, Boeing 737s, and 727s, but even a Lockheed Hercules heavy freighter. It took over Ptarmigan Air and NWT Air. Its network extended as far north as Iqaluit, formerly Frobisher Bay, of Second World War and DEW-Line memory, and further north to Resolute Bay.

Canadian Charters

The Canadian non-scheduled or charter airline industry has not been as clearly regulated into specific categories as in the United States, where Large Irregular Carriers became Supplemental Carriers, many of which moved into scheduled operations. One Canadian charter company, however, was a true success story, even though it was eventually sold to the Pacific Western corporation.

After wartime service with the Canadian Air Force, Maxwell Ward was, in 1945, a highly skilled pilot. He tried his luck as a bush pilot, and formed Polaris Charter at Yellowknife, NWT, which became a partnership, Yellowknife Airways, which lasted until 1949. He then formed **Wardair**, with a new DHC-3 Otter, and obtained his Air Transport Board operating license on 6 June 1953. For a few years, with a Bristol 170 Freighter from 1957, he then added, in 1961, a 91-seat Douglas DC-6A, which he also used mainly for freighting in the north.

This acquisition coincided with the Transport Board's decision to extend the international charter authority to include "affinity rules," allowing charter airlines to carry whole airplane loads of members of approved organizations. Late that year, Ward changed the name of his airline to **Wardair Canada**, and began to operate flights to Europe. Refueling at Sondre Stromfjord, Greenland, the DC-6A took 19 hours each way, but the on-board service was better than any of the other trans-Atlantic charter airlines. Such was his reputation that by 1963, with a DC-6B bought from K.L.M., the flights were always full, and by 1995, the airline carried almost 6,000 satisfied customers across the Atlantic. Ward was still serving the north, and replaced a fleet of DHC-2 Beavers and DHC-3 Otters with DHC-6 Twin Otters.

In 1966, Ward leased a 119-seat Boeing 727-100, to enter the Jet Age. Flying from Vancouver to London, with stops, this was the first crossing of the Atlantic with a Boeing 727. The flight took almost 10 hours, but the fare was half of the International Air Transport Association (IATA) airlines' tourist class. Traffic doubled to 12,000 passengers, which led to Wardair buying a

This Air Canada Airbus A321 celebrated the airline's 70th birthday, when it was Trans Canada Airlines. (McDonough)

183-seat Boeing 707-320C in 1968 and a second one in 1969. In 1970, the veteran fleet of four Bristol Freighters was reduced to two, but not before one of them landed on smooth ice at the North Pole in May 1967.

In that year, Maxwell Ward's popularity with the air-traveling public brought him much support when he experienced "difficulties" with the government over problems with insurance coverage. His fares were 61% below IATA's. For example, in the summer peak season, Wardair's Toronto-London round-trip was C$223 versus C$574 IATA economy, or C$342 excursion. But it lost money in 1970, and fares were raised by 10%. In 1973, realizing along with other countries that the affinity rules were subject to abuse, "ABC" (Advanced Booking Charters) was adopted by the government. Wardair took delivery of its first 456-seat Boeing 747 on 2 May.

Ward still remembered his personal heritage, and developed his base at Yellowknife, but his battle with authorities continued, and they denied his application to establish bases at Inuvik and Norman Wells in the Northern Territories. Yet Wardair was expanding. On 1 December 1975, Wardair Jamaica was registered to operate a beach hotel, and in 1976, other subsidiaries of the parent company were added: Wardair (U.K.) and International Vacations. In the company's annual report of 1976, Max Ward complained about the bureaucracy that restricted his business, such as the amount of paperwork needed for the 60-day ABCs, and rules that fixed the points of origin, denied mixing inclusive tour loads with ABCs, or Canadians with foreign passengers. His views may have born fruit, as in the late 1970s, regulations were eased considerably. In 1977, Wardair's trans-Atlantic charters were flown from the seven main Canadian cities to destinations in Europe, U.S.A., the Caribbean, Mexico, Hawaii, and South America. It moved into an extensive new base at Edmonton, and Ward ordered two more 747s and two Douglas DC-10s. Nevertheless, many Canadian restrictions still applied, and travelers often chose to fly by U.S. charter airlines.

On 16 October 1979, after more than 30 years of association with the bush-flying areas of northern Canada, the Northern Division of Wardair closed down, partly because operations related to a pipeline project were reduced when the project was abandoned. Mining also decreased. So all the small aircraft were sold, but at last, in November 1979, the Canadian Transport Commission removed all the restrictions that Ward had complained about three years earlier. By the end of that year, the Toronto-London route was being flown every day, and in 1980, Wardair participated in the Hajj pilgrimage market, from Cairo to Jeddah. More important, on 8 May of that year, with domestic charters now permitted, the airline inaugurated flights between all major cities of Canada. With a fleet of four 747s and three DC-10s, the world network matched those of the two scheduled airlines, especially to the U.K., where Belfast, Birmingham, and Newcastle were served as well as London.

Disagreements with the authorities still simmered, and the world economic recession of the early 1980s affected the charter airlines more than their scheduled rivals, because of the low revenues from the low-fare market. Wardair lost more than C$10 million in 1981 and in 1982. On 22 February 1984, Ward submitted recommendations to the Air Transport Committee. In effect, they were a protest against the two-airline policy and the designated regionals, of which only Eastern Provincial was completely independent of government support. On 10 May, the Ministry of Transport announced major policy changes, removing all restrictions on both scheduled and charter airlines. Wardair added Dusseldorf and Rome in Europe, Liverpool and Cardiff in Britain, and San Juan in the U.S.A., Los Angeles having already opened the California market in 1983. On 9 May 1985, Max Ward's airline was officially designated as Canada's second carrier to Britain, and it started scheduled services to London and Manchester in December.

Ward had come a long way, quickly. Within three years, since 1982, when his airline carried barely 700 passengers across the Atlantic, it now carried hundreds of thousands annually. The clientèle enjoyed meals on Royal Doulton china. In 1984 Wardair made a record profit of C$50 million, and one writer observed that the incumbent airlines would have nothing to fear from the new levels of efficiency that were being forced upon them. Alas, these had come at a high cost because of Ward's policy of high on-board standards in spite of low fares. In 1988, in a case of "the higher they climb, the harder they fall," Wardair lost C$119 million. The end was in sight. On 18 January 1989, as narrated above, the Pacific Western Corporation, now owner of the former CP Air, bought Wardair for C$210 million.

Canada's two-airline policy—modified in 1986 to a one-airline policy when P.W.A. merged Canadian and Air Canada; then modified again back to a two-airline policy for a short time after Wardair's elevation to scheduled status—was back to one again. The change did not last long. One airline deserves special mention because it enjoyed a level of prominence, though followed by a downfall that was so abrupt as to be almost unprecedented in air transport history. In 1988, **Canada 3000 (C3)** was founded in Toronto as a low-fare charter airline, specializing in what it termed "exotic" destinations in Europe, Mexico, Hawaii, and the Caribbean including Cuba. Originally Air 2000, a Canadian branch of a British company of the same name, it was allowed to start in 1989 after the Deluce family (of Austin-Air Ontario) gave it part-Canadian ownership. The name change prepared it to move into the next century. C3's fleet quickly grew to 20 new 142-seat Airbus A320s and 2 26-seat Boeing 757-200s. It was able to enter the scheduled market and early in the 1990s to challenge Wardair as Canada's second largest airline. On 29 April 1998, it was the first to receive the wide-bodied Airbus A330-200. By 2000, it was carrying 5 million passengers to 90 destinations, and made C$18 million profit. Early in 2001, it purchased Royal Aviation, with its 737-200s, 757-200s, and a 264-seat A310-300; and CanJet (see above). Then, it shared with other airlines the depressing after-effects of the terrorist attacks in the U.S.A. on 11 September 2001, but still, a month later, introduced an Airbus A340-300 series to open a Polar route to India, and financing improved navigational aids across Siberia. In a dramatic succession of events, including competition from Air Canada's Tango low-fare start-up with a fleet of 42 modern airliners, C3 was declared bankrupt on 9 November. All flights were cancelled immediately, 4,800 employees were laid off, the management board resigned, and 50,000 passengers were temporarily stranded all over the world.

While the high-level maneuvering within the airline industry of Canada left some casualties, and Westjet was to emerge as a powerful survivor, the flag carrier continued to hold on to its status and its size. By 2010, by-annual passenger-miles flown, Air Canada ranked among the top dozen airlines in the world.

Part Eight: A Continent Made for Air Transport

Chapter 41: The Sleeping Giant Awakes

Brazil Continues to Lead

The countries of Latin America, including the Central American republics, the Caribbean islands, and the South American continent, did not, until the middle of the 20th century, enjoy all the transportation benefits of advanced industrial nations such as in North America, Europe, or Japan. There were few roads, few railroads, and few navigable rivers, except the Amazon and the Magdalena. One exception was Argentina, where the British had established good railroads; and there were isolated cases of public transport in the south of Brazil, and in Mexico. There were good reasons for the shortcoming. The Andes mountain chain was a formidable physical barrier and a challenge to any engineer or planner, as were the vast jungles of the Amazon basin. Natural resources, such as minerals, oil, and other products, were mainly in the hands of United States or European industrialists, so that the necessary financing of public utilities such as roads and rails was seldom available for local investment.

Such was not the case for air transport. Because of the difficulties of surface communications, and often the distances involved, airline projects enjoyed the attention of several governments, and were given priority in the allocation of funds or the privileges of favorable legislation. Latin America was thus in the vanguard of progress in many aspects of airline development.

In Colombia, for example, the oldest airline in all the Americas, **AVIANCA**, is directly descended from SCADTA, founded in 1921. Argentina started, in the same year, an international airline (across the River Plate) that lasted for a few years, whereas the world's first airline in 1914 in Florida lasted only three months. By the 1940s, in Rio de Janeiro, the downtown airport was within walking distance of the business center, as was the one in Buenos Aires.

Brazil's **Viação Aérea São Paulo (VASP)** was operating turboprops before any airline in the U.S.A., and Aerolíneas Argentinas was operating Comet jets to New York in 1959. The world's first code-sharing experiment was by TACA's subsidiary airlines in Colombia and Venezuela, and in July 1958, the Rio de Janeiro-São Paulo Ponte Aérea set an example as the world's first no-reservation air shuttle service. The major airlines of Brazil cooperated to provide an on-the-hour, every-hour, schedule between two downtown airports—two years before Eastern Air Lines did the same in the United States. When the Jet Age arrived, Latin America was fully prepared.

Half a century later, in a different branch of transport technology, Argentina, Brazil, and Mexico are exploring routes for the first high speed rail networks in the western hemisphere. Buenos Aires-Rosario-Córdoba, Rio de Janeiro-São Paulo, and Mexico City-Guadalajara are too short for normal economic airline operations, yet their large populations demand high volumes of capacity—hence the interest in rail links that cut the city-center journey times to about two hours. In the case of Brazil, the mountainous terrain will present an engineering problem; but this nation has tackled—and solved—many such challenges already. One such achievement owed its initial launch, as chronicled below, to the airlines.

A New Capital City

During the late 1950s, Brazil's President Kubitschek adopted the slogan "I will Awaken the Sleeping Giant." The giant, of course, was Brazil, a country larger than the continental United States but had never fulfilled its potential for benefitting from vast natural resources. 90% of Brazil's people live along its extensive coastline. Around the world, Brazil is known for its coffee and its nuts, and Rio de Janeiro is a marvelous vacation destination for those who could afford to fly there. However, most of its natural resources, indeed most of its wealth, including agricultural products such as sugar and rubber, meat from the south, and precious metals from the State of Minas Gerais: these were little exploited for export. Kubitschek realized that the wealth of Brazil was inland, not on the coast, and to draw attention to this untapped potential, he resurrected a spectacularly ambitious plan. Brazil would build a new capital in the middle of the country, to replace Rio de Janeiro, and to emphasize the vast potential of the inland resources, hitherto untapped. The location chosen, and named Brasília, had been marked with dotted lines on maps for several decades; but nothing had ever been done. To construct this new capital city, a hundred miles from the nearest railroad (but unlike Rio, blessed with a more temperate climate), would demand unprecedented effort. The challenges were enormous. Nevertheless, they were accepted by Brazilian planning, architectural, and construction industries with vision, enthusiasm, and skill. During the second half of the 20th century, Kubitschek was able to preside over one of the most impressive feats of urban development in the modern world.

One industry that could be excluded from the president's implied accusation of lethargy was Brazil's air transport. Its airlines had never been backward in compensating for the lack of surface travel in the land. Pre-war airlines, such as Syndicato Condor, VASP, Panair do Brasil, and VARIG, were recognized and respected overseas. During the immediate post-war years, with fleets composed largely of war-surplus aircraft, they had reached out to every community in the country. One airline, **REAL (Redes Estaduais Aéreas, Ltda)**, had grown prodigiously by absorbing several small ones. Its fleet included 86 Douglas DC-3s, the largest fleet of its type in the world, and during the late 1950s, it ranked, by passenger boardings, as the tenth largest airline in the world. On 3 May 1957, with a Convair 240, it began the first scheduled service to Brasília.

The airlift to Brasília carried everything needed for the massive project, not only those items of specialized freight customarily carried by aircraft, but also basic materials normally carried by surface transport, such as timber, steel, and even cement. There was an element of irony in the achievement. Paradoxically, the Brazilian airline giant was awakening at both ends of the technological scale. While the airlines were, on the one hand, entering the Jet Age, the airlift to the new capital in its embryo stage was carried out almost entirely with Douglas ex-C-47 DC-3s and Curtiss C-46s, some of them well past their shelf-life. Large fleets had been the left-overs from abandoned war-surplus stocks and acquired very cheaply. Their availability had permitted, if not encouraged, the foundation of a proliferation of small airlines. During the first post-war decade, they had survived precariously but by 1955, most of them had either collapsed or had been absorbed by the established pre-war pioneers. Of the newcomers, however, REAL had prospered to the extent that it was a customer for jet airliners. At many of the main airports in the biggest cities, epitomizing the paradox of Brazil's entry into the Jet Age, was the sight of a handsome modern turboprop, or even an international jet, parked next to a well-worn DC-3 of mid-1930s vintage, loading building materials or cement.

Jet Initiatives in Brazil

As early as 20 March 1953, Dr. Paulo Sampaio, head of **Panair do Brasil,** ordered four de Havilland DH-106 Comet 2s. These had longer range than the world's first jet airliner, the Comet 1, which had startled the airline industry in 1952 by flying from London to South Africa in half the time of the fastest propeller-driven type. More important, it proved that jet propulsion was not nearly as inefficient as had been assumed by all the industry experts. Because of the Comet's problems with the then unrecognized structural fatigue, it was withdrawn from service, but Sampaio retained faith in his decision. He was summarily dismissed in 1955, but his action had served notice that Brazil's airlines were in the forefront of technical progress.

This was confirmed in 1957 when **VASP** was among the first to order the world's first turboprop airliner, the British Vickers Viscount. It started service on 3 November 1958, to give VASP a distinct edge on its competitors which had all bought the piston-engined ConvairLiner in its various versions. This success was soon out-shone, however, by a notable effort by the airline from the southern state of Rio Grande do Sul, **Viação Aérea Rio Grandense (VARIG).** The timing of the deliveries of its jet airliner choices for long-haul routes resulted in the French twin-engined Sud Caravelle arriving at Porto Alegre before the long-haul Boeing 707 was delivered. Conscious of the importance of the connection to New York, and the competition from the U.S. Pan American Airways, VARIG took a calculated risk. It put the short-haul Caravelle on the route on 12 December 1959.

The world's first short-haul jet demonstrated commendable versatility by linking Porto Alegre with New York, with stops only at São Paulo, Rio de Janeiro, Port of Spain, and Nassau, and on 20 January 1960, Brasília was also added to the routeing to provide a direct link from the new seat of government to the United States's main center of commerce. This interim example of opportunism lasted only a few months, as VARIG's first Boeing 707-441 (the Rolls-Royce powered variant) started to fly nonstop from Rio to New York on 28 June, with Brasília included on 2 July. Direct service to Los Angeles was added on 18 November, via Lima, Bogota, and Mexico City. The Caravelles were transferred to a stopping service to Miami. Other jets destined for the fleet by airline acquisition (see below) were sold in 1964. Meanwhile, having started service to Europe with Douglas DC-8s on 20 April 1961, Panair do Brasil put the Caravelle VIR variant into mainline domestic service on 15 September 1962. This was followed by **Cruzeiro do Sul** on 12 September 1962. Simultaneously, on 2 September, VARIG put the first of its 100-seat Lockheed L.188 Electra turboprops into service on the coastal route, and was able to operate them from the downtown Santos Dumont airport, where jets were not allowed. For almost the next 30 years, these reliable airliners also became the standard aircraft for the Ponte Aérea (see above), with the revenues and costs shared between the contributing airlines, but with VARIG supplying the fleet.

Putting the Giant's House in Order

Kubitschek's giant may have not have been quite awake, but it was already tossing and turning. Brazil had lived through and survived many decades of continuous familiarity with commercial aviation and airline problems. They had been tackled by an efficient Department of Civil Aviation at Santos Dumont Airport in Rio de Janeiro, rather akin to the Civil Aeronautics Board (C.A.B.) in Washington, D.C. Now, as the Jet Age descended upon South America, it was faced with the problem of reconciling the virtues of spirited free enterprise with a measure of regulatory control over the often aggressive domestic competition. This was encouraged by Brazil's increasingly rapid economic expansion and industrial growth; but the accompanying need for extensive air transport in this huge road- and rail-starved country was enormous. If all these elements were not carefully watched and administered, chaos could result.

So, on 27 November 1961, in association with other government agencies, the Department convened a 12-day conference at the Castelo Country Club at Petrópolis. It was the Brazilian equivalent of the Chicago Conference that had been, in 1944, the foundation of the International Civil Aviation Organization (I.C.A.O.). Brazil's economic expansion had led to a high rate of inflation. With roads being built everywhere, the natural market for the many small airlines was evaporating. If Brazil was to maintain a balanced air transport industry, it had to be helped, which meant some form of government subsidy, direct or indirect.

The precise terms took many months to thrash out, but on 15 October 1963, Decree No. 52,693 created the Rede de Integração National (RIN). Similar to the U.S. Local Service Airline policy, it was to last for 10 years, and the airlines could operate only the trusty DC-3s (or PBY-5 flying boats in the Amazon region). The RIN was complemented on the main inter-city routes by the Rede Aérea Nacional (RAN) and the Rede Aérea International

(RAI), which did not receive direct subsidy, but whose operations were strictly monitored to avoid wasteful and self-defeating competition. This was achieved by specifying exact seating levels for the aircraft, and applying different levels of fares for the different types, according to their standards of service to the public. The underlying motivation behind the provisions of the Conference was to end the proliferation of airlines as Brazil entered the Jet Age. Tax concessions were also made on airport charges and import duties on aircraft and spares. Special encouragement was given to expanding, on 12 March 1962, the Ponte Aérea to include Belo Horizonte (Brazil's third largest city) and Brasília.

Whether or not the Petrópolis decisions were the direct cause of the surge of airline terminations and takeovers, the process of rationalization was successful. By the early 1960s, the main inter-city air services were flown by the same airlines that had been the early pioneers (Syndicato Condor, VARIG, VASP, and Panair do Brasil), plus two newcomers. One of these two led the way to replacing the workhorse DC-3s with modern twin-engined turboprop airliners, to match the efficiency of VASP's four-engined Viscounts.

Transbrasil had been founded, as **Sadia**, in 1955 by Omar Fontana: a man who could truly be described as a maverick. He flew fresh meat from his father's packing plant in the state of Santa Catarina to the high-class butchers in São Paulo, he changed its name in June 1972. By that time, however, Fontana had moved quickly to take advantage of the provisions of the RIN. Late in 1963, he leased two 40-seat Handley Page Dart Herald turboprops and persuaded the authorities to classify them with DC-3s, and thus qualify for subsidy. This started a flurry of orders by the larger airlines to match the Herald. VASP signed up for them, but replaced the order with one for BAC One-Eleven-400 twin-jets, which went into service on 8 January 1968. The next month, its twin turboprop order was for the 60-seat Japanese Nihon YS-11, which Cruzeiro do Sul had already put into service on 14 August 1967. VARIG bought 12 Hawker-Siddeley HS-748s, whose airfield performance was close to the DC-3's, while the other newcomer airline, **Paraense**, founded on 22 February 1952, chose the larger 48-seat Fokker F-27, the Fairchild Hiller-built F-227B, which it called the Hirondelle. This was an unhappy episode. The Belém-based airline received a fleet of five in January 1968, but after two years, only one was still in service. The airline closed down on 29 May 1970, and VARIG used the refurbished four on the Ponte Aérea.

Rise and Fall of a Great Airline

In fulfilment of the objectives of the Petrópolis Conference, one result was the creation of what, in many airline countries elsewhere in the world, was termed the "chosen instrument." The airline did not necessarily have to be state-owned (though many were) but its important role as a public utility was recognized. Concessions were made, or privileges granted, to guarantee its position as a national standard-bearer. Brazil's choice, partially the result of political influence in the corridors of power, was VARIG. At the end of the Second World War, it was the smallest of the pioneers, but its home State, Rio Grande do Sul, populated largely by German immigrants, was affluent and efficient. More important, one of its sons, Getulio Vargas, had become President of Brazil, and for several decades, the VARIG management could always count on a favorable nod from the government.

As a first step to expand beyond national state borders to reach Rio de Janeiro, it had acquired **Aero Geral** in May 1952. It thus became a national airline, rather than a strictly regional one. In 1954 it crossed into Uruguay to Montevideo and across the River Plate to Buenos Aires. The next step was far-reaching. Founded by Linneu Gomes in December 1945 with a fleet of three DC-3s, REAL (see above) had digested numerous other small airlines and an important one, **Nacional**, which doubled it in size. Its purchase of **Aerovias Brasil** on 10 September 1954 added international routes to the United States, and the Miami terminus was extended, first to Chicago in 1956 then, with Lockheed L1049H Super Constellations, to Los Angeles in 1959. It had been the first to offer scheduled flights to Brasília, and on 9 July 1960, achieved an historic first by opening a trans-Pacific rote to Tokyo—a great gift to the million citizens of Japanese descent in REAL's home State of São Paulo.

But Gomes's oversight and financial control of his airline did not live up to his ambition, although his staff struggled to sustain it. REAL outgrew its strength and had to reduce its network, first the Chicago route then a half share of its international division to VARIG on 2 May 1961. A few months later, on 16 August, VARIG bought the whole airline, including a pending order for three Convair 990 four-engined jets, but these were not permanently incorporated into the fleet.

Having spread its international wings to North America and Asia, VARIG's next step was to Europe. Against competiton from Britain and Argentina, Panair do Brasil had, during the post-war years, proudly carried the Brazilian flag to several European capitals and to Beirut. It had been founded on 15 September 1930 as **NYRBA do Brasil**, after the U.S. Pan American Airways had purchased NYRBA on 19 August. After the Second World War, Pan American ownership was gradually eroded, but service maintained to at least the high standards of the U.S. world-embracing airline, especially by the Brazilian cuisine in its cabin service. After the bold initiative of the 1952 Comet (see above), its long-range jet choice was the Douglas DC-8, which opened service to Europe on 20 April 1961. It had also, on 30 October 1960, introduced, with its relegated Douglas DC-7Cs, a pooled service with the Portuguese airline, T.A.P., charging discounted fares for citizens of the two countries who spoke the same language. In 1964, it received authority to extend this privilege to Angola, the Portuguese colony in southern Africa.

With this impressive and creditable record of representing its country in one of the most internationally competitive world industries, the surprising collapse of Panair do Brasil was tinged with a degree of suspicion. On 10 February 1965, all its flights were cancelled, and VARIG took over the operation at three hours' notice. For any airline to accomplish the smooth transition of substituting for another, no matter how efficient, would normally have taken several days, if not weeks. When, six days later, Panair was declared bankrupt, with debts of $62 million, its financial position was described as "irretrievable;" yet many banks, both in Rio and São Paulo, could have made good investments. In May 1966, Panair's appeal to the Brazilian Supreme Court was denied. It was a sad end to a flagship airline that had done so much for Brasil's prestige overseas, and which had built much of the infrastructure all across the country, including the vast reaches of the Amazon. Its maintenance base in Rio was the only one licensed for airframe and engines by the United States. In the struggle for airline dominance, neither Rio's Cariocas nor the Paulistas won. The spoils went to the Gauchos of Rio Grande do Sul.

Having disposed of all the indigenous competition internationally, VARIG's next step was to eliminate the major domestic competition. This was from Cruzeiro do Sul, the airline whose name had changed from the German-sponsored **Syndicato Condor** on 16 January 1943. By that time, even though Condor had, in 1940, operated two Fw-200s, the first four-engined landplanes in all the Americas, and a host of other German types, Brazilians had taken over. Brazil had declared war on Germany in August 1942. While the Amazon Basin had been pioneered by Panair do Brasil, most of the other long-distance routes had been the result of Condor's expansion from its coastal bases with its fleet of Junkers-Ju 52/3m's. After a succession of corporate maneuvers, VARIG acquired control of Cruzeiro on 22 May 1975. The two airlines continued to operate independently, but shared maintenance and stock of spares, while duplication of routes and schedules ended. The airline fleets were coordinated.

Both airlines continued to provide excellent service, adding modern jets early in the manufacturers' delivery schedules. In February 1976, service was inaugurated across the South Atlantic to Johannesburg, and a cargo route supplied meat to Lagos, Nigeria, the latter including passenger service on 26 June 1977. The international services received a setback when, on 4 June, Government Decree No. 1470-76 imposed a deposit of 12,000 cruzeiros (raised to 16,000 on 17 February 1977) equivalent to hundreds of dollars on all overseas travelers (except government employees), refundable only after one year, without interest. Domestic services, however, were not affected. The HS-748s were sold, and the Electra fleet increased to a dozen. This permitted a half-hour frequency on the Rio-São Paulo Shuttle, which was carrying more than a million inter-city commuters a year. On 8 September, VARIG's affiliated regional airline, Rio-Sul, began service, directed by João Lorenz, who had been Rubem Berta's economic director, and one of the team from Porto Alegre who had laid a firm foundation for this great airline.

Berta, VARIG's long-term president, had died on 14 December 1966. His successor, Erik de Carvalho, retired because of illness in February 1979, and Helio Smidt took over on 30 April 1980. "Mr. Erik" died on 4 May 1984, and Smidt on 11 April 1990. They had overseen the acquisition of Airbus A300-B4s, Douglas DC-10s, the Boeing 747-200s, and, in 1987, Boeing 767ERs, for a total fleet of 90 modern airliners. New routes in 1983 had included Maputo, Mozambique, via Luanda, Angola, both ex-Portuguese colonies; Santo Domingo via Costa Rica in 1984; and Montreal via Toronto in 1986. Altogether, and in spite of Brazil's rampant currency inflation, and possibly as a legacy of Berta's fine team organization, VARIG seemed to be weathering all the economic storms that were part of the Brazilian way of life.

But the apparent wave of prosperity did not last. Smidt's successors had to face increased foreign competition, and the late 1980s witnessed a financial decline, even though the government's latest currency rescue effort, the Real Plan, drastically cut the inflation rate, then 50% per month. In 1994, facing an almost $2 billion debt, this prestigious airline cut its staff by almost 4,000, eliminated most of its international routes, closed offices everywhere, and cancelled orders for eight 747s. Acquiring Uruguay's national airline, PLUNA, in March 1997, and joining the Star Alliance on 26 October, did little to stem the negative tide. In 1998, a new government policy, effectively deregulation, did not help either. Until then, the major inter-city routes had been operated by only the four main airlines. Now, newcomers were not only allowed to enter these hitherto privileged markets, but also permitted to offer heavily discounted fares. Another currency devaluation on 12 January 1999 led to VARIG repeating the drastic measures of 1994, cutting overseas routes again, and trimming aircraft fleets to only three types, most of them leased. To add to all these disasters, the 11 September 2001 terrorist attacks in the U.S.A. created a drastic reduction in international ai traffic worldwide. For VARIG it compounded a situation that was already approaching a crisis level.

In 2002, the workforce was again reduced, by 30%, and 20 leased aircraft were returned to the lessors. The only segment of VARIG's entire network still profitable was the Ponte Aérea shuttle service. An attempt in 2003 to merge with TAM, which had been a major discount intruder on the shuttle with Airbus A330s, came to nothing. A rescue plan from Portugal's T.A.P. early in 2005 also failed, a sad commentary on the fate of an airline that a decade or two earlier could easily have swallowed T.A.P. The Brazilian equivalent of the U.S. Chapter 11 bankruptcy proceedings were started in December 2005. In April 2006, VariLog, VARIG's former cargo subsidiary that was sold to Volo do Brasil, offered to buy its former parent company for $350 million. But even a plan to halve the size of the company could not erase a formidable debt of $3.3 billion. In June, the government conceded the $1.4 billion compensation claim for its arbitrary fare-capping in the late 1980s, but all flights were suspended on 17 July. Except for the Ponte Aérea, Volo do Brasil took over, and VARIG began flying again two days later with a skeleton service on its main routes. The final blow came in April 2007 when GOL (see below) bought control of the airline for $98 million, plus 6 million shares.

A brash newcomer had usurped a once-distinguished veteran pioneer. Commercial aviation in Brazil would never be the same again.

No Immunity for São Paulo

Other than the post-war REAL in 1961, VARIG had absorbed the pre-war Panair do Brasil and Cruzeiro do Sul in 1965 and

1975, respectively. But one of the four pre-war pioneers of the industry still flourished. **VASP** (see above) had drawn its support from the wealth of its city, state, and bank of its native São Paulo, which had financed steady and sound progress as Brazil entered the Jet Age. It had not only led the way in 1958 with the first turbine-powered airliner, the Viscount, it had introduced the BAC One-Eleven twin-jet in 1968, in preference to the older Caravelle, which had gone into service with its domestic competitors. When its five Boeing 737-200s were delivered in the summer of 1969, its fleet of Viscounts, One-Elevens, 737s, and YS-11s were all turbine-powered, either jets or turboprops.

By 1975, it had a fleet of 20 737s, and had supported the infant Brazilian manufacturing industry by ordering Embraer EMB-110 Bandeirantes for the feeder routes to its main-line operations. In August of that year, it was stimulated by a government decree that allocated 60% of domestic airline routes and traffic between the VARIG-Cruzeiro do Sul partnership and 40% to VASP and Transbrasil. The latter two were allowed to increase their fleets to qualify for a better share of the market. Also, in February 1976, VASP presented a plan to the government to invest in the third-level airline, **Taxi Aéreo Marília (TAM)** (see below), under the Transportes Aéreos Regionais system. By December, VASP was carrying 35% of all domestic traffic. Another order for 737s gave it the largest fleet of the type in Latin America, and (at the time) the third largest in the world. In March 1977, it ordered two 152-seat 727-200 tri-jets then 12 Airbus A300s, but took delivery of only three, to add to its 26 Boeings. By the mid-1980s, now 95%-owned by the state government, the airline was battling against rampant inflation and severe competition.

In an unprecedented corporate action, VASP was privatized in October 1990. The purchaser was Wagner Canhedo, a successful operator of a large group of bus companies, and known as a bold and ambitious entrepreneur, with a tendency to take big risks to achieve his business goals. Purchasing 40% of VASP's stock, he launched a $2.5 billion expansion program, with $45 million of his own resources and with bank loans. By the end of 1991, the 53-strong fleet included 22 737s, 21 727s, three Airbus A300s, and three long-range McDonnell Douglas MD-11s. These last were for international services. Within two or three years, the map included numerous cities in Europe and North America, and to Tokyo and Seoul, as well as neighboring South American countries. It closely echoed VARIG's former network at the height of its life.

This expansionist program quickly proved to be foolhardy and worse. Within a year, losses amounted to $1.2 billion, and there were even rumors of corruption. On 8 November 1992, a court order restricted the fleet numbers—all leased—to 31. Flights were suspended to 15 Brazilian cities, and the participation in the Ponte Aérea severely reduced. Undeterred, Canhedo sought further loans and against all thoughts of caution, continued to expand, this time by purchasing control of other South American airlines. First, in 1994, he bought 50.1% of Transportes Aéreos Neuquen (TAN), operating SAAB 340s and Fairchild Metros throughout western Argentina and points in Chile; then a 50.1% share of Ecuatoriana, which had not operated for several years; and finally a 49% share of L.A.B., Bolivia. Canhedo fed these airlines with aircraft fleets, including more MD-11s, to rejuvenate them.

But the bubble burst. In 2002, all international services were cancelled, and domestic routes were curtailed as the local competition made itself felt. On 27 January 2005, the Brazilian government grounded this once reputable airline. A recovery plan on 27 August 2007 was too little too late, and the last of the four pre-war pioneer Brazilian airlines was dead.

Last of an Airline Quartet

Dozens of aspirant companies founded after the Second World War had made only temporary inroads into the preeminence of what could be termed the Brazilian Big Four. VARIG, VASP, Cruzeiro do Sul, and Panair do Brasil had shared in the pre-war establishment of the industry But toward the end of the 20th century, their combined dominance was threatened with collapse. As narrated above, VARIG had been favored as a chosen instrument, taking over Cruzeiro, which, however, continued to operate for a few years under its own name. Absorbing Panair gave it routes to Europe, and REAL added widespread domestic routes. VASP had been supported by São Paulo finance. Thus, when one of the newcomers was an exception to the post-war casualty list, four major airlines still dominated the airline networks.

The newcomer was **Transbrasil**, already mentioned above as heralding—the term is appropriate—the introduction of the Handley Page Herald, the first twin-engined turboprop airliners that replaced the large fleets of piston-engined types in Brazil, including more than 100 old Douglas DC-3s. Owner Omar Fontana was a visionary innovator as well as being a charismatic personality who had the physique of a heavyweight wrestler but who could play Rachmaninoff piano concertos. Under his leadership, he had built his airline, founded as Sadia in 1955, from a regional network in the south into a national one by purchasing **Transportes Aéreos Salvador (TAS)** in 1962. The Dart Herald turboprops had led the way in that category, and after starting pure-jet service on 17 September 1970 with BAC One-Elevens, he changed the name in June 1972.

He helped to stimulate the embryo Brazilian aircraft manufacturing industry by being the first to put into service the 15-seat Embraer EMB-110 Bandeirante turboprop on 16 April 1973. When, in 1975, VARIG absorbed Cruzeiro do Sul, the Civil Aviation Department allocated 40% of domestic traffic to that partnership, 40% to VASP, and 20% to Transbrasil. Minority though it was, Fontana's airline was now recognized as one of the national airlines. The next year, under the new SITAR system (see below), he took the statutory 33% shareholding of **Nordeste**, one of the five small designated operators to form the Brazilian "third level." In 1977, he opened a modern maintenance base, the largest in South America, at Brasília, a ranking that also applied to the fleet of 11 Boeing 727s, some of which he piloted himself on their delivery flights from Seattle. During the following years, he introduced multi-colored "rainbow" aircraft paint

BRAZILIAN REGIONAL AIRLINES, 1976

Of the early regional airlines of Brazil, the São Paulo–based TAM developed into a nationwide airline, eventually to succeed the veteran VARIG pioneer.

schemes, night coach fares, family and student discount fares, and a 21-day Air Pass for foreign visitors.

He collected (personally) the first of three 210-seat widebodied Boeing 767-200s, which entered service on 5 July 1983. Two days earlier, Transbrasil had started charter services to Orlando, for families to visit Disneyworld, and on 5 July 1985 to Freeport, the Bahamas vacation resort. Omar then became involved in an episode that ultimately was to benefit all the airlines of Brazil. On 18 August 1988, the government took draconian steps to curb galloping inflation (2,000% in the year) by freezing all domestic fares. On 5 September it replaced Omar with an intervertor who sold all the 727s and some real estate in Rio, and then leased nine 737-200s. Omar sued the government, and in November 1989, in an extraordinary sequel, the Air Minister appealed to him to take back his airline and to convert the international services from charter to scheduled. After assurances that there would be no retaliation against him for suing the government, in June 1990, Transbrasil became Brazil's second international airline, adding Miami to the map and, in July 1991, Washington, D.C. In August, a "Capital to Capital" service from Brasília was followed a year later by an extension to New York, which, on 29 October 1995, was linked nonstop with São Paulo.

Meanwhile, routes to Europe had included services to Vienna in 1993, with Fortaleza as an additional gateway; Amsterdam in June 1995; and London on 27 November 1996. In July 1995, a new subsidiary, Interbrasil-Star, started to serve 20 domestic points with Embraer Brasílias.

Omar Fontana was on the crest of a wave. And an even bigger crest was not far behind. When, on 5 December 1997, the Brazilian Federal Tribunal (Supreme Court) ruled on the issue of the 1988 fare-freezing in his favor, the value of compensation to Transbrasil was about $1 billion. He had, by a protracted and determined battle with the authorities, not only won a great victory for Transbrasil, but for all the airlines, which could make their own claims. But it was not enough to shore up his company, in which full control still remained in the Fontana family, but which was grossly undercapitalized. The airline sought strategic partners, such as Delta, TAM, and TAP Portugal, but to no avail. In 1998, he retired because of ill health, and his son-in-law, Antonio Celso Cipriani, took over. But deregulation allowed newer airlines to provide far more effective competition. The currency was devalued, and most of the debts were in U.S. dollars. Changing the name to TransBrasil simply added a capital letter to the name, but additional capital of the financial kind was not forthcoming.

When Fontana died in January 2001, he did not, mercifully, live to see his beloved airline go out of business, still with a billion-dollar debt, on 19 December of that year.

The New Wave in Brazil

The important regional airline system created in 1976, under Decree 76,590, the Sistema Integrado de Transportes Aéreos Regional (SITAR), established five regional airlines, by granting scheduled air route authority to former air taxi operators, and qualifying them for a subsidy. Technical support was provided by allocating (except for TABA, in the Amazon basin) 33% of the shareholding to existing airlines. The government support may have appeared generous, but without the creation of the Brazilian equivalent of the U.S. Local Service airlines, much of the country, as yet without trunk roads and without a national railroad, would, as one writer explained, have been "back to the mule-train and the river canoe." Within 18 months, the five Brazilian regional airlines were operating 60 aircraft, including 35 Brazilian Bandeirantes, to 121 cities over an area bigger than the 48 contiguous states of the U.S.A.

One of the five resisted the role of apparent subordination to its larger shareholder. **TAM Transportes Aéreos Regional (TAM)** was made of sterner stuff. It had been founded in 1975, as Taxi Aéreo Marília, and had started its SITAR-sponsored scheduled operations on 12 July 1976. It changed its name to the acronym 20 years later. In some ways, the founder, Capt. Rolim Adolfo Amaro, known to all as Captain Rolim, developed his airline as a later-generation Transbrasil, and he himself was as innovative as Omar Fontana, but with a different approach to risk taking and innovation. At first, he operated mainly with nine 15-seat Bandeirantes, inherited from shareholder VASP, within northern São Paulo State. The area included many prosperous medium-sized cities, where businessmen required frequent communication with the São Paulo metropolis. The demographics were ideal to establish a local airline to serve these communities. Rolim set about the task with enthusiasm. Passengers were offered free parking, free mobile telephones, drinks and snacks, and to emphasize TAM's welcoming spirit, they were greeted by the captain after boarding the airplane. Very often, Amaro himself would be the greeter, and from the terminal was on a red carpet.

The business community of the prosperous area of the State responded to such treatment, so that TAM had to introduce larger aircraft. Service with 44-seat Fokker F-27 twin-engined turboprops started on 2 February 1980, quickly expanding the hub network into adjoining States. Shortly after the new Guarulhos International Airport was opened at São Paulo in 1995, to relieve downtown Congonhas, a new regulation, the Vôos Diretos ao Centro (V.D.C.) allowed airlines such as TAM to fly directly into downtown airports, and charge 30% more than the major airlines, which had to use the larger airports. Its standards of service were appreciated by the frequent flyers, who were heard to comment that "democracy is re-established in Brazil."

In 1986, as its F-27s and the red carpets increased its popularity, Amaro expanded TAM by buying **VOTEC (Vôos Técnicos e Executivos)**, one of the other five SITAR Third Level operators. With routes as far north as the Amazon, it was integrated with the existing Brasil Central subsidiary to become TAM Linha Aérea Regional. At the same time, in September 1989, TAM entered the Ponte Aérea, and on 9 September 1990, the first Fokker 100 was introduced as the Congonhas Jet, as its field performance well matched the short runway. As the liberalization of Brazil's domestic airline industry continued, TAM was one of its main beneficiaries. The territorial allocations of the five SITAR airlines were lifted so that they could fly on all routes in the country, except nonstops between the 27 State capitals. TAM circumvented this restriction by following the example of Southwest in the U.S.A. by flying into satellite fields that were often almost as convenient to the city centers as the main airports.

Across the frontier, the Paraguayan airline was ailing. In 1994, Amaro formed **Aerolíneas Paraguayas (APSA)** and started it off by transferring 12-seat Cessna Caravans from a TAM subsidiary, Brasil Central. He followed this in September 1996 by buying an 80% share in **Líneas Aéreas Paraguayas (L.A.P.)** (see below), changing its name to Transportes Aéreos del Mercosur (TAM), and supplying Fokker 100 twin jets. One of these airliners crashed on take-off at Congonhas on 31 October 1996, but this did not slow the airline's momentum as on 12 December, it changed the name of Brasil Central to **Transportes Aéreos Meridionais (TAM)**, which thus became Brazil's fourth international airline.

The headlong growth continued, this time not with route expansion but with an airliner order that was so innovative that it drew media attention all over the airline world. In January 1998, in close coordination (almost by handshakes and little work for the lawyers) Rolim Amaro joined with Federico Bloch of TACA (see below) and Enrique Cueto of LAN-Chile (see also below) to order a total of no less than 90 Airbus A320 series, plus 89

TAM's extensive fleet in 2009 included (left) Airbus A320s (this one noting TAM as the official airline for Brazil's football team) and (right) an A330, used on the long-haul routes. (McDonough)

options, for $4 billion. They could also select the larger A321 or the smaller A319, according to the individual market needs. TAM's order was for 38 of the series and added also were five 213-seat long-range wide-bodied A330s. Stepping boldly into VARIG's territory, TAM opened service to Miami on 10 December 1998 and to Paris on 2 April 1999. Back in Brazil, the first 144-seat Airbus A319s arrived in July, and at the end of the year, TAM introduced ticketless travel. In July 2000, a former tractor factory at São Carlos was converted into the Centro Técnico TAM, which henceforth could fully maintain its aircraft without any outside help. By December of that year, a combination of events promoted this airline, which less than two decades earlier had been at the "third level," to national leadership. Transbrasil ceased operations, VASP was dying by its own hand, and VARIG was in dire straits. Simultaneously, TAM Transportes Aéreos Regionais and TAM Transportes Aéreos Meridionais merged to become **TAM Linhas Aéreos**.

In the spring of 2001, the new national airline promptly replaced VASP on the southern route to Montevideo and Buenos Aires, and in the north, supplemented VARIG to Zurich and Frankfurt. Sadly, the man whose vision had made this success possible did not live to join in the celebrations, for he was killed on 8 July when his helicopter crashed near the Paraguayan border. But he missed the other side of Fortune's commercial balance. On 15 January, a new airline was formed with a policy far different from Amaro's but more competitively innovative, even for a Brazilian airline industry in transformation (see below). Also, the new route to Europe had to be terminated, and on 30 August 2002, two more Fokker 100s were written off.

Prolonged discussions to merge with VARIG dragged on for a few years, but eventually, in June 2006, much of the great Brazilian pioneer airline's assets were auctioned, and though drastically reduced in size, stature, and reputation, managed to survive, a mere shadow of its former self. TAM sustained another serious crash, when on 17 July 2007, an Airbus A320 skidded off the tight runway at Congonhas, killing 183 people. By now,

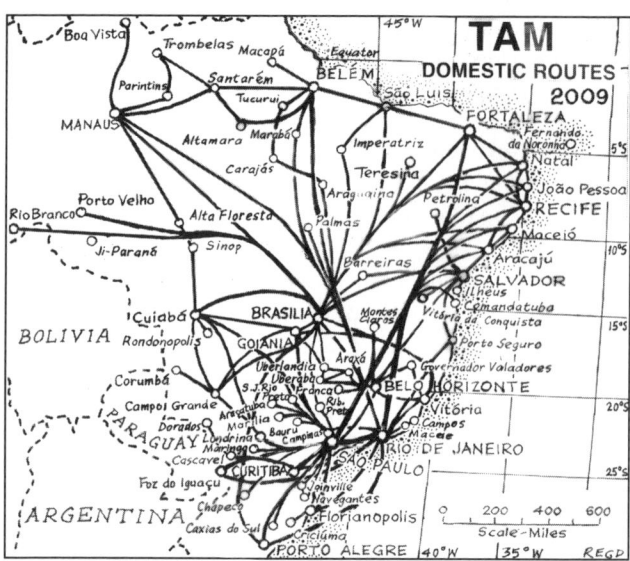

TAM grew from one of the regional airlines formed in 1976 to become Brazil's largest airline. The new budget-fare airline GOL has an almost identical network.

however, since March 2005, it was listed on the New York Stock Exchange, and could take such setbacks in its stride. It had ordered more A320 series and four Boeing 777-300ERs, and, in January 2008, 22 Airbus A350-900s, not yet built. To match the more immediate growing traffic demand, TAM leased two Boeing 767-300ERs in September.

Transformation

Following the easing of regulations in 1996, which led to the entry of TAM, a few new companies tried to start low-fare "budget" airlines. Fly and Brasil Rodo Aéreo (BRA) struggled to survive—unsuccessfully; but **GOL Linhas Aéreas Inteligentes** succeeded beyond its wildest dreams. It was established on 1 August 2000 by the Aurea Group, Brazil's biggest highway bus

Emulating TAM's promotion of Brazil's football team, the name of the new bargain-fare airline was itself a cry to reflect Brazil's leadership of the world-famous sport. (McDonough)

operator (11,000 buses), headed by Constantino de Oliviera. His son, Junior, was president of the airline. The choice of the name was self-advertising; "Goooooal" is a familiar cry by all the radio and television commentators for a public that regards football (i.e., soccer, not American football) almost as a religion. Well capitalized, GOL bought new aircraft, starting on 15 January 2001 with an inaugural flight from Brasília to São Paulo. With an initial fleet of six Boeing 737-700s, the no-frills newcomer was soon linking six State capitals with three flights a day to each city. By the end of the year, it was serving a dozen cities, aided by TransBrasil's demise in December. On 17 March 2002 it entered the Ponte Aérea, and in April flew—after little more than a year of service—its three-millionth passenger.

With its low-fares policy, GOL quickly grew from strength to strength. On 17 May 2004, it ordered 43 Boeing 737-800s, to add to its existing fleet of 20 -700s and -800s. On 24 June, a public stock offering raised $281 million additional capital. In December Buenos Aires became the first international city on the map, which already resembled that of the former Varig at the height of its expansion. In July 2006, GOL took delivery of the first 737-800, which had good airfield performance, especially for operations at Rio de Janeiro's downtown Santos Dumont airport, where the runway is only 4,300 feet long. Another 67 more of the type were on order, some to serve international destinations which now included Santa Cruz, Bolivia; Asuncion, Paraguay; and Montevideo, Uruguay, as well as Buenos Aires. However, GOL did not escape a tragedy that befalls almost every airline in the world. It was unlucky, and likely blameless, on 29 September 2006, when a 737-800 collided in mid-air with a privately owned EMB-135 business jet en route to Manaus, killing 155 passengers and crew. While investigations continued to determine the cause of this setback, GOL moved on, acquiring control of Varig in March 2007 for a reported $275 million. The pioneer airline continued to operate under its own name on a restricted long-haul network, but not as a no-frills low-fare airline. Within a period of only a few years, GOL had usurped the entire airline establishment to claim air transport leadership in Brazil.

Chapter 42: Down Mexico Way

Two National Airlines

"South of the border, down Mexico way," starts the popular song of the 1930s, conjuring up a vision of serenity and siestas, margaritas and tequilas, beaches, and mariachi bands. Traditional associations with Mexico were far from that of technology, and only in the last half-century has this country of more than a 100 million population, and its capital the second largest mega-city in the world, been ranked globally as an industrial nation. Yet its airlines have always been in the vanguard of fleet quality, on-board service, and, within the restrictions of trans-border agreements, route development. Much of this progress was made as airline associates of the U.S. Pan American Airways, but by the beginning of the Jet Age, these were being eroded.

Compañia Mexicana de Aviación (Mexicana) can claim a distant ancestry as one of the earliest airlines in all the Americas, starting in 1921, and with a record of steady expansion ever since. **Aeronaves de Mexico**, the other national airline, grew from an amalgamation of several regional systems in the 1930s, before adopting its present name in 1972 (see below). Both companies entered the Jet Age in different ways, with equally strong initiatives. During their individual courses of development, they have alternately benefitted from, or been the victims of, a dual-airline policy that has been sustained by all Mexican governments, even when changed every six years.

On 31 May 1957, with 20% of its stock owned by Pan Am, Aeronaves de Mexico led the way into the Jet Age when it ordered two 92-seat Bristol Britannia 302 four-engined long-range turboprops. They went into service on the prestigious route from Mexico City to New York on 16 December and thus raised the stature of the airline, hitherto regarded as inferior to Mexicana, still 30% owned by Pan American. The two airlines had shared in the spoils of an important new bilateral agreement with the United States. The award of the route to New York evened things up, to the extent that on 21 November 1958, Mexicana added the Britannia, leased from Aeronaves de Mexico, on its DC-6B route from Los Angeles to Acapulco. The U.S. Civil Aeronautics Board (C.A.B.) protested that this was a device to use the resort city as an intermediate point en route to Mexico City, and the service lasted only two months. Further negotiations were successful, and nonstops to the Mexican capital with Britannias started on 1 September 1959.

The Bristol airliner's hour of jet (strictly turboprop) leadership glory in Mexico was short-lived. Mexicana ordered three 86-seat de Havilland Comet 4Cs on 17 October 1959 and put them into service on the L.A. route on 4 July 1960. During the next few years, they were deployed on other routes to the U.S.A. and to the main routes in Mexico. A leasing arrangement with **Aerovías Guest** permitted Comet service to Paris for a few months. Cooperation between the two national airlines fluctuated between operational courtesies and boardroom rivalries, and these latter had come to a head on 29 January 1959 when a strike paralysed Aeronaves de Mexico. The government took over the airline as a state corporation, with 80% of the capital acquired by the Nacional Financiera, which also took over Pan American's remaining interest on 26 December. Jorge Perez y Bouras was appointed director general, replacing veteran Carlos Ramos. Matching Mexicana's jet initiative, Aeronaves put a 138-seat Douglas DC-8 on the New York route on 15 November 1960, but it crashed on 19 January 1961 and permanent DC-8 service was not resumed until 1 July 1962.

During the late 1950s and early 1960s, most of the smaller airlines in Mexico were either absorbed by the majors or ceased operations. In 1960, Mexicana took over **Aero-Transportes (ATSA)** and **TAMSA**, while Aeronaves absorbed **Aerolíneas Mexicanas** (which had itself formed in 1956) and the routes of **Trans Mar de Cortes**. In August 1962, the Nacional Financiera acquired 88% of the shares of Guest, on behalf of Aeronaves, which thus became an international airline, with service to Central America, Bogota, and Caracas as well as the Atlantic route to Madrid via Miami. Toronto was added on 23 July 1964, At the other end of the distance scale, on 3 May 1965, a no-reservations 11-a-day Puente Aéreo service was established on the popular vacation route from Mexico City to Acapulco. Short-haul Douglas DC-9s began service on the route to Phoenix, with intermediate stops, on 10 June 1967, and provided feeder connections throughout Mexico. Perez y Bouras also formed Aeronaves Alimentadoras (see below), organized regionally in separate divisions. It took over the routes of **Aerolíneas Vega** and **Aeromaya**, whose HS-748 turboprops had been improving air transport in the Yucatan for many years.

As Aeronaves was gaining ground in corporate stature, its rival, Mexicana, was overcoming difficulties. The Comets were ideal to cope with the problems of taking off from Mexico City's 8,000-foot altitude airport, but they were otherwise uneconomical for the medium-haul routes that comprised Mexicana's main network. In October 1965, four 116-seat Boeing 727 tri-jets were purchased, and went into service in 1967. Although two of them crashed in 1969, they were to become the backbone of a rejuvenated airline, under the stewardship of Manuel Sosa de la Vega, who replaced Max Healey as director general in December 1968. A steady hand was certainly needed, as the airline had faced bankruptcy in 1967, a crisis that was resolved when industrialist Crescencio Ballesteros bought the Pan American stock on 15 January 1968. Things then settled down. Aeromexico turned its finances around, started to make modest profits, added to its 727 fleet, and to its destinations in the United States: Denver, San Juan, Dallas, St. Louis, and Kansas City. Havana service started on 22 April 1975. Before the end of the decade, it was called a

Attracting little interest overseas, as Mexican airlines were never prominent on the North Atlantic, the two domestic airlines served their country well, constantly upgrading their fleets with short-haul jets such as (left) Airbus A319s with Mexicana, or (right) Boeing 737-800s with AeroMexico. (McDonough)

"miracle airline" and competing strongly against the U.S. airlines on competitive routes.

Aeronaves de Mexico, meanwhile, changed its name to **Aeromexico** on 28 January 1972 and ordered two 277-seat wide-bodied Douglas DC-10-30s in June. They went into service on the route to Madrid and Paris on 1 May 1974, and (from Acapulco) to New York on 1 June. In 1975, services began to Cancún, the new beach resort in the Yucatán that had been the first to be developed in an innovative program by the Mexican government, not only to stimulate tourism, but also to improve the economies of the poorest states. During the next few years, the little Pacific village of Zihuatenejo was next on the planned list (as Ixtapa), followed by Manzanillo and Cabo San Lucas, all served by Aeromexico's growing fleet of DC-9s. In September 1975, the Madrid service was suspended as a protest against the Spanish dictator Franco's policies, and the DC-10s were then transferred in 1976 to serve Buenos Aires via Bogota and Lima.

In 1977, the Mexican government exercised its dual-airline approach by extending route authority to, and making some exchanges between both airlines, as well as creating an almost "open skies" policy with the U.S.A. Mexicana lost its exclusive rights to the U.S. Pacific coast, but received San Francisco, while Aeromexico was awarded joint service to Monterrey and Mérida, but conceding a share of the Acapulco shuttle. On 28 April 1978, President Carter awarded 13 additional U.S. points to the two Mexican airlines. One result of this liberal policy was that Mexicana became the first Latin American airline to carry five million passengers in one year, at the same time surpassing Brazil's VARIG as Latin America's largest airline.

By the end of the 1970s, Mexico had settled down to its undeclared, but clearly apparent two-airline policy, with both airlines adding aircraft and routes, especially nonstops from U.S. cities to Guadalajara, Acapulco, and Cancún, as well as Mexico City. Aeromexico's jets were all Douglas DC-10s and -9s, while Mexicana's were all Boeing 727s, until it too opened service with 315-seat DC-10s on 1 July 1981. But after steady profits for 15 years, Mexicana started to lose money in 1982, partly because of a devaluation in the peso, and on 15 July of that year, the government increased its interest in the airline to a controlling 54%. Ballesteros and Sosa de la Vega retired but the latter was retained as a special consultant. Sigfrido Paz Paredes, who had guided the tourist resort development program, was appointed director general of Aeromexico in 1984.

La Crisis and (Several) New Deals

During the next few years, things did not go too well for either airline. On 31 March 1986, a Mexicana 727-200 crashed near Mexico City, killing 166 people, and on 31 August, an Aeromexico DC-9 was struck by a private aircraft near Los Angeles, with 82 casualties. An "open skies" agreement with the United States brought more competition from north of the border, although Mexicana did, after 30 years of trying, finally gain a route to New York on 12 May 1989. Two weeks later, on 23 May, the government announced the sale of its majority shareholding. On 18 September, the Corporación Falcon, which included the Xabre group, acquired 58% of Mexicana, at a cost of $140 million, and set up a new holding company, Corporación Mexicana de Aviación.

Aeromexico, meanwhile, was in dire straits. Sparked by a decision to sell 13 DC-9s, and which was opposed by the powerful pilots' union, all the ground personnel went on strike on 12 April 1988. The airline announced bankruptcy six days later. It was grounded for three months amid charges of bad organization, government interference, and old aircraft. Local staff at Ciudad Juarez even started their own local airline. But the problems were acute. By August, half the fleet had been sold, and discussions aimed at privatization were on the way. On a more positive side, a new bilateral with the United States trebled the city-pair authority, granted extensive charter services, and established double-designation on some routes. In October 1988, a new, privately owned, **Aerovías de Mexico**, operating as Aeromexico, emerged. 55% of the shares were held by Mexican investors, 25% by the pilots' union, and 20% by Bancomer, the State bank. In relative airline stature, it was a shadow of its former self. Of the former 12,500 employees, it hired 3,600; the aircraft fleet was reduced from 44 to 28 Douglas jets; the number of city pairs served dropped from 204 to 98. But it did resume many of its international routes.

Both airlines entered the decade of the 1990s against a deregulated airline environment. Mexicana also laid off 4,000 staff, as the Mexican peso was devalued, competition became effective from smaller airlines (see below), and price wars diluted revenues. But essential steps had been taken to supplement ageing aircraft fleets. In June 1990, Mexicana ordered sixteen 130- to 179-seat Airbus A320s, with an option on 14 more, departing from its adherence to Boeing. In contrast, in April 1991, the new Aeromexico introduced two Boeing 767-200s, after decades of dealing with Douglas, which now had no comparable aircraft. It reopened its service to Madrid and Paris on 1 June, with 767s, and put them on the route to Los Angeles, while announcing an expansion program of 26 767s amd 757s. Other than the Airbus order, Mexicana was operating the smaller Fokker 100s on regional routes. In December 1991, it took control of AeroMonterrey, AeroCaribe, and AeroCozumel, while turning southward to start South American routes to Bogotá and Buenos Aires. However, the implied, accepted, and only loosely legislated two-airline policy was falling apart in the face of threats to the two big airlines: financial (further devaluation of the peso) and competitive (international and domestic), with a more liberal policy that permitted the entry of new airlines on trunk routes. Decisions were made without centralized control, and the Mexican air transport industry needed shock treatment. The shocks, though drastic, were only partly effective. In February 1993, the Aeromexico group took a 55% stake in Mexicana, and steps were taken to standardize the two fleets. In May, a plan to take a 47% shareholding in AeroPeru was a prelude only to a Mexican economic crisis in 1994, leading not to the expansion that was attempted during 1995 but to more belt-tightening in 1996, with cancellation of flights, returning of aircraft to lessors, and laying off of staff. The situation was so severe that La Crisis is remembered as a distinct event in the Mexican calendar.

On 13 March 1996, **Alas de America** took flight. This was an alliance of Aeromexico, Mexicana, and AeroPeru, which (with cooperation from Delta, which had taken a 35% stake in AeroPeru) could offer through service from New York or Los Angeles to Buenos Aires or Santiago. On 27 March, a complete recapitalization resolved many outstanding debts, and a reorganization of the corporate structure was possible. This resulted in the formation, by an exchange of shares, of a holding company, the Corporación International de Transporte Aéreo (Cintra). Aeromexico relinquished its control of Mexicana, and service was resumed to Washington.

The convoluted progress continued, as a new broom was beginning to sweep across the Mexican skies. In 1994, a budget-fare airline TAESA (see below) had begun to erode the incumbent establishment's market shares and in short order, reduced Mexicana's from 53% to 25%. Aeromexico's 44% was hardly affected, but TAESA gained 22% in a single year. Then, on 1 June 1998, the government had to take over Aeromexico when the flight attendants went on strike. Within a year, in yet another reversal of official policy, the Competition Commission favored splitting Cintra back to the two airlines. This was delayed when the September 2001 airline terrorist attacks in New York and elsewhere shocked the whole world of air transport.

In 2003, after almost 40 years of service, Mexicana retired its last Boeing 727, and introduced the 767 for long-haul operations. Domestically, as narrated below, it established a low-fare subsidiary in 2005. On 29 November of that year, this airline, one of the oldest in the Americas, was sold to the hotel chain Grupo Posadas for $165 million. Throughout its history, it had maintained a good reputation with its clientele because of excellent cabin service. Even during the years of alternating ownerships, alliances, and code-sharing choices with different foreign airlines, Mexicana still continued to receive commendations from international customer representative agencies.

A New Broom in Mexico

The economic and marketing conditions for the development of air transport in Mexico have been somewhat contradictory, in that progress during the early years of the Jet Age was slow. Though often handicapped by factors beyond their control, such as currency devaluation or labor unrest, the two major airlines were efficient and well liked by their passengers, who appreciated the fine on-board service. But they catered only for businessmen and more affluent tourists, seldom reaching out to the lower levels of the income pyramid. Of the country's population, in 2000 of more than 100 million, only about 5% had ever taken an air journey.

Those independent pioneers who tried to find a geographical niche, to operate local services where Mexicana or Aeromexico did not choose to go, did not last long. Passenger revenues did not match the operating costs, and there were problems in the lack of government support for the airfield infrastructure. During the 1960s, a prime example of an effort to break into the acknowledged two-airline policy was the sequel to Manuel Gomes Mendez's efforts—he who had stopped flying into a community as soon as the first jeep arrived where previously there had been no road. His network was to places west of Mexico City, and on 1 November 1966, he joined forces with Fernando Barbachano, who had provided travel services in the Yucatan since the 1920s, and who had formed **Aero Safari** in 1961. With a small fleet of Hawker Siddeley 40-seat HS-748 turboprops, their Aeromaya was able to offer a kind of domestic "sixth freedom" service from as far west as Puerto Vallarta to as far east as Cozumel by combining operating concessions west and east via Mexico City. Almost revolutionary in the Mexican airline world, Aeromaya offered cheap fares, as low as $56 round-trip from Mexico City to Mérida.

Possibly instigated by political maneuvers, this airline ceased operations on 22 May 1969, and the network was taken over by **Servicos Aéreos Especiales, S.A. (SAESA)**, a government airline that had been formed late in 1968 mainly to carry deportees back from the U.S.A. Also, Aeronaves de Mexico's Perez y Bouras had formed **Aeronaves Alimentadoras** on 28 October 1968 (see also above) to serve smaller communities that did not produce enough traffic for DC-9s. With fleets of Piper Navahos, this feeder organization was subdivided regionally, as Aerovias del Norte, Sur, Este, and Oeste, later acquiring a fifth division, Aerovias del Mayab. With the succession of threats to the survival of Aeromexico, the parent holding company Cintra (see above) was later to form **Aeroliteral**, which, with 27 Fairchild Metros plus Saab 340s, became the largest regional, serving 31 stations.

These regional airlines had semi-official government authority that all but excluded the formation of others by entrepreneurs willing to take risks where others had failed. Nevertheless, in 1970, **Aero California** was operating DC-9s in the Baja California, a once remote territory that was suddenly being discovered by the U.S. vacation industry, and one of the candidates of the Mexican tourist resort development agency that had started with Cancun. **Servicio Aéreo Baja** also opened service to La Paz and other Baja resorts. During the late 1970s, the Yucatan, already a destination for archeology-minded tourists exploring the ruins of the Mayan civilization, was, as described above, fast exploiting the potential of its beaches and crystal-clear Caribbean waters. In the late 1970s, Aerocaribe, Aero Cancun, and AeroCozumel were beneficiaries of this fast-growing market, even operating jet airliners such as the Airbus A320, but were absorbed by Aeromexico on 23 August 1990.

First of the newcomers to join Aero California was the **Concorcio Aviacsa, S.A. de C.V. (Aviacsa)**, established on 5 May 1990 by the government of the southeastern State of Chiapas, at the opposite end of the country. Like Baja California, it lacked good surface transport until recent years, except on its northern and southern fringes and between its two main cities, Tuxtla Gutierrez and Tapachula. Aviacsa filled the gap, starting on 20 September with a 89-seat BAe 146, and with a second aircraft, linking the State with the resorts of Yucatán. Business was so good that in 1991, 108-seat Fokker 100s replaced the 146s, and service was extended to Monterrey and Mexico City, with direct flights to Cancun and Mérida. Further progress led to further expansion in 1994 with 164-seat Boeing 727-200s, while the Fokkers were deployed for charter work. Aviacsa was privatized in that year, sold to Aeroecutivo (Aeroexo) based in Monterrey, and expansion continued. No longer under threat from TAESA (see below) it leased Douglas DC-9-15s in 1997, Boeing 737-200s in 1999, and entered the new century with a fresh image, 26 jet aircraft, and new destinations throughout Mexico and to five cities in the United States. It rose to replace the budget-fare maverick as the third largest airline in Mexico.

Abrupt Rise and Fall

As the air transport world in Mexico came to grips with a more liberal government, one that looked askance on an accepted two-airline system, deregulation did not at first take full effect. But on 27 April 1988, a new company swept onto the scene, the first in the country to echo completely the U.S. Southwest Airlines, with truly bargain-basement fares. **Transportes Aéreos Ejecutivo S.A. (TAESA)** was formed by Captain Alberto Abed, using two Learjets. He realized that there was often only a fine line between charter and scheduled service, and that larger aircraft were needed to take advantage of Mexican deregulation, especially with air freight.

In 1989, he started a cargo division with Boeing 727-100Fs obtained from the Mexican army, and by 1991 was operating scheduled passenger services from Mexico City and a cross-border route to Laredo, Texas, with 737-300s and the first 757-200 to fly in Mexico. Charging fares at about half the rates of other airlines, Abed was a roaring success. By 1992, with fares quoted as being on the level of long-distance buses, TAESA was serving 18 cities in Mexico. Operated almost "round-the-clock," its success was phenomenal, possibly unmatched in the world. In 1988, its passengers numbered about 8,000. In 1992, it claimed to have carried two million, 800,000 of them on charters.

Part of the growth had been underpinned by Hank Rhon, a Mexican financier who had taken a 51% shareholding, but he resigned from the chairmanship in 1993. By this time, however, TAESA was the third largest airline in Mexico, and "was hiring flight crews as fast as Mexicana was laying them off." But then came La Crisis, and a decline followed that was as extreme as had been its growth. Though still holding a 24% market share in 1995, sales dropped by 38%, and losses totaled $148 million. Apparently prepared to take unprecedented risks, flights were made to Japan for two months, and Douglas DC-9s and -10s, plus Airbus A300B4s were added to the previously all-Boeing fleet. Desperate to regain its clientele, ticket sales were offered on credit, but such desperate moves failed to stem the tide of declining fortunes. In April 1997, one of its major creditors, Bancomer, filed to place the airline in bankruptcy. Attempts were made to entice foreign investment, but with no success. On 9 November 1999, a DC-9 crashed near Uruapan, and though the casualties were not high, the consequences were. Questions had already been asked about the standards of maintenance (as well as labor problems), and the airline was grounded two weeks after the accident. The end came quickly. Bankruptcy was

The Boeing company found a good market in Mexico as the new airlines established themselves. Leading them were (left) Aviacsa, with 737-200s, and (right) TAESA, with 737-300s. (McDonough)

MEXICAN REGIONAL AIRLINES (from 1980s)

Airline	Main Bases	Date First Service	Main Fleet Type	Route Network	Remarks
Aero California	La Paz	Jun 82	Douglas DC-9	Baja, CA, Hermosillo	Suspended 23 Jul 08
Aeromar	Mexico City	5 Nov 87	ATR 42/72	Domestic routes	Owned by Grupo Aeromar
Aviacsa	Mexico City Cancún	5 May 90	Boeing 737-200/300	Domestic routes	Founded in Chiapas state, initially with BAe146s, then Fokker 100s. Grounded 6 July 09
Aéreo Calafia	Cabo San Lucas	1993	Cessna 208	Baja California	
Avioquintana	Cancún	1997	Embraer EMB120	Quintana Roo	
Click Mexicana	Yucatian	2005	Fokker F100	Yucatan, northern Mexico, Havana	Formed by Mexicana as a low-cost subsidiary. Re-named Mexicana Click Nov 08
Nova Air	Mexico City	2005	Boeing 737-200	Charters in Latin America	Suspended 5 Aug 08
Avolar	Tijuana	7 Sep 05	Boeing 737-300/500	Domestic routes	Suspended 28 Oct 08
Interjet	Toluca	1 Dec 05	Airbus A320	Domestic routes	Took over from Aero California
Volaris	Toluca	13 Mar 06	Airbus A319/320	Domestic routes	Owned by Grupo Televisa, Inbursa, and TACA
ALMA de Mexico	Guadalajara	12 Jun 06	CRJ 200	Domestic routes	Suspended 7 Nov 08
Aladia	Toluca	Dec 06	Boeing 757-200	Domestic routes	Suspended 21 Oct 08
VivaAerobus	Monterrey	Jul 07	Boeing 737-300	Domestic routes	Part-owned by Ryanair and the IAMSA bus company

declared on 21 February 2000, and all staff and assets were taken over by Lineas Aereas Azteca on 9 May.

The Gates Open

While TAESA was self-destructing, one company, founded only a year earlier on 29 January 1987, survived by a less aggressive posture. **Aeromar** began services from Mexico City on 5 November 1987, and cooperated with, rather than competed with Aeromexico, with which it code-shared on routes to the U.S.A. Operating with a fleet of 40- to 60-seat ATR 42-320 and -500 turboprops, it supplemented the main-line jets on secondary regional services. Other small companies, operating a few local routes but hardly more than as air taxis, were emerging all across Mexico, **Aéreo Calafia**, was founded at Cabo San Lucas in 1993, to fly Cessna 206s and 208s to cities and towns in western Mexico. **Avioquintana** started at Cancun in 1997 with an Embraer Brasília and a Fairchild Metro, did the same in the east.

With an apparent threat to its feeder route system, Mexicana made adjustments to its corporate structure. It had bought Aerocaribe in 1990 (see above), transferred its Fokker 100s, and rebranded it as **Click Mexicana** in July 2005, as a low-cost budget airline. Along with its parent operator, ownership went to the Grupo Posadas in December of the same year. Simultaneously, other entrepreneurs were taking full advantage of perceived complete deregulation, and entered the bargain-fare airline business. **Avolar** started operations from Tijuana on 7 September 2005, with Boeing 737s, and claimed to be the first genuinely low-cost airline in Mexico, as others had only conducted limited experiments. It might also claim to be the first one to fail. After financial losses and flight cancellations, the government closed the airline down on 28 October 2008.

Next to start was on a more solid footing, backed as it was by the affluent and influential Aleman Group. **Interjet** started low-cost operations from Toluca (40 miles west of Mexico City) on 1 December 2005, quickly building a fleet of a dozen or more Airbus A320s. It took over Aero California's Mexico City operations in August 2008, when that airline was obliged to terminate flights because of unpaid debts. Close on the heels of Interjet came **Volaris**, also based at Toluca, and also operating 16 144-seat Airbus A319s. Operations began with a flair on 13 March 2006, to Tijuana, launched by Mexican President Fox, and continued with élan, not only with cheap fares but with commendable on-time service, and various compensations to passengers for delays, and even for standing in line at the check-in counters—an innovation that was possibly a worldwide first. Of all the new low-fare airlines, Volaris's $100-million capital investment was the strongest, shared 25% each by the Spanish Grupo Televisa group, Protego Discovery Fund, the affluent Inbursa insurance company, and—significantly—the Salvadorian airline TACA. This last investor was fulfilling its dream of a Mexican operation that dates back at

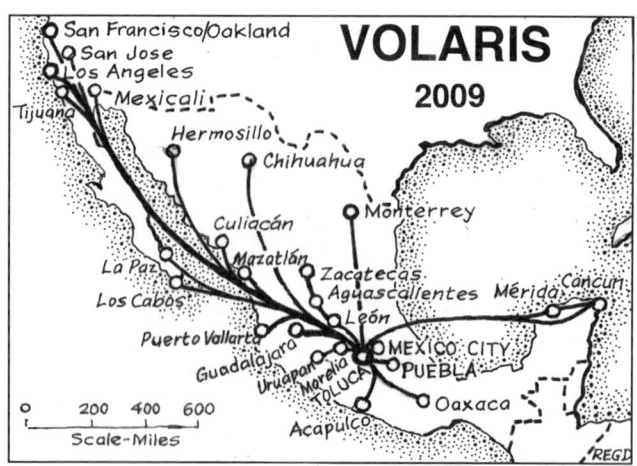

One of the most successful of Mexico's new airlines, Volaris was based at Toluca, a city close enough to Mexico City to share in its traffic potential.

least 60 years, but which has been frustrated by politico-industrial obstruction as well as normal commercial competition.

As indicated above, the year 2006 witnessed much entrepreneurial activity throughout Mexico. In Guadalajara, Mexico's second city, **ALMA de Mexico** started service to Puebla on 12 June 2006 with the first of 20 Bombardier CRJ-200s. It offered an intermodal benefit to its passengers with combined bus services from points such as La Paz, Tijuana, or Puebla to nearby resorts or other destinations. Hard on ALMA's heels was **VivaAerobus**, based in Mexico's third city, Monterrey, with a fleet of 8 Boeing 737-300s. It started service on 30 November 2006 with a capital of $50 million. Significantly, the co-owner with Kite Investments is Ireland's Ryanair, which, within a few years, has become the biggest airline in Europe, based on passenger boardings. A champion of cheap fares—VivaAerobus would challenge all the other Mexican aspirants for the market—it has, as in Europe, specialized (like Southwest in the U.S.) in serving airports that could be termed satellites to the major urban centers. This avoids airport congestion and thus reduces delays and even permits better regularity. Completing the list of low-fare startups, **Aladia**, also based in Monterrey, started in December 2007, with four Boeing 757-200s, but it suspended operations on 21 October 2008.

Throughout its extensive history of air transport, from 1921 to the present, Mexico has been a pioneer. From the days when Charles Lindbergh carried the first mail from Brownsville to Mexico City for Mexicana in 1928, its two-airline policy of the post-war years, its early operations of the first long-range turboprops and jets in 1959, and continued standards of on-board service that included its national cuisine: all these achievements could match those of the bigger airlines north of the border. Today, the industry faces the challenges of airline deregulation. Although the multiplicity of individual operators repeats and reaches the levels of past generations, such proliferation has bred innovation such as fare compensations and the intermodal experiments mentioned above. Mexico has adjusted to the Jet Age in its own individual style.

Chapter 43: Around the Caribbean

Decolonization

Until the early 19th century, almost the whole of the Americas south of the Rio Grande was still under Spanish sovereignty, while Brazil's independence from Portugal came later in mid-century. Exceptionally, except for Cuba and the island of Hispaniola, the islands of the Caribbean remained as colonies of other European nations until well into the 20th century, and some are still remnants of former empires. Cuba, Haiti, and the Dominican Republic have remained independent, while the islands of Guadeloupe and Martinique are now French departments. For airline integration, the three Guiana colonies of northeast South America were linked with the Caribbean. With U.S. sponsorship, Cuba developed its airline before the Second World War, and the entire area, including Central America, was included in the Pan American Airways network. This was operated for political convenience by subsidiaries in all the countries that the U.S. airline regarded as essential for its airline dominance of the region. Other initiatives to create an airline to serve the Caribbean as a whole were by British, Dutch, or French airlines or their surrogates.

The British Hand Over

British West Indian Airways (B.W.I.A.) had been founded in Trinidad on 27 November 1939 by Lowell Yerex, the veteran pioneer of TACA in Central America. Incorporated on 11 May 1943, it extended its network to Jamaica in 1944, to British Honduras (Belize) and Georgetown, British Guiana, then Ciudad Trujillo (now Santo Domingo) in 1945. Together with the West Indies Division of K.L.M., these two airlines were firmly based as the Second World War ended. B.W.I.A. became a wholly owned subsidiary of British South American Airways (B.S.A.A.) in 1947, and this control was transferred to British Overseas Airways Corporation (B.O.A.C.) in 1949, when B.S.A.A. collapsed. The Vickers Viking twin-piston-engined fleet was replaced in 1955 with 40-seat Vickers Viscount turboprops, and the British presence in the Caribbean consolidated by B.W.I.A.'s purchase, in 1956, of a 51% shareholding in Leeward Islands Air Transport (LIAT), based in Antigua (see below) and of British Colonial Airways, of British Honduras.

British interest was still strong throughout the Caribbean, and B.O.A.C. appears to have regarded B.W.I.A. as an instrument to strengthen its presence there. It had purchased **British Caribbean Airways** in Jamaica in October 1949, and merged its operations with Trinidad on 31 March 1950. B.W.I.A. then took over the international services of Bahama Airways, the management of British Guiana Airways, and as a convenience, subleased the local airline in the Cayman Islands to the Costa Rican LACSA.

B.O.A.C. further supported B.W.I.A. to the extent that, in 1959, some Bristol Britannia services to London via Bermuda,

One of Air Jamaica's Airbus A320-200s. (McDonough)

carried B.W.I.A. flight numbers, and from 29 April 1960, the Trinidad airline leased the aircraft, which were also used for the New York route, as well as B.O.A.C. Boeing 707s. After gaining independent status, the Trinidad & Tobago government bought the airline on 1 November 1961 for £520,000, with B.O.A.C. retaining only 10%. Jamaica attained its independence in 1962, and promptly founded its own airline, Air Jamaica, on 27 August 1963. B.O.A.C. held 16% and its new partner, the Cunard shipping line, held 33%. The Jamaican government had the controlling 51%, but the United States regarded the arrangement, as one writer described the action, "a perfidious plot to circumvent the terms of the Bermuda Agreement." The mood of the authorities in those days was far from the "open skies" attitudes of the 21st century. To establish better perceived legitimacy, the Jamaican government founded a new airline, **Air Jamaica** (1968) in November 1968, and which started service on 1 April 1969.

This effectively put an end to any hope that the name B.W.I.A. might have represented all the previous British colonies in the Caribbean. Such cooperation had been highly successful in the world of sports, where the West Indies cricketers combine their joint resources to be, in some years, the world champions. But airlines were businesses. Although it did take a 49% interest in the intra-island Jamaica Air Services, B.W.I.A. adjusted its policy to concentrate on regional routes. It ordered three Boeing 727s, mainly for service to Miami, and on 14 December 1968 leased a Qantas 707-138 for New York. Negotiations with a New York investment banking company resulted in reorganization on 21 February 1969. Service to Toronto began on 3 May. Trans-Atlantic flying carried on with charter contracts, and it disposed of LIAT to the British independent Court Line. Scheduled service to London was resumed from Trinidad and Barbados in April 1974. During the next year or two, additional European destinations were added, but these did not last.

Douglas DC-9s were introduced in 1977, and B.W.I.A. merged with the local **Trinidad & Tobago Air Services**, whose name then appeared on the aircraft to confirm the airline's dual national identity. Major reconstruction took place in 1978 in the wake of a pilots' strike. Wide-bodied Lockheed L-1011-500 TriStars with 237 seats were added in 1980, but the next decade was marred by annual financial losses, and the airline was

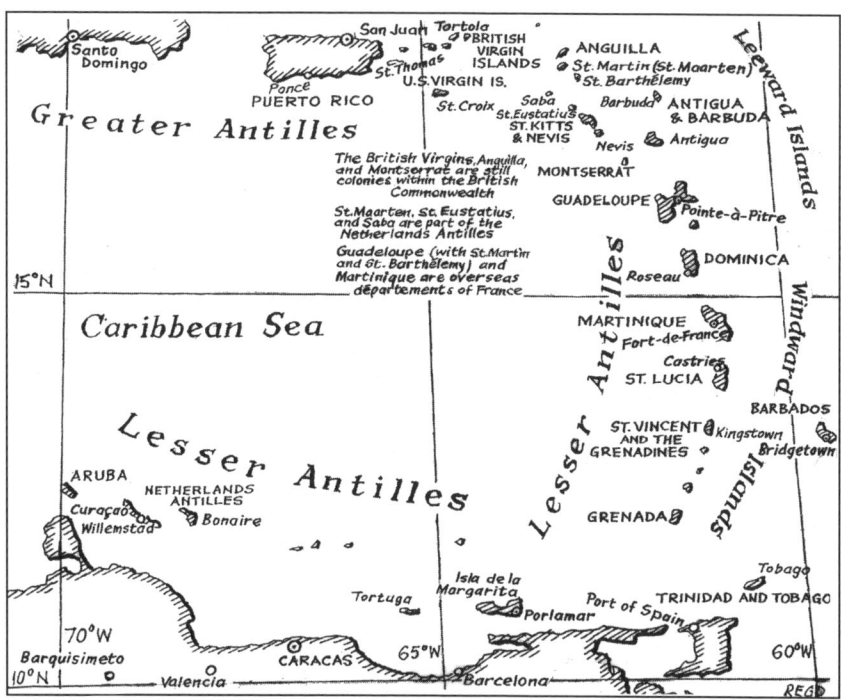

The West Indian islands are variously grouped as the Greater and Lesser Antilles and the Leeward and Windward Islands, administered under almost a score of individual nations or overseas territories.

sustained only by an injection of subsidies from Trinidad's oil resources. Operations were halted briefly in July 1990 by a political coup attempt, but the airline put on a brave face with its three-level (*Golden*, *Silver*, and *Scarlet Ibis*) cabin service.

A Douglas DC-9-50 of B.W.I.A. (Davies)

On 22 February 1995, a new chapter began as the airline was privatized. A U.S. investor group, headed by Ed Acker, formerly head of Pan American, paid £20 million for a controlling 51% of the shares, with the government retaining 33.5% and the employees 15.5%. By this time, the airline was becoming familiarly known as B-Wee.

Meanwhile, the new Air Jamaica had been far from idle. Following its first services to Miami and New York in 1969 (see above), it added Chicago, Philadelphia, Detroit, Toronto, London, Frankfurt and Nassau, Bahamas; and established Montego Bay as a co-terminal in Jamaica. It purchased Boeing 747-200s in 1976, but switched to Airbus A300B4s in 1983, while adding Los Angeles and Atlanta to its U.S. network. Air Jamaica progressed in its expansion with flair—not surprisingly perhaps from a young tropical country that entered a bob-sleigh team for the Olympic Winter Games. The cabin service included free rum bamboozles and elegant fashion shows by the stewardesses.

In November 1994, just before B.W.I.A. did so, Air Jamaica was privatized. With $35 million in cash, and acceptance of some company debt, the Air Jamaica Acquisitions Group (AJAG) acquired 70% of the shares. The AJAG head, Gordon "Butch" Stewart, fired all 1,400 employees, and then rehired 1,000 of them. The airline livery was enlivened with more color, and two MD-83 twin-jets were wet-leased to supplement the Airbuses. Because of the restrictive practice in the United States of categorizing countries according to its F.A.A.'s decisions on levels of safety by the respective national regulatory authorities, Jamaica was ranked as Category 2. This meant that its airline, which had an unblemished safety record, could not add new points in the U.S. to its route system. Stewart responded by strengthening the competition on the routes that he had, upgrading the Airbus fleet with six A310s and four A320s. He also established, on 15 June 1997, the Montego Bay resort as the main hub—a sensible move as tourism was a major Jamaican industry. By 1995, local connections to Kingston, Negril, and the Turks & Caicos Islands had been provided by **Air Jamaica Express** with three Dornier 228-200s, inheriting a tradition that had started with B.W.I.A.'s Jamaica Air Services (see above) in 1963.

Early in 1999, the F.A.A. apparently relented, upgrading Jamaica's safety rating to Category 1. By then, however, Air Jamaica was already on a roll. It had expanded to Barbados (where, in 1997, it had been declared as that independent country's national airline), and to Havana, Nassau, Santo Domingo, and

Grand Cayman. Many of these were served by the Express subsidiary. By 2002, the Airbus fleet had grown to 20.

But "B-Wee" was not doing so well, as Air Jamaica had even encroached into its own back yard, by taking root in Barbados. In May 1995, it started **B.W.I.A. Express**, which quickly became known as B-Wee Express, equipped with 50-seat Bombardier Dash 8s. In so doing, this subsidiary assembled several small local inter-island operators into its network.

While the two airlines at each end of the Caribbean chain of islands vied for international recognition, much had been happening politically in the region in between. **Leeward Islands Air Transport (LIAT)** was formed in 1956 by Frank Delisle in Montserrat, to provide a local service to neighboring Antigua. His airfield was an unprepared strip in front of his hilltop house, and in the early days, at Barbuda, Frank would land in the main street. Although the airline developed from a firmer base in Antigua, some airfields in the chain of Leeward and Windward Islands of the Lesser Antilles were often similar to Frank's. LIAT scheduled services began in 1957 with single-engined Piper Apaches, in conjunction with B.W.I.A., which acquired 57% of the stock. In 1959 it took over the services of the St. Vincent government airline, and by 1960, reached as far as Port of Spain, Trinidad.

Throughout the 1960s, LIAT made steady progress as it became the accepted taxi service between all the islands, still European colonies, but needing links between them. Elsewhere in the world, the Jet Age was in full swing, and tightly regulated, but in the eastern Caribbean, LIAT's single-engined Pipers and Beech Bonanzas would depart from the schedule if a passenger requested an en route stop. Responding to popular local demand, 19-seat de Havilland Herons were added in 1965 and 40-seat HS-748s in 1969.

In November 1971, by which time B.W.I.A. was in control through a 75% shareholding, LIAT was sold to the British Court Line for $4 million. Court was a shipbuilding and travel group that owned two hotels in St. Lucia and one in Antigua, and planned to expand the local operation to link with a trans-Atlantic inclusive tour program. By this time, LIAT had five 748s and five BN-2 Islanders. The Court Line added two more 748s and provided two BAC One-Eleven twin jets for the holiday season. Part of the plan was to extend services to St. Thomas and San Juan, both in U.S. territories and good tourist markets. But the ambitious plan was short-lived. In June 1973, to make ends meet (the 75-mile average stage lengths were quite uneconomical to operate) LIAT sought massive fare increases, and slashed operations, dropping all jet services. This caused some alarm around the islands, and to the airline itself, which in 1974 lost an estimated $25 million. In August of that year, the Court Line collapsed, leaving 40,000 vacationers stranded, many of them in the Caribbean. Emergency aid was provided by Britain and the local governments, and the ensuing crisis further altered LIAT's structure.

On 15 November 1974, a new company, **LIAT (1974)** was formed, following an agreement between the ministers of the eastern Caribbean governments and the Court Line liquidators. The new owners included St. Lucia, St. Vincent, Dominica, Antgua, St. Kitts-Nevis, and Grenada, which inherited six HS-748s and four BN-2s. Trinidad & Tobago, Jamaica, Guyana, and Barbados declined to participate. Funds were provided by a bank loan of $5 million. The airline continued to serve the islands, including San Juan, Puerto Rico, during the next decade, adding DHC-6 Twin Otters, and Dash 8s. Many of the landing fields were still fairly primitive, demanding pilots with certain skills not usually included in the training manuals; so that LIAT's safety record, with a single Twin Otter accident in 1986, was commendable.

In 1992, the shareholders, now numbering eleven, and most of them no longer colonialists but representing small but independent nations, decided to privatize the airline, offering to investors shares in LIAT, whose fleet was now standardized with 12 Bombardier Dash-8-300s. B.W.I.A. returned to the fold, with 29%, and the operational headquarters was transferred to Barbados, which contributed about one-third of the total boardings. In October 2000, B.W.I.A. and LIAT signed a corporation memorandum of understanding, and in March 2001, Barbados also became the operational hub. The following year, B-Wee Express was disbanded to avoid duplication.

Competition to the half-century-old LIAT came in different forms. At one extreme (though hardly a challenge), **Nevis Express** crossed the three-mile strait between St. Kitts and Nevis with an eight-mile route, qualifying as one of the smallest airlines in the world. Like so many other local aspirants, it was short-lived. In contrast, in 2002, a U.S. millionaire, Allen Stanford, started **Caribbean Star**, based in Antigua, with four Dash 8s. On 1 February 2007, its parallel flight schedules were amalgamated with those of LIAT, which acquired the newcomer on 25 October. The combined fleet was 18 Bombardier Dash 8s.

Another British entrepreneur had ventured into this market, which was becoming attractive to European tourists. In September 1970, Norman Ricketts, who had founded International Air Bahama on 2 July 1968, also founded **International Caribbean Airways (I.C.A.)**, operating, from 14 December, from Luxembourg to Barbados, taking advantage of the principality's non-membership of the price-fixing International Air Transport Association (IATA) cartel. Exactly a year later, the route was extended to London. In January 1975, I.C.A. became the international flag carrier for Barbados. Freddy Laker, who leased his Boeing 707s, held 49% of the shares. Douglas DC-10s and Airbus 300s supplemented the fleet.

Because of the nature of the market for freight, much of which consisted of perishable products northbound, and consumer products southbound, several companies operated mainly non-scheduled air cargo services from the United States during the 1980s. Caribbean Air Transport (Douglas DC-6As), Caribbean Air Cargo (Boeing 707s), and Caribbean West (707s and a Lockheed L.188) all identified themselves by name with the market, while Caricargo, was also successful with 707s. All these operated efficiently but seldom for more than a few years. In 1986, **British Caribbean Airways (B.C.A.)** joined the fray, with considerable flair, as an airline of the British Virgin Islands, but with its sights apparently set on expansion throughout the Antilles, it lasted only a few months. It had started from Miami on 17 April, well into the Jet Age, with a veteran DC-3, built in 1944, to cope with the 3,600-foot runway at Tortola. It had visions of modernizing with BAe 146s, but the U.S. authorities decided that its founder, Thomas Strasburger, an American citizen, controlled the airline, and withdrew its certificate.

During the late 1980s, in contrast, regulations were overlooked, ignored, and/or evaded by **St. Lucia Airways**, which had Boeing 707s on "special flights" to Tehran and Israel coinciding with arms and missile shipments to those countries, as well as "relief goods" to Zaïre. In connection with the Iran-contra affair, a U.S. Senate Committee referred to this little airline as a "CIA proprietary." Other small airlines came and went. As each new island-state felt that (as has already been done by larger countries to "show the flag" overseas) it could advertise itself to its neighbors, and even around the Caribbean, with its own airline.

Florida's Offshore Islands

Geographically the Bahamas are not in the Caribbean Sea, but are regarded as part of that region. Consisting of 29 islands and countless cays and rocks, their economy has been weak, as they have never had much produce to export. Even though it was the first landfall for Christopher Columbus, the Spanish made no settlements there, but British interests took over as early as 1647. Because of its proximity, its history has always been closely associated with U.S. affairs. It was a refuge during the American Civil War, and, like Cuba's Havana, was a popular destination after the U.S. Prohibition Act of 1920. By the late 1930s, to add to its illicit export of alcoholic liquor, the Bahamas was becoming a tourist destination, especially from nearby Florida. In 1943, Pan American Airways acquired a 45% interest in **Bahamas Airways**, a small company that had operated local charters since 1933. In February 1948, scheduled services started to Miami, soon followed by the transfer of ownership from Pan Am to British South American Airways (B.S.A.A.), which operated a variety of flying boats, including a veteran Consolidated Commodore. On 23 October of the same year, B.O.A.C. bought all the outstanding stock, having also, on 30 July, taken over B.S.A.A. which had collapsed. 10 years later, when the British flag-carrier formed B.O.A.C.A.C. (Associated Companies) to combine its various overseas subsidiaries into a single organization, it seemed to have lost interest. On 1 April 1959, 80% of the stock was transferred to Eric Ryland's Skyways, a British independent airline, which formed a local holding company. The U.S. Civil Aeronautics Board (C.A.B.) transferred Florida traffic rights, but granted them also to Harold Bamberg's **Eagle Airways** (Bahamas), which, on 1 March 1960, started a service to Miami with a Viscount, chartered from its companion airline in Bermuda.

B.O.A.C. soon had to mount a rescue operation when Skyways also ran into financial difficulties, and the Associated Company took back the 80% holding, reintroduced Viscounts in December 1961, and redistributed the stock as it inherited the Eagle operation, which the Cunard shipping line had acquired. On 7 June 1962, B.O.A.C. (70%) and Cunard Eagle (30%) announced the creation of a joint company, as Cunard had deserted Eagle, with which it had previously collaborated. For some reason, this great opportunity—for the Bahamas to benefit from the substantial tourism potential from the United States—was ignored or neglected, and on 1 October 1968, the Swire Group from Hong Kong, which also owned Cathay Pacific Airways, took over the Bahamas airline. B.O.A.C. retained 15%, and local interests 25%. Headed by Duncan Bluck, Swire introduced 79-seat BAC One-Eleven jets in 1968 and five HS-748 turboprops in 1969. But early in 1973, facing a wave of local nationalism, Cathay closed the airline down.

On 18 June of that year, a new era began. **Bahamasair** was founded as a national airline, merging two local companies, Flamingo Airlines and Out Island Airways, both of which had been flying local charters. With a $2.8-million government investment, operations began again on 1 July. But like its predecessor owners, and in spite of continuing jet service, it could not overcome the handicap of an uneconomic short-haul route structure, aggravated by increased fuel prices, and a surprising local apathy in the face of increased competition from U.S. airlines.

In December 1976, the Irish airline Aer Lingus was brought in as a management consultant, aided by government subsidies in the interests of preserving inter-island communications. This, in turn, subsidized the tourist trade that was essential to the Bahamas economy. The network was expanded domestically and to Atlanta. Boeing 737-200s, with 128-seats, were leased before the Aer Lingus contract ended on 15 May 1980. Gaining confidence, Bahamasair added West Palm Beach and Orlando to its Florida stations in 1984, extended the network to Philadelphia and Newark in 1985, and Washington in 1988. But even though its main U.S. competitor, Eastern Air Lines, went bankrupt in March 1989, and two Boeing 727s were acquired for $2.6 million, the longer routes to the northeast had to be withdrawn. It lost $15 million in 1990 and in April of that year, the first 50-seat DHC-Dash 8-300 began to replace 737s and HS-748s, with Cessna 402s for the short domestic routes.

Over the next decade, in the face of continued U.S. competition, Bahamasair survived by careful husbandry of its routes. It added 36-seat Shorts SD3-60s in May 1994 and leased 737s and even an Airbus A320 for the winter peak. Permanent jet service was restored in December 1997, but the Dash 8s were the backbone of the fleet. In January 2000, a new management cleaned up internal inefficiencies and turned in a modest profit—the first for several years. A restructuring plan included a route to Havana where at least there was no danger of any challenge from a U.S. airline. In August 2004, after a history of competing with the mainland industry, Bahamasair signed a code-sharing agreement with US Airways.

For some reason, the Bahamian national airline never sought to develop a trans-Atlantic market, either to Great Britain or to the European continent. This was left to the initiative of

Norman Ricketts, from the British charter industry, who began flying, as **International Air Bahama**, from Luxembourg to Nassau on 22 July 1968. The fares charged were non-IATA, and the base was chosen because it connected with the established non-IATA Loftleidir. This Icelandic airline took over in August 1969, exchanging a Douglas DC-8-63CF for the single Boeing 707-320C, and adding Freeport as an additional destination. Early in the 1970s, the name was simplified to **Air Bahama**. Such was the growing popularity of the beaches, the fishing, and the vacation ambiance of the Bahamas, a second trans-Atlantic airline joined Air Bahama in the late 1970s. **Bahamas World** leased a DC-8-43, a 707-320, and a Convair 880 at various times, and also flew from Brussels.

Nearer home, the liberal approach by the Bahamian government permitted, in April 2006, seven local charter operators to begin scheduled services within the many islands of the group. Far from regarding this as a loss, the transfer of many loss-sustaining ultra-short routes was of considerable benefit to Bahamasair's balance sheet.

Remnants of the Empire

A wave of nationalism spread throughout the Caribbean during the 1960s and 1970s. Some communities, however, decided to stay with their parent countries, which they regarded as benevolent rulers rather than as commercial exploiters. British exceptions were the British Virgin Islands, Anguilla, Montserrat, the Turks & Caicos Islands, and the Cayman Islands. Except for Aruba, the Dutch possessions in the Lesser Antilles remained with the Netherlands, while Martinique and Guadeloupe, along with the French half of St. Martin and St. Barthélemy, remained as French departments.

Among the exceptions, the Cayman Islands can stake a claim for being the smallest community (population about 20,000) whose airline is able to hold its own alongside major jet competitors from the United States. It has been able to do this because it has been well supported by its affluent colonial residents who sought a tax-free financial haven from Britain. It had started as **Cayman Brac Airways**, in 1955, to replace a previously failed company, to link the main island with Cayman Brac, 98 miles away, with single-engined Cessnas, flown by the Costa Rican LACSA at the request of B.W.I.A. In 1963, with a DC-3, it started service to Kingston, Jamaica. In the summer of 1968, it was reorganized as **Cayman Airways**, with the Grand Cayman government holding 51% and LACSA, with 49%, retaining a management contract. In December of that year, a BAC One-Eleven replaced the DC-3. This aircraft opened service to Miami on 30 April 1972, flown by LACSA as an extension of the Jamaica route, but its lease agreement was terminated on 30 November 1977. The Caymans had voted to remain a British colony, and the local administration purchased LACSA's shares to create a true Cayman Islands flag-carrier. On 1 July 1978, a second BAC replaced a DC-9 that had been leased, and on 29 October, Houston was added as a second U.S. destination. Such was the progress that, in December 1982, two Boeing 737-200s entered service to add more U.S. points: Fort Lauderdale, Tampa, and (seasonally) Chicago, plus Havana.

In 2004, this small airline went through an experience that has had little to equal it in commercial air transport history. The entire airline had to evacuate its base in the Islands and operate temporarily from mainland U.S.A. On 12 September, the eye of Hurricane Ivan passed only 25 miles south of Grand Cayman. With 12–14 inches of rain and ocean storm wave surges of 8–10 feet, the airport, only 8 feet above sea level, was devastated. Three days earlier, the airline president, Michael Adam, had put a contingency plan into action. He evacuated some residents and tourists with a round-the-clock shuttle service with the airline's four 737s to Miami, Tampa, and Houston. Cayman Express's two old DC-6s did the same to Roatan Island, Honduras. The day after the storm had passed, the damage was estimated at $3 billion. Roads were washed away, every tree uprooted or defoliated. The airport terminal floor was covered by four inches of mud. Potable water was in short supply. When, on 14 September, the first 737 arrived back, it began a free evacuation shuttle service for 45,000 people, many of whom had lost everything, including their passports. The Cayman Islands gradually came back to normal. Cayman Airways restored its services and, on 13 December 2008, was able to add Washington, D.C., to its route map.

Flying Dutchmen

The Cayman episode may have been the most dramatic of the occasions when the islands around the perimeter of the Caribbean Sea were attacked by hurricanes. The southern states of the U.S.A. were not immune either, and the 2005 devastation in New Orleans from Hurricane Katrina has gone into the history books. The various airlines of the area, big or small, all have more stories of adventure to tell than many a military organization, and give the lie to the assertion that commercial aviation is not exciting. For example, **Windward Islands Airways (Winair)** (oddly named, as it serves the Leewards) issued a T-shirt for passengers to support a claim that "I survived the Saba landing."

Saba (pronounced "Say-Bah") is a tiny island in the Dutch Antilles, little more than the top of a submerged mountain. Its population of less than 1,500 has always maintained the right to enjoy a local air service, as the ships to the neighboring Dutch islands took at least a day, and landing onto the shore at what passes for a harbor at Saba requires athleticism. Winair was founded on 24 August 1962 to connect Sr. Eustatius and Saba with the main Dutch base at St. Maarten. The airstrip at Saba was completed on 18 September 1963, and at first served by a 7-seat Dornier 228. Described by one passenger, an ex-navy carrier pilot, as a bigger challenge than landing on his aircraft carrier, it is 1,300 feet long, 65 feet wide, and has six windsocks, which often blow in different directions.

Close to the steep hillside, severe turbulence is common, and every Winair pilot used to spend a year in the right-hand seat, under instruction from an ex-Free French Spitfire pilot, Captain "La Pipe" Dormoy. To counteract the turbulence, his advice for the DHC-6 Twin Otter pilots who replaced the Dorniers' was:

Even in the Jet Age, there are airports that jet airliners are wise to avoid. Winair's Twin Otters have to approach the island of Saba with great care. (Davies)

"Approach the runway from about 50° to the left of the runway heading. Keep this diagonal approach, and pass about 200 feet to the left of the runway, aiming for the parking apron. With airspeed at about 66 knots, with full flaps, you will touch down on the runway immediately. Put the engines into reverse, and careful braking will give you a ground roll of about 250 feet."

Other than this almost daily adventure, Winair extended service to other neighboring islands, adding small Beech aircraft, In 1971 it added "International" to its name then leased a 40-seat FH-227 and began to serve the larger Windward Islands, including Guadeloupe and Martinique, and then St. Thomas in the U.S. Virgin Islands. However, "Windies," as it was becoming known, over-reached itself and had to close down briefly on 1 November 1974. With support from the Netherlands Antilles government, A.L.M. (see below) bought the entire stock and put the airline back on its feet, under the direction of Robert Volgers, a former K.L.M. executive.

The Netherlands retained an interest in the West Indies. Before the Second World War, the great Dutch airline, K.L.M., established a West Indies Division, based in Curaçao. By the late 1930s, it was flying around the Caribbean to include Colombia, Venezuela, Trinidad, and Dutch Guiana (Surinam); and during the war, to Miami. It thereby maintained its record of continuous service since its inaugural in 1921 and recovered strongly in the post-war years, with a trans-Atlantic route to the homeland. On 1 August 1964, the Division became a wholly owned K.L.M. subsidiary as **Antilliaanse Luchtvaart Maatschappij (A.L.M.)**.

With a fleet of four 40-seat Convair 340s (hardly appropriate to the Jet Age), this lasted until 1 January 1969, when A.L.M. became completely independent. To emphasize its local identity, it was headed by a native of Aruba, Ciro Yrausquin, who set about modernizing the fleet, to build up tourism, and to reduce its dependence on support from the Royal Dutch Shell's extensive oil refinery interests in Curaçao. The old piston-engined aircraft were replaced with two 80-seat DC-9-10 jets, and two 40-seat Fokker F-27 turboprops. In April 1971, a third DC-9 replaced the F-27s, so that A.L.M. could boast an all-jet fleet. It also chartered a DC-8-63 from K.L.M. to serve New York, and leased a Boeing 727 from Northeast Airlines to link the "A.B.C." islands with St. Maarten, where (see above) it took over the "Windies" operations.

Severe competition from the U.S. Eastern and American airlines, obliged a withdrawal from New York by 1979, but the fleet was improved by adding 131-seat MD-82s. Then, in 1986, Aruba separated from the Netherlands Antilles, but still remained as a Dutch territory. With its beaches and casinos, this island was the major tourist generator of the group, and thus eroded A.L.M.'s major source of overseas revenue, diluting its independent stature. In 1990, it joined with **Air Aruba** (which had just started up) and the Venezuelan Aero Servicios Carabobo (Aserca) to form a local regional alliance; and made an agreement with Surinam Airways. This too was hardly successful, and although a new image was promoted with a name change to Air ALM in December 1997 and a new insignia in January 1998, the Dutch Antillean airline was declared bankrupt in September 2001.

It was succeeded by Dutch Caribbean Airways (D.C.A.) which took over most of the Douglas fleet, and with support from the Belgian Sobelair, Air Holland, and Iceland's Air Atlanta, leased a 234-seat Lockheed TriStar and two 280-seat Boeing 767s to operate to Amsterdam. But this was over-ambitious, and D.C.A. ceased operations in October 2004.

Air Aruba, meanwhile, whose separation from the "A.B.C." partnership had contributed to A.L.M.'s downfall, was itself having problems. It had started service on 18 August 1998, with a small fleet of 60-seat YS-11s for local routes, but its ambition more than equaled A.L.M.'s as, with a mixture of leased Boeing jets, it attempted to build an intercontinental network to include the U.S.A., Europe, and South America. The joint agreement with Air ALM and Aserca did nothing to help, and Air Aruba also declared bankruptcy in November 2000. Equally ambitious was Bonair Exel, which operated briefly before suspending operations on 2 March 2005.

The Guianas

Less than 200 miles away from Trinidad, and separated only by the delta of the Orinoco River in Venezuela, the three Guianas were vestiges of the only region of South America that was colonized by the countries of northern Europe, rather than by Spain or Portugal. To provide airline service to them was operationally convenient for Caribbean airlines whose language was English, Dutch, or French.

Here, as an aside to this account of the Jet Age, mention should be made of the historic heritage of French Guiana, where the first sustained airline in all the Americas was founded on 7 June 1919, and operated local services regularly with small amphibians, from 1920 to 1922. With improved roads, air transport then lay dormant in the colony until after the Second World War, when Air France extended its trans-Atlantic route to the Caribbean, to reach Cayenne with 40-seat Douglas DC-4s, calling at Port of Spain, Georgetown and Paramaribo en route. Local services, echoing those of 30 years previously, were resumed in 1949, by a private enterprise, **Société Aérienne de Transports Guyane-Antilles (SATGA)**, using de Havilland DH-89s. These pre-war wood-and-canvas relics of the 1930s were still operating well into the Jet Age until the late 1960s, when the company had been renamed Guyane Air Transport (GAT) to identify with its location.

Dutch aviation enterprise was created in Suriname (formerly Dutch Guiana) where the local government started operations from Paramaribo to the local bauxite mine with small aircraft and helicopters. It began a coastal route in 1960, and was officially established as **Surinaamse Luchtvaart Maatschappij (Surinam Airways) (S.L.M.)** on 30 August 1962. With DHC-6 Twin Otters, it joined the A.L.M. group and provided cabin service on the route to Curaçao. By 1967, it was operating DC-9s, chartered from A.L.M. When Suriname gained independence from the Netherlands on 25 November 1975, S.L.M. became the national airline.

It had already opened service to Amsterdam on 2 November, with a 242-seat Douglas DC-8-63, and its fleet, all leased, also included two old DC-6 freighters. In November 1978, services began to Miami, Panama City, Belém, and Manaus, but tragedy struck on 7 June 1989 when the DC-8 crashed on approach to Paramaribo, killing 176 on board. The event received additional adverse publicity as 13 Dutch professional footballers, visiting Surinam to help underprivileged children, were among the casualties. The airline took a long time to recover, but by the summer of 2004 was proudly operating to Amsterdam with a Boeing 747-300 Combi.

The largest of the three colonies, British Guiana, possessed more natural resources, mineral and agricultural, than its neighbors. It also had the Kaieteur Falls, a natural wonder, higher than the more famous Niagara or Victoria. Back in 1934, A.J. Williams had founded a local operation which worked for the government. In 1939 this became **British Guiana Airways (B.G.A.)** that operated a short route from 1945 with Grumman Gooses from Georgetown to the bauxite mine at Mackenzie In 1948, by which time two DC-3s had been added to the fleet, Williams developed the idea of slaughtering cattle before transporting them to Georgetown, the capital. This was far more practical than by land, when they would lose much of their marketable beef during several days of driving. B.G.A. also started a service to Trinidad, and in July 1955, the Colonial government took over, and B.W.I.A. provided the management. In 1963, as the colony moved toward independence, the name was changed to Guyana Airways. After free elections in 1953, the socialist leanings of Cheddi Jagan, the chief minister, did not find favor in Britain, which suspended the constitution, and restored it in 1957. After violent riots, Guyana gained its independence in 1966, and **Guyana Airways** became the national airline in 1973. After a period in political opposition, another free election enabled Jagan to become president in 1992. The airline was persuaded to acquire a Tupolev Tu-154B tri-jet in 1985, but like others that had tried the Soviet aircraft, soundly built though they were, the problem of maintenance and spares provision was unworkable. When the airline was declared insolvent in May 2001, it had one Boeing 757-200 and one Airbus A300B4, both leased.

Subsequently, the way toward an airline for Guyana has been an uphill battle. In July 1999, GA2000 wet-leased a Boeing 757, but folded in 2003. **Universal Airlines** was established to replace Guyana Airways in 2001, and started operations on 13 December with a 243-seat Boeing 767-300ER, leased from Poland, for a service to New York. It then had an Airbus A320, leased from TACA, but it was repossessed in 2005, and this was the end of Universal. The only local domestic services have been flown since 1997 by Trans Guyana Airways, with a Shorts Skyvan twin turboprop, two Cessna Grand Caravans, and three Britten Norman Islanders.

The French Caribbean

Far removed from its historic Guiana venture in 1919 (see above), commercial aviation by French enterprise within the islands of the Antilles did not reappear until immediately after the Second World War. Air France then operated its large Latécoère flying boats to restore links with the homeland, as Guadeloupe and Martinique had been under Vichy control during hostilities, and had no airfields. A company named, impressively, **Compagnie Aérienne Antillaise (C.A.A.)** was formed in 1946 by a flying adventurer, Remy De Haenen, at the tiny island of Tintamarre, or Flat Island, less than two miles long and uninhabited. With a fleet of old Stinsons and Vought Kingfishers, and even a

One of Surinam Airways' Boeing 737-300s. (McDonough)

De Havilland Canada DH-6 Twin Otters were much in demand throughout the Caribbean islands. This one of Air Guadeloupe is pictured at Saint Maarten. (Davies)

vintage Sikorsky S-41, the operations carried much inter-island traffic that was of questionable legality, but was popular with the locals because a 10-minute flight, even in an aircraft where a passenger had to hold the door closed, was preferable to hours in a boat. Eventually, the authorities, who must have held the record for regulatory tolerance, suspended C.A.A.'s operations in June 1947, after three fatal crashes in four months.

One of the flying staff was Captain Dormoy, the Capitain La Pipe of Windward Islands Airways (see above), who formed Guadeloupe Air Transport in 1950. He too had difficulty in promoting his venture into a scheduled service, as he complained that, at St. Barthélemy, "you had to pass over the field several times to warn the farmers to clear the sheep." Eventually, some kind of legislative order was established, with the formation of **Air Guadeloupe** on 25 March 1970. Air France held 45% of the shares, with the remainder by the French government and by representatives of all the French Caribbean islands, except

Landing at Saint Barthélemy demanded special skills by the pilots. (Davies)

Martinique. It started with 19-seat DHC-6 Twin Otters, bravely serving Désirade's 700-meter (2,300 feet) strip and making the final approach at Saint Barthélemy ("St. Barth"), where passengers can wave *upward* to people in cars on the parallel road. In 1978, a 44-seat Fokker F-27 turboprop started to operate a shuttle service to Martinique.

The growing fleet included **Air Antilles**, operating DC-3s locally, and which was taken over in 1978; and the airline came to an agreement with Air France. The French flag carrier had been flying between the islands and on to French Guiana, with DC-4s, with a frequent DC-3 shuttle service between Guadeloupe and Martinique. It was now flying Caravelle jets (and later, Airbuses) in the area. Another small company, Air Foyal, with two Bandeirantes, was taken over in 1980, by which time Air Guadeloupe was well established along the island chain as a French competitor to the English-speaking LIAT.

Maintaining a local display of independence, **Air Martinique** was formed as a charter operation in June 1974. With F-27s, it began scheduled service within the Windward Islands to the south, while Air Guadeloupe served the Leewards to the north. Both flew to the French side of St. Martin/St. Maarten. Two Caravelles, introduced in 1980, were too big for the inter-island traffic density, except for the Martinique-Guadeloupe connection, a route that is economically too short.

Not to be outdone, little St. Barth started its own charter flights on **Air St. Barthélemy**, with single-engined aircraft in February 1982, and in 1984 the French government granted permission for local scheduled service, but not to Guadeloupe. Air St. Martin even followed suit. Such self-defeating diversification was resolved in 1990 by merging the four French airlines into **Caraïbes Air Transport (CAT)**, which also ran into financial difficulties. In 2000, the Dubreuil industrial group purchased CAT and renamed it **Air Caraïbes**. Its fleet comprised 50-seat ERJ-145s and ATR-42s, 70-seat ATR-72s, plus smaller Dornier 228s and Cessna Caravans. On 26 March 2001, the hazardous approach into the 2,170-foot strip at St. Barth claimed a victim as 19 people were killed as a Caraïbes aircraft tried to land. This airline was more firmly established than its predecessors, flying a trans-Atlantic route from Paris, with Airbus A340s replacing Air Lib, which had terminated flights.

In December 2002, yet another airline added further capacity to the competitive and booming West Indian aviation environment. Air Antilles Express was a branch of Air Guyane, and by offering cheaper fares, its two ATR-42s made a severe dent in Air Caraïbes's market.

Hispaniola

The great Pan American Airways had come to rule the entire Latin American skies since its first tentative Key West-Havana service in 1928. But after the Second World War, it had little interest in most of the smaller Caribbean islands. It could easily overfly them between San Juan, in the U.S. Territory of Puerto Rico, and on to Trinidad, where the United States had been well established after the airport became part of the wartime

Lend-Lease deal with Great Britain. But it still needed bases in the larger islands, comprising the Greater Antilles, and still retained a minority interest in Cuba (see above) and the island of Hispaniola, shared by Haiti and the Dominican Republic, to the west of Puerto Rico.

On 26 April 1944, it had formed **Compañia Dominica de Aviación (C.D.A.)**, supplying it with two Ford Tri-Motors for local services, and Curtiss C-46s for cargo flights with chilled beef to Puerto Rico, an operation that was to sustain the airlines of the Dominican Republic for several decades. Passenger service to Miami and San Juan was eventually granted, for DC-3s, on 10 March 1955, and Pan Am terminated its interest in C.D.A. on 26 July 1957. This had been negotiated with Leonidas Trujillo, who was the country's dictator from 1930 until he was assassinated in 1961. A period of instability followed, with C.D.A.'s fleet of C-46s, a DC-3, and two DC-4s, all old and unpressurized, taken over by government agencies. The first pressurized DC-6Bs arrived in 1963, and the first jets, DC-9s, leased from Venezuela's VIASA, entered service in 1967. The route to Caracas via San Juan, was a joint operation, with the aircraft carrying the insignia of both airlines.

A Dominicana Douglas DC-9-30. (McDonough)

The airline sustained a set-back on 15 February 1970, when a new DC-9-30 crashed on take-off at Santo Domingo, killing all 103 on board, and this contributed to losses of more than $1 million per year. Operations were not resumed until September, with a leased Lockheed L.188 Electra, followed by a Boeing 707 from Pan Am, and then a 737. On 13 April 1972, the U.S. C.A.B. approved a service to New York, which was promptly inaugurated with two leased Boeing 727s. Expansion continued throughout the 1980s as the country diversified its economy, including the establishment of vacation resorts. The Republic also gained some indirect attention by the prowess of its baseball players, many of whom became stars in the United States. In June 1994, New York (the second largest Dominican city in resident population) was being served by a leased 270-seat Douglas DC-10-40.

Small private airlines emerged from the freedom that followed Trujillo's policy that had given C.D.A. a monopoly. First of these was **Quisqueyana** (the indigenous name for Hispaniola) that was founded with a DC-3 and a Piper Cub in September 1962 to share the meat business to San Juan. It operated spasmodically for a while, with an international service to Curaçao and Aruba, but lost its fleet of two DC-3s that were hijacked by pilots hired by the former owner-creditors. It then acquired, in 1966, two Lockheed Constellation L-749As, but did not put them into service until 1971. Learning by experience, on 26 January of that year, an attempted hijacking was foiled by the crew.

Early in 1974, Quisqueyana received Douglas DC-8 jets, which were used for charter work including Middle East pilgrimage flights to Mecca. Two leased Boeing 707-331s replaced the DC-8s, and on 6 April 1976, the airline optimistically started a service to Madrid and Rome. But this lasted only a few months. Meanwhile, it had been operating the old Constellations, and attained a place in the airline record books when, on 19 January 1978, the last scheduled service by the type flew to San Juan and back. This was 20 years after B.O.A.C. and Pan American had introduced the first sustained jet services and the "Connies" were well past their shelf lives. But the block times on the short routes were not much different from those of the jets, and the clientèle, who benefitted from lower fares, found the accommodation and service to be quite acceptable. But Quisquyana had to declare bankruptcy in May 1978.

When C.D.A. was adjusting to the post-Trujillo conditions, and operating its first jet, together with Quisqueyana, more liberal regulations permitted the entry into the Dominican aviation scene in 1967 of what was described as "a wave of flying truckers." Aéreo Dominicano and Domaire operated cargo C-46s, the former also with a DC-6B leased from Costa Rica, but both had folded by 1973. Alas del Caribe added to its C-46 freighters a fleet of eight Britten Norman BN-2 Islanders in 1972 for domestic services. These were still needed as the Republic did not yet have a good road system, and had never had a railroad. Aeromar had a larger fleet of 10 workhorse C-46s, and was another Constellation operator in 1978–79. It moved into jets in 1978, with two Boeing 720s and four DC-8s. More solidly in the Dominican air trucking business was **ARGO**, which had a DC-6 and a Convair 240, as well as eight C-46s, and acquired two Constellation L 749As in 1978–71. In 1974, among other small companies, Aerochago joined in, also with two Constellations, and added a Convair 240 and then to two Boeing 707s in 1980–82.

The Curtiss C-46 has often been compared unfavorably with the more widely known Douglas DC-3. But for short-haul work from Santo Domingo, each one could carry 15,000 lb. of meat to the restaurants in San Juan. From 1948 to 1951 alone, this regular shuttle service carried 9,000 tons. One C-46 suffered an undignified experience, when, in September 1979, Hurricane David deposited it, upside down, on the roof of a building at Santo Domingo.

This natural disaster would rival the one that would hit the Cayman Islands in 2004 (see above). Santo Domingo was without electricity or piped water for almost a month. It also affected all the airlines, whose fleets were damaged, and in another similar disaster, it contributed to the demise of ARGO in May 1983. This little airline should go into the record books too, as it had retired the last revenue-earning, albeit non-scheduled and all-cargo, operational Lockheed Constellation in February of that year.

The neighboring French-speaking republic of Haiti was far less progressive. At best, its participation in air transport can be described as intermittent. Originally established as the **Aviation Corps de la Garde d-Haiti** on 31 May 1943, it was authorized to carry passengers a year later. After the Second World War, when the country was still ruled by the infamous Francois "Papa Doc" Duvalier, it had the rare distinction of operating an old Boeing 307 Stratoliner. In 1961, its name was changed to the **Compagnie Haïtienne de Transports Aériens (COHATA)**. A private Air Haiti International attempted to start an international route but was disallowed by the government. Finally, **Air Haiti** was formed in December 1969, jointly by Haitian and U.S. interests, and began non-scheduled and cargo C-46 and DC-6 flights from Port au Prince to Miami. In 1973, it was flying with two DC-8-21s to Miami, San Juan, and New York. It provided a domestic service to Cap Haïtien and also operated as Haiti Air International.

Politically Defiant Independence

The airlines of the Caribbean were often handicapped by inadequate infrastructure, attacked by hurricanes, sometimes suffered from excess competition or overambition, and were occasionally the victims of local political interference. In this last category, no airline suffered more than **Cubana**, the national airline of Cuba. It had a respectable history, dating back to the 1920s, when it was founded by the Curtiss aviation group. In 1932, it became a subsidiary of Pan American, which eventually sold it to Cuban interests in 1954. Lockheed Constellation service began from Havana to Madrid on 22 November of that year, and in 1956, Super-G Constellations opened service to New York, with turboprop Viscounts operating to Miami. Forging ahead, more aircraft were added, and 120-seat four-engined Bristol Britannia long-range turboprops ordered in June 1957.

However, when the first Britannia arrived on 19 December 1958, Cubana had already lost a Viscount on 7 November through rebel action. The inaugural Britannia service to Mexico City on 22 December was followed by a prestigious service to New York in March 1959. But celebrations were muted. On 16 February the Cuban communist revolution had installed Fidel Castro as its president, to replace the previous corrupt regime. In May, the new Cuban government took over Cubana, together with two other smaller Cuban airlines. At first, with four Britannias, progress continued, even impressively, with a nonstop route to Madrid starting on 5 June and the New York route scheduled daily on 15 July. But far-reaching changes, both administrative and political, meant that further celebrations were short-lived. Two Boeing 707s that had been ordered were leased to Western Airlines, and the fleet of Viscounts and Constellations was offered for sale, ostensibly to pay off outstanding debts. On 20 September 1960, Cubana's aircraft were impounded in New York, and not released until 3 November.

These actions were far more than the result of financial problems. Castro's government turned its back on the United States, its main trading customer, and aligned itself with the Soviet Union. Diplomatic relations with the United States were severed, and travel, even to nearby Florida, was abandoned by both sides, except for refugees from the communist rule. Lacking maintenance support for the Britannias, Cubana made an agreement with the Czechoslovak airline, C.S.A., to operate to Prague, under Czech colors. Cubana continued to serve Madrid via Bermuda and the Azores. To begin a massive transition from western to eastern (Soviet) equipment, the first of five Ilyushin Il-14 piston-engined twins was delivered for domestic services in October 1961. A year later, on 23 December 1962, the first of seven 100-seat Ilyushin Il-18 four-engined turboprops went into service to Mexico City.

Cubana adjusted to the requirements of Castro political directions, but the spirit and pride of the airline employees remained. Fortunately, many nations other than those in the communist bloc saw no reason to adopt a hostile attitude, and Spain particularly was sympathetic to its former Spanish-speaking colony. The airline survived the turmoil of the October 1962 missile crisis, when the Soviet Union tried to establish a base for nuclear missiles in Cuba. Cubana did its best to maintain "service as usual." In March 1964, Il-14 flights to Bermuda began, while flights to Prague and Madrid continued without much hindrance. Antonov An-24 twin-engined turboprops became the mainstay of the domestic services. This included an Il-18 schedule to Santiago, Chile, where a Communist party had won the election. The service started, via Lima, on 26 June 1971, but was curtailed to Lima when, on 11 September 1973, the Chilean president, Salvador Allende, was assassinated. Cubana had already, on 24 April 1972, introduced the 160-seat Ilyushin Il-62 four-engined long-range jet to Madrid via the Azores. Il-62 service to Prague, also via the Azores and Madrid, followed on 19 September 1972, and to Berlin on 2 April 1973. Feeling its international feet, and in spite of a firm U.S. embargo, Il-18 service began on 3 October to Georgetown, Guiana via Jamaica and Trinidad or Barbados.

The Cuban Communist regime was ostracized by U.S. governments, but most other nations tolerated the system and permitted travel to Havana, where prices were low, and the people friendly, with good food, entertainment, and sunny beaches. Banned from direct flights from the U.S., even from nearby Miami, except for special cultural exchanges, flying to Cuba was attained by connections in Mexico City or Nassau, Bermuda. Canada did not align itself with the firm exclusion policies of the U.S. Thus, in February 1976, Cubana leased three Douglas DC-8s from Air Canada. That country did not share the views

Before Cuba's revolution in 1959, its national airline had set a few local records with its 120-seat Bristol Britannia long-range turboprops. (Davies)

Under the communist government in Cuba, Cubana had to depend on the Soviet Union to supply its fleet. This is one of its Ilyushin IL-62s. (Davies)

of the United States, and its airlines, as did those in Europe and Latin America, flew tourists to Cuba. One of the DC-8s was lost on take-off at Barbados in October of that year when observers claimed that "two bombs blew the DC-8 out of the sky." In March, an An-24 had also been lost in a mid-air collision.

The 1980s saw Cubana consolidating as best it could. The Soviet Union was still the main supplier of its aircraft fleet, but the U.S. blockade ensured that the supply chain for spare parts was long and slow for a fleet that now included 100-seat Yak-42 wide-bodied tri-jets, and 30-seat Yak-40 feeder tri-jets. Curiously, in a parallel situation with Cuba's veteran cars, engineering ingenuity was the product of necessity being the mother of invention. The Soviet aircraft were fuel-hungry, but as they were solidly built, Cubana's maintenance shops could keep the fleet flying.

The 1991 collapse of the Soviet Union was a bitter blow. Cuba lost 85% of its export markets, 70% of its imports, and more than half of its fuel supplies. Cubana's marketing program intensified to tourism, especially to Europe, where the seekers of the sun did not distinguish Varadero Beach from any other, or Havana's food, its bars, or its rum, from any other. Eight Fokker F-27s were purchased from Spain's Aviaco, and two Douglas DC-10s were leased from France's Air OutreMer (A.O.M.) to supply the needs of a growing trans-Atlantic tourist trade. Unlike most of the Caribbean resorts, Cuba was not a tiny island, with limited interests. By 1995, four of Cuba's 16 airports were thriving international gateways, all of them radar-equipped, to cope with almost a million tourists a year. Cubana itself shared in the travel requirements and was described by one observer as "a classic case of how to run a safe operation on a shoestring." By the year 2000, with a fleet now including Airbus A320s, the tourist total rose to almost two million.

Successors to Pan Am

Once a key refueling or transit stop on Pan American Airways' main route from Miami to South America, San Juan, Puerto Rico, had, after the war, changed its status to being one of several airline traffic hubs in the chain of islands, the Greater and Lesser Antilles. In the early 1960s, in an extraordinary transformation of its daily routine, and as 170-seat Boeing 707s and Douglas DC-8 heralded the dawn of the Jet Age, 19-seat de Havilland DH-114 Herons became, in less than a decade, the most frequent visitors to San Juan's busy airport. Founded by Jaime Carrión on 4 July 1964 and named after Puerto Rico's second city, Ponce Air's four-engined Herons symbolized safety to Caribbean travelers. In September 1966, the name was changed to **Puerto Rico International Airlines (Prinair)**, and the uneconomic (and often unreliable) Gypsy Queen engines were replaced by 300-hp Continental 1-520s. With seating at one fewer than the regulatory 20 seats, no flight attendant was required.

This formula was immediately successful. Within months, routes from San Juan included Mayagüez, Puerto Rico; St. Thomas and St. Croix in the U.S. Virgin Islands; Tortola in the British Virgins on 1 March 1969; and St Kitts on 10 May 1971. To service this rapidly growing local network, Carrión had sought out every Heron he could find. In December 1969, he sold Prinair to the Union Corporation of Pennsylvania, headed by James Deresa, who continued the expansion trend with added vigor. By 1971, 20 Herons, each one painted a different color, were flying almost 300 flights a day, including 42 daily round-trips to Ponce. By the summer of 1972, with an annual total of 860,000 passengers, Prinair was among the largest commuter airlines in the world and had extended its route map to include St. Maarten, Aguadilla, and Santo Domingo.

The Herons were so intensely utilized that by the mid-1970s, they were nearing their certified airframe lives of 30,000 hours. In January 1976, a Heron Life Extension Program was approved by the F.A.A. and carried out by the respected Grumman aircraft manufacturer for an additional 30,000 hours. Soon armed with a Supplemental Type Certificate, the fleet grew to 30 Herons, but on 24 July 1979, a clean record was broken when one crashed at St. Croix, killing eight people. On 25 October, the F.A.A. grounded Prinair for three days to ensure that the weight-and-balance procedures for the Heron were modified.

Such was the traffic growth that on 15 January 1981, the first of four 50-seat Convair 580 turboprop twins entered service. Routes were opened to points in the Dominican Republic, but increased competition from Eastern Air Lines, which had absorbed Caribair, signaled a decline of fortunes. In July 1983, seven 23-seat CASA 212s replaced the Convairs, but a few Herons were still retained. Late in April 1985, Air Niagara purchased 80% of the stock, and tried to revive a faltering airline, with a limited Heron service. But the end was near, and this remarkable company's operating rights were revoked on 1 January 1986.

If Puerto Rico's Prinair seemed out of place in an energetic Jet Age, an airline in the neighboring U.S. Virgin Islands could be described as an anachronism. The Herons that frequented San Juan belonged to the pre-jet, post-Second World War piston-engined era; but some of the flying boats of **Antilles Air Boats**, founded on 1 February 1964, belonged to the era before that. Their existence stemmed partly from the past experience of Charlie Blair, a veteran Pan American pilot, and partly because he realized that there were no adequate or convenient airfields in the Virgins at that time. He started with a single 10-seat Grumman G-21A Goose amphibian, based at St. Croix, which at first lacked shore facilities, but was adjacent to downtown Christiansted, the main town on the island, and which was soon equipped with a ramp.

Service to St. Thomas boomed. A route to Fajardo, at the eastern end of Puerto Rico, started in October 1967, and to San Juan and to British Virgin Islands' West End, Tortola, in November 1969. By 1970, more than a dozen Gooses were flying to San Juan's downtown Isla Grande airport, and Road Town, the diminutive capital of the British Virgins. The islanders flocked to the flying boat services because they took them to within walking distance from where they wanted to go. Curiously, the only competition was from inter-island ferry-boat services, such as Bingley Richardson's Bomba Charger, whose 65-foot 90-seat launch covered the short distances in even shorter time.

Business was so good that Blair sought larger flying boats, although his interest was as much because of personal nostalgia as an economic necessity. He had flown the 47-seat Vought-Sikorsky VS-44A on American Export Lines' trans-Atlantic route and had purchased the sole remaining VS-44A in 1968 from Avalon Air Transport, which had operated it from Long Beach to the Catalina Island resort. Then, in the early 1970s, in addition to a few 15-seat Grumman G-73 Mallards and SA-16 Albatrosses, he bought two S-25 Short Sandringhams from Ansett, Australia. These were flown across the Pacific Ocean and the United States, and the only hindrance was when the F.A.A. denied one of them the right to be delivered by air (i.e., fly from San Juan to St. Croix).

The flying boat was "step taxied" across the 90-mile-separation and thus qualified as a boat—or so it was claimed.

In 1977, by which time the airfield and roads in St. Croix had been modernized, and on behalf of American Airlines, Antilles Air Boats operated four 48-seat Convair 440s between St. Thomas and St. Croix. The engines were supplemented by JATO (Jet-Assisted Take-off), an additional power unit, needed to ensure clearance over the high hill that overlooked St. Thomas's airfield, and which was later shaved off at the top. Tragedy then struck this innovative operator. Charlie Blair himself was one of those killed when he flew a Goose into the water at St. Thomas on 2 September 1978. The three passengers who also died were from drowning, and the National Transportation Safety Board (N.T.S.B.)'s report was especially critical of the airline's neglect of regulations and of the lack of F.A.A. oversight. Blair's wife, the former film star, Maureen O'Hara, kept the airline going for a while, but in April 1979, it was sold to Resorts International, which planned to open gambling casinos in the Virgins. But permission was refused, and Resorts drastically reduced the operation. It would have closed down, but on 10 September 1981, Mickey Brounstein, a New York investor, bought the airline and renamed it **Virgin Islands Seaplane Shuttle**, which began service under the new name on 15 March 1982.

Chapter 44: Central America

Pan American Heritage

During the foundation years of the airline industry in the small republics of Central America in the 1930s, Lowell Yerex, an enterprising New Zealand pilot of the First World War, had fashioned some kind of cooperative unity. Beginning in Honduras, he built Transportes Aéreos Centro-Americanos (TACA) (more below), which brought together the divergent interests and ambitions of the individual countries. In this endeavor, he was confronted by an equally ambitious entrepreneur. Juan Trippe, head of the powerful Pan American Airways, needed the cooperation of the same countries to support his airline's domination of the of Latin America airways. To do this (and often by methods that would not have survived an impartial review of the ethical standards involved), Pan American persuaded the republics to transfer mail contracts and operating rights to new companies in which Pan Am held 40% of the shares of each, with either the local governments or private interests holding the balance. The U.S. giant effectively stole Yerex's Central American airline empire.

The first of such transfers was a small company that had started in Guatemala in 1940. Yet, by the turn of events, it was the first to be divorced from Pan Am, when, on 14 November 1944, after a local revolution, AVIATECA was founded as the government's national airline. Compensating for that loss, and in the same year, Compañía Panameña de Aviación (COPA) became a Pan Am affiliate on 21 June, Honduran SAHSA followed on 16 November, Nicaragua's LANICA the next day, and Costa Rica's LACSA on 17 October 1945. (All these airlines are chronicled below.) Pan Am itself still retained full operating rights in Guatemala, and with a base in the U.S. Canal Zone, it reigned supreme throughout Central America during the immediate post-war years. TACA, meanwhile, moved to El Salvador (where Pan Am seemed not to need a foothold), and Yerex, disillusioned, handed over control of the airline that he had created, and departed to Trinidad to found B.W.I.A. (reviewed in Chapter 43).

Central America Finds Its Feet

When Pan American Airways achieved domination of the Central American airways, it introduced a new level of technology and operating efficiency, backed by financial strength, that TACA had not been able to match completely—though with its fast Lockheed 14 twins, it came close. Gradually, such expertise was absorbed by the local airline staff that began to stand on their own feet and reflect the wish of their local administrations to escape from the commercial control of the United States. First to claim the former Pan Am surrogate as its own national airline was Guatemala, whose government, on 14 November 1944 (see also above), instituted legal proceedings against Alfred Denby, Pan American's appointee, who had left the country. **Campañía Guatemalteca de Aviación (AVIATECA)** was at first 70% privately owned, but on 20 July 1946, the government acquired all the shares.

Even though divorced from Pan American, the city of Guatemala was then the largest in Central America, and Pan Am made it a hub for its chain of local international services between the U.S.A. and Panama. Tikal, in the northeast of the country, was one of the most visited of all the Mayan archaeological ruins, so that AVIATECA was able to benefit from the feeder traffic. It inaugurated service to San José, Costa Rica, as early as 7 July 1948. Slow but sometimes intermittent progress thereafter included service to New Orleans and Miami in 1955, and then to Mexico City, San Salvador, and San Pedro Sula in the 1960s. Then, in March 1974, joining other Central American airlines in its choice, it entered the Jet Age with its first 100-seat BAC One-Eleven twin-jet. DC-3s and Convair 440s linked the capital with the landing strip in the shadow of the Tikal pyramid. On 1 May 1976, it ventured across the Atlantic to Madrid, with allocated seating on an Iberia wide-bodied Douglas DC-10, but such ambition was tarnished by a DC-3 crash on 18 November 1975 and a 440 accident in May 1977. Nevertheless, the government airline fulfilled its mission in linking provincial communities to the capital and where surface travel was slow and laborious. It operated as such until 1989, when it joined El Salvador's Grupo TACA (see below).

The Guatemalan airline kept its name alive, even though it was a member of El Salvador's Grupo TACA. This is one of its Boeing 737-200s. (McDonough)

This airline, as chronicled below, has been a modern-day success story. It had won back almost all the Central American routes and traffic that, at the end of the Second World War, it had lost to the Pan American usurper. Now, in the early 2000s, with only a 30% holding in AVIATECA, it met some stout competition in Guatemala. **Tikal Jets** had, since 1990, operated mostly charter flights to Flores (near Tikal) with 25-seat Shorts 360 turboprops. The business was so good that, in 1994, it added a 100-seat BAC One-Eleven jet and a second one two years later. In November 2002, Douglas DC-9s began to replace the One-Elevens, and on 9 October, service began to Cancún, Mexico. The policy was to offer cheap—but not bargain-basement—fares, and still with first-class seats. TACA was operating one-class 40-seat ATR 42 turboprops. On 19 December of that year, service began to Havana, and on 22 March 2004, Mexico City was added. In spite of TACA's presence, Tikal Jets was named as Guatemala's official airline, a distinction it celebrated in October 2004 with services to Belize and San Pedro Sula, Honduras.

Of all the Central American countries that, toward the end of the 20th century, overcame the disparaging "banana republic" description, Costa Rica emerged as the most reputable. The days of revolution were past, and though its police force is well armed, it has no army, as since the invasion of 1948, threats from Nicaragua have evaporated. In 1949, **Lineas Aéreas Costarricenses, S.A. (LACSA)**, still with a Pan American interest, was designated as the country's national airline. In 1952, it acquired TACA de Costa Rica, a non-operating residue of the old TACA consortium, and—still associated with Pan Am—it stabilized as an efficient regional airline. It formed Cayman Brac Airways in 1955, extended services to Panama, San Juan, and Miami in 1956, and to Mexico City in 1961.

It had moved from DC-3s to Convair 340s, and a DC-6B, and on 14 May 1967, it entered the Jet Age with its first BAC One-Eleven twin-jet service. On 14 September 1970, a Costa Rican investment firm bought Pan American's interests, and the now-national airline promptly ordered more One-Elevens, the 99-seat -500 series. In June 1976, its first Lockheed L.188 Electra started a direct freight service from San Juan to Miami. The following year, route expansion took LACSA to Colombia and Venezuela, and on 18 November 1979, traffic volume on the Miami route demanded the addition of 160-seat Boeing 727-200s. Cancun, New Orleans, and Los Angeles were route extensions in 1980.

During the next 10 years, however, the run of success was eroded by increased competition from major U.S. airlines on the Miami route, which accounted for half of LACSA's traffic. In bilateral negotiations, the Costa Rican airline was always at a disadvantage. By 1990, El Salvador's TACA was negotiating to include LACSA into its Grupo organization. In June, this connection led to the delivery to San José of the first 162-seat Airbus A321, and confirmation of the TACA shareholding which, though only 10%, was of great advantage to LACSA. Air service in the homeland was not neglected. In association with the government, which held 49% of the shares, LACSA formed **Servicios Aéreos Nacionales (SANSA)**, replacing its old DC-3s with three 26-seat CASA C-212s in 1980. It served the country well, and survived a much-publicized CASA crash in the mountains south of San José on 15 January 1990. It held a monopoly until 15 January 1991, when Travelair was formed by the brothers Esquivel, operating one 9-seat BN-2 Islander and one 16-seat BN-3 Trislander. This was not an attempt to undercut SANSA's fares or its service to the Costa Rican community. Travelair aimed at higher-income tourists, offering higher standards of comfort and service, and working closely with travel agencies. In August 2001, Alex Khajavi took over and changed the name to NatureAir—reflecting the main interest of many of the tourists—and added three 19-seat DHC-6-300 Twin Otters.

Another airline that was launched with much flair was **Aero Costa Rica**, started by Calixto Chavez, who broke the LACSA monopoly on the San José-Miami route with two Boeing 727-200s on 23 May 1992. In 1995, one was subleased to Islena Airlines, of Honduras, to begin service to Miami from Tegucigalpa and San Pedro Sula. But, like many an airline entrepreneur in the small countries of Central America, the traffic was simply insufficient to cover the operating costs, and this promising effort did not last long.

Honduran Ingenuity

By most statistical measures, Honduras has been the poorest of the Central American countries, which for many years during the 20th century, depended on mining for a few years, as in Nicaragua, or tropical fruit farming. The latter activity earned them the communal descriptor as "banana states," and in the case of Honduras, the U.S. United and Standard Fruit Corporations held extensive citrus fruit plantations along the Caribbean coast. Not unique among the world's nations, but certainly rare, the capital city, Tegucigalpa, far inland in mountainous territory, had no railroad. During the 1920s, for the coastal industry, surface transport to the capital involved an arduous journey, first by a short railroad (attempts to reach very far had failed) then, successively, by road, a ferry across a lake, and finally by road and rail again. Most of the roads were unpaved, and public transport was by crudely built "baronesas"—trucks with improvised and uncomfortable seats.

The 1930s, therefore, witnessed the early development of air transport, with TACA (see below) emerging as a well-organized airline, and providing the foundation for future success. Pan American Airways also ensured that it had a foothold in Honduras, and in 1944, established **Servicio Aéreo de Honduras, S.A. (SAHSA)**, which with a single Douglas DC-2 provided the coast-to-capital link. As with its other associated airlines, it held 40% of the shares, with the Honduran government holding 20%, and private investors the balance.

Operating domestically and only to neighboring Guatemala, El Salvador, and British Honduras, SAHSA acquired TACA de Honduras in 1953, and, in 1957, ex-TACA pilot Joe Silverthorne's Aerovías Nacionales de Honduras (ANHSA), which had two DC-3s. This little operator's main business was transporting the government's monopoly of aguardiente, a potent liquor. One writer claimed that if it was converted to industrial use, Honduras could become a world power.

SAHSA's first overseas routes were to offshore islands, and the first services to supplement DC-3s and C-46s with pressurized equipment were, in 1964, 48-seat Convair 240s, 340s, and turboprop 580s. A genuine overseas route then began to Panama via the Colombian island, San Andrés.

On 21 January 1970, Pan American sold its stock to **Transportes Aéreos Nacionales (TAN)**, which was to make its mark beyond the territory of Honduras. It had been the brainchild of Cornell "Connie" Shelton, an ex-TACA pilot who had flown in China during the Second World War, and who had inherited some wealth from the Chinese Kung family—he had saved Madame Chiang Kai-shek's life during a wartime flight. He founded TAN in 1947, along with a former colleague, Bob Forsblade, and Miguel Brooks, a Honduran businessman. At first a cargo operator, he began scheduled service to Miami, with two Curtiss C-46s, on 12 June 1950. His objective and ambition was to provide air service to ordinary Latin American folk, whom he called the "barefoot people," rather than the affluent U.S. businessmen who comprised almost all Pan American-Panagra's clientele. When, therefore, in June 1954, TAN started international service southward to Lima, Peru, via Managua, Nicaragua, and Guayaquil, Ecuador, at very low fares to compensate for the austerity of the C-46s, this raised eyebrows in Washington, D.C.

The offended airlines claimed that, as a U.S. citizen, Shelton controlled TAN and that as the nationality of ownership was in doubt, it could not provide through service beyond Honduras. The C.A.B. agreed. Shelton then evaded these restrictions in 1957 by forming an ingenious consortium of airlines, recruiting C.E.A. of Ecuador, and APSA, of Peru, to cross-lease his C-46s on those sections of the route to Lima beyond those covered by Honduran traffic rights. A.P.A. of Panama was also involved briefly. During the next few years, as the world's flagship airlines entered the Jet Age, TAN was in constant conflict with the U.S. authorities over the Fifth Freedom issues and of Shelton's non-Honduran control. The real issue, of course, was the erosion of Panagra's market, which it regarded as its birthright, and several decades before the promotion of "open skies" as an airline creed. Shelton died in March 1965.

As mentioned above, by the sale of stock in 1970, SAHSA and TAN worked together. At last, in 1968, Honduras entered the Jet Age as 86-seat Lockheed L.188 Electras went into service to New Orleans and, under TAN colors, to Mexico City and Miami. Traffic then declined as the "football" war with El Salvador interrupted affairs in the summer of 1969, and a Douglas DC-6B crashed at Tegulcigalpa in 1971. But things improved as the first Boeing 737 flew from New Orleans through Honduras to San José on 22 October 1974. In 1977, the shareholders of SAHSA and TAN agreed to a reorganization to further integrate their airlines, by an exchange of shares, both by the two companies and by individual holdings. ANHSA still existed as a local airline and in April 1979, a DHC-6 Twin Otter was acquired to serve communities where the strips were "unprepared." SAHSA lost its Electra during a ferry flight in January 1981, but recovered to replace its 737s with the larger 727-100s, which also had more range, to open a route to Houston. But this success was short-lived, and SAHSA closed down in 1983. TACA promptly formed TACA de Honduras, a true "back to the roots" for the Salvadorian airline, which had started to fly the mail for the fruit companies in 1931. Operations were coordinated with TACA International and in due course, in 1995, it was absorbed in the new Grupo TACA.

The spirit of free enterprise lived on, as Honduras shared in the changing balance of the economies of the Central American region. The banana republics were changing. Tourism was becoming an important source of foreign currency. Some of the main destinations were the ancient Mayan ruins, and Copán, near the Guatemalan frontier, was among them. The offshore islands, especially Roatan, shared in attraction to regular tourists as desirable "off-the-beaten-track" resorts. A number of small companies, seldom more than fixed-base operators, usually with small Cessnas, catered for this business. Among them, from 13 March 1962, **Lineas Aéreas Nacionales (LANSA)**, persisted in operating veteran DC-3s from Tegulcigalpa to the coast, to the jungle outposts, and to the islands, for at least 20 years. Among those which flew shuttle services from La Ceiba to Roatan, Guanaja, and Utila was Isleña de Inversiones, with a fleet of small aircraft that included a Britten-Norman BN-2 Islander (see also below).

Nicaraguan Revivals

By the end of the Second World War, in the 1940s, the Nicaraguan mineral wealth that had financed the early growth of TACA was depleted. Pan American Airways had echoed its methods elsewhere, and had founded **Lineas Aéreas de Nicaragua (LANICA)** on 17 November 1944. It started a DC-3 service to its nearest neighbors at the end of that year, and in 1948, TACA's contract was cancelled. In 1957, it was flying to Miami, and on 17 February 1958, proudly added 40-seat Vickers Viscount turboprops to the route, together with a service to Guayaquil and Lima. But this was a case of delusions of grandeur, as financial problems led to the sale of the Viscounts in 1959-60. LANICA pressed on with four-engined DC-6Bs until, in 1972, relief came from an unexpected source.

Howard Hughes, the famous aviator, film-maker, and aircraft manufacturer, owner of the Hughes Tool corporation, acquired a 25% interest in LANICA, in exchange for two Convair 880s that he had bought and were surplus to his requirements at T.W.A.—in which he had a controlling interest. The deal was negotiated with the manager, Guillermo Somoza, son of the Nicaraguan dictator, Anastasio. Hughes visited Managua (where it was rumored that he was interested in planning an inter-ocean canal to rival Panama's) but departed hastily in December 1972, when Managua was hit by a devastating earthquake, which killed 6,000 people in about 10 minutes.

Nicaragua took some time to recover from this national disaster. The Nicaraguan capital was flattened. The 880s operated only briefly. LANICA ordered two Boeing 727-200s in September 1978, for $32 million, but its days were numbered. In July 1979, Somoza was overthrown by a military coup, and the airline ceased to operate. Flights began again in January 1981, under a wet-lease agreement with Costa Rica's LACSA, but were suspended again on 31 August 1981, after bankruptcy. During the "Iran-Contra" revolution against the left-wing "Sandanista" government, President Reagan severed trade relations with Nicaragua, thereby canceling all air services.

The new government had formed **Aerolíneas Nicaraguenses (Aeronica)** in December 1980 and started service on LANICA's former Central American routes with two Boeing 727-100s early in 1981. Flights to Miami resumed in November 1981, with a

Boeing 720B. The government also attended to improving domestic routes. These included Puerto Cabezas and Bluefields on the Caribbean coast, and with a 24-seat CASA C-212 Aviocar, started flights to the tiny Isla del Maíz (Corn Island), where the pleasures of escaping from a busy commercial world compensated for less than four-star accommodation standards. In 1994, TACA International acquired 49% of the Nica shareholding—another case of that airline returning to its roots.

With a more liberal political administration, other newcomers could now enter the Nicaraguan domestic scene. With a 16-seat Bandeirante, leased from Isleña, La Ceiba, Honduras, and Cessna Grand Caravans, **La Costeña**, founded in 1992, took over the domestic services, especially to Corn Island. After decades of uncertainty, Nicaraguan airline service is at last settling down to welcome stability.

The TACA Phenomenon

The word phenomenon has to be used with discretion, but to describe TACA's revival thus, from close to extinction (several times), to become one of the leading airlines of Latin America is appropriate. Its foundation and development during the 1930s by the New Zealander, Lowell Yerex, until his departure in 1945, would justify a work of fiction, such were the unorthodox methods used to operate succssfully in the mountains and jungles of the Central American republics. At one remote community in Honduras, where **Transportes Aéreos Centro-Americanos (TACA)** was founded, the airstrip included a small wooden bridge which the pilots said was "quite all right as long as you did not land on it."

Drawing much revenue from contracts to serve the gold mines in Nicaragua, TACA moved on to such an extent that its network served more than a hundred cities and communities throughout Central America. It was perceived by Pan American Airways, the U.S. flag carrier, as a threat to its dominance of Latin America. During the mid-1940s, it proceeded to eliminate Yerex by forming its own airlines with the collaboration of all the local governments, which cancelled TACA mail and operating contracts. The threat was real. With subsidiary companies, the TACA "empire" stretched from Miami all the way to Peru and Brazil. The fleet included Lockheed L.10s, L.14s, and L.18s, fast monoplanes which, though smaller than Pan Am's DC-2s and DC-3s, could outpace them.

After a brief wartime and post-war period, when T.W.A. and American Export Lines participated briefly in TACA's ownership, TACA's fortunes were at a low ebb. Rescue came from the Waterman Steamship Company, of Mobile, Alabama, which had been frustrated from supplementing its Caribbean shipping network with a complementary airline because of the United States law that forbade such inter-modal partnership. Waterman evaded the U.S. law by going overseas, buying shares in TACA, which by now was based in San Salvador. It supplemented the depleted fleet of twin-engined aircraft with a 40-seat four-engined Douglas DC-4, which at the time held the world's long-distance record for commercial airliners.

Because of restrictive U.S. regulations, TACA changed hands again, to McLean Industries, also from Mobile, and Southern Industries, which upgraded the fleet by leasing a 44-seat Vickers Viscount turboprop. The controversial issue of national ownership was then solved in 1960, when the Salvadorian Ricardo Kriete purchased a controlling interest and, on 24 March, transferred all the assets of the Corporation to TACA International Airlines. Kriete had ensured the survival of a pioneer airline, and proceeded to develop it. On 14 December 1966, the first 89-seat BAC One Eleven elevated TACA into the true Jet Age, and a new route to Jamaica opened on 1 June 1971.

Nevertheless, the going was tough. Severe competition from powerful U.S. airlines, together with local political problems, earthquakes and volcanoes, and even a local war: these factors combined to present the Kriete family with a challenge to keep TACA alive. They met it by inviting an old friend from university days, Federico Bloch, to join the airline, and to salvage it. Together they applied sound economic principles, while the Krietes increased their shareholdings from 30% to 70%, thus eliminating much time-wasting decision making. Operational curfew restrictions in Salvador were removed, and the first 130-seat Boeing 737-200 arrived on 31 July 1978. To demonstrate the administration's new direction and resolve, when the pilots went on strike in 1985, they were promptly replaced by new crews from Argentina.

By 1990, TACA was flying to eight cities in the United States, including Los Angeles and Washington, which, with their ethnic populations, were respectively the second and third Salvadorian cities. During the next two years, the network was extended through Central America by acquisition, control of, or collaboration with, the regional airlines, except in Panama, where COPA (see below) chose to go elsewhere. This expansion became the Grupo TACA, which adopted an appropriate new insignia, replacing the traditional guacamaya (macaw).

The airline was moving in to the big leagues, and for a few years in the 1990s, expanded its leasing of 224-seat Boeing 767-200s, which arrangements had started in 1986. TACA then transferred its manufacturer affiliation in a dramatic way on 19 March 1998. In partnership with LAN-Chile and Brazil's TAM, Bloch negotiated a tripartite order with Airbus for a joint total of 90 A320 twin-jet series, with the option of choosing the standard 150-seater, the 185-seat A321, or the smaller 124-seat A319, when needed, according to the traffic demand on individual routes. The A319 was used especially in Peru, where TACA established its subsidiary on 1 October 1999. Through Lima, it doubled its international route mileage on 19 July 2000, serving almost the whole of Latin America, either directly, or through close cooperation with national airlines. The corporate name was changed, without altering the now-famous initials, to **Transportes Aéreos del Continente Americano**. Lowell Yerex would have been proud.

Another reflection of a comparison with the pioneering days of TACA was its self-sufficiency. Back in the 1930s, under the direction of Charlie Mathews, the repair shops in Tegulcigalpa were able to sustain the fleet of Ford Tri-Motors and other

In 1998, TACA astounded the airline fraternity in Latin America by ordering a large fleet of the Airbus A320 series. It also modernized its traditional guacamaya (macaw) insignia (left), after a transitional one (right). (Davies)

assorted types, even to the extent of joining the halves of two different Fords to make one. Such ingenuity was not required in the 21st century, but at the Aeroman workshops in San Salvador, a former colleague of Bloch's, Alfredo Shildknecht, organized maintenance and overhaul capabilities to the extent that TACA was contracted by three U.S. airlines to do their work.

Just as Lowell Yerex had done in the 1930s, modern-day TACA still serves the Central American hinterland, even though the clentèle is different. The old TACA did not carry tourists. Today, in Panama, **Aerolíneas de las Perlas (Aeroperlas)**, founded in June 1970, became a TACA affiliate in 2004, serving western Panama and the San Blas Islands with turboprop Twin Otters, Shorts 360s, and even an ATR-42. AVIATECA (see above) still operates within Guatemala, mainly to Flores, near the Mayan ruins at Tikal, with two ATR-42s, while **Inter** provides supporting services with Cessna Grand Caravans. **Isleña de Inversiones (Isleña Airlines)**, founded by Arthur Wood on 16 March 1982, operates domestic routes in Honduras, mostly, as its name suggests, to the offshore islands, with Cessnas, a BN-2, three ATR-42s, and three Shorts 360s. Such was the growing attraction of Roatan that, on 15 July 1995, Isleña leased a Boeing 737 to fly direct from Miami. In Nicaragua, to complete the TACA hierarchy, TACA acquired 49% of Nica in 1994, with La Costeña taking over the domestic routes (see above).

Early in 2010, the Kriete family sold 67% of the TACA shareholding to Colombia's AVIANCA, forming a partnership in which the top-level administration was shared and a holding company was established in the Bahamas. Both airlines continued to operate under their own names.

Not Just a Canal Zone

Throughout the developmental years of commercial airlines in Latin America, the routes of Pan American Airways and its affiliated company, Panagra, met at Balboa, in the 10-mile-wide Canal Zone in 1903, which had been created when the Republic of Panama was hived off from Colombia. It was the ideal geographically central hub for service connections between North and South America. In 1967, when Braniff acquired Panagra, this continued until 1982, when the Texas airline itself collapsed. However, Pan American had retained an interest in Panama through its foundation, on 21 June 1944, **Compañía Panameña de Aviación (COPA)**, one of the chain of companies that it had set up to ensure its dominance throughout the Central American and Caribbean region. Usually, Pan Am's alliances were with the local governments, but Panama was exceptional, as the interest, initially 40%, was with private investors.

Scheduled domestic services began on 15 August 1947, to David and the far northwest of Panama, with two Douglas DC-3s. Other points were added during the next few years, and in 1956, international routes started to Bogotá and San José, with a Curtiss C-46. The fleet was modernized in February 1961, with a 40-seat Martin 4-0-4; then, on 13 October 1965, with an Avro 748 turboprop, which COPA proudly promoted as a Rolls-Royce jet. As the routes were extended to Managua, San Salvador, and Barranquilla, Pan Am progressively reduced its shareholding until it withdrew altogether on 15 March 1971.

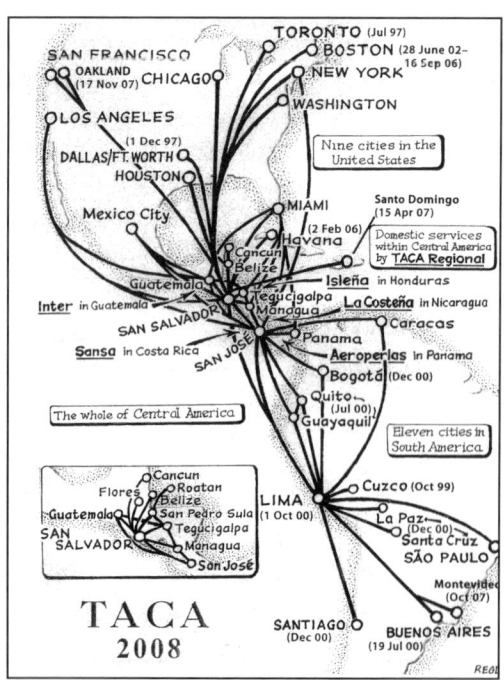

By the early 2000s, the Salvadorean airline had evolved into the Grupo TACA (TACA Group), operating from Canada to Argentina and Chile. It is uncannily similar to the ambitious network planned by TACA's founder, Lowell Yerex, in the 1940s.

Four-engined 100-seat Lockheed L.188 Electras were then introduced, service extended to Guatemala City and to Medellín. By this time, COPA was serving five points in Colombia, although the Cartagena service lasted for only a year or two.

Domestic service was discontinued in 1979, and the routes were transferred to other operators (see below). The airline had other ideas. It began to expand throughout Latin America. Starting in 1988, Pedro Heilbron would steer COPA to greater heights and ensure its survival by shrewd policy decisions, though acquisition of two Boeing 737s was offset by U.S. military action on 20 December 1989 to capture General Manuel Noriega. Air Panama International (A.P.I.) closed down. Once again, in 1992, events cancelled out the prospects. A non-equity partnership with TACA, short of full membership of the Grupo, coincided with a 737 crash on 6 June of that year, in which 47 people were killed—the worst in the country's history.

Recovery during the mid-1990s was slow. Bogotá, Guayaquil, and Caracas were added to the route map, but COPA still approached bankruptcy. Heilbron then took a far-reaching decision. Withdrawing from the association with TACA, he established a broad marketing alliance with the U.S. Continental Airlines, which, on 19 May 1998, acquired a 49% stake in COPA, with Panama's Motta International holding the balance. Compared to TACA, this renegade held some advantages. Geographically, Panama was a better inter-American hub, possibly the best, since the pre-war days of Pan American. The airport was the best in the entire area, with two long runways—unlike San Salvador's one. Code-sharing with Continental gave COPA access to multiple U.S. markets and, for Continental, the whole of Latin America. The exchange more than matched TACA's agreement with American Airlines, which was not so far reaching.

COPA changed its name to **Copa Airlines**. In May 1999, the first of a dozen 124-seat Boeing 737-700s were delivered, in good time to witness, on 31 December 1999, the transfer of control of the Panama Canal from the United States to the Republic of Panama. Within two years, it expanded from being a prominent regional operator to an intercontinental competitor. With the longer range of the new Boeings, the network was far-flung, from Los Angeles in the north to São Paulo in the south. Then, in March 2001, the F.A.A. downgraded Panama's safety rating to Category 2, and on 11 September came the terrorist attack on New York and other centers. Copa recovered rather more quickly than others, and in 2004 announced an order for ten 90-seat Embraer 190s, with more to come; and started service to New York.

On 1 June, it purchased 90% of AeroRepública, by then, Colombia's second largest airline, and on 15 December 2005, the parent company, Copa Holdings, launched an I.P.O. of 14 million shares on the New York Stock Exchange. Continental reduced its investment of 27% and in 2006 further to 10%. The Panamanian airline now claimed to be the fourth largest airline in the whole of Latin America (after LAN-Chile, Brazil's GOL and TAM) and during the next few years expanded its routes to many new destinations throughout South America. In May 2008, the outstanding shares (4.38 million) were sold for $150 million. The fleet comprised 28 Boeing 737-700s and -800s, and 15 Embraer 190s.

Copa Airlines derived some encouragement from the inability of other Panamanian airlines to mount an adequate challenge. **Aerovías Interamericanas de Panama (AVISPA)** was formed in November 1951 by local interests, with a leased Curtiss C-46, operating charter flights to carry shrimps to Miami. This was discontinued in 1952, and the airline than turned to domestic services with a leased DC-3. In March 1954, the U.S. C.A.B. granted permission to operate scheduled services to Miami via Kingston and Havana; so AVISPA changed its name to the more recognizable **Air Panama**. At the end of the year, it rented a Douglas DC-6 from Trans Caribbean Airways (at that time a U.S. non-scheduled airline), to launch *El Panama* services, but the agreement was short-lived. It acquired its own DC-4 at the end of 1955, and extended service southward to Guayaquil and

COPA's Lockheed Electra is parked at San Salvador's early airport (near the city, at 2,000 feet altitude) before the larger airport was built for the big jets 25 miles away (at sea level, near the coast). (Davies)

COPA resisted TACA's persuasions to join its group, and has successfully operated from Panama, geographically placed as a Latin American hub. This is one of its Boeing 737-700s. (McDonough)

Lima in 1957. Its next international association was with Honduras's TAN, which, under C.N. Shelton's direction, was offering, along with Ecuador's C.E.A. and Peru's APSA, bargain fares from Miami to the South American west coast. Meeting predictable objection from the United States, especially as the political situation of the Canal Zone control complicated matters, Air Panama switched its allegiance, late in 1960, to the Colombian R.A.S., and operated to Bogotá instead, with a DC-6B.

It expanded this service, via Barranquilla, to Maracaibo and Caracas, Venezuela; but on 19 January 1965, its certificate was cancelled by the Panamanian government. Another company, Panama Aeronautica, sought a share of the market, starting service to Miami with a DC-7B on 17 March 1962, but was short-lived. On 14 September 1965, a new **Air Panama, S.A. (APASA)** emerged, and resumed operations on the old Air Panama's routes; but it too ceased operations in November 1966. To add to the uncertainty, yet another airline with Panamanian identification, **Panameña de Aviación Internacional (PAISA)** started service on 3 May 1967, but like the other contenders, ceased operations in 1969.

Meanwhile, across the Atlantic, the Spanish flag carrier, Iberia, had been taking an interest in the airline affairs of the Spanish-speaking nations of the Americas. To this end, on 27 April 1967, it supported the foundation of **Air Panama International (A.P.I.)**, which, with two Boeing 727-100s, began operations in 1969 from Mexico City to Lima, adding Bogotá in 1972. By 1975, it had expanded to Los Angeles, New York, and Montreal, and with additional aircraft, three 737-100s, was flying to Caracas and Havana. But by 1978, Iberia had lost its ambition to form a Latin American airline empire, and sold its Panamanian shares to the government. It did not prosper, and on 20 December 1989, when the United States invaded Panama, its sole remaining aircraft was written off. By this time, Heilbron was generating new life into COPA's international network. On 7 November 1991, the government assigned all domestic assets, routes, and liabilities to a *new* **Air Panama International**, which had been founded in 1980 as Turismo Aéreo. It operated Fokker F-27s, DHC-6 Twin Otters, and other small twin-engined types throughout the Republic, with frequent flights to the San Blas and Pearl Islands. Several other small operators of small Cessnas, a few Twin Otters, and even a DC-3, competed for the tourist traffic to the San Blas and Pearl Islands.

One Panamanian airline, founded in January 1967, that only operated internationally, was **Internacional de Aviación (Inair)**. It was an air cargo specialist, and began flights to Miami in December 1969. At first with Curtiss C-46s, and then with Douglas DC-6Bs, it expanded throughout South America. By 1976, it was flying a DC-8 or a Boeing 720 jet to Miami via Belize and Mérida, and to Brazil. Its career came to an abrupt end on 18 June 1984 when its license was canceled. A ton of cocaine, worth $1 billion, was discovered on board one of its aircraft in Miami. The owner was in Spain on a business trip.

The Last Colony

After Spain had lost its empire early in the 19th century, the only vestige of European control in Central America was the foundation of British Honduras as a colony in 1862. It remained as an inactive corner of the British Empire until a century later, when products such as hardwoods and tropical fruits became exportable. Until the early 20th century, there were no roads or railways, and the capital, Belize, was the only urban area in a country the size of New Jersey or Wales. Air transport did not arrive until 1 March 1952, when **British Colonial Airways (B.C.A.)** started local services for the lumbering companies.

On 24 October 1956, B.W.I.A. bought B.C.A. and changed its name to **British Honduras Airways**, controlling it from Jamaica, but ceased operations in the summer of 1961. It was then taken over by a group of local businessmen, as the Mayan Airways Corporation, which expanded service with a Douglas DC-3 to Mérida, Mexico, and San Pedro Sula, Honduras.

In 1973, reflecting the ancient name before colonization, the country was renamed Belize, and on 28 November 1974, **Belize Airways** was founded by Dr. Alfredo Smith, a wealthy Honduran banker. Ambitiously, he acquired five Boeing 720s, a larger fleet of long-range jets than all the other Central American airlines combined. After settling the problem of ownership by transferring 51% of the stock to Belizean citizens, flights began to Miami, San Pedro Sula, and San Salvador on 1 October 1977. But on 17 January 1980, financial losses led to the suspension of services. These were resumed in November with a 100-seat BAC One-Eleven twin-jet, more suited to the traffic demand, and extensions permitted to the Honduran Bay Islands.

In 1981, Belize attained independence from Great Britain, which, however, maintained a friendly presence there, stationing troops and a Royal Air Force contingent of helicopters, as a defense against possible incursions from Guatemala. But an incursion took another form. Like many other countries in the Gulf of Mexico-Caribbean region, Belize is never immune from tropical storms. In 1961, the capital city, Belize (the same name) had been so completely destroyed by a hurricane (190-mph winds) that a new capital had to be created inland at Belmopan. The government moved there in 1970. In spite of such a disaster, this little country was being discovered by tourists, especially scuba divers who enjoyed exploring the largest coral reefs in the western hemisphere.

Chapter 45: Airlines of the Andes

Colombian Heritage

In some respects, air transport history parallels that of Mexico, in that its national airline can trace its history to the dawn of the industry in the western hemisphere. Indeed, the national airline, **Aerovías Nacionales de Colombia (AVIANCA)** can justly claim to be the oldest in all the Americas, having been founded as SCADTA in 1919, and its lineage is more direct and continuous than that of Mexicana. The other similarity is that its base of operations, in the Colombian capital, Bogotá, is at an altitude of 8,400 feet above sea level, and consequently presents a challenge to any aircraft manufacturer wishing to supply its airliners. Mexicana started in July 1960 with the de Havilland Comet (see above), but AVIANCA did not demand its superior take-off performance, ordering instead the Boeing 720B, the specialized modification of the well-established 707. With a shortened fuselage and therefore lighter weight, its take-off performance was adequate for Bogotá.

To match the competition from the United States, however, AVIANCA entered the Jet Age on 16 October 1960 with a Boeing 707 on the route to New York, with aircraft leased from Pan American Airways, pending delivery of the 720Bs, which went into service on 1 December 1961. By January 1962, the Super Constellations were superseded on all its international routes, and jet service began to Mexico City and Buenos Aires in October of that year.

In September 1963, **Sociedad Aeronáutica de Medellín (SAM)**, the only major rival for main-line domestic routes, was acquired so AVIANCA had a near monopoly on routes to Medellín, Barranquilla, and Cali. All with populations exceeding a million, they ensured substantial inter-city traffic where rapid surface transport was close to non-existent because of the mountainous terrain, harsher than Mexico's. Boeing 727s were introduced on these routes on 1 January 1966. Later that year, with unpressurized DC-4s still operating, Manaus, Brazil, was added to the map, via Leticia (Colombia's port on the Amazon), and in 1967, Santiago, Chile, was included en route to Buenos Aires. On 1 April 1968, a 189-seat Boeing 707-320B was introduced for the longest routes, and in December, the first of two 99-seat Boeing 737-100s for local services. The latter were traded back to Boeing for an extra 727, which was adaptable for most of the airline's needs. On 2 July 1969, it opened service to Los Angeles via Mexico City, and after a second -320B was delivered in 1970, the European route was augmented on 28 April 1971 to include Zurich. São Paulo and Rio de Janeiro were added on 17 January 1972.

Since the Second World War, Pan American had owned a substantial interest in AVIANCA, but during the 1970s, its control was gradually reduced to a 25% shareholding in 1965. DC-3 services were suspended, the DC-4s retired, and the lower levels of the domestic market were opened up for smaller operators. In 1976, two 40-seat HS-748s, which had been acquired specifically for the route to Bucaramanga, were also sold. These moves made way for the Colombian flag-carrier to enter the ranks of the wide-bodied jet era with a flourish, even abolishing the Pan Am–based aircraft livery in favor of a bold new paint scheme. On 5 December 1976, a 360-seat Boeing 747 flew from Bogotá to Barranquilla via Cali and Medellín, to mark the 57th anniversary of the founding

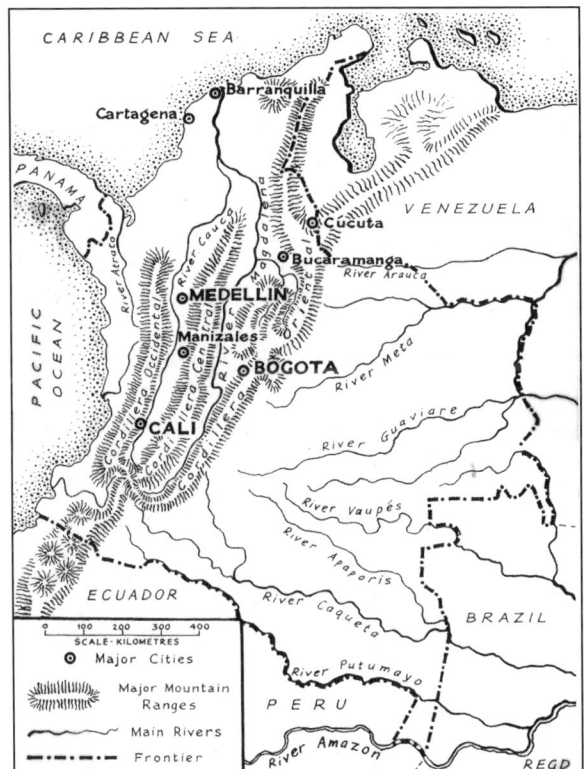

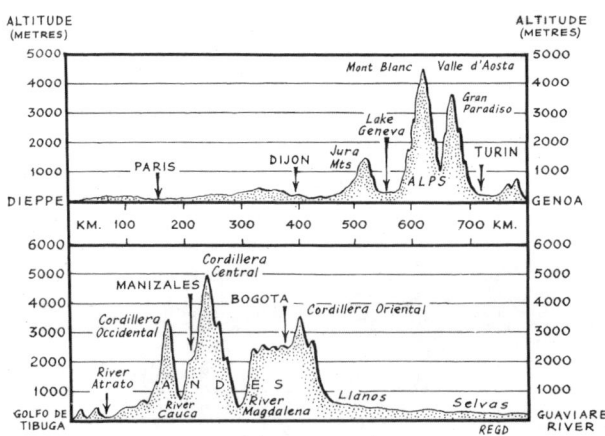

The Colombian terrain presents a challenge to airlines. The formidable Andes mountain range splits into three, and these are three times wider than the European Alps.

of SCADTA, AVIANCA's ancestor; and on the next day, the same aircraft entered scheduled service on the airline's well-established trans-Atlantic route to Frankfurt via San Juan, Madrid, and Paris. 707s started service to La Paz, Bolivia, and to Montevideo, Uruguay, on 26 January 1978, and more destinations added in Europe: London on 3 May, and Rome on 26 October.

The 1980s were a period of steady consolidation with its Boeing fleet, until, in 1991, Colombian airlines were deregulated. AVIANCA and its subsidiary SAM had been receiving complaints for poor service and now faced stronger competition from three airlines (Aces, Aero Republica, and Intercontinental) that had survived the proliferation of earlier years (see below) and acquired jet airliners. The national airline responded with fleets of 147-seat MD-80s and 52-seat Fokker 50s which were able to benefit from improvements made to many of the provincial airports. The competition was such that AVIANCA's domestic market share dropped from 61% in 1990 to 41% in 1997. Its image had been clouded by the memories of three crashes during the 1980s, all involving heavy casualties, even though one near New York on 25 January 1990 was a Boeing 707 that ran out of fuel after being in holding patterns for more than an hour because of weather conditions and traffic congestion. AVIANCA took effective measures to cut costs, reducing staff at all levels, and in 1994, founded a "strategic alliance" with its own affiliates, SAM and Helicol, the latter a helicopter operator. In 1996, it founded Deprisa, a postal services organization (possibly recalling SCADTA's pre-war postal service). Taking advantage of its commercially strategic geographical position, similar to that of Panama, it established a Connections Center at Bogotá, to improve the transfer timings between all the cities served by the airline in North and South America.

Such initiatives were thwarted by the effect of the 11 September 2001 terrorist attacks in the U.S.A. On 20 May 2002, AVIANCA and its affiliate merged their operations completely and absorbed its main independent rival, Aces (see below) to create the Alianza Summa. This solution to the problem did not last long. In November 2003, the Alianza collapsed. ACES was liquidated, and SAM returned to its former status as AVIANCA's regional affiliate.

The struggles continued. A year later, AVIANCA, proud flag carrier with a history (including SCADTA) of more than 80 years of continuous service, filed for Chapter 11 bankruptcy on 10 December 2004. It was forced to seek foreign help in its reorganization, raising $63 million with financial support from the Ocean Air/Synergy Group of Brazil and Colombia's National Federation of Coffee Growers. The determination to retain its reputation as one of the finest of all the South American airlines met yet again with the kind of unforeseen circumstance that was beyond its control. For its order for 10 of Boeing's revolutionary Model 787 Dreamliners, made in March 2007, was followed by a series of manufacturing production problems that has delayed deliveries for more than two years. AVIANCA could not emerge immediately from its financial crisis, and early in 2010. (See TACA history in Chapter 44.) AVIANCA merged with the airline of El Salvador.

Colombian Second Line

The two largest countries of Latin America in size are Brazil and Mexico, followed by Argentina and Peru. The third largest in population is Colombia. As with the other countries, the urban residents are heavily concentrated in the capital city, in this case, Bogotá, home to 8 million people. Three other cities have more than a million, and because of the mountainous terrain (see map), they are relatively separated from each other—unlike Argentina, for example, where the terrain is flat, permitting good railroad and road connections. This circumstance of physical geography has led to a mood of regional independence. Some provinces felt that the flag carrier AVIANCA tended to neglect them, and this feeling expressed itself in a plethora of local airlines.

Prominent among the newcomers as the Jet Age began was SAM, founded in 1945 (chronicled above), which after an association with the Dutch K.L.M., was purchased by AVIANCA through its own subsidiary, Aerotaxi (see also below). As a non–International Air Transport Association (IATA) company, SAM could offer lower fares, and on 15 April 1964, received an operating permit from the United States C.A.B. The transaction removed the taint of monopoly from AVIANCA, and gave Medellín, Colombia's second city, a firm stake in the airline business. Recognizing the severe problems of surface transport in a land where the Andes was split into three ranges, the prospect of an extra airline—any airline—was viewed sympathetically. If a group of investors wished to take a chance and establish a means of travel that compensated for the absence of a national rail system or the poor quality of the roads, then they should be given the chance. The government gave official approval to the application

Oldest airline in all the Americas, Avianca continued to lead Colombia's airlines. Almost nine decades after its foundation it was operating (left) McDonnell Douglas MD-83s and (right) Airbus A330-200s. (McDonough)

of trial-and-error in dealing with market forces. While the succession of names in the airline chronolgy constituted a nightmare for historians, the Colombian public has been well served by a laissez-faire approach, free of excessive or stifling regulations.

Thus, Lloyd Aéreo Colombiano (L.A.C., or Lloyd) tried the system for a decade after 1954; Taxi Aéreo de Santander (Taxader) entered the regular airline field also, after LANSA shut down in 1964; and Aerovías Pilotas Associados (AVISPA) tried its luck in 1956. They all failed. Next in line was a project with more experience and better planning, moving more cautiously into the competitive arena. **Aerocondor** was founded in 1955 by a group of ex- AVIANCA pilots, headed by Juan Millon and Luis Donado. It was based in Barranquilla, where AVIANCA's ancestor started in 1919. At first it carried only air freight, using Curtiss C-46s, the well-tried wartime aircraft with twice the capacity of the DC-3, but moved into passenger operations, with DC-4s and DC-6Bs, on 12 January 1960. It took over the routes of Taxader, but began to concentrate on mainline routes, stimulated in 1964 with a U.S. C.A.B. permit for service to Miami.

On 1 May 1969, Aerocondor introduced 100-seat Lockeed L.188 Electra turboprops, and adopted a bright and attractive color scheme, mainly yellow and red. These were so successful that SAM was obliged to follow the lead, calling its Electras Astrojets, a term described (in Churchillian fashion) as a terminological inexactitude. Three years later, the two airlines sensibly agreed to arrange schedules to avoid self-destructive competition, but such a mutual refinement was only temporary, as Aerocondor introduced a Boeing 720B, which was a real jet. On 15 December 1977, it went further, with a 254-seat Airbus A300B-4, but this time, over-stretched itself, and in May 1980 declared bankruptcy. It will always be remembered, if only because of its refreshingly colorful livery.

Commendable Social Service

Free enterprise had no reason to provide a social service to small communities, and in Colombia no subsidy has ever been granted to any private airline. But the need was vital, as the whole country, not only the big cities, had to be connected to its capital city. By the early 1960s, AVIANCA was retiring its faithful all-weather, all-airfield, DC-3s. The government recognized the public need and came to the rescue. It created the **Servicio Aeronavegación a Territorios Nacionales (SATENA)** as a semi-governmental agency, using Air Force equipment, and charged especially with serving those areas that had not yet achieved provincial status. In short, SATENA had to fly where nobody else wanted to go. It began regular services on 1 June 1962, carrying at first essential supplies and personnel. One of its DC-3s operated as the Aerobanco to provide a service to isolated communities where there was no bank. On 30 December 1968, SATENA was reorganized as a public service, just like any airline, indirectly subsidized. Its aircraft ranged from four-engined C-54s (military DC-4s) and 40-seat HS-748 turboprops to the Swiss 9-seat Pilatus Porter, which could use airstrips where self-respecting birds would take precautions, and at places not even marked on the maps.

AVIANCA's Aerotaxi subsidiary also joined in this aerial social service, with DHC-2 Beavers, and in the mid-1970s took over much of SATENA's network. Even so, that commendable social service advanced to flying, in 1984, 16-seat CASA C-212s, and, in 1985, 65-seat Fokker F-28s.

The Third Line

The spirit of private enterprise has always been very much alive in Colombia, although, with the much-publicized drug traffic, this has too often taken the wrong course. But when specialized opportunities arose, many tried their luck. They entered the Jet Age—although some never made it. They took risks and some paid the penalty for so doing; but for the communities they served and for the potential rewards, the effort was worth the risk.

One of the early risk-takers was Capt. Fernando Henao Jaramillo who, together with his brother Alvaro, founded **Líneas Aéreas La Urraca**. Starting in 1955, they specialized in serving the llanos, the eastern region of cattle-raising plains beyond the Andes. The clientele tended to be demanding, with instances of passengers carrying live boa constrictors, and one who insisted that his cow should be treated as hand baggage. La Urraca is Spanish for magpie, noted for stealing, and Henao enjoyed eroding the traffic of larger airlines. In 1970, he acquired three Handley Page Heralds to add to his four DC-3s. But after two crashes—he himself had been killed on a C-46 ferry flight from Miami and a DC-3 had been hijacked to Cuba—the normally lenient authorities closed down the allegedly thieving magpie in 1979. Nevertheless, as a tribute to the "Benefactor del Vaupés," a plaque on a small obelisk at Mitú, on the eastern frontier, remembers the initiative of the pilot who first connected that community closer to its own capital than with Brazil.

Another small airline served the llanos. Capt. Alejandro Salamanca's **El Venado** (its insignia was a smiling bambi) operated from 1963 to 1981. Its pilots flew without maps or navigational aids. They knew every bend in every river en route, and if necessary would land a DC-3 in a foot of water after a violent storm. From 14 October 1960, **Aeropesca** specialized in hauling freshwater fish from Leticia, the Amazon port. It added passenger service to southern Colombia with turboprop Viscounts in 1971, but was closed down in the 1980s after a series of crashes. **Taxi Aéreo Opita (TAO)**, based in the south at Neiva, Huila Province, also added Viscounts to its DC-3 fleet in 1969. It too terminated in 1974. **Aerotal** had been founded as an air taxi service in 1971, later moving into scheduled service, and finally operated international freight with a Boeing 707-320, and domestic services with Caravelle twin-jets. In the far northeast, in the late 1960s, Dr. Alfonso Sanchez Lopez founded Transportes Aéreos del Cesar (T.A.C.) at Valledupar, capital of the province of that name, first with F-27s and Viscounts then matching Aerotal with Caravelles. By the late 1970s, it claimed to be the fourth largest airline in Colombia (after AVIANCA, SAM, and Aerocondor) and changed its name in January 1980 to simply **Aerocesar**.

By the 1970s, the U.S. market for Colombian fresh flowers was booming, because the climate in the Cauca River region in the Antioquia Province around Medellín was ideal for growing carnations and chrysanthemums all the year round. Several airlines shared in this bounty. The operations were not without problems. One outstanding case provided an example of inspired initiative overcoming a potential disaster. **Transportes Aéreos Mercantiles Panamericano (TAMPA)** had been founded in 1971 by Oscar Posada, formerly the general manager of SAM. It began services with two Douglas DC-6A freighters in 1973, by which time he had been joined by Luis Coulson, who had already been involved in the foundation of SAM and Aces. The Miami fresh flower market in 1975, was so successful that by 1979 TAMPA claimed to be the seventh largest air freight airline in the world. And this was in direct competition with four Colombian and six U.S. airlines.

Small quantities of drugs often escaped detection among shipments of all kinds of cargo, but one day in the early 1980s, two tons of cocaine was discovered by the U.S. Customs on a TAMPA aircraft. The airline could have been grounded, but an agreement was signed with the Customs to set up an efficient security system at both ends of the line, involving precise weighing and X-raying of every box of flowers with video scanners and real-time satellite transmission of data. TAMPA's security stopped many illegal shipments; and although the system cost more than $1 million a year, the airline saved many times that amount in fines—and gained a good reputation with officialdom.

Many airlines reaped shares in the Colombia-Miami air freight harvest, but one new airline took a different approach, specializing in the passenger market, and more than matching the competition with good service and good aircraft. Founded in Manizales on 31 August 1971, **Aerolíneas Centrales de Colombia (Aces)** started service on 20 January 1972 with a single 12-seat Saunders ST-27. Its founders included the Coulson family and other investors from Medellín. Even though it experienced several accidents in its early years, it concentrated on serving provincial cities that had been ignored by other airlines. By 1980, equipped by then with a fleet of five 20-seat DHC-6 Twin Otters and a 48-seat Fairchild FH-227, it was doing well.

At the end of 1981, the Twin Otter fleet had grown to 16 and four Boeing 727-100 jets were introduced. In 1991, the Fokker fleet was replaced by more efficient ATR-42s, and international service to Miami started in 1992. By 1996 Aces was carrying more than two million passengers a year, and doing so in style. In 1997, the capital was doubled, with investment from the Colombian Coffee Growers Federation and the shipping line, also controlled by the coffee growers. This was a solid base for expansion, both in route network and equipment. During the next few years, 150-seat Airbus A320s were flying to an expanded network to cities in Florida; throughout the Caribbean; and to Caracas and Quito. Further success was denied when the 11 September 2001 terrorist attack on the United States brought world air transport to a temporary halt, from which it recovered only slowly.

On 20 May 2002 (see above), Aces merged with AVIANCA and SAM to form the Alianza Summa, and halted its independent operations on 31 August 2003. Of all the Colombian airlines that, through the later years of the 20th century, flew into the Jet Age, Aces will be the best remembered.

Dual Airline Policy in Venezuela

In Venezuela, the two pre-war airlines continued as post-war rivals well into the 21st century. One had been founded by a pioneer of French air transport and still carried its name, even though the originator had been engulfed by Air France in 1933. The other had been an associate of the U.S. Pan American Airways and like its companion airlines belonging to that worldwide organization, retained the same Pan Am winged insignia on its aircraft.

The Venezuelan government had bought the Compagnie Générale Aéropostale on 1 January 1933, and changed the name to **Línea Aeropostal Venezolana (L.A.V.)**. It became independent of French management on 21 May 1937. It served the country well, providing essential contact from Caracas to the more distant provinces which were without surface transport, except along the coast. The main route was to Maracaibo, the second city and center of Venezuela's flourishing oil industry. With complete independence, the fleet was modernized in the late 1930s, as Lockheed 10s supplemented a large fleet of Douglas DC-3s that could land almost anywhere on the primitive strips in the outlying districts. In 1944, the government acquired 23% of the stock of AVENSA (see below), held by the Pan American affiliate, and subsequently canceled the U.S.-controlled airline's cabotage rights on domestic services. Also, in 1944, the Central American airline, TACA, established a branch of its Latin American conglomerate as TACA de Venezuela (see also Chapter 44), which worked closely for a few years with its companion airline in Colombia,

Of the many airlines that entered the field in Colombia in the 1970s, TAMPA (left) became a successful cargo airline, with modern jets such as the Boeing 767-200F. Aces (right) operated Boeing 727s before joining AVIANCA in 2003. (McDonough)

for a direct Caracas-Bogota route, operated alternately by each airline, with an early example of joint ticketing—later becoming known as code-sharing.

On the initiative of Venezuelan Andres (Henry) Boulton, on 13 May 1943, **Aerovias Venezolanas, S.A. (AVENSA)** had been granted a permit to operate domestic services. The Boulton interests held 31%, and the German Vegas group 23%, matching Pan Am's. Services began in May 1944, with Ford Tri-Motors, and the network soon covered the same areas as Aeropostal's. The latter received a subsidy from the government, but AVENSA's was in the form of technical assistance from Pan American. Venezuela's international airline ventures began in July 1945, with an Aeropostal cross-border route to Boa Vista, Brazil, then in 1946, to Aruba, with Douglas DC-4s. On 21 January 1947, in cooperation with Colombia's LANSA, service to Bogotá began, and in March of that year, L.A.V. was serving New York, as well as nearby Trinidad. It operated this prestige route with Lockheed Constellations, and added Martin 202s for domestic routes. AVENSA's overseas involvement, however, did not begin until 1954, when the U.S. C.A.B. granted the rights to serve Miami via the Dutch West Indies and Jamaica, with a stipulation that Pan American's interest could not be mentioned in its advertising.

Aeropostal (L.A.V.) had liquidated its stock in AVENSA in 1948, and embarked on an ambitious program of expansion, backed by a substantial increase in capital—$14 million. The country was not only profiting from its oil riches, its agriculture was also developing well, and L.A.V. increased its DC-3 fleet with seven ex-military C-47s, just to carry fresh meat to Caracas. The 1950s witnessed further evidence of airline strength in Venezuela. In 1951, a direct service to Lima was followed in the following year by purchasing TACA de Venezuela outright, although the two airlines continued to operate separately until 1957.

Still carrying the name that it inherited from the pioneering French airline in the late 1920s, Aeropostal survived the uncertain post-war years and into the Jet Age with McDonnell Douglas MD-82s. (McDonough)

Into the Jet Age

When, in November 1953, L.A.V. boldly joined the ranks of trans-Atlantic operators, it had hoped to fly to Lisbon, Madrid, and Rome via Bermuda and the Azores, with two de Havilland Comet 2 jets. It had ordered these in the summer of 1952, taking note of the dramatic inaugural B.O.A.C. Comet 1 service to Johannesburg on 2 May, when the world's first commercial jet airliner halved the flying time from Europe. L.A.V.'s was one of the first orders for this revolutionary aircraft. Along with Panair do Brasil, which had also ordered the Comet, this South American airline would have made history. But the disasters of 1954 set the Comet production back for four years, and Venezuela's chance for the record books evaporated.

The route to Europe was flown by Constellations, and other routes were added to Miami and New Orleans, but the New York service was withdrawn. L.A.V. moved on, with Super-Constellations replacing the earlier models, but three crashes during 1956–58 were a deterrent to public confidence. Whatever the reason, on 1 March 1958, the Venezuelan flag carrier was declared by decree to be an "Instituto Autónomo," the equivalent to a state corporation.

AVENSA had been less ambitious, concentrating on developing its mainly domestic network with modern aircraft, using a Convair 440 for a route to Miami in November 1954 and to New Orleans a year later. Both airlines also acquired Fokker/Fairchild turboprop F-27s during the latter 1950s, while L.A.V. introduced Vickers Viscount turboprops in 1956. AVENSA bought three Douglas DC-6Bs from Pan American in June 1968.

While the dual airline system was preserved for domestic routes, the time had come to avoid uneconomic duplication in the international field. On 21 November 1960, **Vias Internacionales Aereas, S.A. (VIASA)** was formed to merge the overseas operations L.A.V. and AVENSA, with 55% and 45% of the $3 million capital, respectively. In February 1961, the new airline signed an agreement for the Dutch K.L.M. to act as a general agent in Europe, and to provide technical support, including the wet-lease operation of a Douglas DC-8 jet fleet. Trans-Atlantic services began on 1 April nonstop to Lisbon, and on to Madrid, Paris, London, and Amsterdam, as well as to Bogotá, Lima, and Curaçao. The venture did not start well, as a crash at Lisbon on 29 May killed 62 people.

Undeterred, VIASA introduced the fast Convair 880Ms on 8 August 1961, with its own crew. It developed steadily, with a stop at Las Palmas, Canary Islands, en route to Madrid, and, in June 1965, started a route to Mexico City. Its own DC-8-53s went into service to New York on 5 December of that year, and across the Atlantic on 6 October 1966, when a pooled agreement with Alitalia ended. For the medium-haul routes in the Caribbean area, DC-9-10s were leased from AVENSA in May 1967; a subsidiary, **Transcargo**, was incorporated on 10 January 1968; and direct service to London started on 20 April 1968. Expansion continued in the 1970s, including routes to Los Angeles, Beirut, and Frankfurt, while direct services to Miami were added from Barquisimeto and Maracaibo. The first 160-seat DC-8-63 entered service to New York, an indication of the growth of traffic. In 1972, it took delivery of Douglas aircraft previously ordered by K.L.M.: two DC8-33s and two wide-bodied 269-seat Douglas DC-10-30s. Washington, D.C. was added to the map, but the rate of expansion then slowed down, partly because of increased competition from U.S. airlines. On 1 January 1975, a capacity-sharing agreement with Pan American, to eliminate wasteful duplication, went into effect. In the summer of 1975, VIASA was promoting its Miami-Caracas DC-10 service as *El*

VIASA had been formed in 1960 to merge the international operations of Aeropostal and AVENSA, but it ceased flying in 1997. This was one of its Douglas DC-10s. (Davies)

Grandioso, and Pan Am sold its remaining shares in AVENSA on 28 April 1976. The next month, government participation (through L.A.V.) increased from 55% to 75%, and the DC-10 fleet was increased to six by 1977. More routes included a direct New York-Porlamar service on 5 November 1977, as that island was now joining the list of Caribbean islands for the tourist trade. Service to Santiago, Chile, was added on 1 December 1978 and to Houston 11 days later.

Flag Carrier Crisis

Like all DC-10 operators, VIASA had to ground its fleet after the American Airlines crash in Chicago on 25 May 1979, and soon afterward, bilateral talks with the United States broke down over aspects of what later became known as the "open skies" policy. Venezuela did not wish to prolong Pan American's full traffic rights beyond Caracas, a privilege that the U.S. carrier had enjoyed since the early 1930s. For a while, growing revenue from Venezuelans as well as overseas visitors was supplemented by increased freight traffic, so that a Boeing 747 freighter was leased from Seaboard World in November 1979. But the early 1980s marked the zenith of VIASA's progress, and indeed its prosperity.

The Venezuelan currency, the bolivar, began to fall in value from about four to the U.S. dollar in 1983, down to 33 in 1987. Venezuelans stopped flying overseas, and the airline had to tighten its belt. It lost $75 million in 1983, and this led to the cancellation of leasing contracts, and a reduction of staff and services. To stabilize the situation, in 1987, two twin-engined wide-bodied Airbus A300B4s were leased for the Caribbean and U.S. routes, and in December, a route to Toronto aimed to capture the Canadian market. But VIASA continued on the downward slope, losing money every year.

A rescue attempt by Iberia, with thoughts of building a Latin American airline group affiliation, led to its acquiring 45% of the shares in 1991, with the Venezuelan Investment Fund holding 40% and the Banco Provincial 15%. But the financial drain continued. By 1996, when it was still losing money heavily, its debts had grown to $400 million, and it was forced to stop flying. Iberia offered a plan for survival, but it had problems of its own. It was heavily subsidized by the European Union, which insisted that it should cease its investment into Latin American airlines. After much recrimination and complex negotiation, the government decreed that VIASA's route authorities should be assigned to the original members of the domestic two-airline policy, L.A.V. (Aeropostal) and AVENSA, plus a third airline, the more recently founded Aserca (see below).

The international VIASA had been attracting most attention, but the two domestic airlines had not been idle. In 1965, L.A.V. introduced the Avro (later HS) 748, and preferred to be known as Aeropostal. It introduced Douglas DC-9s in 1970, adding more DC-9-30s and -50s to bring the jet fleet up to 14 by 1977. It also acquired 12 DHC-6 Twin Otters, the latter for services in the south, where the airstrips were all too frequently "unprepared." All the old DC-3s and the Viscounts had been retired. At this time, the airline was reported to be profitable, after a history of continuous losses. Possibly because of this new-found financial stability, on 28 August 1978, a government law converted its Instituto Autónomo status to a limited liability Compañía Anónima Mercantil. But Aeropostal's success did not last long. The 1980s witnessed a gradual deterioration, and a fatal DC-9 crash in 1991 did not help. After depressed finances and the government's failure to privatize it, the airline was grounded in 1994. One of its assets, the fleet of nine DC-9s, however, was maintained as airworthy by the government, so that, in 1996, Nelson Ramiz bought the airline and was able to rejuvenate it, resuming service on 7 January 1997 to nine cities in Venezuela. Emphasizing the break with the previous airline, the new name was Aéropostal Alas de Venezuela. Within two years, and with a 218-seat Airbus A310-300s added to the fleet, Ramiz could claim 42% of the domestic market, and, as narrated above, won the best share of the redistribution of routes of the bankrupt VIASA. It was awarded routes to northern Europe, Canada, Chile, and Cuba.

The other shares went to AVENSA and a third airline (see below). Andres Boulton's airline, which had 45% of VIASA, operated Fokker F-27s and Convair 440s until 1963. AVENSA switched its short-haul twin-engined fleet fo Convair 580 turboprops in August 1964, and at the end of that year introduced Caravelle twin jets, soon to be replaced by Douglas DC-9s, but one of these crashed on 22 December 1974, taking off from Maturin, and killing 77 pople.

Fortunes thereafter fluctuated. In April 1976, in a bold move to cater for the growing tourism industry AVENSA introduced a no-reservation shuttle service from Caracas to Porlamar, on

Whereas Aeropostal's history went back to French sponsorship, AVENSA still carried, in its insignia on the tail of this Boeing 737-300, a reminder of its origins as a Pan American affiliate. (McDonough)

AVENSA's low-cost airline, SERVIVENSA, still carried Pan American's insignia on its Boeing 737-200s long after that airline had ceased operations. (McDonough)

Margarita Island, at least six $50 round-trips a day, some nonstop, some via intermediate points. These Puente Aéreo flights were included in a "Sky Buy" plan, by which visitors could fly anywhere in Venezuela for $120 for 17 days. Financing such an innovation was possible because Pan American sold its remaining 30% in the airline to the Corporación Venezolana de Fomento (C.V.F.) for $6 million. It met the demand for increased traffic by replacing the Convair 580s (one had crashed in March 1978, killing 47) with more DC-9s, and acquired Boeing 727s and 737s in the late 1970s. But yet another crash, a DC-9-32 at Barquisemeto, on 3 November 1983, was the third within 10 years.

As the finances deteriorated, the new aircraft had to be returned, and the fleet was ageing. Some relief came when AVENSA took over some of VIASA's routes when it collapsed in 1997. It founded a low-cost airline, **Servivensa**, but it was declared bankrupt in 2002. It survived as little more than a "paper" airline, with a single EMB 120 Brasilia, before its operations were taken over by **Santa Bárbara Airlines**, founded in Maracaibo on 1 November 1995, and which started flying domestic routes on 1 March 1996. Its fleet comprised turboprop ATR-42s and -72s, which also flew to Miami. Ambitiously, with leased Douglas DC-10s, it offered cheap fares to Madrid and Tenerife, but gained a reputation for poor service to match the fares. The DC-10s were replaced on 2 November 2005 by Boeing 767-300ERs and in September 2006, the airline was sold to Grupo SOAC, a Canary Islands company. But it had out-reached itself, and all long-haul flights were canceled. A further setback was an ATR-42 crash near Mérida on 21 February 2008, killing 46.

A new image in the Venezuelan skies came from oil-rich Maracaibo, where Santa Barbara airlines operated Boeing 757s. (McDonough)

Santa Bárbara had been founded and based in Venezuela's second city, Maracaibo. Not to be outdone, the third city, Valencia (also with more than a million inhabitants) was the base of a third airline that had the stature to join Aéropostal and AVENSA in a bid for the share-out of VIASA's routes in 1997. **Aero Servicios Carabobo (Aserca)**, founded by the García family, started operations in 1988 with small aircraft, and began scheduled services in 1992 with a leased DC-9. In 1994, it moved to Caracas, adding international destinations to Bogotá, Lima, and Miami. From 1995, it had a controlling interest in Air Aruba. Efficiently operated, its fleet had grown to 17 DC-9-30 series by 2008.

Such was Aserca's growth in stature that it qualified for a share in the distribution of VIASA's routes when the Venezuelan flag carrier ceased operations in 1997. It was awarded the important Latin American routes to Brazil and Argentina, while AVENSA received those to Spain, Portugal, and Italy. Although the latter was no longer operating, it claimed that it still owned the rights that had been awarded to it 11 years previously, and the courts upheld the claim. The division of the VIASA heritage was in keeping with President Hugo Chavez's wish to bring back some pride in the country's airline history, and to utilize the current experience was preferable to taking the risk of salvaging a defunct airline. AVENSA got under way almost immediately, starting DC-10 flights to Lisbon, Madrid, Rome, and Milan in December 1998 and to Oporto and Santiago de Compostale in March 1999.

Venezuela's flag carrier, VIASA, had ceased operations in 1997, and some years were to pass before the idea, with some delays, was revived. On 30 March 2004, by decree, the President established a new airline, **Conviasa (Consorcio de Industrias Aeronáuticas y Servicios Aéreos)**, which started service on 10 December. With de Havilland Canada Dash 7s, ATR 42s and 72s, a Cessna Caravan, and Boeing 737s, it operated a domestic network, and inaugurated a route to Madrid with a 269-seat Airbus A340-200 on 11 May 2006. This was later transferred to serve Damascus, Syria, and Tehran, Iran. This direction may have reflected the political leanings of the government, as did the order in 2008 for two Ilyushin Il-96-300s from Russia.

Piston-Engined Postscript

The transition from the old propeller-driven aircraft to the sleek new jets was never more emphasized than in Venezuela. For as VIASA was formed in 1960, the last rights were being prepared for another airline that had been successful for several years. **Rutas Aéreas Nacionales, S.A. (RANSA)** had been formed in September 1948 by private Venezuelan interests as an all-cargo airline, with a large fleet of Curtiss C-46s, to concentrate on exports to Miami via Jamaica and the Netherlands West Indies. After almost two decades of operation, the Venezuelan authorities ordered its suspension, under suspicion of it having carried illegal arms into the country; and the president was put under arrest. The company passed under the control of the government, which added two Douglas DC-6As to the fleet of 13 C-46s. Before RANSA closed down in 1964, it had greeted the onset of the Jet Age in Venezuela by acquiring five piston-engined Boeing B-377 Stratocruisers, converting them to freighters. It was possibly the last operator of this great airliner.

A Constant Resource

Throughout Venezuela's political and economical fluctuations, the country has one resource of benefit to the airlines that is inexhaustible and unaffected by any human intervention, except for visits from airplanes. The world's highest waterfall, with a 3,212-feet drop (or 20 times higher than Niagara) was discovered in 1933 by Jimmy Angel, an American (U.S.) pilot-adventurer. Angel Falls was named after him. At first it was accessible only by bold pilots and hardy passengers, but the airfield at nearby Canaima is now on the Venezuelan airline map.

Equatorial Enterprise

Ecuador is one of the smaller countries of South America, and its airline industry has been at a corresponding disadvantage. Its tourist industry was specialized only for Darwinian enthusiasts going to the Galapagos Islands, and its oil resources were not extensive. Agriculturally, at least, it qualified to be among the so-called banana republics, as it became the world's biggest producer. Like most of its neighbors, surface communications were poor. Of the two big cities, the capital, Quito, is 9,350 feet above sea level; and a railroad journey that linked it to the other big city, the Pacific port, Guayaquil, took all day. Before the Second World War, the U.S. Panagra and the German Lufthansa had set up local airlines, but both closed down, so that by the late 1940s, Ecuador was ready for entrepreneurial initiatives.

Thus, two airlines started services. **Aéreo Transporte Ecuatoriana, C.A. (ATECA)** started in November 1947, while Transandina Ecuatoriana, C.A. joined forces on 15 March 1948. Both airlines provided air service into the eastern jungles where, for many years, the Shell Oil Company had been prospecting, and operating (with much difficulty) its own aircraft. These two early companies were taken over by **AREA**, Ecuatorianas C.A., formed on 8 November 1948, and which began service on 2 February 1949, with small obsolescent wartime aircraft. It improved matters in the summer of 1951 (and attracted attention in the airline world) by adding two four-engined Boeing 307 Stratoliners, also obsolescent, but which could clear the high Andes. With these, AREA was able to open service to Miami via Panama. But these aircraft did not appeal to the public, who preferred the more modern aircraft flown by the U.S. airlines that served Ecuador. The Miami route was suspended in 1954, as were the domestic routes a few months later. Also, a rival airline was founded (see below) in 1957. AREA fought back, supplementing its two veteran DC-3s with a 40-seat Fokker F-27 turboprop on 9 July 1959; but it crashed on 27 November 1960, and the government closed the airline down. Undeterred and with sustained determination, it started flying again with two old Douglas DC-4s, and acquired three DC-7Bs in June 1964. Even though one of these crashed, service was resumed to Miami on 16 August 1965.

Once noted for multi-colored paint schemes on its aircraft, Ecuatoriana's Douglas DC-10s emphasized its ownership. (McDonough)

If this demonstration of resilience to Fate was not enough, AREA entered the Jet Age in June 1966 with a flourish. It added flights to Miami via Bogotá, with an ex-B.O.A.C. Comet 4, which it proudly promoted as its Rolls-Royce Jet. Though outclassed on the world's major trunk routes by the Boeing and Douglas long-range jets, this 83-seat airliner had excellent field performance at high altitudes, and it took Quito's high-altitude runway in its stride. But the Comet was impounded at Miami because of unpaid bills. Yet again, AREA "came up for air" and on 5 May 1968, made one flight to Montevideo via La Paz and Asunción, with a leased Convair 990A, where it was hit by bird strikes. Having been grounded for almost every possible reason, this was the last straw. AREA was forced into receivership in 1968; and as if under a curse, the 990A was written off at Acapulco, Mexico, in August 1970.

The rival airline mentioned above, which was formed on 2 February 1957, by a group of Ecuadoreans and Elly Heckscher, a U.S. citizen with 19% of the shares, had a different aim, other than simply connecting with the U.S. gateway, Miami. The founders of **Compañía Ecuatoriana de Aviación (C.E.A.)** recognized that the smallest of the Andean countries could not sustain a prosperous airline on its own; but it could be a partner in a combined operation with better prospects. Immediately to the south, Peru had twice Ecuador's population, and the capital, Lima, had about three quarters the population of Ecuador. By the end of the year, C.E.A. was a partner in what would now be termed a code-sharing operation: an airline partnership inspired by C.N. "Connie" Shelton from Honduras. His airline, TAN, together with C.E.A. and the Peruvian APSA, which he also founded (see below), operated a through service from Miami to Lima via Panama, alternating with a stop in Cali, Colombia, and Quito and/or Guayaquil, with old 40-seat Curtiss C-46s. Hardly luxury airline travel, the fares were cheap, as Shelton's ambition was to help what he called "the barefoot people" of the Andes to be able to fly.

When AREA introduced DC-7Bs, C.E.A. responded with DC-6Bs and added a twice-daily Quito-Guayaquil domestic service. Then, in April 1967, it introduced 100-seat Lockheed L.188 Electra service and extended the route beyond Lima to Santiago, via Antofogasta. Mexico City was added in March 1968, and Bogotá in June 1972, by which time AREA had succumbed to its Fate. Such was the perceived success that on 15 August 1972, the government acquired 52% of the shares; but the hand of Fate that seemed to have persecuted AREA now turned its attention to C.E.A., as the Electras were grounded worldwide after a series of crashes.

On 16 April 1974, C.E.A. suspended all services, which were taken over by TAME (see below), which, by national decree, acquired all but about 3% of the shares. Leasing two Boeing 720Bs from Israel Aircraft Industries, service was resumed on 1 September, and the airline was henceforth known simply as **Ecuatoriana**, better to identify it with its homeland. The fleet grew to six, and on 6 October 1976, with a Boeing 707-320B, from the same source, inaugurated service to New York—a proud day for this small Andean country. With more prestige routes to Los Angeles and Caracas in December, resumption to Santiago in June 1977, and to Buenos Aires in July of that year, together with interline agreements with Bahamasair and the start of all-freighter services, it was sustained by the country's policy that was echoed by many in Latin America: "A nation's flag carrier is a national resource and must be protected." It also drew much attention, and possibly some traffic, by its new aircraft paint scheme of rainbow-hued colors and artistic design for the whole fuselage, rather than just the conventional tail.

Alas, words could not be supported by deeds. Although Ecuatoriana's was the first Airbus 310-300 wide-bodied twin-jet in the continent, starting service on 24 September 1991, the airline ran into the difficulties that were all too common for a South American airline competing against the corporate strength of those of the United States. In March 1993, the Airbuses were repossessed, and with a debt of $45 million, the airline was grounded in October. To its credit, the 1,300 staff who were laid off received $7 million in severance pay. A reorganization saw a new private-sector company launched on 7 February 1994, with the government holding 25% of the shares. The biggest investor was Brazil's Eljuri Antón, head of Brazil's VASP, who acquired a 50.1% stake as an element of his aim to link several airlines under VASP's control.

The sole asset was one wet-leased Douglas DC-10-30, used briefly in February 1997 to fly to Madrid, while the New York route was revived via Miami with VASP's Boeing 727s, replaced later with A310s. Then, in a spate of international maneuvering, Lan-Chile signed a two-year operating agreement on 1 December 2000 that included taking over the VASP shares and providing two Boeing 767s for the through service to New York. In 2004, the Bolivian L.A.B. operated with Ecuatoriana in a VASP-initiated code-sharing agreement, and a year later, the Chilean airline, going from strength to strength, took charge.

Reference has been made above to TAME's control of Ecuatoriana. With the full approval of the president, **Transportes Aéreos Militares Ecuatorianos (TAME)** was founded on 17 December 1962 by Major José Montesinos, as a division of the Air Force. Domestic services began almost immediately with two DC-3s, charging lower fares than the airlines. It received official status for airline operations on 26 May 1964 and began intermittent flights to the Galapagos Islands, 700 miles to the west. These were becoming a required destination for adventurous tourists with Darwin-related anthropological interests. By April 1967, it was flying regularly once a month, with a Douglas DC-6B, and increased to a weekly frequency on 22 April 1969. TAME cooperated with a tourism agency, which bought a ship that toured the islands and acted as a floating hotel. On 6 December 1969, it had the unusual distinction of having two aircraft hijacked on the same day. One DC-3 was taken to Bogotá, and the other to Havana, where the co-pilot was killed.

Its status as a fully fledged airline was confirmed on 19 January 1970, when, by public notice, it was created as a mixed stock company. At the end of the year, it acquired two 42-seat HS-748 turboprops, and thus modernized, on 23 August 1971, it began to sell stock to private investors. In March 1974, its status as the "chosen instrument" to represent Ecuador's commercial aviation was confirmed when, by government decree, TAME took over Ecuatoriana, but continued to operate separately, and was controlled by a different government department. On 10 August, to celebrate Ecuador's Liberation Day, the first Electra went into service, and on 25 October, to celebrate the anniversary of the Air Force, it started flying to the Galapagos.

In 1981, Boeing 737-200 service began, an indication of growing traffic and strength; but the next few years were marked by no less than five crashes, two 748s, two Electras, and a 737. Three of the crashes were fatal, and TAME's official status must have been a protection to help it to maintain services, with Boeing 727-200s, with which international service began on 30 April 1996 to Santiago, Panama, and Havana. The network expanded to 15 cities, and TAME was carrying 3,000 passengers a day. But the plague of fatal crashes continued, both 727s in Colombia, one near Bogotá, on 20 April 1998, and one near Ipiales, on 28 January 2002, killing a total of 145 people. A Fokker F-28 was also written off.

Undaunted, a new lease of life was undertaken by replacing the F-28 with a series of Embraer airliners, and supplementing the remaining 727s with 162-seat Airbus A320s and an Airbus 319. While the Ecuadorian airline safety record has been a sad one, the repeated phoenix-like recoveries have been a reminder that aviation in the Andes faces severe hazards of terrain and weather that are seldom experienced elsewhere in the world. The crashes are to be profoundly regretted, but credit has to be given to the airmen who have carried out the policy of "protecting the nation's resources" by providing public transportation in a hostile environment.

Such a burden was also carried by two enterprising private airlines which, for several years, did provide such service. Ecuatoriana and TAME were flying Ecuador's flag overseas, but some felt that the key inter-city route between Quito and Guayaquil should be given some priority as well. Late in 1966, a group of army officers in Quito founded **Sociedad Aérea Ecuatoriana de Transportes Aéreos (SAETA)**. Another group in Cuenca, Ecuador's third city, but quite small, had formed **Servicios Aéreos Nacionales (SAN)** as a charter company. SAETA started operations with a single six-seat Piper Aztec from Quito to Cuenca in March 1967, while SAN began with a 25-seat DC-3 from Cuenca

During the late 1960s, two independent airlines in Ecuador came close to operating an hourly shuttle service between Quito and Guayaquil. SAETA survived the competition but terminated its Airbus A320 services in 2000. (McDonough)

to Guayaquil in the following October. Both airlines quickly showed considerable initiative by inroducing turbine-powered equipment. In July 1969, SAN bought two 68-seat Viscount 828 turboprops and started service on the Quito-Guayaquil route, and SAETA did the same with two 52-seat Viscount 785s in April 1970. Such was their success that both upgraded their fleet in 1975, each with 85-seat Caravelle jets, to offer a high-quality air service between the two big cities.

During the next 12 years, six Viscounts—three each by SAETA and SAN—were lost; one was hijacked, but four of them crashed into the formidable Ecuadorian mountains, killing a total of 170 people. Struggling on, by the mid-1990s, SAETA was operating six Airbus A320 series and three Boeing 737s. It became SAETA Air Ecuador, and took over SAN as its domestic affiliate. But with the collapse of the country's economy in 1999, SAETA collapsed in 2000.

Lost Opportunity in Lima

Airline development in South America before the Second World War was mainly under the control of the United States worldwide pioneering giant, Pan American Airways, either by its own network or by surrogate airlines. Concentration was on the east coast, where the major generators of traffic were the big cities in Brazil, including the beaches of Rio de Janeiro, and shopping in Argentina's Buenos Aires, the "Paris of the South." German and French flagship airlines were also present, and a few indigenous companies were beginning to emerge. Brazil in particular was taking its place among the leading airline nations of the world. (See Chapter 41.)

In contrast, most of the countries of the west coast were smaller and less commercially developed. International airline traffic was an accepted monopoly by Pan American-Grace (Panagra), born of a 50-50 shared sponsorship by Pan Am and the W.R. Grace Corporation. The latter was a trading organization that controlled the shipping, and much of the export-import trade, of all the countries from Panama to Chile, and was the only one of Pan Am's scores of affiliates in which it had to concede an equal share, and therefore share the management.

Panagra did found a domestic airline in Peru, but it was not deeply interested in local air services within the Andean countries along its arterial route. Panagra was there to serve North American businessmen. Limited though they were, commercial opportunities existed. In Peru, Elmer "Slim" Faucett, a U.S. citizen who had gone to Lima with the Curtiss company in 1920, realized an opportunity. After exploratory flights, he organized **Compañía de Aviación Faucett** on 4 June 1928 and on 15 September, with two 6-seat Stinson Detroiters, opened service along a 1,100-mile coastal route from Talara, in Peru's far north, to Arequipa, in the far south. Gaining favor with the Peruvian authorities, in 1934 he introduced his own version of the Stinson, modified for high-altitude operations, so as to open services into the Andes mountain regions. In 1938, Panagra suspended its local operations in Peru in exchange for a 20% interest in Faucett.

By 1940, when the Pan American Highway revolutionized surface transport along the Peruvian coastal plain, Faucett was also operating along the Amazonian rivers for the U.S. Rubber Corporation with Catalina flying boats, and in 1945 bought two Douglas DC-4s for nonstop services from Lima to Iquitos and Arequipa. Faucett retired from activity with the airline in 1951 and died in 1960. Even when, in 1960-61, Peru and the U.S. both granted permission to operate internationally to Miami, the airline showed no inclination to do so—curiously a reversal of the former Panagra policy.

Also, in June 1965, another airline had been founded. **Aeronaves del Perú** was organized by ex-Air Force personnel, and after losses from domestic operations, began charter flights to Miami with DC-6s. On 31 January 1967, Braniff bought Panagra and transferred a Boeing 727 to Faucett in 1968. But the traffic potential was not enough to encourage support by another international carrier. APSA and its successor AeroPeru were well established (see below). In the spring of 1970, Faucett DC-4s were flying cargo to Miami, and in 1971, it entered the Jet Age with two BAC One-Eleven twin-jets. But in August 1973, attempts to establish a passenger service to the United States were terminated because the Peruvian government had never granted permission.

Thereafter, Faucett's survival was always at risk. Aeronaves del Perú was expanding with Douglas DC-8s not only to the United States but also to Brazil. A Faucett DC-4 crash on 30 December 1976 did not help, and an enterprising route from Iquitos direct to Miami in 1978 did not succeed. Then, in April 1982, Luis Rupp, the owner, fled the country when his bank was

When Faucett ended its Peruvian career in 1999—it had lasted for 70 years, pioneering the air routes across the Andes—its Lockheed L-1011 Tristars were flying to Miami. (McDonough)

closed down because of "irregularities." But for the airline's long tradition, it would have followed the bank's demise, but it was promptly purchased by the Zanatti family group, which owned 60% of Aeronaves stock.

The once powerful Braniff collapsed on 13 May 1982. Already heavily in debt, and with Eastern Air Lines replacing Braniff, Faucett still struggled. In a bizarre incident, on 11 September 1990, a 727 lost 18 members of aircrew and staff when it ran out of fuel off the shore of Newfoundland during a delivery flight. On 29 February 1996, a Boeing 737 hit a mountain near Arequipa, killing 123 people. On 3 July 1997, Faucett closed down because of a pilots' strike. Resuming service three weeks later, the cherished route to Miami was finally inaugurated on 11 November of that year. But Faucett, a name revered in Peru's older aviation community, declared bankruptcy on 15 November 1999.

South American Hub

A glance at the map of South America indicates that, for a continent-wide airline network, Lima is an obvious choice to establish a hub system. Recognition or acceptance of this fundamental element of airline planning was slow. Theory was not finally transformed into action until 16 September 1956, when **Aerolíneas Peruanas, S.A. (APSA)** was formed by an American, C.N. "Connie" Shelton, who held 99% of the shares. (See TAN of Honduras, A.P.A. of Panama, and C.E.A. of Ecuador above.) Shelton had been approached by Air Force General Carlos Washburn to start a purely Peruvian airline, and APSA was the outcome of a visionary agreement.

The first APSA service, with an old Curtiss C-46, and later with a leased Douglas DC-6, was on 17 June 1957, extending Shelton's multi-national route from Lima to Santiago via Antofagasta. Service began to Buenos Aires, by two routes with intermediate stops, in August 1958, and APSA applied for a direct route to Miami. Predictably, Pan American and Panagra jointly objected to the U.S. C.A.B., claiming that as Shelton was in control, APSA was not a genuine Peruvian airline. But the C.A.B. gave APSA a one-year certificate, as by this time, Shelton's share was a minority, officially 30%, with Dr. Maximo Cisneros, the chairman, holding 51%. The case was reopened on 28 January 1959. APSA did not flinch from challenging the great Pan American, and in February 1960, ordered two Lockheed L.188 Electra turboprops. Unluckily, this attempt to upgrade and modernize the fleet was canceled because of the Electra crashes.

On 12 July 1960, service to Miami via Panama, started with Douglas DC-6s. A solution—or compromise—was reached in the dispute. The C.A.B. Examiner recommended a two-year permit to APSA, subject to adequate record-keeping. The TAN–C.E.A. interchange was to be terminated, and Air Panama withdrew from it. Debts to Shelton were to be fully paid so that the airline would be wholly Peruvian. The C.A.B. no longer had cause to oppose the U.S.-Peru bilateral agreement that had recently been signed on 28 June.

The way was now clear for APSA to fashion a classic intercontinental hub, a long-range geographical X, with New York,

APSA adopted as its symbol the fabled boy, Antarqui, who in ancient Inca legend was reputed to fly.

Los Angeles, Santiago, and Rio de Janeiro forming the four-point pattern. As yet, APSA did not have the aircraft to match words with deeds, and although discussions were held with Brazil's VARIG, the only new route started was to Bogotá with DC-6s in 1961. But on 1 December 1963, a special arrangement was made with Northeast Airlines to provide a through service from New York to Buenos Aires, connecting at Miami. This was the first low-fare jet service from North to South America, taking advantage of the so-called Sixth Freedom. For a round-trip, APSA passengers could save almost 20% on the fare. The service was done in style, although the aircraft was a leased 119-seat Convair 990A, a four-engined jet that was smaller than either the Boeing 707 or the Douglas DC-8, and therefore less economical to operate. But at the time, the airlines were still seeking speed as the most important marketing criterion, and the lease was for seven years. One of its marketing features was its attractive symbol, Antarqui, the mythological youth who could fly.

In 1964, routes were opened to La Paz, Bolivia, extended to Asunción and Montevideo, and culminating, on 7 November, at Rio de Janeiro. On 18 August 1966, Los Angeles was added, via Guayaquil and Mexico City, so that the classic Lima-based X was complete. But Connie Shelton, whose post-war inspiration and ingenuity had created APSA, did not live to enjoy its complete success. He died in March 1965. The next year, São Paulo and Acapulco added further prestige to the network, and the last low-cost DC-6 propeller service ended in March 1968. Its fleet numbered four 990As and one DC-8, leased from Spain's Iberia in May 1970, to operate to Europe via Caracas and Trinidad.

APSA's finances had not kept pace with its ambitions. It was paying high leasing fees, and even though the lessor reduced them, the airline's debts, $22 million, could not be paid. The 990s were impounded at Miami and Los Angeles, and the Peruvian government refused to help in any way. This airline, which had given Peru the opportunity to exploit its geographical location in the highly competitive world of air transport, suspended operations on 3 May 1971.

No doubt there were reasons why the Peruvian government was reluctant to subsidize APSA. For on 22 May 1973, **Empresa de Transportes Aéreo del Perú (Aeroperú)** was founded as a 100% state-owned airline. The first services were domestic—Lima to Cuzco on 3 October, with Fokker F-28s from SATCO; then, in May 1974, to Arequipa and other points with Boeing

When C.N. "Connie" Shelton's TAN code-sharing initiative served Lima, he developed the APSA network into a Latin American hub, based on the Peruvian capital.

727-100s. On 29 July of that year, Aeroperú began international service, with two Douglas DC-8-52s, leased from Venezuela's VIASA, to Santiago, Buenos Aires, and Guayaquil, and adding Miami on 16 September.

This effectively restored a Peruvian airline presence in places that APSA had had to abandon, but early in 1975, a diplomatic log-jam delayed full implementation of the restored network. Peru had restricted Braniff's operational rights through Lima, but on 28 June, Aeroperú was given rights into New York, while Braniff could enjoy onward traffic rights through Lima. This led to the Peruvian national airline flying its DC-8s to Los Angeles via Mexico City, and São Paulo via Rio de Janeiro, on 4 October. The X-pattern hub was back, centered on Lima.

The airline made steady progress. It added Bogotá, Caracas, and Quito to the map, and promoted charter flights from the United States with an additional $99 "Peru for You" anywhere in Peru, incentive. On 16 October 1978, the Peruvian "golden triangle" was completed with a direct Cuzco-Iquitos link. On 14 December, a Lockheed L-1011 wide-bodied jet entered service on the New York route, with an 18-seat luxury lounge in the belly of the aircraft.

During the 1980s, however, the government discovered that running an airline was quite different from running the armed forces. The state airline continued to experience revenue shortfalls and could not cover the extensive costs of supporting a long-distance intercontinental route network, especially with unremitting competition from well-financed and efficient U.S. airlines. Eventually, on 16 December 1992, by public auction, the government sold 70% of Aeroperú, for $41 million, to the shipping company, Naviera Santa S.A., which also, by now, owned Faucett. The State retained 20%. Soon afterward, on 25 January 1993, the privatization was complete, with Aeromexico and Mexicana combining under a code-sharing international consortium, Alas de America (see also Chapter 42). Following their preference, four Boeing 727-200s and two Douglas DC-10s reinforced the fleet.

Aeroperú received a severe setback when, on 2 October 1996, a newly acquired Boeing 757 crashed into the sea near Lima, killing 70 on board. The cause was negligence by the cleaning staff at the airport. A direct service from Miami to Iquitos, which started on 14 June 1997, did not attract enough tourist adventurers to the upper Amazon region. An attempt to cooperate with Delta Air Lines came to nothing, as did more routes into the Caribbean area. The end was near. In March 1999, in the face of a $174-million debt, Aeroperú shut down. Another attempt for cooperation, this time with Continental Airlines, failed on 17 June, and on 18 August, the state successor to APSA met the same fate and was liquidated. The airways of Peru were then invaded from north and south, by El Salvador's TACA, and Chile's LAN, respectively (see below).

While, during the 1990s, attempts to add Peru to the ranks of American intercontinental operators failed, efforts continued within the country to improve domestic services. On 17 May 1990, **Americana** was founded by Leandro Chiok Chang, who followed the almost traditional development pattern of linking the main coastal cities, and also Lima-Cuzco, in May 1991. The first fleet was two Boeing 727-100s, obtained from Aero Chasqui, based in Arequipa, and named after the Inca athletes whose marathon-distance running was Peru's first communication system. The new airline was initially successful, adding more aircraft and more routes, including, in March 1993, additional connections to the Amazon interior. In 1995, now with a fleet of 10 Boeing 727-100s and -200s, an international route began from Lima to Córdoba, Argentina via Tacna and Salta. This innovation, to serve Argentina's second city by a direct route, was not a success, and facing excessive competition—a familiar story for many a promising airline in South America—Americana ceased operations on 2 June 1997.

Some of the competition arose from another company, **Aero Continente**, founded on 4 January 1992 by Carlos Morales in Tarapoto, with two Boeing 737s. He had started flights to the oil regions of northern Peru, receiving tax incentives for

Following the fate of many a South American airline, APSA's successor, Aerperú, closed down in 1999, after operating Boeing 757s, one of which crashed near Lima. (McDonough)

developing transport to isolated locations. On 20 July 1993, under Lupe Zevallos's chairmanship (she was a 38-year-old mother of three), the new upstart entered the scheduled service field, and offered low fares as an incentive. Initially successful, and becoming the leading domestic airline, the fleet had grown to nine aircraft by 1997, with three Boeing 727s, three Boeing 737s, two Fokker F-27s, and one Fokker F-28 providing service according to the traffic demand on individual routes. In December 1999, international service began to Miami, with a bargain fare from Lima of $320 round-trip. The fleet was leased, and an ambitious route map showed future routes to New York and Buenos Aires. But in June 2002, the airline was grounded, all its assets seized, and was declared bankrupt on 12 July.

It revived briefly but then ran into more political problems, when it was accused of drug trafficking. The accusation may have been to protect LAN Chile's recently formed Peruvian subsidiary (see below), by undermining Aero Continente Chile, which had been formed as a subsidiary in June 2002. The revival did not last long. In January 2004, Aero Continente was banned from the United States, a ban that intensified on 1 June 2004 when Fernando Zevallos, among the founders, was named one of the most dangerous drug traffickers in the world. Resourcefully, the airline was almost immediately revived by a consortium of its employees under the name Nueve Continente, but once again, it did not survive.

Peru needed domestic air services. The opportunity to plug the gap was met partly by local attempts. Transperú did not last very long after starting with a Boeing 727 late in 1997. **Transportes Aéreos Nacionales de Selva (TANS)** was another well-meaning attempt, when a military operation serving the trans-Andean areas was converted to civilian control in November 1999. But crashes in 2003 and 2005, respectively, destroyed its small fleet of a Fokker F-28 and a Boeing 737-200. Its license was suspended on 7 January 2006. Aviandina, Aerocondor, and **Transportes Aéreos Andahuaylas (T Doble A)** all operated from 2000—the last of these with an Antonov An-24 and a Yak-40—to link some of the mountain communities, but these, and other small ventures, had neither the finance, nor the expertise, nor the experience to go far. Recalling perhaps the history of previous U.S. involvements, the solution came from beyond the Peruvian frontiers, to the north and to the south.

In July 1998, **LAN Perú** was established by the national airline of Chile, now seven decades old, and respected as a mature leader of the airline industry throughout Latin America. It started domestic operations from Lima to Cuzco and Arequipa on 2 July 1999, and an international route to Miami on 15 November. Thereafter, with a fleet of Airbus A319s and Boeing 767-300ERs, it grew steadily and by 2008, it was serving 28 destinations with 11 front-line jets. In September 2002, it had become a subsidiary of LAN, which held 49% of the shares, while E.R. Larraín held 30% and Inversiones Aéreas 21%.

Almost simultaneously, in July 1999, TransAm, owned by Peruvian veteran airline executive, Daniel Ratti, together with Ernesto Mahle, started operations, and soon changed its name to

One of Peru's new airlines in the Jet Age, Aero Continente, was operating Boeing 767s and serving Arequipa, for tourists en route to the famous Inca ruins at Machu Picchu. This airline lasted eleven tumultuous years from 1993 to 2004. (McDonough)

TACA Perú, with Ratti holding 51%, and TACA (El Salvador) 49%. The agreement was made with TACA's Federico Bloch by a handshake. The fleet was similar to that of its Chilean competitor, Airbuses and 737s, leased from the parent company. The first service, Lima to Iquitos, opened on 1 October 1999, and on 19 July 2000 a Lima-based South American network was inaugurated. Integrated with TACA's own extensive system throughout Central America and to the United States, the TACA organization had recreated the X-pattern that Shelton's APSA had initiated back in the 1960s. Meanwhile, LAN Peru was doing likewise, so that Lima is now a genuine intercontinental airline hub for all the Americas.

The High Flyers

If the mountainous terrain of Ecuador presented a problem for airline operations, because the capital, Quito, high in the Andes, was 9,350 feet above sea level, aviators in Bolivia would take this in their stride. Cochabamba, which was the birthplace of the national airline, is almost at the same altitude, but is considered to be in a valley. The constitutional capital, Sucre, is about 1,000 feet higher (and was the terminus of the airline's first service in 1925). The administrative capital, La Paz, lies at 11,800 feet. Until the late 20th century development of Santa Cruz de la Sierra, in the eastern plain, the two other largest cities were Oruro and Potosí, at 12,100 feet and 13,600 feet, respectively. La Paz is overlooked by two mountains higher than 20,000 feet and by an elevated plateau, the Altiplano, at 13,400 feet. Here was the only place with enough level surface to construct an airport, higher than the cruising height of many a piston-engined airliner, and where first-time visitors have to catch their breath and walk slowly.

The national airline, **Lloyd Aereo Boliviano (L.A.B.)**, therefore, founded as long ago as 1924 by German expatriate residents, has always faced operational problems unlike any other in the world. At first, with German aircraft, it provided faster travel than the limited railroad system and opened links with neighboring countries. The Second World War saw it nationalized and in 1941, the U.S. Panagra took it over, introducing the first of 18 Douglas DC-3s in 1945. In 1950, 10 Boeing B-17 Flying Fortress converted bombers arrived; and in 1951, seven Curtiss C-46s joined an unusual airline fleet. The C-46s have often been compared unfavorably with the DC-3s. Take-offs from La Paz's El Alto airport were hardly spectacular, as they tended simply to accelerate, without climbing, and only seemed to be airborne when the ground fell away beneath them. But a C-46 could carry twice the DC-3's payload and could cope with El Alto.

The early post-war years were a struggle, even with the technical support of Panagra. Venturing across the borders, a route to the Chilean port of Arica on 20 March 1954 was followed by one to Porto Velho, Brazil, in 1958. 42-seat Douglas DC-4s had been acquired in April 1955, and L.A.B. was able to open service to Buenos Aires on 2 July 1959. Possibly because of preference for a Latin American partner, rather than one from the United States, an agreement had been signed with Lloyd Aéreo Colombiano (L.A.C.) on 2 November 1955, for a joint service to Bogota via Riberalta. It started on 19 April 1956, but ended on 3 November. Four crashes in 18 months from September 1955 did not enhance L.A.B.'s reputation, even allowing for the formidable conditions of Andean operations. Pressurized DC-6Bs, added in 1960, improved the comfort levels at the high altitudes, but the Panagra relationship waned and was terminated in 1963.

Still in need of technical support, in October 1963, a new two-year, $800,000 contract was signed with North Central Airlines (N.C.A.), a U.S. Local Service operator, and negotiated with the help of the U.S. Agency for International Development (A.I.D.). By this time, L.A.B. had started service to Lima in March 1961 and, by February 1964, was flying to São Paulo, not only an important destination, but also a direct connection with airlines to Europe. Four-engined 90-seat Lockheed L.188 turboprops brought the Bolivian airline into the Jet Age on 19 September 1968, and for local domestic routes, 36-seat Fairchild F-27s were added on 9 October 1969. These had been purchased on the recommendation of the Systems Analysis Research Corporation (SARC), which had taken over from N.C.A. in 1966.

Relatively remote hitherto from the mainstream of international airline route patterns, the Bolivian flag carrier was growing up, even though it lagged behind the South American leaders. On 14 March 1970, the first 119-seat Boeing 727-100 opened service on the Cochabamba-La Paz main-line domestic route, and subsequently took over all the international routes. The Electras were relegated to the domestics, and in the early 1970s, together with the old DC-6Bs, were transferred to the Bolivian Transporte Aéreo Militar (TAM). A great day dawned on 17 September 1975, when a Boeing 727-100 opened service to Miami, the major U.S. gateway, and on 8 October, the first Boeing 727-200 upgraded the capacity on this important connection with the United States. Significantly, as well as Panama, Santa Cruz de la Sierra was included on the Miami itinerary, an indication of the growing importance of this rapidly growing city of the Bolivian plains. The -200 could also cope better with the 13,400-feet altitude at La Paz.

Further consolidation continued during the late 1970s. On 5 October 1977, service began from Santa Cruz to Caracas, Venezuela, and on 30 November 1978, Manaus, Brazil, was included on this route, which terminated at Miami. The Brazilian stop was to connect with Air France's flights to Paris. A week later, an alternate itinerary to Miami stopped at Lima; Cali, Colombia; and Panama. Buenos Aires and Santiago completed a South American hub network for Bolivia. Two Boeing 707s were also leased from American Airlines for long-distance routes.

On 27 November 1982, a route to Cuzco, Peru, marked the culmination of L.A.B.'s international expansion. The airline was experiencing much difficulty as the government was, to put it mildly, both unsettled and unsettling. The military coup of 1980 had been the 189th in Bolivian history, and such political confusion created rampant inflation, reaching 24,000% in 1985. L.A.B. struggled on, maintaining sporadic services by short-term leases during 1989-91 of a Boeing 767-200, an Airbus A300B2, and A310-300. In 1992, the government decided to privatize its national flag carrier, but at first the only bid, from Iberia, fell through. Eventually, on 19 October 1995, Wagner Canhedo's VASP, Brazil, bought a 49% share for $48 million. But after six years, during which a few new destinations: the Mexican resort, Cancun; Córdoba, Argentina; and Campo Grande, Brazil, were added. VASP sold its shares back to Bolivians in 2001.

The new century witnessed a deterioration of a once pioneering airline to one that had to fight for its survival, even though, in 2004, it operated briefly some of Ecuatoriana's routes. In 2006, it managed to fly some services to Madrid and to New York, but these were more in the nature of charter flights than a scheduled program. L.A.B.'s finances were so bad that all services were suspended on 30 April 2007. The government took over and resumed charter flights with two Boeing 727s.

A Living Aviation Museum

If necessity is claimed to be the mother of invention, in Bolivia, the necessity was extreme, and there were many inventors in the impoverished aviation community where the emphasis for aircraft acquisition was a bargain price. L.A.B. was notorious for its ability to perpetuate the lives of obsolete aircraft types such as the Boeing B-17 bomber, and many a war-weary Curtiss C-46 ended up flying meat between the two-mile-high airfields of the Andean cities and on the even higher *altiplano*. Yet even when the national airline had finished with them, few museums would have opened their doors for them, Many were passed on to valiant operators who prolonged their lives even further. Bolivia

Oldest airline in South America, still operating under its original name, L.A.B. was operating Boeing 737s in the 21st century. (McDonough)

Before being transferred to their final grave, many wartime veteran airplanes ended up in Bolivia, where four engines were welcome for taking off from La Paz's airport at 13,400-feet altitude. This one is an old Boeing B-17 Flying Fortress of Servicio Aéreo Boliviano. (Davies)

became a graveyard for dozens of time-expired commercial aircraft; but they took a long time to expire.

The number of non-scheduled airlines, often with fleets of one or two DC-3s or C-46s, was legion, and the list of airline names in the Bolivian registry between 1950 and 2000 were never the same in any one year, any more than the list of aircraft in the fleets. Only a few carried more than a thousand passengers in any one year, including Aerolíneas Abaroa (ALA), Compañía Boliviana de Aviación (BOA) and Bolivian Air System (BAS), but most companies' lives were short, often only a few months. Air taxi operators were legion, carrying more passengers than the non-scheduled lines, which, however, concentrated on air freight.

One airline, however, deserves mention. In July 1963, **Transportes Aéreos Benianos (TABSA)** was formed and in 1964, was designated as a Bolivian international flag carrier for all-cargo service. Long-drawn out negotiations with the United States delayed the introduction of service, with Lockheed Constellations, until April 1968. Its competition was mainly from the other small Bolivian companies, as well as L.A.B., and it also traded as Transporte Aéreo Boliviano, for better national identification. One other of the many companies that prolonged the lives of the B-17s, and should be recognized, was Fri Reyes, a specialized meat hauler (fresh from the abbatoir) with a fleet that included a more recent DC-6 and a Convair 440. Its claim to historical fame must be that it was the last to operate a Boeing B-17 Flying Fortress. This unpressurized wartime bomber made its last landing at La Paz in 1977, a quarter of a century after the beginning of the Jet Age, and seven years after the Boeing 747 wide-bodied airliner entered service. In this land-locked Andean country, however, wonders will never cease; for in 2008, from Uyuni's gravel strip, 9,300 feet up on the altiplano, Líneas Aéreas Canedo (L.A.C.), operating as AeroSur, started service to Cochabamba with two ex-Navy R4D-8 Super-DC-3s.

Chapter 46: Farthest South

Progress along the Paraná

The establishment of a working air transport service in all the countries of Latin America has invariably been the result of the lack of surface transport. From the Rio Grande to Cape Horn, Argentina alone had an efficient railroad system, while in Brazil, which needed one, multiple companies competed for separated markets. Good roads were rare everywhere. There were no canals, and river services were slow. The only ones of any consequence were along the Amazon, where ocean-going ships could reach Manaus, 1,000 miles from the Atlantic, and even to Iquitos, Peru; or the Magdalena River in Colombia. Solutions to the technical challenge of starting an airline were met by governments that either supported or sponsored local investors, and in some cases, provided air services as branches of the air forces. They were a social benefit for communities that were isolated from all other forms of transport. Customarily, these lasted until the commercial enterprises could eventually fly with reasonable efficiency by themselves; and the air forces often continued as supplementary services.

In Paraguay, this process was particularly necessary. The country was poor, and only the capital, Asunción, had a large enough population to generate minimum demand for travel within the provinces. Consequently, air service was delayed until the beginning of the Jet Age. The Paraguayan Air Force brought the advantages of air travel to the far reaches of the land and survived political changes, including a period of harsh dictatorship.

As early as 1941, as a subsidiary of the Air Force, **Línea Aérea de Transporte Nacional (L.A.T.N.)** was connecting the capital to the outlying districts, using a large variety of small obsolescent aircraft. On 9 October 1944, commercial flying began, to enable the public to participate as well as those on government business. On 10 March 1954, the roles were separated. This was the year when the army general Alfredo Stroessner became president of Paraguay. L.A.T.N. continued to fly military missions, while **Transportes Aéreo Militar (TAM)** offered regular airline service as a second military line. It began scheduled service six days later, and was so popular that the small aircraft were supplemented by five C-47s, (military DC-3s), plus two PBY-5A Catalina flying boats for riverside points. In 1962, the U.S. Military Air Program started to donate more C-47s. By 1970 TAM had 13, and within a few years, this grew to 24 as the network of routes was expanded to serve almost every small community in the land. Such was the lack of infrastructure in Paraguay that when the Brazilian Air Force donated three Douglas DC-6Bs in 1975, Asunción had the only airport with a paved runway where they could be used. At most of the small towns, the strips were subject to flooding after heavy rains, and accessible to grazing cattle, even when aircraft were on final approach. With a capacity of up to 30 seats or three tons of cargo, the C-47s could still use such airfields. When TAM acquired its last of these "Gooney Birds" from Brazil in 1984, wide-bodied jets were flying into Asunción.

The spirit of free enterprise had entered the scene only as late as 1960, when, on 4 September, **Lloyd Aéreo Paraguayo, S.A. (LAPSA)** was formed by local businessmen, with a minority shareholding from the Brazilian airline Paraense. Services began on 24 May 1961, with two Curtiss C-46s from Asunción to Rio de Janeiro via Curitiba and São Paulo. A circuitous train service took three days, and the ships along the Paraná-Paraguay Rivers took even longer, and did not go all the way. LAPSA added two Douglas DC-4s in 1963 and, in 1964, took delivery of a pressurized L-1049 Lockheed Constellation. But it was lost on a ferry flight, and the airline closed down in 1965, by which time the Paraguayan government had stepped in.

On 18 March 1963, it formed **Líneas Aéreas Paraguayas (L.A.P.)**, with a capital of $1 million, and began operations on 20 August, paralleling LAPSA's route, with three Convair 240s. In February 1969, it added three 100-seat turboprop Lockheed L.188 Electras, and although one was lost in an airport collision, it was able to fly its national flag proudly on foreign soil. Montevideo and Santa Cruz, Bolivia, were added on 20 August, Salta, Argentina, on 27 February 1971, Lima on 1 October 1973, and Santiago, Chile, on 10 March 1978. Settling in to the international field, L.A.P. acquired two Boeing 707-320s from Pan American and extended the Lima service to Miami on 17 November 1978. For national identification, the U.S. C.A.B. authorized the use of **Air Paraguay** as a trade name.

Gaining confidence, L.A.P. became a trans-Atlantic airline on 2 November 1979, when it opened service to Madrid and Frankfurt via Rio de Janeiro, adding Brussels in December 1982. During the next few years, the political situation in Paraguay was unsettled, as President Stroessner's dictatorial methods became intolerable and in 1989 he was exiled, and died in 2006. But during his rule, the lifestyle of Paraguay changed as it benefitted from the Itaipu hydro-electric scheme. This was the huge dam across the Paraguay River that provided work throughout the 1980s for thousands of people. When completed, in March 1991, it provided electric power for 20% of Brazil's population (including the 18 million in São Paulo) and 78% of Paraguay's. L.A.P. prospered during the construction period, as technicians and specialists were flown in from far and wide. A larger Douglas DC-8-63 was leased from Canada in 1984, and on 6 May 1992, a 270-seat wide-bodied Douglas DC-10-30 was also leased from Canada. For the regional route to Brazil, it operated a BAe 146-300 from March 1993. It was probably the smallest trans-Atlantic airline in history. But flying Paraguay's flag to Europe and the United States had been costly. After losing $45 million in three years, L.A.P./Air Paraguay ceased operations on 8 March 1994.

Across the River Plate

For international travelers, especially in the business world, the preferred destination of southern South America has always been Buenos Aires which, until the spectacular rise of Brazil's São Paulo, was popular as the "Paris of the Americas." This was not only derived from its being the center of Argentine business, but also from its cultural amenities, befitting a city of many million people. Much of it was built up during the early 20th century by British capital, and before the Second World War, its standard of living, by recognized statistical measures, ranked with those of European countries. Also, across the estuary of the Paraná and Paraguay rivers, the Rio de la Plata, universally known as the River Plate, was Montevideo, the capital of Uruguay. It was less than a tenth of the size of "B.A." but just as sophisticated. As early as 1921, an English entrepreneur had realized the potential for air traffic across the River Plate and had started an air service—one of the first in the world—from the Argentine capital to Colonia, where the Plate was only 50 miles wide.

British influence in Uruguay was also strong (like Buenos Aires, Montevideo even had a cricket field), and Uruguay's first national airline was formed by local importers with the help of de Havilland in Britain. Formed in September 1936, **Primas Líneas Uruguayas de Navigación Aérea (PLUNA)** opened service to the provincial cities of Salta, Artigas, and Rivera on 20 November 1936, with two 3-seat D.H. 90 Dragonflies. The 250-mile lines were short, but the air journey of four hours was a big advantage over the trains' 22 hours. In addition, the frequency was better and the fare was not much higher. The government recognized a national need, and granted a generous subsidy that enabled the airline to purchase larger 12-seat D.H.86B Expresses.

The government then took a 49% interest in the airline in 1943, by which time the fleet also included a 14-seat Potez 62, and two Douglas DC-2s, also 14-seaters. But with a change of government and the loss of subsidies, PLUNA suspended operations until after the Second World War, by which time the government's share was 95%. On 14 May 1948, it was serving with 21-seat DC-3s from Porto Alegre, across the Brazilian border, and also was offering direct service from Punta del Este, a growing coastal beach resort. On 12 November 1951, the government acquired the remaining shares, injected fresh capital, and ordered new equipment. In 1952, with D.H.104 Herons, it reached Asunción, and in January 1955 extended the Porto Alegre route to São Paulo.

One reason why Buenos Aires was not a priority was the strong competition, and an early example of intermodal efficiency. Soon after PLUNA started service, a second Uruguayan airline had been founded by businessman Luis J. Superveille to specialize in flying across the River Plate. With two 12-seat Junkers-Ju 52/3m trimotored floatplanes, **Compañía Aeronáutica Uruguaya, S.A. (CAUSA)** started service on 12 March 1938 from Montevideo to the docks in Buenos Aires, only walking distance from the city. In 1940, it was the first to serve Punta del Este, but replaced that connection in 1943, by starting service to Buenos Aires from Colonia, only 45 miles across the River. The 15-minute flight was much cheaper, as was the bus fare to Montevideo. However, the inter-capital route was so popular that, in December 1947, two ex-B.O.A.C. 24-seat Short S-25 Sandringhams were added to the fleet.

The advantages of the short Colonia connection had not escaped the notice of the ONDA bus company, which joined with some CAUSA employees to found **Aerolíneas Colonia (ARCO)** on 9 January 1957. The inter-modal connection was even better, as ARCO operated landplanes into Buenos Aires's Aeroparque airport, also downtown, starting with ex-CAUSA Curtiss C-46s then with Convair 240s. By the early 1960s, it was able to introduce a 44-seat Convair 600 turboprop. In 1963, when CAUSA started to fly Lockheed Constellations (and the Jet Age was well under way), CAUSA's Sandringhams were retired.

In 1964, there was also a hydrofoil service, with a one-hour trip to Colonia, and cheap fares—half of those of the two airlines. But by this time PLUNA was equal to the competitive threat. In 1958, it had received its first 40-seat Vickers Viscount turboprop and was setting a fast pace, starting to Rio de Janeiro in 1959. In 1964 the Viscounts were flying to Buenos Aires's international airport (Aeroparque could only accept DC-3s), and offering immediate connections to Brazil and Paraguay. But government restrictions on hard currency obliged it to cannibalize aircraft for spare parts, and even though flights to Argentina (where inflation was rampant, and duty-free trade was healthy) were extended to Rosario and Córdoba, those to Brazil were suspended.

Economic recovery enabled PLUNA to acquire a Boeing 737 in March 1970, and to resume service to Brazil. Under a 1974 reorganization, it handed over the responsibility for domestic flights to the military wing of the Air Force, **Transporte Aéreo Militar Uruguayo (TAMU)** which operated DC-3s, Fokker F-27s, and Embraer Bandeirantes. It attained some notoriety when one of its aircraft crashed in the Andes on 13 October 1972, and some passengers, in desperation and by mutual agreement amongst them, survived by resorting to cannibalism.

PLUNA continued to develop its international network, and added more Viscounts and Boeing 727s during the Seventies. By the end of 1979, the Buenos Aires route was operated as a shuttle service, pooled with Aerolíneas Argentinas. Then, as if to emulate the Paraguayan L.A.P., trans-Atlantic flights began to Madrid on 12 May 1981, with a leased 160-seat Boeing 707. Ambitiously, New York and Miami were added. It did not last. In 1986, a route to Santiago, Chile, was more successful. During the early 1990s, PLUNA operated a Boeing 767 and a Douglas DC-10-30 wide-bodied airliners, but its corporate structure underwent a fundamental change, when, on 27 June 1995, Pluna, S.A. was incorporated, with 51% in private ownership. In April 1997, the Brazilian VARIG acquired the remaining shares, but in September 2006, it sold 98% of these to the Uruguayan government. Its national airline seemed destined to fail, but on 4 January 2007, 75% of the shares were negotiated to Leadgate Investment,

Founded in 1936, PLUNA has never yet had a fatal crash. This is one of its Boeing 737s. (McDonough)

a consortium of investors from Germany, the United States, and Argentina, as well as from the home country. A new corporate image was launched on 30 October, and with a new fleet of 90-seat Bombardier CRJ 900s, the old network was restored, including a weekly flight to Bariloche, the Argentine mountain and ski resort. The route to Madrid was maintained by a code-share with Iberia. PLUNA deserves a place in the annals of air transport if only because throughout its entire history, since 1936, it has never had a fatal accident.

Pride of the Pampas

Before the Second World War and largely because of heavy British investment and trade, Argentina was the most prosperous country in Latin America, with a standard of living equal to many European countries, especially in its urban centers. As mentioned above, Buenos Aires was a thriving metropolis (and still is), and a desired destination for businessmen from North America and Europe, and even affluent tourists. As yet, President Kubichek had not awakened Brazil, which, by the middle of the 20th century, was to emerge from its economic slumber to become the South American industrial powerhouse. The Argentine capital was not only a center of business, it was a center of culture and even fashion. Compared to those of other major cities on the continent, its citizens were, on the whole, more educated, more affluent, and lived in a sophisticated environment from which they derived a sense of pride within the Spanish-speaking overseas world. This lifestyle and pride were often perceived in the countries to the north as overconfidence, even arrogance. But such self-esteem was a positive factor in the progress made by its national airline, which led the way in South American commercial aviation progress after the war, and introduced jet service to that continent.

In spite of such an economic and social background, however, Argentina was not immune from political unrest. In 1943, with widespread popular support, the government was overthrown in a military coup, led by General Juan Perón. This led to more than a mere change in administration policy. An admirer of Spain's caudillo, General Franco, Perón created an autocratic regime that was close to being a dictatorship. His intensely nationalist policy led to the expropriation of foreign-based industrial infrastructure, much of it British, handing over control to the Argentine bureaucracy.

Among the decisions was to create a national airline. On 3 May 1949, the Ministry of Transport formed **Aerolíneas Argentinas**, by merging the four existing airlines: FAMA, the international operator; Aeroposta, founded by the French, and the country's oldest; ALFA; and ZONDA, the newest domestic companies. The government agreed to underwrite losses and to guarantee a 5% dividend. At first the integration of four ownerships faced organizational problems, but on 21 March 1950, inaugurating a route to New York, Douglas DC-6s replaced FAMA's unpressurized DC-4s. Short Sandringham flying boats were retained for the route across the River Plate to Montevideo and to Asunción, Paraguay, which did not yet have an international airport. The airline was completely integrated on 7 December 1950, a none-too-difficult task as the four predecessor companies had been regionally distributed. Early in 1953, service opened to Santa Cruz, Bolivia, which at that time still had no railroad connection with the rest of the country. But when this was completed, Aerolíneas, or simply Aero Arg (as the airline was familiarly called) switched to La Paz, and extended the route to Lima, Peru.

On 16 September 1955, another military coup deposed Perón, and the provisional government took steps to restore civil liberties. At first, a plan to award operating certificates to private airlines did not materialize. The disruption of the 1949 merger of the previous airlines could not be patched up immediately. Aerolíneas Argentinas did, however, consolidate its system, adding new British Vickers Vikings to replace DC-3s and other obsolete types on the domestic routes. A Viking crash on 11 January 1957 was the first in Argentina in 10 years, but on 8 December a DC-4 crash at Bariloche killed 59 people, and on the last day of the year, a Sandringham sank at Buenos Aires, and eight passengers drowned. Such incidents no doubt helped to open the door for some competition.

Argentine Newcomers

First off the mark to take advantage of the new law (Decree 12,507/56) was **Aerotransportes Litoral Argentina (A.L.A.)**, formed in 1956 in Rosario by members of the Air Force Command. It operated a small network, at first with small aircraft—Aero Commanders—but moved on to DC-3s in 1958, and by 1964 was flying two DC-6s and two C-46s to all the main cities of Argentina, plus branches to Asunción and Montevideo. In 1966, it began to work closely with Austral and on 26 March 1971, merged with that airline completely.

Austral, Cía Argentina de Transportes Aéreos (CATASA), formed by two big industrial companies in February 1957, was on firmer ground, as a new law (Decree 1256/57) gave better definition to the extent of government control and established a system of state subsidy. The airline was officially registered on 23 June 1957 and started services along the Patagonian coast as far as Rio Gallegos. It was set back when a C-46 crashed on 18 January 1959, killing 50 people, but in November 1960 was able to claim international status by extending its southern terminus to Chile's Punta Arenas. It strengthened its status in November

1961 when it took over the domestic routes of another newcomer that had an impressive name.

Transcontinental had been formed on 5 September 1956 by private interests (originally named Condor, but changed at government request) and was granted a certificate to operate long-distance international routes. Service began to New York via São Paulo, Rio de Janeiro, and Caracas, in September 1958, with Lockheed Super-Constellations, using flight personnel from the United States. Ambitiously, it introduced 104-seat (ex-Northeast Airlines order) four-engined Bristol Britannia turboprops in March 1960. In October, it added Miami as a second U.S. destination, and also Santiago, Chile. In April 1961, 39% of the stock was taken up by the Belgian SABENA; but on 8 November of the same year, its Britannias were impounded in New York. In December, Austral took over the domestic routes which it had opened to the main cities with C-46s; and in May 1962, Aerolíneas Argentinas took over the international route. Transcontinental was declared bankrupt in September.

A brief Argentine Britannia postscript occurred in 1969, when, late in 1969, another airline took over the delivery of a Britannia 312, originally intended for British Eagle. **Aerotransportes Entre Rios (A.E.R.)** was an air freight charter airline, founded in 1962, starting with Constellations to other South American countries. Specializing in transporting livestock, it extended to Miami in November 1965, and later to London. But the Britannia's service life was cut short when it was written off at Buenos Aires when trying to land in dense fog.

Another private venture to challenge Aero Arg was **Aerolíneas Ini**, formed in 1957 by José Ini, a wealthy businessman. On 6 January 1961, he started service to Miami by the west coast route, first with DC-4s then, in September, with DC-6Bs. Ini charged lower fares than the U.S. Panagra but failed to cover its costs and, by the end of 1963, was declared bankrupt. Aerolíneas Argentinas took over the route in May 1964.

Argentine Jet Service

Free elections, the first in 12 years, were held on 22 February 1958. The Aerolíneas Argentinas management resigned, and the new government appointed an entire new team. It quickly made the headlines when, in April, it ordered six de Havilland Comet 4s, the rejuvenated jet airliners that the manufacturer had developed to replace the pioneer Comet 1s that were withdrawn from service in 1954. Services to Europe that began on 19 May 1959, followed by New York on 7 June, were the first jet services in South America. But the airline was bedeviled with more crashes, fortunately non-fatal: in 1959, a Comet at Asunción, and in 1960, another at Buenos Aires. On 7 September of that year, a DC-4 crashed at Salta, killing 30.

Notwithstanding these setbacks, the domestic and regional fleet was revitalized. On 15 February 1962, the first of nine Avro (HS) 748 twin-engined turboprops entered service on the trans-Plata route to Uruguay's Punta del Este resort. The Sandringhams were passed over to CAUSA (see above), which continued to operate them, almost the last of the era of large flying boats, from the Hidropuerto in downtown Buenos Aires. The Avro was able to upgrade service standards on many a provincial route, where some of the airfields were such that one Avro salesman claimed: "I have heard of strips being unprepared, but these were taken by surprise." The new turboprops were joined by Sud Caravelle twin-jets on 1 April 1962, flying to Bariloche and Santiago, Chile.

The international routes were secured as the new airlines, born of the liberalizing policies of 1955, could not continue. Transcontinental and Ini closed down during the early 1960s, and Aerolíneas completed pool agreements with several European airlines. The Lima route was extended to Miami in 1965. The airline had joined the International Air Transport Association (IATA) in 1952, but resigned in 1963, because it was displeased with certain fines imposed, but the problem was resolved, and it rejoined in 1965. Even though the new companies had failed, the Argentine government still believed that Aerolíneas's near-monopoly encouraged inefficiency, and in 1967, decreed, in a Codigo Aeronaútico, that national and private airlines could co-exist.

Inefficient or not, Argentina's flag carrier had moved on. The first Boeing 707-320B went into service to New York on 15 December 1966, and to Europe on 3 April 1967. This larger jet replaced the Comet on all the international routes, eliminating some en route stops, and for a time, the Rio de Janeiro-Rome segment was the longest nonstop air route in the world. On 15 June 1969, the west coast route to Lima was extended to Los Angeles, and the fares were cut to match those of the non-IATA Ecuatoriana (see above). In 1971, 115-seat Boeing 737s replaced the Caravelles and Comets on domestic routes, and on 1 December 1972, an agreement was signed with Austral to end a bitter rivalry.

On 2 April 1973, in cooperation with South African Airways, Aerolíneas started a South Atlantic trans-ocean route from Buenos Aires to Cape Town, and on 6 May began to fly nonstop to New York. President Juan Perón returned from exile to be reelected on 23 September. The pleasure was short-lived, as he died on 1 July 1974, and his wife Isabel became the first woman to rule a country in the western hemisphere. (She was deposed in 1981.) In the next year, when the airline declared a profit, the first in its 25-year history, it took delivery of its first 60-seat Fokker F-28s and followed this in 1976 by leasing two 364-seat Boeing 747s, which went into service on 5 January 1977.

Aerolíneas's traffic figures benefitted in the summer of 1978 when the World Cup was held in Argentina. At the end of the year, three 155-seat Boeing 727-200s were delivered for regional

Aerolíneas Argentinas ("Aero Arg" for short) upheld its role as its country's flag carrier with a fleet of Boeing 747s. (McDonough)

routes, so that the airline was now operating all four of Boeing's then-current airliner types. After much delay because of U.S. concerns about human rights violations in Argentina, a $160 million purchase order for three Boeing 747-200Bs was announced, and the first one went into service to London via Madrid and Paris, on 15 January 1979.

On 7 November 1981, the airline announced a once-a-month Boeing 747 nonstop service from Buenos Aires to Auckland, New Zealand. Advertised as a Trans-Polar service, its itinerary was across the Antarctic in 12 hours, compared to 20 hours by the normal route, at an economy fare of $850. Such a program was cut short, as when Juan Carlos Pellegrini became the Argentine president in February 1982, he launched an invasion of the British Falkland Islands (the Islas Malvinas to the Argentines). After the withdrawal of Argentine forces, many months passed before air services were back to normal. By 1984, however, another 747SP was added, an Exclusive Class was added to the fare structure, and on 19 November of that year, the Trans-Polar service was resumed, twice monthly.

The hopeful rejuvenation did not last. Overseas help was sought, and on 11 August 1988, Scandinavian Airlines System (S.A.S.) agreed to pay $204 million for 40% of the shares. But internal political opposition prevented this deal from going through. Then, on 21 November 1990, an Iberia-led consortium acquired an 85% share of the Argentine national carrier. 49% was foreign, of which Iberia's was 30%; of the domestic shares, 10% was owned by the staff, and 5% by the government. An estimated $2.1 billion in external debt was eliminated. Nevertheless, financial struggles continued, with frequent ownership shares fluctuating. The loss in 1994 was almost $300 million, but the New York route was extended to Toronto on 20 December. Four Airbus A310s were leased, and the market share on the European route improved from 28% to 35%.

Though modest, the 1995 figures encouraged more foreign interest, to the extent that, in July 1997, American Airlines, through its parent company, the AMR Corporation, beat out Continental Airlines for an 8.5% stake in Aerolíneas Argentinas, and a few months later, obtained 9% of Austral. In November 1998, Aerolíneas Argentinas, now headed by David Cush, from American, ordered 12 Airbus A340s for more than $1 billion—a revolutionary change of procurement policy that previously had always favored Boeing.

Since taking over the domestic routes of Transcontinental in 1961 (see above), Austral's fortunes had declined during the next two years, in which it had to comply with a 1963 Decree covering shares of domestic airline routes. A dramatic recovery ensued when, in June 1964, the government authorized direct subsidies for the airlines. Pan American Airways held a 22% interest. It worked closely with A.L.A. (see above) and by the time of its merger in 1971, its fleet had grown sharply to include eight BAC One-Elevens and three Nihon YS-11s. Enterprisingly, it invested in hotels in the Andean resorts, and in inclusive tour groups. On 26 March 1971, the merger with A.L.A. resulted in a change of name to **Austral Líneas Aéreas**, and on 10 May, Decree 1119/71

A Boeing 737-200 of Austral, the leading domestic airline of Argentina. (McDonough)

laid down conditions to ensure a sound administrative structure. It could not engage in other companies' activities, but in compensation, all previous debts to state agencies, including the state oil monopoly, were cancelled.

Subsidies ended in 1973, and Austral made a profit until the political revolution and massive inflation of 1975-76 led to a depression. A One-Eleven crash on 12 December 1978, killing 40 people, may have influenced its decision to turn to the Douglas DC-9, the first delivery of which, on 12 December 1978, signaled a renewed modernization program. In 1987, Cielos del Sur bought the airline, and when Aerolíneas Argentinas was privatized in 1990, Iberia also took a holding in Austral, which continued to fulfill its role as the flag carrier's domestic affiliate. A bad DC-9 crash on 10 October 1987 was the worst in Argentine history.

On 31 October 2001, yet another change of ownership saw the Spanish Grupo Marsans take a majority holding in Aerolíneas Argentinas/Austral, but on 21 July 2008, against strong protests from Marsans, the Argentine government took the airline back under state control, confirmed by the Senate on 18 December.

Throughout the many fluctuations of successes and failures, changes of ownership, and political crises, many small companies had come and gone. One that specialized in bargain fares came close to changing the face of Argentine aviation. **Líneas Aéreas Privadas Argentinas (LAPA)** had originally been founded, modestly enough, in 1976 as a local air-taxi and, on 16 March, was authorized to operate as a commercial airline. It started with Nihon YS-11s, bought from Austral then Shorts 330s, and in 1986, Saab 340s, all turboprops. By this time, the CEO, Andre Deutsch, had acquired the airline and received permission to operate jet airliners.

The first of six 120-seat Boeing 737-200s went into service on 15 March 1993, and before long, LAPA had routes to all major cities and destinations in Argentina. Based at the Jorge Newbery (Aeroparque) downtown airport in Buenos Aires, with fares that were almost half those of the incumbent airlines, it quickly came to the attention of the traveling public, who appreciated, for example, a two-hour flight to the Andean resort, Bariloche, instead of 22-hours on a bus, for little more than the same fare.

Nothing builds a market quicker than discounted prices. Within five years, LAPA's domestic market share was almost half the Argentine total, encouraging further growth. The 737 fleet had doubled and in September 1995, a 227-seat Boeing 757-200ER

Argentina's travelers welcomed LAPA as it offered the first bargain-fare airline services with Boeing 737s-200s in 1993. (McDonough)

started charter flights to destinations in the Caribbean. On 2 August 1988, the first Boeing 737-700 entered service but the justifiable pride took a disastrous fall on 31 August 1999, when a -200 crashed on take-off from Aeroparque's 6,890-foot runway, hitting traffic on a busy road. 71 people were killed, and the airport was closed. LAPA's popularity was shattered, but it recovered enough to be able to order more Boeing aircraft in 2000.

Possibly aiming to erase the faded image, the name was changed to **ARG Argentinas Línea Privada** on 27 September 2001, after Eduardo Eurnekian, main shareholder of the Southern Winds airline, had bought LAPA for $15 million. After a legal battle with Aerolíneas Argentinas (Aero. Arg.), the name was changed to **AIRG** in 2002. This occurred just after the terrorist attacks in the United States on 11 September, and this negative effect on all airlines, together with the devaluation of Argentine currency, led to the suspension of all LAPA's international routes. LAPA was sold to the AeroAndina consortium on 29 August 2002, and on 18 October, the name reverted to the original LAPA, which had retained its affection for reaching out to the Argentine public beyond the non-business community.

The Deepest South

During the early decades of commercial aviation, many countries quickly adapted to the new form of transport because of the timesavings through speed or, in the case of Canada or the Soviet Union, for example, to establish communication into areas where surface transport was next to impossible. Overcoming distance was a common factor even in well-developed countries such as Australia, where Perth was remote from the eastern cities. The transcontinental railway of the early 1930s was doomed to a short period of popularity as the airlines soon took over. The ambitious Cape-to-Cairo railroad, to link South Africa with the north quicker than by sea, was dreamed of, and partially built, but never completed. Imperial Airways and others concentrated on the route to Johannesburg, and filled the need.

In the case of Chile, this was a country made for air transport. Never more than 50 miles or so wide, it was 3,000 miles long, with the capital, Santiago, in the middle. Chile's Antarctic foothold, Base Teniente Marsh, extended that length by another 900 miles. Chile's railroad network was never able to link the extremes of the country.

LAN (Líneas Aéreas Nacional) had ruled the Chilean skies since its founding in 1929. As the Jet Age began in the early 1950s, LAN was facing its first domestic competition. In 1953, a decree permitted private airlines not only to compete with LAN, but also to throw down the gauntlet of cheaper fares to the powerful Panagra, which monopolized the South American Pacific coast route from Panama to Santiago. Compañía Nacional de Turismo Aéreo (CINTA) was founded in 1953 as a subsidiary of a Chilean steamship company. It initially operated domestic routes then, with 55-seat unpressurized Douglas DC-4s, started a route to Havana, paralleling Panagra's. It had the effrontery to paint its aircraft in the same colors as Panagra's, and even to paint the oval windows to look like the rectangular ones of the rival DC-6Bs. CINTA's Latin Americano fare to North America was $394 round-trip, compared to Panagra's Inter-Americano $678 tourist class.

Such enterprise was more than matched in 1954 by **ALA**, Sociedad de Transportes Aéreos, a division of Antofagasta nitrate producers. With 54-seat Lockheed Constellations, it started service to New York in May 1957. Unlike other Latin American bargain-fare operators, such as Honduras's TAN and Peru's APSA, CINTA's and ALA's seating and meal service standards were excellent. Nevertheless, they had to merge in December 1957, handing over the domestic routes to a new company, LADECO, which was just being formed (see below).

Meanwhile, LAN was only then reaching the stage of operating four-engined aircraft, when, on 31 January 1955, it took delivery of its first Douglas DC-6B. On 20 January 1954, a DC-3 had flown nonstop from Punta Arenas to Arica, but this took more than 15 hours, and was irrelevant to commercial operations. LAN reached Lima and Buenos Aires in 1955, and on 22 December 1956, a DC-6B made its first flight to Antarctica, in support of Chile's territorial claims. On 16 August 1958, service began to Miami via Panama, to connect Chile with the United States for the first time, only a few months before Pan American Airways began its worldwide jet services.

With visions of, ultimately, a southern trans-Pacific air service to Australia, a PBY-6A Catalina flying boat flew to Isla Pascua (Easter Island) on 23 January 1963, and extended the survey to Tahiti on 27 August 1965. Both islands would await the construction of airports to receive larger landplanes. Meanwhile, LAN was busy expanding its routes in South America, and introducing jet service, the first, on 18 May 1964, with Sud Caravelles, to Punta Arenas, and prestigiously to Buenos Aires and Montevideo one week later. Progress and expansion were swift, and by the summer of 1965, the French short-haul jet was serving all international routes, while, within Chile, Convair 340s were acquired in 1960 to replace the ageing DC-3s and Doves.

The year 1967 was a banner year for LAN. On 8 April, DC-6B service began to Easter Island, whose unique stone statues added tourist appeal to the island, as well as consolidating it as a potential trans-Pacific refueling stop. For the 2,500-mile route, seating was restricted to 40, to allow for extra fuel tank capacity. On 15 April, service began to New York with a 144-seat Boeing 707, purchased from Lufthansa, and on 19 September, the first of nine twin-turboprop 40-seat Hawker Siddeley 748s (delivered by the northern Polar route via Greenland) opened service to Africa. Maintaining the momentum, on 16 January 1968, the DC-6B Pacific service was extended to Tahiti (to the nearby island of Bora Bora) until the new airport was completed.

The next two years were of mixed fortunes. In 1969, Cali, Colombia; Asuncion, Paraguay; and Rio de Janeiro, Brazil; were added to the network. On 12 November, south of Santiago, a Caravelle was hijacked (but the crew overcame the terrorists and landed safely). On 28 February 1970, Boeing 707s started to fly the Pacific route and, on 26 June, were omitting the stop at Easter Island on some Tahiti flights. Comodoro Arturo Merino Benitez, founder of LAN back in 1929, died on 31 April and did not live to witness the opening of service to Europe. Boeing 707s started to Madrid, Paris, and Frankfurt via Buenos Aires and Rio de Janeiro, on 4 August 1970.

Just when all economic indications were on the ascendant, the political ones were the reverse. In November of that year, in a free election, the communist party, led by Dr. Salvador Allende, won, and immediately revolutionized the government, and indeed the entire economy and lifestyle of the nation. Drastic measures to nationalize all industry, including agriculture and mining, were little short of disastrous. Along with other outstanding debts, the American-owned copper company froze LAN's assets, in default of a loan, but this was quickly settled.

Air fares were drastically reduced in 1972, producing a boom in traffic, including, for some months, travel to Havana, where Fidel Castro had assumed power in 1960. Pressure was exerted on LAN to purchase aircraft from the Soviet Union, and general manager George Hofer was sent to Moscow to buy long-range Ilyushin Il-62s. To his credit, he reported that a combination of range limitations, short engine life, special fuel requirements, and unreliable spares supplies: these combined to render such a purchase economically untenable.

The unsatisfactory situation was resolved when, on 11 September 1973, President Allende died, allegedly by suicide, but strongly suspected of assassination. A new government, headed by General Pinochet, took over, and though oppressive to political opponents, released all restrictions on LAN-Chile, and indeed gave it full support. Three Boeing 707s were added to the fleet, service frequencies increased, and survey flights made to Australia, culminating in an extension of the Tahiti route to Fiji on 5 September 1974. Six DHC-6 Twin Otters were acquired and transferred to the Air Force.

During the 1970s, better administration led to adjustments in the international network to follow traffic requirements more precisely. The Caravelles and HS-748s were replaced by Boeing 727s, including -200s; and Boeing 737-200s entered service to Arica on 3 January 1981. Six months later, on 1 June, a 270-seat Douglas DC-10-30 was introduced on the New York and Buenos Aires routes. On 24 July, Patricio Sepulveda took over as president. Two more DC-10s were purchased from Air New Zealand in 1982, but all services to Europe were suspended on 10 March 1983. The route terminated at Rio de Janeiro, where VARIG took over the traffic to Madrid by special arrangement—what would later be called code-sharing. On 31 December 1983, Sepulveda "cleaned house." Línea Aérea Nacional, Ltda. (later to S.A., on 9 February 1985) was constituted to replace the state-controlled (and subsidized) operation, with emphasis on good service, safety, and a good balance sheet, rather than simply as a social service. The trading name was changed to **Lan-Chile**, to identify the airline's nationality overseas. Under Pinochet, staff numbers had already been halved between 1974 and 1983. They were now, by 1985, halved again.

Four "Three Ocean" southern-hemisphere round-the-world flights were made between April 1985 and August 1986, as a move to publicize the airline, which hitherto had been beyond the vision of most industrialized countries north of the Equator, but which were now beginning to recognize Chile as a tourist destination as well as a source of nitrates and copper. The route to Easter Island and Tahiti had DC-10s from 25 September 1985, while the first Boeing 767 entered service to New York on 8 June 1986, extending to Montreal on 4 July. Lan-Chile even made a special flight to China.

The Chilean airline attracted some international attention in 1987. Ten flights were made to Puerto Williams, in the far south, for the German Antarctic Expedition; and special flights were made to the Base Teniente Marsh with C-130s of the Chilean Air Force. This was later to be serviced regularly by Aerovias DAP (see below), so that Chile was the first country in the world to serve the world's "last continent." In April, Lan-Chile provided all flights for Pope John Paul II's visit to Chile. In July, special schools programs included Vuelos de Fantasia 2000 Boeing 737 sight-seeing flights every Sunday, for $18, or by winning a prize in an aviation-related competition.

Lan-Chile had been the first airline in South America to privatize, with Guillermo Carey's Icrosan and the Scandinavian S.A.S. airline holding 60% of the shares. But the airline's debt reached $140 million by March 1994, when it was sold again to the Hermes and Cueto families for $28 million. In the summer of 1995, Sebastian Pinera invested in Lan-Chile, and then sold his investment for $20 million, which he used to take a 57% stake in LADECO, Chile's other airline. The two airlines worked together until 1996, when the latter was declared bankrupt and ceased operating. **Línea Aérea del Cobre (LADECO)** had taken over the routes of CINTA (see above), formed on 5 September 1958 in association with the Anaconda copper industry. It guaranteed the capacity to serve the huge open-cast copper mine at Chuquicamata and the smelting plant at Potrerillos, initially with two old Douglas DC-3s. It was also backed by affluent Chilean investors. In 1960, it opened a new route to the south, and expanded down the length of the country to compete with Lan-Chile. It prided itself on the high quality of the service, which was even offered on the 10-minute flight from Calamá to Antofagasta—quail eggs, canapés, drinks, plus earphones and cassettes to keep. By the end of the 1980s, LADECO was carrying twice as much domestic traffic as Lan-Chile, and had ventured into the international arena. In May 1989, it was serving New York, nonstop from Santiago, with a Boeing 707-300, and on 26 September 1990 added Washington, D.C. But it had gone too far. Merger negotiations were proposed, with Iberia's support, in November 1993, culminating, as mentioned above, in August 1996, with the termination of independent operations.

In January 1998, Lan-Chile at last gained the headlines in the international press, when it participated in what was described as "the most significant event in commercial aviation in the region during the past 25 years." In cooperation with TACA's Federico Bloch in El Salvador, and TAM's Rolim Amaro in Brazil, Enrique Cueto placed an order with Airbus for 88 firm orders, and 87 options, for airliners of the A320 family, with the flexibility to choose the standard 150-seaters, the larger A321 185-seaters, or the smaller 122-seaters, as required. The entire transaction—reminiscent of bygone days before the Second World War—was conducted with a handshake. During the year, Lan-Chile's three operating units, LAN, LADECO, and the freight line, Fast Air, were consolidated into one.

The united company was flexing its muscles and, by sound planning and efficient service, was gaining strength rapidly—while other Latin American national airlines were declining and even collapsing. In July 1999, it obtained Peruvian government permission to establish **Lan-Peru** for domestic services in that country. On 7 October 2000, with its first long-range Airbus A340, its service to New York was daily and nonstop, followed by the same to Madrid. A month later, it took over Ecuatoriana's international routes, and by May 2003, established **Lan-Ecuador**. **Lan-Argentina** continued the pattern of airline empire-building in the summer of 1995.

Terrorist attacks in the United States on 11 September 2001 did not prevent the formation, one month later, of **LanExpress** with six Airbus A320s, by which time the total fleet of the parent airline was 47 Boeings and Airbuses. LanExpress replaced the extensive LADECO network. In March 2004, the corporate name was changed to **LAN Airlines**, the initials standing for Latin American Network. Its policy of expansion had been to establish new airlines from scratch, rather than to buy local operators which invariably invoked many problems. It had also built up a substantial cargo business, serving all Latin American capitals as far north as Mexico. On 24 March 2009, to crown that successful

LAN celebrated its 80th anniversary in 1999 with emphasis on its Boeing 767-300s. (McDonough)

policy, it opened an all-cargo service to Manaus, with a Boeing 767-300F, carrying a 54-ton payload.

In contrast, because the extended pattern of Chile's population and its urban concentration in Santiago and Valparaiso, there has never been much incentive to start small airlines. Most attempts ended in failure because of the lack of continued travel support. One interesting venture was by **Transportes Aéreos de Chile, S.A. (TRANSA)**, which, in addition to operating Curtiss C-46 freight services to northern South America, flew, in 1957, Consolidated PBY-6A flying boats from Valparaiso to Chile's Juan Fernandez island, to air freight lobsters. It also carried some tourists who wished to set foot on the place that has always been presumed to be the inspiration for Defoe's fictional Robinson Crusoe. The operation was taken over by Aeroservicios Parague, a company specializing in fire-fighting, but which continued to fly to Juan Fernandez, with the PBYs either on floats or on wheels to a precarious landing strip, which was abandoned in 1979.

In 1976, **Aeronorte** was founded by the La Tercira newspaper to carry its papers to the cities of the far north of Chile, and offering service to passengers on its Fokker F-27s. By 1980, it was also operating to the south, as far as Puerto Montt, but a crash in 1982 at La Serena, killing 42 people, led to curtailment of service and eventual termination by the late 1980s. The southern provinces of Chile were relatively isolated by distance from the agricultural center and were dominated by the Andes Mountains, which came close to the sea. Early in 1985, **Aerosur** operated local services from Puerto Montt, to be succeeded, on 2 May 1987, by **Aeroregional, S.A. (A.S.A.)**. Curiously, the small towns in that region were closer to the rail and road termini in Argentina, and A.S.A. became an international airline on 2 November, when it replaced its Cessna 402 with a Fokker F-27 on its route to Bariloche, the Argentine mountain resort

Even further south, at the tip of the South American mainland, a small airline, based at Punta Arenas, operated to Porvenir, on the island of Tierra del Fuego. **Transporte Aereo de Magallenes (TAMA)**, owned by Jorge Freyggang, operated a Beech 18, a Cessna 182, and two Beech Queenairs. He made sight-seeing flights, including the occasional visit to the Antarctic Peninsula, and, with his wife, provided lodge accommodation for adventurist tourists.

The Last Continent

Many an airline has claimed to serve "the six continents" of the eastern and western hemispheres, but none had, until the late 20th century, considered flying to Antarctica, except to supply research stations there. Only in the last decade did cruise ships exploit the areas on the fringe of that vast ice cap, bigger than Australia. They catered for tourists who sought to enjoy the breathtaking panoramas of iceberg-laden seas and to make the acquaintance of colonies of penguins.

The idea of regular air service to Antarctica seemed to be completely uneconomical, for the frigid climate alone was a deterrent to normal travel. But a special initiative on the part of a small Chilean airline turned fantasy into fact. **Aerovías DAP**,

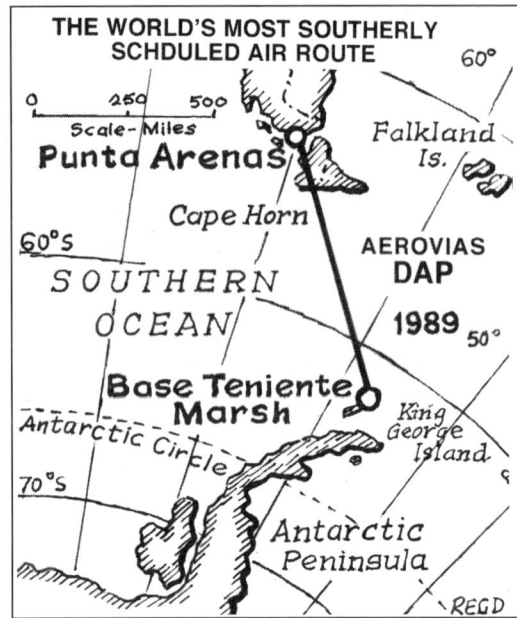
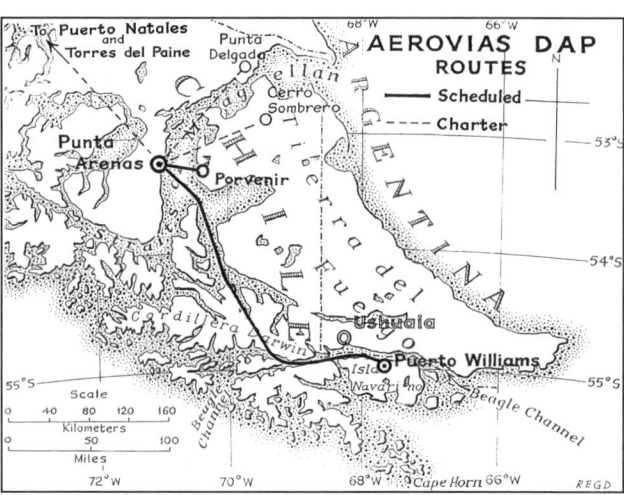

founded by Domingo Andres Pivcevic and his brother Alex, started service on 7 November 1980 from Punta Arénas, the southernmost city of the Chilean mainland, to Puerto Williams, on Navarin Island, even further south. The 19-seat DHC-6 Twin Otters not only served this, the southernmost commercial airport in the world, they also flew to points in Tierra del Fuego and internationally to Rio Gallegos, in Argentina (until restricted by high insurance rates).

As related above, Lan-Chile had already made charter flights to the Chilean Base Teniente Marsh, on King George Island. After receiving operating authority, DAP began regular service, once a month, to the Chilean base on 26 May 1989. Additional fuel for the 900-mile flight from Punta Arenas reduced the available seats to 10. Albeit to the offshore King George Island, this was the world's first scheduled air service to the Antarctic. Subsequently, on 17 September 1990, Pivcevic started a route to the Falkland Islands, taking advantage, no doubt, of the estrangement of the islanders from the closer airports in Argentina, because of the war.

Far-Flung Outpost of Empire

After the end of the Second World War in 1945, Winston Churchill insisted that, were he in power, he would not preside over the dissolution of the British Empire. But this was the twilight period of that political-geographical entity upon which, "the sun never set." Once accounting for hundreds of millions of people (mostly in India) it is now reduced to a few small islands widely distributed around the globe, and on which, curiously, the sun still never sets. The main elements of the former empire, which was renamed the British Commonwealth, departed as self-governing dominions, or, like Burma and Ireland, departed altogether. The Commonwealth today is more of a symbol rather than a political organization. Except for Canada, where ice-hockey reigns supreme, qualification for membership depends on the possession of a world-class cricket team. A few specks of territory, however, decided to stay with London, mainly because their resources for natural subsistence were very limited.

One of these, with a population of less than 2,000, was the Falkland Islands. Until June 1982, when invaded by Argentine armed forces, few Britons even knew where they were. The main islands, East and West Falklands, were mostly uncultivated, there were no roads, and communication between the tiny capital, Port Stanley, and other settlements, was either by sea or by small aircraft. These latter have to be supported by substantial local spares holdings as the British manufacturers are 8,000 miles away. Mainly for medical emergencies, fisheries patrols, or occasional administrative needs, the **Falkland Islands Government Air Service (FIGAS)** made its first flight on 19 December 1948, with a two-seat Auster. Passengers were carried on an ad hoc basis, and other small types were added, including seven Canadian DHC-2 Beaver landplanes and floatplanes. The first Britten-Norman Islander arrived on 4 October 1979, by which time the service had become fairly regular, if not strictly scheduled.

The conflict of 1982 emphasized the need not only for improved air service to the isolated communities, especially the smaller islands; but also for a modern airport—the British air forces during the Falklands conflict had depended on aircraft carriers. Today almost every farm has a landing strip, served on demand by FIGAS, while the field at Port Stanley has been usurped by an international airport at Mount Pleasant, about 30 miles away. This can cope with Boeing 747s, and reflects the importance of this remote territory, now that oil has been discovered in the surrounding seas, and its development observed by the occasional tourist.

Part Nine: Africa

Chapter 47: Across the Mediterranean

More than a Colony

Almost all of northern Africa west of Egypt and the Sudan was colonized by the French. Of the various territories, Algeria had direct shipping lanes across the western Mediterranean Sea so became what could be termed the most French. The climate and terrain were conducive to productive agriculture, especially for semi-tropical fruits, and this encouraged much migration from the home country. By the 20th century, the immigrants outnumbered the indigenous Arabs and Berbers by three to one. They colonized the three northern provinces, but the much larger southern area of present-day Algeria, mostly desert, was extremely remote and close to being unexplored, until the advent of air transport.

Until the end of the Second World War in 1945, airline service had been conducted by French companies. Then, in 1947, the privately owned Compagnie Générale de Transport Aériens (C.G.T.A.), with 11 DC-3s, started non-scheduled services between Algiers and European points. By 1949, as **Air Algérie**, it was operating scheduled routes to France, Switzerland, and between northern Algerian cities, with Sud-Ouest SO-30P Bretagnes. On 23 May 1953, Air France and French shipping interests took control of the airline, at which time 80% of the traffic was trans-Mediterranean. But with the prospect of oil development in the south, domestic services were improved, cutting two-day journeys by road to two hours by air, using Nord 2501 Noratlas cargo aircraft from 1957.

Air Algérie was among the first of Jet Age participants. When it opened a daily Caravelle service on 12 January 1960, it was only the fourth to do so, with the pioneering twin-jet from Algiers to Paris. Not long afterward, when Algeria gained independence from France, the shareholding was modified to include 20% by the Algerian Délégation Nationale. In March 1963, the Algerian government increased its holding to 51%, then to 83% in 1970, and in 1972, acquired the remaining balance. By 1976, the fleet included six Boeing 727-200s and eight Boeing 737-200s, although it was leasing four Airbus A300B2s.

In 1984, the domestic services were separated, as **Lignes Interieures Algériennes (L.A.I.)** and two Airbus A310-200s, leased from Lufthansa, were allocated to serve the country, where the sparsely inhabited south was assimilating more with the north. The main-line fleet had doubled in size as traffic to France was quite intensive, For several years, many French colonists had been returning to their homeland. In 1990, three 235-seat Boeing 767-300ERs were ordered to become the new flagships, mainly for the north African route and for the Hajj.

Progress came to a halt in the mid-1990s, with the outbreak of civil war. The revolution lasted for several years, until 1999, when an amnesty was offered. 6,000 fighters accepted, but an estimated 100,000 had died. Air Algérie had to suspend many of its flights but became a joint stock company in February 1997, following nine years of financial losses. It ordered seven 162-seat Boeing 737-800s and three 108-seat -600s, and in November 2003, to emphasize the recovery, it ordered six ATR-72-500s for domestic and regional routes and five 302-seat long-range Airbus 330-200s to strengthen trans-Atlantic links with French-speaking Canada. These latter inaugurated an Algiers-Montreal route on 15 June 2007.

A Royal Airline

The sovereignty of Morocco was the source of international dispute throughout the 19th century and continued into the 20th, with France maintaining ascendancy. Spain retained territorial enclaves on the northern coast, and Tangier was established as an international zone until 1956, when it reverted to

This Air Algérie Caravelle (7T-VAG) was the first African-owned jet airliner to open service in Africa on 12 January 1960. (Michel Gilliand)

Air Algérie progressed well after its Caravelle debut. This is one of its Boeing 747-400s. (McDonough)

One of Royal Air Maroc's Boeing 737-400s. (McDonough)

Morocco. The sultan, who had survived many local tribal disputes, emerged as the nominal ruler, and the administration functioned as a French protectorate.

Air Maroc (Société Avia Maroc Ligne Aérienne) was organized by private investors in 1947. It began local services in 1948 with DC-3s, and international service in 1949 with DC-4s from Casablanca to Paris, Geneva, and Frankfurt. Another airline, **Air Atlas**, had been formed by French shipping companies, and in 1953, it merged with Air Maroc to form the Compagnie Chérifienne de Transports Aériens (C.C.T.A.). In February 1957, the name was changed to **Royal Air Maroc (R.A.M.)**. The chairman was the personal appointee of King Hassan.

Almost in parallel with Air Algérie, and after replacing the DC-4s with Constellations in 1958, Caravelle jet service was introduced on the Casablanca-Paris route on 20 May 1960, and subsequently extended to other French cities and to Dakar and Bamako, west Africa. By this time, the government held 55% of the shares, Air France 30%, the Société Air Transport 10%, and the Spanish Aviaco 5%. Also, even more than its neighbor's, Morocco's tourist industry was growing apace, partly because of beach resorts and historic cities such as Marrakech, but also because Casablanca had become a major north African hub. Its airport was a convenient port of call for trans-Atlantic airline routes to the Middle East.

In 1970, the domestic services were reorganized, with the formation of **Air Inter** (85% R.A.M.), which linked the Moroccan cities with two Fokker F-27-600s. Two Caravelle crashes, in 1970 and 1973, did not deter R.A.M. from becoming, in 1975, the first Arabic airline to operate to New York, with a leased Boeing 707. In November 1976, it also started flying to Rio de Janeiro and São Paulo. In May 1974, the first order for Boeing 727s heralded a close relationship with Boeing. The fleet grew to include 707s, 727s, 737s, and a 747, all of which were maintained in the airline's own base in Casablanca. The 424-seat 747-200 operated its first R.A.M. service on the Hajj on 11 October 1978, and then went into regular service to Jeddah via Cairo.

The first 219-seat Boeing 757 arrived in the summer of 1986, flying the 5,653 miles nonstop from Seattle to Casablanca in about 10 hours, with 11 tons of payload. "Political" routes were also started to Equatorial Guinea and Gabon, west Africa. R.A.M. acquired a 439-seat 747-400 in October 1993, which unfortunately collided with some ground equipment in Montreal, killing three people, in August 1994. An ATR-42 was deliberately crashed in the same month by a suicidal pilot. But this did not slow the airline's momentum, which by 1995, was owned 94% by the Kingdom of Morocco.

It took a 51% share of Air Sénégal on 7 February 2000, to extend its influence in west Africa, but more than any other airline in north Africa, was seriously affected by the terrorist attacks in the U.S.A. on 11 September 2001. When its August 2001 orders for 20 Boeing 737-700s and -800s and four Airbus A321s were reactivated on 25 March 2002, they marked a return to France as the source of aircraft after a long partnership with Boeing. At the same time, however, two Boeing 767-200ERs were selected to fly the nonstop Montreal route.

The 124-seat A321s were destined for **Atlas Blue**, a low-fare subsidiary, started in July 2004 to meet the new demand for lower-income passengers. The traffic was enough to increase the low-fare fleet with six 737s and a 757.

Tunisian Success

Of the three French north African territories on the Mediterranean, Tunisia was the smallest. Its main assets were the harbor port of Bizerta and the ruins of Carthage, whence two millennia previously, Hannibal had set off to conquer Rome. Compared to those of Algeria and Morocco, the native resources were small, and so was its airline. Founded on 21 October 1948, **Société Tunisienne de l'Air (Tunis Air)** began operations in January 1949 with only two 28-seat Douglas DC-3s, transferred from Air France. The government held 35% of the shares, Air France 35%, and private interests the balance. At first with only a few domestic points, a route to Casablanca in 1951 was not a success, but by 1953, it was able to serve Marseilles and Paris with SE 161 Languedocs. 68-seat DC-4s started in June 1954, and two of these unpressurized propeller aircraft plus four DC-3s were a modest fleet with which to represent the country when it gained independence in 1956. Tunis Air did not then waste time. In September 1961, it was (with Air Algérie and Royal Air Maroc) among the first to open service with the 76-seat Caravelle. By March 1964, it was serving the north African coast from Casablanca to Tripoli, and several cities in France, Italy, and Switzerland. Service to Frankfurt was added in April 1966, for German tourists who discovered Djerba Island.

By this time, Tunis Air was almost entirely government-owned, except for 6% by Air France. Two Cessna 402s and a Nord 262 replaced the DC-3s for local connections to Tunis, and the first of ten 168-seat Boeing 727-200s entered service in

A Tunis Air Airbus A320. (McDonough)

1977. Excellent cabin service, combined with the country's political stability, stimulated the tourist trade. Such was this growth that in 1982 Tunis Air bought a 246-seat Airbus A300B4-200. In 1989, for five weeks, it even leased from Kuwait a wide-bodied Boeing 747 for the Hajj pilgrimage.

To cater for the trans-Mediterranean tourist boom, Tunis Air took a 40% interest in the private company **Tuninter**. With a fleet of two 70-seat ATR-72s and one 48-seat ATR-42, it linked Djerba with Tunis (for the Carthage ruins), and for the shorter regional routes. **Nouvelair** also operated four MD-83s and moved on to an Airbus A320 in 1998, such was the demand for the Tunisian beaches. Tunis Air had become Tunisair and had a fleet of 15 Boeing 737s and 727s, and 8 Airbus A320s, with more of the short-haul Airbus family on order. Tunisair extended its routes as far north as Stockholm, to Abu Dhabi in the Gulf, and to Dakar in Senegal. The ongoing success—it had 35 Airbuses and Boeings in 2002—was marred only by a Tuninter ATR-72 crash into the sea near Palermo on 6 August 2005, leading to a change of the airline name to **Sevenair** on 7 July 2007.

Before changing its name to Sevenair, Nouvelair's Airbus A320s were a familiar sight over the beach at Djerba, Tunisia. (McDonough)

Beyond the Maghreb

The French possessions of the north African coast (formerly known, when part of the Ottoman Empire, as the Arabic Maghreb—the Djezira-el-Maghrib, or Isle of the West), extended as far as Tunisia. The Empire lost Tripolitania and Cyrenaica to Italy in 1912, which provinces, with Fezzan, were united as Libya. After the Second World War, the British controlled the Mediterranean coast, and the French the Fezzan, until Libya became independent on 24 December 1951. In October 1965, the **Kingdom of Libya Airlines** was founded, and for four years operated Caravelles to Europe and a Fan-Jet Falcon for King Idris.

On 1 September 1969, he was deposed by Colonel Muammar al-Qadaffi, and under the new republic, the airline was reconstituted as **Libyan Arab Airlines**.

Getting under way slowly at first, it added 40-seat Fokker F-27s to develop routes into the southern desert regions, where oil had been discovered, and which was to become a dominant factor in Libyan economics. On 21 February 1973, a Boeing 727, wet-leased from Air France, was shot down over the Sinai Desert by the Israeli Air Force, leading to much antagonistic activity in diplomatic circles. Financially, however, the airline was in good shape, benefitting from indirect support from oil revenues. In May 1974 it ordered three more Boeng 727s (making five in the fleet), and in 1981, ordered eight more F-27s (making 18) as services both to the oil wells and along the coast were increased.

A program of expansion began in 1982. **Jamahira Air Transport** was taken over to become a charter airline affiliate, and six Airbus A300B4-200s were ordered, as tourism began to develop in Cyrenaica. But the order was deferred because some of the aircraft content. Engines, for example, were American and suffered from a United States trade embargo. Qadaffi's attitude had been confrontational so that political relations with the West were at a low ebb. These were aggravated further when, on 21 December 1988, a Pan American Boeing 747 crashed at Lockerbie, Scotland. 243 people were killed, including 11 townsfolk, and the cause was a bomb placed on board by two Libyans. The United Nations imposed sanctions on Libya, and in 1992 its airline's international operations ceased as Qadaffi refused to hand over the two men, allegedly government agents, to an international tribunal.

In April 1999, protracted negotiations led to a diplomatic settlement. The Libyan government agreed to a generous monetary compensation to the victims' families; the embargo and the sanctions were lifted; and an international route to Amman, Jordan, was the first to be operated for more than a decade. In 2001, the scheduled and charter branches of the airline were merged as **Libyan Airlines**, and a second reconstruction began. In March 2003, Bombardier CRJ 900Rs began to replace the F-27s on domestic routes, and as relationships with the West improved, code-sharing with Lufthansa, Austrian, and Swiss began.

Such arrangements were also agreed with **Afriqiyah Airways**, which had started in 2001 with a Boeing 747 and an Airbus. It expanded swiftly, with routes across northern Africa as well as to Paris, Brussels, and Geneva. At the June 2007 Paris Air Show, Libyan Airlines announced a large Airbus M.O.U. for seven A320s, four A330-200s, and four A350s, confirming this early in 2009. By this time, in 2008, the two airlines had been grouped under the Libyan African Aviation Holding Company, owned by the Libyan National Social Fund (30%), the Libyan National Investment Company (30%), the Libyan-Africa Investment Fund (former owner of Afriqiyah) (25%), and the Libya Foreign Investment Company (15%). Afriqiyah had already ordered 11 A320s, three A330-200s, and three A319s in 2006, and six A350XWBs in 2007. The memories of the Lockerbie disaster were fading fast, and the European manufacturer was favored in sales to Libya more than Boeing was, because of the easing of political differences.

Service to the Nile

The impressive structures of the pyramids and the tombs of Upper Egypt have fascinated archeologists and tourists alike. To visit these ancient structures, late 19th century tourists of the affluent class spent weeks on ships to Alexandria and additional weeks on boats that paddled their way up the Nile to Aswan and Luxor. A railway ran parallel to the great river, and cut the weeks to days, but could not offer the amenities of the boats. Toward the end of the 1930s, air travel made visits to Egypt within two or three weeks a practical possibility. The traveling public was no longer confined to the so-called landed gentry.

First to explore the potential was a partnership between the British aviation company Airwork and Egyptian interests, which, on 7 June 1932, founded **Misr Airlines** (*Misr* is Arabic for "Egypt"). The Misr Bank held 85% of the capital, Airwork 10%, and the remainder by private interests, mostly Egyptian. The driving force was Alan Muntz of Airwork, who started operations in July 1933 with two de Havilland Dragon biplanes from Cairo to Alexandria and Mersa Matruh. It was the Middle East's first airline. Routes and traffic expanded quickly during the 1930s, and with the outbreak of the Second World War in 1939, the routes were taken over by the government. It did well during the hostilities, serving the Allied forces, but with the return to peace in 1945, a series of crashes led to a strike, and all services were cancelled on 6 February 1946. They resumed in May with a mixture of war-surplus types until, early in 1948, 36-seat Vickers Vikings—the British equivalent of the Douglas DC-3—were introduced. In the following year, the name was changed to **Misrair**, S.A.E., and all capital was now Egyptian. In October 1951, three Languedocs replaced the Vikings on some international routes, until March 1956, when the first 40-seat Viscount turboprop proudly entered service on the Cairo-London route.

Misrair was now establishing itself among the trans-Mediterranean flagship airlines and benefitting from the resurgence of tourist traffic. This was no longer characterized only by the well-to-do scions of stately homes and castles. The accessibility of the Nile through the speed of air transport permitted an influx of middle-class folk further down the income pyramid. Misrair opened a Viscount route to Athens, Rome, and Zurich on 7 July 1958. The negative image from a Viscount crash on 10 April 1960 was relieved when the airline joined the ranks of jet operators on 16 July 1960. On that date, Misrair's first de Havilland 106 Comet 4C went into service from Cairo to London. The airline was eventually to have nine of this type, which soon flew in new colors, as under Gamal Abdel Nasser, Egypt fashioned a political Union with Syria, and Misrair became **United Arab Airlines** on 1 January 1961. The Comets were to be seen as far afield as Moscow (on 21 June 1961), Tokyo (on 19 May 1962), all over Europe, and to west and east Africa on scheduled services; and later, to New York on charters. Five of the Comets crashed or were written off, and Douglas DC-6Bs were acquired to make up the lost capacity.

In August 1964, the United Arab Republic—Egypt still retained the name, even though Syria had withdrawn late in 1961—ordered seven 48-seat Antonov An-24 twin turboprops from the Soviet Union, as Nasser leaned toward Moscow in the international political field. These were for a new **Misrair**, which, on 1 August 1965, was created as the domestic arm of U.A.A., and also to operate regional routes. In January 1967, with the growing accessibility of the Nile destinations through the airlines, Frankfurt and Copenhagen were added to the U.A.A. route map, as Scandinavian and German tourists sought both the sun and the culture.

Misrair's independent status was terminated on 1 January 1968, because it was unprofitable; while the parent airline increased its fleet from sources both east and west. In August, the first two 100-seat Ilyushin Il-18s were delivered from Moscow, for European routes, especially to the Soviet bloc; and later that year, the first 140-seat Boeing 707 went into service to London. Still leaning toward the Soviets, two 160-seat long-range Ilyushin Il-62s were leased on 23 May 1971. Anwar Sadat had succeeded Nasser in 1970, and adopted a policy that was more liberal than confrontational, but the airline could not change its entire fleet overnight, even if it was experiencing difficulties with the aircraft.

On 10 October 1971, the name of the airline was changed once again, to **Egyptair**, by which time the first Il-62 had made its debut on routes to the east, where maintenance and spares support were available. Further association in that direction was a $60-million order, in July 1972, for eight 120-seat Tupolev Tu-154 tri-jets, the Soviet equivalent of the Boeing 727 or the British Trident. But to ensure service continuity, and to retain relationships with the more reliable western sources, four more Boeing 707s, the -320 series, were delivered during 1973, while the first Tu-154 went into service at the end of that year.

Operational and technical factors obliged Egyptair to abandon its ties with the Soviet manufacturers. On 15 October 1973, the leased Il-62s were returned to Aeroflot, and after a Tu-154 crashed on a training flight on 10 July 1974, that fleet was grounded. The Tokyo route was suspended during the 1973-74 winter because of the "October War" with Israel. Early in 1975, the Tu-154s and the An-24s were returned to the U.S.S.R., and in May, Egyptair ordered six Boeing 737-200s, financed with help from the United Arab Emirates and a $60-million government loan. The flirtation with the Soviet Union as a source of equipment was at an end.

Punctuated by a Boeing 737 hijacking on 22 August 1976 (the aircraft was recovered by commandos) and a Boeing 707 crash at Bangkok on 25 December of the same year, Egypt's flagship airline recovered during the late 1970s, adding more services to Europe and to Karachi. On 3 June 1977, a leased 250-seat Airbus A300 made its inaugural flight to Karachi and the first A300B4 was delivered in 1980. In spite of concerns for safety because of the continued problems with Israel, the annual tourist count to the attractions in Upper Egypt had grown to more than two million.

Egyptair seems to have been a particular target for terrorists. On 23-24 November 1985, a Boeing 737 was hijacked en route from Athens to Cairo. The pilot landed at Malta, where, during the night, some passengers were murdered. At noon next day, an

Egyptian Air Force C-130 brought a force of commandos, who stormed the 737 where, however, the hijackers caused a fire, and 60 people, including the perpetrators, were killed.

Then, during a period of relative calm, two wide-bodied 400-seat Boeing 747-300s and three Boeing 767-300s went into service, and orders were placed for five 767-200s and -300s. Early in 1991, the respite was interrupted by the war in Iraq, and a fleet reoganization got under way. In the early 1990s, the older Airbuses were replaced by nine A300-600s and the older 737s by seven A320-200s plus 737-500s. In July 1995, negotiations were finally concluded for three Airbus A340s, and two months later, for three 308-seat Boeing 777-200s. With healthy traffic increases, Egyptair's finances were in good shape.

Fate has not been kind to Egypt's flag-carrying airline. Once again, its list of hijackings and indirect involvement in the Middle East wars was, on 31 October 1999, supplemented by yet another tragedy which attracted worldwide attention. After taking off from New York, a 767-300 crashed into the sea, following what appeared to be deliberate action by a suicidal co-pilot.

In 2006, Egyptair launched **Egyptair Express**, with a fleet of 76-seat Embraer E-170 jets. This was to serve the expanding domestic market, which now attracted tourists not only to the Nile destinations, but also to beach resorts on the Red Sea. Also allocated to it were regional routes across north Africa and across the Mediterranean to Italy. The parent airline, meanwhile, began nonstop service to Beijing (omitting the Bangkok stop) on 29 March 2009, and reintroduced the southern route to Dar es Salaam and Lusaka.

With a population approaching 80 million, Egypt is, after Nigeria, the most populous country in Africa, and in the Middle East. Predominantly Muslim, it is the biggest center of culture and education, so that Cairo, with more than 12 million people, is a hub for international business, commerce, and cultural exchange. Together with the eternal fascination with the architectural remains of ancient Egypt, the national airline seemed destined to maintain healthy growth, in spite of the constant threats to stability beyond its control.

This Airbus A320 left little doubt as to its destination. (McDonough)

The threat of competition from independent airlines in Egypt has not been significant. **Air Cairo**, for example, started operations in 1997, with Soviet Tupolev 204s, but in 2003, control passed to Egyptair, and, as Cairo Aviation, with four Airbus A320s, it became a charter subsidiary of the national airline. Other companies that operated for a few years in the late 1990s and early 2000s were **AMC Aviation**, with two Boeing 737s; **Lotis Air**, with an Airbus A219; **Luxor Air**, with an MD-83; **Flash Airlines**, whose career was cut short by a 737 crash in the Red Sea on 3 January 2004, killing 148; **Shorouk Air**, which operated to Kuwait with A320s and 757-200s from 1993 to 2003; **Transmed Airlines**, with 737s and 707s from 1989 to 1996; and **ZAS Airline of Egypt**, with a fleet of 707s, DC-9s, MD80s, and Airbus A300B4s, from 1982 to 1995, to Europe and on the Hajj. All these, and others, had prospects of profits from supplying the oil-well settlements and the Red Sea resorts; but they were all victims of the continued political uncertainties of the Middle East, in particular the Gulf War of 1991.

One interesting company was **Air Sinai**, which was founded by Egyptair in 1982 to fly between Egypt and Israel on routes which the sensitive politics of the region denied to the parent company. It used a 737-200 and 52-seat Fokker F-27s, lent to it by Egyptair until 2002, when, as the delicate relations between the two countries improved, only the name was retained as a "paper" airline.

Chapter 48: Sub-Saharan Contradictions

The vast area of the African continent south of the Sahara, by far the largest desert in the world, is inhabited only sparsely and sporadically in small regions of fertility and isolated oases. It has never been a preferred destination area of the airlines of Europe, whose countries had colonized the area during the 19th century. Colonial boundaries had been arbitrarily fixed in the corridors of power in Great Britain, France, Belgium, Germany, Italy, Portugal, and Spain. As air transport developed in the late 1920s and the early 1930s, British air routes and services were mainly restricted to connecting points that were geographically situated as technical and refueling stops en route to South Africa, whose climate, dominion status, and mineral wealth gave it a special value. French interests were in west and equatorial Africa and Madagascar; the Belgian interest in the Congo. Few individual colonies or territories in west, east, and central Africa possessed their own airlines. This led to the establishment of airline consortia, as some of the small colonies, which became independent with the wave of nationalism that swept through the continent after the Second World War, combined their individual limited resources.

Commendable Consortium

The British released their African colonies and protectorates in a series of parliamentary decisions, but the French approach was more direct. General Charles de Gaulle, never noted for policies of compromise, came to power as the French president on 1 January 1958. Tunisia and Morocco had already been granted full indpendence. For the remainder of the French territories in West and Equatorial Africa, de Gaulle called a referendum on their future relationship with Paris. Algeria, home of upward of two million Frenchmen, and close to being part of France politically, was excluded, as were Madagascar and Réunion. The choice for the remainder was: (1) complete independence, (2) continue as colonies, or (3) become members of a reconstructed French Community. All except Guinea and Mali, leaning toward communism, accepted the third choice.

On 26 October 1958, President Houphouet-Boigny, of the Côte d'Ivoire (Ivory Coast), in association with Air France and U.A.T. airlines, proposed the creation of a common African airline. This was followed by a second conference on 15–19 December at Brazzaville, French Congo, attended by 12 new heads of state. On 28 March 1961, at Cameroun's new capital, the Treaty of Yaoundé established **Air Afrique**. The shareholdings were 6% each from 11 new states, and 34% from SODETRAF (Société pour le Développement du Transport Aérien en Afrique) that had been formed by U.A.T. (75%) and Air France (25%). The two French airlines had already laid the groundwork by forming Air Afrique in September 1960. By a unanimous vote, Cheikh Fal, from Senegal, was elected as the first president of the new airline. On 1 August all the U.A.T. and Air France services in west and central Africa were taken over by Air Afrique. SODETRAF donated 12 Douglas DC-4s to form a basic fleet. On that day, the first service began from Dakar to other west African cities.

From the start, Air Afrique was dependent upon U.A.T. and Air France for technical support as well as the aircraft. This included engineering bases at Dakar and at the new airline headquarter city, Abidjan. With a solid engineering background, Fal quickly upgraded the fleet from the unpressurized piston-engined DC-4s. On 16 October 1961, the first long-haul service to Paris was inaugurated, linking the main cities—Douala, Cotonou, Abidjan, Dakar, and Port Etienne—with the French capital, with an Air France Lockheed L.1649A Super Constellation. Three days later, the second service added Libreville, Port Gentil, and Nice with a U.A.T. Douglas DC-6B. Jet service began on 4 January 1962, again with leased DC-8s and Boeing 707s, terminating at Brazzaville, French Congo. Air Afrique's own DC-8s were delivered nonstop from Long Beach, California, to Abidjan on 19 October 1963 and 12 January 1964. The airline accepted complete responsibility at all stations and agencies; and on 24 April 1964, the American Civil Aeronautics Board approved a service to New York from six African states and using 45 blocked-space seats on Pan American aircraft. Service to Europe had also been expanded to include Marseilles, on 25 January, and Geneva, on 6 October.

Closer to home, the first short-haul jet, a Caravelle 11R, arrived in July 1967. On 1 January 1968, Togo joined the consortium, with its 6% share reducing SODETRAF's to 28%. But canceling this increase in membership was the departure of Cameroon on 2 September. Possibly feeling that it was not receiving

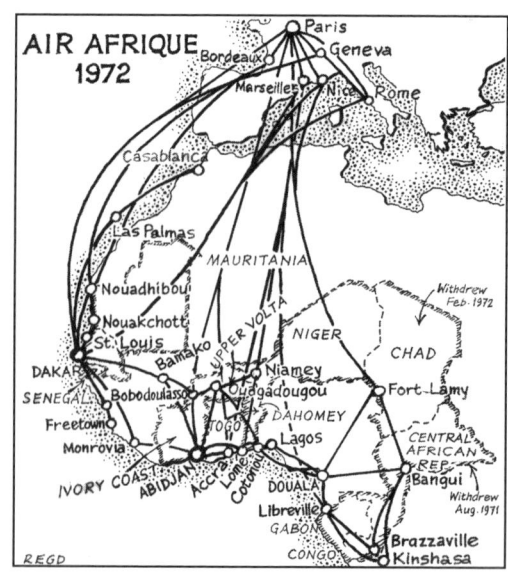

as much attention as the Ivory Coast or Senegal, it had formed Cameroon Airlines on 26 July (see below). For similar reasons, the Central African Republic and Chad both withdrew in August 1971 and February 1972, respectively, but resumed membership after only a few months. Two Nihon YS-11As, purchased in 1969 for local and regional routes, were sold.

Air Afrique acquired its first wide-bodied airliner when, on 2 March 1973, a 251-seat Douglas DC-10-30 was delivered (like the DC-8s previously) nonstop, 6,130 miles, to Dakar. By this time, the shareholding was entirely west African, including 40% SONATRA (Senegal), Air Ivoire 20%, Air Volta (Upper Volta, later Burkina Faso) 20%, and Transgabon (Gabon) 14.5%. Fal retired in September 1973, a few months before the handsome new headquarters building in Abidjan was opened. This was the zenith of Air Afrique's years of existence. During the 1980s, the political structure, rather than commercial necessities, increasingly took precedence. Standards of service, punctuality, and reliability began to deteriorate, and overstaffing was evident. In 1984, facing an operating deficit of $7.15 million and $250 million in debt, 1,600 employees (of 5,600) were dismissed overnight. The trans-African route, started in pool with Ethiopian Air Lines, ended. Successive presidents were unable to stop the decline. A 302-seat Lockheed L.1011 tri-jet and a 137-seat Boeing 737-300 were leased for the peak periods in the early 1970s, but most of the routes to Europe were eliminated. A further factor contributing to the decline was the high proportion of free seats given to governmental personnel and other favored passengers, while paying passenger seats were highly priced. Further changes in management, the addition of Mali (replacing Gabon, which had left), and in 1988 the lease of two Airbus A330s, could not revive an airline that had never been able to operate on strictly commercial principles. One commentator synthesized the negative factors as political favoritism, corruption, and nepotism. In May 2002, Air Afrique closed its doors.

Before its demise, Air Afrique even operated a Boeing 747. (McDonough)

The Refugees from Air Afrique

The subtitle of this section could have used the word remnants, or more harshly, cast-offs, or leftovers. Unkind though this judgment is, it is no more than the cold truth. Under the French, the vast area of northern Africa (other than the Maghreb), from the Atlantic Ocean almost almost to the Nile, had been administered as two territories, French West Africa and French Equatorial Africa. Both were subdivided into divisions. In 1958, each of these divisions became independent countries. Air Afrique had been formed to face the reality that these individual ex-colonies of the French empire had insufficient experience, resources, or prospective traffic potential, each to stand on its own. In 2002, with the collapse of this broad experiment, airline activity in that same area was fragmented, and the individual young republics were "back to square one."

The fragmentation was real. Along the coast, from the westernmost point at Dakar to the Ivory Coast—about the same distance as the length of California—there are six countries. Only two have working railroads, other than for mining. Domestic operations for individual airlines were extremely limited. Sénégal, however, had been developed partly because of the geographical importance of Dakar, the most convenient refueling base for South America-bound airlines from Europe. The first **Air Sénégal** was founded privately in November 1962, and began domestic flights in November 1963 in affiliation with Air France and U.T.A. Its fleet included Fokker F-27s and small Piper aircraft. On 1 July 1971, it was nationalized, with the government holding 50% of the shares, and Air Afrique 40%. It connected Dakar with outlying communities on its far frontiers, including those that were geographically separated by surface transport by the Gambia. On 23 February 2001, Royal Air Maroc acquired a majority stake and added *International* to the name. Financial losses led to the government purchasing up to 75% on 5 November 2007, but operations were suspended on 24 April 2009.

The other French West African province with the potential to survive Air Afrique's demise was the Côte d'Ivoire (Ivory Coast), whose capital, Abidjan, had been the technical base of the consortium. **Air Ivoire** was formed in 1956 by the French T.A.I. (which later merged with U.A.T. to form U.T.A.) and in 1958 began internal routes with 8-seat de Havilland DH-89A Rapides then 14-seat DH-104 Herons, to connect with the trunk route to Paris. Service was discontinued in 1960, when the province gained independence, and after a spell with U.T.A. in 1963/4, resumed operations with Air Afrique in 1964, adding Douglas DC-3s. The government acquired all the shares in 1976, and its president, Felix Houphouet-Boigny, moved to assert leadership of the former French West African colonies. He designated his village birthplace, Yamoussouko, as the new capital, but fast-growing Abidjan remained the commercial and economic center. Côte d'Ivoire's railroad served many provincial towns and ran to Burkina Faso, and there was a network of roads, but Air Ivoire grew to serve almost a score of the towns.

It was suspended with the outbreak of tribal strife in 1999 then resumed in 2001 as Nouvelle Air Ivoire, but soon reverted to its first name. It also survived a rebellion in 2002 that almost split the country into two, but emerged to expand its fleet of Fokker F-28s with two Airbus twins, an A319 and an A321, to operate the former Air Afrique trunk route to Paris.

Some of the French colonies had been reasonably comfortable, if not affluent. Others had few resources that could generate enough interest to start an airline, even with foreign help. But new-found national pride often demanded, after the creation of a national flag, the birth of a national airline. Mauritania was one such impoverished territory, and its area seemed to require air service. But most of it was either desert or scrubland, with only a small area adjacent to Sénégal available for agriculture. Supported by the Spanish airline Spantax, **Air Mauritanie** was founded in September 1962 and began service in October 1963 with a Fokker F-27, from the new capital, Nouakchott, along the coast to Nouadhibou (formerly Pte. Etienne). By 1980, the airline was operating south to Dakar and across the sea to Las Palmas, Canary Islands, with Fokker F-28s, and even, by the 1990s, with a Boeing 737 and two ATR-42s.

By the late 1990s, however, the Mauritanian fleet was reduced to a single F-28. Debts had climbed to almost $5 million, the staff was severely cut, and for a while, in 2003, Tunisair, with a 51% shareholding, kept it going. Then, in August 2006, Royal Air Maroc took over from Tunisair. The end was now in sight, but Air Mauritanie must be remembered for a remarkable episode. On 16 February 2007, it foiled a hijacker who forced the 737 to land at Las Palmas to refuel. The pilot, like the passengers, spoke French, and realized that the hijacker did not. He announced on the public address system that on landing, he would brake suddenly. This threw the hijacker on to the floor, the flight attendants doused him with boiling water, and the passengers beat him up. It was an honorable memory for Air Mauritanie when it was liquidated in October 2007.

As mentioned above, Cameroon had seceded from Air Afrique, and had prepared itself to "go it alone" by forming **Cameroon Airlines** on 26 July—before the secession on 2 September 1968. 70% of the shares were held by the government, and 30% by Air France, which leased a Boeing 707, to open a route to Paris via Rome, on 1 November 1971, and a Boeing 737, for the domestic trunk route from Douala, the port, to Yaoundé, the capital. In July 1972, with more success and wider scope than many of the ex–Air Afrique regions, Cameroon's own 142-seat Boeing 707 joined the fleet, and Geneva and Marseilles were added to the Paris route.

Delivery of a 20-seat DHC-6 Twin Otter in 1974 extended the domestic network to many small towns, and a 40-seat Convair 440 and an HS-748 met an increased demand—until new roads were built. By the early 1980s, international traffic was so good that a Boeing 747-200 was leased for the Paris route, and also for London. But in September 2005, French authorities banned the airline for several months because of poor maintenance and safety records. In March 2008, it suffered from deficiencies in management, operations, and finance. Powerful competition from Europe forced Cameroon Airlines to cease operating.

Some of the French colonies were so small that a domestic operation was impossible. Air Benin, with an Aerospatiale Corvette and a Fokker F-27 had started in 1979, but gave way to **Trans Air Benin** in 2000. With leased aircraft, it operated from Cotonou along the west African coast from Dakar to Brazzaville, and north to Bamako. Neighboring Togo, only half the size of Benin, has never aspired to have an airline flag carrier.

Further north, in Burkina Faso, **Air Burkina** traced its history back to 17 March 1967, when it was called Air Volta (because the French colony was called Upper Volta). The two main cities, 200 miles apart, had some air service, but were connected by railroad. A succession of coups delayed progress, until, on 21 February 2001, the government privatized the airline, which worked closely with Air Ivoire (an Airbus A319) and other companies, mainly to operate across the southern border to coastal cities. Its fleet included a Fokker F-28, a Saab 340, and two McDonnell Douglas MD-87s. These last were acquired through the Celestair Group, which was funded through AKFED, the Aga Khan Fund for Economic Development.

Air Niger linked the capital, Niamey, with the smaller towns of the country, as there are no railroads or river transport, and many of the roads are in the desert. But the distances are long enough to justify Fokker F-27 operations.

To the northeast, **Tournaï Air Chad** is the national airline of Chad, based at N-Djamena (formerly Fort Lamy). Its fleet is headed by four leased Boeing 737-200s. It was handicapped in the late 1990s by hostilities with Sudan when the ruthless oppression in the latter's Darfur province erupted. The U.S. Embassy in Chad banned its employees from flying for safety concerns.

Chad's neighbor, the Central African Republic, which like the other French colonies, had voted for independence in 1960, and its airline, **Air Bangui**, started operations with a single DC-3 in 1966. When Jean-Bedel Bokassa declared himself as Emperor in 1965, he changed the name to **Air Centrafique**, withdrew from Air Afrique, and enlarged the fleet to include a Douglas DC-4 and a Sud Caravelle jet. It served the outlying regions of the Republic under restrictive conditions—described as "a reign of terror"—but was never established as a reliable scheduled airline. Bokassa departed in 1979, but the country lacked the resources and the experience to achieve political stability.

Equatorial Heritage

Further south of the former French Equatorial Africa, Gabon was blessed with more resources than many of the other colonies. Much of its area was productive tropical hardwood forest, and it also had minerals, including manganese and uranium. Its exports were balanced by consumer-goods imports, and it was described as "the Showcase of Young Africa." At first, its airline seemed to reflect that compliment. It had a good heritage, starting as early as 1951, when **Transports Aériens du Gabon (T.A.G.)** connected the capital, Libreville, with inland centers. It used small aircraft, including a de Havilland DH-89A Rapide.

A Cameroon Airlines Big Boss *Boeing 747 SUD. (McDonough)*

In 1968, it was designated as the national carrier, as the first **Cie. Aérienne Gabonaise (Air Gabon)** to extend the domestic routes to all parts of the country, upgrading the equipment to 28-seat DC-3s.

Gabon had been a member of the Air Afrique consortium, but left it in 1977, when it felt that, as it provided 25% of the airline revenues, it should have had more representation. Accordingly, in December of that year, the second Air Gabon was formed. It took over the assets of the first Air Gabon, which had already absorbed other small operators, including Transgabon. 70% of the shares were held by Gabon, 30% by French interests. This time, it was the **Cie. Nationale**, and its ambitions went beyond domestic and local services, with Fokker F-28s from its predecessor. It acquired a Boeing 747 combi for service to France via Rome and Geneva, and a Boeing 737 to west African capitals as far as Dakar.

Relatively prosperous among African countries, a railroad was built to connect Libreville to the far east of Gabon, to transport timber and minerals, while other cargo was carried by Air Gabon in the 747 combi, two Vickers Vanguards, and, from 1985, a Lockheed L-100 for heavy cargo. Oil was discovered off shore, and the airline prospered for close to a decade. For its local routes, 105-seat Fokker 100 jets, the first in Africa, replaced the F-28s. Libreville's high-rise buildings, luxury hotels, and urban freeways suggested prosperity, but the all-too-familiar mismanagement, government interference, and poor service (at least for the paying customers, not the officials and their families) led to an ominous decline in Air Gabon's fortunes in the 1990s. In 2001, Lufthansa Consulting undertook the restructuring of the airline. The government took over Air France's shares (now 80%), absorbed most of a heavy debt, and provided $47 million extra capital. But the task was beyond even the efficient German consultants. The fleet consisted of six Boeing jets, of four types, and an Antonov An-12 cargo aircraft, but like the hubs of other west African capitals, Libreville was now on the maps of European airlines. In 2007, Air Gabon was replaced by a new company, **Gabon Airlines**, which had two Boeing 767-200s.

Possibly because of its relative financial comfort level, Gabon's government took a liberal approach toward airline activity. Like Nigeria, it was one of the few African countries to permit more than a single national airline. Thus, on 26 October 1998, with a 44-seat Hawker-Siddeley HS-748 (ex-air force Andover), **Gabon Express** started operations from Libreville to the oil port, Port Gentil. It then started nonstop services to the north and the southeast, and on 18 July 1999, introduced a 99-seat Sud Caravelle 11R, equipped with a large freight door. It was the last of this, the world's first short-haul twin-jet airliner, to enter scheduled airline service, four decades after the first of the type started in 1958. It operated for a few years, but crashed. The owners were convicted for drug-running.

Gabon's neighbor, the Congo Republic, suffered from a constantly turbulent political history, with a succession of governmental coups, including an assassination and a Marxist administration. **Trans-Air Congo** started service on 24 August 1994, mainly between Brazzaville and the port city of Pointe-Noire, with a small fleet of Soviet airliners. But in 1997, the airline had to move to South Africa to avoid a civil war.

Other than Ethiopia, Liberia was the only independent country in Africa with its economy sustained by productive U.S.-owned rubber plantations. As early as 1949, **Liberian National Airways** was formed to operate limited local services with a DC-3 and a de Havilland DH-89. The French U.T.A. took over the management in 1965, and subsequently, in 1974, the U.S. Hughes Air West added Liberia to its assistance program for third-world countries. It changed its name to **Air Liberia**, and donated two Fairchild F-27s and a Boeing 737 for government work. But operations ceased in 1990.

Of the non-French colonial territories in west Africa, in what was then Portuguese Guinea, a small company was formed in 1960, mainly to connect this remote and unproductive colony with the Cape Verde Islands via Dakar, using de Havilland DH-104 Herons. When, in 1974, guerrilla insurrections led to independence, contact with the islands became irrelevant, and the name **Transportes Aéreos da Guine Portuguesa (T.A.G.P.)** was later simplified to **Air Bissau**, after the local capital. Multi-party elections in 1994 were followed by a civil war in 1998–9, which euphemistically, in one account, caused "severe damage to the infrastructure." To be realistic, there was very little infrastructure when, in 2002, Guine Bissau was founded, and after a military coup in 2002, it was "disestablished."

Guinea had elected to be completely independent from France, and left-wing politics led it to ally itself with the Soviet Union. Thus, when **Air Guinée** was formed on 31 December 1960, its first service, on 18 October 1961, from Conakry to Kankan, and connecting with Bamako in the then Upper Volta, was with a 40-seat twin piston-engined Ilyushin Il-14. On 24 August 1962, a 100-seat Ilyushin Il-18 opened international service north to Dakar, and on 10 May 1963, east to the local capital cities as far as Lagos. But disillusionment with the lack of complete support from the Soviet Union led to a change of heart. With assistance from Alaska Airlines, and, later, Pan American, Douglas DC-4s supplemented (but not replaced) the Il-18s, which still received help from Ilyushin. Antonov An-24s operated the domestic and regional routes. Guinean politics were still in upheaval and repressive rule plunged the country into economic ruin. During the 1970s, however, Boeing aircraft kept the airline going with a 707-138B, a 727-100, and a 737-200. But the path was far from clear. An Il-18 crashed in 1978 and an An-24 in 1980. Then in 1984, after a military coup, a new government took over. The airline recovered enough to be able to acquire an Airbus A300C-4 in 1985, and opened service to Paris and Brussels. A new multi-party administration in 1990 ensured more stability for the operating environment, and the airline was reconstructed in 1992.

Like Guinea, Mali had elected for full independence from France in 1958, and founded its own airline on 27 October 1960. After starting service with three Douglas DC-3s in February 1961, **Air Mali** made an agreement with the Soviet Union, with which it had close political ties, to use aircraft from its manufacturers. In

December 1961, a 100-seat Ilyushin Il-18 started service to Paris via Casablanca, and soon afterward, domestic and local routes were opened with 40-seat Antonov An-24s. They operated quite successfully, but on 12 August 1974, an Il-18 crashed at Ouagadougou, killing 46. There were problems of support and spares supply also, and the Soviet types were replaced by Boeing 727s for the Paris route. The An-24s and even the old DC-3s carried on, until replaced by Fokker F-28s.

A Promising Inheritance Eroded

Unlike the French experience of 1958, in which a consortium was created as a political and economic necessity, the British had already made preparations to link their disconnected colonies in west Africa with a coordinated air service. In 1944, Lord Swinton, then the resident minister, appointed the Stanford Committee to decide what to do with the air transport that had been provided during the Second World War by the Royal Air Force. Accordingly, on 15 May 1946, the **West African Airways Corporation (W.A.A.C.)** was established by Order in Council, with the shareholding held by the colonial governments of Nigeria, the Gold Coast, Sierra Leone, and the Gambia.

Starting service in October 1946 with Douglas DC-3s, it built a network that extended from Dakar, Senegal, to Khartoum, Sudan, including an extensive domestic system in Nigeria and local routes in the Gold Coast. The DC-3s were replaced by a succession of British piston-engined types, de Havilland Doves, Bristol 170s, and the ill-fated Miles Marathons. This last 18-seat feeder airliner was withdrawn because of excessive maintenance problems, and de Havilland 14-seat Herons started service on 16 May 1956. W.A.A.C. was something of a poor relation in the British scheme of things in Africa, as the pioneering Comets had already forged a route from London to Johannesburg in 1952 (though suspended in 1954—see below). The routes to London from Lagos, Nigeria, and Accra, Gold Coast, continued to be flown by B.O.A.C. until May 1957, when W.A.A.C. was able to charter the British flag carrier's DC-4M Argonauts and Boeing Stratocruisers to operate in pool, in its own airline colors.

But in this year, the "wind of change" (to quote Prime Minister Macmillan) was sweeping through Africa. The Gold Coast declared independence, renaming the country as Ghana, to become the first African colony to secede from the old Empire. In June 1958, the trading name of W.A.A.C. was changed to **Nigerian Airways**, and on 30 September the old name was modified to W.A.A.C. (Nigeria) Ltd. The shareholding was 51% Nigerian government, 33% Elder Dempster (the shipping line that had operated its own airline briefly before the war), and 16% B.O.A.C. Associated Companies. The next day, Ghana Airways took over its domestic routes with aircraft chartered from W.A.A.C., and Nigerian Airways took over the route to London, still with aircraft chartered from B.O.A.C., including, from 16 April 1959, a Bristol Britannia four-engined turboprop.

On 1 October 1959, Nigeria too became independent. This was more than a small colony. Its population, then approaching 100 million, was (except India's) far more than that of any of the self-governing dominions of the British Commonwealth, as the Empire had become known. A further difficulty, and unsettling, was that, as with all the European territories that were being liberated, the boundaries had been arbitrarily decided with little regard for tribal or ethnic considerations. In the case of Nigeria, the multitude of both was dominated by three main groups: the Yoruba in the west, the Hausa in the north, and the Ibo in the east, a situation that would be one of the many problems to face the new airline.

It started off confidently. On 25 March 1961, all the shares were sold to the Nigerian government. A fleet of DC-3s, for domestic and regional routes, inherited from Britain, and the Britannia, were soon joined on 1 April 1962 by Vickers VC-10s and Comet 4s, chartered from B.O.A.C., and in March 1963 by Fokker F-27 Friendships. On 1 May of that year, a new long-term agreement with the British airline ensured technical support for the next eight years. In addition, on 4 October 1964, Nigerian was able to announce a trans-Atlantic service to New York through a 25-seat blocked-space agreement with Pan American Airways.

During the next few years, Nigerian Airways fortunes plummeted as the country plunged into a civil war. A military coup on 15 January 1966 was followed by the Biafran War, from 6 July 1967 to 15 January 1970, when the Ibo-inhabited eastern province fought to break from Lagos, whence the Yoruba majority now controlled the country, with cooperation from the Muslim north. The airline managed to keep going sporadically, even adding Madrid, Rome, and Frankfurt to its long-haul routes; but two VC-10 crashes in 1969, one of them fatal (89 killed) was symptomatic of the severe problems that the young airline had to face.

During the early 1970s, it slowly recovered, leasing Boeing 707s and 737s, for its longer routes, and in May 1972, purchased F-28 Fellowships for the regionals. With gradual expansion, its own Boeing 707-320Cs were complemented, late in 1976, by 300-seat Douglas DC-10-30 wide-bodied tri-jets. Nigerian finances, including those of the national airline, were in better shape, as oil had been discovered in the Biafran Gulf, to the benefit of the national purse-strings. Nigerian Airways's network now spread across the whole of sub-Saharan Africa and to 19 domestic points.

But all was not well. Two Fokker crashes led, in 1979, to the engagement of a management team from the experienced K.L.M.—like the crashed aircraft, from the Netherlands. Part of the agreement was to train local personnel in the technical, operational, and administrative disciplines needed for a first-class airline. But in 1984, a military-led coup changed the entire structure of the airline, even dismissing the K.L.M. trainees. Also, in 1984, in a strange Nigerian Airlines incident, the British police thwarted an attempt to kidnap a Nigerian diplomat in a wooden crate at London's Stansted Airport.

Late in the same year, the first (of four) Airbus A320-200s were delivered, to operate on the busiest domestic routes, where the towns and cities were now growing to require increased air service in a country where the railways were slow and roads were not only inadequate but frequently unsafe. Back in the colonial days, Nigerian air travelers were mostly government officials and businessmen. Now, the oil industry was adding wealth to the country at all income levels. This, however, was uncontrolled, and much of it led to the growth of industry, rapid urbanization, and the appearance of many new airlines, offering competition to Nigerian Airlines under a government that seemed unwilling to regulate the industry.

Group-Captain Bernard Banfe was appointed chairman, to face a situation that could only be described as desperate. He started to prune the staff from an inflated 11,000 to a workable 4,500, including management appointments that had been based on political, tribal, and religious preferences, rather than managerial, administrative, or technical experience. Banfe himself cited "inefficiency, declining productivity, and fraud." The airline had had 14 board chairmen since 1958. The accumulated debt was $250 million, with a $15-million loss in 1987 alone.

The decline continued in the 1990s, almost unabated. After drastic cuts, a few routes were resumed in 1989, but in 1992, nine aircraft were grounded, and three were impounded in Europe for non-payment of bills for fuel and airport charges. Worst of all, there were more crashes, the most spectacular in July 1991, a DC-8-61 at Jeddah, killing 261 occupants. More crashes in the mid-Nineties tarnished the image of the airline to the extent that the air-traveling public avoided it. The national airline was not alone in its poor safety record, as the many new African airlines that had been formed were also, as described below, guilty of irresponsible lack of disciplined conduct in their affairs.

The combination of all these factors led to the termination of all Nigerian Airways operations in 2003. The collapse of a national flag carrier left a void that many entrepreneurs had already begun to fill. Since independence, Nigeria has had no less than 105 registered airlines, most of them very small, often with a single airplane, in the role of fixed base operations. Many were charter or cargo operators who were riding the wave of the oil industry boom in the Niger delta region. But some were passenger carriers, and one of the first, from the Muslim north, was a survivor when many failed. **Kabo Air**, owned by Chief Kabo, began operations in April 1981 with five Sud Caravelles, adding three Boeing 727-200s in 1987, and 13 BAC One-Elevens from 1991. 11 more 727s and five Boeing 747s in the late 1990s were used for long-haul international flights and expecially for the Hajj to Mecca. This early independent airline's survival rested partly on its casualty-free record, although it had several relatively minor accidents.

Boeing 747, owned by Chief Kabo, from Kano. (McDonough)

Other newcomers to the Nigerian airline scene were not so successful, nor as safe. A DC-8 ground collision of **Intercontinental Airlines** (1981) at London's Stansted Airport on 5 September 1982 curtailed that airline's career. E.A.S. (Executive Airlines Services) Airlines, carried cargo from 1983 until 1992, and executive charters from November 1993 until starting regular scheduled flights on 12 May 1996 as **EAS Airlines**. Two crashes, one of them serious, a One-Eleven at Kano, on 4 May 2002, killing 154 people, led to its operating certificate being revoked. **Okada Air**, starting in September 1983, had a similar experience. It acquired a Boeing 707-300 and a total of 18 One-Elevens, and later, 727s and two 747s for international services. It too suffered minor crashes and did not last long, and nor did **Oriental Airlines**, from 1989 to 1994, and **Harca Air** (later Hardo Air), from 1991 to 1995.

By the turn of the century, the oil industry was generating much industrial activity in Nigeria, where the population—already exceeding 100 million—was becoming increasingly urbanized. Lagos had become a large, if still developing, metropolis of more than eight million; Kano in the north, and Port Harcourt, the center of the oil and gas region, had grown to be large cities. As mentioned above, the railroads and roads were inadequate, so there was a big demand for domestic air service. During the early 2000s, of the early independents, Kabo Air was still in business, and had been joined by **Bellview Airlines** and **ADC Airlines** in 1992, and **Chanchangi Airlines** in 1997. Bellview and ADC sustained fatal crashes in 2005–2006, both Boeing 737s, the former on 22 October 2005 near Abuja, the latter on 29 October 2006 also at Abuja. Both crashes occurred at the new Federal capital, and ADC's was the second bad one, one of its 727s having crashed at Lagos on 6 November 1996, killing 143. Another newcomer, **Sosoliso Airlines**, which started in July 2000, suffered a DC-9 crash on 29 October 2006. Within 12 months, six crashes had killed 322 people, not including three in a Nigerian Air Force incident. Moreover, the fatalities in the ADC crash in 2006 had included the Sultan of Sokoto, Muhammed Maceido, the spiritual head of the Nigerian Muslim community; while the Sosolito death had included a popular Christian speaker and 50 of his Jesuit colleagues. The Nigerian authorities had had enough. They set a deadline of 30 April 2007 for all airlines operating in the country to be grounded unless they were recapitalized and could demonstrate better service and safety standards. ADC and Sosolito failed the test, but Kabo, Bellview, and Chanchangi made it through.

A crisis of confidence in all Nigerian airlines was predictable, and even during the spell during which the local airlines seemed to be taking turns to crash their aircraft, confidence was somewhat restored from an unexpected quarter. Sir Richard Branson's Virgin Atlantic Airlines had started a London-Lagos Boeing 747-200 service on 16 July 2001, to provide some competition with British Airways. He was approached to help save Nigerian Airways, but felt that his good money should not be chasing bad. So on 28 September 2004, he signed an agreement with President Olusegun Obasanjo to launch **Virgin Nigeria**, backed by a $24.5-million investment, of which Sir Richard held 49% of the shares.

Airbus A340-300 service began from Lagos to London on 28 June 2005. This was followed by Boeing 767 service to New York, and Boeing 737 and Fokker 50s on domestic and regional routes. On 25 September 2008, 94-seat Embraer 190-100ARs were handed over at the Brazilian factory. All was not plain flying, however, as the Nigerian aviation authorities tried to force Virgin to switch its base from Lagos's international airport to another terminal. Flights to London were interrupted briefly but resumed in July 2009.

Of potentially equal stature, to represent Nigeria in the world of international airlines, was **Arik Air**, which Sir Joseph Arumemilkhide had started in July 2004 with a Hawker 800 business jet for his oil and gas company. In 2005, he launched Arik as a commercial airline, taking over, on 3 April 2006, the Nigerian Airways installations at Lagos. On 14 June, it introduced three Bombardier CRJ-900 regional jets, and quickly built up a fleet of Boeing 737s and Fokker F50s. On 15 December 2008, two Airbus A340-500s started a route to London, and with Boeing 777s and 787s on order, Arik Air seemed destined to inherit the privilege of being Nigeria's flagship airline.

A Boeing 737-700 of Arik Air. (McDonough)

In spite of the renewed energy bestowed to the Nigerian airways by Virgin and Arik, there is no substitute for local African experience, as long as it is systematic and disciplined. This quality appears to have rested with **Aero Contractors (Nigeria)**, trading as **Aero**. It was founded in 1959 by the Dutch Schreiner Airways to serve the oil and gas explorations in Nigeria, taking a 40% interest in 1973, increased to 60% in 1976. The Canadian Helicopter Corporation bought 40% of Shreiner's share in 2004, while the Ibro family retained the balance. It started scheduled domestic service with Canadian DHC-8s and Boeing 737s in the fall of 2005, and quickly built up a fleet of 15 aircraft that gained a reputation for reliable and punctual service. It passed the test imposed by the authorities on 30 April 2007 to join the senior ranks of Nigeria's commercial airlines.

Even though personal incomes by the majority of the public are low, by 2010 the country's population exceeded 140 million, which alone guaranteed an air travel market. Urbanization has led to Lagos having about 11 million inhabitants, and Kano and Ibadan each have 4 million. At the beginning of the Jet Age, Port Harcourt was only a small town at the terminus of one of the railroad lines. Today, thanks to the oil boom, it is a thriving city of close to 2 million. Except for Ibadan, close to Lagos, they all have nonstop services to London and other European cities, as does Abuja, the fast-growing Federal capital. With proper discipline, the future for airlines in Nigeria should be assured, if only because of the demographics.

Independence (from Britain) at All Costs

The global conflict that cost tens of millions of lives during the Second World War resulted in a costly victory for the Allied powers over the evil ambitions of the Axis dictatorships. After the war ended in 1945, the policies of democratic government—to quote Lincoln's definition as "of the people, by the people, and for the people"—were embraced by the colonies and protectorates of the European empire-builders of the past. Self-government in Africa had already been achieved in South Africa, Southern Rhodesia was approaching that status, and in east and central Africa, economic progress was sought by cooperative national consortia. In west Africa, however, where the colonies were fragmented along the coast, the urge for complete individual independence was too strong.

First of the many was the Gold Coast, where, in 1958, Kwame Nkrumah led his country away from Great Britain, renaming it Ghana. As became customary, one of the main indications of newly independent status was the creation of a national airline. **Ghana Airways** was formed on 4 July of the same year after an agreement with Britain's B.O.A.C. for pooled services to London. The capital was $112 million, 60% by the government, 40% by B.O.A.C. With a wet-leased Boeing Stratocruiser from its part-owner, the airline proudly showed its country's flag at London's Heathrow Airport on 15 July 1958. On 1 October, it took over domestic routes from West African Airways. For these, the first de Havilland 19-seat four-engined D.H. 114 Heron was delivered at the end of the year, to be supplemented in March 1959 with trusty Douglas DC-3s.

On 13 April 1959 Ghana Airways replaced the Stratocruiser with a turboprop-powered Bristol Britannia 102, also leased from B.O.A.C., and on 2 December 1960, replaced it with its own Britannia 300 series. Ghana's politics were now leaning toward close ties with the Soviet Union, and on the next day the airline took delivery of the first of eight Ilyushin Il-18s, whose performance was similar to the Britannia's. But a service to Moscow was short-lived, and problems of support from the U.S.S.R. led to their return to the manufacturer in 1963. An order for two Boeing 707s was also canceled. On 14 February, the government bought B.O.A.C.'s shareholding, and sought technical support elsewhere. In October 1963, the airline signed an agreement with Swissair, which leased a Convair 990. On 11 November, it started Ghana Airways's first jet service to London.

The choice for its own long-range jet airliner was the Vickers VC-10. Of the three ordered, the first began service to London on 15 February 1965, the second was destroyed by Israeli commandos at Beirut in 1968, and the third was never delivered. Like most of the new African republics, the national airline was primarily a symbol of independence and of national pride. Political requirements took precedence over commercial or financial necessities, so that Ghana Airways had always been able to call upon government subsidy for anything it wanted, including expensive jet aircraft, and inflated staff numbers. But when, in 1966, President Nkrumah was deposed, in favor of Flt. Lt. Jerry Rawlings, the subsidies, estimated to have totaled $20 million, were abolished, and the airline's fleet and its route network were severely reduced. From then on, with aircraft ranging from Hawker-Siddeley 748s and Fokker F-27s to Douglas DC-8s to comprise the operating fleet, Ghana Airways survived by a succession of leased aircraft. In 1980, when Douglas DC-10 wide-bodied airliners were leased from K.L.M., contracts with expatriate foreign pilots were terminated, as in spite of its many problems, the flying personnel, both aircrew and flight attendants, were well up to international standards. But when Group Captain Frank Okyne took over the management in 1983, the airline had had 22 chairmen/managing directors, serving no less than 20 different ministries. One description at the time of the management and administration shortcomings was that "instability (was) the only consistency factor in the airline's past."

The airline staggered on bravely, determined to "show the flag" of Ghana overseas. With a fleet of only four aircraft—one DC-10, one DC-9, and two F-28s—international services were somehow maintained sporadically, and in 1994 one MD-11 was leased for the New York route, and the Harare route extended to Johannesburg. Such actions were gestures of defiance against desperation; for simultaneously, the decision was made to privatize the company. While suitors were being sought, some relief was gained by services to Dusseldorf and Hamburg, where some Ghanain expatriates provided fresh traffic. But by now, Ghana Airways was unattractive to any buyer. During the early 2000s, two Airbus A320s and an Airbus A330 were leased, but the end was near. Described by one reporter as being "plagued by corruption," it had 94 bank accounts, and was $160 million in debt. By 2004, it had only one serviceable airplane. On 28 July of that year, the axe fell, when the United States banned it from flying to the U.S. because of safety concerns with its maintenance procedures. On 13 August 2004, Ghana Airways ceased operations.

On condition that any replacement for the failed national flag carrier had absolutely no links with it, a group of U.S. investors agreed to form a new airline with 49% of the shares. The government would hold 51% and undertake to clear up the old airline's considerable debts. These and other negotiations were more complex than expected, and when **Ghana International Airlines (GIA-USA)** was finally formed, the government's share, from a contribution of $4.9 million, was 70%. The first service, with a wet-leased 160-seat Boeing 757-200, left London's Gatwick Airport for Accra on 29 October 2005.

Another British west African colony did not achieve independence until 1961, but **Sierra Leone Airways** was formed early in 1958, with the help of West African Airways, which in June would become Nigerian Airways. De Havilland DH-89s, followed in October 1961 by Scottish Aviation Twin Pioneers, operated short flights from the capital, Freetown, including one across an estuary to the airport that was four hours away by road. An agreement in November with British United Airways (70% shareholding), following the country's independence from Britain, led to a Bristol Britannia service to London. Political unrest, including tribal confrontations during the 1970s, did not help attempts to promote Freetown's beaches as a tourist destination, even though, with B.U.A. becoming British Caledonian, some flights to London were with Boeing 707s and Vickers VC-10s. Two Britten Norman BN-2A Trislanders improved the tiny domestic operation, but the economics of the operations were insufficient for permanency. Sierra Leone Airlines (S.L.A.) was relaunched in 1982, this time with help from Jordan's Alia, which held 20% of the shares, but it did not last long. S.L.A. folded in 1987, but was reformed as **Sierra National Airlines** and resumed flights on 1 May 1990 with a Boeing 727.

By this time the country was in the throes of considerable political instability. One opposition group, mainly students, calling themselves the Revolutionary United Front, began a campaign that included extensive banditry, resulting from battles for control of the diamond mines. The official period of the civil war was from 23 March 1991 to 18 January 2002, during which time tens of thousands were killed, more than 100,000 refugees fled to neighboring Guinea, and two million were displaced from their homes. The savagery ended only after British forces had intervened to evacuate British subjects in the summer of 2000 and had reinforced the United Nations Mission, which had previously replaced the Nigerian-led west African forces. A series of conferences had resulted in Peace Accords, but these were ineffective. Sierra Leone gradually recovered, and most of the perpetrators were indicted, punished, or had died or been killed. The diamond industry returned to government control, although much smuggling continued, mainly across the border to Liberia, which had its own problems. The environment for a small airline to prosper was far from encouraging.

Even smaller than Sierra Leone is the Gambia, which consists of a narrow strip of territory on each side of the river of that name. It gained its independence from Britain in 1965, retaining an extremely valuable asset: the 12,000-foot airport runway at the capital, Banjul (formerly Bathurst). Its aviation history goes back to the early 1930s, when it was used by Deutsche Luft Hansa as the African base for its flights to South America; and more recently as a vital refueling transit point during the Falklands War, and as an emergency landing site for the U.S. Space Shuttles.

Attempts were made to exploit this valuable aviation asset, but to no avail. Between the late 1980s and the mid-1990s, half a dozen small companies were formed, but none operated more than a few isolated flights. Only one gained any recognition, when in 1989, **Air Gambia** (the second of that name) operated briefly to London with a Boeing 707, in cooperation with Omega Air, which owned 49% of the shares. On 1 December 2000 **Gambia International Airlines**, originally a ground-handling company, started flying to London, in cooperation with Air Namibia, but ceased flying in April 2004. At the end of that year, **Slok Air**

Gambia began service, halted it in 2007, and started again early in 2009. Its prospects for long-term survival are bleak as Gambia alone cannot generate enough traffic from all sources to sustain break-even, much less profitable, airline operations.

The Offshore Islands

The need for air transport in the whole of west Africa was always apparent, because of long distances between cities and the lack of good surface transport. During the colonial period of the 1930s, most of this need was met by long-distance airlines from Europe and the occasional feeder affiliate. After the end of the Second World War, a proliferation of airlines, either as consortia or individually, met an increasing demand for travel to and within Africa. Road and rail construction eroded continued expansion, and indeed replaced the air routes in many areas, not least because surface travel was cheaper than air, because of the higher operating costs of airplanes. Only in east Africa was there a natural demand for foreign tourists, who sought safari expeditions, mountaineering, and beaches. Hundreds of miles of sandy shores in west Africa did not attract large numbers, and local enterprises to attract them were few and far between.

Exceptionally, however, prospects for the islands in the Atlantic Ocean were more favorable, as competition from shipping was slow, often uncomfortable in heavy seas, and sometimes irregular. The Canary Islands, still politically part of Spain, and Madeira and the Azores, politically parts of Portugal, were early beneficiaries of a European tourism boom. But the Cape Verde Islands were 1,000 miles south of the Canaries, which were 800 miles south of Spain. This was at first too far for economical package tours that built the thriving business elsewhere. Also, the Cape Verdes were little developed, even for local people, and its first airline was for them to avoid the ferry boats. Curiously, the airport of one of the islands, Sal, had one of the longest runways in Africa, almost two miles long. It was first built by the Italians in 1938, for their pioneering landplane service to South America then developed after the war as an ideal refueling stop between Europe and Brazil. Sal Island became a valuable asset as the Cape Verde Islands slowly became known to the outside world.

Transportes Aéreos de Cabo Verde (T.A.C.V.) was founded on 27 December 1958—just as Pan American Airways opened its jet service across the Atlantic. A fleet of eight-seat de Havilland Doves connected the eight main islands. Owned by the Portuguese government, it operated until the mid-1960s, when it suspended flights until a reorganization, with support from the Portuguese airline T.A.P. During the 1970s, 10-seat BN-2As and 40-seat HS-748s coped with the inter-island needs.

Independence from Portugal on 5 July 1975 ushered in a new spirit. The Islands' long distance from the homeland had not encouraged the same interest in the potential of tourism as had Madeira. But with jet aircraft able to eliminate the journey time factor, and a program to erect the necessary infrastructure to attract visitors who sought new destinations, Cape Verde emerged from international obscurity. In 1978, the first of two 20-seat DHC-6 Twin Otters arrived to augment the local island

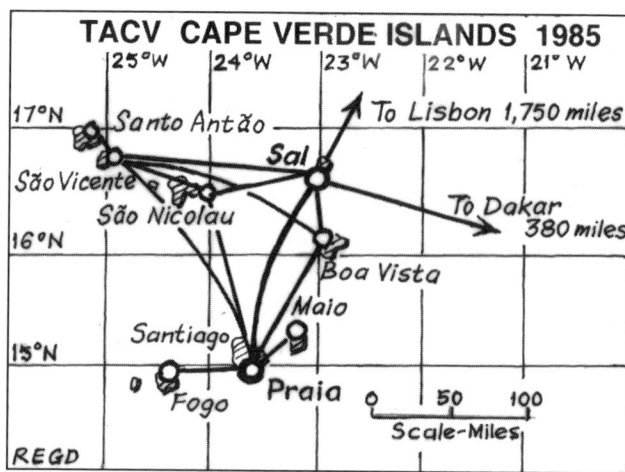

Until the Jet Age began, and unlike the Canary Islands or Madeira, the Cape Verde Islands were too far from Europe, both in distance and in journey time, to rank as a resort destination. This has now changed, and a local airline serves all the islands.

connectors; service to Lisbon started in 1985, with help from T.A.P.; and 30-seat EMB-120 Brasilias began service on 22 January 1990. The next day, T.A.C.V. had the honor to carry Pope John Paul II around the islands, an event that was of more promotional value than all the travel agents' advertising. Purchases of 46-seat ATR-42s in 1994 and 185-seat Boeing 757s in 1996 confirmed the momentum. The run of expansion was interrupted in 1998 when one of the Twin Otters was lost in an accident, and on 7 August 1999, a Coastguard Dornier 228, that T.A.C.V. was operating on its behalf, crashed, killing 18. However, by this time, the 757 was flying to several destinations in Europe, albeit on a fragmented semi-schedule, and the Republic of Cape Verde was no longer beyond the reach of the international traveler.

Promising Colonial Enterprise

At the Berlin Conference in 1884, in what was described by many historians as "The Scramble for Africa," the empire-building countries of Europe decided to split up the continent amongst themselves. Boundaries of new colonies or protectorates were drawn up with little concern for local tribal traditions or territorial rights. Almost all the post-colonial countries of today inherited those artificial boundaries, and have adapted to them. The original motivation for the colonization was far from altruistic; it was mainly to profit from agricultural and mineral resources. But with the passing of the years toward the end of the 19th century, Europeans began to settle in Africa as farmers, miners, and administrators. They introduced stable governments, constructed railroads, opened schools, and established profitable trading with Europe. All of this was not necessarily idealistic, and the motivation was mainly to support commercial activity. But to achieve their goals, the colonists did introduce systems of law and order, even though initially, the objectives were often achieved by force. Eventually, the growing wealth and strength of some colonies led to semi-independence, such as the dominion status of South Africa, after the Boer War had resulted in British rule over the Dutch settlers in the Transvaal. The northern Algerian provinces were like departments of France; and Egypt shared with Britain control over the Sudan. Throughout the period of colonization, only Ethiopia (then called Abyssinia) and Liberia (politically independent, but commercially partnered to the United States) remained free of the colonists. Italian rule over Ethiopia lasted only a few years. In the course of reaching their goals, good communications were essential, and some positive results were achieved. Among these was the establishment of commercial airlines.

Three British territories in east Africa had already formed East African Railways to provide a communal link between the Kenya colony, the protectorate of Uganda, and the mandated territory of Tanganyika. At the end of the Second World War, succeeding the pioneering **Wilson Airways**—the first airline in the world to be owned and managed by a woman—and following the railroad precedent, **East African Airways Corporation (E.A.A.C.)** was organized on 1 January 1946 by the governments of Kenya (68%), Uganda (22%), Tanganyika (9%), and Zanzibar (almost 1%.).

Without any resources or experience, the local committee that organized the airline called upon B.O.A.C. to operate the first local routes to connect the four territories and by 1948, a comprehensive network was being operated by de Havilland 89A Rapides. Lockheed Lodestars and de Havilland Doves followed and the dependable Douglas DC-3s arrived in 1949. In August 1950, this aircraft opened the first route beyond east Africa, to Salisbury, Southern Rhodesia (now Zimbabwe). E.A.A.C. had the honor of flying Queen Elizabeth II from Nanuki to Nairobi on 6 February 1952 on the occasion of the King's death. Steady expansion continued, to Northern Rhodesia (see map). In 1952, Nairobi was introduced to the Jet Age when B.O.A.C.'s Comet 1s opened the world's first jet service, to Johannesburg. Until 1954, after the tragic crashes, the Kenyan capital was an essential refueling stop. On 2 April 1957, with DC-4M Argonauts from B.O.A.C., E.A.A.C. boldly started a route from Nairobi to London via Entebbe, Khartoum, Benghazi, and Rome. This was augmented on 15 September by one to Bombay (Mumbai) via Aden and Karachi, and another on 6 January 1959 to Johannesburg.

This east African airline was now among the ranks of older intercontinental airlines, able to offer service from Great Britain to India, and was also the first to do so from South Africa to India. It had to elevate its flying equipment beyond the level of unpressurized airliners. After flying B.O.A.C. Bristol Britannia 312s from 8 October 1958, it introduced its own Comet 4s on 17 September 1960. By careful scheduling, and with only two jet aircraft, E.A.A.C. joined the Jet Age on all its long-haul routes. Nearer to home, four Fokker F-27 Friendships replaced the DC-3s where the veteran Douglas twin was the only airliner that could cope with the dusty and sometimes muddy short airstrips.

On 12 October 1963, services to South Africa terminated, following political action by the South African transport minister. A successful quadripartite pool with B.O.A.C., Central

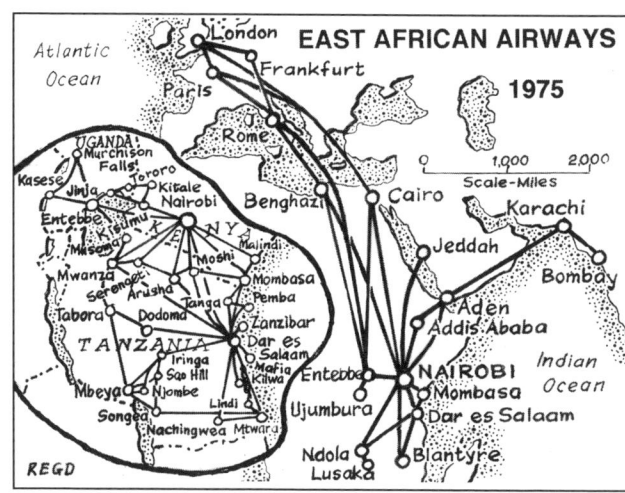

Before the individual territories of European colonial administrations became independent countries, several of them combined to form a cooperative airline. East African Airways, limiting the cooperative airline resources of Kenya, Tanzania, and Uganda, was a successful example.

African Airways, and South African Airways ended, though the British corporation remained as a partner with E.A.A.C. They were joined on 1 May 1964 by Aden Airways and Air India, signifying that Nairobi was valued as a strategically important station on the African continent. This recognition was partly because Kenya's agriculture was expanding, particularly with coffee plantations, and Indian immigrants were developing retail business throughout the area.

On 1 January 1965, B.O.A.C. relinquished its support and Chief A.S. Fundikura, from Tanzania, was appointed chairman of a now wholly African-managed airline. His first move was, on 31 March, to order three Vickers Super VC-10s, for $20 million, and the first one opened service to London in October 1966. Like the Comets, the VC-10s could also cope with Nairobi's 5,400-foot airport altitude. Their arrival released the Comets to fly to Blantyre, Nyasaland (now Malawi), Mauritius, and Mogadishu, Somalia. An African transcontinental route to Lagos and Accra also began, but was suspended in 1970, for lack of traffic. Commercially and socially, east and west Africa are poles apart, divided by jungles that seem as impenetrable in human terms as they are geographically. A similar fate occurred for a weekly flight to New York, inaugurated on 10 December 1970, with a stop at Frankfurt but which had to be withdrawn in June 1971, as was the route to Hong Kong. Some domestic services were cancelled, although standards were improved with DHC-6 Twin Otters in 1967, and three Douglas DC-9s replaced Comets on regional routes from 1970. E.A.A.C. was finding a lucrative cargo business between Britain and east Africa, so in 1971, a Bristol Britannia was chartered for a route from London to Nairobi and terminating in Zambia.

These operational adjustments were carried out against a background of managerial and administrative changes. In December 1967, a decree by the East African Community ensured that no national government (of which there were now three, Zanzibar having been amalgamated with the Tanganyika mandated territory to form the Republic of Tanzania in 1964) should have a disproportionate voice in the airline's affairs. Regrettably, this did nothing to improve what was becoming a corporate crisis, and on 14 January 1972, Alitalia was called in to advise on aspects of operations and marketing. The timing was unlucky, for on 14 January, a VC-10 crashed at Addis Ababa, killing most of the 103 passengers and crew. Then in May, after 13 years of profitability, the airline announced a financial loss, alleged to be caused by uneconomic domestic services and the opening of too many international routes against strong competition.

In 1973, $3.8 million was injected into the accounts "to stave off threatened disaster." This was a case of too little, too late. Foreign airlines were exploiting the new-found tourist opportunities in east Africa, and had the advantage of bigger and more modern aircraft fleets for the European seekers of the sun on Kenya's beaches, the programs for the wildlife safaris, and Tanzania's Mount Kilimanjaro. The worsening decline ended on 14 January 1977, when local political relations had become strained to the limit, and this once idealistic airline consortium suspended all operations.

Post-Colonial Success

The separation of the three partners was far from amicable. Relations with Uganda, not yet recovered from the repressions of Idi Amin, were cool. Tanzania was so disgruntled that it closed the frontier with Kenya for a week after the collapse. At Nairobi, however, Kenya emerged with few problems. For E.A.A.C.'s non-African passenger clientele, the airline had been identified mainly with its fast-growing capital. It was the hub of operations, the base for its aircraft maintenance, and the center of administration and management. All these elements were in place, ready to replace the fallen consortium. On 22 January 1977, the Kenya government founded **Kenya Airways**. With close support from British Midland Airways, a Boeing 707, one of two leased from that airline, arrived on 4 February, to inaugurate service with little interruption of service from its predecessor. It had also inherited a DC-9 and two F-27s from E.A.A.C., bought two 707-320Bs from Northwest, leased a Boeing 720B from Western Airlines, and quickly restored the routes to Europe and neighboring African countries. It kept a much closer watch on its finances, cancelling the short-lived trans-African route to Nigeria and Ghana in 1979, and adding the beach resort of Malindi to cope with the growing tourist demand. The following year, it started a route to Salisbury (now Harare), Zimbabwe, via Lusaka, Zambia. Such was the growing popularity of Kenya as a tourist destination that it leased a wide-bodied Boeing 747 for the peak season, and started a London-Mombasa service.

Such initial success, however, may have led to over-ambitious programs of expansion, for by the mid-Eighties, Kenya Airways was experiencing the same malaise that had affected many an African newcomer to the highly competitive air transport market. It claimed that its growth had been handicapped by government procrastination. Whatever the cause, it soldiered on with a leased DC-10 for the prestige routes to Europe and acquired two 50-seat Fokker 50 jets for local and regional services. But by 1989, to make up for an estimated cumulative loss of $40 million, the new managing director, Joseph Nyagah, dismissed 1,000 of his staff. Nevertheless Kenya's market base was sound, and its airline was resilient. Its government ownership, with advice with K.L.M., ensured continuity. By the early 1990s, the fleet included three 220-seat Airbus 310-300s, and its three Boeing 757s were the first in Africa. It sought help from Britain's Speedwing Consultancy, which described the airline as "operated as a government-run transport business." This description may have been intended as a criticism, but things could not have been all bad, as in 1995, Kenya Airways made a profit of $16 million.

It overcame an Airbus 310 crash at Abidjan on 30 January 2000, when 170 people were killed, and in June 2004, introduced the first of four Boeing 777-767s on the trunk routes from London and Amsterdam through Nairobi to Lusaka, Zambia, and Lilongwe, Malawi. By then it was a solid Boeing customer, with six 767s and eleven 737s. In 2006, it ordered three of the advanced -800 variant of the 737 series, plus six of Boeing's revolutionary new 787 Dreamliner. But once again, the pendulum of fortune swung the other way, as on 4 May 2007, one of the new 737s crashed in Cameroon, killing 114.

A Boeing 777 of Kenya Airways. (McDonough)

Post-Colonial Struggles

The junior-partner territories that had helped to form East African Airways were at a disadvantage, compared to Kenya, which was the base for the airline. Tanzania inherited no more than a Fokker F-27, and it had no local organization like the one based in Nairobi. Its territory was much bigger that those of its former partners. When **Air Tanzania** was founded on 11 March 1977, it had to lease another F-27 and a Boeing 737 from Mozambique's DETA, while it ordered three more F-27s, the Series -600. In 1978, it added four DHC-6 Twin Otters, and included Bujumbura, Burundi, and Kigali, Rwanda, as extensions to its domestic network. Ambitiously, the 737 started flying to Maputo, Mozambique; Lusaka, Zambia; Tananarive, Madagascar; and the Seychelles. By an arrangement with Ethiopia, Air Tanzania reached Bombay late in 1982.

This promising beginning had to face reality during the late 1980s. A fatal DHC-6 crash on 20 December 1984 and further accidents in the early 1990s led it to seek assistance, which was forthcoming from Rwanda's Alliance partnership. By 1999, however, the total fleet was reduced to two Boeing 737s and a grounded F-27. A contest to privatize the failing airline was won in December 2002 by South African Airways, which invested $20 million for a 49% shareholding. On 31 March 2003, Air Tanzania Company Ltd. (A.T.C.L.) was launched, with fresh hope, but with no success. The key route to Nairobi, connecting point for almost all long-distance flights, was suspended on 31 January 2005. The government met the crisis by buying back South Africa's stake on 7 September 2006, and a year later, relaunching the airline with completely new management. The inaugural flight on 1 October was no more than symbolic. In August 2008, Air Tanzania was banned from flying for safety reasons, and in December of that year, grounded by the Tanzanian Civil Aviation Authority. If only to preserve a sense of national pride—in flying its own airline flag—the Tanzanian government allocated $2 million in January 2009 in what could only be described as a desperate bailout.

The other junior E.A.A.C. partner had faced a far different problem, as on 25 January 1971, Uganda had been plunged into a period of oppressive rule, in which the idea of a national airline representing its country was irrelevant. The country itself fast became ostracized by the rest of the world, as Idi Amin seized power in a military coup (while the President was attending a conference in Singapore) and proceeded to exert a dictatorship that shocked the world. Human rights abuses, political repression, ethnic persecution, and mass murders were estimated by Amnesty International to have killed hundreds of thousands of Ugandans. Much of the country's business had been run by Asian immigrants. They were all deported, without compensation, and British-owned businesses were nationalized. In 1973, the United States closed its embassy, but Amin intensified his policies of repression and aggression, not only against his own people but also against his neighbors.

The formation of **Uganda Airlines** in May 1976, as a subsidiary of the Uganda Development Corporation, was a sham. When it began operations in 1977 with a single Boeing 737-200, it was mainly to provide air travel for government officials. Chaos reigned to the extent that there was dissent in the government, even defections. In June, the passengers in a hijacked Air France airliner were held hostage at Entebbe, and rescued by Israeli commandos. In 1978, Amin threatened to annex parts of Kenya and Sudan, but in November of that year invaded Tanzania instead. Such actions were so outrageous and so politically intolerable that he fled the country on 11 April 1979.

Somehow, the airline kept going, maintaining the route to Nairobi, but flying only sporadically elsewhere. For a decade, it did its best to represent its country, taking years to recover from the depredations of its former ruler. The crash of a Boeing 707 in Rome on 17 October 1988, killing 31, did not help, although the atrocious weather—thick fog—was the main cause of the tragedy. Within two more years, debts had risen to $20 million, and the fleet reduced to a single Fokker F-27. In 1996, Uganda Airlines leased two Boeing 737s.

No single country of Africa has been spared the devastations caused by civil wars, revolutions, disease, or natural disasters. But none has suffered more than Rwanda. With another small neighbor, Burundi, its history dates back to 1924, when the area was finally agreed internationally to be a Belgian share of German reparations from the First World War. Hived off German East Africa, most of which became the Tanganyika Territory (later Tanzania), it was mandated to Belgium as Ruanda-Urundi. The division into two came after the Second World War, with decolonization and the creation of separate republics in 1962.

The area of Rwanda is almost equal to that of Massachusetts, but its eight-million population exceeds the U.S. State's six million. Of the many tribes, 84% are Hutu, 15% Tutsi. **Air Rwanda** was formed in 1975, and renamed **Rwandair** in 1994. It had a single Boeing 707 and a DHC-6 Twin Otter, and with the latter, managed to fly from the capital, Kigali, to outlying towns. Any aspirations for permanence were shattered in 1994, when a civil war broke out with unparalleled intensity and brutality. On 6 April, the Presidents of Rwanda and Burundi were both killed when their aircraft was shot down, and the mayor of Gisenyi initiated a program of massacre and rape. On 17 May 1994, the United Nations conceded that "acts of genocide may have been committed," a judgment that was widely considered to be an understatement. The Red Cross estimated the deaths to be more than a million and the rapes more than 250,000. In July the Tutsis defended Kigali to start a civil war, and in 1996, a Tutsi uprising in neighboring Congo started another local war. More than a million refugees returned from Congo and Tanzania. This was no

Together with Kenya Airways, Uganda Airlines and Air Tanzania became their countries' national airlines after the breakup of East African Airways. Both were able to operate Boeing 737-200s. (McDonough)

place for an airline. Yet, amazingly, air transport soon returned to Rwanda.

On the Horn of Africa, three former Italian and British colonies were amalgamated as the republic of Somalia in 1960, and the national airline, **Somali Airlines**, was formed on 5 March 1964. The government held 49% of the shares, and Alitalia the balance. It started operations on 7 July, from Mogadishu to Hargeisa, with four DC-3s, and soon linked most of the small communities between these two cities. On 4 March 1965, it crossed the Red Sea to Aden, in pool with Aden Airways, and in 1977 to Yemen, Oman, and Abu Dhabi. During the 1960s/70s with various leased Boeing 707s, Somali flew to London, Cairo, Rome, and Frankfurt, but these routes were far from regular or frequent.

In 1977, the airline was nationalized, and benefitted somewhat from flying to Europe from Johannesburg, whence South African Airways was unable to fly across Africa, because of the continent's intolerance with that nation's apartheid politics. In 1988, two Airbus A310s were leased, and these flew briefly to west Africa. Fokker F-27s were used for domestic and regional routes, but two crashed, on 20 July 1981 and 28 June 1989. By the late 1980s, political unrest in Somalia, where the republic was really a dictatorship, had developed into a civil war, exacerbated by frontier incursions from Ethiopia. Somali Airlines ceased to operate in 1991.

Almost all the fighting took place in the south, around Mogadishu, but against the deterrent of continued belligerence, another Somali airline started up on 20 March 1992. **Diallo Airlines** filled in with a 100-seat Ilyushin Il-18, the same type that went into service with Aeroflot in 1959.

Whereas Somalia is a thousand miles long from north to south, Djibouti (the former French Somaliland) is barely a hundred miles wide in any direction. Yet it possessed a little airline. The first **Air Djibouti**, formed in April 1963, operated to Aden and Yemen, with a de Havilland DH 89A and a Bristol Freighter, but was taken over by Air Somalia in 1971. The successor **Air Djibouti**, also known as Red Sea Airlines, started up again, with strong French support from various industrial sources, including Air France. After independence as the tiny republic Djibouti in 1977, the new government acquired 90% of the shares in 1981. With a Boeing 727 for regional services, it also managed to fly short services within the country with DHC-6 Twin Otters, but fell into bankruptcy in 1990.

Airline Extraordinary

While the battles were fought over airline ascendancy in the former British East African territories, an almost unnoticed development was unfolding in the offshore island colony, the Seychelles, about 1,000 miles east of Mombasa. Back in the 1950s, East African Airways had formed **Seychelles-Kilimanjaro Air Transport (SKAT)** to operate local services in the coastal area of Tanganyika and to Zanzibar. Its de Havilland DH 89A Rapides never operated regularly to either of the places named in its title. On 1 January 1968, the parent company changed the status of its subsidiary to a charter operator and took over its routes.

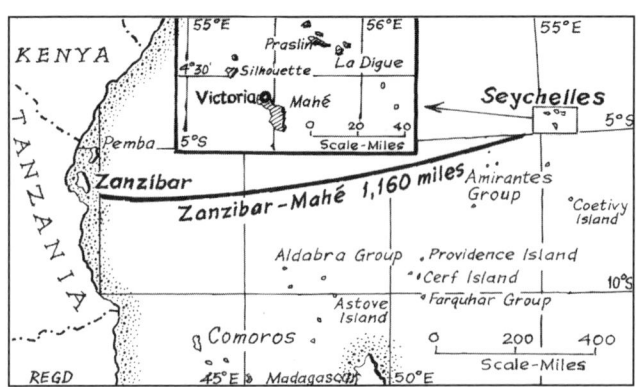

Rather like the Portuguese Cape Verde Islands, in the Atlantic, the British Seychelles were too distant from Europe to be able to benefit from the potential for tourism. The Jet Age brought them within a comfortable day's flight from London.

The name may have foreshadowed a future for the islands that had hitherto been almost unknown except among geographers. For in the 1970s, the rate of growth of the overseas tourist industry in Europe was explosive. The speed of jet airliners was able to extend the radius of a day's journey to the Middle East, to the islands in the Atlantic, to east Africa, and to India and the Indian Ocean. This led to the "discovery" of the Seychelles that, like the Maldives, epitomized the storybook charms of a desert island, far away from the crowds. The story of their elevation from being almost unknown to a sophisticated resort destination has been almost in the realm of fiction.

The total population of the Seychelles, including two other neighboring island groups, is less than 100,000, and in the past the economy was only at subsistence level, with fishing as the main activity. Journeys between the islands were by boat, taking several hours. Then, on 1 July 1972, John Faulkner began an air service from Victoria, the capital on Mahé, to Praslin, the only other island with even a village, with a four-seat Piper Seneca. Named **Air Mahé**, business was so good that a nine-seat Britten-Norman BN-2A3 replaced the smaller aircraft in August and a 12-seat de Havilland DH-89A Rapide in February 1973.

Emerging from its former comparative isolation from the rest of the world, the government opened a new international airport at Mahé in December 1972. Seychelles started to appear on the promotional brochures of European tourist agencies, now that airliners could fly direct. They were encouraged by local support, stimulated by the granting of independence as a republic in June 1976. Reacting promptly, **Inter-Island Airways** was formed on 12 August, with a BN-2 and a 17-seat BN-2A Trislander. It added service to the little Bird Island as well as Praslin. Sensibly, it merged with Air Mahé on 26 May 1978 to form **Air Seychelles**, to be owned by the government.

Surviving an abortive coup by mercenaries in 1981, the islands were now firmly on the European tourist map, so that on 26 October 1983, a direct service from London began via Amsterdam, Frankfurt, and Rome, with a 294-seat Douglas DC-10, leased from British Caledonian. A series of other leases followed, and a flight in January 1986 was the first in the airline's own colors. Late in 1986, another small company, **Lignes Aérienne Seychelles (L.A.S.)** joined in the flourishing tourist trade, with charter flights from southern Africa, Australia, and Singapore, but it too was taken over by Air Seychelles, by now a well-established and prosperous airline, late in 1987.

It proceeded to expand its network, purchasing a Boeing 767-200ER on 26 June 1989 and a 757-200R on 29 March 1993. During the 1990s, services began from Paris, Zurich, Johannesburg, Dubai-Bahrain and -Bombay, Tel Aviv, and Manchester. By 1996, business was so good that it was able to standardize its fleet with two Boeing 767-300ER replacements. In November 2001, a 126-seat Boeing 737-700 was also leased, and for the busy inter-island route to Praslin, a 36-seat Shorts 360-300 supplemented three 20-seat DHC-6s. This "bus service" grew to 26 daily flights each way. A further stimulus to assured progress was the withdrawal of British Airways from its flights to Mahé, because of protective restrictions by the Seychelles government.

Seychelles was not the only island community to emerge from the isolation of the Indian Ocean because of the advent of the Jet Age (see Chapter 50).

A Much-Troubled Land

The largest country in Africa is Sudan, of which the national airline has had to operate (at least since its independence was achieved in 1956) against a continual series of internal uprisings that amounted closely to a civil war. Before independence, it had been governed by a consortium as Anglo-Egyptian Sudan, in which Great Britain and Egypt had solved their respective claims to the region of the upper Nile by a compromise that worked well. From the earliest days of air transport, the capital, Khartoum, was of vital interest to the British airlines as a refueling stop on the route to South Africa.

Sudan Airways was founded in February 1946 as a subdivision of Sudan Railways. Like Egypt's Misrair, it was organized and managed by the British company Airwork and began services with four eight-seat de Havilland DH-104 Doves in the summer of 1947. Its domestic network stretched to areas beyond the reach of the railway or road systems. Five-hour flights to Juba, in the deep south, replaced 12 days by paddle-steamer up the Nile. The airline became independent from the Railways in 1949, and replaced the Doves with the ubiquitous 28-seat Douglas DC-3s, which started international service to Cairo.

Sudan gained its independence in 1956, and—if the operation of a successful airline is an indication of national prestige—Sudan Airways did its job well. Its second decade was marked by some noteworthy events. On 8 June 1959, a 40-seat Vickers Viscount turboprop launched the *Blue Nile* service to London via Athens and Rome. Still crewed and maintained by Airwork, Sudan was nevertheless past the adolescent stage of airline development. Viscounts were flying to Beirut and Asmara within the year, and in January 1962, 40-seat Fokker F-27s replaced the DC-3s on most of the domestic routes. And to crown the program of technical advance, in December 1962, 101-seat de Havilland Comet 4C jets went on to the Blue Nile service, which, in March 1963, was extended to Nairobi. In May, Frankfurt was added as a second European destination; the F-27s started flying to Fort Lamy and Entebbe; and three 20-seat DHC-6 Twin Otters were able to provide service to communities where the Fokkers had difficulty with the landing strips. Two F-27s were based at Port Sudan for the short flights to Jeddah during the annual Hajj pilgrimage.

During the 1970s, at least five aircraft were lost in crashes on the short-haul routes, but the long-haul routes were upgraded, late in 1972, by 160-seat Boeing 707s, leased at first from British Midland then from British United Airways. In 1974, Sudan's own 707s replaced them. In 1975, Boeing 737s replaced the F-27s on the *White Nile* service to the south. But the airline's progress was hindered by increasing political instability. The government in Khartoum was almost entirely Arab, who comprised less than 40% of the population. More than 50% were black Africans in the south or west, including many individual tribes and ethnicities. Troubles in the south did not amount to a revolution, but a large area was effectively a war zone, and not the ideal environment for an airline. This may have excused Sudan Airways for a deterioration from the high points of the 1960s, as there were more crashes during the 1980s, and both the Blue and the White Nile were no longer places for visitors to Sudan to go to. In Khartoum, General Mohammed Nineiri had seized power in 1970 but was deposed in 1985. Another regime took over in 1989, but did not interfere with the airline, which bought its first Airbus in 1992, an A310-304, and subsequently bought A300s and A320s to supplement its Boeing fleet. Its safety record improved, although, on 24 March 1996, an A310 was hijacked en route to Amman and forced to go to Cyprus then to London, where the hijackers surrendered.

Early in the 21st century, the political instability of Sudan made it difficult for its airline to maintain normal service throughout its network. In 2003, some rebel groups in the western province of Darfur—an area as big as France—led the government to take drastic action. It launched a sustained policy of repression, universally described as genocide, in which an estimated 400,000 people were killed by the armed forces and by unofficial mercenaries. Two million people were displaced from their homes.

The government privatized the airline in 2007, retaining 30% of the shares. The next year, two crashes killed 54 people, and Sudan Airways was operating from year to year, if not from month to month. Events beyond its control doomed it further, as unrest in the south revived, a campaign emerged to declare independence for the southern provinces.

Africa's Own

Considering that the potential for political uncertainty and instability was little different from the situation in many other African countries, the success story of **Ethiopian Air Lines** is quite remarkable. Except for the occupation of Mussolini's Italian troops during the late 1930s, Ethiopia had always been independent, resisting the inroads of European colonialism. British troops liberated it in 1941 and subsequently exercised strict control. Britain denied permission in 1945 for an Ethiopian delegation to fly to Cairo en route to the founding conference at the United Nations. The transition back to full independence was thus tainted and may have been the reason why, when the national airline was organized on 26 December 1945, it turned not to Britain but to the United States for the technical, managerial, and operational experience, without which it could never have got off the ground.

Owned by the Emperor, Haile Selassie, it sought help from Transcontinental and Western Airlines (T.W.A.)—soon to become Trans World Airlines. But unlike many other African airlines that needed such a mentor, it took all the advice well, and two T.W.A. representatives were on the board of directors. The partnership was wholly positive, with mutual respect, without fear of any "master-and-servant" suspicions that led to the collapse of others.

Operations began on 8 April 1946, with five 28-seat Douglas DC-3s (ex-C-47s) flying from Addis Ababa to Cairo via Asmara. The veteran twin was ideal, as it could use not only the many dirt strips of the Ethiopian outback, but also the 7,626-foot altitude airport of Addis Ababa, the highest of any African capital city. The versatile DC-3s were to remain in service long after the Jet Age began, in fact until 1988, when they could be seen parked next to Boeing 767s.

Ethiopian could have qualified, by one definition, as being the first jet airline in Africa. For in January 1951, when the first Convair 240 took off from Addis Ababa to restore the route to Karachi (too far for the DC-3's range), it did so with Jet-Assisted Take-Off (JATO) power. The Convairliners were joined by Lockheed Constellations and Douglas DC-6Bs, with which the first European route—to Frankfurt—was extended from Khartoum on 21 June 1958 and the first trans-African route started to Lagos, Accra, and Monrovia on 8 November 1960. An order for Boeing 720B jets was diverted to Saudi Arabia in 1961 because the Addis Ababa airport was not ready, and was further delayed by unrest in the country when in 1963, the Emperor annexed Eritrea, the former Italian colony that had been federated with Ethiopia since 1952 under a United Nations-sponsored agreement.

The Boeing jet service finally began on 16 January 1963, to Nairobi, and the next day to Madrid via Athens, in addition to Frankfurt. T.W.A. was still giving excellent advice to Ethiopia's airline, and was benefitting from the connection with its own trans-Atlantic route at the Spanish capital. The arrangement pre-dated by about two decades the practice of code-sharing that is prevalent today. During the next 10 years, the name was changed slightly—Air Lines became one word—and in 1968, Boeing 707-300s, which could now take-off and land safely at Addis Ababa, joined the fleet. In 1971, in what would later have some significance in both political and commercial developments, Haile Selassie flew to China in an Ethiopian Boeing 707. Such was the maturity of the airline by this time, and so well had it learned from its American mentor, that the management contract with T.W.A. ended amicably. The two events may have been related, as when the first service to Shanghai began on 21 February 1973—one of the first foreign airlines to fly to communist China—the Chinese insisted on all-Ethiopian crews and cabin staff. As mentioned, the Ethiopians had learned well. The airline turned the corner financially, making a profit in 1971, after losses in previous years. On 1 April 1973, it started service to London.

In 1974, the Emperor was dethroned, to be succeeded, under Mengistu Haile Mariam, by an administration that took some years to settle down. In 1980, Capt. Mohammed Ahmed took over as the national airline's general manager, adopting what the *New York Times* described as "the style, corporate culture, inherited from T.W.A." It was a high standard of disciplined efficiency, technical expertise, and commercial acumen that was on a par with any European or American airline. Its maintenance base at Addis Ababa gained overhaul contracts with other airlines in Africa.

In 1982, two DHC-5 Buffalos were delivered for cargo operations, mainly across the Red Sea, where the export of qat, the mild narcotic, to Aden, later Yemen, was a thriving business. Ethiopian was one of the few airlines in the world to operate the Buffalo, which had excellent performance for small airfields. In 1984, Boeing won an important competition with Airbus, when the 767-200 was selected over the A310, because of the stringent performance requirements at hot-and-high Addis Ababa. It also made headlines by flying nonstop from Washington, D.C., almost 7,500 miles to the Ethiopian capital.

Unlike the airlines in many other African countries, the national airline was resilient to factors beyond its direct control, such as political changes. The government transformation from monarchy to communism did no serious damage to Ethiopian Air Lines, as Mengistu appears to have realized its value to the country. London's *Financial Times* commented on "an aggressive company, run exclusively by Ethiopians, on strict capitalist lines, within the ambit of one of the world's most rigid, centrally controlled, Marxist economies." In 1990, it was the first airline outside the United States to operate the Boeing 757 freighter. This was because Ethiopia, with a population exceeding 50 million, with a mountainous terrain, was land-locked, except for a single railroad to the Gulf of Aden through Djibouti. Access to the Red Sea through Eritrea was only by circuitous roads. As a result, air cargo was generating one-third of the airline's revenue.

After three decades of internal conflicts—short of an absolute civil war—the Marxist dictatorship collapsed in 1991. During the crisis, Ethiopian Air Lines lost a 707 and a 767 was sprayed with shrapnel. The national coffers were empty, but the airline was undeterred, as its credit rating was high, and four new Boeing 757-200s were delivered in 1992. On 3 June of that year, the Bombay route was extended to Bangkok. The hijacking of a Boeing 727 to Rome on 28 August 1992 was of little significance but the independence of Eritrea in 1993 (see below) did initiate important changes. Previous administrations had tended to ignore the effects of ethnic and religious concerns in a country where the majority of the population were Christians or Muslims. Most of the latter lived in the eastern Ogaden region where

A Boeing 767-360ER of Ethiopian Air Lines, always a model of operational efficiency, in spite of an operating base of mountainous terrain, high altitudes, and domestically poor airfields. (McDonough)

starvation through droughts every few years is a tragic reality. A new government constitution reorganized local administrations into nine ethnically based regions.

Ethiopian's new chief executive Dr. Ahmed Kellow presided over an airline that seemed immune from political, social, or national economic changes. Profits increased to $30 million by 1995; five Fokker 50 jets replaced Twin Otters and ATR 42s that served the outlying communities; and the crash of a hijacked Boeing 767 in the Comoro Islands, killing 127, in full view of a beach resort, did not reflect negatively on the airline itself. In June 1998, a prestigious service opened to Washington, D.C. via New York, partly to serve about half a million Ethiopian emigrants to the United States. But this coincided with a border war with Eritrea, which killed tens of thousands, and was settled by the United Nations to fix the frontier. In 2002, Amsterdam and Paris were added to the list of European destinations. Cross-border skirmishes and battles continued in the southeast, as Ethiopian troops helped the Somali government to fight off left-wing guerilla revolutionaries.

Throughout all the national trials and tribulations, Ethiopian Air Lines has kept its nerve, maintained discipline, and controlled its own destiny. Late in 2004, to ensure the modernity of its aircraft fleet, it took delivery of the first of six 118-seat Boeing 737-700 Series and six 242-seat 767-300ERs. On 4 February 2005, as if to trump that aviation ace, it ordered five composite-structured Boeing 787 Dreamliners, to enter, along with the major trend-setters of the airline world, the Third Jet Age.

Eritrea

The history of this small country on the Red Sea dates back to the ancient Egyptians. It became the Kingdom of Aksum and then part of the Ottoman Empire until it passed to Italy in 1885. When Mussolini's forces conquered Ethiopia in 1936, it became part of Italy's east African empire, then under British administration in 1943 during the Second World War.

Subsequently, Eritrea's independence was in doubt for many years as Ethiopia took over its administration in 1952. After a war for independence, this was finally achieved in 1993. Further border disputes continued until the frontiers were finally settled by the Algiers Agreement of 2000.

Eritrean Airlines was thus no more than a ground handling agent at Asmara, the capital, and Massawa, the only port. Eventually, in 2002, it was able to start services in 2002, with Boeing 767-300s, to European points, later adding routes to Dubai and Jeddah.

Chapter 49: End of the Empire Airlines

The name of this chapter can be interpreted either geographically or historically. The continent of Africa was a major target of colonialism before the First World War. Aside from the two countries Ethiopia and Liberia, which had not been taken over by the Europeans, only South Africa had achieved self-government, following the Boer War of 1902, that amalgamated the Dutch-speaking Afrikaners with the British. Belgium's only colony, the Congo, was the terminus of SABENA's long-distance route from Brussels (and where one of the world's pioneering airlines had started). Germany's southernmost colony, Southwest Africa (now Namibia), had been lost as reparations after the war. The farthest French outposts, Madagascar and Réunion, were at the end of a route that crossed southern Africa. Most of the Portuguese empire consisted of Angola and Mozambique. With the post–Second World War momentum of decolonization, the airline industry south of the Equator went through a fundamental series of reorganizations.

Central African Cooperative

As with Air Afrique and East African Airways (see above) one solution toward airline independence from London was stronger links between some colonies, short of complete amalgamation. The two Rhodesias, Northern and Southern (now Zambia and Zimbabwe), together with Nyasaland (now Malawi) had close commercial links, because of extensive mining and agricultural resources, dating back to the 1920s. In line with this cooperative policy, the Rhodesian Aviation Company of 1929 had become **Rhodesia and Nyasaland Airways (RANA)** on 12 October 1933. After developing a comprehensive domestic route network with a succession of small de Havilland biplanes, and opening international services to Beira, the Mozambique port, and to Johannesburg, it participated in the historic Empire Air Mail Scheme in 1937, as a feeder service to Imperial Airways.

Of the three colonies, Southern Rhodesia was the richest. On 1 February 1940, in association with the Air Force, RANA assumed control and changed the name to **Southern Rhodesia Air Service (S.R.A.S.)**. After the war, on 1 June 1946, to return to the previous partnership policy, it became **Central African Airways (C.A.A.)**, with shareholdings 50% to Southern Rhodesia, 35% to Northern Rhodesia, and 15% to Nyasaland. On 19 November 1946, 36-seat Vickers Vikings updated the fleet, and services began to Elizabethville, Belgian Congo (now Lubumbashi, Zaïre), and Dar es Salaam, Tanganyika. On 29 July 1950, it was offering package tours to Lake Nyasa, and to the Victoria Falls; and on 10 August 1951, to Lourenço Marques, Mozambique (now Maputo).

In August 1953, the three former colonies formed the Central African Federation. Newcomer though it was to the international aviation stage, its flag carrier, C.A.A., was not about to play second fiddle to the established trunk airlines of Europe. Showing considerable initiative—it had already begun low-fare *Starlight* night flights to Johannesburg in July 1951—it introduced innovative programs such as, on 4 April 1953, the *Zambesi Colonial Coach* service, with Vikings, between Salisbury (now Harare) and London via Nairobi, Wadi Halfa, and Malta. This was in contrast to the B.O.A.C. Comet jet services, which offered only first-class fares from London to South Africa, and attracted a completely different clientele. 40-seat Vickers Viscount turboprops started service on 1 June 1956, and replaced the Vikings on the Zambesi service on 30 August 1957.

Rivalry with B.O.A.C. was muted. On 20 May 1957, C.A.A. accepted the British airline's offer to operate the overseas routes for 10 years, at first with Argonauts. A profit was guaranteed, but the agreement was controversial as the independent airline **Hunting-Clan** was believed to have made a better offer. On 31 July 1958, long-range Britannia 312 turboprops replaced the slow Argonauts, and on 4 December 1959, Comet 4s were designated as C.A.A. flights. A Viscount crashed in Libya on 9 August 1958, killing 36, and the fleet was grounded in January 1961. Meanwhile, low-fare *Skybus* services started between the main cities of the Federation on 1 February 1960.

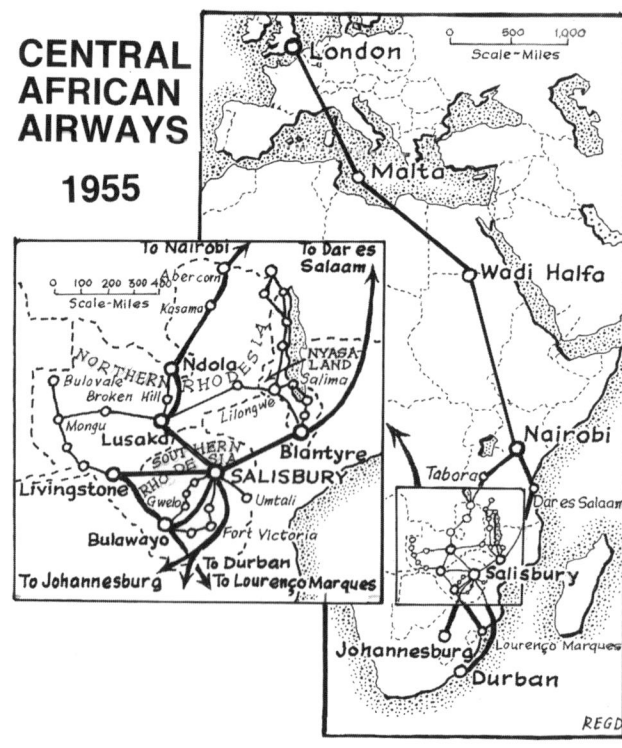

Paralleling the initiatives in East Africa, the two Rhodesias and Nyasaland combined to form Central African Airways. But it too succumbed to the pressures of independence.

This airline consortium was popular among its customers, and its employees enjoyed an enviable esprit de corps. The new airport at Salisbury, opened on 1 July 1956, allowed fiercer competition from the European trunk airlines, but C.A.A. started its (nominally) own jet services on 1 April 1961, when a Rhodesian Comet (still operated by B.O.A.C.) extended the London flights to Johannesburg. In 1958, a pool agreement had been signed with East African Airways, effective on 1 January 1959, to reconcile differences on routes to the north. But sadly, such progressive gestures were overcome by serious political changes in the area. The Central African Federation was dismembered in the face of African demands for independence against intransigence by the white minority leader in Southern Rhodesia. The confrontation led to the break-up of the quadripartite agreement (B.O.A.C., South African Airways, C.A.A., and East African) on 12 October 1963. For practical purposes, the continuation of C.A.A. was assured for a while, with Rhodesia (as it still was) holding 45%, Northern Rhodesia, now Zambia, 45%, and Nyasaland (now Malawi), 10% of the shares. On 4 December 1963, agreements were concluded that preserved C.A.A. for an interim period, while the principle of three separate airlines was established.

Pressured by the political turmoil, the decline of C.A.A., a progressive and efficient airline, continued during 1964. Sir Robert Taylor was appointed chairman to oversee the unhappy dismemberment, which, in spite of governmental confusions, was systematic. The Beaver fleet was handed over to Zambia and Malawi, where services to the African bush were still needed. The DC-3s were transferred also, but hired back to C.A.A. for joint regional operations. C.A.A. retained the Viscounts. In April, inclusive tours were operated for the miners in the Copperbelt from N'dola to Salima, on Lake Nyasa, now Malawi. As a parting gesture, on 23 July, the C.A.A. service to London was upgraded to Vickers VC-10s. But the die was cast.

In November 1965, Rhodesia declared independence from Great Britain. In this case, Macmillan's "wind of change" had become a destructive gale. The confrontation was so intense that overflying Rhodesia was denied to many countries. The British government applied trade sanctions, so that the BAC One-Elevens that would have been allocated to Rhodesia went to Zambia. A sad end to an innovative and potentially successful enterprise, the official dissolution of Central African Airways was signed into law on 31 August 1967.

New Airlines for Central Africa

On 1 September 1967, **Zambia Airways**, as a corporation, took over the former company of the same name that had been a subsidiary of C.A.A. It chose Alitalia to provide technical and managerial assistance, and began operations on 1 January 1968. With its inherited fleet of two BAC One-Elevens, the initial international network from Lusaka included Kinshasa (in Zaïre), Nairobi, Blantyre, and domestically to Livingstone. On 1 November, with a DC-8-43 from Alitalia, Zambia opened service to London via Rome, and a year later added Mauritius. Gradually overcoming the problems of adolescence, it replaced the Italian contract in 1964 with one with the Irish Aer Lingus, and on 1 April, the first of three Boeing 707-320Cs replaced the DC-8s. With Boeing 737s replacing the One-Elevens (like some of the 707s, leased from Ireland), and HS-748 turboprops serving to retire the DC-3s, the infant airline was settling down.

Problems then began. After it started a route to Frankfurt in July 1976, a work-to-rule strike by the pilots in August disrupted services, and a 707 crash at Lusaka on 14 May 1977 was discouraging. Nevertheless, a route to Johannesburg opened in 1980, and the Aer Lingus contract gave way to one with Ethiopian Air Lines. In 1984, Zambia Airways proudly entered the wide-bodied era, with Douglas DC-10s, with which it opened trans-Atlantic service to New York, often via Libreville, Gabon. After heavy losses, it made a small profit in 1985, leased a second DC-10 from SABENA in 1989 then another from Lufthansa, and extended its network to Amsterdam and Bombay. It replaced its four HS-748s with two ATR-42s, and in 1993, leased them to Botswana, in exchange for the lease of BAe 146s. But possibly because the worldwide competition in the copper industry had expanded, and eroded much of Zambia's prosperity derived from the Copperbelt exports—about a third of the world production—the government withdrew its support for the airline. With a worsening economic climate, the airline took the familiar measures of reducing its fleet, staff, and services, all to no avail. Zambia Airways was liquidated in 1995.

When, in the mid-1960s, the political situation had deteriorated to crisis level, the two big copper-mining companies felt that desperate measures had to be taken to maintain and guarantee the flow of the mineral from N'dola, chief city of the Copperbelt. They acted swiftly. In February 1966, they formed **Zambian Air Cargoes (ZAC)** and immediately confirmed an agreement with Lockheed, signed on 15 February, to purchase four L.382B Hercules (commercial C-130s) heavy-lift cargo aircraft. On 23 March, the first flight was made to Dar es Salaam, Tanganyika, and within weeks, this had developed into an intensive operation.

The statistics were amazing. Two 845-mile round-trip daily flights were made, each carrying to the Indian Ocean port more than 20 tons of copper wirebars (ingots), and the same payload in oil-drums or other mining requirements back to N'dola. By December 1967, the Hercules quartet, like their namesake, had indeed performed its labor well, carrying 100,000 tons in less than two years, as much cargo as by leading European airlines. Even so, they were able to account for only about 15% of the requirement. Direct railroad connection to a coastal port, previously either west to Benguela, Angola, through Zaïre, or to Beira, Mozambique, was impeded by the intransigent political conflicts throughout the region. Thus, the construction of a railroad directly to Dar es Salaam, that had been projected in the 1950s was finally undertaken by China, and completed in 1975. The need for ZAC evaporated, but it can claim its place in airline history. Other notable air freight haulers were Guinea Airways of the late 1920s, and Nicaragua's TACA of the 1930s, both of which operated gold-lifts from mines to ports. The U.S. airline Zantop also specialized for many years in the rapid supply of components from the subcontractors to the Detroit car manufacturers. (The Berlin Airlift of 1948–49 was a military operation.) ZAC was thus a member of an unusually elite airline group.

With Zambia Airways designed as the "chosen instrument," other opportunities for airline activity were scarce. Mines Air Services (M.A.S.) was formed in 1948 by the mining companies in the Copperbelt. By 1998 it was operating locally with two 18-seat Beech 1900s. On 28 April of that year, the government took over M.A.S., renamed it **Zambian Airways**, and added three 118-seat Boeing 737-200s, but it ceased operations on 10 January 2009. Aero Zambia started 737 service from Lusaka on 27 March 1995, but was short-lived.

In Southern Rhodesia, the most affluent of the three Central African components, the conflict between the white minority and the black people was so intense that it was often marked by hostilities. The very name was associated with Cecil Rhodes, whose colonial history of exploration was regarded by the indigenous inhabitants as predatory. However, for a few years, after the reconstitution of Central African Airways on 1 January 1964, **Air Rhodesia**, formed on 1 June, was established as a subsidiary, with two DC3s and the four Viscounts, which C.A.A. continued to operate on its behalf. Domestic routes continued, and Gwelo and Fort Victoria (now Masvingo) were added. On 1 September 1967, Air Rhodesia became independent as its government's airline. It took over the allocated C.A.A. fleet, as the former parent airline terminated on 31 December.

Bitter confrontation continued, with Ian Smith's white-minority rule perceived as so extremely biased that sanctions were imposed on Rhodesia by the United Nations. The airline managed to circumvent the trade barriers by acquiring three ex–Eastern Air Lines Boeing 720s through Switzerland. They entered service in September 1973 to Johannesburg, as South Africa's apartheid government policy was sympathetic to Smith. But the unrest grew to dangerous proportions, and two Viscounts were shot down by guerilla fighters on 3 September 1978 and 12 February 1979, killing a total of 97 people. For a while, the airline was renamed Air Zimbabwe Rhodesia, and renamed again on 1 April 1980 as **Air Zimbabwe**. Two days later, with a Boeing 707 leased from South African Airways, it proudly opened a route to London. Zimbabwe was declared as an independent republic on 18 April.

Now that Cecil Rhodes's name was consigned to the history books, Air Zimbabwe proceeded in fine style. It had started service to neighboring Lusaka, Zambia, on 21 January 1980, and now added Nairobi, Kenya, and Gaberone, Botswana, on 3 April and 4 December 1981, respectively. Frankfurt became an additional European destination; Series 800 Viscounts replaced the older ones on 6 March 1981, and Affretair (founded as Air Trans Africa in 1965, as a DC-8 cargo airline) was acquired in 1983. This last action reflected the need for a major air freight uplift as, like Zambia, the nation was land-locked, and dependent on railroads to the ports of other countries for the export of its agricultural and mineral production. Perishable vegetables and fruits and high-value minerals such as diamonds demanded fast transport to the export markets.

Zimbabwe won its spurs among the world of airlines as the memories of the isolation and sanctions receded. On 27 September 1985, the airline leased a 105-seat Boeing 737-200 and then bought three of them late in 1986, to replace a series of leased 707s. In December 1987, a BAe 146 arrived, not for the public, but for presidential use. Service to Mauritius began on 26 March 1988 and the first 203-seat Boeing 767-200ER flew to London on 16 December of that year. Air Zimbabwe was climbing high. President Robert Mugabe, the hero of liberation from colonial rule, was obsessed with—to use a coined term—Africanization, that is, to take over all businesses that had been founded and maintained for many decades by white colonists, and to turn them over to Africans. These included the farming community that had built up a profitable export market, that fed, it was reported, half of Africa. The problem was that the Africans lacked the experience and the competence for industrial management. From an economic status of, in the African context, relative affluence, the late 1990s and the 2000s witnessed a steady decline in the nation, as racial prejudice overwhelmed economic sense. Within two decades, almost systematically, Mugabe's government transformed affluence into poverty. The financial situation was so bad that, after precipitous declines in the value of Zimbabwean currency, inflation rose to global records exceeding, first, hundreds then thousands then millions of percentage increases to the U.S. dollar. In April 2009, the currency was abolished.

In step with this economic and environmental background, Air Zimbabwe's prosperity declined. In 1999, it was carrying a million passengers a year. By 2006, the figure was less than 200,000. Yet even when the country was collapsing around it, in November 2004, it managed to open a service to Beijing via Singapore. In 2005, two 60-seat Xi'an MA-60 turboprops were leased from China, which, for many years, had sought to extend its influence throughout Africa, and was prepared to subsidize efforts to attain that goal. In October 2007, British Airways, whose history of serving the country goes back to 1932, withdrew from Harare. But against all odds, Air Zimbabwe then increased its frequency to London, to pressure essential contacts with Great Britain.

With the country's tourism potential at a low ebb, to start a new airline during Mugabe's program of national self-destruction was to swim against a powerful tide. But Mr. and Mrs. Denver

In spite of the declining economic situation in Zimbabwe, its airline still showed the country's colors. This was one of its Boeing 737-200s. (McDonough)

Hornsby deserved great credit for trying to do just that. On 27 July 1997, with a single 19-seat Beech 1900, their **Expedition Airways** began service from Harare to the preferred destinations that had been abandoned by Air Zimbabwe. Enterprisingly, they also opened a route to Vilankulos, a new beach resort in Mozambique.

As junior partner of Central African Airways, Nyasaland became Malawi, and its independent airline, **Air Malawi**, inherited only two DC-3s and three DHC-2 Beavers. It was registered as a private company on 26 March 1964, and started its first service, from Blantyre to Beira, Mozambique, on 1 July. It became the national government airline on 1 September 1967, by which time it had also added two ex-C.A.A. Viscounts. In 1969, two 40-seat HS-748s replaced the DC-3s, and a 10-seat BN-2 Islander was obtained specifically to operate the short route from Blantyre to Lilongwe, that was to be the new Malawi capital, Junior in size Malawi may have been, but it was keen to assert itself. So in November 1970, with a leased BAC One-Eleven, it started service to Johannesburg and Lusaka, then on 24 February 1972, it bought a -475 version of the One-Eleven, better suited for the route to hot-and-high Nairobi. On 7 December, Air Malawi was the first African airline to serve the Seychelles, where, for some months, it connected with B.O.A.C.'s VC-10s to London and to Asia. This connection was superseded on 19 February 1974, when a blocked space agreement was concluded with British Caledonian, and even better, on 3 December, with its own VC-10 direct to London's Gatwick Airport. With services to Mauritius in April 1975 and to Colombo in 1976, Air Malawi was perhaps aiming too high. This aspiring airline withdrew from the London route on 1 November 1979.

Malawi's economy lacked mineral resources as did Zambia and Zimbabwe, but its agriculture included tea and coffee plantations. In the 1980s, it was able to add tourism as a source of income, as Salima and Makakola, on the shore of Lake Malawi (formerly Lake Nyasa), became resort destinations for South Africans. Through the next decades, the national airline held steady, with a Boeing 737-300 and an ATR-42-320 replacing the One-Elevens and 748s in 1991, and a Let L410UVP for the short domestic routes in 2005. But for a small airline representing a small country, it was an uphill battle, and on 10 September 2008, the government planned to sell its flag carrier to South Africa's British Airways affiliate, Comair.

Portuguese Remembrance

Portugal's contribution to world exploration has often been forgotten. Vasco da Gama and others discovered most of the perimeter of the African continent and much of southern Asia. Brazil—half of South America—was once part of its empire. Remnants of its sovereignty survived until after the Second World War in isolated enclaves in Asia, Atlantic islands (some are still Portuguese), and three colonies in Africa. The combined area of Angola and Mozambique, the two largest of the three, was more than the whole of western Europe. They are rich in mineral and agricultural resources, and, like other European colonialists, large numbers of Portuguese migrated to these colonies as administrators, businessmen, farmers, and miners. During the "wind of change" period of decolonization, most of the colonists returned to their homeland, but in spite of the fervor of nationalism, some elements of the traditional relationships with Lisbon were not completely erased.

Both Angola and Mozambique had active domestic airlines during the late 1930s, before the war, with **Divisão de Exploração dos Transportes Aérea de Angola (D.T.A.)** and **Divisão de Exploração dos Transportes Aéreos (DETA)**, respectively. With small de Havilland aircraft, both had served coastal cities from their capitals. When the war ended, the few years of this modest experience provided the foundations, in infrastructure, personnel, and installations, for post-war development. D.T.A. was first off the mark, in March 1946, from Nova Lisboa to Luanda, and on to Leopoldville, Belgian Congo (later Kinshasa, Zaïre); DETA soon followed, resuming Lourenço Marques (now Maputo)—Johannesburg service in November, and to Salisbury, Southern Rhodesia, in February 1947.

In 1951, the two colonies were incorporated as Portuguese overseas provinces, and the two airlines settled down to consolidate their networks, replacing post-war DC-3 fleets with Fokker F-27s in 1961. But neither could fly to Lisbon as the long-distance route was held by T.A.P., the Portuguese flag carrier. The political situation changed considerably on 11 November 1975, when both colonies gained independence. The transition in Angola was far more difficult than in Mozambique, although neither was straightforward. Conflicts between rival factions were already battling for power, with left-wing forces, backed by the Soviet Union and Cuba, opposed to right-wing forces supported by South Africa, later by the United States. Such was the degree of anti-colonial antagonism in Angola that the Portuguese colonists were at life-threatening risk. As described in Chapter 30, more than 200,000 people were evacuated to Lisbon in the four months from May to August 1975. D.T.A. was transformed into a national airline, **TAAG Angola Airlines**, or **Linhas Aéreas de Angola**. In spite of all the political convulsions, it managed to sustain some services, equipped with Boeing 707s and 737s, Fokker F-27s, and Lockheed L-100 freighters from the West, and Ilyushin Il-62s and Yak-40s from the East. The period of turmoil continued for many years, but the end was in sight with the Battle of Cuito-Cuanavale early in 1987. A Tripartite Accord on 22 December 1988 was inconclusive, as an election in 1991 was a failure, with the rebel UNITA forces resuming the civil war. TAAG tried to return to normality, with an Airbus A300 service from Luanda to Johannesburg in June 1992, but a 737 crash in northern Angola on 8 November 1993, killing 126, was a setback. In 1998, UNITA forces resumed fighting, until 22 February 2002, when its leader, Jonas Savimbi, was killed. Throughout the period of conflict, lasting two decades, an estimated 1.5 million lives were lost, and four million people displaced from their homes.

Angola gradually turned its back on this era of self-destruction, and normal life slowly returned. Its natural resources were extensive, especially in mineral and oil wealth,

Angola recovered well from the political disruptions of the 1990s. By the early 2000s, it was operating Boeing 747-400s. (Bentley)

and this helped to restore the economy. In what was becoming a regular routine, TAAG picked itself up again, this time permanently. In 2005, it signed a billion-dollar deal with Boeing for three 737-700s—the latest variant—and two 777-200ERs. The network of routes was built up again, and the Angola national airline was flying to many African countries, including Portuguese-speaking São Tomé and Sal Island, Cape Verde. These latter were convenient as refueling points en route to Lisbon, service to which started on 12 February 2007. More African destinations were added during 2008, including Maputo, Mozambique. By 2009, with a fleet of thirteen modern Boeings, now including four 747-300s and -400s, TAAG could claim to have the youngest jet fleet in the whole of Africa.

Calmer heads presided in Mozambique, where the 1975 independence was soon followed by a DETA service from Maputo (previously Lourenço Marques) to Lisbon, with leased aircraft, in January 1976. On 19 November 1980, the airline was restructured as **Linhas Aéreas de Mozambique (LAM)**, with a fleet of Boeing 737s, Fokker F-27s, and, for a few years, a leased Douglas DC-10. One of its 737s, delivered in 1969, was still in service 40 years later. Like TAAG, it was able to call at Sal Island, where it offered seats to Lisbon for the local T.A.C.V. airline. In 1998, L.A.M. was transformed into a limited company, as **LAM–Mozambique Airlines**.

Less rigid than Angola, the government allowed a degree of competition, to serve its country whose coast is as long as the west coast of the United States. Rail connections link Mozambique with South Africa, Zimbabwe, and Malawi, but there is no coordinated internal line. An arduous road journey from Maputo to Nampula, in the north, would take several days, In August 2004, free enterprise appeared in Nampula when Momed Akil started **Air Corridor**, with a 108-seat Boeing 737.

The Congo Changes Hands

Because the Belgian Congo was the largest single colonial unit in Africa, political events there tended to be more far-reaching than in other African lands. The events that followed decolonization combined to portray a macrocosm of all that was deficient in the transformation to self-government. Rich in valuable minerals: copper, cobalt, and diamonds, and with the experienced Belgian airline, SABENA, to guide it (and the one that had pioneered its enviable national airline network), the flag carrier of the new nation's checkered history was one of lost opportunities—though not all of its own making.

When independence was achieved on 30 June 1960, the first short-lived administration was politically sponsored by the Soviet Union, which seized the opportunity to augment the spread of the communist creed in Africa. But on 14 September, Joseph-Désiré Mobutu, a well-educated army officer, assumed leadership of the country. His political views were the opposite of Prime Minister Patrice Lumumba's, and they received approval from the West, which overlooked the circumstances of the prime minister's assassination in 1961. Against this background of strife, **Air Congo** was formed on 28 June 1961, with 65% of the shares held by the government, 30% by SABENA, and the remainder by a small airline, Air Brousse, and the Belgian charter airline, Sobelair.

As in the case of decolonization throughout the continent, the animosity between the Europeans and the liberated native population was such that the former left the country en masse. The new airline did not at first take over the route to Brussels, which started in March 1963, with a Boeing 707 leased from SABENA, after emotions had cooled somewhat. Air Congo had started regional services in February 1962 to the capitals of all its neighboring states, with 21 piston-engined Douglas DC-3s, 4s, and 6s, two Curtiss C-46s, and a few small aircraft. The arrangement with the Belgian airline did not last long, as in January 1964, the French independent airline, U.T.A., replaced the 707 Brussels route with one to Paris, and linking it with an onward connection to Johannesburg.

On 25 November 1965, General Mobutu seized power again, this time absolute power. Four of his opponents were publicly hanged. All SABENA property in the Congo, accumulated during decades of infrastructure development, was seized, due debts cancelled, and its interest in Air Congo abolished. By this time, the aircraft fleet was aging, and steps were taken

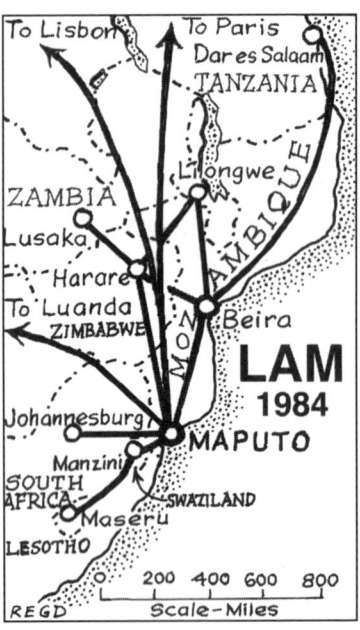

Unlike British colonies that combined to form successful airlines, the Portuguese territories in Africa did not have common frontiers. Their railroads were built to provide access to ports for other countries. But there had been Portuguese airlines in Angola and Mozambique to provide experience and infrastructure. Angola was less handicapped by prolonged civil war, but Mozambique was not so severely affected.

End of the Empire Airlines

This BAC One-Eleven of Air Katanga was never able to "show the flag," as that province's rebellion against Zaïre did not succeed. (McDonough)

to modernize it, at first with two Caravelles and four Fokker F-27s then, on 12 May 1967, with a leased BAC One-Eleven on the African routes, and on 25 November a DC-8 kept the long-haul ones alive. Reflecting a growing friendship with the United States, in October 1970, Pan American Airways signed a three-year management contract with Air Congo.

On 25 October 1971, the country was renamed Zaïre, and simultaneously the airline became **Air Zaïre**. At the time, prospects seemed good. One comment from an African airline director forecast a great future for it, because of its "political stability, natural resources, and its fantastic tourist potential." And for a few years, this prediction (except for the tourism) appeared to be correct. Also, the airline had the technical support from the then-great Pan American, combined with the United States' Technical Assistance Program (T.A.P.), and even more important, the approval of Mobutu, who had renamed himself with a highly complementary title and promoted himself to the rank of Field Marshal. With such encouragement, Air Zaïre moved ahead. On 3 January 1973, it ordered two 252-seat Douglas DC-10s and five 115-seat Boeing 737-200s (with gravel runway kits). It also leased a 360-seat Boeing 747 for one year. During the mid-1970s, the whole area of Central Africa was unstable, with factions in the copper-rich Katanga province stirring up a rebellion, and in 1977, invading Zaïre from Angola. During the same period, from 1974 to 1980, Air Zaïre sustained five crashes, four of them F-27s. These were replaced in 1981 by F-27-500s.

During the 1980s, Mobutu continued to be involved in the maneuvers of world politics. Air Zaïre was struggling, as the DC-10s had been withdrawn from service, and management contracts alternated between U.T.A. and British Caledonian. Mobutu, meanwhile, hired the supersonic Concorde in the summer of 1989 for three special flights: to New York, for a United Nations meeting; to Paris, to meet President Mitterrand; and to Marseille, with the Congolese Youth Choir, from Gbadolite, Mobutu's birthplace in northern Zaïre, where a special runway was built at the airfield to accommodate the aircraft's long take-off run.

The country always seemed doomed to be in a war zone, either internally, or with Angola. Now, in the summer of 1994, with the Rwanda civil war and genocide on its eastern frontier, a million refugees sought survival in Zaïre. This was no place for an airline to flourish, and with a depleted fleet, the domestic network ceased to function, while traffic on the long-haul routes evaporated. At the end of 1994, with huge debts, Air Zaïre was declared bankrupt. After a year's hiatus, **New Air Zaïre** attempted to renew a national air service in February 1996 with two Airbus A310-300s, but it lasted only a few months in the face of the political and ethnic turmoil that seemed to have engulfed much of Africa during the 1990s. In November of that year, a rebellion by Tutsis in the east ravaged its way across the country, and on 16 May 1997, together with other anti-Mobutu groups, captured the capital, Kinshasa. By this time, domination of the all-powerful ruler had diminished; in August 1996, he had gone to Switzerland for cancer surgery and died on 7 September 1997 in Morocco, having embezzled an estimated $5 billion from his country's revenues, deposited mainly into Swiss banks.

Air Zaïre benefitted from its nation's wealth by operating a fleet of Douglas DC-10-30s. (McDonough)

During the three decades of Mobutu's regime, opportunities for entrepreneurship ebbed and flowed, dependent upon his moods and mainly on his personal relationships. But the nature of the host of small airlines that came and went seemed to reflect the wealth of the Congo. Many of them operated turboprop Electras and Viscounts, and One-Eleven, 707, and 727 jets. One company, **Shabair**, based in Lubumbashi, even had a wide-bodied DC-10. They were used mainly for cargo in a large country which had no coordinated railroad system, and in which road haulage was a dangerous way of life. These operators also contributed to Africa's notorious reputation for poor safety standards, especially when the aircraft were used for passenger charters. The accident rate was more than six times that of the world average.

Nepotism under Mobutu soared to a new level in Zaïre. Among the many small airlines, half a dozen were owned by his relatives or his ministers, and engaged in smuggling, including an airlift of arms to assist the UNITA rebel forces in Angola. Illustrative of the tragic results of the complex structure of illegality was the crash of an Antonov 32 cargo aircraft, in January 1996, on take-off from Kinshasa's downtown airport, killing close to 400 people in the adjoining market. The aircraft was operating as Africa Air, rented from Scibe Airlift, which leased it from a Belgian company, which in turn had contracted with Moscow Airways.

Hewa Bora Airways was one of the many short-lived small airlines that operated briefly as Africa came to terms with new-found independence. This was one of its "previous-owned" Boeing 707s. (McDonough)

Even after the Congo's slow recovery from a mountain of political and economic problems, the hazards of airline operation did not return to normal for several years. Connections with Belgium were resumed, generating the essential airlift requirements. The collapse of SABENA left the market open for others, including Air France, which started, in 2001, a Paris-Kinshasa service, with TGV train service from Brussels to Paris. A Congo airline, **Hewa Bora Airways**, started service on the route, with internal connections, but on 15 April 2008, a DC-9 crash at Goma, killing at least 50 people, was a grim reminder of the lack of adequate safety standards. A pilot who survived said that the aircraft may have had a flat tire. These companies also flew to Europe, which began to resume business with the Democratic Republic of the Congo, as Zaïre had been renamed after the departure of Mobutu.

Chapter 50: To the Cape and Beyond

South African Airways

Africa's record of airline progress into the 21st century has been less than satisfactory. There has been little cooperation between the many small countries, especially those that needed it most, and the safety statistics of the continent have fallen well behind those of the rest of the world. The fact that Africa was the first in the globe to experience jet airline travel is therefore something of a paradox. The British state airline, B.O.A.C., boldly started jet service from London to Johannesburg via Rome, Beirut/Cairo, Khartoum, Entebbe, and Livingstone on 2 May 1952. The 36 all-first-class-seat de Havilland Comet 1s were so competitive—the journey time was about half that of the piston-engined aircraft that they replaced—that **South African Airways (S.A.A.)** had to match them. On 4 October 1953, it leased two Comets from B.O.A.C., and introduced its own jet service to London.

The national airline of the Union of South Africa, then a dominion of the British Commonwealth, was thus the second airline in the world to operate jet airliners. Sadly, it was also the second airline in the world to suffer a disaster, when one of them crashed in the Mediterranean on 4 April 1954. B.O.A.C. chose the route because it catered to business executives of the affluent mining corporations of South Africa, especially the diamond industry. The clientele was only white, as black Africans were segregated by the policy of apartheid, introduced in 1948. Almost 90% of South Africa's population of 24 million was black and lived on little more than 10% of the land. Their per capita income was about one-fourteenth of whites, and black passengers were not seen on S.A.A. airliners.

With the departure of the Comets, to supplement the Constellations, S.A.A. ordered Douglas DC-7Bs, and these entered service on the *Springbok* route to London on 21 April 1956. From 4 December, this reached England in 21 hours, with a single stop in Khartoum. Also, on 2 April 1957, a second route started via the west coast, stopping at Leopoldville, Kano, Algiers, and Amsterdam—thus avoiding the more difficult en route stops of the eastern route. On 25 November 1957, in pool with the Australian QANTAS, S.A.A. pioneered the first trans-Indian Ocean route, via Mauritius, to Perth, and on to Sydney. In the following year, on 21 June, it ordered three Boeing 707s, to reenter the Jet Age, and on 24 November, introduced 40-seat Vickers Viscount turboprops on domestic and regional services.

In striking contrast with the high-quality service in a maturing network, and a surprising example of apartheid at an unusual level, on 4 December 1959, a Johannesburg-Durban DC-3 service began for non-whites, at fares 25% lower than standard. Very few of the black majority could afford even the discounted fare. There were none on the inaugural 139-seat Boeing 707-144 jet service to London on 1 October 1960. The weight of oppression generally led to protest marches and assemblies against the pass laws—every non-white person had to carry an identity card and was heavily punished if found without one. At the Sharpeville massacre, many people were killed and hundreds injured. The repercussions aroused indignation worldwide and outright political confrontation throughout Africa. By 1963, the airspace across almost every other country in Africa was closed to South African Airways, at the risk of its airliners being shot down. The only way to fly to Europe was to avoid the continent. Flights were rerouted via Portuguese territories: Luanda, Angola, Sal (Cape Verde Islands), and Lisbon, with technical stops at Brazzaville (Congo), and Las Palmas (see map). The agreement allowed the Portuguese airline, T.A.P., to sell unsold space. On 12 October, the pool partnership on the Springbok route was broken up by mutual agreement.

Undeterred, S.A.A. ordered five 97-seat Boeing 727s in May 1964 for its regional services, and maintained the long western route to Europe. On 1 November 1968, it was able to fly to Blantyre, Nyasaland (Malawi) with Viscounts, and on 23 February 1969, introduced a trans-Atlantic service to New York via Rio de Janeiro. In the fall of 1971, flying this route was made easier with the delivery of three Boeing 747Bs, with more range than the standard ones, and these were soon flying once a week to London via Cape Town, which, at sea level, was more accommodating for take-offs than Johannesburg's 5,500-foot altitude. The 727s, meanwhile, replaced the Viscounts. On 6 November 1972, a Cape Town-Buenos Aires service started, in partnership with Aerolíneas Argentinas, each airline flying once every two weeks. On 3 September 1973, S.A.A. opened the world's longest nonstop air route, Johannesburg-London, 7,020 miles; and in 1974, a trans-Indian Ocean route to Hong Kong via Seychelles, a distance of 6,710 miles. In spite of foreign restrictions overseas, the airline was thus drawing upon aeronautical technical development on its overseas routes. At home, business was booming, partly because of a 50-mph speed limit on the roads, so the 727s were converted from a generous five- to the standard six-abreast seating. In 1976, S.A.A. took delivery of its first Boeing 228-seat 747SP, the shortened version of that highly successful airliner, exchanging seats for extra fuel. Boeing delivered it nonstop from Seattle to Cape Town, 10,240 miles, a new record. Simultaneously, the first 241-seat Airbus A300B2 was delivered. Though the country was by now under siege politically, the airline was forging ahead.

Luck did not favor the airline on 15 January 1980, for a most unusual reason. A third of its fleet was knocked out of service when, for 45 minutes, it was subjected to attack by a hailstorm of "frozen missiles the size of billiard balls." S.A.A. had to lease aircraft from Air Rhodesia and Luxair.

The national administration showed no signs of compromise with international sensitivities toward its apartheid policy. The airline had always been an operating unit of South African

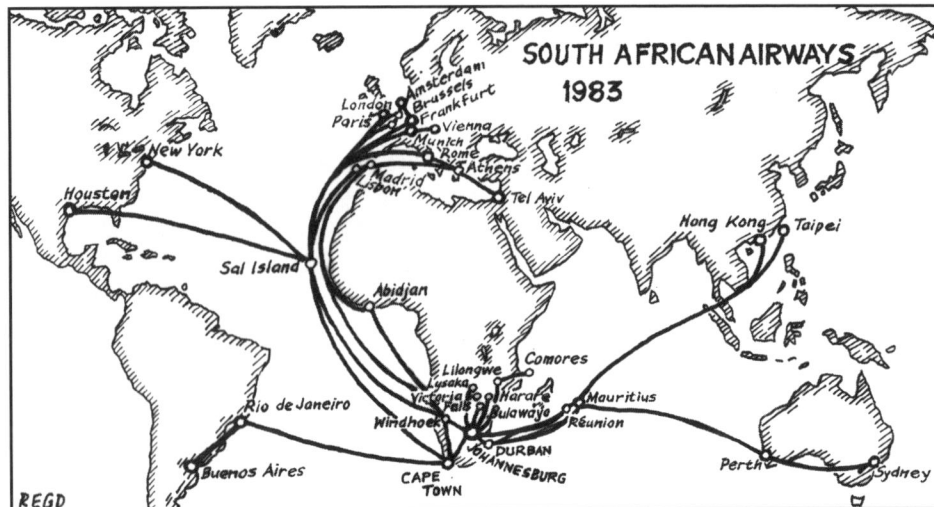

With long-range Boeing 747s, S.A.A. was able not only to bypass the anti-apartheid countries of Africa, but also to cross the Atlantic and Indian Oceans.

Railways and Harbors, and in 1981, this was changed to South African Transport Services (SATS), to include every form of transport, including oil transmission lines. Reflecting the attitude of the government, the name of the airline was altered to Suid-Afrikaanse Lugdiens (S.A.L.), possibly to remind perfidious Albion that the Boer War had not been forgotten. (This name was already used, at least on one side of the aircraft.)

In the face of growing worldwide abhorrence to the human rights infringements of apartheid, this was the last gesture by a recalcitrant extremist government. Nevertheless, the airline had progressed with determination. By 1985 it had 87 jet airliners, and except for seven Airbuses, all were Boeings (seventeen 117-seat 737s had replaced the 727s in 1968). But world opinion forced the issue. In 1978 and 1983, the United Nations had condemned South Africa in a World Conference Against Racism. In November 1986, the United States imposed economic sanctions, and in 1987, Australia followed. S.A.L. had to cancel its routes to New York, Houston, Perth, and Sydney, and had to lease some of its fleet to other airlines.

South Africa finally had to acknowledge the injustice that had prevailed for more than 40 years. On 2 February 1990, President F.W. de Klerk announced that the policy of apartheid was to be abolished. On 11 February, Nelson Mandela, the leader of the African National Congress, was released from 27 years in prison. On 21 March, the military occupation of South-West Africa came to an end, and Namibia became an independent state. South African Airways hastened to make up for lost time. During the next two years, its intercontinental network was restored, notably overflying Africa, for the first time since 1983, to Nairobi on 8 September 1991, to New York (via Sal Island) on 3 November, to Australia on 18 January 1992, and to Hong Kong in April. To cope with growing competition at home, **SAExpress (SAX)** became a low-fare affiliate, for which 12 DHC 40-seat Dash 8s were ordered in December 1993.

The end of the despised apartheid was complete when Nelson Mandela was elected President of South Africa on 10 May 1994. For laying the foundations of the new regime, he and de Klerk had been awarded the Nobel Peace Prize the previous year. In the domestic field, airline competition was permitted, with Flitestar and Comair (the latter, Boeing 737-equipped, associated with British Airways—see below) leading with more low fares. Another interesting new airline was **Sun Air** (formerly Bop Air—see also below), which, on 2 October 1996, began a Douglas DC-9 service to London in association with Virgin Atlantic, always ready to challenge B.A.

South African Airways continued to develop in the face of heavy competition from a host of foreign airlines that was now able and willing to serve the once-ostracised nation. In 1996, services were resumed to Kinshasa, Luanda, and Abidjan, and on 3 April 1997, finally to Osaka, as the rights to Tokyo could not be negotiated. By this time, with the new South African national flag on the tails, and SOUTH AFRICAN, instead of S.A.A. or S.A.L. on the fuselages, the airline was flying to 13 destinations in Africa and 16 intercontinentally. But the bold recovery came

With the Boeing 747SP, S.A.A. was able to avoid the countries that prohibited its overflying privileges because of the apartheid policies of its parent country. In addition to its Boeing, its long-haul services also used Airbus A342s. (McDonough)

To the Cape and Beyond

South African (Airways) operated frequent services on the Johannesburg-Durban-Cape Town triangular network with a fleet of Boeing 737s. (McDonough)

The Jet Age did not reach some of the recruits who were hired for the mines in South Africa. Vintage DC-3 propeller aircraft took them to Francistown, Bechuanaland (now Botswana) and thence by rail to Johannesburg.

at a price, and the rejuvenated airline sought help. On 15 June 1998, Coleman Andrews, an experienced U.S. airline executive arrived to restore order by cutting staff and changing schedules. In September 1999, the Swiss SAir Group, parent of Swissair, acquired a 20% shareholding. In February 2000, the code-sharing agreement with American Airlines, which had been the basis of the route to New York, was exchanged for one with Delta Air Lines and service to Atlanta began. 21 Boeing 737s were ordered, but not taken up, as a complete fleet reorganization was under way. Boeing lost one of its faithful customers. Airbus took over, with a large order for 26 short-medium-haul A319/320s and six long-haul A340s, the first of which was delivered on 24 January 2004. The 340s could carry 30 tons more cargo and burn 28 tons less fuel than the Boeing 747, added to which was better fleet commonality with resultant lower maintenance costs. It was a major victory for Airbus, and the Swiss shareholding was also cancelled.

During this eventful period, major changes were also made in management. Andrews had completely misjudged the business environment in South Africa. In an effort to smother the domestic competition, he made decisions to eliminate Sun Air. They were described as "bludgeoning (the airline) into bankruptcy," an action that was not appreciated by the government, now under non-white African control. Many remembered that Sun Air had been born as an early example of ending apartheid discrimination, and Coleman's policy led to his abrupt dismissal in April 2001, to be replaced by Andre Viljoen. He too was replaced by Khaya Nygala, of impeccable ancestry, in July 2004. In April 2006, South African Airways joined the Star Alliance, an indication that the former political exile was now an honored member of the world airline fraternity. It celebrated by launching its own low-cost airline, Mango, on 15 November 2006 (see below).

Jet Age Paradox

Soon after South African Airways' Comet jet crash in April 1954, but not widely known or publicized in southern Africa or elsewhere, was the nearby debut of a remarkable experiment in air transport. An operation was launched with the veteran—some would say archaic—Douglas DC-3, which first saw service in 1936; and in which, unlike S.A.A.'s first-class fares, the seats were free. In 1952, the Witwatersland Native Labour Association (W.N.L.A.) had chartered aircraft from Africair to carry native labor from neighboring countries to the gold mines in the Transvaal and the Orange Free State. The operation served as a trial for the start, on 1 July 1954, of the **Winela Air Service**.

Based at Francistown, to the far north of Bechuanaland (then a British protectorate, and now, since 1966, Botswana), its DC-3s carried 39 miner recruits with minimal possessions, at no charge, then transferred them by rail or road en route to the South African mines. A year or two later, they returned, this time with accumulated savings to pay their own fare, plus excess baggage, on 25 seats. By 1958, Winela was carrying 80,000 miners a year, and the fleet of eight DC-3s was supplemented by an 80-seat DC-4. But its crash on 4 April 1974, killing 78, accelerated the demise of a highly successful air transport operation whose ancient DC-3s had survived into the era of wide-bodied "jumbo" Boeing 747s.

Comfort at Bargain Fares

Although South Africa regarded South African Airways as its "chosen instrument," it did allow other airlines to operate as long as they did not compete directly with it—and the International Air Transport Association (IATA) rules seemed to rule out direct competition. But—to coin a phrase—in a classic example of inspired enterprise, there was an exception: a case of the sublime to the ridiculous. It began in an unpretentious manner. **Trek Airways** was founded in Pretoria by three pilots on 24 September 1953. Its first flight from Johannesburg was to Amsterdam, on 21 December—in time for Christmas—with a veteran DC-3, which had to stop several times en route. With little thought for regular service, it had been authorized because previous attempts by others had resulted in what were described as "dubious practices." The following year, two 40-seat Vickers Vikings from Eagle Aviation provided better comfort than the old Douglases, and flights began to Dusseldorf. The passengers were mainly immigrants from Europe who appreciated the cheap fares, and unlike the businessmen, were not in a hurry, and did not demand first-class service.

Limited though the service was, and restricted to five per month per aircraft, its popularity demanded more capacity. Trek bought two Douglas DC-4s from Northwest Airlines. Still unpressurized, they were not, however, converted military C-54s, but post-war aircraft, with longer range. The fares were well below IATA levels, but comfort was not compromised. The seats, at 40" pitch, could be reclined, and the catering was first-class. Each round-trip took nine days, with overnight stops at Entebbe and Cairo, reminiscent of the pre-war flying boat days of Imperial Airways, when passengers enjoyed the brief breaks for a little sight-seeing. The DC-4s went into service in April 1958, just a few months before sustained jet services began across the North Atlantic.

One of the DC-4s made a non-fatal crash at Luxor on 3 September 1960, so Trek hired two Lockheed L.749A Constellations from South African Airways. Their faster speed allowed more leisure time at the stops, starting in December 1961. Traffic rights to Dusseldorf were to be rescinded in May 1962, and this had led to an agreement with Luxembourg Airlines to terminate in the Principality. This also allowed for an arrangement with the low-fare Icelandic trans-Atlantic pioneer, Loftleidir, for connections to New York. By this time, Trek was flying 88 flights a year, with most of its seats filled. In October 1963, Douglas DC-6Bs had to be chartered (from U.T.A.) to fly the service, now by the west coast route, because the Constellations had South African registrations, and the dispute over apartheid prevented overflying African countries. Luxair, in partnership, operated Trek's remaining DC-4. This arrangement continued when, on 17 February, the first 98-seat Lockheed L.1649A Super-Constellation arrived, and the second one was registered in Luxembourg.

By 1965, Trek Airways was sufficiently established for the majority of its shares to be sold to investment companies in South Africa. In 1966, charter flights were made to Rio de Janeiro and Tokyo, and in June 1968, Bristol Britannias were leased, with one based at Luxembourg for Luxair to make connecting flights to London. Because of the trans-Africa embargo of South African-registered aircraft, flights were suspended in 1980, after a Boeing 707 had been introduced. They were revived in 1991, in cooperation with Luxair once again, using one of the latter's Boeing 747SPs, but with a Trek identity in the aircraft paint scheme. In 1993, it founded a South African domestic airline, **Flitestar**, with four 134-seat Airbus A320s and two 60-seat ATR-72s. By this time, the restrictions of apartheid were evaporating, but airline deregulation, introduced in 1991, invited competition from other embryo airlines—see below. South African Airways, which had enjoyed close to a monopoly of domestic air service, did not give up easily, resorting to questionable competitive practices. Flitestar lost money heavily, and with its parent, Trek, ceased operations on 11 April 1994. Such innovative marketing deserved a better fate.

South African Domestics

South African Airways had enjoyed close to a monopoly of air services within the Union, in which the routes between the three largest cities, Johannesburg, Cape Town, and Durban, were regarded as the "golden triangle"—busy enough to generate substantial traffic, and long enough to operate at a comfortable profit. One new rival was a long-established company, originally for charter contracts, that was permitted to fly regular short-haul services that S.A.A. did not want. By the late 1950s, however, **Commercial Air Services (Comair)** was flying to the Rhodesias, and by 1963 its small fleet had progressed from small commuter types to Douglas DC-3s. 44-seat Fokker F-27s were added in 1976, and after deregulation, it was serving main domestic markets. On 27 October 1996, Comair became a franchise partner of British Airways, which acquired a 17% minority interest. Its fleet now comprised Boeing 737s, 727s, and ATR-72s. Moving with the times and trends, it then, on 1 August 2001, established a low-cost subsidiary, **Kulula-com** (*kulula* means "easy" in the Zulu language), starting with one of Comair's 175-seat 727s. This colorful airline added six Douglas DC-9-82s, and together with its operating partner, and under the same management, competed well with S.A.A.

Flitestar, backed by Trek, and Comair, backed by British Airways, and a few other companies had been formed after deregulation, but the demographics of South Africa are not conducive to much diversification. Apart from the three large cities of the "Golden Triangle," few others have justified substantial air traffic, at least enough to permit profitable competition for all participants. Thus, as the Jet Age matured, South African Airways, supported by a protective government, faced little competition except from Comair.

During the 1970s, the creation of the 10 "homelands" was a mixed blessing for the non-white peoples of South Africa. Rather in the style of the reservations of Native American peoples in the United States, the homelands were fragmented pieces of territory distant from the developed and industrial areas, and notably with little rail access. Deliberately designed to separate the races,

Comair is the South African affiliate of British Airways, operating Boeing 727s. (McDonough)

Whether intentional or not, "Kulula" in South Africa means "easy", and may have been a reflection of the highly successful easyJet in England. This is one of its Boeng 727s. (McDonough)

For Transkei, the Hawker Siddeley HS-748 was ideal in size, to match the traffic potential; and in performance—it could cope with unprepared airstrips, like the old DC-3. (Davies)

600,000 black, Indian, and Chinese people had been forced to move to them, and about one-third of that number of whites were relocated from the designated areas.

Of the 10 homelands, four were granted independence, while six were self-governing but short of complete self-rule. One area of the former category, Transkei, possibly serving as a "trial balloon," attained self-government as early as 1963 and was able to establish **Transkei Airways**, based at Umtata, on 22 October 1976. Twelve-seat Beech King-Airs provided twice-daily services to Johannesburg, and these were joined by a BN-2 Islander, and later, a 44-seat Hawker Siddeley HS-748. Of the other homelands, Venda and Ciskei were too small to justify regular air service, but Bophuphatswana comprised seven separated enclaves, rich in minerals, game parks, and a new resort, Sun City (formerly Planesburg) close enough to Johannesburg to generate weekend air traffic. Mmabatho was the new capital of a land that was relatively prosperous, and boasting a modern airport with a three-mile-long runway. On 20 July 1979, the government of this new country founded Mafiking Air Services (named after the nearby city of the historic Relief during the Boer War). After renaming as Mmabatho Air Services, it was renamed Bophuthsatswana Air Services, soon called **Bop Air**, if only to make room for the name on the aircraft. The airline prospered, and was again renamed **Sun Air** in 1996, by which time its 18-seat Embraer Bandeirantes had been joined by a BAe (HS) 748 and four 100-seat Douglas DC-9s. It expanded its route network to fly in the Golden Triangle.

In 1991, after airline deregulation, **Nationwide Air** was formed, privately owned, and at first flew charter services for the United Nations. In 1994, it started scheduled service on the main trunk route from Johannesburg to Cape Town, and with a fleet of 11 BAC One-Elevens, expanded to Durban and George. On 28 March 1997, it entered into a code-sharing agreement with SABENA, with a service to Brussels, with Nationwide titles on the aircraft. By 1998, it had two Boeing 727s of its own, and with four Beech King-Airs, claimed to be the second largest airline in South Africa. **Avia Airlines** lasted for less than a year in 1995, and in February 2004, **1-Time (One-Time)** entered the domestic scene, competing with Comair for the low-fare market.

As mentioned above, S.A.A. had reacted to the competition on 1 December 1993 by associating with S.A.Express (SAX) with a 20% interest, and on 15 November 2006, formed its own low-cost subsidiary, **Mango**, with four 186-seat Boeing 737-800s, brightly colored to match its name. Several other airlines have operated from various bases in the Union, but all have met specialized local needs or have provided local commuter or feeder services to the main urban centers.

Airlines on the South African Fringe

Political jurisdiction in southern Africa was not entirely within the sovereignty of the Union of South Africa. One area, almost entirely within the highest mountains, was completely surrounded by the Union. The Basuto nation had resisted its acquisition by the Boers, the British colonists, and the South African government. Eventually, in 1884, it accepted jurisdiction as a British colony. Basutoland is not endowed with many resources, but it contains the headwaters of the Orange River, and a hydro-electric dam exports water to the Union. It has one mile of railroad, connecting its capital, Maseru, with a main line across the border. After independence in 1966, **Lesotho Airways** (named after a traditional name for the colony) was formed as the national airline on 1 January 1970, with a fleet of single-engined Cessnas, a Skyvan, and five 20-seat DHC-6 Twin Otters. Its modest objectives were to connect Maseru with Johannesburg, and to fly to communities in the high mountains, where peaks of the Drakenberg range rise to 10,000 feet. By 1980, it was also operating to Gaberone, Maputo, Manzini, and Durban, and to many mountain strips. Roads improved, surface transport replaced the airline, and operations were suspended on 1 October 1996.

Swaziland also had a checkered history of remaining outside the Union. It was recognized in 1884 by the Boers of Transvaal, who cherished the idea of a mutual route to the sea. But after the Boer War, the British (who had acquired the coastal land) recognized the area as a protectorate. Sovereign rights were granted in 1926, and independence granted in 1968. As early as 1956, as the antithesis of the Jet Age inaugural in 1952 at Johannesburg, **Swazi Air** was founded by an ex-Imperial Airways pilot at Stegi, near the Mozambique border. The owner, A.J.M. "Winkle" Aldwinkle and his wife operated—not too intensively—two 4-seat Cessna 170s. In 1961, the National Airways Corporation bought them out and started a route from Manzini to Durban, later adding Johannesburg and Lourenço Marques.

South African Airways started its low-cost airline affiliate in 2006. Mango's color scheme was appropriately a bright orange. (McDonough)

After complete independence, the country was ruled as an absolute monarchy, and on 1 August 1978, **Royal Swazi National Airways** was formed with 50% state ownership. Its fleet of a single 60-seat Fokker F-28-3000 operated intermittently to neighboring countries. A route to the Seychelles in 1991 had to be cancelled after a hijacking, but traffic was enough to justify the short-term lease of a Boeing 737-200. Most of its revenue was from the link to Johannesburg, whose citizens flew into Swaziland because of its liberal drinking and gaming laws—a South African Las Vegas. Improvements on the 150-mile road from the Transvaal metropolis led to the airline's bankruptcy.

The other British protectorate in South Africa was a much bigger area northwest of the Union, mostly desert or scrub land. Like Basutoland and Swaziland, Bechuanaland had been an area of dispute between the Dutch-immigrant Boers and the British. The former made it a protectorate in 1884, but the British usurped them in 1895, and consolidated their rule after the Boer War at the turn of the century. Its early value to the colonists was the railroad along its eastern rim, as a vital segment to the Rhodesias and beyond, and until the advent of air transport, would have contributed to the dream of a Cape-to-Cairo Railway. With considerable mineral wealth, especially diamonds, it is not a poor country, with a per capita income close to that of the South African Republic.

Shortly before independence was achieved in 1966, **Bechuanaland National Airways** was founded at Francistown on 1 October 1965, and services begun on 15 November with two Douglas DC-3s—hardly Jet Age, but matched to the demand. The route network, with distances suited to air transport, included domestic ones to Gaberone, the capital, and to Maun, far to the northwest, and which is the local center for the Okavango Delta, the seasonal destination for hunters and tourists seeking the "big game" of Africa. At the end of 1966, with the change of the country's name, the services were taken over by **Botswana National Airways**, with a relatively modern fleet of a Viscount and Fokker F-27 turboprops, a BN-2 Islander, and a Beech Baron. It launched enthusiastically into service, adding a Douglas DC-4 to carry 32 tons of fuel per flight to Livingstone, for onward transport by rail to the Copperbelt.

Enthusiasm was not enough. The airline terminated operations in 1971. Its place was taken on 2 July 1972 by **Air Botswana**, controlled by the Botswana Development Corporation. Operations began on 1 August, with a single F-27, and a leased DC-3. It flew the same routes as its predecessor, and by 1981, when it contracted with British Airways for a leased F-27, it also had a Hawker Siddeley HS-748. The next few years were uneventful, except for the lease of a Lockheed L-100 for air cargo, and the lease of a 16-seat Dornier Do-228 from Kalahari Air Service, to carry tourists to that developing tourist destination. On 1 April 1988, with a change in management, the Botswana government took over the airline and replaced the F-27s with two ATR-42-300s and two 46-seat BAe 146s. Air Botswana negotiated cooperation agreements with some other airlines for international connecting services, but failed with others, and still lost money heavily. Then, on 11 October 1999, it tried to economize in conventional fashion by asking for salary reductions. But a pilot with a grievance deliberately flew his ATR-42 into two others, thus destroying all the active airplanes in the fleet. Picking itself up, the airline obtained a Beech 1900D and, on 19 March 2009, received its first of two leased 68-seat ATR-72-500s, and in the following year wet-leased a 75-seat Fokker F-28. By this time, Maun had become an important tourist destination, and direct service from Johannesburg had become Air Botswana's best route.

Further to the west, South Africa had inherited a large slice of territory after the First World War. The severe reparations imposed on Germany by the Treaty of Versailles included the loss of all its colonies, shared among the victors. South Africa's share was South West Africa, a large slice of adjoining territory on the Atlantic coast. In 1946, **South West Air Transport** had revived local services which had been pioneered before the war, and now connecting with S.A.A. at the territorial capital, Windhoek. With small single-engined types such as the Ryan Navion, it had little ambition at first for expansion, except in 1966 to Alexander Bay, near some diamond mines. In 1959, the country's German heritage had favored a change of the airline name to the **Afrikaans Suidwes Lugdienst**, with which they may have felt more affinity. By 1971, it was operating to Cape Town. 28-seat Douglas DC-3s had replaced the light aircraft in 1973, and they, in turn, were replaced by a 40-seat Fairchild FH-227B turboprop on 18 December 1975. Adding a Convair CV580 turboprop on 27 April 1978, this infant nation, still dependent on South Africa for its economy, was on the fringe of the Jet Age.

It took the plunge in 1990, when South West Africa became Namibia, and the name of the airline changed to **Namib Air**, owned by TransNamib, a state corporation. With a Boeing 747SP leased from South African Airways, it boldly opened services from Windhoek to London and to Frankfurt, where some ethnic memories still survived with distant family connections. The flights originated from Johannesburg, and could then fly nonstop across Africa, whereas S.A.A., because of the political opposition to its apartheid policy, had to fly the long way around the continent, offshore from the mainland via Sal Island.

A route to London was added, and the name changed again to **Air Namibia**. In April 1998, it leased a Boeing 767-300ER to replace the SP, but reverted to that aircraft a year later. Growing

Namib Air's Boeing 747SP. (McDonough)

mineral wealth offset the handicap of its geographical location between South Africa and Angola, deeply involved in a civil war, and eroding normal traffic. As hostilities evaporated, however, Namibia was able to benefit from tourism, as it could provide service to all four of the most popular destinations: the Elosha Game Reserve in the north; the Okavanga Delta, just across the border in Botswana; the Victoria Falls, at the end of the odd frontier extension, the Caprivi Strip; and to Cape Town's Table Mountain.

French Jets in the Indian Ocean

Of all the world's great oceans, the last one to be served by commercial airlines was the Indian. German airships had started South Atlantic service in 1931 and the North Atlantic in 1936. Pan American Airways' flying boats had conquered the North Pacific in 1935, the South Pacific in 1940, and the North Atlantic in 1939. Airlines were flying over parts of the Arctic during the Second World War. Because the traffic potential of the scattered islands of the Indian Ocean was insignificant, little attention was paid to them by the world's airlines, and the islands themselves did not have the resources to start their own. Allied air forces had valued them during the Second World War as vital staging posts between Europe and Australia when Japan occupied the southern route across Asia, but post-war development was slow and infrequent.

During the decades of colonial expansion, France had led the way to the Indian Ocean. Beyond the continental mainland was Madagascar, the fourth largest island in the world. Excluded from the "Scramble for Africa" and after some bargaining with the British, it had become a French colony only in 1896, until which time it had been an independent monarchy. As early as 1947, **Air Madagascar** had been established by local capital as an extension of Air France's long route to Antananarivo. A fleet of five 28-seat Douglas DC-3s and six 8-seat de Havilland DH-89s were deployed to serve about two dozen small communities throughout the almost 1,000-mile-long island. There were few railways or paved roads. Other than the capital, there were no other towns of consequence, and there has never been a trunk air route that could generate much traffic.

After independence on 26 June 1960, with cooperation from Air France, the airline name was changed to **Madair**, and on 20 October 1961, it operated its first international route to Paris, with a Douglas DC-7C leased from the French airline, T.A.I. Service was also started to Réunion. At this time, the government held 20% of the capital, and Air France still 44%. The DC-3 fleet had grown to eight, and two larger 60-seat DC-4s were added, as the domestic network had now grown to 58 points, arguably one of the largest local service systems in the world. On 14 October 1962, the airline name reverted to the earlier one, because of the unfortunate English-language connotation of the latter.

In 1963, DC-4s were operating to the French Comoro Islands. Air Madagascar was beginning to assert itself, with the government and the Aeronautical Society of Madagascar each holding 30% of the shares. In July 1964, some of Air France's Boeing 707 flights to Paris were in full Air Madagascar livery, and in 1967, the airline acquired its own Boeing 707. More modern Piper Aztecs and Cherokee 300s replaced the veteran DH-89s for the local routes and a new DC-4 route opened to Johannesburg on 6 August 1967. Further progress was made in 1969, when two Boeing 737-200s developed a regional jet network from Antananarivo to Johannesburg, Nairobi, Dar es Salaam, Lourenço Marques, and the Comoros. By 1972, these jet airliners replaced the DC-4s to points in northern Madagascar.

On 7 November, having ceased operations to Johannesburg because of the apartheid-prompted sanctions from black Africa, Air Madagascar started service to Mauritius (where French was widely spoken), and in 1979, it was operating to European points with a Boeing 747-200B combi. The airline also continued to serve its country well domestically, as the slow pace of road-building still left many of the smaller communities without connections to the capital or to local towns. On 12 September 1997, the first of three ATR-42-320s arrived for service to 40 places, and in June 1999, the first Boeing 767-300ER was delivered to replace the 747. But expansion came at a price. Amid political unrest, including a fiercely contested election that was close to a civil war, Air Madagascar was bankrupt, and the ambitious international network had to be terminated. Air France's role had diminished to a mere 3% shareholding, and in June 2002, Lufthansa Consulting was contracted to put the airline's house in order. In November, under Malagasy law, at a Creditors' Conference, $40 million—half of the airline's debt—was waived.

From a purely business viewpoint, this would not make any financial sense. But in Madagascar, twice the size of Italy, with 12 million people, and with inadequate surface transport, airline service is indispensable to the economic well-being of the nation.

One of Air Madagascar's Boeing 767-300s. (McDonough)

To abandon its airline would have been the equivalent of cutting off the electricity because it did not make money.

The island Réunion lies 400 miles east of Madagascar, and unlike that country, its inhabitants had no strong wish for independence, and it remains a French Overseas Department. **Réunion Air Service** was founded by Gérard Ethève in 1975, and its first service, with a 40-seat HS-748, was to the island of Mayotte, which had, alone among the Comoro Islands, also resisted independence. The founder retired, for health reasons, in 1986, but returned in 1990, when, on 26 October, his operation was reconstituted as **Air Austral**. 34% of the shares were held by SEMATRA, a consortium of Réunion financial interests, 34% by Air France, and 32% by French banks. Before the end of the year, the first of three 115-seat Boeing 737s arrived to consolidate a growing network, augmented in 2000 by three 64-seat ATR-72-500s.

Much as adventurous British vacationers had "discovered" the Seychelles in the 1970s, the French, already determined to retain a vestige of their empire outposts in the Indian Ocean, also realized the tropical attractions of Réunion. On 28 June 2003, Air Austral leased a Boeing 777-200ER for a service to Paris, and this was so popular that in July 2005, Marseille was added as a new destination, and the route extended to Lyon in November. Toulouse was added in March 2007. These innovations were then, in April 2009, transcended by an even bolder addition to the network. Originating in Paris, an Air Austral Boeing 777-300ER flew, via Sydney, Australia, to Noumea, New Caledonia, another French overseas territory in the Pacific Ocean. Jet air transport has put this little island firmly on the world map. On 17 November 2009, this airline set a new record by ordering two Airbus A380s, each with no less than 840 economy seats.

To the west of Madagascar, another French colony, the Comoro Islands, also needed an airline to end its comparative isolation. In 1966, **Air Comores** started charter flights between the islands and to Dar es Salaam with two de Havilland DH-114 Herons and other leased aircraft, but ceased operations in 1974. When independence was achieved, as the Federal Islamic Republic of the Comoros, the airline was revived on 1 March 1975, with Air France holding 90% of the shares. The local government took over in 1977, by which time the fleet consisted of four old Douglas DC-4s and one Fokker F-27-2000 turboprop. Air Inter acquired a 20% shareholding in 1978, and by the late 1980s, the fleet included a Boeing 737-200 and a Fokker 50. But with inadequate traffic to sustain it, the airline ceased operations in September 1995. One of the islands, Mayotte, incidentally, determined to stay French. After a hiatus during which time the Comoros depended on Madagascar and Réunion for its air services, **Air Comores International** was formed in 2004 by the government, holding 60% of the shares, and Air Bourbon, an airline based in Lyon, France. Using Airbus A340-200s, a Boeing 737-400 and a 767-300ER, it aimed to create a new island paradise for French vacationers, as well as to ensure that the Comoro Islands were not longer cut off from the world.

Jet Travel Inspires a Nation

After the end of the Second World War, air service from Europe to the empire outposts in the Indian Ocean were of secondary importance to reestablishing trunk routes to Asia, Australia, the African colonies; and trans-Atlantic destinations. As mentioned above, the small islands had served their purpose during the war as staging points to Australia and the Pacific when Japan occupied southeastern Asia, but little thought was at first given to their development on the world air map. Before the Second World War, Mauritius was an even more remote outpost of the British Empire than most of the islands of the Pacific. It was off the main shipping routes and was not regarded as an essential refueling stop en route to the Antipodes. It had little industry except the production of sugar, which accounted for 90% of its exports. Its potential air travel market comprised a few government administrators and a few businessmen associated with the sugar industry.

Other than military operations, the first visit by a civil airliner was in 1945, when a French airline flew once a week from Madagascar to Réunion and Mauritius, its 15-seat Junkers-Ju 52/3m's taking nine hours each way. In 1947, Air France extended its African empire route to those islands, and in 1948, the British Skyways began a 9-seat Avro Lancastrian service from Nairobi to Mauritius; but this lasted little more than a year. In September 1952, the Australian QANTAS inaugurated the first trans-Indian Ocean service from Sydney to Johannesburg via the Cocos Islands and Mauritius. The Constellations took almost two days, but it was a start. South African Airlines joined QANTAS in 1957, and B.O.A.C. flew from London in 1962, with a turboprop Bristol Britannia, which took a whole day for the journey. Later in 1962, in Comet 4 jets, European passengers could reach Mauritius in 17 hours—at last in less than a day. In November 1966, Air France introduced Boeing 707s from Paris to Réunion and Mauritius via Djibouti. This remote piece of the old British Empire (later the Commonwealth) and with complete independence only two years away, Mauritius was, thanks to jet air transport, joining the mainstream of the world's air routes.

Unlike Air France, which valued its territorial footholds in the Indian Ocean, B.O.A.C. was not yet prepared to match French enterprise. **Air Mauritius** was founded by Amadée Maingard, but it was only a handling agent. Thus, when the island attained its independence on 12 March 1968, it still lacked an airline of its own, or even a British one. Owned 42% by the government, 20% by B.O.A.C. Associated Companies, and 20% by Air France, its beginning was not spectacular. The first service was with a 6-seat Piper Navajo leased from Air Madagascar, to Rodrigues, an island dependency 400 miles east of Mauritius, and to Réunion. But in November 1973, in addition to an Air France service to Paris, Air Mauritius joined the Jet Age by leasing a Super VC-10 from British Airways, still in the latter's colors, to open a route to London via Nairobi. In February 1975, it replaced the Navajo with a 20-seat DHC-6 Twin Otter, and on 7 November a Boeing 737 began service to Johannesburg via Antananarivo. It called at the Malagasi capital because it had cancelled service to South Africa in line with African sanctions against apartheid, and the refueling stop at Lourenço Marques was omitted in 1976, when a 156-seat Boeing 707 was deployed on the route.

On 1 May 1976, the London service, now with Boeing 707s, was more closely identified with Mauritius. On 1 October 1977, a leased aircraft flew in full Air Mauritius colors. In November 1981, a joint service with Air Madagascar linked Mauritius with Nairobi, the Comoros, and Réunion. Traffic was building to such an extent that in November 1984, a Boeing 747SP was leased from South African Airways, for nonstops to Paris en route to London, and to Rome and Zurich. Service to Singapore started in May 1985.

Gaining momentum, the former agrarian economy of Mauritius was changing. In addition to the sugar industry, Mauritius was developing manufacturing—it was gaining a reputation for wrist watch–making, a value-intensive product that was ideal for air freighting. And the tourism industry was growing by leaps and bounds, marked by five-star hotels at its beaches. In April 1988, the airline lease-purchased two Boeing 767-200ERs, and gained some unexpected publicity when the first one was delivered nonstop to Mauritius from Halifax, Nova Scotia: 8,727 miles, in 16 hours, 27 minutes, with 39 people on board. It was a world record for a twin-engined airliner. At the end of the year, a 48-seat ATR-42 replaced the Twin Otter on regional routes.

While Air Mauritius continued to expand, with new routes to Kuala Lumpur in May 1988, to Hong Kong in 1989, and to Perth in 1991, all with Boeing equipment, it apparently decided on a complete change in its airliner supplier. On 14 May 1994, the first of three 301-seat A340-300s was delivered, and during the next two years, more long-distance nonstop routes were opened to European points, to Cape Town, and to Melbourne. Two more A340s were delivered in the late 1990s, and at the end of 2006, the first of three A340-300E (extended-range) Airbuses heralded the retirement of the Boeing fleet, excellent service though they had given. At the regional level, larger 66-seat ATR-72-500s replaced the 42s, and and a 124-seat Airbus A319 was added for the route to Réunion. By 2009, Air Mauritius had a fleet of 10 large Airbuses, two ATR-72s, and three Bell 206B Jet Ranger helicopters for domestic flights on the island. It has been a truly remarkable story. Within five decades, a mere handling agent had grown to join the ranks of well-established intercontinental airlines. The new nation is in complete control, with the government and the Mauritian public or agencies holding all except 6% of the stock, still shared between Air France and Air India.

A prosperous airline is a credit to any country, old or new. Some comparison can be made with the success of Singapore Airlines, from an even smaller country, but with four times the population of Mauritius, and with a long tradition of experience as a major intercontinental hub before its independence. In the case of this Indian island nation, half the size of Rhode Island (smallest state of the U.S.A.), or about the size of an average English county, and with a population of only 1.2 million, the airline that has been the foundation of its prosperity had to start from scratch. Not only is Air Mauritius a Jet Age airline; Mauritius itself is a Jet Age nation.

Part Ten: Transitions

Chapter 51: The Third Jet Age Begins

The First Two Jet Ages

The first Jet Age began in 1952 with the introduction into service of the first pioneering (but short-lived) British de Havilland Comet 1 then of **Aeroflot**'s short-haul Tupolev Tu-104. It was consolidated in 1958, by the larger and far more successful four-engined "big jets" from the United States, followed by the western short-haul jets, beginning with the French Caravelle. At the same time, turboprop airliners were introduced by the Vickers Viscount, and again followed by larger turboprops from the U.S.A., Britain, and the Soviet Union. All the airliners of this generation had four or five-abreast seating.

The second Jet Age began in 1970, with the Boeing 747 widerbodied jets, followed by Douglas and Lockheed tri-jets. These long-haul twin-aisled types were followed by short-haul widebodied aircraft, led by Airbus, as the formerly over-fragmented European aircraft industry combined to create an organization that could match the volume and efficiency of the Americans. The Soviets were not far behind. By the 21st century, technical developments from Boeing, Airbus, and the Soviets had created further advances in size—as many as ten-abreast seating—and range—up to 5,000 miles or more. But increases in speed were limited as attempts to justify commercial supersonic operations were doomed to fail, partly because the "sonic boom" prevented all flights over land, and all operations were hopelessly uneconomic.

In almost every category, developed variants of initial airliner designs were invariably better than their predecessors, mainly because their bigger—"stretched"—fuselages produced better economics, judged by lower seat-mile costs and more seats sold. Jet engine efficiencies progressed beyond all expectations. By the 21st century, range was no longer a problem. Boeing (which acquired Douglas) and Airbus airliners could fly half-way around the world, and thus connect any pair of major cities with nonstop service.

During the closing decades of the 20th century, world-wide passenger traffic grew at an astonishing rate. In the 1960s and 1970s, annual increases averaged as much as 15% per year (doubling the total volume every five years). To cope with the ever-increasing demand, the airlines demanded—and were presented with—ever larger aircraft. By the 1990s Boeing 747-400s were carrying 450 passengers on long-haul routes, and in the more densely traveled routes in Japan, they were carrying up to 530. By the 21st century, to cope with this unremitting requirement for more seats on the world's major inter-city routes, an even bigger airliner was needed.

The airlines were handicapped by airport congestion at the big airports. They could not always answer the call for more flights. Growth was limited by the essential separation of landings and take-offs that were safely possible and legally permitted within a given time. Across the Atlantic, the New York-London route alone was generating two million passenger boardings every year. At New York's JFK Airport, the evening queue for take-offs often exceeded 30 big airliners. One solution was more airports. Newark grew in importance at New York; Gatwick, Stansted, Luton, and London City supplemented Heathrow in London; and Charles de Gaulle relieved Orly in Paris.

The solution, therefore, was larger aircraft, just as with previous generations of airliners. Market research studies confirmed this, and although Boeing looked carefully at the problem, theories were only put into practice by Airbus, which, in 2000, announced its A3XX project, soon to be confirmed as the double-decked A380. Each passenger cabin would seat at least 300 passengers—the combined equivalent of two Boeing 777s, the most efficient airliner then operating across the Atlantic.

A Changing Balance

Supporting the European constructor's confidence in the market potential was substantial traffic growth in the Middle East and Asia. During the first decade of the 21st century, the North Atlantic market was approaching saturation level, partly because almost everyone, businessman or tourist, who needed to fly, was already flying. Meanwhile, "east of Suez," the reverse was the case. In oil-rich countries in the Middle East, adequate rail and road transport had never been developed; air transport filled the need. This was not simply in established regimes. In the independent Emirates in the Persian Gulf, small fishing ports were transformed into centers of commerce, tourism, and wealth.

Around the Pacific Rim, the post-war Japanese economic miracle was spreading throughout neighboring countries. Hong Kong and Singapore, already rich entrepôts of trade, joined Tokyo and Osaka as major destination airports. South Korea was determined to match Japan in its economic growth and consequent airline service. Thailand's Bangkok challenged Hong Kong as the busy hub of southeast Asia. Indonesia, slow to catch up, was nevertheless a potentially major source of traffic.

Above all, China rose to become an industrial nation. It was slow to transform from a tightly controlled centralized administration under Communism. With few roads and a fragmented railroad system, a revolution in transport first took the form of an intensive railroad construction program to unify the nation, and to keep potential war-lords in check. Railroads revitalized China, to the envy of airline administrators, who, for some years, were neglected. But provincially based companies eventually replaced the ponderous state airline. China's billion-strong population was organized to perform an economic miracle that would outshine Japan's. Its airline industry grew to world stature, with individual companies ranking among the world's leaders (see Appendix).

The Growth of China

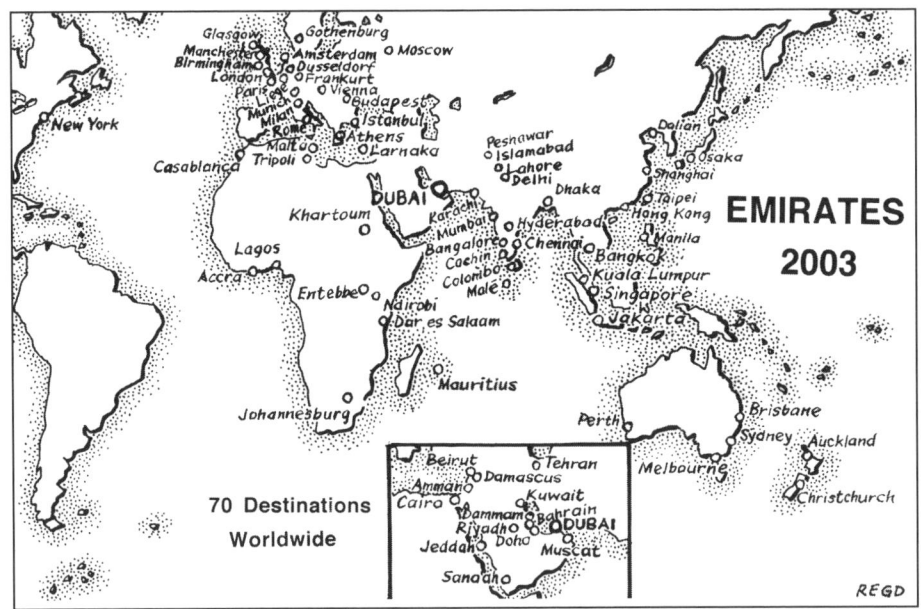

The growth of Emirates, the airline of Dubai, has, in the first decade of the 21st century, been phenomenal. By 2010, measured by annual passenger-miles, it was the sixth largest in the world, serving all continents except South America.

Meanwhile, also with a billion inhabitants, and with a large English-speaking element—second largest in the world—India had inherited much commercial acumen from the British. By the early years of the 21st century, and already the largest supplier of computer software in the world, it now has the world's biggest steel industry, and echoes China in large-scale automobile construction.

All these factors, from Dubai to Shanghai, have created an enormous demand for air travel. A glance at the departure board at London, Paris, or Frankfurt will reveal as many destinations to the East—British Airways alone serving half a dozen in India—as westward across the Atlantic. No longer is a trans-Atlantic inaugural the essential proof of a new airliner's performance and capability. It is now a service across Asia.

Airbus Chooses Size

When, therefore, in 2000, Airbus introduced its 500-seat Airbus A380, its order book looked quite different from the earlier conventional list of European and American airlines. The launch customer was from Dubai-based **Emirates**, which placed a large order, but conceded the privilege of the inaugural service to the second customer, **Singapore Airlines**.

The A380 started service on 25 October 2007, with a route to Sydney, Australia, with a single aircraft. The route, though long, could permit a 24-hour-day round-trip. The airline was able to report that the requirements were minimal. A route to London opened on 18 March 2008. Emirates started its trans-Atlantic A380 service on 1 August 2008, to New York, but soon switched to Toronto. Australia's **QANTAS** began trans-Pacific service,

Emirates matched its ambition for airline leadership by investing in the largest airliner. By 2010, it had in service or on order no less than ninety 500-seat Airbus A380s. It started service in 2008. (Davies; photo by Jay Selman)

First into service with the Airbus A380 was Singapore Airlines, to Sydney, on 25 October 2007. (Photo by Jean Marie Magendie)

Melbourne-Los Angeles, on 20 October of that year. Finally, **Air France** brought the big double-decker, with 530 seats, into New York on 13 November 2009. As yet, no passenger airline from the United States has ordered an A380.

Since the 1950s, no airframe manufacturer has also built its own engines. The 1960s and 1970s witnessed the decline of Great Britain as a leading builder of airliners, although it retained a place in the military field. But in spite of a setback that almost led to its demise, Rolls-Royce continued to build fine engines. They power many of the Airbuses and the Boeings, including the latest A380 and the 787, respectively. Also, when, late in the 1960s, Britain lost its founding 50% share of the Airbus, Hawker-Siddeley retained the responsibility of building the wings. Every Airbus wing is built in north Wales, near Chester then shipped by special barge to Toulouse, via the Gironde estuary, by barge up the Garonne river, and finally by truck. Most of the fuselage is built at Hamburg.

Boeing Chooses Technology

When Boeing decided not to pursue the idea of a double-decked 500-seater, and having discovered that there was no future for a supersonic airliner, it proposed at first the Sonic Cruiser, an aircraft that would fly at the threshold of the speed of sound. But this too had no future, and in 2005, Boeing announced its Model 787, the Dreamliner. It is only half the size of the A380. For the Seattle company, renowned for its engineering and developmental skills, this project has been truly revolutionary, for it represents the biggest advance in construction methods since metal replaced wood in the 1930s.

Designed from the start in three variants—this was also an innovation—the Dreamliner took to the limit the need for outsourcing subassemblies. Other manufacturers had done this before, but not to such an extent. The Dreamliner's wings and part of the fuselage are made in Japan, and another part of the fuselage is made in Italy. They are flown by huge freighters to Boeing's enormous plant at Everett, near Seattle, where the assembly of these parts demands microscopic accuracy.

The major revolutionary element is that about 80% of the aircraft, even the basic structure, is built with composite materials, not metal. Problems with the fasteners, then with the logistics of supplying components from around the globe, and then, in 2009, with de-lamination of the composite sections in the wing, delayed the program for even longer than in Airbus's experience with conflicting computer programs for hundreds of miles of wiring. From the outset, Boeing has won more than 800 orders, and such is the confidence in its integrity that it has lost only a few of these because of contractual delays in deliveries.

Finally, on 15 December 2009, the Boeing 787 Dreamliner made its first flight. It had lost two years in the delivery program, but the similarly sized Airbus A350 was still two years behind. Significantly, Boeing turned across the Pacific instead of across the Atlantic for its launching customers. No doubt related to its

QANTAS opened A380 service across the Pacific in 2008 (QANTAS photo credit: Sunil Gupta), and Air France across the Atlantic in 2009. (Air France photo credit: Jean Marie Magendie)

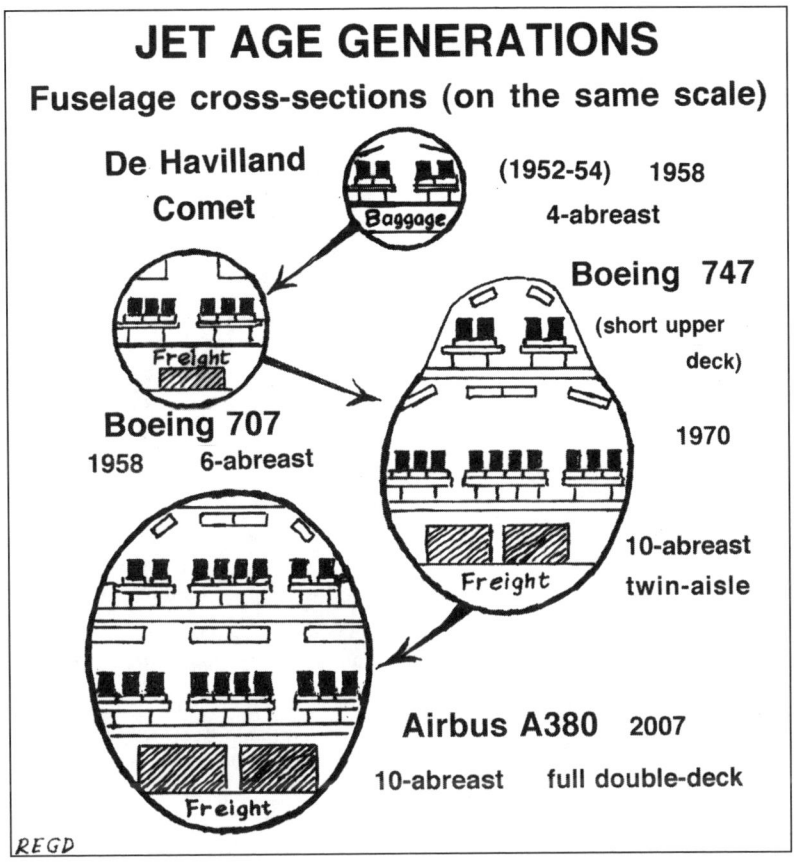

Within half a century, the size of the largest commercial airlines grew quickly to accommodate the demands of the air-traveling public. The Airbus A380 can carry, in all-economy class, as many passengers as ten Comets, five Boeing 707s, or two Boeing 747s.

manufacturing outsourcing, the first orders came from **All Nippon Airways** and **Japan Air Lines**.

On to a Thousand Seats?

The late Juan Trippe, intuitive head of the great Pan American Airways, followed a purchasing principle of ordering airliners that were twice the size of those of the previous generation. In 1958, the Boeing 707s were twice as big as the Douglas DC-7s and Lockheed Constellations; in 1970, the Boeing 747s were twice as big as the 707s. In 2007, the Airbus A380 is twice as big again as the 747. It aims to meet the market for air travel between all the world's major mega-cities. At least a dozen of them each have more than 12 million inhabitants. The world's urban population is growing two or three times as fast as in rural areas. In the year when the A380 entered service, the world crossed an epochal threshold. More than half of its population now live in urban areas.

The International Civil Aviation Organization (I.C.A.O.) statistics show that more than three-quarters of the world's international travelers fly between only 25 of the world's major airports. These are mostly the termini of long-haul intercontinental or transcontinental routes. This is the market for the next generation of airliners that will epitomize the Third Jet Age. When, in 1958, the Boeing 707s and DC-8s entered service, they were just in time to avoid complete congestion at places like New York, Paris, or Frankfurt. In 1970, the Boeing 747, with the smaller Douglas DC-10 and Lockheed TriStar, performed the same role. To satisfy the trans-Atlantic market today with 707s alone is unthinkable. By 2015, fleets of A380s will have at least relieved some of the congestion. One French airline has already ordered two of them, with all-economy seating for 830 passengers on the two decks. A "stretched" -900 is already projected to have 900 seats.

We may yet live to see a thousand-seat airliner in service. As with passenger ships decades ago, such an aircraft will eventually provide the essential transport links between the major international cities that now comprise a high percentage of the world's population. With them, the airlines will provide inexpensive tours to the far ends of the Earth, just as Londoners take a weekend in Florida, New Yorkers a quick visit to San Juan, or the Japanese to Bangkok or Auckland. Airline travel has become the safest mode of travel. In almost an entire decade between the disaster of the terrorist attacks in September 2001, there has been only one major fatal air accident in the entire United States. Airplanes have not made the world a safer place as a whole, but thanks to the technology and operational ingenuity of the aeronautics and airline industry, the world has truly become a smaller one.

Chapter 52: A New Competitor—High Speed Rail

Intra-City Helicopters

Since the earliest days of airline operations, access between city centers and airports has always been a problem. Aircraft were unable to land in downtown areas because of safety measures (the risk of a crash), noise levels (popular objections), and operations (the absence of adequate clearances, free from obstruction, for landing or take-off distances). Exceptions, such as Rio de Janeiro's airport, almost adjacent to the business center, were few.

After the Second World War, the advent of practical helicopter service attracted much interest, especially in the United States. A pre-war autogiro experiment by Eastern Air Lines in Philadelphia had demonstrated the advantages for rapid city-to-airport transit of mail. Further proving and survey flights suggested that helicopters could solve the problem of inconvenient access to airports. Early Bell and Sikorsky small helicopters were soon supplemented by 7-seat S-55s, larger S-58s, 20-seat S-61s, as well as twin-rotor Vertol 44s and 107s.

Though not termed as commuters, these scheduled airline companies served in a similar role, but they were limited in range, and so expensive to operate that they had to be subsidized by the government. The ceiling of $6 million per year was terminated altogether in 1965. This ended the prospects of continued expansion of a helicopter-based commuter industry, although support was provided for a few more years by major airlines such as Pan American, T.W.A., and United.

The pioneering airlines involved were **Los Angeles Airways (L.A.A.)** (mail in 1947, passengers, 1951–1968); Helicopter Air Services—renamed **Chicago Helicopter Services (C.H.A.)** in 1956—(mail in 1949, passengers, 1956–1965); **New York Airways (N.Y.A.)** (mail 1952, passengers, 1953–1979); and **San Francisco & Oakland Helicopter Airlines (S.F.O.)** (passengers 1961–1968). In 1954, National Airlines in Miami and Mohawk Airlines at Newark operated helicopters for a few months.

The tenure of this component of the air transport industry was eroded when, in the early 1960s, a series of accidents occurred, some in full view of New Yorkers. In 1965, N.Y.A. boldly started seven-minute Vertol 107 flights between JFK Airport and the rooftop of the Pan American Building astride Fifth Avenue. This came to an abrupt end in 1977 when a rooftop accident killed several people, including one from a falling rotor blade on the street below.

Other companies in the U.S.A. and elsewhere tried to revive helicopter interest, but these aimed merely to provide interconnection between city airports or short overwater routes. The loss-sustaining economics of regular helicopter services alone ensured that they would never again serve as commuter airlines.

Japan Creates High Speed Rail

Throughout the history of air transport, airlines have had little to fear from surface competition. Express trains across Europe and

In 1964, Japan did more than revolutionize railroad travel. The Shinkansen "Bullet" trains introduced a new form of transport, more than able to compete with airlines. (Davies)

America did not exceed maximum speeds of around 100 mph. In 1938, when the steam locomotive *Mallard* achieved the world speed record of 126 mph on a straight and level stretch of British track, it was done at great risk and with damage to the locomotive. Subsequently, inter-city average rail speeds have seldom exceeded 80 mph, and some airlines could be competitive over distances of only 100 miles.

That was until 1964, when a transportation event, little noticed across the world at first, marked the advent of a new form of surface transport. The Japanese may have been the first to realize that the key to high speed was not in the motive power of the locomotive but on the track. Their rail system (of narrower gauge than the world standard) was also a handicap. To cope with the huge traffic demand between the two mega-cities, Tokyo and Osaka, a new standard-gauge line was built to unprecedented standards of precision. Driving through tunnels and across long viaducts, it is close to being straight and level throughout its entire length. The Shin Kan-sen "Bullet" high-speed rail (H.S.R.) trains started service on 1 October 1964, covering the 321 miles in 3 hrs 10 m. They were the first in the world to exceed a point-to-point average speed of more than 100 mph. Units of 16 coaches, operating at a frequency of 10-minute intervals, were able to cope with the traffic demand of about 40 million passengers a year—a density beyond the capability of even the biggest airliners. Thanks to meticulous track maintenance, they are safe. By the early 2000s, these trains, including extended lines throughout Japan and operation at higher speeds and frequencies, have never killed a passenger.

A New Competitor—High Speed Rail

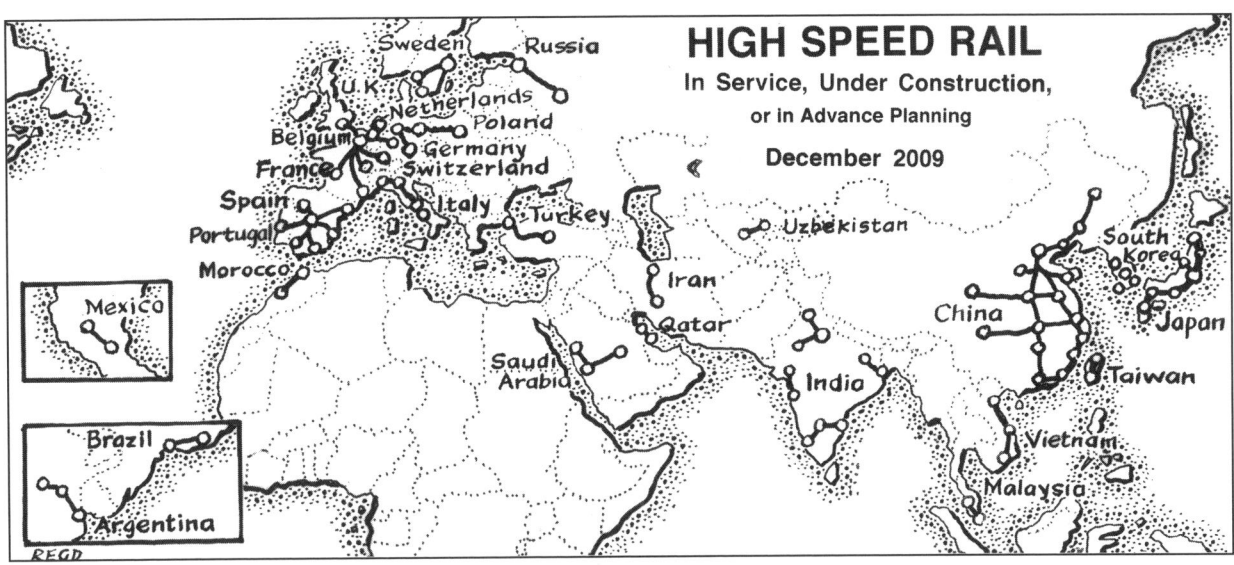

After Japan introduced H.S.R. in 1964, France's Train à Grande Vitesse, in 1981, began this new form of transport in Europe. By the end of 2009, fourteen countries were actively engaged in supplementing, or even replacing, airline services on short-haul routes, and as many others were making detailed route surveys for future construction. In 2010 the United States announced its intention to build several networks.

France Leads Europe into H.S.R.

In 1991, already with a tradition of excellent railroad service, France entered the ranks of high speed. The first Train à Grande Vitesse (T.G.V.) started H.S.R. service from Paris to Lyons on 27 September 1981. The domestic airline Air Inter's frequent air shuttle service immediately declined, and its domestic network considerably diminished, as, during the next few years, France led Europe into the H.S.R. age. The 500-mile Paris-Marseille rail journey is covered in three hours, at an average speed of almost 190 mph. T.G.V. traffic grew from a little more than a million passengers in 1981 to 128 million in 2008. Air services, formerly close to "on the hour, every hour," Paris-Brussels and Paris-Lyons, have ceased. Cross-Channel air routes, formerly dominating surface transport, now account for little more than one-fifth of the total traffic, thanks to the opening of the Channel Tunnel in 1994. *Eurostar* high-speed trains connect London with Paris in 2 hr 15 m, and Brussels in 1 hr 50 m.

T.G.V.s and other high speed trains have been introduced all across western Europe. In northern France, Lille has become the junction for the Cross-Channel route to Britain and for the Thalys trains to Belgium and the Netherlands. In Spain, the Alta Velocidad Española (AVE) system connects Madrid with every major provincial city. The head of Iberia, Spain's national airline, recognized the AVE as beneficial to the nation. He reflected, no doubt, that the short-haul routes of an airline are the money-losers, as a much shorter time is flown on their economical cruising segments than on long-haul arteries. Germany's ICE (Inter City Express) trains started to operate between Hamburg and Munich in 1991. The Frankfurt-Cologne line has eliminated air service on that route. Italy completed the all-important Rome-Milan link on 13 December 2008, with a three-hour journey time on its 380-mile Treno Alta Velocitá (T.A.V.) line. Ninety-two percent of the 50-mile section through the Apennines between Florence and Bologna is through tunnels. Switzerland, France, and Italy are combining to connect their H.S.R.s through longer and straighter tunnels through the Alps. On 17 December 2009, Russia's two largest cities, Moscow and St. Petersburg, were connected by H.S.R.—400 miles in less than four hours. Matching Japan's example, no T.G.V. train has yet killed a passenger in service.

By 2015, the whole of western Europe will enjoy H.S.R. travel between all the major city centers. Londoners will be able to reach Cologne by lunchtime, and Rome within a day. In the winter, Swedes will breakfast in Stockholm, lunch in the comfort

France's Train à Grande Vitesse. (Davies)

of the train in France, and dine in the warmth of Malaga. They will be safe, immune to delays through weather and free from airport congestion. For the first time since their beginning, the hub-based airlines of Europe will suffer from severe competition from this new form of transport.

Asia Follows Japan

A similar acceleration of railroad development has occurred in eastern Asia. On 1 April 2004, South Korea, and early in 2007, Taiwan, joined Japan with H.S.R. These countries have vied with Japan for technological advancement, particularly in high-technology products. South Korea's cars, for example, are to be seen all over the world, competing with Japan's, whose output has overtaken the former dominance of United States and European manufacturers. Taiwan televisions grace homes everywhere.

Yet these innovative achievements have been overtaken by the phenomenal growth of China, as this nation has, during the

TABLE 1: CURRENT HIGH-SPEED RAIL (H.S.R.) NETWORKS

Country	Name of System (or train)	First Service	First Route	Remarks and Subsequent Extensions
Japan	Shin Kan-sen ("Bullet" train)	1964	Tokyo-Osaka via Nagoya, Kyoto	3 levels of service: Hakari (limited stop); Kodama (additional stops) and Nozomi (non-stop). Subsequent extensions: North to Morioka, northeast to Niigata, southwest to Hiroshima, Fukuoka, and Kagoshima (2004).
France	T.G.V. (Train à Grande Vitesse)	1981	Paris-Lyon	Subsequent extensions: north to Lille (1993), west to (near) Le Mans (1989), south to Marseille (2001), east to Strasbourg (2008), and southwest to Montpellier. Paris-Lyon airline service terminated.
Germany	ICE (Inter-City Express)	1991	Mannheim-Stuttgart; Hannover-Würzburg	Additional routes: Frankfurt-Köln (2001), Hannover-Nürnberg, Berlin-Hamburg, Stuttgart-Ulm. Through trains, Paris-Stuttgart. Frankfurt-Köln airline service terminated.
Spain	AVE (Alta Velocidad Española)	1992	Madrid-Seville	Madrid-Barcelona (2008). Madrid-Valladolid, Madrid-Malaga (2009) open. Valencia, Alicante under construction.
Italy	E.T.R. 500	1992	Rome-Florence	Naples/Salerno, Turin "T" network completed. Rome-Milan (3 hrs) inaugurated 2009.
Belgium	Thalys	1996	Lille-Brussels (-Paris)	Extension to Antwerp and to Liège opened 2009. Belgian H.S.R. network complete. Paris-Brussels airline service terminated.
Sweden (Denmark)	X2000	2000	Stockholm-Copenhagen	Includes new bridge-tunnel across the Øresund (marginally high-speed).
China	C.R.H. (China Railway High Speed)	2003	Shenyang-Qinhuangdao	2,000-mile nationwide H.S.R. network planned, with emphasis on Beijing-Shanghai. Wuhan-Guangzhou (600 miles, 3 hours) opened Dec. 2009; Fuzhou-Xiamen also opened as first section of Shanghai-Guangzhou coastal route.
U.K.	T.G.V.	2003	Channel Tunnel-London (St. Pancras)	Opened 17 November 2007. London-Paris 2 hr 15 min, -Brussels 2 hrs. (Eurostar carries more people than all the airlines.)
South Korea	K.T.X. (Korea Train Express)	2004	Seoul-Taegu-Busan	Southwest branch planned to Kwangju.
Netherlands	Thalys	2005	(Antwerp)-Amsterdam	Extension of Paris-Brussels line to Antwerp-Amsterdam, 2010.
Taiwan	T.H.S.R. (Taiwan H.S.R.)	2007	Taipei-Kaohsiung	Opened December 2006. Several airlines terminated.
Turkey	Italian	2009	Ankara-Istanbul	Ankara-Eskisehir opened 13 March 2009.
Russia	Siemens	2009	Moscow-St. Petersburg	Possible extension to Nijni Novgorod; also Omsk-Novosibirsk.

TABLE 2: FUTURE HIGH-SPEED RAIL (H.S.R.) NETWORKS

Country	Name of System (or train)	First Service	First Route	Remarks and Subsequent Extensions
Portugal	AVE	(2010)	(Madrid)-Lisbon planning	Lisbon-Oporto planned (extension of Spanish AVE network).
Switzerland	Various	(2010)	—	New alpine tunnels under construction to connect France and Germany with Italy.
Argentina			Buenos Aires-Rosario-Córdoba	Buenos Aires-Mar del Plata. Argentina may open the first H.S.R. service in the Americas.
Mexico			Mexico City-Guadalajara	Via Queretaro, Irapuato.
Brazil			São Paulo-Rio de Janeiro	Could overtake Argentina as first H.S.R. in the Americas.
Morocco			Casablanca-Rabat	
Poland	Siemens		Warsaw-Lódz	High-speed trials, 2009.
Malaysia			Kuala Lumpur-Singapore	
Vietnam			Hanoi-Ho Chi Minh City	Hue-Da Nang.
India				Planned routes: Bombay-Ahmedabad; Calcutta-Patna; Madras-Bangalore-Cochin; New Delhi-Jaipur; New Delhi-Amritsar.
Saudi Arabia			Mecca-Jeddah-Medina	Planned trans-Arabia route to Riyadh.
Iran			Teheran-Qum-Isfahan	
Egypt			Cairo-Alexandria	
Czech Republic			Prague-Brno-Ostrava	
United States			Several	

early years of the 21st century, systematically created an industrial base that challenges the might of the United States.

China Takes the Lead

Transport in China was revolutionized during the second half of the 20th century. The fragmented railroad system was modernized, enlarged, and coordinated so that every provincial capital was linked with the others and with the capital, Beijing. Moving into the 21st century, the railroads, already improving in speeds and service, have taken a giant step forward. As a preliminary test, China started its first high speed rail line, from Qinhuangdao to Shenyang (a segment of a future trunk line from Beijing to Harbin) on 1 July 2003. Far more significant, as part of a complete expansion, overhaul, and improvement of its entire railroad network, it has accelerated its H.S.R. construction program. On 26 December 2009, it opened a 600-mile line from Wuhan to Guangzhou, a distance that the frequent trains cover in three hours—averaging more than 200 mph. This is about half of the projected north-south Beijing-Guangzhou trunk line. Also in December, sections of a new coastal route from Shanghai to Guangzhou opened, and work is proceeding with high-speed lines to connect most of the major cities of China, including Beijing-Shanghai. A 2,000-mile nationwide network of high-speed lines is planned to be completed by 2012.

Starting in 2003, China's program for H.S.R. will, by 2012, be the longest in the world and, at more than 200 mph, be the fastest. (CSR Sifang Locomotive & Rolling Stock Company)

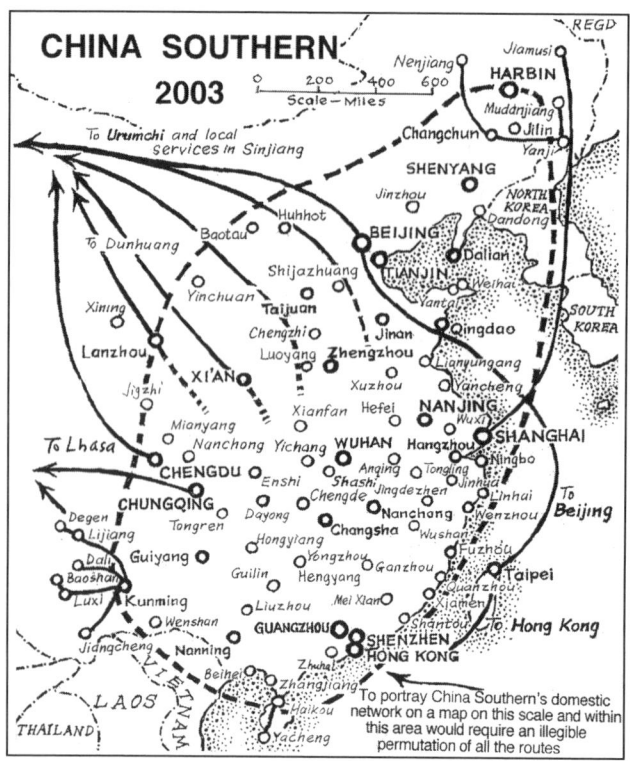

This railroad revolution will undoubtedly intrude into some of the main inter-city air routes. But as this map indicates, China's larger airlines already blanket the map with webs of routes.

Most of the cities shown on the map (left) have populations of more than a million, several of them multi-million. China Southern is one of four large airlines in China. China Eastern, Cathay Pacific, and Air China have similar networks. As the Chinese economy grows, the airlines are also expanding rapidly, but on many inter-city routes, this is slowed by the introduction of H.S.R. (below).

Chapter 53: A New Age Beckons

A Solid Airline Foundation Nevertheless

Similar situations of rail versus air occur in many industrialized countries of the world, where large cities are no more than 500 miles apart. The threat to the airlines is illustrated by the map and the tabulation in the previous chapter. By the end of 2009, 30 countries were operating, building, or in the advanced stage of route planning High Speed Rail. In Europe, a continent-wide network, "seamless" with other railroads everywhere, will substantially erode the traffic on the main-line domestic and cross-border routes of the airlines.

However, during the six decades of progress since the Jet Age began in 1952, the airline industry, and the manufacturers who supplied the tools of their trade, have progressed beyond all expectations. The efficiency of engines, for example, has been almost unbelievable. The time-between-overhauls (T.B.O.s) of the Rolls-Royce Dart turboprops of the infant jet years was around one thousand hours. The big turbofans that propel the Boeings and Airbuses of the 21st century will turn for 15,000 hours (more than four years of average service by the major airlines) before overhaul. The efficiency of the manufacturing process has also improved, in aerodynamics, structures, and systems. Aluminum has been supplemented by lighter-weight titanium of better strength and, in the 1990s, by the selective use of composite materials. This process was at first for nonstructural components, but the Boeing 787 is 80% composite. The longevity is truly impressive. Airliners coming off the production lines in 2010 will still be in service (and paid for) in 2050.

Operationally, the airlines thus serve the public magnificently. They have taken advantage of these technological advances and translated them collectively into a better deal for their passengers. The cost of travel today, related to average income levels, has declined considerably. Most of the airlines that offer lower fares are the most financially successful.

The invention of computers coincided with the birth of the Jet Age, and has been of tremendous benefit, especially in manufacture. The Boeing 777 was designed entirely by computer, and has had fewer problems than any other airliner. The airlines also put computers to good effect in administration, saving thousands of staff numbers, especially in marketing. Expensive downtown ticket offices are now a memory. A printed ticket is now almost a collector's item, as printed timetables are already.

Above all, the level of safety has exceeded all predictions, even by authorities such as the Flight Safety Foundation, which has been understandably cautious. Although all airline disasters are invariably caused by people: pilot misjudgment, traffic controller's error, hijacking or terrorist action, faulty maintenance, or even negligent manufacture the human element in the airline industry of the 21st century is superbly disciplined. As mentioned above, in the United States, since the terrorist attack in September 2001, almost an entire decade has passed with only two fatal crashes (one by a commuter aircraft).

The Other Side of the Coin

Improvements in technology, service, and safety during the Jet Age have thus been truly commendable. But the airlines' inexorable traffic growth has created its own problems for their clientele. Empty seats on the airliners are now rare. Passengers not only feel cramped on the flights, but their processing at airports has become arduous. Exacerbated by the need for additional security precautions (following the emergence of suicide bombing as a constant terrorist threat), passenger check-in times are now as long as three hours. Wheel-chairs appear more frequently to avoid long walking tours of the airports. In most industrialized countries (the U.S.A. excepted), an air journey of up to 400–500 miles can take longer than by taking a train.

The problem facing air transport today is thus not in the air but on the ground. The airliners cannot fly any faster, nor can the manufacturers or the operators make them any more comfortable, except at the expense of economy and therefore higher fares. The outstanding success of bargain-fare airlines in the United States, Europe, southeast Asia, and Brazil (and the failure of most of the airlines that have emphasized luxury) has demonstrated what the mass market will prefer and accept. At the airports, however, passengers on the A380s and the Dreamliners will still have to negotiate the labyrinthine corridors, hallways, and stairs, only occasionally relieved by elevators, escalators, and traveling walkways or trains. Even worse is that if their final destination is distant by only a few miles from the airport, interconnection—or intermodality, to use the preferred term today—is seldom convenient. In few major cities of the world are local bus services, much less local subway services, to be found at short walking distances from the airline baggage claim carousels.

Intermodal Convenience

There are some notable exceptions. London's Heathrow Airport has three underground stations on the Piccadilly Line and there is a 20-minute fast train service to downtown. Gatwick's on-site train station is only half an hour from the city. In Paris, Charles de Gaulle Airport has a T.G.V. station for immediate connection with the rest of France. Passengers arriving at Frankfurt can begin travel to other German cities simply by walking down an escalator to the railroad platforms. It is the same at Zurich if the destination is Lucerne or Berne.

In complete contrast is the situation in the United States, where convenient intermodal transfer is rare. The capital, Washington, D.C., has the best and the worst. Reagan National Airport has its own Metrorail station, only minutes away from downtown or the suburbs. Dulles International Airport is in direct contrast. Passengers with baggage are faced with little choice but a near-monopoly $60 taxi service to cover the 30-mile trip to the city center.

Cooperation, not Competition

During the three Jet Ages reviewed in this book, progress has been possible because of technology advances in airliner design, and engine power and efficiency. Traffic expansion has stimulated continually increasing capacity requirements, thus successively bigger airliners. Advocacy of even higher frequencies of flights ignores the problem of airport congestion, air traffic control limitations, and traveling convenience at all the busiest airports in the world. These airports will be unable to accept operations of any new airliners larger than a stretched A380. And with ever-increasing passenger travel demand, a new solution to cope with the growth will be required.

Ninety Percent on the Ground

Back in 1929, Clement Keys, one of the early American airline promoters, declared "90% of aviation is on the ground." This wise observation is as true today as it was then, although the basic reasons are different. Nevertheless, as the erosion into short-haul airline operations by H.S.R. has already demonstrated, the statement may be the key to the long-term future of air transport.

Except for long-distance trans-ocean or transcontinental travel requirements, airlines should no longer concentrate on direct competition with surface transport on the ground, either from high speed roads or high speed trains. Cooperation should be the main criterion for long-term development.

Intermodality of transport systems must be increasingly recognized as the ultimate solution to solving the problem of moving the world's population, estimated to reach eight billion within the Third Jet Age. People will be increasingly more affluent, and anxious to see the world—the whole world—in which we live. The airlines will not be able to do it alone.

Limitations of Market Forces

As in other industries, excessive competition can sometimes be self-destructive. This has happened in the past and was evident when the dust had settled after the unrestricted deregulation in the United States in the late 1970s. It was a case of survival of the fittest, with no credit given to past accomplishments. Those that survived owed much to the victims of "market forces" at the time. Many airlines that contributed so much to the foundation of the industry—Pan American, Eastern, Western, Braniff, and others—are now only names in history books such as this one. Pioneers such as the Belgian SABENA and the Brazilian VARIG are gone. Northwest Airlines, Continental, and the famous Dutch K.L.M. no longer control their own fates. Delta merged with Northwest Airlines in 2008, being granted a single operative certificate by the F.A.A. on 29 October of that year. Similarly, United and Continental merged to form United Continental Holdings on 1 October 2010.

Throughout the history of airlines worldwide, few have made sustained genuine profits by normal accountancy standards. In the United States, mail subsidies, direct or indirect, ensured positive balance sheets until the 1950s, after which these were maintained by mandatory fare increases—until deregulation in 1978. Elsewhere in the world, they were upheld by government subsidy for prestige purposes, or as essential public utilities. In Canada, Great Britain, and many countries in Latin America, airline ownership by a railroad or a shipping company, or even a bus company, was not against the law.

A curious paradox is that, back in 1934, the United States government turned its back on intermodal transport systems. At that time, there was a good reason: conflict of interest. The automobile manufacturing giant General Motors had substantial shareholdings, amounting to effective control, of almost half the U.S. airline industry. The Pennsylvania Railroad also had shares, as did a smaller railroad in New England, and several shipping companies had interests in international airlines.

Three-quarters of a century later, for a different reason, there is now an advantage for air and surface modes to collaborate once again. If other transport interests can be overcome (for example, long-delayed introduction of high speed rail in the United States), the airlines could be rescued from jeopardy by surface transport.

The Third Jet Age, or generation, reviewed in Chapter 51, is destined to last for several decades. If there is to be another generation, the resources of technology in the manufacture of airliners and their operation by the airlines are now severely limited. In-flight competition is reduced to the number of channels on the video screen, or subtle changes in lighting for the twilight hours. Experienced aviation aficionados find difficulty in identifying individual airliner types. Improvements in design, speed, and comfort have thus reached a stage whereby "a plane—any plane—is a plane."

The Need for Intermodal Transport

Airport congestion is already at saturation levels at many of the busiest international or intercontinental hubs. Further improvements will depend on cooperative activity between different modes of transport, highlighted by increased accessibility to the airports, improved interchangeability between the airlines and surface transport, and better airport-related surface transport itself. In many countries of the world, this problem is being energetically addressed—but not, as yet, in the United States. Air France and the T.G.V. sell tickets to each other. British Airways has a 10% shareholding in the cross-Channel Eurostar high-speed train.

The H.S.R. revolution in railroad practice depended not on the vehicles, but on the track. Existing railroad stations are compatible with any trains, high speed or not. In an analogous situation, the airliner "track" is the air. But with airport congestion already a problem at the airports, air traffic control has to be extremely efficient and disciplined to avoid disasters. And the density of traffic will limit the scope of further expansion.

The Lufthansa Airport Express in 1988. (Davies)

A Fourth Jet Age

Measurable improvements in air travel in the future can be achieved only by innovative cooperation on the ground. This author remembers a journey in 1988 from Washington to Cologne, when the Lufthansa connecting rail journey from Frankfurt was a coupon on the air ticket. Airlines should be in partnership with the railroads and be able to code-share with them. When airline passengers everywhere can disembark from an aircraft and walk to a railroad or subway platform (as in London, Zurich, Frankfurt, and Washington's Reagan National Airport today), and travel onwards using the same ticket, we may witness the beginning of a new era. When airlines and railroads cease to compete, but energetically cooperate, and the policy of intermodality is universally accepted, this could signal the advent of a Fourth Jet Age.

Appendix 1: Selected Aircraft Specifications

(A) Jets

"Normal" range refers to airline routes flown, including worst weather conditions. "Typical" seating refers to average mixed class. "No. Built" column omits some aircraft still in production in 2009.

Manufacturer and Model	No. of Engines	Length (ft)	Max Weight (x1,000 lb)	Cruise Speed (mph)	Normal Range (miles)	Typical Seating	First Service Year	First Service Airline	No. Built	Remarks
Boeing										
707-120	4	145	248	571	3,100	143	1958	Pan Am	} 1,010	First sustained long-range jet airliners. Fuselage width for all models to the -737 and the -757.
-320		153	336	607	4,000	135	1962	Pan Am		
-720		137	234	610	5,200	130	1960	United		
727-100	3	153	170	585	1,500	129	1964	United	} 1,832	World's first tri-jet airliner into service.
-200		173	191	585	2,500	168	1967	Northeast		
737-100	2	94	111	575	1,150	104	1968	Lufthansa	30	
200		100	128	575	2,130	130	1968	United	1,095	737-600, -900 still in production. More than 6,350 already delivered. Several variants through to the -900.
300		110	138	491	3,500	138	1984	Southwest/USAir		
700		110	171	515	3,750	138	1998	Southwest		
747-100	4	232	735	555	6,100	366	1970	Pan Am	} 643	First wide bodied twin-aisled "Jumbo" jet. Still in production. 1,400 already delivered.
-200		232	735	555	7,900	393	1971	K.L.M.		
-400		232	875	567	7,200	416	1989	Northwest		
757-200	2	155	255	528	4,500	200	1963	Eastern	} 1,050	(No 757-100)
-300		179	278	528	3,400	242	1999	Condor		
767-200	2	159	395	530	7,300	181	1982	United		Still in production. More than 970 already delivered.
-300		180	412	530	6,900	218	1986	Japan Air		
-400 ER		201	450	530	5,600	245	2000	Continental/Delta		
777-200	2	209	545	554	5,200	305	1995	United		Still in production. More than 850 already delivered.
-300ER		242	775	554	7,900	305	2004	Air France/JAL		
787-8	2	186	486	554	8,500	237		All Nippon		(Entry into service 2011)
Douglas										
DC-8-10	4	151	273	542	4,300	170	1959	United/Delta	} 294	
-30		151	315	592	5,970	170	1960	Pan Am		
-61		187	328	580	5,300	250	1967	United	88	Re-engined DC-8-60s still in service as DC-8-70s.
-62		157	350	580	5,800	180	1967	Braniff	61	
-63		187	580	580	5,800	250	1968	Seaboard	104	Total of 547 DC-8s built.

Manufacturer and Model	No. of Engines	Length (ft)	Max Weight (x1,000 lb)	Cruise Speed (mph)	Normal Range (miles)	Typical Seating	First Service Year	First Service Airline	No. Built	Remarks
Douglas (cont.)										
DC-9-10	2	104	91	560	1,700	80	1965	Delta	137	⎫
-30		119	108	560	1,700	105	1967	Eastern	662	⎬ Total, all DC-9s, 895 built
-50		133	121	560	1,700	114	1975	Swissair	96	⎭
-80		148	140	560	1,700	142	1980	Swissair	1,191	Re-designated as MD-80 series
-95		124	110	504	1,600	106	1999	Air Tran	156	Later designated as Boeing 717-200
Convair										
880	4	129	193	560	3,000	110	1960	Delta	65	
990	4	139	255	580	2,300	120	1962	American	37	Also named Coronado
Lockheed										
L-1011-1	3	178	430	570	3,000	250	1972	Eastern	⎫ 250	
L-1011-500		164	510	570	5,000	230	1979	British	⎭	Also named TriStar
Airbus										
A300	2	176	347	560	2,500	250	1975	Air France	447	A300-600 had more seats, more range
A310		153	313	560	3,250	214	1983	Swissair	255	
A320	2	123	150	525	2,300	150	1988	Air France		Also A318, A319 smaller, and A321 larger versions. 4,400 delivered by 2009.
A-330	2	209	510	537	5,500	335	1994	Air Inter		300 delivered by end 2009
A340	4	209	610	584	8,500	295	1992	Lufthansa/Air France	246	
A 340-5/600	4	209	820	584	10,000	400	2002	Emirates		120 delivered by end 2009
A-380	4	239	1,250	580	9,400	525	2007	Singapore		World's first fully double-decked airliner
Great Britain										
D.H.Comet 1	4	93	105	490	1,500	36	1952	B.O.A.C.	20	World's first commercial jet airliner
Comet 4	4	112	162	503	3,225	81	1958	B.O.A.C.	76	Total of 114 Comets built. All types.
Vickers VC-10	4	159	312	580	4,000	115	1964	B.O.A.C.	54	Still operating for R.A.F. in 2000s
Trident	3	114	142	610	2,700	115	1964	B.E.A.	117	Trident 3 (150 seats) longer fuselage
BAC One Eleven	2	93	79	548	1,400	89	1963	B.U.A.	247	-500 had (119 seats) longer fuselage
BAe 146	4	93	93	498	1,800	82	1983	DanAir	387	Developed as the Avro RJ
France										
Caravelle 1	2	105	96	480	780	80	1959	Air France	224	World's first rear fuselage–engined airliner
Series V1-R	11	105	110	500	1,000	80	1961	United	56	Longer fuselaged Caravelle
France-Great Britain										
Concorde	4	202	408	1,350	4,000	100	1976	Brit. Airways/ Air France	14	Number built=deliveries only not inc. prototypes/pre-production; 21 total.
Netherlands										
Fokker F-28	2	89	65	528	1,350	65	1969	Braathens	241	World's first feeder jet
Fokker F-100	2	116	95	525	1,500	107	1988	Swissair	283	

Manufacturer and Model	No. of Engines	Length (ft)	Max Weight (x1,000 lb)	Cruise Speed (mph)	Normal Range (miles)	Typical Seating	First Service Year	First Service Airline	No. Built	Remarks
Brazil										
Embraer										
145	2	98	49–53	515	1,200	50	1996	Express Jet	1000	Also built in China by Harbin
170	2	103	83	530	2,000	70	2004	LOT		Still in production, 1100 by 2009. 170 developed as 190 (94 seats).
Canada										
Bombardier										
CRJ 200	2	88	53	503	1,500	50	1992	Lufthansa	1021	Later models in production
U.S.S.R.										
Tupolev										
Tu-104	2	127	167	480	1,650	50	1956	Aeroflot	210	World's first <u>sustained</u> jet services. Numbers built include variants.
Tu-124	2	100	83	480	780	50	1962	Aeroflot	112	Shorter version of Tu-104
Tu-134	2	115	97	500	1,250	72	1967	Aeroflot	852	Single-aisle, 4-abreast (c.f. DC-9)
Tu-154	3	157	198	580	1,770	164	1972	Aeroflot	1,015	Single-aisle, 6-abreast (c.f. B737)
Tu-144	4	216	397	1,500	2,200	70	1975	Aeroflot	16	Short-lived supersonic, 20 built (c.f. Concorde)
Ilyushin										
IL-62	4	174	357	560	4,000	165	1967	Aeroflot	292	Similar design to British VC-10
1L-86	4	195	459	540	1,500	350	1980	Aeroflot		Soviet wide-bodied airliner.
Yakovlev										
Yak-40	3	67	34	340	300	32	1968	Aeroflot	1,011	World's first tri-jet feeder jet.
Yak-42	3	119	125	400	1,320	120	1980	Aeroflot	106	
Antonov										
An-124	4	227	893	500	2,700	—	1982	Aeroflot	58	Known as Ruslan. Freight. (Typical load: 150 tons)
An-225	6	276	1,323	500	5,000	—	2002	Antonov Airlines	1	Known as Mriya (Dream). World's largest fixed-wing aircraft. Freight. (Typical Load: 200 tons)

(B) Turboprops

Manufacturer and Model	No. of Engines	Length (ft)	Max Weight (x1,000 lb)	Cruise Speed (mph)	Normal Range (miles)	Typical Seating	First Service Year	First Service Airline	No. Built	Remarks
Great Britain										
Vickers Viscount										
V700	4	82	65	312	1,700	44	1953	B.E.A.		World's first turboprop airliner.
V800	4	86	72	312	1,200	60	1957	B.E.A.		Larger version of V700.
Avro 748	2	67	46	280	1,000	40	1960	Skyways Coach-Air	380	Avro (A.V.Roe) became HS-(Hawker-Siddeley). Also 89 produced in India.
Handley-Page Dart Herald	2	75	43	270	600	48	1961	Jersey	50	
Bristol Britannia										
100	4	114	175	360	3,000	90	1957	B.O.A.C.	85	"The Whispering Giant"
300	4	124	185	360	3,500	130	1957	Aeron. de Mex.	105	
Shorts										
330	2	58	23	218	1,000	30	1976	Time Air	136	
360	2	71	27	250	740	36	1985	Suburban	164	Known as the Sherpa.
France–Italy										
Avions de Transport Regional										
ATR 42	2	74	42	340	1,000	48	1985	Air Littoral		Still in production. 800 by 2009.
ATR 72		89	45	315	900	70	1989			
France										
Nord 262	2	63	23	220	200	27	1964	Air Inter	110	
Netherlands										
Fokker										
F-27	2	77	42	260	350	40	1958	West Coast	586	F-27s also built under license in U.S.A. by Fairchild, also the larger F-227s.
F-50		83	46	280	1,200	50	1983	DLT	213	Larger version of F-27.
U.S.A.										
Lockheed L-188 Electra	4	105	116	405	2,500	98	1959	Eastern	170	Still in service, until the 2000s.
Convair CV 580	2	82	53	340	650	52	1964	Frontier	170	Turboprop variant of the Convair 240/340/440 series. (Total built includes CV600, etc.)
Japan										
Nihon YS-11	2	86	54	300	700	60	1965	Toa Airways	182	Largest of the twin-engined turboprops.
Spain										
Casa 212	2	53	17	220	820	24	1975	Pelita Air Service	478	Popular name: Aviocar
Casa-Nurtanio CN 235	2	70	35	360	1500	44	1978	Merpati Nusantara	28	Number built: civil only

Appendix 1

Manufacturer and Model	No. of Engines	Length (ft)	Max Weight (x1,000 lb)	Cruise Speed (mph)	Normal Range (miles)	Typical Seating	First Service Year	First Service Airline	No. Built	Remarks
Canada										
De Havilland/Bombardier										
DHC-6	2	52	12	165	1,000	19	1966	(Ontario Dept. Lands)	844	Worldwide versatility.
DHC-7	4	81	44	240	750	50	1978	Rocky Mtn.	113	
DHC-8	2	73	36	320	1,200	50	1984	NorOntair		Still in production (1,000 +).
Canadair										
CL-44	4	137	210	400	5,000	160	1964	Loftleidir	37	Swing-tail version of Bristol Britannia.
U.S.S.R.										
Ilyushin IL-18	4	174	135	390	2,750	100	1959	Aeroflot	585	Known as Moskva. Equivalent to Bristol-Britannia or Lockheed 1011.
Antonov										
An-10A	4	112	122	420	745	90	1959	Aeroflot	600	Number built includes 300 (cargo) AN-10A.
AN-24	2	79	46	280	375	48	1962	Aeroflot	1,000	Equivalent to Fokker F-27.
AN-12	4	109	134	360	1,900	—	1965	Aeroflot	300	
AN-22	4	180	550	380	3,000	—	1968	Aeroflot	55	Cargo only. 8 propellers.
Czechoslovakia										
Let 410	2	47	14	230	330	19	1971	Aeroflot	1,138	
China										
Harbin Y-12	2	49	12	155	830	17	1985			In production.

Appendix 2: Notable Events and Facts

	Date	Event or Fact	Country	Page
FIRSTS (NS = non-sustained)				
	17 Dec 1903	The Wright brothers' flight	U.S.A.	1
	15 Mar 1913	Flight by a transport aircraft	Russia	1
	1 Jan 1914	Scheduled airline service (NS)	U.S.A.	1–3
AIRLINE SERVICES				
Europe	11 Mar 1918	Military airline service (NS)	Austro-Hungary	2
	5 Feb 1919	Deutsche Luft Reederei	Germany	3
N. America	15 May 1918	U.S. Post Office (NS) (Mail)	U.S.A.	7
	15 Oct 1919	Aeromarine (NS)	U.S.A.	8
	17 Apr 1926	Western Air Express	U.S.A.	9 (Chart)
S. America	12 Oct 1919	TAG (NS)	French Guiana	5
	5 Dec 1919	SCADTA	Colombia	6
Africa	May 1920	LARA (NS)	Belgian Congo	5
Oceania	3 Nov 1921	QANTAS	Australia	6
Asia	1922	Royal Aeronautical Service	Siam (Thailand)	6 (Chart)
Antarctica	26 May 1989	Aerovias DAP	Chile	370
OTHER FIRST SERVICES				
	22 Nov 1935	Trans-ocean (excluding Zeppelin)	U.S.A.	15
	29 Jul 1950	Turboprop (NS)	U.K.	37
	5 May 1952	Jet (NS)	U.K.	39
	6 Apr 1953	Turboprop	U.K.	37
	5 Sep 1956	Jet	Russia	42
	5 May 1959	Short-haul jet	France	56
	21 Jan 1976	Supersonic (NS)	France–U.K.	114
	22 Jan 1970	Wide-body	U.S.A.	108
	25 Oct 2007	Full-length double-deck jet	Singapore	409
	4 Nov 1966	Automatic landing	U.K.	195
	1937	Hajj flight to Mecca	Egypt	16
	19 Jul 1961	In-flight movie	U.S.A.	166
	Jul 1959	No-reservations shuttle	Brazil	313
	1 Feb 1985	ETOPS (First FAA-approved)	U.S.A.	166

AIRPORT RECORDS

- **Furthest north:** Longyearbyen, Spitzbergen, p. 228–229
- **Furthest south:** Base Teniente Marsh, King George Island, Antarctica, p. 370
- **Highest altitude:** Qamdo Bangda, Tibet, 14,219 ft. (formerly Potosí, Bolivia, 13,600 ft., p. 359)
- **Lowest altitude:** Atyrau, Kazakhstan, -72 ft.
- **Shortest commercial runway:** Saba, Netherlands Antilles, 1,300 ft., pp. 332, 333p
- **Only constantly moving airstrip:** Tasman Glacier, New Zealand, p. 292

MISCELLANEOUS

- **Oldest airlines in continuous service until present day:** K.L.M. from May 1920, p. 4; AVIANCA from 19 Sep 1921 (SCADTA until 1942), p. 6; QANTAS from 2 Nov 1922, p. 6
- **Shortest route (two miles):** Orkney Islands, p.196
- **Worst fatal tragedy:** K.L.M.–Pan American, Tenerife, 27 March 1977, p. 215
- **Last service by large flying boat:** Ansett to Lord Howe Island, 1974, p. 286
- **Airline route crossing four continents:** Saudia, Jeddah–New York, p. 787p

Appendix 3: Monetary Conversion from 1940 to 2010 (US$) (2010 conversion = $1.00)

$1.00 in	is equivalent in 2010 to
1940	15.58
1950	9.05
1960	7.37
1970	5.62
1980	2.65
1990	1.67
2000	1.27

Source: Consumer Price Index.

Appendix 4: The Five Freedoms of the Air

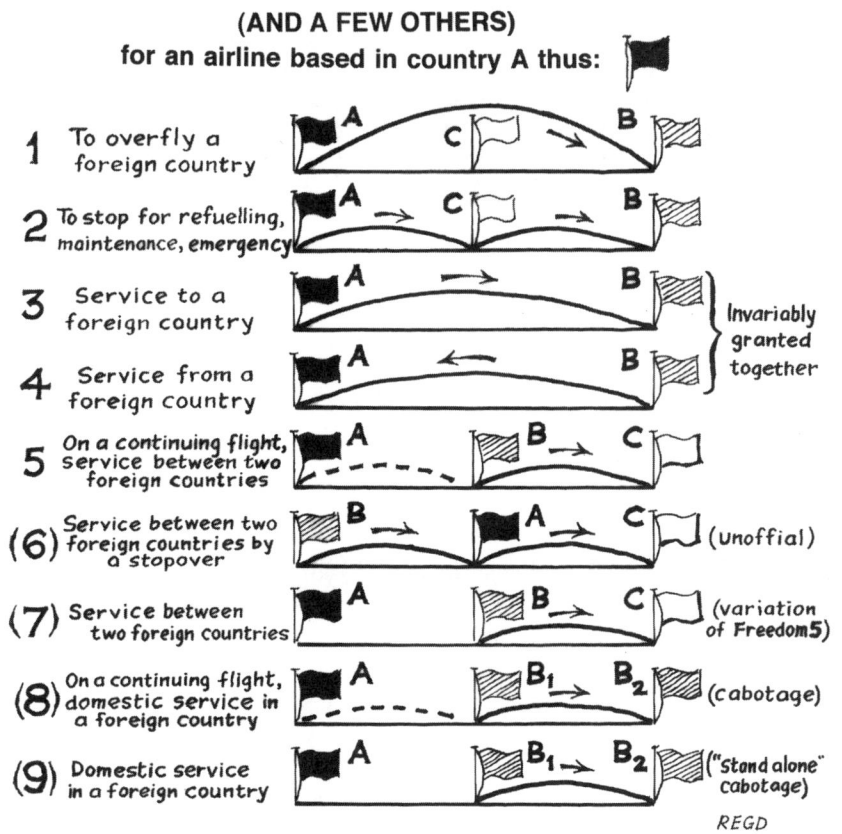

Appendix 5:
The World's Largest Airlines

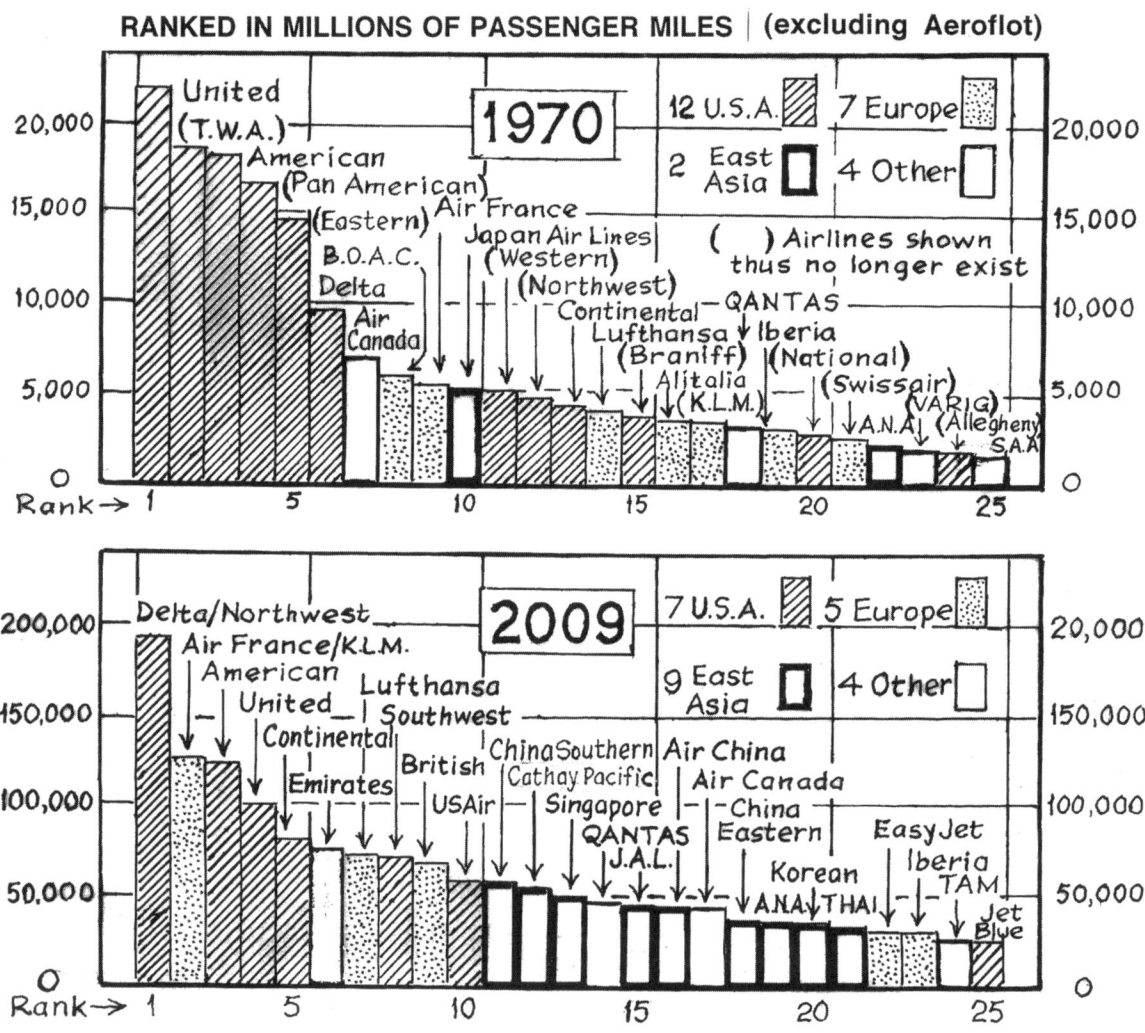

Notes on the Charts

1. Aeroflot, the state airline of the Soviet Union, was, in 1970, more than twice as big as United. The network of "The Greyhound Bus" of the U.S.S.R. covered eleven time zones.
2. The scale of the 2009 chart is ten times that of 1970, reflecting a growth within only four decades. Eleven of the 1970 airlines have either terminated, or have been acquired by others.
3. In 1970 (when the Boeing 747 entered service) airlines of the United States accounted for about 50% of the world's airline traffic. In 2009 this has declined to less than 30%.
4. In 1970, only two airlines from east Asia—both from Japan—were among the top 25. In 2009 there were nine, including four from China. The Middle East airline, Emirates, did not exist, but in 2009, it already ranked eighth, and is still growing fast.
5. Airlines that have entered the lists only during the last few years include low-fare airlines: the U.S. Southwest and Jet Blue, the British easyJet, and the Brazilian Tam.

BIBLIOGRAPHY

Further Reading

This selective resource list emphasizes Jet Age developments since 1952.

Global Air Transport

Brindley, John F. *Wings for the World: IATA 1945–1995.* Montreal: International Air Transport Association, 1995.

Doganis, Rigas. *Flying Off Course: Airline Economics and Marketing.* 4th ed. London: Routledge, 2010.

Graham, Brian. *Geography and Air Transport.* Chichester, England: Wiley, 1995.

Hanlon, Pat. *Global Airlines: Competition in a Transitional Industry.* 3rd ed. Oxford: Butterworth-Heineman, 2007.

Hengi, B.I. *Airlines Worldwide: Over 360 Airlines Described and Illustrated in Colour.* 4th ed. Hinckley, England: Midland, 2004.

———. *Airlines Remembered: Over 200 Airlines of the Past, Described and Illustrated in Colour.* Hinckley, England: Midland, 2000.

Hudson, Kenneth and Julian Pettifer. *Diamonds in the Sky: A Social History of Air Travel.* London: Bodley Head/BBC, 1979.

Jarrett, Philip, ed. *Modern Air Transport: Worldwide Air Transport from 1945 to the Present.* London: Putnam, 2000.

Leary, William M., and William F. Trimble, eds. *From Airships to Airbus: The History of Civil and Commercial Aviation.* 2 vols. Washington, D.C.: Smithsonian Institution Press, 1995.

Pearman, Hugh. *Airports: A Century of Architecture.* New York: Abrams, 2004.

Proctor, John, Mike Machat, and Craig Kodera. *From Props to Jets: Commercial Aviation's Transition to the Jet Age, 1952–1962.* North Bend, Minn.: Specialty Press, 2010.

Sampson, Anthony. *Empires of the Sky: The Politics, Contests and Cartels of World Airlines.* New York: Random House, 1984.

Sealy, Kenneth R. *The Geography of Air Transport.* 2nd ed. London: Hutchinson, 1966.

Serling, Robert J. *The Jet Age.* Alexandria, Va.: Time-Life "The Epic of Flight," 1982.

Wragg, David. *The World's Major Airlines.* 2nd ed. Stroud, England: History Press, 2007.

Zukowsky, John, ed. *Building for Air Travel: Architecture and Design for Commercial Aviation.* Munich: Prestel, 1996.

Specific Regions or Nations

Excludes books on individual airlines.

Davies, R.E.G. *Airlines of the United States Since 1914.* Revised ed. London: Putnam, 1982.

———. *Airlines of Latin America since 1919.* London: Putnam, 1984.

———. *Airlines of Asia since 1920.* London: Putnam, 1997.

Dienel, Hans-Liudger and Peter Lyth, eds. *Flying the Flag: European Commercial Air Transport since 1945.* London: Macmillan, 1998.

Guttery, Ben R. *Encyclopedia of African Airlines.* Jefferson, N.C.: McFarland, 1998.

Halford-McLeod, Guy. *Britain's Airlines, 1946 to Deregulation.* 3 vols. Chalford, England: Tempus Publishing/History Press, 2006–2010.

Hayward, Keith. *Government and British Aerospace: A Case Study of Post-War Technology Policy.* Manchester, England: Manchester University Press, 1983.

Komissarov, Dmitriy, and Yefim Gordon. *Russian Airlines and Their Aircraft.* Hinckley, England: Midland, 2004.

Millberry, Larry. *Air Transport in Canada.* 2 vols. Toronto: CANAV Books, 1997.

Staniland, Martin. *Government Birds: Air Transport and the State in Western Europe.* Lanham, Md.: Rowman & Littlefield, 2003.

U.S. Department of Commerce, Business and Defense Services Administration. *World Survey of Civil Aviation.* 12 booklets on different regions of the world. Washington, D.C.: Government Printing Office, 1960–70.

Airliners

Angelucci, Enzo. *World Encyclopedia of Civil Aircraft.* New York: Crown, 1982.

Bowers, Peter M. *Boeing Aircraft since 1916.* 3rd ed. London: Putnam, 1989.

Brooks, Peter W. *The Modern Airliner.* London: Putnam, 1961.

———. *The World's Airliners.* London: Putnam, 1962.

Brown, Eric. *The Helicopter in Civil Operations.* New York: Van Nostrand Reinhold, 1981.

Donald, David, ed. *The Encyclopedia of Civil Aircraft.* San Diego: Thunder Bay, 1999.

Ellis, Paul. *British Commercial Aircraft: Sixty Years in Pictures.* London: Jane's, 1980.

Gunston, Bill. *Airbus: The Complete Story.* 2nd ed. Yeovil, England: Haynes, 2009.

———, ed. *The Illustrated Encyclopedia of Commercial Aircraft.* New York: Exeter Books, 1980.

Jackson, A. J. *British Civil Aircraft 1919–1972.* 2nd ed. London: Putnam, 1973.

Miller, Ronald and David Sawyers. *The Technical Development of Modern Aviation.* London: Putnam, 1968.

Munson, Kenneth. *U.S. Commercial Airliners.* London: Jane's, 1982.

Newhouse, John. *The Sporty Game.* New York: Knopf, 1982.

———. *Boeing vs Airbus: The Inside Story of the Greatest International Competition in Business.* New York: Knopf, 2007.

Skinner, Stephen. *British Airliner Prototypes since 1945.* Hinckley, England: Midland, 2008.

Smith, Myron J. Jr. *Passenger Airliners of the United States 1926–1995: A Pictorial History.* Missoula, Mont.: Pictorial Histories, 1995.

Stroud, John. *European Transport Aircraft since 1910.* London: Putnam, 1966.

———. *Soviet Transport Aircraft since 1945.* London: Putnam, 1970.

———. *Jetliners in Service since 1952.* London: Putnam, 1994.

———. *Passenger Aircraft and Their Interiors 1910–2006.* Newcastle-Upon-Tyne: Scoval Publishing, 2002.

Trubshaw, Brian. *Concorde: The Inside Story.* Stroud, England: Sutton, 2000.

Wegg, John. *Caravelle: The Complete Story.* Sandpoint, Id.: Airways International, 2005.

Reference

Airbus and Boeing both issue useful annual "Global Market Forecasts" projecting the likely sale of different types of airliners in coming years based on air travel trends.

Groenewege, Adrianus D. *Compendium of International Civil Aviation.* 2nd ed. Montreal: International Aviation Development Corporation, 1999.

International Air Transport Association. *World Air Transport Statistics.* Geneva: IATA: 1957–present, annual.

International Civil Aviation Organization. *Civil Aviation Statistics of the World: The ICAO Statistical Handbook.* Montreal: ICAO, 1974–present, annual.

JP Airline Fleets. Zurich: Buchair, 1966–present, annual.

Roadcap, Roy, ed. *World Airline Record.* 7 eds. Chicago: Roadcap & Assoc, 1948–72.

Smith, Myron J. Jr. *The Airline Encyclopedia, 1909–2000.* 3 vols. Lanham, Md.: Scarecrow Press, 2002.

Stroud, John. *Airports of the World.* London: Putnam, 1980.

Bibliographies

Federal Aviation Administration, Office of Systems Engineering. *Air Transportation Bibliography.* Washington, D.C.: F.A.A., 1978.

Miller, E. Willard and Ruby M. Miller. *Air Transportation.* 5 booklets. Monticello, Ill.: Vance Bibliographies, 1987.

Smith, Myron J. Jr. *The Airline Biography: The Salem College Guide to Sources on Commercial Aviation.* 2 vols. West Cornwall, Conn.: Locust Hill Press, 1986, 1988.

Sterling, Christopher H. *Commercial Air Transport Books: An Annotated Bibliography.* McLean, Va.: Paladwr Press, 1996.

———. *Commercial Air Transport Books: An Annotated Bibliography (Supplement).* McLean, Va.: Paladwr Press, 1998.

INDEX

Index entries do not include appendices. Entries located in graphic or tabular elements are indicated with letters following page numbers: c = chart or exhibit; m = map; p = photograph; t = table. Country of origin/ownership is included after name of airline if not apparent from the airline's name.

11 September 2001, terrorist attacks on United States, 179, 213

AACO. *See* Arab Airline Corporation
A.A.J.C. *See* Associated Airways Joint Committee
Abacus, computerized reservations system, 262
ABAMEL. *See* Associated British Airlines (Middle East)
Abdul Rahman, Abdul Aziz ben, 262
Abed, Alberto, 325
Abeles, Peter, 286
Abraham, Reinhardt, 203
Abramovich, Boris, 154
A.C.A. *See* Association of Commuter Airlines
Aces. *See* Aérolíneas Centrales de Colombia
Acker, C. Edward, 160, 162–163, 329
Adam, Michael, 332
Adastra (Australia), 137c
ADC Airlines (Nigeria), 381
Addoms, Sam, 182
Adelaide Airways (Australia), 137c
Aden Airways, subsidiary of B.O.A.C., 388
   Ceases operations in 1967, 76–77
   Quadripartite pool, 385
Adria Aero Lloyd (Albania), 225
Adria Airways (Slovenia), 224
   See also nex-Adria
Adria Aviopromet (Yugoslavia). *See* Inex-Adria
Advanced Booking Charters (APEX fares), 64, 194
A.E.A. *See* American Export Airlines
AEG biplane, D.L.R. service, 3, 3p
Aegean Airlines, 221, 222m
Aegean Aviation. *See* Aegean Airlines
A.E.R. *See* Aerotransportes Entre Rios
Aer Lingus (Ireland), 43, 188, 198, 393
   Consultant to Bahama Airways, 331
   First Fokker Friendship service in Europe, 84
Aerial Transport Company of Siam, takes over from military air service, 266
Aéreo Calafia (Mexico), 326, 326t
Aéreo Dominicano, 336
Aéreo Transporte Ecuatoriana, C.A. (ATECA), forms AREA, 354
Aerlinte (Ireland), 28t

Aero. *See* Aero Contractors
Aero Belau (Palau), 300
Aero Berlin (Germany), 203
Aero California (Mexico), 325, 326, 326t
Aero Caribe (Mexico), 324
   Rebranded as Click Mexicana, 326
Aero Commuter, ancestor of Golden State, 95m
Aero Continente (Peru), 358–359
Aero Contractors (Nigeria), 382
Aero Costa Rica, 341
Aero Cozumel, 324
Aero Geral (Brazil), 315
Aero Ltd. (U.S.), 8
Aero Monterrey, controlled by Mexicana, 324
Aero O/Y, name change from Finnair, 232
Aero Safari (Mexico), 324
Aero Servicios Carabobo (Aserca) (Venezuela), 333, 352, 353
Aero Transporte Italiani
   Absorbs Aeromediterranea, 210
   Relationship with Alitalia, 209, 210
Aero Zambia, 394
Aerobanco, 349
Aerocesar (Colombia), 349
Aerocondor (Colombia), 349
Aeroflot (Soviet Union), 21
   Aircraft operated, 47, 47p, 48–49, 48p, 49m, 54m, 61, 99–100, 112, 115–116, 116m
   BAM railroad construction, 104, 104m
   Compared to western airlines, 61
   First sustained jet airline service, 42, 42p, 42m
   Glasnost and *perestroika* policies, 150
   Helicopter operations, 103–104
   Local services throughout Soviet Union, 88, 88m
   Organizes regional airline divisions, 131–132
   Regional subdivisions, 91
   Route network, 22m
   Service to Antarctica, 47–48
   Soviet C.I.S. airline, 151t
   Takes over Aviaarktika, 47
Aerolíneas Abaroa (A.L.A.) (Bolivia), 361
Aerolíneas Argentinas ("Aero Arg"), 364–366

Aircraft operated, 87, 365, 365p, 366
   Iberia shareholding, 218
   Investments from S.A.S. Iberia, American Airlines, 366
   South Atlantic and North-South American jet debuts, 52, 52t
   Trans-Polar service, 366
Aerolíneas Centrales de Colombia (Aces), 350
   Joins Alianza Summa, 348, 350
Aerolíneas Colonia (ARCO) (Uruguay), 363
Aerolíneas de las Perlas. *See* Aeroperlas
Aerolíneas Ini (Argentina), 365
Aerolíneas Mexicanas, 322
Aerolíneas Nicaraguenses. *See* Aeronica
Aerolíneas Paraguayas (APSA) (Paraguay), 318
Aerolíneas Peruanas, S.A. (APSA) (Peru), 357
   Arrangement with Northeast Airlines, 357
   Joins TAN low-fare Latin American consortium, 342
   Route map, 378m
Aerolíneas Vega (Mexico), 322
Aeroliteral (Mexico), 324
Aeromar (Dominican Republic), 336
Aeromar (Mexico), 326, 326t
Aeromarine Airways, 2m, 8
Aeromaritime (French charter airline), 64t
Aeromaya (Mexico), 322, 324
Aeromediterranea (Italian charter airline), 210
Aeromexico, 322–324
   Aerovías de Mexico, 323
   Aircraft operated, 323, 324
   Stake in Mexicana, 324
Aeronaves de México, 20, 322–324
   Absorbs Aerolíneas Mexicanas, 322
   Britannia service, 45
   Name change in 1972, 323
   See also Aeromexico
Aeronaves Alimentadoras (Mexico), feeder organization for small regional airlines, 324
Aeronaves del Perú, 356
Aeronica (Nicaragua), 342–343
   Acquired by TACA, 344
Aeronorte (Chile), 369

Aeroperlas (Panama), 344
Aeroperú, 357–358, 358p
   Alas de America alliance, 324
Aeropesca (Colombia), 349
Aeroposta Argentina, 19
Aéropostal Alas de Venezuela, 352
Aéropostale (French pioneer airline), 14
   Argentine subsidiary, 19
   South Atlantic service, 19m
Aeroregional, S.A. (Chile), 369
AeroRepublica (Colombia), 345
Aeroservicios Parague (Chile), 369
Aérospatiale
   Concorde production, 113
   New name for Sud Aviation, 109
Aerosur (Chile), 369
AeroSur. *See* L.A.C.
AeroSvit (Ukraine), 238
Aerotransportes Entre Rios (A.E.R.) (Argentina), 365
Aerotransportes Litoral Argentina (A.L.A.), 364, 366
Aerovías Brasil
   Sold to VARIG, 315
   With REAL, route map, 32m
Aerovías DAP (Chile), 369–370, 370m
Aerovías de Mexico, 323
Aerovías Ecuatorianas (AREA) (Ecuador), 354
   Fokker F-27, crash, 1960, 87
Aerovías Guest (Mexico), 33, 33t, 227, 322
Aerovías Interamericanas de Panama (AVISPA), 345
Aerovías Nacionales de Colombia (AVIANCA), 327–328
   Aircraft operated, 327–328, 348, 348p
   Bankrupt, merges with TACA, 2010, 348
   Forms Alianza Summa, 348
   Name change from SCADTA, 6
   Orders Boeing 787 Dreamliner, 348
   Partnership with TACA, Central America, 244
   South Atlantic route, 1950, 33, 33t
Aerovías Nacionales de Honduras (ANHSA) (Honduras), 341
Aerovias Venezolanas, S.A. (AVENSA) (Venezuela), 87, 351–353
Aerovolga (Soviet C.I.S.), 151t

Affinity groups, low-fare system by charter airlines, 143
Afretair (Air Trans Africa), 394
Africa, post-war wave of nationalism, 67
Africa Air, 397
Afrikaans Suidwes Lugdienst (Namibia), 404
  See also Namib Air
Afriqiyah Airways (Libya), 373
"Aguardiente," Honduran liquor fit for fuel, 341
Aguilo, Miguel, 218
Ahmed, Mohammed, 390
Aigle Azur (France), 279
Air 2000 (Canada), becomes Canada 3000 (C3), 311
Air Afrique (France), 14, 376–377
  Aircraft operated, 376–377, 377p
  Founded as consortium, 30, 68–69, 68m, 376
  Route exchange with SABENA, 14
  Route map, 1972, 376m
  See also Treaty of Yaoundé
Air Algérie (Compagnie Générale de Transports) (C.G.T.A.), 68, 371
  Aircraft operated, 371, 371p, 372p
Air ALM. See Antilliaanse Luchtvaart Maatschappij
Air Antilles Express, 335
Air Aruba, 333
Air Asia (Malaysia), 282, 283m, 283p
Air Astana (Kazakhstan), 157m
Air Atlanta (Iceland), 234
Air Atlantic (Canada), 306
Air Atlas. See Royal Air Maroc
Air Atlas (Algeria), 372
Air Austral, 406
Air Baltic (Latvia), 239
Air Bangui. See Air Centrafique
Air BC (Canada), 310
  Integrated with CP Air, 306, 307
Air Benin. See Trans Air Benin
Air Bissau (Portuguese Guinea), 379
Air Botswana, 404
Air Burkina, 378
Air Cairo, 375
Air Caledonia International (or Air Calin), 302
Air Calédonie, 302
Air California, 172–173
  Douglas DC-9 service, 118
  Sold to American Airlines, 173
Air Calin. See Air Caledonia International
Air Canada
  Aircraft operated, 119, 304, 311p
  Douglas DC-9 service, 118
  Emerges from bankruptcy, 307
  Merger proposal with Canadian International, 306
  Name change from T.C.A., 304
  North Atlantic success, 105
  Privatization, 304
Air Caraïbes, 335

Air Centrafique, 378
Air Ceylon, 254–255, 256p
  See also Air Lanka
Air Chang'an. See Chang'an Airlines
Air Charter (U.K.)
  Merged into B.U.A., 1960, 59
  Flies cars across English Channel, 106
Air Charter (French charter airline), 64t
Air China, 241m, 242t
  Aircraft operated, 241p
  Code-share with Lufthansa, 204
Air Comoros, 406
Air Congo. See Air Zaïre
Air Coral Coast (Fiji), 297
Air Deccan (India), 249–250, 250m
Air Djibouti, 388
Air Europa (Spain), 218
Air Europe, 190
Air Fiji, 296
Air Florida, 160
  Boeing 737 crash, 1982, 160
Air Foyal (Caribbean), 335
Air Foyle (U.K.), 156, 238
Air France, 4
  African service, 35
  Aircraft operated, 51, 110, 199, 199p, 200, 201p
  Atlantic service chronology, 28
  Caravelle introduction, 1956–1959, 56, 56m
  Central Atlantic, services, 1953, 33, 33t
  Comet acquisition and jet service, 1953, 40, 40m
  Concorde crash, Paris, 2000, 198, 201
  Concorde service, 1976, 114, 114m, 114p, 199
  Final alliance with K.L.M., 2003–2004, 216
  First Airbus service (A300B), 1974, 199
  First route to China, 1972, 240
  Interest in Air Laos, 279
  Interest in Air Liban, 72–73
  Introduces Viscount, 1953, 43
  Merger with K.L.M., 201
  Merger with U.T.A. and Air Inter, 200
  North Atlantic success, 1970s, 105
  Partnership with TAM Brazilian Airlines, 200
  Polar service, 34t
  Resumes service to Vietnam, 1954, 277, 277p
  Round-the-world service, 1973, 199
  SABENA proposal, early 1990s, sold to Swissair, 1995, 214
  Shares in Royal Air Maroc, 372
  South and Central Atlantic jet debuts, 52t
  South Atlantic service, 33, 33t
  South Atlantic service, post-war, 334

Supports Air Afrique, 376
  "Wet-lease" agreement with Jersey European, 192
Air Gabon, 378–379
Air Gambia, 383
Air Greece, 221
Air Guadeloupe, 335, 335p
Air Guam, 300
Air Guinea, 379
  First independent French African airline, 67
Air Guinée, 379
Air Haiti, 337
Air Hebrides, 299
Air Iceland, 234
Air Inter (France), 90
  High-speed train, impact, 200
  Merger with Air France and U.T.A., 200
Air Inter (Morocco), 372
Air Inuit (Canada), 309m
Air Ivoire, 377
Air Jamaica, 328
  Aircraft operated, 329
  Privatized, 1994, 329
Air Jamaica Acquisitions Group (AJAG), 329
Air Jamaica Express, 320
Air Jordan, 72
  See also Jordan Airways
Air Jugoslavia (charter airline), 64t
Air Katafanga (Fiji), 297
Air Koryo (North Korea), 276
Air Labrador (Canada), 309m
Air Lanka, 255–256
  Aircraft operated, 256
  Becomes Air Sri Lanka, 256
Air Laos, 279
Air Liban (Lebanon), 55–56, 72–73
Air Liberia, 379
Air Liberté (France)
  Franchised from British Airways, 198
  Virgin bid to buy, 1996, 191
Air Littoral (France), Lufthansa franchise, 204
Air Madagascar, 405–406, 405m, 406p
Air Mahé (Seychelles), 388
"Air Mail Crisis" (1934)
  Resultant route network, 1934 10m
  "Spoils Conferences," 1933, 11
Air Malawi, 395
Air Maldives, 257, 258m
  Aircraft operated, 85
  Malaysian Airways stake, 262
Air Mali, 379–380
Air Mandalay, 257
Air Manila, 85m, 282
Air Manila International (A.M.I.). See Air Manila
Air Maritime, Eastern Provincial affiliate (Canada), 306
Air Maroc (Société Avia Maroc Ligne Aérienne), 68, 372

Air Martinique, 335
Air Mauritanie, 378
Air Mauritius, 406–407
Air Melanésiae, 299
Air Micronesia ("Air Mike"), 300–301
Air Mongol, 276, 276p
Air Moorea (Tahiti), 301
Air Namibia, 404
Air Nauru
  As Norfolk Jet Express, 299
  Renamed Our Airline, 299
Air New England (U.S.), 123c
Air New Zealand (A.N.Z.), 291
  Battles for control of Ansett, 293
  Buys T.N.T. shares of Ansett, 287, 288
  DC-10 crash in Antarctica, 292–293
  Merger with N.A.C., 291
Air Niagara, 338
Air Niger, 378
Air Niugini (A.N.G.), 294–295
Air North (Canada), 309m, 310
Air Nostrum (Spanish domestic airline), 218
Air Nova (Canada), 307
Air One (Italy)
  Bids for Volare, 211
  Code-share with Lufthansa, 204
Air Ontario (Canada), 307, 310
Air OutreMer (A.O.M.) (France)
  Becomes part of SAir Group, 214
  Leases DC-10s to Cubana, 338
Air Pacific (formerly Fiji Airways), 295–298
  Aircraft operated, 296
  Replaces Air Nauru, 299
  Service in Guam, 300
  Service to America, 1993, 296
Air Panama, 345–346
Air Panama International (A.P.I.), 345–346
Air Panama, S.A. (APASA), 346
Air Paraguay, 362–363
Air Philippines, 282
Air Polynésie (Tahiti), 301
Air Portugal
  Island destinations, 220m
  Name change from T.A.P., 220
Air Provence (France), becomes Virgin Express France, 191
Air Rhodesia, 394
Air Rwanda. See Rwandair
Air Saint Pierre (French territorial airline), 309m
Air Sénégal, 372, 377
Air Services of India, Empire service, 21m
Air Seychelles, 388–389
Air Siam, 267
  Aircraft operated, 267
  Assists Air Ceylon, 255
Air Sinai, 375
Air St. Barthélemy, 335
Air Tahiti, 301
Air Tahiti Nui, 302

Air Tanzania, 386–387
Air Trans Africa. *See* Afretair
Air Transport Association (A.T.A.) (U.S.), 65, 138
Air Transport Licensing Board
    Approves inclusive tour programs, 63
    Deals with Laker Skytrain application, approval, 105–106
Air Transportation Oversight System (ATOS), 180
Air Transportation Stabilization Board, 184
Air Travel (N.Z.) (New Zealand air service), 16
Air Tungaru, 298, 299
Air U.K.
    Name change to Buzz, 215
    Code-shares, Jersey European, 192
Air Ukraine (Soviet C.I.S.), 151t, 238
Air Union (France), 4
Air Vanuatau, name change from Air Melanésiae, 29
Air Vietnam, 277–278
Air Volta. *See* Air Burkina
Air Wakaya (Fiji), 297
Air Waves. *See* PeauVava'u
Air West (U.S.), 123c, 124
    Route map, 1969, 278m
Air Zaïre, 69, 396–397
    Aircraft operated, 397, 397p
    Name change from Air Congo, 69
Air Zimbabwe, 394
AirBridge Cargo (U.K.), 156
Airbus
    Announces A3XX project (later became A380), 408
    Formation, shareholding, 1970, 109–110
    Hawker-Siddeley as subcontractor, 32
    See also specific aircraft
Airbus A-300, A300B2, A300B4
    Air Algérie, 1970s, 371
    Air France, first service, 110, 199
    Air Siam, 1970s, 267
    Air Jamaica, 1983, 329
    Air-India, 1982, 246
    Alitalia, 1980, 209
    Angel Airlines, 1998, 269
    Chinese airlines, from late 1990s, 242t
    Compass Airlines, 1990, 289
    Design, first flight, 110
    Eastern Air Lines, 1977, 164
    Egyptair, 1990s, 375
    Finnair, 1988, 233
    Garuda Indonesian, 1982, 263
    Grand Air, 1995, 282
    I.A.C., 1975, 247, 248, 248p
    I.C.A., 1970s, 330
    Korean Air Lines, 1972, 275
    Lufthansa, 1976, 202
    Pan American Airways, 1984, 162
    SABENA, 1984, 214
    Sempati Air Transport, 1991, 266
    Sibir, Russia, 2004, 153
    Singapore Airlines, 1981, 260
    South African Airways, 1976, 399
    Sudan Airways, 1992, 389
    T.A.A., 1981, 286
    Thai International, 1970s, 267p
    US Air, 1998–1999, 169
    Vietnam Airlines, 1993, 278
    ZAS, Egypt, 1990s, 375
Airbus A310
    Aéropostal Alas de Venezuela, 1997, 352
    Air Calin (Air Caledonia), 2000, 302
    Air Mongol, 1998, 276, 276p
    Air Jamaica, 329
    Air-India, 1998, 247
    Austrian Airlines, 1989, 236
    Chinese orders, 1985, 243
    Ecuatoriana, first in continent, 1991, 355
    Kenya Airways, 1990s, 386
    L.A.I., 1984, 371
    Lufthansa order, 1979, 203
    New Air Zaïre, 1996, 397
    SilkAir, 1993, 261
    Somali Airlines, 1988, 388
    Sudan Airways, 1990s, 389
    Swissair, 1983, 212
    Vietnam Airlines, 193, 278
Airbus A320 (and A318, A319, A321)
    A321 launched by Alitalia, 1994, 210
    Afriqiyah Airways, 373
    Air Asia, 2005, 283, 283p
    Air Calin (Air Caledonia), 2004, 302
    Air Canada, 304, 311p
    Air France, 1988 and 1999–2000, 199, 199p
    Air Ivoire, 2002, 377
    Air Jamaica, 328
    Air Malta, 1990, 224
    Air New Zealand, 2003, 293
    Albanian Airlines, 1995, 225
    Bahamasair, 1994, 331
    Braniff, Inc., 160
    C3, 2000s, 312
    Chinese airlines, from late 1990s, 242t
    Cubana, 2000, 338
    Egyptair, 1990s, 375
    Flitestar, South Africa, 1993, 402
    Frontier Airlines, 2001, 182–183
    I.A.C., 1989, 248
    IndiGo Airlines, 2006, 250
    JetBlue, 1999, 181, 182p
    JetStar Asia, 2004, 283
    La Navette shuttle service, 1997, 200
    LACSA, Costa Rica, 1990, 341
    LAN Perú, 1999, 359
    LAN-Chile, 1998, 343
    Lao Airlines, 2003, 280
    Mexican airlines, 1900s–2000s, 326t
    Mexicana, 1970s, 324, 323p
    Nigerian Airways, 1984, 380
    Nouvelair, Tunisia, 1990s, 373
    Philippine Air Lines, 2006, 274
    Royal Air Maroc, 1976–1986, 372
    Royal Bhutan Airlines, 2004, 258
    Royal Brunei, 2003 and 2005, 280
    SAETA, 2000, 356, 356p
    Shorouk Air, Egypt, 1993, 375
    Siem Reap Airways, 2004, 269
    SilkAir, 1997, 261
    South African Airways, 2004, 401
    Spirit Airlines, 2001, 184
    Sudan Airways, 1990s, 389
    TACA, Peru, 1999, 343, 344p
    TAM, 1980, 319p
    TAM, Brazil, 1998, 343
    Tiger Airways, 2003, 284, 284p
    Universal Airlines, Guyana, 334
    US Air, 1998–1999, 169
    Valuair, 2004, 283
    Vietnam Airlines, 1993, 278
Airbus A330
    Afriqiyah Airways, 373
    Air Afrique, 377
    Air Algérie, 2007, 371
    Air Calin (Air Caledonia), 2000s, 302
    Air Lanka, 1998, 256
    Austrian, 1996, 214
    AVIANCA, 2000s, 348
    C3, Canada, 1998, 312
    China Airlines, 2005, 270
    Greenlandair, 2002, 235
    Kingfisher Airlines, India, 2005, 250
    Lauda Air, 1993, 237
    Philippine Air Lines, 2006, 274
    SABENA, 1996, 214
    Swissair, 1996, 214
    TAM, Brazil, 1980, 319; crash, 2007, 320
    THAI, 1995, 268
Airbus A340
    Air Caraïbes, 2000s, 335
    Air France, 2000s, 201p
    Air Lanka, 1994, 256
    Air Mauritius, 1994, 407
    Air Tahiti Nui, 1996, 302
    Arik Air, Nigeria, 2008, 382
    Conviasa, Venezuela, 2006, 353
    Egyptair, 1995, 375
    Jet Airways, India, 2005, 250
    Olympic Airways, 1999, 221
    Philippine Air Lines, 2006, 274
    Singapore Airlines, 1990s, 260
    South African Airways, 2004, 401, 400p
    Virgin Nigeria, 2005, 382
Airbus A350
    Afriqiyah Airways, 373
    Kingfisher Airlines, India, 2005, 250
    Vietnam Airlines order, 2007, 278
Airbus A380 (ex-A3XX)
    Air Austral order, 2009, 406
    Air France plans order for A3XX, 2000, 201, 408
    Air France service, 2009, 410, 410p
    China Southern, 245
    Emirates, first service, 2008, 409, 409p
    Kingfisher Airlines, India, 2005, 250
    Korean Air Lines order, 2003, 276
    Lufthansa order, 2001, 204
    Malaysia Airlines order, 2003, 262
    QANTAS order and service, 288, 409–410, 410p
    Singapore Airlines, A380 inaugural service, 2007, 261, 261p, 409, 410p
    "Stretched" -900 (900 seats) proposed, 411
    THAI order, 2004, 268
Airco. *See* de Havilland Trident
Aircraft Innsbruck (Tyrolean Airways), 237
Aircraft Transport and Travel (A.T.&T.) (U.K.), 3, 3t, 4m
Airfast, Indonesian airliner, 136p
AIRG. *See* Líneas Aéreas Privadas Argentinas
Air-India, 246–247
    Aircraft operated, 246, 247
    Crash near Ireland, 1985, 246
    Decline from world leadership, 247
    Enters North Atlantic route, 51
    Joins quadripartite pool, 385
    North Atlantic airline chronology, 28t
    Orders Boeing 777s and 787s, 247
Air-India Express, 247
Air-India International. *See* Air-India
Airline deregulation
    Japan, 149
    U.K., 142–143
    U.S. *See* Airline Deregulation Act
Airline Deregulation Act, 1978, 65, 118, 122, 126, 140, 149, 158, 159, 166, 167–168, 172, 173, 176, 177, 181, 186
Airline of the Marshall Islands (A.M.I.), 300
Airline Pilots Association (ALPA), U.S. pilots' union, 128, 168
Airlines of New South Wales, 90, 137c, 138, 286, 286p
Airlines of Northern Australia, 286
Airlines of South Australia, 90, 137c, 138, 286
Airlines of Western Australia, 90, 137c, 138, 286
Airspeed AS-57 Ambassador (British airliner)
    Brabazon Committee recommendation, 32
    Service with B.E.A., 43
Airspeed Envoy (British airliner), 18

AirTran Airways (U.S.), 180
　CRJ-200 feeder airliner, 94p
　First service, MD-95, 117
　Merger with ValuJet, 1997, 180
Airwest (U.S.), 123c
　See also Hughes Air West
Airwork (U.K.)
　Buys Laker interests, joins Hunting-Clan to form B.U.A., 106
　Founds Misrair, 67
　Leases aircraft to Sudan Airways, 67
　Merged to form B.U.A., 59
Aisiri, Vikrom, 269
A.L.A. See Aerolíneas Abaroa; Aerotransportes Litoral Argentina
ALA, Sociedad de Transportes Aéreos (Chile), 367
Ala Littoria (Italy), 14, 14m
Aladia (Mexico), 326t, 327
Alamuddin, Najib, 72
Alas de America, Latin American alliance, 324
Alas del Caribe (Dominican Republic), 336
Alaska Airlines, 118
Albanian Airlines, 225
Albatros (Germany), 4m
Alcazar Group, European planned airline group, 212
Alemán, Miguel, 20
ALFA (Argentina), 364
Alia, Royal Jordanian Airlines, 79
Alianza Summa, Colombian airline alliance, 348
Aliblu (Italian third-level airline), 210
Alimentadoras, Aeronaves (Mexico), 322
Alitalia Express, 210
Alitalia–Linee Aeree Italiane (Alitalia), 28t, 98
　Advises East African Airways, 386
　Agreement with K.L.M., 210, 216
　Agreements with Iberia and MALEV, 210
　Aircraft operated, 51, 118, 209, 210, 211p
　And A.T.I., 209, 210
　Bids for Volare, 2006, 211
　Challenges IATA price fixing, 209
　Domestic routes, 210m
　Forms ATLAS partnership, 111
　Launches Airbus A321, 210
　Orders Boeing supersonic 2707, 1960s, 209
　Services in South and Central America, 33, 33t
All-American Aviation (U.S.), 122, 123c
　See also Allegheny Airlines
All Nippon Airways (Japan), 144–149
　Acquisition of other airlines, 1963–1967, 145
　Affinity group charters, inclusive tour charters, 1971, 147

ANA World Tours, 147
　Boeing 737 service, 118
　Cancellation of Douglas DC-10s, 146
　Formed 1958 by merger, rise to prominence in 1960s, 144, 144m
　Growth of "Beam Lines," 1944–1945, 145m
　International charter flights, 146
　Joins IATA, 148
　Miles Marathon, 1950s, Viscount, 1960; F-27, 1961, turboprop services, 144
　Minor shareholding in Austrian Air Lines, 1989, 148
　Operates Fokker Friendship, 85
　Orders Boeing 747SRs, 1977, 147
　Preference for 727 v. DC-9, 61
　Purchases Lockheed TriStars, 1972
　Scheduled international services, 1986, 148
Allegheny Airlines, 122, 168
　All-American Aviation ancestor, 122
　Genealogy, 123c
Allegheny Commuter Airlines
　Commuter system, 94p
　Renamed US Air Express, 168
Allende, Salvador, 368
Allison, U.S. engine manufacturer, 122, 125
A.L.M. See Antilliaanse Luchtvaart Maatschappij
ALMA de Mexico, 326t, 327
Aloha Airlines, 120
　Forms Air Micronesia, 1967, 300
ALPA. See Airline Pilots Association
Alta Velocidad Española (AVE). See High-speed rail, Spain
Amaro, Rolim Adolfo, 319, 320
AMC Aviation (Egypt), 375
AMECO, Air China maintenance company, 244
America West (U.S.)
　Merges with US Airways, 170
　Survives deregulation, 141, 168
American Airlines, 10
　Aircraft operated, 11p, 46, 52, 52t, 57, 108, 110, 110p, 120
　Buys Air California, 118, 173
　Buys London routes from T.W.A., 166
　Buys shares of Iberia, 218
　Genealogy, 9c
　Introduces Douglas DC-3, 1936, 11p
　Introduces Super-Saver fares, 140
　Invests in Aerolíneas Argentinas, 366
　Invests in Canadian International, 306
　Lockheed Electra crash, 1960, 46
　London route from Braniff, 159
　One of U.S. "Big Four," 9c, 122
　Post-war summary, 26t

Post-war U.S. leadership, 28
　Transcontinental route, 1934, 10p
American Airways
　Genealogy, 9c
　Name change to American Airlines, 26t
American Export Airlines (A.E.A.)
　Atlantic service chronology, 28t
　Becomes American Overseas Airlines, 28t
　Owns TACA, 343
　Wartime service, 26
American Flyers Airline (U.S. Supplemental), 64t
American Overseas Airlines (A.O.A.). See American Export Airlines
American SST project, 114–115
American Trans Air (A.T.A.), 183
Americana (Peru), 358
A.M.I. See Air Manila International; Airline of the Marshall Islands
AMR Corporation, invests in Canadian, 306
A.N.A. See All Nippon Airways; Australian National Airways
Andrews, Coleman, 401
Andrews, Floyd, 172
A.N.G. See Air Niugini
Angel Airlines (Thailand), 269
Angel, Jimmy, 354
Angola. See Divisão de Exploração dos Transportes Aéreos de Angola
ANHSA. See Aerovías Nacionales de Honduras
Ansett Airways, Ansett Airlines of Australia, 285–287, 286p
　Australian airline group, 90
　Buys Australian Airlines, 1957, 138
　Buys state regional airlines, 286
　Early purchaser of Boeing 727 and DC-9 jets, 138
　Genealogy, 137c
　Renamed, 287
Ansett, Reginald, 90, 138, 285, 286
Ansett Transport Industries (A.T.I.)
　Battles for control with New Zealand, 293
　Control to industrialists, 286
　Interest in Air Niugini, 294
　Purchases A.N.A., 285
ANT, pre-war Soviet aircraft designs, 48
　ANT-6 bomber, flies to North Pole, 1937, 21
　ANT-7 bomber, flies to North Pole, 1937, 21
　ANT-9 tri-motor, Soviet airliner, 1920s, 20, 20p
　ANT-20 Maxim Gorky and ANT-20bis, 1939, 48
　ANT-25, nonstop transpolar flight, 1937, 21
　See also Andrei Tupolev
Antarctica
　Aerovías DAP, scheduled service, 369

First service, 367
　Special flights, 368
Antarqui, mythical boy who flies, 357p
Antilles Air Boats, 338
Antilliaanse Luchtvaart Maatschappij (A.L.M.), 333, 334
Antón, Eljuri, 355
Antonov Airlines (Ukraine), 238
Antonov An-2 (Soviet biplane)
　Mongolian, 1956, 276
　Resilience, 101
　Tyumen Avia Trans, 154
　Workhorse of regional airlines, 1960s–1970s, 131–132, 132p, 132m
Antonov An-8 (Soviet military turboprop), 102
Antonov An-10 Ukraina (Soviet airliner)
　Aeroflot, 61, 101
Antonov An-12 (Soviet airliner), 102
Antonov An-22 Antheus (Soviet airliner), 102–103, 103p
Antonov An-24 (Soviet turboprop airliner)
　Aeroflot, 89, 89p
　Air Guinée, 1960s, 379
　Air Mali, 1961, 280
　C.A.A.C., China, 58
　Compared to other twin-engined turboprops, 89t
　Cubana, from 1960s, 337
　Mongolian, 1970s, 276
　Record production numbers, 100p
　Regional services, 1960s, 1970s, 131–132
　T Doble A, 2000s, 359
Antonov An-26 (Soviet turboprop airliner)
　Tyumen Avia Trans, 154
Antonov An-32 freighter
　Kinshasa, Zaïre, crash in 1996, 397
Antonov An-124 Ruslan
　Air Foyle, 156
　Antonov Airlines, 1989, 238
　Volga-Dnepr, 155–156, 155p
Antonov An-225, 238
A.N.Z. See Air New Zealand
A.O.A. See American Overseas Airlines
A.O.M. See Air OutreMer
Apartheid, 399–400
APASA. See Air Panama, S.A.
APEX fares, 194
A.P.I. See Air Panama International
APSA. See Aerolineas Paraguayas; Aerolineas Peruanas, S.A.
Aquila Airways, flying-boat services, 220
Arab Airline Corporation (AACO), 76
Arabian American Oil Company (ARAMCO), 74
Archangelsk CAD (Soviet C.I.S.), 151t
ARCO. See Aerolíneas Colonia

Index

Arctic Wings (Canada), merges to form Transair, 134
AREA. *See* Aerovías Ecuatorianas
ARG Argentinas Línea Privada. *See* Líneas Aéreas Privadas Argentinas
ARGO (Dominican Republic), 336–337
Argonaut (Canadian Merlin-engined DC-4)
  East African Airways, 385
  Survives into Jet Age with B.O.A.C., 45
Argosy aircraft. *See* Armstrong-Whitworth Argosy
Argyros, George, 173
Arik Air (Nigeria), 382, 382p
Arizona Airways, 123c, 125, 126m
Armenian Airlines
  National airline, 239
  Soviet C.I.S. airline, 151t
Armstrong-Whitworth Argosy
  Early British airliner, 11
  Imperial Airways, 12–13, 13m
Armstrong-Whitworth Argosy 222 freighter
  Safe Air, New Zealand, 1972, 292, 292p
Armstrong-Whitworth Atalanta
  Christmas mail to Australia, 12
  Early British airliner, 11
Arnarflug. *See* Eagle Air
Arumemilkhide, Joseph, 382
A.S.A. *See* Aeroregional, S.A.
Aserca. *See* Aero Servicios Carabobo
Asia, urban population, 243m
Asian Spirit Airlines (Philippines), 282
Asiana Airlines (Korea), 275–276
Associated Airways Joint Committee, 23
Associated British Airlines (Middle East) (ABAMEL), 74
Association of Commuter Airlines (A.C.A.), 94
A.T.A. *See* Air Transport Association; American Trans Air
Ataturk, Kemal, 79
ATECA. *See* Aéreo Transporte Ecuatoriana
A.T.I. *See* Aero Transporte Italiani; Ansett Transport Industries
Atlantic air services, 28t, 29
Atlantic Airways, 25
Atlantic Coast Airlines, United Airlines partner, 195
Atlantic Excellence, European ailine partnerhip, 212
ATLAS, European airline partnership, 111
Atlas Blue (Morocco), 372
ATOS. *See* Air Transportation Oversight System
ATR-42, ATR-72 (turboprop airliners)
  Aces, Colombia, 1991, 350

Aeromar, Mexico, 1987, 326
Aeroperlas, Panama, 1970s, 344
Air Algérie, 2003, 371
Air Austral, 2000, 406
Air Botswana, 1988, 404
Air Calédonie, 2007, 302
Air Caraïbes, Antilles Air Express, 2000, 335
Air Greece, 1999, 222
Air Madagascar, 1997, 405
Air Malawi, 1991, 395
Air Mandalay, Yangon Airways, 1994–1996, 257
Air Mauritanie, 378
Air Mauritius, 1988, 407
Air Pacific, Fiji, 1980s, 296
Air Tahiti, 1987, 301
Air Vanuatu, 1981, 299
Alitalia group, 210
AVIATECA, 344
Azerbaijan, 2000s, 239
Bangkok Airways, 1994, 268
Cape Verde Islands, 1994, 384
China Xinjiang, 1985, 242t
Comair, South Africa, 1990s, 402
Conviasa, Venezuela, 2004, 353
Croatia Airlines, 1993, 224
Ethiopian Air Lines, 1995, 391
Finnair, 1986, 233
First Air, Canada, 2000s, 310
Flitestar, South Afrca, 1993, 402
Isleñas, Honduras, 1982, 344
Jet Airways, India, 1990s, 249
Lao Airlines, 2003, 280
P.I.A., Pakistan, 2006, 253
Royal Air Cambodge, 1995, 279
Ryanair, 1980s, 188
Santa Barbara, Venezuela, 1995, 353
Siem Reap Airways, 1997, 269
TransAsia Airlines, Taiwan, 1992, 271
Tuninter, Tunis, 1980s, 373
UTair, Siberia, 2004, 154
Vietnam Airlines, 1992, 278, 278p
Zambia Airways, 1980s, 393
ATSA (Mexico), 322
A.T.S.B. *See* Air Transport Stabilization Board
A.T.&T. *See* Aircraft Transport and Travel
Attali, Bernard, 200
Augsburg Airways (Germany), 204
Aurea Group, Brazilian bus operator, 320–321
Austin Airways (Canadian local airline), 310
Austral. *See* Austral Líneas Aéreas
Austral Líneas Aéreas (Argentina), new name for Austral, 364–366
  Aircraft operated, 366
Australia
  Air routes, 1925, 6m
  Airlines Agreement Act, 138, 285
  Australian Federation of Airline Pilots (AFAP) strike, 287

Cross-Charter Agreement, 286
Early order for Viscount turboprop airliner, 138, 285
Genealogy, 137c
Government prize, 6
Regional airlines, 136–138
Takes over QANTAS's domestic routes, 138
Third Level Services, 289
Tripartite Agreement, 246, 287
Two-Airline System, 285, 287
Australian Aerial Services, 137c
Australian Airlines, name change from T.A.A., 1985, 286
Australian National Airlines (A.N.A.), 137
  Assists Air Ceylon, 255
  Empire service, 21m
  Sold to Ansett, 138, 137c, 285
Austria, first airline service, 5
Austrian Air Services (domestic airline), 236
Austrian Air Transport (charter airline), 64t, 236
Austrian Airlines, 236
  Aircraft operated, 117, 236, 237p
  Cooperation with Swissair, 212
  Minor shareholding by All Nippon Airways, 148
  Shares in Lauda Air, 237
Austrian Arrows, name change from Tyrolean Airways, 237
Austro-Hungarian Empire, air service, 2, 3t, 236
Avalon (U.S.), 95m
AVENSA. *See* Aerovias Venezolanas, S.A.
Avia Airlines (South Africa), 403
Aviaarktika (U.S.S.R.), 21, 47, 102
Aviacion Y Comercio (A.Y.C. or Aviaco) (Spain), 64t, 90
  Aircraft operated, 218
  Consolidates with Iberia, 218
  Shares in Royal Air Maroc, 372
Aviaco. *See* Aviacion Y Comercio
Aviacsa (Mexico), 324, 325t
AVIANCA. *See* Aerovías Nacionales de Colombia
Avianova (Italian third-level airline), 210
AVIATECA. *See* Campañía Guatemalteca de Aviación
Aviation Corporation (AVCO), 9c, 10
Aviation Corps de la Garde d'Haiti, 336–337
Aviation Enterprises (U.S.), 123c, 127
Aviation Traders, 102
Avio Linee Italiane-Flotte Reunite (Italy), 98
Aviogenex (Yugoslavian charter airline), 64t, 223
Avion, l' (France), 198
Avioquintana (Mexico), 326, 326t
AVISPA. *See* Aerovías Interamericanas de Panama

Avolar (Mexico), 326, 326t
Avro 748 (British turboprop airliner), 85
  Compared to other twin-engined turboprops, 89
  COPA, Panama, 344
  Indian Airlines, 86
  Philippine Air Lines, 85m, 87p
  Thai Airways, 86
  VIASA, 352
  See also Hawker Siddeley 748
Avro Lancastrian
  Converted from British Lancaster bomber, 27, 31, 34p
  Skyways service to Mauritius, 406
Avro RJ-70
  Air Baltic, 239
Avro Tudor, 31
Avro York (British post-war interim airliner), 27p
A.Y.C. *See* Aviacion Y Comercio
Ayling, Robert, 198
Azerbaijan Airlines
  Founded as national airline, 239
  Soviet C.I.S. airline, 151t
Azzura Air (Italy), 210

B.A. Connect (low-fare airline), 198
B.A. European (British Airways subsidiary), 198
B.A.C. *See* British Aircraft Corporation; Burma Airways Corporation
BAC One-Eleven (British airliner)
  Air Congo, 1967, 397
  Air Katanga, never operated, 1970s, 397p
  Air Malawi, 1970, 395
  Air Siam, 1970s, 267
  American Airlines, 120
  AVIATECA, 1974, 340
  Bahamas Airways, 1968, 331
  Belize Airways, 1980, 346
  Braniff Airways, 120
  British Airways, 1970s, 196
  Cayman Airways, 1968, 332
  Compañía de Aviación Faucett, 1971, 356
  Cyprus Airways, 1970s, 226
  Development, first flight, 60, 60p
  Gulf Air, 76
  Kabo Air, Nigeria, 1990s, 381
  LACSA, Costa Rica, 1967, 341
  LIAT, 1970s, 330
  Mohawk Airlines, 1965, 122
  Nationwide Air, South Africa, 1991, 403
  Ordered by Laker, 106
  Ryanair, easyJet, 1980s–2000s, 187–190
  Service record, 120–121, 121p
  Solair, 1980, 298
  TACA, 1950s, 343
  Tikal Jets, Guatemala, 1994, 340
  Zambia Airways, 1968, 393

BAe. *See specific aircraft (British Aerospace BAe)*
Bahamas Airways, 328
Bahamas World, 328, 331–332
Bahamasair, 331
Baikal-Amur Magistral railroad (BAM), 104, 104m
Baikalavia (Soviet C.I.S.), 151t
Baldanza, Ben, 184
Bali Air, 135
Bali International Air Services, 265
Balkan Bulgarian Airlines (TABSO), 62
Ball, Clifford, 8m, 104, 104m
Ballesteros, Crescencio, 322
Baltensweiler, Armin, 212
Baltic International (Latvia), 239
BAM. *See* Baikal-Amur Magristral railroad
Bamberg, Harold, 46, 59, 105, 331
Banfe, Bernard, 381
Bangkok Airways, 268–269
Bangladesh, 251m, 252, 253
Bangladesh Biman, 84, 253, 253m
 Aircraft operated, 253
 Name change to Bangladesh Airline, 253
Barbachano, Fernando, 324
Barkley, Paul, 172
Barnewell, Reginald, 297
Barratt, Colleen, 179
Barretto, Renato, 272, 282
Barrier Reef (Australia), 137c
Barry, Gordon, 20
Barry, John, 184
Bashkir Airlines (Soviet C.I.S.), 151t
Batik service, P.I.A., 252
Bavaria (Germany), charter airline, 64t
Bay, Rodolfo (Rudi), 218
Bayrischer (Germany), 4m
B.C. Airlines (Canada), flies Queen Elizabeth II, 310
B.C.A. *See* British Caribbean Airways; British Colonial Airways
B.C.P.A. *See* British Commonwealth Pacific Airlines
B.E.A. *See* British European Airways
Bearskin Airlines (Canada), 309m
Beauvais, Edward, 182
Bechuanaland National Airways. *See* Botswana National Airways
Beckman, Robert, 107
Beddoe, Clive, 308
Beech 18 (ex-military aircraft)
 Favored by commuter airlines, 92
 Hagerstown Commuter, 94
 Pacific Missionary Air Service, 300p
Beech 99
 Commuter airlines, 94
Beech 1900
 Air Botswana, 1990s, 404
 Australia, 2000s, 290
 Mines Air Services, Zambia, 394

Beech Baron
 Botswana National Airways, 1960s, 404
 Solair, 1968, 298
Beech Bonanza
 LIAT, 1960s, 330
Beech King-Air
 Nationwide Air, South Africa, 1990s, 403
 Transkei Airways, 1976, 403
Belarus CAD (Soviet C.I.S.), 151t
Belize Airways, 346
Bell 206 Longranger, compared to Mil Mi-2, 103p
Bell helicopters, 412
Bell Jet Ranger
 Air Mauritius, 407
Bellview Airlines (Nigeria), 381
Ben Ari, Mordechai, 77
Benoist XIV flying boat, world's first airline, 1p
Berchtold, Walter, 212
Berlin Accord, 1966, 62
Berlin Conference, 13
Bermuda Agreement, 29
"Bermuda II," 59, 143
Berta, Rubem, 316
Bez, Nick, 124, 125
B.G.A. *See* British Guiana Airways
BIA-COR Holdings, 160
"Big Apple" insignia, New York Airways, 128, 128p, 174
"Big Four," major U.S. airlines, 9c, 10m, 122
"Big Orange," name for Braniff Boeing 747, 159
"Big Six" Russian airlines, 157
Bishop, Ron, 38
Black, Hugo, 11
Black Entertainment Television, 169
Blair, Charlie, 338–339
Blanc, Christian, 200
Bland Line, interests in Gibraltar airlines, 224–225
Blériot, 4
Bloch, Federico, 319–320, 343
Bloch 120
 Air Afrique, 14, 14m
Bluck, Duncan, 331
"Blue Nile," Sudan Airways service, 67, 389
B.M.I. (and *bmibaby*). *See* British Midland International
bmibaby. *See* British Midland International
BOA. *See* Compagñía de Boliviana de Aviación
B.O.A.C. *See* British Overseas Airways Corporation
B.O.A.C. Associated Companies (B.O.A.C.A.C.)
 Diminishing interest in Middle East, 76
 Formation, 74
 Interests in Caribbean, 331

B.O.A.C., Inc., division of British Airways Board, 195
Bodensee (German airship service), 3
Boeing 247
 Introduced by United Air Lines, 10, 10p
 Superseded by Douglas DC-2, 12
Boeing 247D
 Empire Air Lines, 1946, 124
 Zimmerly Air Lines, 1946, 124
Boeing 307 Stratoliner
 AREA, Ecuador, 1951, 354
 Garde d'Haiti, 1943, 337
 Royal Air Cambodge, 1956, 278
 T.W.A., wartime trans-Atlantic service, 25
 Vietnam International Control Commission, 277p
 World's first pressurized airliner, 22
Boeing 377 Stratocruiser
 Boeing reenters commercial market, 30
 Military C-97 origins, 57
 RANSA, Venezuela, last operator, 1960s, 353–354
Boeing 707
 Aerlinte, 51
 Air Afrique, 1962, 376
 Air Florida, 160
 Air France, 51, 277p
 Air Gambia, 383
 Air Guinée, 1970s, 379
 Air Madagascar, 1967, 405
 Air Manila International, 1974–1976, 281
 Air Mauritius, 1976, 407
 Air Siam, 1970s, 267
 Air Zimbabwe, 1980, 394
 American Airlines, first in U.S. with own aircraft, 1959, 52, 52t
 American Trans Air, 1991, 183
 B.O.A.C., 1970s, 194
 B.W.I.A., 1960s, 328
 Bahamas World, 1970s, 332
 Braniff Airways, 158
 Cameroon Airlines, 1971, 378
 China Airlines, 1970, 269–270
 Cyprus Airways, 1970s, 226
 Ecuatoriana, 1976, 355
 Ethiopian Air Lines, 1968, 390
 First flight, orders, and services, 50–51, 51p
 First two years service by Pan American, 1958, 54v
 I.C.A., Caribbean, 1970s, 330
 Kenya Airways, 1977, 386
 L.A.P., Paraguay, 1978, 362
 LADECO, Chile, 1989, 369
 Last Pan American 707 retired, 1981, 162
 Malaysian-Singapore, 1960s, 259
 Malaysian, 1973, 261
 Model -138B, Pacific Western (Canada), 1967, 134
 Okada Air, Nigeria, 1983, 381

 Olympic Airways, 1966, 221
 Prototype, Model 367–80, 50
 QANTAS, 1959, 287
 Royal Air Maroc, 1976–1986, 372
 Rwandair, 1994, 387
 Singapore Airlines, 1972, 259
 Somali Airlines, 1970s, 388
 South African Airways, 1958, 399
 St. Lucia Airways, 1980s, 331
 Sudan Airways, 1972, 389
 Transmed Airlines, 1989–1996, 375
 Trek Airways, 1980, 402
 T.W.A., last 707 retired, 1983, 166
 Uganda Airlines, 1988, 387
 Zambia Airways, 1964, 393
 ZAS, Egypt, 1989, 375
Boeing 707-138B
 Braniff Airways, 158
 B.W.I.A., 1968, 328
 Ethiopian Air Lines, 1961, 390
 Kenya Airways, 386
 Pakistan, 1961, 352
 QANTAS, 1960, 287, 287p
Boeing 717, redesignation of Douglas MD-95, 1997, 117
 AirTran Airways, 1999, 180
 Impulse Airlines, 2000, 290
 Olympic Airways, 2000, 221
 Siem Reap Airways, 2000, 269, 279, 279p
Boeing 720/720B
 Aeromar, 336
 Aeronica, 1981, 343
 Air Malta, 1978, 224
 Air Rhodesia, 394
 American Trans Air, 1981, 183
 AVIANCA, 1968, 347
 Belize Airways, 1974, 346
 Cyprus Airways, 1970s, 226
 Eagle Air, 1976, 234
 Eastern Air Lines, 1963, 164
 Ecuatoriana, 1974, 355
 Korean Air Lines, 1969, 275
 Pakistan International, 1961, 252
Boeing 727
 Aces, 1981, 350, 350p
 Aero Costa Rica, 1992, 341
 Aeronica, 1981, 342
 Aerperú, 1974, 357
 Air Algérie, 1970s, 371
 Air Djibouti, 1963, 388
 Air Florida, 160
 Air Guinée, 1970s, 379
 Air Mali, 1961, 380
 Air Micronesia, 1968, 300
 Air Mongol, 1990s, 276
 Air Tungaru, 1981, 299
 All Nippon Airways, 1964, 145; 1965, 57
 American Airlines, 57
 Americana, 1990–1992, 358–359
 Ansett-A.N.A. and T.A.A., 286
 Aviacsa, 1994, 325
 AVIANCA, 1966, 347
 China Airlines, 1967, 269

Index

Comair, and Kulula.com, South Africa, 1990s, 402
Compañía de Aviación Faucett, 1968, crash, 356
Development history and first services, 57, 57p
Eastern Air Lines, 1963, 164
Eastern Provincial Airways, Canada, 1969, 134
Kabo Air, Nigeria, 1987, 381
Korean Air Lines, 1972, 275
Libyan Arab Airlines, 1970s, 373
Mexicana, 1965, 322–323; crash, 1986, 323
Nationwide Air, South Africa, 1998, 403
Okada Air, Nigeria, 1983, 381
Olympic Airways, 1969, 221
P.S.A. mid-air collision, 1978, 172
People Express, 174–175
PLUNA, Uruguay, 1970s, 363
Royal Air Maroc, 1976–1986, 372
SAHSA, Honduras, 1981, 342
Sierra Leone, 1990, 383
Singapore Airlines, 1972, 259
South African Airways, 1964, 399
"Stretched" to -200 series, 57
TAESA, Mexico, 1989, 325
Texas Air Corporation, Trump Shuttle, 1980s, 174
Toa Domestic, 1972, 149
Boeing 737
  Aero Continente, Peru, 1992, 358–359
  Aero Contractors, Nigeria, 2005, 382
  AeroMexico, 1970s, 323p
  AeroSvit, Ukraine, 239
  Air Algérie, 1970s, 371
  Air Asia (and subsidiaries), from 1996, 282–283, 283p
  Air Austral, 1990, 406
  Air California, 1968, 173
  Air Canada, 307
  Air Comoros, 1980s, 406
  Air Gabon, 1980s, 379
  Air Liberia, 1974, 379
  Air Guinée, 1970s, 379
  Air Madagascar, 1969, 405
  Air Malawi, 1991, 395
  Air Maldives, 1976, 257
  Air Mauritanie, 378
  Air Micronesia, 1990s, 201
  Air Mongol, 2002, 276
  Air Nauru, 1975, 299
  Air North, Canada, 1970s, 310
  Air Pacific, Fiji, 1998, 296
  Air Philippines, 1996, 282
  Air Tanzania, 1977, 386
  Air Vanuatu, 1990, 299
  Air Zaïre, 1973, 397
  Air Zimbabwe, 1985, 394, 394p
  AirTran Airways, 180
  Alaska Airlines, first 737-900 service, 2001, 118
  AMC Aviation, 2000s, 375
  Ansett and T.A.A., Australia, 1964, 286
  Arik Air, Nigeria, 2006, 382, 382p
  Asiana, 1988, 275
  Aviacsa, and TAESA, Mexico, 1997, 325, 325p
  Bahamasair, 1970s, 331
  Bouraq Indonesian Airlines, 1994, 265
  Braathens-SAFE, 1970s–1980s, 230–231, 230p
  Britannia Airways, 118
  C3, Canada, 2000s, 311
  Cameroon Airlines, 1971, 378
  Canadian Airlines International, 1986, 306
  CanJet Airlines, 2000, 310
  Chinese airlines, from late 1990s, 242t
  China Southern, 241p
  Chinese orders, 1985, 243, 245
  Comair, South Africa, 1990s, 402
  Conviasa, Venezuela, 1997, 353
  COPA, Panama, 1999, 345, 346p
  Croatia Airlines, 1993, 224
  Cronus, Greece, 1999, 222
  easyJet, 1980s–2000s, 187–190, 189p
  Egyptair, 1975, 374
  Ethiopian Air Lines, 2004, 391
  FAT, Taiwan, 1976, 270
  First Air, Canada, 2000s, 310
  Flash Airlines, crash, 2004, 375
  Flybe, 2000s, 193
  Frontier Airlines, 1967, 126
  Development history, -100 to -900 series, 118–119, 118p
  GOL, Brazil, 2000, 320–321, 320p
  Helios Airways, crash, 2005, 226
  Jet Airways, India, 1983, 249, 249p
  L.A.M., Mozambique, 1980s, 396
  LAPA, Argentina, 1993, 366, 367p
  Lauda Air, 1985, 237
  Lion Air, Indonesia, 1999, 284, 284p
  Lithuanian Airlines, 2000s, 239
  Maersk Airlines, 1976, 230
  Malaysian-Singapore, 1960s, 259
  Merpati Nusantara, Indonesia, 2000s, 265
  Mexican airlines, 1900s, 2000s, 326t
  Nordair, Canada, 1968, 134
  Pacific Western, Canada, 1970s, 307, 307p
  People Express, 1981, 175
  Piedmont Airlines, 1968, 122
  PLUNA, Uruguay, 1990s, 363, 364p
  Polynesian Airlines, 1978, 297
  Presidential Airlines, 1985, 176
  Record production, trans-ocean range, 118
  Riair, Latvia, 239
  Royal Air Cambodge, 1995, 279
  Royal Air Maroc, 1976–1986, 372
  Royal Brunei, 1975, 280
  Ryanair, 187–190, 188p, 189p
  SAETA, Ecuador, 1990s, 356
  SAHSA, Honduras, 1968, 342
  Sempati Air Transport, 1991, 266
  Servivensa, Venezuela, 1990s, 352p, 353p
  Seychelles, 1990s, 389
  Sibir, Russia, 2005, 153
  Singapore Airlines, 1972, 260
  South African Airways, 1968, 400, 401p
  Southwest Airlines, biggest operator, 118, 118p, 177
  Sterling Airlines, 2000s, 230–231
  Sudan Airways, 1975, 389
  Surinam, 1967, 334p
  TACA, Central America, 1978, 343
  TAESA, Mexico, 1991, 325
  Tournaï Air Chad, 1990s, 378
  Transaero, Russia, 1993, 152
  Transmed Airlines, 1989–1996, 375
  Uganda Airlines, 1977, 387, 387p
  VASP, Brazil, 1969, 317
  Vietnam Airlines, 1992, 278
  Virgin Blue, Australia, 2000, 290
  Virgin Nigeria, 2000s, 382
  WestJet, 1996, 308
  Zambia, 1998–2009, 394
Boeing 747 and 747SP
  Air Afrique, 2000s, 377
  Air Algérie, 372p
  Air Canada, 1971, 304
  Air China, 241p
  Air France, 201p
  Air Gabon, 1980s, 379
  Air Jamaica, 1976, 329
  Air Lanka, 1980s, 256
  Air Mauritius, 1984, 407
  Air Micronesia, 1990s, 301
  Air Pacific, Fiji, 1994, 296
  Air Siam, 1970s, 267
  Air Sinai, 1982, 375
  Air-India, crash near Ireland, 1985, 246
  American Airlines, 1970, 108
  Asiana, 1990s, 275, 275p
  AVIANCA, 1976, 347
  Braniff Airways, 158
  British Airways, 1970s, 196
  C.A.A.C., China, 1981, 240
  Cameroon Airlines, 1980s, 378, 378p
  China Airlines, 1979, 270
  Chinese airlines, from late 1990s, 242t
  Chinese orders, 1985, 243
  Eastern Air Lines, 1970, 164
  Egyptair, 1980s, 375
  Eva Air, 1989, 271
  Garuda Indonesian, 1980, 263
  Kabo Air, Nigeria, 1990s, 381
  Kenya Airways, 1980, 386
  Korean Air Lines, 1973, 275, 275p
  Kuwait Airways, 75p
  Launches Second Jet Age, 108, 108p
  Lufthansa, 1970, 202, 204p
  Namib Air, 1990, 404
  Okada Air, Nigeria, 1980s, 381
  Olympic Airways, 1973, 221
  People Express, 1983, 175
  Philippine Air Lines, 1980, 274
  QANTAS, 1971, 288
  Royal Air Maroc, 1976–1986, 372
  Shorouk Air, 1980s, 375
  Singapore Airlines, 1973, 260
  Solair, 1989, 298
  South African Airways, 1976, 399, 400p
  T.A.C., Thailand, 1970s, 267
  T.A.P., Portugal, 1972, 219
  Trek Airways, 1991, 402
Boeing 757-200
  Aeroperú Boeing 757, 358p
  AeroSvit, Ukraine, 2000s, 239
  Air Micronesia, 1998, 301
  Air Namibia, 1990, 404
  Air Pacific, Fiji, 1990, 296
  American Trans Air, 1991, 183
  Azerbaijan, 2000s, 239
  British Airways, 198p
  Cape Verde islands, 1996, 384
  Eastern Air Lines, 1983, 164
  Ethiopian Air Lines, 1990, 390
  Icelandair, 1990, 234
  Kenya Airways, 1990s, 386
  LAPA, Argentina, 1993, 366
  Phuket Air, Thailand, 2004, 269
  Royal Air Maroc, 1976–1986, 372
  Royal Brunei, 1986, 280
  Santa Barbara, Venezuela, 353, 353p
  Seychelles, 1990s, 389
  Shanghai Airlines, 241p
  TAESA, Mexico, 1991, 325
Boeing 767-200, -300ER
  Aeromexico, 1991, 324
  Air Canada, "The Gimli Glider," 304
  Air Madagascar, 1999, 405
  Air Mauritius, 1988, 407
  Air Pacific, Fiji, 1990, 296
  Air Zimbabwe 1988, 394
  Ansett and T.A.A., 1981, 286
  Asiana, 1990s, 275–276
  Austrian Airlines, 237p
  Chinese orders, 1985, 243
  Egyptair, 1980s, 375
  Ethiopian Air Lines, 1984, 390–391, 391p
  Eva Air, 1989, 271
  Gabon Airlines, 2007, 379
  L.A.I., Algeria, 1990, 371
  LAN Perú, 1999, 359
  Lauda Air, crash in Thailand, 1991, 237

Boeing 767-200, -300ER (*continued*)
  Mexicana, 1990, 324
  Piedmont Airlines, 1987, 124
  PLUNA, Uruguay, 1990s, 363
  Royal Air Maroc, 1976–1986, 372
  Royal Brunei, 1990, 280
  Santa Barbara, Venezuela, 2005, 353, 353p
  Seychelles, 1990s, 389
  T.W.A., 1983–1985, 166
  TAMPA, Colombia, 1970s, 350p
  Transbrasil, 1983, 318
  Ukraine International, 2003; Aero-Svit, Ukraine, 238–239
  Universal Airlines, Guyana, 2001, 334
  Vietnam Airlines, 1993, 278
  Virgin Nigeria, 2000s, 382
Boeing 777
  Air Austral, 2003, 406
  Air France, 1998, 200
  Air New Zealand, 2004, 293
  Alitalia, 2000s, 211p
  Arik Air, Nigeria, 2008, 382
  British Airways order, 1991, 197
  Egyptair, 1995, 375
  Kenya Airways, 2004, 386, 386p
  P.I.A., Pakistan, 2006, 253
  Singapore Airlines, 1999, 260
  Vietnam Airlines, 2001, 278
  Virgin Australia, 2007, 290
Boeing 787 Dreamliner, 261, 410
  Air Canada order, 2005, 307
  Air New Zealand order, 2004, 293
  Arik Air order, 2008, 382
  Ethiopian Air Lines order, 2005, 391
  Korean Air Lines order, 2005, 275
  Singapore Airlines order, 2006, 261
Boeing 2707
  Alitalia order, 1960s, 209
  Supersonic airliner project, 114
  Wins competition but cancelled by Congress, 1971, 115
Boeing Air Transport, 8m, 9c
Boeing B-17 bomber
  Atlantic service chronology, 28t
  Fri Reyes, Bolivia, last B-17 landing, 1977, 361
  L.A.B., Bolivia, 1950, 360
  Servicio Aereo Boliviano, 1950s, 361p
  SILA service to Africa, 1946, 35
Boeing B-314 flying boat
  Atlantic and Pacific service at outbreak of war, 23
  B.O.A.C. service, 1941, 23
  Pan American Airways, 1939, 15, 15p, 29
  "Return Ferry Service," 28t
Boeing Company, U.S. aircraft manufacturer
  Boeing-Boeing (movie), 54
  Forms ATLAS partnership, 111
  Forms United Air Lines, 9

Genealogy, 9c
  Merges with McDonnell-Douglas Corporation, 117
  Model 787 Dreamliner, 410
  Proposes Sonic Cruiser, 410
  Supersonic airliner project, 114
  Takes over de Havilland Canada, 95
  See also specific aircraft
Bolivian Air System (BAS), 361
Bolshoi Baltisky. See Russian Knight
Bomba Charger, competes with Antilles Air Boats, 339
Bombardier, Canadian aircraft manufacturer
  Buys de Havilland Canada (from Boeing) and Canadair, 95
  B.W.I.A. Express, 1995, 330
  Jersey European, 1999, 192
  See also de Havilland Canada Dash-8
Bonanza Air Lines (U.S.), 124
  Claims first all-jet airline (with F-27 fleet), 124, 124p
  Douglas DC-9 service, 118
  Genealogy, 123c
  Orders jet airliners, 60
Bond, William Langhorn, 18
Bop Air (South African homelands), 403
Boreal Airways (Canadian local airline), 134
Borman, Frank, 164–165
Boston-Maine Airways, becomes Northeast Airlines, 1940, 26t
Botswana National Airways, 404
Bouilloux-Lafont, Marcel, 18, 19
Boulton, Henry, 87, 351
Bouraq Indonesian Airlines, 84, 135, 265
  Aircraft operated, 136p, 265
Braathens-SAFE (Norwegian airline), 230–231, 230p
  Charter airline, 64t
  First service to Spitzbergen, northernmost airport, 231, 235m
  Partnership with Loftleidir, 30
  S.A.S. stake, 229
Brabazon Committees, 32, 44
Bradley Air Service, 310
Brain, L.J., 285
Brando, Marlon, 301
Braniff Airlines International, 160
Braniff Airways (and Braniff International), 158–159
  Aircraft operated, 114, 120, 158–159
  Buys PANAGRA, 1967, 158, 356
  Electra service and crash, 46
  Genealogy, 9c
  Post-war summary, 26
Branson, Richard, 191, 197, 290
Brasil Central, name change to TAM, 319
Brazil
  Brasilia, capital city stimulates air transport growth, 313

Early airline history, 18
  Fragmented transport, emergence of airline categories, 129–131
  Overseas travel deposit restricts airlines, 316
  Pays compensation to airlines, 318
  Regional airline routes, 318m
  See also Sistema Integrado de Transportes Aéreos Regional
Brazilian Blue, first Embraer 190 JetBlue, 2005, 182
Breech, Ernest, 165
Breguet, French aircraft manufacturer, 4
Breguet 14
  Latécoère Mission to Brazil, 1925, 18
Breguet Deux-Ponts, post-war double-decker transport aircraft, 55
Breguet-Nord, French aircraft manufacturer, 56, 109
Bremmer, Herbert, 236
Brenner, Mel, 166
Bretagne (French airliner), 371
Brierley Investments, 293
Bristol, British aircraft manufacturer, 59
  Brabazon Committees recommendation, 32
  Post-war development, 30
  See also specific aircraft
Bristol 170 Freighter/Wayfarer
  Air cargo, car ferry, 101, 102p, 105
  Air Djibouti, 1963, 388
  Post-war British airliner, 27, 32
  SAFE, New Zealand, 1951–1972, 292
  Wardair, Canada, 1950s, 310
  West African Airways, 1940s, 380
Bristol 175 Britannia
  B.O.A.C. round-the-world service. 45
  B.W.I.A., 1959, 328
  Brabazon Committee recommendation, 32
  Central African Airways, 1958, 392
  Compared to Lockheed Electra and Ilyushin Il-18, 48t
  Canadian Pacific Airlines, 1958, 305, 305p
  Cubana, 1958–1960, 337–338, 337p
  Cyprus Airways, 1970s, 226
  East African Airways, 1958, 385
  El Al service, 1957, 45, 45m, 77, 77p
  Entry into service, B.O.A.C., 1957, 45
  First flight, 44, 44p
  First London-New York nonstop service, 45
  "Flame-out" problem, 45
  Ghana Airways, 1959, 382
  Malayan-Malaysian, 1960s, 259
  Sierra Leone, 1960s, 383

Transcontinental and Entre Rios, Argentina, 1960–1969, 364
Trek Airways, 1968, 402
Bristol 200, wide-bodied twin design, 119
Bristol Brabazon, 31
Bristol Centaurus engine
  Airspeed Ambassador, 1948, 43
Bristol Britannia, 44
Bristol Olympus 593 engine, powers Concorde, 113
Bristol Proteus engine, powers Bristol Britannia, 44
Bristol Type 200, short-haul jet design, 57
Bristol Type 223, preliminary design for Concorde, 113
Britannia Airways (British charter airline), 64t, 118
Britavia group, 59
British Aerospace BAe 146 feeder jet, 90
  Aer Paraguay, 1993, 362
  Air Botswana, 1988, 404
  Air Zimbabwe, 1987, 394
  Albanian Airlines, 1990s, 225
  Aviacsa, Mexico, 1990, 325
  Buzz, Netherlands, 2000s, 192
  China Northwest, 1989, 242t
  Orders by Chinese companies, 1985, 243
  Debonair, 1994, 190
  Druk-Air, Bhutan, 1988, 258
  Jersey European, 1980s, 192
  Makung Airlines, 1990, 271
  P.S.A. service, 1984, 172
  Presidential Airlines, 1986, 176
British Aerospace BAe RJ-100
  Aegean Airlines, 1999, 221
British Air Tours (charter airline), 64t
British Aircraft Corporation (B.A.C.)
  Joint production of Concorde, 113
  Merger of British aircraft manufacturers, 59, 60
  See also BAC One-Eleven
British Airways, 194–198
  Buys British Caledonian, 187
  Buys shares of Iberia, partnership, 218
  Ceases to be a national corporation, 142
  Concorde grounded, Air France crash, 198
  Concorde service, 114, 113p, 114m
  Deutsche B.A., 191, 197
  Go, 191, 198
  Invests in, sells shares of US Air, 168–169
  Merger of B.O.A.C. and B.E.A., 105, 142
  SABENA proposal, 1989–1990, 214
  Stock offering, 142
  Success with Vickers Super-VC-10, 105
  Sued by R. Branson, 197

British Airways (pre-war), 21m
British Airways Associated Companies, 195
British Airways Board, 195
British Airways Engine Overhaul, division of British Airways Board, 195
British Airways Helicopters, division of British Airways Board, 195
British Airways Regional, division of British Airways Board, 195
British Asia, 271
British Caledonian Airways (B-Cal)
  Affinity groups, 143
  Charter airline, 64t
  Created by merger, 59
  Edwards Report and Bermuda II route benefits, 144, 194
  Leases to Sierra Leone, 383
  Sold to British Airways, 197
British Caribbean Airways (B.C.A.), 328, 330
  U.S. certificate withdrawn, 331
British Colonial Airways (B.C.A.) (Belize), 346
British Commonwealth Pacific Airlines (B.C.P.A.), 40, 137c, 305
British Eagle International Airways
  Inclusive tours, 63
  Moves into the Jet Age, 105
  Operates Britannias, agreement with Cunard shipping, 46
  Remains independent, 59
British European, 192–193
British European Airways (B.E.A.)
  BAC One-Eleven service, 120–121, 121p
  B.E.A. as division of British Airways Board, 195
  B.E.A. Airtours, 195
  B.E.A. Helicopters, 195
  Comet 4B service, 47
  Compromises de Havilland Trident sales prospects, 119
  Consortium with Olympic Airways, 221
  First fully automatic touch-down, 195
  Formation of British Airways, 105, 196
  Operates Trident 1C, 1E, 2E, and 3B, 58
  Operations with Cyprus Airways, 80
  Opposes closed group operators, 1950s, 1960s, 63
  Partnerships with Malta, Gibraltar, Cyprus, 1950s, 224–225
  Post-war Viking service, 27, 28p
  Promotes Viscount airliner, 37, 37p
  Separates domestic services, 90
  Trident, 1964, 57, 57p
  Vanguard service, 1961, 47
  Viscount 700, 1953, 37–38, 38m
  Viscount 801 service, 1957, 44

British Guiana Airways (B.G.A.), 328, 334
British Honduras Airways, change of name from British Colonial, 1956, 346
British International Airlines (B.I.A.L), subsidiary of B.O.A.C., 74
British Latin American Airlines (BLAIR), name change to B.S.A.A., 33
British Mediterranean, franchised from British Airways, 1990s, 198
British Midland and British Midland International (B.M.I.)
  Charter airline, 1975, 64t
  B.M.I. starts low-fare subsidiary bmibaby, 2001, 192
  Sells shares to Lufthansa, 204
  Eurocity Express, 1987, 214
British Overseas Airways Corporation (B.O.A.C.) (U.K.), 23
  Acquisition of other airlines, 328
  Aids Eagle Air, Iran, 71
  Assists Air Ceylon, 255
  Comet 4 service and routes, 1958–1960, 53, 53m
  Comet jet airliner, 40
  Cunard shipping, 46, 331
  Formation of British Airways, 105, 196
  Interest in M.E.A., 72
  Middle East subsidiary. See ABAMEL
  Nonstop London-New York round-the-world service, 45
  North Atlantic service chronology, 28
  North Atlantic, Europe-East Asia, Europe-trans-Africa jet debuts, 52t
  Obliged to buy American aircraft, 31
  Operates Canadian DC-4 into Jet Age, until 1960, 45
  Overtaken by Pan American, 108
  Polar service, 1960, 34t
  Post-war service to Africa, 35
  Quadripartite pool with East African, C.A.A., and South Africa, 1960s, 385
  Super-VC-10s, 194–195, 195p
  Vickers VC-10 destroyed by P.F.L.P., 1970, 212
  Wartime "Horseshoe" route, 24, 24m
  Withdraws from Gulf Air, 76
  World's first jet airline services, 39, 39m, 40m
British Post Office, 12
British Regional, 198
British South American Airways (B.S.A.A.), 33, 33t, 328, 331
British United Airways. See B.U.A.

End of the Second Force, 197
Formed, 59, 105
Inclusive tours, 63
Launches BAC One-Eleven, 60
Moves into the Jet Age, 105
Vickers VC-10 service, 120
British West Indian Airways (B.W.I.A.) (West Indian airline), 328
  Atlantic service chronology, 28t
Britt Airways (U.S.), 175
Britten-Norman BN-2 Islander
  Air Calédonie, 1980s, 302
  Air Hebrides, 1970s, 299
  Air Mahé, 1970s, 388
  Air Malawi, 1964, 395
  Air Moorea, Air Tahiti, 1968, 301
  Air Seychelles, 1970s, 388
  Alas del Caribe, 1972, 336
  Botswana National Airways, 1990s, 404
  Cape Verde Islands, 1970s, 384
  FIGAS, Falkland Islands, 1979, 370
  Fiji Air, 2000s, 297p
  Indonesian Air transport, 136p
  Isleña, Honduras, 1960s, 342, 344
  LIAT, 1970s, 330
  Malaysian, 1973, 261
  Operations in Indonesia, 84
  Pacific Sun, 2008, 296p
  PATI, Philippines, 1978, 273
  Polynesian Airlines, 1978, 297
  Solair, 1968, 298
  Sun Air, South Africa, 1996, 403
  Sunflower Airlines, Fiji, 296
  Trans Guyana, 1997, 334
  Transkei Airways, 1976, 403
  Travelair, Costa Rica, 1991, 341
Britten-Norman Trislander
  Air Hebrides, 1970s, 299
  Air Pacific, Fiji, 1974, 295
  Air Tungaru, 1978, 299
  Bali Air, Indonesia, 136p
  Inter-Island Airways, Seychelles, 1976, 388
  Travelair, Costa Rica, 1991, 341
Bronner, David, 169
Brounstein, Mickey, 339
Brown, Walter F., 9, 10, 11
Brown, Sam, 140
Bruggisser, Philippe, 212
Brymon (U.K.), 198
B.S.A.A. See British South American Airways
B.U.A. See British United Airways
Buch, Francisco, 20
Buchanan, Dennis, 294, 299
Buffett, Warren, 168
"Bullet train" (Japan). See Shin Kan-sen
Burma, independence (as Myanmar), 251, 251m
Burma Airways Corporation (B.A.C.), 256
Burr, Donald, 174

Bush Pilots Airways (Australia), 289, 289p
Busy Bee, low-fare affiliate of Braathens, 231
Butler Air Transport, becomes Airlines of New South Wales, 90, 137, 137c, 286
Butler, C.A., 137
Buzz, low-fare Cityhopper, 192, 216
B.W.I.A. See British West Indian Airways.
B.W.I.A. Express, 330
By Love Possessed, first on-board movie, 166

C3. See Canada 3000
C.A.A. See Central African Airways; Civil Aviation Authority (Britain); Civil Aviation Authority (U.S.); Compagnie Aérienne Antillaise
C.A.A.C. See Civil Aviation Administration of China
C.A.A.K. See Air Koryo
C.A.B. See Civil Aeronautics Board
Cable Commuter, ancestor of Golden State, 95m
C.A.L. See China Airlines
Calder, Alexander, 159
Caledonian Airways (British independent airline), 59, 197
Califano, Joseph, 115
California Central Airlines (intra-state airline), 171
Calm Air (Canada), 306
Cambodian International Airlines, 279
Cambrian Airways, partial division of British Airways Board, 195
Cameroon Airlines, 378, 378p
Cammacorps, builds Douglas DC-70 series, 52
Campañía Guatemalteca de Aviación (AVIATECA), 340–341
  Aircraft operated, 340p, 344
  Joins Grupo TACA, 340
Campbell, John, 296
C.A.N. See Correio Aéreo Nacional
Canada
  Bilateral agreement with United States, 1995, 306
  Post-war classification of nine airline categories, 309
  Public Participation Act, 304
  Regional airlines, 133–134, 134m, 309m
  Remove restrictions on charter airlines, 1984, 311
Canada 3000 (C3), 311–312
Canadair Air (Micronesia), 300
Canadair CL-44
  Cyprus Airways, 226
  Loftleidir, 233
Canadian Airlines International (C.A.I.), 306

Canadian Airways, ancestor of
    C.P.Air, 304
Canadian Colonial Airlines, 9c
Canadian North, 309m
Canadian Pacific Airlines (C.P.A.),
    133, 304–307, 305m
  Absorbs local airlines, 306
  Bristol Britannias, 1958, 305, 305p
  de Havilland Comet 1A, crash,
    1953, 305
  Name change to CP Air, 1968, 306
  Polar service, 34t
  Route map, 1957, 305m
  Transfers routes to Pacific Western,
    1957–1959, 134
  Upgrades fleet with Britannias, 46
Canadian Regional, 307
Canhedo, Wagner, 317
CanJet Airlines (Canada), 308, 310,
    312
Cannibalism, TAMU, Uruguay, 363
Cant Z506 (Italian airliner), 14
Canteen Company, 166
Cape Air (Guam), 301
Cape-to-Cairo
  Basis for British air services, 14, 69
  Railway never completed, 35
Capital Airlines
  First coach-class fares, 139
  Introduces Viscount to U.S.,
    43–44, 43p
  Name change from P.C.A., 26t
  Post-war emergence as competitor,
    28
  See also Nighthawk fares
Capitol International (U.S. Supple-
    mental airline), 65t
Caraïbes Air Transport (CAT). See Air
    Caraïbes
Caravelle, Sud-Est SE-210 (French
    airliner)
  Aero O/Y, Finland, 1960, 232
  Aerotal, Aerocesar, Colombia,
    1960s–1970s, 349
  Air Afrique, 1967, 376
  Air Algérie, 1960, 56, 371, 371p
  Air Centrafique, 1965, 378
  Air Congo, 1960s, 397
  Air Liban, 55–56
  Air Vietnam, 1958, 277, 278p
  Alitalia, 98
  Austrian Airlines, 1963, 236
  AVENSA, Venezuela, 1964, 352
  Development history, first flight,
    services, 56, 56m
  Filipinas Orient Airways, 1972,
    282
  Gabon Express, last scheduled
    airline service, 1999, 379
  Kabo Air, Nigeria, 1981, 381
  LAN, Chile, 1964, 367
  Promotion, 32
  Royal Air Cambodge, 1969, 278,
    279p
  Royal Air Lao, 1969, 280

Royal Air Maroc, 1960, 56, 372
Tunisair, 1961, 372
SAETA, Ecuador, 1975, 356
T.A.P., Portugal, 1962, 220
Thai International, 1964, 266
Transasian Airlines, 1970s, 282
Carco Air Service (U.S.), 92
Carey, Guillermo, 368
Cargo aircraft, 101–102
Cargolux Airlines International
    (Luxembourg), 234
Caribbean Air Cargo, 330
Caribbean Air Transport, 330
Caribbean Star, 330
Caribbean West, 330
Caricargo (Caribbean), 330
Carlson, Jon, 228
Carney, Robert, 127
Carr, Hal, 125
Carrington, Lord, 111
Carrión, Jaime, 338
Carter, James ("Jimmy"), 106, 127,
    140, 161, 172
Carvair (car-carrying aircraft)
  Devised by Freddie Laker, 102
  Flies cars across the Channel, 105
Carvalho, Erik de ("Mr. Erik"), 316
CASA, Spanish aircraft manufacturer,
    135
  See also specific aircraft
CASA 212 Aviocar
  Aeronica, 1981, 343
  Prinair, 1983, 338
  SANSA, Costa Rica, 1980, 341
  SATENA, Colombia, 1984, 349
Casey, John, 159
Cassani, Barbara, 191
Castro, Fidel, 45, 337
CAT. See Air Caraïbes
C.A.T. See Civil Air Transport
Catair (French charter airline), 64t
Catalina Air Transport
  Ancestor of Golden State, 95m
  Name change from Wilmington-
    Catalina, 26t
Catalina flying boat. See Consolidated
    PBY-5
CATASA, Argentine industrial
    company, 364
Cathay Pacific Airlines, 244m
CATIC, Chinese purchasing agency,
    240
CAUSA. See Compañía Aeronaútica
    Uruguaya
Cayman Airways, 332
Cayman Brac Airways, 332
Cayman Islands (local airline), 328
C.C.A.A. See China Civil Aviation
    Administration
C.C.N.A. See Compañía Colombiana
    de Navegación Aérea
C.C.T.A. See Compagnie Chérifienne
    de Transports Aériens
C.D.A. See Compañía Dominica de
    Aviación

C.E.A. See Compañía Ecuatoriana de
    Aviación; Cunard-Eagle Airways
Cempella, Domenico, 210
Central African Airways (C.A.A.),
    392–393
  Aircraft operated, 392–393
  Comet 4 service, 53
  Founded 1946, 30
  Long-range service, 67
  Quadripartite pool with East
    African, B.O.A.C., S.A.A., 385,
    392
  Route map, 1955, 392m
Central Air Lines, 9c
Central Airlines (U.S.), 123c, 126
Central Atlantic Routes, 33, 33t
Central Intelligence Agency (C.I.A.)
    (U.S.)
  C.A.T., Taiwan, 269
  St. Lucia Airways, 331
Central Japan Airlines, sold to All Nip-
    pon Airways, 145
Central Mountain Air (Canada),
    309m
Central Transport (U.S.), 92
Century 21, real estate company, 166
Cereti, Fausto, 210
Ceskoslovenske Statni Aerolinie
    (C.S.A.) (Czechoslovakia), 42,
    45–46, 62, 201, 211, 337
  Central Atlantic route, 33t
  Jet service, Tu-104, 42
  Member of Six-Pool, operates
    Tu-134, 62
  Supports Cuban Britannias, 1959,
    45–46
Cessna 206, 208s
  Aéreo Calafia, Mexico, 1993, 326
Cessna 402
  A.S.A., Chile, 1987, 369
  Air Ontario, 1987, 310
  Bahamasair, 1990s, 331
  Bush Pilots, Australia, 1970s, 289,
    289p
  Freedom Air, Guam, 1978, 300
  Island Air, Guam, 1976, 300
  Tunisair, 1960s, 372
Cessna Bobcat, P.B.A. service, 92
Cessna Caravan and Grand Caravan
  Air Caraïbes, 2000, 335
  Conviasa, Venezuela, 2004, 353
  Inter, Guatemala, 344
  Trans Guyana Airways, 1997, 334
Ceylon, name change to Sri Lanka,
    1972, 251, 251m
C.F.R.N.A. See Compagnie Franco-
    Roumaine de Navigation
    Aérienne
C.G.E.A. See Compagnie des Grands
    Express Aériens
C.G.T.A. See Air Algérie
C.H.A. See Chicago Helicopter
    Services
Chalk, "Pappy," 92
Chalk's Flying Service (U.S.), 92

Challenger Airlines (U.S.), forms
    Frontier Airlines, 123c, 125,
    126m
Chanchangi Airlines (Nigeria), 381
Chang, Leandro Chiok, 358
Chang'an Airlines, 241m, 242t
Channel Airways, de Havilland Tri-
    dent service, 119
Channel Islands Airways, partial
    division of British Airways
    Board, 195
Channel Tunnel
  Effect on airlines, 214
  Effect on high-speed rail, 412
  Opened 1994, 413
Chaplin Air Line, 2m
Chaplin, Syd, 8
Charter One (U.S.), name change to
    Spirit Airlines, 183
Chase Manhattan Bank, retains Jet
    Capital Corporation, 127
Chatrachai Bunya-Ananta, 267–268
Chavez, Calixto, 341
Chavez, Hugo, 353
Checchi, Alfred, 215
  Chiang Kai-shek, 17
Chicago & Southern Airlines (C&S),
    26, 26t
Chicago Express, 183
Chicago Helicopter Services
    (C.H.A.), 412
China
  Airlines of China, 1990s,
    ex-C.A.A.C., 241m, 242t
  High-speed rail, 414–415, 414t,
    415p, 416m
  Political uncertainties during
    1920s, 17
China Airlines (C.A.L.)
  Aircraft operated, 269–270
  Dynasty class service, 270
  Series of crashes, 1992–2007, 270
  Trans-Pacific route, 269
China Airways Federal (China), 17
China Civil Aviation Administra-
    tion (C.C.A.A.), first airline of
    China, 132
China Eastern, 241m, 242t
  Formed 1984, 243
  MD-82, 241p
China Flying Dragon, 241m, 242t
China General, 241m, 242t
China National Aviation Corporation
    (C.N.A.C.) (China), 17, 17m,
    17p, 18
China Northern, 241m, 242t, 243
China Northwest, 241m, 242t, 243
China Southern, 241m, 242t, 243
  Boeing 737-500, 241p
  Route map, 2003, 416m
China Southwest, 241m, 242t, 243
China United, 241m, 242t, 243
China Xinhua, 241m, 242t, 243
China Xinjiang, 241m, 242t, 243
China Yunnan, 241m, 242t, 243

Index

Chinische-Deutsche Luftverkehrs-gesellschaft. *See* Eurasia
Chkalov, Valery, 21
Chodrow, Jeffrey, 160
"Chosen Instrument," government-favored airlines, 14
Chou En-lai, 99, 132
Churchill, Winston, 24
C.I.A. *See* Central Intelligence Agency
Cimberair (Denmark), 227, 230
CINTA. *See* Compañía Nacional de Turismo Aéreo
Cintra (Corporación International de Transporte Aéreo), Mexican airline holding company, 324
Cipriani, Antonio, 318
C.I.S. *See* Commonwealth of Independent States
Cisneros, Maximo, 377
CitiExpress, British Airways consolidation of franchised airlines, 198
Citizen's League against the Sonic Boom, 115
City Jet, Lufthansa's Boeing 737 service, 202
CityFlyer (U.K.), 198
Cityhopper, K.L.M. subsidiary, 215
  Changes name to Buzz, 192
Civil Aeronautics Board (C.A.B.)
  Advisory Committee on Procedural Reform, 140
  Approves Laker's Skytrain service, 1977, 140
  Categories of U.S. airlines, 122
  Deregulation, 127, 139–140
  Dispute with APSA, 377
  Faces increase in tourist traffic, 82
  Opposes Supplemental airlines, 65
  Pacific Route Case, Braniff, 158
  Recognizes term *third level*, 93
  Reviews status of air taxi services, 92
  "Use-it-or-lose-it," instruction, 94
Civil Air Transport (C.A.T.) (Taiwan), 269, 269m
Civil Aviation Administration of China (C.A.A.C.), 119, 135, 225, 240–245, 241m, 242t, 269, 270
  Aircraft operated, 58, 240
  Boeing 747SP service to U.S.A., 1981, 240–241
  Handicapped by "Cultural Revolution," 90
  Reaches Lhasa, Tibet, 1980s, 243
  Renamed from Civil Aviation Bureau, 1962, 133
  Trident 2E and 3B operations, 58, 58m, 58p
Civil Aviation Authority (England), 196
Civil Aviation Authority (U.S.), 122
  See also Federal Aviation Administration

CL-600 Challenger (Bombardier business jet), 95
Clarkson, Richard, 38, 90, 109
Click Mexicana, 326t
  Rebranded from Aerocaribe, 326
Cloud Nine, upper deck lounge on Philippine Airlines, 274
C.M.A. *See* Compagnie des Messageries Aériennes; Compañía Mexicana de Aviación
C.M.T.A. *See* Compañía Mexicana de Transportación
C.N.A.C. *See* China National Aviation Corporation
Coast-to-Coast Travel Costs, air, rail, and bus fares compared, 1950s, 65t
Coates, Sam, 290
Cobham, Alan, 13
COHATA. *See* Compagnie Haïtienne de Transports Aériens
Cohen, Arthur, 160
Cojuanco, Antonio, 274
Colgan Airways (U.S.), 176
Colodny, Edwin, 168
Colombia, terrain, 347m
Colonial Air Transport (and Airlines)
  Contract air mail route (CAM 1) 1926, 8m
  Contract air mail route (FAM 1) 1926, 8
  Genealogy, 9c
  Post-war summary, 26t
Colonial Western Airlines, 9c
Colorado Airways
  Contract air mail route (CAM 12), 8m
  Genealogy, 9c
Comair (Commercial Air Services) (South Africa), 402
  Aircraft operated, 402, 402p
  Franchised from British Airways, 198, 402
Commercial Aviation (Australia), becomes MacRobertson-Miller, 137c
Common Market Commuter, SABENA, 213–214
Commonwealth of Independent States (post–U.S.S.R. collapse), 150, 150t
  Airlines, 151t
Commuter airlines
  Definition of passengers, 122
  Growth in U.S., 96m-97m
  Impact of U.S. highway system, 94
  Formerly "Third Level" or "Scheduled Air Taxi," 122
  Origins, 92
  U.S. Local Service airlines, 123c
Comoros. *See* Air Comoros
Compagnie Aérienne Antillaise (C.A.A.), 334–335
Compagnie Aériennes Gabonaise. *See* Air Gabon

Compagnie Chérifienne de Transports Aériens (C.C.T.A.), early name for Royal Air Maroc, 68, 372
Compagnie des Grands Express Aériens (C.G.E.A.) (France), 4
Compagnie des Messageries Aériennes (C.M.A.) (France), 4
Compagnie Franco-Roumaine de Navigation Aérienne (C.F.R.N.A.) (France), 4
Compagnie Générale de Transports (C.G.T.A.). *See* Air Algérie
Compagnie Haïtienne de Transports Aériens (COHATA) (Haiti), 336–337
Compagnie Nationale. *See* Air Gabon
Compañía Aérea Cubana, 5, 377–378
  Britannia service, link with C.S.A., 45
  Central Atlantic service, 1949, 33, 33t
Compañía Aeronaútica Uruguaya (CAUSA), 363
Compañía Boliviana de Aviación (BOA), 361
Compañía Colombiana de Navegación Aérea (C.C.N.A.) (Colombia), country's first airline, 5
Compañía de Aviación Faucett (Peru), 19m, 356, 356p
  Aircraft operated, 356p
Compañía Rio-Platense de Aviación, 6
Compañía Dominica de Aviación (C.D.A.), 336
  Aircraft operated, 336
  Douglas DC-9s, crash, 1970, 336, 336p
Compañía Ecuatoriana de Aviación (C.E.A. or Ecuatoriana) (Ecuador), 354–355
  Douglas DC-10, 354p
  Joins TAN consortium, 354
  LAN-Chile takeover, 355
  Lockheed L.188s grounded, 354–355
  VASP shareholding, 317
Compañía Mexicana de Aviación (C.M.A. or Mexicana) (Mexico), 322–324, 323p, 326
  Aeromexico stake, 324
  Britannia service, 45, 322
  Sold to Grupo Posadas, 324
  Takes over ATSA and TAMSA, 322
  Takes over C.M.T.A., 6
Compañía Mexicana de Transportación (C.M.T.A.), 6
Compañía Nacional de Turismo Aéreo (CINTA) (Chile), 367
Compañía Panameña de Aviación (COPA), 340, 344
  Name change to Copa Airlines, 345
Compass Airlines (Australia), 289–290

Compass Mark II (Australia), 290
Conair (Scandinavian charter airline), 64t
Concorde
  Braniff Airways, 114, 159
  First service, Air France, 199
  First service, British Airways, 196
  Fleet withdrawn, 2003, 198
  Grounded after Air France crash, 2000, 198, 201
  History, 1954–2003, 113–114, 113p
  Mobutu, special flights, 397
  Ordered by IranAir, 71
  QANTAS order, 287
  Restricted service, v. turboprop "workhorses," 89
  Service record, 1976–2003, 114M
"Concordski." *See* Tupolev Tu-144
Condor Luftreederei/ Flugdienst (German charter airline), 63–64, 64t, 205
Condor Syndikat (German aircraft export company), 6
  Linha da Lagôa, Brazil, 1927, 18
  See also Syndicato Condor
Connellan, E.J., 137, 137c
Connellan Airways, 137, 137c, 286
Conquest Sun Holdings, acquired by AirTran Holdings, 180
Consolidated Commodore (U.S. flying boat), 14, 18, 331
  Bahamas Airways, 1940s, 331
Consolidated Coronado (U.S. military flying boat), 27
Consolidated Liberator, wartime trans-Indian Ocean service, 24
Consolidated PBY-5 and -6 (Catalina flying boats)
  Canadair Air, Micronesia, 300
  Compañía de Aviación Faucett, 356
  In the Brazilian Amazon, 314
  LAN, to Easter Island, 357
  TRANSA, to Juan Fernandez Island, 369
  Trans-Indian Ocean service, 24
Consorcio de Industrias Aeronáuticas y Servicios Aéreos (Conviasa) (Venezuela), 353
Construction, aircraft
  Composite materials, 417
Continental Air Micronesia, 301
Continental Airlines (U.S.)
  Bankruptcy, 128
  Bermuda II route benefits, 144
  Buys People Express, 175–176
  Contract air mail route (CAM 16), 8m
  Controls COPA, 345
  Forms Air Micronesia, 300
  Genealogy, 9c, 123c
Continental Airlines (ex-Varney), post-war summary, 26t
Continental Connection (Guam), 301

Continental Express
  Partnership with Presidential Airlines, 176
  Takes first delivery of Embraer 145 jet, 95
Convair 540, Napier-engined trials with Allegheny Airlines, 122
Convair 580 (turboprop airliner)
  Afrikaans Suidwes, 1959, 404
  Air Ontario, 1987, 310
  Allegheny Airlines and Lake Central, 1966, 122
  AVENSA, 1964, 87, 352
  Frontier Airlines, 1964, 126
  North Central Airlines, 1967, 125
  Peau Vava'u, 2005, 298
  Prinair, 1981, 338
Convair 600 (Rolls-Royce Dart-engined twin airliner)
  ARCO, Uruguay, 363
  Central Airlines, 126
  Trans Texas Airways, 127
Convair 640 turboprop
  Pacific Western Airlines, 1967, 134
Convair 880
  Bahamas World, 1970s, 332
  C.A.T., Taiwan, 1961, 269
  LANICA, Nicaragua, 1972, 242
  T.W.A., 1961, 165
  VIASA, Venezuela, 1961, 351
Convair 990 and 990A
  APSA, Peru, 1963–1970, 377
  AREA, Ecuador, 1968, 354
  Garuda Indonesian, 1963, 263
  Ghana Airways, 1963, 382
  REAL/VARIG, 1961, 315
  Spantax, 1967, 219
  Thai International, 1962, 266
Converse, Ed, 124, 125
Conviasa. *See* Consorcio de Industrias Aeronáuticas y Servicios Aéreos
Conway, Michael, 184
Cook, Thomas, 204
Cook Island Airways, 298
Coolidge, Calvin, 9
COPA. *See* Compañía Panameña de Aviación
Corfield, Frederick, 111
Corporación Falcon, 323
Corporación International de Transporte Aéreo. *See* Cintra
Corr, Joseph, 180
Correio Aéreo Nacional (C.A.N.) (Brazilian military airline), 87
Costeña, La (Nicaragua), 344
Coulson, Luis, 350
Court Line (U.K.), buys LIAT, 328
CP Air. *See* Canadian Pacific Airlines
CP Commuters, Canadian airline group, 306
C.P.A. *See* Canadian Pacific Airlines
Crashes, deliberate
  Egyptair, 1999, 375
  Royal Air Maroc, ATR-42, 1995, 372
Crisis, La, 323–324

"Critter," ValuJet logo, 179–180
CRJ-200
  Adria, Jugoslavia, 1991, 224
  ALMA de Mexico, 2006, 327
  Canadian commuter airliner, 94p, 95
  China Yunnan, Shandong Airlines, 1990s, 242t
  Jazz, 2000s, 307
  Jersey European, 1999, 192
CRJ-900
  Arik Air, Nigeria, 2006, 382
  Libyan Airlines, 2003, 373
Croatia Airlines, 224
Cronus Airlines (Greece), 222
Crossair (Swiss charter airline), 212
Crowley, Karl, 11
Crowley, Lawrence, 298
Cruz, Ramon, 273
Cruz Airways (Philippines), 281
Cruzeiro do Sul (Brazil)
  Acquired by VARIG, 1975, 129, 316
  Operates Nihon YS-11s, 1967, 88
C.S.A. *See* Ceskoslovenske Statni Aerolinie
C.T.A. *See* Cyprus Turkish Airlines
Cueto, Enrique, 319–320, 369
Culmann, Herman, 203
Cunard, shipping line, 46, 331
  Shares in Air Jamaica, 328
Cunard-Eagle Airways (C.E.A.), 46
Cunningham, John, 38, 39, 40, 50
Curtiss Aeroplane & Motor Company, 9c, 17, 79
  See also specific aircraft
Curtiss C-46 (U.S. twin-engined airliner)
  At high altitude, La Paz, Bolivia, 360–361
  Dominican Republic, post-war use, 336
  RANSA, Venezuela, 1948–1964, 353–354
  TAN consortium, Latin American low-fare fleet, 342, 354
  Wartime supply route to China, 26
Curtiss JN-4H biplane, 3, 7
Curtiss 75 (military F-5L), 8
Curtiss-Wright, post-war development, 30
Cush, David, 366
Cutter-Clark Flying Service (U.S.), 92
Cyprus Airways, 80–81, 225–226
  de Havilland Trident, Comet 4B service, 119, 226
  Problems of a divided island, loss of fleet, 225–226
  Resumption of service, 1975, 226
Cyprus Turkish Airlines (C.T.A.), 226
Czechoslovakia
  Assists Cubana, 337
  First airline service, 5

Dai Nippon Koku (D.N.K.) (Greater Japan Airlines), 18, 25

Daimler car company, and early British airlines, 3
Daly, Ed, 66
Danair (British charter airline)
  Big Comet operator, 64, 64t
  Demise, 190
  Purchased by British Airways, 197
Danzig Free State (first airline service), 5
DAP. *See* Aerovías DAP
Dart-Dakota
  First service as B.E.A. freighter, 1951, 37
Dassault Falcon
  Air Nauru, 1970, 299
Davis, Tom, 122
Davis, Tony, 284
Davis & Newman Holdings. *See* Danair
DC Air, proposed airline, 2000, to buy US Airways, 2000, 169
D.C.A. *See* Dutch Caribbean Airways
De Gaulle, Charles, 114, 376
De Haenen, Remy de, 334
de Havilland, Geoffrey, 38
de Havilland, Geoffrey (son), 38
de Havilland Australia, Drover
  Fiji Airways, 1954, 295
de Havilland Canada Dash-7, 95
  Asian Spirit Airlines, 1996, 282
  Conviasa, Venezuela, 353
  Eurocity Express, 1987, 214
  Greenlandair, 1979, 235
  Tyrolean Airways, 1980, 237
de Havilland Canada Dash-8, 95
  Aero Contractors, Nigeria, 2005, 382
  Air Niugini, 2006, 295
  Albanian Airlines, 1992, 225
  Bahamasair, 1990, 331
  Bangkok Airways, 1989, 268
  Great China Airlines, Taiwan, 1987, 271
  Presidential Airlines, 1989, first in U.S., 176
  See also Bombardier
de Havilland Canada DHC-2 Beaver
  Air Malawi, 1964, 395
  Canadian post-war bush workhorse, 310
  FIGAS, Falkland Islands, 1948, 370
de Havilland Canada DHC-5 Buffalo
  Ethiopian Air Lines, 70, 390
de Havilland Canada DHC-6 Twin Otter
  Aces, Colombia, 1980s, 350
  Aeroperlas, Panama, 1970, 344
  Aervías DAP, Chile, 1980, 370
  Air Calédonie, 1980s, 302
  Air Djibouti, 1980s, 388
  Air Guadeloupe, 1970s, 335
  Air Maldives, 1980s and 1990s, 257
  Air Mauritius, 1975, 407
  Air Tanzania, 1978, 386
  Air Vanuatu, 1980, 299

Austin Airways, Canada, from 1958, 310
  Canadian post-war bush workhorse, 310
  Cape Verde Islands, 1978, 384
  China Flying Dragon, 242t
  Commuter airlines, 92p, 94
  Ethiopian Air Lines, 1980s, 391
  Greenlandair, 1960, 235
  Indonesian airlines, 84
  L.A.V., Venezuela, 1970s, 352
  Merpati Nusantara, Indonesia, 1960–1970s, 135, 135p; 2000s, 265
  NaturAir, Costa Rica, 2001, 341
  Pacific Sun, Fiji, 2008, 296
  Panama, 1980, 346
  R.A.I., Tahiti, 1970, 301
  Rwandair, 1994, 387
  Sudan Airways, 1960s, 389
  SunAir, South Africa, 1996, 400
  Sunflower Airlines, Fiji, 1990s, 296
  Surinam, 1962, 334
  T.A.L., New Guinea, 1972, 294
  Wideroe, Norway, 1968, 231
de Havilland Comet 3, ordered by Pan American Airways, 40
de Havilland Comet 4 and 4C
  Aerolíneas Argentinas, 1959, 365
  Air Ceylon, 1960s, 255
  AREA, Ecuador, 1966, 354
  B.O.A.C. routes, 1958–1960, 53m
  Central African Airways, 1961, 393
  East African Airways, 1960, 385
  Excellent field performance, 53
  Malayan-Malaysian, 1960s, 259
  Mexicana, 1960, 322
  Nigeria Airways, 1962, 380
  Sudan Airways, 1962, 389
  World's first trans-ocean jet airline service, 1958, 50, 50p
de Havilland DH-4 biplane fighter
  A.T.&T., 1919, 3
  First World War, 38
de Havilland DH-4B
  U.S. Post Office air mail service, 7p
de Havilland D.H. 66 Hercules (British airliner), 11
de Havilland D.H. 88 Comet, wins England–Australia Air Race, 12
de Havilland D.H. 89A Rapide
  biplane, 1930s popularity, 23p
  Air Djibouti, 1963, 388
  Air Gabon, 1951, 378
  Air Ivoire, 1958, 377
  Air Madagascar, 1940s–1960s, 405
  Air Mahé, 1970s, 388
  B.E.A. Scilly Islands service, pre-1964, 195
  Fiji Airways, 1951, 295
  Liberian National, 1949, 379
  PLUNA, Uruguay, 1930s, 363
  SATGA, French Guiana, 1949, 334
  Sierra Leone, 1958, 383
  Transpac, Melanesia, 1950s, 302

Index 443

de Havilland D.H. 91 Albatross
  B.O.A.C. Lisbon service, 1940, 23, 24p
de Havilland D.H. 104 Dove
  All Nippon Airways, 144
  Brabazon Committee recommendation, 32
  Cape Verde Islands, 1958, 384
  Megapode Airways, 1963, 298
  SATA, Azores, 1947, 219
  Sudan Airways, 1947, 389
  TAG Airlines, and crash, 92
  Toa Airways, 148
  W.A.A.C., 1940s, 380
de Havilland D.H. 106 Comets 1 and 2 (world's first jet airliner)
  CP Air, order, crash, 1953, 305
  Comet 2, Avon-powered Comet 1, 40
  Disasters, temporary return to service, 1953–1954, 41
  Early study, 1944, 38c
  First flight, 1949, 38
  L.A.V., Venezuela, order, 1952, 351
  Metal fatigue revealed, 1954, 41, 41c
  Ordered by Japanese Airlines, 1952, 98
  Panair do Brasil order, 1953, 314
  Sets pace on B.O.A.C. routes, 40
  South African Airways, crash, 399
  Survey flights, 1949, 39
  World's first jet airline service, 1952, 39, 39m
de Havilland D.H. 106 Comet 4B
  B.E.A., 47
  Cyprus Airways, 80
  Olympic Airways, 1960, 221
  T.A.P., Portugal, 1961, 219
de Havilland D.H. 108, attempts first supersonic flight, 38
de Havilland D.H. 114 Heron
  Air Bissau, 1960s, 370
  Air Comoros, 1966, 406
  Air Ivoire, 1958, 377
  Air Pacific, Fiji, 1974, 300
  Air Tungaru, 1980, 299
  Fiji Airways/Air Pacific, 1959, 295
  Ghana Airways, 1958, 382
  LIAT, 1965, 330
  Prinair, large fleet, 1960s–1980s, 338
  Toa Airways, 1953, 148, 149p
  W.A.A.C., 1956, 380
de Havilland D.H. 121 Trident
  Air Ceylon, 1960s, 255
  Airline sales, 119
  British Airways, 1970s, 196
  Initial problems, eventual service with B.E.A., 1964, 57, 57p, 119
  P.I.A., Pakistan, 1966, 252
  Service with C.A.A.C., China, 1973, 58, 58m, 58p, 240
  Trident 1C, 1E, 2E, 3B versions, 58
  Trident 2, Cyprus Airways, 80

Trident 2Es and 3Bs to China, 1960s, 119
  World's first tri-jet airliner, 32
de Havilland D.H.-126, short-haul jet project, 1960s, 90
de Havilland D.H. Mosquito, 38
de Havilland Ghost engine
  Powers Comet airliner, 38
  Superseded by Rolls-Royce Avon, 39–40
  World's first commercial jet engine, 38
De Klerk, E.W., 400
Debonair (U.K.), 190–191
Del Sur, Cielos, 366
DELAG
  German airship service, 3
  Route map, 1919, 4m
Delfort Corporation, 159
Delisle, Frank, 330
Delta Air Lines
  Bermuda II route benefits, 1971, 144
  First DC-8 service, 52, 52p
  First DC-9 order, 60
  First Douglas DC-9-10 service, 117, 118
  Lockheed TriStar order and entry into service problem, 111
  Post-war summary, 26t
  Takes over Pan American routes, 203
  Wartime service, 26
Delta Air Transport (Belgium), 214
Deluce, Stan, 310–311
Denby, Alfred, 340
Denmark, first airline service, 5
Denver Hornsby, Mr. and Mrs., 394–395
Department of Civil Aviation conference (Petrópolis, Brazil), 314–315
  Creation of airline categories, 130
  Creation of RIN, 130
  VARIG as "chosen instrument," 315
Deprisa, Colombian postal service, 348
Derby Aviation, original name of British Midland International, 192
Deregulation. See Airline deregulation
Deresa, James, 338
Deruluft (U.S.S.R./Germany), 20
DETA. See Divisão de Exploração dos Transportes Aéreos
Deutsche, Andre, 366
Deutsche B.A., British Airways German subsidiary, 191
Deutsche Luft Hansa (name prior to Second World War)
  Condor, Brazil, 18, 18m
  Establishes Eurasia in China, 1931, 17
  Founded 1924, 4
  Last wartime flight, 25

Liquidation, 25
Route maps, 4m, 14m, 21m, 24m
Service curtailed by war, 22, 24
South Atlantic route, 33, 33t
South Atlantic service, 19, 19m
Technical prowess, 15
Use of depot ships, 19, 33
Deutsche Luft Reederei (D.L.R.)
  First air service, 1919, 3, 3t
  "Flying crane" symbol, 3
  Route map, 1919, 4m
Deutsche Lufthansa (name after Second World War). See Lufthansa
Deutsche Lufthansa Sucursal Perú, 20
Deutsche Luftverkehr GmbH (D.L.T.) (German domestic airline), 203
Deutsche Zeppelin Reederei (D.Z.R.)
  South Atlantic Service, 1932–1937, 19m
Deutscher Aero Lloyd (Germany), 3
Devlet Hava Yollari (D.H.Y) (Turkey), 79
Diallo Airlines (Somalia), 388
Dickenson, contract air mail route (CAM 9). See Northwest
Dietrich, Marlene, 105
Dietrick, Ralph, 92
"Dirty tricks" campaign, British Airways v. Virgin Atlantic, 197
Divisão de Exploração dos Transportes Aéreos (DETA) (Mozambique), 69, 395
  Origin of Linhas Aéreas de Moçambique (L.A.M.), 395
Divisão de Exploração dos Transportes Aéreos de Angola (D.T.A.), 69, 395
  Origins of TAAG, 395
Dix, William, 288
Djohan, Robby, 264
D.L.T. See Deutsche Luftverkehr GmbH
D.N.K. See Dai Nippon Koku
Dobrolot (U.S.S.R.), 20
Domaire (Dominican Republic), 336
Domodedovo Airlines (Soviet C.I.S.), 151t, 157
  Aircraft operated, 153, 153p
  One of Russia's "Big Six," 157
Donado, Luis, 349
Donbasaero (Ukraine), 239
Dormoy, Jose "La Pipe," 332–333, 335
Dornier, German aircraft manufacturer, 4, 18
Dornier 228 (STOL aircraft)
  Air Botswana, 1980s, 404
  Air Caraïbes, 2000, 335
  Cape Verde Islands, 1999, 384
  Druk-Air, Bhutan, 1983, 258, 258p
  Formosa Airlines, 1983, 271
  Royal Brunei, 1995, 280
  Tradewinds, Singapore, 1984, 261
  Vayadoot, 1980s, 249
  Windward Islands, to Saba, 1963, 332

Dornier 328
  Tianjin Airlines, 242t
Dornier Wal (German flying boat)
  Deutsche Luft Hansa, 1930, 19, 19m, 33
  In Japan, 1930s, 18
"Double Sunrise Service." See Qantas Empire Airways
Douglas Aircraft Company
  Considers long-range turboprop airliner, 50
  K.S.S.U. partnership, 111
  Merges with McDonnell, 60
  "Stretches" DC-6 into DC-7, 37
  Supersonic airliner project, 114
  See also specific aircraft
Douglas DC-1, 10
Douglas DC-2
  C.N.A.C., 17p, 18
  Developed from DC-1, 10
  England–Australia Air Race, 12, 13p
  Introduced by T.W.A., 10, 11p
  Supersedes Boeing 247, 12
Douglas DC-3
  Air Madagascar, 1940s–1960s, 405
  Air Niugini, 1973, 294
  Air Tonga, last DC-3 in scheduled service, 2004, 298
  "Airbus" service in East Pakistan, 252
  Bouraq Indonesian Airlines, 136p
  Ethiopian Air Lines, 1946–1980s, 390
  Friedkin, 1949, 171
  Gibraltar, 225
  Highest flying hours, 92
  Introduced by American Airlines, 1936, 11p
  Operations perpetuated in New Guinea, 1960–1970s, 135
  Provides 85% of U.S. airline capacity, 1930s, 11
  REAL, Brazil, fleet of 86, 1950s, 313–314
  Resists oblivion in Canada, 310
  Rough-field performance, 87
  Supplements DC-2, 12
  Survives into the Jet Age, 31
  Winela Air Service, Bechuanaland, 1954–1974, 401, 401m
  Zamrud, Indonesia, 1980s, 136, 136m, 136p
Douglas DC-4
  Air Comoros, 1977, 406
  Air Madagascar, 1940s–1960s, 405
  Botswana National Airways, 1990s, 404
  First flight, 1942, 23
  Loftleidir, 30, 30p
  Reconverted from wartime C-54 role, 27, 28p, 29
  Restores TACA, Central America, 1940s, 343
  Trek Airways, 1950s and 1990s, 402

Douglas DC-4 (*continued*)
  Winela Air Service, Bechuanaland, 1954–1974, 401, 401m
Douglas DC-4E, experimental service, 23
Douglas DC-4M. *See* Argonaut; North Star
Douglas DC-5, operated by K.L.M., 51
Douglas DC-6, rushed into production, 29, 102
Douglas DC-6A, first modern freighter, 102
  Wardair, Canada, 1960s, 310
Douglas DC-6B, thoroughbred airliner, 102
Douglas DC-7, uses Pratt & Whitney R-3400 engine, 30
Douglas DC-7Bs
  South African Airways, 1956, 399
Douglas DC-7C
  B.O.A.C. service, 1960, to compensate for Britannia delay, 45
  Enters service with Pan American, 1956, 37
  Japan Air Lines, trans-Pacific service, 1954, 98
  S.A.S. Polar route, 1954, 34, 34m
Douglas DC-8-10, -30, -50 series
  Aeromar, Dominican Republic, 336
  Aeroperú, 1974, 378
  Air Afrique, 1962, 376
  Air Congo, 1967, 397
  Air Haiti, 1973, 337
  Air New Zealand, 1965, 291
  Air Paraguay, 1984, 362
  Bahamas World, 1970s, 332
  Cargolux, 1970, 234
  Cubana, 1976, 337
  DC-8 Jet Trader, T.C.A., 304
  Eastern Air Lines, 1960, 164
  First orders and services, 1955–1960, 50–51, 52p
  Garuda Indonesian, 1966, 263
  Korean Air Lines, 1972, 275
  Surinam, 1975, crash in 1989, 334
  U.T.A., with Air Ceylon, 1960s, 255
  VIASA, 1965, 351
  Zambia Airways, 1968, 393
Douglas DC-8-61, -62, -63, -70 series, 52
  Braniff Airways, 158
  Eastern Air Lines, 1969, 164
  Finnair, 1969, 232
  VIASA, 1970s, 351
Douglas DC-9-10, -20, -30, -40, -50 series
  Aeronaves de Mexico, 322, mid-air collision, 1986, 323
  Air California, DC-9-80s, 1981, 173, 173p
  Air Canada, 1964, 304
  Allegheny Airlines, 1966, 122

Ansett and T.A.A., Australia, 1967, 286
AVENSA, 1970s, 352
Aviaco, Iberia, 1973, 218
Built by Shanghai Aircraft Factory, 1980s, 241
B.W.I.A., 1977, 328, 329p
Cyprus Airways, 1970s, 226
Developed as MD-80, 61
Eastern Air Lines, 1963, 164
Full development, 117, 117p
Garuda Indonesian, 1968, 263
J.A.T., 1970s, 222
Kenya Airways, 1977, 386
Korean Air Lines, 1967, 275
Kulula.com, South Africa, 2000s, 402
Launched, 60, 61p
L.A.V., Venezuela, 1970s, 352
Marshall Islands, DC-9-62, 1980s, 300
MD-90, MD-95 redesignated as Boeing 717, 117
Merpati Nusantara, Indonesia, 1989, 264
North Central Airlines, 1976, 125
Ryanair, 1980s, 187–188
S.A.S., 1960s, 227
Sun Air, South Africa, 1990s, 400, 403
Surinam, 1967, 334
TAESA, Mexico, 1990s, 325
Toa Domestic, 1973, 149
Transbrasil, 61
ValuJet, 1992, 179
VIASA, Venezuela, 1967, 351
ZAS, Egypt, 1982, 375
See also MD-95, DC-9 development
Douglas DC-10
  Aerperú, 1993, 358
  Air Ceylon, 1976, 255
  Air Florida, 1980, 160
  Air Liberté, 198
  Air Micronesia, 1990s, 301
  Air New Zealand, 1973, 291
  Air Pacific, Fiji, 1983, 296
  Air Paraguay, 1992, 362
  Air Seychelles, 1983, 388
  Air Zaïre, 1973, 397
  American Airlines, 1971, 110, 110p
  Ansett, T.A.A., 1967, 286, 286p
  AVENSA, 1998, 353
  Canadian Airlines International, 1986, 306
  Cubana, 1990s, 338
  Development, first flight, service, 110, 110p
  Ecuatoriana, 1997, 355
  Finnair, 1975, 232
  Garuda Indonesian, 1976, 263
  I.C.A., Caribbean, 1970, 330
  Icelandair, 1979, 234
  Kenya Airways, 1990s, 386
  Korean Air Lines, 1975, 275

Kras Air, Russia, 152–153
Laker Skytrain service, 1977, 106, 106p
LAM, Mozambique, 1980s, 396
Lufthansa, 1971, 202
Malaysian, 1976, 261
Pan American Airways, 1978, 161
PLUNA, Uruguay, 1990s, 363
Santa Barbara, Venezuela, 1990s, 353
S.A.S., 1974, 228
Singapore Airlines, 1977, 260
Sun Country Airlines, 1986, 184
Swissair, 1982, 212
Thai International, 1977, 267, 267p
Tikal Jets, Guatemala, 2002, 340
Toa Domestic, Japan Air System, 1986, 149
Transaero, Russia, 1994, 152–153
VIASA, 1970s, 351, 352p
Zambia Airways, 1984, 393
Douglas Super DC-3, ex-Navy R4D-8
  L.A.C., in Uyuni, Bolivia, 2008, 361
Dovair (Fiji), 297
Dowty-Rotol, British propeller manufacturer, 31
Druk-Air (Bhutan), 258, 258p, 258m
D.T.A. *See* Divisão de Exploração dos Transportes Aéreos de Angola
Dubreuil, industrial group, 335
Durrett, R. Lamar, 306
Dutch Caribbean Airways (D.C.A.), 333
Dymond, Lew, 125–126
Dynasty class service, China Airlines, 270

E.A.A.C. *See* East African Airways Corporation
Eagle Air (Iceland), 234
Eagle Airlines (Iran), 71
Eagle Airways (Bahamas), 331
Eagle Nest, T.W.A. wartime training center, 25
EAS Airlines (Nigeria), 381
East African Airways Corporation, 30, 67, 285
  Aircraft operated, 120, 385–386
  Comet 4 service, 1959, 53
  Operates SKAT, 388
  Qhadripartite pool, 385
  Route map, 385m
  Vickers VC10 crash, 1972, 386
East Line (Russian cargo airline), 153
East-West Airlines (Australia), 90, 137c, 289
East-West Airlines (India), 249
East-West Scheduled Aviation Society (T.T.K.K.) (Japanese airline), 7m
Easter Island, first services, 367
Eastern Air Lines, 122, 163–165
  Aircraft operated, 164
  Buys Caribair, 164

Buys Mackey Airlines, 164
Douglas DC-8 service, 1959, 52
Douglas DC-9-10 service, 1967, 117, 118
Electras on Shuttle services, 47
Enters Jet Age, 164
First Boeing 727 service, 1964, 57, 57p
First service with Lockheed Electra, 1959, 46, 46p
Genealogy, 9c
Introduces coach-class fares, 140
Latin American routes sold to American Airlines, 165
Leadership, 164
Lockheed TriStar order, 111
Machinists Union strike, 165
One of U.S. "Big Four," 9c, 167, 177
Picks up former PANAGRA routes from Braniff, 159
Post-war summary, 26t, 28
Sells Shuttle to Donald Trump, 165
Sold to Texas Air Corporation, 165
Trans-Atlantic service, 164
Wartime service, 25
Eastern Air-Shuttle, 164
Eastern Air Transport, former name of Eastern Air Lines, 9c, 26t
Eastern Provincial Airways (E.P.A.) (Canada), 134
  Boeing 727s, 1969, 134
  Integrated with CP Air, 306
  Route network, 1969, 134m
Eastern Timor, last T.A.P. flights, 220
EasyJet, 189–190, 189p, 190m, 191, 192, 193, 198, 204, 205, 213, 249
EasyJet Switzerland (Switzerland), name change from T.E.A., 189
Economy fares, introduced by IATA, 1958, 143
Ecuatoriana. *See* Compañía Ecuatoriana de Aviación (C.E.A.)
Eddington, Rod, 198
Edwards, George, 31, 37, 47, 60
Edwards Committee, appointed by British government, 59
Egyptair, 374–375
  Renamed from United Arab Airlines, 1971, 70, 374
Egyptair Express, 375
Eisenhower, Dwight, 83–84, 138
El Al (Israel), 77
  Atlantic airline chronology, 28t
  Operates Bristol Britannia, 45, 45m, 77, 77p
El Economico, Philippine night air service, 272
El Panama, Air Panama service, 345
El Venado (Colombia), 349
Elders Colonial Airways, Empire service, 21m
Eliasson, Alfred, 234

Index

Elizabethan, B.E.A. class name for Airspeed Ambassador, 43
Ellis, Ray, 92
EMB 110 Bandeirante, turboprop commuter/feeder airliner, 95
   Air Fiji, 1995, 296
   Bangkok Airways, 1985, 268
   Finnaviation, 1979, 232, 232p
   First service, 1973, 131, 132p
   Island Air, Guam, 1976, 300
   Ryanair, 1985, 187
   Sun Air, South Africa, 1996, 403
   TAM, Brazil, 319
EMB 120 Brasilia (turboprop commuter airliner), 95
   Avioquintana, Mexico, 326
   Cape Verde Islands, 384
   D.L.T., 1978, 203
   Servivensa, Venezuela, 2000s, 353
EMB 145, first Embraer jet, 95
   Air Caraïbes, 2000, 335
EMB 170
   Egyptair Express, 2006, 375
   Solair, Solomons, 2007, 299
EMB 190
   Copa Airlines, Panama, 2004, 345
   JetBlue sale, 2001, 182
   Virgin group, Australia, 2006, 290
   Virgin Nigeria, 2008, 382
EMB 195
   Flybe, 2005, 193
   Swiss, 213p
Embraer, Brazilian aircraft manufacturer, 95, 130–131
See also specific aircraft (EMB)
Embry-Riddle Company, 9c
Emerald Air, certificate acquired by Braniff Airlines International, 160
Emergency Loan Guarantee Act, 1971, rescues Lockheed, 111
Emirates (Dubai)
   Assists revival of Sri Lankan Airlines, 1998, 256
   Launch customer for Airbus A380, 2000, 409
   Route map, 2003, 409m
   Starts A380 service, 2008, 409, 409p
Empire Air Lines (U.S.), 123c
   Sold to West Coast Airlines, 124
Empire Air Mail Scheme (U.K.), 12
"Empire," Short S-23 flying boat, 13
Employee Stock Ownership Plan (ESOP), 166
Empresa de Transportes Aéreo del Perú. *See* Aeroperú
Engines
   Armstrong-Siddeley Mamba, 37
   CF6-6D, for Douglas jets, 111
   CFM56, for Douglas DC-8-70, 52
   First jets and turboprops, 36–42
   GE/SNECMA CFM56, for Boeing 737, 118
   I.A.E. engine for MD-80 series, 117

Junkers Jumo, 36c
See also specific engines
England–Australia Air Race, 1934, 12
   See also de Havilland D.H. 88 Comet; Douglas DC-2; Grosvenor House; K.L.M.; Moll, J.J.; Parmentier, K.D.; Robertson, Macpherson
English Electric, British aircraft manufacturer, 59
English Electric Canberra, first jet-powered crossing of Atlantic, 40
E.P.A. *See* Eastern Provincial Airways
Ernoul (France), 4m
ESOP. *See* Employee Stock Ownership Plan
Esquivel brothers, 341
Essair (U.S.), becomes Pioneer Airlines, 123c
Estonia, first airline service, 5
Estonian Air, Maersk shareholding, 239
Ethève, Gérard, 406
Ethiopian Air Lines, 69, 389–391
   Advice and cooperation with TWA, 389–390
   Aircraft operated, 390, 391
   Route to China, 240
ETOPS navigation system, 77
Euralair (French charter airline), 64t
Eurasia (or Chinesische-Deutsche Luftverkehrs-gesellschaft) (China), 17, 17m
Eurnekian, Eduardo, 367
Euro Berlin (Germany), 200, 203
Euro-Belgian Airlines, 191
Eurocity Express (U.K.), 214
Eurofly (Italian local airline), 210
Europa Jet, Lufthansa's Boeing 727 service, 202
European Quality Alliance, 212
Eurostar, cross-Channel high speed trains, 413
Eurowings (Germany), 204, 210
Eva Air (Taiwan), 271
Evanson, Richard, 297
Everest Air (Nepal), 254
Evergreen Marine, shipping company, 271
Expediton Airways (Zimbabwe), 395
Express Air Service (U.K.), taken over by Intra Airways, 192

F.A.A. *See* Federal Aviation Administration
Fairchild F-27, U.S. license-built Fokker F-27
   Air Vanuatu, 1981, 299
   Piedmont Airlines, 1958, 122
Fairchild-Hiller FH-227 (turboprop airliner)
   Mohawk Airlines, 1966, 122
   Paraense, Brazil, 1967, crashes, 88
   Piedmont Airlines, 1967, 122

Fairchild Metro
   Aerocaribe, Mexico, 1997, 326
   Aeroliteral, Mexico, 1970s, 324
   Avioquintana, Mexico, 1997, 326
   TAN, Argentina, 1994, 317
Fairey, British aircraft manufacturer
   Pre-war (FC-1) design, 23
Faisal, King (Saudi Arabia), 78
Fal, Cheikh, 376
Falcon Jet Corporation, Pan American-Dassault agency for Dassault business jet, 161–162
Falkland Islands Government Air Service (FIGAS), 370
FAMA. *See* Flota Aérea Mercante Argentina
Fansler, Percy, 1
Far Eastern Airlines, merges to form All Nippon Airways, 144, 144m
Far Eastern Avia (Soviet C.I.S.), 151t
Far-east Air Transport (FAT) (Taiwan), 85, 270
Farley, James, cancels air mail contracts, 11
Farman (France)
   First service, 1919, 3, 3t
   Name change, 4
   Route map, 4m
Farman 2200 (French airliner)
   South Atlantic, 1938, 33
FAST (Fleming A.S.T.) Philippine cheap-fare airline, 281
FAT. *See* Far-east Air Transport
Faucett, Elmer "Slim," 356
Faulkner, John, 388
F.B.O.s. *See* Fixed-base operators
Federal Aviation Administration (F.A.A.), 43–44, 77, 114, 161, 171
   Category 2 policy, Air Jamaica, 329
   Commuter airlines records, 92
   Institutes ATOS, safety inspection system, 180
   Watches over navigational, operational requirements, 122
Fernandes, Tony, 282
Ferreira Lima, Manuel, 220
Fifth Freedom
   Air Nauru, Pacific operations, 299
   Bone of contention, 29
   Braathens, Loftleidir, evasions, 231–233
   Challenged by TAN Latin American consortium, 342
   North Atlantic route operations, 1959–1960, 51
FIGAS. *See* Falkland Islands Government Air Service
Fiji Air (ex-Air Pacific), renamed Air Fiji, 296, 297p
Fiji Airways. *See* Air Pacific
Filev, Vladislav, 153
Filipinas Orient Airways (Philippines), 282

Finland, first airline service, 5
Finnair, 232–233
Finnaviation, succeeds Karhumaki, 232, 232p
Firefly (Malaysia), 262
First Air (Canada), 310
   Route map, 2009, 309m
First-class fares, abolished in Europe, 1972, 195
Five Freedoms (of the air), 29, 100, 143, 187, 190, 231, 233, 247, 299, 324, 357
Fixed-base operators (F.B.O.s)
   Origin of commuter airlines, 92, 92m
   Role in U.S. smaller airline postwar development, 171
FL Group, Iceland, 230
Flash Airlines (Egypt), 375
Fleming, James, 272, 281
Flight magazine (U.S.), Third Level commuter airlines, 93
Flitestar (South Africa), 402
Florida Airways
   Contract air mail route (CAM 10), 1926, 8m
   Genealogy, 9c
Florida Airways, 123c
Florida West Indies Airways, 2m
Flota Aérea Mercante Argentina (FAMA)
   Leases aircraft to L.A.I., 28t
   South Atlantic service (with Iberia), 33, 33t, 364
Flugfélag Islands, changed name to Icelandair, 234
Flugleidir, merger of Loftleidir and Icelandair, 234
Flybe (U.K.), 193, 193m
"Flying Colors of America," Calder art designs for Braniff aircraft, 159
Flying crane, Lufthansa insignia, 98
FlyNiu Airlines (Tonga), 298
Focke-Wulf Fw 200 (German airliner)
   Final flight at war's end, 1945, 25
   Record trans-Atlantic flight, 16, 16p
   Serves notice to end flying-boat era, 23, 24, 29
   Sydicato Condor, 1940s, 316
Fokker, Dutch aircraft manufacturer, 5
   Interest in Western Air Express, 9
Fokker XVIII, supplements F-XII, 12
Fokker 50
   Air Comoros, 1980s, 406
   Arik Air, Nigeria, 2006, 382
   AVIANCA, 1991, 348
   D.L.T., 1978, 203
   Ethiopian Air Lines, 1995, 391
   Firefly, Malaysia, 2007, 262
   Icelandair, 1992, 234
   Kenya Airways, 1980s, 386
   Virgin Nigeria, 2000s, 382
Fokker 100
   Air Gabon, 1985, 379
   Air Greece, 1999, 222

Fokker 100 (*continued*)
  Air Niugini, 2006, 295
  Aviacsa, 1991, 325
  Bangkok Airways, 1992, 288
  Merpati Nusantara, Indonesia, 2000s, 265
  Mexicana, 1980s, 324
  Sempati Air Transport, Indonesia, 1991, 266
  Swissair, 1986, 212
  TAM, Brazil, 319
Fokker F-III, Deruluft, 20
Fokker F-VII
  Japan–Manchuria, 18
  SABENA, route to Africa, 14
Fokker F-VIIb/3m, airliner of the 1920s, 5
Fokker F-XII, historic K.L.M. flight to Batavia, 11–12
Fokker F-27 Friendship
  Aercesar, Colombia, 1960s, 349
  Aero Continente, Peru, 1990s, 359
  Aeronorte, and A.S.A, Chile, 1976, 369
  Air Benin, 1979, 378
  Air Comoros, 1977, 406
  Air Guadeloupe, 1978, 335
  Air Liberia, 1974, 379
  Air Martinique, 1974, 335
  Air Mauritanie, 378
  Air Niger, 378
  Air Niugini, 1973, 294
  Air Polynésie, 1970, 301
  Air Sinai, 1982, 375
  Air Tanzania, 1977, 386
  Air Vanuatu, 1980, 299
  Air Zaïre, 1981, 397
  AREA, Ecuador, 1959, 354
  AVENSA, Venezuela, 1950s–1960s, 352
  Aviaco, 1980s, 218
  Botswana National Airways, 1990s, 404
  Bouraq Indonesian Airlines, 1972, 265, 265p
  Comair, South Africa, 1950s, 402
  Compared to other twin-engined turboprops, 89t
  Crashes in Ecuador, 1960, 87
  Crashes in Philippines, 1987, 86
  Cubana, 1990s, 338
  D.T.A., Angola, 1961, 395–396
  DETA, 1961, 395–396
  East African Airways, 1950s, 385
  First all-jet airline in the world (Bonanza), 1959, 124, 124p
  Garuda Indonesian, 1969, 263
  Jersey European, 1980s, 192
  Kenya Airways, 1977, 386
  LAM-Mozambique, 1961, 395–396
  Libyan Arab Airlines, 1970s, 373
  Malaysian Airways, 1971, 259, 261
  N.A.C., New Zealand, 1960, 291
  Nigerian Airways, 1963, 380
  P.I.A., Pakistan, 1960s, 252, 252m; crashes, 253
  Panama, 1980, 346
  Sempati Air Transport, Indonesia, 266
  Somali Airlines, 1980s, 388
  Sudan Airways, 1962, 389
  T.A.A., Australia, 1955, 285
  TAM, Brazil, 1980, 319
  U.S. Local Service, worldwide operations, 84
  Uganda Airlines, 1980s, 387
  Vayudoot, India, 1981, 249
Fokker F-28 Fellowship
  Aero Continente, Peru, 1990s, 359
  Air Botswana, 1972, 404
  Air Burkina, 2001, 378
  Air Gabon, 1951 and 1977–2007, 378–379
  Air Ivoire, 2002, 377
  Air Mali, 1980s, 380
  Air Mauritanie, 378
  Air Nauru, 1972, 299
  Air New South Wales, 1960s, 286
  Air Niugini, 1977, 294
  Air Ontario, 1987, 310
  B.A.C., Burma, 1976, 256
  Braathens, 1969, 231
  First feeder jet, 1969, 89
  Garuda Indonesian, 1971, 263
  Iberia, 1970, 217
  Linjeflyg, 1973, 232
  Merpati Nusantara, Indonesia, 1989, 264
  Nigerian Airways, 1972, 380
  SATENA, Colombia, 1985, 349
  SilkAir, 1996, 261
Fokker FH-227
  Aces, Colombia, 1980s, 350
  Afrikaans Suidwes, 1959, 404
  Paraense, Brazil, 1952–1970, 315
Fokker Universal
  Japan–Manchuria, 18
Fontana, Omar, 61, 88, 315, 318
Força Aérea Brasileira, 87, 130
Ford Motor Company
  Contract air mail routes (CAM 6 and 7), 8m
  Geneology, 9c
Ford Tri-Motor
  At Port Columbus, T.A.T. inaugural, 10p
  Dominicana, terminated Pan Am interest, 336
  Superseded by Boeing 247, 10
Formosa Airlines, 271
Fornaro, Robert, 180
Forsblade, Bob, 342
Fort, Daniel, 20
Foshing Airlines (Taiwan), 269
  Renamed TransAsia Airlines, 271
Foulois, Benjamin, 11
France
  Initial shareholding in Airbus, 1970, 110
  Recovery from Second World War, 55
Franz, Anselm, 36c
Freberg, Stan, 124
Fred Olsen Flyselskap, Norwegian shipping line, 230–232
  Shares in Austrian Airlines, 236
Freedom Air (Guam), 300
Freight, all-cargo aircraft, 101–102
Freyggang, Jorge, 369
Fri Reyes (Bolivia), 361
Friedkin, Kenny, 171, 187
Frontier Airlines (U.S.), 123c, 125–126, 126m, 175, 182
Frye, Jack, 10, 29
Fuji Airlines (Japan), merges to form J.D.A., 146
Fujian Airlines (China), 241m, 242t
Fujita Airlines (Japan), sold to All Nippon Airways, 145
Fundikura, Chief A.S., 385

Gabon Airlines, 379
Gabon Express, 379
Galapagos Islands, air service, 355
Galion, Sud Aviation design for wide-bodied twin airliner, 109
Gallagher, Maurice, 179
Gambia International Airlines, 383
GAMCO. *See* Gulf Air Aircraft Maintenance Company
GAMECO. *See* Guangzhou Aircraft Maintenance Corporation
Gandhi, Mahatma, 251
Gangwal, Rakesh, 169
Garuda Indonesian Airways, 262–264
  Aircraft operated, 84, 89, 263
  Buys DC-9s, 61
  Crashes, 2006–2007, 264
  Establishes Indonesian airline network, 135
  Name change to Garuda Indonesia, 263
  Orders Boeing 787 Dreamliner, 264
Gatchalian, William, 282
Gates, Richard, 297
Gatty, Harold, 295
G.B. Airways (Gibraltar), franchised from British Airways, 198
G.C.S. *See* German Cargo Services
General Air Lines, brief name change from Western Air Express, 26t
General Dynamics
  B-58 supersonic bomber, 115
  Supersonic airliner project, 1959, 114
General Electric, CF6–6D engine. *See* Engines
General Motors, interest in T.W.A., 9c
Georgian CAD (Soviet C.I.S.), 151t
German Cargo Services (G.C.S.), 203
Germanair (German charter airline), 64t, 207
Germany
  First air mail services, 1917, 2
  Initial shareholding in Airbus, 110
  Reunification, 1991, 200
GE/SNECMA, European engine manufacturer, 118
CFM56. *See* Engines
Ghana Airways, 382–383
  Operates Britannias, 46
  Takes over from West African Airways, 67
Ghana International Airlines (GIA-USA), 383
Ghost engine. *See* de Havilland Ghost engine
GIA-USA. *See* Ghana International Airlines
Gibbes, Bobby, 294
Gibbes-Sepik (New Guinea), 137c, 294
Gibraltar Airways (or Gibair), name change to GBairways, 225
"Gimli Glider," Air Canada, 304
Gitner, Gerald, 175
Glasnost, Soviet political policy, 150
Global Airlines Corporation, offers to buy US Airlines, 169
Gloster E28/39, first British jet aircraft, 36c
Gloster Meteor, first British jet fighter aircraft, 36
Go (Go-Fly, Ltd.) (British low-fare airline), 191
Goa, last flights, 220
GOL Linhas Aéreas Inteligentes (Brazilian low-fare airline), 320–321
  Controls VARIG, 316
Golden State Airlines (U.S.), 95m
Goldfield Corporation, buys Frontier Airlines, 126
Goldrick, P.J., 188
Goliath (French airliner), 3
Gomez, Linneu, 31, 315
Gonilga, Institute (Soviet C.I.S.), 151t
Gonzales, José, 274
Gonzales, Manuel, 20
Gopinath, G.R., 249–250
Goyal Naresh, 249
Grace, W.R., 14, 356
Graf Zeppelin (German dirigible airship), 15, 19
Grand Air (Philippines), 282
Grand Metropolitan, British hotel corporation, 162
"Grandfather rights," U.S. airline regulations, 65
Gray, Harold, 109
Great Baltic, world's first transport airplane, 1913, 1
Great Britain. *See* U.K.
Great China Airlines (Taiwan), 271
Great Lakes Aviation (U.S.), 182
Great Lakes Local Service Case, 125
Great Northern Airways (Canadian local airline), 134
Great Wall Airlines, 241m, 242t

Index 447

Greatamerica Corporation, buys control of Braniff, 1964, 158
Greater Japan Airlines. *See* Dai Nippon Koku
Greenlandair (Greenlandsfly), 234–235
Grey, Brian, 289
Gromov, Mikhail, 20p, 21
Grosvenor House, wins 1934 England–Australia Air Race, 12
Grumman G-73 Mallard
    Antilles Air Boats, 1970s, 339
Grumman Goose amphibian
    Antilles Air Boats, 1964, 338
    British Guiana Airways, 1945, 334
    Mount Cook, New Zealand, 1972, 292
Grumman SA-16 Albatross (U.S. flying boat)
    Airfast, Indonesia, 136p
    Antilles Air Boats, 1970s, 339
    Service in Micronesia, 300
Grumman Widgeon amphibian
    T.A.T., New Zealand, 1960s, 292
"Guacamaya," TACA's insignia, 343, 344p
Guadeloupe Air Transport, 335
Guangxi Airlines (China), 241m, 242t
Guangzhou Aircraft Maintenance Corporation, 244
"Guest workers"
    Air routes to Europe and Middle East, 83, 83m
    Turkish airline traffic, 80
Guine Bissau, 379
Guinea Airways, 294
    Becomes Airlines of South Australia, 90
    Empire service, 1939, 21m
    Genealogy, 137,137c
    Pioneer services to gold mines, 16
    Sold to Ansett, 138, 286
Guizhou Airlines (China), 241m, 242t
Gulf Air (Bahrain), name change from Gulf Aviation, 76, 76m
Gulf Air (U.S.), 176
Gulf Air Aircraft Maintenance Company, 76
Gulf Air Lines, 9c
Gulf Aviation (Bahrain), 75
    See also Gulf Air
Gurtovoi, Gregori, 238
Guyana Airways, 334
Guyane Air Transport (GAT), new name for SATGA, 334

Haddaway, George, 93
HAECO. *See* Hong Kong Engineering Company
Hagerstown Commuter, 94, 94p, 94m
Hagg, Arthur, 43
Hagrup, Knut, 228
Haidir, Munir Abu, 73
Haile Selassie, 69–70, 389

Hainan Airlines (China), 241m, 242t
Haiti Air International. *See* Air Haiti
Haji-Ioannou, Stelios, 189
Hajj pilgrimage, Saudia builds infrastructure, 78
Halaby, Najib, 161, 176
Halford, Frank, 38
Hall, Arnold, 32, 41, 110, 113
Hall, Floyd, 164
Hamburg-Amerikanische Packetfahrt A.G. (HAPAG) (German airship company), 1
Hamiata (Soviet–Chinese wartime airline), merges into Minhaiduy, 132
Hamilton-Standard, U.S. propeller manufacturer, 31
Handley Page (U.K.), 3, 4
    See also specific aircraft
Handley Page 0/400 (bomber aircraft), imported to China, 7
Handley Page Halton, 31
Handley Page Herald and Dart Herald
    Compared to other twin-engined turboprops, 89t
    Eastern Provincial Airways, Canada, 134
    FAT, Taiwan, 1966, 270
    La Urraca, Colombia, 1970, 349
    Transbrasil, 1964, 88
Handley Page Hermes, 27, 31
    B.O.A.C. Africa, 1950, 35
Handley Page HP 42, 11, 12p
    Imperial Airways African route, 1932, 13m
Handley Page Marathons
    All Nippon Airways, 144
Hanford's Tri-State Airlines, 26t
Hàng-Không Viêt-Nam. *See* Air Vietnam
Hanjin Group, 275
Hansen, Hans Erik, 266
Hanshue, H.S., 9c
HAPAG. *See* Hamburg-Amerikanische Packetfahrt A.G.
Hapag-Lloyd (German charter airline), 64t
    First Boeing 737-800 service, 1998, 118
Harbin Y-12 (Chinese airliner)
    Air Fiji, 1995, 296
    Lao Airlines, 2000s, 280
Harca Air (Nigeria), 381
Hasan, Mohamed (Bob), 266
Haughton, Daniel, 111
Hawkair (Canada), 309m
Hawker 800
    Arik Air, Nigeria, 2004, 382
Hawker Siddeley, British aircraft manufacturer, 57, 59, 86–87, 109
    See also specific aircraft
Hawker Siddeley 748
    Aero Safari, Mexico, 1961, 324
    Aeromaya, Mexcio, 1960s, 322

Air Botswana, 1981, 404
Air Ceylon, 1960s, 255
Air North, Canada, 1970s, 310
Austin Airways, Canada, 310
Austrian Airlines, 1966, 236
Bahamas Airways, 1969, 331
Bahamasair, 1990, 331
Bangkok Airways, 1986, 268
Bouraq Indonesian Airlines, 1970, 135; 1973, 265
Cameroon Airlines, 1974, 378
Cape Verde Islands, 1970s, 384
Fiji Airways, 1967, 295
First Air, Canada, 2000s, 310
Gabon Express, 1999, 379
Jersey European, 1980s, 192
LIAT, 1969, 330
Marshall Islands, 1980s, 300
Mount Cook Airways, 1970, 292
Polynesian Airways, 1970s, 297p
Réunion Air Service, 1975, 406
SATENA, Colombia, 1970s, 349
Sun Air, South Africa, 1996, 403
T.A.C., Thailand, 1970s, 267
Transair, Canada, 1970s, 134
Transkei Airways, 1970s, 403, 403p
VARIG, Brazil, 1967, 315
Vayudoot, India, 1980s, 249
    See also Avro 748
Hawker-Siddeley HS-136, short-haul jet project, 90
Hawker-Siddeley HS-146, becomes BAe 146, 90
Hawker-Siddeley Trident. *See* de Havilland Trident
Hazelton, Max, 289
Hazelton Airlines (Australia), 289
HBN-100, initial design for wide-bodied twin airliner, 109
He 178, first German jet aircraft, 36c
He 280, development from He 178, 36c
Healey, Max, 322
HeavyLift (U.K.), operates Antonov An-124s, 155, 238
Hebredair (New Hebrides), 299
Heckscher, Elly, 354
Heilbron, Pedro, 345
Heinkel, Ernst, 36
Heinkel He-116 (German airliner), 25
Helgason, Sigurdur, 234
Helgstrand, Anders, 229
Helicopter Air Services, renamed Chicago Helicopter Services, 412
Helicopter airlines, 412
Helios Airways (Cyprus), 226
Henao Jaramillo, Fernando and Alvaro, 349
Henson, Dick, 94, 94p
Heschel, Anton, 236
Hewa Bora Airways (Zaire), 398, 398p
Highlands Division, British Airways, 196–197
High-speed rail, 413m
    Argentina, 415t
    Belgium (Thalys), 414t

    Brazil, 415t
    China, decelerates airline growth, 245, 414–415, 414t, 415p, 416m
    Competition with Turkish airline, 80, 414t
    Competition with Saudia, 78
    Czech Republic plan, 415t
    Denmark (X2000), 414t
    Egypt, 415t
    English Channel Tunnel opening, 214, 414t
    France (T.G.V.), 200, 213, 413, 413p, 414t
    Germany, ICE trains, 203, 414t
    India, 415t
    Iran, 415t
    Italy (T.A.V.), 210m, 413, 414t
    Malaysia, 415t
    Mexico, 415t
    Morocco, 415t
    Netherlands, 414t
    Poland, 415t
    Portugal, 415t
    Russia, 413, 414t
    Saudi Arabia, 415t
    South Korea (K.T.X.), 276, 414, 414t
    Spain (AVE), 217, 413, 414t
    Sweden (X2000), 414t
    Switzerland, 415t
    Taiwan, 271, 272, 414, 414t
    U.K., 414t
    Vietnam, 415t
Hijacking
    Air France, in Uganda, 1977, 387
    Air Mauritanie (foiled), 2007, 378
    Egyptair, 1976 and 1985, 374
    Ethiopian Air Lines, 1992 and 1995, 290–291
    Garuda, 1981, 263
    I.A.C., India, 1998, 249
    LAN, Chile, 1969, 368
    Philippine Air Lines, 1973, 1976, 1982, 273–274
    P.S.A., 1972, 172
    SAETA, Ecuador, 1970s, 356
    Sudan Airways, 1996, 389
    Swissair, 1970, 212
    TAME, Ecuador, 1969 (twice in one day), 355
Hikari, Japanese high-speed train, 99
Himalayan Helicopters, 254
Hindenburg (German dirigible airship), 15, 16p, 29, 36
Hi-Plains Airways, first use of *third level* term, 93
Hofer, George, 368
Holden's Air Transport (New Guinea), 137c
Holt, F.V., 7
Holt Thomas, George, 3
Holyman, Ivan, 137, 137c
Holyman's Airways, becomes Australian National, 137c

Hong Kong Engineering Company (HAECO), replaced by GAMECO, 244
Houphouet-Boigny, 68, 376, 377
Hovercraft service, S.A.S., 228
HS-748. *See* Hawker-Siddeley
Hu Yishao, 243
Huat Lye, Saw, 262
Hub operation, at Zagreb, 222
Hubbard, Edward, 2m, 8, 9c
Hughes, Howard, 28, 29, 45, 51, 124–125, 165–166, 342
Hughes Airwest (and Hughes Air West) (U.S.)
    Aids Air Liberia, 379
    Final confirmation of merger, 125
    Genealogy, 123c
    Strengthens fleet, 125
Hughes Tool Company, buys Air West, 124–125
Hummingbird Helicopters (Maldives), 257
"Hump," wartime supply route to China, 26
Hungary, first airline service, 5
Hunting Aircraft, designs H.107, 60
Hunting-Clan (U.K.)
    Competes with Central African Airways, 392
    Merged to form B.U.A., 59
Hurricane Ivan, Cayman Airways, 2004, 332
Hussein, Jordanian King, 79
Hwoo, T.C., 270
Hyatt Corporation, invests in Braniff, 159

I.A.C. *See* Indian Airlines Corporation
I.A.E. V2500. *See* Engines
IATA. *See* International Air Transport Association
Iberia (Spain), 33, 33t, 217–218
    Agreement with Alitalia, 210, 217
    Aircraft operated, 217, 218
    British Airways, American Airlines, buy shares, 218
    Douglas DC-8 service, 51, 217
    Douglas DC-9 service, 118, 217
    Interest in Latin American airlines, 346
    Invests in Aero Argentinas, 366
    North Atlantic airline chronology, 28t
    VIASA rescue attempt, 1991, 352
I.C.A. *See* International Caribbean Airways
Icahn, Carl, 166
I.C.A.O. *See* International Civil Aviation Organization
ICE. *See* Inter City Express
Icelandair, 234
    Buys shares in easyJet, 190
Idris, King of Libya, 373
Ikarus, Hungarian bus manufacturer, 101

Iliaronov, Vladimir, 154
Il'ya Muromets (pioneer Russian transport airplane), 2, 2p
    Flies St. Petersburg–Kiev, 1914, 2
    Victim of Bolshevik Revolution, 2, 20
    Wartime bomber, 2
Ilyushin, Sergei, 47, 112
Ilyushin Il-2 Shturmovik (tank buster), 99
Ilyushin Il-14, first Soviet aircraft for Cubana, 1961, 337
Ilyushin Il-18 Moskva (Soviet airliner)
    Air Guinée, 1962, 279
    Air Mali, 1961, 380
    C.A.A.C., China, 58; 1965, 240
    Compared to Bristol Britannia and Lockheed Electra, 48t
    Cubana, 1962, 337
    Diallo Airlines (Somalia), 1992, 388
    Enters service, 1959, 47, 47p
    Ghana Airways, 1960, 382
    Misrair, Egypt, 1968, 374
    Record production numbers, 100
    Survives in to Jet Age, 54
    Workhorse of Aeroflot, 1950s, 61
Ilyushin Il-62 and Il-62M (Soviet jet airliner), 54p
    Aeroflot, 1967, 100
    Air Ukraine, 1991, 238
    C.A.A.C., China, 58; 1971, 240
    Considered by LAN, Chile, 1970s, 368
    Cubana, 1972, 337, 338p
    Japan Air Lines, 1970, 99
    Kras Air, 153
    Misrair, Egypt, 1971, 374
    Similarity to Vickers VC-10, 100
    UKAMPS, North Korea, 1950s, 276
Ilyushin Il-76 (Soviet freighter aircraft)
    Armenian Airlines, 2000s, 239
    Developed into Il-86, 112
    Domodedovo Airlines, 153
    Kras Air, 153
Ilyushin Il-86 (Soviet wide-bodied jet airliner)
    China Xinjiang, 1985, 242t
    Development, first flight, service, 1980, 112, 112p
    Pulkovo, 156
    Transaero, Sibir, 1990s, 152, 152p
Ilyushin Il-96 (wide-bodied jet airliner)
    Conviasa, Venezuela, 2008, 353
    Domodedovo Airlines, 153, 153p
Imperial Airways (U.K.), 3, 12–14, 22–23, 24p, 25, 35, 40, 285, 367, 392, 42–43
    Intense competition from K.L.M. during 1930s, 11
    Maintains wartime service, 22
    Orders fleet of Short S-23 flying boats, 1934, 12
    Reaches Karachi, 1929, 1

Route maps, 12m, 13m
    Short S.23 "Empire" flying boat service, 13, 13m, 13p
    Train service, 13m
    Transcontinental, 1933, 11
    World routes, 1939, 21m
Impulse Airlines (Australia), 290
Inair (Internacional de Aviación), 346
Inclusive Tour Charters (ITC), 64
Inclusive tours
    Introduced in Europe, 1952, 63
    Success in Spain, 217
Independence Air (U.S.), 185
Independent United (Soviet C.I.S.), 151t
India
    Builds Avro 748s, 86
    Confrontation with China, 248
    First air mail service in Asia, 1
    Revokes Air Corporations Act, 1994, 247
    Tripartite Agreement, 246, 287
Indian Airlines Corporation (I.A.C.), 86, 86m
    Aircraft operated, 247–249
    Assists Maldives, 257, 257p
    Competition from railroads, 248
    Ends Night Air Mail Service, 248
    Hijacking, 1998, 249
    Separates route categories, 90
    Tupolev Tu-154 crash, 1993, 248
Indian National Airways, Empire service, 21m
Indian Transcontinental Airways, 11
IndiGo Airlines (India), 250
Indigo Partners, founds Tiger Airways, 284
Indonesia, regional airlines, 134–136, 135p, 136p
Indonesia Air Asia, 283
Indonesian Air Transport
    Britten-Norman BN-2 Islander, 136p
Indonesian Airways, ancestor of Garuda, 262
Inex-Adria (Yugoslavia)
    Name change from Adria Aviopromet, 223
    Charters, 64t
    DC-9 vacation traffic, 61, 223m
Ini, José, 365
I.N.I., Spanish investment corporation, 218
Inland Air lines (U.S.), post-war autonomous division of Western, 26t
Inouye, Choichi, 7
Inter (Guatemala), 344
Inter Atoll Air (Maldives), 257
Inter City Express (ICE) (Germany's high-speed rail), 203, 413
Intercontinental Airlines (Nigeria), 381
Interflug (East Germany)
    Absorbed by Lufthansa, 203
    Member of Six-Pool, 62

Inter-Island Airways. *See* Air Seychelles
Interjet (Mexico), 326, 326t
Intermodality, air and surface transport, 418–419, 419p
Internal German Service (I.G.S.), sold to Lufthansa, 163, 203
International Aero Engines, I.A.E. V2500. *See* Engines.
International Air Bahama (and Air Bahama), 332
International Air Transport Association (IATA), 29–30, 32, 44, 59, 62, 78, 100, 106, 132, 142–144, 148, 149, 190, 194, 202, 207, 209, 217, 228, 231, 233–234, 236, 238, 260, 262, 270, 288, 310–311, 330, 332, 348, 365, 401–402
    Denies flexible tariffs, 32, 44
    Evaded by Braathens, Lolftleidir, 231–233
    Evaded by Trek Airways, 401–402
    Faces increase of tourist traffic, 82
    Fare structure challenged by tour groups, 1959
    Inclusive tour market in Spain, 1950s–1960s, 217
    Introduces tourist fares and economy fares, 143
International Caribbean Airways (I.C.A.), 330
International Civil Aviation Organization (I.C.A.O.), 29, 51, 83, 155, 187, 226, 233, 2 40, 245, 253, 260, 270, 314, 411
International Radio, division of British Airways Board, 1972, 195
Interstate Airlines, 9c
"Inter-Wing" services between East and West Pakistan, 252
Intra Airways (U.K.), becomes Jersey European, 192
Iowa Airlines (U.S.), becomes Midwest, 123c
Irala, Xavier de, 218
Iranian Airways Company (Iranair), 71
    Route to China, 240
Iraqi Air Force, as airline, 75
Iraqi Airways, 75–76
    de Havilland Trident service, 119
Irelandia Investments, founds Tiger Airways, 284
"Irregulars" (U.S. non-scheduled airlines), 65, 92
    Origin of commuter airlines, 92
Isaikin, Alexei, 155–156
Isitt, Leonard, 291
Island Air (Fiji), 297
Island Air (Guam), 300
Island Air Ferries (U.S.), 123c
Island Sky Ferries (U.S.), 92
Isleña de Inversiones (Isleña Airlines) (Honduras), 341, 342, 344

Index

Italy
  First air mail services, 2
  First airlines, 5
  Minor shareholding in Airbus, 110
  Route to Africa, 14, 14m

J.A.A. *See* Japan Asia Airways
J.A.C. *See* Japan Air Commuter
J.A.L. *See* Japan Air Lines
Jamahira Air Transport (Libya), 373
Jamaica Air Services, 328
Jamall, Enver, 252
Jamieson, Donald, 133
Jannus, Tony, 1
Japan
  Builds Douglas DC-2s under license, 18
  Early airline history, 18
  Enters Second World War, 25
  Innovative high-speed rail introduced, 412, 414t
  Pioneer airlines, 7m
  Wartime scheduled services of navy, 25m
Japan Air Commuter (J.A.C.), formed by All Nippon Airways, 149
Japan Air Lines (J.A.L.) (post-war)
  Boeing 727 service, 57
  Concentrates on main-line routes, 85, 145
  Dominates trans-Pacific travel, 99
  Japan's "chosen instrument," 145
  Operates Tupolev Tu-114, 49
  Orders Concorde, 114
  Polar service, 34t
  Prefers 727 v. DC-9, 61
  Reorganized formation, jet service, 98
  Round-the-world service, 99
  Route map, 1991, 280m
  Service to China, 99
  Use of Soviet aircraft, 99
Japan Air System
  First MD-90 service, 117
  Name change from Toa Domestic, 149
  Route map, 1991, 147m
Japan Air Transport Company (N.K.Y.K.K.), 18
Japan Asia Airways, formed to serve Taiwan, 147
Japan Domestic Airlines (J.D.A.), 146, 149
Japan Helicopter and Aeroplane Transport Company, 144, 144m
Japanese Air Lines, earliest airline of Japan, 7m, 98
  See also Japan Air Lines
J.A.T. *See* Jugoslovenski Aerotransport
JATO. *See* Jet-Assisted Take-off
Jazz
  Acquires Air Ontario, 310
  Air Canada affiliate, 307, 307p
J.D.A. *See* Japan Domestic Airlines
J.E.A. *See* Jersey European Airways

"Jelly bean jets," Braniff's innovative paint scheme, 158
Jensen, Henry, Thai International, 1962, 266
Jersey European Airways (J.E.A.), 192
Jet Age Generations, 411, 411c
Jet aircraft debuts, 52t
Jet Airways (India), 247, 249, 249p
  Buys Sahara, 250
  International service, first by Indian independent, 250
Jet-Assisted Take-off (JATO)
  Antilles Air Boats, 339
  Ethiopian Air Lines, 390
Jet Blue, 181–182, 182p, 185–186
Jet Capital Corporation, acquired by Chase Manhattan Bank, 127
"Jet Commuter," United Air Lines, 171
JetStar Asia (Singapore), 283, 290
Jetstream 31 (U.K.), 210
Johansson, Angrimur, 234
John Paul II (Pope), 294, 368, 384
Johnson, Lyndon B., 115, 124, 154
Johnson, Robert, 169
Johnson Flying Service (U.S. Supplemental airline), 65t
Jones, Aubrey, 113
Jordan, Lewis, 180
Jordan Airways, 72, 79
Jordanian World Airways, subsidiary of Jordan Airways, 79
Jugoslovenski Aerotransport (J.A.T.) (Yugoslavia), 222, 223
  DC-9 vacation traffic, 61, 223m
Junkers, German aircraft manufacturer
  Aircraft in Brazil, 18
  Benefits from all-metal construction, 6
  Builds F13, 1919, 3
  License-built in Soviet Union, 20
  Restricted by Versailles Treaty, 3
  South Africa, pre-war fleet, 16
  See also specific aircraft
Junkers Jumo engine. *See* Engines
Junkers-G 31 (German cargo aircraft), 16
Junkers-Ju 52/3m (German airliner), 5
  Deutsche Luft Hansa inter-war fleet reliability, 15, 15p
  Gibbes-Sepik, New Guinea, 1955, 294
  In Brazil, 19
  Last flight at war's end, 25
  Réunion and Mauritius, 1945, 406
  Service to far east, 25
  Syndicto Condor, Brazil, 1930s and 1940s, 316
  Use by British during war, 24
Junkers-Ju 86 (German landplane), 24
Junkers-Ju 90, European service, 25
Junkers-W34 (and 33) (German floatplanes), 5p, 6

Kabo, Chief, 381
Kabo Air (Nigeria), 381, 381p
Kahn, Alfred E., 140
K.A.L. *See* Korean Air Lines
Kalahari Air Service (Botswana), 404
Kalinin K-5 (Soviet airliner) Dobrolot, 1929, 20
Kamov, Nikolai, 104
Kamov Ka-26 (Soviet helicopter), 104, 104p
Kampuchea Airlines, 279
Karhumaki (or Kar-Air) (Finnish charter airline), 64t, 232–233
Kazakh CAD (Soviet C.I.S.), 151t
Kelleher, Herb, 118, 118p, 141, 177, 187
Kellow, Ahmed, 391
Kendell, Don, 289
Kendell Airlines (Australia), 289
Kenya Airways, 386, 386p
Key Airlines (U.S.), 176
Keys, Clement, 7, 9c, 17, 418
Khademi, Ali, 71
Khajavi, Alex, 341
Khan, Rahim, 253
Kharafi, Mohammed al-, 225
Khomeini, Ayatollah, 1980
Kibris Turk Hava Yollari (K.T.H.Y.) (Cyprus), 80–81, 226
King, Lord, 142, 197
King, Rollin, 177
Kingdom of Libya Airlines, 373
Kingfisher Airlines (India), 250
Kingsford-Smith, Charles, 137, 295
Kingsley, Major Shirley, 6
Kirana, Rusdi, 184
Kirghizi CAD (Soviet C.I.S.), 151t
Kirtleside, Lord Douglas of, 37
Kissinger, Henry, 146
Kita Nihon Koku. *See* North Japan Airlines
K.L.M. *See* Koninklijke Luchtvaart Maatschappij voor Nederland en Kolonien
K.L.M.-U.K., owned by Air France–K.L.M., 201
K.N.I.L.M. *See* Koninklijke Nederlandsch-Indische Luchtvaart Maatschappij
Kochian, Carl, 146
Kodama, Japanese high-speed train, 99
Kolkholsnik, familar name for the Antonov An-2 biplane, 131
Komi Ave (Soviet C.I.S.), 151t
Koninklijke Luchtvaart Maatschappij voor Nederland en Kolonien (K.L.M.) (Netherlands)
  Agreement with Alitalia, 1997, 210, 216
  Aircraft operated, 51, 61, 118, 215
  Assists Air Ceylon, 255
  Assists Philippine Air Lines, 272
  Buys Electras, 47
  Central and South Atlantic service, 33, 33t
  Final alliance with Air France, 216

Historic flight to Batavia, 12
  Intense competition with Imperial Airways, 11
  Interests in Kenya Airways, Malaysian Airlines, 216
  Interests in local airlines, 215
  K.S.S.U. airline partnership, 110–111
  Management team to Nigerian Airways, 380
  Merger prospects with Northwest Airlines, 215–216
  Merger with Air France, 2003, 201
  North Atlantic service chronology, 28t
  North Atlantic success, 105
  Polar service, 34t
  Post-war Silk Road to the far east, 34
  SABENA proposal, 214
  Second place in England–Australia Air Race, 12, 13p
  Subsidiary, Cityhopper, changes name to Buzz, 192, 215
  Tenerife, deadliest airline disaster, 215
  West Indian Division, 328, 333
Koninklijke Nederlandsch-Indische Luchtvaart Maatschappij (K.N.I.L.M.) (Netherlands), 12
Kooka, "Bobby," 246
Korean Air Cargo, 275
Korean Air Lines (K.A.L.), 85, 275
Korean National Airlines (K.N.A.), 275
Korotkonogiy, "Short-Legged," nickname for the Mil Mi-10K, 103
Kras Air
  Name change from Krasnoyarskavia (Krasnoyarsk Airlines), 153–154
  One of Russia's "Big Six," 157
Krasnoyarskavia (Krasnoyarsk Airlines) (Soviet C.I.S.), 151t
  See also Kras Air
Kriete, Ricardo, 343, 344
Krogager, Ejlif, 64, 229
K.S.S.U. Group, European airline consortium, 111, 202
  K.L.M., 215
  S.A.S., 228
  Swissair, 211
  U.A.T., 111
K.T.H.Y. *See* Kibris Turk Hava Yollari
K.T.X., South Korean high-speed rail, 414t
Kubitschek de Oliveira, Juscelino, 129, 313
Kuk Ho, Korean business group, 275
Kulula.com (South Africa), 402, 402p
Kuwait National Airways, becomes Kuwait Airways, 75, 75p
de Havilland Trident service, 119
Kyokuto Koku. *See* Far Eastern Airlines

L.A.A. *See* Los Angeles Airways
L.A.B. *See* Lloyd Aereo Boliviano
L.A.C. *See* Lloyd Aéreo Colombiano; Líneas Aéreas Canedo
LACSA. *See* Lineas Aéreas Costarricenses, S.A.
LADECO. *See* Línea Aérea del Cobre
L.A.I. *See* Lignes Interieures Algériennes; Linee Aeree Italiane
La Navette (France), shuttle service, 200
Lake Central Airlines (U.S.)
 Founded as Turner Airlines, name change, 122
 Genealogy, 123c
 Operates Nord 262, 1965, 122
Lakefield, Bruce R., 169–170
Laker, Freddie, 59, 102, 105–107, 106p, 106c, 140, 144, 187
Laker Airways (British charter airline), 64t, 106, 194
 End of the Second Force, 197
 Foreclosure, anti-trust suit, settlement, 106–107
L.A.M. *See* Linhas Aéreas de Mozambique
LAM-Mozambique. *See* Linhas Aéreas de Mozambique
LAN Perú, established by LAN-Chile, 359
Lancastrian, conversion of British bomber, 27
LAN-Chile. *See* Líneas Aéreas Nacional
Lane, Lloyd, 127
LANICA. *See* Lineas Aéreas de Nicaragua
LANSA. *See* Lineas Aéreas Nacionales
LANSA (Colombia), cooperates with AVENSA, 351
Lao Aviation/Airlines, 279–280
L.A.P. *See* Líneas Aéreas Paraguayas
LAPA. *See* Líneas Aéreas Privadas Argentinas
LAPSA. *See* Lloyd Aéreo Paraguayo, S.A.
LARA. *See* Ligne Aérienne du Roi Albert
Larkin Aerial Supply Company (Australia), 6, 6m, 137
Larrain, E.R., 359
L.A.S. *See* Ligne Aérienne Seychelles
Latavio (Latvia), 239
Latécoère, French aircraft manufacturer
 African route pioneer, 14
 Aircraft status at outbreak of war, 23
 Founds early French airline, 4, 4m
 Post-war Atlantic service, 334
Latécoère Mission to Japan, 18
LATI. *See* Linee Aeree Transcontinentali Italiane
L.A.T.N. *See* Línea Aérea de Transporte Nacional

Lauda, Andreas Nikolaus ("Niki"), 237
Lauda Air (and Lauda Air Italy), 237
Laurentide Air Services (Canada), 20
L.A.V. *See* Línea Aeropostal Venezolana
Lawrence, Harding, 158–159
Le Grand. See Russian Knight
Leadgate Investment, 363
Lebanese International Airlines, 72
Leeward Islands Air Transport (Caribbean), 329, 329m
 Aircraft operated, 330
 B.W.I.A. control, 330
 Newly named after Court Line collapse, 330
 See also Court Line
Lembaga Urusan Tabung Haji (LUTH), Malaysian agency, 261
Lend-Lease program, Pan American involvement, 25
Leningrad ACA (Soviet C.I.S.), 151t
Leonard, Joe, 180
Let L410 (Czech turboprop feeder airliner)
 Aeroflot service, 1971, 101
 Air Malawi, 2005, 395
 Regional services, 1960s, 1970s, 131–132
Levine, Michael, 174
Levy Lepen hydroplane
 LARA service in Congo, 1920, 13
Li, Victor Y.K., 307
L.I.A. *See* Lebanese International Airlines
LIAT. *See* Leeward Islands Air Transport
Liberian National Airways. *See* Air Liberia
Libyan Airlines. *See* Libyan Arab Airlines
Libyan Arab Airlines, 373
Lighted airway, 7, 18
Ligne Aérienne du Roi Albert (LARA) (Belgian Congo), first African airline, 5, 13
Ligne Aérienne Seychelles (L.A.S.), 389
Lignes Interieures Algériennes (L.A.I.) (Algeria), 371
Lim Chin Beng, 283
Lindbergh, Charles, 9, 10p, 11, 115
Lindegard, Joergen, 229
Línea Aérea de Transporte Nacional (L.A.T.N.) (Paraguay), 362
Línea Aérea del Cobre (LADECO) (Chile), 368–369
 Iberia shareholding, 218
Línea Aeropostal Santiago-Arica (Chile), 19
 Renamed LAN-Chile, 1985, 368
 See also Líneas Aéreas Nacional
Línea Aeropostal Venezolana (L.A.V. or Aeropostal), 350–352
 Central Atlantic route, 33, 33t

Liquidates stock in AVENSA, 351
Operates Avro 748s, 67
Operates MD-82s, 351
Orders Comet jet, 87, 350
Starts service (as French Aéropostale) 1931, 19
Lineas Aereas Azteca, and TAESA, 325–326
Líneas Aéreas Canedo (or Aerosur) (Bolivia), 361
Lineas Aéreas Costarricenses, S.A. (LACSA) (Costa Rica), 340–341
 Aircraft operated, 341
 Forms Cayman Brac Airways, 332, 340
 Forms SANSA, 341
 TACA shareholding, 341
Líneas Aéreas de Nicaragua (LANICA), 340, 342
Líneas Aéreas La Urraca (Colombia), 349
Líneas Aéreas Nacional (LAN-Chile), 19, 367–369
 Aircraft operated, 368, 369, 369p
 Consolidates Chilean airlines, 369
 Order for Airbus A320 series 319–320, 343
 Takes over VASP shares in Ecuatoriana, 355
Líneas Aéreas Nacionales (LANSA) (Honduras), 342
Líneas Aéreas Paraguayas (L.A.P.)
 Name change to Air Paraguay, 362
 Name change to ARG Argentinas Línea Privada, 367
 TAM investment, 319
Líneas Aéreas Privadas Argentinas (LAPA), 366–367
Linee Aeree Italiane (L.A.I.), 28t, 98
Linee Aeree Transcontinentali Italiane (LATI), 33, 33t
Linee Imperiale, 14, 14m
Linha da Lagôa, experimental flights in Brazil, 18
Linhas Aéreas de Angola (TAAG or Angolan Airlines), 69, 395–396
 Aircraft operated, 396, 396p
 Survives civil war, 395
Linhas Aéreas de Mozambique (L.A.M. or LAM-Mozambique), 69, 395, 396
 Aircraft operated, 395–396
 Route map, 396m
Linjeflyg (Sweden), 90, 232
 S.A.S. half-share, 227, 232
Lion Air (Indonesia), 284, 284p
Lisunov Li-2 (Soviet Douglas DC-3)
 Minhaiduy, China, 1954, 132
 Mongolian, 1956, 276
Lithuanian Airlines, 239
"Little Amy," Marshall Islands HS-748, 300
Lloyd Aereo Boliviano (L.A.B.) (Bolivia), 6, 359–360

 Aided by North Central Airlines, 360
 Aircraft operated, 360, 360p
 Cooperation with SEDTA, Ecuador, 20
 LAN-Chile controls, 355
 Shares sold to VASP, 317, 359–360
Lloyd Aéreo Colombiano (L.A.C.), 349, 360
Lloyd Aéreo Paraguayo, S.A. (LAPSA) (Paraguay), 362
Local Service airlines, U.S.
 Establishment, territories served, 83, 84m
 Genealogy, 123c
 Renamed Regional, 60, 122
 See also Commuter airlines
Lockheed 100 and C-130 Hercules freighter, 102
 Air Botswana, 1980s, 404
 Air Gabon, 1985, 379
 First Air, Canada, 2000s, 310
 Pacific Western, Canada, 1970s, 307
 Zambian Air Cargoes, 1966–1975, 393
Lockheed Aircraft Company
 Fixes Electra problem, 46
 Loses competition to Boeing, 115
 "Stretches" Constellation into L-1649A Starliner, 37
 Supersonic airliner project, 114
 See also specific aircraft
Lockheed Constellation
 Nonstop transcontinental flight, 1944, 29
 Sets post-war pace, 27
 Sponsorship by Hughes's T.W.A., 28
 Trek Airways, 1960, 402
Lockheed L10 Electra
 Trans Canada (inaugural), 1939, 20, 20p, 303
 Wisconsin Central Airlines, 1944, 125
Lockheed L-188 Electra, 46, 46p
 Aerocondor, Colombia, 1969, 349
 Air California, 1967, 172
 Air Ceylon, 1960, 255–256
 Air Florida, 1973, 160
 Air Lanka, 1991, 255–256
 Air Manila International, 1971, 282
 C.E.A./Ecuatoriana, 1972, 354
 Compared to Bristol Britannia and Ilyushin Il-18, 48t
 COPA, Panama, 1970s, 345, 345p
 FAT, Taiwan, 1980, 270
 Garuda Indonesian, 1961, 263
 L.A.P., Paraguay, 1969, 362
 Mandala, Indonesia, 135–136
 QANTAS, 1959, 287
 SAHSA, Honduras, 1968, 342
 Survives into Jet Age, 54
 TEAL, New Zealand, 1959, 291
Lockheed L-1011 TriStar
 Air Canada, 1973, 304
 Air Lanka, 1980s, 256

Index

Air-India, 1998, 247
British Airways, 1970s, 196
B.W.I.A., 1980, 328
Development, first flight, 111, 112p
Eastern Air Lines "Whisperjets," 1972, 164
Gulf Air, 76
Pan American Airways, 1978–1982, 161–162
P.S.A., 1974, 172
Sale to All Nippon Airways, scandal, 146
Saudia, 78
Lockheed Model 18 Lodestar
  B.O.A.C., 35
  SABENA, 35
Lockheed Super Constellation
  Pratt & Whitney R-3400 engine, 30
  Trek Airways, 1963, 402
Lockwood, Joseph, 111
Loepfe, Otto, 212
Loftleidir (Iceland), 233
  Atlantic airline chronology, 28t
  Connection with International Air Bahama, takeover, 332
  Cooperation with Trek Airways, South Africa, 402
  First service, 1948, 30p, 30m
  Pioneer of Sixth Freedom traffic, 143
Loke Wan Tho, 259
Lombardo, Diaz, 20
Long Beach, JetBlue service to Los Angeles satellite airport, 182
Longyearbyen, world's most northerly airport, 235m
Lorenz, João, 316
Lorenzo, Frank, 127–128, 128p, 140, 140p, 161, 165–166
Los Angeles Airways, helicopter airline, 412
LOT. *See* Polskie Linie Lotnicze
L.R.E. (Long Range Empire) airliner, became Britannia, 32
L.T.U. *See* Lufttransport Unternehmen
LTV Corporation, buys interest in Braniff, 159
Luftag, lays foundations for post-war Lufthansa, 98
Lufthansa (or Deutsche Lufthansa), 98, 202–204
  Boeing 707 service, 51, 98, 202
  Boeing 727 service, 57, 98, 202
  Boeing 737-100, 118, 202
  Boeing 747 service, 202, 204p
  Buys Pan American Internal German Service, 163
  Consulting branch restructures Air Gabon, 379
  Douglas DC-10 service, 202
  First service, 1968, 118, 202
  Government sells remaining stake, 204
  Increases stake in Swiss International, 2005, 213

Joint venture, AMECO, 244
Lufthansa Airport Express, 419
Management team for Garuda, 264
Management team for Philippine Air Lines, 274
Member, ATLAS Group, 202
North Atlantic service, 28t, 105
Orders Airbus A380s, 204
Post-war name change, 202
Shares in Lauda Air, 237
South Atlantic service, 33t
Viscount Service, 202
See also Deutsche Luft Hansa
Lufttransport Unternehmen (L.T.U.) (Germany), 63
  Charters, 64t
  Control by SAir Group, 212
  First order for Fokker F-28, 89
  Sold to Rewe retail giant, 212
Lumenta, R.A.J., 263–264
Lumholdt, Niels, 266
LUTH. *See* Lembaga Urusan Tabung Haji
Luxair (Luxembourg), cooperation with Trek Airways, 402
Luxor Air (Egypt), 375, 375p
Lyon, William, 173

Macair (Solomon Islands), 274, 298
Macao, last flights, 220
Macchia, Bill, 185
Machinists Union, 1989 strike, 165
Mackenzie Air Service, ancestor of CP Air, 304
Macmillan, Harold, 67
MacRobertson-Miller Aviation (M.M.A.) (Australia)
  Becomes Airlines of Western Australia, 90, 138, 286
  Sold to Ansett, 137, 137c
Madair. *See* Air Madagascar
Madang (New Guinea), 137c
Maddux Air Lines, 9c
Maersk (Scandinavian charter airline), 64t
Maersk Air (Denmark), 233
  Merger to form Sterling Airlines, 230
  Stake in Estonian Air, 239
  With S.A.S., forms Danair, 227
Maersk Air (U.K.), franchised from British Airways, 198
Mafiking Air Services (South African homelands), 403
Magadan Avia (Soviet C.I.S.), 151t
Magyar Legikozlekedesi Vallalat (MALEV) (Hungary)
  Alitalia interest, 210
  Cold War service to Albania, 225
  Member of Six-Pool, 62
Maingard, Amadée, 406
Makaris III (Archbishop of Cyprus), 80
Makung Airlines (Taiwan), 271
Malayan Airways, predecessor of Malaysian Airways, 259

Malaysian Airways. *See* Malaysian Airways System
Malaysian Airways System (M.A.S.), 246, 259, 261–262
  Operates Fokker Friendship, 85
  Orders Airbus A380s, 262
  Renamed Malaysia Airways, 262
  Tripartite Agreement, 1967, 246
Malaysian Helicopter Services (M.H.S.), 262
Malaysian-Singapore Airlines (M.S.A.), 259
Maldives, independence, 251, 251m, 258m
Maldives International Airlines (M.I.A.). *See* Air Maldives
Maldivian Air Taxi, 257, 258m
MALEV. *See* Magyar Legikozlekedesi Vallalat
Mallya, Vijay, 250
Malmö Aviation, merges with Transwede, 231
Malta Airways, becomes Air Malta, 224
Mancilla, Francisco, 20
Mandala Airlines (Indonesia), 84, 135, 265–266
Mandarin, airline service by C.A.T., 269
Mandarin Airlines, 271
  MD-11 crash, 1999, 270
Mandated Airlines (New Guinea), 137c
  Acquires Gibbes-Sepik, 294
Mandela, Nelson, 400
Mango (South Africa), 403, 403p
Manshu Koko Kabushiki Kaisha (M.K.K.K.) (Japan), 18
Manx (U.K.), franchised then sold to British Airways, 198
Mao Tse-tung, 133
Marcos, Ferdinand, 86
Maritime Central Aiways (Canada), merges into Eastern Provincial, 134
Marking, Henry, 196
Marsans Grupo (Spain), 1966
Marshall, Colin, 142, 168–169, 197
Martin 202
  Japanese Airlines, 1952, 98
  Pioneer Airlines, 1952, 84
Martin 404
  Southern Airways, 125
Martin M-130 flying boat
  Pan American service, 1935, 15, 15p
Martinair (Netherlands), 201, 215
Martins, Fernando Augusto dos Santos, 220
Martirosov, Andrei, 155
M.A.S. *See* Malaysian Airways System; Mines Air Services
Mascarenhas, Michael, 247
MASCO. *See* Mideast Air Service Company

Masefield, Peter, 37
Mass production, U.S. v. U.K., 32
Master Cooperation Agreement (M.C.A.), 216
"Material diversion," charter airline competition, 63
Mathews, Charlie, 343
Maya, Philippine low-fare service, 272
Mayrhuber, Wolfgang, 204
Maytag, Lewis B. (Bud), 126–127
McAdoo, Bob, 184
McConachie, Grant, 304–306
McDonnell. *See* McDonnell Douglas Aircraft Corporation
McDonnell Douglas Aircraft Corporation, U.S. aircraft manufacturer
  Formed by merger, 60
  Merged with Boeing Company, 117
  See also specific aircraft (MD)
McGowan, Gerry, 290
McGregor, Gordon, 304
McIntyre, Malcolm, 164
McKaughan, Earl, 127
McLean Industries, 343
McQuay, Michael, 296
MD-11, "stretched" Douglas DC-10
  Eva Air, 1989, 271
  Korean Air Lines, 1990, 275
  Mandarin Air, crash, 1999, 270
  Swissair order, 1995; crash, 1998, 212
  VASP, Brazil, 1990s, 317
MD-80, DC-9 development, 61
  AVIANCA, 1991, 348
  Croatia Airlines, 1991, 224
  New York Air, 1984, 174
  ZAS, Egypt, 1982, 375
MD-81
  Swissair, 1980, 212
MD-82-83
  Air Jamaica, 1994, 329
  A.L.M., Curaçao, 1979, 333
  AVIANCA, 2000s, 348
  Bouraq Indonesian Airlines, 1978, 265
  Built by Shanghai Aircraft Factory, 1980s, 241
  China Eastern, 241p
  China Northern, 1990, 242t
  Compass Mark II, Australia, 1992, 290
  L.A.V., Venezuela, 351p
  Lion Air, Indonesia, 2000s, 284
  Nouvelair, Tunis, 1990s, 373
MD-87
  Air Burkina, 2001, 378
  Tradewinds, Singapore, 1989, 261
MD-95, DC-9 development
  Designated as Boeing 717, 1997, 180, 180p
  ValuJet, 1995, 179p, 180
M.E.A. *See* Middle East Airlines
Megapode Airways (Solomon Islands), 298

Melanesian Airways. *See* Macair
Melgosa, Luis, 20
Mendez, Manuel Gomes, 324
Mendis, Padwan "Paddy," 255
Mengistu, Haile Mariam, 70
Mercury-Singapore Airlines (M.S.A.), 259
Meridiana (Sardinia), 210
Merino Benítez, Arturo, 368
Merpati Nusantara Airlines (Indonesia), 135, 264–265
  Aircraft operated, 84, 135, 135p, 264
  CASA-Nurtanio aircraft, 264–265
  Domestic routes, 85m
  Douglas DC-3 operations in New Guinea, 135
  "Six Lives," 264
  Transfer to Garuda, 1978, 263
Mesa Airlines (U.S.), low-fare airline, 182
Messerschmitt 262 (German fighter aircraft), 36, 36c
Metal fatigue, problems revealed by Comet disasters, 41
Metro Manila (Philippines), 294
Metrojet, formed by US Airways, 169
Metroliner (Canada), 306
Mexicana. *See* Compañía Mexicana de Aviación
Mexico, dual-airline policy, 323
M.I.A. *See* Maldives International Airlines; Myanmar International Airways
MIAT (Mongolyn Irgeniy Agaaryn Teever). *See* Air Mongol
Mid-Atlantic Airways (U.S.), low-fare airline, 170
Mid-Continent Airlines (U.S.), 26t
Middle East Airlines (M.E.A.) (Lebanon), 71–72
Mideast Air Service Company (MASCO), engine servicing depot, 72
"Midnight Flyer," P.S.A. service, 172
Midway Airlines
  Acquires Air Florida, 160
  Suspends operations, 1991, 178
Midwest Airlines (U.S.), 123c
Mikelsons, J. George, 183
Mil, Mikhail, 103
Mil Mi helicopters, 103, 103p
  Mil Mi-6, 40-ton helicopter, 103, 154
  Mil Mi-8, 12-ton versatile helicopter, 103, 104p, 131–132
  Mil Mi-10 and Mil Mi-10Ks, 103, 154
  Mil Mi-26, 20-ton payload, 103, 154
Miles Marathon (British airliner)
  All Nippon Airways, 1950s, 144
  Brabazon Committee recommendation, 32
  W.A.A.C., 1950s, 380

Miller, Ross, 92
Millon, Juan, 349
Milton, Robert, 306
Minabatho Air Services (South African homelands), 403
Mineralvodskoe PO (Soviet C.I.S.), 151t
Minerva (Italy), local airline, 210
Mines Air Services (Zambia), renamed Zambian Airways, 394
Minhaiduy (China), 132
Mini-skirts, flight attendant uniforms, 171
Minnesota Enterprises, 127
Misrair, 374
  First Hajj pilgrims by air, 1937, 16
  Name change to United Arab Airlines, 70, 374
Miss Indy, American Trans Air's first aircraft, 183
Mr. Citizen, Air Deccan's insignia, 250
"Mr. Erik." *See* Carvalho, Erik de
M.K.K.K. *See* Manshu Koko Kabushiki Kaisha
M.L.T. Vacations, forms Sun Country Vacations, 184
M.M.A. *See* MacRobertson-Miller Aviation
Mobutu, Joseph- Désiré, 396–397
Modern Air Transport (U.S. Supplemental airline), 65t
Mohawk Airlines (U.S.), 60, 122, 168, 412
  Genealogy, 123c
  Merger with Allegheny Airlines to create USAir, 1972, 122
Moldavian CAD (Soviet C.I.S.), 151t
Moll, J.J., 12
Monarch (U.K.), 64t
Monarch Airlines (U.S.), forms Frontier Airlines, 123c, 125m
Mongolian Airlines. *See* Air Mongol
Mongolyn Irgeniy Agaaryn Teever (MIAT) (Mongolia). *See* Air Mongol
Mont Laurier Aviation (Canada), 134
Montesinos, Major José, 355
Morales, Carlos, 358
Morgan, Marien, 113
Morris Air (U.S.), 181
Moskva. *See* Ilyushin Il-18
Mount Cook Airways (New Zealand), 292, 292p
"Mountain Flights," Nepal, 254, 254t, 254m
Movies in flight, 166
Mozambique. *See* Divisão de Exploração dos Transportes Aéreos
M.R.E. (Medium Range Empire) airliner, became Britannia, 32
M.S.A. *See* Malaysian-Singapore Airlines; Mercury-Singapore Airlines
Murdoch, Rupert, 286, 293

Muse, Lamar, 126
Myanmar. *See* Burma, independence
Myanmar International Airways (M.I.A.), 257

Nacional (Brazil), sold to REAL, 315
Nagasaki Airlines (Japan), sold to All Nippon Airways, 145
Naka Nihon Koku. *See* Central Japan Airlines
Namib Air (Namibia), 404, 404p
  See also Air Namibia
Napier, British engine manufacturer, 122
Nasser, Abdel, 70, 374
National Air Lines (U.S.), 26t, 52, 52t
  Aircraft operated, 46, 52, 110
  Helicopter service, 412
  Name revived, 1998, 184
National Air Transport
  Contract air mail route (CAM 3), 1926, 8
  Genealogy, 9c
National Airways Corporation (N.A.C.) (former N.Z.N.A.C.), 291, 292
National Jet Italia, franchised from British Airways, 198
National Transportation Safety Board (N.T.S.B.), 180, 339
Nationwide Air (South Africa), 403
Naviera Santa, S.A., Peruvian ship company, 358
N.C.A. *See* Nippon Cargo Airlines; North Central Airlines
Neckerman, German department store, 64
Neeleman, David, 181
Nelson, Orvis, 66, 67p
Nepal Airways, 254
Nepcon Air (Nepal), 254
Nerungi Sakha Corp. (Soviet C.I.S.), 151t
Nether-Lines (Netherlands), 215
Nevis Express, 330
New Air, provisional name for JetBlue, 181
New Air Zaïre, 397
New Airline, Inc. (U.S.), 184
New England Airways (Australia), 137c
New Guinea
  Importance of air transport, 293–294
  Pioneer air services, 16
New Guinea Gold, becomes Guinea Airways, 137c
New Hebrides Airways (Australia), 288, 294, 295, 299
New York Air, 128, 128p, 174
New York Airways (N.Y.A.), helicopter airline, 412
New York, Rio and Buenos Aires Line (NYRBA) (U.S.–Latin America)
  Renamed Panair do Brasil, 18
  Routes, 5m

New York Silk Express, THAI service, 268
New Zealand
  Early air services, 16
  Tripartite Agreement, 1967, 246
Newman, David, 38
Newman's Air (New Zealand), 286
News Corporation, 286, 293
N.H.Y.K.K. *See* Japan Helicopter and Aeroplane Transport Company
Nicholson, David, 195
Nigeria, series of crashes, 381
Nigerian Airways, 380–381
  Kidnapping attempt, 1984, 380
  Operates Britannias, 1959, 46
  Takes over West African Airways, 67
Night Mercury, Philippine Air Lines service, 272
Nighthawk fares, Capital Airlines, 139
Nihon Herikoputa Yuso Kabushiki Kaisha (N.H.Y.K.K.). *See* Japan Helicopter and Aeroplane Transport Company
Nihon Koku Kabashiki Kaisha (N.K.K.K.). *See* Japanese Air Lines
Nihon Koku Yuso Kabushiki Kaisha (N.K.Y.K.K.). *See* Japan Air Transport Company
Nihon YS-11 (Japanese turboprop)
  Air Aruba, 1998, 333
  Air Philippines, 1996, 282
  All Nippon Airways, 1965, 146
  Bouraq Indonesian Airlines, 1971, 265
  Compared to other twin-engined turboprops, 89t
  Cruzeiro do Sul, 1967, 88
  Filipinas Orient Airways, 85m
  LAPA, Argentina, 1976, 366
  Merpati Nusantara, Indonesia, 1970, 264
  Olympic Airways, 1970, 221
  Piedmont Airlines, 1968, 123p
  Transair, Canada, 1960s, 134
  VASP, Brazil, 1968, 315
Nippeli, familiar name for N.H.Y.K.K., 144
Nippon Cargo Airlines (N.C.A.), 148
Nitto Airlines (Japan), 146
Nixon, Richard, 111, 125, 146
N.K.K.K. *See* Japanese Air Lines
N.K.Y.K.K. *See* Japan Air Transport Company
Nok Air (Thailand), 269, 283
Nomad (Australian aircraft)
  Island Air, Guam, 1976, 299
  Marshall Islands, 1986, 300
  Polynesian Airlines, 1978, 297
Norcanair (Canada), 306
Nord 262 (French turboprop airliner)
  Lake Central Airlines, 1965, 122
  Linjeflyg, 1962, 232
  Tunisair, 1960s, 372

Nord Noratlas (cargo aircraft)
  Air Algérie, 1950s, 271
Nordair (Canada), 134, 134m
Nordair Metro (Canada), 306
Nord-Deutscher Lloyd, 3
Nordeste (Brazil), 131m
  Routes, 1976, 318m
  Transbrasil buys shares, 317
Nordio, Umberto, 209
Norfolk Jet Express. *See* Air Nauru
Norris, Ralph, 293
North American, U.S. aircraft manufacturer
  B-70 Mach 3 bomber, 115
North American Airlines (U.S.), Supplemental airline, 65, 66c
North American Aviation and Eastern Air Lines Divisions, 9c
North Atlantic jet service, 52, 104
  Sea v. air traffic, 53c
North Central Airlines (N.C.A.), 125
  Becomes main unit of Republic Airlines, 123c
  Douglas DC-9 service, 118
  Orders jet airliners, 60
  Sold to Northwest Orient Airlines, 125
North Japan Airlines, 90
  Merges to form J.D.A., 146
North Pole, Soviet landings, 21
North Queensland Airways, 137c
North Star (Douglas DC-4M), CP Air trans-Pacific service, 1949, 304–305
Northeast Airlines (U.S.), 26t
  And APSA, Peru, 1963, 377
  Boeing 727-200, first airline service, 57
  Wartime trans-Atlantic service, 25
Northeast Airlines, partial division of British Airways Board, 195
Northern Air Lines (U.S.), 9c
Northern Airways (Australia), sold to Guinea Airways, 137c
Northwest Airlines (formerly Northwest Airways) (U.S.), 26t
  Buys North Central Airlines, 125
  Contract air mail route (CAM 9), 1926, 8m
  Electra service, and crash, 1960, 46
  Merger prospects with K.L.M., 215–216
  Wartime service, 25
Nouvelair (Tunisia), name change to Sevenair, 373, 373p
Nova Air (Mexico), 326t
Novozhilov, Genrikh, 112
NPO PANKH (Soviet C.I.S.), 151t
N.T.S.B. *See* National Transportation Safety Board
Nur Khan, 252
Nurtanio 212/235/250
  Bouraq Indonesian Airlines, 1978, 265, 265p
  License-built by Spanish CASA, 1978, 135
  Merpati Nusantara, Indonesia, 1980s, 264
Nusantara Air Service, 265
  See also Bali International Air Service
NWT Air (Canada), taken over by First Air, 310
N.Y.A. *See* New York Airways
Nygala, Khaya, 401
NYRBA. *See* New York, Rio and Buenos Aires Line
NYRBA do Brasil, 315
N.Z.N.A.C. (New Zealand National Airways Corporation). *See* National Airways Corporation

Obregon, Alvaro, 87
O'Hara, Maureen, 339
Okada Air (Nigeria), 381
OLAG. *See* Osterreichische Luftverkehr A.G.
O'Leary, Michael, 188
Oliviera, Constantino de, 320–321
Olsen, Fred, 230, 231–232
Olympic Airways (Greece), 221
  Local service to the Greek islands, 221, 222m
  Renamed Olympic Airlines, 221
O.N.A. *See* Overseas National Airways
Onassis, Aristotle, 221
O'Neill, Ralph, 18
One-Time (1–Time) (South Africa), 403
One-Two-Go (Thailand), 269, 283
Onex Corporation, bid to acquire Air Canada, 306
Opal Air (Australia), 289
Open Skies, British Airways subsidiary, 198
"Open skies" policy, 29
Orcas Island Air Service, 92
Orient Express Air. *See* Orient Thai Airlines
Orient Thai Airlines (Thailand), 269
Oriental Airlines (Nigeria), 381
Orlandini, Sergio, 215
Orlando Airlines, becomes Florida Airways, 123c
Ornstein, Jonathan, 191
Oshibori, hot towels introduced by J.A.L., 98
Osterreichische Luftverkehr A.G. (OLAG) (Austria), 236
Ost-Europa Union (Germany), 3
Ottoman Empire, sponsors 1912 air race, 79
Our Airline. *See* Air Nauru
Overseas National Airways (O.N.A.), 40
  Orders Comet jet, denied operation, 40
  U.S. Supplemental airline, 65t
Oxley Airlines (Australia), 290

Ozark Airlines, 118, 123c, 166
Ozjet, replaces Air Nauru, 299

Pacific Aerial Transport (New Guinea), 137c
Pacific Air Lines (U.S.), 124
  Genealogy, 123c
  Name change from Southwest, 124
Pacific Air Transport (U.S.)
  Contract air mail route (CAM 8), 1926, 8m
  Genealogy, 9c
Pacific Blue (New Zealand/Australia), 290
Pacific Island Air (Fiji), 297
Pacific Island Airways, temporary name for Air Pacific, 295
Pacific Marine Airways (U.S.), 9c
Pacific Missionary (Ponape), 300p
Pacific Overseas Airlines (Siam), merges to form Thai Airways, 266
Pacific Seaboard Air Lines (U.S.), name change to Chicago & Southern Air Lines, 26t
Pacific Southwest Airlines (P.S.A.) (U.S.), 118, 123c, 159, 160, 168, 171–172
  Aircraft operated, 118, 171–172, 172p
  Boeing 727 mid-air collision, 1978, 172
  Delegation from Southwest Airlines, 172
  Sold to US Airways, 172
Pacific Sun (Fiji), 296
Pacific Western Airlines (P.W.A.) (Canada), 306, 307–308
  Boeing 737 service, 118, 307p
  Buys Transair, 307
  Buys Wardair, 306, 311
  Route network, 1969, 133, 133m
Pagas Air (Australia), 289
P.A.I.C., 9c
PAISA. *See* Panameña de Aviación Internacional
Pakistan, independence, 251, 251m
Pakistan International Airways (P.I.A.)
  Aircraft operated, 119, 251, 252
  Batik service to Indonesia, 252
  Enters North Atlantic route, 51
  First Asian jet service, 252
  First non-Communist airline to China, 240, 252
  North Atlantic service chronology, 28t
  Service to Himalaya Mountains, 252m
  Services between East and West Pakistan, 252
  Stake in Air Malta, 224, 252
P.A.L. *See* Philippine Air Lines
Palau Micronesia Air, 300
Palestine Airways, Empire service, 21m

Palestine Liberation Organization (P.L.O.)
  Attacks affect El Al, 77
  Fighting closes Beirut Airport, 72
Pan Adria (Croatia), 224
Pan Am Express, shuttle in Germany, 162
Pan Am Shuttle, U.S. east coast shuttle, 162
Pan American Airways, 14, 128, 141, 143
  Aircraft operated, 15, 15p, 29
  Blocked-space agreement with Nigerian Airways, 380
  Boeing 747 destroyed by P.F.L.P., 1970, 212
  Buys NYRBA, 1930, 14, 18
  Comet 3 orders, 40, 50
  Concorde order, 114
  Contract air mail route (FAM 4), 1926, 8
  Final decline, 162–163
  First Boeing 707 order and service, 1955–1958, 50, 51p
  First service, 1928, 14
  Founds affiliates in Central America, 340
  In the Middle East, 71–72, 79, 80
  Interest in COPA, Panama, 344–345
  Launches second Jet Age, 108–109, 111, 114–115
  Leasing of aircraft, 52, 52t
  Lockerbie disaster, 163, 373
  North Atlantic route, 105
  PA1 and PA2 round-the-world service, 35
  Passes interest in M.E.A. to B.O.A.C., 72
  Polar service, 34t
  Post-war U.S. leadership, 28
  Role in Boeing 747 development, 108,109
  Route maps, 5m, 22m, 54m
  Selling/termination of routes and interests, 197, 203, 326, 331, 353
  Tenerife collision with K.L.M., 161
  Tenerife disaster, 215
  Trans-ocean services, 15, 28t
  Wartime service, 23, 24, 25
  See also Pan Am Express; Pan Am Shuttle; Pan American II; PANAGRA; Panagra
Pan American II, reconstituted airline, 184
Pan American-Grace Corporation (PANAGRA), 14
  Challenged by TAN low-fare consortium, 342
  Declining interest in Peru, 356
  Sold to Braniff. *See* Panagra
PANAGRA. *See* Pan American-Grace Corporation

Panagra, 158, 159, 342, 344, 354, 356, 367
  Routes, 1930, 5m
  See also Pan American-Grace Corporation
Panair do Brasil
  Aircraft orders, 87, 314
  Renamed from NYRBA do Brasil, 18
  Sold to VARIG, 315–316
  South Atlantic service, 33, 33t
Panama Canal Zone, transfer of control, 345
Panameña de Aviación Internacional (PAISA), 345
Panga Airways (Solomon Islands), 294
Panini, Carlos, 20
Papousek, Hubert, 236
Paraense (Brazil), 315
  Aircraft operated, 88, 315
Paramount Airways (India), 250
Pareti, Harold, 175
Park, Sum Koo, 275
Parker, James, 179
Parks Air Transport (U.S.), 123c
Parmentier, K.D., 12
P.A.S. *See* Persian Air Services
PATI, Philippine government air service, 273
Patrick Corporation, buys into Virgin Blue, 290
Paul, Eugene, 297
Paz Paredes, Sigfrido, 323
PB Air (Thailand), 269
P.B.A. *See* Provincetown-Boston Airline
P.C.A. *See* Pennsylvania-Central Airlines
"Peanuts Fares," 127, 140, 173
Pearson, Robert, 304
Peau Vava'u (Tonga), 298
Peiser, Robert, 182
Peking Syndicate, 7
Pelita Air, airline division of Indonesian oil company, 266
Pennsylvania Railroad, interest in T.A.T., 9c
Pennsylvania-Central Airlines (P.C.A.), 26
  Name change to Capital Airlines, 26t
People Express (trading as PEOPLExpress), 174–175
Percival Prince (British aircraft)
  Polynesian Airlines, 1959, 297
Perestroika, 150
Perez y Bouras, Jorge, 322, 324
Perimeter Air (Canada), 309m
Persian Air Services (P.A.S.), 71
Peruvian air routes, 1929, 19m
Peruvian Airways, 19m
Peruvian Naval Air Service, 19m
P.F.L.P. *See* Popular Front for the Liberation of Palestine

P.G.A.-Portugália (or P.G.A.), 220–221
  Island destinations, 220m
Philadelphia Rapid Transit Service (P.R.T.)
  Contract air mail service routes (CAM 13 and 15), 1926, 8m
Philippine Air Lines (P.A.L.), 272–275
  Aircraft operated, 87p, 272, 273, 274
  DC-3 rough-field services, 87p
  Early service to Europe, 34–35
  Role in Philippine economy, 281
  Route maps, 86m, 272m
  Series of bombs, hijackings, 1968–1994, 273–274
  Special services, 1950s–1960s, 272
Phnom Penh Airlines, 279
Phuket Air (Thailand), 269
P.I.A. *See* Pakistan International Airways
Pickering, E.H., 93
Pickersgill, J.W., 133
"Piddle-packs," provided by Bush Pilots Airways, 289
Piedmont Airlines (U.S.), 122, 123–124, 123p, 125
  Sold to US Airways, 124, 123c, 168
Piedmont Aviation, 123c
Pilatus Porter (Swiss short-field aircraft)
  SATENA, Colombia, 1960s, 349
Pilgrims Management and Fund Board. *See* Lembaga Urusan Tabung Haji
Pillay, J.V.M., 260
Pinera, Sebastian, 368
Pinochet, Augusto, 368
Pioneer Airlines (U.S.)
  Genealogy, 123c
  Operates first modern airliner, 1952, 84
Piper Apache
  LIAT, 1957, 330
Piper Aztec
  Air Madagascar, 1960s, 405
Piper Cherokee
  Air Madagascar, 1960s, 405
  Freedom Air, 1978, 300
Piper Navaho
  Aeronaves Alimentadores, 1968, 324
  Air Mauritius, 1968, 40
  Air Pacific, Fiji, 1974, 300
Piper Seneca
  Air Mahé, 1972, 388
Piquet, Henri, 1
Pitcairn Aviation (U.S.), 9c
Pivcevic, Alex, 370
Pivcevic, Domingo, 370
Pleshakova, Olga, 152
P.L.O. *See* Palestine Liberation Organization
PLUNA. *See* Primas Líneas Uruguayas de Navigación Aérea

Poland, first airline service, 5
Polaris Charter (Canada), 310
Polski Linie Lotnicze (LOT) (Poland)
  Member of Six-Pool, 62, 62p
  Swissair acquires interest, 212
Polynesian Airlines (Western Samoa), 297–298, 297p
Polynesian Blue Airlines, Virgin group, 290, 297
PolyPass, code-sharing venture, 297
Ponape, air service, 300, 300p
Ponce Air (Puerto Rico), 338
Ponte Aérea. *See* Shuttle services
Popular Front for the Liberation of Palestine (P.F.L.P.), 212
Porodisa, Indonesian timber business, 125, 265
Posada, Oscar, 350
Posadas Group, Mexican hotel chain, 324, 326
Potez, French aircraft manufacturer, 4
Prasarttong-Osoth, Prasert, 268
Pratt & Whitney, U.S. engine manufacturer, 9c, 30, 111
Pratt & Whitney JT8D, for Boeing 737s, 118
Pratt & Whitney PT6 turboprop, for DHC-6 Twin Otter, 94
Pratte, Yves, 304
Presidential Airlines (U.S.), 176
Pressed Steel Plate (P.S.P.), paves wartime runways, 24
Priddy, Robert, 179, 180
Primas Líneas Uruguayas de Navigación Aérea (PLUNA) (Uruguay), 363–364
  Sold to VARIG, 1997, 316, 363
Prinair, 338
"Prince Nicky." *See* Varanand
Privatair (Germany), 204
"Promenade lounge," in Short flying boat, 12
Propellers
  Survivival into the Jet Age, 31
  See also turboprop aircraft
Provincetown-Boston Airline (P.B.A.), 92–93, 93p
  Sold to People Express, 175
Provincial Airlines (Canada), 309m
P.R.T. *See* Philadelphia Rapid Transit Service
P.S.A. *See* Pacific Southwest Airlines
Ptarmigan Air (Canada), taken over by First Air, 310
Puente Aéreo (Mexican shuttle service), 322
Puerto Rico International Airlines. *See* Prinair
Pulkovo Air Enterprise (Russia), 156–157
  One of Russia's "Big Six," 157
Pulsifer, Roy, 140
Purdue Airlines (U.S.), Supplemental airline, 65t

Putnam, Howard, 159, 177
P.W.A. *See* Pacific Western Airlines

Qadaffi, Muammar al-, 373
QANTAS. *See* Queensland and Northern Territory Aerial Services
Qantas Airways, 12, 24, 283, 288
Qantas Empire Airways (Q.E.A.). *See* Qantas Airways
QantasLink (Australia), 290
Q.E.A. *See* Qantas Airways
Quadripartite agreement, 385, 393
Qualifier Group
  European airline group, 212
  SABENA founding member, 214
Quebecair (Canada), 134, 134m, 306
Queen Charlotte Airlines (Canada), sold to Pacific Western Airlines, 134
Queen Elizabeth II
  Flies with B.C. Airlines, late 1950s, 310
  Flies with East African, 1952, 385
  Flies with T.C.A., 1964, 304
Queen Mary, British ocean liner, 172
Queensland Airlines (Australia), 90, 286
Queensland and Northern Territory Aerial Services (QANTAS) (Australia), 6, 285–290
  Aircraft operated, 287, 287p, 409–410, 410p
  Aircraft orders, 47, 287, 288
  Assists Air Lanka, 1984, 256
  Atlantic service chronology, 28t
  Empire service map, 1939, 21m
  Europe-Australia jet service, 53
  Forms Qantas Empire Airways, 12
  Founds JetStar Asia, 283
  Genealogy, 137, 137c
  Interest in Air Niugini, 294
  Interest in Air Pacific, 296
  North Atlantic route, 51
  Round-the-world service, 287
  Route map, 1925, 6m
  Shares in Air Melanésiae, 299
  Trans-Pacific jet debut, 52t
  World's longest pre-war route, 24
Quesada, Pete, 46
Quisqueyana (Dominican Republic), 336

R.A.E. *See* Royal Aircraft Establishment
Rafelghem, Carlos van, 214
Raffles service, Singapore Airlines, 260
RAI. *See* Rede Aérea International
R.A.I. *See* Reseau Aérien Interinsulaire
Raj, Raghu, 246
R.A.M. *See* Royal Air Maroc
Rama, King (Siam), 266
Ramiz, Nelson, 352
Ramos, Oscar, 272
RAN. *See* Rede Aérea Nacional

Index

RANA. *See* Rhodesia and Nyasaland Airways
RANSA. *See* Rutas Aéreas Nacionales, S.A.
Ransome Airlines (U.S.), 162
"Rapidair," Air Canada program, 304
Ratti, Daniel, 359
REAL. *See* Redes Estaduais Aéreas, Ltda.
Rebulka, Mario, 236
Red Sea Airlines. *See* Air Djibouti
Rede Aérea International (RAI), 314–315
Rede Aérea Nacional (RAN), Brazilian inter-city route system, 314
Rede de Integração Nacional (RIN) (Brazil), 130–131,131m, 314
Redes Estaduais Aéreas, Ltda. (REAL) (Brazil), 313–314
 DC-3 operator, 31
 Route map, 1955, 32m
 Sold to VARIG, 315
Regional airlines, U.S., 60, 122
 See also Local Service airlines, U.S.
Renschler, F. (Pratt & Whitney), 9c
Republic Airlines (U.S.), 123c
Reseau Aérien Interinsulaire (R.A.I.), 301, 301p
 See also Air Polynésie
Resorts International, Antilles Air Boats, 339
Retirement Systems of Alabama, and US Airways, 169
Réunion Air Service, 406
 See also Air Austral
Rhodesia, Empire service, 21m
Rhodesia and Nyasaland Airways (RANA), ancestor of Central African Airways, 392
Rhon, Hank, 325
Riair (Latvia), 239
Richardson, Bingley, 339
Rickenbacker, Eddie, 164
Ricketts, Norman, 330–332
Riddick, Merrill, 8
 Early air mail contract (FAM 3), 1923, 2m
Rimouski Aviation Syndicate (Canada). *See* Quebecair
RIN. *See* Rede de Integração Nacional
Rio-Sul (Brazil), 316, 318m
River Plate Aviation, early South American airline, 6
Riverso, Renato, 210
R.N.A.C. *See* Royal Nepal Airline Corporation
Roberts, Dick, 184
Robertson, Macpherson, 12
Robertson Aircraft
 Contract air mail route (CAM 2), 1926, 8m
 Genealogy, 9c
Robinson Airlines (U.S.), 123c
Robson, John, 140

Rockhampton Aerial Services, sold to Guinea Airways, 137c
Rolim. *See* Amaro, Rolim Adolfo
Rolls-Royce, British engine manufacturer
 Financial crisis, receivership, 111
 Post-war engine development, 30
Rolls-Royce Avon, first axial-compressor jet engine, 40
Rolls-Royce Dart, turboprop engine, 126
Rolls-Royce 400s, so-called by Loftleidir, 233
Rolls-Royce Ltd. (1971), 111
Rolls-Royce Merlin, Second World War piston engine, 31
Rolls-Royce RB162, supplementary booster engine, 58, 119
Rolls-Royce RB-211, engine for Lockheed TriStar, 111
Rolls-Royce Spey, 58, 60, 89, 119, 120
ROMBAC, Romanian aircraft manufacturer
 Builds BAC One-Elevens, 121
Romueldez, Eduardo, 272–274
Roosevelt, Franklin D., 11
Roots (Canada), 308
Royal Aeronautical Air Service of the Siamese Army, 6m
Royal Air Cambodge, 278–279
 Aircraft operated, 85, 279
 Malaysian Airways stake, 262
Royal Air Force (U.K.)
 Aircraft ordered and/or operated, 40, 119, 120
 Military presence, operations, 73, 74, 225
 Presence in Belize, 346
 Repurposed aircraft, 7, 37, 380
 Wartime service in Africa, 35
Royal Air Lao, 279, 280p
Royal Air Maroc, 68, 371
 Air Maroc and Air Atlas merger, 68
 Aircraft operated, 56, 372
 Control of Air Sénégal, 372
 See also Air Maroc (Société Avia Maroc Ligne Aérienne)
Royal Aircraft Establishment (R.A.E.)
 Comet salvage operation, 41, 41c
 Preliminary studies for Concorde, 113
Royal Aviation (Canada), 308, 312
 Sold to C3, 312
Royal Bhutan Airlines, 258
Royal Brunei Airlines, 280
Royal Canadian Air Force, buys Comet 1As, 41
Royal Navy, Comet salvage operation, 41
Royal Nepal Airline Corporation (R.N.A.C.), 253–254, 254m, 254p, 255p

Aircraft operated, 85, 254
Royal Orchid Service, Thai International Airways, 267
Royal Phnom Penh Airways, 279
Royal Tongan Airlines, 298
Rubicon Corporation, controls Philippine Air Lines, 272–273
Ruhnau, Heinz, 203
Rural Air Service, Philippines, 272
Russian Knight (Russky vityaz), world's first transport airplane, 1
Russo-Baltic Wagon Company, builds world's first transport airplane, 1
Rutas Aéreas Nacionales, S.A. (RANSA) (Venezuela), all-cargo airline, 353–354
Rwanda Alliance, assists Air Tanzania, 387
Rwandair, 387
Ryan, Tony, 187, 284
Ryan Airline (U.S.), 8
Ryan Navion (single-engined airplane)
 South West Air Transport, Namibia, 404
Ryanair (Ireland), 187–189, 188p, 190, 191, 192–193, 204, 213, 229, 249, 282, 326c, 327
Ryland, Eric, 331

SAAB 340 (Swedish airliner)
 Aeroliteral, Mexico, 1970s, 324
 Air Baltic, 1995, 239
 Air Burkina, 2001, 378
 Finnair, 1988, 233
 LAPA, Argentina, 1986, 366
 TAN, Argentina, 1994, 317
Saba, Caribbean island, 332, 333p
SABENA. *See* Société Anonyme Belge d'Exploitation de Navigation Aérienne
Sablatnig (Germany), 4m
Sachsische (Germany), 4m
Sadia (Brazil), 315
SAESA. *See* Servicios Aéreos Especiales, S.A.
SAETA. *See* Sociedad Aéreos Ecuatoriana de Transportes
SAExpress (SAX) (South Africa), low-fare airline, 400
SAFE. *See* South America and Far East; Straits Air Freight Express
Sahara India Airlines, 249
 Sold to Jet Airways, 250
SAHSA. *See* Servicio Aéreo de Honduras
SAir Group, restructured Swissair, 212–213
 Collapse, 213–215
 Porugália, 220
Salamanca, Alejandro, 349
Salazar, Antonio, 220
Sales, Javier, 218
Salim, M.M., 253

SAM. *See* Sociedad Aeronáutica de Medellín
S.A.M. (Italy), charter airline, 64t, 90
Sampaio, Paulo, 314
SAN. *See* Servicios Aéreos Nacionales
San Francisco & Oakland Helicopter Airlines (S.F.O.), 412
Sanchez Lopez, Alfonso, 349
SANSA. *See* Servicios Aéreos Nacionales
Santa Barbara Airlines (Venezuela), 353, 353p
Sapphire service, Air Ceylon, 255
S.A.S. *See* Scandinavian Airline System
SATA. *See* Sociedad Açoriana de Transportes Aéreos
Satellite airports, usage policy, Southwest Airlines, 178
SATENA. *See* Servicio Aeronavegación a Territorios Nacionales
SATGA. *See* Société Aérienne de Guyane-Antilles
Saturn Airways (U.S.), Supplemental airline, 65t
Saudi Arabian Airlines. *See* Saudia
Saudia, 78, 78p
Saunders ST-27
 Aces, Colombia, 1980s, 350
Saunders-Roe Princess (British flying boat), 27
Savoia-Marchetti SM-73 (Italian airliner)
 Ala Littoria, 1935, 14, 14m
 SABENA, 1935, 14, 14m
Savoia-Marcheti SM-83A (Italian airliner)
 South Atlantic service, LATI, 1939, 33, 33t
SAX. *See* SAExpress
SCADTA. *See* Sociedad de Transportes Aéreos Colombo-Alemana
Scanair, Scandinavian charter airline, 64t
Scandinavian Airline System (S.A.S.), 30, 227–228
 Aircraft operated, 51, 56, 228, 229
 First Boeing 737-600 service, 1998, 118
 First Douglas DC-9-20 and DC-9-40 services, 1968, 117, 118
 First European electronic reservations, first female pilot, 227
 Forms THAI, 86
 Forms Thai International, 266
 K.S.S.U. airline partnership, 110–111
 Lufthansa franchise, 204
 Majority stake in Spanair, 229
 North Atlantic service chronology, 28t
 Polar services, 34, 34p, 34m, 227–228
 S.A.S.-Braathens, 231

Scandinavian Airline System (S.A.S.) (*continued*)
   Shares in Air Baltic, 239
   Shares in Austrian Airlines, 236
   Shares in LAN-Chile, 368
   South American service, 33t
   Stakes in Wideroe's and Braathens, 229
   Trans-Siberian Express, 228, 228p, 229p
   World's most northerly route, Spitzbergen, 235m
   World's only successful airline consortium, 227
Scheduled Air Taxis (U.S.), develops into commuter airlines, 92
Schildnecht, Alfredo, 344
Schisano, Roberto, 210
Schoen, Bob, 92
Schofield, Seth, 168
Schreiner Airways, founds Aero Contractors, Nigeria, 382
Schturmovik (Soviet tankbuster). *See* Ilyushin Il-2
Schwaben (airship), 1, 1p
Scottish Airways, partial division of British Airways Board, 195
Scottish Aviation Twin Pioneer
   Malaysian, 1973, 261
   Philippine Air Lines, 1960, 272
   Sierra Leone Airways, 1961, 383
"Scramble/Struggle for Africa," 19th century political settlement, 13, 35
Seawell, William T., 160
"Second Force," British airline policy, 59
"Second Level"
   U.S. Local and Regional airlines, 60
   Worldwide acceptance, 90
Sedalia-Marshall-Boonville Stage Lines, Beech 18, 92p
SEDTA. *See* Sociedad Ecuatoriana de Transportes
SEMATRA, Réunion consortium, 406
Sempati Air Transport (Indonesia), 84, 266
Sepulvada, Patrício, 368
Servicio Aéreo Baja (Mexico), 325
Servicio Aéreo de Honduras (SAHSA) (Honduras), 340, 341–342
Servicio Aeronavegación a Territorios Nacionales (SATENA) (Colombia), government airline, 349
Servicio Bolivariano, Colombian air service, 5m
Servicios Aéreos Especiales, S.A. (SAESA) (Mexico), 324
Servicios Aéreos Nacionales (SAN) (Ecuador), 355–356
Servicios Aéreos Nacionales (SANSA) (Costa Rica), 341
Servivensa (Venezuela), 353, 353p

Seulawah Air Services (Indonesia), 84, 135
   Merged with Mandala Airlines, 265
Seven States Area Case (U.S.), 125, 126
Sevenair. *See* Nouvelair
Seychelles-Kilimanjaro Air Transport (SKAT), 388–389
S.F.O. *See* San Francisco & Oakland Helicopter Airlines
S.G.T.A. *See* Société Générale de Transport Aérien
Shabair (Zaïre), 397
Shandong Airlines, 241m, 242t
Shanghai Airlines, 241m, 242t, 245
   Boeing 757, 241p
Shanghai Aviation Industrial Corporation, 117, 241
Shanghai-Chengtu Air Mail Line, 17
Shanxi Airlines (China), 241m, 242t
Shavit, Abraham, 77
Sheen, Kerry, 185
Shelton, Cornell "Connie," 341–342, 354, 357
Shen Tu, 240–243
Shenzhen Airlines, 241m, 242t
Shidlovsky, Mikhail, 1
Shin Kan-sen, Japanese "Bullet Train," 85, 98, 145, 412, 412p, 414t
Shore, Peter, 106, 144
Shorouk Air (Egypt), 375
Short 330, 360, and Skyvan
   Aeroperlas, Panama, 1970s, 344
   Bahamasair, 1994, 331
   British Airways, 1970s, 196
   Commuter airliner, 94, 94p
   D.L.T., 1978, 203
   Freedom Air, Guam, 1992, 300
   Isleñas, Honduras, 1982, 344
   Jersey European, 1980s 192
   LAPA, Argentina, 1970s, 366
   Maldives International, 1976, 257
   Olympic Airways, 1980, 221
   Philippine Air Lines, 1987, 274
   Seychelles, 1990s, 389
   Sunflower Airlines, Fiji, 1990s, 296
   T.A.C., Thailand, 1970s, 267
   Tikal Jets, 1990s, 340
   Tradewinds, Singapore, 1984, 261
   Trans Guyana Airways, 1997, 334
Short Calcutta (flying boat), 11
   Imperial Airways African route, 1932, 13m
Short S.23 (flying boat)
   Maintains wartime service, 23
   Ordered by ImperialAirways, 12
   Service to Alexandria, Karachi, Singapore, Sydney, 1937–1938, 12
   Several lost to Japanese at outbreak of war, 24
   Tasman Empire Airways, 16
Short S-25 Sunderland/Sandringham flying boats, 27
   Aerolíneas Argentinas, 1950s, crash, 364, 365

   Antilles Air Boats, 1970s, 339
   CAUSA, Uruguay, 1947, 363, 365
   Last service, 1970, by large flying boats, 301, 301p
Short S.26 G-Class flying boat, 23
Short Scipio (flying boat)
   Imperial Airways, 1932, 13
Short Solent
   B.O.A.C. African route. 1948, 35
Short Take-off and Landing (STOL), 93p, 176, 213, 237, 254
Shorts, British aircraft manufacturer, 23
Shugrue, Martin, 165
Shurcliff, William, 115
Shuttle services
   Air Canada "Rapidair," 304
   AVENSA, Caracas-Porlamar, 352
   Eastern, New York-Washington/Boston, 47
   Iberia, Spain, 217
   Indonesia, Jakarta-Surabaya, Semarang, 263
   La Navette, France, 200
   Mexico City-Acapulco, 322
   Pacific Western Chieftan Airbus, 307
   P.G.A. Express, Portugal, 221
   Ponte Aérea, Brazil, 164, 313, 314–315, 316, 317, 319, 321
   Puente Aéreo, Mexico, 322, 359
   Seychelles "bus service," 389
   Tahiti, 301
   Taiwan, 270
   Tradewinds, Malaysian, Singapore-Kuala Lumpur, 261, 262
   Trump Shuttle, 165, 168–169, 174, 183
S.I.A. *See* Singapore Airlines
Siam Kampuchea Airlines. *See* S.K. Air
Siamese Aeronautical Service, 6m, 7
Siao, K.T., 270
Sibavia (Soviet C.I.S.), 151t
Siberia, reliance on Aeroflot, 102
Siberian Airlines. *See* Sibir
Sibir, 152–153
   One of Russia's "Big Six," 157
   Tu-134s shot down, crashed, 2001–2004, 153
Sichuan Airlines, 241m, 242t
Siegel, David N., 169
Siem Reap Airways (Cambodia), 279, 279p
Sierra Leone Airways, 67, 383
   Renamed Sierra National Airlines, 383
Sihanouk, Prince, 278–279
Sikorsky, Igor, 1, 20
Sikorsky S-38 (U.S. flying boat)
   Pan American, 14p
Sikorsky S-40 (U.S. flying boat)
   Pan American, 15, 15p
Sikorsky S-41 (U.S. flying boat)
   Antilles, 1946, 335
Sikorsky S-42 (U.S. flying boat)
   Pan American, 15, 15p

Sikorsky S-55 (helicopter)
   Greenlandair, 1963, 235
   U.S. helicopter airlines, 1940s–1960s, 412
Sikorsky S-58 (helicopter)
   U.S. helicopter airlines, 1950s–1960s, 412
Sikorsky S-61 (helicopter)
   B.E.A. Helicopters, 1964, 195
   Hummingbird Helicopters, 1989, 257
   P.I.A., East Pakistan, 1963, 252
   U.S. helicopter airlines, 1950s–1960s, 412
SILA (Sweden), 28t, 35
SilkAir, Singapore Airlines subsidiary, renamed from Tradewinds, 261
Silver Wing, B.E.A. London-Paris service, 43
Silverthorne, Joe, 341
Simigdalás, Nick, 221
Singapore Airlines (S.I.A.), 259–260
   Establishes Tradewinds and SilkAir subsidiaries, 261
   Inaugural services, Airbus A380 and Boeing 747-300, 260, 261, 261p, 409, 410p
   Voted world's best airline, 143
Sino-Soviet Joint Stock Company. *See* SKOGA
Sistema Integrado de Transportes Aéreos Regional (SITAR), 130, 317, 319–320
Six, Robert, 128
Six-Day War, 1967
   Effect on United Arab Airlines, 70
   Subsequent effect on M.E.A., 72
"Six-Pool," cooperative airline system 62
Sixth Freedom, circumvented by Aeroflot, 100
S.K. Air (Cambodia), 279
SKAT. *See* Seychelles
SKOGA, China's first airline, 132
Skybus service, Central African Airways, 392
Skymark, ancestor of Golden State, 95m
Skyteam, airline alliance, 201
Skytrain
   Freddie Laker's innovative North Atlantic service, 105–106, 106c, 194
   Receives U.S. C.A.B. approval, 140
Skyways (U.K.)
   Buys Bahamas Airways stock, 1949, 331
   Charters Avro Yorks to T.M.A., 1953, 73
   Remains independent, 59
   Service to Mauritius, 406
Slattery, William D., 159
"Sleeping Giant," Brazil, 129
Slok Air Gambia, 383–384
Smidt, Helio, 316

Index

Smith, Alfredo, 346
Smith, C.R., 46
Smith, Ross, 6
SN Brussels Airlines (S.N.B.A.), 191
SNECMA. *See* GE/SNECMA
Snowflake, low-fare subsidiary of S.A.S., 229
Sobelair (Belgium), 64t
    Becomes part of SABENA, 214
Sociedad Açoriana de Transportes Aéreos (SATA) (The Azores), 219–220, 219m
Sociedad Aéreos Ecuatoriana de Transportes (SAETA) (Ecuador), 355–356, 356p
Sociedad Aeronáutica de Medellín (SAM) (Colombia), 347–348
Sociedad de Transportes Aéreos Colombo-Alemana (SCADTA), 5m, 6
Sociedad Ecuatoriana de Transportes (SEDTA) (Ecuador), 20
Société Aérienne de Guyane-Antilles (SATGA) (French Guiana), 334
Société Anonyme Belge d'Exploitation de Navigation Aérienne (SABENA) (Belgium)
    Association with Air Congo, 69, 213, 396
    ATLAS partnership, 111
    British Airways–K.L.M. proposal, 214
    Buys stock in Transcontinental, Argentina, 365
    Code-shares with Nationwide, South Africa, 403
    Common Market Commuter, 1976, 213–214
    Controls Delta Air Transport, 1986, 214
    Final days, 215
    First European operator of Boeing 707, 51
    First services, 4
    Forms SABENA Group with Sobelair, 214
    Interest sold to Swissar, 212, 214
    North Atlantic service chronology, 28t
    Post-war service to Africa, 35
    Route exchange with Air France, 14
    SAir deal, 212, 213
    Starts African route, 14, 14m
    Starts Persian Air Services, 71
Société Avia Maroc Ligne Aérienne. *See* Air Maroc
Société Générale de Transport Aérien (S.G.T.A.) (France), 4
Société Tunisienne de l'Air. *See* Tunisair
SODETRAF, French airline agency, 68, 376
Soedjono, Hasan, 266
Soeparno, Mohammed, 263
Soepono, Wiweko, 262–263

Soet, Jan de, 215
SOKAO, Soviet–North Korean airline, 276
Solair (Solomon Island Airways), 298
Solovlev D-30KU, Soviet engine for Tu-154, 101
Somali Airlines, 388
Somosa, Guillermo, 342
Sonic Boom, supersonic shock wave, 114
Soriano, Andres, 272
Soros, George, 181
Sosa de la Vega, Manuel, 322
Sosolito Airlines (Nigeria), 381
South African Airways (S.A.A.), 399–401, 400m
    Aircraft operated, 399–401, 400p
    Comet jet service, 1953, 40, 40m, 399
    Effects of Apartheid, 67, 388, 399–400, 400p
    Empire service, 21m
    German aircraft commandeered, 24
    Hailstrom, 1980, 399
    Pool with QANTAS, 399
    Quadripartite pool, 385
    Service to London, 35
    Swissair acquires interest, 212
South America and Far East (SAFE), 230, 230p
    See also Braathens-SAFE
South Coast Airlines (Australia), 137c, 289
South Pacific Airlines of New Zealand (SPANZ), 292
    Ansett attempt to buy, 1960, 286
South Pacific Island Republics (and Overseas Territories), 298m
South West Air Transport. *See* Air Namibia
Southern (Australia), 137c
Southern Air Transport (U.S.), 9c
Southern Air Transport (U.S.), Supplemental airline, 65t
Southern Airlines (Soviet C.I.S.), 151t
Southern Airways (Philippines), 281
Southern Airways (U.S.)
    Genealogy, 123c
    Merges with North Central to form Republic Airlines, 125
Southern Industries, owns TACA, Central America, 343
Southern Rhodesia Air Service (S.R.A.S.), ancestor of Central African Airways, 392
Southern Winds (Argentina), buys LAPA, 367
Southwest Airlines, 118–119, 141, 160, 169–170
    Benefits from airline deregulation after 1981, 141
    Biggest operator of Boeing 737, 118p
    Buys American Trans Air stock, 183

    Delegation to P.S.A., 172
    First Boeing 737-700 service, 1998, 118
    Original name, 177
Southwest Airways (1941)
    Genealogy, 123c
    Name change to Pacific Air Lines, 1958, 124
South-Western Aviation Corporation (China), 18
Soviet C.I.S. airlines, 151t
Soviet Union (Union of Soviet Socialist Republics)
    Collapse, 150
    Early airlines, 20
    First airline service, 1923, 5
    Pre-war output, 21
Spain
    First airline service, 1921, 5
    Minor shares in Airbus, 110
Spanair (Spain), 218
    S.A.S. majority stake, 229
Spantax (Spain), 64, 218–219
SPANZ. *See* South Pacific Airlines of New Zealand
"Speedbird" emblem, on B.O.A.C. Comets, 40
Spice Jet (India), 250
Spinetta, Jean-Cyril, 200
Spirit Airlines (U.S.), name change from Charter One, 183, 184p
Spitzbergen (Swedish Svalbard), world's furthest north airport, 228, 228p, 229p
"Spoils Conferences," 1933, 11
Springbok route, London-South Africa, 399
S.R.A.S. *See* Southern Rhodesia Air Service
Sri Lanka, independence (as Ceylon), 251, 251m
Sri Lankan Airlines
    Fleet damaged by civil action, 2001, 256
    Name change from Air Lanka, 1998, 256
St. Barthélemy, 335p
St. Lucia Airways (U.S.), 331
St. Petersburg-Tampa Airboat Line, first airline, 1, 2m, 3t
St. Tammany-Gulf Coast Airlines, 9c
S.T.A.C. *See* Supersonic Transport Aircraft Committee
Stainton, Ross, 196
Standard Airlines (U.S.), 9c
Standard Airways (U.S.), Supplemental airline, 65t
Standard biplane
    Ryan Airline, 8
    U.S. Post Office service, 3
Stanford, Alan, 330
Star, bargain-fare Philippine air service, 272
Starlight, Central African Airways low-fare service, 392

Staubl, Robert, 212
Sterling Airways (Denmark), 64, 229–230
Sterling European, merger forms Sterling Airlines, 230
Sterling Philippines, 282
Sternberg, Jan, 229
Stewart, Gordon "Butch," 329
Stinson (aircraft)
    Antilles, 1946, 334
Stinson Voyager (U.S.), 92
STOL. *See* Short Take-off and Landing
Stout Air Services
    Contract air mail route (CAM 14), 8m
    Genealogy, 9c
Straits Air Freight Express (SAFE) (New Zealand), name change to Safe Air Ltd., 292, 292p
Strong, James, 286
Stroud, John, 101
Sud, French aircraft manufacturer, 56
    Becomes Aerospatiale, role in formation of Airbus, 109
Sud Aviation, supersonic airliner project, 113
Sudan Airways, 67, 389
Sud-Est, French aircraft manufacturer
    Becomes Sud Aviation, 55, 56, 109
    Builds SE-210 Caravelle, 109
Sud-Est SE-210 Caravelle. *See* Caravelle
Sudflug (Germany), sold to Lufthansa, 202
Sud-Ouest (France), 4m
Sud-Ouest SO-30. *See* Bretagne
Sumendap, J.A. "Gerry," 135, 265
Summa Corporation, 125
Summit (U.S.), 123c
Sun Air (Fiji), sold to Air Pacific, renamed, 296
Sun Air (South Africa), 400, 403
Sun Country Airlines (U.S.), 184
"Sun Living," Air Canada program, 304
Sun-Air (Scandinavia), 198
Sunflower Airlines (Fiji), 296
Super-Caravelle. *See* Sud Aviation
Superior Airways (Canada), 310
Super-Saver fares, introduced by American Airlines, 140
Supersonic Transport Aircraft Committee (S.T.A.C.), study group for Concorde, 113
Surinam Airways (Surinaamse Luchtvaart Maatschappij), 333, 334, 334p
Suter, Moritz, 213
Svalbard. *See* Spitzbergen
Swarovski, Christian Schwemberger-, 237
Swarovski, Gernot Langes-, 237
Swearingen Metros
    Texas International, 1971, 126
    Trans Adria, Croatia, 1979, 224

"Sweaty palms," Pacific Air Lines survival kit, 124
Swenson, Robert, 180
Swinton, Lord, 380
Swiss International Airlines, 213, 213p
Swissair
　Aircraft operated, 211, 212
　Bankruptcy, 2001, 215
　Buys control of SABENA, 212
　Convair 990 bombed, DC-8 hijacked, 1970, 212
　Douglas DC-8 service, 1960, 5
　First Douglas DC-9-50 and DC-9-80 services, 117, 118
　K.S.S.U. airline partnership, 111, 211
　North Atlantic airline chronology, 28t
　Orders Airbus A330s, 212
　Route to China, 240
　South American service, 33, 33t
　Suspends operations, 213
　See also SAir Group
Switzerland, first airline service, 5
Syndicato Condor (Brazil), 18, 316
　Name change to Cruzeiro do Sul, 316
　Trans-Atlantic service, 19, 19m
Syrian Arab Airlines, joint service with Jordanian, 79

T.A.A. See Trans-Australia Airlines
TAAG. See Linhas Aéreas de Angola
TABA (Brazil), 318m
TABSA. See Transportes Aéreos Benianos
TABSO. See Balkan Bulgarian Airlines
T.A.C. See Aerocesar; Thai Airways Company
TACA. See Transports Aéreos Centro-Americanos; Transportes Aéreas del Continente Americano
TACA de Honduras, 341, 342
TACA Perú, 359
T.A.C.V. See Cabo Verde
Tadzhik CAD (Soviet C.I.S.), 151t
TAE (Spain), 64t
TAESA. See Transportes Aéreos Ejecutivo, S.A.
T.A.G. See Transports Aériens Guyanais; Transportes Aéreas du Gabon
TAG Airlines (U.S.), 92
T.A.G.P. See Air Bissau
Tague, John, 184
T.A.I. See Transports Aériens Intercontinentaux
Taiwan Airlines, sold to Eva Air, 271
T.A.L. See Territory Air Lines
Talair. See Territory Air Lines
TALOA. See Transocean Airlines
TAM. See Taxi Aéreo Marília; Transportes Aéreos del Mercosur; Transportes Aéreos Meridionais

TAMA. See Transporte Aéreo de Magallenes
TAME. See Transportes Aéreos Ecuatorianos Militares, Ecuador
TAMPA. See Transportes Aéreos Mercantiles Panamericano
TAMSA (Mexico), 322
TAMU. See Transporte Aéreo Militar Uruguayo
TAN. See Transportes Aéreos Nacionales; Transportes Aéreos Neuquen
Tan, Lucio, 274
Tanaka Giichi, 146
Tango, Air Canada's low-fare affiliate, 307
TANS. See Transportes Aéreos de Nacionales de Selva
TAO. See Taxi Aéreo Opita
T.A.P. See Transportes Aéreas Portuguesas
TAROM (Romania)
　Member of Six-Pool, 62, 121p
　Route to China, 1974, 240
TAS. See Transportes Aéreos Salvador
Tasman Empire Airways, Ltd. (TEAL) (New Zealand), 16, 291
　Buys Electras, 47
Tasmanian Aerial Services, 137, 137c
T.A.T. See Tourist Air Travel; Transcontinental Air Transport; Tyumen Avia Trans
Tata, J.R.D., 246, 246p
Tata Airlines (India), Empire service, 21m
Tatarstan Airlines (Soviet C.I.S.), 151t
Tauvasa, Joseph, 294
T.A.V. See Treno Alta Velocitá
Taxi Aéreo de Santander (Colombia), 349
Taxi Aéreo Marília (TAM) (Brazil), 317, 319
Taxi Aéreo Opita (TAO) (Colombia), 349
Taylor, Robert, 393
T.B.O. (Time Between Overhauls), 39, 417
T.C.A. See Trans Canada Airlines
T.D.A. See Toa Domestic Airlines
T Doble A. See Transportes Aéreos Andahuaylas
T.E.A. (Switzerland), becomes part of easyJet group, 189
Teague, John, 183
TEAL. See Tasman Empire Airways, Ltd.
Temasek Holdings, 283–284
Tenerife disaster, 1977. See K.L.M.; Pan American Airways
Territory Air Lines (T.A.L.) (New Guinea), 294
　Name change to Talair, 294
　Takes over Macair, 298
Texas International Airlines (T.X.I.) (U.S.), 127–128
　Acquires Continental Airlines, 1986, 123c

Applies for slots at New York's airports, 174
Introduces "Peanut" fares, 140
Name change from Trans-Texas Airways, 123c, 127
THAI. See Thai Airways International; Thai International
Thai Air Asia, 269, 282
Thai Airways Company (T.A.C.), 86, 266–267
　Route network, 268m
Thai Airways International (THAI), 268, 268m
Thai International (THAI)
　Aircraft operated, 266–267
　Establishes Nok Air, 283
　Formed, S.A.S. partnership, 86, 266
　Pioneers trans-Asian routes, 267, 267m, 267p
Thatcher, Margaret, 59
Third Level (commuter airlines)
　Brazilian system founded 1975, 130–131
　Name changes, 122
　U.S. airlines, 93
　See also Pickering, E.H.
Thomas, Miles, 39
Thomas Nationwide Transport, Ltd. (T.N.T.), Australian investment group
　Battles for control of Ansett, Air New Zealand, 1990s, 293
　Controls Ansett, 1970s, 286
　Sells shares to Air New Zealand, 287
Thompson, Adam, 105, 197
Thompson, Bruce R., 125
Thorsteinsson, Magnus, 234
T.H.Y. See Turk Hava Yollari
T.I.A. See Trans International Airlines
Tianjin Airlines (China), 241m, 242t
Tiger Airways (Singapore), 284, 284p
Tikal Jets (Guatemala), 340
Tillinghast, Charles, 165
Time Air (Canada), 306
Timoner, Eli, 160
Tito, Marshal, 222
Tjaereborg Rejser, Danish travel bureau, 229
T.M.A. See Trans Mediterranean Airways
T.N.T. See Thomas Nationwide Transport, Ltd.
Toa Airways (Japan), 90, 149p
　Merges with J.D.A. to form Toa Domestic, 149
　Orders Nihon YS-11s, 148
Toa Domestic Airlines, 147m, 149
Toda, Benigno "Benny," 272–274
Tolmachevo State Aviation Enterprise, becomes Sibir, 152
Toomey, Gary, 293
Tourism, rise of tourist travel in Europe, 63

Tourist Air Travel (T.A.T.) (New Zealand), 292
Tourist fares, introduced by IATA, 143
Tournaï Air Chad, 378
Tradewinds, renamed SilkAir, 261
Train à Grande Vitesse (T.G.V.). See High-speed rail, France
Trans Adria (Croatia), changes name to Croatia Airlines, 224
Trans Air Benin, 378
Trans Canada Airlines (T.C.A.), 20, 20p, 29, 303–305, 303p, 310
　Aircraft operated, 43–44, 43p, 47
　Empire service, 1939, 21m
　Name change to Air Canada, 304
　North Atlantic service, 28t, 51
Trans Europa (Spain), 64t
Trans Guyana Airways, 334
Trans International Airlines (T.I.A.) (U.S.), Supplemental airline, 65t
Trans Mar de Cortes (Mexico), 87, 322
Trans Mediterranean Airways (T.M.A.) (Lebanon), 73, 73m
Trans World Airlines (T.W.A.), 10–11, 12, 26t, 28, 33–34, 50–51, 52, 56, 105, 108–109, 166
　Aid to other airlines, 69, 71, 78
　Aircraft operated, 51, 52, 108, 111, 166
　Boeing 707 destroyed by P.F.L.P., 1970, 212
　Buys/sells airlines and/or routes, 166
　Eagle Nest Flight training center, 25
　First on-board movie, 166
　Founded as Transcontinental and Western Air, 10
　Genealogy, 9c
　Introduces coach-class fares, 140
　Introduces Douglas DC-2, 11p
　Negotiates to buy US Airways, 169
　Nonstop transcontinental flight, 29
　North Atlantic service chronology, 28t
　One of U.S. "Big Four," 9c, 122
　Overhauls Pan American on the North Atlantic, late 1950s, 105
　Owns TACA, Central America, 343
　Polar service, 34t
　Post-war U.S. leadership, 28
　Trans-Atlantic services, 25, 166
　Transcontinental route, 1934, 10m
　See also Hughes, Howard
TRANSA. See Transportes Aéreos de Chile, S.A.
Transaero (Soviet C.I.S.), 151t, 152
　Aircraft operated, 152, 152p
　One of Russia's "Big Six," 157
Transair (Canada), 134, 134m
Trans-Air Congo, 379
Transandina Ecuatoriana, C.A., forms AREA, 354

Index

TransAsia Airlines, renamed from Foshing Airlines, 271
Transasian Airlines. *See* Sterling Philippines
Trans-Australia Airlines (T.A.A.), 43, 63, 138, 285–290
   Becomes Australian Airlines, 1985, 286
   Genealogy, 137c
   Interest in Air Niugini, 1973, 294
   Introduces Viscount, 1954, 43
Transavia (Netherlands), 64t
   Owned by Air France–K.L.M., 201, 215
Transbrasil, 315, 317–318
   Aircraft operated, 61, 88, 131, 131p, 317
   Name changes, 318, 319
   Shares in Nordeste, 317
Transcargo (Venezuela), 351
Trans-Caribbean Airlines, 65, 139
Transcontinental (Argentina), 365
Transcontinental Air Transport (T.A.T.)
   Genealogy, 9c
   Inaugural at Port Columbus, 10, 10p
   Merger to form T.W.A., 1930, 10
Transcontinental & Western Air (T.W.A.). *See* Trans World Airlines
Trans-Europa Union (Germany), 3
Trans-European (Belgium), 64t
Transgabon, 379
Transkei Airways (South African homelands), 403, 403p
Transmed Airlines (Egypt), 375
Transocean Airlines (U.S.), Supplemental airline, 66, 71
Trans-Oceanic (Australia), 137c
Transpac–Société Caledonienne de Transports Aériens. *See* Air Calédonie
Transperú (Peru), 359
Trans-Polar routes, 33, 33t
Transporte Aéreo de Magallenes (TAMA) (Chile), 369
Transporte Aéreo Militar (TAM) (Paraguay), 360, 362
Transporte Aéreo Militar Uruguayo (TAMU), 363
Transportes Aéreas del Continente Americano (TACA). *See* Transports Aéreos Centro-Americanos (TACA)
Transportes Aéreas du Gabon (T.A.G.). *See* Air Gabon
Transportes Aéreas Portuguesas (T.A.P.), 219–220
   Aircraft operated, 219–220
   Forms ATLAS partnership, 111
   Island destinations, 220m
   Service to African colonies, 35
   Shuttle service, 221
Transportes Aéreos Andahuaylas (T Doble A) (Peru), 359
Transportes Aéreos Benianos (TABSA) (Bolivia), 361
Transportes Aéreos de Cabo Verde (Cape Verde Islands), 384, 384m
Transportes Aéreos de Chile, S.A. (TRANSA), 369
Transportes Aéreos de Guine Portuguesa (T.A.G.P.). *See* Air Bissau
Transportes Aéreos de Nacionales de Selva (TANS) (Peru), 359
Transportes Aéreos del Cesar. *See* Aerocesar
Transportes Aéreos del Mercosur (TAM) (Paraguay), 319, 362
   See also Líneas Aéreas Paraguayas
Transportes Aéreos Ecuatorianos Militares, Ecuador (TAME), 355
Transportes Aéreos Ejecutivo, S.A. (TAESA) (Mexico), 324–326, 325p
Transportes Aéreos Mercantiles Panamericano (TAMPA) (Colombia), 350, 350p
Transportes Aéreos Meridionais (TAM) (Brazil), 319–320
   Airbus A320 series order, with TACA and LAN-Chile, 319–320, 343
   Forms TAM Linhas Aéreos, 320
   Partnership with Air France, 200
   Route maps, 318m, 320m
   VASP investment, 317
Transportes Aéreos Nacionales (TAN) (Honduras), 341–342
Transportes Aéreos Neuquen (TAN) (Argentina), 317
Transportes Aéreos Salvador (TAS) (Brazil), 317
Transports Aéreos Centro-Americanos (TACA) (Central America), 340–346, 344m, 344p, 346p
   Airbus A320 series (with TAM, Brazil, and LAN-Chile), 319
   Buys into Volaris, Mexico, 326
   Change of corporate name, 343
   Move from Honduras to El Salvador, 340
   Partnership with AVIANCA, Colombia, 344
   Route map, 2008, 344m
Transports Aériens Guyanais (T.A.G.) (France), first airline in South America, 5
Transports Aériens Intercontinentaux (T.A.I.) (France), 301–302
   Forms Air Ivoire, 377
   Pacific operatons, 301
   With U.A.T., French Europe–Africa jet airline debut, 52t
Trans-Siberian Express, S.A.S. route, 227
Trans-Siberian Railway, v. air transport in Soviet Union, 61
Trans-Texas Airways (U.S.), 127
   See also Texas International Airlines
Transwest (Canada), 309m
Travel Group Charters (TGC), introduced, 1970s, 64
Travelair (Costa Rica), 241
Treaty of Potsdam, 98
Treaty of Rapallo, 20
Treaty of Yaoundé, 68, 376
Trek Airways (South Africa), 401–402
   Cooperation with Lioftleidir, Luxair, 401–402
   Founds Flitestar, 402
Trinidad & Tobago, government buys B.W.I.A., 328
Trinidad & Tobago Air Services, merges with B.W.I.A., 328
Tripartite agreements, 211, 246, 287, 294, 314, 395
Trippe, Juan, 14, 24, 28, 50–51, 108, 109, 162
Trujillo, Leonidas, 336
Trump, Donald, 165, 168–169, 174, 183
T.T.A. *See* Trans-Texas Airways
T.T.K.K. *See* East-West Scheduled Aviation Society
Tuninter (Tunis), 72s, 373
Tunis Air. *See* Tunisair
Tunisair, 68, 372–373, 373p
Tupolev, Andrei, 20, 47
Tupolev Tu-104
   Aeroflot, 1950s, 61
   Debut, 42, 42m, 42p, 99, 408
Tupolev Tu-104A
   C.S.A. jet service, 42
Tupolev Tu-114 Rossiya (turboprop airliner), 48–49, 48p, 49m
   Aeroflot long-range routes, 99–100
   Japan Air Lines, 99
   Survives into Jet Age, 54
Tupolev Tu-124
   Aeroflot service, 1962, 61
Tupolev Tu-134
   Aeroflot, 1967, 62, 62p, 100p
   Air Vietnam, 1980s, 277–278
   Aviogenex, 1968, 223
   Baltic International, 239
   Estonian Air, 1991
   Pulkovo, 156
   Sibir losses, 2001–2004, 152
   Tyumen Avia Trans, 154
Tupolev Tu-144 (supersonic airliner), 115–116, 115p, 116m
   Aeroflot obliged to operate, 61
   Crash at Paris air show, 1973, 116
Tupolev Tu-154
   Air Mongol, 1987, 276
   Albanian Airlines, 1990s, 225
   China Northwest, 1989, 242t
   Chinese orders, 1985, 243
   Egyptair, 1972, 374
   Enters service, Aeroflot, 1972, 101, 101m, 101p
   Guyana Airways, 1985, 334
   Kras Air, Russia, 153
   Pulkovo, 156
   Tyumen Avia Trans, 154
   UKAMPS, North Korea, 1950s, 276
Tupolev Tu-204
   Air Cairo, 1997, 375
   Kras Air, Russia, 1998, 153
   Rolls-Royce engine powered, 153–154
Turk Hava Yollari (T.H.Y.) (Turkey), 80
Turkey, high-speed rail, 2009, 414t
Turkmenavia (Soviet C.I.S.), 151t
Turner, Roscoe, 122, 123c
Turner Airlines (U.S.), 122, 123c
Turtle Airways (Fiji), 297
Tuvalu, air service, 196, 299
T.W.A. *See* Trans World Airlines; Transcontinental & Western Air
T.X.I. *See* Texas International Airlines
Tyrolean Airways, 237
Tyumen Airlines, division of T.A.T., 154
Tyumen Avia Trans (T.A.T.)
   Simplifies name to UTair, 154
   Soviet C.I.S. helicopter airline, 103,151t

U.A.A. *See* United Arab Airlines
U.A.T. *See* Union Aeromaritime de Transport
U.B.A. *See* Union of Burma Airways
Uganda Airlines, 387
Ugats (Soviet C.I.S.), 151t
Ugorsk Transport. *See* UTair
U.K. (U.K.)
   Creates "Second Force" airline, 59
   Empire routes, 21
   Initial shareholding in Airbus, 110
   Loses technical leadership to the U.S., 50
   Tourist routes, 1960s–1970s, 63m
   Tripartite Agreement, 246, 287
   Wartime bomber conversions, 27
UKAMPS (North Korea), 276
Ukraine International Airlines (U.I.A.), 237, 248
   See also Tyrolean Airways
Ukrainian-Mediterranean Airlines (UM Air), 239
Ukrvozdukhput (Ukraine), 238
UM Air. *See* Ukrainian-Mediterranean Airlines
UMCA (Colombia), 5m
UNI Air (Taiwan), 271
Union Aéromaritime de Transport (U.A.T.) (France)
   Comet 1A service, 40, 40m
   K.S.S.U. airline partnership, 111
   Supports Air Afrique, 376
Union Airways (South Africa), 16
Union Airways of New Zealand
   Empire service, 1939, 21m
   Starts service, 1936, 16

Union de Transports Aériens (U.T.A.) (France), 199–200
  Assists Air Ceylon, 1960s, 255
  Comet 1A service, 40, 40m
  K.S.S.U. airline partnership, 111
  Merger with Air France and Air Inter, 200, 200m
  Supports Air Afrique, 376
  With T.A.I., French Europe–Africa jet airline debut, 52t
Union of Burma Airways, 256–257
  Aircraft operated, 84–85, 256
  Name change to Burma Airways Corporation, 256
Union of Soviet Socialist Republics. *See* Soviet Union
United Air Lines, 9
  Aircraft operated, 52, 57, 110, 118
  Alliance with Lufthansa, 1993, 203
  Bankruptcy, 2002, 185
  Buys Pacific route system from Pan American, 1985–1986, 162
  Buys Pan Am's route to London, 1991, 197
  Genealogy, 9c
  Introduces Boeing 247, 1933, 10, 10p
  One of U.S. "Big Four," 9c, 122
  Post-war summary, 26t
  Post-war U.S. leadership, 28
  Transcontinental route map, 1934, 10m
  Wartime service, 25
United Aircraft & Transport Corp., 9c
United Arab Airlines (U.A.A.), 70, 374
United Arab Emirates, emerge from Ottoman Empire, 74, 74m
United Breweries (India), founds Kingfisher Airlines, 250
United Iranian Airlines (IranAir), 71, 240
United Kingdom Society of California, representative affinity group, 143
United Micronesia Development Association, forms Air Micronesia, 300
United States (U.S.)
  Air Commerce Act, 1926, 9
  Air Mail Act, 1925 ("Kelly"), 9
  Air Mail Act, 1934, 11
  Air Mail Act of 1930 ("McNary-Watres"), 9
  Aircraft grounded, September 11, 2001, 179
  Bilateral agreement with Canada, 1995, 306
  Commuter airlines, 92, 123c
  Deregulation, 139–141
  Effect of mail payments during 1930s, 11
  Emergency Loan Guarantee Act, 1971, 111
  First airlines, 1914–1923, map series, 2m
  Interstate highway program v. local airlines, 138
  Lighted airway, 7
  Local Service Operations, 83
  Low-fare airlines, 171–175
  Post Office Mail Contracts, 1925–1927, 8m
  Supersonic technology, 114–115
  Supplemental airlines, 65–66, 66t
  Transcontinental route map, 1934, 10m
Universal Air Transport, 9c
Universal Airlines (Guyana), 334
Universal Airlines (U.S.), 65t
Urals CAD (Soviet C.I.S.), 151t, 153
US Air. *See* US Airways
US Air Express, name change from Allegheny Commuter, 1989, 168
US Air Shuttle, 168, 174, 183
US Airways, 168–170
  Aircraft operated, 169
  Bankruptcy, 169–170
  British Airways investment, 168–169
  Buys P.S.A., 118, 124, 172
  Buys Piedmont Air Lines, 124
  Forms Metrojet, 1997, 169
  Merges with America West, 2004, 170
  Name change from Allegheny Airlines to US Air, 1979, 122, 123c, 169
  Name change from US Air, 1996, 169
  Orders 400 Airbuses, 169
  United Airlines offer, 2000, 169
U.S. Army Air Corps
  Carries air mail during 1934 crisis, 11
  First U.S. air service, 1918, 3
U.S. Department of Transport, 141
U.S. Post Office
  Forms air service, 1918, 3, 3T, 7
  Backs Pan American Airways, 14
  "Use-it-or-lose-it," C.A.B. direction, 94
U.S.S.R. *See* Soviet Union
U.T.A. *See* Union de Transports Aériens
UTair, 153
  Name change from Tyumen Avia Trans, 155
  One of Russia's "Big Six," 157
Uzbeki CAD (Soviet C.I.S.), 151t
  Crash-landing at Delhi, India, 1993, 248

Vachet, Paul, 18
Valuair (Singapore), 283
ValuJet (U.S.), 179–180
  DC-9 crash, 117
  MD-95s, 179p
  Merger with AirTran Airways, 1997, 180
Van Arsdale, John, 92–93
Vance International (U.S.), Supplemental airline, 65t
Vanguard Airlines (U.S.), 184
Vannukul, Virachai, 268
Varanair Siam. *See* Air Siam
Varanand (Prince), 267
Vardhan, Harsh, 249
Vargas, Getulio, 315
VARIG. *See* Viação Aérea Rio-Grandense
VariLog, VARIG subsidiary, 316
Varney Air Transport
  Contract air mail route (CAM 5), 1926, 8m
  Genealogy, 9c
  Name change to Continental Air Lines, 1937, 26t
VASP. *See* Viação Aérea São Paulo
Vassilakis Group (Greece). *See* Aegean Airlines
Vayudoot (India), 249
Velangair (Tonga), sold to Macair, 294
Vertol 44 and 107 helicopters, 412
VFR (visiting friends and relations) traffic, 143
Yugoslavia, 1970s, 222
Viação Aérea Rio-Grandense (VARIG) (Brazil), 18, 315–316
  Acquires Cruzeiro do Sul, 1975, 129, 314
  Aircraft operated, 88, 314, 315–316
  Buys Electras, 47
  Buys Uruguay's PLUNA, 316, 363
  Caravelle service, 56–57
  "Chosen instrument" status, 1950s, 315
  Sold to GOL, 2007, 316
Viação Aérea São Paulo (VASP) (Brazil), 18, 313–314
  Aircraft operated, 131, 315, 317
  Collapse, 2007, 317
  Invests in TAM, third-level airline, 1976
  L.A.B. purchase, 360
  Privatized, 317
  Sold to GOL, 2007, 321
Vias Internacionales Aéreas, Venezuela (VIASA), 351–353
  Aircraft operated, 351, 352p, 352
  End of services, 1997, 218
  Iberia rescue attempt, 1994, 352
  Orders Comet jets, 1952, 351
VIASA. *See* Vias Internacionales Aéreas, Venezuela
Vickers, British aircraft manufacturer, merged to form B.A.C., 59
Vickers Super-VC-10
  Air Mauritius, 1973, 407
  B.O.A.C., 1975, 105, 195p
  British Airways, 1970s, 196
  E.A.A.C., 1970, 120; 1972, 386
Vickers Valiant bomber, 119
Vickers Vanguard, 47
  Air Canada, 119, 304
  B.E.A., 119, 119p
Merpati Nusantara, Indonesia, 84
T.C.A., 1961, 304
Transgabon, 1980s, 379
Vickers Vanjet, jet airliner project, 119
Vickers Viceroy (turboprop), 37
Vickers Viking
  Post-war airliner, 27, 28p
  Trek Airways, South Africa, 1954, 401–402
Vickers Vimy bomber
  Flies to Australia, 1919, 6
  Imported to China, 1919, 7
Vickers V-630 (renamed Viscount), 37
Vickers V-1000, 50, 119
Vickers VC-7, 119
Vickers VC-10
  Air Ceylon, 1960s, 255
  Air Malawi, 1974, 395
  B.O.A.C., 105, 120
  British Airways, 1970s–1980s, 195
  B.U.A. order, 1960, 106, 120, 120p
  Central African Airways, 1964, 393
  Delayed introduction, 50
  Ghana Airways, 1965, 120, 382
  Nigeria Airways, 1962, 380
  Sierra Leone, 1960s, 383
  With Gulf Air, 76
Vickers Viscount
  Aerocesar, Colombia, 1971, 349
  Aeropesca, Colombia, 1960s, 349
  Air Canada, 304
  Air Zimbabwe, 1980s, 394
  Bahamas Airways, 1961, 331
  B.E.A. success during 1950s, 43
  Botswana National Airways, 1990s, 404
  Bouraq Indonesian Airlines, 1977, 265; 1982, 135
  Brabazon Committee recommendation, 32
  Central African Airways, 1956, 392
  Debut, 37
  Eagle Airways (Bermuda), 1960, 331
  FAT, Taiwan, 1970, 270
  I.A.C., India, 1957, 247
  LANICA, Nicaragua, 1958, 342
  Lufthansa, 98
  Malayan-Malaysian, 1960s, 259
  Merpati Nusantara, Indonesia, 1960s, 135, 135p
  Misrair, Egypt, 1956, 374
  N.A.C., New Zealand, 1958, 291
  PLUNA, Uruguay, 1958, 363
  SAETA, Ecuador, 1970, 356
  Series 700, first sustained turboprop service, 37–38, 38m
  Series 800, 44
  South African Airways, 1958, 399
  Sudan Airways, 1959, 389
  TACA, Central America, 1950s, 343
  TAO, 1969, 349
  T.C.A., 1955, 303–304, 303p
  To China, 1961, 132; in service, 1963, 240

Index

U.B.A., Burma, 1958, 256
VASP, Brazil, 1968, 315
World's first turboprop, 31
Vietnam Airlines, 278
Viljoen, Andre, 401
Virgin Atlantic Airlines, 191
    Agreements with SABENA, Air Liberté, 1996, 191
    Granted rights to U.S.A., 1991, 197
    Launches Virgin Nigeria, 2004, 381–382
    Sues British Airways, 1993, 197
    See also Branson, Richard; Euro-Belgian Airlines; *other Virgin-owned airlines*
Virgin Australia, 290
Virgin Blue (Australia), 290
Virgin Express France, 191
Virgin Express Ireland, 191
Virgin Islands Seaplane Shuttle, renamed Antilles Air Boats, 339
Virgin Nigeria, 381–382
VivaAerobus (Mexico), 327, 326t
Vladivostok Avia (Russia), 157m
Vnokovo Airlines (Soviet C.I.S.), 151t
    Aircraft operated, 152
Volare (Italy), 211
Volaris (Mexico), 326, 326m, 326t
Volga-Dnepr (Russia), 155–157, 155p
Volgers, Robert, 333
Volo do Brasil, takes over VARIG, 316
von Marvil, A.B., 2
von Ohain, Hans, 36, 36c
von Zeppelin, Ferdinand, 1
Vôos Técnicos e Executivos (VOTEC) (Brazil)
    Integrated with TAM, 319
    Routes, 1976, 318m
VOTEC. *See* Vôos Técnicos e Executivos
Vought Kingfisher
    C.A.A., Antilles, 1940s, 334–335
Vought-Sikorsky VS-44 flying boat
    A.E.A., wartime trans-Atlantic service, 26
    Antilles Air Boats, 1968, 339
    Avalon Air Transport, 1960s, 339

W.A.A.C. *See* West African Airways Corporation
Walker, C.C., 39
Walker, Jack, 192
Wall Street Crash, 1929, 9
Walsh, Willie, 198
Waltrip, William, 161
Ward, Maxwell, 310

Wardair (U.K.), 311
Wardair Canada (formerly Wardair), 310–312
    Name change from Wardair, 310
    Sold to Pacific Western, 306, 311
    Trans-Atlantic charters, 310
Wardair Jamaica, 311
Wasaya Airways (Canada), 309m
Waterman Steamship Company, buys TACA, 343
Wearne's Air Services (Malaya), 21m
Weber, Juergen, 203
Wedding, Air Atlanta 1996, 234
Weiss, Stan, 65, 66c, 67p
Wells, Mary, 158
West African Airways Corporation (W.A.A.C.), 380
    Long-range service overtaken by Nigeria Airways, 67
West Australian Airways, 6, 6m, 137, 137c
West Coast Air Transport, 9c
West Coast Airlines (U.S.), 124
    Buys Empire Air Lines, 124
    First Fokker F-27 Friendship service, 1958, 84, 124
    Genealogy, 123c
    Orders airliners, 1966, 60
Western Air Express (U.S.), 26t
    Contract air mail route (CAM 4), 1926, 8m
    Genealogy, 9c
    Merger to form T.W.A., 10
Western Airlines (U.S.)
    Electra service, 1960, 46
    Name change from Western Air Express, 26t
    Wartime service, 25
Western Pacific Airlines (W.P.A.) (U.S.), 182
Westgate California Corporation, control of Air California, 173
WestJet (Canada), 308
"Wet-leasing," Air Atlanta, 234
Wexford Management, takes over Western Pacific Airlines, 182
Wheatcroft, Stephen, 195
Wheeler Airlines (Canada), 310
Wheless, R.F., 128
"Whispering Giant," name for Bristol Britannia, 44–45, 44p
"Whisperjets," Eastern Air Lines Lockheed TriStars, 164
White, Harry, 124
White River Air Service (Canada), 310

Whitehall Travel, 63
Whittle, Frank, 36, 36c
Wideroe, Turi, 227
Wideroe, Viggo, 231
Wideroe's Flyveselcap (Norway), 231–232, 231p
    Only airline completely north of Arctic Circle, 231
    S.A.S. stake, 1997, 229
Wigar, Azim, 253
Wiggins, E.W. (U.S.), 123c
Wigley, Harry, 292
Wigley, Rodolph, 291
Wikramanayake, S.K. "Captain Wik," 255–256
Williams, A.J., 334
Williams, J.E.D., 77
Williams, Syd, 289
Wilmington-Catalina Airline, 26t
Wilson, Harold, 113
Wilson Airways (Africa), 21m, 385
Winair. *See* Windward Islands Airways
Windward Islands, Caribbean, 329m
Windward Islands Airways (Winair), 332–333
    Known as "Windies," 333
Winela Air Service (Bechuanaland), 401, 401m
Wings Holdings, owned by Alfred Checchi, 215
Wisconsin Central Airlines (U.S.), 123c, 125
    See also North Central Airlines
Wolf, Stephen, 169
Wood, Arthur, 344
Woods (Australia), once world's shortest route, 137c, 289
Woodside, "Peck," 20
Woolman, C.E., 60
World Airways (U.S. Supplemental airline), 65t, 66
    Malaysian Airways stake, 262
W.P.A. *See* Western Pacific Airlines
W.R. Carpenter (New Guinea), 137c
Wright, U.S. engine manufacturer, builds R-3400, 30
Wright Amendment, 178
Wright brothers, first flight, 1
Wuhan Airlines (China), 241m, 242t

Xabre group, acquires control of Mexicana, 323
Xiamen Airlines (China), 241m, 242t
Xian Y-7, Chinese An-24
    Lao Airlines, 2000s, 280

Yakovlev Yak-40 (Soviet feeder airliner), 100
    Aeroflot regional services, 1960s–1970s, 131–132
    Albanian Airlines, 1990s, 225
    Cubana, 1980s, 338
    Estonian Air, 1991, 239
    T Doble A, Peru, 2000s, 359
    Tyumen Avia Trans, 154
Yakovlev Yak-42
    AeroSvit, and crash, 1998, 238
    China General, 1989, 242t
    Cubana, 1980s, 338
    Lithuanian, 1991, 239
    UM Air, and crash, 2003, 239
Yakutavia (Soviet C.I.S.), 151t
Yangon Airways (Burma), 257
Yellow Cab, taxi group, 123c
Yellowknife Airways (Canada), 310
Yerex, Lowell, 326, 340
Yrausquin, Ciro, 333
YS-11. *See* Nihon (NAMCO) YS-11
Yukon Southern Airlines, ancestor of CP Air, 304
"Yukon's Airline" (Air North), 310
Yung Shing Airlines (Taiwan), becomes Formosa Airlines, 271
Yunnan Airlines. *See* China Yunnan

ZAC. *See* Zambian Air Cargoes
Zambezi Colonial Coach, C.A.A. low-fare service, 1953, 392
Zambia Airways, 393
Zambian Air Cargoes (ZAC), heavy-lift records, 393
Zambian Airways, takes over Mines Air Services, 394
Zamrud Aviation (Indonesia), 84, 136, 136m, 136p
Zarate, Alfredo, 20
ZAS Airline of Egypt, 375
Zeppelin, Luftschiffbau GmbH, 1
Zevallos, Fernando, 359
Zhao Ziyang, 245
Zhejiang Airlines (China), 241m, 242t
Zhongyuan Airlines (China), 241m, 242t
Zhukovsky Institute, Moscow, 20
Ziegler, Henri, 109
Zimmerly Air Lines (U.S.), 123c, 124
Zinzer, Julio, 20
Zip, Air Canada affiliate, 307
ZONDA (Argentina), 364

ABOUT THE AUTHOR

Born in England, Ron Davies started a civil service career in 1938, spent six years in the British Army during the Second World War, and then joined the new Ministry of Civil Aviation. He moved on to British European Airways then to the Bristol, de Havilland, and Hawker-Siddeley aircraft manufacturing companies, specializing in market research and traffic analysis.

Davies developed innovative procedures for airline traffic forecasting and, at Bristol, established probably the world's first air transport market research department. His work supported the sales of British commercial aircraft such as the Viscount, Britannia, Comet, and Trident. In 1968, he joined the Douglas Aircraft Company, where he helped to sell DC-8s, DC-9s, and DC-10s and participated in many areas of market and economic research, specializing in Eastern Europe and China. Davies advocated twin-engine and stretched versions of the DC-10 and opposed, on the basis of careful traffic and operational analysis, a supersonic airliner project.

Davies left the industry in 1981 when he accepted the Lindbergh Chair of Aerospace History at the Smithsonian Institution's National Air and Space Museum. He later became the Curator of Air Transport at that museum.

Ron Davies' first book, *A History of the World's Airlines*, was published in 1964. He has since written 24 other books. He is a Fellow of three Royal Societies: Aeronautical, Arts, and Geographical. He is an Associate of the Academie Nationale de l'Air et de l'Espace. He is a Fellow National of the Explorers Club and a member of New York's Wings Club and Washington's Cosmos Club. From Brazil, he has received the Santos Dumont Medal and the Aeronautics Order of Merit. Davies has traveled to more than 120 countries and all seven continents.

In the year 2000, Davies delivered the 37th "Sight" (Hindsight, Insight, and Foresight) Lecture at New York's Wings Club. He has subsequently presented the lecture, "Directions of Air Transport in the 21st Century—Lessons from History," to agencies, universities, and conferences on both sides of the Atlantic. A supplemental lecture subtitled "On to a Thousand Seats" is Davies' prediction for an airliner that will match the capacity of the double-decked high-speed trains.